A TEXT-BOOK

OF

CHURCH HISTORY.

BY DR. JOHN C. L. GIESELER.

Translated from the Fourth Revised German Edition,

BY SAMUEL DAVIDSON, LL.D.,

PROFESSOR OF BIBLICAL LITERATURE AND ECCLESIASTICAL HISTORY IN THE LANCASHIRE INDEPENDENT COLLEGE.

A NEW AMERICAN EDITION, REVISED AND EDITED

BY HENRY B. SMITH,

PROFESSOR IN THE UNION THEOLOGICAL SEMINARY, NEW YORK.

VOL. I. A.D. 1–726.

NEW YORK:
HARPER & BROTHERS, PUBLISHERS,
PEARL STREET, FRANKLIN SQUARE.
1857.

INTRODUCTORY NOTE.

In this new edition of Gieseler's Church History a thorough revision of the translation has been made, with additional references to the English and later German works. The alterations are numerous, giving more exactly the sense of the original, and correcting frequent mistranslations.

The entire history to the epoch of the Reformation will be comprised in three volumes, following the divisions of the original German. The subsequent history, to 1848, can probably be embraced in two additional volumes. At the time of Gieseler's decease, his work was completed to the year 1648, in three volumes, subdivided into six parts, each of which was separately issued. The history is to be continued under the editorial supervision of his colleague, Dr. E. R. Redepenning. The volume for the period from 1814 to 1848 is just published; we have taken from it, with slight abridgments, an account of Gieseler's life and writings. The narrative of the ecclesiastical events of this period was written out by Gieseler himself; unlike the previous volumes, it is an extended history, with comparatively few notes. The intervening volume, for the period from the Peace of Westphalia, 1648 to 1814, is promised for the next year. Thus the work will form a complete and authentic history of the Christian Church, to A.D. 1848, composed with abundant and careful learning, especially adapted to the wants of students, and indispensable as a guide to any who would examine the original sources. The aid it gives in the critical investigation of the original authorities is its chief merit, apart from its use as a text-book for classes in Theological Seminaries. It is cold, but cautious; it is more rational than sympathetic; it has not the warmth of Neander's incomparable work, but it is more complete; it has not the vividness of Hase's delineations, but it is more full, and gives copious extracts from the sources, such as can nowhere else be found.

The first three volumes of the present edition correspond with volumes one and two of the original. The first extends to the year 726. The second will be from 726 to 1305; the third from 1305 to 1517. The whole period, 726 to 1517, was published by Gieseler as his second volume, in four subdivisions. The third volume of the German, in two parts, will be the fourth in this translation; and a fifth volume will probably embrace the fourth and fifth of the original.

In the German edition, both parts of the first volume, and also the first two divisions of the second volume (to 1305), are in their fourth edition; the third division of the second volume has reached a second edition; its fourth division, and the whole of the third volume (1517 to 1648), are still in their first edition; and the publisher states that a new one is not to be expected, as a sufficiently large number of copies was struck off to meet the demand.

The first English translation of Gieseler's work was well executed from the third edition of the earlier volumes by Francis Cunningham, and published in Philadelphia, in 1836, in three volumes, extending to the Reformation. The version published in Clark's Library, from which this edition is in part reprinted, is by different translators: the first and second volumes are by Dr. Davidson; the third and fourth by Rev. J. W. Hull. The Edinburgh edition is inconveniently arranged; the first volume breaks off in the middle of the second period; the second, in the midst of the third period; and the fourth, about two hundred pages short of the Reformation. This defect is remedied in the present edition, and a translation added of the portion needed to complete the history to the Reformation. This will be followed, as soon as practicable, by a translation of the additional volumes.

The least satisfactory portion of Dr. Gieseler's work is undoubtedly that of the first century. It is disproportionately concise; and the bias of the author is more marked. But here, too, the sources for correcting his opinions are near at hand to all our students.

NEW YORK, *Sept.* 1, 1855.

THE LIFE AND WRITINGS OF GIESELER.

Both the father and grandfather of Dr. Gieseler were clergymen. His grandfather, John Arend Gieseler, born at Minden in 1726, was a pastor at Lahde, and afterward at Hartum, in the principality of Minden. He received his theological education at Halle. The family records describe him as wholly in sympathy with the practical Christian tendencies reintroduced by Franke and Spener, though not devoted to the peculiarities of "pietism;" as a true adherent of the symbols of Lutheranism; as a very earnest, active, and orderly man, yet cheerful, and of great hilarity with the right sort of people. These characteristics reappear in the grandson. The grandmother, of the family of Haccius, shared her husband's piety and love of order.

These qualities also distinguished their son, George Christopher Frederick Gieseler, born in 1770, who was a preacher in Petershagen, near Minden, and afterward in Werther, not far from Bielefeld. He was a man of a marked intellectual character. Though deaf from his fourteenth year, so that in the University he was often obliged to transcribe from his neighbor's manuscript, and though thus almost deprived in later life of social intercourse, he yet attained the most thorough culture and self-discipline. His infirmity seemed to forbid his entering the clerical profession; but, as if born for a minister, he would be that, and nothing else. In his eleventh and twelfth years he held meetings on Sunday afternoons, in a garden-house of his father, which were attended in large numbers from the village, and not without good results. When only thirteen, he took for a time the place of a sick teacher in the chapel at Holtzhausen, conducting the singing and catechetical exercise. He, too, was educated at the University of Halle, and taught in several private families, until he became a pastor at Petershagen in 1790. He was devoted to his congregation, yet ever earnest in his studies. He published several works, but more remain in manuscript, upon Theology, or rather Theosophy, the Revelation of John, and Education. With much that is original, these writings contain also one-sided and erratic views.

John Charles Louis Gieseler was born at Petershagen the third of March, 1793, the oldest of ten children. When four years old, death deprived him of the faithful and loving care of his mother, whose maiden name was Berger, a woman of great practical sagacity. His earliest instruction was from his grandfather, who taught him in an easy, sportive way, to be a good reader in his fourth year. His father's peculiarities contributed to the formation of that independence of character which in early life distinguished him, and in later years came to his aid in so many difficult circumstances. In his tenth year he was sent to the Latin school of the Orphan-house at Halle. Here he soon enjoyed the counsels and care of Niemeyer, whose friendship in after years never deserted him. He aided him in his studies, and after their completion promoted him to the post of teacher in the Orphan School. He had hardly been a year in this position, when, in October, 1813, he followed the call of his father-land, became a volunteer in the war for Germany's freedom, and was present at the raising of the siege of Magdeburg. After the peace in 1815, he resumed his office as teacher; two years later he received the degree of Doctor of Philosophy: he became co-rector of the gymnasium at Minden in the same year, and in 1818 director of the gymnasium at Cleve. At Michaelmas, in 1819, he was appointed "professor ordinarus" of Theology in the newly-established Frederick-William's University of Bonn, having already received from that University, on the third of April of the same year, the doctorate of divinity through Augusti's influence.

This rapid promotion he owed to his "Critical Essay upon the Origin and earliest History of the written Gospels," published in 1818. This exposition set aside the hypothesis of one written original Gospel as the common source of the synoptical Gospels, and confirmed the positions laid down by Herder, Lessing, and others, which are at the basis of the whole recent criticism of the Gospels. This important work of Gieseler was soon out of print; yet he could never decide upon issuing a second edition. He shunned that confusion of hypotheses, many of them wholly groundless, which afterward sprung up on this subject, and also thought that the time had not come for new and definitive results.

His thorough philological culture is proved by his treatises published in the second volume of Rosemüller's "*Repertorium*," which helped to enrich the science of the grammar of the New Testament, then in its infancy. His Essay upon the "Nazarenes and the Ebionites," in Stäudlin and Tzschirner's "*Archiv*" (Bd. iv. St. 2), showed his peculiar talent in disentangling confused problems. From this time forth he dedicated his powers almost exclusively to his loved studies in church history. Neander's "*Genetic Development of the Gnostic Systems*" was the occasion of his penetrating review (in the "*Hallische Lit. Zeitung*, 1823), which cast much new light upon this chaos. The next year he commenced the publication of his "Text-book of Church History." With Lücke, he also edited the "*Zeitschrift für gebildete Christen*," four numbers being issued in the years 1823, 4.

At that time the yet youthful University of the Rhine enjoyed a fresh and free life; Protestants and Catholics were not rent asunder; Gratz and Seber still taught without hinderance their independent exegesis and theology, assailed only by Hermes; they, with Ritter, the Roman Catholic church historian, were in constant intercourse with Gieseler; all were of one heart and one soul; robust powers were working peaceably together; the University was in the perfect blossom of its spring-time. In his family Gieseler was blessed in a high degree, attached with incomparable truth and devotion to his early loved and early lost wife, Henrietta, of the Feist family in Halle. The blessing of many children was theirs, and with these came many a care. But trusting in God, relying upon his own power of labor, untiringly active, most conscientious in all his work, not troubled by little things, in the midst of his cares he kept his heart open to every joy.

For twelve and a half years he stood in this post of special influence as a teacher of church history, and enjoying the confidence of his colleagues, who had just committed to him the rectorship of the University, when the Georgia Augusta called him to her service; and certainly, in no other University could he have been so wholly in his place as at Göttingen. In its fundamental character, as the nurse of the empirical and historical sciences, and in the manifold practical services to which it called him, it corresponded entirely with his own bias. Mere learned investigation would not have filled up the measure of his activity. It is difficult to say which in him was predominant, his capacity for learning, or his practical sagacity and inward fitness to organize and govern; both, without doubt, went hand in hand. As he was in life, so was he in science, clear, definite, foreseeing, conscientious; in expression concise, at times laconic, in all things a man of one piece —a man in every sense of the word. This was felt as soon as you came in contact with him and put confidence in him. The University frequently committed to him, and in times of trial almost always to him alone, the dignity of pro-rector; with hardly an interruption, he was a member of one or several academical courts. His counsel must be sought upon propositions for the revisal of the University statutes, or in making new regulations. He was a constant member of the Library Commission. The city corporation chose him for its speaker, an office, however, which he afterward declined. He was curator of the Göttingen Orphan-house, and had the administration of many other charitable foundations, especially the scholarships. The Göttingen Academy of Sciences, of which he was a member, committed to him the direction of the Wedemeyer prizes. In union with Lücke, he directed the Theological Ephora. But the Orphan-house was the special joy of his heart. With few exceptions, he was there every day, and hence knew exactly the disposition, conduct, and faults of each child, had for every one friendly words and counsel, and kept the pupils in his eye long after they had left the institution. They, in return, were attached to him, and manifestly eager to give him pleasure; only in a very few cases did he fail of success in his noble efforts for the rescue of the abandoned, undertaken with so bold a faith.

He gave much time to the lodge of the Order of Free-masons, and undoubtedly knew why he did this. In his last days he was violently assailed on this account, in a way which detracts as little from his good name as from the prosperity of the order.

The interests of his country were ever dear to his heart. The last volume of his church history, embracing the period from

1814 to 1848, shows in many passages what his wishes were. His judgment upon the revolutionary movements of 1848 runs through the whole narrative, in which is also seen the calm hope with which he looked to the future in the midst of the storms that robbed so many of their self-possession.

In the affairs of the Church, as well as of the State, he loved to see a constant and ever judicious advance; he would not have any of the threads severed which bind together the new and the old. Hence he declared against the so-called "Constituent Synods," projected in 1848; and these, in fact, would only have done injury, had they been, as he conceived them to be, courts sitting in judgment upon what was henceforth to be received as the doctrines of the Church. But such a tendency might have been easily avoided; and when we think how much has been lost by nearly forty years of neglect, and the difficulty of its restoration, we can only desire that efforts for the building up of our Protestant Church should not again be undervalued; there may at least be progress in the ecclesiastical order and arrangement of the individual churches, so that, when there is greater clearness in doctrine, we may find the foundations ready for the future structure.

The question whether Gieseler was a rationalist, was answered in the negative, immediately after his death, by a Theologian of high standing, his colleague, Dr. Dorner;* and he certainly was never what we now most commonly understand by that word. From the beginning to the end of his literary career, he held immovably to the truth of justification through faith alone, the fundamental idea of the Protestant system, understanding by this, the free personal reception of the divine truth and grace that come through the mediation of Christ, and are manifested in Him. He did not put the knowledge given by human reason above the divine truth given us in Christ; he acknowledged him only to be a Christian who saw in Christ the sum of all the highest truth, never to be surpassed by any one here below. But when, on the other hand, any one detracted from the right and obligation of human reason to appropriate, examine, and grasp this truth, to free

* Dorner, "Abwehr der hengstenbergscher Angriffe auf Gieseler und Lucke." Gottingen, 1854.

it from the letter and receive it as spirit and truth, he became a bold and strong champion for this right, which no one ever undervalued without punishment; for reason is that light in us which can not become darkness, without plunging the whole man into darkness (Matth. vi. 22. 23; Luke, xi. 34. 35). In this sense Gieseler was a rationalist, and had in full measure the claim to be honored with that appellation by those who so readily give it to all who hold to clear and logical thinking, and to a wise separation between what is scientifically certain and all arbitrary fancies. He was ever averse to what some love to call profundity of doctrine, to that empty speculation which is either ignorant of or overthrows the empirical basis on which it should rest, and which runs a tilt against all logic without respect; he laughed in a quiet way at one and another who, without the capacity, considered themselves to be speculative theologians. Every philosophical position had for him value only in the degree of its real certainty; it was one of his prime convictions, that in theology nothing is now more important than the difficult, yet not impossible sundering of the spheres of faith and knowledge (πίστις and γνῶσις), of that which is the object of faith, and that which is but a human elaboration of the materials, necessarily changing with the progress of time, and always developing itself with many a fluctuation.

His whole treatment of church history rests upon this distinction. His sole aim was to exhibit the historical developments as they were: he combined in one view whatever was internally connected; he made the agencies and counter-agencies apparent, and pointed out the aim and tendencies of events; but he held himself aloof from the construction of arbitrary schemes and divisions, and from all merely subjective judgments. Starting from the position to which the investigations had already advanced, he penetrated to the problems under the guidance of previous leaders, and had a singular gift of quickly finding the way that led to the goal, without taking any fruitless step. It might be said that the intellectual traits of his Westphalian father-land—where is ever found so much unperverted practical sense, quickly seizing upon the right point—were his own in the highest perfection in his scientific explorations. To the outward form he assigned a subordinate value, as well in his own writings as in his critical investigations. He was sagacious in conjecturing the right words of original documents; many such emendations of high value are due to him. Perhaps, however, in the question of the genuineness of this or that work, he allowed too little influence to its external form—its diction.

The plan and arrangement of his church history are not one symmetrical whole, or, rather, a change in the original plan was made with the second volume. At first intended to be in three volumes of about the same size, the work in the second was so extended, that it lost in some measure its original destination as a guide in the University lectures. The disproportion was to be made up by a more concise history of the period from the Peace of Westphalia, 1648, to the year 1814. But who laments this enlargement of the work? In the very form which the author gave it, it has become the mine from which is drawn so much learning in church history; without it a mass of our later outlines of church history would, doubtless, not have appeared, or at least would not have offered so rich materials.

In another place will be found a designation of the more salient parts of this church history.* In the history of the ancient church Gieseler's assiduity and preference were specially devoted to the Greek Theology. Our acquaintance with it has been materially enlarged by his Programmes upon the opinions of the "Alexandrian Clement and of Origen as to the Body of the Lord," upon the pseudepigraphic "Vision of Isaiah," upon the doctrines of the "Monophysites," as well as by his edition of the "History of the Manichees" by Petrus Siculus, and of the "Panoply" of Euthymius Zygadenus (Tit. 23). In the medieval times he entered into the most thorough and successful examination of the sources of the history of the Cathari, of the Waldenses, of the reforming parties and tendencies before the Reformation, of the cultus, and even of many portions of political history, so far as involved in that of the Papacy. But the crown of his labors in church history is the second division of the third volume (in the German), which exhibits the doctrinal development in the period of the Reformation to the Peace of Westphalia. We there find in the most

* In the "Protestant. Kirchenzeiting für das evangelische Deutschland," Jahrg. i. 1854, No. 30.

compressed expression, in many points exhausting all the sources, rich instruction upon the mutual relations of the two great branches of the Reformation, the Swiss and the German, upon the growth of Luther's views, upon the clerical office and the shaping of the Protestant church government.

Gieseler also wrote upon ecclesiastical matters of immediate interest. During the controversy of the Prussian State with the Archbishop of Cologne, he published a work, enumerating the concessions which each party must make to re-establish permanent peace. He gave these counsels under the name of Irenaeus. He retained the same name in another pamphlet, in which he exposed the wondrous perverseness of the times, as seen in those who, in their zeal for so-called "confessional truth," insisted upon it that even their ecclesiastical opponents should be equally zealous for their own confessions; as when, for example, a Lutheran maintained that Calvinists or Catholics must hold stiffly to the distinguishing doctrines of their own communions, while he at the same time rejected them himself as soul-destroying poison. Under his own name he published his acute investigations upon the "Lehnin Prophecy," whose warning words seem still to announce to Prussia impending misfortunes in the perilous position in which that great state is now entangled.

Gieseler also took the liveliest interest in the neighboring Dutch and French Churches. In 1840 he introduced to the German public a work on the "Disturbances in the Dutch Reformed Church," whose author did not wish to be named; and in 1848, a still larger work, the "History of the Protestant Church in France, from 1787 to 1846." His last literary labor was a discriminating review of the Essays of Chastel and Schmidt, to which the French Academy of Moral Sciences awarded prizes, upon the "Influence of Christianity on the Social State of the Roman Empire," a subject which also involves the question of the restorative means offered by Christianity for the social oppressions and perils of our own times.

This question was one which he examined in the most various aspects. He was a man with a clear eye and an open heart for all who are straitened and in distress: science did not take him away from life, it was rather a means of his better preparation for the most various and useful practical service. From manifold experience Gieseler had become acquainted with the life and the relations of the laboring classes, the difficulties and deprivations with which so many are now contending, and not through their own fault; his strong and manly sense of right made him sympathize with all human needs, even those of the guilty. He first called into life in Göttingen a society for the aid of dismissed convicts; he wrote the statutes for the large funds of the "Von Hugo Stipends," which were under his direction as long as he lived; and so wisely did he administer them, that they can now be completely and permanently applied to many a beneficent object. There have probably never lived many men who have rendered more efficient aid than he, or in a more unassuming, sympathizing, and obliging way.

He possessed in a high degree the faculty of order and practical organization, and was wise in the direction of entangled affairs. He seemed born to take the lead. In the critical state of the University fifteen years ago, he showed his discretion and firmness to the full satisfaction of all who were able to understand without prejudice the actual state of the case. Gieseler was also willing to rule, but, we must add, he was without any trace of lordliness; he gave his reasons, he convinced, and if at any time outvoted, he seemed to question again for a moment his own opinion, which, however, he seldom changed, even when he did not refer to it anew. He gave his counsel only when asked; he helped and cared for many a one before they came to him.

He was a very faithful friend. He did not lightly withdraw his confidence from any one to whom he ever gave it.

He never seemed proud of the numerous honors which were bestowed upon him during his life. Far from all vanity, he had a noble, manly self-respect; he felt his own worth without being distinctly conscious of it. He stood firm for the right good cause, not troubled by the sacrifices it might cost. He took the most lively part in the struggle for the maintenance of the Union (between the Reformed and Lutheran Churches), and rejoiced with all his heart in the new light that seemed to break in upon the darkness before his departure. He felt assured that in the kingdom of the Lord new and fair days of prosperity would come, though they be delayed.

Faithful to the welfare of the Church and of his country, and ministering with love to the necessities of others, he was also visited with many a care in his own house. After the death of his first wife in the year 1831, which soon followed his transference to Göttingen, he found compensation for a loss he ever deplored, in his second marriage with a relative of the deceased, Amelia Villaret, whom he chose as his companion and the guardian of his children. This marriage, too, was unusually fruitful in children. Care for their education was added to the necessity of providing for his other sons and daughters, already grown up. But to the last day of his life he had constant experience of the truth of Him who has said to his house, My eyes shall be open upon it both night and day.

On his dying bed he saw all his sons and daughters gathered around him, with the exception of two, who could not come for the distance, and took his last farewell of them, comforted by that firm trust in God which was the leading trait of his character. Until that time sound in soul and body as are few, retaining a vigorous manly form of youthful freshness even to his sixty-third year, he sank only by slow degrees under the violence of the abdominal disease by which he was suddenly attacked. His vigorous body resisted long the pangs of the assault, till its powers were exhausted, and a still and peaceful decease brought to its close his active life on the eighth of July, 1854, in the earliest dawn of morning. Three days later he was interred. Both the city and the University equally felt his loss. The long funeral retinue showed that a place was vacant which another would not soon fill with equal power and honor.

The name of Gieseler will not be forgotten in the history of Göttingen, in science, or in the Church. Whoever knew him as he was, preserves his memory thankfully and faithfully, as a costly treasure among his dearest memories. He, however, separated from us, and regretted with deep sorrow in the ranks of his fellow-champions for the dear and noble freedom and unity of our Evangelical Church, still acts among us by his works and by his life, and thus, like the oldest of all the witnesses for God (Heb. xi. 4), although he is dead, he yet speaketh.

CONTENTS OF VOL. I.

INTRODUCTION.

PAGE

§ 1. Definition of the Church 13
2. Definition of Ecclesiastical History—its Departments—General History of the Christian Church 14
3. Relation of Church History to other Historical Studies 19
4. Of the Sources of Ecclesiastical History 21
5. The Inquiries peculiar to Ecclesiastical History 23
6. Arrangement of the Materials of Ecclesiastical History—Historical Representation 24
7. Value of the History of the Christian Church 25

FIRST PERIOD.

TO THE SOLE REIGN OF CONSTANTINE, BY WHICH THE ACKNOWLEDGMENT OF THE CHURCH IN THE ROMAN EMPIRE WAS SECURED, I. E. TILL 324.

Sources 27
Works 28

FIRST DIVISION.

TO THE TIME OF HADRIAN, 117.

INTRODUCTION.

ON THE CONDITION OF THE NATIONS, ESPECIALLY THEIR RELIGIOUS AND MORAL CONDITION AT THE TIME OF CHRIST'S BIRTH, AND DURING THE FIRST CENTURY.

I. Condition of the Heathen Nations, § 8 30
§ 9. Of the Religious and Moral Character of the ancient Nations generally 31
10. Religion and Morals of the Greeks 33

PAGE
§ 11. Religion and Morals of the Romans to the Time of Augustus 34
12. Religious Tolerance of the Romans 35
13. Relation of Philosophy to the popular Religion............................. 36
14. Revolution in the Mode of religious thinking under the Emperors........... 40

II. CONDITION OF THE JEWISH PEOPLE.

§ 15. In Palestine 44
16. Sentiments of the Heathen Nations toward Judaism........................ 47
17. Condition of the Jews out of Palestine.................................... 49
18. Samaritans 53
19. Relation of the Times to Christianity in its Growth......................... 57

FIRST CHAPTER.

THE LIFE OF JESUS.

§ 20. Chronological Data relative to the Life of Jesus........................... 59
21. Early History of Jesus.. 62
22. John the Baptist 63
23. Public Ministry and Doctrines of Jesus................................... 64
24. Alleged contemporary Notices of Jesus not in the New Testament........... 68

SECOND CHAPTER.

APOSTOLIC AGE TO THE DESTRUCTION OF JERUSALEM.

§ 25. Early History of the Community of Christians till the Time of Paul's Conversion.. 72
26. Paul 76
27. History of the other Apostles and their immediate Disciples................ 80
28. Reception of Christianity among Jews and Heathen........................ 83
29. Internal Development of Christianity 85
30. Constitution of Churches... 90
31. Time of the Jewish Troubles 95

THIRD CHAPTER.

AGE OF JOHN. FROM 70–117.

§ 32. Fate of the Jewish Christians in Palestine 98
33. External Fortunes of the Christians in the other Provinces of the Roman Empire.. 101
34. Arrangements of the Churches.. 104
35. Apostolic Fathers.. 108
36. Development of Doctrines during this Period 111

SECOND DIVISION.

FROM HADRIAN TO SEPTIMUS SEVERUS. FROM 117–193.

INTRODUCTION.

PAGE
§ 37. Condition of Heathenism 114
38. Fate of the Jews 115

FIRST CHAPTER.

EXTERNAL FORTUNES OF CHRISTIANITY.

§ 39. Its Diffusion 117
40. Opposition to Christianity by Writers 118
41. Popular Disposition in the Roman Empire toward Christianity 119
42. Persecutions of Christianity 125

SECOND CHAPTER.

HERETICS.

§ 43. Jewish Christians 128
44. Gnostics 129
45. (Continuation.) 1. Alexandrian Gnostics—Basilides—Valentinus—Ophites—Carpocrates 133
46. (Continuation.) 2. Syrian Gnostics—Saterninus—Bardesanes—Tatian 137
47. (Continuation.) 3. Marcion and his School 138
48. Montanists and Alogi 140

THIRD CHAPTER.

Internal History of the Catholic Church, § 49 144
§ 50. Apologies for Christianity against Heathens and Jews 145
51. Controversy with Heretics — Catholic Church — Canon of the New Testament 148
52. Development of Doctrines—Supposititious Writings 153
53. Ecclesiastical Life 159

THIRD DIVISION.

FROM SEPTIMUS SEVERUS TO THE SOLE DOMINION OF CONSTANTINE.
FROM 193-324.

INTRODUCTION.

PAGE
§ 54. Condition of Heathenism 171

FIRST CHAPTER.

EXTERNAL FORTUNES OF CHRISTIANITY.

§ 55. Disposition of the Heathen toward it 174
56. Conduct of the Emperors toward the Christians 176
57. Spread of the Church 187

SECOND CHAPTER.

HERETICS.

§ 58. Elcesaitism of the Clementines 188
59. Struggle in Rome against Montanism, and the Asiatic Mode of celebrating Easter 193
60. Monarchians 197
61. Manichaeans 203

THIRD CHAPTER.

THEOLOGY OF THE CATHOLIC CHURCH.

I. In the East.
§ 62. Alexandrian School 208
63. (Continuation.) View of the Alexandrian Theology, particularly that of Origen 211
64. (Continuation.) Adherents and Opponents of Origen 220
65. Other distinguished Teachers of the Oriental Church 223
II. In the West, § 66 225

FOURTH CHAPTER.

PAGE

ECCLESIASTICAL LIFE, § 67 231

§ 68. History of the Hierarchy 234

69. (Continuation.) Hierarchy in the separate Churches 240

70. Public Worship 244

71. Ecclesiastical Discipline 248

72. (Continuation.) Controversies respecting the Objects of Ecclesiastical Discipline. Felicissimus—Novatian—Baptism of Heretics—Meletius—Donatus 253

73. Asceticism 258

74. Moral Character of Christianity in this Period 263

SECOND PERIOD.

FROM CONSTANTINE TO THE BEGINNING OF THE IMAGE-CONTROVERSY. FROM A.D. 324–726.

FIRST DIVISION.

TO THE COUNCIL OF CHALCEDON. A.D. 324–451.

Sources 268

FIRST CHAPTER.

STRUGGLE OF CHRISTIANITY WITH PAGANISM.

§ 75. The Advantages conferred on Christianity by Constantine and his Sons 271

76. Julian the Apostate 278

77. General Toleration till the Year 381 281

78. Suppression of Paganism by Theodosius 282

79. Complete Suppression of Paganism in the East—its Struggles in the West, after Theodosius 285

SECOND CHAPTER.

HISTORY OF THEOLOGY.

§ 80. Introduction 292

I. PERIOD OF THE ARIAN CONTROVERSY.

§ 81. Beginning of the Arian Controversy to the Synod of Nice (A.D. 325) 294

PAGE

§ 82. Resistance of the Eusebians to the Nicene Council till the second Synod at Sirmium (A.D. 357) 298
83. Divisions among the Eusebians till the Suppression of Arianism (A.D. 381) . 302
84. History of the Theological Sciences during the Arian Controversy 314

II. Period of the Origenistic and Pelagian Controversies.

§ 85. Origenistic Controversy 323
86. Controversies with Heretics in the West 326
87. Pelagian Controversy 330

III. Controversies respecting the Person of Christ.

§ 88. Nestorian Controversy 343
89. Eutychian Controversy 355
90. On the Theological Authority of Oecumenical Councils 359

THIRD CHAPTER.

HISTORY OF THE HIERARCHY.

§ 91. Growing Importance of the Clergy 361
92. Dependence of the Hierarchy on the State 363
93. Origin of Patriarchs, especially in the East 371
94. History of the Roman Patriarchs and of the higher Hierarchy in the West. 377

FOURTH CHAPTER.

HISTORY OF MONACHISM.

§ 95. Origin and History of Monachism in the East 397
96. Monachism in the West 408
97. Relation of the Monks to the Clergy 412

FIFTH CHAPTER.

History of Public Worship, § 98 415
§ 99. New Objects of Worship 416
100. Places and Times of Public Worship 429
101. Rites and Ceremonies of Worship 432

SIXTH CHAPTER.

HISTORY OF MORALS.

§ 102. History of Christian Ethics 439
103. Morals of the Clergy 441
104. Moral Influence of the Church on the People 445
105. Influence of the Church on Legislation 453

SEVENTH CHAPTER.

PAGE
ATTEMPTS AT REFORMATION, § 106 455

EIGHTH CHAPTER.

SPREAD OF CHRISTIANITY.

§ 107. In the East 458
108. In the West 460

SECOND DIVISION.

FROM THE COUNCIL OF CHALCEDON TO THE BEGINNING OF THE MONOTHELITIC CONTROVERSIES, AND THE TIME OF MUHAMMED, A.D. 451–622.

Sources 463

FIRST CHAPTER.

ENTIRE SUPPRESSION OF PAGANISM IN THE ROMAN EMPIRE, § 109 .. 464

SECOND CHAPTER.

HISTORY OF THEOLOGY.

§ 110. Monophysite Controversies 466
111. Controversies under Justinian I. 475
112. Development of Monophysite Churches 481
113. Controversy between Augustinism and Semipelagianism 483
114. History of the Theological Sciences 486

THIRD CHAPTER.

HISTORY OF THE HIERARCHY.

§ 115. Privileges of the Clergy 492
116. Dependence of the Hierarchy on the State 494
117. History of the Patriarchs 495

FOURTH CHAPTER.

HISTORY OF MONACHISM, § 118 506
§ 119. Benedictines 507
120. Relation of the Monks to the Clergy 510

FIFTH CHAPTER.

PAGE
HISTORY OF PUBLIC WORSHIP, § 121 512

SIXTH CHAPTER.

SPREAD OF CHRISTIANITY, AND ITS CONDITION WITHOUT THE ROMAN EMPIRE.

I. IN ASIA AND AFRICA, § 122 517
II. AMONG THE GERMAN NATIONS, § 123 519
§ 124. Hierarchy in the German Empire 521
125. Moral Influences of Christianity among the German Nations 525
III. OLD BRITISH CHURCH, § 126 529

THIRD DIVISION.

FROM THE BEGINNING OF THE MONOTHELITIC CONTROVERSY, AND FROM THE TIME OF MUHAMMED TO THE BEGINNING OF THE CONTROVERSY CONCERNING THE WORSHIP OF IMAGES. FROM 622–726.

FIRST CHAPTER.

RESTRAINING OF THE CHURCH IN THE EAST, § 127 534

SECOND CHAPTER.

HISTORY OF THE GREEK CHURCH.

§ 128. Monothelitic Controversy 537
129. Concilium Quinisextum 541
130. Fortunes of Monothelitism 543

THIRD CHAPTER.

HISTORY OF THE WESTERN CHURCH.

§ 131. Ecclesiastical State of Italy 545
132. Ecclesiastical State of France and Spain 548
133. Ecclesiastical Condition of the British Islands 552
134. Spread of Christianity in Germany 557

Additions to the Literature and Notes, by the Editor 559

PREFATORY NOTICE.

Dr. Gieseler's Compendium of Ecclesiastical History is marked by peculiar excellencies. It occupies an important position of its own. The text is very brief and condensed, marking the results at which the learned author has arrived; while the accumulated materials in the notes enable the reader to see at once the basis on which the statements of the text rest. If the student be not convinced of the correctness of the assertions made by the historian, he can easily draw his own conclusion by the help of what is presented to him. The work is characterized by immense research, and by striking impartiality. In the latter respect, indeed, the author has been blamed by some, his spirit of impartiality preventing him from expressing a decided opinion, where it would be desirable to throw the weight of his authority into the side of truth. There is also an air of dryness diffused over the work, inseparable perhaps from its exceeding brevity, but also indicating a deficiency in vivid sketching. The excellencies, however, far outweigh any minor faults that may be supposed to belong to it. Its rigid impartiality is its chief recommendation; and the abundant references and quotations in the notes supply the want of a library such as very few have within their reach.

The work in the original consists of several volumes published at different times. The first division of the last volume, containing a portion of the history of the Reformation in different lands, appeared in 1840. In 1844 and 1845 a fourth edition of the first volume was published, one part in each year, greatly improved and enlarged. The author states, in the preface, that this volume first appeared twenty years ago, and that during the interval he has not been inattentive to the subject, but has endeavored to conform his book to the latest investigations. On comparing this edition with the third, we have observed a great improvement, and a large number of new notes.

It may be proper to apprize the reader, that an American translation of the history, down to the time of the Reformation, appeared at Philadelphia in 1836, *professedly* taken from the third edition of the original, the fourth, however, is so different from the third (if, indeed, Cunninghame's version was made from the latter), that it was deemed desirable to make a new version.

The Translator has adhered closely to the original text. His simple aim has been to give the sense of his author. He has not endeavored to make the narrative smooth or elegant, for in that case he should have been compelled to resort to paraphrase, Professor Gieseler being by no means an elegant writer. On the contrary, his style is loose, and his sentences evidently constructed without any view to effect. It must be always remembered, that the book is a *text-book*, not an extended history, like Neander's. As such, the Translator reckons it invaluable. In truth, there are only two ecclesiastical histories at the present time that deserve to be read and studied, viz. those of Neander and Gieseler, both *ex fontibus hausti*, as Bretschneider once remarked to the writer. Guerike's is one-sided; and Hase's, alas is too short. The Translator, on looking about for a text-book which he could put into the hands of his students as the substratum of lectures on ecclesiastical history, could find none so suitable to his purpose as the present; and he accordingly recommended the enterprising publishers to bring out a new version of the new edition, that students might not be obliged to apply to the American translation, the cost of which is very considerable.

It is almost superfluous to state, that the Translator does not coincide with all the sentiments of Dr. Gieseler. He has occasionally inserted in brackets a reference to books with which the German professor is probably unacquainted.

INTRODUCTION.

§ 1.

THE CHURCH.

Stäudlin über den Begriff der Kirche und Kirchengeschichte (in the Göttingen Bibliothek d. Neuesten Theolog. Literatur i. 600). C. G. Bretschneider's systemat. Entwickelung aller in der Dogmatik vorkommenden Begriffe (4te Auflage, Leipzig, 1841), S. 749. Dr. H. F. Jacobson, über die Individualität des Wortes u. Begriffes Kirche (in his Kirchenrechtlichen Versuchen, i. 58).

The Christian Church[1] (ἡ ἐκκλησία τοῦ Χριστοῦ, Matt. xvi. 18, ἡ ἐκκλησία τοῦ Θεοῦ, 1 Cor. x. 32, Gal. i. 13) is a religious-moral society, connected together by a common faith in Christ, and which seeks to represent in its united life *the kingdom of God* announced by Christ (τὴν βασιλείαν τοῦ Θεοῦ, τοῦ Χριστοῦ, τοῦ οὐρανοῦ). This kingdom it hopes to see at one time realized, and strives to prepare itself for becoming worthy of having a part in it.[2] The church bears the same relation to the kingdom

[1] The German word Kirche, which was originally applied to the building alone, is most probably derived from the Greek, τὸ κυριακόν. Walafrid Strabo (about 840), De rebus ecclesiasticis, c. 7. Quomodo theotisce domus Dei dicatur (in Melch. Hittorp. de Divinis Cathol. Eccles. officiis varii vetust. Patrum libri. Colon. 1568, fol. p. 395): Ab ipsis autem Graecis Kyrch a Kyrios—et alia multa accepimus.—Sicut domus Dei Basilica, i. e. Regia a Rege, sic etiam Kyrica, i. e. Dominica a Domino nuncupatur.—Si autem quaeritur, qua occasione ad nos vestigia haec graecitatis advenerint, dicendum,—praecipue a Gothis, qui et Getae, cum eo tempore, quo ad fidem Christi, licet non recto itinere, perducti sunt, in Graecorum provinciis commorantes, nostrum, i. e. theotiscum sermonem habuerint. It appears from Ulphilas, that Greek appellations of Christian things were generally adopted by the Goths (see Zahn's Ulphilas, Th. 2, S. 69, ff.; also aikklesjon, ἐκκλησία, Phil. iii. 6. in the fragments published by Maius). The Greek origin of the word is favored not only by its occurrence in all German dialects (Swedish Kyrka, Danish Kyrke, &c.), but also in the dialects of the Slavonian nations converted by the Greeks (Bohemian cyrkew, Polish cerkiew, Russian zerkow). Other derivations of the word are Kieren (Kiesen), from the Gothic, Kelikn, a tower, &c. Compare Jacobson's work, p. 68, ff.

[2] The idea of the church is an individual idea, given historically, for which we can not substitute the *general* notion (viz. that of a religious society) under which it falls. See Jacobson, p. 116. Ullmann in the Studien und Kritiken, 1835, iii. 607.

of God as the Israelitish *church* (קְהַל יְהוָה, Numb. xx. 4) had to *the ideal theocracy* expected by it. And as the divine kingdom of Christ is the purified and spiritual antitype of the theocracy, so is the Christian church the antitype of the Jewish. Differences relating to the objects of Christian faith and ecclesiastical life early separated the church into various distinct societies, each of which commonly assumed to itself exclusively the name of the "true church of Christ," and branded the others with the titles *heresy* and *schism* (haeresis, schisma).

While the old unreformed church associations are continually prejudiced by this *particularism*, Protestants, on the contrary, acknowledge every ecclesiastical society which holds Christian truth in greater or less purity and clearness, to be a preparatory institution for the kingdom of God, and as such belonging to *the universal Christian church*, whose true essence is *the invisible church*, the entire number of all true believers throughout the world.

§ 2.

DEFINITION OF ECCLESIASTICAL HISTORY—ITS PARTS—GENERAL HISTORY OF THE CHURCH.

Casp. Royko Einleit. in die christl. Religions- und Kirchengeschichte. Aufl. 2. Prag. 1791. 8.—Ch. W. Flügge Einleit. in das Studium u. in die Literatur der Religions- u. Kirchengeschichte, besonders der christlichen. Göttingen. 1801. 8.

The object of ecclesiastical history is to give a *pragmatic view* of all the changes and developments through which the Christian church has passed, and the influences which it has exerted on other human relations, and thus to lay the foundation for an *ethical* and *teleological* estimate of it. As time consists of moments, so is history made up of circumstances connected together as cause and effect. Every condition of the church rests on a two-fold relation. To its *internal* relations belongs, first of all, that *religious faith* which forms its bond of union, both in its scientific development and in its life in the members; next the character of *the public religious exercises;* and thirdly, *the form of government.* To the *external* relations of the church belong *its diffusion* and its *relation to other associations*, particularly to the state. Though these several relations are not independent of one another, but are developed by constant mutual action, they admit of separate historical developments. We have, therefore,

I. A history of the church's external relations (*external church history*), viz. :—

1. History of its spread and limitation.[1]
2. History of its relation to the state.[2]

II. A history of its internal relations (*internal history of the church*), viz. :—

1. History of the teaching of the church.

(*a*.) As an object of science.

History of doctrines (Dogmengeschichte).[3]

History of ethics.[4]

[1] Jo. Al. Fabricii salutaris lux Evangelii toti orbi exoriens, s. notitia propagatorum christ. sacrorum. Hamburgi. 1731. 4to. P. Ch. Gratianus Versuch einer Geschichte über den Ursprung und die Fortpflanzung des Christenthums in Europa. Tübingen. 1766, 73. 2 Th. 8vo. The same author's Geschichte der Pflanzung des Christenthums in den aus den Trümmern des röm. Kaiserthums entstandenen Staaten Europens. Tübingen. 1778, 9. 2 Th. 8vo. Ch. G. Blumhardt Versuch einer allgemeinen Missionsgeschichte. Basel. 1828, ff. 3 Th. 8vo.

[2] Petri de Marca Dissertationum de concordia sacerdotii et imperii s. de libertatibus ecclesiae gallicanae, libb. viii. ed. Steph. Baluzius. Paris. 1663. fol. cum observationibus ecclesiasticis J. H. Boehmeri. Lips. 1708. fol. G. J. Planck's Geschichte der christlich-kirchlichen Gesellschaftsverfassung. Hannover. 1803–1809. 5 Bde. 8vo. The following work is written from a Catholic standpoint: Geschichtlich. Darstellung des Verhältnisses zwischen Kirche und Staat von Casp. Riffel. Theil. 1 (to Justinian 1st). Mainz. 1836. 8vo.

[3] Dion Petavii Dogmata Theologica. Paris. 1644–50. 4 Theile. 4to. cum praefat. et notis Theophili Alethini (Jo. Clerici). Amst. 1700. 6 Theile. fol. W. Münscher's Handbuch der Christlichen Dogmengeschichte. Marburg. 1797–1809. 4 Thle. 8vo, incomplete. The same author's Lehrbuch d. christl. Dogmengeschichte, 3te Auflage, mit Belegen aus den Quellenschriften, Ergänzungen d. Literatur, hist. Noten u. Fortsetzungen versehen von Dr. D. v. Cölln und Dr. Ch. G. Neudecker, 3 Bde. Cassel. 1832–38. Dogmengeschichte von Dr. J. G. V. Engelhardt. 2 Theile. Neustadt a. d. Aisch. 1839. Lehrbuch d. Dogmengeschichte von Dr. K. R. Hagenbach. 2 Thle. in 3 Bden. Leipzig. 1840, 1841. Other text books by Chr. D. Beck (Commentarii historici decretorum rel. christ. Lips. 1801). J. Chr. W. Augusti (3te Ausg. Leipzig, 1820). L. F. O. Baumgarten-Crusius. 2 Abth. Jena. 1832. (The same author's Compendium d. Dogmengesch. Leipz. 1840.) F. K. Meier. Giessen. 1840.

[4] Stäudlin's Geschichte der Sittenlehre Jesu. 4 Bde. Göttingen 1799–1823 (reicht bis 1299). The same author's Gesch. d. christl. Moral seit dem Wiederaufleben d. Wissenschaften. Göttingen. 1808. W. M. L. de Wette christliche Sittenlehre, 2ter Theil: Allgemeine Geschichte der christlichen Sittenlehre, in 2 Hälften. Berlin 1819–21. 8. Stäudlin's Monographieen: Gesch. d. Vorstellungen v. der Sittlichkeit des Schauspiels. Gött. 1823. Gesch. d. Vorstell. u. Lehren vom Selbstmorde. Ebend. 1824. v. Eide. Ebend. 1824. v. Gebete. Ebend. 1824. v. Gewissen. Halle. 1824. v. d. Ehe. Gött. 1826. v. d. Freundschaft. Hannover. 1826. 8.

History of the theological sciences.[5]

(*b*.) As living and working in men.

History of religious and moral life.[6]

2. History of ecclesiastical worship.[7]

3. History of the internal constitution of the church.[8]

A description of *the worship*, *ecclesiastical usages*, and *constitution* of the ancient church, is included in the somewhat vague appellation, *ecclesiastical antiquities*, or *archaeology*,[9] although these departments do not embrace merely one point of time, but a longer or shorter period, and ought, therefore, to belong to history.

The materials of ecclesiastical history are also divided by a reference to particular *countries*, and to separate *ecclesiastical societies*,[10] whose special developments are presented in *special*

5 Ch. W. Flügge's Geschichte der theol. Wissenschaften. Halle. 1796–98. 3 Thle. 8 (as far as the Reformation). K. F. Stäudlin's Gesch. der theol. Wissenschaften seit der Verbreitung der alten Literatur. Göttingen. 1810–11. 2 Thle. 8.

6 The history of religious and moral life among Christians is difficult, and has been neglected down to the latest times. Formerly there appeared only one-sided representations of the life of the first Christians, for example, by W. Cave, Gottfr. Arnold, Peter Zorn. The history of morals is interwoven with it in Stäudlin's history of the moral teaching of Christ. (Geschichte der Sittenlehre Jesu; see note 4.) For the history of Christian life see Neander's Denkwürdigkeiten aus der Geschichte des Christenthums und des christlichen Lebens. Berlin. 1823, ff. 3 vols. [A third edition of the first volume has been lately published.]

7 Edm. Martene De antiquis Ecclesiae Ritibus. 3te sehr verm. Aufl. Antverp. 1736–38. 4 Thle. fol. C. Shöne Geschichtsforschungen über die kirchl. Gebräuche u. Einrichtungen der Christen. Berlin. 1819, ff. [Only three volumes are yet published.]

8 L. Thomassini Vetus et Nova Ecclesiae Disciplina circa beneficia et beneficiarios. Lucae. 1728. 3 Thle. fol. Planck's Gesch. der Christl. kirchl. Gesellschaftsverfassung (see above, note 2).

9 Origines Ecclesiasticae, or the Antiquities of the Christian Church, by Joseph Bingham. A new edition, 8 vols. 8vo. London. 1839, ff. Jos. Binghami Origines sive Antiquitates Ecclesiasticae ex. angl. lat. redditae a J. H. Grischovio. Halae. 1724–38. 11 vol. 4. J. C. W. Augusti's Denkwürdigkeiten aus d. Christl. Archäologie. Leipz. 1817, ff. 12 Bde. The same author's Handbuch d. Christl. Archäologie. Ebend. 1836, ff. 3 Bde. F. H. Rheinwald's Kirchl. Archäologie. Berlin. 1830. Böhmer's Christl. Kirchl. Alterthumswissenschaft. Breslau. 1836. 2 Bde. From Catholic authors we have F. Th. Mamachii Originum et Antiquitatum Christianorum, libb. xx. There have only appeared libb. iv. Romae. 1749–55. 4. J. L. Selvaggii Antiquitatum Christianarum Institutiones libb. iii. in 6 partibus. Neapoli. 1772–74. 8. Alex. Aur. Pelliccia de Christ. Ecclesiae primae, mediae et novissimae aetatis politia libb. vi. Neapoli. 1777. 3 Bde. 8. ed. nova, cura J. J. Ritterii et Braunii. 2 T. Colon. 1829. 38. 8. A German translation by A. J. Binterim: Die Vorzüglichsten Denkwürdigkeiten der Christ-Kathol. Kirche, mit bes. Rücksichtnahme auf d. Disciplin d. Kath. K. in Deutschland. Mainz. 1825, ff. 7 Thle. in 17 Bden. Locherer Lehrb. d. Christl. Archäologie. Frankf. 1832.

10 The history of parties separated from the catholic Church has been confined with too much one-sidedness merely to their controversies with the catholic Church. C. W. F. Walch's Vollständige Historie der Ketzereien, Spaltungen u. Religionsstreitigkeiten bis

histories. But yet in the progress of development, the separate ecclesiastical relations, and also the national and separate ecclesiastical societies of particular lands, are constantly acting upon each other in a greater or less degree; so that no special history, or description of individual ecclesiastical relations, can be wholly separated from the rest of the history. It is the object of *the general history of the Christian church*[11] to exhibit the general steps in its progress, so that its relation to the ideal of the church,

auf die Reformation. Leipzig. 1762. 11 Thle. 8 (reaching as far as the image-controversy). [Lardner's History of the Heretics. Burton's Inquiry into the Heresies of the Apostolic Age, being the Bampton Lecture for 1829.]

[11] Works on the general history of the Christian Church.

I.—BY PROTESTANT WRITERS.

Ecclesiastica historia—congesta per aliquot studiosos et pios viros in urbe Magdeburga. Basil. 1559–74. 13 Bde. fol. (embraces thirteen centuries), usually called Centuriae Magdeburgenses. The new edition by Semler (Norimb. 1757, ff. 6 voll. 4) is incomplete.

J. H. Hottingeri Hist. Ecclesiastica Novi Testamenti. Hanov. et Tiguri. 1655–67. 9 Thle. 8, to the end of the sixteenth century.

J. L. Mosheim Institutionum Historiae Ecclesiasticae Antiquae et Recentioris libb. iv Helmst. 1755. 4 (Mosheim's Vollständige Kirchengeschichte, frei übersetzt u. mit. Zusatzen von J. A. Cp. v. Einem. Leipzig. 1769–78. 9 Thle. 8. Von J. R. Schlegel. Heilbr. u. Rothenb. 1770–96. 7 Bde. 8). [Translated into English by Maclaine, with notes, and frequently reprinted. Also by James Murdock, D.D., 3 vols. 8vo, fifth edition, 1854.]

J. S. Semler Historiae Eccles. selecta capita cum epitome canonum, excerptis dogmaticis et tabulis chronologicis. Halae. 1773–78. 3 Bde. 8, to the end of the fifteenth century.

H. Venema Institutiones Hist. Ecclesiae Vet. et Novi Testam. Lugd. Batav. 1777–83. 7 Thle., to the end of the sixteenth century.

J. Matth. Schröckh's Christl. Kirchengeschichte bis zur Reformation. Leipzig. 1768–1803. 35 Thle. 8. The same author's Kirchengesch. seit der Reformat. Ebend. 1804–10. 10 Thle. 8 (ninth and tenth parts by H. G. Tzschirner).

H. P. C. Henke's Allgemeine Gesch. der Christl. Kirche, fortgesetzt von J. S. Vater. Braunschweig. 1788–1820. 8 Thle. 8, of the first and second parts, the fifth edition, 1818-20; of the third and fourth, the fourth edition, 1806. The history since the Reformation (parts 3–8) is comprised in a third volume by Vater, 1823.

J. E. Ch. Schmidt's Handbuch der Christlichen Kirchengeschichte. Giessen. 1801–20. 6 Thle. (Th. 1–4, 2te Aufl. 1825–27), continued by F. W. Rettberg. Th. 7, 1834, reaches to 1305.

A. Neander's Allgem. Geschichte der Christl. Religion u. Kirche. Hamb. 1825, ff. 8, bis Bd. 5. Abth. 1, in 9 Thlen. geht bis 1300 (new edition, of Bd. 1, Abth. 1, in 2 Bden. 1842 u. 43). [Two volumes, embracing the first three centuries, have been translated from the first edition, by Henry John Rose.]

H. E. F. Guerike's Handb. der Allgem. Kirchengesch. 2 Bde. Halle. 1833 (8te Aufl. 1854).

J. G. V. Engelhardt's Handbuch der Kirchengesch. 4 Bde. Erlangen. 1833, 34.

A. F. Gfrörer's Allgem. Kirchengesch. für die Deutsche Nation. 4 Bde. (Stuttgart. 1841—5.)

Manuals by J. M. Schröckh (Hist. Relig. et Eccles. Christ. 1777. ed. 7, cura Ph. Marheinecke. Berol. 1828). L. T. Spittler (Gött. 1782. 5te Aufl. bes. v. G. J. Planck. 1812). J. E. Chr. Schmidt (Giessen. 1800. 3te Aufl. 1826). W. Münscher (Marburg. 1804. 2te Aufl v. L. Wachler. 1815. 3te Aufl. v. M. J. H. Beckhaus. 1826). K. F. Stäudlin (Hann. 1806

the kingdom of God, may be perceived. Accordingly, such historical data alone as refer to this general progress, are important in its view; while those data which have only a more limited significance, are left to special histories.

5te Aufl. v. Holzhausen. 1833). J. T. L. Danz (2 Thle. Jena. 1818–26). K. Hase (Leipz. 1834. 7te Aufl. 1854). P. Hofstede de Groot. Groningae. 1835. H. J. Royaards fasc. 2. Traj. ad Rh. 1840.

J. S. Vater's Synchronist. Tafeln der Kirchengesch. Halle. 1803. 4te Aufl. 1825. fol.

[English works are, Priestley's General History of the Christian Church to the present time, 6 vols. 8vo. London. 1780–1803. Milner's Church History, continued by J. Scott. Jones's History of the Christian Church. Waddington's History, originally published in the Library of Useful Knowledge; to which was afterward added, a History of the Reformation, in 3 vols. See also Campbell's Lectures on Ecclesiastical History.]

II. BY CATHOLIC WRITERS.

Caes. Baronii Annales Ecclesiastici. Romæ. 1588–1607. 12 Bde. fol. reaches to 1198; the edition of Mogunt. 1601, was improved by the author himself, and has, consequently, been made the basis of succeeding editions. Among the continuators of Baronius, has been most valued Odoricus Raynaldus Ann. Eccles. Tom. xiii.-xxi. Rom. 1646–77. (Tom. xxi. was suppressed by Romish censorship till 1689. Of Tom. xiii.-xx. a new and improved edition was published by the author at Colon. 1693, ss.), reaches to 1565. This was continued by Jac. de Laderchio. Ann. Eccl. T. xxii.-xxiv. Rom. 1728–37, embracing the years 1566–71.

Other continuations of Baronius are those of Abr. Bzovii. Rom. 1616. Tomi viii. to 1564 (improved edition. Colon. 1621, ss.), and that of Henr. Spondani. Paris. 1640–41. Tomi ii. to 1640. Critiques: Is. Casauboni Exercitationes XVI. ad Card. Baronii prolegom. Londini. 1614. fol. continued by Sam. Basnagius: Exercitationes—in quibus Card. Baronii Annales ab anno Christi XXXV., in quo Casaubonus desiit, expenduntur. Ultraj. 1692, also 1717. 4. Anton. Pagi critica historico-chronologica in annales Baronii ed. Franc. Pagi. Antverp, properly Geneva, 1705, also 1727. T. iv. fol.

A great edition of Baronii Annales, Raynaldi continuatio, Pagi critica, and of other smaller writings, by Dom. Ge. and Dom. Jo. Mansi. Lucæ. 1738–59. 38 Bde. fol.

Natalis Alexandri Hist. Eccles. Vet. et Novi Testamenti. Paris. 1699. 8 Bde. fol. (reaches to the end of the 16th century). Claude Fleury Histoire Ecclesiastique. Paris. 1691–1720. 20 Bde. 4 (reaches to 1414), continued by Jean Claude Fabre. Paris. 1726–40. 16 Bde. 4. Casp. Sacharelli Historia Ecclesiastica. Rom. 1772–95. 25 voll. 4. Fr. L. Graf v. Stolberg: Geschichte der Religion Jesu. Hamburg. 1806–19. 15 Bde. 8, continued by F. v. Kerz. Mainz. 1825, ff. Th. 16–38, down to the 12th century. Th. Katerkamp's Kirchengeschichte. Münster. 1819–34. 5 Bde. to 1153. J. N. Locherer's Gesch. d. Christl. Rel. u. Kirche. 9. Thle. Ravensburg. 1824, ff. to 1073. J. N. Hortig's Handbuch d. Christl. Kirchengesch. beendigt von J. J. J. Döllinger. 2 Bde. Landshut. 1826–28. A new working up of the materials: Döllinger's Gesch. d. Christl. Kirche. Bde. 1 in 2 Abtheil. Landshut. 1833, 35, partly to 680. J. J. Ritter's Handb. der Kirchengesch. Elberfield. 1826, ff. 3 Bde. to 1792 (Bd. 1 u. 2, 5te Aufl. Bonn. 1854). J. O. Ritter v. Rauscher Gesch. der Christlichen Kirche. Salzburg. 1829. 2 Bde. to 313. Jac. Ruttenstock Instit. Hist. Eccl. N. T. 3 T. Viennæ. 1832, ss. to 1517. J. Annegarn Gesch. d. Christl. Kirche. Münster. 1842, f. 3 Thle. to 1841.

Manuals by Matthias Dannenmayr (Institutt. h. e. N. T. Viennæ. 1788, ed. 2, 1806. 2 voll.). Fr. Xav. Gmeiner (Epitome h. e. N. T. 2 voll. ed. 2. Grätz. 1803). Ant. Michl. (Christl. K. G. 2 Bde. München. 1807, 11. 2te Aufl. 1811, 19.) Döllinger. Landshut. 1836, ff. (Bd. 1 u. Bd. 2. Abthl. 1, partly to 1517). Joh. Alzog (5te Aufl. Mainz. 1854).

§ 3.

RELATION OF CHURCH HISTORY TO OTHER HISTORICAL STUDIES.

Ecclesiastical history forms a part of *the general history of culture*[1] and *of religion*,[2] and requires attention to other departments of study, that we may judge rightly of the importance of Christianity in relation to general culture, and of its contests with other religions. It is scientifically co-ordinate with *political history*,[3] *the history of philosophy*,[4] and *the history of literature*,[5] with which it stands in so close relationship, that, to be fully understood, it can as little dispense with their aid as they can dispense with it. Besides, it requires, as other histor-

[1] J. G. Herder's Ideen zur Philosophie der Geschichte d. Menschheit. Riga u. Leipzig. 1784–91. 4 Thle. 8. J. G. Gruber's Gesch. des Menschl. Geschlechts a. d. Gesichtspunkte der Humanität. Leipzig. 1806, 7. 2 Bde. 8.

[2] Bernh. Picard Cérémonies et Coutumes Religieuses de tous les peuples du monde. Amsterd. 1723–53. 9 vols. fol. F. H. St. Delaunaye Histoire générale et particulière des Religions et du Culte de tous les peuples du monde. Paris. 1791. 2 T. 4. Ch. Meiners Allg. Krit. Geschichte der Religionen. Hannover. 1806, 7. 2 Bde. 8. F. Mayer Gesch. aller Religionen, als Mythologisches Taschenbuch. Weimar. 1811. 8.

[3] Universal History, 60 vols. 8vo. London. 1747–63. Translated into German by Baumgarten and Semler, and continued by a society of learned men in Germany and England (A. L. Schloezer, L. A. Gebhardi, E. Tozen, J. G. Meusel, J. F. Le Bret, F. Rühs, and others). 1771–1810. A collection of explanatory writings and additions to the Universal History was published at Halle, 1747–65, in 6 Theile 4to.

History of the European States, published by A. H. L. Heeren and F. A. Ukert. Hamburg. 1829, ff. Up to the present time have appeared—History of the Germans, by J. C. Pfister, 5 vols.; of the Austrian empire, by J. Count Mailath, 5 vols.; of the Prussian empire, by G. A. H. Stenzel, 5 vols.; Saxony, by C. W. Boettiger, 2 vols.; Portugal, by H. Schaefer, 5 vols.; Spain, by F. W. Lembke, 1 vol.; France, by E. Al. Schmidt, 4 vols.; France in the time of the Revolution, by W. Wachsmuth. 4 vols.; Italy, by H. Leo, 5 vols.; England, by J. M. Lappenberg, 2 vols.; the Netherlands, by Van Kampen, 2 vols.; Denmark, by F. C. Dahlmann, 3 vols.; Sweden, by E. G. Geijer, 3 vols.; Poland, by R. Röpell, 2 vol.; Russia, by Ph. Strahl, 2 vols.; the Osmans, by Zinkeisen, 1 vol. C. F. Schlosser's Weltgeschichte in zusammenhängender Erzählung, 4 volumes are already published in seven parts (down to the year 1409). Frankf. on the Maine, 1815–41. 8vo.

[4] Jac. Bruckeri Historia Critica Philosophiae. Lips. 1741–67. 6 Bde. 4. D. Tiedemanns's Geist der Speculativen Philosophie. Marb. 1791–97. 6 Bde. 8. J. G. Buhle's Lehrbuch der Gesch. der Philosophie. Gött. 1796–1804. 8 Thle. 8. The same author's Gesch. der neuern Philosophie seit der Epoche d. Wiederherstellung d. Wissensch. Ebend. 1800–5. 6 Bde. 8. W. G. Tennemann's Gesch. d. Philosophie. Leipzig. 1798–1820. 11 Bde. 8. H. Ritter's Gesch. der Philosophie. (Th. 5 u. 12. Gesch. der Christl. Philosophie.) Hamburg. 2te Aufl. 1837—1854.

[5] L. Wachler's Allgem. Gesch. der Literatur. 3te Umarbeitung. Frankf. a. M. 1833. 4 Thle. gr. 8.

ical studies do, *historical geography*,[6] *chronology*,[7] *philology*,[8] *diplomatics*,[9] *numismatics*, *heraldry*, and derives *special assistance from ecclesiastical geography and statistics*.[10]

[6] For this the following are useful:—Chr. Kruse's Atlas zur Gesch. aller Europ. Länder u. Staaten von ihrer ersten Bevölkerung an bis auf die neuesten Zeiten. 6te Ausg. Halle. 1841. Hfte. fol. K. v. Spruner's Historisch-Geographischer Handatlas. Gotha. 1837, ff. bis jetzt 6 Lieferungen in 47 Charten.

[7] The general works on chronology: J. Ch. Gatterer's Abrisz der Chronologie. Göttingen. 1777. 8. L'Art de vérifier les Dates des Faits Historiques, &c., par un religieux Bénédictin. Paris. 1750. 3 Thle. 4. In the latest edition it appeared par M. Viton de Saint-Alais in two parts; L'Art, &c. avant l'ère Chrétienne, 5 Tomes; L'Art, &c. depuis la Naissance de notre Seigneur, 18 Tomes. Paris. 1818 u. 19. 8. Dr. L. Ideler's Handbuch der mathemat. u. technischen Chronologie. 2 Bde. Berlin. 1825, 26. The same author's Lehrbuch der Chronologie. Ebend. 1831. Dr. Ed. Brinckmeier's prakt. Handbuch der Histor. Chronologie. Leipzig. 1843.

In addition to the well-known chronological distinctions ab urbe condita, according to the consuls, emperors, &c., the following eras are important in church history. Aera contractionum or Seleucidarum, beginning B.C. 312, 1st October, formerly the most common in the east, and to this day the ecclesiastical era of the Syrian Christians. Aera Hispanica begins 716 A.U.C., 38 B.C., abolished in Spain in the fourteenth century, in Portugal not until 1415. Aera Diocletiana or aera Martyrum, begins 29th August, A.D. 284, used in the Christian Roman empire, and still current among the Copts. Cyclus indictionum, a fifteen years' cycle constantly recurring, which first began on the 1st September, 312, but in the middle ages assumed the usual commencement of the year. Aera Constantinopolitana reckons after the creation of the world, the 1st September, 5508 B.C., since the council of Trulla (692), in civil use among the Greeks, among the Russians abolished in 1700. Besides the different commencements of the year must be noticed in the reckoning of time. Comp. Ideler's Handbuch ii. 325, ff.

[8] For the later Greek and Latin generally: C. du Fresne Glossarium ad Scriptores mediae et infimae Graecitatis. Lugd. 1688. 2 Tom. fol. C. du Fresne Glossar. ad Scriptores mediae et infimae Latinitatis. Edit. nova operâ et stud. Monachorum ord. S. Bened. Paris. 1733–36. 6 voll. fol. P. Carpentier Glossar. novum ad Scriptores med. aevi cum Latinos tum Gallicos. Paris. 1766. 4 voll. fol. Glossar. manuale ad Scriptores mediae et infimae Latinitatis, (by J. C. Adelung.) Hal. 1772–84. 6 voll. 8. Here also belong all glossaries for the dialects of the middle ages. As every department of life and science has its peculiar ideas and expressions, so in like manner the Christian church. For this ecclesiastical and theological terminology, which can not, indeed, fitly lay the foundation of an ecclesiastical philology as a peculiar study, comp. J. C. Suiceri Thesaurus Ecclesiasticus e patribus Graecis. Second edition. Amsterd. 1728. 2 vols. fol. C. L. Baueri Glossarium Theodoreteum, appended to Schulz's edition of Theodoret (Halle. 1774), and Index latinitatis Tertullianeae, by Schütz and Windorf, annexed to Semler's edition of Tertullian (Halle. 1776).

[9] General works on Diplomatics: J. Mabillon De Re Diplomatica, ed. 2. Paris. 1709. Supplem. 1704. Nouveau Traité de Diplomatique par deux relig. Bénédictins de la Congr. de St. Maur. (Toustain et Tassin.) Paris. 1750–65. 6 voll. 4. Gatterer's Abriss der Diplomatik. Gött. 1798. 8. K. T. G. Schönemann's Vollständiges System der Allgemeinen Diplomatik. Hamb. 1801. 2 Bde. 8.

[10] Caroli a S. Paulo Geographia Sacra s. notitia antiqua dioeceseon omnium veteris ecclesiae, cur. J. Clerico. Amstel. 1703. fol. Fr. Spanhemii Geograph. Sacra et Eccles. (Opp. T. i. Lugd. Bat. 1701.) Bingham Origg. Eccl. lib. ix. For later times: K. F Stäudlin's Kirchl. Geographie u. Statistik. Tübingen. 1804. 2 Thle. 8. Kirchl. Statistik von Dr. Jul. Wiggers. 2 Bde. Hamburg u. Gotha. 1842.

Atlas Antiquus Sacer, ecclesiasticus et profanus, collectus ex tabulis geographicis Nic.

§ 4.

OF THE SOURCES OF ECCLESIASTICAL HISTORY.

The sources of ecclesiastical history, like those of every other history, may be traced back to *private testimony*, *original documents*, and *monuments*. To the first belong not only *the records of ecclesiastical events which are original to us*,[1] and *biographies* of remarkable persons in the history of Christianity, particularly of hierarchs[2] and saints,[3] but also other *works of Christian writers*, especially *the theological*,[4] and even *many*

Sansonis. Tabulas emendavit J. Clericus. Amstel. 1705. fol. Atlas Sacer s. Ecclesiasticus descriptus a J. E. Th. Wiltsch. Gotha. 1843. fol.

1 Literary History of Ecclesiastical History, see C. Sagittarii Introductio in Historiam Ecclesiasticam. Jenae. 1718. Tom. i. 4, with the supplements in Tom. ii. (curante J. A. Schmidio, 1718, p. 1–706.) Ch. W. F. Walch's Grundsätze der zur Kirchenhistorie des N. T. nöthigen Vorbereitungslehren u. Bücherkenntniss. Gött. 1773. 8. Schröckh's Kirchengesch. Bd. 1. S. 141, ff. C. F. Stäudlin's Geschichte u. Literatur der Kirchengesch. herausgeg. v. J. T. Hemsen. Hannover. 1827. 8. Comp. the works about to be quoted in Note 4 below.

2 Especially of the popes. The oldest collection of the biographies of them is Anastasii Bibliothecarii (abbot in Rome about 870) Liber Pontificalis. This, together with the following collections, has been inserted in Muratorii Rerum Ital. Scriptores, T. iii.

3 Existing in great numbers, but only to be used with great caution. Acta Sanctorum, quotquot toto orbe coluntur. Antverp. 1643–1794. 53 vols. fol. A work of the Antwerp Jesuits—Jo. Bolland (he began it; hence the publishers are called Bollandists), God. Henschenius, Dan. Papebrochius, &c., arranged according to the days of the month. The 53d volume contains the 6th of October. The apparatus collected for the work, which was long unknown, to which alone about 700 MSS. belong, came to Brussels from the abbey Tongerloo, in the Bibliothèque de Bourgogne. Since 1839 the Jesuits have been working upon the continuation in Tongerloo at the expense of the Belgian government. De Prosecutione Operis Bollandiani, quod Acta Sanctorum inscribitur. Namur. 1838. 8. Mémoire sur les Bollandistes par M. Gachard, in the Messager des Sciences et des arts de la Belgique. T. iii. (Gand. 1835), p. 200. On the history of the Bollandists, see what is written in the Bonn. Zeitschrift für Philos. u. kath. Theol. Heft. 17. S. 245, ff. Heft. 20. S. 235, ff.

4 Literary collections relating to the fathers : Nouvelle Bibliothèque des Auteurs Ecclésiastiques, par L. Ellies du Pin. Paris. 1686–1714. gr. 8, with the continuations : Bibliothèque des Auteurs séparés de la Communion de l'Eglise Romaine, du 16 et 17 siècle par Ell. du Pin. Paris, 1718–19. 2 vols., and the Bibliothèque des Aut. Eccles. du 18 siècle, par Claude Pierre Goujet. Paris. 1736–37. 3 vols. gr. 8. Comp. Remarques sur la Biblioth. de M. du Pin par Matthieu Petitdidier. Paris. 1691, ss. 3 Tom. 8, and Critique de la Biblioth. de M. du Pin, par Rich. Simon. Paris. 1730. 4 Tom. 8.

Histoire des Auteurs Sacrés et Ecclésiastiques, par R. Ceillier. Paris. 1729, ff. 24 Thle 4 (reaching to the thirteenth century). W. Cave, Scriptorum Ecclesiasticorum Historia Literaria. Oxon. 1740. Basil. 1741. 2 voll. fol. (to the Reformation). Casp. Oudini Commentarius de Scriptoribus Ecclesiast. Antiquis. Lips. 1722. 3 voll. fol. (to the year 1460). J. A. Möhler's Patrologie, herausgegeben v. Reithmayer. Bd. 1. Regensburg,

writings proceeding from persons not Christians, who came in contact with Christians.

Among the *original documents* the following must be particularly examined: *the laws of different states*, as far as they have exerted an influence on the Christian church, or have themselves arisen under the influences of the church itself; *the acts and ordinances of ecclesiastical councils*;[5] *the official writings of the heads of churches, especially of the popes*;[6] *the rules of monastic orders*;[7] *confessions of faith, liturgies, &c.*[8] *Monuments* are *ecclesiastical buildings, monuments of the dead*,

1840. J. Chr. F. Bähr die christl. römische Theologie. Carlsruhe. 1837, and his Gesch. de römischen Literatur im karolingischen Zeitalter, 1840 (a second and third supplementary volume, to his History of Roman Literature).

J. A. Fabricii Bibliotheca Ecclesiastica. Hamb. 1718. fol. Ejusd. Biblioth. Latina mediae et infimae Aetatis. Hamb. 1734–46. 6 vols. 8 (enlarged by Mansi. Patav. 1754. 3 vols. 4), also Fabricii Biblioth. Graeca (Hamb. 1705, ss. voll. xiv. 4, ed. nova variorum curis emendatior curante G. Ch. Harless. Hamb. 1790–1809. vol. xii. 4, incomplete), and Biblioth. Latina (ed. 4. Hamb. 1722. 3 Tomi. 8. auct. ed. J. A. Ernesti. Lips. 1773, 74. 3 Tom. 8), contain accounts of ecclesiastical authors. A Supplement to the last work is presented in C. T. G. Schoenemanni Biblioth. Hist. Literaria Patrum Latin. a Tertulliano usque ad Gregor. M. Tomi ii. Lips. 1792, 94. 8.

Patres ecclesiae are, in the opinion of Catholics, the orthodox ecclesiastical writers as far as the thirteenth century (these, however, are not of normal authority, like the Doctores Ecclesiae, Ambrose, Augustine, Jerome, Gregory the Great, Thomas Aquinas, and Bonaventura). Protestants usually restrict the appellation to the first six centuries, as the purer period of the church. The works of the fathers not included in separate collections are found in the large collections, such as: Magna Bibliotheca vett. Patrum. Paris. 1654. 17 Tomi. fol. Maxima Bibliotheca vett. Patrum. Lugdun. 1677. 27 Tomi. fol. Andr. Gallandii Biblioth. vett. Patrum. Venetiis. 1765, ss. 14 Tomi. fol.

5 Chr. W. F. Walch Entwurf einer Vollständigen Geschichte der Kirchenversammlungen. Leipzig. 1759. 8. Sagittarianae Introductionis in Histor. Eccl. Tom. ii. curante J. A. Schmidio (Jenae. 1718), p. 707.

Collections of the proceedings of general councils: Conciliorum omnium collectio Regia. Paris. 1644. 37 vols. fol. Sacrosancta Concilia—stud. Ph. Labbei et Gab. Cossarti. Paris. 1672. 18 vols. fol. (with a supplementary volume by Baluzius. Paris. 1683). Conciliorum collectio Regia maxima stud. J. Harduini. Paris. 1715. 12 vols. fol. Sacrosancta Concilia —curante Nicol. Coleti. Venet. 1728, ss. 23 vols. fol. (with the supplementum, by J. Dom. Mansi. Lucae. 1748. 6 vols. fol.) Sacrorum Conciliorum nova et amplissima collectio. Cur. J. D. Mansi. Florent. et Venet. 1759, ss. 31 vols. fol., extending to 1509.

6 Bullarium Romanum. Luxemb. 1727. 19 vols. fol. Bullarium amplissima collectio op. Car. Coquelines, from the seventh volume onward, with the title, Bullarium Romanum s. novissima collectio Apostolicarum Constitutionum. Romae. 1739, ss. 14 Tomi in 28 Partt. fol., with the continuation, Bullarium Magnum Romanum Summorum Pontificum Clementis XIII. et XIV., Pii VI. et VII., Leonis XII., et Pii VIII. Romae. 1833, ss. 89 fasc. fol.

7 Lucae Holstenii Codex Regularum Monasticarum. (Rom. 1661. 3 voll. 4), auctus a Mar. Brockie. Aug. Vind. 1759. 6 voll. fol.

8 J. A. Assemani Codex Liturgicus Ecclesiae Universae. Rom. 1749. 13 voll. 4. L. A. Muratorii Liturgia Romana vetus. Venet. 1748. 2 voll. fol. Eus. Renaudot Liturgiarum Orientalium Collectio. Paris. 1716. 2 voll. 4.

stone inscriptions, and other works which art has produced in the service of the church.

§ 5.

USE OF THE SOURCES.

The object of investigations in church history is to reproduce, directly from the original sources, the facts belonging to the sphere of the church, in its external and internal life, in their manifestations as well as their grounds, and also in their causal connections. For this purpose the historian requires not only a penetrating and unbiased *interpretation* of the sources which present themselves, but also *historical criticism*, to enable him to judge of the *genuineness*, *integrity*, and *credibility* of the sources, not only in general, but in each particular case.[1] This criticism must be the more watchful, since distortions of historical truth frequently appear in the province of ecclesiastical history, produced by credulity and ignorance, by prejudice and partisanship, by the desire to adapt it to certain ends, and even by deceit. In those cases in which the sources afford nothing at all, or what is false, relative either to single facts or their causal connection, the inquirer must have recourse to *historical conjectures*, whose probability may border very nearly on truth, but often, perhaps, may rise very little above other possibilities. In forming such historical conjectures, he must be guided by a careful consideration of existing relations, of the character of the period and persons, by analogy, and even by the false data of the sources. The ecclesiastical historian must renounce party interest, as well as prejudices arising from the peculiarities of his time. On the other hand, he can not penetrate into the in ternal character of the phenomena of church history without a Christian religious spirit, because one can not generally comprehend aright any strange spiritual phenomenon without reproducing it in himself. It is only investigation of this nature that can discover where the Christian spirit is entirely wanting,

[1] Ernesti de fide historica recte aestimanda (in his Opusculis Philologico-Criticis, ed. 2. Lugd. Bat. 1776. p. 64, ss.) Griesbachii Diss. de fide hist. ex ipsa rerum quae narrantur natura judicanda (in his Opusc. Acad. ed Gabler. Jenae. 1824. vol. i. p. 167, ss.)

where it is used merely as a mask, and what other spirit has taken its place. Wherever it exists it will not be mistaken, although it should manifest itself in such ways as are foreign to the spirit of our own times.

§ 6.

ARRANGEMENT OF THE MATERIALS OF ECCLESIASTICAL HISTORY.—HISTORIC REPRESENTATION.

The old methods of arranging the materials of ecclesiastical history according to years, or of dividing them into centuries, have been rightly abandoned. The division into *periods*, by means of *epochs*, has been generally adopted, although great difference prevails in fixing these periods. We assume four periods: *the first*, To the time of Constantine, the first development of the church under external oppression; *the second*, Till the beginning of the image controversies, the development of Christianity as the prevailing religion of the state; *the third*, Till the Reformation, the development of the Papacy prevailing over the state; *the fourth*, The development of Protestantism.[1] The contents of each period may be arranged either chronologically or according to a general scheme taken from the different relations of the church. (§ 2.) Both methods used exclusively have their advantages and disadvantages. In the chronological arrangement things similar are often too widely separated, and the lines of development are torn asunder. In the other arrangement, when the periods are large, the mutual influence which the development of separate ecclesiastical relations has on each other at different times is obscured, and the survey of the entire condition of one particular time is rendered difficult. We must therefore endeavor, as far as possible, to unite the advantages of both methods, and to avoid their disadvantages. Although every period has its definite ecclesiastical character, yet this

[1] The following have been used as epochs by different ecclesiastical historians, for the purpose of limiting their periods:—The destruction of Jerusalem, 70; Commencement of Constantine's reign, 306, or the Council of Nice, 325; Gregory the Great, 604, or Muhammed, 622; Boniface, the Apostle of the Germans, 715, or the beginning of the image controversy, 725; Charlemagne, 800; Gregory VII., 1073; Removal of the papal residence to Avignon, 1305; Reformation 1517: Founding of the University of Halle, 1693.

character undergoes many modifications during the lapse of the whole period. Hence the division of periods into small sections of time is justified. The materials of these smaller sections are best arranged chronologically, as long as the church in its first beginnings has not yet formed its internal relations; afterward they may be disposed according to a division taken from these internal relations. In every section of time there prevails the development of one or of several ecclesiastical relations, so that the development of all the other relations of the church is thereby controlled. It is therefore suitable to dispose the history of the different relations in the church in every minor period, according to their relative importance, and their influence on the whole.

The mode of writing ecclesiastical history must be worthy of the subject. The phenomena make a continual demand upon our moral and religious feelings. Where moral greatness is manifested, they excite our admiration; where they bear witness to errors, they excite our compassion; where they evince immoral designs and motives, they stir up our indignation; but they never furnish a fit subject for ridicule.

§ 7.

VALUE OF ECCLESIASTICAL HISTORY.[1]

Church history has a universal interest for men, as it forms the most important part of the religious history of humanity. For the Christian it has a peculiar interest, since it discloses to him the later transformations of Christianity, with their causes and effects, and guides him to a safe judgment with regard to what is original and essential in it. On this account, it is indispensable to the Christian theologian who desires to acquire a scientific knowledge of Christianity.[2] It is also of importance

[1] J. J. Griesbach De Historiae Ecclesiasticae nostri seculi usibus sapienter accommodatae utilitate. Jen. 1776. 4 (in his Opusc. Acad. ed. Gabler. vol. i. p. 318). Respecting the influence of the study of church history on the culture of the mind, and the life, see Dree Vorlesungen von Dr. F. A. Koethe. Leipzig. 1810. 4.

[2] J. A. Ernesti De Theologiae historicae et dogmaticae conjungendae necessitate et modo universo (in his Opuscc. Theoll. p. 565). Niemeyer's Abhandl. über die hohe Wichtigkeit u. die zweckmässige Methode eines fortgesetzten Studiums der Religions- u. Kirchengeschichte für prakt. Religionslehrer (prefixed to Fuhrmann's Handwörterbuch der Christl. Religions- und Kirchengesch. Bd. 1. Halle. 1826. 8).

to the scholar, because of its essential connection with the history of learning, philosophy, morals, and the arts. It is obvious, that a fundamental acquaintance with ecclesiastical law, and the legislative enactments of Christian states, is impossible without it.[3]

[3] J. H. Boehmer Diss. de necessitate et utilitate Stud. Hist. Ecclesiast. in juris ecclesiastici prudentia (in the Observatt. sell. ad Pet. de Marca libr. de concordia sacerdotii et imperii. Francof. 1708. fol.)

FIRST PERIOD.

TO THE SOLE REIGN OF CONSTANTINE, BY WHICH THE RECOGNITION OF THE CHURCH WAS SECURED IN THE ROMAN EMPIRE.
FROM THE YEAR 1–324.

SOURCES.

I. The Scriptures of the New Testament.

II. Ecclesiastical historians. Fragments of Hegesippus (about 170 A.D.) ὑπομνήματα τῶν ἐκκλησιαστικῶν πράξεων (with a commentary in *Routh Reliq. Sacr.*, vol. i. p. 187, ss.).

Eusebius (bishop of Caesarea † about 340) ἐκκλησιαστικὴ ἱστορία in ten books,[1] ed. H. Valesius. Par. 1659. fol. (an incorrect reprint, Mogunt. 1672), ed. ii. 1677 (reprinted Amsterdam, 1695. fol.). Convenient smaller editions by F. A. Stroth. Hal. 1779. Tom. i. 8. E. Zimmermann. PP. II. Francof. ad M. 1822. 8., cum Valesii commentario aliorumque observationibus edidit, suas animadversiones, excursus et indices adjecit F. A. Heinichen. T. iii. Lips. 1827, 28. 8. ad codd. Mss. rec. Ed. Burton. Oxon. 1838. T. ii. 8. The Latin version of Eusebius's Church History, by Rufinus (about A.D. 400), in nine books (the tenth was not translated by him), with its continuation in two books (*Rufini hist. eccl. libb.* xi.), which was very common in the fifteenth and sixteenth centuries, but of which there is no edition since that of Petr. Thom. Cacciari. Romae. 1740–41. Tomi ii. 4to.,

[1] With regard to the credibility of Eusebius, which has been too much depreciated by Scaliger, Baronius, Masch (Abh. v. d. Grundsprache d. Evangel. Matth. Halle. 1755. S. 191), Gibbon and Semler (Novae Observatt., p. 17, and often), see J. Moeller de fide Eusebii Caesar. Hafnae. 1813. 8. (reprinted in Stäudlin's and Tzchirner's Archiv. f. Kirchengesch. Bd. 3. St. 1). J. T. L. Danz de Eusebio Caes. ejusque fide hist. recte aestimanda. P. i. Jenae. 1815. 8. Ch. A. Kestner Comm. de Eusebii auctoritate et fide diplomatica. Goetting. 1817. 4. H. Reuterdahl de Fontibus Hist. Eccles. Eusebianae. Londini Gothor. 1826. 8. Bern. Rienstra de Fontibus, ex quibus hist. eccl. opus hausit Eusebius Pamph. et de ratione, qua iis usus est. Traj. ad Rhen. 1833. 8. Dr. C. R. Jachmann's Remarks on the Church History of Eusebius, in Illgen's Zeitschrift für die histor. Theol. ix. ii. 10.

which was founded on critical principles, is frequently a work upon Eusebius rather than a translation. Still it is not unimportant in the criticism of the original (comp. E. J. Kimmelii de Rufino Eusebii interprete, libb. ii. Gerae. 1838. 8). With the history of Eusebius are connected, even in the editions of Valesius and Zimmermann, his εἰς τὸν βίον τοῦ μακαρίου Κωνσταντίνου τοῦ βασιλέως λόγοι δ',[2] ed. F. A. Heinichen. Lips. 1830. 8.

III. All the Christian writers of this period. The fragments of those whose works have been lost are collected in J. E. Grabe spicilegium SS. Pàtrum ut et haereticorum saeculi i. ii. et iii. Tom. i. s. Saec. i. ed. 2. Oxon. 1700. Saec. ii. t. i. 1700. 8. (A new edition in 3 Tom. Oxon. 1714.) M. Jos. Routh reliquiae sacrae, sive auctorum fere jam perditorum secundi tertiique saeculi fragmenta, quae supersunt Oxonii. 1814–18. 4 voll. 8. vol. 5, 1848.

IV. Acts of the martyrs. Theod. Ruinart acta primorum Martyrum sincera et selecta. Edit. 2. Amstelod. 1713. fol. (ed. Bern. Galura. August. Vindel. 1802, 3. P. iii. 8). [Fox's Book of Martyrs.]

V. Certain passages of writers not Christian, namely, Josephus, Suetonius, Tacitus, Plinius the younger, Scriptores historiae Augustae, Dio Cassius, and others, are collected in Nath. Lardner's Collection of the Jewish and Heathen Testimonies of the Christ. Relig. Lond. 1764–67. 4 vols. 4.

WORKS.

Sebastien le Nain de Tillemont Mémoires pour servir à l'Histoire Ecclésiastique des six premiers siècles, justifiés par les citations des auteurs originaux. Paris. 1693–1712. 16 Thle. 4; reaches to 513. [Tillemont's Ecclesiastical Memoirs of the first six centuries, translated from the French.

[2] The doubts that were raised against the genuineness of these books by Jac. Gothofredus (Diss. ad Philostorg. Hist. Eccl., lib. vii. c. 3) and Chr. Sandius (de Scriptt. Eccl., p. 92) have been refuted by J. A. Bosii, exercit. posterior de Pontificatu max. Imp. Rom. C. 8. § 5. M. Hankius de Byzantin. rerum scriptoribus graecis. § 174. Balth. Bebelii Antiquitt. Eccl. t. i. p. 213. In regard to the historical character of this work even Socrates (hist eccl. i. c. 1) designates Eusebius as τῶν ἐπαίνων τοῦ βασιλέως καὶ τῆς πανηγυρικῆς ὑψηγορίας τῶν λόγων μᾶλλον ὡς ἐν ἐγκωμίῳ φροντίσας, ἢ περὶ τοῦ ἀκριβῶς περιλαβεῖν τὰ γενόμενα.

2 vols. fol. Lond. 1733.] Joh. Laur. Moshemii commentarii de Rebus Christianorum ante Constantinum Magn. Helmst. 1753. 4. [Vol. i. translated by Vidal; vol. ii. by Dr. Murdock, New York, 1852.] Joh. Sal. Semleri commentarius hist. de antiquo Christ. statu. Halae. 1771, 72. T. 2. 8. Ejusd. Observatt. novae, quibus Historia Christianorum studiosius illustratur usque ad Const. M. Halae. 1784. 8.

On the spread and persecution of Christianity:

[Gibbon's Decline and Fall of the Roman Empire.] Ed. Gibbon die Ausbreit. des Christenthums aus natürl. Ursachen, übers. v. A. F. v. Walterstern. Hamb. 1788. 8. J. B. Lüderwald Ausbreitung der Christl. Religion. Helmst. 1788. 8. J. Andreä Entwickel. der natürl. Ursachen, welche die schnelle Ausbreit. des Christenth. beförderten. Helmst. 1792. 8.

Chr. Kortholt de Persecutionibus Eccles. primaevae. Kiloni. 1689. 4. C. W. F. Walch de Persecutionibus Christian. non solum politicis sed etiam religiosis. (Nov. Comment. Soc. Goett. T. ii.) J. G. F. Papst de ipsorum Christianorum culpa in vexationibus motis a Romanis. 3 Progr. Erlangen. 1789, 90. 4. C. D. A. Martini Persecutiones Christianorum sub Impp. Romanis, causae earum et effectus. Rostochii. 1802, 1803. Comm. iii.

FIRST DIVISION.

TO THE TIME OF HADRIAN. FROM 1-117.

Joh. Laur. Moshemii Institutiones Historiae Christianae Majores, Saec. 1. Helmst. 1739. 4. J. S. Semler's neue Versuche die Kirchenhistor. des ersten Jahrhunderts aufzuklären, Leipzig. 1788. 8. (J. A. Starck's Geschichte der christlichen Kirche des ersten Jahrhunderts Berlin und Leipzig. 1779-80. 3 Bde. 8.

INTRODUCTION.

OF THE CONDITION OF THE WORLD, ESPECIALLY ITS RELIGIOUS AND MORAL STATE, AT THE TIME OF CHRIST'S BIRTH, AND DURING THE FIRST CENTURY.

I.

CONDITION OF THE HEATHEN NATIONS.

C. I. Nitzsch üb. den Religionsbegriff der Alten, in the theol. Studien und Kritiken, Bd. 1 S. 527, ff. 725, ff. F. V. Reinhard's Versuch über den Plan, den der Stifter der christl. Religion zum Besten der Menschheit entwarf. Wittenberg. 1781. 4te Aufl. 1798. 8. [Translated into English, and published at Andover, 1831, 12mo.] A. Tholuck über das Wesen und den sittlichen Einfluss des Heidenthums, besonders unter den Griechen u. Römern, mit Hinsicht auf das Christenthum (in A. Neander's Denkwürdigkeiten aus der Geschichte des Christenthums und des christlichen Lebens. Bd. 1. Berlin. 1823. [Translated in the American Biblical Repository for 1832, by Professor Emerson.] Neander's Kirchengesch. I. I. 7, ff. Especially: Der Fall des Heidenthums von Dr. H. G. Tzschirner, herausg. v. M. C. W. Niedner. Bd. 1. (Leipzig. 1829) S. 13, ff. [Leland's Advantage and Necessity of the Christian Revelation.]

§ 8.

The Roman empire, in the first century, extended not only over the whole civilized world, but almost over the known world. Beyond it little was known besides the Germanic tribes in the north, and the Parthians in the east. In the western half of that great empire, the language and customs of the Romans had become prevalent; but in the eastern, Greek cultivation asserted the superiority it had obtained since Alexander's conquests, and under the emperors penetrated more and more even into Rome.[1]

[1] Cicero pro Archia, c. 10: Graeca leguntur in omnibus fere gentibus, Latina suis finibus, exiguis sane, continentur. How the Greek had incorporated itself with the language of conversation among cultivated Romans, may be seen in Cicero's Letters to Atticus, and

It is obvious, how much the union of so many nations under one government, and the general diffusion of the Greek language, must have favored the heralds of Christianity.

§ 9.

OF THE RELIGIOUS AND MORAL CHARACTER OF THE ANCIENT NATIONS IN GENERAL.

Polytheism can not, from its very nature, be favorable to morality. Its deities can only be finite beings, and resembling man, because it separates the divinity into many parts. Every nation gives expression to its character, its virtues, and its vices, in the deities it worships; and therefore the divinity, so disfigured, can not lead men to a higher moral elevation. The heathen stand only in an external relation to their gods; and their entire religion is consequently nothing more than an external worship, which leaves untouched not only theological speculation, as long as it does not attack existing forms, but also moral sentiment. Human deities will be worshiped, propitiated, and reconciled, in the way of men; and for this purpose moral elevation is not needed so much as a kind of prudence. They can not inspire respect and love, but fear only. Their worship is nothing more than a barter, in which man expects mercy, protection, and greater gifts, in exchange for demonstrations of respect, and offerings. This general character of polytheism is found in all heathen religions at the time of Christ. A mythology partly immoral, sanctified many vices by the example of the gods. The worship of several deities was attended with immoral deeds. Thus, the worship of *Bel* in Babylon, of *Amun* in Thebes, of *Aphrodite* in Cyprus, Corinth, and many other places, elevated lewdness to the position of a religious service;[1] and the

in Augustus's letters in Suetonius, &c., Claudius c. 4. Comp. Ovidii ars amandi ii. 121, Dial. de oratoribus c. 29. Juvenal. Satyr. iii. 58. xv. 110, vi. 185, ss. speaking of the Roman ladies:—

> Nam quid rancidius, quam quod se non putat ulla
> Formosam, nisi quae de Tusca Graecula facta est?
> Hoc sermone pavent, hoc iram, gaudia, curas,
> Hoc cuncta effundunt animi secreta.

[1] Clemens Alex. Cohort. ad Gentes, cap. 2. Arnobii Disputatt. adv. Gentes, lib. v Tholuck, as above. S. 171, ff.

worship of other deities excited, at least, sensuality in a high degree.[2] In like manner, human sacrifices were customary, in several places, as yearly expiations; but every where, on occasion of extraordinary threatening dangers, for the purpose of propitiating the enraged deities.[3] Religious motives existed only to promote the exercise of the duties belonging to citizens;[4] and whatever of a higher nature appears in the case of individual Greeks and Romans was owing, not to the religion of the people, but to their better moral nature.[5] In general, the feeling of man's dignity and rights was wanting, while in place of it was found nothing but a partial national conceit, joined to a profound contempt for every thing foreign, and propped up by religion, since every nation had but the expression of its own nationality in its deities. Hence the horrible debasement of man as a slave.[6] When the national pride was humbled by subjugation and oppression, the people readily lost along with it every noble feeling of self-respect, and sank into slavish abjectness. Woman lost among the Greeks the respect due to her, because of her political insignificance, since *public* virtue was deemed of the highest importance with that people.[7] Among eastern nations, polygamy had the same effect to a much greater extent.

[2] Tholuck, as above, S. 143, ff.

[3] Tholuck, S. 221, ff. Octavian caused 300 men to be slaughtered on the altar of Caesar. (Sueton. Oct. c. 15, Dio Cassius, 48, 14). Sextus Pompeius ordered that persons should be thrown into the sea as a sacrifice to Neptune (Dio Cassius, 48, 48). According to Porphyry, de abstin. carnis, ii. c. 56, human sacrifices ceased to be offered in different nations at the time of Hadrian; but even in his day (about 280 A.D.) a human victim was yearly offered to Jupiter Latialis in Rome. Lactantius (about 300) Divin. Institt. i. c. 21: Latialis Jupiter etiam nunc sanguine colitur humano. Comp. Lipsius de Amphith. c. 4. (Opp. iii. 1003), van Dale de Oraculis Gentilium, p. 442. Lamb. Bos, Heidenreich, Pott ad 1 Cor. iv. 13.

[4] Cicero de Legibus, ii. c. 7: Utiles esse autem opiniones has, quis neget, cum intelligat, quam multa firmentur jurejurando; quantae salutis sint foederum religiones; quam multos divini supplicii metus a scelere revocarit; quamque sancta sit societas civium inter ipsos, diis immortalibus interpositis tum judicibus, tum testibus.

[5] As Cicero, de fin. ii. c. 25, judges of Epicurus and his philosophy.

[6] Tholuck, S. 197, ff. Gladiators. As late as the time of Claudius, that emperor was obliged to forbid the exposing or putting to death sick slaves. Suetonius in Claudius, cap. 25.

[7] Tholuck, S. 203, ff.

§ 10.

RELIGION AND MORALS OF THE GREEKS.

Histoire de la civilisation morale et religieuse des Grecs par P. van Limburg Brouwer. Tom. 8. Groeningen, 1833–43. 8vo.

The Greek deities were ideal Greeks, whose sentiments and conduct were Grecian. By their will and example they exhorted to those virtues to which the Grecian character was disposed, or which were found necessary for the state and for social life. But so far were they from imaging forth a pure morality, and so little freed from the national vices of the Greeks,[1] that the mythology granted even by the Greek philosophers was able, for the most part, to influence morality only in the way of injury.[2] After the subjugation of Greece, when national honor, love of country, and patriotism had ceased to be powerful motives, we find Greece in the condition of the deepest moral degradation. Religion became with the people scarcely any thing but an enjoyment of art, wanting too often in all that partakes of a moral spirit. Hence it was unable to elevate the deteriorated nation above their external destiny. How much the cultivation of the intellect and taste was preferred to morality, even in the flourishing times of Greece, is proved by the general estimation in which clever courtesans were held; while the rest of the female sex were, for the most part, neglected, as far as

1 In opposition to Tholuck, in the work already quoted, who traces the corruption of religion and morality to Grecian art, see Fr. Jacobs über die Erziehung der Hellenen zur Sittlichkeit, in his vermischte Schriften, Th. 3. An intermediate course is taken by Dr. C. Grüneisen über das Sittliche der bildenden Kunst bei den Griechen, in Illgen's Zeitschrift f. d. hist. Theologie, iii. ii. 1. But another aspect must not be overlooked. Though it be possible that so much elevation and dignity as is represented by some was reflected in the divine forms, yet they necessarily referred the beholder to their mythology, and the impression that so much immorality could be united with such external excellence must have been highly corrupting to the morals. Cf. Augustinus de civ. Dei. iv. 31: Varro dicit etiam, antiquos Romanos plus quam annos centum et septuaginta deos sine simulacro coluisse. Quod si adhuc, inquit, mansisset, castius dii observarentur. Cujus sententiae suae testem adhibet inter caetera etiam gentem Judaeam, nec dubitat eum locum ita concludere, ut dicat, qui primi simulacra deorum populis posuerunt, eos civitatibus suis et metum dempsisse, et errorem addidisse.

2 Plato (de repub. ii.) wishes to banish the immoral mythology from his republic; Aristotle (Politic. vii. 8) proposes that the young at least should be excluded from witnessing immoral rites.

their spiritual culture was concerned.[3] The love of boys, which was so general, and inspired so many poets, shows how art ministered even to unnatural vices. *The mysteries* were far from presenting a better esoteric religion than that of the people.[4] They offered nothing but a secret mythology which attached itself to the popular religion—a secret ritual to be practiced in worshiping the gods—directions for the purification of the initiated, accompanied, it is true, by several moral precepts, but all for the purpose of making the deities peculiarly propitious to the initiated.

§ 11.

RELIGION AND MORALS OF THE ROMANS TO THE TIME OF AUGUSTUS.

Ch. D. Beck über den Einfluss der röm. Religion auf die Charakter des Volks und des Staats (prefixed to his translation of Ferguson's History of the Roman Republic, Bd. 3, Abth. 2, S. 5, ff.). Du polytheisme romain. Ouvrage posthume par Benj. Constant. Paris. 1833. Die Religion der Römer aus den Quellen dargestellt von J. A. Hartung. 2 Theile, Erlangen. 1836. 8vo.

The religion of the Romans was of a more grave and moral character, although in it the Grecian element was mixed up with the Etrurian. We find the ancient Romans distinguished not only for their political but their domestic virtues, and for a chastity rarely found in the bosom of heathenism. As long as Grecian art was unknown at Rome, so long, too, did the Grecian mythology with its poisoning influence remain unknown;[1] but after the destruction of Carthage and Corinth, the national character generally, and the Roman religion along with it, underwent by degrees a great alteration for the worse.[2] The riches which flowed into the city, the knowledge of Asiatic lux-

[3] Compare the restricting discussions of Fr. Jacobs (Beiträge zur Gesch. d. weibl. Geschlechts in Griechenland: 1. allgem. Ansicht der Ehe; 2. die hellen. Frauen; 3. von. den Hetären), Vermischte Schriften. Thl. 3. S. 157.

[4] As Warburton (the Divine Legation of Moses. Lond. 1742. Translated into German by J. Chr. Schmidt. Frankf. u. Leipz. 1751. 3 Bde.), Thl. 1. Bd. 2, and many after him assume. On the other side see especially Chr. Aug. Lobeck, Aglaophamus s. de theogiae mysticae Graecorum causis, libb. iii. t. i. Regiomontii Pruss. 1829. 8.

[1] Polyb. hist. vi. c. 54. Dionys. Halicarn. Antiquitt. Roman. ii. c. 67, 69. Hartung, i. 244. J. A. Ambrosch, Studien u. Andeutungen im Gebiete des altrömischen Bodens und Cultus. Heft i. (Breslau. 1839). S. 63.

[2] Hartung, i. 249. Ambrosch, S. 69.

uries, and the mode of instruction followed by Greek masters, led to licentiousness and excesses; while the Grecian mythology, incorporated with Grecian art, was diffused by the poets, and entirely extinguished the old Roman character with its rigid virtue.[3]

§ 12.

RELIGIOUS TOLERATION OF THE ROMANS.

It was an universal principle among the ancients, that the gods themselves had arranged the peculiar form of their worship in every country. Hence all polytheistic religions were tolerant toward each other, as long as every worship confined itself to its own people or country. This toleration was also observed by the Romans.[1] On the other hand, to introduce strange gods and modes of worship without the sanction of the state was tantamount to the introduction of a superstition prejudicial to the interests of the community.[2] When, therefore, after the extended conquests of the Romans, foreign modes of worship were more and more introduced into the city, partly lessening, by that means, attachment to the national religion, and partly promoting even immoral practices, the laws against the *sacra peregrina* were frequently renewed.[3] Religious societies of foreign

[3] Compare Terentii Eunuch. Act iii. Scen. 5, v. 35. Ovid. Tristium ii. v. 287, ss. Martialis, lib. xi. Epigr. 44. Seneca de brevit. vitae, c. 16: Quid aliud est vitia nostra incendere, quam auctores illis inscribere deos, et dare morbo, exemplo divinitatis, excusatam licentiam? Compare de vita beata, c. 26. C. Meiner's Gesch. des Verfalls der Sitten und der Staatsverfassung der Römer. Leipz. 1782. 8.

[1] Hartung, i. 231. Dr. K. Hoeck's röm. Geschichte vom Verfalle d. Republik bis zur Vollendung der Monarchie unter Constantin. (Braunschwieg. 1842, ff.) Bd. 1. Abth. 2. S. 216 u. 371.

[2] Cicero de leg. ii. c. 8: Separatim nemo habessit deos; neve novos, sed ne advenas, nisi publice adscitos, privatim colunto.

[3] Compare, in particular, the extirpation of the Bacchanalian rites in the year 185 B.C Livius xxxix. c. 8, ss., and the Senatusconsultum de tollendis Bacchanalibus, in the treatise about to be quoted of Bynkershoek. Valerius Maximus i. 3, de peregrina religione rejecta. Cf. Corn. van Bynkershoek de cultu religionis peregrinae apud veteres Romanos (in ejusd. opp. omn. ed. Ph. Vicat. Colon. Allobr. 1761. fol. Tom. i. p. 343, ss.) Chr. G. F. Walch de Romanorum in tolerandis diversis religionibus disciplina publica (in novis commentariis Soc. Reg. Scient. Goettingensis. Tom. iii. 1773). De Burigny mémoire sur le respect, que les Romains avoient pour la religion, dans lequel on examine, jusqu'à quel degré de licence la tolérance étoit portée à Rome. (Mémoires de l'Acad. des Inscript. T. 34, hist. p. 48, ss.). Hartung, i. 232.

origin could not easily hold out against such prohibitions, since, coming under the Roman idea of *collegia*,[4] they were also opposed by the laws against *collegia illicita*,[5] and since all nocturnal associations were forbidden under pain of death.[6] On the other hand, the private worship of strange gods was not so easily eradicated.

§ 13.

RELATION OF PHILOSOPHY TO THE POPULAR RELIGIONS.

As soon as philosophy was cultivated in Greece, the unity of

[4] Collegia, sodalitia, sodalitates, ἑταιρεῖαι. The Greeks and Romans were fond of such connections, which had their basis partly in relationship (comp. the Roman gentes and curiae, the Athenian φρατρίαι), partly in similarity of profession (so the collegia tibicinum, aurificum, architectorum, &c., at Rome). They had both their own sacred rites, a common fund, and secret meetings and feasts (ἔρανοι). Thus the priests of the same deities not only formed collegia of this nature (comp. sodales Augustales, Aureliani, &c.), but unions for the worship of certain deities were also reckoned collegia (for example, for the solemnization of the rites of Bacchus, see note 3). So Cato says, in Cicero de senectut., c. 13: Sodalitates me quaestore constitutae sunt sacris Idaeis Magnae Matris acceptis. So speaks Philo, in Flaccum, of the ἑταιρείαις καὶ συνόδοις in Alexandria, αἳ ἀεὶ προφάσει θυσιῶν εἱστιῶντο τοῖς πράγμασιν ἐμπαροινοῦσαι. Cf. Salmassii observatt. ad jus Rom. et Atticum, c. 3 u. 4. J. G. Stuckii antiquitatum convivialium, lib. i. c. 31. (Opp. tom. i. Lugd. Bat. et Amstel. 1695. fol. p. 173, ss.) H. E. Dirksen, histor. Bemerkungen über den Zustand der juristischen Personen nach röm. Recht, in his civilist. Abhandlungen (Berlin. 1820). Bd. 1. S. 1, ff.

[5] Besides the prohibitions in the time of the Republic, compare that of Julius Caesar (Sueton. Caesar, c. 42), Augustus (Sueton. Octavian. c. 32), &c. Compare the later jurists in the Pandects: Gajus (about 160), lib. iii. (Digest. lib. iii. tit. 4. l. 1): Neque societas, neque collegium, neque hujusmodi corpus passim omnibus habere conceditur: nam et legibus et Senatusconsultis, et Principalibus constitutionibus ea res coërcetur, &c. Particularly Dig. lib. xlvii. tit. 22, de collegiis et corporibus illicitis, Lex 1 (Marcianus, about 222): Mandatis Principalibus praecipitur Praesidibus Provinciarum, ne patiantur esse collegia sodalitia. § 1. Sed religionis causa coire non prohibentur: dum tamen per hoc non fiat contra Senatusconsultum, quo illicita collegia arcentur. Lex 2 (Ulpianus † 228): Quisquis illicitum collegium usurpaverit, ea poena tenetur, qua tenentur, qui hominibus armatis loca publica vel templa occupasse judicati sunt (consequently according to Dig. xlviii. tit. 4, l. 1, like those convicted of high treason). Lex 3 (Marcianus), § 1: In summa autem, nisi ex Senatusconsulti auctoritate, vel Caesaris, collegium, vel quodcunque tale corpus coïerit, contra Senatusconsultum, et Mandata, et Constitutiones collegium celebratur. Cf. Jac. Cujacii Observationum, lib. vii. Observ. 30. Barn. Brissonii antiquitatum ex jure civili selectarum, lib. i. c. 14.

[6] Tab. ix. Lex 6: Sei quei endo urbe coitus nocturnos agitasit, capital estod. This determination was renewed by the lex Gabinia (Leges xii. Tabularum restitutae et illustratae a J. N. Funccio. Rintelii. 1744. 4. p. 400).

God was expressed in most of the schools,[1] and morality was placed on a more becoming and a religious foundation.[2] But while philosophy could not fail of producing a high religious feeling in the narrow circle of the initiated, it occasioned a crude skepticism among the more numerous class of the half instructed. Although Plato and Aristotle directly expressed their sentiments regarding the popular religion in a reserved and cautious manner, and even conformed externally to its requirements,[3] yet their theology afforded a standard by which, when many parts of the popular faith were judged, they must necessarily vanish into nothing. *The Stoic pantheism* endeavored to preserve the current mythology by considering the deities as the fundamental powers of the universe, and explaining the myths allegorically; but it destroyed, at the same time, all religious feeling by its spirit of pride.[4] The *Epicurean philosophy*, as far as it removed all connection between the gods and the world, making the latter originate in chance, destroyed all religion and morality; and though this was not its tendency in the eyes of the founder, it was certainly the aim of his later disciples. The skepticism of *the middle and new academy* exerted no better influence, at least in the larger circles.

Soon after Greek literature had been introduced at Rome after the time of *Livius Andronicus* (about 240 B.C.), skeptical doubts manifested themselves there also.[5] Subsequently, *the*

[1] Cf. Cicero de Nat. Deorum, i. c. 10, ss. Rad. Cudworthi systema intellectuale, vertit et illustr. J. L. Moshemius. (Jenae. 1733. fol.) p. 730, ss. [Ralph Cudworth's Intellectual System of the Universe. London, folio, 1678.] Chr. Meiner's hist. doctrinae de vero Deo. Lemgov. 1780. p. ii.

[2] Stäudlin's Gesch. der Moralphilosophie, Hannover, 1822, in many passages. Limburg Brower's work already quoted in § 10.

[3] F. A. Carus hist. antiquior sententiarum Ecclesiae graecae de accommodatione Christo imprimis et Apostolis tributa, diss. Lips. 1793. 4. p. 13, ss. For the manner in which the Grecian states judged respecting every departure from the public religion, see F. W. Tittmann's Darstellung der griechisch. Staatsverfassungen. Leipzig. 1822. S. 27, ff.

[4] For example, Seneca, epist. 73.: Jupiter quo antecedit virum bonum? diutius bonus est. Sapiens nihilo se minoris aestimat, quod virtutes ejus spatio breviori clauduntur. Sapiens tam aequo animo omnia apud alios videt, contemnitque quam Jupiter: et hôc se magis suspicit, quod Jupiter: uti illis non potest, sapiens non vult. Schwabe über das Verhältniss der stoischen Moral zum Christenthum, in the Zeitschrift für Moral, by C. F. Böhme and G. Ch. Müller, Bd. 1. St. 3. S. 38, ff. G. H. Klippel comm. exhibens doctrinae Stoicorum ethicae atque christianae expositionem et comparationem. Goetting. 1823. 8.

[5] They appeared first of all in Ennius (239–168 B.C.) Cf. Cicero de Nat. Deor. i. 42;

academy, *the porch*, and *epicureanism*, finding a more general reception, from the time of the famous Athenian embassy, (Carneades, Diogenes, Critolaus, 155 B.C.), the flourishing philosophy tended not only to weaken the popular religion,[6] but to destroy the religious faith of many.[7] But although skepticism spread more and more, yet the unbelieving politicians and philosophers themselves agreed, that the native religion must be upheld with all their powers, as the support of the state, and of all the relations of life.[8] With the multitude, no philosophy could take the place of the religious motives which lay in the popular religion;[9] and of foreign religious rites the opinion was, that they destroyed national feeling, and produced an inclination to foreign customs and laws.[10] Hence, even *Scaevola* (about 100 B.C.) wished to confirm anew the religion of the state by separating it from philosophy and mythology, whence proceeded its

Euhemerum noster et interpretatus et secutus est praeter caeteros Ennius. Ab Euhemero autem mortes et sepulturae demonstrantur deorum. Besides Ennius translated Epicharmus's representation of the Pythagorean doctrine respecting God, nature, and the soul; comp. Dr. L. Krahner's Grundlinien zur Gesch. des Verfalls d. röm. Staatsreligion bis auf die Zeit des August (a school-programme). Halle. 1837. 4. S. 20, ff. Ennius's own religious views are given in Cic. de Divin. ii. c. 50 :

> Ego Deum genus esse semper dixi, et dicam caelitum :
> Sed eos non curare opinor, quid agat humanum genus.

[6] Cic. de invent. i. 29 : In eo autem, quod in opinione positum est, hujusmodi sunt probabilia :—eos, qui philosophiae dent operam, non arbitrari Deos esse. Idem pro Cluentio, c. 61. De Nat. Deor. ii. c. 2. Tuscul. Quaest. i. c. 5, 6.

[7] In Sallustius in Catilina, c. 51, Caesar says: In luctu atque miseriis mortem aerumnarum requiem, non cruciatum esse : eam cuncta mortalium mala dissolvere : ultra neque curae neque gaudio locum esse. And Cato says, in reference to Caesar's speech, c. 52 : Bene et composite C. Caesar paulo ante in hoc ordine de vita et morte disseruit; falsa, credo, existimans, quae de inferis memorantur: diverso itinere malos a bonis loca tetra, inculta, foeda atque formidolosa habere.

[8] Cicero de leg. ii. 7. See above § 9, note 4, de Divin. ii. 33 : Non sumus ii nos augures, qui avium reliquorumve signorum observatione futura dicamus. Erravit enim multis in rebus antiquitas, quas vel usu jam, vel doctrina, vel vetustate immutatas videmus. Retinetur autem et ad opinionem vulgi, et ad magnas utilitates reipublicae mos, religio, disciplina, jus augurum, collegii auctoritas.

[9] Strabo, in geograph. i. c. 2, pag. 19: *Οὐ γὰρ ὄχλον τε γυναικῶν, καὶ παντὸς χυδαίου πλήθους ἐπαγαγεῖν λόγῳ δυνατὸν φιλοσόφῳ, καὶ προσκαλέσασθαι πρὸς εὐσέβειαν, καὶ ὁσιότητα καὶ πίστιν, ἀλλὰ δεῖ καὶ διὰ δεισιδαιμονίας· τοῦτο δ' οὐκ ἄνευ μυθοποιΐας, καὶ τερατείας.*

[10] Comp. the advice of Maecenas to Augustus, according to Dio Cassius, lib. lii. : *τὸ μὲν θεῖον πάντη πάντως αὐτός τε σέβου κατὰ τὰ πάτρια, καὶ τοὺς ἄλλους τιμᾷν ἀνάγκαζε· τοὺς δὲ δὴ ξενίζοντάς τι περὶ αὐτὸ καὶ μίσει καὶ κόλαζε, μὴ μόνων τῶν θεῶν ἕνεκα, ὧν καταφρονήσας οὐδ' ἄλλου ἄν τινος προτιμήσειεν, ἀλλ' ὅτι καινά τινα δαιμόνια οἱ τοιοῦτοι ἀντεισφέροντες, πολλοὺς ἀναπείθουσιν ἀλλοτριονομεῖν· κἀκ τούτου καὶ συνωμοσίαι καὶ συστάσεις ἑταιρεῖαί τε γίγνονται, ἅπερ ἥκιστα μοναρχίᾳ συμφέρει· μήτ' οὖν ἀθέῳ τινὶ, μήτε γόητι συγχωρήσῃς εἶναι.*

corruption;[11] and *M. Terentius Varro*, abiding by that separation (about 50 B.C.), endeavored to prepare for it a new basis out of the doctrine of the Stoics.[12]

[11] Augustin. de civit. Dei, iv. 27: Relatum est in literis, doctissimum pontificem Scaevolam disputasse tria genera tradita deorum; unum a poëtis, alterum a philosophis, tertium a principibus civitatis. Primum genus nugatorium dicit esse, quod multa de diis fingantur indigna: secundum non congruere civitatibus, quod habeat aliqua supervacua, aliqua etiam quae obsit populis nosse (namely, non esse deos Herculem, Aesculapium, &c.—eorum, qui sint dii, non habere civitates vera simulacra—verum Deum nec sexum habere, nec aetatem, nec definita corporis membra). Haec pontifex nosse populos non vult, nam falsa esse non putat. Comp. Krahner, S. 45.

[12] According to Augustinus de civ. Dei vi. 2, Varro said in his Rerum Divinarum, lib. xvi., the second part of his Antiquitates: se timere, ne (dii) pereant, non incursu hostili, sed civium negligentia: de qua illos velut ruina liberari a se dicit, et in memoria bonorum per hujusmodi libros recondi atque servari. He also distinguishes (l. c. vi. 5) tria genera theologiae, namely, mythicon, quo maxime utuntur poëtae, physicon, quo philosophi, civile, quo populi. Primum, quod dixi, in eo sunt multa contra dignitatem et naturam immortalium ficta. Secundum genus est, quod demonstravi, de quo multos libros philosophi reliquerunt. In quibus est: dii qui sint, ubi, quod genus caet. (Augustine adds: Nihil in hoc genere culpavit. Removit tamen hoc genus a foro i. e. a populis: scholis vero et parietibus clausit. Illud autem primum mendacissimum atque turpissimum a civitatibus non removit). Tertium genus est, quod in urbibus cives, maxime sacerdotes, nosse atque administrare debent. In quo est, quos deos publice colere, quae sacra et sacrificia facere quemquam par sit. Prima theologia maxime accommodata est ad theatrum, secunda ad mundum, tertia ad urbem. (Plutarch also, Amator, c. 18, and de placitis philosoph. i. 6, distinguishes this threefold theology, τὸ μυθικόν, τὸ φυσικόν and τὸ πολιτικόν). Respecting the religion of the Roman state, Varro, as reported by Augustine, l. c. iv. 31, said: non se illa judicio suo sequi, quae civitatem Romanum instituisse commemorat; ut, si eam civitatem novam constitueret, ex naturae potius formula deos nominaque deorum se fuisse dedicaturum non dubitet confiteri. Sed jam quoniam in vetere populo essent accepta, ab antiquis nominum et cognominum historiam tenere ut tradita est debere se dicit, et ad eum finem illam scribere ac perscrutari, ut potius eos magis colere, quam despicere vulgus velit. L. c. vii. 6: Dicit ergo idem Varro adhuc de naturali theologia praeloquens, Deum se arbitrari esse animam mundi, quem Graeci vocant κόσμον, et hunc ipsum mundum esse Deum. Hic videtur quoquo modo confiteri unum Deum, sed ut plures etiam introducat, adjungit, mundum dividi in duas partes, caelum et terram; et caelum bifariam in aethera et aëra, terram vero in aquam et humum. Quas omnes quatuor partes animarum esse plenas, in aethere et aëre immortalium, in aqua et terra mortalium: a summo autem circuitu caeli usque ad circulum lunae aethereas animas esse astra ac stellas, eosque caelestes deos non modo intelligi esse, sed etiam videri. Inter lunae vero gyrum et nimborum ac ventorum cacumina aëreas esse animas, sed eas animo, non oculis videri, et vocari heroas, et lares, et genios. Haec est videlicet breviter in ista praelocutione proposita theologia naturalis, quae non huic tantum, sed et multis philosophis placuit. Tertullian's second book, ad Nationes, is directed against this theology of Varro. Comp. Hartung, i. 274. Krahner, S. 49.

§ 14.

REVOLUTION OF RELIGIOUS MODES OF THINKING UNDER THE EMPERORS.

C. Meiners Gesch. des Verfalls der Sitten, der Wissenchaften und Sprache der Römer in den ersten Jahrhunderten nach Christi Geburt. Wien u. Leipzig 1791. 8. S. 268, ff. P. E. Müller de hierarchia et studio vitae asceticae in sacris et mysteriis Graecorum Romanorumque latentibus. Hafn. 1803. 8. (translated in the Neuen Biblioth. der schönen Wissench. Bd. 69 u. 70). To this topic belongs the first section, viz., Origin of the—superstition—till the time of Domitian.

In the reign of the emperors the national deities, who were obliged to divide their honors with the most miserable of men,[1] sank by degrees still lower in the faith of the people.[2] The attachment to traditional customs and institutions, decaying along with liberty, could no longer afford these gods a protection. Politics and habit secured them nothing more than a lukewarm, external worship.[3] The relations of the times did not lead men away from the error that had been abandoned, toward a somewhat purer religion, but to a still grosser superstition. The cowardly weaklings,[4] who were the offspring of a luxury surpass-

1 According to Polybius, 5, the custom of honoring benefactors with sacrifices and altars appeared first among the Asiatics, the Greeks, and Syrians. Similar honors were frequently paid to proconsuls in their provinces. (Cicero ad Atticum v. 21. Sueton. Oct. c. 52. Mongault, in the Mémoires de l'Acad. des Inscr. t. i. p. 353, ss.) Caesar caused these honors to be decreed to him by the senate in Rome also. (Suet. Caes. 76). Augustus accepted in the provinces temples and colleges of priests (Tacit. Annal. i. 10, Suet. Oct. c. 52); and so did all his successors, with the single exception of Vespasian. Domitian even began his letters with: Dominus et Deus noster hoc fieri jubet (Suet. Domit. 13). J. D. Schoepflini comm. de apotheosi s. consecratione Impp. Romanorum (in ejusd. commentt. hist. et. crit. Basil. 1741. 4. p. 1, ss.).

2 Senecae Ep. 24. Juvenal. Satyr. ii. v. 149:

Esse aliquos manes, et subterranea regna
Et contum, et stygio ranas in gurgite nigras,
Atque una transire vadum tot millia cymba,
Nec pueri credunt, nisi qui nondum aere lavantur.

3 Seneca de superstitionibus, apud Augustin. de civit. Dei, vi. c. 10: Quae omnia sapiens servabit tanquam legibus jussa, non tanquam Diis grata. Omnem istam ignobilem Deorum turbam, quam longo aevo longa superstitio congessit, sic adorabimus, ut meminerimus, cultum ejus magis ad morem quam ad rem pertinere.

4 Juven. Sat. vi. 292–300 (comp. Meiners, l. c. S. 85):

Nunc patimur longae pacis mala. Saevior armis
Luxuria incubuit, victumque ulciscitur orbem.
Nullum crimen abest, facinusque libidinis, ex quo
Paupertas Romana perit: hinc fluxit ad istos
Et Sybaris colles, hinc et Rhodos et Miletos,
Atque coronatum et petulans madidumque Tarentum,
Prima peregrinos obscoena pecunia mores
Intulit, et turpi fregerunt secula luxu
Divitiae molles.

ing all bounds, must have stood open to every superstition, especially as dangers daily threatened them from those in power. Curiosity, and an inordinate longing for the secret and the awful, contributed to increase the superstition. To this must be added the decline of the earnest study of the sciences (law and juridical eloquence being almost the only studies of the time); but, above all, the excessive corruption of the age.[5] Cowardly vice sought partly to make magical rites subservient to its will,[6] while it was, in part, driven to more powerful purifications by the stings of conscience. Already had the religions of the east, by their mysterious, fantastic worship, and the asceticism of their priests, made an impression on the superstitious disposition of the Romans, so that they had been restricted and opposed by the laws. But the current of the time that set in now broke through all laws. Foreign modes of worship and priests found their way into the state with a power that could not be repressed. In addition to them, a great number of astrologers (mathematici), who pretended to be initiated into the secret sciences of the east, interpreters of dreams, and magicians, spread themselves through the empire.[7] The object of such per-

[5] Compare especially the satires of Persius and Juvenal. Seneca de Ira, ii. 8: Omnia sceleribus ac vitiis plena sunt: plus committitur, quam quod possit coërcitione sanari. Certatur ingenti quodam nequitiae certamine: major quotidie peccandi cupiditas, minor verecundia est. Expulso melioris aequiorisque respectu, quocunque visum est, libido se impingit. Nec furtiva jam scelera sunt: praeter oculos eunt: adeoque in publicum missa nequitia est, et in omnium pectoribus evaluit, ut innocentia non rara, sed nulla sit. Numquid enim singuli aut pauci rupere legem? undique, velut signo dato, ad fas nefasque miscendum coorti sunt.

—— Non hospes ab hospite tutus,
Non socer a genero. Fratrum quoque gratia rara est.
Imminet exitio vir conjugis, illa mariti.
Lurida terribiles miscent aconita novercae.
Filius ante diem patrios inquirit in annos.

(from Ovid. Metam. i. v. 144, ss.) Et quota pars ista scelerum est! &c. Comp. ejusd. Epist. 95. Pauli Epist. ad Rom. i. 21, ss. Comp. Corn. Adami de malis Romanorum ante praedicationem Evangelii moribus (in his Exercitationes exegeticae. Groening. 1712. 4, the fifth exercit.). Meiners ubi supra. Schlosser's Universalhist. Uebersicht der Gesch. der alten Welt. iii. i. 122, ff. 326, ff. Hoeck's röm. Gesch. vom Verfall der Republik bis zur Vollendung der Monarchie unter Constantin. i. ii. 301, ff.

[6] Diodorus Sic. bibl. hist. xx. c. 43, p. 755: Δεισιδαίμονες γὰρ οἱ μέλλοντες ἐγχειρεῖν ταῖς παρανόμοις καὶ μεγάλαις πράξεσι.

[7] Of foreign deities Serapis and Isis (43 B.C.) were the first who had a temple in the city. The fruits of superstition were shared with the priests of Isis, who was particularly revered by the Galli, the priests of Dea Syra, the Magi, Chaldaei (s. Genethliaci, qui de motu deque positu stellarum dicere posse, quae futura sunt, profitentur, Gellius, Noct. Att. xiv. 1, where a copious refutation of these arts may be found), Mathematici (genus hominum potentibus infidum, sperantibus fallax, quod in civitate nostra et vetabitur

sons was to turn the prevailing superstition, as much as possible, to their own advantage, and at the same time to strengthen it. The laws of the first emperors against foreign customs were of less avail, because they themselves believed in their efficacy, followed them in private, and were only afraid that they should be abused to the prejudice of their own persons.[8]

This superstition was promoted in no slight degree by philosophy making it subservient to its purpose.[9] The more boldly philosophical skepticism had attacked not only the popular religions, but also the general truths of religion, so much the more zealously did the later dogmatism endeavor to put together systems framed in part from earlier ones, and in part from the materials themselves of the popular religion. In these newly-invented systems every superstition found shelter. Under Augustus, the long-forgotten doctrines of Pythagoras were suddenly revived in the most wonderful form by *Anaxilaus*, who was soon followed by the still more adventurous *Apollonius of Tyana*.[10]

semper, et retinebitur. Tacit. Hist. i. 22), and even the vagrant Jews. Comp. Diet. Tiedemann disputat. de quaestione, quae fuerit artium magicarum origo. &c. Marburg. 1787. 4. p. 56, ss. Hoeck i. ii. 378. How much the female sex, in particular, was given to this superstition is strikingly described by Juvenal Sat. vi. 510–555. Cf. Strabo vii. c. 3, § 4: *῞Απαντὲς τῆς δεισιδαιμονίας ἀρχηγοὺς οἴονται τὰς γυναῖκας. αὗται δὲ καὶ τοὺς ἄνδρας παρακαλοῦνται πρὸς τὰς ἐπίπλεον θεραπείας τῶν θεῶν, καὶ ἑορτὰς καὶ ποτνιασμούς· σπάνιον δε εἴ τις ἀνὴρ καθ' αὑτὸν ζῶν εὑρίσκεται τοιοῦτος.* On the superstition of this period generally, see Plinii Nat. Hist. ii. c. 5: Vix prope est judicare, utrum magis conducat generi humano, quando aliis nullus est Deorum respectus, aliis pudendus. Externis famulantur sacris, ac digitis Deos gestant: monstra quoque, quae colunt, damnant et excogitant cibos, imperia dira in ipsos, ne somno quidem quieto, irrogant. Non matrimonia, non liberos, non denique quidquam aliud nisi juvantibus sacris deligunt. Alii in Capitolio fallunt, ac fulminantem pejerant Jovem: et hos juvant scelera, illos sacra sua poenis agunt.

[8] Meiners, l. c. S. 276, ff. The example of the elder Pliny shows how unbelief and superstition united in the educated class. He says, Nat. Hist. ii. c. 5: Irridendum vero, agere curam rerum humanarum illud quicquid est summum. Anne tam tristi atque multiplici ministerio non pollui credamus dubitemusve? vii. c. 56: Omnibus a suprema die eadem, quae ante primum: nec magis a morte sensus ullus aut corpori aut animae, quam ante natalem. He speaks, however, in his Second Book in a very believing tone respecting portenta, ex. gr., cap. 86: Nunquam urbs Roma tremuit, ut non futuri eventus alicujus id praenuntium esset. Comp. Tacit. Ann. vi. c. 22.

[9] Tzschirner, Fall des Heidenthums. Bd. 1. S. 127, ff.

[10] Apollonius lived from 3 B.C. till 96 A.D. Celsus does not name him among the wonder-workers (Aristeas, Abaris, &c.), whom he compares with Christ (Origen against Celsus, iii.). In the second century Lucian (in Alexander) and Apuleius (Apologia, Opp. ed. Elmenhorst, p. 331) describe him as a famous magician. In the same light did he also appear to his oldest biographer, Möragenes, who speaks besides of his influence with the philosophers (Origenes c. Cels. vi. ed. Spencer, p. 302), so that he appears to have given a philosophical basis to magic. From the beginning of the third century, when a religious eclecticism gained ground, the memory of Apollonius became prominent.

While these men endeavored to restore, out of its own sources, the Pythagorean philosophy, as if it had proceeded from the mysteries of Egyptian priests, and looked upon Platonism as an efflux of the doctrine of Pythagoras, a singular, heterogeneous philosophy of religion grew up under their hands, in which all popular religions, no less than all magic arts, found their justification. From this time onward even the Platonic school forsook the skepticism of the new academy, attaching itself to those modern Pythagoreans, though it sought to assimilate its dogmatism to other systems also, particularly the Aristotelian. The mode of life among the Pythagoreans was not attractive to many, and consequently this *new Platonism* formed the prevailing philosophy. With it, as the philosophy of superstition,[11] *Epicureanism* almost alone, as the philosophy of unbelief,[12] divided the dominion over the minds of men generally. Of the pure *Peripatetics* there was always but a small number; and though the *Stoics* could boast of so distinguished men at this time (*Seneca*, *Dio of Prusa*, *Epictetus*), yet their system of morality excited admiration, instead of exerting an influence on the life.[13] The Cynics had lowered themselves so much by

Caracalla dedicated a sanctuary to him (Dio Cassius, lxxvii. 18); Severus Alexander set him up in his collection of household gods (Aelius Lamprid. in vita Sev. Al. c. 29). Julia Mammaea, in particular, was a great admirer of him. Into her hands came the memorabilia of Damis, a companion of Apollonius, which Philostratus the elder, in his life of Apollonius (Philostratorum opera gr. et lat. ed. G. Olearius. Lips. 1709. fol.), wished to bring into a more acceptable form (vita Ap. i. 3) by using a work of Maximus of Aege. Here Apollonius appears as a wise man and a favorite of the gods, furnished with wonderful powers in working miracles, and commissioned by the gods themselves to reform the popular religions. On the other hand, the older representation of Möragenes is designated as almost useless. Dio Cassius, however, continually enumerates Apollonius among the magicians and impostors. That the work of Damis is spurious, and originated probably in the third century, may be proved not only from the absurdity of the contents, but also from anachronisms (Prideaux's Connection, Hug's Introduction to the N. T.) Cf. Mosheim de existimatione Apollonii Tyanaei (in his Commentationes et Orationes varii argumenti, ed. J. P. Miller. Hamburgi. 1751. 8. p. 347), de scriptis A. T. (l. c. p. 453), de imaginibus telesticis A. T. (l. c. p. 465). Apollonius v. Tyana u. Christus, od. d. Verhältniss d. Pythagoreismus zum Christenthum von Dr. Baur (in the Tübingen Zeitschr. f. Theol. 1832. Heft. 4, also printed separately).

[11] These Platonists also exercised the profession of astrology. So Thrasybulus, the soothsayer of Tiberius (Sueton. in Tib. c. 14. 62. Tac. Ann. vi. 20).

[12] See above note 8. Juvenal. Satyr. xiii. 86, ss.

Sunt, in fortunae qui casibus omnia ponant,
Et nullo credant mundum rectore moveri,
Natura volvente vices et lucis et anni;
Atque ideo intrepidi quaecunque altaria tangunt.

[13] Cicero, Orat. pro Murena, c. 30: arripuit—disputandi causa—magna pars. Respecting the customs of the philosophers of this time generally compare in Seneca, epist. 29,

their shamelessness that their influence on the age was of little consequence.

II.

CONDITION OF THE JEWISH PEOPLE.

SOURCES—Writings of the New Testament. Flavii Josephi (born 37 n. Chr. † about 93) Opera (Antiquitatum Judaicarum libb. xx.—de Bello Judaico libb. vii.—de Vita sua—contra Apionem libb. ii.) ed. Sigeb. Havercamp. Amstel. 1726. 2 Bde. fol. Smaller editions by Franc. Oberthür. Wirceburgi. 1782-85. 3 Thle. 8, and C. E. Richter. Lips. 1826, s. 6 voll. 8.

J. M. Jost Geschichte der Israeliten seit der Zeit der Maccabäer bis auf unsere Tage. Berlin. 1820-28. 9 Thle. 8.

§ 15.

IN PALESTINE.

After the Babylonish captivity the Jews were successively subject to the Persians, Egyptians, and Syrians, and then formed (from 167–63 B.C.) an independent state under the Maccabees, till the last of that race, *Hyrcanus*, was obliged to acknowledge the Roman sovereignty. After his death *Herod*, the Idumean (from 40–4 B.C.), ruled over the land in dependence on the Romans, and afterward divided it among his three sons, so that *Archelaus* was ethnarch of Judea, Idumea, and Samaria, while *Philip*, and *Herod Antipas*, as tetrarchs, received possession—the former, of Batanea, Ituraea, and Trachonitis—the latter of Galilaea and Peraea. After the banishment of *Archelaus* (6 A.D.), his territories became a Roman province, and were governed under the proconsul of Syria, by a procurator, (the fifth, *Pontius Pilate* from 28–37 A.D.) The tetrachy of *Philip* did not continue long after his death in the hands of the Romans, but was consigned to *Herod Agrippa* (37), who

the reason why he doubts of gaining over a wit, Marcellinus, to philosophy: Scrutabitur scholas nostras, et objiciet philosophis congiaria, amicas, gulam: ostendet mihi alium in adulterio, alium in popina, alium in aula. Hos mihi circulatores, qui philosophiam honestius neglexissent, quam vendunt, in faciem ingeret. Juvenal. Sat. ii. init.

united it to the tetrarchy (39) of the banished *Herod Antipas*, and was finally elevated by Claudius even to be king of all Palestine (41). After his death, his entire kingdom again became a Roman province, managed by procurators, (*Cuspius Fadus*, *Tiberius*, *Alexander*, *Ventidius Cumanus*, *Claudius Felix*, *Porcius Festus*, *Albinus*, *Gessius Florus*). His son, Agrippa II., afterward obtained the kingdom of Chalcis (47), which he was soon obliged to change for the tetrarchy of Philip (52); while, at the same time, the superintendence of the temple at Jerusalem was intrusted to him as a Jew. With him the race of Herod became extinct († 100 at Rome).[1]

Oppression under a foreign yoke, and especially the persecution of religion by Antiochus Epiphanes, had produced among the Jews a strict separation from all that was unjewish, inflaming their contempt and hatred for all foreign customs, and, at the same time, raising to a high degree their national feelings and attachment to the religion of their fathers. But, alas! a spiritual feeling for religion had expired with the spirit of prophecy. The priesthood, finding no longer any opposing obstacle, connected, with one-sided aim, the renovated zeal of the people with the external law, and, in particular, with the Levitical worship which was always enlarging itself, in which alone the priests, as such, had an interest. Even *the synagogues* that arose after the Babylonish captivity,[2] adapted as they were to promote a more spiritual religion, served still more to advance the legal spirit of the Levitical code. Hence, there arose at this time the most obstinate attachment—yea, a fanatical zeal for the Mosaic ceremonial, apart from any real religious feeling and moral improvement, and accompanied rather by a more general and deeper corruption of the people.[3] With this disposition, which was directed only to the external, their pride in

[1] Christ. Noldii hist. Idumea, s. de vita et gestis Herodum. Franeq. 1660. 12, also in Havercamp's edition of Josephus, t. ii. Appendix, p. 331, ff. E. Bertheau's zur Gesch. der Israeliten zwei Abhandlungen. Göttingen. 1842. S. 437.

[2] Cf. Camp. Vitringa de Synagoga vetere, libb. iii. Franeker. 1696. ed. 2, Leucopetr. 1726. 4.

[3] Comp. Josephus in several passages; for example, de B. J. v. 10, 5, he declares: *μήτε πόλιν ἄλλην τοιαῦτα πεπονθέναι, μήτε γενεὰν ἐξ αἰῶνος γεγονέναι κακίας γονιμωτέραν.* Ibid. v. 13, 6. Ibid. vii. 8, 1: *ἐγένετο γάρ πως ὁ χρόνος ἐκεῖνος παντοδαπῆς ἐν τοῖς Ἰουδαίοις πονηρίας πολυφόρος, ὡς μηδὲν κακίας ἔργον ἄπρακτον καταλιπεῖν, μηδ' εἴ τις ἐπινοίᾳ διαπλάττειν ἐθελήσειεν ἔχειν ἂν τι καινότερον ἐξευρεῖν. οὕτως ἰδίᾳ τε καὶ κοινῇ πάντες ἐνόσησαν, καὶ πρὸς ὑπερβαλεῖν ἀλλήλους ἔν τε ταῖς πρὸς τὸν θεὸν ἀσεβείαις, καὶ ταῖς εἰς τοὺς πλησίον ἀδικίαις ἐφιλονείκησαν.*

transmitted privileges, and in the peculiar favor of Jehovah, increased equally with the hope that God would soon free his favorite people from the yoke of the heathen, and under the dominion of Messiah elevate them to be the rulers of the earth. These earthly expectations and views, which the people painted to themselves in a highly sensuous degree, must have been very prejudicial to the inward religious feelings.[4] At the same time, the opinion was not rare, that it was unworthy of the people of God to obey a foreign power.[5] On the other hand, the prejudices and national pride of a people despised by the Romans, infused hatred into the minds of the procurators and other Roman officials, which was often exhibited in provocations and oppressions. Hence arose frequent rebellions against the Roman power, till at last the general insurrection under *Gessius Florus* (65) led to the devastation of the whole land, and the destruction of Jerusalem, (70). By this means the strength of the people was broken for a time, but their disposition and aims were not changed.

It remains for us to notice three sects of the Jews:[6] *the Pharisees*,[7] in whom the Judaism of that time, with the new doctrinal sentiments acquired in exile, and its own continued culture of the Levitical law, presented itself in a completed form. All the traits of the national character were presented by this sect in a still more cultivated degree, and hence it was the greatest favorite among the people. *The Sadducees*[8] en-

[4] Respecting the Judaism of this time, see De Wette's biblische Dogmatik (2te Aufl. Berlin. 1818), § 76, ff. Baumgarten-Crusius, Grundzüge der bibl. Theologie. Jena. 1828, S. 117, ff. C. H. L. Poelitz dissert. de gravissimis theologiae seriorum Judaeorum decretis. Lips. 1794. 4. The same author's pragmatische Uebersicht der Theologie der spätern Juden. Leipz. 1795. Th. 1. 8. A. F. Gfrörer's das Jahrhundert des Heils. 2 Abth. Stuttgart. 1838. On the ideas entertained of the Messiah: Bertholdt christologia Judaeorum Jesu Apostolorumque aetate. Erlang. 1811. 8. C. A. Th. Keil historia dogmatis de regno Messiae Christi et Apostolorum aetate. Lips. 1781 (in Keilii opusculis, ed. J. D. Goldhorn. Lips. 1821. Sect. i. p. 22, ss.) Bertholdt and Gfrörer have ventured to throw too much of the later Rabbinism backward into this period.

[5] Judas Galilaeus and his adherents, *μόνον ἡγεμόνα καὶ δεσπότην τὸν θεὸν ὑπειληφότες* (Jos. Ant. xviii. 1, 6). *Ἰούδας εἰς ἀπόστασιν ἐνῆγε τοὺς ἐπιχωρίους, κακίζων, εἰ φόρον τε Ῥωμαίοις τελεῖν ὑπομένουσι, καὶ μετὰ τὸν θεὸν οἴσουσι θνητοὺς δεσπότας* (de B. J. ii. 8, 1) cf. Deut. xvii. 15.

[6] Trium scriptorum illustrium (Drusii, Jos. Scaligeri, et Serarii) de tribus Judaeorum sectis syntagma, ed Jac. Triglandius. Delphis. 1703. 2 voll. 4. De Wette's hebräisch-jüdische Archäologie, § 274, 275. Peter Beer's Geschichte, Lehren und Meinungen aller bestandenen und noch bestehenden religiösen Secten der Juden, und der Geheimlehre oder Cabbalah. Brünn. 1822, 23. 2. Bde. 8.

[7] Winer's bibl. Realwörterbuch, ii. 289.

[8] Chr. G. L. Grossmann, de philosophia Sadducaeorum, Part iv. Lips. 1836–38. 4, is of

deavored to give prominence to the old Hebraism, as it appears in the written law of Moses. *The Essenes* led an ascetic life in retirement,[9] and exerted but little influence over the people.

§ 16.

SENTIMENTS OF THE HEATHEN NATIONS TOWARD JUDAISM.

Judaism was respected by the heathen as an old, popular religion; and Jehovah, as the God of the Jews, received, particularly from the different rulers of this country, the honors due to the deity of the land.[1] But the Jews did not respect the religions of other people in the same manner, inasmuch as they treated their deities as nonentities, avoided all intercourse with foreigners as unclean, and expected that their own only true God would one day triumph over all other nations.[2] Hence

opinion that, though Philo does not mention the Sadducees, there are many references to them in his works, whereas the parties whom Philo combats are to be looked for in Alexandria (comp. Schreiter in Keil's u. Tzschirner's Analecten i. 1, u. ii. 1). Comp. Winer ii. 415.

9 Respecting them see Philo quod omnis probus sit liber, Josephus in several places, Plinius Nat. Hist. v. 15. J. J. Bellerman's geschichtl. Nachrichten aus dem Alterthume über Essäer u. Therapeuten. Berl. 1821. 8. Jos. Sauer de Essenis et Therapeutis disqu. Vratislav. 1829. 8. A. Gfrörer's Philo und die alexandrinische Theosophie, ii. 299. A. F. Dähne's geschichtl. Darstellung der jüdisch-alexandr. Religionsphilosophie i. 469. Neander's K. G. 2te Aufl. i. i. 73. According to Gfrörer, they were Therapeutae who had come into Palestine, and whose opinions were there modified. According to Baur (Apollonius of Tyana, p. 125), they were Jewish Pythagoreans. Dähne is of opinion that the Essenes had at least an Alexandrian basis for their sentiments. Neander, on the contrary, thinks that the peculiar tendency which characterized them had been formed independently of external circumstances out of the deeper religious meaning of the Old Testament, but that subsequently it received foreign, old-oriental, Parsic, and Chaldean, but not Alexandrian elements.

1 Even Alexander is said to have offered sacrifice in the temple at Jerusalem according to the direction of the high priest (Joseph. Ant. xi. 8, 5). So also Ptolemy Euergertes (c. Apion. ii. 5). Seleucus Philopator (2 Macc. iii. 1–3) and Augustus (Philo de Legat. ad Cajum. p. 1036) appointed a revenue for the daily sacrifices. Vitellius sacrificed in Jerusalem (Jos. Ant. xviii. 5, 3). Tertullian. Apolog. c. 26: cujus (Judaeae) et deum victimis, et templum donis, et gentem foederibus aliquando, o Romani, honorastis.

2 Certainly the Jewish idea of the Messiah was known to the heathens in general, but we must not derive the measure of this knowledge from the passages: Sueton. Vespas. c. 4: Percrebuerat Oriente toto vetus et constans opinio, esse in fatis, ut eo tempore Judaea profecti rerum potirentur. Tacit. Hist. 5, 13: Pluribus persuasio inerat, antiquis sacerdotum literis contineri, eo ipso tempore fore, ut valesceret oriens, profectique Judaea rerum potirentur. Both these historians have here manifestly copied Josephus (de B. J. vi. 5, 4: *ἦν χρησμὸς ἀμφίβολος ὁμοίως ἐν τοῖς ἱεροῖς εὑρημένος γράμμασιν, ὡς κατὰ τὸν καιρὸν ἐκεῖνον ἀπὸ τῆς χώρας τὶς αὐτῶν ἄρξει τῆς οἰκουμένης*), as is proved not

they were despised and hated, especially since antiquity was accustomed to estimate the power of the gods by the condition of the people that served them.[3] They were most hated by the neighboring nations, particularly the Egyptians. In the eyes of the proud Romans, they were rather an object of contempt.[4] We find, therefore, no attempt, under the dominion of the Romans, to extinguish this hostile religion, such as that made by Antiochus Epiphanes, although, once and again, there seems to have been a design to make Roman customs universal in opposition to the national prejudices. This hatred and contempt produced singular stories respecting the origin and history of the Jews,[5] as well as absurd notions of their religion;[6] and

only by the similarity of the words and the common reference to Vespasian, but also the express mention of Josephus and his prophecy in Sueton. Vesp. c. 5. But Josephus, in this case, gave a Grecian expression to the Jewish notion of the Messiah, and the flattering application to Vespasian was made for the purpose of giving importance to the writer's nation and himself, and to remove suspicion from them, for the present at least. Tacitus makes frequent use of Josephus in his history of the Jews, though he always takes a Roman point of view.

3 Cicero pro Flacco, c. 28. Sua cuique civitati religio, Laeli, est, nostra nobis. Stantibus Hierosolymis, pacatisque Judaeis, tamen istorum religio sacrorum a splendore hujus imperii, gravitate nominis nostri, majorum institutis abhorrebat: nunc vero hoc magis, quod illa gens, quid de imperio nostro sentiret, ostendit armis: quam cara diis immortalibus esset, docuit, quod est victa, quod elocata, quod servata. Apion ap. Joseph. contra Apionem, ii. 11. Minucii Felicis Octavius, c. 10: The heathen Caecilius says, Judaeorum sola et misera gentilitas unum—Deum—coluerunt; cujus adeo nulla vis nec potestas est, ut sit Romanis numinibus cum sua sibi natione captivus.

4 Of Apollonius Molon, a rhetorician of Rhodes, B.C. 70, Josephus says (c. Apion. ii. 14), *ποτὲ μὲν ὡς ἀθέους καὶ μισανθρώπους λοιδορεῖ, ποτὲ δ' αὖ δειλίαν ἡμῖν ὀνειδίζει καὶ τοὔμπαλιν ἔστιν ὅπου τόλμαν κατηγορεῖ καὶ ἀπονοίαν· λέγει δὲ καὶ ἀφυεστάτους εἶναι τῶν βαρβάρων.* Tacit. Hist. v. 5, apud ipsos fides obstinata, misericordia in promptu, sed adversus omnes alios hostile odium; c. 8, despectissima pars servientium—teterrima gens. Diodor. Sic. xxxiv. p. 524. Philostratus in vita Apollonii, v. c. 33. Juven. Sat. xiv. 103. According to Philo (in Flacc. p. 969), there remained among the Egyptians *παλαιὰ καὶ τρόπον τινὰ γεγεννημένη πρὸς 'Ιουδαίους ἀπέχθεια.* Jos. c. Apion. i. 25, *τῶν δὲ εἰς ἡμᾶς βλασφημιῶν ἤρξαντο Αἰγύπτιοι—αἰτίας δὲ πολλὰς ἔλαβον τοῦ μισεῖν καὶ φθονεῖν*, caet.

5 The oldest sources of these fables are the fragment of Hecataeus Milesius (doubtless Abderita), in Photius's bibl. cod. 154, and the more malignant representation of the Egyptian Manetho (about 280 B.C., ap. Joseph. c. Apion. i. 26, comp. 14). The saying afterwards repeated with manifold remodelings by the Egyptian Chaeremon (at the time of Augustus, ap. Jos. l. c. c. 32), by Lysimachus (about 100 B.C., ibid. c. 34), Justin (Hist. 36, 2), and Tacitus (Hist. v. c. 2). Comp. J. G. Müller in the theol. Studien u. Kritiken. 1843, iv. 893. Josephus wrote his two books against Apion in refutation of these calumnies against his countrymen.

6 Particularly concerning the object of their worship. Many, indeed, saw in Jehovah their Zeus or Jupiter: Varro ap. Augustin. de consensu evangel. i. 22. Aristeas de legis divinae interpr. historia, p. 3, *τὸν γὰρ πάντων ἐπόπτην καὶ κτίστην θεὸν οὗτοι σέβονται, ὃν καὶ πάντες, ἡμεῖς δὲ μάλιστα, προσονομάζοντες ἑτέρως Ζῆνα.* According to another opinion the Jews worshiped the heaven (Juvenal. Sat. xiv. 97, nil praeter nubes et coeli

these in their turn contributed to increase the contempt of which they were the offspring.

§ 17.

CONDITION OF THE JEWS OUT OF PALESTINE.

J. Remond Geschichte der Ausbreitung des Judenthums von Cyrus bis auf den gänzlichen Untergang des jüd. Staats. Leipz. 1789. 8. Jost's Gesch. d. Israeliten. Th. 2. S. 262.

The Jewish people were by no means confined to Palestine. Only the smaller part of them had availed themselves of the permission of Cyrus to return to their native land, and therefore numbers had remained behind in *Babylonia*, who, doubtless, spread themselves farther toward the east, so that in the first century they were very considerable (*οὐκ ὀλίγαι μυριάδες, Jos. Ant.* xv. 3, 1). In Arabia, the kings of the *Homerites* (about 100 B.C.) had even adopted the Jewish religion, and subsequently it had reached the throne of *Adiabene*, by the conversion of King *Izates*, (about 45 A.D., comp. Jos. Ant. xx. 2). At the building of *Alexandria*, Alexander the Great brought a colony of Jews to settle there, (Jos. de B. J. ii. 36); more were brought by Ptolemy Lagus to *Egypt*, *Cyrene*, and *Lybia*, (Jos. Ant. xii. 2, 4); and the Jews were very numerous in these places, (1,000,000, Philo in Flacc. p. 971. In Alexandria two-fifths of the population, ibid. p. 973). By trade they soon became rich and powerful.[1] Many Jewish colonists had also been carried into *Syria* by Seleucus Nicanor (Jos. Ant. xii. 3, 1), especially to *Antioch*, where, in after times, a great part of the population consisted of Jews (Jos. de B. J. vii. 3, 3). Antiochus the Great was the first who sent a Jewish colony to *Phrygia* and *Lydia* (Jos. l. c.), and from these two countries they had spread themselves not only over the whole of *Asia*

numen adorant). Others thought that they worshiped Bacchus (Plutarch Sympos. iv. Qu. 5, Tacit. Hist. 5. 5). According to others, the object of adoration was an ass's head (Apion ap. Jos. c. Ap ii. 7. Tacit. Hist. 5. 4. Plut. l. c.) According to others, a swine (Plutarch l. c. Petronius in fragm.: Judaeus, licet et Porcinum numen adoret, &c.) Comp. the fable of the Jews sacrificing every year a Greek, and eating of his flesh (Joseph. c. Apion. ii. 8). Jo. Jac. Huldrici gentilis obtrectator s. de calumniis gentilium in Judaeos et in primaevos Christianos. Tiguri. 1744. 8.

[1] C. E. Varges de statu Aegypti provinciae Romanae I. et II. p. Chr. n. saeculis. Gottingae. 1842. 4. p. 18, 39, 46.

Minor, but also over *Greece*. The first Jews in Rome had been brought as prisoners of war by Pompey. They afterward obtained their freedom (therefore they were styled *libertini*, Philo de legat. ad Caj. p. 1014, Tacit. Ann. ii. 85), received permission from Julius Caesar to erect synagogues (Jos. Ant. xiv. 10, 8), and soon occupied the greatest part of the city beyond the Tiber (Philo l. c.). Thus, at the time of Christ it was not easy to find a country in the whole Roman empire in which the Jews did not dwell (Strabo, xiv. c. 2, Philo legat. ad Caj. p. 1031).

All these widely dispersed Jews (*ἡ διασπορά*) considered Jerusalem as their common capital, the sanhedrim of that place as their ecclesiastical supreme court; and sent not only yearly contributions in money (*δίδραχμα*), and offerings to the temple (Philo de Monarch. lib. ii. p. 822, in Flacc. 971, legat. ad. Caj. 1014, 1023, 1031, Cicero pro Flacc. 12, Tacit. Hist. 5, 5), but also frequently repaired thither to the great festivals (Philo de Monarch. lib. ii. p. 821), without detriment being done to this common sanctuary by the temple built in Leontopolis (152 B.C.) by Onias.[2] They obtained peculiar privileges, not only in the places where they settled as colonists at the desire of the princes of the country, but Caesar had allowed them the free exercise of their religion,[3] in a series of regulations enacted for the purpose, while he granted them several favors in relation to their law.[4] But these very distinctions merely served to make them still more hated by their fellow-citizens, with whom, therefore, they had frequent quarrels.

[2] The temple of Onias was as far from causing a schism among the Jews as the dispute between the Pharisees and Sadducees, although the building of it was disapproved by the Palestinian Jews.

[3] By this, therefore, their synagogues were put into the class of collegia licita (see above, § 12). Comp. the decree of the Praetors C. Julius ap. Joseph. Ant. xiv. 10, 8: *Γάϊος Καῖσαρ, ὁ ἡμέτερος στρατηγὸς καὶ ὕπατος, ἐν τῷ διατάγματι κωλύων θιάσους συνάγεσθαι κατὰ πόλιν, μόνους τούτους οὐκ ἐκώλυσεν οὔτε χρήματα συνεισφέρειν, οὔτε σύνδειπνα ποιεῖν. ὁμοίως δὲ κἀγὼ τοὺς ἄλλους θιάσους κωλύων τούτους μόνους ἐπιτρέπω κατὰ τὰ πάτρια ἔθη καὶ νόμιμα συνάγεσθαί τε καὶ ἵστασθαι.* So also Augustus (Philo de legat. ad Cajum, p. 1035, 1036).

[4] Comp. Jos. Ant. xiv. 10, 2, ff. Claudius, in his edict, gives briefly what was granted them, and what was required of them, (Jos. Ant. xix. 5, 3): *'Ιουδαίους τοὺς ἐν παντὶ τῷ ὑφ' ἡμᾶς κόσμῳ τὰ πάτρια ἔθη ἀνεπικωλύτως φυλάσσειν,—καὶ μὴ τὰς τῶν ἄλλων ἐθνῶν δεισιδαιμονίας ἐξουθενίζειν.* Decreta Romana et Asiatica pro Judaeis ad cultum div.—secure obeundum—restituta a Jac. Gronovio. Lugd. Bat. 1712. 8. Decreta Romanorum pro Judaeis e Josepho collecta a J. Tob. Krebs. Lips. 1768. 8. Dav. Henr. Levyssohn disp. de Jud. sub Caesaribus conditione et de legibus eos spectantibus. Lugd. Bat. 1828. 4.

In the mean time, Judaism had been introduced in many ways among the heathen. It is true that only a few became complete converts to it by submitting to circumcision (proselytes of righteousness);[5] but several, particularly women,[6] attached themselves to it for the purpose of worshiping Jehovah as the one true God, without observing the Mosaic law (proselytes of the gate),[7] which was sufficient for those who were not Jews, according to the opinion of the more liberal Jewish expositors.[8] Others, on the contrary, especially in Rome, which longed after foreign rites, felt themselves attracted, not so much by the religion, as by the religious ceremonial of the Jews. These individuals observed Jewish ceremonies without separating themselves on that account from heathen forms of worship, kept Jewish festivals, and trusted in Jewish conjurations. There

5 I. e., right, complete proselytes. Of such speaks Tacitus, Hist. v. 5: Circumcidere genitalia instituere, ut diversitate noscantur. Transgressi in morem eorum idem usurpant, nec quidquam prius imbuuntur, quam contemnere deos, exuere patriam; parentes, liberos, fratres vilia habere. Juvenal. Sat. xiv. 96, ff. ?

Quidam sortiti metuentem sabbata patrem,
Nil praeter nubes, et coeli numen adorant:
Nec distare putant humana carne suillam,
Qua pater abstinuit, mox et praeputia ponunt.
Romanas autem soliti contemnere leges,
Judaicum ediscunt, et servant, ac metuunt jus,
Tradidit arcano quodcunque volumine Moses.

A list of existing proselytes is given by Causse in the Museum Haganum I. 549.

6 So almost all the women in Damascus, Joseph. de B. J. ii. 20, 2; so was Fulvia in the time of Tiberius, at Rome, *νομίμοις προσεληλυθυῖα τοῖς Ἰουδαϊκοῖς*, Ant. xviii. 3, 5. So were many Judaizers in Syria, de B. J. ii. 18, 2, comp. the inscriptions in Hug, Einl. in d. N. T. 3te Aufl. ii. 339. Act. xiii. 50, xvii. 4. Comp. Strabo above, § 14, note 7.

7 Such was the name originally given to those who were not Jews, but to whom permission was granted to dwell as sojourners in Palestine, under the condition of observing certain laws (Levit. xvii. 8, ff., גֵּרְךָ אֲשֶׁר בִּשְׁעָרֶיךָ, Exod. xx. 10; Deut. v. 14). But now, under altered circumstances all heathens who attached themselves to Judaism by the voluntary observance of those precepts, received the same appellation. These precepts, which, in the opinion of the Jews, were delivered even to Noah (comp. Genesis, ix. 4, ff.), and in him to the whole human race, are said to be seven. 1. A prohibition of idolatry; 2. Blasphemy; 3. The shedding of human blood; 4. Incest; 5. Theft; 6. The command to practice righteousness; 7. To eat no blood, and no animal in which the blood still remains. See Seldenus de jure nat. et gent. lib. 1, c. 10. In the New Testament these proselytes are called *φοβούμενοι τὸν θεόν, σεβόμενοι τ. θ.*

8 The school of Hillel, to which Gamaliel, Paul's preceptor, belonged, allowed these proselytes a part in the kingdom of the Messiah; the school of Shammai excluded them from it—both with reference to Ps. ix. 18. See E. M. Roeth epistolam vulgo ad Hebraeos inscriptam non ad Hebraeos sed ad Ephesios datam esse. Francof. ad M. 1836. 8. p. 117. 126, ss. At the conversion of King Izates, Ananias was of the milder, Eleazer of the stricter views, Joseph. Ant. xx. c. 2. The later rabbins follow the opinion of Hillel, as they do in all disputes between these two schools. Othonis lexicon rabbin. p. 243. Roeth, p. 129.

soon appeared, also, Jewish jugglers, who ministered to this heathen superstition as conjurors and soothsayers.[9]

At the same time, intercourse with the pagans could not exist without exerting some influence on the Jews. It must have partly smoothed away many rough points of their national character, and have partly communicated to them a great portion of the cultivation of the nations among whom they lived. A philosophical mode of treating their religion was developed especially at *Alexandria*, under the Ptolemies, in consequence of the study of Grecian philosophy, and thence a peculiar philosophy of religion, which may be traced from *Aristobulus* (about 160 B.C.), through *the Book of Wisdom*,[10] and *the Therapeutae*,[11] to its most distinguished representative *Philo*

[9] On account of many impostors of this kind, Tiberius expelled the Jews from Rome, Jos. Ant. xviii. 3, 5. The Jewish festivals were kept by the heathen, Horat. Sat. i. 9, 69 :

> —— hodie tricesima sabbata: vin' tu
> Curtis Judaeis oppedere? Nulla mihi, inquam,
> Religio est. At mi: sum paulo infirmior, unus
> Multorum.

The women in particular frequented them.

Cultaque Judaeo septima sacra Syro (Ovid. Art. Amat. i. 75), cf. Selden de jure nat. et gent. lib. iii. c. 15, ss. Gottl. Wernsdorf de gentilium sabbato. Viteb. 1722. 4. For examples of Jewish conjurors see Acts xix. 13. Joseph. Antiq. viii. 2, 5 (Eleazer, who before Vespasian gave proofs of exorcism). Plinii Natur. Hist. xxx. c. 2: Est et alia magices factio a Mose et Janne et Jotape Judaeis pendens. Celsus accused the Jews (Orig. c. Cels. i. p. 21), *αὐτοὺς σέβειν ἀγγέλους, καὶ γοητείᾳ προσκεῖσθαι, ἧς ὁ Μωϋσῆς αὐτοῖς γέγονεν ἐξηγητής*. In regard to Jewish soothsayers see Juven. Sat. vi. 543:

> Arcanam Judaea tremens mendicat in aurem,
> Interpres legum Solymarum, et magna sacerdos
> Arboris, ac summi fida internuntia coeli:
> Implet et illa manum, sed parcius. Aere minuto
> Qualiacunque voles Judaei somnia vendunt.

In this way the Jewish names for deity came into the formulae of heathen impostors, though at a later period; and were supposed to possess a peculiar magical power in union with the heathen appellations of God (Origines c. Cels. iv. p. 183, v. p. 262), and were found on gems; see my remarks in the Theol. Stud. u. Kritiken. 1830, Heft 2, p. 403. To this influence of Judaism Seneca refers, de superstitionibus (ap. Augustin. de civit. Dei, vi. 11): Cum interim usque eo sceleratissimae gentis consuetudo convaluit, ut per omnes jam terras, recepta sit, victi victoribus leges dederunt. Illi tamen causas ritus sui noverunt, sed major pars populi facit, quod cur faciat ignorat. It might be expected that with this heathen tendency many should make a mere external profession of Judaism. Hence we can explain why the Talmudists passed so severe a judgment on the Pharisees, although the latter were still very zealous in making proselytes at the time of Christ (Matth. xxiii. 15): Proselyti impediunt adventum Messiae, sunt sicut scabies Israeli, &c. Othonis lexicon rabbin. p. 491. Wagenseilii Sota, p. 754.

[10] In regard to those traces, see generally, Gfrörer's Philo, ii. and Dähne's jüdisch-alex. Religionsphilosophie, ii.

[11] Philo de vita contemplativa. The writings of Bellermann and Sauer mentioned in § 15, note 9. Gfrörer ii. 280. Dähne, i. 443. Later writers, by drawing unhistorical conclusions, have discovered Christian ascetics in the Therapeutae. So Eusebius Hist. eccles. ii. 17,

(† 41 A.D.)[12] Though Philo's Platonic Judaism in this complete form was only the property of a few, yet the general ideas contained in it were widely diffused among the Hellenic Jews at that time, and afterward gained an important influence over the philosophy of religion which formed itself within the bosom of Christianity. This is especially the case with regard to the doctrine of Philo concerning *the Logos*, the God revealing himself in the finite, in whom the Mosaic creative word, and the Platonic ideal world, were united.[13]

§ 18.

THE SAMARITANS.

The mixed people[1] who had grown up into a society after the

and all succeeding authors except Photius, cod. 104. The same opinion was held after the Reformation by most of the older historians of the Catholic and Episcopal English church (see the writings on both sides in Triglandii syntagma, see above, § 15, note 6), even Bern. de Montfaucon (not. ad Philon. de vit. contempl.), and L. A. Muratori (anecdot. graec. p. 330). The dispute of the former respecting this point, with Jo. Bouhier: Lettres pour et contre sur la fameuse question, si les solitaires appellez Therapeutes étoient Chrétiens. Paris. 1712. 8. Even Philo is said to have been on friendly terms with Peter at Rome, under Claudius (εἰς ὁμιλίαν ἐλθεῖν Πέτρῳ, Euseb. l. c. Hieron. catal. 11), from which afterward arose the fable that he had embraced Christianity and afterward forsook it (Photius cod. 105). Cf. Mangey praef. in Phil. Opp.

12 Opp. ed. A. Turnebus, Paris. 1552, in an improved edition by Dan. Hoeschelius. Col. Allobrog. 1613. Paris. 1640. Francof. 1691. fol. (citations are usually made according to the pages of the last two editions, which coincide in this respect). Thom. Mangey. Lond. 1742. 2 voll. fol. A manual edition by A. F. Pfeiffer. Erlang. 1785. 5 voll. 8, incomplete. In late times Angelo Mai found in the Greek language the writings of Philo de festo cophini and de parentibus colendis (Philo et Virgilii interpretes. Mediol. 1818, 8vo); and J. B. Aucher published in Latin several treatises preserved in an Armenian version (de providentia and de animalibus. Venet. 1822. fol. Philonis Jud. paralipomena Armena. ibid. 1826. fol.) All this has been taken into the latest manual edition by E. Richter. Lips. 1828–30. 8. tom. 8. Comp. F. Creuzer zur Kritik der Schriften des Juden Philo, in the theol. Studien u. Krit. 1832. i. 1. Dähne's Bemerkungen über die Schriften des Philo. das. 1833, iv. 984. Philo's Lehrbegriff von E. H. Stahl (in Eichhorn's Bibl. d. bibl. Lit. iv. 5, 770). C. G. L. Grossmann quaestiones Philoneae. Lips. 1829. 4. A. Gfrörer's Philo u. die alexandrin. Theosophie. 2 Thle. Stuttgart. 1831. 8. A. F. Dähne's geschichtl. Darstellung der jüdisch-alexandrin. Religionsphilosophie. 2 Abthl. Halle. 1834. 8.

13 I can not agree with the prevailing view, that the strictly monotheistic Philo thought of the Logos as hypostatically different from God. Since the infinite can not be revealed in the finite, God was under the necessity, so to speak, of making himself finite for this purpose, i. e., of separating from his own infinite perfections a finite measure of ideas and powers. God, in this aspect, is the Logos. Accordingly, the Logos is less than God, the revealed God less than deity in himself, but not, on that account, a hypostasis different from God.

1 In opposition to Hengstenberg, who (Beitr. zur Einleit. ins. A. T. ii. 1, 3) affirms, that

destruction of the kingdom of Israel, in the tract belonging to it (2 Kings xvii. 24, ff., כּוּתִים, Σαμαρεῖται), had constantly been an object of detestation to the Jews, because of their religion, which had been at first compounded of Judaism and heathenism. The Samaritans, indeed, under the direction of the Jewish priest Manasseh, supported by the Persian viceroy *Sanballat*, had retained the Pentateuch, (409 B.C.), erected a temple on Gerizim, established a levitical priesthood—in short, the whole of Judaism as it then was;[2] but all served merely to increase the hatred of the Jews against them, although they were united from this time onward, not only by neighborhood, but also by a similar religion, and a series of like fortunes. This hatred entertained by the Jews, which the Samaritans seemed not to have returned with like virulence, was not abated in their native land by the destruction of the temple on Gerizim by *John Hyrcanus* (109 B.C.); it was transferred to Egypt where Jewish and Samaritan colonies had been planted by Alexander and Ptolemy Lagus,[3] and has continued to the latest times.

The Samaritans held fast by Judaism, as it had come to them by Manasseh, with rigid strictness; and therefore the later developments of it among the Jews remained unknown to them, as they did also to the Sadducees.[4] Besides, in the history of

the Samaritans were originally a heathen people, who accommodated themselves by degrees to the Mosaic institution, see Dr. Kalkar's treatise, die Samaritaner ein Mischvolk, in Pelt's theolog. Mitarbeit. Jahrg. 3, Heft 3. (Kiel. 1840) p. 24.—[Kitto's Cyclopaedia of Biblical Literature, art. *Samaritans*.]

[2] Nehem. xiii. 28. Comp. Joseph. Ant. xi. 7, 2. 8, 2. 4. 6, who places incorrectly the defection of Manasseh under Darius Codomannus, instead of Darius Nothus. Prideaux hist. des Juifs. ii. 397. Jahn bibl. Archäologie, ii. 1, 278. G. Gesenius de pentateuchi Samaritani origine, indole et auctoritate. Halae. 1815. 4.

[3] Samaritan warriors were transplanted into Thebais by Alexander (Joseph. Ant. xi. 8, 6), into Lower Egypt and Alexandria by Ptolemy Lagus (Jos. l. c. xii. 1). A controversy between the Jews and Samaritans at Alexandria is related by Josephus, l. c. xiii. 3, 4.

[4] Concerning their doctines see Philastrius de haer. cap. 7. Epiphanius de haer. 9. Leontius de sectis, c. 8. Their pentateuch was printed along with the Samaritan translation in the Paris Polyglott, 1629. A more accurate knowledge of their condition and doctrines in modern times has been obtained from the letters of the Samaritans to Jos. Scaliger, 1589; to men at Oxford, through the medium of Robert Huntingdon, 1671; to Job Ludolf, 1684 (see these letters in Eichhorn's Repertorium ix. and xiii.); and to De Sacy (since 1808), comp. Sylv. de Sacy mémoire sur l'état actuel des Samaritains. Paris. 1812 (translated into German in Stäudlin's and Tzschirner's Archiv. for Kg. I. iii. 40). These were revised, and along with the recent letters containing two of 1820, republished by De Sacy in the Notices et Extraits des manuscrits de la Bibl. roy. T. xii. Paris. 1829. In addition, a letter of 1700 was made known by Hamaker in the Archief voor kerkelijke Geschiedenis door Kist en Royaards, v. 1 (Leiden. 1834). Besides this, Samaritan poems exist, which

this people there was no ground for the same degree of national arrogance and hatred of every thing foreign as existed among the Jews.[5] And while among the Jews the extravagant national feeling fostered a more sensuous apprehension of the doctrine of a special Divine providence in favor of their nation, and of the Messiah, and by this means favored a worldly view of the doctrines of religion; that smaller measure of national pride existing among the Samaritans was the cause of their looking at Judaism more in its spiritual aspect.[6] This tendency was certainly promoted by the connection of the Samaritans with those of the same faith who had settled in Alexandria, and who were then partakers of Grecian culture. Still, however, the spiritual tendency which characterized the constantly oppressed people received no scientific improvement. But yet in Samaria there appeared in the first century in succession three founders

belong to the times of the Arabs, and were first used in Gesenius de Samaritanorum theologia ex fontibus ineditis comm. (Weihnachtsprogramm, Halle. 1822. 4), and subsequently published: Carmina Samaritana e codd. Londinensibus et Gothanis ed. et illustr. Guil. Gesenius. Lips. 1824. 8.

5 Hence Josephus blames them (Ant. xi. 8, 6): *εἰσὶν οἱ Σαμαρεῖς τοιοῦτοι τὴν φύσιν, ἐν μὲν ταῖς συμφοραῖς ὄντας τοὺς Ἰουδαίους ἀρνοῦνται συγγενεῖς ἔχειν, ὁμολογοῦντες τότε τὴν ἀλήθειαν. ὅταν δέ τι περὶ αὐτούς λαμπρὸν ἴδωσιν ἐκ τύχης, ἐξαίφνης ἐπιπηδῶσιν αὐτῶν τῇ κοινωνίᾳ, προσήκειν αὐτοῖς λέγοντες, καὶ ἐκ τῶν Ἰωσήπου γενεαλογοῦντες αὐτοὺς ἐκγόνων Ἐφραΐμου καὶ Μανασσοῦ.* So, too, they are said to have professed themselves to Alexander, *Ἑβραῖοι μὲν εἶναι, χρηματίζειν δ' οἱ ἐν Σικίμοις Σιδώνιοι* (Joseph. l. c.). On the contrary, to Antiochus Epiphanes as *ὄντες τὸ ἀνέκαθεν Σιδώνιοι* (Joseph. Ant. xii. 5, 5). In like manner, they are said to have escaped threatening danger under this king by calling their temple *ἱερον Διὸς Ἑλληνίου*, but without making other change in their worship, Joseph. l. c. cf. 2 Macc. vi. 2.

6 In the later Samaritan writings a progressive development of several doctrines by the influence of the Alexandrian peculiarities can not be mistaken. The characteristics of Samaritan theology are strict Monotheism, aversion to all Anthropomorphism (Gesenius de theol. Sam. p. 12, ss.), both which were manifested even in their Pentateuch (Gesenius de pentat. Sam. p. 58, ss.). According to Leontius de sectis, they denied the doctrine of angels, i. e., the improved Jewish doctrine regarding them. In the later poetical writings angels appear as uncreated influences proceeding from God חֵילִין (חֲיָלִים *δυνάμεις*), comp. Gesenius de theol. Sam. p. 21, which belongs to a gnostic development, of which the first trace appears to be in Acts viii. 10. They magnified Moses and the law, rejecting all the later prophetic writings. The Sabbath and circumcision were regarded as the most important pledges of the covenant with Jehovah. The temple on Gerizim was the only true one (Deuteron. xxvii. 4, עֵיבָל altered into גְּרִזִים. Gesen. de Pent. Sam. p. 61). According to the fathers, they denied immortality and the resurrection, i. e., they maintained the insensible state of the soul in Sheol. We find among them afterward a ressurection to a life entirely different from the present (Gesenius de theol. Sam. p. 38). The Messiah (הַשָּׁהֵב or הַתָּהֵב Ges. l. c. p. 44: reductor, conversor), probably a בֶּן יוֹסֵף, will lead the people to repentance, and then to happiness, the nations will believe in him, and by him will be won over to the law, and to the temple on Gerizim. (Compare John iv. 25.)

of sects, of whom *Dositheus*[7] departed from the prevalent Samaritan Judaism in a very few particulars. *Simon Magus*[8] drew the germ of his syncretic magical system from the philosophical opinions then current, probably at Alexandria, and unfolded them farther, instigated, perhaps, by Christianity, which had lately appeared. In the third place, *Menander*,[9] the disciple of Simon Magus, departed little from the footsteps of his master. All three left behind them sects which continued for several centuries. The followers of Simon and Menander were often confounded with Christians by the heathen,[10] and actually endeavored to insinuate themselves into the Christian church after Christianity had become the prevailing religion.[11]

7 Moshemii institt. hist. Christ. majores, Saec. i. 376, ss. דּוֹסְתָּאי gave himself out to be the prophet promised in Deut. xviii. 18. The church fathers falsely ascribe to him many peculiar doctrines which were held by all the Samaritans. (According to Jewish tradition, the priest sent by Sennacherib, 1 Kings xvii. 27, 28, was one R. Dosthai. Drusius de tribus sectis Jud. iii. 4. It is probable, therefore, that the two persons were confounded. (A strict, ascetic life, and an overscrupulous observance of the Sabbath were peculiar to him. Origen. de princ. iv. c. 17, quo quisque corporis situ in principio sabbathi inventus fuerit, in eo ad vesperum usque ipsi permanendum esse, manifestly a literal interpretation of Exod. xvi. 29. As late as the year 588, the Dositheans and Samaritans had a controversy in Egypt about Deut. xviii. 18. (Eulogius ap. Phot. bibl. cod. 230.)

8 Mosheim, l. c. p. 289–432. Walch's Historie der Ketzereien, i. 135, ff. Neander's gnostische Systeme. Berlin. 1818. S. 338, ff. Leben u. Lehre Simons d. Magiers, by Dr. A. Simson (in Illgen's Zeitschr. für histor. Theol. 1841, iii. 15). Act. viii. 9, 10, *Σίμων—μαγεύων καὶ ἐξιστῶν τὸ ἔθνος τῆς Σαμαρείας, λέγων εἶναί τινα ἑαυτὸν μέγαν.* By the people he was looked upon as *ἡ δύναμις τοῦ θεοῦ ἡ μεγάλη* (חַיִל cf. not. 6). Probably the *Σίμων Ἰουδαῖος, Κύπριος δὲ γένος, μάγος εἶναι σκηπτόμενος* apud Joseph. Ant. xx. 7, 2. Fabulous accounts of his death at Rome (first found in the Apostol. Constitut. vi. 9, and in Arnobius, ii. c. 12) were perhaps occasioned by the occurrence related in Sueton. in Nerone, c. 12. Juvenal. Sat. iii. 79, 80. The statue on the island in the Tiber, as Justin relates, Apol. maj. c. 26 and 56, with the inscription Simoni sancto Deo, was found in 1574, and has on it, Semoni Sanco Deo Fidio Sacrum, &c. (See Baronius ad ann. 44 no. 55.) On Semo Sancus or Sangus, comp. Ovid. Fast. vi. 213. Justin's mistake is apparent, although Baronius, Thirlby, Maranus, especially Fogginius de Romano Divi Petro itinere et episcopatu, Florent. 1741. 4to, p. 247, ss., wish to justify his account; and Braun (S. Justini M. Apologiae. Bonnae. 1830. p. 97) has promised a new defense of it. The followers of Simon must be regarded as Samaritan Gnostics (Justin M. Apol. maj. c. 26: *καὶ σχεδὸν πάντες μὲν Σαμαρεῖς, ὀλίγοι δὲ καὶ ἐν ἄλλοις ἔθνεσιν, ὡς τὸν πρῶτον θεὸν ἐκεῖνον ὁμολογοῦντες, ἐκεῖνον καὶ προσκυνοῦσι*), whose system may have been developed parallel with the Christian Gnosis. Among Christians Simon has always been looked upon as the master and progenitor of all heretics (Irenaeus adv. haer. i. 27, ii. praef.), and although he never was a Christian, yet, in later times, he was thought to be the first heresiarch. In the Clementines he is the representative of Gnosis generally, and the system there attributed to him is a compound of the most striking Gnostic positions, and must not be considered genuine (see Baur's christl. Gnosis, p. 302).

9 Mosheim, l. c. 432–438.

10 Justin. Apol. ii. p. 70.

11 Regarding the Simonians see Euseb. Hist. eccl. ii. 1, 4. For the Menandrians, iii. 26, 2.

§ 19.

RELATION OF THE TIMES TO CHRISTIANITY IN ITS INFANCY.

From the view that has been given it may be seen, that the popular religions of the heathen had become superannuated at the time of Christ, and that unbelief and superstition were on the point of putting an end to all true religion. It is further apparent, that Judaism, losing more and more its spiritual character, threatened to sink down in externalities. Under these circumstances many heathens must have longed for a religion which put an end to their doubts and agitations, satisfied the demands of their moral nature, and afforded them consolation and inward peace. The circumstance of Christianity coming from the East, whose mystical religions had at that time attracted general attention to itself, must have facilitated at least the introduction of it. Not could it be otherwise than that many Jews felt the emptiness of their ceremonial service, especially as they had been already guided to a more spiritual worship of God by many passages in their own prophets. On the other hand, expectations of the Messiah prepared the way for Christianity among the Jews.

But however much there was in the circumstances of these times which must have promoted Christianity, there was not less to obstruct it. Among the Jews, national pride, earthly hopes of Messiah, and habituation to an almost external religion; among the heathen, unbelief as well as superstition, which prevailed at this time, the stain attaching to Jewish origin, and the political grounds which, in the universal opinion, rendered it necessary to abide by the national religion. Christianity could reckon on toleration on the part of the state, agreeably to the principles of the Romans, only as long as it was confined to the Jewish people. But a religion which, like the Jewish, did not only declare all other national religions false, but was likewise gathering adherents among all nations in a more suspicious degree than the Jewish, and was threatening to extinguish all others, could not be endured by the Roman government without an abandonment of the old state religion. The toleration which all philosophical systems and foreign superstitions found at Rome could not, therefore, be expected by Christianity ;[1] for an external observance of the state religion was at least consistent with the nature of such systems and superstitions.[2]

FIRST CHAPTER.

THE LIFE OF JESUS.

J. J. Hess Lebensgeschichte Jesu, 3 Bde. 8te Aufl. Zürich. 1822 u. 23. 8. The same : Lehre, Thaten, und Schicksale unseres Herrn, v. verschiedenen Seiten beleuchtet. 2 Hälften. 3te Aufl. Zürich. 1817. 8. J. G. Herder vom Erlöser der Menschen nach unsern 3 ersten Evangelien. Riga. 1796. 8. The same : von Gottes Sohn der Welt Heiland, nach Johannis Evangel. Riga. 1797. 8. J. Ch. Greiling das Leben Jesu von Nazareth. Halle. 1815. 8. H. E. G. Paulus das Leben Jesu, als Grundlage einer reinen Gesch. d. Urchristenthums. Heidelb. 1828. 2 Bde. 8. Dr. A. Hase das Leben Jesu. Ein Lehrbuch zunächst für akadem. Vorlesungen. Leipz. 1829. 3te Aufl. 1840. 8.—Dr. Strauss's Leben Jesu has given a new impulse to a scientific treatment of the subject. Tübingen. 1835, 36. 4te Aufl. 1840. 2 Bde. 8. The fruits of it are especially A. Neander's Leben Jesu Christi. Hamburg. 1837 (4te Aufl. 1845). 8. Chr. F. v. Ammon Gesch. d. Lebens Jesu mit steter Rücksicht auf die vorhandenen Quellen. Bd. 2. Leipzig 1842—4. 8.

F. V. Reinhard Versuch über den Plan, den der Stifter der christl. Religion zum Besten der Menschen entwarf. 5te Ausg. with additions by Heubner. Wittenb. 1830. 8. G.

[1] Although the Christian apologists often appeal to it, Justini M. Apol. maj. c. 18, 24, 26. Tertulliani Apologeticus, c. 24, 46.

[2] In opposition to the wrong views taken by Voltaire Traité sur la tolérance, 1763, c. 8–10, (Oeuvres éd. Deux-Ponts. Tom. 40, p. 271, ss.), relative to the toleration of the Romans, and the exclusive fault of the Christians in bringing persecutions on themselves, Hegewisch made very just remarks in his treatise on the epoch in Roman history most favorable to humanity. Hamburg. 1800. p. 173.

J. Planck Gesch. d. Christenth. in der Periode seiner ersten Einführung in die Welt durch Jesum und die Apostel. Göttingen. 1818. 2 Bde. 8.

J. A. G. Meyer Versuch einer Vertheidigung und Erlaüterung der Geschichte Jesu und der Apostel allein aus griech. und röm. Profanscribenten. Hannover. 1805. 8.

§ 20.

CHRONOLOGICAL DATA RESPECTING THE LIFE OF JESUS.

J. F. Wurm's astron. Beiträge zur genäherten Bestimmung des Geburts u. Todesjahres Jesu, in Bengel's Archiv. für d. Theol. II. 1, 261. R. Anger de temporum in Actis Apost. ratione diss. c. 1, de anno quo Jesus in coelum ascenderit. Lips. 1830. 8. F. Piper de externa vitae J. Chr. chronologia recte constituenda. Gottingae. 1835. 4. K. Wieseler's chronolog. Synopse der vier Evangelien. Hamburg. 1843. 8.[1]

The only definite date in the evangelical history[2] is in Luke iii. 1, relating to the appearance of John the Baptist.[3] On the supposition that Jesus appeared in public half a year after John, as he was born half a year after him, the designation of his age in Luke iii. 23 gives nearly the time of his birth, which, perhaps, may be still more closely determined by the circumstance that it must have happened before the death of Herod († shortly

[1] According to Wieseler, Christ was born in February 750 A.U. (4 B.C.), baptized in spring or summer 780, (27 A.D.), crucified on the 7th April 783 (30 A.D.). A work so acute and learned as that of Wieseler can not be sufficiently characterized in a few words. The exact coincidence, however, of different investigations produces more doubt than conviction, since the separate data may be bent, on account of their vacillating nature, in subservience to one object, without completely removing scruples in regard to them. In particular, ὡσεί, in Luke iii. 23, p. 126, appears to be taken too strictly; it is incredible that the chronological designation of Luke iii. 1, should reach to the captivity of the Baptist, p. 197; and the computation of the Jewish calendar, taken from Wurm for the purpose of ascertaining the year of Jesus' death, appears to be wholly uncertain, according to Wurm's explanations.

[2] Doubtful chronological dates are: Luc. i. 5, ἐφημερία 'Αβιά (cf. 1 Chron. xxiv. 10. Jos. Scaliger de emendat. temporum. App. p. 54. Wieseler, S. 140. Comp. Paulus Comm. über die drei ersten Evang. i. 36, ff. Luc. ii. 2, the Census of Quirinus (cf. Jos. Ant. xviii. i. 1. Paulus i. 141, ff. On the contrary, P. A. E. Huschke über den zur Zeit d. Geburt J. Chr. gehaltenen Census. Breslau 1840. 8. Wieseler, S. 49. Comp. Hoeck's röm. Gesch. vom Verfall d. Republik b. Constantin. i. ii. 412).—Joh. ii. 20. The building of the temple (cf. Jos. Ant. xv. 11, 1, xx. 9, 7. Lampe, Paulus, and Lücke on John. Wieseler, S. 165).

[3] Augustus died 19th August, the year 14 of our era. and thus the 15th year of Tiberius's reign fell between the 19th August, 28, and the 19th August, 29 (781-2, A.U.C.), Wurm in Bengel's Archiv. ii. 5.

before the passover, 750 A.U.), Matth. ii. 1, 19.[4] Even in the first centuries accounts of the year of Jesus' birth are given;[5] but the Romish abbot Dionysius Exiguus (525) reckoned, independently of them, the period of the incarnation for the purpose of fixing by it the years in his table for Easter, making the first year from the incarnation coincide with the year 754 A.U. of the Varronian computation.[6] This Dionysian era, applied first of all under the Anglo-Saxons,[7] then by the Frankish kings Pepin and Charlemagne, begins at least four years after the true date of Christ's birth.[8] The day of birth can not be determined.[9]

The ministry of Jesus was supposed by many of the older church fathers, after the example of the Alexandrians, to have

[4] On the year of Herod's death see Klaiber's Studien d. evangel. Geistlichkeit Wirtemberg's, i. 1, 50. Wurm in the same, i. ii. 208. A list of the various opinions concerning the year of Christ's birth may be seen in Fabricii bibliographia antiquaria, ed. 2, Hamb. 1716, 4to, p. 187, ss., continued in F. Münter's der Stern der Weisen u. s. w. Kopenh. 1827, p. 109. The latest important investigations unite in the year 747 A.U. So Henr. Sanclementii de vulgaris aerae emendatione libb. iv. Romae. 1793. fol., solely on historical grounds. Münter, on the same grounds, and, also, because he regards with Keppler the star of the wise men as the great conjunction of the planets Jupiter and Saturn in Pisces. which happened on that year. Ideler Chronol. ii. 394, ff., Piper l. c., Schubert Lehrb. d. Sternenkunde, s. 226, Winer bibl. Realwörterbuch, ii. 614, assent to these results. Compare, however, on the other side, Wurm in Klaiber's Studien, i. ii. 211, ff.

[5] Irenaeus, iii. 25, and Tertull. adv. Jud. 8, give the 41st year of Augustus, 751 A.U. On the other hand, Clemens. Alex. Strom. i. p. 339, the 28th year (namely, after the conquest of Egypt), with whom agrees Euseb. hist. eccl. i. 5, Epiphan. haer. li. 22, and Orosius histor. i. 1, the 42d year, 752 A.U.—Sulpicius Severus hist. sacr. ii. 27, gives the 33d year of Herod, Coss. Sabinus and Rufinus (which does not suit, as Sab. and Ruf. were consuls 751 A.U. Herod died after a reign of 37 years, 750 A.U. An Egyptian monk, Panodorus (after 400), placed the birth of Christ in the year 5493 of his aera, i. e., 754 A.U. (Ge. Syncelli chronographia, ed. Paris, p. 25, 326).

[6] The Incarnatio, σάρκωσις, always means in the fathers the annunciation. Dionysius, therefore placed the birth of Christ in the conclusion of the first year of his era. When first about the time of Charlemagne, the beginning of the year was made to coincide with the 25th of December, the incarnation appears to have been taken as synonymous with the nativity. See Sanclementius, iv. c. 8. Ideler's Chronologie, ii. 381, ff.

[7] Ethelbert, king of Kent, dated first of all an original document anno ab incarnatione Christi DCV. cf. Codex diplomaticus aevi Saxonici, opera J. M. Kemble. T. i. (Lond. 1839. 8.) p. 2. Afterward the venerable Bede used this era in his historical works.

[8] G. A. Hamberger de epochae christianae ortu et auctore. Jenae. 1688. 4 (in Martini thesaur. dissertatt. T. iii. P. i. p. 241). Jo. G. Jani. historia aerae Dionysianae. Viteb. 1715. 4 (also in his opuscula ad hist. et chronolog. spectantia ed. Klotz. Halae. 1769). Ideler's Chronologie, ii. 366, ff.

[9] Clem. Alex. Strom. i. p. 340, relates that some regarded the 25th of Pachon, (20th May), others the 24th or 25th Pharmuthi, (the 19th or 20th April), as the birth-day. After the 6th of January, solemnized as a day of baptism by the followers of Basilides, was kept by the Oriental Christians since the third century as the day of baptism and birth, people began to keep this day as the true day of birth, (Epiphan. haer. li. 21). After the 25th December was solemnized in the fourth century in the west, as the birth-festival, this day came soon to be looked upon as the day of birth, (Sulpic. Sever. hist. sacr. ii. 27).

continued one year, agreeably to Isaiah lxi. 1, 2, comp. Luke iv. 19 (ἐνιαυτὸν κυρίου δεκτόν).[10] On this was founded the hypothesis, which became almost traditional in the ancient church, that Jesus was crucified in his thirtieth year, in the consulship of Rubellius Geminus and Fufius Geminus[11] (in the fifteenth year of Tiberius, 29th of the Dionysian era). But, according to the gospel of John ii. 13 (v. 1), vi. 4, xi. 55, three, or perhaps four passovers occurred during the public ministry of Christ. It must, therefore, have continued more than two years, and may, perhaps, have extended over three. Thus, the year of his death falls between 31 and 33 aer. Dionys., making his age from thirty-four to thirty-eight years. Even if we could agree on the preliminary question whether the Friday on which Jesus died was the day before the passover, or the first day of the passover,[12] yet, amid the uncertainty of the Jewish calendar of that time, an astronomical reckoning of the year of his death can scarcely be established.[13]

[10] So the Valentinians, (Irenaeus, ii. 38, 39), in opposition to whom Irenaeus puts forth the singular assertion that Jesus was baptized in his thirtieth year, but did not appear as a teacher till between his fortieth and fiftieth (John viii. 57), and then taught three years. One year, however, was adopted by Clem. Alex. Strom. i. 340. Origenes, hom. 32 in Lucam, and de princip. iv. On the other hand, c. Cels. ii. p. 397, and Comment. in Matth. xxiv. 15, he says, that Judas was not three entire years with Jesus. Auct. Clementin. hom. 17 in fine. Julius Africanus (ap. Hieronym. in Dan. ix.). Philastrius haer. 106. Cyrill. Alex. in Esaiam, c. 32. Some moderns have attained to a simular result in another way. Priestley's Harmony of the Evangelists in Greek, 1777. Haenlein progr. de temporis quo Jesus cum apostolis versatus est duratione. Erlang. 1796. 4to.

[11] Tertull. adv. Jud. 8 (but comp. adv. Marcion. i. 15). Lactant. institutt. iv. 10. Augustin. de civ. Dei. xviii. 54, de trinit. iv. 5 (according to Tertull. and August. ll. cc. and according to the old Acta Pilati in Epiphan. haer. l. 1, he was crucified the 8th of the Kalends of April, on the 25th of March the day of the vernal equinox, comp. Thilo cod. apocr. N. T. i. 496. Wieseler, S. 390). That Christ was thirty years old: Hippolytus Portuensis in canone paschali. Chronicon anonymi (in Canis. lect. antiq. T. ii.) c. 17 u. 18. Hieronym. epist. 22. ad Eustochium. Augustin. epist. 80 and 99. Comp. Petavii rationarium temporum (ed. Ludg. 1745). P. ii. p. 266, ss.

[12] The first three evangelists designate the last supper as the passover (Matth. xxvi. 17, ss., Mark xiv. 12, Luke xxii. 7), and hence it has been usually assumed in the Western Church that Christ was crucified on the first day of the passover. On the contrary, the day of Christ's death was according to John xiii. 1, 29, xviii. 28, xix. 14, 31, the day before the passover. The latter is followed by Tertullian, adv. Jud. c. 8, the Greeks, Scaliger, Casaubon, Capellus, Lampe, Kuinoel, &c. It is strongly in favor of the latter hypothesis that the first day of the passover can never fall on a Friday, at least according to the present calendar of the Jews. See Ideler's Chronologie, Bd. i. p. 519. Probably the account of the first three evangelists is to be explained by the circumstance, that they took the last supper of Jesus to be the Christian passover; see Theile in Winer's Krit. Journal der Theol. Literat. ii. 153, ff., v. 129, ff. Comp. Hase's Leben Jesu, p. 167. [Bibliotheca Sacra, new series, 1845, an article by Robinson.]

[13] Bynaeus de morte J. C. libb. 3. Amstel. 1691, 98. 3 voll. 4. Paulus über die Möglich-

§ 21.

HISTORY OF THE YOUTH OF JESUS.

The history of Jesus' life before his public appearance is very obscure,[1] and affords no disclosures in relation to the important question of the mode and progress of his spiritual development. Modern scholars have endeavored to supply this deficiency by conjectures, and have attributed a decided influence on his character, sometimes to the doctrines of the *Essenes*,[2] sometimes to those of the *Sadducees*,[3] sometimes to a combination of *Pharisaism* and *Sadduceism*,[4] sometimes to the *Alexandrian-Jewish* education.[5] But such a spirit could not have received its direction from any school, and least of all from the schools of those times, which were better adapted to fetter the spirit, partly by their literal externality, partly by their fanatical idealism, than to prepare it for a clear and great self-development.[6] On the contrary, the reading of the prophets of the Old Testament must have quickened in his kindred spirit a religious feeling as spiritual as that of the time was literal and carnal, and must have

keit Jesu Todesjahr zu bestimmen, in his Comment. über das N. T. iii. 784. Wurm in Bengel's Archiv. ii. 261.

[1] Chr. Fr. Ammon's bibl. Theologie. Bd. 2, (2te Ausg. Erlangen 1801) s. 244, ff. Paulus Commentar über das neue Testament, Th. 1. Schleiermacher on the writings of Luke, Th. 1. Berlin. 1817. S. 23, ff. [Translated by Thirlwall, Lond. 8vo, 1825.]

[2] So first the English Deists (see against them Prideaux's Connection). From them Voltaire borrowed this idea, as well as many others, (Philosophical Dictionary, under Esséniens). Frederic the Great, Oeuvres ed. de Berlin, T. xi. p. 94. Stäudlin Geschichte der Sittenlehre Jesu, Th. 1. S. 570, ff. The same hypothesis has been enlarged in J. A. C. Richter das Christenthum und die ältesten Religionen des Orients. Leipzig. 1819. Christianity is supposed to be the public revelation of the Essene doctrines, and that these were connected with the ancient schools of the prophets, with Parsism, the Egyptian and Grecian mysteries, and through them with Brahmaism! According to Gfrörer, (das Heiligthum u. die Wahrheit. Stuttgart. 1838, S. 382), Jesus was educated among the Essenes, and afterward followed his own course, but continued to hold what was sound in their doctrines and customs. On the other side see Bengel über d. Versuch Christenth. a. d. Essenismus abzuleiten, in Flatt's Magazine, vii. 148, ff. Heubner in the 5th appendix to his edition of Reinhard's Versuch über d. Plan Jesu. V. Wegnern über das Verhältniss des Christenthums zum Essenismus, in Illgen's Zeitschrift für die histor. Theol. 1841, ii. 1.

[3] Des-Cotes Schutzschrift für Jesum v. Nazereth. Frankf. 1797.

[4] Versuch den Ursprung der Sittenlehre Jesu historisch zu erklären (in Henke's Magazin. Bd. 5. S. 426.)

[5] Bahrdt's Briefe über die Bibel im Volkstone. Berlin. 1784, ff.

[6] So in John vii. 15, all higher cultivation in any school is denied to Jesus

given it a standard for estimating the condition of the Jewish nation at that period, and for judging of the means by which alone it could be elevated, very different from the usual view.

§ 22.

JOHN THE BAPTIST.

William Bell's Inquiry into the divine mission of John the Baptist and Jesus Christ. Lond. 1761. 8vo. Translated into German by Henke, Braunschweig. 1779, 8vo. J. G. E. Leopold Johannes d. T., eine biblische Untersuchung. Hannover. 1825. 8. Joh. d. T. in s. Leben u. Wirken dargestellt nach den Zeugnissen d. h. Schrift von L. v. Rohden. Lübeck. 1838. 8.

Before Jesus, appeared one of his relatives John, in the wilderness of Judea, with the solemn call, "Repent, for the kingdom of heaven is at hand," and dedicating his followers to this altered state of mind by a symbolical washing of the body.[1] It is certain that John and Jesus had been earlier acquainted with one another; but it is improbable that there existed a close connection between them, or the concerting of a common plan. The peculiarities of John point to an earlier connection with the Essenes.[2] The same character was possessed by his disciples, who, after Jesus' appearance, continued apart from the disciples of the latter (John iii. 26; Luke v. 33; Matth. ix. 14; xi. 2, ff.),[3] and of whom we meet with remains in Asia Minor, long

1 Was the baptism of John an imitation of Jewish proselyte baptism? The question is answered in the affirmative by Buxtorf Lexic. talmud. p. 408. Lightfoot, Schoettgen, Wetstein ad Matth. iii. 6. J. A. Danz baptismus proselytorum Judaicus ad illustrandum baptismum Joannis, and his antiquitas baptismi initiationis Israelitarum vindicata (both contained in Meuschen N. T. ex talmude illustratum. Lips. 1736. 4, p. 233 u. 287, ss.). W. C. L. Ziegler über die Johannistaufe als unveränderte Anwendung der jüdischen Proselytentaufe (in his theol. Abhandlungen. Bd. 2. Göttingen. 1804, S. 132, ff.). E. G. Bengel über das Alter der jüd. Proselytentaufe. Tübingen. 1814. 8. On the other hand, others deny that Jewish proselyte baptism existed so early. Among the moderns, Paulus Comment. Th. 1, S. 278. De Wette comment. de morte J. C. expiatoria. Berol. 1813. p. 42, ss. J. G. Reiche de baptismatis origine et necessitate necnon de formula baptismali. Goeting. 1816. 8. D. M. Schneckenburger über das Alter der jüdischen Proselytentaufe. Berlin. 1828. 8. Washing, as a symbol of moral cleansing, is mentioned as early as in the writings of the prophets, Ezek. xxxvi. 25, Zech. xiii. 1.

2 Even the place of his appearance *ἐν τῇ ἐρήμῳ τῆς Ἰουδαίας* (Matth. iii. 1), where, according to Plin. Nat. Hist. v. c. 17, the Essenes also dwelt.

3 There is a remarkable testimony concerning John in Jos. Ant. xviii. 5, 2 (first mentioned by Orig. c. Cels. i. p. 35). *Κτείνει τοῦτον (Ἰωάννην) Ἡρώδης, ἀγαθὸν ἄνδρα, καὶ τοὺς Ἰουδαίους κελεύοντα, ἀρετὴν ἐπασκοῦντας, καὶ τῇ πρὸς ἀλλήλους δικαιοσύνῃ καὶ πρὸς τὸν θεὸν εὐσεβείᾳ χρωμένους, βαπτισμῷ συνιέναι· οὕτω γὰρ καὶ τὴν βαπτισιν*

after John himself had fallen a sacrifice to his intrepidity (Acts xviii. 25, xix. 1, ff.).[4]

§ 23.

THE PUBLIC LIFE AND MINISTRY OF JESUS.

Jesus also came out of Galilee to Jordan to be baptized by John, and was recognized in such a way by the latter that he considered it more befitting to receive baptism from Jesus than the contrary. The import of this is, that the Baptist looked upon the rite as a call to higher purity. This baptism was to Jesus the consecration to his Messianic activity. It is true that he began with the same call to his nation as John the Baptist (Matth. iv. 17); but he soon unfolded a far more comprehensive system in the discharge of his ministry, which, though it directly affected the Jewish people only, yet in its very nature belonged to all humanity. The Jewish people at that time

ἀποδεκτὴν αὐτῷ φανεῖσθαι, μὴ ἐπί τινων ἁμαρτάδων παραιτήσει χρωμένων, ἀλλ' ἐφ' ἁγνείᾳ τοῦ σώματος, ἅτε δὴ καὶ τῆς ψυχῆς δικαιοσύνῃ προεκκεκαθαρμένης· καὶ τῶν ἄλλων συστρεφομένων, καὶ γὰρ ἤρθησαν ἐπὶ πλεῖστον τῇ ἀκροάσει τῶν λόγων, δείσας Ἡρώδης τὸ ἐπὶ τοσόνδε πιθανὸν αὐτοῦ τοῖς ἀνθρώποις μὴ ἐπὶ ἀποστάσει τινὶ φέροι, πάντα γὰρ ἐῴκεσαν συμβουλῇ τῇ ἐκείνου πράξοντες, πολὺ κρεῖττον ἡγεῖται, πρίν τι νεώτερον ἐξ αὐτοῦ γενέσθαι, προλαβὼν ἀναιρεῖν, ἢ μεταβολῆς γενομένης εἰς τὰ πράγματα ἐμπεσὼν μετανοεῖν. καὶ **ὁ** *μὲν, ὑποψίᾳ τῇ Ἡρώδου, δέσμιος εἰς τὸν Μαχαιροῦντα πεμφθεὶς—ταύτῃ κτίννυται· τοῖς δὲ Ἰουδαίοις δόξα, ἐπὶ τιμωρίᾳ τῇ ἐκείνου τὸν ὄλεθρον ἐπὶ τῷ στρατεύματι γενέσθαι, τοῦ θεοῦ κακῶς Ἡρώδῃ θέλοντος.*

[4] Cf. Recog. Clem. i. 54 and 60. In the middle of the 17th century, the existence of a sect was made known by Carmelite missionaries, whose head-quarters were Basrah and Suster, calling themselves Nazoreans (not to be confounded with the Muhammedan sect Nasaireans), or Mendeans, but by the Muhammedans they were named Sabians (Sabaei, probably the name was borrowed from the star-worshipers of the Koran). They got the name Christians of St. John from the missionaries. Cf. Ignatii a Jesu narratio originis, rituum et errorum Christianorum S. Johannis. Rom. 1652. 8vo. After one of their holy books was published entire (Codex Nasireaeus, liber Adami appellatus, Syriace transcriptus latineque redditus a Matth. Norberg. 3 Thle. Lond. 1815, 1816. 4to) fragments of two others (the Divan and the book of John) communicated to the world, and many accounts furnished by travelers, Gesenius gave a critical survey of their system in the Universal Encyclopaedia of Ersch and Gruber (Leipzig. 1817), article Zabier, from which it appears that the system is Gnostic-ascetic, nearly related to that of the Valentinians and Ophites, John appearing as an incarnate aeon. The language of their sacred books is an Aramaean dialect, which occupies a middle position between the Syriac and Chaldee. They allege that they came from Jordan, from whence they were driven by the Muhammedans. Most scholars assume the descent of this sect from the disciples of John the Baptist. Les Nazoréens, thése de Theologie historique par L. E. Burckhardt. Strasbourg. 1840. 8vo. On the other side, see O. G. Tychsen in the Deutsches Museum, 1784, Th. 2. S. 414 (who, however, confounds the Nazoreans with another sect, Burckhardt, p. 11. 107). Baumgarten-Crusius bibl. Theol. S. 143.

presented an aspect the most deserving of compassion. In the deepest external degradation, always cherishing the most extravagant hopes in regard to the immediate future, they were led by their very religious views in the road to their destruction. And yet this very religion, when judged, not by the partial, priestly form which it had then received, but as drawn from its original documents, and pervaded by the living prophetic spirit which animated it as there described, must have marvelously revealed itself to every human breast as directly certain, as the only true source of human happiness. It was the aim and object of Jesus to awaken, by his life and doctrine, this prophetic element of the Mosaic religion, but in a purer form and in greater development, among his countrymen; and to bring it into the hearts of men as a spontaneous principle of action. By such spiritual regeneration alone could the Jewish people be delivered even from external corruption; and we can not doubt that Jesus would gladly have effected this outward deliverance also. But his plan extended far wider, although the germs which lay in the compass of his ministry proceeded forth and became visible, for the most part, only after he had left our world. Jesus appeared first in Galilee, and resided not at Nazareth (Luke iv. 24), but usually at *Capernaum.* From this place, however, he not only traversed Galilee, but often abode for a long time in Judea in his journeys to the festivals in Jerusalem. He was only in Samaria occasionally as he went through it; and we find him but once beyond the confines of Judea (Mark vii. 24, ff.). By degrees he drew around him twelve young men, illiterate (Matth. xi. 25), and from the lower orders of society, for the purpose of initiating them into his spirit and plan, by their living with him and continually receiving his instructions. They accompanied him in his smaller journeys on which he appeared, sometimes among small domestic circles, sometimes in synagogues, sometimes among great multitudes under the canopy of heaven; and much as he attracted to himself universal attention by the extraordinary works he wrought, he excited no less astonishment and wonder by his doctrine, which directly convinced and carried captive the hearer (Matth. vii. 28, 29; Luke iv. 32). At first he avoided observation (Matth. ix. 30); he even forbade his disciples to make him known as the Messiah (Matt. xvi.

20); but afterward he declared himself to be the promised Messiah, with a firmness that forbids the idea of mere accommodation (Matth. xxvi. 64). But the religious ideas of the Old Testament had obtained within him a new and higher life, reaching far beyond the local and temporal form handed down among the Jews by tradition.[1] The Old Testament conception of a *Theocracy* was transformed in him into the high idea of the *kingdom of God*, in which men, animated by the Spirit of God, should be united with Deity and one another in moral unity. This kingdom of God he wished, as the Messiah, to establish on earth; on which account he required of his cotemporaries, sunk as they were in the external and the literal, first of all, *change of heart*, that they might be susceptible of the Spirit of God; next, *faith* in himself as the Christ, that by yielding itself up to the higher spirit, even the weaker mind might be elevated to free communion with God. It follows, of course, that nothing stood more in his way than that *Pharisaic righteousness* which rested on works. Hence he leveled his attacks chiefly against *it*. He did not indeed abolish the ceremonial law of Moses, constantly observing it himself; but he could not look upon it in any other light than as an expression of inward religious feeling; and all value attached to religious external observances, independently of true devotional feelings, was worthless in his eyes (Matth. xii. 1, ff.; xv. 1, ff.; v. 24; xii. 9). So far as he designated the free development of this internal religious feeling as the only genuine religious culture, it necessarily followed from his doctrine, and must have been sooner or later expressed publicly by his disciples, that no religious law for men can be in the form of a rule that requires something *merely external*. Thus the abolition of the ceremonial law necessarily followed his teachings. In like manner Jesus confined his immediate efforts to the Jews alone, and avoided coming in contact with those who were not Jews, out of regard to the very prejudices of his nation (Matth. x. 5; xv. 21–28). But still there lay always in his doctrine, which rejected all reliance on externalities, an adaptation for all mankind, as he himself often intimated with sufficient distinctness (Matth. viii. 11, 21, 43).

[1] Chr. F. Böhme die Religion Jesu Christi aus ihren Urkunden dargestellt. Halle. 1825. 2te Aufl. 1827. 8.

While Jesus endeavored to guide his disciples to this purer religion and moral communion in the kingdom of God, he also drew them gradually away from the common notion of retribution which prevailed among the Jews (Luke xiii. 2, ff.; John ix. 2, 3), announced to them the forgiveness of sins in the way of repentance and faith, and then taught them, in this inward communion with God, to meet all external fortunes with submission and confidence, and the firmest trust in God (Matth. vi. 33; x. 28). The kingdom of God, as it was then begun, was only an inward thing (Luke xvii. 21), in continual conflict with the world and with evil; but Jesus promised that he should appear again, to judge the evil, and to place piety and happiness in their natural relation, in the kingdom of God (Matth. xxiv. 30; xxv. 31). The notion of such a triumphant kingdom of God had been already set forth, though in a sensuous form, in the description given of Messiah's reign; and since it could be spoken of generally only in figures, Jesus borrowed his figures from it, giving at the same time sufficient intimation of a more spiritual, universal, and purer view (Matth. xxii. 30). It could not be otherwise than that these figures should be more or less spiritually understood, according to the different degrees of religious culture: but the leading idea on which all depended, the idea of a future adjustment of the relation of happiness to piety in the kingdom of God triumphant, must have always been maintained. The disciples, accustomed to entertain the conception of an earthly Messianic kingdom, not only took all those images in a sensuous acceptation, but also introduced into them many more definite points. Thus, although Jesus had declared the point of time when he should come again to be a secret with God the Father (Matth. xxiv. 36), yet they annexed to the admonition to be always ready (Matth. xxiv. 43, 44), the expectation of the near approach of his coming (Matth. xvi. 27). These sensuous expectations could not at once be eradicated from their minds, without at the same time endangering their faith in Jesus; but they were gradually purified and spiritualized by a series of events. Probably the closing fortunes of Jesus' life, though even they did not destroy those sensuous hopes, were required to convince the disciples that God's ways are very different from man's expectations, and to confirm their faith in the Divine mission of

Jesus; while at the same time they furnished the highest example of a mind renouncing the earthly, entirely devoted to God, and of a self-sacrificing love.[2]

The Pharisees cotemporary with Jesus, affected and exasperated by the truth of his doctrine, did not rest till they had brought him to the death he had long foreseen (Matth. ix. 15; xvi. 21, *et seq.*). Delivered up to them by a disciple, after he instituted, shortly before, a *covenant-supper*, as a symbol of internal union with him, and of unity among his disciples themselves, he was accused by them of insurrection before *Pontius Pilate*, and condemned by him through unworthy views. The courage of the disciples, which had almost vanished away, returned after his resurrection with so much strength and purity, that an unshaken attachment to Jesus was now to be expected from them, even amid outward renunciations and self-denial. It was still reserved, however, for later occurrences to correct many remaining prejudices. Thus it was some time before they fully understood the last commission of Jesus to carry the glad news of the beginning of God's kingdom on earth to all nations, to invite all into it, and to initiate them into it by baptism.

§ 24.

ALLEGED COTEMPORARY NOTICES OF JESUS, NOT IN THE NEW TESTAMENT.

The testimony concerning Christ in Josephus, Ant. xviii. 3, 3, is regarded with the greatest probability as genuine, but interpolated.[1] On the contrary, *the correspondence of Christ*

[2] Chr. F. Boehme de spe Messiana apostolica. Halae. 1826. 8.

[1] *Γίνεται δὲ κατὰ τοῦτον τὸν χρόνον* Ἰησοῦς, *σοφὸς ἀνὴρ [εἴγε ἄνδρα αὐτὸν λέγειν χρή· ἦν γάρ], παραδόξων ἔργων ποιητής [διδάσκαλος ἀνθρώπων τῶν σὺν ἡδονῇ τἀληθῆ δεχομένων], καὶ πολλοὺς μὲν τῶν* Ἰουδαίων *πολλοὺς δὲ καὶ ἀπὸ τοῦ* Ἑλληνικοῦ *ἐπηγάγετο.* [Ὁ Χριστὸς *οὗτος ἦν.*] Καὶ *αὐτὸν ἐνδείξει τῶν πρώτων ἀνδρῶν παρ' ἡμῖν σταυρῷ ἐπιτετιμηκότος* Πιλάτου *οὐκ ἐξεπαύσαντο οἱ τὸ πρῶτον αὐτὸν ἀγαπήσαντες.* [Ἐφάνη *γὰρ αὐτοῖς τρίτην ἔχων ἡμέραν πάλιν ζῶν, τῶν θείων προφητῶν ταῦτά τε καὶ ἄλλα μυρία περὶ αὐτοῦ θαυμάσια εἰρηκότων.*] Εἰσέτι *τε νῦν τῶν* Χριστιανῶν *ἀπὸ τοῦδε ὠνομασμένων οὐκ ἐπέλιπε τὸ φῦλον.* This passage was first mentioned and cited by Eusebius (Hist. eccles. i. 11, demonstr. Evangel. iii. 5), and for a long time repeated by succeeding writers without any hesitation. The first who entertained doubts of its authenticity were Hubert Gifanius, ICtus (the letter in refutation of Sebastianus Lepusculus dd. Basileae the 24. Febr. 1559. See in Melch. Goldasti centuria epistolarum philologicarum, Nro. 61), and

with Abgarus, toparch of Edessa,[2] and the apocryphal narratives of the birth, youth, and last days of Jesus,[3] are un-

Lucas Osiander (in Epitome hist. eccles. Centur. i. lib. 2, cap. 7. Tubing. 1592). More searching investigations of various scholars, respecting the matter from 1646–1661, first occasioned by the Altdorf Professor Sebastian Snellius, who denied the authenticity, are collected in: Epistolae xxx. philol. et. hist. de Fl. Jos. testim., quod. J. C. tribuit, rec. Christoph. Arnold. Noriberg. 1661. 12 (also in Havercamp's edition of Josephus, tom. ii. Append. p. 233). Here the reasons against it are developed with superior skill, especially by Dav. Blondel and Tanaquil Faber. Later defenders are: Carol. Daubuz pro testimonio Flavii Josephi de Jesu Christo, libb. ii. Londini. 1706. 8 (also in Havercamp's Josephus, tom. ii. Append. p. 187). Houteville erwiesene Wahrheit der christl. Religion durch ihre Geschichte. Frankf. 1745. 4. S. 275, ff. Oberthür in der Vorrede zum 2ten Theile der Uebersetzung des Josephus v. Friese. Altona. 1805. C. G. Bretschneider πάρεργον super Jos. de J. C. testimonio (hinter s. capit. theolog. Jud. dogm. e Fl. Josephi scriptis collect. Lips. 1812. 8. pag. 59). C. F. Böhmert über des Flav. Joseph. Zeugniss von Christo. Leipz. 1823. 8 (comp. on the other side, the review in Winer's and Engelhardt's theolog. Journ. Bd. 2. S. 95, ff.). F. H. Schoedel Flav. Josephus de J. Chr. testatus. Vindiciae Flavianae. Lips. 1840. 8. Opponents of the genuineness are: (Abbé de Longuerue) sur le passage de Joseph en faveur de Jésus-Christ (against Daubuz) in Clericus biblioth. ancienne et moderne, t. vii. p. 237. God. Lessii disertt. ii. super Josephi de Christo testimonio. Goetting. 1781, 82. Eichstaedt Flaviani de J. C. testimonii αὐθεντία quo jure nuper defensa sit, quaestt. vi. Jenae. 1813–41. Arguments for the genuineness: 1. The agreement of all MSS. from the time of Eusebius. 2. The number of Christians was too great to allow Josephus to pass over their origin without mention. 3. Josephus mentions John the Baptist. Against the genuineness: 1. The silence of the fathers before Eusebius, while Josephus, in Orig. c. Cels. i. p. 35, is said to be ἀπιστῶν τῷ Ἰησοῦ ὡς Χριστῷ. 2. The passage interrupts the connection. 3. The contents betray a Christian. 4. The other Jewish historian, Justus Tiberiensis, has not mentioned Christ. Photii bibl. cod. 33. The assumption of interpolations which found their way into all the MSS. of Josephus out of the far more extensively circulated church history of Eusebius, is the most probable, since Josephus was read and copied only by Christians. Chrysostom appears, however, not to have been acquainted with these interpolations, since he mentions Josephus several times, and in hom. in Joann. 12, quotes his testim. de Joanne, but is silent in regard to this passage. Remarkable is the silence of Photius in his accounts regarding Jos., Archaeol. (bibl. cod. 76 and 238), especially as he remarks respecting Justus, cod. 33, that he being a Jew, and encumbered with Jewish prejudices, does not mention Jesus and his miracles. The following writers have decided in favor of an interpolation formed by altering single expressions: Knittel (nova biblioth. phil. et crit. vol. i. i. 118. Goetting. 1782. 8), and Paulus (Heidelb. Jahrb., August 1820, S. 734). In favor of an interpolation formed by inserted glosses are: Steph. le Moyen varia sacra, ii. 931, l'Abbé de Fontaines in the Journ. des Savans, ann. 1723, Juill., p. 10, Paulus Comm. über die 3 ersten Evang. iii. 740, H. Olshausen hist. eccl. vet. monumenta praecipua, vol. 1. Berol. 1820. 8. p. 3, Heinichen Excursus in his edition of Eusebius, tom. iii. p. 331. I have indicated above, by parenthetic marks, in what light I look upon the interpolation.

[2] Euseb. Hist. eccl. i. 13, and Moses Chorenensis (about 440) Hist. Armen. ii. 29–31, found these letters in the Archives of Edessa, and gave them to the public in a Greek and Armenian translation. At the time of Christ, Abgarus Uchomo: about 170, there was a Christian Abgarus. These letters, therefore, may have been forged long before Eusebius. Cf. Assemani bibl. Orient. t. i. p. 554. t. iii. p. 2. p. 8. Bayer historia Osrhoëna et Edessena. Petrop. 1734. 4. p. 104. Semler de Christi ad Abgarum epistola. Hal. 1768. 4. The genuineness of the letters is defended by W. F. Rinck, in Illgen's Zeitschrift f. d. histor. Theol. 1843. ii. 3.

[3] Two classes of apocryphal gospels may be distinguished: I. The older, which contained much the same cycle of narrations as the canonical; for example, the gospels of the

questionably spurious. Still more modern are the pretended authentic *likenesses* of Jesus;[4] and the epistle of *Lentu-*

Hebrews and the Egyptians, &c. II. The later, which refer to the youth, the parents, and the last fortunes of Christ. A. Respecting the history of Christ's youth, we find fabulous writings first of all among the Marcosians in the second century. (Irenaeus, i. c. 17.) The orthodox, at the same time, received a doctrinal interest in maintaining the miraculous stories of Jesus' youth in opposition to those Gnostics who asserted that the aeon was first united with the man at the baptism of the latter. (Ephiphan. haer. li. c. 20.) Several of these traditions are found in the Koran (comp. Augusti christologiae Coranicae lineamenta. Jen. 1799). Gospels of the infancy still extant are the gospel of Thomas, an Arabic gospel of the infancy, and a Latin history of the nativity of Mary and the infancy of the Saviour. At a later period the virgin Mary also began to invite men to similar fabrications. Compounds of the two are exemplified in the Protevangelion of James, the Arabic history of Joseph the carpenter, and the Latin gospel of the nativity of Mary. B. Respecting the last days of Jesus, Justin Martyr, Apol. i. c. 35 and 48, refers to the τὰ ἐπὶ Ποντίου Πιλάτου γενόμενα ἄκτα; in the same way he himself alludes, c. 34, and also Chrysostom, hom. 31. de natali Christi, to the acts regarding the census of Quirinus; not that he had seen them himself, but because he pre-supposes their existence in the Roman archives. Hence arose Christian traditions in relation to the contents of these acts, out of which Tertullian, Apolog. c. 5, 21, draws the fabulous. During the persecution of Maximin, the heathen, taking occasion from these traditions, produced wicked Acta Pilati (Euseb. H. E. ix. c. 5), to which the Christians of that day had none others to oppose. The latter, however, soon made their appearance afterward (Epiphan. haer. l. c. 1), and were fashioned and molded in various ways. One of these fabrication has received in later times the name, gospel of Nicodemus. Cf. Henke de Pilati actis probabilia. Helmst. 1784 (opusc. academ. Lips. 1802. p. 199). W. L. Brunn de indole, aetate, et usu libri apocr. vulgo inscripti Evangel. Nicodemi. Berol. 1794. 8. Editions are: J. A. Fabricii codex apocryphus N. T. partes iii. ed. 2. Hamb. 1719. 8. J. C. Thilo codex apocryphus N. T. t. i. Lips. 1832 (containing the apocryphal gospels). [Jones on the canon of the New Testament. Lond. 3 vols. 8vo.] Die apokryph. Evangelien u. Apostelgeschichten, übers. mit Einleit. und Anmerk. v. Dr. K. F. Borberg. Stuttgart. 1841. Cf. C. J. Nitzsch de apocryphorum Evangeliorum in explicandis canonicis usu et abusu. Viteb. 1808. 4. F. J. Arens de Evangell. apocr. in canonicis usu historico, critico, exegetico. Goetting. 1835. 4.

[4] The first traces of likenesses of Christ are to be found among the Carpocratians (Iren. i. 25), and in the lararium of Severus Alexander (Lamprid. c. 29). The persecuted church of the first centuries needed in Christ the pattern of a sufferer. Hence arose the general opinion that he was of unsightly form, according to Isaiah liii. 2, 3. (So Tertullian de carne Christi 9, adv. Jud. c. 14, and often. Clem. Alex. Paedeg. iii. 1, Strom. ii. p. 308. Origenes contra Cels. vi. p. 327, δυσειδὲς τὸ Ἰησοῦ σῶμα.) At the same time all representations were forbidden, according to Exodus xx. 4. As soon as art began to represent Jesus, it must also have sought to express his excellence even in external form. Hence, from the fourth century onward, Jesus was supposed to have had a body of external beauty, something divinely majestic in his exterior, according to Psalm xlv. 3. (Hieron. comm. in Matt. ix. 9). Yet they confessed still that there was no authentic likeness of Jesus to be seen. (Augustin de trinitate, viii. 4. Nam et ipsius dominicae facies carnis innumerabilium cogitationum diversitate variatur et fingitur, quae tamen una erat, quaecunque erat, and c. 5, qua fuerit ille facie, nos penitus ignoramus). Eusebius (H. E. vii. c. 18. Comp. the excursus in Heinichen's edition, tom. iii. p. 396, ss.) relates concerning a statue at Paneas that it was there supposed to point to Jesus and the occurrence in Matt. ix. 20. All later writers repeat the story after him, and John Malala (600 A.D.), in his Chronog. p. 305, gave the name of the woman Beronice. This monument was destroyed by Julian (Sozom. v. 21. Philostorg. vii. 3), or according to Asterius, bishop of Amasia (about 400, in Photii bibl. cod. 271 in fine), by Maximin at a time when copies of it

lus to the Roman senate,[5] containing a description of his person.

were hardly taken. Judging by the analogy of many coins, the memorial had been erected in honor of an emperor (probably Hadrian), and falsely interpreted by the Christians, perhaps on account of a σωτῆρι or θεῷ appearing in the inscription (cf. Th. Hassaei diss. ii. de monumento Paneadensi. Bremae. 1726. 4, and in ejusd. sylloge dissertt. ii. 314. Beausobre über die Bildsäule zu Paneas in Cramer's Sammlungen zur Kirchengesch. und theolog. Gelehrsamk. Th. 1. Leipzig. 1748). Later imagines Christi non manu factae (cf. J. Gretser syntagma de imagg. non manu factis. Ingolst. 1622, and appended to Georg. Codinus ed. J. Goar. p. 289. Is. Beausobre des images de main divine, in the Biblioth. Germanique, xviii. 10. Comp. also the controversial writings in the succeeding volumes of that work). 1. The *θεότευκτος εἰκὼν, ἣν ἀνθρώπων χεῖρες οὐκ εἰργάσαντο* (Evagrius Hist. eccl. iv. 27), sent to King Abgarus, and often mentioned in the image controversy, came from Edessa to Constantinople. Rome and Genoa now contend for the honor of its possession. A new miraculous copy of it on a brick was brought by order of the Emperor Nicephorus from Edessa to Constantinople, 968 A.D. Bayer hist. Osrhoëna et Edess. p. 112. Cf. Leo Diaconus (prim. ed. Hase, Paris. 1819), lib. iv. c. 10. 2. Sudarium St. Veronicae, still in the middle ages rightly named Veronica, i. e., vera icon. Cf. Gervassi Tilberiensis (about 1210) otia imperialia, c. 25 (Leibnit. scriptt. Brunsv. t. i. p. 968) : De figura Domini, quae Veronica dicitur. Est ergo Veronica pictura Domini vera. Matth. Paris, ad ann. 1216 : effigies vultus Domini, quae Veronica dicitur. Now in Jaen, Milan, and Rome. (Cf. Act. SS. ad d. 4. Febr. Lambertini de servorum Dei beatificatione, lib. iv. p. 2, c. 31). John VII. (705 A.D.) is said to have erected a house of St. Maria in Beronica. 3. Sudarium Christi (first mentioned by Bede in lib. de locis sanctis) in Besançon, and the Sindon Christi in Turin. Pretended pictures of Christ made by his cotemporaries : 1. A picture of Christ, painted by Luke. Perhaps the first mention of it is by Theodorus Lector (about 518) apud Nicephorum Callistum (about 1333) Hist. eccles. ii. 43, who also mentions pictures of Mary and the principal Apostles, painted by Luke, Gregorius III., in epist. ad Leonem Imp., Simeon Metaphrastes (about 900) in vita S. Lucae. There is a picture of Christ, as a boy of thirteen years of age, by Luke, in the Sancta Sanctorum in the church of St. John Lateran at Rome. 2. An image of Christ, cut out of cedar-wood by Nicodemus, which was before at Berytus, as is pretended (cf. (Pseudo-) Athanasius de passione imaginis D. n. J. Chr. qualiter crucifixa est in Syria in urbe Beryto), appears first in the Acta Synod. Nicaenae, ii. (787) sess. iv., was brought to Constantinople by the emperor Nicephorus (Leo Diac. x. c. 5), and is now at Lucca (vultus Lucanus in Gervasius, c. 24, in Leibnitii script. Brunsv. t. i. p. 967). Cf. Joh. Reiskii exercitatt. hist. de imaginibus J. Chr. Janae. 1685. 4. Jablonski de origine imaginum Christi, in Opuscul. ed. te Water. t. iii. p. 377. (Lugd. Bat. 1809). F. Münter Sinnbilder und Kunstvorstellungen der alten Christen (2 Hfte. Altona. 1825. 4) ii. 3. Junker üb. Christusköpfe, in Meusel's Miscellaneen artist. Inhalts. xxv. 28. Ammon über Christusköpfe in his Magazin für christl. Prediger, i. ii. 315.

[5] (J. B. Carpzov) de oris et corporis Jesu Christi forma Pseudolentuli, Joh. Damasceni et Nicephori prosopographiae. Helmstad. 1777. 4. In *αὐθεντίαν* epistolae P. Lentuli ad Sen. Rom. de Jesu Chr. scriptae denuo inquirit J. Ph. Gabler. Jen. 1819. (Pfingstprogr.) [American Bibl. Repository, 1832.]

SECOND CHAPTER.

APOSTOLIC AGE TO THE DESTRUCTION OF JERUSALEM.

SOURCES: Acts of the Apostles,[1] and Epistles of the New Testament. Scattered notices in the fathers of the first period, collected by Eusebius.[2]

WORKS: Lud. Capelli historia apostolica illustrata. Genev. 1634. 4. ed. Jo. A. Fabricius, Lips. 1691. 8. (William Cave's History of the Apostles. London. 1677). Ph. Jac. Hartmann comm. de rebus gestis Christianorum sub Apostolis. Berol. 1699.' 4. J. Fr. Buddei ecclesia apostolica s. de statu ecclesiae christ. sub Apostolis. Jenae. 1729. 8. (G. Benson's Planting of the Christian religion. London. 1756. 4to.) J. J. Hess Geschichte u. Schriften d. Apostel Jesu. 3 Bde. 4te Aufl. Zürich. 1820–22. 8. F. Lücke comm. de eccl. christ. apostolica. Goetting. 1813. 4. Planck's Gesch. d. Christ. u.s.w. See § 20. A. Neander's Gesch. d. Pflanzung u. Leitung der christl. Kirche durch die Apostel. 2 Bde. 3te Aufl. Hamburg. 1841.

G. Ch. R. Matthäi der Religionsglaube der Apostel nach s. Inhalte, Ursprunge u. Werthe. Bd. 1. Gött. 1826. Chr. Fr. Böhme die Religion der Apostel Jesu Christi aus ihren Urkunden dargestellt. Halle. 1829.

§ 25.

EARLY HISTORY OF THE CHRISTIAN COMMUNITY TILL THE CONVERSION OF PAUL.

The adherents of Jesus, more than 500 in number (1 Cor. xv. 6), and among them the twelve disciples, *Simon* (Cephas, Peter), and *Andrew*, sons of Jonas, *James* and *John*, sons of Zebedee (Boanerges, sons of thunder, Mark iii. 17),[1] *Philip*,

[1] For an account of the numerous Acts of the Apostles which are found in antiquity especially among single heretical parties, see the list in Fabricii cod. apocr. Nov. Test. tom. ii. p. 743, ss. Thus the Ebionites had the *περίοδοι Πέτρου διὰ Κλήμεντος γραφεῖσαι* (Epiphan. haer. xxx. c. 15, comp. below, § 59), and *πράξεις ἄλλαι Ἀποστόλων* (l. c. c. 16). The Manichaeans, the Actus Apostolorum or *τῶν Ἀποστόλων περίοδοι*, composed by one Leucius Charinus (Augustin. de fide contra Manich. c. 38, and often. Photii bibl. cod. 114), &c. One of the most modern and copious productions of this kind is the Abdiae (this Abdias, it is pretended, was a disciple of the Apostles, and first bishop of Babylon) historia certaminis apostolici (belonging to the eighth or ninth century), published in Latin in Fabricii cod. apocryph. New Test. t. ii. p. 388, ss. Respecting the apocryphal productions of this kind, printed and unprinted, see Thilo acta Thomae in the Notitia, p. lii. ss.

[2] Later records are: Synopsis de vita et morte Prophetarum, Apostolorum, et lxx. discipulorum Christi, spuriously ascribed to Dorotheus Tyrius, who lived about 303 (Latin in Bibl. PP. max. tom. iii., Greek fragments in Cave histor. literar. t. i. p. 164, ss., and in the Chronicon paschale ed. du Fresne, p. 426, ss.). Hippolytus (not Portuensis, about 230, perhaps Thebanus, about 930) de xii. Apostolis, ubinam quisque eorum praedicaverit, et consummatus sit (in Combefisii auctario, t. ii. Paris. 1648).

[1] According to Wieseler (theol. Studien u. Krit. 1840, iii. 648), the sons of Zebedee were cousins of the Lord, their mother Salome the sister of Mary.

Thomas (called Didymus, John xx. 24), *Bartholomew* (Nathanael? John i. 46), *Matthew* (Matthew ix. 9; Levi, the son of Alphaeus, Mark ii. 14), *James* (the son of Alphaeus, Matthew x. 3, and of Mary, Matthew xxvii. 56, the wife of Cleopas, John xix. 25),[2] *Thaddeus* (Lebbaeus surnamed Thaddeus, Matth. x. 3, Jude the brother of James, Luke vi. 16; Acts i. 13), *Simon Zelotes* (the Canaanite, Matth. x. 4), and *Matthias*, who was chosen in place of Judas Iscariot, to whom were now added the brethren of Jesus who had become believers,[3] spent the first days after Christ's ascension in retirement in Jerusalem, till the Divine Spirit, who had been in the prophets and in Jesus, began to manifest his living power in them in an extraordinary manner on the day of Pentecost. Furnished with power and courage, the apostles now appeared more publicly, and the number of Christ's confessors increased every day. The community, however, did not renounce Judaism and the Jewish law, but rather considered themselves to be the society of genuine Israelites (*μαθηταί, ἀδελφοί, πιστεύοντες, σωζόμενοι, φοβούμενοι τὸν θεόν*, called in derision by the Jews *Nazarenes and Galileans*) who, having been saved from that untoward generation (Acts ii. 40), were preparing themselves for the unfolding of the Messiah's kingdom in its excellency. It must certainly be admitted, however, that sensuous expectations and erroneous opinions of the near approach of Christ's return (Acts i. 6, iii. 19–21), were mixed up with their better principles.[4] The conditions of reception into this kingdom were repentance and faith in Christ, on which forgivenes of sin was promised in baptism, and the Holy Spirit imparted by the imposition of hands. Though they knew that the heathen also were admitted into the kingdom of God, still more that they should be invited, they yet believed that these Gentiles should first be incorporated among the Jewish people as *proselytes of righteousness*, and necessarily observe

[2] He is generally reckoned the same person with the *ἀδελφὸς τοῦ κυρίου*, Gal. i. 19. Comp. especially Pott prolegg. in epist. Jacobi (ed. iii. 1816), p. 58, ss. Schneckenburger annotatio ad. epist. Jac. (Stuttg. 1832), p. 144. On the other side see Dr. C. F. W. Clemen die Brüder Jesu, in Winer's Zeitschr. für wissenschaftl. Theol. iii. 329. Credner's Einl. in d. N. T. i. ii. 571. Neander's apost. Kirche, ii. 422. E. Th. Mayerhoff's Einleit. in d. petrin. Schriften (Hamb. 1835), S. 43. A. H. Blom de *τοῖς ἀδελφοῖς* et *ταῖς ἀδελφαῖς τοῦ κυρίου*. Lugd. Bat. 1839. 8. Neudecker's Einl. in d. N. T. S. 656. Wieseler in the theol. Studien u. Krit. 1842, i. 71. Comp. Winer's bibl. Realwörterbuch, i. 620.

[3] Act. i. 14, comp. John vii. 5.

[4] Chr. Fr. Boehme de spe Messiana apostolica. Halae. 1826. 8.

the entire Mosaic law. With this opinion they could not be in haste to invite the heathen also to embrace Christianity.

But although the community did not separate itself from the religion of the Jews, yet they were more closely connected together by the peculiar direction which their religious feelings naturally took, and by their peculiar hopes. Thus there arose by degrees a regularly constituted society among the brethren. For this the Jewish synagogue presented itself as the most natural model.[5] At first, the apostles themselves performed the duties of the society, but by degrees special officers were appointed. The apostles caused seven *distributors of alms* to be chosen (Acts vi. 1–6),[6] inasmuch as the brethren showed very great liberality toward their poor,[7] and because the administration of these gifts threatened to be detrimental to the proper calling and ministry of the twelve. Soon after this, we find πρεσβύτεροι, elders (Acts xi. 30 = זְקֵנִים), chosen not so much for the purpose of teaching, as for the management of common concerns, and for maintaining the ordinances of the church. In all these appointments of the society, the apostles did not act despotically, but allowed the church to determine them (Acts vi. 2; xv. 22, 23).

The bold appearance of the apostles, and the enlargement of their party, soon excited attention. The *Sadducees* were now

[5] The chief work is: Campeg. Vitringa de synagoga vetere, lib. iii., quibus tum de synagogis agitur, tum praecipue formam regiminis et ministerii earum in ecclesiam christ. translatam esse demonstratur. Franequerae. 1696, and Leucopetr. 1726. 4.

[6] Luke calls them simply the seven (οἱ ἑπτά), Acts xxi. 8. In later times they have for the most part been regarded as the first deacons. So Cyprian, as early as his time; Epist. 65, ad Rogatianum. They are, however, distinguished from the deacons by Chrysostom, Hom. 14 in Acta § 3 (ed. Montfaucon. ix. 115), and the council of Trulla, canon 16. Vitringa de syn. vet. lib. iii. p. ii. cap. 5, compares them with the גַּבָּאִים of the synagogue; and on the other hand, the διακόνοι of Paul with the חַזָּנִים. Boehmer, diss. jur. eccl. ant. diss. vii. p. 377, actually looked upon them as the first presbyters. See on the other side Mosheim de rebus Christ. ante Const. p. 122. Without doubt the deacons arose from the seven, by an enlargement of the circle of duties required. See Mosheim, l. c. p. 120. Neander's apost. Kirche, i. 142. R. Rothe's Anfänge d. christl. Kirche, i. 162. Another opinion of Vitringa (l. c.), supported by Mosheim (l. c. p. 118), is, that those seven were appointed for the Hellenist poor. But the Grecian names do not necessarily indicate Hellenists; comp. the names of the apostles Andrew and Philip. Perhaps three were Hebrew, three Hellenistic Jews, and one a proselyte.

[7] The opinion that the kingdom of Messiah would soon appear contributed, doubtless, very much to promote this liberality (comp. Matth. xxv. 34, ff.). It is not a community of goods that is taught in Acts ii. 44, 45; iv. 33–35; but a voluntary equalizing of property, according to the precept laid down in Luke xii. 33. Cf. Mosheim de vera natura communionis bonorum in eccl. Hierosol. in his dissertatt. ad hist. eccles. pertinentium, ii. i. Ananias's crime was a meanly calculating selfishness, assuming withal the appearance of enthusiastic brotherly love.

the bitterest enemies of those who confessed the name of one risen from the dead (Acts iv. 2; v. 17; xxiii. 6). On the other hand, *priests* (Acts vi. 7) and *Pharisees* (xv. 5) joined the Christians. After threatenings had been used with the apostles in vain (Acts iv.), the Sadducean party in the Sanhedrim wished to apply violent measures (v. 17, ff.), but were restrained by the prudent counsel of the Pharisee Gamaliel (v. 34, ff., comp. xxiii. 6). Some Hellenists, however, provoked by the zeal of Stephen, stirred up the popular fury, to which the Sanhedrim soon gave way. Stephen fell as the first martyr (vi. 8–vii. 60); but the very persecution that now set in was the first means of spreading Christianity still farther. The Christians, driven from Jerusalem, preached the gospel in Judea, Samaria (viii. 1–4), even as far as Damascus (ix. 10, 19), Phoenicia, Cyprus, and Antioch, but yet only to the Jews (xi. 19). In the mean time they had cast off the Pharisaic prejudice against the Samaritans; and in Samaria itself *Philip* gained many converts to Christianity. The same individual preached the gospel in the towns on the sea-coast of Palestine, and finally took up his abode in Caesarea, probably as the founder of a church there (viii. 40, comp. xxi. 8). The apostles, who had hitherto remained always in Jerusalem, now sent Peter and John to Samaria, in order to carry on the work there begun (viii. 14, ff.). Peter then went to the towns on the sea-coast, where he was commanded by Heaven to baptize a pious proselyte of the gate, the centurion Cornelius, in Caesarea (Acts x.). He quieted, indeed, the believers in Jerusalem who were not pleased with this transaction (xi. 1–18); but the greatest part of them did not proceed farther than to allow that the heathen should be baptized before being circumcised. In this sense alone the church at Jerusalem approved of the conduct of some Hellenistic Jews in Antioch who had converted Gentiles also to Christianity (xi. 20, comp. ver. 22). They still maintained the view, that the Mosaic law was absolutely binding on all nations,[8] which was held particularly by some believing Pharisees (xv. 5), regarding the universal and strict observance of that law as an essential characteristic of the times of Messiah (according to Isaiah lii. 1, lxvi. 17, 20; Zech. viii. 21–23, xiv. 16, &c.).

[8] Above, § 17, note 8. My treatise respecting the Nazarenes and Ebionites in Staüdlin's u. Tzschirner's Archiv. f. K. G. iv. 2, 308.

§ 26.

PAUL.

W. Paley's Horae Paulinae. Translated into German, from the English, by Henke. Helmstadt. 1797. 8vo. J. T. Hemsen der Apostel Paulus, herausgeg. v. Lücke. Göttingen. 1830. 8. K. Schrader der Apostel Paulus. 3 Thle. Leipzig. 1830. f. 8. (Chronology, history, creed.) Winer's bibl. Realwörterbuch, ii. 245.

On the chronology see J. Pearson annales Paulini (prefixed to his Opp. posthumis chronol. Lond. 1688. 4). Keil de definiendo tempore itineris Pauli Hierosolymitani Gal. ii. 1, 2, commemorati. 1798 (also in Keilii opuscul. academ. ed. J. D. Goldhorn. i. 160). Vogel Versuch chronolog. Standpunkte in der Lebensgesch. Pauli (in Gabler's theol. Journ. i. ii. 243), Süskind Versuch chronol. Standpunkte für die Apostelgesch. u. f. d. Leben Jesu (in Bengel's Archiv. für d. Theol. i. 156, ff. 297 ff.). J. E. C. Schmidt Chronologie d. Apostelgeschichte (in Keil and Tzschirner's Analecten, iii. i. 128). On the other side, Keil über die Zeit, in welcher der Brief an die Galater geschrieben ist (Analecten, iii. ii. 55, and in Latin in Keilii opusculis, i. 351). C. G. Küchler de anno quo Paulus Apost. ad sacra christ. conversus est. Lips. 1828. 8. H. A. Schott's Erörterung einiger wichtiger chronolog. Punkte in d. Lebensgesch. d. Ap. Paulus. Jena. 1832. 8. R. Anger de temporum in actis App. ratione. Lips. 1833. 8. J. F. Wurm über die Zeitbestimmungen im Leben d. Ap. Paulus, in the Tübingen Zeitschrift f. Theol. 1833, i. 3.

In the mean time, however, that man had been previously converted to Christianity, to whom the mystery was to be announced that the Gentiles should be fellow-heirs of the promises (Ephes. iii. 3–6). *Saul*, born at *Tarsus* in Cilicia, and a Roman citizen,[1] but educated in Jerusalem under Gamaliel, a Pharisee, from being a dangerous enemy of Christianity suddenly became a zealous adherent to it (37–40 A.D.). After a three years' abode in Damascus and Arabia he came to Jerusalem, where *Barnabas*[2] introduced him to the apostles Peter and James (Gal. i. 17–19; Acts ix. 19–27). The very same person conducted him also to the great scene of his apostolic labors; for, having been sent by the apostles to Antioch in order to establish the infant church there, he recalled Paul from Tarsus, and took him as his assistant (Acts xi. 22–26). After this, when *Herod Agrippa* (41–44), for the purpose of ingratiating himself with the people, persecuted the church at Jerusalem, when James the elder was put to death, and Peter was saved from a like fate only by a miracle (Acts xii.), Jerusalem ceased to be the secure seat of the apostles;[3] and *James*, the brother

[1] On the rights of Roman citizenship, see Winer's bibl. Realwörterbuch, i. 235.

[2] Gu. H. Haverkorn van Rysewyk diss. de Barnaba. Arnhemiae. 1835. 8.

[3] With this agrees Apollonius (about 190), who (Euseb. H. E. v. 18) ὡς ἐκ παραδόσεως

of the Lord, and a Nazarite, appeared at the head of the church with a reputation equal to that of an apostle.[4] In the mean time, Barnabas and Saul at Antioch gathered from among Jews and Gentiles a church so numerous, even in wealthy members (*χριστιανοί*, Acts ii. 26),[5] that they were able to bring contributions thence to the brethren at Jerusalem when a famine occurred (44 A.D., Acts xi. 27–30; xii. 25). After this, the two entered on the first large missionary journey through *Cyprus*, *Pamphylia*, *Pisidia*, *Lycaonia*, during which the gospel was preached to Jews and Gentiles. After they had again abode for a long time in Antioch, Hebrew Christians came thither who excited divisions in the church, by the assertion, that the

τὸν σωτῆρά φησι προστεταχέναι τοῖς αὐτοῦ ἀποστόλοις ἐπὶ δώδεκα ἔτεσι μὴ χωρισθῆναι τῆς Ἱερουσαλήμ. So also the *Κήρυγμα Πέτρου* in Clem. Alex. Strom. vi. 762. Comp. Credner's Beiträge zur Einl. in die bibl. Schriften, i. 353, 363.

[4] Hegesippus in Euseb. H. E. ii. 23: *Διαδέχεται τὴν ἐκκλησίαν μετὰ τῶν ἀποστόλων ὁ ἀδελφὸς τοῦ κυρίου Ἰάκωβος, ὁ ὀνομασθεὶς ὑπὸ πάντων δίκαιος.—Οὗτος δὲ ἐκ κοιλίας μετρὸς αὐτοῦ ἅγιος ἦν. Οἶνον καὶ σίκερα οὐκ ἔπιεν, οὐδὲ ἔμψυχον ἔφαγε· ξυρὸν ἐπὶ τὴν κεφαλὴν αὐτοῦ οὐκ ἀνέβη· ἔλαιον οὐκ ἠλείψατο, καὶ βαλανείῳ οὐκ ἐχρήσατο. Τούτῳ μόνῳ ἐξῆν εἰς τὰ ἅγια εἰσιέναι· οὐδὲ γὰρ ἐρεοῦν ἐφόρει, ἀλλὰ σινδόνας. Καὶ μόνος εἰσήρχετο εἰς τὸν ναὸν, ηὑρίσκετό τε κείμενος ἐπὶ τοῖς γόνασι, καὶ αἰτούμενος ὑπὲρ τοῦ λαοῦ ἄφεσιν, ὡς ἀπεσκληκέναι τὰ γόνατα αὐτοῦ δίκην καμήλου, διὰ τὸ ἀεὶ κάμπτειν ἐπὶ γόνυ προσκυνοῦντα τῷ θεῷ, καὶ αἰτεῖσθαι ἄφεσιν τῷ λαῷ. Διά γέ τοι τὴν ὑπερβολὴν τῆς δικαιοσύνης αὐτοῦ ἐκαλεῖτο δίκαιος, καὶ Ὠβλίας, ὅ ἐστιν ἑλληνιστὶ περιοχὴ τοῦ λαοῦ καὶ δικαιοσύνη, ὡς οἱ προφῆται δηλοῦσι περὶ αὐτοῦ.* (*Ὠβλίας* עַם עֹפֶל according to Reines. Var. lect. lib. iii. On the other hand, Fuller, Misc. sacr. lib. iii., *Ὠζλίαμ* עֻזָּלְעַם after Ps. xxix. 11. Comp. Routh Reliq. sacr. i. 214. Heinichen ad h. l. Kimmel de Rufino, p. 278.) Here the principles of the Essenes are mixed with the Nazarite, doubtless in the traditional account of the later Ebionites, who fathered their asceticism upon James. Clement of Alexandria related, in the sixth book of his Hypotyposes (Euseb. ii. 1), *Πέτρον καὶ Ἰάκωβον καὶ Ἰωάννην μετὰ τὴν ἀνάληψιν τοῦ σωτῆρος, ὡς ἂν καὶ ὑπὸ τοῦ κυρίου προτετιμημένους, μὴ ἐπιδικάζεσθαι δόξης, ἀλλ' Ἰάκωβον τὸν δίκαιον ἐπίσκοπον Ἱεροσολύμων ἑλέσθαι.* The three apostles selecting are also those named in Matth. xvii. 1, 26, 37: consequently the James specified is the son of Zebedee. It has been disputed whether the person chosen, the same who appears at the head of the church in Jerusalem (Acts xii. 17; xv. 13; xxi. 18; Gal. i. 19; ii. 9), was the son of Alphaeus, or the brother of our Lord, or both (comp. § 25, note 2). Hegesippus manifestly points out the brother of the Lord, different from the apostle. So also the Apost. Constit. ii. 55; vi. 12. In vi. 14, they give a list of the twelve apostles, and then put in equal rank with them: *Ἰάκωβός τε ὁ τοῦ κυρίου ἀδελφὸς καὶ Ἱεροσολύμων ἐπίσκοπος, καὶ Παῦλος ὁ τῶν ἐθνῶν διδάσκαλος;* a testimony which deserves consideration as belonging to the third century and to Syria. It need not appear remarkable that James the son of Alphaeus, as well as most of the apostles, should disappear from the record of the New Testament, and that Luke and Paul did not consider it necessary to separate from him and to characterize particularly the James who is conspicuous in all Christendom.

[5] This was probably at first a name of derision in the mouth of the inhabitants of Antioch, who were famous for their wit (Lucian. de Saltat. c. 76: *οἱ γὰρ Ἀντιοχεῖς εὐφυεστάτη πόλις.* Julianus Misopog. p. 314. Ammian. Marcell. xxii. 14. Zosimus, iv. p. 258. Procop. Pers. ii. 8).

newly converted Gentile Christians must also necessarily become Jewish *proselytes of righteousness*. Hence Paul and Barnabas were sent to Jerusalem, where they received from the collective apostles, and the assembled church, a decision to the effect that the Gentiles should only be required to accede to proselytism of the gate (Acts xv.).[6] They were also, at the same time, recognized as *apostles of the Gentiles* by Peter, James, and John, who resolved to continue their labors among the Jews (Gal. ii. 9, A.D. 52). Soon after, Barnabas and Mark made *a second journey* to Cyprus, while Paul and Silas repaired to the churches of Asia Minor. In Lystra, Paul took Timothy with him, traveled through *Phrygia* and *Galatia*, passed over into *Macedonia*, where churches were founded at Philippi, Thessalonica, and Beroea, and came by Athens to *Corinth* (*Epistles to the Thessalonians*).[7] After remaining there a year and a half, he returned by Ephesus, Caesarea, and Jerusalem, to An-

[6] The injunctions in Acts xv. 29 are the so-called precepts of Noah. See above § 17, note 7. So Origen in comment. ad epist. ad Rom. lib. ii. (ad Rom. ii. 26, ed Lommatzsch, p. 128): Vides ergo (out of Levit. xvii. 10–12), hanc de observatione sanguinis legem, quae communiter et filiis Israel et advenis data est, observari etiam a nobis, qui ex gentibus per Jesum Christum credimus Deo. Nos enim proselytos et advenas Scriptura nominare consuevit: cum dicit (Deut. xxviii. 43): Advena qui est in te, ascendet super te sursum; tu autem descendes deorsum. Ipse erit tibi caput, tu autem eris ejus cauda. Ideo ergo legem de observatione sanguinis communem cum filiis Israel etiam gentium suscepit ecclesia. Haec namque ita intelligens in lege scripta, tunc beatum illud Apostolorum Concilium decernebat, dogmata et decreta gentibus scribens, ut abstinerent se non solum ab his, quae idolis immolantur, et a fornicatione, sed et a sanguine et a suffocato. Tertull. de Monogam. c. 5: In Christo omnia revocantur ad initium—et libertas ciborum et sanguinis solius abstinentia, sicut ab initio fuit. Initium tibi et in Adam censetur, et in Noe recensetur. Constitt. apost. vi. 12, says of those prohibitions: *ἅπερ καὶ τοῖς πάλαι νενομοθέτητο τοῖς πρὸ τοῦ νόμου φυσικοῖς* 'Ενῶς, 'Ενὼχ, Νῶε *κ. τ. λ.* My treatise respecting the Nazarenes and Ebionites in Stäudlin's u. Tzschirner's Archiv. f. K. G. iv. ii. 309. This explanation is also given by W. Schickard de jure regio Ebraeorum (Argentor. 1625), cap. 5, p. 129. Hammond and Alex. Morus ad Act. xv. 20. Sandius in nucleo hist. eccl. p. 54. It is otherwise explained by Spencer de legibus Hebr. ritualibus ed. Pfaff. p. 595, ss. Nitzsch de sensu decreti apostolici Act. xv. 29, Viteb. 1795 (also in Commentatt. theol. ed. a Velthusen, Ruperti et Kuinoel, vi. 403). Nösselt diss. de vera vi et ratione decreti Hierosolymitani Act. xv. (in ejusd. exercitt. ad. sacr. script. interpret. p. 95.) When many writers assume that the abstaining from flesh offered in sacrifice to idols, from blood, and things strangled, was enjoined on the Gentile Christians, because the Jews held those things in greatest abhorrence, it should be remarked that this greater abhorrence of them had its foundation in the circumstance of those things being forbidden of God, according to the Jewish opinion, not merely to the Jews, but to all men.

[7] The conduct of Gallio, the brother of Seneca, toward Paul, Acts xviii. 12, and Phil. iv. 22, gave rise to the subsequent fabrication of a correspondence between Seneca and Paul. Hieron. Catal. c. 12. Fabric. cod. apocr. N. T. t. ii. p. 880, ss. Cf. Gelpke tract. de familiaritate, quae Paulo Apost. cum Seneca philosopho intercessisse traditur, verisimillima. Lips. 1813.

tioch (Acts xv. 36–xviii. 22). But he soon entered on the *third great journey* to Asia Minor, where he passed at *Ephesus* the first two years and three months. Here, and in the vicinity, he established Christianity more firmly (*Epistle to the Galatians? First Epistle to the Corinthians*), and then traveled through *Macedonia* (*Second Epistle to the Corinthians*) to *Corinth* (*Epistle to the Romans*). After a three months' abode in this city, he returned to Jerusalem by Miletus (Acts xviii. 23, xxi. 17). Here, having been taken in the temple (58 A.D.), he was brought to Caesarea, and thence to Rome (60–61 A.D., Epistles to the *Ephesians*, *Philippians*, *Colossians*, and to *Philemon*). The Acts of the Apostles closes with the second year of the Roman captivity (63 A.D.); but according to later, though ancient testimonies, he was again liberated from this bondage, made several other journeys (*First Epistle to Timothy*,[8] *Epistle to Titus*), and then fell into a second captivity at Rome (*Second Epistle to Timothy*), which terminated in his death (67 A.D.).[9] Among Paul's disciples the most distinguished were *Silas*, or *Silvanus* (Acts xv. 40, ss., as far as xviii. 5; 2 Cor. i. 19), who was afterward with Peter (1 Peter v. 12); *Timothy*, who, commissioned by Paul, abode for a long time at Ephesus, in

[8] So according to Ussher, Mill, Pearson, Le Clerc, and Paley: Heydenreich die Pastoralbriefe Pauli. Bd. 1. (Hadamar. 1826). S. 36, ff. G. Böhl über die Zeit der Abfassung u. d. Paulin. Charakter der Briefe an Timoth. u. Titus. Berlin. 1829. S. 204, ff. If the pastoral letters had been a forgery of the second century, as Baur thinks (die Sogen. Pastoralbriefe d. Ap. Paulus. Stutt. and Tüb. 1835), it would be an inexplicable thing that the writer should lay at the basis of the history certain situations in which the apostle was placed, which can not be pointed out in the New Testament.

[9] So Eusebius, H. E. ii. c. 22, supported by Clemens Rom. Ep. i. § 5: *Διὰ ζῆλον ὁ Παῦλος ὑπομονῆς βραβεῖον ἄπεσχεν.—Κήρυξ γενόμενος ἔν τε τῇ ἀνατολῇ καὶ ἐν τῇ δύσει, τὸ γενναῖον τῆς πίστεως αὐτοῦ κλέος ἔλαβεν. Δικαιοσύνην διδάξας ὅλον τὸν κόσμον, καὶ ἐπὶ τὸ τέρμα τῆς δύσεως ἐλθὼν, καὶ μαρτυρήσας ἐπὶ τῶν ἡγουμένων, οὕτως ἀπηλλάγη τοῦ κόσμου, καὶ εἰς τὸν ἅγιον τόπον ἐπορεύθη.* Even the fragmentum de canone in Muratorii antiquitt. ital. medii aevi, iii. 854, which belongs to the third century, mentions the departure of Paul setting out from the city for Spain. A single captivity of Paul in Rome, ending with his death, is assumed by Petavius, Lardner, J. E. C. Schmidt, Eichhorn, E. F. R. Wolf (de altera Pauli Ap. captivitate, diss. ii. Lips. 1819. 20. 8.), Schrader (Paulus, i. 227), Hemsen, Baur, Reuss (Gesch. d. Schriften d. N. T. § 54), Matthiä (Pastoralbr. S. 185, 593), de Wette (Einl. in d. N. T. § 122), Schenkel (theol. Studien u. Krit. 1841, i. 53). On the contrary, the older view is defended by P. E. Jablonski diss. de ultimis Pauli Ap. laboribus a Luca praetermissis (Opusc. ed. J. G. te Water, iii. 289), J. P. Mynster de ultimis annis muneris apostolici a Paulo gesti (kleine theol. Schriften. Kopenhagen. 1825. S. 189), Heydenreich (Pastoralbriefe, ii. 6), Böhl (a. a. O. S. 81), Wurm (Tübing. Zeitschr. f. Theol. 1833, i. 81), Schott (Erörterung einiger chronol. Punkte in d. Lebensgesch. d. Ap. Paulus. S. 116), Neander (apost. Kirche, i. 389), Credner (Einl. in d. N. T. i. i. 317), Neudecker (Einl. in d. N. T. S. 397).

order to arrange the affairs of the church at that place; *Titus*, who had been left for the same purpose in Crete (both considered in later times as the first bishops of these churches, *Euseb* iii. 4); and *Luke*.

§ 27.

HISTORY OF THE OTHER APOSTLES AND THEIR DISCIPLES.

J. A. Fabricii salutaris lux evangelii toti orbi exoriens (Hamburg. 1731, 4to), page 95, ss.

The history of the other apostles, and their early pupils, is involved in great obscurity, and has frequently been much disfigured by mistakes and fabrications. Among these distortions may be reckoned principally, the traditions respecting the apostles determining by lots to what countries they should go from Jerusalem,[1] the joint composition of the *apostles' creed*,[2] and their unmarried state,[3] as well as the tradition that they all suffered martyrdom except John.[4] And when the apostles, who

[1] First advanced by Rufinus in Hist. Eccl. i. 9. Cf. Act. SS. ad d. 15, Jul. Thilo acta Thomae, p. 87, ss.

[2] First advanced by Rufinus in Exposit. symboli apostolici. A homily de symbolo, falsely ascribed to Augustine, gives a still more particular account. *Cf.* Fabricii cod. apocr. N. T. vol. iii. p. 339, ss. The story is defended by Natalis Alex. Hist. Eccl. saec. i. diss. xii.; Acta SS. ad. d. 15, Jul. u. J. Chrys. Trombellius tract. de sacramentis. Bonon. 1770. t. ii. diss. 4, qu. 3. On the contrary, Du Pin and Tillemont, with all Protestant theologians, acknowledge the fiction.

[3] Comp. against this 1 Cor. ix. 5. Hence also Ignatius ad Philadelph. c. 4. mentions *Πέτρου καὶ Παύλου—καὶ τῶν ἄλλων ἀποστόλων τοῖς γάμοις προσομιλησάντων*. Clem. Alex. Strom. iii. p. 448: *Πέτρος καὶ Φίλιππος ἐπαιδοποιήσαντο· καὶ Παῦλος οὐκ ὀκνεῖ ἔν τινι ἐπιστολῇ τὴν αὐτοῦ προσαγορεύειν σύζυγον, ἣν οὐ περιεκόμιζεν διὰ τὸ τῆς ὑπερεσίας εὐσταλές*. See J. A. Theiner and A. Theiner die Einführung der erzwungenen Ehelosigkeit bei den christl. Geistlichen und ihre Folgen (Altenburg. 1828. 2 Bde. 8). Bd. 1. S. 26. On the other hand, the Montanist Tertullianus de Monogam. c. 8: Petrum solum invenio maritum; caeteros cum maritos non invenio, aut spadones intelligam necesse est aut continentes. Nec enim—Paulum sic interpretabimur, quasi demonstret uxores apostolos habuisse. In later times, 1 Cor. ix. 5, was explained of female friends who served: Ambrosiaster ad h. l. Hieronymus ad Matth. xxvii. 55. Theodoret. ad 1 Cor. ix. 5, who adds, however, *τινὲς οὕτως ἡρμήνευσαν*. (Cf. Suiceri thesaur. ecclesiasticus, ed. ii. Amstel. 1728. T. i. p. 810, s. v. *γυνή*.) Even when it was conceded, as by Ambrosiaster ad 2 Cor. xi. 2: Omnes apostoli, exceptis Johanne et Paulo, uxores habuerunt: the view was usually held, Hieron. Epist. 30 (al. 50) ad Pammachium (ed. Martianay, t. iv. p. ii. p. 242): Apostoli vel virgines, vel post nuptias continentes. On the whole subject, see G. Calixtus de conjugio Clericorum (ed. ii. ed. H. Ph. C. Henke. Helmst. 1783). P. ii. p. 147, ss.

[4] Heracleon (ap. Clem. Alex. Strom. iv. p. 502) says that Matthew, Philip, Thomas, and Levi (Thaddeus ?), did not suffer martyrdom.

continued a long time in single churches, were considered as the first bishops of them, this is also liable to be misunderstood. *Peter* was still found in Jerusalem in the year 52 (Acts xv.), then in *Antioch* (Gal. ii. 11), also in *Babylon* (1 Peter v. 13), and, according to other ancient testimonies, he suffered martyrdom in Rome (67 A.D.)[5] Since the end of the 4th century, the fabrication of the Clementines, that Peter was first bishop of Antioch, and then of Rome, obtained more general

[5] Clemens, Rom. Epist. i. c. 5, testifies merely to his martyrdom; Ignatius, Ep. ad Rom. cap. 4, alludes to it. The Praedicatio Petri (which was known even to Heracleon, and consequently belongs to the beginning of the second century; see the Clementines by A. Schliemann. Hamb. 1844, P. 253), comp. Lib. de non iterando bapt. appended to Cypriani opp. ed. Rigalt. p. 139: Liber, qui inscribitur Pauli praedicatio, in quo libro—invenies, post tanta tempora Petrum et Paulum, post conlationem evangelii in Hierusalem et mutuam altercationem et rerum agendarum dispositionem, postremo in urbe, quasi tunc primum, invicem sibi esse cognitos. (The Praedicatio Pauli seems to have formed the last part of the Praed. Petri. Credner's Beiträge zur Einleit. in die bibl. Schriften, i. 360.) Dionysius Corinth. (about 170) Ep. ad Romanos (in Euseb. ii. 25): Ἄμφω (Πέτρος καὶ Παῦλος) καὶ εἰς τὴν ἡμετέραν Κόρινθον φυτεύσαντες ἡμᾶς, ὁμοίως ἐδίδαξαν· ὁμοίως δὲ καὶ εἰς τὴν Ἰταλίαν ὁμόσε διδάξαντες, ἐμαρτύρησαν κατὰ τὸν αὐτὸν καιρόν. Irenaeus adv. Haer. (written 176 or 177) iii. 1: Ὁ μὲν δὴ Ματθαῖος ἐν τοῖς Ἑβραίοις τῇ ἰδίᾳ διαλέκτῳ αὐτῶν καὶ γραφὴν ἐξήνεγκεν εὐαγγελίου, τοῦ Πέτρου καὶ τοῦ Παύλου ἐν Ῥωμῃ εὐαγγελιζομένων, καὶ θεμελιούντων τὴν ἐκκλησίαν. Μετὰ δὲ τὴν τούτων ἔξοδον Μάρκος κ. τ. λ. Tertullianus de Praescr. haereticorum, c. 36: Felix ecclesia (Romana), cui totam doctrinam apostoli cum sanguine suo profuderunt; ubi Petrus passioni dominicae adaequatur, ubi Paulus Johannis (baptistae) exitu coronatur. Cajus Romanus (about 200) in Euseb. ii. 25: Ἐγὼ δὲ τὰ τρόπαια τῶν Ἀποστόλων ἔχω δεῖξαι· ἐὰν γὰρ θελήσῃς ἀπελθεῖν ἐπὶ τὸν Βατικανὸν, ἢ ἐπὶ τὴν ὁδὸν τὴν Ὀστίαν, εὑρήσεις τὰ τρόπαια τῶν ταύτην ἱδρυσαμένων τὴν ἐκκλησίαν. In the middle ages the Waldenses denied (Moneta adv. Catharos et Waldenses. Romae. 1743, fol. p. 411) Marsilius Patavinus, Michael Caesenas, &c. (cf. Spanheim de ficta profectione Petri Ap. in urbem Romam, Opp. ii. 337) that Peter had ever been at Rome. In this they were followed by Matth. Flacius, Claud. Salmasius, and Fred. Spanheim (l. c.), all obviously entangled by party feeling. Several moderns, resting on a scientific basis, have made the same assertion, particularly Eichhorn (Einl. in d. N. T. i. 554), Baur (Tübinger theol. Zeitschr. 1831. iv. 136. 1836. iii. 163) and Mayerhoff (Einl. in die Petrin. Schriften, Hamburg. 1835. S. 73). Neander (apost. Kirche, ii. 458) and Winer (bibl. Realwörterbuch, ii. 281) waver. On the contrary, the old tradition is defended by Credner (Einleit. in d. N. T. i. ii. 628. Hall. A. L. Z. 1836, July, S. 370), Bleek (theol. Studien und Krit. 1836 iv. 1061) and Olshausen (Einleit. zum Römerbriefe, and theol. Stud. und Kritik. 1838, iv. 916). There is a new rejoinder by Baur (über den Ursprung des Episcopates, s. 43). A violent catholic defense is presented in Frid. Windischmanni vindiciae Petrinae. Ratisb. 1836. If, according to Baur, this tradition proceeded from Judaizing Christians at Rome for the purpose of exalting Peter above Paul, we can not understand how the fabrication did not forthwith meet with a decided contradiction from the adherents of Paul at Rome, nor how Caius, a disciple of Paul, is a leading witness for its truth. Comp. Drey, Herbst, and Hirscher theol. Quartalschrift. Tübingen 1820, iv. 567. Mynster's Kleine theol. Schriften. Kopenhag. 1825, s. 141. On the manner of Peter's death Tertullian speaks (l. c.): Petrus passioni dominicae adaequatur. On the other hand, Origen (in Euseb. H. E. iii. c. 1): Πέτρος—ἀνεσκολοπίσθη κατὰ κεφαλῆς, οὕτως ἀξιώσας παθεῖν, according to Rufinus' version: crucifixus est deorsum capite demerso, quod ipse ita fieri deprecatus est, ne exaequari domino videretur.

currency.[6] *Philip* spent the last years of his life in Hierapolis in Phrygia (*Polycrates*, about 190, *ap. Euseb.* H. E. iii. 31, and v. 24). *John* also went to Asia Minor, and a great part of his life belongs to the following period. The traditions are ancient respecting *Thomas* preaching the gospel in Parthia,[7] *Andrew* in Scythia (*Origines ap. Euseb.* iii. 1), *Bartholomew* in India[8] (*Euseb.* v. 10), and it is reported that *John Mark*, first the companion of Paul and Barnabas, then of Peter, was the founder of the church in Alexandria (*Euseb.* ii. 16). The later traditions respecting the apostles, and apostolic men, which have been partly indebted for their origin to the wish of many nations to trace their Christianity up to the apostolic age, are, to say the least, uncertain, and in part so marvelously forged, that they sufficiently betray their own falseness.[9]

6 Die Clementinen von A. Schliemann. Hamburg. 1844. S. 115. Eusebius, iii. 2, says: *Μετὰ τὴν Παύλου καὶ Πέτρου μαρτυρίαν πρῶτος κληροῦται τὴν ἐπισκοπὴν Λῖνος*, and according to him, iii. 4, Clement is *τῆς Ῥωμαίων ἐκκλησίας τρίτος ἐπίσκοπος καταστάς* (Linus, Anacletus, Clemens). Rufini praef. in recognitiones Clementis: Linus et Cletus fuerunt quidem ante Clementem episcopi in urbe Roma, sed superstite Petro, videlicet ut illi episcopatus curam gererent, ipse vero apostolatus impleret officium. Epiphanius also has the correct opinion respecting the episcopate of the apostles, Haer. xxvii. 6: *Ἐν Ῥώμῃ γὰρ γεγόνασι πρῶτοι Πέτρος καὶ Παῦλος οἱ ἀπόστολοι αὐτοὶ καὶ ἐπίσκοποι.*—Peter is named the first bishop of Antioch, first of all by Chrysostom. Hom. xlii. in Ignat. Mart. Hieronymus Catal. c. 1, and Comm. in ep. ad Gal. c. 1, the first bishop of Rome by Optatus Milev. de schism. Donatist. ii. 2. Hieron. Catal. c. 1. Augustin. Ep. liii. ad Generosum and contra lit. Petilian. iii. Jerome was the first that knew that he had been twenty-five years bishop of Rome. The tradition of the modern Roman church is most fully developed in Gregor. Cortesii de Romano itinere gestisque principis Apostolorum libri ii. Vinc. Al. Constantius recensuit, notis illustravit, annales SS. Petri et Pauli et appendicem monumentorum adjecit. Rom. 1770. 8.

7 Later accounts make Thomas go to India. So first Gregor. Nazianz. Orat. xxv. ad Arian. p. 438, ed. Paris. Ambrosius in Psalm xlv. 10. Hieronym. Epist. 148, and so the Syrian Christians in India (Thomas-Christians) consider him to be the founder of their church (Assemani bibl. orient. iii. ii. 435), comp. Acta Thomae apostoli ed. J. C. Thilo. Lips. 1823, p. 97, 121. These Manichaean Acta Thomae render it probable that the tradition is of Manichaean origin. On this account Theodoret Haer. fab. i. c. 26, declares that the Thomas sent to the Indians was a disciple of Manes.

8 Probably Yemen. Rufinus H. E. x. 9: Thomae Parthia, et Matthaeo Aethiopia, eique adhaerens exterior India Bartholomaeo dicitur sorte decreta. Inter quam Parthiamque Media, sed longo interior tractu India ulterior jacet. So also Philostorgius H. E. ii. 6, calls the Sabaeans, or Homerites, *τοὺς ἐνδοτάτω Ἰνδούς*.

9 Thus the Spaniards pretend that James the elder was seen in their country (his body is said to be in Compostella since A.D. 816); the French claim Dionysius the Areopagite, Lazarus, Mary Magdalene, and others; the English, Simon Zelotes, and especially Joseph of Arimathea; the Germans, Maternus, Eucherius, and Valerius, as legates of Peter; the Russians, Andrew, &c. The real but later founders of churches have been frequently transferred to the times of the apostles by tradition.

§ 28.

RECEPTION OF CHRISTIANITY AMONG JEWS AND GENTILES.

(COMP. § 19.)

Neander's Kirchengesch. 2te. Auflage i. i. 117, ff.

With the Jews, their earthly expectations of the Messiah always presented a special obstacle to Christianity. When the Christians not only took into their society the Samaritans, but when Paul admitted the very heathen into it, without requiring of them circumcision, the fact appeared to the Jews to afford sufficient proof that the confessors of Christ could not be followers of a true Messiah; and Christianity now appeared to them only a form of Judaism profaned by a mutilated impartation of it to the heathen, as is expressed even in the appellation of the Christians, כּוּתִים, which originated, perhaps, somewhat later. On this account Paul and his disciples were most violently hated by the Palestinian Jews (Gal. v. 11, Rom. xv. 31), who could even spread the report concerning him, that he had introduced heathen into the temple, the uproar arising from which caused his imprisonment (Acts xxi. 27, ff.). Among the Hellenistic Jews Paul found once and again much susceptibility of mind in relation to Christianity, as in *Berea* (Acts xvii. 11, 12), *Ephesus* (xviii. 19, 20), and *Rome* (xxviii. 17). In other places these very Jews were his most dangerous enemies, as in *Thessalonica* (xvii. 5, ff.), and *Corinth* (xviii. 12, ff.), partly from the usual national prejudice, and partly, also, perhaps, from fear lest the publication of their Messianic hopes might injure them in the eyes of the Romans (Acts xvii. 6–8).

In addition to the inward power of Christian truth on the human spirit, the miraculous origin of Christianity and the prevailing inclination to foreign superstitions, influenced the heathen in its favor. On the contrary, with the higher classes, and especially the philosophers (1 Cor. i. 18, ff.), its Jewish origin, the simple form in which it appeared (Acts xvii. 18, ff.), and the doctrine of the resurrection of the body (l. c. 32) hindered its reception. Christianity was looked upon at this time by the heathen only as a Jewish sect,[1] an opinion which from many indeed may have drawn upon it contempt, but which secured for it, notwithstanding, the protection of the civil government (Acts xviii. 12, ff.); for now, the Christian societies, like the Jewish, passed for *Sodalitia licita* (comp. § 12). The circumstance that even some heathens were drawn away from their own religion by means of these communities, served, indeed, to raise complaints against them (Acts xvi. 20, ff.; xvii. 18); these, however, were generally overlooked by the Roman magistrates, just as the circumstance of many heathens becoming *proselytes of the gate* had been formerly passed over, since, amid the general inclination to foreign superstitions,[2] the old religious laws were not strictly enforced. When *Claudius*, on account of a dispute between the believing and unbelieving Jews at Rome, expelled both parties from the city, this act can not naturally be reckoned a persecution of the Christians.[3] As little were the Christians persecuted on account of their religion by *Nero*, when, to turn from himself the suspicion of setting fire to the city, he gave up the despised sectaries to all kinds of torture (64).[4] Probably the Neronian persecution was confined to Rome,[5] though it appears to have continued with some inter-

[1] J. G. Kraft proluss. ii. de nascenti Christi ecclesia sectae judaicae nomine tuta. Erlang. 1771–72.—J. H. Ph. Seidenstücker diss. de Christianis ad Trajanum usque a Caesaribus et Senatu Romano pro cultoribus religionis Mosaicae semper habitis. Helmst. 1790.

[2] When Tertullian relates that Tiberius wished Christ to de admitted among the Roman deities (Apologeticus, c. 5: Detulit ad Senatum cum praerogativa suffragii sui. Senatus,quia non ipse probaverat, respuit. Caesar in sententia mansit comminatus periculum accusatoribus Christianorum), this is in contradiction to the Roman spirit, the character of Tiberius (Sueton. Tiber. c. 36: Externas ceremonias, Aegyptios Judaicosque ritus compescuit. C. 69: Circa deos ac religiones negligentior: quippe addictus mathematicae, plenusque persuasionis, cuncta fato agi), and the historical relations; while the silence of the Roman historians in regard to it would be inexplicable. The less credit is to be given to Tertullian's single testimony, inasmuch as he falsely ascribes to his cotemporary Marcus Aurelius, partiality for the Christians, in a passage subsequent to the one in which he speaks of Tiberius. Yet the account is defended by J. W. T. Braun de Tiberii Christum in Deorum numerum referendi consilio comm. Bonnae. 1834. 8.

[3] Sueton. in Claudio, c. 25: Judaeos impulsore Chresto assidue tumultuantes Roma expulit, cf. Act. xviii. 2. A play on the word, Χριστός, Χρηστός, sometimes used by the Christians (Justin. Apol. maj. p. 45. Athenag. Leg. 281, 282), sometimes declined (Tertull. Apolog. 3: perperam Chrestianus pronuntiatur a vobis). Comp. the programm. of Ammon, 1803: Illustratur locus Suetonii de Judaeis imp. Chr. ass. tum. Credner's Einl. in d. N. T. i. ii. 380.

[4] Tacit. Ann. xv. 44. Sueton. Nero, c. 16.

[5] First extended to the provinces also by Orosius, vii. 7, whose opinion gained the assent of many till H. Dodwell in dissertt. Cyprianicarum (Oxon. 1684. 8.), dissert. xi. de paucitate martyrum, § 13, proved the opposite. Yet Theod. Ruinart in praefat. ad acta

ruptions till the death of the tyrant (*Peter* and *Paul* suffered under him).[6]

§ 29.

INTERNAL DEVELOPMENT OF CHRISTIANITY.

The assembly of the apostles and church at Jerusalem had allowed the Gentile Christians to neglect the Mosaic law, but in so doing they had tacitly recognized its binding force on the posterity of Abraham. Since, therefore, on this account the Jewish Christians must have avoided intimate intercourse with the Gentile Christians, for the sake of Levitical purity; and since the one party looked upon *James*, the Lord's brother, and on *Peter*, as their leaders, while the other took *Paul* for their head (Gal. ii. 9), a certain wall of partition necessarily stood between them, and perfect incorporation into one brotherhood was impossible. This must have been first felt in many churches gathered from among Jews and Gentiles by Paul out of Palestine (Gal. ii. 11, ff.). The very circumstance, however, contrib-

Martyr. sincera, § 3, still defended the opinion of Orosius. The inscription pretending to have been found in Spain or Portugal: Neroni ob provinciam latronibus et his qui novam generi humano superstitionem inculcabant, purgatam (Jan. Gruteri inscriptt. t. i. p. 238, n. 9), is spurious, and was forged perhaps by Cyriacus of Ancona. See Ferreras histoire d'Espagne, i. 192. Defended by J. E. J. Walch persecutionis Christianorum Neronianae in Hispania ex ant. monumentis probandae uberior explanatio. Jenae. 1753. 4. But compare especially the epistola Hagenbuchii, p. 31–60, there given.

[6] Since the Christians constantly expected Antichrist, as the forerunner of Christ, to be near at hand, it is not to be wondered at that Nero, during his persecution, should appear to them as Antichrist, and that they entertained the opinion after his death that he had not actually died, but should soon return again to undertake a final persecution. Hence the Apocalypse (written about 69) xiii. 3; xvii. 10, 11, and the Sybilline oracles, iv. 116 (which verses, according to Bleek in Schleiermacher's, De Wette's, and Lücke's theol. Zeitschrift, i. 244, were composed about the year 80 A.D.) That the like report among the heathen originated in that sentiment of the Christians, is at once apparent from the form of it, comp. Sueton. Nero, c. 40: Praedictum a mathematicis Neroni olim erat, fore, ut quandoque destitueretur. Spoponderant tamen quidam destituto Orientis dominationem, nonnulli nominatim regnum Hierosolymorum. Hence the Pseudoneronen. Sueton. l. c. c. 57. Tacit. Hist. ii. 8. Dio Cassius, lxiv. 10. Among the Christians that expectation survived for several centuries. Lactant. de Morte persecut. c. 2. Sulpic. Sever. Hist. sacr. ii. 28, § 1, 29, § 6, dial. ii. c. 14. Hieronym. in Daniel xi. 28, in Esaiam xvii. 13, ad Algasiam, qu. xi., and it was believed that Paul referred to Nero in 2 Thess. ii. 7. Chrysostom., Theodoret, Theophyl., and Oecumen. on this passage. Augustin. de civ. Dei, xx. c. 19. Compare Corodi's krit. Gesch. d. Chiliasmus, ii. 309. Lücke's Einl. in d. Offenb. Johannis, S. 248. Credner's Einl. in d. N. T. i. ii. 704.

uted in no small degree, to lead that apostle to a more spiritual development of Christianity and one freer from the national prejudices of the Jews.[1] He attained, accordingly, to the inward perception of the truth, that spiritual communion with God by faith in Christ alone constitutes the essence of Christianity. In this conviction, he was not afraid to overstep those rules of the council at Jerusalem in a twofold manner, both by declaring the obligation of the Jews to observe the Mosaic law invalid (Romans vii. 1, ff.; 1 Cor. ix. 20, 21; Gal. ii. 15, ff.), since he regarded that law merely as preparatory to Christ (Gal. iii. 24); and also by denying the absolute binding force of the laws regarding food given to the Gentile Christians (1 Cor. viii. 10, 23, ff.), while with reference to all such external institutes he merely required some regard for the consciences of weaker brethren, and practiced himself such forbearance (1 Cor. viii. 9, ff.; x. 32; Acts xxi. 26). The other national prejudice of the Jewish Christians, viz. carnal millennarianism, likewise disappeared from his mind along with an overweening estimate of the Mosaic law. He thought, indeed, of the return of Jesus as near at hand (Phil. iv. 5), but he expected the triumph of God's kingdom in a state above the earthly (1 Thess. iv. 16, 17; 2 Cor. v. 1, 2). Christ himself was conceived of by Paul, who had seen him in the clouds of heaven, more in his spiritual and divine aspect; while the Jewish apostles, in consequence of the personal intercourse with him which they had enjoyed, dwelt more on his human appearance.

The Palestinian Christians might have overlooked the new development of doctrine, inasmuch as they had been accustomed to much more important doctrinal differences springing up in Judaism, without forfeiting the privileges of ecclesiastical fellowship. On the other hand, they attributed to Paul's loose view of the law, by which he drew away so many Jews from the observance of its precepts, in the Gentile-Christian churches, so much the greater mischief, because the other apostles conformed to the stricter view (Acts xxi. 20, ff.). Nor, on the other side, could the Palestinian appear to the Pauline Christians in any

[1] G. W. Meyer Entwickelung des Paulin. Lehrbegriffs. Altona. 1801. (J. G. F. Leun) reine Auffassung des Urchristenthums in den Paulin. Briefen. Leipzig. 1803. L. Usteri Entwickelung des Paul. Lehrbegriffs. Zürich. 1832. 4te Aufl. Neander apost. K. ii. 503. A. F. Dähne Entwickelung des Paulin. Lehrbegriffs. Halle. 1835. 8.

other light than as obtuse persons, who had not at all penetrated into the essence of Christianity (Heb. v. 11, 12).

The difference between these two parties is still more strongly manifested in the aberrations into which individuals fell from the respective positions of the parties. Among the Jewish Christians,[2] a party always continued, who asserted the absolutely-binding nature of the Mosaic law in relation to the Gentiles. By this means many belonging to Gentile-Christian churches were led astray, so that Paul felt the necessity of combating the error (*Ep. to the Galatians; Phil.* iii. 2). And when persecutions befell the Christians in Palestine, shortly before the destruction of Jerusalem, many of them were on the point of falling away entirely from Christianity (Hebrews vi. 4, ff.; x. 25, ff.),[3] having been rendered impatient, partly by the long-continued disappointment of their millenarian expectations, partly because they could not decide upon a complete separation from Judaism, such as now appeared necessary.

Among the Gentile Christians, on the contrary, philosophy early began to mingle itself with Christianity. As far as we know, *Apollos*, a cultivated Alexandrian Jew, was the first who looked at Christianity from a more speculative point of view, and first preached it in this form with great eloquence at Corinth.[4] Little as he desired to appear in an antagonist position to Paul, the latter declined in reputation, notwithstanding, among many of the Corinthians, and divisions arose in the church (1 Cor. i.–iv.).[5] Paul wishes to leave it to time to disclose the value of such a philosophical system erected on the foundation of Christian faith (1 Cor. iii. 11, ff.); but he blames the divisions occasioned by it, agreeably to his manner of inculcating toleration even in regard to errors, provided they be not practically scandalous or claim for themselves exclusive adoption (Rom. xiv. 1, ff.). Afterward, however, there appeared among

[2] Dav. van Heyst diss. de Judaeo-Christianismo ejusque vi et efficacitate, quam exseruit in rem christianam saec. primo. Lugd. Bat. 1828. 8. C. E. Scharling de Paulo Apostolo ejusque adversariis. Havniae. 1836. 8.

[3] Brief a. d. Hebräer erläutert v. F. Bleek, i. 60, ff.

[4] Bleek, l. c. p. 423, ff.

[5] Comp., in addition to the commentators, Baur on the Christ-party, in the Tübingen Zeitschr. für Theol. 1831, iv. 83. Comp. 1836, iv. Neander's apost. Kirche, i. 292. Dan. Schenkel de ecclesia Corinthiaca primaeva factionibus turbata. Basil. 1838. 8. A. F. Dähne die Christuspartei in d. apost. Kirche zu Korinth. Halle. 1841. 8. Die Partei ungen in d. Gem. zu Korinth, v. F. Becker. Altona. 1842. 8. Th. F. Kniewel ecclesiae Corinthiorum vetustissimae dissensiones. Gedani. 1842. 4. [Eclectic Review, May, 1846].

the Gentile Christians actual errors, and those, too, of an important moral bearing, which Paul was obliged to combat with all his might.

The Christians considered themselves, in opposition to the rest of the world (*ὁ κόσμος, ὁ αἰὼν οὗτος*, under the *κοσμοκράτωρ*, Eph. vi. 12, the *θεὸς τοῦ αἰῶνος τούτου*, 2 Cor. iv. 4) hastening in their perversity to destruction, a chosen people dedicated to God, *ἅγιοι*,[6] *ἐκλεκτοί, κλητοί*. In these appellations there was no claim to moral perfection, but a remembrance of their high calling in Christ. Though it is certain that Christianity in its first beginning imparted spiritual enlightenment to many of its adherents, and transformed them in a moral view, yet it could so much the less purify them all from the imperfections of the education belonging to their nation and time, because it is certain that many of them had been led to embrace it by superstitious or other interested motives.[7] This explains the reason why Paul found that he had continually to contend with even gross vices among the Gentile Christians, particularly at *Corinth* (1 Cor. v. 6), and in *Crete* (Titus i. 10, ff.); why James saw himself obliged to condemn the moral abuse of the Pauline doctrine relative to the power of faith, as that alone which brings salvation (*Ep. of James*); and why the Apocalypse (written 69 A.D.) denounces seducers in Pergamus (*the Nicolaitanes*),[8] who

[6] As the later Jews עַם־קְדוֹשִׁים Dan. viii. 24, cf. vii. 18, ss.

[7] One-sided laudatory descriptions are given in William Cave's Primitive Christianity, or the religion of the ancient Christians in the first ages of the gospel, ed. 5. Lond. 1689 (translated into German by Frauendorf, Leipz. 1694 and 1723. 8), and Gottfr. Arnold's erste Liebe, d. i. wahre Abbildung der ersten Christen. Frankf. 1696. fol. Leipz. 1732. 4. Sometimes unjust to the Christians, but otherwise worth reading, is L. A. Paetz comm. de vi, quam religio christ. per iii. priora saecula ad hominum animos, mores, ac vitam habuit. Gotting. 1799. 4. Comp. A. Neander das christl. Leben der drei ersten Jahrhunderte, in his Denkwürdigkeiten aus d. Gesch. des Christenth. Bd. 1. Berlin. 1823. J. G. Stickel et C. F. Bogenhard biga commentationum de morali primaevorum Christianorum conditione. Neostad. ad Orlam. 1826. 8.

[8] Apoc. ii. 6, 14, 15. Those who *κρατοῦντες τὴν διδαχὴν* Βαλαάμ (cf. Numb. xxxi. 16, and those who *κρατοῦντες τὴν διδαχὴν τῶν* Νικολαϊτῶν are the same. בִּלְעָם is derived from בָּלַע עָם, even among the Rabbins. Buxtorf. Lex. talmud. p. 314, to which corresponds *νικᾷν τὸν λαόν*. So first Chr. A. Heumann in Actis erudit. an. 1712, p. 179. Ejusd. Poecile, ii. 392. Münscher in Gabler's Journal für theol. Liter. v. 17. Eichhorn and Ewald in their commentaries on Apoc. ii. 6. Hence the appellation Nicolaitanes was not the common name for a sect, but one invented by the Apocalyptic writer. As the names of sects were usually formed after the name of the founder, the fathers thought of Nicolaus, Acts vi. 5, who, according to Irenaeus, i. 26, iii. 11, and Tertullian de Praescr. haer. c. 46, is said to have been the founder of the party; but according to Clemens Alex. Strom. ii. p. 490, iii. p. 522, he was merely the unconscious cause of the appellation on

paid no regard to the regulations respecting food enjoined on the Gentile Christians, nor even to the prohibition of lewdness (Acts xv. 29). But after a philosophical treatment of Christianity had procured friends in many churches of the Gentile Christians, the superstitious philosophy of the times also speedily crept in among the Christians, first of all, as it would appear, in Asia Minor, and threatened morality with still greater danger by recommending chimerical, mysterious doctrines, and an arbitrary asceticism, as the true mode of purifying the soul. Against such errorists as united a Jewish-heathen asceticism with a peculiar philosophy, Paul had first to warn the Colossians (Col. ii. 8, 16, ff.).[9] The same tendency spread itself as far as Ephesus, where it manifested itself in high-flying speculations, in prohibitions of marriage and meats (1 Tim. i. 5–7; iv. 3, 7; vi. 20), and manifestly contributed to the immorality of that place (2 Tim. iii. 6). The attempt, also, of *Hymeneus* and *Philetus* to explain spiritually (2 Tim. ii. 18) the doctrine of the resurrection of the body, so offensive to the heathen (1 Thessal. iv. 13, ff.; 1 Cor. xv. 12, 35, ff.), an attempt that proceeded from the same tendency, was not destitute of a moral influence at this time, when the doctrine was most intimately connected with that of retribution.[10] That Paul did not reject philosophy as such, he has proved in his conduct toward Apollos; *the philosophy* against which he warns his readers (Col. ii. 8) is that *science, falsely so called* (1 Tim. vi. 20) which, as Paul had be-

account of his words which were misunderstood by others, ὅτι παραχρήσασθαι τῇ σαρκὶ δεῖ. (παραχρᾶσθαι is, 1. to abuse, used particularly, according to Suidas de concubitu immodico; 2. equiv. to διαχρᾶσθαι, to put to death, as Justin. Apol. maj. c. 49.)

[9] Matth. Schneckenburger über die Irrlehrer zu Colossä, annexed to his treatise Ueber das Alter der jüd. Proselytentaufe. Berlin. 1828. 8. S. 187, ff. The same author's Beiträge zur Einl. ins N.T. Stuttgart. 1832. S. 146. The same author's Bemerkungen über die Irrlehrer zu Colossä, theol. Studien. u. Krit. 1832, iv. 841. Neander apost. K. i. 474. F. H. Rheinwald de pseudodoctoribus. Bonnae. 1834. 4. Osiander über die colossischen Irrlehrer, in the Tübingen Zeitschrift f. Theol. 1834, iii. 96. [Eclectic Review, March 1845.]

[10] That consciousness and feeling could not be conceived of apart from bodies, was a very common notion of antiquity. Comp. the Epicurean Vellejus in Cic. de Nat. deor. ii. c. 12: Quod (Plato) sine corpore ullo Deum vult esse—id quale esse possit, intelligi non potest. Careat enim sensu necesse est, careat etiam prudentia, careat voluptate. The heathen Caecilius in Minucius Felix, c. 11, says: Vellem tamen sciscitari, utrumne sine corpore an cum corporibus, et corporibus quibus, ipsisne an innovatis, resurgatur? Sine corpore? hoc, quod sciam, neque mens, neque ani a, nec vita est. Ipso corpore? sed jam ante dilapsum est. Alio corpore? ergo homo novus nascitur, non prior ille reparatur. Justini dial. c. Tryph. c. 1: ἀπαθὲς γὰρ τὸ ἀσώματον. Tertulliani Apologeticus, c. 48: Ideo repraesentabunter et corpora, quia neque pati quicquam potest anima sola sine stabili materia, i.e., carne caet.

fore anticipated, was only the first beginning of still greater errors, of the later gnostic reveries (2 Tim. iii. 1, ff.).[11]

In strong relief to these defects of the time, the brotherly love, the benevolence (2 Cor. viii. 1, ff.; Heb. vi. 10; xiii. 1, ff.), the patient endurance of the hostility of the unbelieving (Phil. i. 29; 1 Thess. i. 6; ii. 14; 2 Thess. i. 4, ff.; Heb. x. 32, ff.), and the holy zeal for Christianity, form the bright part of the picture presented by the first Christians. The church at Philippi, in its tender attachment to the apostle Paul, appears to us particularly attractive. (Comp. *the Ep. to the Philippians.*)

§ 30.

CONSTITUTION OF THE CHURCH.

Die Anf. d. christl. Kirche u. ihrer Verfassung von R. Rothe. Bd. i. Wittenb. 1837. S. 141.

The new churches out of Palestine formed themselves after the pattern of the mother church in Jerusalem. Their presidents were *the elders* (πρεσβύτεροι, ἐπίσκοποι),[1] officially of equal

[11] The traces of Gnosis in the N.T. are exaggerated, particularly by Henr. Hammond diss. de Antichristo (in his diss. iv. quibus episcopatus jura adstruuntur. Lond. 1651), and in his Annot. ad N. T. (lat. per J. Clericum. Amst. 1698, fol.) But, on the other side, C. Chr. Tittmann (tract. de vestigiis Gnosticorum in N. T. frustra quaesitis. Lips. 1773. 8), goes too far. Comp. Joh. Horn über die biblische Gnosis. Hannover. 1805. 8.

[1] That both appellations are the same follows from Acts xx. 17, 28; Tit. i. 5, 7; Phil. i. 1; 1 Tim. iii. 1, 8. Acknowledged by Hieronymus Epist 82, (al. 83) ad Oceanum: Apud veteres iidem episcopi et presbyteri, quia illud nomen dignitatis est, hoc aetatis. Epist. 101, ad Evangelum see below, § 34, note 2.—Idem ad Tit. i. 7: Idem est ergo presbyter, qui episcopus: et antequam diaboli instinctu studia in religione fierent, et diceretur in populis: ego sum Pauli, ego Apollo, ego autem Cephae, communi presbyterorum consilio ecclesiae gubernabantur. Postquam vero unusquisque eos, quos baptizaverat, suos putabat esse, non Christi; in toto orbe decretum est, ut unus de presbyteris electus superponeretur caeteris, ad quem omnis ecclesiae cura pertineret, et schismatum semina tollerentur. Putat aliquis non scripturarum, sed nostram esse sententiam, episcopum et presbyterum unum esse, et aliud aetatis, aliud esse nomen officii: relegat apostoli ad Philippenses verba, dicentis. Here follow the above cited passages; then: Haec propterea, ut ostenderemus apud veteres eosdem fuisse presbyteros, quos et episcopos: paulatim vero ut dissensionum plantaria evellerentur, ad unum omnem sollicitudinem esse delatam. Sicut ergo presbyteri sciunt, se ex ecclesiae consuetudine ei, qui sibi praepositus fuerit, esse subjectos: ita episcopi noverint se magis consuetudine, quam dispositionis dominicae veritate, presbyteris esse majores, et in commune debere ecclesiam regere. Augustini Epist. 82, ad Hieron. c. 33: Quamquam secundum honorum vocabula, quae jam ecclesiae usus obtinuit, episcopatus presbyterio major sit: tamen in multis rebus Augustinus Hieronymo minor est. Cf. Chrysostomi Hom. i. in Ep. ad Philipp. Theodoret. comm. in Philipp. i. 1. It is remarkable how long afterward persons maintained this view of the original identity of bishops and presbyters. Isidorus Hispal. Etymol. vii. c. 12, transcribes that passage from Hieron. Epist. ad Oceanum. Bernaldus Constantiensis (about 1088) the most zealous defender of

rank, although, in many churches, individuals among them had a personal authority over the others.[2] Under the superintend-

Gregory VII. appeals on this subject, in his de presbyterorum officio tract. (in monumentorum res Allemannorum illustrantt. S. Blas. 1792. 4. t. ii. p. 384, ss.), to the New Testament and Jerome, and then continues: Quum igitur presbyteri et episcopi antiquitus idem fuisse legantur, etiam eandem ligandi atque solvendi potestatem et alia nunc episcopis specialia habuisse non dubitantur. Postquam autem presbyteri ab episcopali excellentia cohibiti sunt, coepit eis non licere, quod licuit, videlicet quod ecclesiastica auctoritas solis pontificibus exequendum delegavit. Even a pope, Urbanus II., in Conc. Benevent. ann. 1091, can. 1: Sacros autem ordines dicimus diaconatum et presbyteratum. Hos siquidem solos primitiva legitur ecclesia habuisse: super his solum praeceptum habemus apostoli (pretty nearly the same words are found in Petri Lomb. Sentent. lib. iv. dist. 24, c. 8), Hence even Gratian receives the above passages of Jerome ad Tit. i. (dist. xcv. c. 5), epist. ad Evangel. (dist. xciii. c. 24).u. Isidori Hisp. (dist. xxi. c. 1) without scruple. The same view is maintained by the Glossa ad Gratiani decret. dist. xciii. c. 24, Cardinalis S. Marci at the Costnit. Concilium 1414 (v. d. Hardt. Concil. Const. ii. 228), Nicolaus Tudeschus, archiepiscop. Panormitanus (about 1428) super prima parte Primi cap. 5 (edit. Lugdun. 1547. fol. 112, b.: Olim Presbyteri in commune regebant ecclesiam et ordinabant sacerdotes), Nicolaus Cusanus (about 1435) de Concordantia cath. lib. iii. c. 2, (in Schardii syntagma tractatuum, p. 358), where he remarks, in opposition to the genuineness of the Pseudo-Isidore letters of Clement: Invenitur insuper in ipsis epistolis de episcoporum a sacerdotibus differentia, quae longo tempore post hoc, ut Hieronymo placet et Damaso, in ecclesia orta est. Even the papal canonist Jo. Paul Lancelottus, in his Institutt. juris canon. lib. i. tit. 21, § 3, unfolds the same view (1563) with a sunt, qui affirment, without adding any thing in refutation of it. Since no value was set, during the middle ages, on the distinction between the institutio divina and ecclesiastica, a distinction on which modern Catholics insist, that view could not disturb ecclesiastical practice. But after the Council of Trent, sess. xxiii. (July, 1563) cap. 4, had declared, episcopos, qui in apostolorum locum successerunt,—positos—a spiritu sancto, regere ecclesiam Dei, eosque presbyteris superiores esse etc., the old view became suspicious, although the council did not expressly or definitely maintain the institutio divina. Michael de Medina (about 1570) de Orig. sacr. homin. did not hesitate to declare, illos patres materiales fuisse haereticos, sed in his patribus ob eorum reverentiam hoc dogma non esse damnatum. But Bellarmin de Clericis, lib. i. c. 15, calls this sententiam valde inconsideratam, and would rather resort to the expedient of an interpretation. Although, afterward, among Catholic theologians, Edmundus Richerius (Defensio libelli de eccles. et polit. potest, t. ii. p. 52, ss.) defended the view of Jerome, and John Morin (de sacris ecclesiae ordinationibus, p. iii. Exerc. iii. c. 3) at least asserted, that the opinion was not heretical, episcopos non jure divino esse presbyteris superiores; yet, since the Tridentine council, the institutio divina of episcopacy, and its original distinction from presbyteratus became the general doctrine of the Catholic church, which the English Episcopalians also followed in this particular, while the other Protestant churches returned to the most ancient doctrine and regulation on the subject. The first leading works in favor of the modern Catholic view are Petavii de Ecclesiastica hierarchia, libb. v. and dissertatt. theologic. lib. i. in his Theolog. dogmat. tom. iv. p. 164. On the other side, Walonis Messalini (Claud. Salmasii) diss. de episcopis et presbyteris. Lugd. Bat. 1641. 8. Dav. Blondelli apologia pro sententia Hieronymi de episcopis et presbyteris. Amstelod. 1646. 4. Against these H. Hammond wrote dissert. iv. quibus episcopatus jura ex sacra scriptura et prima antiquitate adstruunter. Lond. 1651. The controversy was still continued; on the side of the Episcopalians by Jo. Pearson, William Beveridge, Henr. Dodwell, Jos. Bingham, Jac. Usserius. The view of the Presbyterians was defended by Jo. Dallaeus, Camp. Vitringa; also the Lutherans, Joach. Hildebrand, Just. Henn. Boehmer, Jo. Franc. Buddeus, Christ. Matth. Pfaff, &c. Jo. Phil. Gabler de episcopis primae ecclesiae Christ. eorumque origine diss. Jenae. 1805, 4. Rothe's Anf. d. christl. Kirche, i. 171.

[2] So Epaphras appears to have had a certain superiority for a length of time in Colossæ

ence of these elders were *the deacons* and *deaconesses* (Rom. xvi. 1; 1 Tim. v. 9, 10).[3] All these officers received their support, in so far as they needed, as well as the poor, from the free-will contributions of the church (1 Tim. v. 17; 1 Cor. ix. 13). The duty of teaching as an office was by no means incumbent on the elders,[4] although the apostle wishes that they should be *διδακτικοί, apt to teach* (1 Tim. iii. 2; 2 Tim. ii. 24). The capacity for instructing and edifying in the assemblies was rather considered as a free gift of the Spirit (*χάρισμα πνευματικόν*), which manifested itself in many Christians, although in different modes (*προφήτης—διδάσκαλος—γλώσσῃ λαλῶν*, 1 Cor. xii. 28–31, c. xiv.). Still less was a distinct priestly order known at this time; for the whole society of Christians formed a royal priesthood (*βασίλειον ἱεράτευμα*, 1 Peter ii. 9), God's peculiar people (*κλῆρος*, נחלה, 1 Peter v. 3; *cf. Deut.* iv. 20; ix. 29).[5] The Christians met in private houses; in many cities the churches were divided into several smaller communities meeting in different places.[6]

(Col. i. 7, iv. 12); then Archippus, supported by the reputation of his father Philemon (Col. iv. 17; Philemon i. 2). Comp. the *σύζυγος γνήσιος*, Phil. iv. 3.

[3] Respecting Deaconesses see Rothe, i. 243.

[4] Against the division into presbyteros docentes and regentes (first made by Calvin. Institutt. christ. relig. lib. iv. c. 3, § 8: verbi ministros s. episcopos and gubernatores s. seniores ex plebe delectos—afterward made a part of the constitution of the Presbyterian church) see Vitringa de Synag. vetere, lib. ii. c. 2. Neander apost. Kirche, i. 186. Rothe, i. 221.

[5] Tertullianus de Exhort. castit. c. 7: Differentiam inter ordinem et plebem constituit ecclesiae auctoritas. Ambrosiaster (Hilarius Diaconus), about 380, in comment. ad Ephes. iv. 11: Primum omnes docebant et omnes baptizabant, quibuscunque diebus vel temporibus fuisset occasio; nec enim Philippus tempus quaesivit aut diem, quo ennuchum baptizaret neque jejunium interposuit.—Ut ergo cresceret plebs et multiplicaretur, omnibus inter initia concessum est et evangelizare et baptizare et scripturas in ecclesia explanare. At ubi omnia loca complexa est ecclesia, conventicula constituta sunt, et caetera officia in ecclesiis sunt ordinata, ut nullus de clericis [perhaps ceteris] auderet, qui ordinatus non esset, praesumere officium quod sciret non sibi creditum vel concessum. Et coepit alio ordine et providentia gubernari ecclesia, quia si omnes eadem possent, irrationabile esset, et vulgaris res et vilissima videretur. Hinc ergo est, unde nunc neque diaconi in populo praedicant, neque clerici vel laici baptizant, neque quocunque die credentes tinguntur, nisi aegri. Ideo non per omnia conveniunt scripta apostoli ordinationi, quae nunc in ecclesia est, quia haec inter primordia sunt scripta.

[6] *ἐκκλησίαι κατ' οἶκον*, Rom. xvi. 5; 1 Cor. xvi. 19; Philem. ver. 2; Col. iv. 15. N. Chr. Kist über den Ursprung der bischöfl. Gewalt, (aus d. Archief voor Kerkerlijke Geschiedenis, Deel. 2, translated into German in Illgen's Zeitschrift für die hist. Theol. ii. 2, 54), thinks that these churches in houses, belonging to one town, were established by different teachers, and without a common government. Baur (Pastoralbriefe, S. 78, ff.) infers from Titus i. 5, that every church had but one elder, and that where several elders are represented as being in one city each governed independently a particular church. The analogy of the synagogue, however is in favor of the plurality of elders in a church; for the connection of the elders of one city into a college, and, consequently, of the churches in houses into one

In their assemblies, there was an interchange of reading out of the Old Testament, explanation of what was read, free discourse, singing,[7] and prayer (Col. iii. 16; 1 Tim. iv. 13). The letters of Paul also were read, and sent from one church to another (Col. iv. 16; 1 Thess. v. 27). The covenant-supper of Jesus was solemnized in an actual evening meal (ἀγάπη, 1 Cor. xvi. 20).[8] The kiss of charity was customary—the token of brotherly love in the assemblies (φίλημα ἀγάπης, φίλημα ἅγιον, Rom. xvi. 16; 1 Pet. v. 14). The other regulations of the churches were left free to each society, innocent national customs being observed (1 Cor. xi. 4); and therefore they differed in separate communities. While the Jewish Christians of Palestine retained the entire Mosaic law, and consequently the Jewish festivals, the Gentile Christians observed also *the Sabbath* and *the passover* (1 Cor. v. 6–8), with reference to the last scenes of Jesus' life, but without Jewish superstition (Gal. iv. 10; Col. ii. 16). In addition to these, Sunday, as the day of Christ's resurrection (Acts xx. 7; 1 Cor. xvi. 2; Apoc. i. 10, ἡ κυριακὴ ἡμέρα[9]), was devoted to religious services. All bodily asceticism was valued only as a means of virtue, and left to the free discretion of individuals. Thus, fasting was looked upon as a suitable preparation for prayer (Acts xiii. 2, 3; xiv. 23); celibacy was regarded by Paul desirable on account of the distressing times impending (1 Cor. vii. 26); but this very apostle requires that all these abstinences should be left to the free choice of every one (Romans xiv. 17; 1 Cor. viii. 7; 1 Tim. iv. 3). Immoral members were excluded from the church (1 Cor. v. 2-13), repentance and improvement forming the conditions of restoration (2 Cor. ii. 5–8).

church, (even if every house-church, as every synagogue, had its particular elders), those passages speak in which the collected elders of one city appear and act as a united whole. Comp. Acts xv. 4, xx. 7; Phil. i. 1; James v. 14. Comp. Rothe, i. 180, ff.

7 On the nature of the singing see Isidor. Hispal. de eccles. offic. i. 5: Primitiva ecclesia ita psallebat, ut modico flexu vocis faceret psallentem resonare, ita ut pronuntianti vicinior esset quam canenti (out of Augustini Confess. X. xxxiii. 2: [Alexandrinus episcopus Athanasius] tam modico flexu vocis faciebat sonare lectorem psalmi, ut pronuntianti vicinior esset quam canenti).

8 J. Th. Fr. Drescher de veterum Christian. agapis. Giessae. 1824. 8.

9 These passages furnish valid proof, when taken in connection with the fact, that the observance of Sunday is presupposed as an established custom, in Epist. Barnab. c. 15: Ἄγομεν τὴν ἡμέραν τὴν ὀγδόην εἰς εὐφροσύνην, ἐν ᾗ καὶ ὁ Ἰησοῦς ἀνέστη ἐκ νεκρῶν καὶ φανερωθεὶς ἀνέβη εἰς τοὺς οὐρανούς. Cf. C. Chr. L. Franke de diei dominici apud veteres Christianos celebratione comm. Halae. 1826. 8. Neander apost. K. i. 198.

The idea set forth by Christ of the union of his people with himself, and with one another in one joint body (John x. 16; xv. 1, ff.), was kept alive by the apostles (σῶμα τοῦ Χριστοῦ, Romans xii. 5; 1 Cor. x. 17; xii. 13; Ephes. ii. 16; iv. 4; xii.; xvi.; Col. iii. 15: ἐκκλησία, Acts ix. 31; xx. 28; 1 Cor. x. 32; xii. 28; Ephes. iii. 10).[10] This unity did not, indeed, obtain, for a long time, the corresponding external form; but it had an external opposition in the unbelieving, and an external center-point in the apostles,[11] who exercised a general survey over all the churches (2 Cor. xi. 28), and were co-overseers in every single church (συμπρεσβύτεροι, 1 Peter v. 1). As they had themselves divided the large sphere of their activity by the separation into apostles of the Jews and of the Gentiles (Gal. ii. 7–9); so, again, did each one find in the churches he had himself founded, his narrower field of labor (Romans xv. 20), without, however, being prevented by this circumstance from being zealous for Christianity in other churches also. The first arrangement in the newly planted churches, even the appointment of elders in them, was made by the apostles themselves (Acts xiv. 23). Afterward, the officers belonging to societies of Christians were appointed by elders with the consent of the churches.[12] In the newly established churches, Paul was accustomed to transfer the first arrangement and superintendence to one of his assistants (Acts xvii. 14; 1 Tim. i. 3, ff.; Titus i. 5, ff.), who then had a routine of duties similar to those of the later bishops, though not bound to any particular church.[13] They belonged rather to the class of teachers who, without being confined in one place, preached the gospel as opportunity offered (εὐαγγελισταί, 2 Tim. iv. 5). *James*, the Lord's brother, occupied a peculiar position. He stood in Jerusalem, where he continued to reside, at the head of the church, in equal esteem with the apostles, and with extensive influence and reputation, quite in the relation of a later bishop, but without the appellation.[14]

[10] Rothe, i. 282.

[11] Rothe, i. 302.

[12] Clement of Rome, Epist. i. 44, says, that the presbyters were at first appointed (κατασταθέντες) by the apostles, afterward ὑφ' ἑτέρων ἐλλογίμων ἀνδρῶν, συνευδοκησάσης τῆς ἐκκλησίας πάσης, as according to Cyprian, Epist. 52, the bishop was chosen de clericorum testimonio, de plebis suffragio.

[13] Rothe, i. 305.

[14] Gal. i. 19, ii. 12; Acts xii. 17, xv. 13, xxi. 18. (Comp. § 25, note 2. § 26, 6, note 4.) Rothe, S. 264

§ 31.

TIME OF THE JEWISH DISTURBANCES.

The Jewish expectations of the Messiah had constantly been most lively under the oppression of foreign rulers, and had expressed themselves among the Palestinian Jews in an Apocalyptic literature, shaped after the old Hebrew prophecies, but far surpassing these in definiteness and richness in imagery, viz.: *the book of Daniel*[1] (under Antiochus Epiphanes); *the book of Enoch*[2] (under Herod the Great). The times of oppression, in like manner, before and after the destruction of Jerusalem, furnished new nourishment to such expectations (*4th book of Ezra*).[3] Alexandrian Jews,

[1] Bleek über Verf. u. Zweck des B. Daniel, a review of the inquiries made into these points in the theol. Zeitschrift v. Schleiermacher, De Wette und Lücke, iii. 171. Against Hengstenberg (die Authentie des Daniel u. die Integrität des Sacharjah. Berlin. 1831) and Hävernick (Comm. über d. B. Daniel. Hamburg. 1832) comp. C. v. Lengerke d. B. Daniel. Königsberg. 1835, Redepenning in the theol. Studien u. Krit. 1833, iii. 831, 1835, i. 163.

[2] Preserved in an Ethiopic version first translated into English by R. Laurence. Oxford, 3d edition, 1838. A. G. Hoffmann's Buch Henoch in vollständiger (translated from the English as far as the 55th chapter, the remainder from the Ethiopic) Uebersetzung, mit Commentar, Einleitung und Excursen. 2 Abth. Jena. 1833, 38. 8vo. According to Laurence, Hoffmann, i. 23, Gfrörer (Jahrhundert des Heils, i. 96) and Wieseler (die 70 Wochen und die 63 Jahrwochen des Proph. Daniel. Göttingen. 1839, S. 163), it belongs to the first year of the reign of Herod the Great; according to Hoffmann's later opinion (ii. Vorr. S. 11), to the conclusion of the Maccabean period. Lücke (Einl. in die Offenbar. Johannis, S. 60) places it in the time of the Jewish war, probably after the destruction of Jerusalem. So, in like manner, Credner (Einl. in d. N. T. i. ii. 712), in the time about which the Apocalypse was written. Unquestionably, Christian elements have been pointed out by Lücke (S. 75) in the book, which, however, came into it by means of a later revision. [Kitto's Cyclopaedia of Biblical Literature, book of Enoch.]

[3] The Greek original is lost. There are preserved an old Latin translation (in J. A. Fabricii codex pseudepigraphus V. T. iii. 173), an Ethiopic (Primi Ezrae libri, qui apud Vulgatum appellatur quartus, versio aethiopica, nunc primo in medium prolata, et latine angliceque reddita a R. Laurence. Oxon. 1820. 8), and a paraphrasing Arabic one (translated into English in Whiston's Primitive Christianity, iv.; its variations are also found in Fabricus, l. c. On the book comp. Corodi's Krit. Gesch. des Chiliasmus, i. 179; Lücke a. a. O. S. 78; Gfröfer a. a. O. i. 69; Wieseler a. a. O. S. 206. Ch. J. van der Vlis disp. crit. de Ezrae libro apocrypho, vulgo quarto dicto. Amstelod. 1839. 8. Laurence fixes the time of its writing between 28 and 25 B.C. Mick. Merkel (Vermischte Anmerkungen aus d. Philologie, Kritik, und Theologie, Erste Samm. Leipz. 1772, S. 75, ff.) places it in the time of Vespasian. On the other hand, Corodi, Lücke, Gfröfer, and Wieseler, in the end of the first century. It was written by a Jew, but interpolated by a Christian hand. From the latter proceed cap. i. ii. xv. and xvi. entirely.

on the other hand, made use of the widely spread form of the *sybilline* oracles,[4] in order to oppose idolatry, and to procure respect among the heathen for their people and their destiny. The more the Christians were inclined to see the beginning of the end in the oppressions of that time, the easier access to them did such writings obtain, and the more readily were they imitated (first *Christian sybillines.*)[5]

When Jewish fanaticism pressed severely on the Christians of Jerusalem immediately before its destruction, and even *James*, the Lord's brother (69 A.D.), fell a sacrifice to it;[6] the most of

4 After the genuine sybillines had been burnt along with the capitol, 74 B.C., and persons began to collect new sybillines, they sprang up in so great numbers that the loss in the capitol was not only replaced very soon, but Augustus could even cause such writings to be deposited in the temple of Apollo on the Palatine (Sueton. Aug. c. 31). Although at that time the possession of all soothsaying books was forbidden, yet numerous sybilline predictions were constantly circulated among the people (Tacit. Ann. vi. 12). The first certain trace of Jewish sybillines is to be found in Joseph. Ant. i. 4, 3 (cf. orac. Sybill. iii. 35). The sybillines now extant (Sybillinorum oraculorum lib. viii. ed. Jo. Opsopoeus. Paris. 1589, ed. 3, 1607, gr. 8vo. Servatius Gallaeus. Amst. 1689. 4. Gallandius in his Bibl. pp. i. 133: to these have been lately added, lib. xi.-xiv. in Ang Maji scriptorum vett. nova collectio, t. iii. p. 3. Romae. 1828. 4) were usually before this time assigned to the second century, and to the Montanists; by many (Casaubon, Scaliger, Blondel) to Montanus himself. Huet conjectured their authors to be the Gnostics; Cave, Alexandrian Christians; Semler, Tertullian. Grotius regarded them as Jewish productions, afterward interpolated by Christians. G. J. Vossius, however, perceived that they proceeded from several authors at different times. Birger Thorlacius (libri Sybillistarum veteris ecclesiae crisi, quatenus monumenta christiana sunt, subjecti, Hann. 1815. 8, and Conspectus doctr. christ. qualis in Sibyllistarum libris continentur, 1816, also in F. Münter Miscellanea Hafniensia 1, i. 113) assumed that they had been for the greater part composed between 100 and 170 A.D., in Phrygia—some of them, too, by Alexandrians. According to Bleek (über die Entstehung u. Zusammensetzung d. sib. Or. in Schleiermacher's, De Wette's u. Lücke's theol. Zeitschrift, i. 120, and ii. 172) the oldest of them are Jewish oracles belonging to the second century before Christ; the youngest, Christian oracles of the fifth century after Christ. The greatest part of the third book, and several sections in the fifth (l. c. i. 198, ii. 182, 194), proceed from Alexandrian Jews. Gfrörer (Philo. ii. 121) agrees with him in this opinion, and points out Jewish-Alexandrian dogmas in these sections.

5 According to Bleek (l. c. i. 240, ii. 232), the fourth book was composed by a Christian, about 80 A.D., probably in Asia Minor.

6 Josephus Antiq. xx. 9, 1 (also in Eusebius, ii. 23), relates: "The high-priest Ananus, a Sadducee, a severe and cruel man, made use of the time in which, after the death of Festus, the procurator, his successor Albinus had not yet entered on office (63 A.D.): *καθίζει συνέδριον κριτῶν· καὶ παραγαγὼν εἰς αὐτὸ [τὸν αδελφὸν Ἰησοῦ τοῦ λεγομένου Χριστοῦ, Ἰάκωβος ὄνομα αὐτῷ, καὶ] τινας [ἑτέρους], ὡς παρανομησάντων κατηγορίαν ποιησάμενος, παρέδωκε λευσθησομένους.* Many pious and zealous Jews were much displeased with this proceeding, and accused Ananus before King Agrippa and Albinus. Agrippa, therefore, deposed him from the office of high-priest." Le Clerc, however, Art. crit. ii. 223, Lardner Suppl. vol. iii. cap. 16, sect. 5, and Credner (Einl. u. d. N. T. i. ii. 581) regard, on important grounds, the bracketed words as spurious. On the other hand, Hegesippus, in Euseb. ii. 23, according to the passage given in a preceding note (4, § 26), narrates the death of James in this manner: "By his preaching he had gained over many

the members of the church fled to Pella.[7] About this time also *John* repaired to Asia Minor, and there, full of the impressions which he had taken along with him from Palestine, and perceiving in these oppressions the beginning of the last events, wrote the *Apocalypse* (69 A.D.).[8] This was the commencing point of a rich apocalyptic literature among the Christians.

of the people to Christ, and stood generally in the highest repute as the righteous one. Hence the scribes and Pharisees demanded of him a solemn denial of Christ: *Ἔστησαν οὖν τὸν Ἰάκωβον ἐπὶ τὸ πτερύγιον τοῦ ναοῦ, καὶ ἔκραξαν αὐτῷ καὶ εἶπον· δίκαιε, ᾧ πάντες πείθεσθαι ὀφείλομεν, ἐπεὶ ὁ λαὸς πλανᾶται ὀπίσω Ἰησοῦ τοῦ σταυρωθέντος, ἀπάγγειλον ἡμῖν, τίς ἡ θύρα Ἰησοῦ τοῦ σταυρωθέντος.* (*θύρα* as in Rabbinic שַׁעַר estimate, value. See Credner in the new Jena A. L. Z. August, 1843, S. 795. "What is the disclosure, the truth of Christ?") *Καὶ ἀπεκρίνατο φωνῇ μεγάλῃ· τί με ἐπερωτᾶτε περὶ Ἰησοῦ τοῦ υἱοῦ τοῦ ἀνθρώπου; καὶ αὐτὸς κάθηται ἐν τῷ οὐρανῷ ἐκ δεξιῶν τῆς μεγάλης δυνάμεως, καὶ μέλλει ἔρχεσθαι ἐπὶ τῶν νεφελῶν τοῦ οὐρανοῦ.* Since now many agreed with him, the scribes and Pharisees resolved to put him to death. *Ἀναβάντες οὖν κατέβαλον τὸν δίκαιον—καὶ ἤρξαντο λιθάζειν αὐτόν.* He was not, however, killed instantaneously, but still prayed for his murderers: *Καὶ λαβών τις ἀπ' αὐτῶν εἷς τῶν κναφέων τὸ ξύλον, ἐν ᾧ ἀπεπίεζε τὰ ἱμάτια, ἤνεγκε κατὰ τῆς κεφαλῆς τοῦ δικαίου. καὶ οὕτως ἐμαρτύρησεν. Καὶ ἔθαψαν αὐτὸν ἐπὶ τῷ τόπῳ παρὰ τῷ ναῷ, καὶ ἔτι αὐτοῦ ἡ στήλη μένει παρὰ τῷ ναῷ. Καὶ εὐθὺς Οὐεσπασιανὸς πολιορκεῖ αὐτούς.* In opposition to Josephus, who places the death of James in the year 63, there agree with the designation of time by Hegesippus, agreeably to which the siege of Jerusalem took place immediately after James's death, Eusebius, iii. 11 (Symeon was chosen successor to James, *μετὰ τὴν Ἰακώβου μαρτυρίαν καὶ τὴν αὐτίκα γενομένην ἅλωσιν τῆς Ἱερουσαλήμ*), although in his chronicle he places the death of James and the inauguration of Symeon, after Josephus, in the seventh of Nero; the Clementines (so far the Ep. Clemen. Rom. ad Jacob, c. 1, in Cotelerii Patres ap. i. 611, and Clementina Epitome de gestis S. Petri, c. 147, l. c. p. 798, announce that Peter died before James), and the Paschal Chronicle, which (ed. Bonn. i. 460) places the death of James in the first year of Vespasian's reign. Comp. Credner Einleit. in d. N. T. i. ii. 580. Rothe Anfänge d. christl. Kirche, i. 275.

[7] Euseb. H. E. iii. 5. Epiphanius Haer. xxix. 7, de mensuris et ponderibus, c. 15.

[8] This time is specified by Ewald Comm. in Apoc. p. 48, and Lücke Einleit in d. Offenbar. Joh. S. 244. I can not, however, bring myself to refuse to the apostle John the authorship of the book. The author designates himself as the apostle; the oldest witnesses declare him to be so. Had the book been forged in his name thirty years before his death, he would certainly have contradicted it, and this contradiction would have reached us through Irenaeus from the school of John's disciples. On the contrary, the later contradictions of the apostolic origin proceed from doctrinal prepossession alone. The internal difference in language and mode of thought between the Apocalypse, which John, whose education was essentially Hebrew, and his Christianity Jewish-Christian of the Palestinian character, wrote, and the gospel and epistles which he had composed after an abode of from twenty to thirty years among the Greeks, is a necessary consequence of the different relations in which the writer was placed, so that the opposite would excite suspicion. There is much at the same time that is cognate, proving continuousness of cultivation in the same author. Comp. F. Lücke Versuch einer vollständigen Einleitung in die Offenbarung Johannis, und in die gesammte apokalyptische Literatur. Bonn. 1832. 8vo.

THIRD CHAPTER.

AGE OF JOHN: FROM 70-117.

§ 32.

FATE OF THE JEWISH CHRISTIANS IN PALESTINE.

Although a Jewish Christian church soon formed itself among the ruins of Jerusalem,[1] and again selected a relative of Jesus, Symeon,[2] to be its head, yet, after the judgment which had befallen Judaism,[3] this church could no longer continue to be a model mother-church, and the center of Christendom. We have a proof that these Christians were continually hated by the Jews, in the composition of the work called בִּרְכַּת הַמִּינִים,[4] and in the crucifixion of *Symeon* at the age of 120[5] (107). After the

[1] Epiphanius de mensuris et ponderibus, c. 15. According to c. 14, the small Christian church on Mount Zion was among the few buildings that were spared.

[2] Euseb. iii. 11. See § 31, note 6. Hegesippus apud Euseb. iv. 22: *Καὶ μετὰ τὸ μαρτυρῆσαι Ἰάκωβον τὸν δίκαιον—πάλιν ὁ ἐκ θείου αὐτοῦ Συμεὼν ὁ τοῦ Κλωπᾶ καθίσταται ἐπίσκοπος· ὃν προέθεντο πάντες, ὄντα ἀνεψιὸν τοῦ Κυρίου, δεύτερον.* Clopas, the father of Symeon, was, according to Hegesippus in Euseb. iii. 11, a brother of Joseph. (Sophron. in app. ad Hieronymi Catal. § 6, represents this Symeon as Judas, the brother of James, and moreover the apostle Simon Zelotes. In opposition to this, see Sam. Basnage Annales politico-ecclesiastici ad ann. 31, no. 72.) These Jewish Christians generally preferred to choose relatives of our Lord as presidents of their churches. So Hegesippus relates (in Euseb. iii. 20) that the grandchildren of Judas, a brother of Christ, after they had been set free by Domitian, *ἡγήσασθαι τῶν ἐκκλησιῶν, ὡς ἂν δὴ μάρτυρας ὁμοῦ καὶ ἀπὸ γένους ὄντας τοῦ Κυρίου.*

[3] The feeling of this is plainly expressed in the writings of this period. Barnabae Epist. c. 9: *ἡ περιτομή, ἐφ' ᾗ πεποίθασι, κατήργηται* even for the Jews. The law of Moses had only a typical meaning, particularly the laws regarding meats (c. 10); the Jews are not heirs of the promises, but the Christians (c. 13, 14); the Jewish Sabbaths are not agreeable to the Lord, but Sundays are (c. 15); in place of the destroyed Jewish temple appears a spiritual temple (c. 16).

[4] Samuel, the Little, is said to have composed it at the instigation of R. Gamaliel in Jafne, where the Sanhedrim met after the destruction of Jerusalem (Talmud. Hierosol. et Babylon. in tract. Berachoth). Hence this Gamaliel can not be the elder Gamaliel, but his grandson. Cf. Vitringa de Synagog. vet. p. 1047. Respecting the name מינים, see Fulleri Miscellan. theologic. lib. ii. c. 3. G. E. Edzardus in not. ad Avoda Sara, p. 253, ss. Hieronym. Ep. 89, ad Augustin.: Usque hodie per totas Orientis synagogas inter Judaeos haeresis est, quae dicitur Minaeorum et a Pharisaeis nunc usque damnatur, quos vulgo Nazaraeos nuncupant, qui credunt in Christum, filium Dei, natum de virgine Maria, et eum dicunt esse, qui sub Pontio Pilato passus est et resurrexit: in quem et nos credimus, sed dum volunt et Judaei esse et Christiani, nec Judaei sunt nec Christiani.

[5] Hegesippus in Eusebii H. E. iii. 32: *Ἀπὸ τούτων τῶν αἱρετικῶν κατηγοροῦσί τινες*

death of this man, there also arose an internal division among them. An opposition in the church, which had existed since the apostolic council at Jerusalem (Acts xv.), but had been hitherto restrained, now broke out openly (*Thebuthis*);[6] and from *the Nazaraeans*,[7] who remained steadfast in the apostolic faith, a party separated which held the Mosaic law to be binding in all cases, and Jesus to be the son of Joseph and Mary. To them the name *Ebionites* was afterward for the most part applied—an appellation originally given by the Jews, in derision, to the Christians generally.[8] A new party also arose among the Jew-

Συμεῶνος τοῦ Κλωπᾶ, ὡς ὄντος ἀπὸ Δαβὶδ καὶ Χριστιανοῦ. These heretics can only have been the adherents of the seven Jewish αἱρέσεις, of which Hegesippus in Euseb. ii. 23, and iv. 22, speaks. In the Chronographia of Jo. Malala (about 600—ed. Oxon. 1691, 8vo, p. 356) is the following Relatio Tiberiani, or Relation of Tiberianus, a president of Palestine, communicated to Trajan, which, if it be genuine, must belong to this time: 'Απέκαμον τιμωρούμενος καὶ φονεύων τοὺς Γαλιλαίους, τοὺς τοῦ δόγματος τῶν λεγομένων Χριστιανῶν, κατὰ τὰ ὑμέτερα θεσπίσματα· καὶ οὐ παύονται ἑαυτοὺς μηνύοντες εἰς τὸ ἀναιρεῖσθαι. ὅθεν ἐκοπίασα τούτοις παραινῶν καὶ ἀπειλῶν, μὴ τολμᾶν αὐτοὺς μηνύειν μοι ὑπάρχοντας ἐκ τοῦ προειρημένου δόγματος· καὶ ἀποδιωκόμενοι οὐ παύονται. Θεσπίσαι μοι οὖν καταξιώσατε τὰ παριστάμενα τῷ ὑμετέρῳ κράτει τροπαιούχῳ. But Dodwell Dissertt. Cypr. diss. xi. § 23, and Tillemont, note 2, sur la persécut. de Trajan (in the Mémoires, ed. Bruxelles. 8, tom. ii. p. ii. p. 433, s.) have sufficiently proved the spuriousness of this relation.

[6] Hegesippus, in Eusebius, iii. 32, says that the church enjoyed a profound peace from the death of Symeon, till the time of Trajan, and continued to be παρθένος καθαρὰ καὶ ἀδιάφθορος. When he designates Thebuthis as the person who corrupted it (Euseb. iv. 22), the connection does not render it necessary to understand the death of James as the point of time at which Thebuthis appeared; and we must therefore refer to the point of time which was before announced in obvious terms. Least of all can the opinion of Schliemann (Clementinen, S. 460) be justified, according to which, iv. 22 should be understood of the first beginnings of heretical views immediately after the death of James; iii. 32 of the open breaking out of these heresies in the second century. The influence of a Thebuthis, because he was not a bishop, can only have been an open opposition. The first beginnings of heretical views among the Jewish Christians are to be found long before the death of James in the opponents of Paul. It is still more remarkable that Schleimann, p. 488, f. did not farther consider this point of time given by Hegesippus as that in which the sects arose, but places the separation of the Ebionites from the Nazaraeans in the year 136. Comp. my treatise on the Nazaraeans and Ebionites in Stäudlin's and Tzschirner's Archiv. iv. ii. 320. Θέβουθις, according to Credner (Einl. in d. N. T. i. ii. 619), is not a person, but a collective idea, Chald. תיובתא תְיוּבָא, opposition, reluctance, especially abhorrence of the stomach, nausea, hence vomitus, and then generally filth, dirt, much the same as σπιλάδες, Jude 12; σπῖλοι καὶ μῶμοι, 2 Peter ii. 13.

[7] Comp. Epiphanii Haer. 29. According to c. 7, they lived at the time of Epiphanius, toward the end of the fourth century, in Beroea, in Syria, in Coele-Syria, in Decapolis about Pella, and in Cocabe in Basanitis (now a village, Cocab, between Damascus and Nablús, nearer the latter. See Burckhardt's Travels, German edition, edited by Gesenius, p. 591).

[8] Origenes c. Cels. ii. init.: 'Εβιωναῖοι χρηματίζουσιν οἱ ἀπὸ 'Ιουδαίων τὸν 'Ιησοῦν ὡς Χριστὸν παραδεξάμενοι. V. 61: Οἱ διττοὶ 'Εβιωναῖοι, ἤτοι ἐκ παρθένου ὁμολογοῦντες ὁμοίως ἡμῖν τὸν 'Ιησοῦν, ἢ οὐχ οὕτω γεγεννῆσθαι, ἀλλ' ὡς τοὺς λοιποὺς ἀνθρώπους. C. 65: 'Εβιωναῖοι ἀμφότεροι. These two classes can not, as Schliemann supposes, be the

ish Christians about the time of Trajan, in the countries lying eastward of the Dead Sea, by means of the diffusion of Essenism, which united with the asceticism of the Essenes the peculiar opinion that the Spirit of God associated himself differently with man, that, as the true prophet (Adam, Enoch, Noah, Abraham, Isaac, Jacob, Moses, Jesus), he might announce the same truth, and restore it when obscured.[9] This party became

Gnostic and the common Ebionites. He has himself shown, p. 207, that the former could not think of a birth of Christ by a virgin; Origen also calls them Elcesaites; see below, note 10. They are the Nazaraeans and Ebionites whom even Eusebius, H. E. iii. 27, groups together under the common appellation Ebionites, and at the same time obviously draws a distinction between them. The Ebionites, in a stricter sense, arose, according to Epiphanius Haer. xxx. 2, at Cocabe, and lived in his day (l. c. c. 18), in Nabathea, Paneas, Moabitis, and Cocabe. Respecting their adherents in Asia Minor, Rome, and Cyprus, of which he also speaks, see below, note 10. The derivation of the name from one Ebion, occurs first in Tertullian de Praescript. haeret. c. 33. In the Talmud. Hierosolymit. tract. Joma, fol. 4, col. 3, appears no אֶבְיוֹן, as Lightfoot Parergon de excid. urbis, Opp. t. ii. p. 148, asserts, but a ר׳ אָבוּן. Comp. my treatise, p. 297, ff. 306, ff.

[9] Comp. Credner "On the Essenes and Ebionites, and a partial connection between them," in Winer's Zeitschrift f. wissensch. Theol. i. 211, 277. A. Schliemann's die Clementinen nebst den Verwandten Schriften, und der Ebionitismus. Hamburg. 1844. According to Epiphanius, the Ἐσσηνοί (Haer. x.) lived in Samaria; on the other hand, the Ὀσσηνοί (Haer. xix.) in Nabathea, Iturea, Moabitis, and Areilitis. Hence he takes the former as a Samaritan, the latter as a Jewish sect. Doubtless the names were different merely by provincial pronunciation. The Essenes had withdrawn into these districts during the Jewish wars, in order to avoid the importunity of the Jews insisting on their carrying arms along with them. To the Ossenes, i. e. the Essenes living to the east of the Dead Sea, Ἠλξαΐ, Ἠλξαῖος attached himself in the reign of Trajan (Epiphan. Haer. xix. 1); and remains of the party which he modified were still existing in the time of Epiphanius as a Christian sect, under the name of Σαμψαῖοι, living in Nabathea and Moabitis (l. c. c. 2), also in Iturea. They were also called Ἐλκεσαῖοι (Haer. liii. 1); and by Origen (in Euseb. H. E. vi. 38) Ἐλκεσαΐται. That Elxai also attached himself to the Ebionites, and a part of them followed him (Epiphan. Haer. xxx. 3). Epiphanius professes even to have read the prophetic book left by Elxai (Haer. xix. 1, 3); and he had heard besides of another writing, belonging to a brother of Elxai (Haer. liii. 3) called Ἰεξξέος (Haer. xix. 1). The name Ἠλξαΐ signified, according to his followers, *δύναμις κεκαλυμμένη*, from חֲיִל and כַּסָּה (Haer. xix. 2). Modern writers have conjectured that this name first originated from the name of the party, and have declared the name Elcesaite equivalent to אַלְכְּחָשִׁין (from כחש, to deny), apostate. Baumgarten's Geschichte der Religionsparteien, pag. 271; from אֵל שַׁדַּי, Nitzsch de Testamentis xii. patriarcharum, p. 5. But according to Scaliger, Ἐλξαΐ אל חסאי ὁ Ἐσσαῖος (Petavii comm. ad Epiphan. Haer. xix.) According to Delitzsch (in Rudelbach's and Guerike's Zeitschrift, 1841, i. 43), the Elcesaites derived their name from the town Elcesi, in Galilee. I believe that חֵיל כְּסָי is an appellation of the Spirit of God which made the true prophet, and which is also called in the Clementines, Hom. xvii. 16, *δύναμις ἄσαρκος*. The Elcesaites praised this secret power as their teacher; hence arose the error of Epiphanius. If the title of the work which he possessed was חֵיל כְּסָי, and he heard of another יָהּ כְּסָי, the latter treating of the concealed deity as the former did of his concealed power, he may have made out of this two brothers. That this development proceeded from a confounding of the Essenes with Jewish Christians is shown by Credner, l. c. p. 312. When Schliemann denies this, because the similarity of

known beyond their own country by means of the *Clementines*, toward the end of the second century;[10] and they were called sometimes *Elcesaites* or *Sampsaeans*, sometimes *Ebionites;* which latter was the general appellation of heretical Jewish Christians.

§ 33.

EXTERNAL FORTUNES OF THE CHRISTIANS IN THE OTHER PROVINCES OF THE ROMAN EMPIRE.

(COMP. § 16.)

After the destruction of Jerusalem, the heathen Christians were every where so numerous that it was no longer possible to mistake the distinction between Christianity and Judaism. Still, however, the Christians were looked upon as a Jewish sect.[1] All the prejudices entertained against the Jews, and the hatred of the heathen, which had been strengthened against them since their rebellion, were transferred in like manner to the

the Essene creed to the Elcesaite can not be demonstrated, he forgets that the former is completely unknown to us, since it was guarded as a mysterious doctrine under the sanction of an oath, a thing which the Elcesaites had also to do (Credner's Beiträge zur Einl. in d. bibl. Schriften, i. 369). When Schliemann, on the other hand, designates this tendency as Gnostic Ebionitism, no objection can be made to the assertion, if Gnosis be taken as synonymous with theosophy generally. In this sense the Essenes, too, were Gnostics. But that theosophy which is in historical possession of the name Gnosis was opposed by the Elcesaites, as Schliemann, p. 539, himself shows. When, moreover, this same writer refers to the incorporation of the old oriental elements into Judaism, in order to explain Gnostic Ebionitism, and quotes Neander, he lays claim to the same source for it as that from which Neander derives Essenism (see above § 15, note 9). Regarding the name of the party, I do not believe with Credner (Beiträge, S. 367) that Ossenes, Sampsaeans, and Elcesaites were the names of the three highest classes of the Essenes. The Ossenes were the Essenes east of the Dead Sea, who by degrees became Christians. These Essene Christians were styled Elcesaites from the חֵיל כְּסִי, which they confessed; Sampsaeans (Epiphan. Haer. liii. 2: *Σαμψαῖοι ἑρμηνεύονται Ἡλιακοί* from שֶׁמֶשׁ), probably because they turned while praying toward the rising sun, as did the Essenes. The name Ebionites which was given to them, if we may rely on the authority of Epiphanius, is with him the general appellation for all heretical Jewish Christians, and is therefore least of all adapted for a strict description.

10 See below § 58. From this time onward the party appears to have obtained adherents in Asia Minor, Rome, and Cyprus. Hence Origen, in Euseb. H. E. vi. 38, distinguishes the *αἵρεσιν τῶν Ἑλκεσαϊτῶν* as *νεωστὶ ἐπανισταμένην*. On the other hand, it is very doubtful whether the doctrine of this party be represented in its pure unadulterated form in the Clementines.

1 Hence in Tacitus (Hist. v. 5), while describing the Jews, traits appear which are manifestly borrowed from the Christians: Animas proelio aut suppliciis peremptorum aeternas putant. Hinc generandi amor et moriendi contemptus.

Christians. At the same time Christianity appeared far more dangerous than Judaism, inasmuch as it was not confined, like it, to one people, but propagated itself every where with immense rapidity.[2] Yet the persecutions which the Christians had to suffer from individual emperors were only partial. *Vespasian* (70–79) did not at all persecute the Christians as such, although they may have been harassed under his reign and that of *Titus* his successor (79–81) by the demand of the tax imposed on every Jew. This was still more the case under *Domitian* (81–96),[3] who caused some Christians to be put to death even in Rome,[4] and search to be made in Palestine for the posterity of David.[5] Under *Nerva* (96–98), all these provocations ceased.[6] At the time of *Trajan* (98–117), appear the first traces of that popular rage against them to which, in succeeding times, so many must frequently have fallen sacrifices (Eusebius iii. 32). *Pliny* the younger, governor of Bithynia, where the

[2] Notions of this time concerning the Christians: Tacit. Annal. xv. 44: Quos per flagitia invisos, vulgus Christianos appellabat. Auctor nominis ejus Christus, Tiberio imperitante, per procuratorem Pontium Pilatum supplicio affectus erat. Repressaque in praesens exitiabilis superstitio rursus erumpebat non modo per Judaeam originem ejus mali, sed per Urbem etiam, quo cuncta undique atrocia aut pudenda confluunt celebranturque. Odio humani generis convicti sunt. Sueton. in Nerone, c. 16: Christiani, genus hominum superstitionis novae ac maleficae.

[3] The *δίδραχμος* now to be paid to Jupiter Capitolinus. Joseph. de B. J. vii. 6, 6. Sueton. in Domitiano, c. 12: Praeter caeteros Judaicus fiscus acerbissime actus est: ad quem deferebantur, qui vel improfessi Judaicam viverent vitam, vel dissimulata origine imposita genti tributa non pependissent. Interfuisse me adolescentulum memini, quum a procuratore frequentissimoque consilio inspiceretur nonagenarius senex, an circumsectus esset. Petri Zornii historia fisci Judaici sub imperio vett. Roman. Alton. 1734.

[4] Xiphilini epitome Dionis Cass. lxvii. 14: *Τὸν Φάβιον Κλήμεντα ὑπατεύοντα, καίπερ ἀνεψιὸν ὄντα, καὶ γυναῖκα καὶ αὐτὴν συγγενῆ ἑαυτοῦ Φλαβίαν Δομιτίλλαν ἔχοντα κατέσφαξεν ὁ Δομιτιανός· ἐπηνέχθη δὲ ἀμφοῖν ἔγκλημα ἀθεότητος· ὑφ' ἧς καὶ ἄλλοι ἐς τὰ τῶν Ἰουδαίων ἤθη ἐξοκέλλοντες πολλοὶ κατεδικάσθησαν· καὶ οἱ μὲν ἀπέθανον, οἱ δὲ τῶν γοῦν οὐσιῶν ἐστερήθησαν. ἡ δὲ Δομιτίλλα ὑπερωρίσθη μόνον εἰς Πανδατέρειαν.* (*ἄθεος*, i. e., *ὁ μὴ σεβόμενος τοὺς θεούς*). Euseb. Chron. lib. ii. ad Olymp. 218: *Πολλοὶ δὲ Χριστιανῶν ἐμαρτύρησαν κατὰ Δομετιανὸν, ὡς ὁ Βρέττιος* (Hieron. Brutius. Chron. pasch. *ὁ Βρούττιος*) *ἱστορεῖ, ἐν οἷς καὶ Φλαυία Δομετίλλα ἐξαδελφὴ Κλήμεντος Φλαυίου ὑπατικοῦ, ὡς χριστιανὴ εἰς νῆσον Ποντίαν φυγαδεύεται· αὐτός τε Κλήμης ὑπὲρ Χριστοῦ ἀναιρεῖται.* Cf. Ejusd. Hist. Eccl. iii. c. 18, § 2. According to Hieronymi Epist. 86 (al. 27) ad Eustochium Virg. epitaphium Paulae matris, Paula had seen on the Island Pontia the little cells in quibus illa (Flavia Domitilla) longum martyrium duxerat.

[5] As Vespasian had already done (Hegesipp. ap. Euseb. iii. 12), Hegesippus, in Euseb. iii. 20, relates how the grandchildren of Judas, the brother of Christ, were brought before Domitian.

[6] Xiphilini epit. Dionis, lxviii. 1: *Ὁ Νερούας τούς τε κρινομένους ἐπ' ἀσεβείᾳ ἀφῆκε, καὶ τοὺς φεύγοντας κατήγαγε· τοῖς δὲ δὴ ἄλλοις οὔτ' ἀσεβείας, οὔτ' Ἰουδαϊκοῦ βίου καταιτιᾶσθαί τινας συνεχώρησε.* A coin of the senate: Fisci Judaici calumnia sublata. S. Eckhel Doctrina nummor. veter. vi. p. 405.

number of Christians had unusually increased, applied against them the general laws, which had been lately revived by Trajan, against *forbidden societies* (*hetaeriae*) which were really dangerous (*cf. Plin. Epist.* x. 42, 43; 110 *or* 111 A.D.). He adopted that course because no special laws had been enacted with regard to them. His account of the Christians, addressed to Trajan, which is of the highest importance toward understanding their condition at that period, led to the first legal enactment relative to the course which should be adopted,[7] to

[7] Plinii lib. x. Epist. 96 (al. 97): C. Plinius Trajano. Solemne est mihi, Domine, omnia, de quibus dubito, ad Te referre. Quis enim potest melius vel cunctationem meam regere, vel ignorantiam instruere? Cognitionibus de Christianis interfui nunquam: ideo nescio, quid et quatenus aut puniri soleat, aut quaeri. Nec mediocriter haesitavi, sitne aliquod discrimen aetatum, an quamlibet teneri nihil a robustioribus differant: deturne poenitentiae venia, an ei, qui omnino Christianus fuit, desisse non prosit: nomen ipsum, si flagitiis careat, an flagitia cohaerentia nomini puniantur. Interim in iis, qui ad me tanquam Christiani deferebantur, hunc sum secutus modum. Interrogavi ipsos, an essent Christiani: confitentes iterum ac tertio interrogavi, supplicium minatus: perseverantes duci jussi. Neque enim dubitabam, qualecunque esset quod faterentur, pertinaciam certe et inflexibilem obstinationem debere puniri. Fuerunt alii similis amentiae: quos, quia cives Romani erant, annotavi in urbem remittendos. Mox ipso tractatu, ut fieri solet, diffundente se crimine, plures species inciderunt. Propositus est libellus sine auctore, multorum nomina continens, qui negarent, esse se Christianos aut fuisse. Cum praeeunte me Deos appellarent, et imagini Tuae, quam propter hoc jusseram cum simulacris numinum afferri, thure ac vino supplicarent, praeterea maledicerent Christo, quorum nihil cogi posse dicuntur, qui sunt revera Christiani, dimittendos esse putavi. Alii ab indice nominati, esse se Christianos dixerunt, et mox negaverunt: fuisse quidem, sed desisse, quidam ante triennium, quidam ante plures annos, non nemo etiam ante viginti quoque. Omnes et imaginem Tuam, Deorumque simulacra venerati sunt: ii et Christo maledixerunt. Affirmabant autem, hanc fuisse summam vel culpae suae, vel erroris, quod essent soliti stato die ante lucem convenire, carmenque Christo, quasi Deo, dicere secum invicem: seque sacramento, non in scelus aliquod obstringere, sed ne furta, ne latrocinia, ne adulteria committerent, ne fidem fallerent, ne depositum appellati abnegarent; quibus peractis morem sibi discedendi fuisse, rursusque coëundi ad capiendum cibum, promiscuum tamen et innoxium (non singularem maleficae superstitionis); quod ipsum facere desisse post edictum meum, quo secundum mandata Tua hetaerias esse vetueram. Quo magis necessarium credidi, ex duabus ancillis, quae ministrae dicebantur, quid esset veri, et per tormenta quaerere. Sed nihil aliud inveni, quam superstitionem pravam et immodicam: ideoque dilata cognitione ad consulendum Te decurri. Visa est enim mihi res digna consultatione, maxime propter periclitantium numerum. Multi enim omnis aetatis, omnis ordinis, utriusque sexus etiam, vocantur in periculum, et vocabuntur. Neque enim civitates tantum, sed vicos etiam atque agros superstitionis istius contagio pervagata est. Quae videtur sisti et corrigi posse. Certe satis constat, prope jam desolata templa coepisse celebrari, et sacra solemnia diu intermissa repeti, pastumque venire victimarum, cujus adhuc rarissimus emtor inveniebatur. Ex quo facile est opinari, quae turba hominum emendari possit, si sit poenitentiae locus.

Ibid. Ep. 97 (al. 98): Trajanus Plinio. Actum, quem debuisti, mi Secunde, in executiendis causis eorum, qui Christiani ad te delati fuerant, secutus es. Neque enim in universum aliquid, quod quasi certam formam habeat constitui potest. Conquirendi non sunt: si deferantur et arguantur, puniendi sunt, ita tamen, ut qui negaverit se Christianum esse, idque re ipsa manifestum fecerit, i. e., supplicando Diis nostris, quamvis suspectus in

which, among others, Ignatius also, bishop of Antioch (116), fell a sacrifice.[8]

§ 34.

REGULATIONS OF THE CHURCH.

Of the apostles we find at this time only *Philip* in Hierapolis (*Polycrates ap. Euseb. H. E.* iii. 31 and v. 24) and *John*[1] in

praeteritum, veniam ex poenitentia impetret. Sine auctore vero propositi libelli in nullo crimine locum habere debent; nam et pessimi exempli, nec nostri seculi est. (This text is after the edition of J. C. Orelli, prefixed to the Zürich Lectionscataloge. Mich. 1838.) Even Tertullian (Apologet. c. 2) and Eusebius (Hist. Eccl. iii. 33) mention these letters. Against the doubts of Gibbon, Semler, and Corodi, concerning their genuineness, see H. C. Haversaat's Vertheidigung der Plinischen Briefe über die Christen. Göttingen. 1788. 8, and Gierig, in his edition of Plinii Epist. tom. ii. (Lips. 1802), p. 498, ss. Against Dr. J. Held prolegomena ad librum epistt. quas mutuo sibi scripsisse Plinium jun. et Trajanum Caes. viri docti credunt (Schweidnitz. 1835, 4), who looks upon the entire tenth book as a forgery, see the Munich gel. Anz. Sept. 1836. No. 186. Commentaries on these epistles are in: Franc. Balduini comm. ad edicta veterum principum Rom. de Christianis. Basil. s. a. (and appended to his Constantinus Magnus, Lips. 1727), p. 26–69. Just. Henn. Boehmeri xii. dissertatt. juris eccles. ant. ad Plin. sec. et Tertullianum. ed. 2. Halae. 1729. Gierig, l. c.

8 Euseb. H. E. iii. 36. Trajan's conduct toward Ignatius is not inexplicable, as Baur (Ursprung des Episcopats, S. 149) supposes, but was well considered. He sent him to be executed at Rome, partly for the sake of not provoking the fanaticism of the Christians at Antioch, by looking upon his martyrdom; partly because he thought that the tedious hardships endured on the way to the place of execution might effect a change of mind, for the apostasy of this head of the Christians must have been of the greatest consequence; partly for the purpose of terrifying the Christians on the way when they saw the sufferer. Among the various texts of the Acta martyrii Ign., that of the old Latin version is the most ancient (Cotelerii Patr. apost. ii. 171); the Greek is (l. c. p. 161) a revision, which first proceeded, perhaps, from Simeon Metaphrastes. Both may also be found in Ruinart Acta mart. selecta.

1 John's exile to Patmos, an inference from Apoc. i. 9. Clemens Alex. quis dives salvetur, c. 42. Cf. Tertull. de Praescr. haer. 36: Apostolus Johannes posteaquam in oleum igneum demersus nihil passus est, in insulam relegatur. That he drank off a poison-cup without injury (as Justus Barsabas after Papias ap. Euseb. iii. 39, comp. Mark xvi. 18) is first related by Augustin in Soliloquiis. Cf. Fabricii Cod. apocr. N. T. ii. 576. Thilo acta Thomae, in the notitia uber. p. 73. Tradition gave rise to the fabrication of the story concerning the cup and the baptism, that Matth. xx. 23 might be fulfilled. His death was under Trajan (Iren. ii. 29, iii. 3), according to Euseb. Chron. and Hieron. Catal. c. 9, in the third year of Trajan, 100 A.D. Traditions growing out of John xxi. 22: the one that John placed himself alive in the grave, and is only sleeping in it, Fabric. l. c. p. 588, Thilo, l. c. lxxiv.; the other, that he was translated like Enoch and Elias, Pseudo-Hippolytus de consummat. mundi (in Hippol. opp. ed. Fabricius, append. p. 14) and Ephraemius Antioch. about 526 (in Photii bibl. cod. 229, ed. Rothomag. p. 798, ss.)—Surnames: virgo, παρθένος (so ran at first the subscription to the first and second epistles of John: ἐπιστ. Ἰωανν. τοῦ παρθένου. The Latins, afterward misunderstanding it, made out of it Epistolam ad Parthos), after the council of Nice especially θεολόγος.—Credner's Einl. in d. N. T. i. i. 217.

Ephesus. While the latter superintended the churches of Asia Minor, and laid the foundation of a peculiar development of doctrine, by instructing able disciples and by his writings, the churches of other countries lost that superintendence which they had hitherto enjoyed, by the death of the apostles and their immediate disciples. The need of unity required something to compensate for this loss; it was presented in *the episcopate*,[2]

[2] Comp. § 30, not. 1. Hilarius Diaconus (usually called Ambrosiaster), about 380, in comment. ad 1 Tim. iii. 10: Episcopi et presbyteri una ordinatio est. Uterque enim sacerdos est; sed episcopus primus est; ut omnis episcopus presbyter sit, non tamen omnis presbyter episcopus: hic enim episcopus est, qui inter presbyteros primus est. The traces of this relation were longest preserved in Alexandria. Hieronym. Epist. 101 (al. 85) ad Evangelum (in the old editions falsely styled ad Evagrium, also in Gratianus dist. xciii. c. 24): Apostolus perspicue docet eosdem esse presbyteros, quos episcopos.—Quaeris auctoritatem? Audi testimonium. Then Phil. i. 1, Acts xx. 28, &c., are cited. Quod autem postea unus electus est, qui caeteris praeponeretur, in schismatis remedium factum est, ne unusquisque ad se trahens Christi ecclesiam rumperet. Nam et Alexandriae a Marco evangelista usque ad Heraclam et Dionysium episcopos (about 240 A.D.) presbyteri semper unum ex se selectum, in excelsiori gradu collocatum, episcopum nominabant. Quomodo si exercitus imperatorem faciat, aut diaconi eligant de se, quem industrium noverint, et archidiaconum vocent (comp. on this letter Chr. Waechtler, acta eruditorum ann. 1717, p. 484, ss. 524, ss. With a Catholic bias P. Molkenbuhr, and after him Binterim Denkwürdigk. d. christkath. Kirche, ii. i. 78, ff., have pronounced the letter spurious). Hilarius Diac. comm. ad Ephes. iv. 11: Primum presbyteri episcopi appellabantur, ut uno recedente sequens ei succederet. Denique apud Aegyptum presbyteri consignant, si praesens non sit episcopus. Sed quia coeperunt sequentes presbyteri indigni inveniri ad primatus tenendos, immutata est ratio, prospiciente concilio, ut non ordo, sed meritum crearet episcopum, multorum sacerdotum judicio constitutum, ne indignus temere usurparet, et esset multis scandalum.—Pseudo-Augustini (probably also Hilarii Diaconi) Quaestiones vet. et nov. testamenti (in the appendix tom. iii. p. ii. of the Benedictine edition), quaest. 101: Presbyterum autem intelligi episcopum probat Paulus apostolus, quando Timotheum, quem ordinavit presbyterum, instruit, qualem debeat creare episcopum (1 Tim. iii. 1). Quid est enim episcopus, nisi primus presbyter, hoc est summus sacerdos? Nam in Alexandria et per totam Aegyptum, si desit episcopus, consecrat [Ms. Colb. consignat] presbyter. In like manner, Eutychius (Said Ibn Batrik about 930) patriarcha Alex. in Ecclesiae suae origg. (ed. Joh. Selden p. 29): Constituit Marcus evangelista xii. presbyteros, qui nempe manerent cum patriarcha, adeo ut cum vacaret patriarchatus, eligerent unum e xii. presbyteris, cujus capiti reliqui xi. manus imponerent, eique benedicerent, et patriarcham eum crearent (comp. 1 Tim. iv. 14).—Neque desiit Alexandriae institutum hoc de presbyteris, ut scilicet patriarchas crearent ex presbyteris duodecim, usque ad tempora Alexandri patriarchae Alexandrini, qui fuit ex numero illo cccxviii. Is autem vetuit, ne deinceps patriarcham presbyteri crearent. Et decrevit, ut mortuo patriarcha convenirent episcopi, qui patriarcham ordinarent. In this account the part, at least, which contradicts the later discipline has certainly not been interpolated in later times (but still Gulielmus Autissiodorensis, about 1206, Comm. ad sent. l. iv. qu. 1, de sacram. ord. sub finem, says: Quod si non essent in mundo nisi tres simplicis sacerdotes, oporteret quod aliquis illorum consecraret alium in episcopum et alium in archiepiscopum), and so far it has a historical value. Attempts to remove from the passage what is offensive to preconceived opinions have been made by Morin, Pearson, Le Quien, Renaudot, Petavius, especially by Abrah. Echellensis Eutychius patriarcha Alex. vindicatus et suis restitutus orientalibus, s. responsio ad Jo. Seldeni origines, &c. Romae. 1661. 4. Mamachii Origg. et antiquitt. Christian. tom. iv. p. 503, ss. See on the contrary sides, J. F. Rehkopf Vitae

which had been adumbrated for a considerable time in the mother-church of Jerusalem, by the position of *James* and his successors.[3] This example was imitated especially in the neighboring churches, at *Antioch* in particular.[4] It is true, that in the more remote churches the chief presbyters, as presidents of the college of presbyters, occupied a similar position; but they had not been as yet elevated above the other presbyters by independent privileges peculiar to themselves.[5] Ignatius, through

patriarcharum Alexandrinorum saec. i. et ii. Specim. iii. Lips. 1759. 4. p. 28, s.—On the accounts of Jerome and Hilary rests the usual Protestant view of the origin of episcopacy, which is developed among the moderns (for the older literature see § 30, note 1), with different modifications by Zeigler Gesch. d. Kirchl. Verfassungsformen, p. 7. Gabler de Episcopis primae eccl. Christ. eorumque origine diss. Jenae. 1805. 4to. Neander K. G. i. i. 324. Episcopacy is said to have been established as a point of union between the ἐκκλησίαι κατ' οἶκον, which may have stood independently of each other in towns (see § 30, note 6), by J. F. Gruner de Origine episcoporum exerc. Halae. 1764. 4to. Münscher Dogmengeschichte, ii. 376, and especially by N. Chr. Kist. über den Ursprung der bisch. Gewalt (in Illgen's Zeitschrift für d. hist. Theol. ii. ii. 47). See on the other side Rothe die Anfänge d. christl. Kirche and ihrer Verfassung, i. 194. According to Rothe (p. 392) episcopacy was introduced as an instrument of Christian unity by the still remaining apostles at the council of Jerusalem, at which they chose Symeon bishop of Jerusalem (Euseb. iii. 11). But when the memory of this synod is preserved how can its most important transaction be forgotten? According to Baur (über d. Ursprung des Episkopats. Tübingen. 1838. 8), the heresies which first appeared in full power under the Antonines, which brought the idea of the Catholic church into a clear point of view, gave rise to the outward manifestation of this idea by establishing the episcopate, which was looked upon as a matter of pressing necessity. The Petrine and Pauline parties were united on this point; and in the endeavor to realize the measure, the influence of the Clementines, which proceeded from the Petrine party, as well as the Acts of the Apostles, the pastoral epistles, and the later Ignatian letters, which now proceeded from the Pauline party, were working in the one direction.

[3] See above, § 26, note 4. § 32, note 2.

[4] Comp. the epistles of Ignatius, Rothe Anfänge d. christl. Kirche, i. 467. It is worthy of notice, that the bishop is always here represented as Christ's representative; the presbyters as the representatives of the apostles (ad Trallianos c. 2: Τῷ ἐπισκόπῳ ὑποτάσσεσθε ὡς Ἰησοῦ Χριστῷ.—ὑποτάσσεσθε καὶ τῷ πρεσβυτερίῳ, ὡς τοῖς ἀποστόλοις Ἰησοῦ Χριστοῦ, cf. c. 3, ad Magnes. c. 6, ad Smyrn. c. 8); whereas, according to the view which soon after prevailed in the church, the bishops are the successors and representatives of the apostles. The Ignatian apprehension of this relation appears to have had its origin in Jerusalem, where James, the brother of Jesus, might be reckoned the representative of the latter; and in like manner, the other relatives of Jesus who were subsequently chosen presidents by the churches in Palestine, see § 52, note 2.

[5] Clemens Rom. in Epist. i. ad Corinth, c. 42, names only ἐπίσκοποι καὶ διάκονοι, and finds these two classes of the clergy prophetically announced as early as Isaiah lx. 17. Hermae Pastor, i. vis. ii. 4: Seniores, qui praesunt ecclesiae. Vis. iii. 5: Apostoli, et episcopi, et doctores, et ministri. Here the bishops are the seniores, the doctores, the teaching presbyters and evangelists, and not as Rothe, p. 408, supposes, the presbyters merely. Polycarp. ad Philipp. c. 5, admonishes, ὑποτάσσεσθαι τοῖς πρεσβυτέροις καὶ διακόνοις, ὡς τῷ θεῷ καὶ Χριστῷ. Polycarp designates himself as president among the presbyters in the beginning of the epistle: Πολύκαρπος καὶ οἱ σὺν αὐτῷ πρεσβύτεροι τῇ ἐκκλησίᾳ τοῦ θεοῦ τῇ παροικούσῃ Φιλίπποις κ. τ. λ.

the instrumentality of his epistles, recommended episcopacy universally, as a condition of unity, and that, too, in the most urgent terms;[6] and thus the first presbyters soon generally moved up to the higher step as ἐπίσκοποι,[7] although they retained besides, for a long time, the title πρεσβύτεροι.[8] When the attempt was made, at a later period, to carry up the series of bishops, as the successors of the apostles, to the apostles themselves, the most distinguished presbyters of the earlier times were reckoned as the first bishops.[9] In this way we explain the different accounts of the order of the first Romish bishops.[10] The universal right to teach in the public assemblies having occasioned improprieties very early (James iii. 1), it seems to have been already in this period so limited by custom, that usually

[6] Ignatius recommends submission to the episcopal authority, as something new, or at least not yet sufficiently settled, see Kist in Illgen's Zeitschrift, ii. ii. 68. In his Epist. ad Polycarpum he addresses the latter as ἐπίσκοπον different from the πρεσβυτέροις (c. 6), and exhorts him to the exercise of his episcopal rights and duties; although Polycarp himself, in his epistle written not long afterward, designates himself merely as the principal presbyter (see note 5). Thus Ignatius represents the first presbyters of the churches as bishops, and wishes to induce them to appropriate the idea of the episcopate. Thus he addresses Onesimus as bishop of Ephesus (Ep. ad Ephes. c. 1), Polybius as bishop of Tralles (ad Trall. c. 12), Dumas as bishop of Magnesia (ad Magnes. c. 2), and an unknown person as bishop of Philadelphia (ad. Philadelph. c. 1).

[7] The προεστώς, who, in Justini Apol. maj. c. 65, is supposed to be in all churches, is doubtless the bishop.

[8] Because they always possessed as yet the character of the presiding presbyter. Thus the bishops are included among the πρεσβυτέροις in Irenaeus, iii. 2, 2 (successiones presbyterorum; on the other hand, iii. 3, 1 and 2, successiones episcoporum), iv. 26, 2, 3, 5. v. 20, 2. In Irenaei Epist. ad Victorem ap. Euseb. v. 24, the earlier bishops are called οἱ πρεσβύτεροι, οἱ προστάντες τῆς ἐκκλησίας. Tertullianus in Apologet. c. 39, calls bishops and presbyters together, seniores.

[9] In Alexandria: (Marcus) Annianus, Abilius, Kerdon (Euseb. ii. 24, iii. 14, 21). In Antioch: Evodius, Ignatius, Heros (Euseb. iii. 22, 36).

[10] Comp. § 27, note 6. First of all, Irenaeus adv. Haer. iii. 3, followed by Eusebius, iii. 2, 13, 14, 31, gives it thus: Linus (2 Tim. iv. 21 ?) † 80, Anencletus, Anacletus or Cletus † 92, Clemens (Philipp. iv. 3 ?) † 102, Evarestus † 110. According to the Clementines, on the contrary, Clement, the constant attendant of Peter, was consecrated by that apostle bishop of Rome. This opinion is followed by Tertullian de Praescr. c. 32. Accordingly, the Apostol. constitutt. vii. 46, give the following order: Linus nominated by Paul, Clement by Peter, &c. In like manner, Optatus Milev. de schism. Donatist. ii. 2. Augustini Ep. 53, ad Generosum. On the other hand, Epiphanius, xxvii. 6, represents Clement as ordained bishop by Peter, but not as having entered on his office till after the death of Linus and Anacletus. Rufinus praef. in Recognit. says that Linus and Cletus were bishops in the lifetime of Peter; and that after the death of the latter, Peter appointed Clement, shortly before his own death. According to Jerome (Catal. c. 15), most of the Latins looked upon Clement as the immediate successor of Peter. The modern Romish church assumes the following order: Peter, Linus, Clemens, Cletus, Anacletus, Evarestus. Comp. Jo. Pearsonii and Henr. Dodwelli Diss. de successione primorum Romae episcoporum, in Pearsonii opp. posthum. Lond. 1688. 4. J. Ph. Baraterii Disquisitio chronol. de successione antiquissima episcoporum Rom. Ultraj. 1740. 4.

only the officers of the congregation spoke in public, although it was not formally abolished.[11]

§ 35.

APOSTOLIC FATHERS.

SS. Patrum, qui temporibus apostolicis floruerunt, opera ed. J. B. Cotelerius. Paris. 1672 recud. curavit J. Clericus, ed. 2. Amst. 1724. 2 voll. fol. SS. Patrum apostolic. opera genuina ed. Rich. Russel. Lond. 1746. 2 voll. 8. S Clementis Rom., S. Ignatii, S. Polycarpi, patrum apostt., quae supersunt. Accedunt S. Ignatii et S. Polycarpi martyria. Ad fidem codd. rec., adnotationibus illustravit, indicibus instruxit Guil. Jacobson. 2 tomi. Oxon. 1838. ed. 2. 1840. 8. Patrum apostt. opera (genuina). Textum recognovit, brevi adnotatione instruxit, et in usum praell. acadd. ed. C. J. Hefele. Tubingae. 1839. ed. 2. 1843.

Apostolic fathers is a title given to those who were the immediate and genuine disciples of the apostles, and in a stricter sense, to such of them as have left works behind. To the school of Paul belong *Barnabas* (comp. § 26)[1] *Clement of Rome* (comp.

[11] Dr. K. F. W. Paniel's pragm. Gesch. d. christl. Beredsamkeit u. d. Homiletik. Bd. 1. Abth. 1. Leipzig. 1839. p. 75.

[1] The epistle of Barnabas, which was regarded even by Clement of Alexandria, Origen, and Jerome, as genuine, remained entirely unknown till, after Ussher's edition had been burned in the printing-office at Oxford, 1643, it was first published by Hugo Menardus, Paris, 1645, 4to, and with a corrected text by Iss. Vossius appended to the epistles of Ignatius. Amstel. 1646. 4to. For a long time the predominant opinion was against its authenticity, see especially Tentzel ad Hieron. Catal. cap. 6, in Fabricii Bibl. eccles. p. 38, ss. Yet Isaac Vossius, Cave, Grynaeus, Gallandius, declared it genuine. Since J. E. Chr. Schmidt K. G. 437, Münscher Dögmengesch. i. 111, Rosenmüller Hist. interpret. libb. sacr. i. 42, decided in its favor, this became almost the prevailing opinion, and has been defended with ingenuity, particularly by D. E. Henke de epistolae quae Barnabae tribuitur authentia, Jenae. 1827. 8vo; Bleek Brief a. d. Hebräer, i. 416; and J. Chr. Rördam Comm. de authentia epist. Barnabae. Partic. I. Hafn. 1828. 8vo. Gu. H. Haverkorn von Rysewyk Diss. de Barnaba, Arnhemiae. 1835. 8vo, has also declared in favor of the genuineness. Recently, however, certain important voices have been raised again in opposition to the epistle, as Neander (K. G. i. ii. 1133), Twesten (Dogmatik, i. 104), Ullmann (theol. Studien u. Kritiken, i. ii. 382), and Hug (Zeitschrift für d. Geistlichkeit d. Erzbistb. Frieburg. ii. 132, ff.; iii. 208, ff.). Dan. Schenkel (über d. Brief d. Barn. in d. theol. Stud. u. Kritik. 1837, iii. 652) believes that § 1-6, 13, 14, 17, constitute the genuine original letter, and that § 7-12, 15, 16, were afterward inserted by a therapeutic Jewish Christian. On the other hand, C. J. Hefele, in the Tübing. theol. Quartalschr. 1839, i. 50, affirms the integrity of the epistle, but denies the authenticity of it in the work entitled, "das Sendschreiben des Apostels Barnabas aufs neue untersucht, übersetzt und erklärt, Tübingen. 1840. 8."—The chief ground urged against the genuineness, that the absurd mystical mode of interpretation could not have proceeded from a companion of the apostle Paul, seems to me untenable. That Barnabas was not a man of spiritual consequence, is clear even from the Acts of the Apostles. There he is at first the more prominent by virtue of his apostolic commission, in company with Paul (Acts xi. 22; xii. 2, Barnabas and Saul), but he soon falls entirely into the background behind Paul, after a freer sphere of

§ 34, note 10),[2] to whom, in later times, many writings were falsely ascribed,[3] and *Hermas*, whose work (ὁ ποιμήν)[4] inculcates moral precepts in visions and parables, in order to promote the

activity has commenced (xiii. 13, 43, Paul and Barnabas). The epistle was written soon after the destruction of Jerusalem, according to chapters iv. and xvi.; and the ancient testimony of Clement, that Barnabas was the author, can not be derived from a partiality of the Alexandrian in favor of a production of kindred spirit, because the millennarianism of the letter (c. 15) could not have pleased the Alexandrian, and besides, all the interpretations do not agree with Clement, who in his Paedag. ii. p. 221 refutes one of them, and in his Stromata, ii. p. 464 prefers another view of Psalm i. 1 to that given in the epistle before us.

[2] His epistle to the Corinthians, which was usually read in the religious assemblies at Corinth, as early as the second century (Dionys. Corinth. in Euseb. H. E. iv. 23, 6. Iren. iii. 3), is called in question without reason by Semler (histor. Einleit. zu Baumgarten's Unters. theol. Streitigkeiten. Bd. 2. S. 16) and Ammon (Leben Jesu, i. 33), but it has been looked upon as interpolated, by H. Bignon, Ed. Bernard, H. Burton, Jo. Clericus (see Patrum apost. Cotelerii ed. Clerici, ii. p. 133, 478, 482, and in the notes to the letter), Ittig, Mosheim, and Neander. It seems to belong to the end of the first century. In opposition to Schenkel (theol. Studien und Krit. 1841, i. 65), who places it between 64 and 70, see Schliemann's Clementinen, p. 409. The so-called second epistle, a mere fragment, is spurious (Euseb. iii. 38). These two letters, preserved only in the Cod. Alexand., were first published by Patricius Junius, Oxon. 1633. 4to, and his incorrect text has been repeated in most editions. After a careful comparison of the MS., a more correct text was given first of all by Henr. Wotton, Cantabr. 1718.

[3] Namely, 1. Two letters in the Syriac language, see below § 73, note 5. 2. Constitutiones and Canones apostolorum, see § 67, note 3. 3. Recognitiones Clementis and Clementina, see § 58.

[4] Partly an imitation of the 4th book of Ezra (see § 31, note 3, comp. Jachmann, p. 63), it professes to be a writing of the Hermas mentioned in Romans xvi. 14 (lib. i. vis. ii. c. 4), and is quoted as scripture even by Irenaeus, iv. 3. When the opposition to Montanism began in the west toward the close of the second century (see below § 59), it lost its reputation there with those who were inclined to Montanist views, because it allowed a repentance once after baptism, and with the opponents of Montanism it fell into disrepute, on account of its apocalyptic form (Tertull. de Pudic. c. 10: Cederem tibi, si scriptura pastoris, quae sola moechos amat, divino instrumento meruisset incidi, si non ab omni concilio ecclesiarum, etiam vestrarum, inter apocrypha et falsa judicaretur. C. 2: Ille apocryphus pastor moechorum), and now it is declared by the Fragmentum de canone in Muratorii Antiquitt. Ital. iii. 853: Pastorem vero nuperrime temporibus nostris in urbe Roma Hermas conscripsit, sedente cathedra urbis Romae ecclesiae Pio episcopo, fratre ejus. This assumption, which Irenaeus can not have known, became afterward the usual one in the west. On the contrary, the work remained in repute among the Alexandrians, and is cited by Clement of Alex. and Origen frequently, by Athanasius several times as an authority (see Jachmann, p. 37). Origenes in Ep. ad Rom. comm. lib. x. c. 31: Puto tamen, quod Hermas, iste (Rom. xvi. 15) sit scriptor libelli istius, qui Pastor appellatur, quae scriptura valde mihi utilis videtur, et, ut puto, divinitus inspirata. But when in later times the Arians appealed to it (Athanasii Epist. ad Afros in Opp. i. ii. 895) its reputation sank in the Greek church also. Hieronymus in Catal. c. 10: Herman, cujus apostolus Paulus ad Romanos scribens meminit—asserunt auctorum esse libri, qui appellatur Pastor, et apud quasdam Graeciae ecclesias etiam publice legitur. Revera utilis liber, multique de eo scriptorum veterum usurpavere testimonia, sed apud Latinos paene ignotus est. Lücke Einl. in die Offenbarung Joh. p. 141, places it in the middle of the second century, Jachmann der Hirte des Hermas, Königsb. 1835, in the beginning of it, and regards the Hermas of Paul as the author.

completeness of the church. The disciples of John are *Ignatius*, bishop of Antioch (see § 33, note 8),[5] *Polycarp*, bishop of Smyrna († 167),[6] and *Papias*, bishop of Hierapolis,[7] of whose writings

[5] Seven epistles ad Smyrnaeos, ad Polycarpum, ad Ephesios, ad Magnesios, ad Philadelphienses, ad Trallianos, ad Romanos (Polycarp Ep. c. 13, mentions the epistles of Ignatius in general, Iren. v. 28 cites that to the Romans, Origenes prol. in Cant. Cant. and Hom. vi. in Lucam those to the Romans and Ephesians; Eusebius, iii. 36 mentions all the seven) are extant in a longer and in a shorter recension. (The latter was first published by Is. Vossius, at Amstel. 1649. 4to.) The controversy concerning their genuineness was interwoven with that respecting the origin of Episcopacy. In the older literature, which is rich in notices of the epistles, the chief work in favor of the authenticity is: Jo. Pearson. Vindiciae epistol. S. Ignatii. Cantabr. 1672. 4. The leading work against the authenticity is: Jo. Dallaeus de scriptis, quae sub Dionysii Areop. et Ignatii Antioch. nominibus circumferuntur. Genev. 1666. 4. Recently Rothe (Anfänge p. 715) defended the authenticity. But in opposition to him, Baur (über die Ursprung des Episkopats, S. 148, ff.) asserted that those letters were composed at Rome in the second half of the second century, on the side of the pure Pauline Christianity against the Petrine Judaizing tendency which had found expression in the Clementines. Dr. J. E. Huther again defended the authenticity with reference to these doubts (Illgen's Zeitschrift für die histor. Theol. 1841, iv. 1). As regards the two recensions, W. Whiston (Primitive Christianity revived. Lond. 1711) is the only person who has declared the longer to be the original one; while Dr. F. K. Maier (theol. Stud. u. Krit. 1836. ii. 340) is of opinion that it comes much nearer the original text. Against the latter see Rothe, l. c. p. 739, and Arndt (theol. Stud. u. Krit. 1839. i. 136). J. E. Chr. Schmidt (in Henke's Magazin. iii. 91) thought that both recensions arose from a thorough revision of the genuine text, but yet he admitted (in his Biblioth. für Kritik. u. Exegese d. N. T. ii. 29) that the shorter comes nearest to the genuine text. Netz (theol. Stud. u. Kritik. 1835. iv. 881) has repeated the same opinion. Against him see Arndt (theol. Stud. u. Krit. 1839. i. 742). The latest investigations have all turned out in favor of the shorter recension (see Rothe, Arndt, Huther, ll. cc. F. A. Chr. Düsterdieck, quae de Ignatianarum epistolarum authentia, duorumque textuum ratione et dignitate hucusque prolatae sunt sententiae enarrantur et dijudicantur. Gottingae. 1843. 4. Worthy of attention are the remarks of Arndt, S. 139, respecting the necessity of revising the text of the shorter recension after the best MSS. and other existing critical helps. Eight other pretended letters of Ignatius are certainly spurious. [See particularly "The ancient Syriac version of the epistles of St. Ignatius to St. Polycarp, the Ephesians, and the Romans; together with extracts from his epistles collected from the writings of Severus of Antioch, Timotheus of Alexandria, and others. Edited with an English translation and notes. Also the Greek text of these three epistles, corrected according to the authority of the Syriac version. By William Cureton, M.A., London. 1845. 8vo.

[6] Epist. ad Philippenses, mentioned so early as by Irenaeus, iii. 3 (ap. Euseb. iv. 14, 3), frequently, however, controverted by the opponents of the Ignatian epistles, doubted of by Semler and Rössler, and recently declared to be spurious by Schwegler (der Montanismus und d. Christl. Kirche. Tübingen. 1841. S. 260). On the other side, Schliemann's Clementinen, S. 418.

[7] *Ἰωάννου μὲν ἀκουστής, Πολυκάρπου δὲ ἑταῖρος γεγονώς*, Iren. v. 33, is said to have suffered martyrdom in 163, in Pergamus (Chronic. pasch. ed. Bonn. i. 481), wrote *λογίων κυριακῶν ἐξήγησις*; fragments in Grabe, ii. p. 26. Routh, i. p. 1. In Euseb. H. E. iii. 36, he is called: *ἀνὴρ τὰ πάντα ὅτι μάλιστα λογιώτατος, καὶ τῆς γραφῆς εἰδήμων* (respecting the omission of these words in some MSS. after Rufin's example, see Kimmel de Rufino, p. 236). But because he expressed very gross millennarianism in his writings (although that doctrine was older), Eusebius passes a very severe judgment upon him, H. E. iii. 39: *Χιλιάδα τινά φησιν ἐτῶν ἔσεσθαι μετὰ τὴν ἐκ νεκρῶν ἀνάστασιν, σωματικῶς τῆς τοῦ Χριστοῦ βασιλείας ἐπὶ ταυτησὶ τῆς γῆς ὑποστησομένης—σφόδρα γάρ τοι σμικρὸς ὢν τὸν*

nothing but fragments are extant. The compositions attributed to *Dionysius the Areopagite* (Acts xvii. 34) are spurious.[8]

§ 36.

DEVELOPMENT OF DOCTRINE IN THIS PERIOD.

While the stricter party of Jewish Christians maintained the Jewish particularism, and therefore constantly indeavored to impose on the Gentile Christians the observance of the Mosaic law,[1] that speculation which strove to comprehend Christianity in its peculiar nature was always becoming more powerful in other quarters. Inasmuch as a speculative basis was not yet firmly established, great freedom was allowed for it; but as soon as it trenched upon the moral and religious interests of Christianity, it was resisted, and not till then.[2] It was principally with the wonderful person of Christ, which it endeavored to understand, that speculation occupied itself. Even here the most different tendencies were indulged in, as long as they left unimpaired the divine and human in Christ, by the union of which the atoning and model character of the life of Jesus was necessarily constituted. Hence, *the Shepherd of Hermas*, with its peculiar Christology, gave no offense.[3] On the contrary, the doctrine of

νοῦν.—πλὴν καὶ τοῖς μετ' αὐτὸν πλείστοις ὅσοις τῶν ἐκκλησιαστικῶν τῆς ὁμοίας αὐτῷ δόξης παραίτιος γέγονε—ὥσπερ οὖν Εἰρηναίῳ κ. τ. λ. With what right Eusebius, who in his Chronicon (Olymp. 220) allows Papias without hesitation to have been a disciple of the apostle John, declares in this work that he was only the pupil of a certain presbyter John, is examined by Olshausen, die Echtheit der vier kanon. Evangelien. Königsb. 1823. S. 224, ff.

8 Respecting them see below § 110, note 4.

1 Against this party is directed Epist. Barnabae, c. 1–16.

2 Thus an error which threatened to turn Christian liberty into licence is combated in the Epistle of Jude, which was written after the destruction of Jerusalem (Credner's Einl. in d. N. T. i. ii. 611), and in the 2d Epistle of Peter, which is an imitation of that of Jude (Credner, i. ii. 650). The false teachers mentioned in the latter epistle denied the return of Christ and the judgment (2 Peter iii. 3, ff.).

3 Hermae Pastor, iii. 5, 5: Filius Spiritus sanctus est. iii. 9, 1: Spiritus filius Dei est. iii. 9, 12: Filius Dei omni creatura antiquior est, ita ut in consilio patri suo adfuerit ad condendam creaturam. C. 14: Nomen filii Dei magnum et immensum est, et totus ab eo sustentatur orbis. This spirit dwells in men, i. 5, 1: *Τὸ πνεῦμα τὸ ἅγιον κατοικοῦν ἐν σοί.* iii. 5, 6: Accipiet mercedem omne corpus purum ac sine macula repertum, in quo habitandi gratia constitutus fuerit Spiritus sanctus. The Holy Spirit is the essence of all virtues, which, iii. 9, 13, are designated under the title of virgins, and even called Spiritus sancti: non aliter homo potest in regnum Dei intrare, nisi hae (virgines) induerint eum

the Docetae was rejected, which represented Christ's humanity as a mere appearance, in the way that the Jews conceived of the manifestations of angels (δοκηταί).[4] In the mean time, however, speculation relative to the higher nature of Christ and the essence of Christianity, attached itself to the more general questions respecting the creation of the world and the origin of evil. Here the Alexandrine Jewish philosophy presented itself as a pattern. The idea of the λόγος in particular was borrowed from it for the purpose of explaining the higher nature of Christ.[5] John followed this speculation in his gospel, in order to divert it from the region of a fruitless hyper-naturalism into a consideration of *the moral efficacy* of the Logos.[6] It went astray, how-

veste sua. Quicunque nomen filii Dei portat, harum quoque nomina portare debet: nam et Filius nomina portat earum. Respecting the person of Christ, iii. 5, 2: A master intrusts a faithful servant with the care of a vineyard, praecipiens, ut vitibus jungeret palos. The servant does for him still more than he had been ordered. The master consults about rewarding him adhibito filio, quem carum et haeredem habebat, et amicis, quos in consilio advocabat, and concludes: volo eum filio meo facere cohaeredem. The explanation, c. 5: The master is God, Filius autem Spiritus sanctus est: servus vero, ille Filius Dei est. Vinea autem populus est, quem servat ipse. Pali vero Nuncii (angels) sunt, qui a Domino praepositi sunt ad continendum populum ejus. C. 6: Quare autem Dominus in consilio adhibuerit Filium de haereditate et bonos Angelos? Quia Nuncius (Christ) audit illum Spiritum sanctum, qui infusus est omnium primus, in corpore, in quo habitaret Deus. Cum igitur corpus illud paruisset omni tempore Spiritui sancto; placuit Deo—ut et huic corpori—locus aliquis consistendi daretur, ne videretur mercedem servitutis suae perdidisse. A useful application, c. 7: Corpus hoc tuum custodi mundum atque purum; ut Spiritus ille qui inhabitabat in eo, testimonium referat illi, et tecum fuisse judicetur. The eternal Son of God is here the Holy Spirit, and there is no account of a personal union of him with the man Jesus. Against Jachmann Hirte des Hermas, S. 70, and Schliemann Clementinen, S. 423, who wish to defend the orthodoxy of Hermas, see Baur Lehre von der Dreieinigkeit, i. 134.

[4] Later names: Phantasiastae, Phantasiodocetae, Opinarii. Perhaps even 1 Joh. iv. 2; 2 Joh. 7 (see Lücke's Comm. zu Johannes, 2te Aufl. iii. 66). Distinctly and often in Ignatius ad Ephes. vii. 18, ad Trallianos ix. 10, ad Smyrn. 1-8: Ἰησοῦν τὸ δοκεῖν (δοκήσει, φαντασίᾳ) πεπονθέναι, and in the Evang. Petri (Serapion apud Euseb. vi. 12). Cf. Hieronymus adv. Luciferianos (ed. Martian. tom. iv. p. ii. p. 304): Apostolis adhuc in saeculo superstitibus, adhuc apud Judaeam Christi sanguine recenti, phantasma Domini corpus asserebatur. So thought the Jews about the appearances of angels, Tob. xii. 19. Philo de Abrah. p. 366: Τεράστιον δὲ καὶ τὸ μὴ πεινῶντας πεινώντων, καὶ μὴ ἐσθίοντας ἐσθιόντων παρέχειν φαντασίαν. (Comp. Neander's gnostische Systeme, S. 23.) Josephus Antt. i. 11, 2, v. 6, 2: Φαντάσματος δ' αὐτῷ (Gideoni) παραστάντος νεανίσκου μορφῇ. The church fathers had the very same idea of the appearances of angels, comp. Keilii opusc. ed. Goldhorn ii. 548. H. A. Niemeyer comm. de Docetis. Halae, 1823. 4.

[5] So also in the κήρυγμα Πέτρου. Clem. Alex. Strom. i. p. 427, Credner's Beiträge zur Einl. in die bibl. Schriften, i. 354.

[6] Lücke's Comm. über d. Evangel. d. Johannes. 3te Aufl. i. 202. C. L. W. Grimm de Joanneae christologiae indole Paulinae comparata. Lips. 1833. 8. K. Frommann's der Johanneische Lehrbegriff in his Verhältnisse zur gesammten biblisch-christl. Lehre. Leipzig, 1839. 8. K. R. Köstlin's Lehrbegriff des Evang u. der Briefe Johannis. Berlin, 1843. 8.

ever, even at that time, falling into that false *Gnosis* which denies the fundamental principles of Christianity, and which the apostle Paul had already predicted in its germs. The first Christian-Gnostic system was that of Cerinthus, in which, however, the Gnosis did not yet attain a consistent development, but was obliged to accommodate itself to many Jewish opinions.[7]

[7] According to him, the God of the Jews (*δημιουργός*) is separated from the highest God by a series of Aeons, and the highest God was first revealed by the Aeon Christ. The Mosaic law, however, must be observed, a resurrection and thousand years' reign be expected. J. E. Ch. Schmidt Cerinth ein judaisirender Christ, in his Bibliothek fur Kritik u. Exegese des N. T. i. 181. H. E. G. Paulus historia Cerinthi in his Introductionis in N. T. capita selectiora. Jenae. 1799. 8. Neander's Kirchengesch. 2te Aufl. i. ii. 683.

SECOND DIVISION.

FROM HADRIAN TO SEPTIMUS SEVERUS. FROM 117-193.

INTRODUCTION.

§ 37.

STATE OF PAGANISM.

P. E. Müller de hierarchia et studio vitae asceticae in sacris et mysteriis Graecorum Romanorumque latentibus. Hafn. 1803. 8, in the second section (translated in the Neue Biblioth. der schönen Wissenschaften. Bd. 69. S. 207, ff.). Tzschirner's der Fall des Heidenthums. Bd. 1. S. 124-164.

Although the emperors of this time preserved to the Roman empire external security, maintained internal order and justice, and favored the sciences,[1] yet the old Roman morality and religious sobriety could not be restored among the degenerate people. The propensity to theosophic mysteries, consecrations, and purifications (§ 14), produced new institutions which ministered to superstition. They were no longer satisfied with the wandering priests of Isis and Cybele, the Chaldeans and Magic. In the second century, many secret rites or mysteries were spread abroad over the Roman empire in addition to the former (those of the *Dea Syra*, of *Isis*, of *Mithras*). Besides these, the old Eleusinian and Dionysian mysteries also came again into greater repute, though it would appear that they were variously accommodated to the spirit of the time. Abstinence from sensual pleasures was a universal condition of initiation, by which it was supposed that the people obtained a nearer communion with the deities as they passed through the different gradations of the mysteries. This period was conscious of its godless condition, but mistaking the religious moral way, it sought to obtain

[1] Schlosser's universalhist. Uebersicht d. Geschichte d. alten Welt, iii. ii. 167. Bernhardy's Grundriss d. röm. Literatur. S. 126. The same author's Grundriss d. griech. Literatur. i. 406.

purity by magic, with the aid of all kinds of external observances. We have a proof, in the horrible *Taurobolium* and *Kriobolium* which now appeared, of the extreme ingenuity of superstition. The prevailing philosophy continued to be that *Platonic eclecticism* which adopted and defended all superstitions,[2] although by it a certain monotheism was elevated above polytheism, even in the view of the people generally.[3] Among the Platonics of this time, the most distinguished are *Plutarch* of *Chaeronea* [† 120], *Apuleius* of *Madaura* [about 170] and *Maximus* of *Tyre* [about 190]. In opposition to this dogmatic philosophy, skepticism, too, was always rising to a higher degree of strength. *Sextus Empiricus.*

§ 38.

FATE OF THE JEWS.

Dio Cassius, lxviii. c. 32, lxix. c. 12–14. Euseb. Hist. eccl. iv. c. 2 u. 6.—F. Münter der jüd. Krieg unter den Kaisern Trajan u. Hadrian. Altona u. Leipz. 1821. 8. Jost's Gesch. d. Israeliten, Th. 3, S. 181, ff.

The hatred of the Jews against the Romans was still more increased by the destruction of Jerusalem, and the great oppression that followed, and soon began to manifest itself in new acts of rebellion. An insurrection first broke out in *Cyrenaica* (115), which spread over *Egypt* also, and raged longest in *Cyprus.* Another was kindled simultaneously in *Mesopotamia.* Even Hadrian found relapses of these rebellions, which required

[2] Numenius (about 130) *περὶ τἀγαθοῦ* lib. i. (apud Eusebii Praep. evang. ix. 7): *Εἰς δὲ τοῦτο δεήσει εἰπόντα, καὶ σημηνάμενον ταῖς μαρτυρίαις τοῦ Πλάτωνος, ἀναχωρήσασθαι καὶ ξυνδῆσασθαι τοῖς λόγοις τοῦ Πυθαγόρου· ἐπικαλέσασθαι δὲ τὰ ἔθνη τὰ εὐδοκιμοῦντα, προσφερόμενον αὐτῶν τὰς τελετὰς, καὶ τὰ δόγματα, τας τε ἱδρύσεις συντελουμένας Πλάτωνι ὁμολογουμένως, ὁπόσας Βραχμᾶνες, καὶ Ἰουδαῖοι, καὶ Μάγοι, καὶ Αἰγύπτιοι διέθεντο.*

[3] Maximus Tyrius Diss. xvii. (al. i.) ex rec. J. Davisii. Lond. 1740. 4. p. 193, with reference to the different opinions of men respecting divine things: *Ἐν τοσούτῳ δὴ πολέμῳ, καὶ στάσει, καὶ διαφωνίᾳ, ἕνα ἴδοις ἂν ἐν πάσῃ γῇ ὁμόφωνον νόμον καὶ λόγον, ὅτι Θεὸς εἶς πάντων βασιλεὺς, καὶ πατὴρ, καὶ θεοὶ πολλοὶ, Θεοῦ παῖδες, συνάρχοντες Θεῷ. Ταῦτα δὲ ὁ Ἕλλην λέγει, καὶ ὁ βάρβαρος λέγει, καὶ ὁ ἠπειρώτης, καὶ ὁ θαλάττιος, καὶ ὁ σοφὸς, καὶ ὁ ἄσοφος. κἂν ἐπὶ τοῦ ὠκεανοῦ ἔλθῃς τὰς ἠϊόνας, κἀκεῖ θεοὶ, τοῖς μὲν ἀνίσχοντες ἀγχοῦ μάλα, τοῖς δὲ καταδυόμενοι.* Accordingly we now frequently meet with the view that the numerous names of the deities designated nothing but the same being under different aspects. Apuleii Metamorph. lib. xi. ed. Elmenhorst. p. 258, ss. Lobeck Aglaophamus, t. i. p. 460, ss. To this also the figurae pantheae, frequently found on gems, point.

to be combated, and appears to have been led by them to entertain the idea of doing away the dangerous and exclusive nationality of this people, by prohibiting circumcision.[1] As he resolved, at the same time, to restore Jerusalem by means of a Roman colony, a pretended Messiah soon made his appearance, who, under the title of *Bar Cochab* (Numb. xxiv. 17),[2] obtained many adherents, especially by the recognition of *Rabbi Akiba*, elevated the fortress *Bether* to be the seat of his kingdom, and endeavored from it to drive the Romans out of the land (132). His conquests had already extended beyond Syria, when *Julius Severus* appeared, and, after a bloody war, put an end to the insurrection by taking possession of Bether (135). Palestine became a complete wilderness. The colony of *Aelia Capitolina* rose on the ruins of Jerusalem, but access to it was prohibited to the Jews on pain of death. Hadrian's prohibition of circumcision was first abolished by *Antoninus Pius*.[3]

1 Spartianus in Hadriano, c. 14. Moverunt ea tempestate et Judaei bellum, quod vetabantur mutilare genitalia.

2 Called after his want of success, בַּר כּוֹזִיבָא filius mendacii.

3 Modestinus JCtus (about 244) in Dig. lib. xlviii. tit. 8. l. 11: Circumcidere Judaeis filios suos tantum rescripto Divi Pii permittitur: in non ejusdem religionis qui hoc fecerit, castrantis poena irrogatur. Ulpianus in Dig. lib. L. tit. 2. l. 3. § 3: Eis, qui Judaicam superstitionem sequantur, D. Severus et Antoninus honores (namely, decurionum) adipisci permiserunt: sed et necessitates (the onera functiones et munera incumbent on the decuriones) eis imposuerunt, quae superstitionem eorum non laederent. Julius Paulus (about 222) in his sententiis receptis (in Schultingii Jurisprudentia vetus antejustinianea and Hugo Jus civile antejustin. tom. i.) lib. v. tit. 22. de seditiosis 3: Cives Romani, qui se Judaico ritu vel servos suos circumcidi patiuntur, bonis ademptis in insulam perpetuo relegantur. Medici capite puniuntur. 4. Judaei si alienae nationis comparatos servos circumciderint, aut deportantur aut capite puniuntur. Even the Samaritans were not allowed to practice circumcision, Origenes c. Celsum, ii. c. 13. p. 68. ed. Spencer.

FIRST CHAPTER.

EXTERNAL HISTORY OF CHRISTIANITY.

§ 39.

ITS DIFFUSION.

Although the Christian writers of this time manifestly speak in exaggerated terms of the spread of Christianity,[1] yet the extraordinary progress it made can not be mistaken. In the west, it extended from Rome to western *Africa*, where *Carthage* was its chief seat.[2] In *Gaul*, we find churches at *Lyons* and *Vienne*, immediately after the middle of the second century (Euseb. V. c. 1). From this country Christianity may have spread into *Ger-*

[1] Justin. Dial. c. Tryph. c. 117: *Οὐδὲ ἓν γὰρ ὅλως ἐστὶ τὸ γένος ἀνθρώπων, εἴτε βαρβάρων, εἴτε Ἑλλήνων, εἴτε ἁπλῶς ᾡτινιοῦν ὀνόματι προσαγορευομένων, ἢ ἁμαξοβίων, ἢ ἀοίκων καλουμένων, ἢ ἐν σκηναῖς κτηνοτρόφων οἰκούντων, ἐν οἷς μὴ διὰ τοῦ ὀνόματος τοῦ σταυρωθέντος Ἰησοῦ εὐχαὶ καὶ εὐχαριστίαι τῷ πατρὶ καὶ ποιητῇ τῶν ὅλων γίνονται.* Irenaeus, i. 3: *Καὶ οὔτε αἱ ἐν Γερμανίαις ἱδρυμέναι ἐκκλησίαι ἄλλως πεπιστεύκασιν, ἢ ἄλλως παραδιδόασιν, οὔτε ἐν ταῖς Ἰβηρίαις, οὔτε ἐν Κελτοῖς, οὔτε κατὰ τὰς ἀνατολὰς, οὔτε ἐν Αἰγύπτῳ, οὔτε ἐν Λιβύῃ, οὔτε αἱ κατὰ μέσα τοῦ κόσμου ἱδρυμέναι.* Tertullianus adv. Judaeos c. 7: In quem enim alium universae gentes crediderunt nisi in Christum, qui jam venit? Cui enim et aliae gentes crediderunt: Parthi, Medi, Elamitae, et qui inhabitant Mesopotamiam, Armeniam, Phrygiam, Cappadociam, et incolentes Pontum et Asiam, Pamphyliam, immorantes Aegyptum et regionem Africae, quae est trans Cyrenen, inhabitantes Romam, et incolae tunc et in Hierusalem Judaei et caeterae gentes (according to Acts ii. 9, 10): etiam Getulorum varietates, et Maurorum multi fines, Hispaniarum omnes termini, et Galliarum diversae nationes, et Britannorum inaccessa Romanis loca, Christo vero subdita, et Sarmatarum et Dacorum et Germanorum et Scytharum et abditarum multarum gentium, et provinciarum et insularum multarum, nobis ignotarum, et quae enumerare minus possumus. In the Roman empire: Tertulliani Apol. c. 37: Si enim hostes exertos, non tantum vindices occultos agere vellemus, deesset nobis vis numerorum et copiarum? Plures nimirum Mauri et Marcomanni ipsique Parthi, vel quantaecunque, unius tamen loci et suorum finium, gentes, quam totius orbis? Hesterni sumus, et vestra omnia implevimus, urbes, insulas, castella, municipia, conciliabula, castra ipsa, tribus, decurias, palatium, senatum, forum. Iren. iv. 49, mentions fideles, qui in regali aula sunt et ex iis, quae Caesaris sunt, habent utensilia.

[2] Fr. Münteri Primordia eccl. Africanae. Hafn. 1829. 4. p. 6, ss. The numbers of the Christians here, even so early as the end of the second century, may be inferred from Tertullian Apologet. c. 37: Hesterni sumus et vestra omnia implevimus, urbes, insulas, castella, municipia etc., and adv. Scapul. c. 5, when it is said that, in case of a persecution of the Christians, Carthage would have to be decimated. About 200 A.D. a synod was held under Agrippinus, bishop of Carthage (Cyprian. Epist. 71 and 73), which, according to Augustin. de Baptism. ii. c. 13, consisted of seventy African and Numidian bishops.

many (Cisrhenana)[3] and *Britain*, but only by the efforts of individuals. In the east, we find it firmly established in *Edessa*, so early as the middle of the second century;[4] and from this city it had also extended itself, as it seems, into the countries lying eastward.[5] In northern Arabia,[6] there must likewise have been Christians so early as this period. About 180, *Pantaenus* went from Alexandria to India,[7] to preach the gospel in that region (Euseb. H. E. v. 10).

§ 40

OPPOSITION TO CHRISTIANITY BY WRITERS.

Tzchirner's der Fall des Heidenthums. Bd. 1. S. 313, ff.

The principal opponent of Christianity at this period was the Epicurean *Celsus* (about 150), who, in a work styled "ἀληθὴς λόγος," and perhaps in others now lost, collected all that could be said against it with any appearance of probability.[1] The

[3] C. J. Hefele's Gesch. d. Einführung des Christenthums in südwestl. Deutschland. Tübingen. 1837. S. 42.

[4] The Christian scholar Bardesanes, about 160–170, was highly esteemed by the prince of Edessa, Abgar Bar Manu. According to the Chronicon of Edessa in Assemani Bibl. orient. i. 391, the church of the Christians in Edessa was destroyed by an inundation as early as 202 A.D. Comp. Bayer Historia Osrhoena et Edessena. Petrop. 1734. 4. p. 170.

[5] Bardesanes de Fato (in Eusebii Praep. evang. vi. c. 10): Οὔτε οἱ ἐν Παρθίᾳ Χριστιανοὶ πολυγαμοῦσι, Πάρθοι ὑπάρχοντες, οὔθ' οἱ ἐν Μηδίᾳ κυσὶ παραβάλλουσι τοὺς νεκρούς· οὐχ οἱ ἐν Περσίδι γαμοῦσι τὰς θυγατέρας αὐτῶν, Πέρσαι ὄντες· οὐ παρὰ Βάκτροις καὶ Γάλλοις φθείρουσι τοὺς γάμους· οὐχ οἱ ἐν Αἰγύπτῳ θρησκεύουσι τὸν Ἆπιν, ἢ τὸν Κύνα, ἢ τὸν Τράγον, ἢ Αἴλουρον· ἀλλ' ὅπου εἰσὶν, οὔτε ὑπὸ τῶν κακῶς κειμένων νόμων, καὶ ἐθῶν νικῶνται.

[6] Arabia Petraea, since the time of Trajan a Roman province under the name Arabia, its chief city being Bostra, or Nova Colonia Trajana. So early as the middle of the third century there were many bishops here, Euseb. vi. 33, 37.

[7] Probably Yemen, see § 27, note 28. Comp. Redepenning's Origines, i. 66.

[1] Celsus and his work are known only by the refutation of Origen (contra Celsum libb. viii. ed. G. Spencer. Cantabrig. 1677. 4to, translated by Mosheim, Hamburg. 1745. 4to, cf. C. R. Jachmann de Celso philosopho disseruit, et fragmenta libri, quem contra Christianos edidit, collegit, a Koenigsberg Easter-programm. 1836. 4). Origen calls him an Epicurean (i. p. 8, εὑρίσκεται ἐξ ἄλλων συγγραμμάτων Ἐπικούρειος ὤν), who merely kept back his Epicureanism in his work (iv. p. 163, μὴ πάνυ ἐμφαίνων διὰ τοῦ συγγράμματος τὸν Ἐπικούρειον, ἀλλὰ προσποιούμενος πρόνοιαν εἰδέναι), and assumed the mien of a Platonic philosopher (iv. p. 219, ἐν πολλοῖς πλατωνίζειν θέλει); doubtless because he was able to influence the religious heathen only in this way. In opposition to the opinion that Celsus was really a Platonist, which has become common on Mosheim's authority (preface to his version of Origen, p. 22, ff.), his Epicureanism is asserted by J. F. Fenger de Celso, Christianorum adversario, Epicureo comm. Havn. 1828. 8. Tzschirner's Fall des Heiden-

Cynic philosopher *Crescens*, and the rhetorician *M. Cornelius Fronto* (about 150), are known as the enemies of Christianity only by detached passages.[2] *Lucian* of Samosata (about 180) also considered Christianity in no other light than as one of the many follies of the time, which deserved the satirical lash.[3]

§ 41.

DISPOSITION OF THE PEOPLE IN THE ROMAN EMPIRE TOWARD CHRISTIANITY.

Christ. Kortholt Paganus obtrectator. Kilon. 1698. 4. J. J. Huldrici Gentilis obtrectator. Tigur. 1744. 8. G. F. Gudii Paganus Christianorum laudator et fautor. Lips. 1741. 4. Tzschirner der Fall des Heidenthums, i. 225, ff. 335, ff. G. G. S. Koepke de statu et conditione Christianorum sub impp. Romanis alterius p. Chr. saeculi. Berol. 1828. 4. (A school-programm.)

In proportion as the peculiar nature of Christianity, as a different system from Judaism, became better known, so much the

thums, i. 325. According to F. A. Philippi de Celsi, adversarii Christianorum, philosophandi genere. Berol. 1836. 8, he was an eclectic with a special leaning to Epicurus. According to C. W. I. Bindemann (über Celsus u. seine Schrift gegen die Christen, in Illgen's Zeitschr. für d. hist. Theol. 1842, ii. 58), he was a Platonic philosopher of a more liberal tendency, who agreed with Epicurus in many points. According to Origen, i. p. 28, Celsus lived κατὰ Ἀδριανὸν καὶ κατωτέρω. It is certain that he wrote in the second half of the second century, for he recognizes the whole of the Gnostic sects, and even the Marcionites (v. p. 272), as parties completely formed. Probably he is the same Celsus to whom Lucian dedicates his Alexander, as is assumed by the ancient scholiast (see Luciani Alexander ed. C. G. Jacob, Colon. 1828, p. 8. Fenger p. 40, ss. Bindemann, l. c. 99). Origen does not know (i. p. 53, iv. p. 186) whether he is the same Celsus who wrote several books against magic, and two other books against the Christians.

2 Respecting Crescens comp. Euseb. iv. 16, where also the passages Justin. Apol. ii. c. 3. Tatian. Orat. c. 19, are quoted. Respecting Fronto see Minucius Fel. c. 9 and c. 31.

3 In his works de morte Peregrini, c. 11–16, Alexander c. 25, 38, de vera Historia, i. 12, 30, ii. 4, 11, 12, cf. Walchii Rerum christianarum apud Lucianum de morte Peregr. explicatio, in the Novis commentariis Soc. Reg. scient. Gotting. t. viii. p. 1, ss. Lucianus num scriptis suis adjuvare religionem christianam voluerit diss. scripsit H. C. A. Eichstädt. Jenae. 1820. 4 (also in Luciani Opp. ed. Lehmann, t. i. p. lxxv. ss.). Tzschirner's Gesch. d. Apologetik, i. 200, ff. The same author's Fall des Heidenthums, i. 315, ff. K. G. Jacob's Charakteristik Lucian's v. Samosata. Hamburg. 1832, S. 155. Baur's Apollonius von Tyana u. Christus, S. 140. The dialogue Philopatris according to J. M. Gesneri de aetate et auctore dialogi Lucianei, qui Philopatris inscribitur, ed. 3. Gotting. 1741 (also in Luciani Opp. ed. Reitz. iii. 708, ss.), is usually placed in the time of Julian. According to Niebuhr it was first composed under the emperor Nicephorus Phocas, in the year 968 or 969, see Corporis scriptt. hist. Byzant. Bonnensis, P. xi. (Leo Diaconus, &c.) praef. p. ix. On the other side, see Bernhardy in the Berlin Jahrbücher, Juli, 1832, S. 131, and Neander K. G. ii. i. 190. A new opinion is advanced by Ehemann in Stirm's Studien der ev. Geistlichk. Wirtemberg's, 1839, S. 47.

more must it have appeared, when viewed from the position of a heathen citizen, as a hostile threatening power, whose rapid diffusion was highly suspicious. The Christians saw only evil demons in the gods of the heathen; and since the worship of the gods had pervaded all forms of life, they were compelled entirely to withdraw themselves from the public and the domestic life of the heathen, from their amusements, and their works of art.[1] Hence Christianity appeared to the heathen in the light of a misanthropic superstition.[2] But the Christians refused even to the emperors the usual marks of divine honor paid them.[3] They cherished among them the expectation that a near destruction was impending over all the kingdoms of the earth;[4] and many would not assume the civil and military offices to which they were called.[5] It was natural, therefore, that they should be looked upon as bad citizens; and however solemn was their asseveration that Christianity demanded still greater obedience

[1] Hence from the games (cf. Tertulliani de Spectaculis liber), festivities, and banquets (even the wearing of garlands was not permitted. Tertull. de Corona militis. Clemens Alex. in Paedagogo, ii. c. 8), from certain professions, &c., cf. Tertull. de Idololatria liber. Neander's Antignosticus. Berlin. 1825, S. 22, ff. The same author's Kirchengesch. i. i. 450, ff. Fr. Münter's die Christinn im heidnischen Hause vor den Zeiten Constantin's d. G. Kopenh. 1828, 8.

[2] Minucii Felicis Octavius, c. 12, the heathen Caecilius says: Vos vero suspensi interim atque solliciti honestis voluptatibus abstinetis: non spectacula visitis, non pompis interestis: convivia publica absque vobis; sacra certamina, praecerptos cibos et delibatos altaribus potus abhorretis. Sic reformidatis deos, quos negatis. Non floribus caput nectitis, non corpus odoribus honestatis: reservatis unguenta funeribus, coronas etiam sepulcris denegatis, pallidi, trepidi, misericordia digni et nostrorum deorum. C. 8: Latebrosa et lucifuga natio, in publicum muta, in angulis garrula.

[3] Theophil. ad Autolycum, i. 11: Ἐρεῖς μοι· διὰ τί οὐ προσκυνεῖς τὸν βασιλέα; Tertullianus ad Nationes, i. 17: Prima obstinatio est, quae secunda ab eis religio constituitur Caesarianae majestatis, quod irreligiosi dicamur in Caesares: neque imagines eorum repropitiando, neque genios dejerando hostes populi nuncupamur. Tertull. de Idololatr. c. 13–15, is zealous even against the illumination and decoration of the doors in honor of the emperors, cf. c. 15: Igitur quod attineat ad honores regum vel imperatorum, satis praescriptum habemus, in omni obsequio esse nos oportere, secundum Apostoli praeceptum, subditos magistratibus et principibus et potestatibus: sed intra limites disciplinae, quousque ab idololatria separamur.—Accendant igitur quotidie lucernas, quibus lux nulla est, adfigant postibus lauros postmodum arsuras, quibus ignes imminent: illis competunt et testimonia tenebrarum, et auspicia poenarum. Tu lumen es mundi, et arbor virens semper. Si templis renuntiasti, ne feceris templum januam tuam.

[4] How this was expressed in a manner exasperating to the heathen, especially by the Montanists, see below § 48, note 5. On this account, it appeared to the heathen politically dangerous. Justini Apol. i. 11: Καὶ ὑμεῖς ἀκούσαντες βασιλείαν προσδοκῶντας ἡμᾶς, ἀκρίτως ἀνθρώπινον λέγειν ἡμᾶς ὑπειλήφατε, ἡμῶν τὴν μετὰ θεοῦ λεγόντων.

[5] Especially Tertull. de Idol. c. 17, 18. Idem de Cor. militis, c. 11. Origen. c. Celsum. viii. p. 427: Still, however, there were many Christian soldiers at this time. Neander's K. G. i. i. 464.

to the powers under which they lived,[6] it appeared, notwithstanding, in the eyes of the heathen, accustomed as they were to a religion subordinate to political objects, a circumstance so much the more suspicious, that the Christians were constantly obliged to annex a condition, viz., that the commands of the magistrate should not contradict the Divine law.[7] The moral impression which the doctrine and customs of the Christians must have made on the unbiased, was weakened by prejudices. The Jews, in whom an accurate knowledge of Christianity was presupposed, contributed to increase the disposition which was adverse to it.[8] Many of the heathen recognized in the Christian doctrine much that was true, but believed that they possessed it still purer in their philosophy,[9] and took offense at its positive doctrines.[10] Credulous persons allowed themselves to be deceived by ridiculous fabrications respecting the objects which the Christians wor-

[6] Epist. eccl. Smyrn. ap. Euseb. iv. 15, 9. Justinus M. Apol. i. 17. Irenaeus, v. 24. Theophil. ad Autolycum, i. 11.

[7] Tertulliani Apologet. c. 2: Christianum hominem omnium scelerum rerum, deorum, imperatorum, legum, morum, naturae totius inimicum existimas. C. 35: Publici hostes Christiani,—nos nolunt Romanos haberi, sed hostes principum Romanorum. Ad Scapulam, c. 2: Circa majestatem imperatoris infamamur.—Christianus nullius est hostis, nedum imperatoris: quem sciens a Deo suo constitui, necesse est ut et ipsum diligat, et revereatur, et honoret, et salvum velit cum toto Romano imperio, quousque saeculum stabit. Tamdiu enim stabit. Colimus ergo et imperatorem sic, quomodo et nobis licet, et ipsi expedit, ut hominem a Deo secundum, et quicquid est, a Deo consecutum, solo Deo minorem. Cf. contra Gnosticos, c. 14.

[8] Justinus M. Dial. c. Tryph. 17 and 108, speaks of Jewish emissaries, who had gone out from Jerusalem into all the world, in order to calumniate Christ and the Christians. Accordingly, the Jews were particularly active about the execution of Polycarp, Epist. eccl. Smyrn. ap. Euseb. iv. 15, 11: *Μάλιστα Ἰουδαίων προθύμως, ὡς ἔθος αὐτοῖς, εἰς τοῦτο ὑπουργούντων.* Respecting the cursings of the Christians in the synagogues, see Justinus Dial. c. Tryph. c. xvi. 47, 96, 108, 117, 137. Hieronymus in Es. v. 18; xlix. 7, lii. 5, in Amos. i. 11. Semisch Justin d. Märtyrer, i. 28.

[9] Celsus, in particular, often reverts to this (Orig. c. Cels. v. p. 274): *Βουλόμενος τὰ καλὰ—καὶ βέλτιον καὶ τρανότερον εἰρῆσθαι παρὰ τοῖς φιλοσοφοῦσιν.* (vi. p. 275): *Καὶ χωρὶς ἀνατάσεως καὶ ἐπαγγελίας τῆς ἀπὸ θεοῦ, ἢ υἱοῦ θεοῦ.* So he remarks (vii. p. 370) regarding the Christian prohibition of revenge, Matth. v. 39: *Ἀρχαῖον καὶ τοῦτο εὖ μάλα πρόσθεν εἰρημένον, ἀγροικότερον δ' αὐτὸ ἀπεμνημόνευται· ἐπεὶ καὶ Πλάτωνι πεποίηται Σωκράτης Κρίτωνι διαλεγόμενος τάδε κ. τ. λ.* He assumes, in plain terms, that the Christians had borrowed these doctrines from the Greek philosophers, particularly from Plato (vi. p. 283–288). Tertull. Apolog. c. 46.

[10] The heathen said, apud Arnobius, i. c. 36: Sed non iccirco dii vobis infesti sunt, quod omnipotentem colatis Deum: sed quod hominem natum, et, quod personis infame est vilibus, crucis supplicio interemptum, et Deum fuisse contenditis, et superesse adhuc creditis, et quotidianis supplicationibus adoratis. The doctrines of the resurrection of the body, and the judgment, were particularly offensive, comp. Celsus (Teller Fides dogmatis de resurrect. carnis per iv. priora secula. Halae. 1776. 8. p. 270). Tertull. Apologet. c. 18: Haec et nos risimus aliquando. De vestris fuimus: fiunt, non nascuntur Christiani.

shiped;[11] the superstitious inferred from their oppressed condition the impotence of their God;[12] and, finally, the foreign origin of Christianity,[13] as well as the humble lot of most of its votaries,[14] were as offensive to all as the idea of an universal religion was absurd.[15] The external morality of the Christians could not fail to be perceived by the heathen;[16] and the brotherly love prevailing among them had unquestionably attracted many a feeling heart to Christianity, although it sometimes also allured low selfishness;[17] but the secret meetings of both sexes[18] gave occasion to hatred, and furnished a ground for mis-

[11] Tertulliani Apologet. c. 16: Somniastis, caput asininum esse Deum nostrum,—crucis nos religiosos.—Alii plane humanius et verisimilius solem credunt deum nostrum.—Sed nova jam Dei nostri in ista civitate proximo editio publicata est, namely, pictura cum ejusmodi inscriptione: Deus Christianorum Ononychites (according to E. A. Schulzii Exercitt. philolog. fasc. i. p. 30: Ononychotus; according to Havercamp and Münter Primord. eccl. Afr. p. 167: Onokoitis). Is erat auribus asininis, altero pede ungulatus, librum gestans, et togatus (see Münter's Christinn im heidn. Hause, S. 18), Minucius Felix, c. 9, below note 19. Comp. above § 16, note 6.—Other fictions respecting the person of Jesus are referred to by Celsus, Orig. c. Cels. i. p. 22, ss.

[12] The heathen Caecilius says, apud Minuc. Felix. c. 12: Ecce pars vestrum et major et melior, ut dicitus, egetis, algetis, ope, re, fame laboratis: et Deus patitur, dissimulat, non vult aut non potest opitulari suis, ita aut invalidus, aut iniquus est. Nonni Romani sine vestro Deo imperant, regnant, fruuntur orbe toto, vestrique dominantur?

[13] Celsus, therefore, calls it *βάρβαρον δόγμα*, Orig. c. Cels. i. p. 5.

[14] Caecilius apud Minuc. Felix, c. 5: Indignandum omnibus, indolescendumque est, audere quosdam, et hoc studiorum rudes, literarum profanos, expertes artiam etiam nisi sordidarum, certum aliquid de summa rerum ac majestate decernere, de qua tot omnibus saeculis sectarum plurimarum usque adhuc ipsa philosophia deliberat. Cap. 12: Proinde si quid sapientiae vobis aut verecundiae est, desinite coeli plagas, et mundi fata et secreta rimari: satis est pro pedibus adspicere, maxime indoctis, impolitis, rudibus, agrestibus: quibus non est datum intelligere civilia, multo magis denegatum est disserere divina. How the Christians drew over to themselves ignorant, humble, and immoral men, is described by Celsus with hostile exaggeration, apud Origines adv. Cels. iii. p. 144, ss.

[15] Celsus (Orig. c. Cels. viii. p. 425): *Εἰ γὰρ δὴ οἰόντε εἰς ἕνα συμφρονῆσαι νόμον τοὺς τὴν 'Ασίαν, καὶ Εὐρώπην, καὶ Λιβύην, Ἕλληνάς τε καὶ βαρβάρους, ἄχρι περάτων νενεμημένους!—ὁ τοῦτο οἰόμενος οἶδεν οὐδέν.*

[16] The famous physician Claudius Galen (about 160) said in one of his last works (the passage is cited in a Syriac translation in Bar-Hebraei Chron. Syr. ed. Bruns et Kirsch, p. 55, from Gal. comm. in Phaedonem Platonis; more copiously in Arabic in Abulfedae Historia anteislamica, ed Fleischer, p. 109, from Gal. de Sententiis politiae Platonicae): Hominum plerique orationem demonstrativam continuam mente assequi nequeunt, quare indigent, ut instituantur parabolis. Veluti nostro tempore videmus, homines illos, qui Christiani vocantur, fidem suam e parabolis petiisse. Hi tamen interdum talia faciunt, qualia qui vere philosophantur. Nam quod mortem contemnunt, id quidem omnes ante oculos habemus; item quod verecundia quadam ducti ab usu rerum venerearum abhorrent. Sunt enim inter eos et foeminae et viri, qui per totam vitam a concubitu abstinuerint; sunt etiam, qui in animis regendis coërcendisque et in acerrimo honestatis studio eo progressi sint, ut nihil cedant vere philosophantibus.

[17] Lucianus de morte Peregrini, c. 11-16.

[18] Particularly nightly meetings, which were strictly forbidden by the law (see § 12, note 6), and constantly awakened suspicion.

interpreting that love, by representing it as being of an impure character, and several Christian practices as crimes,[19] just as they had appeared in their own mysteries, and other secret societies.[20] The steadfastness of the martyrs must, indeed, have invited every unbiased mind to a nearer acquaintance with the source of this lofty spirit;[21] but yet an unfavorable opinion was

[19] Tertull. Apologet. c. 39: Sed ejusmodi vel maxime dilectionis operatio notam nobis inurit penes quosdam. Vide, inquiunt, ut invicem se diligant; ipsi enim invicem oderunt: et ut pro alterutro mori sint parati; ipsi enim ad occidendum alterutrum paratiores. Sed et quod fratrum appellatione censemur—infamant. The heathen Octavius ap. Minucius Felix, c. 9: Occultis se notis et insignibus (according to c. 31, § 9, notaculo corporis: the Carpocratians actually marked themselves on the ear, Iren. i. 24. Epiphan. Haer. xxvii. 5) noscunt, et amant mutuo paene ante quam noverint: passim etiam inter eos velut quaedam libidinum religio miscetur: ac se promiscue appellant fratres et sorores, ut etiam non insolens stuprum, intercessione sacri nominis, fiat incestum. Ita eorum vana et demens superstitio sceleribus gloriatur. Nec de ipsis, nisi subsisteret veritas, maxime nefaria et honore praefanda sagax fama loqueretur. Audio, eos turpissimae pecudis, caput asini consecratum inepta nescio qua persuasione venerari: digna et nata religio talibus moribus. Alii eos ferunt ipsius antistitis ac sacerdotis colere genitalia, et quasi parentis sui adorare naturam: nescio an falsa, certe occultis ac nocturnis sacris apposita suspicio: et qui hominem, summo supplicio pro facinore punitum, et crucis ligna feralia, eorum caerimonias fabulatur congruentia perditis sceleratisque tribuit altaria, ut id colant, quod merentur. Jam de initiandis tirunculis fabula tam detestanda, quam nota est. Infans farre contectus, ut decipiat incautos, apponitur ei, qui sacris imbuitur. Is infans a tirunculo, farris superficie quasi ad innoxios ictus provocata, caecis occultisque vulneribus occiditur: hujus (proh nefas!) sitienter sanguinem lambunt: hujus certatim membra discerpunt: hac foederantur hostia.—Et de convivio notum est (passim omnes loquuntur), id etiam Cirtensis nostri testatur oratio; ad epulas solemni die coëunt, cum omnibus liberis, sororibus, matribus, sexus omnis homines et omnis aetatis. Illic post multas epulas, ubi convivium caluit, et incestae libidinis fervor ebrietate exarsit, canis, qui candelabro nexus est, jactu offulae ultra spatium lineae, qua vinctus est, ad impetum et saltum provocatur: sic everso et extincto conscio lumine impudentibus tenebris nexus infandae cupiditatis involvunt per incertum sortis, &c. (Cf. Tertull. Apolog. c. 8, ad Nationes, i. 16: also Apulejus Metam. ix. p. 223, ed. Elmenhorst, alludes to the same subject. Clemens Alex. Strom. iii. c. 2, relates the same thing of the Carpocratians, from whom it was falsely transferred to all Christians, cf. Euseb. H. E. iv. 7, 5). According to Athanagoras Apol. c. 4, the heathen brought three charges in particular against the Christians: *ἀθεότητα, Θυέστεια δεῖπνα* and *Οἰδιποδείους μίξεις*.

[20] So among the Bacchanals in Rome, A.D. 185. Comp. the expressions of Livy xxxix. 13: Ex quo in promiscuo sacra sint, et permixti viri feminis, et noctis licentia accesserit, nihil ibi facinoris, nihil flagitii praetermissum, plura virorum inter sese, quam feminarum esse stupra. Si qui minus patientes dedecoris sint, et pigriores ad facinus, pro victimis immolari, &c. Catiline employed human blood as pignus conjurationis (Sallust. Catil. 22), quo inter se fidi magis forent, alius alii tanti facinoris conscii. Dio Cassius, xxxvii. 30, relates of the same person: *Παῖδά τινα καταθύσας, καὶ ἐπὶ τῶν σπλάγχνων αὐτοῦ τὰ ὅρκια ποιήσας, ἔπειτα ἐσπλάγχνευσεν αὐτὰ μετὰ τῶν ἄλλων.*

[21] Justinus M. Apol. ii. c. 12, speaks of the impression which they had made upon him. Tertull. Apologeticus, c. 50: Nec quicquam tamen proficit exquisitior quaeque crudelitas vestra, illecebra est magis sectae; plures efficimur, quoties metimur a vobis; semen est sanguis Christianorum.—Illa ipsa obstinatio, quam exprobratis, magistra est. Quis enim non contemplatione ejus concutitur ad requirendum, quid intus in re sit? Quis non, ubi requisivit, accedit? ubi accessit, pati exhortat?

entertained regarding that, too, even by the cultivated, agreeably to preconceived notions.[22] The Jews were still protected by their peculiar national character.[23] But the Christians were looked upon merely as ignorant and wild fanatics, who wished to destroy all established order. The cultivated laughed contemptuously at them on account of the confidence and obstinacy of their religious faith;[24] the *goetae* (impostors) were inimical to them as opponents of their interest;[25] the people hated them as despisers of their gods (*ἄθεοι, ἀσεβεῖς*), and in the public misfortunes saw nothing but admonitions from heaven to exterminate them.[26]

22 Tertull. Apolog. c. 27: Quidam dementiam existimant, quod cum possimus et sacrificare in praesenti, et illaesi abire, manente apud animum proposito, obstinationem saluti praeferamus. C. 50: Propterea desperati et perditi existimamur. Arrianus Comm. de Epicteti disputationibus, iv. c. 7: *Εἶτα ὑπὸ μανίας μὲν δύναταί τις οὕτω διατεθῆναι πρὸς ταῦτα (θάνατον κ. τ. λ.) καὶ ὑπὸ ἔθους ὡς οἱ Γαλιλαῖοι, ὑπὸ λόγου δὲ καὶ ἀποδείξεως οὐδεὶς δύναται;* Schweighäuser in his edition, Th. 2, S. 915, looks upon the words *ὡς οἱ Γαλ.* as a gloss. Marc. Aurel. *εἰς ἑαυτόν*, xi. c. 3: *Οἵα ἐστὶν ἡ ψυχὴ ἡ ἕτοιμος, ἐὰν ἤδη ἀπολυθῆναι δέῃ τοῦ σώματος, καὶ ἤτοι σβεσθῆναι σκεδασθῆναι, ἢ συμμεῖναι; τὸ δὲ ἕτοιμον τοῦτο, ἵνα ἀπὸ ἰδικῆς κρίσεως ἔρχηται, μὴ κατὰ ψιλὴν παράταξιν, ὡς οἱ Χριστιανοί, ἀλλὰ λελογισμένως, καὶ σεμνῶς, καὶ ὥστε καὶ ἄλλον πεῖσαι, ἀτραγώδως.* Eichstädt (Exercit. Antoniniana, iii.) conjectures that the words *ὡς οἱ Χρ.* were a later interpolation in this place.

23 Celsus ap. Origen. contra Celsum lib. v. p. 247, 259: *Εἰ μὲν δὴ κατὰ ταῦτα περιστέλλοιεν Ἰουδαῖοι τὸν ἴδιον νόμον, οὐ μεμπτὰ αὐτῶν, ἐκείνων δὲ μᾶλλον, τῶν καταλιπόντων τὰ σφέτερα, καὶ τὰ Ἰουδαίων προσποιουμένων.*

24 How the Jews and Christians had become a proverb on this account, see Galenus de Pulsuum differentiis, lib. ii. (ed. Kühn, viii. 579): *Κάλλιον δ' ἂν ἦν πολλῷ προσθεῖναί τινα —ἀπόδειξιν,—ἵνα μή τις εὐθὺς κατ' ἀρχὰς, ὡς εἰς Μωϋσοῦ καὶ Χριστοῦ διατριβὴν ἀφιγμένος, νόμων ἀναποδείκτων ἀκούῃ.* Lib. iii. (p. 657): *Θᾶττον γὰρ ἄν τις τοὺς ἀπὸ Μωϋσοῦ καὶ Χριστοῦ μεταδιδάξειεν, ἢ τοὺς ταῖς αἱρέσεσι προστετηκότας ἰατρούς τε καὶ φιλοσόφους.*

25 Thus spoke the false prophet Alexander of Abonoteichos (Luciani Alex. c. 25) to the inhabitants of Pontus, *ἀθέων ἐμπεπλῆσθαι καὶ Χριστιανῶν τὸν Πόντον,—οὓς ἐκέλευε λίθοις ἐλαύνειν, εἴγε ἐθέλουσιν ἵλεω ἔχειν τὸν θεόν.* And he began his consecrations with the formula (c. 37): *Εἴ τις ἄθεος ἢ Χριστιανὸς ἢ Ἐπικούρειος ἥκει κατάσκοπος τῶν ὀργίων, φευγέτω.*

26 Tertull. Apologet. c. 37, to the Romani imperii antitistes: Quoties in Christianos desaevitis, partim animis propriis, partim legibus obsequentes? Quotiens etiam praeteritis vobis suo jure nos inimicum vulgus invadit lapidibus et incendiis? Ipsis Bacchanalium furiis nec mortuis parcunt Christianis, quin illos de requie sepulturae, de asylo quodam mortis, jam alios, jam nec totos, avellant, dissecent, distrahant. C. 40: Existimant omnis publicae cladis, omnis popularis incommodi Christianos esse causam. Si Tiberis ascendit in moenia, si Nilus non ascendit in arva, si coelum stetit, si terra movit, si fames, si lues, statim: Christianos ad leonem.

§ 42.

PERSECUTIONS OF CHRISTIANITY.

The laws against *religiones peregrinae* and *collegia illicita* still remained in force, even in reference to the Christians;[1] but they were by no means universally and uniformly enforced. The persecutions of this period were rather the effects of the people's hatred, to which the magistrates gave way, and also of personal malevolence in those possessing official power. Hence all the persecutions of the period were confined merely to single cities or provinces. Under *Hadrian* (117–138) the people first began to clamor for the execution of some Christians at the public festivals. But at the representation of Serenius Granianus, proconsul of Asia Minor, Hadrian issued a rescript to the successor of the proconsul, interdicting such tumultuous proceedings.[2] The tradition regarding this emperor, that he caused temples to be dedicated to Christ, is the more improbable, because he entertained very erroneous and unfavorable notions of the Christians.[3] Under *Antoninus Pius*, the Christians were

[1] Hence Caecilius apud Minuc. Fel. c. 8, calls them homines deploratae, inlicitae ac desperatae factionis. Tertulliani Apologetic. c. 38: Inter licitas factiones sectam istam deputari oportebat, a qua nihil tale committitur, quale de illicitis factionibus timeri solet, etc.

[2] Originally preserved in Latin by Justin Martyr. Apol. i. c. 69: then translated into Greek by Eusebius (H. E. iv. 9). Rufinus (Hist. eccl. iv. 9) has probably preserved the Latin original (cf. Alexii Symmachi Mazochii disquisitio in Gallandii biblioth. vett. Patr. T. i. p. 728): Exemplum epistolae imperatoris Adriani ad Minucium Fundanum Proconsulem Asiae: Accepi literas ad me scriptas a decessore tuo Serenio Graniano clarissimo viro: et non placet mihi relationem silentio praeterire, ne et innoxii perturbentur, et calumniatoribus latrocinandi tribuatur occasio. Itaque si evidenter provinciales huic petitioni suae adesse valent adversum Christianos, ut pro tribunali eos in aliquo arguant, hoc eis exsequi non prohibeo: precibus autem in hoc solis et acclamationibus uti, eis non permitto. Etenim multo aequius est, si quis volet accusare, te cognoscere de objectis. Si quis igitur accusat, et probat adversum leges quidquam agere memoratos homines, pro merito peccatorum etiam supplicia statues. Illud mehercle magnopere curabis, ut, si quis calumniae gratia quemquam horum postulaverit reum, in hunc pro sui nequitia suppliciis severioribus vindices. Cf. F. Balduinus ad edicta vett. Princip. Rom. de Christianis, p. 72.

[3] Lampridius in vita Sev. Alexandri, c. 43. Christo templum facere voluit, eumque inter deos recipere. Quod et Adrianus cogitasse fertur, qui templa in omnibus civitatibus sine simulacris jusserat fieri, quae ille ad hoc parasse dicebatur. On the other hand, Spartianus in vita Hadriani, c. 22: Sacra Romana diligentissime curavit, peregrina contempsit. Flav. Vopiscus in vita Saturnini, c. 8, from a work of Phlegon, a freedman of Hadrian: Hadrianus Augustus Serviano Cs. S. Aegyptum, quam mihi laudabas, Servi-

disturbed afresh once and again (138–161).[4] But the reign of *Marcus Aurelius* (161–180) was still more unfavorable to them, for in it the frequent misfortunes that befell the empire caused many outbursts of the popular fury against them; while the emperor himself endeavored right earnestly to maintain the ancient reputation of the state religion.[5] Hence the Christians in Asia Minor[6] suffered persecutions, to which even *Polycarp*

ane carissime, totam didici levem, pendulam et ad omnia famae momenta volitantem. Illi, qui Serapin colunt, Christiani sunt, et devoti sunt Serapi, qui se Christi episcopos dicunt. Nemo illic archisynagogus Judaeorum, nemo Samarites, nemo Christianorum presbyter, non mathematicus, non haruspex, non aliptes. Ipse ille patriarcha cum Aegyptum venerit, ab aliis Serapidem adorare, ab aliis cogitur Christum. Unus illis Deus nullus est. Hunc Christiani, hunc Judaei, hunc omnes venerantur et gentes, etc.

⁴ Dionysius Corinth. ap. Euseb. iv. p. 23, concerning a persecution in Athens, in which Bishop Publius, the predecessor of Quadratus, suffered. Melito in Apolog. ad Marc. Aurel. ap. Euseb. iv. c. 26, § 5: Ὁ δὲ πατήρ σου—ταῖς πόλεσι περὶ τοῦ μηδὲν νεωτερίζειν περὶ ἡμῶν ἔγραψεν· ἐν οἷς καὶ πρὸς Λαρισσαίους, καὶ πρὸς Θεσσαλονικεῖς καὶ Ἀθηναίους, καί πρὸς πάντας Ἕλληνας. This writing may have given rise to the opinion that the Edictum ad commune Asiae proceeded from Antoninus, although it is manifestly spurious. This edict has been appended by a later hand to Justini Apol. i. c. 70, and has been communicated in a different text by Eusebius, iv. c. 13, with a reference to Melito (probably to the above passage, which he misunderstood). All that can be said with plausibility in defense of that edict may be seen in T. G. Hegelmaier Comm. in edictum Imp. Ant. P. pro Christianis. Tubing. 1767. 4. The spuriousness of it, before asserted by J. J. Scaliger, Moyle, Thirlby, has been convincingly proved by Is. Haffner de edicto Antonini Pii pro Christianis ad commune Asiae. Argentor. 1781. 4. Cf. Eichstädt exercitatio Antoniniana v. in the Annales acad. Jen. i. 286. The edict contains that explanation of the edict issued by Hadrian, which had arisen among the Christians. They believed that the expression adversus leges quidquam agere should not be referred to the exercises of Christian worship, and accordingly this edict explains it as an ἐπὶ τὴν ἡγεμονίαν Ῥωμαίων ἐγχειρεῖν. From this, therefore, it followed that whoever accused a Christian as such, without being able to prove against him such a crime, was liable to punishment as a false accuser.

⁵ Modestinus (Dig. lib. xlviii. Tit. 19, l. 30): Si quis aliquid fecerit, quo leves hominum animi superstitione numinis terrerentur, Divus Marcus hujusmodi homines in insulam relegari rescripsit. Julii Pauli Sententt. receptt. lib. v. Tit. 21, § 2: Qui novas, et usu vel ratione incognitas religiones inducunt, ex quibus animi hominum moveantur, honestiores deportantur, humiliores capite puniuntur. On the religious views of Marcus Aurelius and his sentiments toward the Christians, see Neander's K. G. i. i. 177.

⁶ Melito in Apolog. ad Marc. Aurel. ap. Euseb. iv. 26: Τὸ γὰρ οὐδὲ πώποτε γενόμενον, νῦν διώκεται τὸ τῶν θεοσεβῶν γένος, καινοῖς ἐλαυνόμενον δόγμασι κατὰ τὴν Ἀσίαν· οἱ γὰρ ἀναιδεῖς συκοφάνται καὶ τῶν ἀλλοτρίων ἐρασταὶ, τὴν ἐκ τῶν διαταγμάτων ἔχοντες ἀφορμὴν, φανερῶς λῃστεύουσι, νύκτωρ καὶ μεθημέραν διαρπάζοντες τοὺς μηδὲν ἀδικοῦντας.—εἰ δὲ καὶ παρὰ σοῦ μὴ εἴη ἡ βουλὴ αὕτη καὶ τὸ καινὸν τοῦτο διάταγμα,—δεόμεθά σου, μὴ περιϊδεῖν ἡμᾶς ἐν τοιαύτῃ δημώδει λεηλασίᾳ. Neander K. G. i. i. 184, is of opinion that this διάταγμα was certainly issued by the emperor, and is preserved in in the Acta Symphoniani apud Ruinart, p. 69. But the very inscription, Aurelius Imp. omnibus administratoribus suis atque rectoribus, throws suspicion on the law there given. The emperor could not open his proclamation with the name Aurelius. See Semisch, in the Theol. Studien u. Kritiken, 1835, iv. 934; administratores is not an official designation of the governors, and the emperor could not call them administratores suos. The emperor could have issued no edict against Christians before 177. See Semisch, l. c. S. 935, ff.

(167) fell a sacrifice,[7] while *Justin* (166) became a martyr at Rome.[8] But the recently formed churches at Lyons and Vienne (177)[9] suffered most. The supposed miracle of the *legio Melitina* (κεραυνοβόλος, *fulminatrix*) (174) could have had the less influence on the emperor in favor of the Christians, since so many parties ascribed the merit of it to themselves.[10] Under the barbarous *Commodus* (180–192), the Christians lived in peace.[11]

[7] Ecclesiae Smyrnensis de martyrio Polycarpi epistola encyclios ap. Euseb. iv. c. 15, first published by Ussher, 1647, in a form somewhat longer, then printed in Cotelerii Patr. apost. and in Ruinart. On the relation of the two recensions, see Danz de Eusebio, p. 130, ss.

[8] Acta martyrii Justini Philos. apud Ruinart, nova interpretatione, annotationibus atque disquisitionibus illustrata ab A. S. Mazochio in Gallandii Bibl. vett. patr. T. i. p. 707, ss. Semisch on the year of Justin Martyr's death in the Theol. Stud. u. Krit. 1835, iv. 907.

[9] Ecclesiarum Viennensis et Lugdunensis epistola ad ecclesias Asiae Phrygiaeque de passione martyrum suorum ap. Euseb. H. E. v. 1-3. To what a height the rage of the heathen proceeded, is proved, c. i. § 6, by the violation of the ancient law, de servo in dominum quaeri non licere, Cic. pro Dejot. c. 1. Tacit. Annal. ii. 30. Digest. lib. xlviii. Tit. 18, de quaestionibus.

[10] The heathen writers ascribe the phenomenon partly to the conjurations of the Aegyptian Arnuphis (Dio Cassius in excerpt. Xiphilini, lxxi. 8. Suidas s. v. Ἰουλιανός), partly to the prayer of Marcus (Capitolinus in vita Marc. Aurel. c. 24. Themistius in Orat. xv. p. 191, ed. Harduini). The emperor himself expresses his opinion on a coin on which Jupiter is represented hurling his lightning against the barbarians lying on the ground (Eckhel Numism. iii. 61). Cf. Claudianus de sexto consulatu Honorii, v. 342. Similar occurrences are related of Alexander, Curt. iv. 7, 13; of Marius, Orosii Hist. v. 15; and Hosidius, Dio Cass. lx. § 9. The Christians, in like manner, ascribed the merit to themselves, cf. Claudius Apollinaris ap. Euseb. v. 5. Tertulliani ad Scapul. c. 4, and especially Apologet. c. 5: At nos e contrario edimus protectorem, si litterae M. Aurelii—requirantur, quibus illam Germanicam sitim, Christianorum forte militum praecationibus impetrato imbri, discussam contestatur. Qui sicut non palam ab ejusmodi hominibus poenam dimovit, ita alio modo palam dispersit, adjecta etiam accusatoribus damnatione, et quidem tetriore. This writing, falsely ascribed to M. Aurelius, was afterward annexed to Justin Martyr's Apolog. i. In it all accusation of the Christians is forbidden under punishment of death by fire. The same thing is found in Edictum ad commune Asiae, note 4.

[11] Marcia, concubine of Commodus, was favorable to the Christians (Dio Cassius, lxxii. 4). On the martyrdom of Apollonius, see Euseb. H. E. v. 21; Hieron. Catal. c. 42. According to Jerome, he was betrayed by a slave Severus; according to Eusebius, his accuser was immediately put to death, ὅτι μὴ ζῆν ἐξὸν ἦν κατὰ βασιλικὸν ὅρον τοὺς τῶν τοιῶνδε μηνυτάς. M. de Mandajors (Histoire de l'acad. des inscript. tom. 18, p. 226) thinks that the slave was put to death as the betrayer of his master, according to an old law renewed by Trajan; but that the occurrence had been misunderstood by the Christians, and had given rise to the tradition which is found in Tertullian and in the Edictum ad comm. Asiae (see above note 10), that an emperor at this period had decreed the punishment of death for denouncing a Christian. So also Neander K. G. i. i. 201. Certainly such a law against the denunciation of masters by slaves was passed under Nerva (Dio Cassius, lxviii. p. 769. Cf. Capitolinus in vita Pertinac, c. 9. Digest. lib. xlix. tit. 14, l. 2, § 6): on the contrary, it was also a law (Julius Paulus Sententt. receptt. tit. 16, § 4): servo, qui ultro aliquid de domino confitetur, fides non accommodatur (cf. Digest. lib. xlviii. tit. 18, l. 1, § 5 u. § 16, l. 9, § 1); and though the case of high treason (causa Majestatis) was

SECOND CHAPTER

HERETICS.

§ 43.

JEWISH CHRISTIANS.

(Comp § 32.)

Gieseler's Abhandl. v. d. Nazaräern u. Ebioniten, Stäudlin's u. Tzschirner's Archiv. Bd. 4. St. 2, S. 325, ff.

The Jewish Christians in Palestine were severely persecuted by *Bar Cochab* (§ 38), because they would not attach themselves to him;[1] and they must afterward also undergo the same oppression as the Jews generaly, from whom they were not externally distinguished. These circumstances caused many of them, now that a church of heathen converts had been collected in Jerusalem, where *they* were forbidden to remain, to separate themselves entirely from Judaism, and to join the Christian community.[2] Still, however, the different parties of Jewish Christians[3] continued down to the fourth century, and even later. In what way the *Nazarenes* and the Gentile Christians still looked upon one another as orthodox, is evident from the expla-

excepted, yet then the punishment of the slaves also was remitted, if they had made a well-grounded accusation (Cod. Justinian. lib. ix. tit. 2, l. 20). Comp. on all these laws, Gothofredus in comm. ad Cod. Theodos. lib. x. tit. 10, c. 17. J. A. Bachii D. Trajanus, sive de legibus Trajani Imp. Lips. 1747. 8. p. 73, ss. According to these principles of law, therefore, either Apollonius only, or his slave only, could have been put to death, but in no case both. Jerome does not say either that Severus was the slave of Apollonius, or that he was executed; and since Eusebius grounds this execution expressly on a supposititious law, it may have belonged only to the oriental tradition, which may have adduced this instance in support of the alleged law.

1 Justin. Apol. i. c. 31. Euseb. in Chronico. Hieron. Catal. c. 21.

2 Euseb. iv. 5, enumerates down to this time fifteen bishops of Jerusalem belonging to the circumcision. Probably during the dispersion of the church several of them were contemporary. Ibid. c. 6. Cf. Sulpic. Sever. Hist. sacr. ii. 31. Militum cohortem (Hadrianus) custodias in perpetuum agitare jussit, quae Judaeos omnes Hierosolymae aditu arceret. Quod quidem christianae fidei proficiebat, quia tum paene omnes Christum Deum sub legis observatione credebant. Nimirum id Domino ordinante dispositum, ut legis servitus a libertate fidei atque ecclesiae tolleretur. Ita tum primum Marcus ex gentilibus apud Hierosolymam episcopus fuit.

3 See respecting them above, § 32.

nations of *Hegesippus* on his journey to Rome, whither he arrived under bishop Anicetus (157–161).[4] But since the Gentile Christians looked upon the Nazarenes as weak Christians, on account of their adherence to the Mosaic law,[5] the connection between them became less and less intimate, the knowledge of their creed more indistinct; but at the same time, since they did not keep pace with the progressive development of doctrine in the catholic church, the actual difference between the two parties was greater, until at length Epiphanius (about 400) went so far as to include the Nazarenes in his list of heretics (Haer. xxix.).

§ 44.

GNOSTICS.

Sources. Irenaeus adv. Haereses (especially against Valentinus). Tertullianus adv. Marcionem libb. v.; de Praescriptionibus haereticorum; adv. Valentinianos; contra Gnosticos scorpiacum. Epiphanius adv. Haereses. Clemens Alex. and Origen in many passages. The work of the neo-Platonic Plotinus *πρὸς τοὺς γνωστικούς*, i. e., Ennead. ii. lib. 9 (ed. G. A. Heigl. Ratisbonae. 1832. 8. Comp. Creuzer in the theol. Stud. u. Krit. 1834, ii. 337. Baur's Gnosis, S. 417).

Isaac de Beausobre Histoire critique de Manichée et du Manichéisme. Amsterd. 1734 and 39, 2 T. 4. J. L. Moshemii de rebus Christian. ante Const. M. comm. p. 333, ss. Walch's Ketzerhistorie, i. 217. (F. Münter's) Versuch über die kirchl. Alterthümer der Gnostiker. Anspach. 1790. 8. E. A. Lewald Comm. de doctrina gnostica. Heidelberg. 1818. 8. Aug. Neander's genetische Entwickelung d. vornehmsten gnostischen Systeme. Berlin. 1818. 8. (Comp. my Review in the Hall. A. L. Z. April, 1823, S. 825, ff.). Neander's K. G. i. ii. 632. Histoire critique du Gnosticisme par J. Matter, 2 tom. Paris. 1828. 8. (Comp. my Review in the theol. Studien u. Kritiken, 1830, ii. 378, ff.). Die christl. Gnosis, od. d. christl. Religionsphilosophie in ihrer geschichtl. Entwicklung v. Dr. F. Baur. Tübingen 1835. 8. Dr. H. Ritter's Gesch. d. christl. Philosophie (Hamburg. 1841) i. 111. [An Inquiry into the heresies of the apostolic age, by E. Burton, D.D. Oxford. 1829.]

The tendency of theological speculation, which was before apparent in Cerinthus (§ 36), appeared, at the commencement of this period, completely developed in the different Syrian and Egyptian systems.[1] The philosophical basis of this speculation

4 Eusebius iv. 22. Hegesippus had conferred with many bishops, particularly with Primus in Corinth and Anicetus at Rome and testifies on this point: *ἐν ἑκάστῃ δὲ διαδοχῇ καὶ ἐν ἑκάστῃ πόλει οὕτως ἔχει, ὡς ὁ νόμος κηρύττει καὶ οἱ προφῆται καὶ ὁ Κύριος.* The Nazarenes might find the life of the Gentile Christians conformed to the law, because the latter observed the precepts of Noah, see § 17, note 7, § 26, note 6, An Ebionite would have required the observance of the Mosaic law. Against Baur (Tübinger Zeitschr. 1831, iv. 171) and Schwegler (Montanismus, S. 276), who thinks that he was an Ebionite, see Schliemann's Clementinen, S. 428.

5 Justin. Dial. cum Tryphone, c. 47.

1 Sources of Gnosis, Lewald, l. c. p. 60, ss. The church fathers derived it from the hea-

was the old question, *πόθεν τὸ κακόν*.[2] In proportion as the idea of the highest divinity had developed itself, the less did philosophy believe itself right in venturing[3] to consider him as a world-creator (*δημιουργός*),[4] and the more strongly was it disposed to derive the imperfect good in the world from lower beings, but

then philosophy, especially from Platonism (Tert. adv. Hermog. c. 8: haereticorum patriarchae philosophi. De anima, c. 23: Plato omnium haereticorum condimentarius), and class the theosophic fantasies with the heathen myths. Down to Mosheim, most writers were in favor of the Platonic origin of Gnosis. So also Tiedemann Geist der speculativen Philosophie, iii. 96. Derivation from the Jewish Cabbala, Jo. Croji conjecturae in quaedam loca Origenes, Irenaei, &c., appended to Grabe's Irenaeus. F. Buddei diss. de haeresi Valentiniana, annexed to the Introd. ad histor. philos. Hebraeorum, ed. 2. Halae. 1720. 8. p. 619, ss. Jac. Basnage Histoire des Juifs, liv. iii. p. 718, ss. From an oriental philosophy (= x), especially Mosheim: comp. F. Lücke in Schleiermacher's, De Wette's, u. Lücke's theol. Zeitschr. ii. 138. From the Zend-system, Lewald, l. c. p. 106, ss. Comp. on the other side, A. L. Z. April, 1823, S. 828. The writings of Zoroaster, to which some Gnostics appeal (Porphyrius in vita Plotini, p. 10. Clemens Alex. Strom. i. 304), are unquestionably of Greek origin. From the Buddhist doctrines, by J. J. Schmidt über die Verwandtschaft der gnostisch-theosoph. Lehren mit d. Religionssystemen des Orients, vorzüglich des Buddhaismus. Leipzig. 1828. 4to. Comp. his treatises on Buddhism in the Mémoires de l'Académie impériale des sciences de S. Petersbourg vi. Série. Sciences polit. Histoire, Philologie. T. i. livr. ii. (1830), p. 89; livr. iii. p. 221, T. ii. livr. i. (1832) p. 1, 41. (See theol. Studien u. Krit. Jahrg. 1830, ii. 374.) According to Möhler (Vers. über d. Ursprung d. Gnosticismus, in his Schriften u. Aufsätzen, i. 403), Gnosis proceeded directly and entirely from Christianity, and from a practical motive, viz. from an exaggerated contempt of the world, which afterward endeavored to lay a speculative foundation for itself, and for this purpose applied all that was useful in the older systems of philosophy, theosophy, and mythology. According to Baur (Gnosis, S. 36), Gnosis, has borrowed its material substance from the religions which were given historically, its chief object being to inquire into and define the relation in which those historical elements stood to one another. Its first elements were formed among the Alexandrian Jews. Persian dualism, platonism, and Alexandrian philosophy of religion, have had their influence in originating the Christian Gnosis. It is an attempt to conceive the entire course of the world as a series of elements in which the absolute spirit becomes objective to himself, and is reconciled with himself, and has therefore nothing more similar than the Hegelian philosophy of religion. (Comp. this author's Krit. Studien über d. Begriff d. Gnosis, in the theol. Stud. u. Krit. 1837, iii. 511.) [An Inquiry into the Heresies of the apostolic age. By E. Burton, D.D. Oxford. 1829. 8vo.]

[2] Tertull. de Praescript. haeret. c. 7: Eaedem materiae apud haereticos et philosophos volutantur, iidem retractatus implicantur, unde malum et quare? et unde homo et quomodo? et quod proxime Valentinus proposuit, unde deus? Euseb. Hist. eccl. v. 27, *πολυθρύλλητον παρὰ τοῖς αἱρεσιώταις ζήτημα τὸ πόθεν ἡ κακία.*

[3] Even according to Plato (Timaeus p. 41), only the divine in man was created by the highest God, who then leaves it to the *τοῖς νέοις θεοῖς ἀθανάτῳ θνητὸν προσυφαίνειν*. So also Philo (de mundi opif. p. 16, de ling. conf. p. 346, de profug. p. 460), in speaking of the creation of man, makes the *τὸ ἄλογον, τὸ θνητὸν ἡμῶν τῆς ψυχῆς μέρος* be created by angels. But Lucretius (70 B.C.) de rerum natura v. 196 ss.:—

Quod si jam rerum ignorem primordia quae sint,
Hoc tamen ex ipsis coeli rationibus ausim
Confirmare, alieisque ex rebus reddere multeis,
Nequaquam nobis divinitus esse paratam
Naturam rerum: tanta stat praedita culpa.

4 *Δημιουργός* is the former of the world even in Xenoph. Memorab. i. 4, 7, and in Plato Timaeus, p. 41, more frequently in the younger Platonists.

the evil from an evil principle.[5] Among the speculating Christians, these ideas obtained some hold from the Christian view taken of Christianity, Judaism, aud heathenism, as the complete, the incomplete, and the evil. These three religions appeared as revelations of three corresponding principles, which were first perceived in their true light from the position of Christianity. Matter (ὕλη) was the evil principle, which had revealed itself in heathenism, and was there conceived as having sometimes an undeveloped, sometimes a developed consciousness.[6] The creation of the world belonged, according to Gen. i., to the God of the Jews, who, commonly regarded as the first of the seven planet-princes,[7] proceeded from the highest God only at an infinite distance, and was as incapable of willing the perfect as of restraining the opposition of matter.[8] On the other hand, Christ revealed the high-

[5] Plutarchus de Iside et Osiride, c. 45: *Οὔτε γὰρ ἐν ἀψύχοις σώμασι τὰς τοῦ παντὸς ἀρχὰς θετέον, ὡς Δημόκριτος καὶ Ἐπίκουρος· οὔτε ἀποίου δημιουργὸν ὕλης ἕνα λόγον καὶ μίαν πρόνοιαν, ὡς οἱ Στωϊκοὶ, περιγινομένην ἁπάντων καὶ κρατοῦσαν· ἀδύνατον γὰρ ἢ φλαῦρον ὅτιοῦν, ὅπου πάντων, ἢ χρηστὸν, ὅπου μηδενὸς ὁ θεὸς αἴτιος, ἐγγενέσθαι.* Hence the ancient opinion of the wise men is this: *Ἀπὸ δυεῖν ἐναντίων ἀρχῶν, καὶ δυεῖν ἀντιπάλων δυνάμεων—ὅ, τε βίος μικτὸς, ὅ, τε κόσμος—ἀνώμαλος καὶ ποικίλος γέγονε καὶ μεταβολὰς πάσας δεχόμενος.* C. 46: *Καὶ δοκεῖ τοῦτο τοῖς πλείστοις καὶ σοφωτάτοις. Νομίζουσι γὰρ οἱ μὲν θεοὺς εἶναι δύο, καθάπερ ἀντιτέχνους, τὸν μὲν γὰρ ἀγαθῶν, τὸν δὲ φαύλων δημιουργόν· οἱ δὲ τὸν μὲν ἀμείνονα Θεὸν, τὸν δὲ ἕτερον Δαίμονα καλοῦσιν.* Zoroaster calls the former Ormuzd, the latter Ahriman, *μέσον δὲ ἀμφοῖν τὸν Μίθρην εἶναι· διὸ καὶ Μίθρην Πέρσαι τὸν μεσίτην ὀνομάζουσιν· ἐδίδαξε μὲν τῷ εὐκταῖα θύειν καὶ χαριστήρια, τῷ δὲ ἀποτρόπαια καὶ σκυθρωπά.* C. 48: *Χαλδαῖοι δὲ τῶν πλανητῶν τοὺς θεοὺς γενέσθαι, οὓς καλοῦσι, δύο μὲν ἀγαθουργοὺς, δύο δε κακοποιοὺς, μέσους δὲ τοὺς τρεῖς ἀποφαίνουσι καὶ κοινούς.* This dualism is found also among the philosophers, even in Plato, who speaks in the clearest manner concerning it, *ἐν τοῖς νόμοις* (Leg. x. p. 669, and Tim. p. 528) *οὐ μιᾷ ψυχῇ κινεῖσθαι τὸν κόσμον, ἀλλὰ πλείοσιν ἴσως, δυοῖν δὲ πάντως οὐκ ἐλάττοσιν· ὅθεν τὴν μὲν ἀγαθουργὸν εἶναι, τὴν δὲ ἐναντίαν ταύτῃ, καὶ τῶν ἐναντίων δημιουργόν· ἀπολείπει, δὲ καὶ τρίτην τινὰ μεταξὺ φύσιν, οὐκ ἄψυχον, οὐδὲ ἄλογον, οὐδὲ ἀκίνητον ἐξ αὑτῆς,—ἀλλ' ἀνακειμένην ἀμφοῖν ἐκείναις, ἐφιεμένην δὲ τῆς ἀμείνονος ἀεὶ, καὶ ποθοῦσαν, καὶ διώκουσαν.* Similar to it is the Egyptian doctrine, in which Osiris is the good, Typhon the evil principle, and Isis that third nature. Numenius *περὶ τἀγαθοῦ* (in Euseb. Praep. evang. xi. 18) shows that the Demiurgus must be distinguished from the highest God, who, as he thinks, resembles the Logos of Philo: *Τὸν μὲν πρῶτον θεὸν ἀργὸν εἶναι, ἔργων ξυμπάντων καὶ βασιλέα, τὸν δημιουργικὸν δὲ θεὸν ἡγεμονεῖν, δι' οὐρανοῦ ἰόντα. διὰ δὲ τούτου καὶ ὁ στόλος ἡμῖν ἐστι, κάτω τοῦ νοῦ πεμπομένου ἐν διεξόδῳ πᾶσι τοῖς κοινωνῆσαι συντεταγμένοις.* And in a preceeding passage: *Καὶ γὰρ οὔτε δημιουργεῖν ἐστι χρεὼν τὸν πρῶτον, καὶ τοῦ δημιουργοῦντος δὲ θεοῦ χρὴ εἶναι καὶ νομίζεσθαι πατέρα τὸν πρῶτον θεόν.*

[6] Analogous to the Jewish-Christian view, according to which the heathen gods were evil angels. Keilii Opusc. ii. 584, 601.

[7] The Jewish-Christian opinion of the division of the world among angels corresponded to this. Keil. l. c. p. 480.

[8] Origen de Princ. l. iv. (Philocalia, ed. Spencer, p. 6): *Οἵ τε ἀπὸ τῶν αἱρέσεων ἀναγινώσκοντες τό· πῦρ ἐκκέκαυται ἐκ τοῦ θυμοῦ μου* (Jer. xv. 14, then: Exod. xx. 5, 1 Reg. xv. 11, Es. xlv. 8, Am. iii. 6, Mich. i. 12, 1 Reg. xvi. 15), *καὶ μυρία ὅσα τούτοις παραπλήσια, ἀπιστῆσαι μὲν ὡς θεοῦ ταῖς γραφαῖς οὐ τετολμήκασι, πιστεύοντες δὲ*

est divinity, which, elevated above all being, had produced out of himself only the world of light, a world of blessed spirits. Human spirits, *πνεύματα*, are rays of light proceeding from this blessed spirit, whose object is consequently to free themselves from the fetters of the Demiurgus and matter, in order that they may return into the world of light. To effect this was the object of Christ, who was thought by most Gnostics to be one of the highest spirits of light. As the means of doing so, he left behind to his genuine disciples, the *γνῶσις*. These general ideas were carried out in special ways in the separate schools, on which account they received different forms and modifications. Among the *Alexandrian* Gnostics, traces of the Platonic philosophy are most obvious;[9] among the *Syrian*, the influence of Parsism was superadded. Among the former, the emanation doctrine was pre-eminent; among the latter, *dualism*.[10] In all the schools, however, there remained a wide field for the play of fancy in making vivid to the perception the internal relations of the world of light, the origin of the Demiurgus from it, and the creation of the world. For this purpose the Alexandrian Gnostics employed, but only as an insecure guide, a representation which was borrowed from the Platonic doctrine of ideas, that the visible world, with its germs of life, is only an image and impression of the world of light.[11] With this view the allegorical

αὐτὰς εἶναι τοῦ δημιουργοῦ, ᾧ 'Ιουδαῖοι λατρεύουσιν, ᾠήθησαν ὡς ἀτελοῦς καὶ οὐκ ἀγαθοῦ τυγχάνοντος τοῦ δημιουργοῦ, τὸν σωτῆρα ἐπιδεδημηκέναι τελειότερον καταγγέλλοντα θεόν, ὅν φασι μὴ τὸν δημιουργὸν τυγχάνειν, διαφόρως περὶ τούτου κινούμενοι, καὶ ἅπαξ ἀποστάντες τοῦ δημιουργοῦ, ὅς ἐστιν ἀγέννητος μόνος θεὸς, ἀναπλασμοῖς ἑαυτοὺς ἐπιδεδώκασι, μυθοποιοῦντες ἑαυτοῖς ὑποθέσεις, καθ' ἃς οἴονται γεγονέναι τὰ βλεπόμενα, καὶ ἕτερά τινα μὴ βλεπόμενα, ἅπερ ἡ ψυχὴ αὐτῶν ἀνειδωλοποίησεν. New Testament passages also may have been cited by the Gnostics in favor of the distinction, ex. gr. Joh. xii. 31, xiv. 30; 2 Cor. iv. 4; Gal. iii. 19; 1 Cor. ii. 6, 7; Eph. iii. 9, ff.

9 Plotin. cont. Gnost. c. 6: *Ὅλως γὰρ αὐτοῖς τὰ μὲν παρὰ τοῦ Πλάτωνος εἴληπται· τὰ δὲ, ὅσα καινοτομοῦσιν, ἵνα ἰδίαν φιλοσοφίαν θῶνται, ταῦτα ἔξω τῆς ἀληθείας εὕρηται.*

10 Neander divides the Gnostics into such as adhered to Judaism, and anti-Jewish: see the Hall. A. L. Z. April, 1823, S. 831, and Baur's Gnosis, S. 97, ff. The latter assumes three classes; 1. Those who brought Christianity into closer connection with Judaism and heathenism; 2. Those who made a strict separation of Christianity and Judaism from heathenism; 3. Those who identified Christianity and Judaism, and opposed both to heathenism in the form of Gnosis (the pseudo-Clement. system).

11 Philo de Somniis, p. 593: *Τὸν ἐκ τῶν ἰδεῶν συσταθέντα—κόσμον νοητὸν οὐκ ἔνεστιν ἄλλως καταλαβεῖν, ὅτι μὴ ἐκ τῆς τοῦ αἰσθητοῦ καὶ ὁρωμένου τούτου μεταναβάσεως.* So, according to Hebr. ix. 23, the earthly sanctuary contains *ὑποδείγματα τῶν ἐν τοῖς οὐρανοῖς*. Clem. Alex. Strom. iv. p. 593: *Εἰκὼν τῆς οὐρανίου ἐκκλησίας ἡ ἐπίγειος* So, particularly in the system of the Valentinians, Iren. ii. 7. It is the Sophia, quae emittit similitudines et imagines eorum, quae sursum sunt. C. 8: In honorem eorum, quae sursum sunt, facta sunt haec secundum illorum imaginem.

interpretation of holy scripture already current could be readily united, and employed in an arbitrary manner. Moreover, all the Gnostics appealed particularly to a secret doctrine handed down to them from the apostles. The principle of the gnostic morality, *freedom from the fetters of the Demiurgus, and of matter*, led to rigid abstinence, and a contemplative life. But when the pride of dogmatism among the later Gnostics had stifled the moral sense, a part of them fell upon the expedient of giving out the moral law to be only a work of the Demiurgus, for the sake of indulgence in sensual excesses.[12]

§ 45.

(CONTINUATION.) 1. ALEXANDRIAN GNOSTICS.

I. Basilides of Alexandria (about 125) represented seven *δυνάμεις* in particular, as emanating from the great original (*θεὸς ἄῤῥητος*), viz., *νοῦς, λόγος, φρόνησις, σοφία, δύναμις, δικαιοσύνη, εἰρήνη*. These composed the first kingdom of spirits (*οὐρανός*). From this emanated a second, and so on until there were 365 kingdoms of spirits, each of which was successively an imperfect impression of the preceding. The total idea of these spiritual kingdoms, i. e., *God so far as he has revealed himself*, in contradistinction from *God in himself*, he called Ἀβρασάξ.[1] The seven angels of the lowest heaven, and especially the first among them, *ὁ ἄρχων*, the God of the Jews, are the creators of the world. To effect the return of human spirits to the world of

12 Clement Alex. Strom. iii. p. 529: *Αἱρέσεις—ἢ—ἀδιαφόρως ζῆν διδάσκουσιν, ἢ τὸ ὑπέρτονον ἄγουσαι, ἐγκράτειαν διὰ δυσσεβείας καὶ φιλαπεχθημοσύνης καταγγέλλουσι.* Cf. ii. 411: Plotinus contra Gnosticos, c. 15: *Ὁ δὲ λόγος οὗτος (τῶν Γνωστικῶν)—τὴν πρόνοιαν μεμψάμενος, καὶ πάντας νόμους τοὺς ἐνταῦθα ἀτιμάσας, καὶ τὴν ἀρετὴν—τό, τε σωφρονειν τοῦτο ἐν γέλωτι θέμενος, ἵνα μηδὲν καλὸν ἐνταῦθα δὴ ὀφθείη ὑπάρχον, ἀνεῖλε τό, τε σωφρονεῖν καὶ τὴν ἐν τοῖς ἤθεσι σύμφυτον δικαιοσύνην, τὴν τελουμένην ἐκ λόγου καὶ ἀσκησέως—ὥστε αὐτοῖς καταλείπεσθαι τὴν ἡδονὴν, καὶ τὸ περὶ αὐτοὺς, καὶ τὸ οὐ κοινὸν πρὸς ἄλλους ἀνθρώπους, καὶ τὸ τῆς χρείας μόνον.*

1 J. J. Bellermann Versuch über die Gemmen der Alten mit dem Abraxas-Bilde. Berlin 1817–19. 3 Stücke. U. F. Kopp Paleographia critica, P. iii. et iv. Manhemii. 1829. 4. Good impressions of many Abraxas-gems are appended to Matter's Hist. du Gnosticisme; but many of them are not of Gnostic origin. See theol. Studien u. Kritiken, 1830. Heft. 2. S. 403, ff. Ἀβρασάξ appears as a powerful incantation-name of God, as well as the Jewish Jao, Sabaoth, Adonai, even in magical formulae whose origin is obviously heathen-Egyptian, see C. J. C. Reuvens lettres à M. Letronne sur les Papyrus bilingues et grecs du Musée de Leide (à Leide. 1830. 4). Prem. lettre, p. 22, 64.

light (ἀποκατάστασις), the νοῦς united itself with the man Jesus at his baptism. Hence the followers of Basilides celebrated the festival of the baptism as *the epiphany* (τὰ ἐπιφάνια, on the 11th Tybi, the 6th of January).[2] The man alone endured the sufferings, which, like all human sufferings, were expiations of guilt contracted, though in a former period of existence. The ἄρχων of Basilides is not evil, but only circumscribed; and therefore he subjects himself to the higher arrangement of the world, as soon as it is made known to him. The later followers of Basilides,[3] on the contrary, conceived him to be an open adversary of the world of light, and thus rejected Judaism entirely; in which, however, Basilides could perceive types and preparations for something higher. In like manner, they received into their system the views of the Docetae, and contrived by sophisms to make their moral doctrine more loose. They rendered themselves particularly odious, by supposing that they could deny the crucified One; thus they escaped persecution. The party was still in existence about 400.[4]

II. Still more ingenious is the system of *Valentinus*, who came from Alexandria to Rome about 140, and died in Cyprus about 160.[5] From the great original (according to him βυθός, προπάτωρ, προαρχή), with whom is the consciousness of himself (ἔννοια, σιγή) emanate in succession male and female *aeons*[6] (νοῦς

[2] According to Jablonski de origine festi nativitatis Christi diss. ii. § 8, ss. (Opuscul. ed. te Water, iii. 358), they borrowed this day from the Egyptians, who celebrated on it the inventio Osiridis. This application of the Egyptian festival, however, rests on an unfortunate alteration of the text in Plut. de Isis et Osir. c. 39. The festival of the inventio Osiridis occurred in November. See Wyttenbach. animadverss. in Plut. Moralia, ii. i. 225. Wieseler's Chronolog. Synopse der Evang. S. 136. In like manner Jablonski incorrectly infers from Clem. Alex. Strom. iii. p. 340, that the followers of Basilides celebrated not only the baptism, but also the birth of Jesus, on the Epiphany.

[3] The genuine system of Basilides is given in Clemens Alexandrinus; that of his later adherents in Irenaeus, see Neander gnost. Systeme, S. 31.

[4] The sources of information concerning Basilides are: the tradition of Glaukias, an interpreter (ἑρμηνεύς) of the apostle Peter, and a tradition of the apostle Matthias.—Prophets Βαρκάβας, Βαρκώφ, Παρχώρ.—He wrote twenty-four books ἐξηγητικά, which may have also been called his gospel.

[5] J. F. Buddeus de Haeresi Valentiniana appended to Introductio ad historiam philos. Ebraeorum. ed. 2. Halae. 1720. 8, p. 573–736. It is remarkable that Valentinus not only received the New Testament, but made constant allegorical use of it in his system. Thus he formed his system of Aeons for the most part after John i. Irenaeus i. 8, 5.—His secret doctrine is from Theodades, a disciple of Paul; his hymns, discourses, and letters are for the most part lost. From the work preserved in Coptic, entitled Fidelis Sophia, has been published D. Fr. Münter Odae gnosticae, thebaice et latine. Havniae. 1812.

[6] On *αἰών* see Numenius ap. Euseb. Praep. evang. xi. 10: Τὸ ὂν οὔτε ποτὲ ἦν, οὔτε ποτὲ γένηται· ἀλλ' ἔστιν ἀεὶ ἐν χρόνῳ μὴ ὡρισμένῳ, τῷ ἐνεστῶτι μόνῳ. τοῦτον μὲν

or *μονογενής* and *ἀλήθεια, λόγος* and *ἀλήθεια, λόγος* and *ζωή, ἄνθρωπος* and *ἐκκλησία*, &c.), so that 30 aeons together (distinguished into the *ὀγδοάς, δεκάς* and *δωδεκάς*) form the *πλήρωμα*.[7] From the passionate striving of the last aeon, the *σοφία*, to unite with *Bythos*, itself, arises an untimely being (*ἡ κάτω σοφία, ἐνθύμησις, Ἀχαμώθ, i. e.*, הַחָכְמוֹת), which, wandering about outside the pleroma, communicates the germ of life to matter, and forms the *δημιουργός* of psychical material, who immediately creates the world. In this three kinds of material are mixed—*τὸ πνευματικόν, τὸ ψυχικόν, τὸ ὑλικόν*. The goal of the course of the world is, that the two first should be separated from the last, and that *τὸ πνευμ.* should return to the pleroma, *τὸ ψυχικόν* into the *τόπος μεσότητος*, where the *Achamoth* now dwells. In the mean time, two new aeons, Christ and the Holy Spirit, had arisen, in order to restore the disturbed harmony in the pleroma; then there emanated from all the aeons, Jesus (*σωτήρ*), who, as future associate (*σύζυγος*) of the Achamoth, shall lead back into the pleroma this and the pneumatic natures. The *σωτήρ* united itself at the baptism with the psychical Messiah promised by the Demiurgus. Just so is the letter of the doctrines of Jesus for *psychical* men. On the other hand, the spirit introduced by the Soter or Saviour, is for the *spiritual*. These theosophic dreams were naturally capable of being molded in many different ways; and, accordingly, among Valentinus's disciples are found many departures from their teacher. The most important of his followers were *Heracleon*,[8] *Ptolemy*,[9] and *Marcus*.

III. To the system of Valentinus was nearly allied that of the *Ophites*,[10] who, perhaps, existed as a party in Egypt even before the Valentinians.[11] Their pleroma is simpler than that of

οὖν τὸν ἐνεστῶτα εἴ τις ἐθέλει καλεῖν αἰῶνα, κἀγὼ συμβούλομαι. (I have believed it necessary to place the *μή*, which stands in the usual text before *γένηται*, before *ὡρισμένῳ*). Thus among the Gnostics *αἰῶνες* are developments of the Divine Being, who, as such, are elevated above the limitations of time.

7 On *πλήρωμα* see Baur's Gnosis, S. 157.

8 Of his Commentary on John there are numerous fragments in the commentary of Origen.

9 His epistola ad Floram apud Epiphanius Haer. xxxiii. A. Stieren de Ptolemaei Gnostici ad Floram epist. P. 1, Jenae. 1843, distinguishes in the letter two parts proceeding from different authors, both which, however, could not have been written by Ptolemy.

10 J. L. v. Mosheim Versuch einer unparteiischen u. gründlichen Ketzergeschichte. Geschichte der Schlangenbrüder der ersten Kirche. 2te Aufl. Helmstädt. 1748. 4. A. H. L. Fuldner Comm. de Ophitis. Part 1. Rintelli. 1834. 4. (A school programm.)

11 Origen c. Celsum. vi. § 28, ed. Spenc. p. 294: Ὀφιανοὶ τοσοῦτον ἀποδέουσι τοῦ

Valentinus. From the Bythus emanate *the first man*, *the second man* or *the son of man*, *the Holy Spirit*. The last gives birth, by means of the first two, to the perfect masculine light-nature, *the Christ*, and the defective female σοφία, Ἀχαμώθ, προύνεικος. The creator of the world (Ἰαλδαβαώθ, probably יַלְדָּא בָּהוּת, son of chaos), the first of the seven planet princes, is ambitious and malevolent, and is therefore involved in continual strife with his mother Sophia, who endeavors to deprive him of the pneumatic natures. The Ὀφιόμορφος, the ruler of Hyle, and the cause of all evil, is an image of him. The christology of the Ophites is altogether like that of Valentinus, with this difference, that *Jesus* is the *psychical*, *Christ* the *pneumatic* Messiah.[12] The Ophites were divided into various sects (ex. gr. *Sethians*, *Cainites*). One of them looked for the Sophia in the serpent of Genesis, and hence the name of the whole party. This continued the longest of all the Gnostic sects. (So late as 530 A.D. Justinian enacted laws against them, Cod. lib. i. tit. v. 1, 18, 19, 21).

IV. *Carpocrates* struck out an entirely different way.[13] In his view, *Jesus* was a mere man, like Pythagoras, Plato, and Aristotle, who had set an example of the mode in which the Gnostic must free himself from the Demiurgi (ἄγγελοι κοσμοποιοί), and unite with the highest divinity (μονάς). As the Carpocratians had portraits of those Grecian philosophers and of Jesus in their sanctuaries, so they built in Cephalenia a temple to *Epiphanes*,[14] a youth seventeen years old, the son of

εἶναι Χριστιανοὶ, ὥστε οὐκ ἔλαττον Κέλσου κατηγορεῖν αὐτοὺς τοῦ Ἰησοῦ. καὶ μὴ πρότερον προσίεσθαί τινα ἐπὶ τὸ συνέδριον ἑαυτῶν, ἐὰν μὴ ἀρὰς θῆται κατὰ τοῦ Ἰησοῦ. Mosheim (l. c. S. 19 and S. 127) infers from this that the Ophites formed a more ancient Jewish sect, which afterward adopted Christianity only in part. On the other side see A. L. Z. April, 1823. S. 846.

[12] On the *διάγραμμα* of the Ophites apud Origines c. Celsum, vi. ed. Spencer. p. 291, ss. see Mosheim, l. c. S. 79, ff. 178, ff.

[13] G. H. F. Fuldner de Carpocratianis, in Illgen's historischtheolog. Abhandlungen, dritte Denkschrift der hist. theol. Gessellschaft zu Leipzig. 1824. S. 180, ff. G. Gesenius de inscriptione Phoenicio-Graeca in Cyrenaica nuper reperta ad Carpocratianorum haeresin pertinente. Halae. 1825. 4.

[14] Fragments of this work *περὶ δικαιοσύνης* preserved by Clemens Alex. Strom. iii. p. 512, s. His moral principles: *Οἱ νόμοι, ἀνθρώπων ἀμαθίαν κολάζειν μὴ δυνάμενοι, παρανομεῖν ἐδίδαξαν· ἡ γὰρ ἰδιότης τῶν νόμων τὴν κοινωνίαν τοῦ θείου νόμου κατέτεμεν καὶ παρατρώγει.—Κοινῇ ὁ θεὸς ἅπαντα ἀνθρώπῳ ποιήσας, καὶ τὸ θῆλυ τῷ ἄρρενι κοινῇ συναγαγὼν, καὶ πάνθ' ὁμοίως τὰ ζῶα κολλήσας, τὴν δικαιοσύνην ἀνέφηνεν κοινωνίαν μετ' ἰσότητος.* Hence, according to page 514, at the conclusion of their agapae, concubitus promiscui.

their founder, after his death. The sects of the *Antitactes* and the *Prodiciani*,[15] allied to the Carpocratians, were branded like it by immoral principles.[16]

§ 46.

(CONTINUATION.) 2. SYRIAN GNOSTICS.

The Syrian Gnostics developed the doctrine of dualism more decidedly than the Egyptian, to which the neighborhood of Persia may have largely contributed. With this was connected their fanatical asceticism, in which they exceeded the Egyptians, and their *Docetic* views.[1] *Saturninus* in Antioch, a cotemporary of Basilides, taught that by the original cause (πατὴρ ἄγνωστος) the world of spirits was created by successive steps, and placed in the lowest gradation the spirits of the seven planets (ἄγγελοι κοσμοκράτορες). In opposition to them stood the evil principle (ὁ Σατανᾶς), who set in antagonism to the race of men of light animated by the highest divinity, a race of evil men, so that both kinds of men are continued beside one another. In order to avoid all contact with the evil principle, the followers of Saturninus abstained from marriage and the eating of flesh. The wide diffusion of the Gnostic opinions in Syria and the countries lying eastward of it may be seen in the case of *Bardesanes* in Edessa (about 172),[2] who, although he believed

[15] On the 'Αντιτάκται cf. Clemens Strom. iii. p. 526. Theodoret. Haer. fab. comp. i. c. 16: Respecting Πρόδικος Clemens, l. c. p. 525. Theodoret, l. c. i. c. 6.

[16] The inscriptions which, as pretended, were found in Cyrene, and brought to Malta, were regarded at first as Carpocratian (cf. G. Gesenius, l. c.), but were afterward shown to be recent fabrications, like many other spurious productions, particularly Eumali Cyrenaici Hist. Libycae, lib. vi., all of which were made known by the Marquis Fortia d'Urban in Avignon. They were meant to confirm the hypotheses which this person had formerly put forth respecting an island, Atlantis, in the Mediterranean Sea, which was sunk at the flood, in which island a St. Simonian community of goods and wives is said to have prevailed. See Boeckh preface to the Berlin Lectionskataloge, Easter, 1832. Gesenius in the Hallische A. L. Z. 1835, August, S. 462. When M. J. R. Pacho, Relation d'un voyage dans la Marmarique, la Cyrénaique, &c. Paris. 1827. 4. p. 128, believed that he had found in a pit at Lameloudèh, in Cyrenaica, traces referring to a place where the Carpocratians assembled, he was led astray by the opinions at first pronounced on those inscriptions. A cross with a serpent is a common Christian symbol, according to John iii. 14; and Catholic Christians may as well have used that pit as a place of meeting, like those at Massakhit, p. 114.

[1] A. L. Z. April, 1823. S. 833, ff.

[2] Bar daizon (Bayer hist. Osrh. et Edess. p. 13) lived under the prince Abgar bar Maanu, and gave up his book, περὶ εἱμαρμένης. to Antoninus Verus, of which Euseb.

in two eternal principles, derived evil from the Hyle, and held many other Gnostic tenets, was still looked upon as orthodox in that place. Cotemporary with him was the Assyrian *Tatian*,[3] who had been a disciple of Justin Martyr, but after his death had returned to his native land, and founded there a Gnostic sect, which was chiefly distinguished by abstinence (Ἐγκρατῖται, Ὑδροπαραστάται, *Aquarii*),[4] and continued till after the fourth century.

§ 47.

(CONTINUATION.) 3. MARCION AND HIS SCHOOL.[1]

The Gnosis of *Marcion*, the son of a bishop of *Sinope*, who attached himself to the Syrian *Cerdo* at Rome (between 140 and 150), and developed there a system of his own, has a character quite peculiar. He assumed three moral principles (ἀρχαί), viz., the θεὸς ἀγαθός, the δημιουργὸς δίκαιος, and the ὕλη (ὁ πονηρός, ὁ διάβολος). To free men—who had only to expect from

praep. Evang. vi. 10, has preserved a fragment (republished in Alexandri Aphrodisiensis, Ammonii, Plotini, Bardesanis et Gemisti Plethonis de fato quae supersunt graece, rec. et notas adjecit J. C. Orellius. Turici. 1824. 8. p. 202, ss.). He gained over many adherents by his hymns. The fifty-six hymns of Ephraem Syrus against heretics are important for the knowledge of his system. Cf. Bardesanes Gnosticus Syrorum primus hymnologus, comm. historico-theol. quam scripsit Aug. Hahn. Lips. 1819. 8. C. Kuehner Astronomiae et astrologiae in doctrina Gnosticorum vestigia, p. i. Bardesanis Gnostici numina astralia. Hildburghusae. 1833. 8.

[3] Tatianus d. Apologet v. Dr. H. A. Daniel. Halle. 1837. S. 253. Respecting his εὐαγγέλιον διὰ τεσσάρων, see Credner's Beiträge zur Einl. in d. biblisch. Schriften, i. 437.

[4] These names, as well as the appellation Docetae, certainly designate a heresy, which was common to many parties; but they appear to have been specially given to the followers of Tatian, because a particular sect-name for them does not appear.

[1] Particular sources: Tertull. adv. Marcionem libri v.—(Pseudo-) Origenis διάλογος περὶ τῆς εἰς θεὸν ὀρθῆς πίστεως s. dial. contra Marcionitas (ed. J. R. Westein. Basil. 1674. 4). The credibility of the fathers respecting Marcion is too much doubted by H. Rhode Prolegomenorum ad quaestionem de Evangelio Apostoloque Marcionis denuo instituendam, cap. i.–iii. Vratislav. 1834. 4. See on the other side Ch. E. Becker Examen crit. de l'évangile de Marcion. Première partie. Strasbourg. 1837. 4. Works on the subject: Neander gnost. Syst. S. 276, ff. Aug. Hahn Diss. de gnosi Marcionis antinomi. Regiomonti. 4. (Two Christmas programmes of 1820 and 1821.) Ejusd. Antitheses Marcionis Gnostici liber deperditus, nunc quoad ejus fieri potuit restitutus. Regiom. 1823. 8. The same author's das Evangelium Marcion's in seiner ursprünglichen Gestalt, nebst dem vollständigsten Beweise dargestellt, dass es nicht selbstständig, sondern ein verstümmeltes und verfälschtes Lucas-Evangelium war. Königsb. 1823. 8. Compare my review in the Hall. A. L. Z. Oct. 1823, S. 225, ff.

the Demiurgus, according to the principles of strict justice, either condemnation or at most a limited happiness—to free them, I say, from such a yoke, Christ suddenly descended into Capernaum with the appearance of a body, and proclaimed to men the good deity hitherto unknown. Those who believe in Christ, and lead a new, holy life, from love to the good deity, will be blessed with happiness in his heavenly kingdom, while others are left to the strict justice of the Demiurgus. Marcion required of the perfect Christians a strictly ascetic life, abstinence from marriage, avoidance of all earthly pleasures, and restriction to a few simple articles of diet. But all the disciples of this school were not "faithful" (fideles); many continued catechumens for a long time. Marcion's gospel (*εὐαγγέλιον*) was that of Luke, mutilated according to his system; in addition to which, he used ten of the Pauline epistles (*ὁ ἀπόστολος*), not, however, without corruption.[2] In a work entitled "Antitheses," he endeavored to prove the different characters of Judaism and Christianity, by means of positions from both set over against one another.

Respecting metaphysical relations, as far as they do not affect the moral interests of men, no declarations are found in Marcion. His disciples, therefore, borrowed such principles partly from the Syrian Gnostics, partly, like *Apelles*, from the Valentinians, so that the school of Marcion was afterward divided into many branches.[3]

[2] The adulteration was first doubted by J. S. Semler in his paraphrasis epist. ad Galatas. Hal. 1779. 8. Prolegom. § 2, 3. Then by Chr. F. J. Loeffler Diss., qua Marcionem Pauli epistolas et Lucae evangel. adulterasse dubitatur Traj. ad. Viadr. 1788. 4 (reprinted in the Commentatt. theol. coll. a Kuinoel et Ruperti, vol. i. p. 180, ss.). On this the hypothesis was built upon by H. Corodi, J. G. Eichhorn, and J. E. Ch. Schmidt. Of another opinion is Dr. Gratz krit. Untersuchung über Marcion's Evangel. Tübing. 1818. 8. Comp. especially Hahn's Evang. Marcion's, &c. Ejusd. Diss. de canone Marcionis. P. i. Regiom. 1824. 4. Ejusd. Evang. Marcionis ex auctoritate vett. monumentorum descriptum, in J. C. Thilo Cod. apocryph. N. T. i. 401. Becker, l. c.

[3] Even Rhodon (ap. Euseb. v. 13) says: *Διὰ τοῦτο καὶ παρ' ἑαυτοῖς ἀσύμφωνοι γεγόνασιν, ἀπὸ γὰρ τῆς τούτων ἀγέλης Ἀπελλῆς μὲν—μίαν ἀρχὴν ὁμολογεῖ·—ἕτεροι δὲ, καθὼς καὶ αὐτὸς ὁ ναύτης Μαρκίων, δύο ἀρχὰς εἰσηγοῦνται·—ἄλλοι δὲ πάλιν ἀπ' αὐτῶν ἐπὶ τὸ χεῖρον ἐξοκείλαντες, οὐ μόνον δύο, ἀλλὰ καὶ τρεῖς ὑποτίθενται φύσεις.* Comp. A. L. Z. l. c. S. 226, ff. The thoroughly practical tendency of the true Marcionites is expressed particularly in what Apelles said to Rhodon (l. c.): *Μὴ δεῖν ὅλως ἐξετάζειν τὸν λόγον, ἀλλ' ἕκαστον ὡς πεπίστευκε διαμένειν. σωθήσεσθαι γὰρ τοὺς ἐπὶ τὸν ἐσταυρωμένον ἠλπικότας ἀπεφαίνετο, μόνον ἐὰν ἐν ἔργοις ἀγαθοῖς εὑρίσκωνται. τὸ δέ πάντων ἀσαφέστατον ἐδογματίζετο αὐτῷ πρᾶγμα—τὸ περὶ τοὺ θεοῦ.* Thus it is not incredible that, as Tertullian, de Praescr. c. 30, relates, Marcion at the close of his life wished to return to the catholic Church. He may have perceived that the practical interests of Christianity were more

§ 48.

MONTANISTS AND ALOGI.

Defenders of the Montanists are: Nic. Rigaltius in praefat. ad Tertulliani opp. Arnold's Kirchen und Ketzerhistorie, Th. 1, Bd. 2, K. 4, § 44. Gottlieb Wernsdorf de Montanistis saeculi secundi haereticis comm. Gedani. 1751. 4. More impartial are: Mosheim de rebus Christ. ante Const. M. p. 410, ss. Walch's Ketzerhist. i. 611. Full of peculiar combinations is: Dr. F. C. A. Schwleger's der Montanismus u. d. christl. Kirche d. 2ten Jahrhund. Tübingen. 1841. 8.—M. Merkel's hist. krit. Aufklärung der Streitigkeit der Aloger über die Apokalypsis. Frankf. u. Leipz. 1782. 8. F. A. Heinichen de Alogis, Theodotianis atque Artemonitis. Lips. 1829. 8. Dr. L. Lange's Gesch. und Lehrbegriff der Unitarier. Leipzig. 1831. S. 156.—Neander's K. G. i. ii. 877.

As a peculiar impress is stamped on Christianity in all countries by the national character, so also in Phrygia it could not but experience the influence of the popular tendency to a sensuous, enthusiastic worship of deity. The doctrines of supernatural gifts of the Spirit,[1] the renunciation of the earthly, and the millennial reign, were susceptible of such development.[2] These subjects appear to have been peculiar favorites in Phrygia very early,[3] where the oppression of persecution, and opposition to the speculations of the Gnostics, may have accelerated their one-sided development. Accordingly, *Montanus*,[4] at *Pepuza* (about 150),[5] in an ecstatic state,[6] began to announce, that the

injured than promoted by his opposition, and that they had a sufficient support even in the catholic Church.

[1] As they continued among the Christians even after Justin and Irenaeus. Schwegler, S. 94.

[2] As far as Montanism proceeded out of these doctrines, Schwegler designates it as a development of Ebionitism, which had been prevalent up to that time in the church; but he arbitrarily understands by Ebionitism the entire Jewish basis of Christianity.

[3] Ex. gr. Philip and his daughters in Hierapolis (to whom the Montanist Proculus against Caius refers, Euseb. iii. 31), Papias (§ 35, not. 7).

[4] According to Didymus de Trin. lib. iii. cap. penult., he had formerly been ἱερεὺς εἰδώλου. Jerome Ep. 27 ad Marcellam calls him abscissum et semivirum. He appears accordingly to have been a priest of Cybele, a circumstance which must have become of importance in respect to his conception of Christianity. Schwegler, S. 243, would have Montanus to be a mythic personage, but younger contemporaries, the anonymous writer in Euseb. v. 17, and Apollonius, l. c. v. 18, mention him.

[5] According to Apollonius, who wrote under Commodus, Montanus had appeared forty years before (apud. Euseb. v. 18). This is the oldest and safest account. Eusebius in his Chronicle places the commencement of Montanism in the year 172; Epiphanius Haer. li. 33, in the year 135; and Haer. xlviii. 1, in the year 157.

[6] Following the example of Philo, Justin and Athenagoras also consider the state of prophetic inspiration as an ecstasis. The former (Coh. ad. Graecos p. 9) compares the prophets during it to a lyre which is touched by the Holy Spirit as the plectrum; the

Paraclete had imparted itself to him for the purpose of giving the church its manly perfection. Two fanatical women, *Maximilla* and *Priscilla*, attached themselves to him as prophetesses; and thus a party was formed, the adherents of which, vainly presuming that they alone possessed the last revelations of the Spirit,[7] as *πνευματικοί*, full of spiritual arrogance, looked down upon other Christians as *ψυχικοί*. These new prophets did not wish to alter the received creed, but to confirm it anew.[8] On the other hand they prescribed new and rigorous fasts,[9] forbade second marriage, attributed extraordinary value to celibacy and martyrdom, manifested profound contempt for every thing earthly, and taught that incontinence, murder, and idolatry, though they did not exclude from the grace of God (*Tertullian de pudic.* c. 3), shut a person out forever from the church.[10] At the same time, they were not afraid to proclaim

latter (Legat. p. 9) compares them in the same sense to a flute (Schwegler, S. 100). In like manner the Holy Spirit, through Montanus, describes the ecstasy of the Montanist prophets, apud Epiphan. Haer. xlviii. 4: *Ἰδοὺ ἄνθρωπος ὡσεὶ λύρα, κἀγὼ ἵπταμαι ὡσεὶ πλῆκτρον· ὁ ἄνθρωπος κοιμᾶται, κἀγὼ γρηγορῶ· ἰδοὺ κύριός ἐστιν ὁ ἐξιστάνων καρδίας ἀνθρώπων, καὶ διδοὺς καρδίας ἀνθρώποις*. Tertullian calls the ecstasis which he explains by amentia (lib. de anima c. 11) Sancti Spiritus vis, operatrix prophetiae. That which he describes bears a striking resemblance to magnetic clairvoyance (l. c. c. 9): Est hodie soror apud nos revelationum charismata sortita, quas in Ecclesia inter dominica solemnia per ecstasin in spiritu patitur, conversatur cum angelis, aliquando etiam cum Domino, et videt et audit sacramenta, et quorundam corda dinoscit, et medicinas desiderantibus submittit, &c. A similarity also to the speaking with tongues among the Corinthians (1 Cor. xiv.) can not but be noticed. Schwegler, S. 83.

[7] The Montanists had not an uninterrupted series of prophets. The Anon. ap. Euseb. v. 17, wrote in the 14th year after the death of Maximilla, and says that since then none had boasted of the gift of prophecy. But in the time of Tertullian there was again a Montanist prophetess in Africa, see note 6.

[8] So Tertullian adv. Praxeam, c. 2, § 13, appeals to the prophecies of the Paraclete in favor of his doctrine of the Trinity. Schwegler, S. 8.

[9] At first there were two yearly, each one continuing a week, with the exception of Saturday and Sunday (Tertullian de jejun, c. 15) afterward three (Hieron. Ep. 27 ad Marcellam), in case the third be not the usual ecclesiastical quadragesimal fast, as Valesius ad Euseb. v. 18, and Schwegler suppose, and which, therefore, Tertullian has not reckoned.

[10] Tertull. de virginibus velandis c. 1: Regula quidem fidei una omnino est, sola immobilis, et irreformabilis.—Caetera jam disciplinae et conversationis admittunt novitatem correctionis:—cum propterea Paracletum miserit Dominus, ut, quoniam humana mediocritas omnia semel capere non poterat, paulatim diregeretur et ordinaretur et ad perfectum perduceretur disciplina ab illo vicario Dei Spiritu Sancto. From John xvi. he draws the conclusion that the administratio Paracleti is, quod disciplina dirigitur, quod scripturae revelantur, quod intellectus reformatur, quod ad meliora proficitur. Just as in nature every thing ripens gradually, sic et justitia—primo fuit in rudimentis, natura deum metuens. Dehinc per legem et prophetas promovit in infantiam. Dehinc per Evangelium efferbuit in juventutem. Nunc per Paracletum componitur in maturitatem. Compare the other writings of Tertullian in defense of single monastic institutions, de exhortat. castitatis, de monogamia, de fuga in persecutione, de jejunio adv. Psychicos, de pudicitia.

aloud the end of the world, and the millennial reign as near at hand.[11] By this means they excited first of all dislike and opposition in their vicinity. Their opponents were satisfied for the most part with disputing their prophetic gift as not genuine;[12] and on this ground alone they were excluded from communion by the churches of Asia Minor.[13] Some, however, led on by opposition to farther inquiry, began to reject even the support which Montanism had in the doctrines of the church at that time.[14] In this respect, those afterward called *Alogi* went

[11] Maximilla announced, according to Euseb. v. 16, 8: *Πολέμους ἔσεσθαι καὶ ἀκαταστασίας*, according to Epiph. Haer. xlviii. 2: *Ὅτι μετ' ἐμὲ προφῆτις οὐκέτι ἔσται, ἀλλὰ συντέλεια.* Priscilla or Quintilla apud Epiph. Haer. xlix. 1: *Ἐν ἰδέᾳ γυναικὸς ἐσχηματισμένος ἐν στολῇ λαμπρᾷ ἦλθε πρός με Χρίστὸς, καὶ ἐνέβαλεν ἐν ἐμοὶ τὴν σοφίαν, καὶ ἀπεκάλυψέ μοι, τουτονὶ τὸν τόπον (τὴν Πεπούζην) εἶναι ἅγιον, καὶ ὧδε τὴν Ἱερουσαλὴμ ἐκ τοῦ οὐρανοῦ κατιέναι.* A collection of Montanist predictions in Wernsdorf de Montanistis, § 4, others besides in Didymus Alex. de trinit. lib. iii. cap. penult. Cf. Tertullian. de resurrect. carnis, c. 63: At enim Deus omnipotens—effundens in novissimis diebus de suo spiritu in omnem carnem, in servos suos et ancillas, et fidem laborantem resurrectionis carnalis animavit, et pristina instrumenta manifestis verborum et sensuum luminibus ab omni ambiguitates obscuritate purgavit.—(Spiritus sanctus) jam omnes retro ambiguitates et quas volunt parabolas, aperta atque perspicua totius sacramenti praedicatione discussit, per novam prophetiam de paracleto inundantem. The same, in a fragment in the Praedestinatus haer. 26: Hoc solum discrepamus (a Psychicis), quod secundas nuptias non recipimus, et prophetiam Montani de futuro judicio non recusamus. How fanatical they were in their expectations may be seen in Tertullian. de spectaculis, c. 30: Quale autem spectaculum in proximo est, adventus Domini jam indubitati, jam superbi, jam triumphantis!—Quid admirer, quid videam, ubi gaudeam, ubi exultem, tot spectans reges, qui in coelum recepti nuntiabantur, cum ipso Jove et ipsis suis testibus in imis tenebris congemiscentes! item praesides, persecutores dominici nominis, saevioribus quam ipsi contra Christianos saevierunt flammis insultantibus liquescentes! praeterea sapientes illos philosophos coram discipulis suis una conflagrantibus erubescentes, &c. Tertullian's lost work, de spe fidelium, mentioned by him, adv. Marcion iii. c. 24, was exclusively devoted to this object.

[12] Eusebius, iv. 27, and v. 16-19, mentions the polemic writings of Claudius Apollinaris, Miltiades, an anonymous person (who, according to Jerome, Cat. c. 37 and 39, was Rhodon; by several modern authors incorrectly supposed to be Asterius Urbanus, cf. Wernsdorf de Montanistis, p. 4), Apollonius, and Serapion, and gives extracts from the last three.—The *ἔκστασις* of the Montanist prophets gave special offense. It was asserted in opposition that all *ἔκστασις* is an inspiration proceeding from demons, cf. Anonymus apud Euseb. v. 16, 3, and Miltiadis *σύγγραμμα περὶ τοῦ μὴ δεῖν προφήτην ἐν ἐκστάσει λαλεῖν* (Euseb. v. 17, 1). Tertull. adv. Marcion. iv. c. 22: Defendimus, in causa novae prophetiae, gratiae ecstasin, id est amentiam, convenire. In spiritu enim homo constitutus, praesertim cum gloriam Dei conspicit, vel cum per ipsum Deus loquitur, necesse est excidat sensu, obumbratus scilicet virtute divina: de quo inter nos et Psychicos quaestio est. According to Jerome, Cat. c. 53, Tertullian wrote de ecstasi libros vi.

[13] Anonymus ap. Euseb. v. 16, 5.

[14] To this number appear to belong the rejecters of Chiliasm, of whom Irenaeus, v. c. 31, says: Quidam ex his, qui putantur recte credidisse, supergrediuntur ordinem promotionis justorum,—haereticos sensus in se habentes; and 32: Transferunter quorundam sententiae ab haereticis sermonibus, &c. Farther, the rejecters of the Apocalypse, of whom Dionysius Alex. *περὶ ἐπαγγελιῶν* apud Euseb. vii. c. 25, says: *Τινές μὲν οὖν τῶν πρὸ ἡμῶν ἠθέτησαν καὶ ἀνεσκεύασαν πάντῃ τὸ βιβλίον κ. τ. λ.*, who went so far as to hold Cerinthus to be the author.

farthest, who not only denied the continuance of charismata in the church, and millennarianism, but rejected the Apocalypse, and even the gospel of John.[15]

This very mode of opposition, against which, even in Asia Minor, *Melito*, bishop of Sardis, presented himself as an antagonist,[16] contributed largely, perhaps, to procure Montanism many friends in the west.[17] The western churches never declared themselves exclusively in favor of any of the conflicting parties in Asia;[18] and thus the principles of the Montanists, which were, after all, only the carrying out of orthodox doctrines, could be diffused there,[19] without the necessity of a Montanist party separating itself from the rest of the church.

The Montanists in Asia, who had their peculiar ecclesiastical

[15] Compare especially the above cited work of Merkel, whom also Olshausen (Aechtheit der vier canon. Evang. S. 254, ff.) follows. Irenaeus, iii. c. 11: Alii vero, ut donum Spiritus frustrentur, quod in novissimis temporibus secundum placitum patris effusum est in humanum genus illam speciem non admittunt, quae est secundum Joannis evangelium, in qua Paracletum se missurum Dominus promisit; sed simul et evangelium et propheticum repellunt Spiritum. Infelices vere, qui pseudoprophetae [leg. pseudoprophetas] quidem esse volunt, prophetiae vero gratiam ab ecclesia repellunt; similia patientes his, qui propter eos, qui in hypocrisi veniunt, etiam a fratrum communicatione se abstinent. Datur autem intelligi, quod hujusmodi neque apostolum Paulum recipiant. In ea enim epistola, quae est ad Corinthios, de propheticis charismatibus diligenter locutus est, et scit viros et mulieres prophetantes. Per haec igitur omnia peccantes in Spiritum Dei, in irremissibile incidunt peccatum. The name Ἄλογοι appears first in Epiphanius Haer. li. adv. Alogos, comp. especially the passage cap. 33, according to the following correction of the text (so Merkel, S. 35, ff.): Ἐνοικησάντων γὰρ τούτων ἐκεῖσε (εἰς Θυάτειρα) καὶ τῶν κατὰ Φρύγας, [οἱ μὲν] δίκην λύκων ἁρπαξάντων τὰς διανοίας τῶν ἀκεραίων πίστων, μετήνεγκαν τὴν πᾶσαν πόλιν εἰς τὴν αὐτῶν αἵρεσιν· οἱ δὲ ἀρνούμενοι τὴν Ἀποκάλυψιν, τοῦ λόγου τούτου εἰς ἀνατροπὴν, κατ' ἐκεῖνον καιροῦ ἐστρατεύοντο.

[16] To this subject sppear to belong, his works περὶ πολιτείας, καὶ προφητῶν, λόγος περὶ προφητείας, περὶ τῆς ἀποκαλύψεως Ἰωάννου (comp. Lücke's Einl. in d. Offenb. Johan. S. 289). They were naturally very welcome to the Montanists, and hence Melito was praised by Tertullian even in the Montanist period of the latter's life (Hieronymus, in Catal. c. 24: Hujus elegans et declamatoriam ingenium laudans Tertullianus in septem libris, quos scripsit adversus ecclesiam pro Montano, dicit, eum a plerisque nostrorum prophetam putari). But it does not follow from this, as Danz, Heinichen, and Schwegler (S. 223) would have it, that Melito was a Montanist. See Piper's Melito, in the theol. Stud u. Krit. 1838, i. 86.

[17] Cf. Irenaeus above, not. 14 and 15. The account of Praedestinatus, Haer. 26: Scripsit contra eos (Montanistas) librum s. Soter Papa urbis is highly improbable, and is perhaps nothing more than a conclusion from Tertullian adv. Prax. c. 1, praecessorum ejus auctoritates defendendo.

[18] The Christians of Lyons and Vienne had added to their account of the persecution they endured, a judgment on the controversy with the Montanists, which Eusebius unfortunately omitted, (Euseb. v. 3, 2): Ἐκθέμενοι καὶ τῶν παρ' αὐτοῖς τελειωθέντων μαρτύρων διαφόρους ἐπιστολὰς, ἃς ἐν δεσμοῖς ἔτι ὑπάρχοντες τοῖς ἐπ' Ἀσίας καὶ Φρυγίας ἀδελφοῖς διεχάραξαν· οὐ μὴν ἀλλὰ καὶ Ἐλευθέρῳ, τῷ τότε Ῥωμαίων ἐπισκόπῳ, τῆς τῶν ἐκκλησιῶν εἰρήνης ἕνεκα πρεσβεύοντες. Comp. the Praefatio of Maranus to the Opp. of the Apologists, P. iii. c. 14, § 2, ss.

[19] An instance below, § 53, note 39.

constitution,[20] continued down to the tenth century.[21] Besides their usual names, *Montanistae*, *Cataphryges* (οἱ κατὰ Φρύγας), other appellations were applied to them, some of which may have referred to particular sections, while others were mere names of derision.[22]

THIRD CHAPTER.

INTERNAL HISTORY OF THE CATHOLIC CHURCH.

§ 49.

The internal development of the orthodox church depended in a great degree on its external relations, the persecution of the heathen, and the attacks of heretics. Christian literature had been confined till now solely to didactic and admonitory letters, seven of which in this period also, proceeded from the pious *bishop of Corinth*, *Dionysius*;[1] but now it developed itself in other directions, particularly in defending Christianity against the heathen, and in combating heretics. It was corrupted, however, by a mass of spurious writings. Those external relations could not be without an influence on the formation of doctrines, since they led of necessity to the exhibition and support of particular dogmas. In like manner, ecclesiastical usages received from them a more definite character. At the same time, it was a circumstance of great importance, that several Platonic philosophers had now come over to Christianity, by

[20] Hieronym. Ep. 27, ad Marcellam: Habent primos de Pepusa Phrygiae Patriarchas: secundos, quos appellant Cenonas: atque ita in tertium, i. e., paene ultimum locum Episcopi devolvuntur.

[21] The last laws against them proceeded from Justinian, A.D. 530 and 532, see Cod. lib. i. tit. 5, l. 18-21.

[22] Quintilliani, Priscillianistae, Ἀρτοτυρῖται (see on this Noesselt de vera aetate scriptt. Tertulliani, § 47), Tascodrugitae (πασσαλορυγχῖται). The following are mere corruptions of words: Tascodrocitae (Cod. Theod. xvi. 5, 10), Ascodrogitae (Philastr. c. 75), Ascodrogi (Theodos. jun. novella iii. in fine), Ascodrutae, Ascodrupitae, (which, however, are enumerated among the Marcosians by Theodoret Haer. fab. comp. i. 10), Ascitae (Augustin de Haer. 62), cf. Gothofredus ad novellam iii. Theodosii jun. From such corrupted names, however, new heresies have been etymologically deduced.

[1] Ἐπιστολαὶ καθολικαί to the churches of Rome, Nicomedia, Gnossus, Athens, Lacedaemon, Gortyna, and in Pontus. Fragments are given by Euseb. ii. 25, iv. 23.

means of whom Platonism continued to gain more friends among the Christians. Besides, the Greek language was almost the only ecclesiastical tongue.[2] Although several Latin translations of the Bible were made,[3] yet the writers even of the western church wrote in Greek. But Christian ideas had a freshness of life only in the people who spoke the language of the New Testament. In the west, they merely received what the east produced.

§ 50.

APOLOGIES FOR CHRISTIANITY AGAINST HEATHEN AND JEWS.

J. A. Fabricii Delectus argumentorum et syllabus scriptorum, qui veritatem relig. christ. asseruerunt. Hamb. 1725. 4. H. G. Tzschirner's Geschichte der Apologetik. Leipz. Th. 1. 1805. 8. The same author's Fall des Heidenthums, i. 202, ff. A list of apologetic works may be found in Danz de Eusebio Caes. p. 93, ss.—The best edition of all the apologists is given by Prudentius Maranus. Paris. 1742. fol.

The pressure of circumstances gave rise at this time to various apologies for Christianity, which are supposed in part to have been presented to emperors;[1] the first to Hadrian (126), in Athens, by *Quadratus* and *Aristides* (*Euseb.* iv. 3; *Hieron. Catal.* 19, 20).[2] The first apology of *Justin Martyr* († 166)[3]

[2] At this period originated the custom of the Roman Church, which continued down to the middle ages, of requiring those who were to be baptized to recite the creed first in Greek then in Latin. Cf. Edm. Martene de antiquis eccl. ritibus, ed. 2, t. i. p. 88; A. Gavanti Thesaurus sacr. rituum ed. G. M. Meratus, t. i. p. 42, and the other works quoted in Walchii Biblioth. symbol. vetus, p. 57.

[3] Augustin. de Doctr. christ. ii. 11: Qui scripturas ex hebraica lingua in graecam verterunt, numerari possunt, latini autem interpretes nullo modo. Ut enim cuivis primis fidei temporibus in manus venit codex Graecus, et aliquantulum facultatis sibi utriusque linguae habere videbatur, ausus est interpretari. C. 16: In ipsis autem interpretationibus Itala caeteris praeferatur; nam est verborum tenacior cum perspicuitate sententiae. L. van Ess Gesch. d. Vulgata. Tübingen. 1824. 8.

[1] First doubted by Bayle, s. v. Athenagore. Semler Introduction to Baumgarten's Polemik, ii. 43. Henke, i. 129. In opposition to these doubts, see Tzschirner Fall des Heidenthums, i. 233. Semisch Justin d. M. i. 63.

[2] The apology of Quadratus was still extant in the beginning of the seventh century (Photius, cod. 162). That Ado (about 860) had the apology of Aristides does not follow from his Martyrolog. ad d. 5, Nov. (cf. J. Dallaei de scriptis, quae sub Dionysii Areop. et Ignatii Antioch. nominibus circumferunter, p. 90, s.): and the account of de la Guilletière Athènes anciennes et nouvelles, Paris. 1676, p. 146, of its being still preserved at that time in the monastery of Medelli at Athens, is as little worthy of credit as all the rest of the narrative of this pretended journey (see on it Spon Voyage d'Italie et Dalm. Chateaubriand's Travels from Paris to Jerusalem, part i. p. 33.

[3] According to Dr. A. Stieren in Illgen's Zeitschr. für d. hist. Theol. 1842, i. 21, the year

is addressed to Antoninus Pius (138 or 139), the second and smaller belongs, according to the usual opinion, to Marcus Aurelius and Lucius Verus (161–166).[4] The other apologetic writings designed for the heathen, which are attributed to him, are of more doubtful origin.[5] To Marcus Aurelius, *Athenagoras* addressed his πρεσβεία περὶ Χριστιανῶν;[6] and *Melito*, bishop of Sardis,[7] and *Claudius Apollinaris*, bishop of Hierapolis,[8] their apologies since lost (*Euseb.* iv. 26; *Hieron. Cat.* 24, 26). At the same time appeared the apology of *Miltiades* (*Euseb.* v. 17; *Hieron. Cat.* 39); of *Theophilus*, bishop of Antioch, in three books to *Autolycus*;[9] and of *Tatian*, the λόγος πρὸς Ἕλληνας.[10] On the other hand, the epistle to Diognetus is older.[11] Per-

of Justin's death was 161. On the credibility of the ancient narrative of Justin's death, see Semisch Justin d. M. i. 16.

[4] So according to Pagi, Tillemont, Mosheim, and Semisch. On the other hand, according to Valesius, Longuerue, and Neander (K. G. i. ii. 1144), it was also written under Antoninus Pius. F. Chr. Boll, in Illgen's Zeitschrift, 1842, iii. 3, assumes that both apologies made up originally one whole, which may have been written about 150. Apologiam primam ed. J. E. Grabe. Oxon. 1700, alteram H. Hutchin. ib. 1703, utramque C. Gu. Thalemann. Lips. 1755. J. W. J. Braunius. Bonnae. 1830. 8. In the older editions before Grabe the smaller apology is incorrectly placed first. Comp. Justin d. Märtyrer von C. Semisch. 2 Thle. Breslau. 1840–42. 8. J. C. Th. Otto de Justini M. scriptis et doctrina comm. Jenae. 1841. 8. S. Justini philosophi et M. opera rec., prolegomenis, adnotatione ac versione instruxit indicesque adjecit J. C. Th. Otto. 2 tomi. Jenae. 1842. 8.

[5] The λόγος παραινετικὸς πρὸς Ἕλληνας was first denied to be Justin Martyr's by Oudinus, lately by Herbig (comm. de scriptis, quae sub nomine Justini phil. et mart. circumferuntur. Vratisl. 1833), Arendt (krit. Untersuchungen uber die Schriften Just. d. M. in the Tübinger theol. Quartalschr. 1834, ii. 256), and Moehler (Patrologie, i. 224), but it is defended by Semisch, i. 105. The λόγος πρὸς Ἕλληνας is pronounced unauthentic by most writers, even by Semisch, i. 163. On the fragment περὶ ἀναστάσεως opinions are divided. Herbig, l. c. p. 74, endeavors at great length to prove the spuriousness; Semisch, i. 146, the genuineness of it. There is also great difference of sentiment respecting the work περὶ μοναρχίας. Herbig, p. 69 and Semisch, i. 167, regard it as spurious. In the mean time, however, all these works belong to this period.

[6] I. e. supplicatio, not legatio, according to Mosheim de vera aetate apologetici, quam Ath. pro Christ. scripsit, diss. (in dissert. ad hist. eccl. pertin. vol. i. p. 269, ss.) written in the year 177. ed. J. G. Lindner. Longosal. 1774, ejusd. curae posteriores in Athen. ibid. 1775. 8. Περὶ ἀναστάσεως τῶν νεκρῶν ed. L. A. Rechenberg. Lips. 1685. 8. Th. Adr. Clarisse Comm. de Athenagorae vita et scriptis et ejus doctrina de relig. christ. Lugd. Bat. 1819. 8 Guerike de schola Alexandrina, i. 21, ii. 6, 50, 97, 403.

[7] Melito, by licentiate F. Piper in the theol. Stud. u. Krit. 1838, i. 54.

[8] The fragments in the Catenae, especially in the Σειρὰ εἰς τὴν Ὀκτάτευχον—ἐπιμελείᾳ Νικηφόρου τοῦ Θεοτόκου, Lips. 1772, 2 voll. fol., attributed to one Apollinaris, deserve a closer examination. The most of them belong to Apollinaris, bishop of Laodicea in the fourth century; but many might be referred even to the bishop of Hierapolis. See Schwegler's Montanismus, S. 203.

[9] Ed. J. C. Wolf. Hamb. 1724. 8, translated by M. W. F. Thienemann. Leipzig. 1834.

[10] Ed. Worth. Oxon. 1700. 8. Tatianus d. Apologet, von Dr. H. Daniel. Halle. 1837. 8.

[11] Formerly attributed falsely to Justin. On the other side, see Tillemont, Mémoires, ii. 371; C. D. a Grossheim de epist. ad Diognetum comm. Lips. 1828. 4to, who fixes the

haps also *M. Minucius Felix*, a lawyer in Rome, who defended Christianity in a dialogue called *Octavius*,[12] belongs to the age of Marcus Aurelius, and is in this view the oldest Latin apologist. On the contrary, the *διασυρμὸς τῶν ἔξω φιλοσόφων* of *Hermias* must be placed in a later period.[13]

All these defenders aim principally to show the groundlessness of the accusations adduced against Christianity,[14] the reasonableness of it contrasted with the absurdity and immorality of heathenism, and the nothingness of the heathen deities.[15] While they refer to the fact that Christianity agrees with the wisest philosophers, they represent the latter again as having drawn their wisdom from the Old Testament. In proving the divine origin of Christianity, they attach special value to the predictions of the Old Testament, the miracles of Jesus and the apostles, the miraculous powers continuing among Christians,[16]

epistle about the year 132; Moehler (Schriften u. Aufsätze, i. 19. Patrologie, i. 154), who places it in the time of Trajan; Semisch (Justin d. M. i. 172), who puts it in the time of Justin. It has been published with an introduction and remarks by Lic. G. Böhl in Opuscula Patram selecta. Berol. 1826. p. i. p. 109, ss.

[12] In the three only known MSS., and in the older editions, it appears as the eighth book of Arnobius (lib. octavus, a misunderstanding of the title Octavius). It has been very frequently published, among other forms cum integris Woweri, Elmenhorstii, Heraldi, et Rigaltii notis, aliorumque hinc inde collectis, ex rec. Jac. Gronovii. Accedunt Cyprianus de Idol. van. et Jul. Firm. Maternus. Lugd. Bat. 1709. 8. J. G. Lindner. Longosalissae. 1760, ed. ii. emend. 1773. 8, translated with an introduction and remarks by J. G. Russwurm, Hamburg. 1824. 4, newly published, explained and translated by Dr. J. H. B. Lubkert. Leipzig. 1836. 8, ad fidem codd. regii et Bruxell. rec. ed. D. Muralto. Turici. 1836. 8. The earlier more prevailing opinion that Minucius belongs to the interval between Tertullian and Cyprian, 220–230, rested particularly on the testimony of Jerome, who Catal. cap. 53, says: Tertullianus presbyter nunc demum primus post Victorem et Apollonium Latinorum ponitur; and first mentions Minucius in cap. 58. On the other hand, Blondell (de l'Eucharište, p. 119), Dallaeus (against whom see Bayle's Dictionn. s. v. Fronton), J. D. ab Hoven (in Lindner's second edition, p. 261), Oelrichs (de scriptt. eccl. lat., p. 24) place him, from internal grounds, and because, cap. 9, Fronto (see § 40, note 2) is mentioned as still living, in the age of Marcus Aurelius. This view has been lately adopted by Kestner (Agape, S. 356), H. Meirer (comm. de Minucio Felice, Turici. 1824. 8), Russwurm, and v. Muralt l. c., and even Tzschirner (Fall des Heidenthums, i. 219), who had formerly defended the old opinion in the Geschichte der Apologetik, i. 279.

[13] Ed. Worth (annexed to his Tatian), J. Ch. Dommerich, Hal. 1764. 8. Gu. F. Menzel, Lugd. Batt. 1840. 8. According to Menzel, the work belongs to the fifth century.

[14] Ch. F. Eisenlohr, Argumenta ab apologetis saec. ii. ad confirmandam rel. christ veritatem usurpata. Tubing. 1797. 4. (recus. in Pottii Sylloge comm. theologg. vol. ii. p. 114, ss.) Tzschirner's Fall des Heidenth. i. 237, ff. F. Wurm, in Klaiber's Studien der evangel. Geistlichkeit Wirtemberg's, i. ii. 1. Semisch, Justin d. M. ii. 56.

[15] Here an important preparation had been already made for them by the heathen philosophers, especially by the view that had originated with Euhemerus, that the deities were dead men. See above § 13, note 5. Cf. Athenagoras, Leg. p. 35. Theoph. ad Autol. p. 75, 70. Minucius Felix, Oct. c. 21, appeals expressly to Euhemerus.

[16] Tholuck on the miracles of the Catholic Church in his verm. Schriften, i. 28.

the rapid spread of Christianity, and the steadfastness of its followers in times of persecution. They demand, in fine, the same protection for Christians, which other philosophical sects enjoyed.

In defense of Christianity against Judaism, there appeared at this period two dialogues; under Hadrian the ἀντιλογία Παπίσκου καὶ Ἰάσονος, which was afterward, but certainly without reason, ascribed to *Aristo of Pella;*[17] and διάλογος πρὸς Τρύφωνα Ἰουδαῖον, of *Justin Martyr.*[18]

§ 51.

COMBATING OF HERETICS—CATHOLIC CHURCH—CANON OF THE NEW TESTAMENT.

The writings of the earlier opponents of heretics, the work of *Justin Martyr* against all heresies;[1] the books of *Agrippa Castor* (about 135), who wrote against Basilides; of *Justin Martyr*, *Theophilus* of *Antioch*, *Rhodon*, *Philip* bishop of Gortyna, and of *Modestus*, who all wrote against Marcion; of *Miltiades*, *Claudius Apollinaris*, *Serapion* bishop of Antioch, and *Apollonius*, who all wrote against the Montanists, have been lost, except a few fragments. On the other hand, we still possess the work of *Irenaeus* (bishop of Lyons, 177–202), ἔλεγχος καὶ ἀνα-

[17] This ἀντιλογία or διάλεξις, cited so early as by Celsus (Orig. c. Cels. iv. p. 199), is lost, and even of the Latin translation of one Celsus the Praef. ad Vigilium (in opp. Cypriani) is alone extant. Maximus († 662) comm. ad. Dionys. Areop. de myst. theol. c. 1, is the first who names Ariston as the author, but adds that Clement of Alex., Hypotyposeon, lib. vi., ascribes this dialogue to Luke. On the other hand, Hieron., in quaest. in Genes., says: In principio fecit Deus coelum et terram. Plerique existimant, sicut in altercatione quoque Iasonis et Papisci scriptum est—in Hebraeo haberi: in filio fecit Deus coelum et terram. Quod falsum esse ipsius rei veritas comprobat. A Hebrew Jewish-Christian like Aristo could never have written that. The Chron. paschale ad Olymp. 228, ann. 2, says that Ἀπελλῆς and Ἀρίστων (probably ὁ Πελλαῖος Ἀρίστων) handed over an apology to Hadrian. Since this is not found, it seems that some conjectured they discovered it in the dialogue in question.

[18] Ed. Sam. Jebb. Lond. 1719. 8. The doubts of its authenticity raised by C. G. Koch (Justini M. cum Tryph. Jud. dial.—suppositionis convictus. Kilon. 1700. 8. The controversial writings on the subject, see in Walchii Bibl. patrist. p. 216), Wetstein, Semler (Wetst. prolegg. in N. T. ed. Semler, p. 174), and S. G. Lange (Gesch. d. Dogmen d. christl. Kirche, i. 137), have been answered by G. Münscher, an dialogus cum Tryphone Justino M. recte adscribatur. Marb. 1799. 4 (also in Commentatt. theoll. edd. Rosenmüller, Fuldner et Maurer, i. ii. 184), and Semisch, Justin d. M. i. 75.

[1] Σύνταγμα κατὰ πασῶν τῶν γεγενημένων αἱρέσεων cited by himself, Apol. i. c. 26.

τροπὴ τῆς ψευδωνύμου γνώσεως in five books, but for the most part merely in an old Latin translation.[2]

The discordant opinions of the philosophical schools (*αἱρέσεις*), which were to have been removed by the one, certain, Christian truth, had again appeared within the province of Christianity at this period, in the different parties. The ecclesiastical idea of *αἵρεσις* was formed from thence chiefly by the characteristics of separation from the unity implied in the true church, and of insecure subjective presumption;[3] but since Christian truth appeared not likely to be mistaken without blame attaching to the individuals, it was generally believed that the sources of the heresies must be looked for in nothing else than self-will, pride, ambition, desire of rule, and want of love.[4] To the opposition presented to unbelievers, in which alone the church had been engaged till the present time,[5] there was now added the other opposition directed against heretics. By this means the idea of *the church* being farther developed, there arose the expression *ἐκκλησία καθολική*,[6] i. e., *the only*

[2] Ed. J. E. Grabe. Oxon. 1702. fol. Renatus Massuet. Paris. 1710. fol. Lib. iii. capita 1–4, in graecum sermonem restituta, criticisque annotationibus illustrata per H. Gu. J. Thiersch in the theol. Stud. u. Krit. 1842. ii. 512. A. Stieren de Irenaei adv. haer. operis fontibus, indole, doctrina, et dignitate. Gottingae. 1836. 4. In favor of the authenticity, in regard to which doubts were raised by Semler (especially in the dissert. in Tertull., in his edition of Tertullian, vol. v. p. 261, 300, ss.), see Chr. G. F. Walch de *αὐθεντίᾳ* librorum Iren. adv. haer. in nov. commentariis soc. scient. Gotting. t. v. p. 1. Respecting the fragments of Irenaeus found by Pfaff in the Turin Library (S. Irenaei fragmenta anecdota ed. Chr. M. Pfaff, Hagae Com. 1715. 8, reprinted in his Syntagma dissertt. theoll. Stuttgard. 1720. 8. p. 573), whose authenticity was doubted, chiefly from a Catholic bias, by Scip. Maffei, see Rothe's Anfänge d. christl. Kirche, i. 361.

[3] Irenaeus, v. 20, 2: Tales sunt omnes haeretici—semper quaerentes et nunquam verum invenientes. Tertullianus de Praescr. 6: Haereses dictae graeca voce ex interpretatione electionis, qua quis, sive ad instituendas, sive ad suscipiendas eas utitur. Nobis vero nihil ex nostro arbitrio inducere licet, sed nec eligere quod aliquis de arbitrio suo induxerit. Apostolos Domini habemus auctores, qui nec ipsi quidquam ex suo arbitrio, quod inducerent, elegerunt, sed acceptam a Christo disciplinam fideliter nationibus adsignaverunt. Comp. Rothe's Anf. d. christl. Kirche, i. 563.

[4] Irenaeus, iii. 3, 2: Confundimus omnes eos, qui quoquo modo, vel per sibiplacentiam vel vanam gloriam, vel per caecitatem et malam sententiam praeterquam oportet colligunt. iv. 33, 7: Ἀνακρινεῖ δὲ τοὺς τὰ σχίσματα ἐργαζομένους, κενοὺς ὄντας τῆς τοῦ θεοῦ ἀγάπης, καὶ τὸ ἴδιον λυσιτελὲς σκοποῦντας, ἀλλὰ μὴ τὴν ἕνωσιν τῆς ἐκκλησίας. Clemens Alex. Strom. vii. p. 887: Αἱ φίλαυται καὶ φιλόδοξοι αἱρέσεις.

[5] See above § 30.

[6] The name first appears in Ignatii epist. ad Smyrn. c. 8, and in the epist. Eccl. Smyrn. de martyr. Polycarpi ap. Eusebius, iv. c. 15, § 1. Tertull. de Praescr. haeret. c. 20: (Apostoli) ecclesias apud unamquamque civitatem condiderunt, a quibus traducem fidei et semina doctrinae caeterae exinde ecclesiae mutuatae sunt, et quotidie mutuantur, ut ecclesiae fiant. Ac per hoc et ipsae apostolicae deputantur, ut soboles apostolicarum ecclesiarum. Omne genus ad originem suam censeatur necesse est: itaque tot ac tantae

church,[7] out of which there is no salvation,[8] which is destined to become universal, and has already given practical proof of this destination.[9]

The writers against heresies certainly went into the peculiar doctrines of the heretics, for the purpose of refuting them; but they particularly combated their pretensions in alleging that their doctrine was the genuine doctrine of Christ and the apostles, by proving, from the agreement of the apostolic churches, that the doctrine of the apostles had been preserved without alteration in the catholic church.[10] The common interest which

ecclesiae una est, illa ab apostolis prima, ex qua omnes. Sic omnes prima, et omnes apostolicae, dum una; omnes probant unitatem. The words can not refer to a formal founding of the catholic Church, as is assumed by J. E. Ch. Schmidt in his Bibliothek für Krit. u. Exegese, ii. 1. The idea first arose, and it afterward gave expression to itself by degrees, in the constitution and ordinances of the church. Comp. Münscher's Dogmengeschichte, ii. 379. Twesten's Dogmatik, i. 109. Rothe's Anf. d. christl. Kirche, i. 555.

[7] In opposition to the sects which designed to form churches also, but which were only schools, διατριβαί (Clem. Alexandrin. Strom. vii. p. 889), ἀνθρώπιναι συνηλύσεις (l. c. p. 898).

[8] Irenaeus, iv. 26, 2. Haeretici alienum ignem afferentes ad altare Dei, i.e., alienas doctrinas, a coelesti igne comburentur, quemadmodum Nadab et Abiud. iv. 33, 7. Tertull. de Baptismo, c. 8. Ecclesia est arca figurata (cf. 1 Petr. iii. 20, 21).

[9] Irenaeus, i. 10, 1. Ἡ ἐκκλησία καθ' ὅλης οἰκουμένης ἕως περάτων τῆς γῆς διεσπαρμένη. Cf. i. 10, 2, iii. 11, 8, iv. 36, 2, v. 20, 1.

[10] Tertullian. de Praescr. haer. c. 21. Quid autem (apostoli) praedicaverint, id est, quid illis Christus revelaverit: et hic praescribam, non aliter probari debere, nisi per easdem ecclesias, quas ipsi apostoli condiderunt, ipsi eis praedicando, tam viva (quod aiunt) voce, quam per epistolas postea. Si haec ita sunt, constat proinde omnem doctrinam, quae cum illis ecclesiis apostolicis, matricibus et originalibus fidei conspiret, veritati deputandam. C. 36. Percurre ecclesias apostolicas, apud quas ipsae adhuc cathedrae apostolorum suis locis praesident, apud quas authenticae literae eorum recitantur, sonantes vocem et repraesentantes faciem uniuscujusque. Proxima est tibi Achaia? habes Corinthum. Si non longe es a Macedonia, habes Philippos, habes Thessalonicenses. Si potes in Asiam tendere, habes Ephesum. Si autem Italiae adjaces, habes Romam, unde nobis quoque auctoritas praesto est. Ista quam felix ecclesia, cui totam doctrinam apostoli cum sanguine suo profuderunt, ubi Petrus passioni dominicae adequatur, ubi Paulus Johannis exitu coronatur, ubi apostolus Johannes, posteaquam in oleum igneum demersus nihil passus est, in insulam relegatur. Videamus quid dixerit, quid cum Africanis quoque ecclesiis contesserarit, &c. (Comp. Neander's Antignosticus, S. 313, ff.) In the west the Roman was the only apostolic church. Hence they naturally appealed to it there chiefly, Iren. iii. 3. Traditionem itaque apostolorum in toto mundo manifestatem, in omni ecclesia adest perspicere omnibus, qui vera velint videre, et habemus annumerare eos, qui ab apostolis instituti sunt Episcopi in ecclesiis et successores eorum usque ad nos, qui nihil tale docuerunt.—Sed quoniam valde longum est, in hoc tali volumine omnium ecclesiarum enumerare successiones; maximae et antiquissimae et omnibus cognitae a gloriosissimis duobus apostolis, Petro et Paulo, Romae fundatae et constitutae ecclesiae eam, quam habet ab apostolis, traditionem et annunciatam hominibus fidem, per successiones episcoporum pervenientem usque ad nos, indicantes confundimus omnes eos, qui quoquo modo—praeterquam oportet colligunt. Ad hanc enim ecclesiam propter potentiorem (so all MSS., Massuet was the first that altered it into potiorem) principalitatem

was felt against heretics, and the feeling of oneness, strengthened by the idea of *a catholic church*, led to a closer union, of which the apostolic churches were regarded as a center, though without the existence of an external subordination among them.

As the heretics appealed to apostolic traditions, and even used pretended apostolic writings in justification of their sentiments, the attention of catholic Christians was by this means more directed to the genuine writings of the apostles scattered among them. The apostolic epistles had always been read in the places to which they were addressed, and in the neighboring congregations; but there was no universally received collection of the

necesse est omnem convenire ecclesiam, hoc est, eos qui sunt undique fideles, in qua semper ab his, qui sunt undique, conservata est ea, quae est ab apostolis, traditio. Irenaeus wishes to prove that the doctrine of the catholic Church is apostolic, preserved by the successors of the bishops ordained by the apostles. Since it is too prolix to point out this connection of the apostles with all churches, he wishes to limit his proof to the Church of Rome alone, and finally to represent the doctrine of the Roman Church as necessarily agreeing with that of the whole remaining church. Necesse est (*ἀνάγκη*) must not be confounded with oportet (*δεῖ*): the former expresses a natural necessity, the latter an obligation, duty. Potentior is *ἱκανώτερος* (cf. iii. 3, 3: potentissimas literas, *ἱκανωτάτην γραφήν*), principalitas probably *πρωτεία* (iv. 38, 3: *πρωτεύει μὲν ἐν πᾶσιν ὁ θεός*, principalitatem quidem habebit in omnibus Deus). Accordingly the Greek text may have been: *πρὸς ταύτην γὰρ τὴν ἐκκλησίαν διὰ τὴν ἱκανωτέραν πρωτείαν ἀνάγκη πᾶσαν συμβαίνειν τὴν ἐκκλησίαν, τούτ' ἔστι τοὺς πανταχόθεν πιστοὺς, ἐν ᾗ ἀεὶ τοῖς πανταχόθεν συντετήρηται ἡ ἀπὸ τῶν ἀποστόλων παράδοσις.* "For with this church must the whole church, i.e., the believers of every place, agree, of course, on account of its more important pre-eminence." A pre-eminence belonged to all apostolic churches; to the Roman Church a more important pre-eminence, on account of its greatness, and its having been founded by the two most distinguished apostles. In the rest of the sentence, I conjecture that the Latin translator was mistaken. Supposing the Greek text to have stood as above, the translator took the words *τοῖς πανταχόθεν* for *ὑπὸ τῶν παντ.* which was certainly grammatically correct; "in which the apostolic tradition was always preserved by believers from all places," referring to the many foreigners who constantly belonged to the Roman community, and who afforded a warrant for the uninterrupted agreement of the Roman tradition with that of the rest of the church. But Irenæus meant to say: "in which the apostolic tradition has been always preserved in fellowship with the believers of all places." Hence he adduces, in what follows, Clement's epistle to the Corinthians, and Polycarp's abode at Rome, as proofs of this uninterrupted fellowship. Many other explanations may be seen in Grabe and Massuet on the passage. Paulus, in Sophronizon, Heft 3. 1819. S. 141, ff. On the other side, Th. Katerkamp über den Primat. d. Apost. Petrus u. s. Nachfolger. Münster. 1820. S. 30, ff. Griesbach de potentiore Eccl. Rom. principalitate comm. Jen. 1778 (reprinted in his Opuscula Academ. ed. Gabler, vol. ii. p. 136, ss.) H. W. J. Thiersch in the Theol. Stud. u. Krit. 1842, ii. 525. J. Wolff in Rudelbach's and Guerike's Zeitschrift für d. luther. Kirche, 1842, iv. 7. Thiersch reads *πᾶσαν ἐκκλησίαν*, and refers to it the *ἐν ᾗ* in the sense: unaquaeque alia ecclesia idem testabitur de traditione apostolorum, dummodo in ea a fidelibus, cujusvis sint loci, pure conservata sit tradita ab apostolis veritas. On the contrary, Neander, K. G. i. i. 349, says that the expression, qui undique sunt fideles, is not synonymous with omnis ecclesia, if the latter mean "every single church," but only if it mean "every church," i.e., all churches: and in the single churches the tradition was not preserved ab iis qui sunt undique.

evangelical narratives, and the existing ones (comprehending, besides our canonical gospels, also *the gospel of the Hebrews*, that *of the Egyptians*, &c.) served in their spheres only for private use. After the churches had now come into closer connection, they communicated to one another, in their common interest against heretics, the genuine apostolic writings; and thus the canon began to be formed, in the first half of the second century, in two parts (τὸ Εὐαγγέλιον or τὸ Εὐαγγελικόν, and ὁ Ἀπόστολος or τὸ Ἀποστολικόν), although in the different congregations there continued to be other writings, which were valued almost, if not altogether, as much as those which were universally received (ὁμολογούμενα, ἐνδιάθηκα).[11]

Instigated by the bold speculation of the Gnostics, which sought to lay an entirely foreign basis under Christianity, the catholic Christians began to establish as the unalterable *regula fidei*,[12] that summary of doctrine which could be shown, as well in the consciousness of all Christian communities, as also in the apostolic writings, to be the essential basis of Christianity, and which must remain untouched by, and be necessarily laid at the foundation of, every speculation. Accordingly, even the originally simple statements of the baptismal confession (πίστις, σύμβολον)[13] were secured by additions against misunderstandings and perversions; but as the different wants of the church required this or the other doctrine to be made more clear, or to be emphatically exhibited, so the form of the baptismal confession became longer or shorter in different places.[14]

[11] Compare my essay über die Entstehung und die frühesten Schicksale der schriftl. Evangelien. Leipz. 1818. S. 142, ff. 179, ff. 190, ff.

[12] ὁ κανὼν ἐκκλησιαστικός Clemens Alex. Strom. vi. p. 803. ὁ κανὼν τῆς ἀληθείας, Iren. i. 1, in fine. This rule of faith, therefore, as it is found, for example, in Irenaeus, i. 10, 1, was not a formula handed down to the apostles (cf. Tertull. de Praescr. c. 13: Haec regula a Christo, ut probabitur, instituta; particularly c. 21: Omnis doctrina, quam ecclesiae ab apostolis, apostoli a Christo, Christus a Deo accepit; c. 37: Regula, quam ecclesia ab apostolis, apostoli a Christo, Christus a Deo traditit), and was not placed above the interpretation of Scripture (for according to Tertullian de Corona militis, c. 3, it was a Catholic fundamental principle, etiam in traditionis obtentu exigenda est auctoritas scripta), as was asserted, after Lessing's example, by Delbrück, Philip Melancthon der Glaubenslehrer. Bonn. 1826. S. 17, ff. 145, ff. Comp. on the authority of Holy Scripture, and its relation to the rule of faith, three theological epistles to Herr Prof. Delbrück by Sack, Nitzsch, and Lücke. Bonn. 1827.

[13] Maximus Turinensis (about 430) homil. in Symb. p. 239: Symbolum tessera est et signaculum, quo inter fideles perfidosque secernitur. These additions are referred to by Tertull. de Corona mil. c. 3: Ter mergitamur, amplius aliquid respondentes, quam Dominus in Evangelio determinavit.

[14] Cf. Ch. G. F. Walchii biblioth. symbolica vetus. Lemgov. 1770. 8. Dr. Aug. Hahn,

§ 52.

DEVELOPMENT OF DOCTRINES—SPURIOUS WRITINGS.

A speculative treatment of Christian doctrine was generally indispensable, if Christianity was to be accessible to the philosophical culture of the times, and it was rendered unavoidable by the progress of the Gnostics. It could only proceed from Platonism, which of all philosophical systems stood the nearest to Christianity.[1] While many Platonic philosophers were brought over to Christianity by this internal relation, they received the latter as the most perfect philosophy,[2] and retained, with their philosophical mantle,[3] their philosophical turn of mind also. They set out with these positions, both that the Logos has constantly communicated to men the seeds of truth,[4] and that the truth taught by Plato was derived from Moses and the prophets.[5] The arbitrary mode of interpretation then current fur-

Bibliothek d. Symbole u. Glaubensregeln d. apostolischkatholischen Kirche. Breslau. 1842. 8. P. Kingii Hist. symboli apostolici ex angl. serm. in latinum translata (by Olearius). Basil. 1750. 8. J. R. Kiesling Hist. de usu symbolorum. Lips. 1753. 8.

¹ (Stäudlin) de philosophiae Platonicae cum doctrina religionis judaica et christiana cognatione (a Göttingen Whitsuntide programm. 1819. 4.) D. C. Ackermann, das Christliche im Plato u. in d. platon. Philosophie. Hamburg. 1835. D. F. Chr. Baur, das Christliche des Platonismus, od. Sokrates u. Christus, in the Tübinger Zeitschr. f. Theologie, 1837. Heft 3.

² Comp. the remarkable history of Justin Martyr's conversion in his Dial. c. Tryph. c. 3, ss.: which he, c. 8, concludes with the words, *ταύτην μόνην εὕρισκον φιλοσοφίαν ἀσφαλῆ τε καὶ σύμφορον. Οὕτως δὴ καὶ διὰ ταῦτα φιλόσοφος ἐγώ.* Thus Christianity is designated by Melito, ap. Euseb. iv. 26, 4, as *ἡ καθ' ἡμᾶς φιλοσοφία.* Keilii Opusc. ii. 463.

³ *τρίβων, τριβώνιον*, pallium. C. G. F. Walchii Antiquitates pallii philosophici vett. Christian. Jen. 1746. 8. Semisch, Justin d. M. i. 23.

⁴ Justin M. Apol. ii. c. 13: *Οὐκ ἀλλότριά ἐστι τὰ Πλάτωνος διδάγματα τοῦ Χριστοῦ, ἀλλ' οὐκ ἔστι πάντη ὅμοια, ὥσπερ οὐδὲ τὰ τῶν ἄλλων, Στωϊκῶν τε, καὶ ποιητῶν, καὶ συγγραφέων· ἕκαστος γάρ τις ἀπὸ μέρους τοῦ σπερματικοῦ θείου λόγου τὸ συγγενὲς ὁρῶν καλῶς ἐφθέγξατο.—ὅσα οὖν παρὰ πᾶσι καλῶς εἴρηται, ἡμῶν τῶν Χριστιανῶν ἐστί.* According to c. 10, Christ was apprehended *καὶ ὑπὸ Σωκράτους ἀπὸ μέρους· λόγος γὰρ ἦν και ἔστιν ὁ ἐν παντὶ ὤν.*

⁵ So the Jews had already asserted, Josephus contra Apion, ii. 8; and Aristobulus apud Clemens Alex. Strom. i. p. 410, according to whom Plato is said to have employed even the Old Testament in an ancient version. The heathen philosopher Numenius (l. c.) goes so far as to say: *Τί ἐστι Πλάτων, ἢ Μωσῆς ἀττικίζων.* The fathers derived all that was true and good in the Greek poets and philosophers from Moses and the prophets, Justin Apolog. i. 44, ii. 13. Coh. ad Graecos, c. 14. Theoph. ad Autol. ii. 37. Because they found most truth in Plato, they represented him especially as drawing from this source. Hence he is called in Clemens Alex. Paed. ii. p. 224, *ὁ ἐκ Μωσέως φιλόσοφος*, Strom. i. p.

nished them with the means of proving their views even from numerous passages of the Old Testament, which they could use, indeed, only in the Septuagint version.[6] Thus, then, they over-valued even the actual agreement of Plato with Christianity,[7] and believed that they found many a Platonic idea in the latter, which in reality they themselves had first introduced into it.[8] The Christian philosophers of this time with which we are acquainted are *Aristides*, *Justin Martyr*, *Athenagoras*, *Tatian*, *Pantaenus* (§ 39), and *Maximus* (about 196).[9] The questions with which they were chiefly occupied were the same as those the Gnostics set out with, respecting the origin of evil, and its overthrow by Christ, but especially regarding the divine in Christ.[10] They found the latter designated by John as the *λόγος*, and in the development of this idea took Philo for their guide; since, like him, they thought the Logos was met with every where in the Old Testament.[11] Most difficult were the

321, ὁ ἐξ 'Εβραίων φιλόσοφος. Cf. H. N. Clausen Apologetae Eccl. christ. antetheodosiani Platonis ejusque philosophiae arbitri. Havn. 1817. 8. p. 187, ss. Clausen himself attributes to Plato (p. 196) some knowledge of the law and of the doctrine of the Hebrews.

[6] Comp. Justini Coh. ad Graecos, c. 20, ss. According to c. 29, Plato is said to have borrowed his doctrine of ideas from the passages Exod, xxv. 9, 40; xxvi. 30, incorrectly understood; and according to c. 31, to have imitated Ezek. x. 18 in the winged chariot of Zeus, &c. See Clausen, l. c. p. 191.

[7] Justin finds in him the doctrine of the Son and Spirit; Clemens Alex. Strom. v. p. 710, the whole Christian Trinity. Clausen, l. c. p. 84.

[8] The Platonism of the fathers was perceived even by Petavius, Dogm. Theol. t. ii. lib. i. c. 3. The dogma of the Trinity was derived from it by (Souverain) le Platonisme devoilé, ou Essai touchant le verbe Platonicien. Cologne (Amsterdam). 1700 (translated by Löffler: Versuch über d. Platonismus d. KV. Züllichau. 1782. 2te Aufl. 1792. 8), and Jo. Clericus epist. crit. et eccles. (Artis criticae, vol. iii. Amst. 1712), especially ep. vii. and viii. On the other side, the matter was exaggerated by the Jesuit Baltus, Défense des saints pères, accusés de Platonisme. Paris. 1711. 4. Keil, de doctoribus veteris ecclesiae, culpa corruptae per platonicas sententias theologiae liberandis, comm. xxii. in ej. opusc. t. ii. Lips. 1821, has copiously given the literature of the subject.

[9] Fragments of his work περὶ τῆς ὕλης are preserved in Eusb. Praep. Ev. vii. 22.

[10] Ch. D. A. Martini Vers. einer pragm. Gesch. des Dogma v. d. Gottheit Christi in den vier ersten Jahrh. Th. 1. Rostock. 1800. 8. Dr. F. Chr. Baur's die christl. Lehre v. d. Dreieinigk. u. Menschwerdung Gottes (3 Th. Tübingen. 1841–43. 8). i. 163. G. A. Meier's Lehre v. d. Trinität in ihrer hist. Entwickelung (Hamburg u. Gotha. 1844), i. 53.

[11] So particularly Proverbs viii. 22, ss., but also Psalm xxxiii. 6; xlv. 1; civ. 24. The doctrine that God created the world by the Logos was also naturally sought for in the Mosaic account of creation, where it was found: Gen. i. 1, ἐν ἀρχῇ is equivalent to διὰ τῆς ἀρχῆς, and ἀρχή is, according to Proverbs viii. 22, ἡ σοφία or ὁ λόγος. Theophil. ad Autol. ii. 10, 13. Tatian. Apol. c. 7. Tertull. adv. Hermog. c. 20. This explanation was repeated in later times by Origenes, Hom. 1, in Gen., Basilius, Hom. 1, in Hexaëmeron, Augustinus de Genesi lib. i. Others believed that they might venture to presuppose the existence of that doctrine as still more obviously contained in the Hebrew original, which they did not know. According to the Altercatio Iasonis et Papisci, the original expressed

questions respecting the essence of the Logos in relation to the Father, and his agency in relation to that of the Holy Spirit. With regard to the former point, there were several who did not assume a personal distinction of the Logos from the Father.[12] But the view was more generally adopted, that he was a divine person, less than the Father, and produced out of his essence according to the will of the latter.[13] Agreeably to both views, the Logos was the God working all in the finite, so that no room appeared to be left for the agency of the Holy Spirit. Accordingly, the doctrine of the Holy Spirit still remained entirely undeveloped.[14] These speculations, whose object was to

this idea, in filio fecit Deus coelum et terram (see above § 50, note 17); or as others believed (Tertull. adv. Praxeam c. 5), in principio Deus fecit sibi filium.

[12] Justini Dial. c. Tryph. c. 128: *Γινώσκω τινὰς—λέγειν,—ἄτμητον καὶ ἀχώριστον τοῦ πατρὸς ταύτην τὴν δύναμιν* [*τὸν λόγον*] *ὑπάρχειν, ὅνπερ τρόπον τὸ τοῦ ἡλίου φασὶ φῶς ἐπὶ γῆς εἶναι ἄτμητον καὶ ἀχώριστον ὄντος τοῦ ἡλίου ἐν τῷ οὐρανῷ· καὶ ὅταν δύσῃ, συναποφέρεται τὸ φῶς· οὕτως ὁ πατὴρ, ὅταν βούληται, λέγουσι, δύναμιν αὐτοῦ προπηδᾷν ποιεῖ· καὶ ὅταν βούληται, πάλιν ἀναστέλλει εἰς ἑαυτόν. Κατὰ τοῦτον τὸν τρόπον καὶ τοὺς ἀγγέλους ποιεῖν αὐτὸν διδάσκουσιν.* Athenagoras represents the Logos in the very same way as Philo to be the manifest God, not personally distinct from the concealed deity. Legat. c. 9: *Ἔστιν ὁ υἱὸς τοῦ θεοῦ ὁ λόγος τοῦ πατρός ἐν ἰδέᾳ καὶ ἐνεργείᾳ· πρὸς αὐτοῦ* [leg. *αὐτὸν*] *γὰρ καὶ δι' αὐτοῦ πάντα ἐγένετο· ἑνὸς ὄντος τοῦ πατρὸς καὶ τοῦ υἱοῦ, ὄντος δὲ τοῦ υἱοῦ ἐν πατρὶ, καὶ πατρὸς ἐν υἱῷ, ἑνότητι καὶ δυνάμει πνεύματος· νοῦς καὶ λόγος τοῦ πατρὸς ὁ υἱὸς τοῦ θεοῦ. Εἰ δὲ δι' ὑπερβολὴν συνέσεως σκοπεῖν ὑμῖν ἔπεισιν, ὁ παῖς τὶ βούλεται, ἐρῶ διὰ βραχέων, πρῶτον γέννημα εἶναι τῷ πατρὶ, οὐχ ὡς γενόμενον (ἐξ ἀρχῆς γὰρ ὁ θεὸς, νοῦς ἀΐδιος ὢν, εἶχεν αὐτὸς ἐν ἑαυτῷ τὸν λόγον, ἀϊδίως λογικὸς ὢν), ἀλλ' ὡς, τῶν ὑλικῶν ξυμπάντων ἀποίου φύσεως καὶ γῆς ὀχείας* [leg. *ἀχρείας*] *ὑποκειμένωι δίκην, μεμιγμένων τῶν παχυμερεστέρων πρὸς τὰ κουφότερα ἐπ' αὐτοῖς, ἰδέα καὶ ἐνέργεια εἶναι προελθών. Συνᾴδει δὲ τῷ λόγῳ καὶ τὸ προφητικὸν πνεῦμα· Κύριος γάρ, φησιν, ἔκτισέ με ἀρχὴν ὁδῶν αὐτοῦ εἰς ἔργα αὐτοῦ* (Proverbs viii. 22). *καί τοι καὶ αὐτὸ τὸ ἐνεργοῦν τοῖς ἐκφωνοῦσι προφητικῶς ἅγιον πνεῦμα ἀπόῤῥοιαν εἶναι φαμὲν τοῦ θεοῦ, ἀποῤῥέον καὶ ἐπαναφερόμενον, ὡς ἀκτῖνα ἡλίου.* Comp. Münscher's Dogmengesch. i. 407. Martini, l. c. S. 54. Clarisse comm. de Athenagora p. 98. Others supposed that the divine in Christ was exactly one with the Father: Scriptor xii. Testam. Patriarch: *Κύριος ὁ θεὸς μέγας τοῦ Ἰσραὴλ φαινόμενος ἐπὶ γῆς ὡς ἄνθρωπος* (Sym. 6). *τὸ πάθος τοῦ Ὑψίστου* (Lev. 4). Cf. Nitzsch de Testam. xii. Patriarch. p. 29. Epiphanius Haer. lxii. c. 2, respecting the Evangelium Aegyptiorum: *Ἐν αὐτῷ πολλὰ τοιαῦτα ὡς ἐν παραβύστῳ μυστηριωδῶς ἐκ προσώπου τοῦ Σωτῆρος ἀναφέρεται, ὡς αὐτοῦ δηλοῦντος τοῖς μαθηταῖς, τὸν αὐτὸν εἶναι Πατέρα, τὸν αὐτὸν εἶναι Υἱὸν, τὸν αὐτὸν εἶναι ἅγιον Πνεῦμα*, comp. Neander's Antignosticus, S. 467, ff. According to Baur (Lehre v. d. Dreieinigkeit, i. 173) even Irenaeus had no definite ideas of the Son as personally distinct from the Father. On the other side see Licentiate L. Duncker's des h. Irenaeus Christologie. Göttingen. 1843. 8. S. 32.

[13] Semisch, Justin d. M. ii. 277. Tertull. adv. Praxeam c. 8 calls this emanation *προβολὴν* veritatis in opposition to the false *προβολαῖς* of the Gnostics. The Montanists believed this latter theory confirmed by the revelation of the Paraclete, l. c. c. ii. 8, 13. The Alogi, on the contrary, rejected the doctrine of the Logos. Epiphan. Haer. li. L Lange's Gesch. u. Lehrbegriff d. Unitarier vor der nicänischen Synode. Leipz. 1831. S. 156.

[14] Accordingly, the fathers of this period represent the prophets to be inspired sometimes by the Logos, sometimes by the Holy Spirit, and call both the Logos and the Holy

fathom the depths of the Godhead, might certainly at first wound the feelings of many, and Irenaeus openly expresses his disapprobation of the inconsiderate curiosity they manifest;[15] but, on the other hand, ecclesiastical orthodoxy could still endure diversities in doctrine and customs, which did not injure the religious basis of Christianity.[16]

Notwithstanding this philosophical tendency, and although in other respects the Pauline mode of surveying Christianity predominated, yet *the millennarianism* of the Jewish Christians,[17] presenting a sensuous counterpoise to the external pressure of persecution, which had been announced in so many apocalyptic writings,[18] and for which the reputation of John (Apoc. xx. 4–6; xxi.) and his peculiar followers, afforded a warrant—this millennarianism became the general belief of the time, and met with almost no other opposition than that given by the Gnostics,[19]

Spirit σοφίαν, &c. Semisch, Justin. d. M. ii. 305, 311. Note.—Theophilus ad. Autol. ii. 23, gives the members of the Divine triad thus: Θεός, ὁ λόγος αὐτοῦ, καὶ ἡ σοφία αὐτοῦ, and says, ii. 14: Ἔχων οὖν ὁ θεὸς τὸν ἑαυτοῦ λόγον ἐνδιάθετον ἐν τοῖς ἰδίοις σπλάγχνοις, ἐγέννησεν αὐτὸν μετὰ τῆς ἑαυτοῦ σοφίας ἐξερευξάμενος πρὸ τῶν ὅλων. Τοῦτον τὸν λόγον ἔσχεν ὑπουργὸν τῶν ὑπ' αὐτοῦ γεγενημένων καὶ δι' αὐτοῦ τὰ πάντα πεποίηκεν.—Οὗτος οὖν ὢν πνεῦμα θεοῦ, καὶ ἀρχὴ, καὶ σοφία, καὶ δύναμις ὑψίστου κατήρχετο εἰς τοὺς προφήτας, καὶ δι' αὐτῶν ἐλάλει τὰ περὶ τῆς ποιήσεως τοῦ κόσμου, καὶ τῶν λοιπῶν ἁπάντων. οὐ γὰρ ἦσαν οἱ προφῆται, ὅτε ὁ κόσμος ἐγίνετο, ἀλλὰ ἡ σοφία ἡ ἐν αὐτῷ οὖσα ἡ τοῦ θεοῦ, καὶ ὁ λόγος ὁ ἅγιος αὐτοῦ ὁ ἀεὶ συμπαρὼν αὐτῷ. Here the Holy Spirit is the immanent wisdom of God, but the Logos the revealed God, who emanated from the Father.

[15] Irenaeus adv. Haer. ii. 28, 6: Si quis itaque nobis dixerit: quomodo ergo Filius prolatus a Patre est? dicimus ei, quia prolationem istam, sive generationem, sive nuncupationem, sive adapertionem, aut quolibet quis nomine vocaverit generationem ejus inenarrabilem existentem, nemo novit, non Valentinus—neque Angeli—nisi solus qui generavit Pater, et qui natus est Filius. Inenarrabilis itaque generatio ejus cum sit, quicunque nituntur generationes et prolationes enarrare, non sunt compotes sui, ea quae inenarrabilia sunt, enarrare promittentes. Quoniam enim ex cogitatione et sensu verbum emittitur, hoc utique omnes sciunt homines: non ergo magnum quid invenerunt, qui emissiones excogitaverunt, neque absconditum mysterium, si id quod ab omnibus intelligitur, transtulerunt in unigenitum Dei Verbum: et quem inenarrabilem et innominabilem vocant, hunc, quasi ipsi obstetricaverint, primae generationis ejus prolationem et generationem enunciant, adsimilantes eum hominum verbo emissionis (λόγῳ προφορικῷ). Comp. Duncker's des h. Iren. Christologie, S. 36.

[16] This doctrinal latitudinarianism is shown in the fact of the Nazarene Hegesippus, being recognized as orthodox in the churches of Corinth and Rome, these churches agreeing with his orthodoxy. See above § 43, note 4. The same latitudinarianism may be seen in Justin's declaration respecting those who denied the personality of the Logos (above note 12), in the estimation in which the Shepherd of Hermas was held. (See § 35, note 4, § 36, note 3).

[17] (H. Corodi's) krit. Geschichte des Chiliasmus, 3 Bde. Zürich. 1781–83. 8.

[18] See above § 31.

[19] To the question of Trypho, whether Justin really believes in a millenial reign, Justin replies. Dial. cum Tryph. c. 80: 'Ωμολόγησά σοι καὶ πρότερον, ὅτι ἐγὼ μὲν καὶ ἄλλοι

and subsequently by the antagonists of the Montanists.[20] The thousand years' reign was represented as the great Sabbath which should begin very soon; or, as many supposed, after the lapse of the six thousand years of the world's age,[21] with the first resurrection, and should afford great joys to the righteous.[22] Till then the souls of the departed were to be kept in the under world,[23] and the opinion that they should be taken up to heaven immediately after death, was considered a gnostic heresy.[24]

In reference to the advancement of the various Christian interests, and in like manner also to the confirmation of those developments of doctrine already mentioned, *the spurious literature* which had arisen and continually increased among Jews and Christians, was of great importance. The Christians made use of such expressions and writings as had already been falsely attributed by Jews, from partiality to their religion, to honored persons of antiquity,[25] and altered them in part to suit their own

πολλοὶ ταῦτα φρονοῦμεν, ὡς καὶ πάντως ἐπίστασθε (you Jews), τοῦτο γενησόμενον· πολλοὺς δ' αὖ καὶ τῶν [μὴ ?] τῆς καθαρᾶς καὶ εὐσεβοῦς ὄντων Χριστιανῶν γνώμης τοῦτο μὴ γνωρίζειν ἐσήμανά σοι. Τοὺς γὰρ λεγομένους μὲν Χριστιανοὺς, ὄντας δὲ ἀθέους καὶ ἀσεβεῖς αἱρεσιώτας, ὅτι κατὰ πάντα βλάσφημα καὶ ἄθεα καὶ ἀνόητα διδάσκουσιν, ἐδήλωσά σοι.—Εἰ γὰρ καὶ συνεβάλετε ὑμεῖς τισὶ λεγομένοις Χριστιανοῖς, καὶ τοῦτο μὴ ὁμολογοῦσιν, ἀλλὰ καὶ βλασφημεῖν τολμῶσι τὸν θεὸν Ἀβραὰμ, καὶ τὸν θεὸν Ἰσαὰκ, καὶ τὸν θεὸν Ἰακὼβ, οἳ καὶ λέγουσι μὴ εἶναι νεκρῶν ἀνάστασιν, ἀλλὰ ἅμα τῷ ἀποθνήσκειν τὰς ψυχὰς αὐτῶν ἀναλαμβάνεσθαι εἰς τὸν οὐρανὸν, μὴ ὑπολάβητε αὐτοὺς Χριστιανούς.—Ἐγὼ δὲ, καὶ εἴ τινές εἰσιν ὀρθογνώμονες κατὰ πάντα Χριστιανοὶ, καὶ σαρκὸς ἀνάστασιν γενήσεσθαι ἐπιστάμεθα, καὶ χίλια ἔτη ἐν Ἱερουσαλὴμ οἰκοδομηθείσῃ καὶ κοσμηθείσῃ καὶ πλατυνθείσῃ, ὡς οἱ προφῆται Ἰεζεκιὴλ (xxxvii. 12, ss.) καὶ Ἡσαΐας (lxv. 17, ss.) καὶ οἱ ἄλλοι ὁμολογοῦσιν. Dallaeus, Münscher, Münter, Schwegler, and others, have regarded the insertion of μὴ as necessary in the first sentence. On the other side see Semisch, Justin d. M. ii. 468, and Otto ad h. l.

[20] See above § 48, note 14.

[21] Apoc. xx. 4–6. This calculation was based on Ps. xc. 4. Cf. Barnabas, c. 15. Justin. Dial. c. Tryph. c. 81. Iren. v. 23; and is also found in the Rabbins of this period, see Corodi's Gesch. d. Chiliasmus, i. 328.

[22] See the descriptions in Justin. Dial. c. Tryph. c. 80, after Is. lxv. 17, ss. Iren. v. 25–36. Tertull. adv. Marc. iii. 24.

[23] In the Greek fathers Ἅιδης (the שְׁאוֹל of the Hebrews), cf. Tertull. de Anima, c. 7: Si quid tormenti sive solatii anima praecerpit in carcere seu diversorio inferum; in igni vel in sinu Abrahae: probata erit corporalitas animae. Adv. Marcion, iv. c. 34: Eam itaque regionem sinum dico Abrahae, etsi non coelestem, sublimiorem tamen inferis, interim refrigerium praebituram animabus justorum, donec consummatio rerum resurrectionem omnium plenitudine mercedis expungat. A copious description of Ἅιδης, χωρίον ὑπόγειον, ἐν ᾧ φῶς κόσμου οὐκ ἐπιλάμπει, see in Hippolytus adv. Platon. (Opp. ed. Fabricius, i. 220). Cf. J. A. Dietelmaieri Hist. dogm. de desc. Christi ad inf. ed. 2. Altorf. 1762. 8, c. i. ii.

[24] Justinus above, note 19, Tertull. below § 53, note 40.

[25] See above § 31. Thus, verses were falsely attributed to Orpheus, respecting the unity of God, in which even Abraham and Moses appeared (L. C. Valckenaeri diatr. de Aristobulo Judaeo, ed. J. Luzac. Lugd. Bat. 1806. 4, p. 13; Lobeck, Aglaophamus, i. 438, ss.), to Linus, Homer, and Hesiod, in favor of the Sabbath (Valckenaer, p. 8, 116. Valckenaer

wants, such as *the book of Enoch* and *the fourth book of Ezra.*[26] But writings of this kind were also fabricated anew by Christians, who quieted their conscience respecting the forgery, with the idea of their good intention,[27] for the purpose of giving greater impressiveness to their doctrines and admonitions by the reputation of respectable names, of animating their suffering brethren to steadfastness, and of gaining over their opponents to Christianity.[28] Hence there now appeared, in particular *the Testaments of the twelve Patriarchs,*[29] and the Ἀναβατικὸν Ἡσαΐου,[30] the latter so peculiar in its contents, that in later times heretics only could still use it. To make an impression on the heathen, supposititious predictions, relating especially to Christ and the last things, were constantly ascribed to *the Sybil.*[31] To them were added those of *Hystaspes.*[32]

regards Aristobulus as the deceiver, though without sufficient reason), to Sophocles, Æschylus, and Euripides, respecting the unity, power, and righteousness of God (Graecae tragoediae principum, Aeschyli, Sophoclis, Euripidis, num ea, quae supersunt, et genuina omnia sint. Scrips. Aug. Boeckhius. Heidelb. 1808. 8, p. 146). Justin Martyr, Athenagoras, and Clement of Alexandria, make use of these productions.

26 See above § 31, notes 2 and 3.

27 The anecdote respecting the Acta Pauli et Theclae is characteristic, apud. Tertull. de Baptismo c. 17: Quod si quae Paulo perperam adscripta sunt ad licentiam mulierum docendi tinguendique, defendunt, sciant in Asia presbyterum, qui eam scripturam construxit, quasi titulo Pauli de suo cumulans, convictum atque confessum id se amore Pauli fecisse, loco decessisse.

28 A one-sided view is given by Mosheim de causis suppositorum librorum inter Christianos saec. i. et ii. (Dissertt. ad hist. eccl. pertin. vol. i. p. 217, ss.) Comp. C. J Nitzsch de Testamentis xii. Patriarcharum, p. 1, ss.

29 In Fabricii Cod. pseudepigraphus v. t. i. 496. Comp. Veesenmeyer's Beiträge zur Gesch. d. Literatur u. Reformation. Ulm. 1792. 8, S. 1, ff. In their apocalyptic part, they are modeled after the Apocalypse of John, Daniel, and especially the Book of Enoch. See Lücke's Einl. in die Offenb. Joh. S. 123. Wieseler's die 70 Wochen u. die 63 Jahrwochen d. Proph. Daniel. S. 226. C. J. Nitzsch de Test. xii. Pariarcharum comm. Viteberg. 1810. 4.

30 Extant in an Ethiopic version, Ascensio Isaiae vatis aethiop. cum versione lat. anglicanaque, ed. Rich. Laurence. Oxon. 1819, 8: the old Latin fragments which Angelo Maius, Nova collectio scriptorum veterum, iii. ii. 238, has published, are corrected and criticised by Nitzch in the Theol. Stud. u. Krit. 1830, ii. 209. Another Latin translation preserved entire (ed. Venetiis. 1522. 8), has been recently published by me, together with the Greek fragment in Epiphanius, and the Latin in Mai: Vetus translatio latina Visionis Jesaiae, ed. atque praefatione et notis illustra (a Göttingen Easter Programm). That the work was not necessarily written before 68, as Laurence supposes, is shown by Gfrörer Jahrhundert des Heils, i. 66. Comp. Gesenius Commentar über den Jesaias, i. 45, ff Lücke, l. c. S. 125.

31 See above § 31, note 4. According to Bleek in Schleiermacher's, De Wette's, and Lücke's theol. Zeitschrift, ii. 231, old Jewish and Christian oracles were composed under Hadrian by an Egyptian Christian, and, after several enlargements, put together so as to constitute books iii.-v. The eighth book belongs to the time of Marcus Aurelius, books vii. and vi. to the third century, i. and ii. to the middle of the fifth.

32 Ammianus Marcellinus, xxiii. 6: Magic is divinorum incorruptissimus cultus, cujus

§ 53.

ECCLESIASTICAL LIFE.

As the prevailing desire was now to compare the Mosaic institute with the Christian, of which it was regarded as the type, and to trace out an analogy even in their individual features, the idea soon occurred to the mind, of comparing the Christian officers in the church with the Mosaic priesthood,[1] and of giving them the very same titles (summus sacerdos, sacerdotes, Levitae). As a body, they were called, by way of eminence, *κλῆρος*, viz., *τοῦ θεοῦ, κληρικοί;*[2] among the Latins, ordo;[3] in opposition

scientiae saeculis priscis multa ex Chaldaeorum arcanis Bactrianus addidit Zoroastres: deinde Hystaspes rex prudentissimus Darii pater. The latter traveled into India to the Brahmins, eorumque monitu rationes mundani motus et siderum, purosque sacrorum ritus quantum colligere potuit eruditus, ex his quae didicit, aliqua sensibus magorum infudit: quae illi cum disciplinis praesentiendi futura, per suam quisque progeniem, posteris aetatibus tradunt. Ch. G. F. Walch de Hystaspe ejusque vaticiniis apud Patres i. d. Commentationes Soc. Reg. Gotting. i. 3.—So early as in the Praedicatio Petri (which belongs to the beginning of the second century, see § 27, note 5) the Sybil and Hystaspes are recommended (cf. Clemens Alex. Strom. vi. p. 761), and by Justin Martyr several times quoted. According to Celsus ap. Orig. c. Cels. vii. p. 368, they were adulterated and used by a Christian party, whom he thence calls *Σιβυλλισταί*, lib. v. p. 272.

1 The whole Christian world is called, in 1 Pet. ii. 5, *ἱεράτευμα ἅγιον*: v. 9, *βασίλειον ἱεράτευμα*. The passage in Clem. Rom. Ep. 1, c. 40, speaks of the Old Testament economy, and does not belong here. On the contrary, traces of a peculiar Christian priesthood appear in the Test. xii. Patr., cf. Nitzsch de Test. xii. Patr. p. 19. Also in Polycratis Ep. ad Victorem apud Euseb. v. 24, § 1: *Ἰωάννης, ὃς ἐγενήθη ἱερεὺς τὸ πέταλον πεφορηκώς*, although *πέταλον* (cf. Exod. xxix. 6; Lev. viii. 9) stands here only tropically; cf. J. F. Cotta de lamina pontificali App. Joannis, Jacobi et Marci. Tubing. 1775. 4. The idea is first found in a distinct form in Tertullian.

2 1 Pet. v. 3, Christians are called *κλῆροι*, a band belonging to God. In like manner, Ignatius, Ep. ad Eph. c. 11: *ὁ κλῆρος Ἐφεσίων τῶν χριστιανῶν*. In a narrower sense *κλῆρος τῶν μαρτύρων* in Epist. Eccl. Vienn. et Lugd. ap. Euseb. v. 1, § 4. The clergy are called so early as in Tertullian, clerus, and they afterward cited in their own favor, Numb. xviii. 20, Deut. x. 9, xviii. 1, 2: *κύριος αὐτὸς κλῆρὸς τοῖς Λευίταις;* though here God is *κλῆρος*, not the Levites. In like manner, they appropriated to themselves in the fourth century, the names christiani and christianitas as their peculiar right (cf. Cod. Theod. v. 5, 2; xii. 1, 50 and 123; xii. 1, 123, du Fresne glossar. ad h. v.) cf. J. H. Boehmer de differentia inter Clericos et Laicos diss. (xii. dissertt. juris eccl. ant. ad Plinium, &c., p. 340, ss.). A different view is given by Neander, K. G. i. i. 333.

3 Borrowed from the town councillors in the municipal boroughs, who, according to the analogy of the Roman senate, were styled ordo Decurionum, or ordo, in opposition to plebs and plebeii; cf. Digest. lib. l. Tit. 2. de Decurionibus. Boehmer, l. c. p. 342. Hoeck's röm. Gesch. vom. Verfall der Republ. i. ii. 159. Even the verb ordinare, i. e., ordinem dare (Sueton. Vespas. c. 23), had already received in Cyprian an ecclesiastical use.

to the λαός, plebs, λαϊκοί.[4] The idea, however, of a universal Christian priesthood was still maintained.[5] The influence of the bishop necessarily increased when *synods* began to be common,[6] at which the bishop chiefly represented his congregation (παροικία),[7] although the presbyters also had a voice along with him.[8] All congregations were independent of one another, although some had a peculiar reputation more than others, on account of many circumstances, ex. gr. their apostolic origin, the importance of the city to which they belonged, or because they were mother churches. Many such circumstances united in procuring for *Rome*, particularly in the west, an especial reputation, even so early as the period of which we are speaking.[9]

4 So λαός stands also in opposition to the Jewish priests, 2 Chron. xxxvi. 14; Luke i. 10, 21

5 Iren. iv. 20. Omnes enim justi sacerdotalem habent ordinem. Tertullian. de Exhortat. Castitatis c. 7: Nonne et laici sacerdotes sumus? Differentiam inter ordinem et plebem constituit ecclesiae auctoritas, et honor per ordinis concessum sanctificatus. Adeo ubi ecclesiastici ordinis non est consessus, et offers et tinguis, et sacerdos es tibi solus. Sed ubi tres, ecclesia est, licet laici. Igitur si habes jus sacerdotis in temet ipso, ubi necesse est, habeas oportet etiam disciplinam sacerdotis, ubi necesse est, habere jus sacerdotis. (Cf. de Baptismo c. 17, de Monog. c. 7, 12, de Corona mil. c. 3. See Neander's Antignosticus, S. 154.) Against the impartial explanation of this language given by Nic. Rigaltius: Gabr. Aubespine (Albaspinaeus) de l'eucharistie. Controversy concerning offerre in this place (see on it below note 15), and de jure laicorum sacerdotali. For Rigaltius (Hugo Grotius) de administratione coenae, ubi pastores non sant. 1638. Claudius Salmasius and others. On the other side are D. Petavius, H. Dodwell, and others. The history of the controversy may be found in Chr. M. Pfaffii diss. de consecratione veterum eucharistica § 23 (in his Syntagma dissertt. theologg. p. 533). Cotta and Gerhardi loc. theol. x. 21. Cf. Boehmer, l. c. p. 272, 485. Neander's Denkw. i. 179.

6 The first synods held against the Montanists (160-170), Euseb. v. 16, regularly returned, and are first mentioned in Tertullian de Jejun: Aguntur praeterea per Graecias illa certis in locis concilia ex universis ecclesiis, per quae et altiora quaeque in commune tractantur, et ipsa repraesentatio totius nominis Christiani magna veneratione celebratur. Perhaps an imitation of the Amphictyonic Council, which still continued (Pausan. x. 8). Comp. Ueber den Ursprung der Kirchenversammlungen in (J. M. Abele) Magazin für Kirchenrecht u. K. G. Leipzig. 1778. St. 2. S. 479, ff.; W. L. C. Ziegler in Henke's neuem Magazin für Religionsphilosophie, &c. i. 125, ff.

7 Irenaeus apud Euseb. v. 24, § 5. The Christians considered themselves on this earth as πάροικοι, according to 1 Peter, i. 17; ii. 11. Comp. Epist. ad Diognet. c. 5: Πατρίδας οἰκοῦσιν ἰδίας, ἀλλ' ὡς πάροικοι,—ἐπὶ γῆς διατρίβουσιν, ἀλλ' ἐν οὐρανῷ πολιτεύονται. Hence the churches designated themselves companies of strangers, Clemens Rom. init. Epist. i. Ἡ ἐκκλησία τοῦ θεοῦ ἡ παροικοῦσα Ῥώμην τῇ ἐκκλησίᾳ τοῦ θεοῦ τῇ παροικούσῃ Κόρινθον. In like manner Epist. Eccl. Smyrn. apud Euseb. iv. 15, § 1.

8 The ancient form is apparent from the introduction of the Conc. Eliberitani, ann. 305: Cum concedissent sancti et religiosi Episcopi—item Presbyteri—residentibus cunctis, adstantibus diaconibus et omni plebe, Episcopi universi dixerunt.

9 To these belonged also the support of other churches. Dionys. Corinth. ad Rom. Epist. (ap. Euseb. iv. 23): Ἐξ ἀρχῆς γὰρ ὑμῖν ἔθος ἐστὶ τοῦτο, πάντας μὲν ἀδελφοὺς ποικίλως εὐεργετεῖν, ἐκκλησίαις τε πολλαῖς ταῖς κατὰ πᾶσαν πόλιν ἐφόδια πέμπειν· ὧδε μὲν τὴν τῶν δεομένων πενίαν ἀναψύχοντας, ἐν μετάλλοις δὲ ἀδελφοῖς ὑπάρχουσιν ἐπιχορηγοῦντας.

Public worship was extremely simple. Without temples, altars, or images, the Christians assembled in houses appointed for the purpose, and, in times of persecution, in solitary places,[10] sometimes even in the night, particularly on the night before Easter.[11] The members of the church brought with them voluntary offerings, from which was taken what was necessary for the solemnization of *the Lord's supper* (εὐχαριστία), and *the agape*,[12] which was still usually connected with it. The remainder belonged to the clergy and the poor, for whom also they provided by monthly contributions.[13] After the clergy had be-

[10] Celsus ap. Orig. c. Cels. viii. p. 389: *Βωμοὺς καὶ ἀγάλματα καὶ νεὼς ἱδρύσθαι φεύγουσι.* Minucii Felicis Octavius, c. 10: Cur nullas aras habent, templa nulla, nulla nota simulacra? Toward the end of the second century, buildings appear to have been devoted here and there exclusively to the worship of God. Tertull. de Idolol. c. 7: Ab idolis in ecclesiam venire, de adversarii officina in domum Dei venire. Comp. Chron. Edessen. above, § 39, note 4. The expression, *ἐκκλησία*, is frequently used even so early of the places of assembling, ex. gr., Tertull. de Cor. mil. c. 3, below, note 25. Clem. Alex. Strom. vii. p. 846.

[11] Tertull. ad Uxor. ii. c. 4: Quis (infidelis maritus uxorem christianam) nocturnis convocationibus, si ita oportuerit, a latere suo adimi libenter feret? Quis denique solemnibus paschae abnoctantem securus sustinebit? Lactant. Institt. vii. 19: Haec est nox, quae a nobis propter adventum regis ac dei nostri pervigilio celebratur. Cujus noctis duplex ratio est, quod in ea et vitam tum recepit, quum passus est, et postea orbis terrae regnum recepturus est. Hieronymus comm. in Matth. lib. iv. ad Matth. xxv. 6: Traditio Judaeorum est, Christum media nocte venturum in similitudinem Aegyptii temporis, quando pascha celebratum est, et exterminator venit, et Dominus super tabernacula transiit, et sanguine agni postes nostrarum frontium censecrati sunt. Unde reor et traditionem apostolicam permansisse, ut in die vigiliarum Paschae ante noctis dimidium populos dimittere non liceat, exspectantes adventum Christi. Et postquam illud tempus transierit, securitate praesumta, festum cuncti agunt diem.

[12] Not always, indeed, on account of the persecutions. According to Tertull. de Corona militis, c. 3, the eucharist was celebrated even in antelucanis coetibus. Also in Justin's description, Apol. i. c. 85. the *agape* is not mentioned: *Ἔπειτα* (after the common prayers) *προσφέρεται τῷ προεστῶτι τῶν ἀδελφῶν ἄρτος, καὶ ποτήριον ὕδατος καὶ κράματος. καὶ οὗτος λαβὼν αἶνον καὶ δόξαν τῷ πατρὶ τῶν ὅλων διὰ τοῦ ὀνόματος τοῦ υἱοῦ καὶ τοῦ πνεύματος τοῦ ἁγίου ἀναπέμπει, καὶ εὐχαριστίαν ὑπὲρ τοῦ κατηξιῶσθαι τούτων παρ' αὐτοῦ ἐπὶ πολὺ ποιεῖται. Οὗ συντελέσαντος τὰς εὐχὰς καὶ τὴν εὐχαριστίαν, πᾶς ὁ παρὼν λαὸς ἐπευφημεῖ λέγων ἀμήν.—ἐπευφημήσαντος παντὸς τοῦ λαοῦ οἱ καλούμενοι παρ' ἡμῖν διάκονοι διδόασιν ἑκάστῳ τῶν παρόντων μεταλαβεῖν ἀπὸ τοῦ εὐχαριστηθέντος ἄρτου καὶ οἴνου τῶν ὕδατος, καὶ τοῖς οὐ παροῦσιν ἀποφέρουσι.* A description of the *agape* is given in Tertullian's Apologet. c. 39: Coena nostra de nomine rationem sui ostendit, id vocatur quod dilectio penes graecos. Quantiscunque sumptibus constet, lucrum est pietatis nomine facere sumptum, siquidem inopes quosque refrigerio isto juvamus. Non prius discumbitur. quam oratio ad Deum praegustetur; editur quantum esurientes cupiunt, bibitur quantum pudicis est utile. Ita saturantur, ut qui meminerint etiam per noctem adorandum deum sibi esse; ita fabulantur, ut qui sciunt dominum audire. Post aquam manualem et lumina, ut quisque de scripturis sanctis vel de proprio ingenio potest, provocatur in medium Deo canere; hinc probatur quomodo biberit. Aeque oratio convivium dirimit, &c.

[13] Tertull. Apolog. c. 39: Modicam unusquisque stipem menstrua die, vel quum velit, et si modo velit, et si modo possit, apponit. Hence Cyprian. Ep. 28 and 34: divisiones

come a priestly caste, it was the more necessary to look for a sacrifice in Christianity, because the ancient world generally could not conceive of divine worship without sacrifice. For this purpose the solemnity of the supper presented several points of comparison. First of all, *the prayer*, which, indeed, had always been considered spiritual sacrifice.[14] But next, the gifts of the church members, as also the bread and wine set apart by the bishop by prayer as holy food, might be considered as offerings dedicated to God. Of both the same expressions were used, *προσφέρειν*, *προσφορά*, offerre, oblatio: both were compared with the Old Testament sacrifices and first fruits.[15] As, accordingly,

mensurnae, sportulae presbyterorum. Ep. 66: sportulantes fratres. Ziegler über die Einkünfte des Klerus u. d. Kirche in den ersten drei Jahr., in Henke's neuem Magazin für Religionsphilosophie. Bd. 4, S. 1, ff. Münter primord. Eccl. Afric. p. 63, ss.

[14] 1 Peter ii. 5, Justin. M. Dial. c. Tryph. c. 116: *Ἡμεῖς—ἀρχιερατικὸν τὸ ἀληθινὸν γένος ἐσμὲν τοῦ θεοῦ.—οὐ δέχεται δὲ παρ' οὐδενὸς θυσίας ὁ θεὸς, εἰ μὴ διὰ τῶν ἱερέων αὐτοῦ.* C. 117: *Πάσας οὖν διὰ τοῦ ὀνόματος τούτου θυσίας, ἃς παρέδωκεν Ἰησοῦς ὁ Χριστὸς γίνεσθαι, τουτέστιν ἐπὶ τῇ εὐχαριστίᾳ τοῦ ἄρτου καὶ τοῦ ποτηρίου τὰς ἐν παντὶ τόπῳ τῆς γῆς γενομένας ὑπὸ τῶν Χριστιανῶν, προλαβὼν ὁ θεὸς, μαρτυρεῖ εὐαρέστους ὑπάρχειν αὐτῷ.—Ὅτι μὲν οὖν καὶ εὐχαὶ καὶ εὐχαριστίαι, ὑπὸ τῶν ἀξίων γινόμεναι, τέλειαι μόναι καὶ εὐάρεστοί εἰσι τῷ θεῷ θυσίαι, καὶ αὐτός φημι. Ταῦτα γὰρ μόνα καὶ Χριστιανοὶ παρέλαβον ποιεῖν, καὶ ἐπ' ἀναμνήσει δὲ τῆς τροφῆς αὐτῶν ξηρᾶς τε καὶ ὑγρᾶς, ἐν ᾗ καὶ τοῦ πάθους, ὃ πέπονθε δι' αὐτοὺς ὁ υἱὸς τοῦ θεοῦ, μέμνηται.*

[15] Justin. M. Dial. c. Tryph. c. 41: *Περὶ δὲ τῶν ἐν παντὶ τόπῳ ὑφ' ἡμῶν τῶν ἐθνῶν προσφερομένων αὐτῷ θυσιῶν, τουτέστι τοῦ ἄρτου τῆς εὐχαριστίας καὶ τοῦ ποτηρίου ὁμοίως τῆς εὐχαριστίας προλέγει τότε* (namely, Mal. i. 10–12). Irenaeus iv. 17, 5: Sed et suis discipulis dans consilium, primitias Deo offerre ex suis creaturis, non quasi indigenti sed ut ipsi nec infructuosi, nec ingrati sint, eum, qui ex creatura est panis, accepit, et gratias egit, dicens: Hoc est corpus meum. Et calicem similiter, qui est ex ea creatura, quae est secundum nos, suum sanguinem confessus est: et novi Testamenti novam docuit oblationem, quam Ecclesia ab apostoli accipiens, in universo mundo offert Deo, ei qui alimenta nobis praestat, primitias suorum munerum in novo Testamento, de quo in XII. Prophetis Malachias sic praesignificavit (Mal. i. 10, 11), &c. Cap. xviii. 1: Igitur Ecclesiae oblatio, quam Dominus docuit offerri in universo mundo, purum sacrificium reputatum est apud Deum, et acceptum est ei: non quod indigeat a nobis sacrificium, sed quoniam is qui offert glorificatur ipse in eo quod offert, si acceptetur munus ejus. Irenaei fragm. II. ed. Pfaffii: *Προσφέρομεν γὰρ τῷ θεῷ τὸν ἄρτον καὶ τὸ ποτήριον τῆς εὐλογίας, εὐχαριστοῦντες αὐτῷ, ὅτι τῇ γῇ ἐκέλευσε ἐκφύσαι τοὺς καρποὺς τούτους εἰς τροφὴν ἡμετέραν, καὶ ἐνταῦθα τὴν προσφορὰν τελέσαντες ἐκκαλοῦμεν τὸ πνεῦμα τὸ ἅγιον, ὅπως ἀποφήνῃ τὴν θυσίαν ταύτην καὶ τὸν ἄρτον σῶμα τοῦ Χριστοῦ καὶ τὸ ποτήριον τὸ αἷμα τοῦ Χριστοῦ, ἵνα οἱ μεταλαβόντες τούτων τῶν ἀντιτύπων τῆς ἀφέσεως τῶν ἁμαρτιῶν καὶ τῆς ζωῆς αἰωνίου τύχωσιν.* Cf. Chr. M. Pfaffii Diss. de oblatione Veterum eucharistica, in his Syntagma dissertt. theologg. Stutt. 1720, p. 219, ss. Stäudlin's History of the dogma of the sacrifice of the Lord's Supper, in Schleusner's u. Stäudlin's Götting. Biblioth. d. neuesten theol. Literatur, ii. ii. 163. This idea of oblations is expressed not only in the sacrificial prayers of the old liturgies (see Constitt. Apost. viii. c. 12, comp. Pfaffii Syntagma, p. 378, ss.), but also even now in the commencing words of the canon missae of the Romish church: Te igitur, clementissime pater—supplices rogamus ac petimus, uti accepta habeas ac benedicas haec dona, haec munera, haec sancta sacrificia illibata (i. e., the still unconsecrated bread and wine).

the Mosaic law of first fruits, and soon, in consequence, the law of tithes also, appeared to be still valid,[16] the Christians obtained in them a rule for their oblations, without, however, any kind of external compulsion being used for enjoining the observance of them. The eucharist being considered the symbol of the intimate communion of the church with itself and with Christ, it was also sent to the absent as a token of this communion,[17] and taken by those who were present to their homes.[18]

Baptism was preceded by instruction,[19] fasting, and prayer. The baptism of children was not universal, and was even occasionally disapproved.[20] While Christians were supposed to be engaged in constant warfare with the world and the devil under the banner of Christ,[21] they generally used the sign of the cross,[22]

[16] Irenaeus, iv. 18, 1: Offerre igitur opportet Deo primitias ejus creaturae, sicut et Moyses ait: Non apparebis vacuus ante conspectum Domini Dei tui (Deut. xvi. 16).— 2: Et non genus oblationum reprobatum est: oblationes enim et illic, oblationes autem et hic: sacrificia in populo, sacrificia in Ecclesia: sed species immutata est tantum. quippe cum jam non a servis, sed a liberis offeratur. Origenes in Num. Hom. xi. 1: Primitias omnium frugum, omniumque pecudum sacerdotibus lex mandat offerri.—Hanc ergo legem observari etiam secundum literam, sicut et alia nonnulla, necessarium puto. 2: Quomodo abundat justitia nostra plus quam scribarum et Pharisaeorum, si illi de fructibus terrae suae gustare non audent, priusquam primitias sacerdotibus offerant, et Levitis decimas separent: et ego nihil horum faciens, fructibus terrae ita abutar, ut sacerdos nesciat, Levites ignoret, divinum altare non sentiat? Constitutt. Apost. ii. c. 25: *Αἱ τότε θυσίαι, νῦν εὐχαὶ, καὶ δεήσεις, καὶ εὐχαριστίαι· αἱ τότε ἀπαρχαὶ, καὶ δεκάται, καὶ ἀφαιρέματα καὶ δῶρα, νῦν προσφοραὶ, αἱ διὰ τῶν ὁσίων ἐπισκόπων προσφερόμεναι κυρίῳ τῷ θεῷ διὰ Ἰησοῦ Χριστοῦ τοῦ ὑπὲρ αὐτῶν ἀποθανόντος.*

[17] Cf. Justin above, note 12. Irenaeus ap. Euseb. v. 24, § 5: The presbyters of one church *ἔπεμπον εὐχαριστίαν* to those of another.

[18] Tertull. ad Uxorem, ii. c. 5. De Orat. c. 14.

[19] On the creed see above, § 51, note 13.

[20] Tertull. de Baptismo, c. 18: Itaque pro cujusque personae conditione ac dispositione, etiam aetate, cunctatio baptismi utilior est: praecipue tamen circa parvulos. Quid enim necesse est, sponsores etiam periculo ingeri? quia et ipse per mortalitatem destituere promissiones suas possunt, et proventu malae indolis falli. Ait quidem Dominus: Nolite illos prohibere ad me venire (Matth. xix. 14). Veniant ergo, dum adolescunt, veniant dum discunt, dum, quo veniant, docentur: fiant Christiani, quum Christum nosse potuerint. Quid festinat innocens aetas ad remissionem peccatorum? Cautius agetur in saecularibus, ut cui substantia terrena non creditur, divina credatur. Norint petere salutem ut petenti dedisse videaris. Non minore de causa innupti quoque procrastinandi, in quibus tentatio praeparata est tam virginibus per maturitatem, quam viduis per vagationem, donec aut nubant, aut continentiae corroborentur. Si qui pondus intelligant baptismi, magis timebunt consecutionem quam dilationem: fides integra secura est de salute. Cf. G. Walli Hist. baptismi infantum, lat. vertit, J. L. Schlosser (P. i. Bremae. 1748, P. ii Hamb. 1753. 4). P. i. p. 57, ss.

[21] Tertull. ad Martyres, c. 3: Vocati sumus ad militiam Dei vivi jam tunc, cum in sacramenti verba respondimus, &c. De Corona mil. c. 11.

[22] Tertull. adv. Marc. iii. 18, de Cor. militis, c. 3. But no adoration of the cross. Minucius Fel. c. 29: Cruces etiam nec colimus, nec optamus.

and often exorcism,[23] as a powerful defense against the machinations of evil spirits. Probably they already began to apply the latter in the case of those persons who, renouncing the prince of this world, prepared themselves for baptism.[24] Many new usages were connected with baptism itself toward the end of the second century.[25]

The concluding of a marriage was announced by the bishop of the church; and with this was very naturally connected the giving of his blessing on the new union.[26] Second marriages were condemned by many in all cases,[27] and began to be expressly disallowed in the case of the clergy.[28] But when *the*

23 Tertull. de Idololatr. c. 11, of the Christian Thurarius: Qua constantia exorcizabit alumnos suos (i. e., the demons, ironically), quibus domum suam cellariam praestat? De Cor. milltis, c. 11, of the Christian soldiers: Quos interdiu exorcismis fugavit, noctibus defensabit, incumbens et requiescens super pilum, quo perfossum est latus Christi?

24 Barnabas Epist. c. 16: *Πρὸ τοῦ ἡμᾶς πιστεῦσαι τῷ θεῷ, ἦν ἡμῶν τὸ κατοικητήριον τῆς καρδίας φθαρτὸν καὶ ἀσθενὲς—οἶκος δαιμόνων, διὰ τὸ ποιεῖν ὅσα ἦν ἐναντία τῷ θεῷ.* From this view, the application of exorcism in the case of candidates for baptism resulted as a matter of course.

25 The ceremony of baptism was still very simple, as described in Justin Apol. i. c. 79. Otherwise in Tertull. de Cor. mil. c. 3: Aquam adituri, ibidem, sed et aliquanto prius in ecclesia, sub antistitis manu contestamur, nos renunciare diabolo (*ἀποτάσσεσθαι διαβόλῳ*) et pompae et angelis ejus. Dehinc ter mergitamur, amplius aliquid respondentes quam dominus in Evangelio determinavit. Inde suscepit lactis et mellis concordiam praegustamus (qua infantamur, adv. Marc. i. c. 14): exque ea die lavacro quotidiano per totam hebdomadam abstimemus. There is an opinion that the last-mentioned rite was borrowed from the heathen mysteries; see Mosheim de rebus Christ. ante Const. M. p. 321. An excursus to the whole passage is given in Neander's Antignosticus, S. 149, ff.—Tertull. de Baptismo, c. 7: Exinde egressi de lavacro perungimur benedicta unctione (*χρίσματι*) de pristina disciplina, qua ungi oleo de cornu in sacerdotium solebant. (This anointing, according to Thilo Acta Thomae, p. 177, was of Gnostic origin.) Cap. 8: Dehinc manus imponitur, per benedictionem advocans et invitans spiritum sanctum (*χειροθεσία*). Jo. Dallaeus de duobus Latinorum ex unctione sacramentis. Genev. 1659. 4, p. 126, ss. Neander's K. G. i. i. 543.

26 Ignat. Epist. ad Polycarp. § 5. Tertull ad Uxor. ii. c. 9: Unde sufficiam ad enarrandam felicitatem ejus matrimonii, quod ecclesia conciliat, et confirmat oblatio, et obsignatum angeli renunciant, pater rato habet? De Pudicit. c. 4: Penes nos occultae quoque conjunctiones, i. e., non prius apud Ecclesiam professae, juxta moechiam et fornicationem judicari periclitantur. Cf. Jo. Seldeni uxor Ebraica, lib. ii. c. 28. Concerning the marriage of the first Christians see in (Abele) Mag. f. Kirchenrecht. Bd. 1, S. 261, ff. Münter's Sinnbilder d. alten Christen. Heft 2, S. 112, ff.

27 Athenagoras Deprec. c. 28: *Ὁ δεύτερος (γάμος) εὐπρεπής ἐστι μοιχεία.* On the other hand, Hermae Past. lib. i. mand. iv. 4: Si vir vel mulier alicujus decesserit, et nupserit aliquis illorum, numquid peccat? Qui nubit non peccat, inquit, sed si per se manserit, magnum sibi conquirit honorem apud Dominum. So also Clem. Alex. Strom. iii. p. 548. Cf. Cotelerius ad Hermae, l. c.

28 Tertull. ad Uxor. i. 7: Disciplina ecclesiae et praescriptio apostoli—digamos non sinit praesidere. Yet de Monagam. 12: Quot enim et digami praesident apud vos, insultantes utique apostolo! Derived from 1 Tim. iii. 2. Tertullian read also in Lev. xxi.: Sacerdotes mei non plus nubent (de Exhort. castit. 7). Comp. Heydenreich's Pastoralbriefe Pauli, Bd. 1, S. 166, ff.

Montanists forbade them universally, they met with opposition. *Fasts*, which were looked upon as a suitable preparation for prayer, and *celibacy*, were valued, but continued to be left to the free choice of every one,[29] although the opinion of Philo, that the marriage intercourse was something that rendered a person unclean, had been already introduced.[30] Many Christians devoted themselves to a certain abstinence (ἀσκηταί);[31] but all forced and artificial asceticism was disapproved.[32] The only custom of the kind which was universal was the celebration of the passion-time of Jesus by a fast; but this was observed in very different ways. In other cases, for voluntary fasting and prayer (stationes, stationum semijejunia, *Tert. de Jejun.* c. 13) they chose *Wednesday* and *Friday*.[33] *Sunday* and *the Sabbath*

29 Even for the clergy: G. Calixti de Conjug. clericorum. Helmst. 1631, ed. Henke, ibid. 1783. 4. ii. 181. Theiner's Einführung der erzwungenen Ehelosigkeit bei den Geistl. i. 69

30 Semisch, Justin d. M. i. 199.

31 This appellation formerly applied to the athletae (Plato de Republ. iii. p. 297), was afterward by Philo (de Praem. et Poen. 914, 917, 920) to the exercises of virtue in the wise. So also among the heathen philosophers (Arrian. diss. in Epict. iii. c. 12, περὶ ἀσκήσεως. Artemidorus, about 100, Oneirocrit. iv. c. 33, says of a philosopher, Alexander: Ἔμελε δὲ αὐτῷ ὄντι ἀνδρὶ ἀσκητῇ οὔτε γάμου, οὔτε κοινωνίας, οὔτε πλούτου). Athenagorae Deprec. c. 28: Εὕροις δ' ἂν πολλοὺς τῶν παρ' ἡ μῖν καὶἄνδρας καὶ γυναῖκας καταγηράσκοντας ἀγάμους, ἐλπίδι τοῦ μᾶλλον συνέσεσθαι τῷ θεῷ. Tertull. de Cultu foem. 11: Non enim et multi ita faciunt, et se spadonatui obsignant propter regnum Dei (Matth. xix. 12), tam fortem et utique permissam voluptatem sponte ponentes (continentes, ἐγκρατεῖς, cf. de Vel. virg. 3)? Numquid non aliqui ipsam Dei creaturam sibi interdicunt, abstinentes vino et animalibus esculentis, quorum fructus nulli periculo aut sollicitudini adjacent, sed humilitatem animae suae in victus quoque castigatione Deo immolant? Galenus, see above, § 41, note 16; cf. Sal. Deyling de Ascetis veterum, in ejusd. Observatt. sacr. lib. iii.

32 Dionys. Corinth. (ap. Euseb. iv. 23), in his letter to the Gnossians, exhorts bishop Pinytus, μὴ βαρὺ φορτίον ἐπάναγκες τὸ περὶ ἁγνείας τοῖς ἀδελφοῖς ἐπιτιθέναι, τῆς δὲ τῶν πολλῶν καταστοχάζεσθαι ἀσθενείας.—Ex epist. Eccl. Vienn. et Lugd. ap. Euseb. v. 3: Ἀλκιβιάδου γάρ τινος ἐξ αὐτῶν, πάνυ αὐχμηρὸν βιοῦντος βίον, καὶ μηδενὸς ὅλως τὸ πρότερον μεταλαμβάνοντος, ἀλλ' ἢ ἄρτῳ μόνῳ καὶ ὕδατι χρωμένου, περιωμένου τε καὶ ἐν τῇ εἱρκτῇ οὕτω διάγειν, Ἀττάλῳ μετὰ τὸν πρῶτον ἀγῶνα, ὃν ἐν τῷ ἀμφιθεάτρῳ ἤνυσεν, ἀπεκαλύφθη, ὅτι μὴ καλῶς ποιοίη ὁ Ἀλκιβιάδης, μὴ χρώμενος τοῖς κτίσμασι τοῦ θεοῦ καὶ ἄλλοις τύπον σκανδάλου ὑπολειπόμενος. πεισθεὶς δὲ Ἀλκιβιάδης πάντων ἀνέδην μετελάμβανε καὶ ηὐχαρίστει τῷ θεῷ.

33 Respecting the stationes, watches of milites Christi, which were usually continued till three o'clock in the afternoon, see Hermae Pastor iii. Sim. 5, and Fabricius ad h. l. Gu. Beveregii Cod. canonum eccl. primitivae vindicatus, lib. iii. c. 10.—Tertull. de Jejun. c. 2: Certe in evangelio illos dies jejuniis determinatos putant (Psychici), in quibus ablatus est sponsus (Matth. ix. 15): et hos esse jam solos legitimos jejuniorum christianorum. (De Orat. 14: Die Paschae communis et quasi publica jejunii religio est),—sic et apostolos observasse, nullum aliud imponentes jugum certorum et in commune omnibus obeundorum jejuniorum: proinde nec stationum, quae et ipsae suos quidem dies habeant, quartae feria et sextae, passim tamen currant, neque sub lege praecepti, neque ultra supremam dici, quando et orationes fere hora nona concludat, de Petri exemplo, quod actis refertur. (De Orat. 14: Statio de militari exemplo nonem accipit: nam et militia Dei sumus). C. 13 ·

were observed as festivals; the latter, however, without Jewish superstition. In the celebration of the passover, there was a difference between *the churches of Asia Minor* and *those of the west.*[34] The former adhered to the Jewish passover feast, giving it a reference to Christ;[35] the latter, on the other hand, kept

Bene autem, quod et Episcopi universae plebi mandare jejunia assolent—ex aliqua sollicitudinis ecclesiasticae causa.—Irenaeus ad Victorem ap. Euseb. v. 24. 4: *Οὐδὲ γὰρ μόνον περὶ τῆς ἡμέρας ἐστὶν ἡ ἀμφισβήτησις, ἀλλὰ καὶ περὶ τοῦ εἴδους αὐτοῦ τῆς νηστείας· οἱ μὲν γὰρ οἴονται μίαν ἡμέραν δεῖν αὐτοὺς νηστεύειν, οἱ δὲ δύο, οἱ δὲ καὶ πλείονας, οἱ δὲ τεσσαράκοντα ὥρας ἡμερινάς τε καὶ νυκτερινὰς συμμετροῦσι τὴν ἡμέραν αὐτῶν.* On the last words see the Excursus in Heinichen. Euseb. t. iii. p. 377, ss. I am inclined to read *τῇ ἡμέρᾳ αὐτῶν.* "Others measure off forty hours along with their day" (*μετροῦσι σὺν τῇ ἡμέρᾳ*), i. e., they fast the day which they celebrate as the passover, or the day of Christ's death (for in this there was a difference), and begin with the hour of the death (three o'clock, afternoon), a new forty hours' fast till the resurection.—Cf. Jo. Dallaeus de Jejuniis et quadragesima. Daventr. 1654. 8.

34 The older historians in taking the passover as the festival of the resurrection, misunderstood the celebration practiced in Asia Minor. Different opinions of the moderns: Gabr. Daniel de la discipline des Quartodécimans pour la célébration de la Pacque (in his Recueil de divers ouvrages philos., theolog., histor. Paris. 1724. 4. iii. 473). Chr. A. Heumann Vera descriptio priscae contentionis inter Roman et Asiam de vero Paschate (in ejusd. Nova sylloge dissertat. i. 156, ss). J. L. Mosheim de reb. Christ. ante Const. M. p. 435, ss. Neander im kirchenhist. Archiv. 1823, Heft 2, S. 90, ff. Kirchengesch. i. i. 511, ff. J. W. Rettberg's Paschastreit der älten Kirche, in Illgen's Zeitschr. f. d. hist. Theol. ii. ii. 91. (Comp. my remarks in the theol. Studien u. Krit. 1833, iv. 1149).

35 The most important in this festival was the passover day, the 14th of Nisan, which, after it had been probably spent in fasting, closed with a Christian paschal meal (love-feast and Eucharist). (Epiphan. Haer. l. 1, *ἅπαξ τοῦ ἔτους μίαν ἡμέραν τοῦ πάσχα φιλονείκως ἄγουσι.* Polycrates, bishop of Ephesus, who defended, in the year 196, this solemnity against the Romish bishop Victor, designates it in Euseb. v. 24, as a *τηρεῖν τὴν ἡμέραν τῆς τεσσαρεσκαιδεκάτης τοῦ πάσχα κατὰ τὸ εὐαγγέλιον.* The whole day, therefore, was kept, but it might be observed merely by fasting. Comp. Tertull. de Orat. c. 14, see above, note 33). In favor of this they appealed to a passage of the law, (Epiphan. Haer. l. 1): *ὅτι ἐπικατάρατος, ὃς οὐ ποιήσει τὸ πάσχα τῇ τεσσαρεσκαιδεκάτῃ ἡμέρᾳ τοῦ μηνός.* They said (apud Hippolytus in chron. Pasch. p. 6): *ἐποίησε τὸ πάσχα ὁ Χριστὸς τότε τῇ ἡμέρᾳ καὶ ἔπαθεν· διὸ κἀμὲ δεῖ ὃν τρόπον ὁ κύριος ἐποίησεν, οὕτω ποιεῖν.* In it they ate unleavened bread, probably like the Jews, eight days through; they said (Chrysostomus contra Jud. Orat. iii. ed. Montfaucon, i. 610): *ὅτι μετὰ τοῦ ἀζύμου τὸ πάσχα ἐστίν.* On the contrary, there is no trace of a yearly festival of the resurrection among them, for this was kept every Sunday. Since the Christians of Asia Minor appealed in favor of their passover solemnity on the 14th Nisan to John, (Polycrates, l. c.), and yet, according to his gospel Christ partook of the last supper with his disciples so early as the 13th Nisan; an argument has been lately deduced from this fact against the authenticity of John's gospel, (Bretschneider Probabilia, p. 109, after him Strauss and Schwegler). To judge correctly of this matter we must set out with that which is remarked very truly respecting it by Socrates, Hist. eccl. v. 22: *Οὐδαμοῦ τοίνυν ὁ ἀπόστολος, οὐδὲ τὰ εὐαγγέλια ζυγὸν δουλείας τοῖς τῷ κηρύγματι προσελθοῦσιν ἐπέθηκαν· ἀλλὰ τὴν ἑορτὴν τοῦ πάσχα καὶ τὰς ἄλλας ἑορτὰς τιμᾶν, τῇ εὐγνωμοσύνῃ τῶν εὐεργετηθέντων κατέλιπον.—σκοπὸς μὴν οὖν γέγονε τοῖς ἀποστόλοις, οὐ περὶ ἡμερῶν ἑορταστικῶν νομοθετεῖν, ἀλλὰ βίον ὀρθὸν καὶ τὴν θεοσέβειαν εἰσηγήσασθαι· ἐμοὶ δὲ φαίνεται, ὅτι ὥσπερ ἄλλα πολλὰ κατὰ χώρας συνήθειαν ἔλαβεν, οὕτω καὶ ἡ τοῦ πάσχα ἑορτὴ παρ' ἑκάστοις ἐκ συνηθείας τινὸς ἰδιάζουσαν ἔσχε τὴν παρατήρησιν, διὰ τὸ μηδένα τῶν ἀποστόλων, ὡς ἔφην, μηδενὶ νενομοθετηκέναι περὶ αὐτῆς.* In the Christian assemblies the Jewish passover was at first kept up, but observed with

up the recollection of the death and resurrection of Christ, as in every week, so with greater solemnity every year, at the passover festival, on the corresponding days of the week, so that the passover Friday was always regarded by them as *dies paschae*. When *Polycarp* visited Rome, about 160, he had a conference on this point with the Romish bishop *Anicetus* (*Epist. Iren. ap. Euseb.*, v. 24). Both remained of the same opinion as before, but separated in perfect friendship. Among the Christians of Asia Minor themselves, there was a controversy in Laodicea respecting the passover, about 170; but the proper point debated is not certainly known.[36]

Public sinners were excluded from the church, and the way for restoration could only be prepared by public repentance.[37]

reference to Christ, the true passover, (1 Cor. v. 7, 8). Thus John, too, found it in Ephesus and allowed it to remain unaltered. He corrected it in his gospel only so far as it proceeded on the supposition that Christ had eaten with the Jews the passover on the day before his death, by making it apparent that Christ was crucified on the 14th Nisan. But that solemnity needed not to have been changed on this account; on the contrary, if the 14th Nisan was the true Christian passover day, the fulfillment of the typical pasch took place on the same day with it.

[36] Melito *περὶ τοῦ Πάσχα* ap. Eusebius iv. 26, 2: *'Επὶ Σερουϊλίου Παύλου, ἀνθυπάτου τῆς 'Ασίας, ᾧ Σάγαρις καιρῷ ἐμαρτύρησεν, ἐγένετο ζήτησις πολλὴ ἐν Λαοδικείᾳ περὶ τοῦ πάσχα, ἐμπεσόντος κατὰ καιρὸν ἐν ἐκείναις ταῖς ἡμέραις· καὶ ἐγράφη ταῦτα.* Eusebius adds, that Clement of Alexandria was induced to write his book on the passover by this work of Melito. Since now Melito is quoted by Polycrates (Euseb. v. 24, 2) as an authority for the custom as observed in Asia Minor, but since the Paschal Chronicle, p. 6, s., quotes the writings of the contemporaneous Apollinaris, bishop of Hierapolis, and Clement of Alexandria, on the passover, together in favor of the view that Christ had not eaten the Jewish passover on the day before his death, it has been inferred that Apollinaris had attacked the Asiatic practice, and that Melito defended it. But no trace of this is found in Eusebius; on the contrary, both writers are named by him beside one another as working together harmoniously, (iv. 26.) In the fragments of Apollinaris's work which remain, those persons are combated who said: *ὅτι τῇ ιδ´ τὸ πρόβατον μετὰ τῶν μαθητῶν ἔφαγεν ὁ Κύριος, τῇ δὲ μεγάλῃ ἡμέρᾳ τῶν ἀζύμων αὐτὸς ἔπαθεν*, and appealed to Matthew in their favor. This view, says Apollinaris, contradicts the law (so far as the passover, and consequently also Christ as the passover, must be offered the 14th) and the gospels, and he asserts in opposito it: *ἡ ιδ´ τὸ ἀληθινὸν τοῦ Κυρίου πάσχα, ἡ θυσία ἡ μεγάλη, ὁ ἀντὶ τοῦ ἀμνοῦ παῖς θεοῦ, κ. τ. λ.* Hence he does not combat the keeping of the 14th as the paschal day, but merely intends to vindicate the right significance of it against erroneous conceptions. This day was to be celebrated as the Christian passover, not because Christ had eaten on it the typical passover with the Jews, but because he himself, as the true passover, had offered himself to God.

[37] *ἐξομολόγησις.* Iren. i. c. 9 of a female penitent: *αὐτὴ τὸν ἅπαντα χρόνον ἐξομολογουμένη διετέλεσε πενθοῦσα καὶ θρηνοῦσα.* Tertull. de Poenit. c. 9: Exomologesis —, qua delictum Domino nostrum confitemur: non quidem ut ignaro, sed quatenus satisfactio confessione disponitur, confessione poenitentia nascitur, poenitentia Deus mitigatur. Itaque exomologesis prosternendi et humilificandi hominis disciplina est, conversationem injungens misericordiae illicem. De ipso quoque habitu atque victu mandat, sacco et cineri incubare, corpus sordibus obscurare, animum moeroribus dejicere; illa, quae peccavit,

After baptism only a public repentance was generally allowed.[38] In the African church they proceeded so far as frequently to exclude forever those who had been guilty of incontinence, murder, and idolatry. This was done in pursuance of Montanist principles.[39]

Those persons were highly honored who endured persecutions for the sake of the Christian faith. The death of *a martyr* (μάρτυρ, Acts xxii. 20; Heb. xii. 1; Apoc. xvii. 6) was supposed, like baptism, to have the efficacy of destroying sin (lavacrum sanguinis, τὸ βάπτισμα διὰ πυρός, Luke xii. 50; Mark x. 39), supplied the place even of baptism (according to Matthew x. 39), and alone introduced the person immediately to the presence of the Lord in paradise (Matt. v. 10–12; Apoc. vi. 9: hence ἡμέρα γενέθλιος, γενέθλια τῶν μαρτύρων, natales, natalitia martyrum.[40] But the surviving *confessors* also (ὁμολογῆται, confessores, Matt. x. 32; 1 Tim. vi. 12, 13) were held to be chosen members of Christ. People were zealous in visiting them in

tristi tractatione mutare. Caeterum pastum et potum pura nosse; non ventris scilicet, sed animae causa. Plerumque vero jejuniis preces alere, ingemiscere, lachrymari, et mugire dies noctesque ad dominum Deum tuum, presbyteris advolvi, et caris Dei adgeniculari, omnibus fratribus legationes deprecationis suae injungere.—In quantum non peperceris tibi, in tantum tibi Deus, crede, parcet.

[38] Hermae Pastor ii. Mand. 4, § 1. Servis enim Dei poenitentia una est. (Cf. Cotelerius ad h. l.) Then he softens, § 3, the principle afterward asserted by the Montanists, quod alia poenitentia non est nisi illa, cum in aquam descendimus, et accipimus, remissionem peccatorum, so far: quod post vocationem illam magnam et sanctam, si quis tentatus fuerit a Diabolo, et peccaverit, unam poenitentiam habet. So too Clemens Alex. Strom. ii. c. 13, p. 459, s. Cf. Bingham, lib. xviii. c. 4, vol. viii. p. 156, ss.

[39] Tertull. de Pudic. c. 12, appeals in favor of this to Acts xv. 29. Cyprian. Epist. 52: Apud antecessores nostros quidam de Episcopis istic in provincia nostra dandam pacem moechis non putaverunt, et in totum poenitentiae locum contra adulteria clauserunt. Non tamen a Coëpiscoporum suorum collegio recesserunt, aut catholicae Ecclesiae unitatem vel duritiae vel censurae suae obstinatione ruperunt; ut, quia apud alios adulteris pax dabatur, qui non dabat, de ecclesia separaretur. Manente concordiae vinculo et perseverante Catholicae Ecclesiae individuo sacramento, actum suum disponit et dirigit unusquisque Episcopus, rationem propositi sui Domino redditurus. Though this severity was afterward relaxed in reference to the Moechi (see below, § 59, note 4), yet they still remained at first united with the Montanists in asserting this principle, Tertull. de Pudic. c. 12: Quod neque idololatriae neque sanguini pax ab Ecclesiis redditur.

[40] Hermas (Pastor. iii. Simil. ix. 28) says to the martyrs: Vitam vobis donat Dominus, nec intelligitis. Delicta enim vestra vos gravabant: et nisi passi essetis hujus nominis causa, propter peccata certe vestra mortui eratis Deo. Tertull. de Resurr. carnis, 43: Nemo enim peregrinatus a corpore statim immoratur penes Dominum, nisi ex martyrii praerogativa scilicet paradiso, non inferis diversurus. (In like manner, according to the ancient Greeks, only heroes attained to the Ἠλύσιον or the μακάρων νῆσοι, of whose situation similar ideas were entertained as of Paradise, see Dissen de Fortunatorum insulis disp. Gotting. 1837. On Paradise see Uhlemann in Illgen's Zeitschr. f. d. hist. Theol. i. i. 146.) Clemens Alex. Strom. iv. p. 596: ἔοικεν οὖν τὸ μαρτύριον ἀποκάθαρσις εἶναι ἁμαρτιῶν μετὰ δόξης.

the prisons, and taking care of them;[41] and this was enjoined on the deacons as a peculiar duty.[42] If the lapsed (lapsi)[43] had been admitted by them to communion, there was a general aversion any longer to refuse them restoration to the privileges of the church.[44] As it was an important point in the estimation of Christians generally to keep up the consciousness of enduring communion with their departed, this communion, accordingly, with the blessed martyrs, was especially valuable and dear to them. In this sense, families celebrated the remembrance of their departed members,[45] churches that of their martyrs yearly on the day of their death,[46] by prayers at the

[41] Tertull. ad Martyres, c. 1, init.: Inter carnis alimenta, benedicti martyres designati, quae vobis et domina mater ecclesia de uberibus suis, et singuli fratres de opibus suis propriis in carcerem subministrant, capite aliquid et a nobis, quod faciat ad spiritum quoque educandum. Carnem enim saginari et spiritum esurire non prodest. The excess of care which he here only refers to (cf. Lucian. de morte Peregrini, c. 12), he afterward censured with bitterness in the Psychics, de Jejunio c. 12: Plane vestrum est in carceribus popinas exhibere martyribus incertis, ne consuetudinem quaerant, ne taedeat vitae, ne novi abstinentiae disciplina scandalizenter. He even accuses them of endeavoring to put courage into the prisoners before their judges, condito mero tanquam antidoto.

[42] Cypriani Ep. 11: Semper sub antecessoribus nostris factum est, ut Diaconi ad carcerem commeantes Martyrum desideria consiliis suis et scripturarem praeceptis gubernarent. So Perpetua relates in the Passio Perpetuae Felicitatis c. 3: Ibi tunc Tertius et Pomponius, benedicti Diaconi, qui nobis ministrabant, constituerunt praemio, ut paucis horis emissi in meliorem locum carceris refrigeraremus.

[43] In opposition to the stantes, as Romans xiv. 4, 1 Cor. x. 12.

[44] Epist. Eccl. Vienn. et Ludg. ap. Euseb. v. 2, § 3. Tertull. ad Mart. c. 1: Quam pacem quidam in ecclesia non habentes a martyribus in carcere exorare consueverunt. Idem de Pudicitia, c. 22: Ut quisque ex consensione vincula induit adhuc mollia, in novo custodiae nomine statim ambiunt moechi, statim adeunt fornicatores, jam preces circumsonant, jam lacrymae circumstagnant maculati cujusque, nec ulli magis aditum carceris redimunt, quam qui Ecclesiam perdiderunt.

[45] Tertull. de Exhort. Cast. c. 11, to the man who had married a second time: Neque enim pristinam poteris odisse, cui etiam religiosiorem reservas affectionem, ut jam receptae apud Deum, pro cujus spiritu postulas, pro qua oblationes annuas reddis. Stabis ergo ad Deum cum tot uxoribus, quot in oratione commemoras, et offeres pro duabus, et commendabis illas duas. De Monogamia c. 10: Enimvero et pro anima ejus (mariti mortui) orat (uxor), et refrigerium interim adpostulat ei, et in prima resurrectione consortium, et offert annuis diebus dormitionis ejus.

[46] Epist. Eccl. Smyrn. de martyr. Polyc. ap. Euseb. iv. 15, 15: *Χριστὸν μὲν γὰρ υἱὸν ὄντα τοῦ θεοῦ προσκυνοῦμεν· τοὺς δὲ μάρτυρας ὡς μαθητὰς τοῦ κυρίου καὶ μιμητὰς ἀγαπῶμεν ἀξίως, ἕνεκα εὐνοίας ἀνυπερβλήτου τῆς εἰς τὸν ἴδιον βασιλέα καὶ διδάσκαλον, ὧν γένοιτο καὶ ἡμᾶς συγκοινωνούς τε καὶ συμμαθητὰς γενέσθαι.—οὕτως τε ἡμεῖς ὕστερον ἀνελόμενοι τὰ τιμιώτερα λίθων πολυτελῶν καὶ δοκιμώτερα ὑπὲρ χρυσίον ὀστᾶ αὐτοῦ* (Πολυκάρπου), *ἀπεθέμεθα ὅπου καὶ ἀκόλουθον ἦν. ἔνθα ὡς δυνατὸν ἡμῖν συναγομένοις ἐν ἀγαλλιάσει καὶ χαρᾷ, παρέξει ὁ κύριος ἐπιτελεῖν τὴν τοῦ μαρτυρίου αὐτοῦ ἡμέραν γενέθλιον, εἴς τε τῶν προηθληκότων μνήμην, καὶ τῶν μελλόντων ἄσκησίν τε καὶ ἑτοιμασίαν.* Tert. de Corona mil. 3: Oblationes pro defunctis, pro natalitiis annua die facimus, Cyprian. Epist. 34: Sacrificia pro eis (martyribus semper, ut meministis, offerimus, quoties martyrum passiones et dies anniversaria commemoratione celebramus. Comp. Cyprian's

graves,[47] and by *agapae*. So high an estimation of martyrdom induced many Christians to give themselves up to the authorities, thus furnishing cause for the charge of fanatical enthusiasm brought against them by the heathen.[48] This mode of proceeding, however, was for the most part discountenanced, in consequence of the express command of Christ (Matt. x. 23).[49]

instructions to his clergy how they should take care of the confessors. Epist. 37: Officium meum vestra diligentia repraesentet, faciat omnia quae fieri oportet circa eos, quos in talibus meritis fidei ac virtutis illustravit divina dignatio. Denique et dies eorum quibus excedunt annotate, ut commemorationes eorum inter memorias Martyrum celebrare possimus —et celebrentur hic a nobis oblationes et sacrificia ob commemorationes eorum quae cito vobiscum Domino protegente celebrabimus. Further notices of the martyrs were the affairs of private individuals; and the representation of Anastasius (liber Pontificalis in vita Clementis) originated in the respect paid to saints in later times. Hic fecit vii. regiones dividi Notariis fidelibus Ecclesiae, qui gesta Martyrum sollicite et curiose, unusquisque per regionem suam, perquirerent (cf. vitae Anteri and Fabiani), which was afterward copied into martyrologies. How few genuine histories of the martyrs may be expected from this age is evident from Augustini sermo xciii. de diversis: Hoc primum primi Martyris (Stephani) meritum commendatum est charitati vestrae: quia, cum aliorum Martyrum vix gesta inveniamus, quae in solemnitatibus eorum recitare possimus, hujus passio in canonico libro est. Gregorius M. lib. viii. ep. 29, ad Eulogiam Episc. Alex.: Praeter illa quae in Eusebii libris de gestis SS. Martyrum continentur, nulla in archivo hujus nostrae Ecclesiae, vel in Romanae urbis bibliothecis esse cognovi, nisi pauca quaedam in unius codicis volumine collecta. Nos autem paene omnium martyrum, distinctis per dies singulos passionibus, collecta in uno codice nomina habemus, atque quotidianis diebus in eorum veneratione missarum solemnia agimus. Non tamen in eodem volumine, quis qualiter sit passus indicatur, sed tantummodo nomen, locus, et dies passionis ponitur. The cause of this may not indeed have been that assigned by Prudentius *περὶ στεφάνων*, i. v. 75:

Chartulas blasphemus olim nam satelles abstulit,
Ne tenacibus libellis erudita saecula
Ordinem, tempus, modumque passionis proditum,
Dulcibus linguis per aures posterorum spargerent.

Cf. Casp. Sagittarius de natalitiis martyrum in primitiva ecclesia. Jen. 1678, auctius ed. J. A. Schmid. 1696. 4.

47 Hence the cry of the heathen: Areae non sint. s. Tertull. ad Scapul. c. 3.

48 Tertull. ad Scapulam, c. 5. Arrius Antoninus (at the time of Hadrian) in Asia cum persequeretur instanter, omnes illius civitatis Christiani ante tribunalia ejus se manu facta obtulerunt, cum ille, paucis duci jussis, reliquis ait: *ὦ δειλοί, εἰ θέλετε ἀποθνήσκειν, κρημνοῖς ἢ βρόχοις ἔχετε.* In like manner, Justin makes the heathen say to the Christians, Apol. ii. 4: *πάντες οὖν ἑαυτοὺς φωνεύσαντες πορεύεσθε ἤδη παρὰ τὸν θεὸν, καὶ ἡμῖν πράγματα μὴ παρέχετε.* Afterward the Montanists especially, see Tertull. l. c. de fuga in persec. &c. Cf. S. F. Rivini diss. de professoribus veteris Ecclesiae martyribus. Lips. 1739. 4.

49 Epist. Eccl. Smyrn. c. 4: *Οὐκ ἐπαινοῦμεν τοὺς προσιόντας ἑαυτοῖς, ἐπειδὴ οὐχ οὕτως διδάσκει τὸ εὐαγγέλιον.* (Eusebius, an admirer of such transactions, has omitted this sentence). Clemens Alex. Strom. iv. p. 597, vii. p. 871, ed. Potter.

THIRD DIVISION.

FROM SEPTIMUS SEVERUS TO THE SOLE DOMINION OF CONSTANTINE.
A.D. 193–324.

INTRODUCTION.

§ 54.

CONDITION OF HEATHENISM.

While the Roman empire appeared hastening to its fall, the throne being occupied by soldiers, the provinces devastated by barbarians, and the government changed into the most arbitrary despotism, the kingdom of superstition, in which alone the men of that time sought for peace and security from the dangers that surrounded them, had established itself firmly. Not only were the emperors themselves addicted to this superstition, but they also openly confessed it, and in part introduced even foreign rites into Rome.[1] The Platonic philosophy, which had confined itself till now to a defense of the popular religions, and to securing for the wise a more elevated worship of deity, endeavored, since the beginning of the third century, to give to the people's religion a higher and more spiritual form, under the pretense of bringing it back to its original, purer state. This philosophy had been unquestionably forced to this by the spiritual preponderance of Christianity. With this view, *Philostratus*

[1] P. E. Müller de hierarchia et studio vitae asceticae in sacris et mysteriis Graec et Rom. latentibus, Hafn. 1803. Abschn. 3 (translated in the N. Bibl. d. schön. Wissensch. Bd. 70. S. 3, ff.) The Jewish religion also was continually incorporated into this religious mixture (comp. above, § 17, note 9), see Commodiani (about 270) instructiones adv. gentium deos pro christiana disciplina (in Gallandii Biblioth. vett. Patr. T. iii.):

> Inter utrumque putans dubie vivendo cavere,
> Nudatus a lege decrepitus luxu procedis?
> Quid in synagoga decurris ad Pharisaeos,
> Ut tibi misericors fiat, quem denegas ultro?
> Exis inde foris, iterum tu fana requiris.

the elder composed the life of *Apollonius* of Tyana (220), in which the latter was represented as the reformer of heathenism.[2] But all the preceding tendencies of philosophy, and this also, were perfected in the so-called *new-platonic* school.[3] The founder of it, *Ammonius Saccas*, Σακκᾶς (*i. e.*, σακκοφόρος) of Alexandria († about 243), an apostate from Christianity to heathenism,[4] appears to have borrowed the pattern of his heathenism defending philosophy principally from the Christian Gnostics. He communicated his system only as a secret; but by his disciple, the Egyptian *Plotinus* († 270), it was farther developed, and spread abroad with incredible rapidity. With no less renown, Plotinus was followed by his disciple, *Porphyry* of Tyre (*Malchus* † 304), and he by *Jamblichus* of Chalcis († 333), who survived the overthrow of paganism.[5]

The leading principles of the theology of these philosophers, who wished to find the absolute, not by a process of thought, but by immediate intuition, like the Christian Gnostics, are the following: From the highest existence (τὸ ἕν) arises intelligence (ὁ νοῦς), and from this the soul (ἡ ψυχή). The highest world of intelligence or understanding (κόσμος νοητός), is the totality of all intelligences, of the gods as well as of human spirits. By the soul of the world (hence called the δημιουργός), the visible world was formed. The gods are divided into *those dwelling above the world* (ἄϋλοι, νοητοί, ἀφανεῖς), and *those inhabiting the world* (περικόσμιοι, αἰσθητοί, ἐμφανεῖς). To the latter the different parts of the world are intrusted for oversight (hence θεοὶ μερικοί, μέρισται, ἐθνάρχαι, πολιοῦχοι); and from them the various nations

[2] Comp. § 14, note 10, and Baur's treatise there quoted. Tzschirner's Fall. d. Heidenthums, i. 405, 461.

[3] Concerning this comp. Tiedemann's Geist der specul. Philosoph. iii. 262. Tennemann's Gesch. d. Philos. vi. Ritter's Gesch. d. Philos. iv. 535. C. Meiner's Beitrag zur Gesch. d. Denkart d. ersten Jahrh. n. Chr. G. Leipzig 1782. 8, S. 47, ff. Imm. Fichte de philosophiae novae Platonicae origine. Berol. 1818. F. Bouterwek Philosophorum Alexandrinorum ac Neo-Platonicorum recensio accuratior in the Commentatt. Soc. Reg. Scient. Gotting. recentiores, vol. v. (1823) p. 227, ss. Tzschirner's Fall. d. Heidenth. i. S. 404, ff. K. Vogt's Neoplatonismus u. Christenthum. Th. i. Neoplatonische Lehre. Berlin. 1836. 8.

[4] Porphyrius contra Christianos ap. Euseb. vi. 19: Ἀμμώνιος μὲν γὰρ Χριστιανὸς ἐν Χριστιανοῖς ἀνατραφεὶς τοῖς γονεῦσιν, ὅτε τοῦ φρονεῖν καὶ τῆς φιλοσοφίας ἥψατο, εὐθὺς πρὸς τὴν κατὰ νόμους πολιτείαν μετεβάλετο. On the other hand, Eusebius: τῷ Ἀμμωνίῳ τὰ τῆς ἐνθέου φιλοσοφίας ἀκέραια καὶ ἀδιάπτωτα καὶ μέχρις ἐσχάτης τοῦ βίου διέμενε τελευτῆς. Here Eusebius evidently refers to another Ammonius, probably to the author of the Gospel Harmony.

[5] Vita Plotini by Porphyrius in Fabric. Bibl. Gr. vol. iv. Eunapii (about 395) vitae Sophistarum, rec. et illustr. J. F. Boissonade. Amst. 1822. 8.

have derived their peculiar character. Lower than the gods stand the *demons*, some good, and others bad. While the people worship the highest god only in their national deities, and that with propriety, the wise man must, on the contrary, endeavor to attain to immediate union with the highest deity. While Neo-platonism endeavored in this way both to prop up heathenism, and to give it a higher and more spiritual character, it adapted itself, on the one hand, to the grossest popular superstitions, and, on the other, adopted the purest ideas respecting the supreme deity. Accordingly, it communicated, at the same time, the most excellent precepts regarding the moral worship of God, and recommended asceticism and theurgy,[6] in order to elevate its votaries to communion with the deity, and to obtain dominion over the demons. It can not well be doubted, that Christianity influenced the development of the purer aspect of the neo-platonic doctrines, when we look at the striking agreement of many of these doctrines with those of Christianity.[7] This source, however, was not acknowledged by the new Platonists, who wished that the root of their doctrine should be considered as existing only in the national philosophy, and, along with it, in the oldest Chaldean and Egyptian wisdom. In consequence of this view, neo-platonic productions appeared sometimes in the form of *Chaldean oracles*,[8] and in the name of *Hermes Trismegistus.*[9]

6 Lobeck Aglaophamus, i. p. 104, ss.

7 Mosheim, Diss. de studio ethnicorum Christianos imitandi, in his Diss. ad hist. eccl. pertinentes, i. 351. Ullmann über den Einfluss des Christenth. auf Porphyrius, in the theol. Stud. u. Krit., 1832, ii. 376.

8 Respecting the Χαλδαϊκὰ λόγια among the New Platonists, see J. C. Thilo, Comm. de coelo empyreo, pp. iii. Halae. 1839, 40. 4.

9 Hermes Trismegistus was the concentration of the old Egyptian wisdom, in whose name works of very different kinds were composed. The philosophic portion of them belongs to the New Platonism: Asclepius and Poemander are the most important (Opp. gr. lat. ed. Adr. Turnebus. Paris. 1554. 4. Colon. 1630. fol. Hermes Trismegists Poemander, von D. Tiedemann. Berlin. 1781). Even in them we find many ideas borrowed from Christianity, so that they are erroneously, in part, attributed to Christian authors. Comp. Casauboni exercitatt. ad Baronium, p. 69. Chr. Meiner's Religionsgeschich. d. aeltesten Voelker, bes d. Aegyptier. Göttingen. 1775. S. 202. Tennemann's Gesch. d. Philos. vi. 464. Baumgarten-Crusius de librorum Hermeticorum origine atque indole (a Jena Easter-programm), 1827. 4to.

FIRST CHAPTER.

EXTERNAL FORTUNES OF CHRISTIANITY.

§ 55.

DISPOSITION OF THE HEATHEN TOWARD IT.

Though the reports of secret abominations said to be practiced by the Christians in their assemblies vanished by degrees among the *heathen people*,[1] yet other prejudices against them remained unchanged. Every public calamity was continually regarded as a token of the wrath of the gods against the Christians, and excited fresh hatred and persecution.[2] The *cultivated heathen* held fast by the old view, that whatever truth they could not avoid perceiving in the Christian religion, was disfigured by a barbarous form, and the admixture of rude enthusiasm, and was found in a purer form in their national traditions. From this point of view began, from the commencement of the third century, the efforts which were made to reform the popular religion, that it might be elevated to the same height as Christianity. In this way either both religions might be blended together, or greater power would be given to heathenism to withstand Christianity. *Philostratus*, in his life of Apollonius of Tyana, might have had in view this *syncretistic* object,[3] but Neo-platonism, on the contrary, appeared in an attitude decidedly hostile to Christianity.[4] The new Plato-

[1] Origenes c. Cels. vi. p. 294: Ἥτις δυσφημία παραλόγως πάλαι μὲν πλείστων ὅσων ἐκράτει,—καὶ νῦν δὲ ἔτι ἀπατᾷ τινας. Eusebius, iv. 7, 5: Οὐκ εἰς μακρόν γε μὴν αὐτῷ (δαίμονι) ταῦτα προὐχώρει.

[2] Comp. above, § 41, note 26. The constant reproach of the heathen may be found in Cyprianus lib. ad Demetrianum: Dixisti, per nos fieri, et quod nobis debeant imputari omnia ista, quibus nunc mundus quatitur et urgetur, quod dii vestri a nobis non colantur. Origenes in Matth. commentariorum series, c. 39 (on Matth. xxiv. 9), Arnobius adv. gentes i. c. 1: Postquam esse in mundo christiana gens coepit, terrarum orbem periisse, multiformibus malis affectum esse genus humanum: ipsos etiam Coelites derelictis curis solennibus, quibus quondam solebant invisere res nostras, terrarum ab regionibus exterminatos, c. 3, iii. 36, iv. 47. Cf. Maximini Epist. ap. Euseb. ix. 7, 4.

[3] Comp. § 14, note 10. Baur's Apollonius u. Christus, in the Tübingen Zeitschr. f. Theol. 1832, iv. 123, ff.

[4] Mosheim de turbata per recentiores Platonicos ecclesia, in his Dissert. ad hist. eccl. pert. i. 120, 173. Keil de Causis alieni Platonic. recent. a rel. Christ. animi Opusc. acad. ii. 393, ss.). Tzschirner's Fall d. Heidenth. i. 560.

nists, for the most part, regarded Christ as the most distinguished sage and theurgist. On the other hand, however, they asserted that the doctrine of Christ perfectly agreed with theirs at first, but that it had been in many ways corrupted by his disciples, especially by the doctrine of Christ's deity, and forbidding the worship of the gods.[5] In this manner the Christians appeared to be a crowd of misguided enthusiasts who had strayed from their leader, in contrast with whom, the heathen in their philosophy, and in their purified popular worship, possessed the purer truth, and occupied a higher position. The contest of these philosophers with Christianity, which continued till the sixth century, had thus a more earnest character than the earlier attacks. In the works of *Plotinus* many passages are aimed at the Christians, without their name being introduced.[6]

[5] Porphyrius *περὶ τῆς ἐκ λογίων φιλοσοφίας* (a book which Ficinus had read even in the fifteenth century. See his Comment. in Plotini Ennead. ii. lib. iii. c. 7, p. 121, and frequently, and which is probably still preserved in some Florentine library) apud Augustin. de civ. Dei, xix. 23: Praeter opinionem profecto quibusdam videatur esse quod dicturi sumus. Christum enim Dii piissimum pronunciaverunt et immortalem factum, et cum bona praedicatione ejus meminerunt (namely by oracles). Christianos autem pollutos et contaminatos et errore implicatos esse dicunt, et multis talibus adversus eos blasphemiis utuntur.—De Christo autem interrogantibus si est Deus, ait Hecate: "Quoniam quidem immortalis anima post corpus ut incedit, nosti: a sapientia autem abscissa semper errat: viri pietate praestantissimi est illa anima, hanc colunt aliena a se veritate." The same in Euseb. Demonstr. evang. iii. c. 8:—

"Οττι μὲν ἀθανάτη ψυχὴ μετὰ σῶμα προβαίνει,
Γιγνώσκει σοφίῃ τετιμημένος. ἀλλάγε ψυχὴ
'Ανέρος εὐσεβίῃ προφερεστάτη ἐστὶν ἐκείνου.

Sunt spiritus terreni minimi loco terreno quodam malorum Daemonum potestati subjecti Ab his sapientes Hebraeorum, quorum unus iste etiam Jesus fuit, sicut audisti divina Apollinis oracula, quae superius dicta sunt: ab his ergo Hebraei Daemonibus pessimis et minoribus spiritibus vetabant religiosos, et ipsis vacare prohibebant: venerari autem magis coelestes Deos, amplius autem venerari Deum patrem. Hoc autem et Dii praecipiunt, et in superioribus ostendimus, quemadmodum animadvertere ad Deum monent, et illum colere ubique imperant. Verum indocti et impiae naturae, quibus vere fatum non concessit a Diis dona obtinere, neque habere Jovis immortalis notionem, non audientes et Deos et divinos viros Deos quidem omnes recusaverunt, prohibitos autem Daemones non solum nullis odiis inseque, sed etiam revereri delegerunt. Aug. de Cons. Ev. lib. i. c. 7, § 11. Honorandum enim tamquam sapientissimum virum putant, colendum autem tamquam Deum negant. Ibid. c. 9, § 14: Ita vero isti desipiunt, ut illis libris, quos eum (Christum) scripsisse existimant, dicant contineri eas artes, quibus eum putant illa fecisse miracula, quorum fama ubique precrebuit: quod existimando se ipsis produnt, quid diligant, et quid affectent. Ibid. c. 15: Vani Christi laudatores et christianae religionis obliqui obtrectatores—continent blasphemias a Christo, et eas in discipulos ejus effundunt. Ibid. c. 34: Ita enim volunt et ipsum credi, nescio quid aliud scripsisse, quod diligunt, nihilque sensisse, contra Deos suos, sed eos potius magico ritu coluisse, et discipulos ejus non solum de illo fuisse mentitos, dicendo illum Deum, per quem facta sint omnia, cum aliud nihil quam homo fuerit, quamvis excellentissimae sapentiae: verum etiam de Diis eorum non hoc docuisse, quod ab illo didicissent.

[6] Vogt's Neoplatonismus u. Christenthum, S. 137, ff.

Direct attacks against them were the κατὰ Χριστιανῶν λογοί, fifteen books of *Porphyry*;[7] and the λόγοι φιλαλήθεις πρὸς Χριστιανούς, in two books of *Hierocles*, governor of Bithynia under Diocletian.[8] The lives also of Pythagoras by *Jamblichus* and *Porphyry*, had a hostile reference to Christianity.[9]

§ 56.

CONDUCT OF THE EMPERORS TOWARD THE CHRISTIANS.

After Christianity had been favorably regarded by several emperors in the first half of this period, and had been introduced into the general religious syncretism, there arose in the second half, not only new persecutions, but such as partook of a far more hazardous character than any of the earlier, since they were generally commanded by the emperors, and aimed at nothing less than the complete annihilation of Christianity. *Septimus Severus* (193 till 211) was, indeed, not unfriendly to the Christians at first (*Tertull. ad Scapulam*, c. 4); but they had much to suffer in the provinces from the popular rage[1] and the avarice of the governors.[2] These persecutions increased considerably after the emperor (203), changed, perhaps, by the excesses of the Montanists, had forbidden the adoption of Christ-

[7] Whether he was an apostate from Christianity, as Socrates, iii. 23, Augustin. de civit. Dei, x. 28, say, is questionable. See the correspondence between Siberus and Thomas in Miscellan. Lips. tom. i. p. 331, ss. Ullmann in the theol. Stud. u. Krit. 1832, ii. 380.—Fragments of his writings have been collected by Luc. Holstenius Diss. de vita et scriptis Porphyrii. Rom. 1630. 8 (reprinted in Fabrici Bibl. Gr. t. iv. p. 207, ss.). The works written against him by Methodius, bishop of Tyre, Eusebius, bishop of Caesarea, and (the best) by Apollinaris, bishop of Laodicea, have also been lost.

[8] Cf. Lactant. Institutt. div. v. c. 2 and 3. Agaist his comparison of Christ with Apollonius of Tyana see Eusebius contra Hierocl. lib. appended to his Demonstratio Evangelica ed. Paris 1628, and Colon. 1688. Baur's Apollonius von Tyana und Christus, S. 1. Even in Chrysostom's time, the writings of the heathen philosophers against Christianity were for the most part lost (Chrys. de S. Babyl. Opp. ed. Montf. ii. 539). According to a law of Valentinian III. and Theodosius II., A.D. 449, they were enjoined to be burnt (Cod. Justin. i. 1, 3).

[9] Jamblichus de vita Pythagorae gr. et lat. ed. Theoph. Kiessling. Acc. Porphyrius de vita Pyth. 2 Partes. Lips. 1815, 16. 8. Comp. Mosheim, Dissertt. ad hist. eccl. pert. i. 151 Tzschirner's Fall d. Heidenth. i. 465. Baur's Apollonius, S. 208.

Tertullian. de Fuga in persecut. c. 12: Persecutionem—non esse—redemptio nummaria fuga est.

[1] Tertullian. de Fuga in persecut. c. 12: Persecutionem—non esse—redimendam—redemptio nummaria fuga est.

[2] Tertull. Apologet. (written 198) c. 7, 12, 30, 37, 49. Cf. Mosheim de aetate apologet. Tertull. et initio persecut. Christ. sub Severo (Dissertt. ad hist. eccl. pert. vol. i. p. 1, ss.).

ianity.[3] Under *Caracalla*, however (211–217), they gradually ceased.[4] *Elagabalus* (218–222) went so far as to think of blending the Christian religion with the worship of his god.[5] *Severus Alexander* (222–235), and his mother, Julia Mammaea, were addicted to a similar but more rational syncretism, and gave the Christians many proofs of their good-will.[6] But *Maximin the Thracian* (235–238), persecuted the Christian clergy, and overlooked the persecutions in which the people of some provinces, excited against the Christians by an earthquake,

[3] Cf. Tertull. de Corona militis.—Spartian. in Severo c. 17: In itinere Palaestinis pluri ma jura fundavit. Judaeos fieri sub gravi poena vetuit. Idem etiam de Christianis sanxit. Ulpiamus in lib. sing. de officio Praefecti Urbi (Dig. lib. i. tit. 12, § 14): Divus Severus rescripsit, eos etiam, qui illicitum collegium coisse dicuntur, apud Praefectum Urbis accusandos. Euseb. vi. 7: (Ἰούδας συγγραφέων ἕτερος) τὴν θρυλλουμένην τοῦ ἀντιχρίστου παρουσίαν ἤδη τότε πλησιάζειν ᾤετο· οὕτω σφοδρῶς ἡ τοῦ καθ' ἡμῶν τότε διωγμοῦ κίνησις, τὰς τῶν πολλῶν ἀνετάραττε διανοίας. Martyrs in Alexandria: Leonides (Euseb. vi. 1), Potamiaena (Ibid. c. 5), in Africa: Martyres Scillitani, Perpetua et Felicitas (Acta apud Ruinart and in Münter primord. Eccl. Afr. p. 219, ss. On Severus generally see Münter, l. c. p. 172, ss.).

[4] Not in Africa at first, Tertull. ad Scapulam liber.—In this book, c. 4, Caracalla is said to be lacte christiano educatus.—Under this emperor, as appears from Dig. lib. i. tit. 16, l. 4, Domitius Ulpianus wrote his Libb. x. de officio Proconsulis. Cf. Lactant. Institutt. v c. 11: Domitius de officio Proconsulis libro septimo rescripta principum nefaria collegit, ut doceret, quibus poenis affici oporteret eos, qui se cultores Dei confiterentur.

[5] Lampridius in Heliogabal. c. 3: Heliogabalum in Palatino monte juxta aedes imperatorias consecravit, eique templum fecit, studens et Matris typum et Vestae ignem et Palladium et ancilia et omnia Romanis veneranda in illud transferre templum, et id agens, ne quis Romae Deus, nisi Heliogabalus coleretur. Dicebat praeterea, Judaeorum et Samaritanorum religiones, et christianam devotionem illuc transferendam, ut omnium culturarum secretum Heliogabali sacerdotium teneret. Baur's Apollonius v. Tyana u. Christus, in the Tübingen Zeitschrift f. Theol. 1832, iv. 127.

[6] Origen was called by Julia Mammaea to Antioch, Euseb. vi. 21. On this account, later writers (first Orosius, vii. 18) make her a Christian.—Lampridius in Sev. Alex. c. 22: Judaeis privilegia reservavit, Christianos esse passus est. C. 28: Quodam tempore festo ut solent, Antiochenses, Aegyptii, Alexandrini lacessiverant eum conviciolis, Syrum Archisynagogum eum vocantes, et Archierea. C. 29: Matutinis horis in larario suo, in quo et divos Principes, sed optimos electos, et animas sanctiores, in queis et Apollonium, et, quantum scriptor suorum temporum dicit, Christum, Abraham et Orpheum, et hujusmodi caeteros habebat, ac majorum effigies, rem divinam faciebat. C. 43: Christo templum facere voluit, eumque inter Deos recipere, quod et Hadrianus cogitasse fertur:—sed prohibitus est ab iis, qui consulentes sacra repererant omnes Christianos futuros, si id optato evenisset, et templa reliqua deserenda. (On the religious syncretism of the emperor see two dissertations in Heyne Opusc. acad. vol. vi. p. 169.) C. 45: Ubi aliquos voluisset vel rectores provinciis dare, vel praepositos facere, vel procuratores, id est rationales ordinare, nomina eorum proponebat, hortans populum, ut si quis quid haberet crminis, probaret manifestus rebus; si non probasset, subiret poenam capitis: dicebatque grave esse, cum id Christiani et Judaei facerent in praedicandis sacerdotibus, qui ordinandi sunt, non fieri in provinciarum rectoribus, quibus, et fortunae hominum committerentur et capita. C. 49: Cum Christiani quendam locum qui publicus fuerat, occupassent, contra popinarii decerent, sibi eum deberi, rescripsit, melius esse, ut quomodo cunque illic Deus colatur, quam popinariis dedatur.

indulged.[7] After the reign of *Gordian* (238–244), and *Philip the Arabian* (244–249),[8] during which they were unmolested, *Decius* (249–251), immediately after he had ascended the throne, gave the signal by an edict for a fearful (the first really general) persecution,[9] in which many Christians suffered martyrdom,[10] while many others, enervated by long quietude, apostatized (*sacrificati*, *thurificati*, *libellatici*).[11] *Gallus* also (251–253), after a short interruption, continued this persecution.[12]

[7] Eusebius, vi. 28, Firmilianus ad Cyprian. (in Epp. Cypr. 75) Origenes Commentar. in Matth. xxiv. 9 (tom. 28).

[8] Euseb. Hist. eccl. vi. 34: *Τοῦτον κατέχει λόγος Χριστιανὸν ὄντα ἐν ἡμέρα τῆς ὑστάτης τοῦ Πάσχα παννυχίδος τῶν ἐπὶ τῆς ἐκκλησίας εὐχῶν τῷ πλήθει συμμετασχεῖν ἐθελῆσαι· οὐ πρότερον δὲ ὑπὸ τοῦ τηνικάδε προεστῶτος* (according to Leontius, bishop of Antioch, about 350, in the Chronic. Pasch. ad Olymp. 257, it was Babylas, bishop of Antioch) *ἐπιτραπῆναι εἰσβαλεῖν, ἢ ἐξομολογήσασθαι, καὶ τοῖς ἐν παραπτώμασιν ἐξεταζομένοις, μετανοίας τε χώραν ἴσχουσιν, ἑαυτὸν καταλέξαι·—καὶ πειθαρχῆσαί γε προθύμως λέγεται.* Hieron. in Chron. ad ann. 246. Philippus primus omnium ex Romanis imperatoribus Christianus fuit. First contradicted by Jos. Scaliger ad Euseb. Chron. and Is. Casaubonus ad Jul. Capitolin. p. 201, especially Frid. Spanheim de Christianismo Phil. Ar. (Opp. t. ii. p. 400, ss.). It looks like a disposition of this emperor toward the Christians, that Origen wrote letters both to him and his spouse. Severus, Eusèbius, vi. 36.

[9] Of the earlier persecutions, it is said by Origenes, contra Celsum iii. p. 116: *Ὀλίγοι κατὰ καιροὺς καὶ σφόδρα εὐαρίθμητοι περὶ τῆς Χριστιανῶν θεοσεβείας τεθνήκασι.*

[10] Gregor. Nyssenus in vita Gregor. Thaumaturgi (Opp. t. iii. p. 567): *Πέμπει πρὸς τοὺς τῶν ἐθνῶν καθηγουμένους πρόσταγμα, φοβερὰν κατ' αὐτῶν τὴν ἀπειλὴν τῆς τιμωρίας ὁρίζων, εἰ μὴ παντοίοις αἰκισμοῖς τοὺς τὸ ὄνομα τοῦ Χριστοῦ προσκυνοῦντας διαλωβήσαιντο, καὶ προσαγάγοιεν πάλιν αὐτοὺς φόβῳ τε καὶ τῇ τῶν αἰκισμῶν ἀνάγκῃ τῇ πατρῴᾳ τῶν δαιμόνων λατρείᾳ.* Descriptions by contemporaries Dionys. Alex. (apud Euseb. vi. 40–42) and Cyprian in his letters and de Lapsis lib.—Martyrs: Fabian, bishop of Rome, Babylas of Antioch, Alexander of Jerusalem, Pionius, presbyter at Smyrna (Cyprian. Epist. 52: Tyrannus infestus sacerdotibus Dei).

[11] Cypriani lib. de Lapsis: Ad prima statim verba minantis inimici maximus fratrum numerus fidem suam prodidit, nec prostratus est persecutionis impetu, sed voluntario lapsu se ipse prostravit.—Non exspectaverunt saltem, ut interrogati negarent, ut accenderent, apprehensi. Ante aciem multi victi, sine congressione prostrati, nec hoc sibi reliquerunt, ut sacrificare idolis viderentur inviti. A later pretext of the libellatici sec Cypriani Epist. 52: Ego prius legeram et Episcopo tractante cognoveram, non sacrificandum idolis:—et idcirco ne hoc facerem, quod non licebat, cum occasio libelli fuisset, oblata, quem nec ipsum acciperem, nisi ostensa fuisset occasio, ad magistratum vel veni, vel alio eunte mandavi, Christianum me esse, sacrificare mihi non licere, ad aras diaboli me venire non posse; dare me ob hoc praemium, ne quod non licet faciam. Different kinds of them, Cypr. Ep. 31: Sententiam nostram—protulimus adversus eos, qui se ipsos infideles illicita nefariorum libellorum professione prodiderant,—quo non minus, quam si ad nafarias aras accessissent, hoc ipso quod ipsum contestati fuerant tenerentur; sed etiam adversus illos qui acta fecissent, licet praesentes, cum fierent, non affuissent, cum praesentiam suam utique, ut sic scriberentur mandando, fecissent. Id. lib. de Lapsis: Nec sibi quominus agant poenitentiam blandiantur, qui etsi nefandis sacrificiis manus non contaminaverunt, libellis tamen conscientiam polluerunt. Et illa professio denegantis contestatio et Christiani: [est Christiani], quod fuerat abnuentis. Fecisse se dixit quidquid alius faciendo commisit. Cf. Mosheim de reb. Chr. ante Const. M. p. 483.

[12] Dionys. Alex. ap. Euseb. vii. 1.—Cypriani Epist. 57, 58, et lib. ad Demetrianum

Valerian (253–260), gave the Christians rest for some time, but was induced by his favorite *Macrianus* (257) to renew the persecution.[13] *Gallienus* (260–268), first put a stop to it;[14] and in the stormy times that now succeeded, the emperors had too much to do with antagonist emperors, rebellions, and barbarians, to think of persecuting the Christians. Only *Aurelian* (270–275) issued an edict against them, the execution of which was prevented by his murder that immediately followed. When the empire of *Diocletian* had received (284–305) four rulers (285, *Maximian*, Augustus of the west;—292, the Caesars, *Galerius* and *Constantius Chlorus*), the church was at first undisturbed, notwithstanding the enmity of *Galerius.* The Christians attained to the most important offices, and the church was raised to a condition externally prosperous (*Euseb.* viii. 1). The alleged persecution of *Maximian* in Gaul and Rome is very improbable.[15] But in February 303,

[13] Dionys. Alex. ap. Euseb. vii. 10, 11.—Cypriani Epist. 82, according to the report of his messengers sent to Rome: Quae sunt in vero ita se habent. Rescripsisse Valerianum ad Senatum, ut Episcopi et Presbyteri et Diacones in continenti animadvertantur, Senatores vero et egregii viri et equites Romani, dignitate amissa, etiam bonis spolientur, et si ademptis facultatibus Christiani esse perseveraverint, capite quoque multentur; matronae vero ademptis bonis in exsilium relegentur, Caesariani autem, quicunque vel prius confessi fuerant, vel nunc confessi fuerint, confiscentur, et vincti in Caesarianas possessiones descripti mittantur. Martyrs: Cyprian (Vita et Passio Cypr. scripta per Pontium diaconum ejus, and Acta proconsularia ejusd. apud Ruinart), Sixtus II. bishop of Rome, and Laurentius his deacon (Prudentius *περὶ στεφάνων* Hymn 2).

[14] The first laws of toleration. Two rescripts addressed on this subject to Christian bishops are quoted by Eusebius, vii. 13. The first is that by which Gallienus, after he had conquered Egypt (261), makes known to the bishops in that country the toleration which had been already announced to the rest of the empire: *Τὴν εὐεργεσίαν τῆς ἐμῆς δωρεᾶς διὰ παντὸς τοῦ κόσμου ἐκβιβασθῆναι προσέταξα. ὅπως ἀπὸ τῶν τόπων τῶν θρησκευσίμων ἀποχωρήσωσι. καὶ διὰ τοῦτο καὶ ὑμεῖς τῆς ἀντιγραφῆς τῆς ἐμῆς τῷ τύπῳ χρῆσθαι δύνασθε, ὥστε μηδένα ὑμῖν ἐνοχλεῖν.* The other he issued *τὰ τῶν καλουμένων κοιμητηρίων ἀπολαμβάνειν ἐπιτρέπωι χωρία.*

[15] Legio Thebaea, leg. felix Agaunensis, Thebaei with their leader (primicerius) Mauricius (286?) massacred in Acaunensibus angustiis (Agaunum, St. Maurice in Wallis). Eusebius, Lactantius, Prudentius, Sulpicius Severus, are silent on the subject. The first mention of it is about 520, in vita S. Romani (Acta SS. Februar. t. iii. p. 740). Then by Avitus, archbishop of Vienne († 523), dicta in Basilica SS. Agaunensium in innovatione monasterii ipsius vel passione martyrum. By Eucherius, bishop of Lyons (about 530), Passio SS. Mauricii ac sociorum ejus (apud Ruinart). These Latin acta appear to have been transferred, with arbitrary alterations, by Simeon Metaphrasta (Acta SS. Februar. t. iii. p. 237) to a Greek martyr, Mauricius (Theodoret Graec. affect. curat. disput. viii. in fine), who, as tribunus milit. is said to have been executed along with seventy soldiers in Apamea, in Syria, by the command of Maximianus. Against this narrative: Jean Dubordieu Diss. hist. et crit. sur le martyre de la Légion Thébéene. Amst. 1705. 12. For it: Jos. de L'Isle Défense de la vérité de la Légion Thébéene. Nancy. 1737. 12. Later additions respecting Thebans, who are said to have suffered in other places, ex. gr. Gregor. Turon.

Diocletian, moved by superstition[16] and the persuasions of *Galerius* and *Hierocles*, caused the splendid church in Nicomedia to be destroyed, and then issued in succession three edicts against the Christians,[17] which were finally succeeded by a *fourth* in 304, by virtue of which all Christians without exception were compelled to worship the gods.[18] Thus there arose in the entire Roman empire, with the exception of Gaul, where *Constantius Chlorus* was even now well-disposed toward the Christians,[19] the most violent persecution against them, abundant both in martyrs and in apostates (a new class called *traditores*). After the two Augusti had laid down their dignity (305), the persecution continued to rage in *the east* under the new Augustus, *Galerius* and his Caesar, *Maximin.*[20] In *Gaul*

de gloria martyr. i. 62. Est apud Agrippinensem urbem basilica, in qua dicuntur L. viri ex illa legione sacra Thebaeorum pro Christi nomine martyrium consummasse. Ado (about 860) has, on the other hand, even: Gereon et alii cccxviii. Pavia has had the whole scene transferred to its neighborhood in later times (Act. SS. September, t. vi. p. 377, 908, ss.). Perhaps the misunderstood expression, milites Christi, gave rise to most of these legends.

16 Constantine, ap. Euseb. de Vita Constant. ii. 50, 51, speaks of this from report.

17 Concerning all these persecutions comp. the contemporaries, Lactantius de Mortibus persecutorum, c. 7, ss., and Eusebius, Hist. Eccl. libb. viii.–x. First edict, Euseb. viii. 2: *Τὰς μὲν ἐκκλησίας εἰς ἔδαφος φέρειν, τὰς δὲ γραφὰς ἀφανεῖς πυρὶ γενέσθαι· καὶ τοὺς μὲν τιμῆς ἐπειλημμένους, ἀτίμους· τοὺς δὲ ἐν οἰκετίαις, εἰ ἐπιμένοιεν ἐν τῇ τοῦ Χριστιανισμοῦ προθέσει, ἐλευθερίας στερεῖσθαι.* (Rufin. Ne, se quis servorum permansisset Christianus, libertatem consequi posset.) Lactant. de Mort. persec. c. 13. Postridie propositum est edictum, quo cavebatur, ut religionis illius homines carerent omni honore ac dignitate, tormentis subjecti essent, ex quocunque ordine ac gradu venirent, adversus eos omnis actio caleret; ipsi non de injuria, non de adulterio, non de rebus ablatis agere possent; libertatem denique ac vocem non haberent. For explanation of this edict, see Mosheim de rebus Christ. ante Const. M. p. 925, s.—Second edict, Euseb. viii. 6, 8 (cf. viii. 2, 3): *Τοὺς πανταχόσε τῶν ἐκκλησιῶν προεστῶτας εἱρκταῖς καὶ δεσμοῖς ἐνεῖραι.* Third edict, Euseb. viii. 6, 10: *Τοὺς κατακλείστους, θύσαντας μὲν, ἐᾷν βαδίζειν ἐπ' ἐλευθερίας, ἐνισταμένους δὲ μυρίαις καταξαίνειν βασάνοις.* (Cf. Euseb. viii. 2, 3: *Πάσῃ μηχανῇ θύειν ἐξαναγκάζειν.*)

18 Fourth edict, Eusebius de martyribus Palaestinae, c. 3: *Καθολικῷ προστάγματι πάντας πανδημεὶ τοὺς κατὰ πόλιν θύειν τε καὶ σπένδειν τοῖς εἰδώλοις ἐκελεύετο, κ. τ. λ.*

19 Lactant. de Mort. persec. c. 15: Constantius, ne dissentire a majorum (i. e., Augustorum) praeceptis videretur, conventicula, id est parietes, qui restitui poterant, dirui passus est, verum autem Dei templum, quod est in hominibus, incolume servavit. C. 16: Vexebatur ergo universa terra, et praeter Gallias ab oriente usque ad occasum tres acerbissimae bestiae saeviebant. Hence the Donatist bishops, A.D. 313, wrote to Constantine (Optat. Milevit. i. c. 22): Pater inter caeteros imperatores persecutionem non exercuit, et ab hoc facinore immunis est Gallia.

20 Martyrs in Palestine: Eusebius de mart. Palaest. liber (Pamphilus, presbyter in Caesarea); in other countries, Euseb. H. E. viii. 7–13. (Peter, bishop of Alexandria; Lucian, presbyter in Antioch), Ruinart Acta primorum martyrum. Respecting the martyrs in Egypt comp. the Coptic acts, which, at least in later times, have been greatly overstated, in De miraculis S. Coluthi et reliquis actorum S. Panesniv martyrum thebaica fragmenta duo opera A. A. Georgii. Romae. 1793, 4. In the praef. p. cxl. ss. there is a chronological survey of the persecution, and of the Egyptian martyrs.

and *Spain*, however, it ceased entirely under the Augustus *Constantius Chlorus;* and in *Italy* and *Africa* under the Caesar *Severus*, it at least abated. After the death of *Constantius Chlorus* (306), his son *Constantine* not only granted full liberty of worship to the Christians in Gaul and Spain; but the two Augusti also, *Maxentius* and *Maximian*, caused persecution to cease in Italy and Africa.[21] In the east, the persecution had been terminated by the edict which *Galerius* issued shortly before his death (311);[22] but in the Asiatic east, six months after, *Maximin* caused it to be renewed.[23] When *Constantine*, after conquering Maxentius (312), had become sole lord of the west, he issued, in conjunction with *Licinius*, ruler of the European east, an *edict of universal toleration for all religions.* This was soon followed by a particular *edict in favor of the Christians*, issued from Milan (313).[24] This edict became valid

21 Lactant. de Mort. persecut. c. 24: Suscepto imperio Constantinus Augustus nihil egit prius, quam Christianos cultui ac Deo suo reddere. Haec fuit prima ejus sanctio sanctae religionis restitutae (i. e. restitutionis). Euseb. viii. 14: *Μαξέντιος—ἀρχόμενος μὲν τὴν καθ' ἡμᾶς πίστιν ἐπ' ἀρεσκείᾳ καὶ κολακείᾳ τοῦ δήμου Ῥωμαίων καθυπεκρίνατο· ταύτῃ τε τοῖς ὑπηκόοις τὸν Χριστιανῶν ἀνεῖναι προστάττει διωγμόν.*

22 Lactant. de Mort. persecut. c. 34. Euseb. viii. 17: Imp. Caesar Galerius Valerius Maximianus, caet., et Imp. Caesar Flavius Valerius Constantinus, caet., et Imp. Caesar Valerius Licinius, caet. Provincialibus S.—Inter caetera, quae pro reipublicae semper commodis atque utilitate disponimus, nos quidem volueramus antehac juxta leges veteres et publicam disciplinam Romanorum cuncta corrigere, atque id providere, ut etiam Christiani, qui parentum suorum reliquerant sectam, ad bonas mentes redirent. Siquidem quanam ratione tanta eosdem Christianos voluntas invasisset, et tanta stultitia occupasset, ut non illa veterum instituta sequerentur, quae forsitan primum parentes eorundem constituerant (cf. § 55): sed pro arbitrio suo, atque ut hisdem erat libitum, ita sibimet leges facerent, quas observarent, et per diversa varios populos congregarent? Denique cum ejusmodi nostra jussio extitisset, ut ad veterum se instituta conferrent, multi periculo subjugati, multi, etiam deturbati sunt. Atque cum plurimi in proposito perseverarent, ac videremus, nec Diis eosdem cultum ac religionem debitam exhibere, nec Christianorum Deum observare; contemplatione mitissimae nostrae clementiae intuentes et consuetudinem sempiternam, qua solemus cunctis hominibus veniam indulgere, promtissimam in his quoque indulgentiam nostram credidimus porrigendam, ut denuo sint Christiani, et conventicula sua componant, ita ut ne quid contra disciplinam agant. Alia autem epistola judicibus significaturi sumus, quid debeant observare. Unde juxta hanc indulgentiam nostram debebunt Deum suum orare pro salute nostra, et reipublicae, ac sua, ut undiqueversum respublica perstet incolumis, et securi vivere in sedibus suis possint.

23 See the description in Euseb. xi. 1–8.

24 Ap. Lactant. de Mort. persec. c. 48. The beginning has been preserved only in the Greek version apud Euseb. x. 5: *Ἤδη μὲν πάλαι σκοποῦντες τὴν ἐλευθερίαν τῆς θρησκείας οὐκ ἀρνητέαν εἶναι, ἀλλ' ἑνὸς ἑκάστου τῇ διανοίᾳ καὶ βουλήσει ἐξουσίαν δοτέον τοῦ τὰ θεῖα πράγματα τημελεῖν κατὰ τὴν αὐτοῦ προαίρεσιν, ἕκαστον κεκελεύκειμεν, τούς τε Χριστιανοὺς, τῆς αἱρέσεως καὶ τῆς θρησκείας τῆς ἑαυτῶν τὴν πίστιν φυλάττειν. Ἀλλ' ἐπειδὴ πολλαὶ καὶ διάφοροι αἱρέσεις* (i. e., conditiones, as below) *ἐν ἐκείνῃ τῇ ἀντιγραφῇ, ἐν τῇ τοῖς αὐτοῖς συνεχωρήθη ἡ τοιαύτη ἐξουσία, ἐδόκουν προστεθεῖσθαι σαφῶς, τυχὸν ἴσως τινὲς αὐτῶν μετ' ὀλίγον ἀπὸ τῆς τοιαύτης παραφυλάξεως ἀνεκρούοντο.* (Quamob-

through the whole Roman empire after the overthrow of Maximin, which soon followed.

With regard to the history of *Constantine's* religious development,[25] till the time when he fully embraced Christianity, we

rem) cum feliciter tam ego Constantinus Aug., quam etiam ego Licinius Aug. apud Mediolanum convenissemus, atque universa, quae ad commoda et securitatem publicam pertinerent, in tractatu haberemus; haec inter cetera, quae videbamus pluribus hominibus profutura, vel imprimis ordinanda esse credidimus, quibus divinitatis reverentia continebatur: ut daremus et Christianis et omnibus liberam potestatem sequendi religionem, quam quisque voluisset, quo quicquid est divinitatis in sede coelesti, nobis atque omnibus, qui sub potestate nostra sunt constituti, placatum ac propitium possit existere. Itaque hoc consilio salubri ac rectissima ratione ineundum esse credidimus, ut nulli omnino facultatem abnegandam putaremus, qui vel observationi Christianorum, vel ei religioni mentem suam dederet, quam ipsi sibi aptissimam esse sentiret, ut possit nobis summa divinitas, cujus religioni liberis mentibus obsequimur, in omnibus solitum favorem suum benevolentiamque praestare. Quare scire dignationem tuam convenit, placuisse nobis, ut amotis omnibus omnino conditionibus (Euseb. τῶν αἱρέσεων), quae prius scriptis ad officium tuum datis super Christianorum nomine videbantur, nunc caveres, ut simpliciter unusquisque eorum, qui eandem observandae religionis Christianorum gerunt voluntatem, citra ullam inquietudinem ac molestiam sui id ipsum observare contendant. Quae solicitudini tuae plenissime significanda esse credidimus, quo scires, nos liberam atque absolutam colendae religionis suae facultatem hisdem Christianis dedisse. Quod cum hisdem a nobis indultum esse pervideas, intelligit dignatio tua, etiam aliis religionis suae vel observantiae potestatem similiter apertam et liberam pro quiete temporis nostri esse concessam, ut in colendo, quod quisque delegerit, habeat liberam facultatem, quia [nolumus detrahi] honori neque cuiquam religioni aliquid a nobis. Atque hoc insuper in persona Christianorum statuendum esse censuimus; quod si eadem loca, ad quae antea convenire consueverant, de quibus etiam datis ad officium tuum literis certa antehac forma fuerat comprehensa, priore tempore aliqui vel a fisco nostro vel ab alio quocunque videntur esse mercati, eadem Christianis sine pecunia et sine ulla pretii petitione, postposita omni frustratione atque ambiguitate, restituantur. Qui etiam dono fuerunt consecuti, eadem similiter hisdem Christianis quantocius reddant. Et vel hi, qui emerunt, vel qui dono fuerunt consecuti, si putaverint, de nostra benevolentia aliquid vicarium postulent, quo et ipsis per nostram clementiam consulatur. Quae omnia corpori Christianorum protinus per intercessionem tuam ac sine mora tradi oportebit. Et quoniam iidem Christiani non ea loca tantum, ad quae convenire consueverunt, sed alia etiam habuisse noscuntur, ad jus corporis eorum, id est ecclesiarum, non hominum singulorum, pertinentia: ea omnia lege, qua superius, comprehendimus, citra ullam prorsus ambiguitatem vel controversiam hisdem Christianis, id est corpori et conventiculis eorum, reddi jubebis; supra dicta scilicet ratione servata, ut ii, qui eadem sine pretio, sicut diximus, restituerint, indemnitatem de nostra benevolentia sperent. In quibus omnibus supra dicto corpori Christianorum intercessionem tuam efficacissimam exhibere debebis, ut praeceptum nostrum quantocius compleatur; quo etiam in hoc per clementiam nostram quieti publicae consulatur. Hactenus fiet, ut sicut superius comprehensum est, divinus juxta nos favor, quem in tantis sumus rebus experti, per omne tempus prospere successibus nostris cum beatitudine publica perseveret. Ut autem hujus sanctionis benevolentiae nostrae forma ad omnium possit pervenire notitiam, prolata programmate tuo haec scripta et ubique proponere, et ad omnium scientiam te perferre conveniet, ut hujus benevolentiae nostrae sanctio latere non possit.

25 Concerning him Franc. Balduini Constantinus M. s. de Const. Imp. legibus eccl. et civ. libri ii. Basil. 1556. Hal. 1727. 8. C. D. A. Martini Ueber die Einführung der christl. Rel. als Staatsrelig. durch den Kaiser Const. München. 1813. 4. J. C. F. Manso Leben Constantins d. G. Breslau. 1817. 8. (Hug's Denkschrift zur Ehrenrettung Constantin's, in the Zeitschrift f. d. Geistlichk. d. Erzbisth. Freiburg. 1829, Heft 3, S. 1, ff. Heinichen Excurs. i. appended to his edition of Euseb. do vita Constant. p. 507, ss.

have only isolated intimations and hints. His first religious sentiments, like those of his father, were essentially the new-platonic. He acknowleged one supreme God who had revealed himself in many ways among men,[26] and honored Apollo in particular, as the revealer of this Being.[27] As this idea of Apollo and the Christian idea of Christ were obviously similar,[28] so Constantine may have thought that he found in it very soon a point of union between Christianity and heathenism. That the phenomenon which appeared to him in the war against Maxentius, respecting which the accounts of his contemporaries are so different,[29] did not yet bring him over exclusively to Christian-

[26] According to Euseb. de vita Const. i. c. 27, when he first began the expedition against Maxentius: Εὖ δ' ἐννοήσας, ὡς κρείττονος ἢ κατὰ στρατιωτικὴν δέοι αὐτῷ βοηθείας, διὰ τὰς κακοτέχνους καὶ γοητικὰς μαγγανείας τὰς παρὰ τῷ τυράννῳ σπουδαζομένας, θεὸν ἀνεζήτει βοηθόν.—'Εννοεῖ δῆτα ὁποῖον δέοι θεὸν ἐπιγράψασθαι βοηθόν. ζητοῦντι δ' αὐτῷ ἔννοιά τις ὑπεισῆλθεν· ὡς πλειόνων πρότερον τῆς ἀρχῆς ἐφαψαμένων, οἱ μὲν πλείοσι θεοῖς τὰς σφῶν αὐτῶν ἀναρτήσαντες ἐλπίδας—τέλος οὐκ αἴσιον, εὕραντο·—μόνον δὲ τὸν ἑαυτοῦ πατέρα--τὸν ἐπέκεινα τῶν ὅλων θεὸν διὰ πάσης τιμήσαντα ζωῆς, σωτῆρα καὶ φύλακα τῆς βασιλείας, ἀγαθοῦ τε παντὸς χορηγὸν εὑρέσθαι. Ταῦτα παρ' ἑαυτῷ διακρίνας —τὸ μὲν περὶ τοὺς μηδὲν ὄντας θεοὺς ματαιάζειν—μωρίας ἔργον ὑπελάμβανε· τὸν δὲ πατρῷον τιμᾶν μόνον ᾤετο δεῖν θεόν. The Panegyricus incerti, c. 26 (ed. Jaeger, i. 548), addressed to the emperor in 313, corresponds with tolerable accuracy to his religious views at the time: Te, summe rerum sator, cujus tot nomina sunt, quot gentium linguas esse voluisti, quem enim te ipse dici velis, scire non possumus: sive in te quaedam vis mensque divina est, qua toto infusus mundo omnibus miscearis elementis, et sine ullo extrinsecus accedente vigoris impulsu per te ipse movearis: sive aliqua supra omne caelum potestas es, quae hoc opus tuum ex altiore naturae arce despicias; te, inquam, oramus, caet.

[27] Umenius in the Panegyric received by Constantine, 310, at Treves, c. 21: Vidisti enim, credo, Constantine, Apollinem tuum, comitante Victoria, coronas tibi laureas offerentem:—vidisti, teque in illius specie recognovisti, cui totius mundi regna deberi vatum carmina divina cecinerunt. Quod ego nunc demum arbitror contigisse, quum tu sis, ut ille, juvenis, et laetus, et salutifer, et pulcherrimus imperator. Merito igitur augustissima illa delubra tantis donariis honestasti, ut jam vetera non quaerant. Jam omnia te vocare ad se templa videantur, praecipueque Apollo noster, caet. On several coins of Constantine is found the inscription, Soli invicto, Soli invicto comiti. See Ez. Spanheim's remarks on the Césars de l'empereur Julien, p. 285, and Remarques, p. 973.

[28] On the idea of Apollo, see Baur's Apollonius v. Tyana u. Christus, S. 168. So Julian accuses the Alexandrians (Epist. 51, ed. Spanheim, p. 434) of believing 'Ιησοῦν χρῆναι θεὸν λόγον ὑπάρχειν, and exhorts them, on the contrary, to worship τὸν μέγαν "Ηλιον, τὸ ζῶν ἄγαλμα καὶ ἔμψυχον, καὶ ἔννουν, και ἀγαθοεργὸν τοῦ νοητοῦ πατρός. That Christ was frequently compared with Apollo, may be seen from Poetae latini minores, ed. J. Chr. Wernsdorf, iv. 767.

[29] Lactant. de Mort. persec. c. 44: Commonitus est in quiete Constantinus, ut coeleste signum Dei notaret in scutis, atque ita proelium committaret. Fecit, ut jussus est, et traversa x. littera, summo capite circumflexo, Christum in scutis notat. On the contrary, the heathen Nazarius in Panegyr. ad Constantinum, c. 14: In ore denique est omnium Galliarum, exercitus visos, qui se divinitus missos prae se ferebant. Haec ipsorum sermocinatio, hoc inter audientes ferebant, Constantinum petimus, Constantino imus auxilio. Constantine, immediately after his entry into Rome, caused a cross to be put into the

ity, is proved by the edict of Milan, which breathes entirely the former syncretistic spirit. But he acted only in the spirit of this decree when he bestowed favors on the *Christian* church, such as the old religion had always enjoyed. Thus he released their clergy from the burdensome municipal offices (312;[30] made valid the manumission of slaves in the churches (prior to 316);[31]

hand of the statue erected to him, with the inscription, *τούτῳ τῷ σωτηριώδει σημείῳ, τῳ ἀληθινῷ ἐλέγχῳ τῆς ἀνδρίας, τὴν πόλιν ὑμῶν ἀπὸ ζυγοῦ τοῦ τυράννου διασωθεῖσαν ἠλευθέρωσα* (Euseb. H. E. ix. 9). It was not till he was an old man that he related to Eusebius the story of a cross, which appeared to him at clear mid-day, with the inscription, hac vince, *τούτῳ νίκα*. Euseb. de vit. Const. i. 28–32. Sozomen, however, i. 3, and Rufin. ix. 9, suppose it to have been a mere dream. The heathen, of course, derided all these stories. See Gelasius Cyzic. Hist. Conc. Nicaeni, i. 4. Cf. Mosheim de rebus Christ. ante Const. M. p. 978, ss. Concerning the cipher of Christ's name, see Münter's Sinnbilder der alten Christen, Heft i. S. 33, ff. The imperial standard, bearing this cipher, was afterward called Labarum. See Du Cange Diss. de nummis infer. aevi, § 20. It is certain that Constantine, even before the battle, supposed that he was directed to the cross as to a propitious sign, and that this could not have happened in a way to attract general notice. If the later narrative of the emperor be not an invention, a light cross of clouds may have appeared to him while in a musing and hesitating mood, and have led him to decide; a phenomenon which was of importance, for this very reason, only to himself, and which remained unobserved by all others. Thus a purple cross, Christmas, 1517, was looked upon as a divine sign at Weimar, under the important circumstances of the time (Oratio de Joanne Duce Sax. in Melanthonis Opp. ed. Bretschneider, xi. 958). In like manner a white cross, which appeared at the entrance of John Frederick, the elector, into Weimar, when he returned from captivity (Hortleder vom teutschen Kriege, Th. 2, S. 966). Several like traditions owed their origin at this time to the feeling that the decisive struggle between heathenism and Christianity, between Christ and demons, was come. Thus it is related that a victory-bringing prayer was taught by an angel to Licinius before the battle with Maximin (Lactant. de Mort. persecut. c. 46). Thus, according to Gregory of Nazianzum, an army of demons accompanied Julian on his Persian expedition; but according to Libanius, it was an army of gods. See Ullmann's Gregor. v. Nazianz. S. 100.

[30] The first law ad Anulinum Procons. Africae apud Euseb. H. E. x. c. 7, confirmed by a second, Cod. Theod. xvi. tit. ii. l. 1, A.D. 313, and repeated in the third, l. c. l. 2, A.D, 319. The last: Qui divino cultui ministeria impendunt, i. e., hi qui Clerici appellantur, ab omnibus omnino muneribus excusentur, ne sacrilego livore quorundam a divinis obsequiis avocentur. Here Constantine merely transferred to the Christian clergy a privilege enjoyed by heathen priests. Cf. Symmachus, lib. x. Ep. 54: Insigne ducitur Sacerdotii vacare muneribus. Cod. Theod. xii. tit. 1, l. 75, and Gothofred. ad h. l. The presidents of the Jews also enjoyed this immunity. Cf. Cod. Theod. xvi. tit. viii. l. 3, A.D. 321. Decurionibus Agrippinensibus: Cunctis Ordinibus generali lege concedimus, Judaeos vocare ad Curiam. Verum, ut aliquid ipsis ad solatium pristinae observationis relinquatur, binos vel ternos privilegio perpeti (i. e., perpetuo) patimur nullis nominationibus occupari. Lex. 2, A.D. 330: Qui devotione tota Synagogis Judaeorum Patriarchiis vel Presbyteriis se dederunt, et in memorata secta degentes legi ipsi praesident, immunes ab omnibus tam personalibus quam civilibus muneribus perseverent. Lex. 4, A.D. 331: Hiereos, et Archisynagogos, et Patres Synagogarum, et caeteros, qui Synagogis deserviunt, ab omni corporali munere liberos esse praecipimus.

[31] According to Sozomen, i. 9, he issued three laws on this subject. The first is lost. The second may be seen in Cod. Justin. i. tit. 13, l. 1, A.D. 316. The third, ibid. l. 2, and Cod. Theod. iv. tit. 7, l. unic. A.D. 321. That this manumission was transferred from the heathen temple to the churches, is shown by Gothofredus on the last law.

allowed legacies to be left to the catholic churches,[32] and contributed a considerable sum himself to the support of the African clergy.[33] Other regulations in favor of the Christians owed their immediate origin to that syncretistic tendency of the emperor. Thus he set bounds to the enmity of the Jews against the Christians, their rigid inflexibility not at all agreeing with his feelings.[34] He abolished several regulations offensive to the Christians (315);[35] and decreed the general observance of Sunday (321).[36] It can not appear strange that, although he

[32] Cod. Theod. xvi. tit. 2, l. 4, and Cod. Just. i. tit. 2, l. 1: Habeat unusquisque licentiam, sanctissimo catholico venerabilique concilio decedens bonorum quod optaverit relinquere.

[33] Namely, 3000 folles (upwards of 70,000 thalers). Cf. Const. Epist. ad Caecilianum Episc. Carthag. in Euseb. H. E. x. c. 6.

[34] Cod. Theod. xvi. tit. 8, l. 1, A.D. 315: Judaeis, et Majoribus eorum, et Patriarchis volumus intimari, quod si qui, post hanc legem, aliquem, qui eorum feralem fugerit sectam, et ad Dei cultum respexerit, saxis aut alio furoris genere (quod nunc fieri cognoscimus) ausus fuerit adtemptare, mox flammis dedendus et cum omnibus suis participibus concremandus. Si quis vero ex populo ad eorum nefariam sectam accesserit, et conciliabulis eorum se adplicaverit, cum ipsis poenas meritas sustinebit.

[35] Cod. Theod. ix. tit. 40, l. 2, A.D. 315: Si quis in ludum fuerit, vel in metallum damnatus, minime in ejus facie scribatur:—quo facies, quae ad similitudinem pulchritudinis coelestis est figurata, minime maculetur. Probably in the same year vetus veterrimumque supplicium patibulorum et cruribus suffringendis primus removit (Aur. Victor de Caes. c. 41; Sozom. i. 8. Cod. Theod. viii. tit. 15, l. 1, A.D. 320: Qui jure veteri caelibes habebantur: imminentibus legum (namely L. Julia and Papia Poppaea) terroribus liberentur, &c. (Cf. Euseb. de vit. Const. iv. 26.)

[36] The first law of March, 321, is in Cod. Justin. iii. tit. 12, l. 3: Omnes judices, urbanaeque plebes, et cunctarum artium officia venerabili die Solis quiescant. Ruri tamen positi agrorum culturae libere licenterque inserviant; quoniam frequenter evenit, ut non aptius alio die frumenta sulcis, aut vinae scrobibus mandentur (as agricultural labors of this kind had been permitted on festivals, according to a Roman custom, Virgil. Georg. i. v. 268, ss. Cato de Re rust. c. 2; cf. Erycius Puteanus de Nundinis Romanis, c. 10 in Graevii Thes. Antiquitt. Rom. t. viii. p. 658). The second of June, in the same year, in the Cod. Theod. ii. tit. 8, l. 1, with the addition: Emancipandi et manumittendi die festo cuncti licentiam habeant, et super his rebus actus non prohibeantur. The Egyptian week, the seven days of which were dedicated to the planets, had been made known to the Romans by the astrologers even since the first century. In the second, the days were frequently named after the planets (Dio Cassius, xxxvii. c. 18. S. Mursinna de hebdomade gentilium et dierum a planetis denominatione in Jo. Oelrichs Germaniae literatae opuscula historico-philologica-theologica. Bremae. 1772. i. 113). As Christ was often compared with Sol, or Apollo (see above, note 28), so Constantine believed, perhaps, that in the festival of the dies solis, as a festival of Christ and the sun at the same time, he found a point of friendly union between both religions, directly opposed though they were to each other. He transferred the Nundines to Sunday: comp. the stone inscription apud Erycius Puteanus de Nundinis Romanis, c. 26: Constantinus—provisione etiam pietatis suae Nundinas die solis perpeti anno constituit. Still the Nundines and weeks were both in use, and both are found in a calendar composed about 354 (in Graevii Thes. t. viii. p. 97) beside each other, until Theodosius I. made the law respecting the observance of Sunday strict, Cod. Theod. viii. tit. 8, l. 3. Eusebius de vit. Constant. iv. 18, and Sozomen, i. 8, relate that Friday was also observed, as well as Sunday, by order of Constantine.

allowed exactly the same freedom to heathenism, and not only so, but even, in his capacity of emperor, observed the heathen practices at the same time that he gave so many privileges to Christianity,[37] he should notwithstanding prejudice the minds of the heathen people by those very measures, inasmuch as he gained over the affections of the Christians toward himself. In the mean time, the successful issue of his undertakings must have strengthened him in the direction he took, in accordance with his peculiar mode of thinking; and it could not escape his political sagacity, that it would be most advantageous for him to have on his side even the smaller party, since it was the more closely united, and more animated by a living soul. In this manner the Christians formed the nucleus of Constantine's party when the relation between him and Licinius became looser. Hence, for this very reason, Licinius sought to obtain a more decided party by renewed attention to the religion of the pagans, and by persecution of the Christians.[38] Accordingly, the struggle that arose between Licinius and Constantine, A.D. 323, was at the same time a struggle between Christianity and heathenism. Licinius was defeated, and Constantine openly professed the Christian faith,[39] though he still put off baptism.[40]

[37] Cod. Theod. ix. 16, 1, 2 (A.D. 319), xvi. 10, 1 (A.D. 321), Zosimus, ii. 29, Ἐχρῆτο δὲ ἔτι καὶ τοῖς πατρίοις ἱεροῖς.

[38] Euseb. H. E. x. 8, de vita Constant. ii. 3, ss.

[39] Euseb, de vita Const. iii. 2: Τὸν Χριστὸν τοῦ θεοῦ σὺν παῤῥησίᾳ τῇ πάσῃ πρεσβεύων εἰς πάντας διετέλει, μὴ ἐγκαλυπτόμενος τὴν σωτήριον ἐπηγορίαν. After the year 323, heathen symbols disappear from Constantine's coins. J. Eckhel Doctrina Numorum veterum, p. ii. vol. viii. (Vineb. 1798. 4,) p. 79.

[40] Modern Catholic Church historians no longer maintain what was asserted as late as Baronius, Schelstraten, and others, that Constantine was baptized in Rome, by Sylvester, A.D. 324. Comp. Euseb. de vita Constant. iv. 61, 62. That Constantine made donations to Sylvester on this occasion is related first in the Acta Sylvestri, then by Hadrian I. A.D. 780 (see below, in volume second. Div. 1, § 5). In the ninth century an original document respecting a great gift of land came to light. The supposititious character of both authorities was perceived so early as 999, by Otto III., and in 1152 by the Romans (vol. ii.). The spirited attack of Laurentius Valla (about 1440, vol. ii. Div. 5, § 154) did not produce much effect till after the Reformation. Since then the investiture has been defended merely by some of the older Catholic scholars, especially the Jesuits J. Gretser and Nic. Schaten; but the deed of investiture has been generally given up as spurious.

The number of persecutions has been fixed at ten since the fourth century, agreeably to Exod. vii. 10, and Apoc. xvii. 1–14. Different calculations: Sulpicius Severus Hist. sacr. ii. 33: Sacris vocibus decem plagis mundum afficiendum pronunciatum est: ita quum jam novem fuerint, quae superest, ultima erit. On the other side, Augustin. de civ. Dei, xviii 52: Nonnullis visum est, vel videtur, non amplius ecclesiam passuram persecutiones usque ad tempus Antichristi, quam quot jam passa est, id est decem, ut undecima novissima sit ab Antichristo. The enumeration in Augustine l. c. is the following (the devia-

§ 57.

SPREAD OF CHRISTIANITY.

In this division of time also, the progress of Christianity was considerable,[1] especially in *Gaul.*[2] In the end of it we find the first traces of bishops *on the Rhine.*[3] About the same time

tions in Sulpicius Severus, ii. 29–32, are inclosed in parentheses): I. Neronis, II. Domitani, III. Trajani, (IV. Hadriani): IV. (V.) Marci Aurelii, V. (VI.) Sept. Severi, VI. Maximini, VII. (VII.) Decii, VIII. (VIII.) Valeriani, IX. Aureliani, X. (IX.) Diocletani. Augustinus l. c. adds: Sed ego illa re gesta in Aegypto istas persecutiones prophetice significatas esse non arbitror, quamvis ab eis, qui hoc putant, exquisite et ingeniose illa singula his singulis comparata videantur: non prophetico spiritu, sed conjectura mentis humanae, qui aliquando ad verum pervenit, aliquando fallitur.

[1] Origines c. Cels. iii. p. 116, points to this: *Χριστιανοὺς μὴ ἀμελεῖν τοῦ πανταχοῦ τῆς οἰκουμένης ἐπισπείρειν τὸν λόγον. Τινὲς γοῦν ἔργον πεποίηνται ἐκπεριέρχεσθαι οὐ μόνον πόλεις, ἀλλὰ καὶ κώμας, καὶ ἐπαύλεις.* Respecting the extension of Christianity about 300, see Arnobius, i. c. 16. Si Alamannos, Persas, Scythas (Dii) iccirco voluerunt devinci, quod habitarent et degerent in eorum gentibus Christiani; quemadmodum Romanis tribuere victoriam, cum habitarent et degerent in eorum quoque gentibus Christiani? Si in Asia, Syria iccirco mures et locustas effervescere prodigialiter voluerunt, quod ratione consimili habitarent in eorum gentibus Christiani: in Hispania, Gallia cur eodem tempore horum nihil natum est, cum innumeri viverent in his quoque provinciis Christani? Si apud Getulos, Tinguitanos hujus rei causa siccitatem satis ariditatemque miserunt, eo anno cur messes amplissimas Mauris Nomadibusque tribuerunt cum religio similis his quoque in regionibus verteretur?

[2] Passio Saturnini Episc. Tolosani, c. 2, apud Ruinart: Postquam sensim et gradatim in omnem terram Evangeliorum sonus exivit, parique progressu in regionibus nostris Apostolorum praedicatio coruscavit: cum rarae in aliquibus civitatibus ecclesiae paucorum Christianorum devotione consurgerent;—ante annos L. sicut actis publicis (Codd. alii: ante annos satis plurimos), i. e., Decio et Grato Consulibus (i. e., 250, A.D.) sicut fideli recordatione retinetur, primum et summum Christi Tolosa civitas s. Saturninum habere coeperat sacerdotem. From this Gregorius Turonensis (about 590) Hist. Franc. i. c. 28: Decii tempore septem viri Episcopi ad praedicandum in Gallias missi sunt, sicut historia passionis s. martyris Saturnini denarrat. Ait enim: Sub Decio et Grato Consulibus, &c., as above. Hi ergo missi sunt: Turonicis Gratianus Episcopus, Arelatensibus Trophimus Episc., Narbonae Paulus Episc., Tolosae Saturninus Episc., Parisiacis Dionysius Episc., Arvernis Stremonius Episc., Lemovicinis Martialis est destinatus Episcopus. This is evidently an arbitrary combination of several traditions. Trophimus must have been first bishop of Arles even before Decius, for in 254 Marcian had been for a long time bishop of the place. See Cypriani, Ep. 67, Pearson Annales Cypriciani ad ann. 254, § 7, ss. With this also agrees Zosimi P. Epist. i. ad Episcopos Galliae, A.D. 417 (apud Constant): Metropolitanae Arelatensium urbi vetus privilegium minime derogandum est, ad quam primum ex hac sede Trophimus summus Antistes, ex cujus fonte totae Galliae fidei rivulos acceperunt, directus est.

[3] First, in the commission appointed by Constantine to decide upon the Donatist controversy in Rome, in the year 313, Optat. Milev. de schism. Donatist. i. c. 23: Dati sunt judices Maternus ex Agrippina civitate: then among the names subscribed to the acts of the Concil. Arelatense, in the year 314: Maternus episcopus, Macrinus diaconus de

they also appear in *Britain*.[4] The first traces of Christianity are now seen in *Vindelicia*.[5] Even among the Goths it had become known by means of captives.[6]

SECOND CHAPTER.

HERETICS.

§ 58.

ELCESAITISM OF THE CLEMENTINES.

Clementina, primum edita in Cotelerii Patribus apostolicis, i. 597. D. v. Cölln in Ersch u. Grubers Encyclopädie, xviii. 36. (Art. Clementinen.) Die Clementinen nebst den verwandten Schriften u. der Ebionitismus von Adolph Schliemann. Hamburgh. 1844. 8.

As Christianity had come to the west from the east, so the occidental church continued in the second century to be entirely dependent on the oriental. Without a peculiar development of doctrine and literature of its own, it merely received the product of the east; but in this way it also drew within itself the different parties of the east. Rome in particular, the capital of the empire and seat of a great church, presented an alluring field to all parties to call forth their activity. The different Gnostic sects,[1] like the Montanists, labored with emulation to gain over this important church to themselves; and all found in it more or less sympathy and adherence. Accordingly, Romish Christendom in the second century was internally divided in many ways; a condition which was calculated not only to lead many Christians astray, and to induce them to waver, but to

civitate Agrippinensium.—Agroecius episcopus, Felix exorcista de civitate Treverorum. Nic. ab Honteim Hist. diplom. Trevirana in prodromo, t. i. p. 64, ss. Walch de Materno uno, in the Commentationes Soc. Gotting. vol. i. (1779) p. 1, ss.

[4] Names subscribed to the Concil. Arelat.: Eborius episcopus, de civitate Eboracensi, provincia Britannia.—Restitutus episcopus, de civitate Londinensi, provincia suprascripta. Adelfius episcopus, de civitate colonia Londinensium (perhaps Colonia Lindi, i. e., Lincoln); comp. Jac. Usserii Britannicarum ecclesiar. antiquitt. Lond. 1687. Bingham Origg. eccl. tom. iii. p. 557, ss.

[5] Afra burnt in Augsburg A.D. 304. See the Acta in Ruinart.

[6] Sozomen. H. E. ii. 6. Philostorg. H. E. ii. 5.

[1] Valentinus (§ 45) and Marcion (§ 47) came in person to Rome.

lay open a dangerous unprotected side to the attacks of heathenism. There, a philosophically educated Christian of Rome,[2] toward the end of the second century, took up the idea that Christianity in its original state must be preserved among the Jewish Christians as the descendants of the oldest church. Probably he sought out this church in its isolation, and found it divided into several parties, but he also discovered among the *Elcesaites*[3] a speculative doctrinal creed already formed, which seemed to him perfectly adapted both to vanquish heathenism and to remove the multiplicity of Christian sects. He received it, therefore as the original Christian doctrine which had obtained its central point in James,[4] and in Peter its most important defender, and appropriated all the more readily the Elcesaite rejection of Paul, who, insomuch as he was not an immediate disciple of Christ, could not have been a genuine apostle,[5] because the Pauline development of Christianity had run out into so great a state of disunion, and appeared to have attained its height in the Marcionite errors. Hence he composed *the Clementines* (τὰ Κλημέντια) consisting of three prologues and twenty (but now only 19) homilies, that he might be able to proclaim to Christendom at large the apostolic truth which had long been concealed, by apostolic lips also. The historical form in which he clothed the whole work, he took in part from the events of his own life. But he reckoned upon it also for the purpose of procuring apostolic authority to his doctrine, and obtaining an introduction for it into Rome in particular. As he himself prosecuted the search, so he represents the apostolic *Clement* (who was highly esteemed in the recollection of the Roman church, and who appears here in the char-

[2] For evidence to show that the author of the Clementines was a Roman, see Baur's Christuspartei in der korinth. Gemeinde, in the Tübingen Zeitschr. f. Theol. 1831, iv. 199 Schliemann, p. 549.

[3] See above, § 32.

[4] In the Clementines, James appears as the chief bishop of all Christendom, to whom Peter must constantly give an account of his doings, Schliemann, S. 86, 213. In the letters prefixed to the Clementines, Peter writes to him as *τῷ κυρίῳ, καὶ ἐπισκόπῳ τῆς ἁγίας ἐκκλησίας*. Clement writes: *Ἰακώβῳ, τῷ κυρίῳ, καὶ ἐπισκόπων ἐπισκόπῳ, διέποντι δὲ τὴν Ἱερουσαλὴμ ἁγίαν Ἑβραίων ἐκκλησίαν, καὶ τὰς πανταχῇ θεοῦ προνοίᾳ ἱδρυθείσας καλῶς*.

[5] What Peter, Hom. xvii. 19, says against Simon Magus, is said to refer to Paul: *Εἰ τις δὲ δι' ὀπτασίαν πρὸς διδασκαλίαν σοφισθῆναι δύναται; Καὶ εἰ μέν ἐρεῖς, δυνατόν ἐστιν· διὰ τί ὅλῳ ἐνιαυτῷ ἐγρηγορόσιν παραμένων ὡμίλησεν ὁ δικάσκαλος;* Schliemann, S. 96.

acter of a distinguished Roman, whose mind had received a philosophical culture)[6] as journeying in the East, impelled by thirst for the truth long vainly sought,[7] there meeting with Peter, and obtaining full satisfaction from him. Peter, the only one of the immediate disciples of Christ who had come to Rome, appears here in opposition to Paul, as the proper apostle of the Gentiles,[8] as the founder of the Romish church, and the first bishop of Rome.[9] He triumphantly refutes all kinds of error which had been advocated by different persons; not only the popular faith and philosophy of the heathen,[10] but also the Christian aberrations of the second century. The Gnostics in particular are combated in the person of Simon Magus;[11] and in addition to them the Montanist prophesying,[12] the hypostatic doctrine of the Trinity,[13] and millennarianism.[14] On the other

[6] He is manifestly confounded with Flavius Clemens, the relation of Domitian (§ 33, note 4). See Baur in the Tübingen Zeitschr. f. Theol. 1831, iv. 199. Schliemann, p. 109.

[7] The narrative in Hom. i., in its essential features, may have been modeled after the experiences of the author.

[8] Peter says, Hom. ii. 17, with reference to the law of syzygies: *Ἐν γεννητοῖς γυναικῶν πρῶτος ἦλθεν* (John the Baptist, Matt. xi. 11), *εἶτα ὁ ἐν υἱοῖς ἀνθρώπων δεύτερος ἐπῆλθεν. Ταύτῃ τῇ τάξει ἀκολουθοῦντα δυνατὸν ἦ νοεῖν, τίνος ἐστὶν Σίμων ὁ πρὸ ἐμοῦ εἰς τὰ ἔθνη πρῶτος ἐλθὼν, καὶ τὶνος ὢν τυγχάνω, ὁ μετ' ἐκεῖνον ἐληλυθώς, καὶ ἐπελθὼν ὡς σκότῳ φῶς, ὡς ἀγνοίᾳ γνῶσις, ὡς νόσῳ ἴασις. Οὕτως δὴ, ὡς ἀληθὴς ἡμῖν προφήτης εἴρηκεν, πρῶτον ψευδὲς δεῖ ἐλθεῖν εὐαγγέλιον ὑπὸ πλάνου τινὸς, καὶ εἶθ' οὕτως μετὰ καθαίρεσιν τοῦ ἁγίου τόπου εὐαγγέλιον ἀληθὲς κρύφα διαπεμφθῆναι εἰς ἐπανόρθωσιν τῶν ἐσομένων αἱρέσεων.*

[9] In the letter prefixed to the Clementines, of Clement to James, Peter is designated, *ὁ τῆς δύσεως τὸ σκοτεινότερον τοῦ κόσμου μέρος, ὡς πάντων ἱκανώτερος, φωτίσαι κελευσθεὶς, καὶ κατορθῶσαι δυνηθείς,—μέχρις ἐνταῦθα τῇ Ῥώμῃ γενόμενος, θεοβουλήτῳ διδασκαλίᾳ σώζων ἀνθρώπους.* It is then related how he transferred his *καθέδρα* to Clement, shortly before his own martyrdom.

[10] Schliemann, S. 101.

[11] Schliemann, S. 90. In particular, the doctrine of Marcion, see Baur's christliche Gnosis, S. 313.

[12] Hom. iii. 12, ss.; xvii. 13, ss. Schwegler's Montanismus, S. 142. Schliemann, S. 547.

[13] Hom. xvi. 12: *Εἷς ἐστιν, ὁ τῇ αὐτοῦ σοφίᾳ εἰπών· ποιήσωμεν ἄνθρωπον· ἡ δὲ σοφία, ὥσπερ ἰδίῳ πνεύματι, αὐτὸς ἀεὶ συνέχαιρεν· ἥνωται μὲν ὡς ψυχὴ τῷ θεῷ, ἐκτείνεται δὲ ἀπ' αὐτοῦ, ὡς χεὶρ δημιουργοῦσα τὸ πᾶν·—κατὰ γὰρ ἔκτασιν καὶ συστολὴν ἡ μονὰς δυὰς εἶναι νομίζεται.* (In explanation of the *ἐκτείνειν*, cf. Philo de somniis, p. 577: *ὁ ἀνθρώπινος νοῦς,—καθάπερ ἥλιος, τὰς αὐτοῦ δυνάμεις ὥσπερ ἀκτῖνας εἰς ὅλον τείνει.* De nominum mutat. p. 1048, *τὸ ὂν—δυνάμεις ἔτεινεν εἰς γένεσιν ἐπ' εὐεργεσίᾳ τοῦ συσταθέντος.* Quod deterius potiori insidiari solet, p. 172: *τέμνεται οὐδὲν τοῦ θείου κατ' ἀπάρτησιν, ἀλλὰ μόνον ἐκτείνεται*). Hom. xvi. 15: *Ὁ κύριος ἡμῶν οὔτε θεοὺς εἶναι ἐφθέγξατο παρὰ τὸν κτίσαντα τὰ πάντα, οὔτε αὐτὸν θεὸν εἶναι ἀνηγόρευσεν.* Comp. Baur in the Tüb. Zeitschr. f. Theol. 1831, iv. 134.

[14] It is the false feminine prophesying which, *τὸν παρόντα ἐπίγειον πλοῦτον ὡς προῖκα δώσειν ἐπαγγέλλεται* (Hom. iii. 23): on the contrary, the male prophesying *τοῦ μέλλοντος αἰῶνος τὰς ἐλπίδας μηνύαν* (c. 26).

hand, Peter proclaims[15] and supports by mighty miraculous deeds the following doctrine: God, a pure, simple being of light, has allowed the world to be formed in antagonisms, and so also the history of the world and of men runs off in antagonisms (*συζυγίαι*) connected by pairs, in which the lower constantly precedes the higher. From the beginning onward God has revealed himself to men, while his Holy Spirit (*σοφία, υἱὸς θεοῦ, θεῖον πνεῦμα, πνεῦμα ἅγιον*) from time to time in the form of individual men (Adam, Enoch, Abraham, Isaac, Jacob, Moses, Jesus), as the true prophet (*ὁ προφήτης τῆς ἀληθείας*), constantly announced the very same truth, and in Jesus caused it also to be communicated to the heathen.[16] According to the law of "*syzgies*," false prophets also are always produced in addition to the true (*γεννητοὶ γυναικῶν* Matth. xi. 11),[17] who corrupt the truth. Thus the original doctrines of Mosaism are perfectly identical with Christianity;[18] though they have not been preserved in their purity in the Pentateuch,[19] which was not composed till long after Moses; and in the present form of Judaism have been utterly perverted. In general, the truth has been constantly maintained in its purity only by a few by means of secret tradition.[20] Man is free, and must expect after death a

[15] Neander's Entwickelung der gnost. Systeme, S. 361, ff. Dr. K. A. Credner über Essäer u. Ebioniten, in Winer's Zeitschr. f. wissenschaftl. Theologie, i. 237, ff. and 277, ff. Baur's christl. Gnosis, S. 300. Schliemann, S. 130.

[16] Hom. iii. 20: *Ἐκεῖνος,—ὃς ἀπ' ἀρχῆς αἰῶνος ἅμα τοῖς ὀνόμασιν μορφὰς ἀλλάσσων, τὸν αἰῶνα τρέχει, μέχρις ὅτε ἰδίων χρόνων τυχὼν, διὰ τοὺς καμάτους θεοῦ ἐλέει χρισθεὶς, εἰς ἀεὶ ἕξει τὴν ἀνάπαυσιν.* The original unpersonal Holy Spirit united himself in Adam with a human person, which appeared, constantly the same, as the true prophet successively in different forms (Baur's Gnosis, S. 362), and is destined for the government of the everlasting kingdom. If one abides by this view, he will not have to assume with Schliemann, S. 142, that a variation prevails in the Clementines respecting the doctrine of the Spirit of God, because he is represented sometimes as an unpersonal energy, sometimes as an hypostasis.

[17] Hom. iii. 23: *Δύο ἡμῖν γενικαὶ ἔστωσαν προφητεῖαι· ἡ μὲν ἀῤῥενική· ἡ δὲ δευτέρα, θῆλυς οὖσα, πρώτη ὡρίσθη ἔρχεσθαι ἐν τῇ τῶν συζυγιῶν προελεύσει. Ἡ μὲν οὖν ἐν γεννητοῖς γυναικῶν οὖσα, ὡς θήλεια, τοῦ νῦν κόσμου ἐπαγγελλομένη, ἀρσενικὴ εἶναι πιστεύεσθαι θέλει· διὸ κλέπτουσα τὰ τοῦ ἄρσενος σπέρματα, καὶ τοῖς ἰδίοις τῆς σαρκὸς σπέρμασιν ἐπισκέπουσα, ὡς ὅλα ἴδια συνεκφέρει τὰ γεννήματα, τοῦτ' ἔστιν τὰ ῥήματα, καὶ τὸν παρόντα ἐπίγειον πλοῦτον, ὡς προῖκα δώσειν ἐπαγγέλλεται.*

[18] Hom. viii. 6: *Μιᾶς δι' ἀμφοτέρων* (Moses and Christ) *διδασκαλίας οὔσης, τὸν τούτων τινὰ πεπιστευκότα ὁ θεὸς ἀποδέχεται.* C. 7: *Πλὴν εἴ τις καταξιωθείη τοὺς ἀμφοτέρους ἐπιγνῶναι, ὡς μιᾶς διδασκαλίας ὑπ' αὐτῶν κεκηρυγμένης, οὗτος ἀνὴρ ἐν θεῷ πλούσιος κατηρίθμηται, τά τε ἀρχαῖα νέα τῷ χρόνῳ καὶ τὰ καινὰ παλαιὰ ὄντα νενοηκώς.* Cf. Hom. xviii. 14.

[19] Hom. iii. 47.

[20] Hom. iii. 19: Christ designated as *τὰ ἀπ' αἰῶνος ἐν κρυπτῷ ἀξίοις παραδιδόμενα κηρύσσων, μέχρις αὐτῶν ἐθνῶν τὸν ἔλεον ἐκτείνων, καὶ ψυχὰς πάντων ἐλεῶν.*

spiritual continuation of life, with rewards and punishments. The conditions of happiness are love to God and man, and struggling against the demons which draw away to evil, through sensuality. For this last purpose these sectaries prescribed abstinence from animal food, frequent fastings and washings, recommended early marriage[21] and voluntary poverty, but rejected all sacrifices.

While the author of the Clementines, from the position of the Elcesaite doctrine, combats parties with which the Elcesaites had never come into contact, he must necessarily go into many new developments of doctrine. How free his movements were in these may be seen from the fact that he frequently used for his purpose our four gospels, unknown to the Elcesaites, with great critical and exegetical arbitrariness.[22] On this very account we might indeed doubt whether he left the Elcesaite doctrine itself entirely untouched.

Although the doctrine here presented could not calculate on any general dissemination, and found several adherents only in *Rome* and *Cyprus*,[23] yet many felt themselves attracted by the historical contents of the production, and its refutation of the heathens and the Gnostics; and since the author knew how to account for the late appearance of his work, which pretended to proceed forth from the apostolic age,[24] they rather thought of it as the corruption of a genuine writing by heretics than a forgery. Hence, another person was soon found, probably an Al-

[21] Hom. iii. 26: ('Ο *ἀληθὴς προφήτης*) *γάμον νομιστεύει, ἐγκράτειαν συγχωρεῖ, εἰς ἁγνείαν πάντας ἄγει.* C. 68: (*Οἱ πρεσβύτεροι*) *νέων μὴ μόνον κατεπειγέτωσαν τοὺς γάμους, ἀλλὰ καὶ τῶν προβεβηκότων, μὴ πως ζέουσα ἡ ὄρεξις προφάσει πορνείας ἢ μοιχείας λοιμὸν προσενέγκοι τῇ ἐκκλησίᾳ.*

[22] A complete collection of the passages from the gospels in the Clementines may be found in Credner's Beiträge zur Einleit. in d. bibl. Schriften, i. 284. According to him the Gospel of Peter lies at the foundation of it. But the passages characteristic of John that appear in the work, can hardly be referred to another gospel; and, if we take these as the standard, we can not expect that the gospel citations generally should be made verbatim.

[23] Epiphanius, Haer. xxx. 18, says, that Ebionites were in Cyprus (by this general appellation for all heretical Jewish Christians he here means this party). Origen (ap. Euseb. vi. 38) calls the heresy of the Elcesaites, *νεωστὶ ἐπανισταμένην*. Since no trace is found of it in the second century beyond Palestine, we may assume that it was first established in those places by the Clementines.

[24] Peter entreats James, in his letter prefixed to the Clementines, to communicate his sermons (*τὰς βίβλους μου τῶν κηρυγμάτων*) only to faithful persons under the seal of secrecy; and James guarantees the secrecy by a *διαμαρτυρία* added, according to which those books should be made known only to tried brethren, after they had agreed by an oath to keep the secret. Comp. Hom. ii. 17, above, note 8.

exandrian, who conceived the idea of purifying it from heretical depravations, by altering it entirely according to the standard of orthodoxy in his day. In this way arose the production which appears under different names among the ancients,[25] and which still exists, but only in the Latin translation of Rufinus, under the title *Recognitiones Clementis*, libb. x.[26] The requirements of a much later orthodoxy gave rise to the ἐπιτομή.[27]

§ 59.

OPPOSITION AT ROME TO MONTANISM, AND THE ASIATIC TIME OF CELEBRATING EASTER.

About the time when the Clementines appeared, there was generally apparent at Rome a lively striving after unity by removing all elements whose tendency was to disturb it.

Montanism had not only obtained many friends in the western church, without giving rise to an external division,[1] but had even gained besides an important influence over the prevailing ecclesiastical principles.[2] The bishop of Rome was already on the point of entering into ecclesiastical communion with the Asiatic Montanists, who had been excluded from the churches of their native country, when *Praxeas*, a confessor, came from Asia to Rome (about 192), and so altered the disposition toward them, that all communion with them was renounced.[3]

25 Περίοδοι Πέτρου or Κλήμεντος (Origenes in Genesin, t. iii. c. 14), Πράξεις Πέτρου (Photius Bibl. cod. 112 and 113), Historia Clementis (Opus imperf. in Matth. ad xxiv. 24), Gesta Clementis, vera disputatio Petri Ap. contra falsitatem Simonis Magi (in Codd.).

26 Schliemann's die clementin. Recognitionen eine Ueberarbeitung der Clementinen (reprinted from Pelt's Theolog. Mitarbeiten. Jahrg. 4, Heft. 4). Kiel. 1843. The same author's Clementinen, S. 265, ff. According to him the composition of them took place in the period between 212 and 230. But the reasons adduced in favor of Rome, as the place of writing, can not be regarded as decisive. The Christology of the Recognitions (Schliemann, S. 331) obviously points to Alexandria.

27 Schliemann, S. 334.

1 See above, § 48, note 17–19, below, note 4.

2 See above, § 53, note 39.

3 Tertull. adv. Praxeam, c. 1. Nam idem (Praxeas) tunc episcopum Romanum, agnoscentem jam prophetias Montani, Priscae, Maximillae, et ex ea agnitione pacem ecclesiis Asiae et Phrygiae inferentem, falsa de ipsis prophetis et ecclesiis eorum adseverando, et praecessorum ejus auctoritates defendendo, coëgit et literas pacis revocare jam emissas, et a proposito recipiendorum charismatum concessare. Victor is usually regarded as that Romish bishop (185–197); but Neander (Antignosticus, S. 485) and Schwegler (Montanismus,

Thus, then, there began in the west also a controversy concerning the distinguishing doctrines of Montanism, which was conducted with violence, especially in Africa.[4] At the head of the Montanist party stood *Quintus Septimius Florens Tertullianus*, presbyter in Carthage, and the earliest Latin ecclesiastical writer of note—a man whose modes of thought were strict and severe, of a violent character, and of a rich though somewhat too sensuous imagination. In his writings it may be seen that he developed his Montanist tendency in a way increasingly rug-

S. 250) declare themselves in favor of Eleutherus (170–185), because an incipient yielding to the Montanists does not appear like the stiff hierarchical character of Victor. That character has been inferred merely from his conduct toward the Quartodecimani. But since experience shows that those who renounce certain views, become the most violent opponents of them, Victor's violent measures against every thing which appears to coincide with Montanism, may be best explained on the supposition that he was at first favorably disposed toward them. Chronology is in favor of Victor; for, by the supposition that Eleutherus was the person, there is too long an interval between the first appearance of Praxeas in Rome, and of Tertullian's, lib. adv. Praxeam (composed according to Noesselt 204 or 205).

[4] An important particular of it is given by Tertullian de Pudicit. c. 1: Audio etiam edictum esse propositum, et quidem peremptorium: Pontifex scilicet Maximus, Episcopus Episcoporum, edicit: ego et moechiae et fornicationis delicta poenitentia functis dimitto Cap. 5: Quid agis mollissima et humanissima disciplina? Idololatram quidem et homicidam semel damnas, moechum vero de medio excipis? Comp. above, § 53, note 39 According to Petavius (not. ad Epiph. Haer. 59. p. 228), it is usually assumed that this Pontifex Maximus is the Romish bishop Zephyrinus (197–217). But the appellation in question does not refer to a real, but to an usurped dignity. It points ironically to the circumstance, that the bishop who had made the regulation arrogated to himself, by so doing, the prerogatives of the only high-priest, Christ. Most probably the allusion is to the bishop of Carthage. Particularly important for the history of the controversy is Tertullian. lib. de Velandis virginibus. In support of his demand, virgines nostras velari oportere, ex quo transitum aetatis suae fecerint, in order to set aside the argument brought against him from custom, cap. 2, Tertullian appeals to the consuetudo of the apostolic churches in Greece, and some barbarous countries: Non possumus respuere consuetudinem, quam damnare non possumus, utpote non extraneam, quia non extraneorum: cum quibus scilicet communicamus jus pacis et nomen fraternitatis. Una nobis et illis fides, unus Deus, idem Christus, eadam spes, eadem lavacri sacramenta. Semel dixerim, una ecclesia sumus. Hence this book was written before the division in the church, when both contending parties still belonged to the same church. Cap. 3 describes how the controversy sprung up from a peaceful living together, and how the parties gradually became more and more embittered. Tamen tolerabilius apud nos ad usque proxime: utrique consuetudini communicabatur. Arbitrio permissa res erat, ut quaeque voluisset aut tegi aut prostituti, sicut et nubere: quod et ipsum neque cogitur, neque prohibetur. Contenta erat veritas pacisci cum consuetudine, ut tacite sub consuetudinis nomine frueretur se vel ex parte. Sed quoniam coeperat agnitio proficere, ut per licentiam utriusque moris indicium melioris partis emergeret: statim ille adversarius bonorum multoque institutorum opus suum fecit. Ambiunt virgines hominum, adversus virgines Dei, nuda plane fronte, in temerariam audaciam excitatae, et virgines videntur.—Scandalizamur, inquiunt, quia aliae aliter incedunt: et malunt scandalizari quam provocari, etc. Soon after, a complete separation took place, adv. Praxeam, c. 1: Et nos quidem postea agnitio paracleti, atque defensio disjunxit a Psychicis.

ged, being heated more and more by controversy (*Spiritalium contra Psychicos*).[5] Others also followed him in the same spirit, till at length in the west also separate Montanist churches were formed.[6] In the mean time, Montanism had become too deeply rooted in the western church; and now also the circumstance operated in its favor (comp. p. 143) that its most zealous opponents, as *Praxeas*[7] and the Roman presbyter *Caius*,[8] fell into other serious errors. Thus, though from this time onward, Montanism was rejected in name even in the western church, yet all Montanist elements were by no means expelled from that church.[9] Not only do we find remaining that

[5] Accordingly he admits of a repentance after baptism, de Poenitentia, c. 7, ss. On the contrary, in his treatise de Pudicitia, c. 16, he writes: Nemo seducat seipsum, i. e., nemo praesumat vitiatim Deo redintegrari denuo posse :—delicta ista—post lavacrum irremissibilia, although, in c. 1, he confesses that he had formerly been of another opinion. In like manner, he allows of flight under persecution, ad Uxorem, i. cap. 3, but rejects the sentiment in his lib. de Fuga in persecutione. Comp. Hieronymus in Catal. c. 53, de Tertull. Hic cum usque ad mediam aetatem presbyter Ecclesiae permansisset, invidia postea et contumeliis clericorum Romanae Ecclesiae ad Montani dogma delapsus. From the historical connection already noticed, it may be seen how this change took place. Comp. J. G. Hoffmann Tertulliani, quae supersunt, omnia in Montanismo scripta videri. Vitemb. 1738. 4. Moshemii Dissertt. ad. hist. eccl. pertinent. vol. i. p. 54, note. J. A. Noesselt de vera aetate ac doctrina scriptorum quae supersunt Q. Sept. Tertulliani dissertt. iii. Hal. 1757, ss. 4 (reprinted in Ejusd. Tres commentationes ad hist. eccl. pertinentes. Halae. 1817, 8, p. 1, ss.). Neander's Antignosticus, Geist des Tertullianus, und Einleitung zu dessen Schriften. Berlin. 1825. 8.

[6] Augustinus, de Haer. c. 86, relates, that in his time the remnant of the Tertullianists in Carthage had returned to the catholic church. Hence the Montanists in Carthage were named after their leader. But they neither gave themselves this appellation, nor can it be inferred from the difference of names, as the Praedestinatus, Haer. 86, does, that the followers of Tertullian had formed a peculiar sect separated from the other Montanists.

[7] See below, § 60.

[8] A cotemporary of Zephyrinus according to Eusebius H. E. ii. 25. Fragments of his διάλογος πρὸς Πρόκλον (τῆς κατὰ Φρύγας αἱρέσεως ὑπερμαχοῦντα, Euseb. vi. 20), are found in Eusebius, ii. 25. iii. 28, 31. Comp. Photii Bibl. cod. 48. Routh Reliqu. Sacr. vol. ii. p. 1, ss. He attributed the doctrine of the millennium and the Apocalypse to Cerinthus. Euseb. iii. 28, comp. Lücke's Einleit. in d. Offenb. Joh. S. 307.

[9] It is a remarkable phenomenon that the Montanists, Perpetua and Felicitas, who were martyred in Carthage in 202, and their Acta composed by a Montanist (see apud Ruinart, and in Münteri Primordia eccl. Afric. p. 227, ss.), were always highly valued in the African church. Cf. Augustini Sermo i. in natali Perpetuae et Felicitatis. The Montanist character of the acts is satisfactorily shown by Valesius (Acta SS. Perpet. et Felicit. Paris. 1664. 8, in the preface), Sam Basnage (Annales polit. Eccl. t. ii. p. 224, ss.), and by Th. Ittig (Diss. de haeresiarchis aevi apostol. et apostolico proximi. Lips. 1690. 4to, sect. ii. c. 13, § 28). Even Jos. Aug. Orsi Diss. apolog. pro SS. Perpetuae et Felicitatis orthodoxia adv. S. Basnagium. Florent. 1728. 4, admits the Montanist principles of the author of the Acta. Comp. particularly Act. cap. 1: Viderint, qui unam virtutem Spiritus unius Sancti pro aetatibus judicent temporum: cum majora reputanda sint novitiora quaeque, ut novissimiora secundum exuberationem gratiae in ultima saeculi spatia decreta. In novissimis enim diebus, dicit Dominus, effundam de Spiritu meo super omnem carnem, &c. (Joel ii. 28, and Acts ii. 17). Itaque et nos, qui sicut prophetias, ita et visiones novas

strictness and tendency to lay stress on external rules of piety,[10] but what is still more striking, even the writings of the Montanist *Tertullian* (about 220) were always valued very highly, and became the model of succeeding Latin ecclesiastical writers.[11]

With the rejection of Montanism in Rome was probably connected *Victor's* opposition to the Asiatic mode of celebrating easter (see p. 166).[12] He called upon the bishops of Asia Minor

pariter repromissas et agnoscimus et honoramus, &c. Cap. 4. Pastor (Christus)—de caseo quod mulgebat dedit mihi quasi buccellam, et ego accepi junctis manibus, et manducavi, et universi circumstantes dixerunt Amen (cf. § 48, not. 22). The enigma, that those Montanizing martyrs should have been constantly considered as members of the catholic church, is accounted for by supposing, that although at the time of their death the controversy between the two parties had begun, yet the separation had not taken place. But, undoubtedly, the Montanist spirit must have been fostered in the church by the high estimation in which such writings were held.

[10] For instance, the principle which was maintained in the African church till the time of Cyprian (Tertull. de Pudic. c. 12), quod neque idololatriae neque sanguini pax ab Ecclesiis redditur. See above, note 4, below, § 71. Neander's Antignosticus, S. 262. The Spanish church, which seems to have adopted the African as its model, expressed the same view in its greatest strictness as late as the Concil. Illiberitanum (about the year of our Lord 305). This council ordains, with regard to those who have defiled themselves with such crimes as idolatry, magic, adultery, incest, placuit nec in fine communionem accipere (can. 1, 2, 6, 7, 8, 10, &c.—The error against which Cyprian, Ep. 63 ad Caecilium, inveighs, quod aliquis existimet, sequendam esse quorundam consuetudinem, si qui in praeteritum in calice Dominico aquam solam offerendam putaverint, may also have sprung from Montanist asceticism.

[11] Hieron. Catal. c. 53: Numquam Cyprianum absque Tertulliani lectione unum diem praeterisse: ac sibi (notario) crebro dicere, Da magistrum, Tertullianum videlicet significans. His works, written from 197–211, are, 1. Against unbelievers, Apologeticus adv. gentes (written about 198, Moshemii de aetate apologetici Tert. comm. in his Dissertt. ad hist. eccl. pert. i. 1. Hefele Tertullian als Apologet, in the Tübingen theol. Quartalschr. 1838, i. 30), libri ii. ad nationes, de testimonio animae, ad Scapulam, adv. Judaeos. 2. Against heretics, adv. Praxeam, adv. Marcionem libb. v., adv. Valentinianos, de Praescriptione haereticorum, adv. Hermogenem. 3. Ascetic writings, the later of them expressly against the Psychics: ad Martyres, de Spectaculis, de Idololatria, de Oratione, de Baptismo, libb. ii. ad Uxorem—de Corona militis, libb. ii. de Cultu feminarum, de Fuga in persecutione, de Patentia, de Virginibus velandis, de Jejuniis, de Pudicitia, caet. Compare the works quoted in note 5. Bähr's christl. römische Theologie, S. 15. Möhler's Patrologie, S. 701.—Ed. Nic. Rigaltius. Paris. 1641. Rep. Ph. Priorius. Par. 1695. fol. J. S. Semler. Hal. 1770–76, 6 Bde. 8. E. F. Leopold, pp. iv. Lips. 1839–41. 8.

[12] Some details relating to this matter are given, perhaps, in the Appendix ad Tertull. de Praescript. haeret. c. 53: Est praeterea his omnibus etiam Blastus accedens, qui latenter Judaismum vult introducere. Pascha enim dicit non aliter custodiendum esse, nisi secundum legem Moysi quartadecima mensis. But this Blastus appeared in Rome (Euseb. v. 15), and Irenaeus wrote to him an ἐπιστολὴ περι σχίσματος (Euseb. v. 20). From Eusebius, it is clear that he did not entirely coincide in sentiment with the Gnosticizing Florinus; he appears to have been an Ultra Montanist. Comp. Pacianus (bishop of Barcelona about 370) Epist. i. ad Sympron. in Gallandii Biblioth. vii. 257: Phryges plurimis nituntur auctoritatibus, nam puto et Graecus Blastus ipsorum est. The Asiatic Montanists have always retained the mode of celebrating easter which he advocates. See Anonymi Orat. vii. in Pascha in Chrysostomi opp. ed. Montfaucon. t. viii. App. p. 276. Schwegler's Montanismus, S. 251.

(about 196) to adopt the custom of the west on this point, and after their refusal, when he had been assured of the assent of the bishops in Palestine, Pontus, Gaul, and Corinth, broke off church communion with them.[13] Several bishops, however, and Irenaeus himself among them, admonished him on account of his too great haste;[14] peace was again restored, and both parties continued undisturbed in the observance of their own customs till the council of Nice.[15]

§ 60.

MONARCHIANS.

Walch's Ketzerhist. i. 537, ii. 3. Martini's Gesch. des Dogma v. d. Gottheit Christi in den vier ersten Jahrh. Rostock. Th. i. 1800. 8. S. 128, ff. F. Schleiermacher über den Gegensatz zwischen der Sabellianischen und der Athanasianischen Vorstellung von der Trinität (in Schleiermacher's, De Wette's, und Lücke's theol. Zeitschrift. Heft 3, Berlin. 1822. S. 295, ff.) [translated into English with notes by Professor Stuart, in the American Biblical Repository for April, 1835.] Neander's K. G. i. ii. 991. L. Lange's Gesch. u. Lehrbegriff d. Unitarier vor der nic. Synode (Beiträge zur ältesten Kirchengesch. Bd. 2). Leipzig. 1831. 8. The same author's Lehre d. Unitarier, v. heil. Geiste, in Illgen's Zeitschr. f. hist. Theol. iii. i. 65. Baur's die christl. Lehre v. d. Dreieinigkeit u. Menschwerdung Gottes, i. 243. G. A. Meier's die Lehre v. d. Trinität. (Hamb. u. Gotha. 1844) i. 74.

The doctrine which regarded the divine in Christ as a personality not distinct from the Father, had subsisted without opposition in the second century alongside of the emanation-doctrine,[1] since it was capable of being united with it in the confession which alone was important in relation to the faith,

[13] Euseb. H. E. v. 23–25.

[14] Euseb. v. 24: Ἀλλ' οὐ πᾶσί γε τοῖς ἐπισκόποις ταῦτ' ἠρέσκετο. ἀντιπαρακελεύονται δῆτα αὐτῷ, τὰ τῆς εἰρήνης καὶ τῆς πρὸς τοὺς πλησίον ἑνώσεως καὶ ἀγάπης φρονεῖν· φέρονται δὲ καὶ αἱ τούτων φωναὶ, πληκτικώτερον καθαπτομένων τοῦ Βίκτορος. Ἐν οἷς καὶ ὁ Εἰρηναῖος ἐκ προσώπου ὧν ἡγεῖτο κατὰ τὴν Γαλλίαν ἀδελφῶν ἐπιστείλας,—τῷ γε μὴν Βίκτορι προσηκόντως, ὡς μὴ ἀποκόπτοι ἕτερα παραινεῖ. Then follow fragments from this letter. Irenaeus expresses his opinion of such disputes very plainly in the Fragm. iii. ed. Pfaff.: Ἔταξαν οἱ Ἀπόστολοι, μὴ δεῖν ἡμᾶς κρίνειν τινὰ ἐν βρώσει καὶ ἐν πόσει [καὶ ἐν μέρει] ἑορτῆς ἢ νεομηνίας ἢ σαββάτων. Πόθεν οὖν ταῦται αἱ μάχαι; πόθεν τὰ σχίσματα; ἑορτάζομεν, ἀλλ' ἐν ζύμῃ κακίας καὶ πονηρίας, τὴν ἐκκλησίαν τοῦ θεοῦ διαῤῥίπτοντες, καὶ τὰ ἐκτὸς τηροῦμεν, ἵνα τὰ κρείττονα τὴν πίστιν καὶ ἀγάπην ἀποβάλλωμεν. Ταύτας οὖν ἑορτὰς καὶ νηστείας ἀπαρέσκειν τῷ κυρίῳ ἐκ τῶν προφητικῶν λόγων ἠκούσαμεν.

[15] According to Athanasius de Syn. c. 5, it was one reason for summoning the council of Nice, that *οἱ ἀπὸ τῆς Συρίας, καὶ Κιλικίας, καὶ Μεσοποταμίας ἐχώλευον περὶ τὴν ἑορτὴν, καὶ μετὰ τῶν Ἰουδαίων ἐποίουν τὸ Πάσχα.* Cf. Euseb. de vita Const. iii. c. 5.

[1] See above § 52, note 12.

viz., that God is in Christ. It found a welcome reception particularly among the Antimontanists, who were averse to all sensuous ideas of Godhead;[2] and on this very account was first combated by the zealous Montanist, Tertullian, in his treatise against Praxeas. In the controversies which extend from this time onward through the third century, and terminate in the ecclesiastical rejection of this doctrine, it developed itself more definitely in different forms, which may be reduced to two great classes. The one looked upon the divine in Christ as continually teaching and acting through him; the other looked upon it as acting only on the human person, so that according to the former, the entire agency of Christ was divine, derived from God; according to the latter, a human agency directed by God.[3] To the first class belonged *Praxeas*,[4] who,

[2] See § 48, notes 14, 15. Neander's K. G. i. ii. 1003, F. A. Heinichen de Alogis, Theodotianis, atque Artemonitis. Lips. 1829. 8. Epiphan. Haer. liv. c. 1, calls Theodotus *ἀπόσπασμα ἐκ τῆς Ἀλόγου αἱρέσεως, τῆς ἀρνουμένης τὸ κατὰ Ἰωάννην εὐαγγέλιον, καὶ τὸν ἐν αὐτῷ ἐν ἀρχῇ ὄντα θεὸν λόγον.*

[3] Novatianus de Trinitate, c. 30: Tam illi, qui Jesum Christum ipsum Deum patrem dicunt, quam etiam illi, qui hominem illum tantummodo esse voluerunt, erroris, sui et perversitatis origines et causas inde rapuerunt, quia, cum animadverterent, scriptum esse, quod unus sit Deus, non aliter putaverunt, istam tenere se posse sententiam, nisi aut hominem tantum Christum, aut certe Deum patrem putarent esse credendum. In like manner Origen. comm. in Joh. tom. ii. c. 2, divides the *εὐλαβουμένους δύο ἀναγορεῦσαι θεοὺς, καὶ παρὰ τοῦτο περιπίπτοντας ψευδέσι καὶ ἀσεβέσι δόγμασιν* into two classes, *ἤτοι ἀρνουμένους ἰδιότητα υἱοῦ ἑτέραν παρὰ τὴν τοῦ πατρὸς ὁμολογοῦντας θεὸν εἶναι τὸν μέχρι ὀνόματος παρ' αὐτοῖς υἱὸν προσαγορευόμενον, ἢ ἀρνουμένους τὴν θεότητα τοῦ υἱοῦ, τιθέντας δὲ αὐτοῦ τὴν ἰδιότητα, καὶ τὴν οὐσίαν κατὰ περιγραφὴν τυγχάνουσαν ἑτέραν τοῦ πατρός.*

[4] Tertullianus adv. Praxean, c. 1: Nam iste primus ex Asia hoc genus perversitatis intulit homo.—Duo negotia diaboli Praxeas Romae procuravit: prophetiam expulit, et haeresin intulit, Paracletum fugavit et patrem crucifixit.—C. 20: Nam sicut in veteribus nihil aliud tenent quam: Ego deus et alius praeter me non est (Es. xlv. 5): ita in Evangelio responsionem domini ad Philippum tuentur: Ego et pater unum sumus, et: Qui me viderit videt et patrem, et: Ego in patre et pater in me (Joh. x. 30, xiv. 9, 10). His tribus capitulis totum instrumentum utriusque testamenti volunt cedere.—C. 3: Itaque duos et tres jam jactitant a nobis praedicari, se vero unius Dei cultores praesumunt.—Monarchiam, inquiunt, tenemus (c. 10, vanissimi isti Monarchiani).—C. 5: Duos unum volunt esse, ut idem pater et filius habeatur.—C. 2: Itaque post tempus pater natus, et pater passus: ipse Deus, dominus omnipotens, Jesus Christus praedicatur. On the other hand, c. 27, aeque in una persona utrumque distinguunt, patrem et filium, dicentes filium carnem esse, id est hominem, i. e., Jesum: patrem autem spritum, i. e., Deum, i. e., Christum, and c. 29: Ergo, inquis, et nos eadem ratione dicentes patrem, qua vos filium, non blasphemamus in Dominum Deum: non enim ex divina sed ex humana substantia mortuum dicimus. Baur (Lehre v. d. Dreieinigkeit, i. 246) and Meier (Lehre v. d. Trinität, i. 77) are of opinion that Praxeas held the view that God connected himself immediately with the flesh, without the medium of a rational human soul. But Tertullian, in express terms, explains carnem by hominem; and when Praxeas said, filium carnem esse, he could not possibly declare a body animated by a mere *ψυχή* to be filius Dei.—Comp. Neander's Antignosticus, S. 481.

notwithstanding the opposition of Tertullian, appears to have been unmolested in Rome on account of his doctrine.[5] But *Theodotus* (ὁ σκυτεύς) who had come to Rome from Byzantium about the same time, was excluded from church-communion by Victor, when he declared Christ to be a mere man; and his disciples (Theodotus ὁ τραπεζίτης, Asclepiades, Natalius Confessor) continued to exist in Rome for some time separated from the church.[6] By means of these Theodotians, however, the Monarchian doctrine generally became so notorious, that *Artemon* (*Artemas*) under bishop Zephyrinus, although he did not agree with the Theodotians, was included in the same class with them, and attacked in various writings.[7] Hence this theory was rendered suspicious every where, even in Asia where it took its rise; and *Noetus* was excommunicated in Smyrna (about 230) on account of his doctrine, which harmonized with that of Praxeas.[8] On the other hand, Origen succeeded in

[5] Tertull. adv. Prax. 1. Denique caverat pristinum doctor de emendatione sua: et manet chirographum apud Psychicos, apud quos tunc gesta res est: exinde silentium. App. l. de Praescr. 53: Post hos omnes etiam Praxeas quidam haeresin introduxit, quam Victorinus (Victor?) corroborare curavit. Cf. note 7.

[6] Comp. the extracts from the anonymous work against Artemon apud Euseb. v. 28, which designates Theodotus as the πρῶτον εἰπόντα ψιλὸν ἄνθρωπον τὸν Χριστόν. Append. l. de Praescr. 53: Ex Spiritu quidem Sancto natum, ex virgine, sed hominem solitarium atque nudum, nullo alio prae ceteris nisi sola justitiae auctoritate. Alter post hunc Theodotus (Trapezita) haereticus erupit, qui et ipse introduxit alteram sectam, et ipsum hominem Christum—inferiorem esse quam Melchisedech, eo quod dictum sit de Christo: Tu es sacerdos in aeternum secundum ordinem Melchisedech (Hebr. vii. 21). Nam illum Melchisedech praecipuae gratiae coelestem esse virtutem: eo, quod agat Christus pro hominibus, deprecator et advocatus ipsorum factus, Melchisedech facere pro coelestibus angelis atque virtutibus. (Melchisedeciani.) According to Theodoret (Haer. fab. comp, 2, 5), even ὁ σμικρὸς Λαβύρινθος accused them of corrupting the Holy Scriptures.

[7] From the σπούδασμα κατὰ τῆς Ἀρτέμωνος αἱρέσεως extracts are given in Euseb. v. 28, in which Artemon, without a clearer explanation of his doctrine, is compared with Theodotus. But the Artemonites asserted, l. c., τοὺς μὲν προτέρους ἅπαντας καὶ αὐτοὺς τοὺς ἀποστόλους παρειληφέναι τε καὶ δεδιδαχέναι ταῦτα, ἃ νῦν οὗτοι λέγουσι· καὶ τετηρῆσθαι τὴν ἀλήθειαν τοῦ κηρύγματος μέχρι τῶν Βίκτορος χρόνων,—ἀπὸ δὲ τοῦ διαδόχου αὐτοῦ Ζεφυρίνου παρακεχάραχθαι τὴν ἀλήθειαν. According to these extracts they must have propounded a doctrine different from that of Theodotus, who was excommunicated by Victor, and such a doctrine, too, as might be reconciled with the earlier doctrine of the Roman church still indefinitely expressed. In the same work, § 5, they are reproached with their dialectic tendency (οὐ τί αἱ θεῖαι λέγουσι γραφαὶ ζητοῦντες, ἀλλ' ὁποῖον σχῆμα συλλογισμοῦ εἰς τὴν τῆς ἀθεότητος εὑρεθῇ σύστασιν, φιλοπόνως ἀσκοῦντες), and with their preference for Aristotle and Theophrastus. Theodoret (Haer. fab. comp. 2, 5) gives extracts frem the σμικρὸς Λαβρύρινθος, written against Theodotus and Artemon, which some falsely ascribe to Origen. When Nicephorus (Hist. eccles. iv. 21) looks upon that σπούδασμα of Eusebius as identical with the Λαβύρινθος of Theodoret, and when Photius (Cod. 48) makes Caius to be the author of both works they advance nothing but conjectures.

[8] Theodoret Haer. fab. comp. iii. 3, names Epigonus and Cleomenes as Noetus's prede-

drawing off *Beryllus*, bishop of *Bostra*, from that view, at a council held in that place, in 244 A.D.[9] *Sabellius*, presbyter in Ptolemais (250–260) renewed it in a form still farther developed.[10] Dionysius, bishop of Alexandria, endeavored in vain

cessors. His doctrine: *Ἕνα φασὶν εἶναι θεὸν καὶ πατέρα, τῶν ὅλων δημιουργόν· ἀφανῆ μὲν ὅταν ἐθέλῃ, φαινόμενον δὲ ἡνίκα ἂν βούληται· καὶ τὸν αὐτὸν ἀόρατον εἶναι καὶ ὁρώμενον, καὶ γεννητὸν καὶ ἀγέννητον· ἀγέννητον μὲν ἐξ ἀρχῆς, γεννητὸν δὲ ὅτε ἐκ παρθένου γεννηθῆναι ἠθέλησε· ἀπαθῆ καὶ ἀθάνατον, καὶ πάλιν αὖ παθητὸν καὶ θνητόν. ἀπαθὴς γὰρ ὢν, φησὶ, τὸ τοῦ σταυροῦ πάθος ἐθελήσας ὑπέμεινε. τοῦτον καὶ υἱὸν ὀνομάζουσι καὶ πατέρα, πρὸς τὰς χρείας τοῦτο κἀκεῖνο καλούμενον.* He is opposed by Hippolytus contra haeresin Noëti [ed. Fabricii, t. ii. p. 5], which is transcribed by Epiphanius Haer. 57, comp. note 9.

[9] Euseb. vi. 33. His doctrine was: *Τὸν σωτῆρα καὶ κύριον ἡμῶν μὴ προϋφεστάναι κατ' ἰδίαν οὐσίας περιγραφὴν πρὸ τῆς εἰς ἀνθρώπους ἐπιδημίας· μηδὲ μὴν θεότητα ἰδίαν ἔχειν, ἀλλ' ἐμπολιτευομένην αὐτῷ μόνην τὴν πατρικήν.* Comp. Origenis fragm. ex libro in epist. ad Titum (from the apology of Pamphilus, Origenis Opp. ed Lommatzsch, v. 287): Sed et eos, qui hominem dicunt Dominum Jesum praecognitum et praedestinatum, qui ante adventum carnalem substantialiter et proprie non extiterit, sed quod homo natus Patris solam in se habuerit deitatem, ne illos quidem sine periculo est ecclesiae numero sociari: sicut et illos, qui superstitiose magis, quam religiose, uti ne videantur duos deos dicere, neque rursum negare Salvatoris deitatem, unam eandemque subsistentiam Patris ac Filii asseverant, i. e., duo quidem nomina secundum diversitatem causarum recipientem, unam tamen *ὑπόστασιν* subsistere, i. e., unam personam duobus nominibus subjacentem, que latine Patripassiani appellantur. The first opinion is that of Beryllus, the second that of Noetus. C. Ullmanni de Beryllo Bostreno ejusque doctrina comm. Hamb. 1835. 4. (in Halle Christmas programm.)

[10] His doctrine according to Basilius Epist. 210: *Τὸν αὐτὸν θεόν ἕνα τῷ ὑποκειμένῳ* [*τῇ ὑποστάσει*, Ep. 214] *ὄντα, πρὸς τὰς ἑκάστοτε παραπιπτούσας χρείας μεταμορφούμενον* (*μετασχηματιζόμενον*, Ep. 235: *προσωποποιούμενον*, Ep. 214), *νῦν μὲν ὡς πατέρα, νῦν δὲ ὡς υἱὸν, νῦν δὲ ὡς πνεῦμα ἅγιον διαλέγεσθαι.* Cf. Athanas. c. Arian. Or. iv. 11: *Τὸν θεὸν σιωπῶντα μὲν ἀνενέργητον, λαλοῦντα δὲ ἰσχύειν*). Theodoret. Haer. fab. comp. ii. 9, *Ἐν μὲν τῇ παλαιᾷ ὡς πατέρα νομοθετῆσαι, ἐν δὲ τῇ καινῇ ὡς υἱὸν ἐνανθρωπῆσαι· ὡς πνεῦμα δὲ ἅγιον τοῖς ἀποστόλοις ἐπιφοιτῆσαι.*—(*τρία πρόσωπα*). Pseudo-Greg. Thaumat. *ἡ κατὰ μέρος πίστις* (in Ang. Maji Scriptt. vett. nova collectio, vii. 1, 171): *Ἀποφεύγομεν τὸν Σαβέλλιον λέγοντα τὸν αὐτὸν πατέρα, τὸν αὐτὸν υἱὸν· πατέρα μὲν γὰρ λέγει εἶναι τὸν λαλοῦτα, υἱὸν δὲ τὸν λόγον ἐν τῷ πατρὶ μένοντα, καὶ κατὰ καιρὸν τῆς δημιουργίας φαινόμενον, ἔπειτα μετὰ τὴν ἁπάντων πλήρωσιν τῶν πραγμάτων εἰς θεὸν ἀνατρέχοντα. Τὸ αὐτὸ δὲ καὶ περί τοῦ πνεῦματος λέγει.* Athanas. c. Arian. Or. iv. 12: *Ἡ μονὰς πλατυνθεῖσα γέγονε τρίας.* Ib. 13: *Συστέλλεσθαι καὶ πάλιν ἐκτείνεσθαι τὸν θεὸν*, respecting this *ἔκτασις καὶ συστολή*, see the Clementinen und Philo above, § 58, note 13). Ib. 25: *Ὥσπερ διαιρέσεις χαρισμάτων εἰσὶ, τὸ δὲ αὐτὸ πνεῦμα, οὕτω καὶ ὁ πατὴρ ὁ αὐτὸς μὲν ἐστι, πλατύνεται δὲ εἰς υἱὸν καὶ πνεῦμα.* Arii epist. ad Alexandrum Alex. ap. Epiphan. Haeres. 69: *Σαβέλλιος τὴν μονάδα διαιρῶν υἱοπάτορα εἶπεν.* (Gregorius Nyss. contra Arium et Sabellium in Ang. Maji Scriptt. vett. nova coll. viii. ii. 1: *Οἱ κατὰ Σαβέλλιον—ἀναιρεῖν μὲν πειρῶνται τὴν ὑπόστασιν τοῦ υἱοῦ, αὐτὸν δὲ τὸν πατέρα ἕνα ὄντα δυσὶν ὀνόμασι γεραίροντα οἰόμενοι, υἱοπάτορα προσαγορεύουσιν*). According to Epiphanius Haer. lxii. 1, he compared the Godhead to the sun, *ὄντι μὲν ἐν μιᾷ ὑποστάσει, τρεῖς δὲ ἔχοντι τὰς ἐνεργείας*, namely, *τὸ τῆς περιφερείας σχῆμα*, or *τὸ εἶδος πάσης τῆς ὑποστάσεως, τὸ φωτιστικόν*, and *τὸ θάλπον*. The Monas is the divine essence in itself, in its concealed state, which reveals itself in the trias, by interchangeably assuming three characters (*πρόσωπα*) according to the nature of the revelations. These three *πρόσωπα* are *ὁ πατήρ, ὁ υἱός, τὸ πνεῦμα*. The Logos is never called a second prosopon, but it is the Logos which became man, and, as such, took the name *ὁ υἱός* (Athanas. c. Arian. Or. iv. 22: *Ἐν ἀρχῇ μὲν λόγον*

to refute him by personal interviews and letters, and in unfolding antagonist views, went so far as to make new and objectionable assertions. Sabellians were found so late as the fourth century, in Rome and Mesopotamia. Still greater offense was given by *Paul of Samosata*, who, being at the same time bishop of Antioch (from 260) and holding a civil office,[11] exhibited a vanity and love of display hitherto unexampled in a Christian bishop. While he maintained with strictness the unity of God, he declared Jesus to be a man begotten by the Holy Spirit, on whom the Divine wisdom descending exerted its influence in a peculiar manner.[12] Three councils

ἁπλῶς· ὅτε δὲ ἐνηνθρώπησε, τότε ὠνομάσθαι υἱόν). Hence Baur's opinion (Dreieinigkeit, i. 261) is very probable that, in the sense of Sabellius, the Logos, in opposition to the Monas, is the manifested God generally, and that the three *πρόσωπα* are to be considered as the changing forms of the Logos. If in some accounts the divine essence is styled *ὁ πατήρ* generally, this may have been done by Sabellius, as well as, according to the Catholic doctrine, *ὁ πατήρ* may even designate the triune God *οὐσιωδῶς*. Finally, with regard to the question whether Sabellius considered the *πρόσωπον* of the Son as a transitory appearance united to the earthly existence of Jesus (as Baur, l. c. p. 266, thinks), or whether he believed that the person of Christ should cease to be only with the final consummation (according to Neander, i. ii. 1031), Gregory of Nyssa decides in favor of the former view, contra Arium et Sabellium in Ang. Maji Coll. viii. ii. 4: *Οἱ δὲ κατὰ Σαβέλλιον—εἰς τὴν μεγίστην τῆς ἀσεβείας ἐκπεπτώκασι πλάνην, οἰόμενοι διὰ μὲν λειποταξίαν ἀνθρωπίνην προεληλυθέναι τὸν υἱὸν ἐκ τοῦ πατρὸς προσκαίρως· αὖθις δὲ μετὰ τὴν διόρθωσιν τῶν ἀνθρωπίνων πλημμελημάτων ἀναλελυκότα ἐνδύναι τε καὶ ἀναμεμίχθαι τῷ πατρί.*

[11] He was a Ducenarius, Euseb. vii. 30. We must not here think of the Ducenarii whom Augustus created as the fourth decuria of knights, so called because they must have property to the amount of ducena sestertia (Sueton. Octav. c. 32), but the ducenarii procuratores, officers of a higher rank, who had so much yearly revenue, to whom Claudius granted the ornamenta consularia (Sueton. Claud. c. 24), and who still continued under Constantine (Cod. Justin. x. 19, 1).

[12] His history is given in Euseb. vii. 27–30. Here also, cap. 30, is found the historical part of the circular letter of the last council of Antioch which was held against him. Doctrinal fragments of the same are given in Leontii Byz. contra Nestor. et Eutych. lib. iii. in the Greek original from a Bodleian MS. apud J. G. Ehrlich diss. de erroribus Pauli Samos. Lips. 1745. 4, p. 23. Among other original documents put together in the collection of councils (apud Mansi, i. 1033), the Epist. Episcoporum ad Paulum is still the most trustworthy. The others are partly suspicious, partly spurious beyond a doubt; such as the epistle of Dionysius Alex. ad Paulum.—Fragments of Paul himself are found in the Contestatio ad Clerum Constantinop. in the Acts of the council of Ephesus apud Mansi v. 393, ap. Leontius, l. c. In Greek from a Paris MS. in J. G. Feuerlini diss. de haeresi Pauli Sam. Gotting. 1741. 4, p. 10, and in Justiniani Imp. lib. contra Monophysitas in Ang. Maji Nova collect. vii. i. 299: The texts contain much that agrees word for word, and may be supplemented and improved by each other. Besides fragments of Paul *ἐκ τῶν πρὸς Σαβιανὸν* (or *Σαβῖνον*) *λόγων* from a Clermont MS. in Feuerlini diss. p. 15, more correctly from a Vatican MS. in Ang. Maji Nova coll. vii. i. 68.—The doctrine of Paul was, according to Epiphanius Haer. lxvi. 1: *Ἐν θεῷ ἀεὶ ὄντα τὸν αὐτοῦ Λόγον, καὶ τὸ Πνεῦμα αὐτοῦ, ὥσπερ ἐν ἀνθρώπου καρδίᾳ ὁ ἴδιος λόγος· μὴ εἶναι δὲ τὸν υἱὸν ἐνυπόστατον, ἀλλὰ ἐν αὐτῷ θεῷ* (*ἐπιστήμην ἀνυπόστατον*, Epist. Episc. ad Paul)—*ἐλθόντα δὲ τὸν Λόγον καὶ ἐνοικήσαντα ἐν Ἰησοῦ ἀνθρώπῳ ὄντι* (Epist. synodi Antioch. apud Leontius: *οὐ συγγεγεν-*

were held in Antioch on his account. At the last of them (269), he was convicted of heresy, by Malchion, his opinion having been hitherto disguised under ambiguous expressions, and deposed from his office.[13] But his newly elected successor, bishop Domnus, could not take possession of his office until Zenobia, the patroness of Paul, had been defeated by Aurelian (272).[14] The party of Paul (Samosateniani, Pauliani, Paulianistae) existed till the fourth century.[15]

ῆσθαι τῷ ἀνθρωπίνῳ τὴν σοφίαν, ὡς ἡμεῖς πιστεύομεν, οὐσιωδῶς, ἀλλὰ κατὰ ποιότητα).—οὐ φάσκει δὲ οὗτος κατὰ τὸν Νόητον τὸν πατέρα πεπονθέναι, ἀλλὰ φησὶ, ἐλθὼν ὁ λόγος ἐνήργησε μόνος, καὶ ἀνῆλθε πρὸς τὸν πατέρα. Fragments of Paul's writings: *Συνῆλθεν ὁ λόγος τῷ ἐκ Δαβὶδ γεγενημένῳ, ὅς ἐστιν Ἰησοῦς Χριστὸς ὁ γεννηθεὶς ἐκ πνεύματος ἁγίου· καὶ τοῦτον μὲν ἤνεγκεν ἡ παρθένος διὰ πνεύματος ἁγίου, ἐκεῖνον δὲ τὸν λόγον ἐγέννησεν ὁ θεὸς ἄνευ παρθένου καὶ ἄνευ τινὸς οὐδενὸς ὄντος, πλὴν τοῦ θεοῦ· καὶ οὕτως ὑπέστη ὁ λόγος.—Ἄνθρωπος χρίεται, λόγος οὐ χρίεται·—καὶ γὰρ ὁ λόγος μείζων ἦν τοῦ Χριστοῦ· Χριστὸς γὰρ διὰ σοφίας μέγας ἐγένετο· τὸ ἀξίωμα τῆς σοφίας μὴ καθέλωμεν. Λόγος μὲν γὰρ ἄνωθεν, Ἰησοῦς δὲ Χριστὸς ἄνθρωπος ἐντεῦθεν* (Epist. Syn. Antioch. apud Euseb. vii. 30, *Ἰ. Χρ. κάτωθεν*). *Μαρία τὸν λόγον οὐκ ἔτεκε—τὸν λόγον ὑπεδέξατο—ἔτεκεν ἄνθρωπον ἡμῖν ἴσον, κρείττονα δὲ κατὰ πάντα, ἐπειδὴ ἐκ πνεύματος ἁγίου.—(Ἡ σοφία) ἐν προφήταις ἦν, μᾶλλον δὲ καὶ ἐν Μωσῇ· καὶ ἐν πολλοῖς κυρίοις, μᾶλλον δὲ καὶ ἐν Χριστῷ, ὡς ἐν ναῷ θεοῦ.* Ex Pauli sermonibus ad Sabinum: *Τῷ ἁγίῳ πνεύματι χρισθεὶς προσηγορεύθη Χριστὸς, πάσχων κατὰ φύσιν, θαυματουργῶν κατὰ χάριν· τῷ γὰρ ἀτρέπτῳ τῆς γνώμης ὁμοιωθεὶς τῷ θεῷ, καὶ μείνας καθαρὸς ἁμαρτίας ἡνώθη αὐτῷ, καὶ ἐνηργήθη ποιεῖσθαι τὴν τῶν θαυμάτων δυναστείαν, ἐξ ὧν μίαν αὐτῷ καὶ τὴν αὐτὴν πρὸς τῇ θελήσει ἐνέργειαν ἔχων δειχθεὶς, λυτρωτὴς τοῦ γένους καὶ σωτὴρ ἐχρημάτισεν.—Ἅγιος καὶ δίκαιος γέγονεν ἡμῶν ὁ σωτὴρ, ἀγῶνι καὶ πόνῳ τῆς τοῦ προπάτορος ἡμῶν κρατήσας ἁμαρτίας· οἷς κατορθώσας τὴν ἀρετὴν, συνήφθη τῷ θεῷ, μίαν καὶ τὴν αὐτὴν πρὸς αὐτὸν βούλησιν καὶ ἐνέργειαν ταῖς τῶν ἀγαθῶν προκοπαῖς ἐσχηκώς· ἣν ἀδιαίρετον φυλάξας, τὸ ὄνομα κληροῦται τὸ ὑπὲρ πᾶν ὄνομα, στοργῆς ἔπαθλον αὐτῷ χαρισθέν.—Μὴ θαυμάσῃς, ὅτι μίαν μετὰ τοῦ θεοῦ τὴν θέλησιν εἶχεν ὁ σωτήρ· ὥσπερ γὰρ ἡ φύσις μίαν τῶν πολλῶν καὶ τὴν αὐτὴν ὑπάρχουσαν φανεροῖ τὴν οὐσίαν, οὕτως ἡ σχέσις τῆς ἀγάπης μίαν τῶν πολλῶν καὶ τὴν αὐτὴν ὑπάρχουσαν φανεροῖ τὴν οὐσίαν, οὕτως ἡ σχέσις τῆς ἀγάπης μίαν τῶν πολλῶν καὶ τὴν αὐτὴν ἐργάζεται θέλησιν διὰ μιᾶς καὶ τῆς αὐτῆς φανερουμένης εὐαρεστήσεως.—Τὰ κρατούμενα τῷ λόγῳ τῆς φύσεως οὐκ ἔχουσιν ἔπαινον· τὰ δὲ σχέσει φιλίας κρατούμενα ὑπεραίνετα, μίᾳ καὶ τῇ αὐτῇ γνώμῃ κρατούμενα, διὰ μιᾶς καὶ τῆς αὐτῆς ἐνεργείας βεβαιούμενα, καὶ τῆς κατ' ἐπαύξησιν οὐδέποτε παυομένης κινήσεως. Καθ' ἣν τῷ θεῷ συναφθεὶς ὁ σωτὴρ οὐδέποτε δέχεται μερισμὸν εἰς τοὺς αἰῶνας, μίαν αὐτῷ καὶ τὴν αὐτὴν ἔχων θέλησιν καὶ ἐνέργειαν ἀεὶ κινουμένην τῇ φανερώσει τῶν ἀγαθῶν.*—J. B. Schwab diss. de Pauli Samos. vita atque doctrina. Herbipoli. 1839. 8. Baur, i. 293. Neander, i. ii. 1035. Meier's Lehre v. d. Trinität, i. 115.

[13] It was established by the council: *μὴ εἶναι ὁμοούσιον τὸν υἱὸν τοῦ θεοῦ τῷ πατρι*, first mentioned in a letter of the Semiarians about 358, allowed by Athanasius de Synod. 43. Hilarius de Synod. 86. Basilius Epist. 52. On the other side, Prudentius Maranus diss. sur les Semiariens (in Voigtii bibl. hist. haeresiologicae, t. ii. p. 159), Feuerlini diss. Dei filium patri esse *ὁμοούσιον*, antiqui ecclesiae doctores in Conc. Ant. utrum negarint. Goetting. 1755. 4. Döllinger's K. G. i. i. 269.—Schleiermacher, l. c. 387, note, thinks that Sabellius first used that expression. That it certainly occurs in the Sabellian controversy is shown below, § 64, note 8.

[14] A remarkable command of Aurelian, Euseb. vii. 30, 9: *Τούτοις νεῖμαι τὸν οἶκον, οἷς ἂν οἱ κατὰ τὴν Ἰταλίαν καὶ τὴν Ῥωμαίων πόλιν ἐπίσκοποι τοῦ δόγματος ἐπιστέλλοιεν.*

[15] The most usual names for all those who asserted *τὸν αὐτὸν εἶναι πατέρα καὶ υἱὸν καὶ*

§ 61.

MANICHAEANS.

SPECIAL SOURCES—Archelai (bishop of Cascar about 278). Acta disputationis cum Manete (first in L. A. Zaccagnii collectaneis monumentor. vet. eccl. Graecae et Lat. Romae. 1698. 4; then in J. A. Fabricii ed. opp. Hippolyti vol. ii. Gallandii bibl. Patr. vol. iii. Routh Reliqu. Sacr. vol. iv. p. 119, ss.).—Titi Bostrensis (about 360) libb. iv. contra Manichaeos (in Hen. Canisii lection. antiquis, ed. Basnage, t. i.).—Augustini Hipponensis contra Fortunatum, contra Adamantum, contra Faustum libb. 33, de actis cum Felice Man. libb. 2, and other writings collected in the 8th vol. of the Benedictine edition.

WORKS—Is. de Beausobre Hist. crit. de Manichée et du Manicheisme. Amst. 1734, 39. 2 Bd. 4. J. L. Moshemii comm. de rebus Christian. ante Constantin. M. p. 728, ss. Walch's Ketzerhist. Th. 1. S. 685, ff. J. S. Semler's Einleitung zu Baumgarten's Untersuch. Theologischer Streitigkeiten, Bd. 1. Halle. 1762. 4. S. 266, ff. K. A. Freih. v. Reichlin Meldegg die Theologie d. Magiers Manes und ihr Ursprung. Frankf. a. M. 1825. 8. Manichaeorum indulgentias cum brevi totius Manichaeismi adumbratione e fontibus descripsit A. F. V. de Wegnern. Lips. 1827. 8. Neander's Kirchengesch. i ii. 824 (Comp. my review of the last three works in the theol. Studien u. Kritiken, Bd i. Heft 3. S. 599, ff.). Das manich. Religionssystem nach den Quellen neu untersucht u. entwickelt von Dr. F. Chr. Baur, Tübingen. 1831. 8. (Comp. Scheckenburger's review in the Theol. Stud. u. Krit. 1833. iii. 875).

Since the Syrian Gnosis, which had spread even to Persia,[2] presented so many points of union with the doctrine of Zoroaster,[3] it is not surprising that the Persian Gnostics should have been led to connect their Christianity still more closely with the Zend doctrine.[4] After the spiritual aspect of the religion of Zoroaster had declined under the *Arsacidae*, and become a rude dualism and mere ceremonial worship, the *Sassanides* (from 227) did every thing in their power to restore its ancient splendor. In the assemblies of the Magi a supreme principle was acknowledged (Zeruane akerene); and, on the other hand, unqualified dualism with its adherents (*Magusaeans*, al thanavia) condemned. These commotions in the bosom of Parsism prob-

ἅγιον πνεῦμα were, according to Athanas. de Synodis, c. 7, Πατροπασσιανοὶ μὲν παρὰ Ῥωμαίοις, Σαβελλιανοὶ δὲ παρ' ἡμῖν.

[1] Fragments of the Greek original are given by Epiphanius (Haer. 66). Respecting their spuriousness, see Beausobre, i. p. 129, ff. Yet even by Jerome they were regarded as authentic (Catal. c. 72). Cf. Fabricii bibl. Graeca ed. Harles, vol. vii, p. 275, ss.

[2] Comp. § 39, note 5, § 46, Sim. de Vries de orig. et progressu Relig. Christ. in vet. Persarum regno, in Barkey Museum Haganum, t. iii. p. 288, ss.

[3] Die Theologie Zoroaster's nach dem Zend-Avesta v. A. Hölty, in Illgen's Zeitschr. f Hist. Theol. viii. i. 1.

[4] In opposition to Baur, who in the work already quoted, p. 433, assumes Buddhism as a third element, and with whom even Neander, l. c. second edition, p. 827, agrees, see the apposite objections of Scheckenburger in the theolog. Studien u. Kritiken. 1833, iii. 890

ably gave rise to the attempt of *Manes* to unite Christianity with the system of these Magusaeans.[5] Eastern and western writers differ from one another not only in the name of this sect-founder (*Mani—Cubricus*, *Manes*, *Manichaeus*), but also in their accounts of him.[6] They agree only in this, that he was hated by the Magi, persecuted by the Persian kings, compelled to flee, and lastly, at the command of a king (according to the orientals, *Baharam* or *Bararanes* I., from 272–275) barbarously put to death, as a corrupter of religion, in a fort or castle (according to the oriental writers, *Dascarrah*, according to the occidental, *Arabion*).

His system of religion rests on the assumption of two everlasting kingdoms coexisting and bordering on each other, *the kingdom of light* and *the kingdom of darkness*, the former under the dominion of God, the latter under the *demon* or *Hyle*. After the borders had been broken through by a war between the two kingdoms, and the material of light had been mixed with the material of darkness, God caused the world to be formed by *the living spirit* (*ζῶν πνεῦμα*, spiritus vivens) out of this mixed material, in order that by degrees the material of light here captured (anima and Jesus patibilis) might be again separated and the old boundaries restored. Two exalted natures of light, *Christ* (whom Mani calls in preference dextra luminis, *τοῦ ἀϊδίου φωτὸς υἱός*, &c.) and *the Holy Spirit*, the former dwelling in the sun and moon (naves), the latter in the air, conduct this process of bringing back the material of light; while the demon and the evil spirits, fettered to the stars, endeavor to hinder them. In every man there dwells an evil soul besides the soul of light;[7] and it is his commission to secure to the latter the sway over the former, to unite with it as many as

[5] Thom. Hyde Historia religionis vett. Persarum et Parthorum et Medorum. Oxon. 1700 (new ed. Lond. 1760), 4. p. 280, ff. Abbé Foucher on the system of Manes, in J. F. Kleuker's appendix to the Zend-Avesta, Bd. i. Th. 2, S. 186, ff. Silv. de Sacy Mémoires sur diverses antiquités de la Perse. Paris. 1793. 4. p. 52.

[6] The orientals are given in Herbelot Bibliothèque orientale. Paris. 1697. fol. (new edition, Haag. 1777, 78. 3. T. in 4.) Art. Mani. The western have all borrowed from Archelai Act. disput. cum Manete.

[7] An old Persian notion: so says the Persian Araspas in Xenoph. Cyrop. vi. c. 1, § 21: *Δύο γὰρ σαφῶς ἔχω ψυχάς.—οὐ γὰρ δὴ μία γε οὖσα ἅμα ἀγαθή τέ ἐστι καὶ κακὴ, οὐδ' ἅμα καλῶν τε καὶ αἰσχρῶν ἔργων ἐρᾷ, καὶ ταὐτὰ ἅμα βούλεταί τε καὶ οὐ βούλεται πράττειν· ἀλλὰ δηλονότι δύο ἐστὸν ψυχὰ, καὶ ὅταν μὲν ἡ ἀγαθὴ κρατῇ, τὰ καλὰ πράττεται· ὅταν δὲ ἡ πονηρὰ, τὰ αἰσχρὰ ἐπιχειρεῖται.* On the later Persians, see Kleuker's Appendix to the Zend-Avesta, Bd. 1, Th. 1, S. 261.

possible of the elements of light, which are scattered in nature, especially in certain plants, and thus to free it from the fetters of the evil principle, and prepare the way for its return to the kingdom of light.[8] After men had long been led astray by the demon, by means of false religions (Judaism and Heathenism), *Christ* descended from the sun to earth in the appearance of a body, to lead them to the worship of the true God, and by his doctrine to help the souls of light in their struggles for liberty. But his instructions were not fully understood even by the apostles, and after his death were still more falsified by the Christians.[9] Hence he promised a still greater apostle, the παράκλητος, who should separate all that was false, and announce the truth in perfection and purity.[10] This person appeared in *Mani*. The Manichaeans accordingly rejected entirely the Old Testament.[11] All that they thought they could make use of in favor

[8] Manes in Epist. ad filiam Menoch (in Augustini Op. imperf. lib. iii. c. 172): Sicut animae gignuntur animabus, itaque figmentum corporis a corporis natura digeritur. Quod ergo nascitur de carne, caro est, et quod de spiritu, spiritus est: spiritum autem animam intellige.—(C. 177.) Sive enim bonum geramus, non est carnis—sive malum geramus, non est animae. Hence the Manichaeans had other definitions of freedom and sin. Fortunatus Disp. ii. cum Augustino, c. 21: Id est peccatum animae, si post commonitionem Salvatoris nostri et sanam doctrinam ejus a contraria natura et inimica sui stirpe se non segregaverit anima. Secundinus Epist. ad Augustin, § 2: (Anima) carnis commixtione ducitur, non propria voluntate. At si, cum se ipsum cognoverit, consentiat malo, et non se armet contra inimicum, voluntate sua peccavit. Quam se iterum pudeat errasse, paratum inveniet misericordiarum auctorem. Non enim punitur, quia peccavit, sed quia de peccato non doluit.

[9] Contemptuously called Γαλιλαῖοι by Manes in Epist. ad Oddam (in Fabricii Bibl Graeca, vol. v. p. 285).

[10] Mani begins his Epistola fundamenti (ap. Augustinum contra epist. Manichaei, c. 5) thus: Manichaeus Apostolus Jesu Christi providentia Dei patris. Haec sunt salubria verba de perenni et vivo fonte, quae qui audierit et eisdem primum crediderit, deinde quae insinuant custodierit, numquam erit morti obnoxius, verum aeterna et gloriosa vita fruetur, caet.—The Manichaean Felix (Augustin. de Act. cum Felice, i. 9): Paulus in altera epistola dicit: "Ex parte scimus et ex parte prophetamus: cum venerit autem quod perfectum est, abolebuntur ea, quae ex parte dicta sunt." (1 Cor. xiii. 9, 10.) Nos audientes Paulum hoc dicere, venit Manichaeus cum praedicatione sua et suscepimus eum secundum quod Christus dixit: "Mitto vobis spiritum sanctum."—Et quia venit Manichaeus, et per suam praedicationem docuit nos initium, medium et finem: docuit nos de fabrica mundi, quare facta est, et unde facta est, et qui fecerunt: docuit nos, quare dies et quare nox: docuit nos de cursu solis et lunae: quia hoc in Paulo non audivimus, nec in caeterorum Apostolorum scripturis: hoc credimus, quia ipse est Paracletus Itaque illud iterum dico, quod superius dixi: si audiero in altera scriptura, ubi Paracletus loquitur, de quo voluero interrogare, et docueris me, credo et renuntio.—Without doubt, Manes made a distinction between the Holy Spirit and the Paraclete, but was misunderstood by the Catholics (for example Euseb. H. E. 7, 31: Τοτὲ μὲν τὸν Παράκλητον καὶ αὐτὸ τὸ ἅγιον αὐτὸς ἑαυτὸν ἀνακηρύττων).

[11] Baur's Manich. Religionssystem, S. 358. F. Trechsel über den Kanon, die Kritik u Exegese d. Manichäer. Bern. 1832. 8. S. 11.

of their doctrine belonging to the canonical and apocryphal writings of the New Testament, was regarded by them as a remnant of the original truth. Whatever was opposed to their views was supposed to be error which had been subsequently mixed up with the truth.[12] Thus, they appealed, where it served their purpose, to the canonical gospels[13] and the epistles of St. Paul as well as to apocryphal gospels without entirely adopting these writings,[14] but at the same time, without attempting to purge them from error, as Marcion did. Since they found least truth in the history of the apostles written by Luke, they confronted this canonical production with another, under the name of Lucius or Leucius.[15] All these writings could not be *canonical* in their estimation, meaning by that term, absolutely authoritative. The works of Mani alone were canonical.[16]

Their morality had for its object to procure for the good the

[12] Baur, S. 378. Trechsel, S. 27. Faustus Manich. (ap. Augustin c. Faust. xxxii. 6): Nobis Paracletus, ex novo Testamento promissus, perinde docet, quid accipere ex eodem debeamus, et quid repudiare.

[13] Faustus (ap. Augustin. c. Faust. xxxiii. 3): Nec ab ipso (Christo), haec (Evangelia) sunt, nec ab ejus apostolis scripta: sed multo post eorum assumptionem a nescio quibus, et ipsis inter se non concordantibus Semijudaeis per famas opinionesque comperta sunt: qui tamen omnia eadem in apostolorum Domini conferentes nomina, vel eorum, qui secuti apostolos viderentur errores ac mendacia sua secundum eos se scripsisse mentiti sunt.

[14] Cyrillus Hieros. Catech. iv. and vi. pronounces the gospel of Thomas to be a Manichaean production, and many have followed him; but the Manicheans may have quoted it for particular sentiments, without entirely adopting it (see Thilo Cod. apocr. N. T. Proleg. p. lxxx.). The gospel of Philip was of Gnostic origin, which document is said to have been used also by the Manichaeans, Trechsel, S. 59.—A catalogue of such writings, which in part at least may have been first used by the later Manichaeans, may be found in Timotheus (presb. Constantinop. about 511) l. de iis qui ad ecclesiam accedunt, in J. Meursii Varia divina. Lugd. Bat. 1619. 4. p. 117.

[15] Leucii Acta Apostolorum (Augustin. de Actis c. Felice, ii. 6): *Αἱ τῶν Ἀποστόλων περίοδοι* (Photius Bibl. cod. 114), written by Leucius Charinus, containing the *Πράξεις Πέτρου, Ἰωάννου, Ἀνδρέου, Θωμᾶ, Παύλου*. Several of them exist in MS. There have been published Acta S. Thomae Apostoli ed. J. C. Thilo. Lips. 1823. 8. Comp. the Prolegomena to this work, p. lx. Respecting the person of Leucius, the most contradictory accounts are given (Trechsel, S. 61). It is highly probable that he is a mythic collective for all heretical histories of the apostles, and that the name was modeled after that of Luke.

[16] *Βίβλος τῶν μυστηρίων* (Syriac in 22 divisions. Fragments apud Titus Bostrensis and Epiphan. Haer. lxvi. 14), B. *τῶν κεφαλαίων, τὸ ζῶν εὐαγγέλιον* (Oriental. Erteng ?), *ὁ θησαυρὸς τῆς ζωῆς* (Fragments in Augustin. de Natura boni, 44, de Act. cum Felice, i. 14, and in Evodius de Fide). These four works Manes is said to have appropriated from the remains of Scythianus. Besides these there are several letters of his: Epist. fundamenti (Augustini lib. contra epist. Manichaei, quam vocant fundamenti), Ep. ad filiam Menoch (Fragments in August. Opus imperfect. lib. iii.). Fragments of the letters ad Zebenam, ad Scythianum, ad Odan, ad Cudarum in Fabricii Bibl. Graeca, vol. v. p. 284, ff. ed. nov. vol. viii. p. 315, also scattered here and there in Ang. Maji Scriptt. vett. nova coll. vii. i. 17, 69, 70, 277, 304.

dominion over the bad soul, by a rigid self-denial. It was divided into the signaculum oris, sign. manus, and sign. sinus. It imposed on the baptized members (electi, perfecti, τέλειοι) so great privations, that most adherents of the sect remained catechumens (auditores) as long as possible, for the sake of being released from the observance of the most stringent laws. The worship of the Manichaeans was very simple. They celebrated Sunday by fasting; the day of Mani's death by a yearly festival (βῆμα). Baptism, which was administered with oil,[17] and the Lord's Supper belonged to the secret worship of the electi.

Mani himself sent out twelve apostles to propagate his doctrine, in like manner afterward electi were constantly dispatched for this purpose. Hence the party remained in very close union. At the head of them was one person, to whom 12 magistri immediately, and next the 72 bishops of the churches, were subordinate. Many followers were attracted by the historical form in which Mani endeavored to explain so much that is incomprehensible,[18] and by the asceticism of his adherents. Accordingly, the Manichaeans spread, soon after the death of their founder, into proconsular Africa, and even further in the Roman dominions, although they were opposed with vehemence, not only by the catholic church, but were also persecuted by heathen emperors,[19] who enacted bloody laws against them as a sect derived from the hostile Persians.

[17] Theol. Studien u. Kritiken, i. iii. 620. Baur, S. 277.

[18] Augustinus de Utilitate credendi, c. 1. (Opp. ed. Bened. viii. 34): Nosti enim, Honorate, non aliam ob causam nos in tales homines incidisse, nisi quod se dicebant, terribili auctoritate separata, mira et simplici ratione eos, qui se audire vellent, introducturos ad Deum, et errore omni liberaturos, etc.

[19] Diocletian's edict to Julian, proconsul of Africa, against the Manichaeans, dat. prid. Kal. April. (287 ?) Alexandriae, mentioned also by Ambrosiaster ad. 2 Tim. iii. 7, and preserved in the Lex Dei s. Mosaicarum et Romanarum legum collatio (best edition by F. Blume. Bonnae. 1833. 8) tit. xv. c. 3, and in the Codicis Gregoriani fragmentis (ed. G. Haenel. Bonnae. 1837. 4. p. 44):—De quibus Solertia tua Serenitati nostrae retulit Manichaeis, audivimus eos nuperrime, veluti nova inopinata prodigia, in hunc mundum de Persica, adversaria nobis gente, progressa vel orta esse, et multa facinora ibi committere: populos namque quietos turbare, nec non et civitatibus maxima detrimenta inserere: et verendum est, ne forte, ut fieri adsolet, accedenti tempore conentur (per) excecrandas consuetudines et scaevas leges Persarum innocentioris naturae homines, Romanam gentem modestam atque tranquillam, et universum orbem nostrum veluti venenis suis malevolis inficere.—Jubemus namque, auctores quidem ac principes una cum abominandis scripturis eorum severiori poenae subjici, ita ut flammeis ignibus exurantur; consentaneos vero et usque adeo contentiosos capite puniri praecipimus, et eorum bona fisco nostro vindicari sancimus. Si qui sane etiam honorati, aut cujuslibet dignitatis, vel majoris, personae ad hanc inauditam et turpem atque per omnia infamem sectam, vel ad doctrinam Persarum

THIRD CHAPTER.

THEOLOGY OF THE CATHOLIC CHURCH.

I. IN THE EAST.

§ 62.

ALEXANDRIAN SCHOOL.

J. G. Michaelis de Scholae Alexandrinae sic dictae catecheticae origine, progressu ac praecipuis doctoribus (Symbolae literariae. i. iii. 195. Bremae. 1745). J. F. Hilscher de Schola Alexandrina. Lips. 1776. 4. H. E. F. Guerike de Schola, quae Alexandriae floruit, comm. hist. et theol. (Pp. ii. Halis Sax. 1824, 25. 8.) Pars prior: de externa Scholae Historia. C. F. G. Hasselbach de Schola, quae Alexandriae floruit, catechetica. Part. i. A Stettin School-programm of the year 1826. Neander's Kirchengesch. i. ii. 909, ff. Redepenning's Origenes, i. 57.

In the present period, Christian theology was cultivated especially at *Alexandria*, at that time the seat of all the sciences, where the catholic teachers, even by their external relations to the heathen and Gnostics, were compelled to enter philosophically into the doctrines of Christianity.[1] Here began to be very soon felt the necessity of an instruction beyond the usual one given to catechumens, as well for the philosophical proselytes as for those who were to become teachers. After many persons thirsting for knowledge had been in this way collected about some distinguished man, the institution of the *Alexandrian catechetical school*[2] attached itself to those prior individual efforts

se transtulerunt, eorum patrimonia fisco nostro adsociari facies: ipsos quoque foenensibus vel proconensibus metallis dari. Ut igitur stirpitus amputari mala haec nequitia de saeculo beatissimo nostro possit, Devotio tua jussis ac statutis Tranquillitatis Nostrae maturius, obsecundare (festinet). Explanations of this passage may be found in Bynkershoek de Relig. peregrina, diss. ii. (Opusc. ii. 207.) Cannegieter ad Fragm. vet. jurisprud. c. 24.

[1] Origenes ap. Eusebium, vi. 19, 5.

[2] Euseb. v. 10 (speaking of the time of Commodus): Ἡγεῖτο δὲ τηνικαῦτα τῆς τῶν πιστῶν αὐτόθι (κατ' Ἀλεξάνδρειαν) διατριβῆς ἀνὴρ κατὰ παιδείαν ἐνδοξότατος, ὄνομα αὐτῷ Πάνταινος· ἐξ ἀρχαίου ἔθους διδασκαλείου τῶν ἱερῶν λόγων παρ' αὐτοῖς συνεστῶτος, ὃ καὶ εἰς ἡμᾶς παρατείνεται, καὶ πρὸς τῶν ἐν λόγῳ καὶ τῇ περὶ τὰ θεῖα σπουδῇ δυνατῶν συγκροτεῖσθαι παρειλήφαμεν. This account is given more fully by Jerome, in Catal. 36: Pantaenus, stoicae sectae philosophus, juxta quandam veterem in Alexandria consuetudinem, ubi a Marco Evangelista semper ecclesiastici fuere doctores, tantae prudentiae et eruditionis tam in Scripturis divinis, quam in saeculari literatura fuit, ut in Indiam quoque—mittere-

shortly before the present period. The height of its prosperity falls under this very time, and its distinguished teachers (κατηχήσεων magistri, Hieron. Cat. c. 38), *Pantaenus*, *Clemens Alexandrinus*, *Origenes*, *Heraclas*, *Dionysius*,[3] (*Pierius* and *Theognostus* ?) are the only persons by whom Christian theology was now advanced. The Alexandrian school took its peculiar direction from its very first teachers. *Pantaenus*, a Stoic philosopher, is otherwise unknown; and we can only judge of him by his pupil *Titus Flavius Clemens*. The peculiarity of the Alexandrian school is already stamped on the writings of the latter, who was president of the catechetical institution from about 191 till 202, then fled in the persecution raised by Severus, and probably returned to Alexandria († about 220).[4] But the characteristics of the school were completely developed and matured by the great *Origen* (ὁ χαλκέντερος, ὁ ἀδαμάντιος) the son of the martyr *Leonides*, who died in 202. When a youth of eighteen he was a catechist at Alexandria,[5] and procured for

tur. Names: τὸ τῆς κατηχήσεως διδασκαλεῖον (Euseb. H. E. vi. 3, 1, vi. 26) τὸ ἱερὸν διδασκαλεῖον τῶν ἱερῶν μαθημάτων (Sozom. H. E. iii. 15), ecclesiastica schola (Hieron. Cat. c. 38), schola κατηχήσεων (ibid. c. 69).

[3] This is the order according to Eusebius and others. On the other hand, Philippi Sidetae (about 420) fragm. in Henr. Dodwelli dissertatt. in Irenaeum. Oxon. 1689. 8. p. 490, ss.: Athenagoras, Pantaenus, Origenes, Heraclas, Dionysius, Clemens, Pierius, Theognostus, Serapion, Petrus Martyr, Macarius πολιτικός, Didymus, Rhodon. Even Socrates Hist. eccl. vi. c. 27, finds fault with the Christian history of Philip ὅτι τοὺς χρόνους τῆς ἱστορίας συγχέει.

[4] Writings: λόγος προτρεπτικὸς πρὸς Ἕλληνας—παιδαγωγός 3 books—στρώματα or στρωματεῖς libb. viii. (cf. Photii. Cod. cx. λόγος, τίς ὁ σωζόμενος πλούσιος (c. comment. C. Segaar. Traj. ad Rh. 1816. 8). With others of his writings have been also unfortunately lost the ὑποτυπώσεις in 8 books, in which later orthodoxy found many ἀσεβεῖς καὶ μυθώδεις λόγους (See Photius Cod. 109). The fragments of it have been collected by Potter in his edition of Clement, vol. ii. p. 1006, ss. A small portion of it, Remarks on the Catholic epistles, has been preserved in a Latin translation under the title of Adumbrationes Clem. Alex. (best ed. Potter, l. c.); probably the same of which Cassiodorus de Institut. div. lit. c. 8, says, that he had prepared it ut exclusis quibusdam offendiculis purificata doctrina ejus securior possit hauriri. Comp. Lücke's Comm. über die Schriften Johannis, 2te Auflage, iii. 77. Perhaps also the ἐκ τῶν προφητικῶν (prophetic interpretations) ἐκλογαι apud Potter, p. 989, are remains of the Hypotyposes.—Opp. omnia ed. J. Potter. Oxon. 1715. 2 voll. fol. R. Klotz. Lips. 1831–34. 4 voll. 8.—P. Hofstede De Groot Disp. de Clemente Alex. Groningae. 1826. 8. v. Cölln's article on Clemens in Ersch and Gruber's Encyclop. Th. 18. S. 4, ff. A. F. Daehne de γνώσει Clementis Alex. Lips. 1831. 8. Bedeutung des Alex. Clemens f. d. Entstehung d. christl. Theologie, by D. Kling, in the theol. Stud. u. Krit. 1841. iv. 857. Ritter's Gesch. d. christl. Philos. i. 421. Redepenning's Origenes, i. 70. [See the article on Clement in Smith's Dict. of Biography and Mythology.]

[5] His self mutilation, related by Eusebius, vi. 2, is questioned by Schnitzer (Origenes über die Grundlehren, Einleit. S. xxxiii.). On the other side see Engelhardt in the theol. Stud. u. Kritik. for 1838, i. 157, and Redepenning's Origines, i. 202.—According to Porphyry Origen was also a hearer of Ammonius Saccas (Euseb. vi. 19), which appears to be con

himself a great reputation even in other places. But he displeased his bishop, *Demetrius*, by being consecrated presbyter at *Caesarea* (228), went thither in 231, and was then excluded from communion with the church by Demetrius on account of his peculiar opinions. The churches in Palestine, Arabia, and Achaia, paid no regard, however, to this excommunication; and Origen not only continued to fill the office of presbyter in Caesarea, but likewise gave instruction in the sciences. Besides this, the revision of the corrupted Septuagint (τὰ ἑξαπλᾶ) occupied him for twenty-eight years. During this time he was twice invited to synods which were held in Arabia against heretics; and both times he succeeded in convincing them of their errors (*Beryllus* of *Bostra*, 244—Arabici, 248). So distinguished a teacher of Christianity could not be overlooked in persecutions. He escaped from *Maximin the Thracian* by fleeing to his friend *Firmilian*, bishop of Caesarea in Cappadocia. But in the *Decian* persecution he suffered so much ill usage in Tyre, that he died there some years after († 254).[6]

firmed by himself in a fragment there given. In opposition to Ritter (Gesch. d. Philos. iv. 576, Gesch. d. christl. Phil. i. 467), who denies it, see Redepenning, i. 230, and L. Krüger über das Verhältniss d. Orig. zu Amm. Sakkas, in Illgen's Zeitschr. f. hist. Theol. 1843, i. 46.—That in addition to the famous Origen, there was a cotemporary heathen philosopher of the same name is proved, in opposition to many writers, by Redepenning, i. 421, and Krüger, S. 51.

[6] On Origen's life, theology, and writings, see Pet. Dan. Huetii Origeniana libb. iii., prefixed to his edition of the commentaries, and in de la Rue, vol. iv. App. p. 79, ss. Ceillier Histoire des auteurs sacrés et eccles. t. ii. p. 584, ss. Origenes, eine Darstellung s. Lebens u. s. Lehre v. C. R. Redepenning. Abth. 1. Bonn. 1841. A development of his doctrine alone in: Origenes, ein Beitrag zur Dogmengeschichte der dritten Jahrhundert. von G. Thomasius Nürnberg. 1837. Writings: 1, exegetical, the model and source for all succeeding Greek commentators: σημειώσεις, scholia—τόμοι, commentarii—ὁμιλίαι. (On these three kinds of explanatory writings, see Rufinus Invectiv. in Hieronym. lib. ii. in Hieronym. Opp. ed. Martianay, t. iv. P. ii. p. 426. On the homilies, Tzschirneri Opusc. academ. p. 206, ss.) Origenes in Sacr. script. commentaria, quaecunque graece reperiri potuerunt, ed. P. D. Huetius, 2 voll. Rothomagi. 1668, also Paris. 1679, and Coloniae (Frankfurt). 1685. fol. Most of the expository writings are extant only in the Latin translations of Rufinus and Jerome. 2, κατὰ Κέλσου τόμοι η′ (ed. G. Spencer, Cantabrig. 1658. 4). 3, περὶ ἀρχῶν lib. iv. only fragments of the Greek are extant, but Rufinus's Latin version is entire (Orig. de Principiis, ed. et annotatione instruxit E. R. Redepenning. Lips. 1836. 8). Origenes über die Grundlehren der Glaubenswissenschaft Wiederherstellungsversuch von Dr. K. F. Schnitzer. Stuttgart. 1835. 8. Cf. Rufini praef.: Interpretando sequor regulam praedecessorum, et ejus praecipui viri, cujus superius fecimus mentionem (Hieronymi), qui cum ultra lxx. libellos Origenis—transtulisset in Latinum, in quibus cum aliquanta offendicula inveniantur in Graeco, ita elimavit omnia interpretando, atque purgavit, ut nihil in illis, quod a fide nostra discrepit, latinus lector inveniat. Hieron. adv. Rufin. lib. i. ed. Martian. t. iv. P. ii. p. 355. Concerning this translation of Rufinus: Quum—contulissem cum Graeco, illico animadverti, quae Origenes de Patre et Filio et Spiritu Sancto impie dixerat, et quae romanae aures ferre non poterant, in meliorem partem ab interprete

§ 63.

(CONTINUATION).—REPRESENTATION OF THE ALEXANDRIAN THEOLOGY, PARTICULARLY THAT OF ORIGEN.

Guerike de Schola Alex. catech. (s. notice prefixed to § 62). Pars posterior: de Scholae Alex. catecheticae theologia. Halis. 1825, and the works relating to the doctrine of Clement and Origen which have been already quoted, § 62 notes 5 and 6. [Davidson's Sacred Hermeneutics. Edinburgh. 1843.]

The Alexandrians set a very high value on philosophy, both because it was formerly among the heathen what the law was among the Jews, a preparation for Christianity, and because by it alone a deeper knowledge of Christian doctrine is opened up, (*γνῶσις*, hence *γνωστικοί*, in Origen *σοφία*, *ἡ θεία σοφία*).[1] This *γνῶσις* was certainly different from the *ψευδώνυμος γνῶσις* of the errorists; since the received doctrines of the church (*πίστις*),[2]

commutata. Caetera autem dogmata, de angelorum ruina, de animarum lapsu, de resurrectionis praestigiis, de mundo vel intermundiis Epicuri, de restitutione omnium in aequalem statum, et multo his deteriora, quae longum esset retexere, vel ita vertisse, ut in Graeco invenerat, vel de commentariolis Didymi, qui Origenis apertissimus propugnator est, exaggerata et firmiora posuisse. Ejusd. Epist. 94, ad Avitum: Quae insania est, paucis de Filio et Spiritu Sancto commutatis, quae apertam blasphemiam praeferebant, caetera ita ut scripta sunt protulisse in medium? Respecting his own and other earlier versions, Ejusdem Epist. 41, ad Pammach. et Oceanum: Ego omnia, quae vitiata fuerunt, correxi. Nec disertiores sumus Hilario, nec fideliores Victorino, qui ejus tractatus, non ut interpretes, sed ut auctores proprii operis transtulerunt. Nuper S. Ambrosius sic Hexaëmeron illius compilavit, ut magis Hippolyti sententias Basiliique sequeretur. . On the translation of Rufinus, see Redepenning Prolegomena, p. xlv. To the lost writings also belong the *στρωματεῖς* in ten books. Philocalia a Basilio M. et Gregorio Theol. ex variis Origenis commentariis excerpta, primum graece ed. Jo. Tarinus. Paris. 1618. 4. Orig. Opp. omnia ed. Car. et Car. Vinc. de la Rue. Par. 1740–59. 4 voll. fol. denuo recensuit C. H. E. Lommatzsch, till the present time, 17 Tomi. Berolini, 1831–44 small 8 (containing the whole of his exegetical and smaller writings).

[1] Clemens in Strom. (ed. Potter) i. p. 331: *Ἦν μὲν οὖν πρὸ τῆς τοῦ Κυρίου παρουσίας εἰς δικαιοσύνην Ἕλλησιν ἀναγκαία φιλοσοφία· νυνὶ δὲ χρησίμη πρὸς θεοσέβειαν γίνεται, προπαιδεία τις οὖσα τοῖς τὴν πίστιν δι' ἀποδείξεως καρπουμένοις.—ἐπαιδαγώγει καὶ αὐτὴ (ἡ φιλοσοφία) τὸ Ἑλληνικὸν, ὡς ὁ νόμος τοὺς Ἑβραίους εἰς Χριστόν.* P. 337: *Θεόθεν ἧκεν εἰς ἀνθρώπους.* (Cf. vii. p. 832: *Ὁ Κύριος ἐστὶν ὁ διδοὺς καὶ τοῖς Ἕλλησι τὴν φιλοσοφίαν διὰ τῶν ὑποδεεστέρων ἀγγέλων.*) P. 338: *Φιλοσοφίαν δὲ οὐ τὴν Στωϊκὴν λέγω, οὐδὲ τὴν Πλατωνικὴν, ἢ τὴν Ἐπικούρειόν τε, καὶ Ἀριστοτελικήν· ἀλλ' ὅσα εἴρηται παρ' ἑκάστῃ τῶν αἱρέσεων τούτων καλῶς, δικαιοσύνην μετὰ εὐσεβοῦς ἐπιστήμης ἐκδιδάσκοντα, τοῦτο σύμπαν τὸ ἐκλεκτικὸν φιλοσοφίαν φημί.* Hence his zeal against those who asserted (Strom. i. p. 326), *πρὸς κακοῦ ἂν τὴν φιλοσοφίαν εἰσδεδυκέναι τὸν βίον ἐπὶ λύμῃ τῶν ἀνθρώπων, πρός τινος εὑρετοῦ πονηροῦ*, namely (vi. p. 773 and 822), *τοῦ διαβόλου*. Origenes in Genesin Hom. 14, § 3: Philosophia neque in omnibus legi Dei contraria est, neque in omnibus consona. Moralis et physica, quae dicitur philosophia, paene omnia, quae nostra sunt, sentiunt.

[2] Clem. Strom. vii. p. 864: *Ἔστιν γὰρ, ὡς ἔπος εἰπεῖν, ἡ γνῶσις τελείωσίς τις ἀνθρώπου,*

as molded and modified in express opposition to the Gnostics, were adopted as an immutable basis for the orthodox Gnosis. Yet these orthodox Gnostics were led by the connection of certain general philosophical principles and opinions with Christianity, to many speculations which were very like those of their heretical brethren. Like them too, they believed that their Gnosis[3] had been handed down as a mysterious doctrine;[4] and that it should be communicated only to the initiated.[5] Hence Origen writes about such doctrines with visible hesitation, and warns in particular, against bringing them before the people.[6] Toward the uninitiated, the Alexandrians regarded

ὡς ἀνθρώπου, διὰ τῆς τῶν θείων ἐπιστήμης συμπληρουμένη, κατὰ τε τὸν τρόπον καὶ τὸν βίον καὶ τὸν λόγον σύμφωνος καὶ ὁμόλογος ἑαυτῇ τε καὶ τῷ θείῳ λόγῳ. Διὰ ταύτης γὰρ τελειοῦται ἡ πιστις, ὡς τελείου τοῦ πιστοῦ ταύτῃ μόνως γιγνομένου. P. 865: *Ἡ μὲν οὖν πίστις σύντομος ἐστιν, ὡς εἰπεῖν, τῶν κατεπειγόντων γνῶσις· ἡ γνῶσις δὲ ἀπόδειξις τῶν διὰ πίστεως παρειλημμένων ἰσχυρὰ καὶ βέβαιος, διὰ τῆς κυριακῆς διδασκαλίας ἐποικοδομουμένη τῇ πίστει.* ii. p. 445: *Στοιχείων γοῦν τῆς γνώσεως τῶν προειρημένων ἀρετῶν* (hope, repentance, abstinence, patience, love), *στοιχειωδεστέραν εἶναι συμβέβηκε τὴν πίστιν, οὕτως ἀναγκαίαν τῷ γνωστικῷ ὑπάρχουσαν, ὡς τῷ κατὰ τὸν κόσμον τόνδε βιοῦντι πρὸς τὸ ζῆν τὸ ἀναπνεῖν. Ὡς δ' ἄνευ τῶν τεσσάρων στοιχείων οὐκ ἔστι ζῆν, οὐδ' ἄνευ πίστεως γνῶσιν ἐπακολουθῆσαι· αὕτη τοίνυν κρηπὶς ἀληθείας.* Origines c. Celsum lib. vi. (ed. Spencer. p. 284): *Ἡ θεία τοίνυν σοφία, ἑτέρα οὖσα τῆς πίστεως, πρῶτόν ἐστι τῶν καλουμένων χαρισμάτων τοῦ θεοῦ· καὶ μετ' ἐκείνην δεύτερον, τοῖς ἀκριβοῦν τὰ τοιαῦτα ἐπισταμένοις, ἡ καλουμένη γνῶσις· καὶ τρίτον (ἐπεὶ σώζεσθαι χρὴ καὶ τοὺς ἁπλουστέρους, προσιόντας κατὰ δύναμιν τῇ θεοσεβείᾳ) ἡ πίστις*, with reference to 1 Cor. xii. 8, 9. De Principiis, i. praef. § 3: Illud autem scire oportet, quoniam sancti Apostoli fidem Christi praedicantes de quibusdam quidem, quaecunque necessaria crediderunt, omnibus—manifestissime tradiderunt, rationem scilicet assertionis eorum relinquentes ab his inquirendam, qui Spiritus dona excellentia mererentur: de aliis vero dixerunt quidem, quia sint; quomodo autem, aut unde sint, siluerunt, profecto ut studiosiores quique ex posteris suis, qui amatores essent sapientiae, exercitium habere possent, in quo ingenii sui fructum ostenderent, hi videlicet qui dignos se et capaces ad recipiendam sapientiam praepararent. Neander's K. G. i. ii. 912, ff. A. F. Daehne de *γνώσει* Clem. Al. Lips. 1831. 8. Redepenning's Origenes, i. 335.

[3] And still earlier, Philo. See Grossmann de Judaeorum disciplina arcani, p. i. (a Leipzig programme at the Reformation-anniversary, 1833. 4).

[4] Clemens Strom. vi. p. 771: *Γνωστικὴ παράδοσις.—ἡ γνῶσις δὲ αὐτὴ, ἡ κατὰ διαδοχὰς εἰς ὀλίγους ἐκ τῶν Ἀποστόλων ἀγράφως παραδοθεῖσα κατελήλυθεν.* Idem Hypotyp. vii. (ap. Euseb. H. E. ii. 1, 2): *Ἰακώβῳ τῷ δικαίῳ καὶ Ἰωάννῃ καὶ Πέτρῳ μετὰ τὴν ἀνάστασιν παρέδωκε τὴν γνῶσιν ὁ κύριος· οὗτοι τοῖς λοιποῖς ἀποστόλοις παρέδωκαν, οἱ δὲ λοιποὶ ἀπόστολοι τοῖς ἑβδομήκοντα.* Origines, c. Cels. vi. p. 279: *Ἰησοῦς, ὅτι μὲν ἐλάλει τὸν τοῦ θεοῦ λόγον τοῖς μαθηταῖς κατ' ἰδίαν, καὶ μάλιστα ἐν ταῖς ἀναχωρήσεσιν, εἴρηται· τίνα δ' ἦν, ἃ ἔλεγεν, οὐκ ἀναγέγραπται· οὐ γὰρ ἐφαίνετο αὐτοῖς γραπτέα ἱκανῶς εἶναι ταῦτα πρὸς τοὺς πολλοὺς, οὐδὲ ῥητά.*

[5] Clem. Strom. i. p. 324: *Τὰ μὲν ἑκὼν παραπέμπομαι, ἐκλέγων ἐπιστημόνως, φοβούμενος γράφειν, ἃ καὶ λέγειν ἐφυλαξάμην. οὔ τί που φθονῶν, οὐ γὰρ θέμις, δεδιὼς δὲ ἄρα περὶ τῶν ἐντυγχανόντων, μή πη ἑτέρως σφαλεῖεν, καὶ παιδὶ μάχαιραν, ἥ φασιν οἱ παροιμιαζόμενοι, ὀρέγοντες εὑρεθῶμεν.* Origen. c. Cels. i. p. 7: In Christianity let there be *τινὰ οἷον μετὰ τὰ ἐξωτερικὰ, μὴ εἰς τοὺς πολλοὺς φθάνοντα.*

[6] Thus the doctrine of the termination of future punishment. Respecting his views de

a certain accommodation as necessary, which might venture even to make use of falsehood for the attainment of a good end, yea, which was obliged to do so;[7] and hence they did not scruple to acknowledge in many ecclesiastical doctrines such an accommodation.[8]

The Alexandrian theology set out with the most elevated idea of God, and strove to keep far away from it all anthropopathic limitations. In like manner it declared the freedom of the rational being to be inalienable; and asserted for the purpose of removing from the Deity every idea of groundless caprice, that the external circumstances of all morally free beings can be conditioned only by their moral state. Since, at the same time, this theology assumed that the world was created only on account of rational beings, and conformably to their moral

fine vel consummatione, he says, de Princ. i. 6, § 1: Quae quidem a nobis etiam cum magno metu et cautela dicuntur, discutientibus magis et pertractantibus quam pro certo ac definito statuentibus, etc.

[7] Plato de Republ. iii. had long before allowed untruth in certain cases *ἐν φαρμάκου εἴδει* as useful. So also Philo, who speaks just as the Christian Alexandrians, of a two-fold mode of religious instruction, Quod Deus sit immutabilis, p. 302: *Οἱ μὲν οὖν εὐμοίρου φύσεως λαχόντες καὶ ἀγωγῆς ἀνυπαιτίου—ἀληθείᾳ συνοδοιπόρῳ χρῶνται, παρ' ἧς μυηθέντες τὰ περὶ τοῦ ὄντος ἀψευδῆ μυστήρια, τῶν γενέσεως οὐδὲν προσαναπλάττουσιν αὐτῷ* (*τῷ θεῷ*). *Τούτοις οἰκειότατον πρόκειται κεφάλαιον ἐν τοῖς ἱεροφαντηθεῖσι χρησμοῖς, ὅτι οὐχ ὡς ἄνθρωπος ὁ θεὸς, ἀλλ' οὐθ' ὡς οὐρανὸς, οὐθ' ὡς κόσμος.—Οἱ δὲ γε νωθεστέρᾳ μὲν καὶ ἀμβλείᾳ κεχρημένοι τῇ φύσει, περὶ δὲ τὰς ἐν παισὶ τροφὰς πλημμεληθήντες, ὀξὺ καθορᾷν ἀδυνατοῦντες ἰατρῶν δέονται νομοθετῶν οἳ πρὸς τὸ παρὸν πάθος τὴν οἰκείαν ἐπινοήσουσι θεραπείαν.—Μανθανέτωσαν οὖν πάντες οἱ τοιοῦτοι τὰ ψευδῆ, δι' ὧν ὠφεληθήσονται, εἰ μὴ δύνυνται δι' ἀληθείας σωφρονίζεσθαι.* Clemens Al. Strom. vi. p. 802: *Ψεῦσται τῷ ὄντι οὐχ οἱ συμπεριφερόμενοι δι' οἰκονομίαν σωτηρίας—ἀλλ' οἱ εἰς τὰ κυριώτατα παραπίπτοντες καὶ ἀθετοῦντες μὲν τὸν Κύριον τὸ ὅσον ἐπ' αὐτοῖς ἀποστεροῦντες δὲ τοῦ Κυρίου τὴν ἀληθῆ διδασκαλίαν.* Origines Strom. vi. (in Hieronymi Apol. i. adv. Rufin. c. 18) brings forward that passage of Plato in defense of this kind of accommodation, and adds: Homo autem, cui incumbit necessitas mentiendi, diligenter attendat, ut sic utatur interdum mendacio, quomodo condimento atque medicamine, ut servet mensuram ejus. Ex quo perspicuum est, quod nisi ita mentiti fuerimus, ut magnum nobis ex hoc aliquod quaeratur bonum, judicandi simus quasi inimici ejus, qui ait: "Ego sum veritas." Cf. Historia antiquior sententiarum Eccl. graecae de accommodatione Christo inprimis et Apostolis tributa, diss. scripsit F. A. Carus. Lips. 1793. 4.

[8] Origines c. Cels. iii. p. 159, in allusion to the Christian eschatology attacked by Celsus: *Ἐὰν δέ τις ἐν τούτοις δεισιδαιμονίαν μᾶλλον ἢ πονηρίαν περὶ τοὺς πολλοὺς τῶν πιστευόντων τῷ λόγῳ εἶναι φαντάζηται, καὶ ἐγκαλῇ ὡς δεισιδαίμονας ποιοῦντι τῷ λόγῳ ἡμῶν· φήσομεν πρὸς αὐτὸν, ὅτι ὥσπερ ἔλεγέ τις τῶν νομοθετῶν* (Solon) *πρὸς ἐρωτῶντα, εἰ τοὺς καλλίστους ἔθετο τοῖς πολίταις νόμους, ὅτι οὐ τοὺς καθάπαξ καλλίστους, ἀλλ' ὧν ἐδύναντο τοὺς καλλίστους. Οὕτω λέγοιτο ἂν καὶ ἀπὸ τοῦ πατρὸς τοῦ Χριστιανῶν λόγου, ὅτι, ὧν ἐδύναντο οἱ πολλοὶ εἰς βελτίωσιν ἠθῶν, τοὺς καλλίστοὺς ἐθέμην νόμους καὶ διδασκαλίαν, πόνους οὐ ψευδεῖς ἀπειλῶν καὶ κολάσεις τοῖς ἁμαρτάνουσιν, ἀλλ' ἀληθεῖς μὲν καὶ ἀναγκαίους, εἰς ἐπανόρθωσιν τῶν ἀντιτεινόντων προσαγομένους· οὐ μὴν καὶ πάντως τὸ τοῦ κωλάζοντος βούλημα, καὶ τὸ τῶν πόνων ἔργον· καὶ τοῦτο γὰρ πρὸς τὸ χρήσιμον, καὶ κατὰ τὸ ἀληθὲς, καὶ μετ' ἐπικρύψεως συμφερόντως λέγεται.*

necessities, the existence of evil in the present world was thereby explained, and the necessity of a succession of worlds was established, so far as the moral conditions of those beings change. The most remarkable of their principles which result from these premises, and appear fully unfolded in Origen, are the following:

1. The Godhead can never be idle. Before the present world there was an endless series of worlds, and an infinite succession of them will follow it.[9]

2. All intellectual beings (angels, stars, men, demons) were originally created alike, but they were never without bodies, since incorporeality is a peculiar prerogative of Deity. After a great moral inequality had arisen among them by their difference of conduct, God created the present world, which affords a dwelling-place to all classes in correspondence with their moral condition. The fallen intellectual beings he put into bodies more or less gross, according to the measure of their sinfulness.[10] Still they all retain their moral freedom, so that they may rise again from the degraded circumstances in which they exist. Even the punishments of the condemned are not eternal, but only remedial; the devil himself being capable of amelioration and pardon.[11] When the world shall have answered its purpose, as the abode of fallen spirits, it will then be destroyed by fire; and by this very fire souls will be completely purified from all stains contracted by intimate union with the body [12]

[9] Still earlier Clement in the Hypotyposes *ὕλην ἄχρονον,—ἔτι δὲ μετεμψυχώσεις, καὶ πολλοὺς πρὸ τοῦ Ἀδάμ κόσμους τερατεύεται* (Phot. Cod. 109). Origines de Princ. iii. 5, 3 In like manner Plato and the Stoics.

[10] That Clement also taught this, Strom. iv. p. 640, is asserted by Keil. Opp. vol. ii. p. 652, but denied by Hofstede de Groot Disp. de Clem. Alex. p. 60: Both accordingly interpret the word *μετεμψυχώσεις* in Photius, note 9, differently. On the other hand, Origen advances this doctrine plainly, de Princ. ii. 9, § 6. Cf. Keil. p. 654, ss. A similar doctrine of Basilides, see Neander's Gnost. Systeme, S. 41, 50, ff.

[11] That Clement. Strom. i. p. 367, s., *ὁ δὲ Διάβολος αὐτεξούσιος ὢν, καὶ μετανοῆσαι οἷοις τε ἦν καὶ κλέψαι*, did not hold this point, is proved by Hofstede de Groot, p. 71. On the contrary, Origen de Princip. i. 6. § 2: Hi vero, qui de statu primae beatudinis moti quidem sunt, non tamen irremediabiliter moti, illis, quos supra descripsimus, sanctis beatisque ordinibus dispensandi subjecti sunt ac regendi: quorum adjutorio usi, et institutionibus ac disciplinis salutaribus reformati, redire ac restitui ad statum suae beatitudinis possint.—§ 3: Ex quo, ut opinor, hoc consequentia ipsa videtur ostendere, unamquamque rationabilem naturam posse ab uno in alterum ordinem transeuntem per singulos in omnes, et ab omnibus in singulos pervenire, dum accessus profectuum defectuumve varios pro motibus vel conatibus propriis unusquisque pro liberi arbitrii facultate perpetitur.

[12] Clemens Strom. vii. c. 6, in fine p. 851. (Cf. Hofstede de Groot Disp. de Clem. Alex. p. 108, ss.) Origines in Exod. xv. 5 (Hom. vi. in Exod. ed. de la Rue, t. ii. p. 148): Idcirco igitur qui salvus fit, per ignem salvus fit, ut si quid forte specie plumbi habuerit admixtum,

But as spirits always retain their freedom, they may also sin again, in which case a new world like this will be again necessary.

3. The Alexandrians speak of the Logos,[13] the mediator of all Divine agency, in very exalted, but not always definite expressions. Evidently, however, they place him beneath the supreme God.[14] Their endeavor to remove all ideas unworthy of God

id ignis decoquat, et resolvat, ut efficiantur omnes aurum bonum. Veniendum est ergo omnibus ad ignem, veniendum est ad conflatorium. Sedet enim Dominus, et conflat, et purgat filios Juda (Mal. iii. 3). Sed et illuc cum venitur, si quis multa opera bona, et parum aliquid iniquitatis attulerit, illud parum tanquam plumbum igni resolvitur ac purgatur, et totum remanet aurum purum. Et si quis plus illuc plumbi detulerit, plus exuritur, ut amplius decoquatur ut etsi parum aliquid sit auri, purgatum tamen resideat. Quod si aliquis illuc totus plumbeus venerit, fiet de illo hoc quod scriptum est, demergetur in profundum, tanquam plumbum in aquam validissimam. Homil. xiv. in Lucam (t. iii. p. 948): Ego puto, quod et post resurrectionem ex mortuis indigeamus sacramento eluente nos atque purgante: nemo enim absque sordibus resurgere poterit. C. Celsum, v. p. 240, s. against Celsus, who derided the notion of a conflagration of the world, *οὐ συνιδὼν, ὅτι, ὥσπερ Ἑλλήνων τισὶν ἔδοξε (τάχα παρὰ τοῦ ἀρχαιοτάτου ἔθνους Ἑβραίων λαβοῦσι), τὸ πῦρ καθάρσιον ἐπάγεται τῷ κόσμῳ· εἰκὸς δ' ὅτι καὶ ἑκάστῳ τῶν δεομένων τῆς διὰ τοῦ πυρὸς δίκης ἅμα καὶ ἰατρείας.*

[13] Comp. with reference to Clement of Alexandria Martini's Gesch. d. Dogma v. d. Gottheit Christi, S. 74, ff. Guerike de Schola Alex. P. ii. p. 131, ss. Hofstede de Groot, p. 47, ss. Redepenning's Origines, i. 109, with references to Origen: Martini, S. 151, ff. Guerike, 197, ss. Schleiermacher in his theolog. Zeitschrift, Heft 3, S. 342, ff. Rettberg. doctrina Originis de *λόγῳ* divino, in Illgen's Zeitschr. f. hist. Theolog. iii. 1, 39. Origenes v. Thomasius, S. 129. On both see Baur's Lehre v. d. Dreieinigkeit, i. 186. Meier's Lehre v. Trinität, i. 93.

[14] Clem. Strom. vii. p. 831: *Τελειωτάτη δὴ καὶ ἁγιωτάτη, καὶ κυριωτάτη, καὶ ἡγεμονικωτάτη, καὶ βασιλικωτάτη, καὶ εὐεργετικωτάτη ἡ υἱοῦ φύσις, ἡ τῷ μόνῳ παντοκράτορι προσεχεστάτη.* Paedag. iii. p. 251: *Μεσίτης ὁ λόγος, ὁ κοινὸς ἀμφοῖν, θεοῦ μὲν υἱὸς, σωτὴρ δὲ ἀνθρώπων· καὶ τοῦ μὲν διάκονος, ἡμῶν δὲ παιδαγωγός.* Strom. vii. p. 838: *Τὸ δεύτερον αἴτιον.*—Origines Comm. in Johannem, tom. ii. 2: *Τίθησι* (*Ἰωάννης*) *τὸ ἄρθρον, ὅτε ἡ θεὸς ὀνομασία ἐπὶ τοῦ ἀγεννήτου τάσσεται τῶν ὅλων αἰτίου, σιωπᾷ δὲ αὐτὸ, ὅτε ὁ λόγος θεὸς ὀνομάζεται.—αὐτόθεος* (*ἀληθινὸς θεὸς*) *ὁ θεός ἐστι, διόπερ καὶ ὁ σωτήρ φησιν ἐν τῇ πρὸς τὸν πατέρα εὐχῇ, ἵνα γινώσκωσί σε τὸν μόνον ἀληθινὸν θεόν* (Jo. xvii. 3), *πᾶν δὲ τὸ παρὰ τὸ αὐτόθεος μετοχῇ τῆς ἐκείνου θεότητος θεοποιούμενον, οὐχ ὁ θεὸς ἀλλὰ θεὸς κυριώτερον ἂν λέγοιτο. ᾧ πάντως ὁ πρωτότοκος πάσης κτίσεως ἅτε πρῶτος τῷ πρὸς τὸν θεὸν εἶναι, σπάσας τῆς θεότητος εἰς ἑαυτὸν, ἐστὶ τιμιώτερος τοῖς λοιποῖς παρ' αὐτὸν θεοῖς κ. τ. λ.* (how loose the Alexandrians were in the use of *θεός* may be seen below, note 26), *εἰ πάντα διὰ τοῦ λόγου ἐγένετο, οὐχ ὑπὸ τοῦ λόγου ἐγένετο, ἀλλ' ὑπὸ κρείττονος καὶ μείζονος παρὰ τὸν λόγον.* C. Cels. viii. p. 387: *Ἔστω δὲ, τινὰς—διὰ τὴν προπέτειαν ὑποτίθεσθαι τὸν Σωτῆρα εἶναι τὸν ἐπὶ πᾶσι θεόν· ἀλλ' οὔτιγε ἡμεῖς τοιοῦτον, οἱ πειθόμενοι αὐτῷ λέγοντι, ὁ πατὴρ ὁ πέμψας με, μείζων μου ἐστί* (Jo. xiv. 28). Hence he is called, lib. v. p. 258, *δεύτερος θεός.* Comm. in Joh. tom. xiii. 25: *Τὸν σωτῆρα, καὶ τὸ πνεῦμα τὸ ἅγιον ὑπερεχόμενον τοσοῦτον ἢ καὶ πλέον ἀπὸ τοῦ πατρὸς, ὅσῳ ὑπερέχει αὐτὸς καὶ τὸ ἅγιον πνεῦμα τῶν λοιπῶν.—ὁ υἱὸς οὐ συγκρίνεται κατ' οὐδὲν τῷ πατρί. Εἰκών γάρ ἐστι τῆς ἀγαθότητος αὐτοῦ, καὶ ἀπαύγασμα οὐ τοῦ θεοῦ, ἀλλὰ τῆς δόξης αὐτοῦ, καὶ τοῦ ἀϊδίου φωτὸς αὐτοῦ, καὶ ἀτμὶς οὐ τοῦ πατρὸς, ἀλλὰ τῆς δυνάμεως αὐτοῦ, καὶ ἀπόρροια εἰλικρινὴς τῆς παντοκρατορικῆς δόξης αὐτοῦ, καὶ ἔσοπτρον ἀκηλίδωτον τῆς ἐνεργείας αὐτοῦ, δι' οὗ ἐσόπτρου Παῦλος καὶ Πέτρος, καὶ οἱ παραπλήσιοι αὐτοῖς βλέπουσι τὸν θεὸν, λέγοντος· ὁ ἑωρακὼς ἐμὲ ἑώρακε τὸν πατέρα, τὸν πέμψαντά με.* De Princ. i. 2, 13: *Οὕτω*

from the generation of the Son, was completed by Origen in his assertions that the Logos did not proceed from the essence of the Father,[15] but as a constant ray of the Divine glory[16] was brought forth, *i. e.*, created, or generated[17] by the will of God,[18] and that from eternity.[19] But he taught that

τοίνυν ἡγοῦμαι καὶ ἐπὶ τοῦ σωτῆρος καλῶς ἂν λεχθήσεσθαι, ὅτι εἰκὼν ἀγαθότητος τοῦ θεοῦ ἐστιν, ἀλλ' οὐκ αὐτοαγαθόν· καὶ τάχα καὶ υἱὸς ἀγαθὸς ἀλλ' οὐχ ὡς ἁπλῶς ἀγαθός. καὶ ὥσπερ εἰκών ἐστι τοῦ θεοῦ τοῦ ἀοράτου, καὶ κατὰ τοῦτο θεὸς, ἀλλ' οὐ περὶ οὗ λέγει αὐτὸς ὁ Χριστὸς "ἵνα γινώσκωσί σε τὸν μόνον ἀληθινὸν θεόν." οὕτως εἰκὼν ἀγαθότητος, ἀλλ' οὐχ ὡς ὁ πατὴρ ἀπαραλλάκτως ἀγαθός.

[15] Orig. Comm. in Joh. p. 306: *Ἄλλοι δὲ τό, ἐξῆλθον ἀπὸ τοῦ θεοῦ, διηγήσαντο ἀντὶ τοῦ, γεγέννημαι ἀπὸ τοῦ θεοῦ, οἷς ἀκολουθεῖ ἐκ τῆς οὐσίας φάσκειν τοῦ πατρὸς γεγέννησθαι τὸν υἱὸν, οἱονεὶ μειουμένου, καὶ λείποντος τῇ οὐσίᾳ, ᾗ πρότερον εἶχε.—ἀκολουθεῖ δὲ αὐτοῖς καὶ σῶμα λέγειν τὸν πατέρα καὶ τὸν υἱὸν, καὶ διῃρῆσθαι τὸν πατέρα, ἅπερ ἐστι δόγματα ἀνθρώπων, μηδ' ὄναρ φύσιν ἀόρατον καὶ ἀσώματον πεφαντασμένων, οὖσαν κυρίως οὐσίαν, κ. τ. λ.* De Princ. i. 2, 6, iv. 28. The Logos is indeed *ἀπόῤῥοια τῆς δόξης τοῦ θεοῦ*, but not *ἀπόῤῥοια τοῦ θεοῦ*, Comm. in Joh. tom. xiii. 25, see above, note 14.

[16] Origines in Jerem. Hom. ix. 4: he is *ἀπαύγασμα δόξης. Τὸ ἀπαύγασμα τῆς δόξης οὐχὶ ἅπαξ γεγέννηται καὶ οὐχὶ γεννᾶται· ἀλλὰ ὅσον ἐστὶ τὸ φῶς ποιητικὸν τοῦ ἀπαύγασματος, ἐπὶ τοσοῦτον γεννᾶται τὸ ἀπαύγασμα τῆς δόξης τοῦ θεοῦ.* De Princ. i. 2, 4: Est ita aeterna ac sempiterna generatio, sicut splendor generatur ex luce.

[17] Orig. de Princ. i. 2, 6: Filius utique natus ex patre est, velut quaedam voluntas ejus ex mente procedens. Et ideo ego arbitror, quod sufficere debeat voluntas patris ad subsistendum hoc quod vult pater. Volens enim non alia via utitur, nisi quae consilio, voluntatis profertur. Ita ergo et filii subsistentia generatur ab eo. Idem in Justiani Epist. ad Mennam (Mansi Collect. concill. ix. p. 525): *Οὗτος δὲ ὁ υἱὸς ἐκ θελήματος τοῦ πατρὸς γεννηθείς.*

[18] So already Clement, Redepenning's Origines, i. 109, Origines in Genesin (ap. Eusebius contra Marcellum, i. c. 4, ap. de la Rue ii. p. 1): *Οὐ γὰρ ὁ θεὸς πατὴρ εἶναι ἤρξατο, κωλυόμενος, ὡς οἱ γενόμενοι πατέρες ἄνθρωποι, ὑπὸ τοῦ μὴ δύνασθαί πω πατέρες εἶναι. Εἰ γὰρ ἀεὶ τέλειος ὁ θεὸς, καὶ πάρεστιν αὐτῷ δύναμις τοῦ πατέρα αὐτὸν εἶναι, καὶ καλὸν, αὐτὸν εἶναι πατέρα τοῦ τοιούτου υἱοῦ· τί ἀναβάλλεται, καὶ ἑαυτὸν τοῦ καλοῦ στηρίσκει, καὶ, ὡς ἔστιν εἰπεῖν, ἐξ οὗ δύναται πατὴρ εἶναι υἱοῦ. Τὸ αὐτὸ μέντοιγε καὶ περὶ τοῦ ἁγίου πνεύματος λεκτέον.* But according to Methodius ap. Photium Cod. 235, Origen also asserted on like grounds *συναΐδιον εἶναι τῷ—θεῷ τὸ πᾶν.* Comp. de Princ. i. 2, 2, iv. 28. The fragment of Origen ap. Athanasius de Decretis syn. Nic. c. 27, is very like the last passage: *Ὁμοιότης τυγχάνων τοῦ πατρὸς (ὁ υἱὸς) οὐκ ἔστιν ὅτε οὐκ ἦν. Πότε γὰρ ὁ θεὸς—ἀπαύγασμα οὐκ εἶχε τῆς ἰδίας δόξης, ἵνα τολμήσας τις ἀρχὴν δῷ εἶναι υἱοῦ πρότερον οὐκ ὄντος; κατανοείτω γὰρ ὁ τολμῶν καὶ λέγων "ἦν ποτε ὅτε οὐκ ἦν ὁ υἱός," ὅτι ἐρεῖ καὶ τό· σοφία ποτὲ οὐκ ἦν, καὶ λόγος οὐκ ἦν, καὶ ζωὴ οὐκ ἦν.* Orig. Comm. in Joh. p. 33: *Τό· υἱός μου εἶ σὺ, ἐγὼ σήμερον γεγέννηκά σε, λέγεται πρὸς αὐτὸν ὑπὸ τοῦ θεοῦ ᾧ ἀεί ἐστι τὸ σήμερον.—ὁ συμπαρεκτείνων τῇ ἀγεννήτῳ καὶ ἀϊδίῳ αὐτοῦ ζωῇ—χρόνος ἡμέρα ἐστὶν αὐτῷ σήμερον, ἐν ᾗ γεγέννηται ὁ υἱός.* In Jeremiam Hom. ix. (t. iii. p. 181): *Οὐχὶ ἐγέννησεν ὁ πατὴρ τὸν υἱὸν, καὶ ἀπέλυσεν αὐτὸν ὁ πατὴρ ἀπὸ τῆς γενέσεως αὐτοῦ, ἀλλ' ἀεὶ γεννᾷ αὐτόν.* So, according to Plotinus, the *νοῦς* also has originated eternally from the One, and the expression generation denotes merely *αἰτίαν καὶ τάξιν*, Tennemann's Gesch. d. Philos vi. 89.

[19] Every human term to express this production could not be a fit representative, but only an incomplete symbol. Thus, as far as the Logos was a being like to God, his origination was a *γεννᾷν*, so far as he was produced by the will of God, a *ποιεῖν, κτίζειν.* Respecting Clement, see Photius Cod. 109: *τὸν υἱὸν εἰς κτίσμα κατάγει* (namely, in the Hypotyposes). Even Rufinus de Adulterat. libb. Origenis confesses: Interdum invenimus aliqua in libris ejus (Clementis) capitula, in quibus filium Dei creaturam dicit; although

the Holy Ghost was a creature created by the Son, as all other things.[20]

4. The human body assumed by the Logos was a real body, but could not have been a common one. According to Clement, it was united immediately with the Logos, and therefore, as is required by the Divine *ἀπάθεια* of the latter, without *πάθη*.[21] Origen taught expressly a human soul in the person of Christ, with which the Logos united itself directly.[22] Thus those *πάθη* were

he would fain regard these passages as spurious. Clemens Strom. v. p. 699: Ἡ *σοφία ἡ πρωτόκτιστος τῷ θεῷ*. So also Origines Comm. in Joh. tom. i. 22: *Κτίσας—ἔμψυχον σοφίαν ὁ θεός*. Contra Celsum, v. p. 357, the Son is *πρεσβύτατον πάντων τῶν δημιουργημάτων*. So also Justinian, l. c. accuses Origen of calling the Son *κτίσμα*, de Princip. lib. iv. These expressions were now generally used by others since in Prov. viii. 22: *Κύριος ἔκτισέ με ἀρχὴν ὁδῶν αὐτοῦ* was a cardinal passage relating to the Logos. See Münter's Dogmengesch. i. 445.—The question whether the Son was of the divine essence was capable of receiving a twofold answer from the standing-point of Origen. De Princip. iv. 36, according to the translation of Jerome (Epist. ad Avitum): Intellectualem rationabilemque naturam sentit Deus et unigenitus Filius ejus et Spiritus sanctus; sentiunt angeli et potestates, caeteraeque virtutes; sentit interior homo qui ad imaginem et similitudinem Dei conditus est. Ex quo concluditur, Deum et haec quodammodo unius esse substantiae. Fragm. ex libris in Epist. ad Hebr. in the apology of Pamphilus: Christus—secundum similitudinem ejus vaporis, qui de substantia aliqua corporea procedit, sic etiam ipse ut quidam vapor exoritur de virtute ipsius Dei.—Sic nihilominus et secundum similitudinem corporalis aporrhoeae esse dicitur aporrhoea gloriae Omnipotentis pura quaedam et sincera. Quae utraeque similitudines manifestissime ostendunt, communionem substantiae esse Filio cum Patre. Aporrhoea enim *ὁμοούσιος* videtur, i. e., unius substantiae cum illo corpore, ex quo est vel aporrhoea, vel vapor. Selecta in Psalm 135: Ὁ *σωτὴρ οὐ κατὰ μετουσίαν, ἀλλὰ κατ' οὐσίαν ἐστὶ θεός*. On the other hand de Oratione c. 50: Ἕτερος *κατ' οὐσίαν καὶ ὑποκείμενόν ἐστιν ὁ υἱὸς τοῦ πατρός*. Comp. Comm. in Joh. tom. ii. 18. The Son was of the divine essence, but did not partake of the divine essence of the Father.

[20] Origines in Johann. i. 3. (de la Rue iv. p. 60): *Οἶμαι γὰρ, ὅτι τῷ μὲν φάσκοντι γενητὸν τὸ πνεῦμα τὸ ἅγιον εἶναι, καὶ προϊεμένῳ τό "πάντα δι' αὐτοῦ ἐγένετο," ἀναγκαῖον παραδέξασθαι, ὅτι τὸ ἅγιον πνεῦμα διὰ τοῦ λόγου ἐγένετο, πρεσβυτέρου παρ' αὐτὸ τοῦ λόγου τυγχάνοντος.—Ἡμεῖς τρεῖς ὑποστάσεις πειθόμενοι τυγχάνειν, τὸν πατέρα, καὶ τὸν υἱὸν, καὶ τὸ ἅγιον πνεῦμα, καὶ ἀγέννητον μηδὲν ἕτερον τοῦ πατρὸς εἶναι πιστεύοντες, ὡ. εὐσεβέστερον καὶ ἀληθὲς, προσιέμεθα τό, πάντων διὰ τοῦ λόγου γινομένων, τὸ ἅγιον πνεῦμα πάντων εἶναι τιμιώτερον, καὶ τάξει πάντων* [perhaps *πρῶτον*] *τῶν ὑπὸ τοῦ πατρὸς διὰ Χριστοῦ γεγενημένων. Καὶ τάχα αὕτη ἐστὶν ἡ αἰτία τοῦ μὴ καὶ αὐτὸ υἱὸν χρηματίζειν τοῦ θεοῦ, μόνου τοῦ μονογενοῦς φύσει υἱοῦ ἀρχῆθεν τυγχάνοντος, οὗ χρήζειν ἔοικε τὸ ἅγιον πνεῦμα, διακονοῦντος αὐτοῦ τῇ ὑποστάσει, οὐ μόνον εἰς τὸ εἶναι, ἀλλὰ καὶ σοφὸν εἶναι, καὶ λογικὸν καὶ δίκαιον, κ. τ. λ.* De Princ. i. 3, 5: *Μείζων ἡ δύναμις τοῦ πατρὸς παρὰ τὸν υἱὸν καὶ τὸ πνεῦμα τὸ ἅγιον. πλείων δὲ ἡ τοῦ υἱοῦ παρὰ τὸ πνεῦμα τὸ ἅγιον, καὶ πάλιν διαφέρουσα μᾶλλον τοῦ ἁγίου πνεύματος ἡ δύναμις παρὰ τὰ ἄλλα ἅγια.*

[21] Strom. vi. p. 775: *Ἐπὶ μὲν τοῦ σωτῆρος τὸ σῶμα ἀπαιτεῖν ὡς σῶμα τὰς ἀναγκαίας ὑπηρεσίας εἰς διαμονὴν, γέλως ἂν εἴη. Ἔφαγεν γὰρ οὐ διὰ τὸ σῶμα, δυνάμει συνεχόμενον ἁγίᾳ· ἀλλ' ὡς μὴ τοὺς συνόντας ἄλλως περὶ αὐτοῦ φρονεῖν ὑπεισέλθοι, ὥσπερ ἀμέλει ὕστερον δοκήσει τινες αὐτὸν παφανερῶσθαι ὑπέλαβον· αὐτὸς δὲ ἁπαξαπλῶς ἀπαθὴς ἦν, εἰς ὃν οὐδὲν παρεισδύεται κίνημα παθητικὸν, οὔτε ἡδονὴ, οὔτε λύπη.* Comp. my Comm. qua Clem. Alex. et Origenis doctrinae de corpore Christi exponuntur. Gottingae. 1837. 4.

[22] Origenes de Princip. ii. 6, § 3: Hac ergo substantia animae inter Deum carnemque mediante (non enim possibile erat Dei naturam corpori sine mediatore misceri) nascitur

no stumbling-block to him, since the soul was affected only through them. On the contrary, in his opinion, the body of Christ, as an appropriate instrument of revelation, was so constituted as, according to the degree of their merit, either to conceal the majesty of the Logos from men, or to allow it to shine through with more or less radiance.[23] Clement, as well as Origen, decidedly opposed the docetic views.[24]

5. The Christian sage (ὁ γνωστικός), in the way the Alexandrians represent him as a pattern, is said to be elevated above the simple believer, not merely by higher perception, but also by a higher virtue which is entirely dispassionate.[25] The aim of this virtue is likeness to God,[26] its basis, freedom from all the restraints of sensuality,[27] its character the highest disinterestedness.[28]

Deus homo, illa substantia media existente, cui utique contra naturam non erat corpus assumere.

[23] In Matth. Comment. series, § 100: Venit traditio talis ad nos de Jesu, quoniam non solum duae formae in eo fuerunt, una quidem secundum quam omnes eum videbant, altera autem secundum quam transfiguratus est coram discipulis suis in monte:—sed etiam unicuique apparebat secundum quod fuerat dignus. Et non mihi videtur incredibilis esse traditio haec, sive corporaliter propter ipsum Jesum, ut, alio et alio modo videretur hominibus, sive propter ipsam Verbi naturam, quod non similiter cunctis apparet. Contra Celsum, iv. 16: Εἰσὶ γὰρ διάφοροι οἱονεὶ τοῦ Λόγου μορφαί, καθὼς ἑκάστῳ τῶν εἰς ἐπιστήμην ἀγομένων φαίνεται ὁ Λόγος, ἀνάλογον τῇ ἕξει τοῦ εἰσαγομένου, ἢ ἐπ' ὀλίγον προκόπτοντος, ἢ ἐπὶ πλεῖον, κ. τ. λ. My Comm. p. 15.

[24] Both have often been accused of holding docetic views even in ancient times. Thus according to Photius Cod. 109, Clement in his Hypotyposes is said to have taught directly, μὴ σαρκωθῆναι τὸν λογον, ἀλλὰ δόξαι. Modern writers, too, have discovered doceticism in the words of Clement, Coh. ad Graec. p. 86: Τὸ ἀνθρώπου προσωπεῖον ἀναλαβὼν καὶ σαρκὶ ἀναπλασάμενος τὸ σατήριον δρᾶμα τῆς ἀνθρωπότητος ὑπεκρίνετο. See on the other side my Comm. quoted in note 21.

[25] Clem. Strom. vi. p. 775: Κἂν γὰρ μετὰ λόγου γινόμενα τὰ προειρημένα (τὰ δοκοῦντα ἀγαθὰ τῶν παθητικῶν κινημάτων, οἷον θάρσος, ζῆλον, χαρὰν, ἐπιθυμίαν) ἀγαθά τις ἐκδέχηται, ἀλλ' οὖν γε ἐπὶ τοῦ τελείου οὐ παραδεκτέον. P. 825; Ἡ ἐπίτασις τῆς κατὰ τὸν νόμον δικαιοσύνης τὸν γνωστικὸν δείκνυσιν.—Τὶς—ἐπὶ τὴν ἀκρότητα τῆς πίστεως χωρήσας, τὴν γνῶσιν αὐτὴν—ἀκροτάτης ὁμοίως τεύξεται τῆς κληρονομίας.

[26] Clem. Strom. iv. p. 632: Δυνατὸν, τὸν γνωστικὸν ἤδη γενέσθαι θεόν· Ἐγὼ εἶπα, θεοί ἐστε καὶ υἱοὶ ὑψίστου (Psalm cii. 6). vi. p. 816: Τοὺς ἐπιγνόντας αὐτὸν υἱοὺς ἀναγορεύει καὶ θεούς. Hence he calls the gnostic θεοειδής, θεοείκελος, θεούμενος, θεοποιούμενος, ἐν σακρὶ περιπολῶν θεός (Strom. vii. p. 894), see Potter ad Cohort. ad gentes p. 88, ad Strom. iv. p. 633. Hofstede de Groot de Clem. Alex. p. 78, 86. Redepenning's Origenes, i. 171.

[27] The body is called by Clem. Strom. iv. p. 626, τάφος, vii. p. 854, δεσμὸς σαρκικός, by Origen, according to Methodius ap. Photium Cod. 234, δεσμὸς τῆς ψυχῆς, Orig. de Princ. i. 7, 5, see Hofstede de Groot, p. 59, ss. Clem. Strom. iv. p. 569: Ὁ τοίνυν τοῦ σώματος ἀπὸ τῆς ψυχῆς χωρισμὸς, ὁ παρ' ὅλον τὸν βίον μελετώμενος τῷ φιλοσόφῳ, προθυμίαν κατασκευάζει γνωστικήν. Hence Clement requires of the Gnostic ἐγκρατείαν, i. e., striving after ἀπάθεια, Keilii Opusc. acad. ii. p. 761, ss. Daehne de γνώσει Clementis, p. 105.

[28] Clem. Strom. iv. p. 576: Δεῖν δ' οἶμαι μήτε διὰ φόβον κολάσεως, μήτε διά τινα ἐπαγ

6. The Alexandrians could not but be averse to sensual chiliasm. Clement does not allude to it. Origen, however, expressly opposes the chiliast expectations; and would have all the passages which appear to favor it interpreted allegorically.[29]

7. Since, in the view of the Alexandrians, the body is merely a prison of the true *Me*, they also assumed that souls, at the time of the resurrection, would not resume the gross material body, but one of fine, incorruptible texture.[30]

To establish this system from the Holy Scriptures the Alexandrians availed themselves of the allegorical mode of interpretation which had been in use before. But after the interpretation of Scripture had been thus made a mere arbitrary play of fancy till now, Origen gained for himself the merit of reinstating the grammatical interpretation in its rights, by a more accurate distinction between the *literal*, the *moral*, and the *mystical* (*mystic-anagogic* and *mystic-allegorical*) sense.[31] In his commentaries he has furnished rich contributions toward the grammatical interpretation, by which means he became the chief source for succeeding commentators.

γελίαν δόσεως, δι' αὐτὸ δὲ τὸ ἀγαθὸν, προσεληλυθέναι τῷ σωτηρίῳ λόγῳ. P. 626: Εἴ γ' οὖν τις καθ' ὑπόθεσιν προθείη τῷ γνωστικῷ, πότερον ἑλέσθαι βούλοιτο τὴν γνῶσιν τοῦ θεοῦ, ἢ τὴν σωτηρίαν τὴν αἰώνιον—οὐδὲ καθοτιοῦν διστάσας, ἕλοιτ' ἂν τὴν γνῶσιν τοῦ θεοῦ. De Wette christl. Sittenlehre, Th. 2, Erste Hälfte. S. 221.

29 A spiritualizing of chiliasm in the excerptis ex scriptis Theodoti (Clem. Opp. vol. ii. p. 1004): Οἱ γὰρ ἐξ ἀνθρώπων εἰς ἀγγέλους μεταστάντες χίλια ἔτη μαθητεύονται ὑπὸ τῶν ἀγγέλων, κ. τ. λ. Orig. de Princip. ii. 11, § 6: Puto enim, quod sancti quique discedentes de hac vita permanebunt in loco aliquo in terra posito, quem paradisum dicit scriptura divina velut in quodam eruditionis loco, et, ut ita dixerim, auditorio vel schola animarum, etc. On the other hand, ibid. § 2: Quidam ergo laborem quodammodo intelligentiae recusantes, et superficiem quandam legis literae consectantes, et magis delectationi suae quodammodo ac libidini indulgentes, solius literae discipuli, arbitrantur repromissiones futuras in voluptate et luxuria corporis exspectandas: et propterea praecipue carnes iterum desiderant post resurrectionem tales, quibus manducandi, et bibendi, et omnia quae carnis et sanguinis sunt agendi numquam desit facultas, apostoli Pauli de resurrectione spiritalis corporis sententiam non sequentes. Cf. Prologus in Cant. Cant.

30 Clemens Paedag. ii. p. 230: Αὐτῇ καθαρᾷ τῇ σαρκὶ ἐπενδυσάμενοι τὴν ἀφθαρσίαν. Orig. de Princ. ii. 10, 3 and c. 11 (see note 29). Cf. Guerike, l. c. p. 164, 285.

31 The leading principle of his hermeneutics. Homil. v. in Levit. § 5: Triplicem in scripturis divinis intelligentiae inveniri saepe diximus modum, historicum, moralem, et mysticum. Unde et corpus inesse ei et animam et spiritum intelleximus. (Comp. Valentinus above, § 45.) His hermeneutical principles are laid down most fully in de Princip. lib. iv. Porphyry's judgment on his allegories apud Eusebius H. E. vi. 19, 2. 3, among others: Ἐχρῆτο δὲ καὶ Χαιρήμονος τοῦ Στωϊκοῦ, Κορνούτου τε ταῖς βίβλοις· παρ' ὧν τὸν μεταληπτικὸν τῶν παρ' Ἕλλησι μυστηρίων γνοὺς τρόπον, ταῖς Ἰουδαϊκαῖς προσῆψε γραφαῖς. Cf. Mosheim Comm. de rebus Christ. ante Const. M. p. 629. J. A. Ernesti de Orig. interp. librorum SS. grammaticae auctore (Opusc. philol. et crit. Lugd. Bat. 1764. p. 288, ss.). Redepenning's Origines, i. 290. [Davidson's Hermeneutics, p. 97, ff.]

§ 64.

(CONTINUATION.)—ADHERENTS AND OPPOSERS OF ORIGEN.

Origen's peculiar opinions met, even in his lifetime, with as many opponents as friends,[1] and excited suspicion in many bishops.[2] He and his disciples, however, succeeded in combating and refuting many sensuous views and expectations which were then current among Christians. Thus some overvalued the importance of the body in the personality of man, so much as to suppose that the soul dies, and is again raised along with it.[3] Origen overthrew this error, when it appeared in *Arabia*.[4] To his most distinguished disciple *Dionysius* (president of the catechetical school from 233, from 248 bishop in Alexandria, † 265)[5] belongs the merit of having victoriously continued in the east the opposition to chiliasm begun by his master. An opportunity for this was furnished to him by an Egyptian bishop, *Nepos*, who, in the ἔλεγχος Ἀλληγοριστῶν, insisted particularly on the literal acceptation of the Apocalypse, and the description of the millennium contained in it. Doubtless the Decian persecution, which soon followed, contributed to procure many advocates to a view which furnished so strong motives to Christian steadfastness, especially in the province of *Arsinoe*. But after the persecution, Dionysius succeeded by oral representations and

[1] Origines Hom. xxv. in Lucam: Plerique dum plus nos diligunt quam meremur, haec jactant et loquuntur, sermones nostros doctrinamque laudantes, quae conscientia nostra non recipit. Alii vero tractatus nostros calumniantes, ea sentire nos criminantur, quae numquam sensisse nos novimus. Sed neque hi qui plus diligunt, neque illi qui oderunt, veritatis regulam tenent, et alii per dilectionem, alii per odium mentiuntur.

[2] Euseb. H. E. vi. 36: Γράφει δὲ καὶ Φαβιανῷ τῷ κατὰ Ῥώμην ἐπισκόπῳ, ἑτέροις τε πλείστοις ἄρχουσιν ἐκκλησιῶν περὶ τῆς κατ' αὐτὸν ὀρθοδοξίας. Hieron. Ep. 41, ad Pammach. et Oceanum: Ipse Origenes in epistola, quam scribit ad Fabianum Romanae urbis episcopum, poenitentiam agit cur talia scripserit, et causas temeritatis in Ambrosium refert, quod secreto edita in publicum protulerit.

[3] So also Tatian (Orat. ad Gr. c. 21). Comp. Daniel's Tatianus, p. 226.

[4] Eusebius, vi. 37: Ἔλεγον, τὴν ἀνθρωπείαν ψυχὴν τέως μὲν κατὰ τὸν ἐνεστῶτα καιρὸν ἅμα τῇ τελευτῇ συναποθνήσκειν τοῖς σώμασι καὶ συνδιαφθείρεσθαι· αὖθις δέ ποτε κατὰ τὸν τῆς ἀναστάσεως καιρὸν σὺν αὐτοῖς ἀναβιώσεσθαι. On the origin of this opinion see § 29, note 10. The name Arabici first appears in Augustin. de Haeres. c. 85 θνητοψυχῖται apud Joann. Damasc. Haer. 90.

[5] The fragments of his writings are collected by Gallandius Bibl. PP. t. iii. p. 481, ss. Simon de Magistris. Romae. 1796. fol.

his work *περὶ ἐπαγγελιῶν*, not only in convincing that party of their error, but also in banishing chiliasm entirely among the theologians of the eastern church.[6] Similar opposition he presented to *Sabellius*. It is true, that in trying to develop more precisely the Origenist distinctions as adverse to Sabellius' doctrine of the Trinity, he gave offense by designating the Logos a creature of the Father,[7] and was therefore blamed by *the Romish Dionysius;* but the many-sided views which he had from Origen permitted him to cloak his view of the Logos as a created being without altering it.[8] This convenient pliableness of expression, in which Origen himself had led the way, is also found in other followers. *Theognostus* simply repeats the Origenist doctrine of the Logos in its different forms of presentation.[9] On the other hand, as used by the opponent of Paul of Samosata, *Gregory* (bishop of Neo-caesarea from 244, † about 270), for whom later traditions have procured the surname *Thaumaturgus*,[10] this doctrine of the Logos appears to

[6] Euseb. H. E. vii. 24, 25. Dionysius thought that the Apocalypse was written by a presbyter called John. Mynster Diss. de Dionysii Alex. circa Apoc. Joann. sententia, hujusque vi in seriorum libri aestimationem. Hafn. 1826. Lücke's Einl. in die Offenb. Joh. S. 321, 397.

[7] Omitted by Euseb. vii. 26. On the contrary, Athanasii *περὶ Διονυσίου τοῦ 'Επ. 'Αλ.* liber. In the letter of Dionysius to Ammon bishop of Berenice and to Euphranor, it is said, Athanas. l. c. cap. 4: *Ποίημα καὶ γενητὸν εἶναι τὸν υἱὸν τοῦ θεοῦ· μήτε δε φύσει ἴδιον, ἀλλὰ ξένον κατ' οὐσίαν εἶναι τοῦ πατρός· ὥσπερ ἐστὶν ὁ γεωργὸς πρὸς τὴν ἄμπελον* (cf. Joh. xv. 1), *καὶ ὁ ναυπηγὸς πρὸς τὸ σκάφος· καὶ γὰρ ὡς ποίημα ὤν, οὐκ ἦν πρὶν γενηται.* According to chap. 14, the Arians also attributed to him the following assertions: *Οὐκ ἀεὶ ἦν ὁ θεὸς πατὴρ, οὐκ ἀεὶ ἦν ὁ υἱός·—ἀλλ' ἦν ποτε ὅτε οὐκ ἦν.* Comp. Martini Gesch. d. Dogma v. d. Gottheit Christi, S. 198. Schleiermacher in his Zeitschrift, iii. 402. Baur's Dreieinigkeit, i. 309.

[8] Fragments of his *ἔλεγχος καὶ ἀπολογία*, libb. iv., addressed to the Roman Dionysius, preserved in Athanasius and Basil, are collected by Gallandius, iii. 495, Routh Reliq. Sacr. iii. 194 (in the second fragment of the first book, the variation in the text from Euthym. Zygab. Panoplia apud Gallandius, t. xiv. App. p. 118, is to be compared). Dionysius declares here, lib. i.: *Οὐ γὰρ ἦν ὅτε ὁ θεὸς οὐκ ἦν πατήρ.* Then he asserts it is a fabrication of his opponents that he ever denied, *τὸν Χριστὸν ὁμοούσιον εἶναι τῷ θεῷ· εἰ γὰρ καὶ τὸ ὄνομα τοῦτό φημι μὴ εὑρηκέναι, μηδ' ἀνεγνωκέναι που τῶν ἁγίων γραφῶν, ἄλλα γε τὰ ἐπιχειρήματά μου τὰ ἑξῆς, ἃ σεσιωπήκασι, τῆς διανοίας ταύτης οὐκ ἀπᾴδει.* Comp. § 63, note 19. Martini, S. 203, ff.

[9] Photii Bibl. cod. 106: in his Hypotyposes *υἱὸν δὲ λέγων, κτίσμα αὐτὸν ἀποφαίνει, και τῶν λογικῶν μόνον ἐπιστατεῖν.* Respecting the origin of the Logos a fragment apud Athanasius de Decretis Syn. Nicaenae, c. 25: *Οὐκ ἔξωθέν τίς ἐστιν ἐφευρεθεῖσα ἡ τοῦ υἱοῦ οὐσία, οὐδὲ ἐκ μὴ ὄντων ἐπεισήχθη· ἀλλὰ ἐκ τῆς τοῦ πατρὸς οὐσίας ἔφυ, ὡς τοῦ φωτὸς τὸ ἀπαύγασμα, ὡς ὕδατος ἀτμίς· (οὔτε γὰρ τὸ ἀπαύγασμα, οὔτε ἡ ἀτμὶς αὐτὸ τὸ ὕδωρ ἐστὶν, ἢ αὐτὸς, ὁ ἥλιος οὔτε ἀλλότριον·) ἀλλὰ ἀπόρβοια τῆς τοῦ πατρὸς οὐσίας οὐ μερισμὸν ὑπομεινάσης τῆς τοῦ πατρὸς οὐσίας.*

[10] Writings: *Εἰς 'Ωριγένην προσφωνητικὸς καὶ πανηγυρικὸς λόγος. 'Επιστολὴ κανονική.* Fragments in Ang. Maji Spicilegium Rom. vol. iii. Two confessions of faith

oscillate between entirely opposite modes of description.[14] It is highly probable, also, that *Hierax* of Leontopolis, at the end of this century, was formed in the school of Origen. His allegorical interpretation, his rejection of the resurrection of the body, and of sensual notions of a future life, as also his disapprobation of marriage and the use of flesh and wine, point rather to a maintenance of Origenist principles carried out to extremes, than to a Manichaean origin, which latter Epiphanes has inferred only from a few external points of resemblance.[12] At the end of this period appeared *Methodius*, bishop of *Olympus* (or Patara), afterward of *Tyre* (martyred 311) as a violent opponent of Origen, defending in a work, *περὶ ἀναστάσεως*, the doctrine of the resurrection of the present body, and in another, *περὶ τῶν γενητῶν*, attacking the notion of an endless succession of worlds.[13] But on the other hand, Origen found warm defenders in *Pamphilus* (martyred 309) and *Eusebius Pamphili*, both presbyters in Caesarea.[14] Among the multitude, report had often distorted already the peculiar principles of Origen, and by that means awakened blind hatred against him;[15] but among

have been also attributed to him, although without doubt they are supposititious, a short Symbolum which he is said to have received from the apostle John who appeared to him (Walchii Bibl. symbol. vetus, p. 14. Martini, S. 231), and *ἡ κατὰ μέρος πίστις* (i. e., plenior ac particulatim concepta, which was formerly known only in the Latin translation of Turrianus, and published in Greek by Sirmond in not. ad Facundam, x. 6, and in Maji Scriptt. vett. nova coll. vii. i. 170), whose genuineness Salig de Eutychianismo ante Eutychen, p. 136, sought in vain to defend. See Martini, S. 233. His life by Gregory Nyssene. Opp. omnia una cum vita, ed. G. Vossius. Mogunt. 1604. 4.

11 Basilii M. Epist. 210 (al. 64) § 5: (Sabelliani) *καθήκαν δέ τινα πεῖραν δι' ἐπιστολῆς, καὶ πρὸς τον ὁμόψυχον ἡμῶν Ἄνθιμον τὸν Τυάνων ἐπίσκοπον, ὡς ἄρα Γρηγορίου εἰπόντος ἐν ἐκθέσει πίστεως, πατέρα καὶ υἱὸν ἐπινοίᾳ μὲν εἶναι δύο, ὑποστάσει δὲ ἕν. τοῦτο δὲ, ὅτι οὐ δογματικῶς εἴρηται, ἀλλ' ἀγωνιστικῶς ἐν τῇ προς Αἰλιανὸν διαλέξει, οὐκ ἠδυνήθησαν συνιδεῖν.—διὸ δὴ καὶ πολλὰς ἂν εὕροις ἐκεῖ φωνὰς, τὰς νῦν τοῖς αἱρετικοῖς μεγίστην ἰσχὺν παρεχομένας, ὡς τὸ κτίσμα, καὶ τὸ ποίημα, καὶ εἴ τι τοιοῦτον.* Martini, S. 233, ff.

12 Only authority Epiphan. Haer. 67. Mosheim de Rebus Christ. ante Const. p. 903, ss.

13 Fragments in Epiphan. Haer. 64. Photii Bibl. cod. 234–236, in Maji Scriptt. vett. nova coll. vii. i. 49, 92, 102. Walch's Ketzerhist. vii. 404. In a later dialogue, *Ξένων*, he is said to have changed and become the admirer of Origen (Socrat. H. E. vi. 13). Other works: *περὶ αὐτεξουσίου*. Symp. dec. virg. etc. Opp. ed. Fr. Combefisius. Paris. 1644. fol

14 Pamphilus wrote in captivity. See Apologia pro Origene, in five books, to which Eusebius added a sixth book. Only the first book is extant in Rufinus's Latin translation, and Greek fragments in Photius Cod. 118 (see Origenis Opp. ed de la Rue, t. iv. App. p. 17.). Pamphilus and Eusebius published conjointly the hexaplar Septuagint—Pamphilus's library in Caesarea.

15 Pamphili Apologiae praefatio ad Confessores ad metalla Palaestinae damnatos: Nihil mirum, fratres, videmini mihi esse perpessi, quod ita vos Origenis subterfugit intellectus, ut vos quoque ea aestimetis de illo, quae et alii nonnulli: qui sive per imperitiam sui, qua non valent sensus ejus altitudinem contueri, sive pravitate mentis, qua studium gerunt non

the learned, respect for this great man was pretty general. Particularly in Egypt, he appears to have enjoyed undivided esteem.[16]

§ 65.

OTHER DISTINGUISHED TEACHERS OF THE EASTERN CHURCH.

While at Alexandria Scripture interpretation was made to subserve the purpose of speculation, we find in Syria and the neighboring provinces, favored by the linguistic relations of these lands, the first traces of that more independent historico-grammatical and critical treatment of the Scriptures, by which the east was so much distinguished in the fourth and fifth centuries.[1] Of such writers we are acquainted, though very imperfectly, with *Julius Africanus* in *Nicopolis* (*Emmaus*), probably a presbyter (about 230), a friend of Origen, the first Christian chronographer;[2] and two presbyters of Antioch, *Dorotheus*

solum dicta ejus incusare, verum etiam adversus eos, qui haec legunt, hostiles inimicitias sumere, tam pertinaciter id agentes, ut nulla prorsus venia eos dignos haberi putent, ne ea quidem quam impertire solent, verbi gratia, his qui vel Graecorum saecularium libros, vel nonnunquam etiam haereticorum, percunctandi atque agnoscendi studio decurrunt. Miramur in tantum temeritatis aliquos esse provectos, ut qui se ita humilitate judicat, adstruant, quod ab illis dicta ejus vel libri pro sermonibus apostolicis vel dictis propheticis habeantur, aut quod ille ipse vel Prophetis vel Apostolis ab aliquo comparetur. Multos invenias, quos si interroges, in quibus libris aut in quibus locis dicta sint haec, quae arguunt, confitentur, se quidem nescire ea, de quibus affirmant, nec legisse unquam, audisse autem alios dicentes. The calumnies which Pamphilus refuted are these (cap. 5): Prima, ille est, quod aiunt, eum innatum dicere filium Dei. Secunda, quod dicunt per prolationem, secundum Valentini fabulas, in subsistentiam venisse filium Dei dicere. Tertia, quae his omnibus valde contraria est, quod dicunt eum, secundum Arteman vel Paulum Samosatenum, purum hominem, id est, non etiam Deum dicere Christum filium Dei. Post (iv.), ista est, quae istis omnibus adversatur (caeca enim est malitia), quod dicunt eum dicere, δοκήσει, i. e., putative tantum et per allegoriam, non etiam secundum ea, quae per historiam referuntur, gesta esse omnia, quae a Salvatore gesta sunt. Alia (v.), quoque criminatio est, qua asserunt, eum duos Christos praedicare. Addunt (vi.), illud quoque, quod historias corporales, quae per omnem S. Scripturam referuntur de gestis Sanctorum, penitus deneget. Sed et (vii.), de resurrectione mortuorum, et de impiorum poenis non levi impugnant eum calumnia, velut negantem peccatoribus inferenda esse supplicia. Quidam vero (viii.), disputatione ejus vel opiniones, quas de animae statu vel dispensatione disseruit, culpant. Ultima vero, omnium (ix.), est criminatio illa, quae cum omni infamatione dispergitur, μετενσωματώσεως, i. e., quod humanas animas in muta animalia, vel serpentes vel pecudes asserat transmutari post mortem, et quod etiam ipsae mutorum animalium animae rationabiles sint.

16 In Justiniani Epist. ad Mennam (apud Mansi, ix. p. 504) very unfavorable statements are made respecting Origen by Bishop Peter of Alexandria (martyred 311); but they have been borrowed from the uncertain Actis Petri Alex. See Tillemont Mémoires, t. iii. p. 589.

1 Münter on the Antiochenian school in Stäudlin's and Tzschirner's Archiv. f. Kirchengesch. Bd. 1. St. 1. S. 1, ff.

2 Χρονογραφιῶν πέντε σπουδάσματα—Ἐπιστολὴ περὶ τῆς κατὰ Σωσάνναν ἱστορίας

(about 290),[3] and *Lucian*, who suffered martyrdom in Nicomedia, A.D. 311.[4] Because *Arius* and his most distinguished friends[5] proceeded from the school founded by Lucian at Antioch, the latter has often in later times been considered the father of Arianism.[6] Of the critical merits which belonged to him and his cotemporary *Hesychius*,[7] in settling the text of the Holy Scriptures, after the example of Origen, it is to be regretted that very imperfect accounts have been preserved.[8]

To this oriental literature appears also to belong most nearly the literary labors of *Hippolytus* (about 240).[9]

(together with the reply of Origen appended to the Dial. c. Marcionitas, ed. Wetstein)—'Επιστολὴ πρὸς 'Αριστείδην (on the genealogies of Christ in Matthew and Luke partly preserved in Euseb. H. E. i. c. 7; another fragment, ex. Mss. Vindob. et Coisl., first printed in Routh Reliqu. Sacr. ii. p. 114). All these remains in Routh, l. c. p. 105, ss. Later oriental writers also attribute to him a Comm. in Evang. Assemani Bibl. Orient. p. 129, 158.

3 Euseb. vii. 32, 1: *Λόγιος ἀνήρ.—φιλόκαλος δ' οὗτος περὶ τὰ θεῖα γεγονὼς, καὶ τῆς 'Εβραίων ἐπεμελήθη γλώττης· ὡς καὶ αὐταῖς ταῖς 'Εβραϊκαῖς γραφαῖς ἐπιστημόνως ἐντυγχάνειν. ἦν δ' οὗτος τῶν μάλιστα ἐλευθερίων [παιδειῶν] προπαιδείας τε τῆς καθ' Ἕλληνας οὐκ ἄμοιρος.* § 2: *Τούτου [μὴ] μετρίως τὰς γραφὰς ἐπὶ τῆς ἐκκλησίας διηγουμένου κατηκούσαμεν.*

4 Euseb. viii. 13, ix. 6. *'Ανὴρ τὰ πάντα ἄριστος βίῳ τε ἐγκρατὴς καὶ τοῖς ἱεροῖς μαθήμασι συγκεκροτημένος.* Hieronymus Catal. c. 77: Lucianus, vir disertissimus, Antiochenae Ecclesiae presbyter, tantum in Scripturarum studio laboravit, ut usque nunc quaedam exemplaria Scripturarum Lucianea nuncupentur. Feruntur ejus de fide libelli, et breves ad nonnullos epistolae.

5 The bishops Eusebius of Nicomedia, Maris of Chalcedon, Theognis of Nicaea, Leontius of Antioch, Antonius of Tarsus, &c. See Philostorgius, ii. 14.

6 Alexander bishop of Alexandria, writes of him (about 320, in Theodoreti Hist. eccl. i. 3): *"Ον (Παῦλον τὸν Σαμοσατέα) διαδεξάμενος Λουκιανὸς, ἀποσυνάγωγος ἔμεινε τριῶν ἐπισκόπων πολυετεῖς χρόνους. ὧν τῆς ἀσεβείας τὴν τρύγα ἐῤῥοφηκότες—"Αρειός τε καὶ 'Αχιλλᾶς, κ. τ. λ.* The Eusebians appealed to a confession of faith by Lucian, Sozomen, iii. 5. Still he is considered by Eusebius, Athanasius, Jerome, Chrysostom (comp. his panegyric on him, tom. i. Hom. 46), etc., as a holy martyr, and is so regarded by the Romish church at this day.

7 Probably the Egyptian Bishop Hesychius, who, according to Eusebius, H. E. viii. 13, 4, suffered martyrdom in the year 311.

8 Hieron. adv. Rufin. lib. ii. (ed. Martian. t. iv. p. ii. p. 425): Alexandria et Aegyptus in Septuaginta suis Hesychium laudat auctorem Constantinopolis usque ad Antiochiam Luciani Martyris exemplaria probat. Mediae inter has provinciae Palaestinos codices legunt quos ab Origene elaboratos Eusebius et Pamphilus vulgaverunt; totusque orbis haec inter se trifaria varietate compugnat. Comp. Eichhorn's Einleit. in das A. T. (4te Aufl. 1823) Bd. 1. S. 506, ff. Hieron. praef. in iv. Evang. ad Damasum: De novo nunc loquor Testamento. Praetermitto eos codices, quos a Luciano et Hesychio nuncupatos, paucorum, hominum asserit perversa contentio: quibus utique nec in toto veteri Instrumento post lxx. interpretes emendare quid licuit: nec in Nova profuit emendasse, cum multarum gentium linguis Scriptura ante translata doceat, falsa esse, quae addita sunt. Comp. Hug's Einl. in d. N. T. (3te Aufl. 1826) Th. 1. S. 196, ff. 231, ff.

9 Concerning him and his numerous writings, among which the treatise *περὶ τοῦ Πάσχα*, which set forth the first Canon paschalis (see on it Ideler's Chronologie, ii. 213), was the most important, see Eusebius, vi. 20, 22. Hieronymus in Catal. c. 61. Both call him bishop, but do not know in what place. Jerome also designates him as a martyr, Comm.

II. THEOLOGY IN THE WEST.

§ 66.

The Latin church, which had been hitherto little more than an appendage to the Greek, now attained to more independence and individuality, after it had materially enlarged itself, and since the Latin language had been more adapted, particularly

ad Matth. praef., and so also later writers call him Episcopum et Martyrem. Prudentius περὶ στεφάνων hymn. xi. relates the martydom of one Hippolytus. The same person was a presbyter among the Novatians, stood in high repute with his own party (the heathen called out, v. 80: Ipsum Christicolis esse caput populi, but in view of death he repented of his taking part in the schism, and exhorted his own disciples, who accompanied him in great numbers, to return to the catholic communion (v. 27, ss.). Thus he became a Catholic martyr at Portus Romanus (probably under Valerian, 258), and his bones were dug up in the vicinity of Rome (v. 151). At the time of Prudentius a splendid martyrium was here dedicated to him (v. 183), and his memory was celebrated on the ides of August (v. 232). In the eighth century Hadrian I. restored this Coemeterium b. Hippolyti Martyris (Liber pontificalis in vita Hadr. I.) At the same place the statue of Hippolytus was found, 1551, on whose cathedra the Canon Paschalis and a catalogue of his writings are inscribed. It belongs probably to the sixth century (Beschreibung der Stadt Rom von Platner, Bunsen Gerhard, u. Röstell, ii. ii. 329), and proves that at that time the ancient writer and the martyr were looked upon as the same person. In the later martyrologies a fragment of genuine tradition may be preserved concerning him. Usuardus, Ado, Notker, and others, have the following on the 30th January:—Apud Antiochiam passio b. Hippolyti Martyris, qui Novati schismate aliquantulum deceptus, operante gratia Christi correctus, ad caritatem ecclesiae rediit, pro qua et in qua illustre martyrium consummavit. Petrus Damianus lib. i. Epist. 9, ad Nicolaum ii. says: Beatus quoque Nonus Martyr, qui et Hippolytus—postquam denique nonnullos sanctarum expositionum libros luculenter explicuit, tandem Episcopatum deseruit, de Antiochenis partibus, unde erat oriundus, abscessit, Romanos fines appetiit; and then relates his death and burial in Portus Romanus. The result of our inquiry into the history of Hippolytus may be stated: Novatian found great favor particularly in Antioch. The bishop Fabius, and many others were friendly to him (Euseb. vi. 44, 46, see below, § 72, note 8). One of them, the presbyter Hippolytus, determined to travel in person to Rome. Probably, since he traveled through Alexandria, he is the same Hippolytus who took with him to Rome the ἐπιστολὴ διακονικὴ of Dionysius of Alexandria (Euseb. vi. 46. Eusebius here names him without any other specifying circumstance, after having spoken before of only one Hippolytus). In Rome he attached himself to the Novatians, and attained to great repute. The separation from the church, however, made him suspicious, until the prospect of immediate death decided him to return to the catholic church. His memory was celebrated at Antioch, his native city, on the 30th January; at Rome on the 13th August. The later martyrologies have adopted both days, and so made two Hippolytuses out of one. The great reputation which Hippolytus enjoyed as an ecclesiastical writer misled Eusebius, when he represents him to have been a bishop. Jerome followed him in this particular. The clerk who was martyred at Portus Romanus may have been previously a bishop somewhere in the East. Although, however, Prudentius correctly designates Hippolytus a presbyter, yet all later writers call him bishop, and conjecture different places where he was such. The Greeks naturally looked for this place in the part where he had suffered, and regarded him sometimes as a bishop of Rome,

by *Tertullian*,[1] to the expression of Christian ideas, and had become the usual written language of the western Christians. As the speculative tendency of the Greeks prevailed in the Greek church, so the practical character of the Romans gave expression. to itself in the Latin church, in the inclination to cultivate chiefly ecclesiastical government and law. While the Greek language now disappeared from the western church, the lively interest of the latter in the new developments of the theology of the east also ceased. As the Greek theology of the second century had been understood and represented with material grossness in the writings of Tertullian, so was it held fast in the western church, in the third century. Phi-

after the example of Leontius; sometimes as a bishop of Portus Romanus, according to the Paschal Chronicle, Georgius Syncellus, Zonaras, and Nicephorus Callistus. The Romish bishop Gelasius, misled by Rufinus's translation of Euseb. vi. 20 (Beryllus—episcopus fuit apud Bostram, Arabiae urbem maximam. Erat et nihilominus Hippolytus, qui et ipse aliquanta scripta dereliquit, Episcopus), thought that he was a metropolitan of Arabia, but maintained at the same time as an indubitable fact that he had come to Rome, and suffered martyrdom there. (The later legend dressed out this with other additions: Petrus Dam. l. c.: Qui, postquam triginta millia Saracenorum ad Christi fidem efficacissima praedicatione convertit, etc.) In order to find a middle way between these different accounts Steph. le Moyne conjectured that he was bishop of Portus Romanus (Aden, in Arabia Felix, and in this several have followed him; but this attempt to reconcile errors could only be a new error itself, since Christianity came for the first time into Arabia Felix in the fourth century. With the results already given, agrees very well what may be gathered from the writings of Hippolytus. 1. Novatianism is as little found in them as in the works of Novatian himself. They were probably composed earlier. 2. According to Phot. Cod. 121, Hippolytus's *σύνταγμα κατὰ αἱρέσεων* was an extract from the work of Irenaeus. But Photius infers too much from a passage of that writing, when he makes him a disciple of Irenaeus. 3. Jerome, Cat. c. 61, enumerates among the works of Hippolytus *προσομιλίαν* de laude Domini Salvatoris, in qua praesente Origene se loqui in Ecclesia significat. (What follows: In hujus aemulationem Ambrosius—cohortatus est Origenem, in scripturas Commentarios scribere, is founded merely on a misunderstanding of the expression *ἐξ ἐκείνου* scil. *χρόνου*, which forms a transition in Euseb. vi. c. 22 to chapter 23.) 4. The numerous exegetical writings (see apud Jerome) point to the east. 5. The *'Απολογία ὑπὲρ τοῦ κατὰ 'Ιωάννην εὐαγγελίου καὶ ἀποκαλύψεως* and *περὶ χαρισμάτων*, marked upon the cathedra, are either directed against the Alogi in Asia Minor (§ 48, note 15), or against the opponents of the Montanists in Rome (§ 59, note 9). For this last supposition appears to speak the notice of Ebedjesu († 1318, in Assemani Bibl. orient. t. iii. p. i., that among the Chaldeans Hippolyti capita adv. Caium were in existence. (Comp. Lücke's Einl. in d. Offenb. Joh. S. 316.) C. Gu. Haenell de Hippolyto comm. Gottingae 1838. 4 (looks upon him has a bishop of Bostra). E. J. Kimmel de Hippolyti vita et scriptis, p. i. Jenae. 1839. 8 (according to him, Hippolytus was an oriental, educated in Alexandrian learning (?), and bishop of Portus Romanus at Rome). L. F. W. Seinecke über d. Leben u. die Schriften des Bisch. Hippolytus, in Illgen's Zeitschr. f. d. hist. Theol. 1842, iii. 48 (he also supposes him bishop of Portus Romanus). Hipp. Op. ed. J. A. Fabricius. Hamb. 1716, 18. 2 voll. fol.

[1] Respecting him see above, § 59. He wrote in Greek, de baptismo (Tert. de Bapt. c. 15), de spectaculis (de Cor. mil. c. 6), and de virginibus velandis (de Virg. vel. c. 1). None of these works are now extant. M. E. F. Leopold über die Ursachen der verdorbenen Latinität der Kirchenväter, bes. des Tertullians, in Illgen's Zeitschr. f. hist. Theol. viii. ii. 12.

losophy was too much hated by the *westerns*,[2] and their interpretation of Scripture, from ignorance of the original languages, was too imperfect to enable them to develop the Grecian theology intelligently. Hence there arose in the occidental church an aversion to all theological speculation,[3] and such *a doctrinal stability* that the influence of the Greek church could produce only negative and unconscious advances. It is true that Montanism, having continued for a long time unmolested in the west, had been condemned, as far as its peculiar doctrines were concerned, in the beginning of this period; but its spirit had found so firm a sympathy in the disposition of the westerns to cultivate external ecclesiastical ordinances, that its continuance may be still recognized in a sensuous acceptation of Christianity, and the high value set upon external discipline. *Thascius Caecilius Cyprianus*, at first a rhetorician in Carthage (converted to Christianity from 245, bishop at Carthage 248, suffered martyrdom 258), left behind several small works, apologetic and admonitory, and many

[2] Although they had unconsciously received many Platonic ideas in the Greek theology of the second century. Tertullianus de Praescr. haeret. c. 7: Quid ergo Athenis et Hierosolymis? quid Academiae et Ecclesiae? quid haereticis et Christianis? Nostra institutio de porticu Salomonis est: qui et ipse tradiderat, dominum in simplicitate cordis esse quaerendum. Viderint, qui stoicum, et platonicum, et dialecticum Christianismum protulerunt. Nobis curiositate opus non est post Christum Jesum, nec inquisitione post Evangelium. Cum credimus, nihil desideramus ultra credere. Hoc enim prius credimus, non esse, quod ultra credere debemus. De anima c. 3: Philosophis—patriarchis, ut ita dixerim, haereticorum. De carne Christi c. 5: Natus est dei filius: non pudet, quia pudendum est. Et mortuus est dei filius: prorsus credibile est, quia ineptum est. Et sepultas, resurrexit: certum est, quia impossibile. Cf. de anima lib., Apologet. c. 46, adv. Marcion. v. c. 19, de testimonio animae, c. 1. Ritter's Gesch. d. christl. Philos. i. 362.

[3] Tertull. de Praescript. c. 7 (see note 2). Cap. 9: Unius porro et certi instituti infinita inquisitio non potest esse: quaerendum est, donec invenias: et credendum, ubi inveneris: et nihil amplius nisi custodiendum, quod credidisti: dum insuper credis, aliud non esse credendum. Cap. 14: Caeterum manente forma ejus (regulae fidei) in suo ordine, quantum libet quaeras et tractes, et omnem libidinem curiositatis effundas, si quid tibi videtur vel ambiguitate pendere, vel obscuritate obumbrari. Est utique frater aliquis doctor, gratia scientiae donatus: est aliquis inter exercitatos conversatus aliquid tecum, curiosius tamen, quaerens: novissime ignorare melius est, ne quod non debeas noris. Fides, inquit, tua te salvum fecit (Luc. xviii. 42): non exercitatio scripturarum. Fides in regula posita est, habens legem et salutem de observatione legis: exercitatio autem in curiositate consistit, habens gloriam solam de peritiae studio. Cedat curiositas fidei, cedat gloria saluti. Certe aut non obstrepant, aut quiescant. Adversus regulam nihil scire omnia scire est. A decided rejection of all secret tradition, ibid. c. 22: Solent dicere (haeretici), non omnia Apostolos scisse: eadam agitati dimentia, qua rursus convertunt, omnia quidem Apostolos scisse, sed non omnia omnibus tradidisse. In utroque Christum reprehensioni injicientes, qui aut minus instructos, aut parum simplices Apostolos miserit. Cf. cap. 25 and 26.

letters which refer for the most part to matters of church government and discipline.[4] There is still preserved a perfectly orthodox work *de Trinitate*,[5] by his cotemporary *Novatian*, a Roman presbyter and founder of a sect. Eighty moral precepts in verse by the African *Commodianus* (about 270) are not unimportant in the history of morals.[6] *Arnobius*, a rhetorician in *Sicca*, formerly an enemy to Christianity, wrote (about 303) his Disputationes adv. Gentes libb. vii.[7] His pupil in rhetoric, *L. Caelius Lactantius Firmianus* (Cicero Christianus) an Italian by birth, wrote in Nicomedia, during the Diocletian persecution, his Institutionum Divinarum libb. vii.[8] He was afterward preceptor of Crispus, eldest son of Constantine the Great († about 330).

The tendency of the western church to a stable unity could effect so little in the province of dogmatic theology, that even gnostic doctrines were still in many instances tolerated as

[4] Vita et passio Cypriani per Pontium ejus diaconum scripta, in Ruinart, and prefixed to the editions of Cyprian. Jo. Pearsonii Annales Cyprianici, prefixed to Fell's edition. Prudentii Marani vita S. Cypr. prefixed to Baluzius's edition. La vie de St. Cyprien (par Jacq. Gervaise). Paris. 1717. 4. Th. C. Cyprianus, dargestellt von D. F. W. Rettberg. Göttingen. 1831. 8. Bähr's christl. römische Theologie, S. 50. Möhler's Patrologie, i. 809.—His works: In the year 246: Lib. ad Donatum.—247: de Idolorum vanitate.—248: Testimoniorum ad Quirinum adv. Judaeos, libb. 3; de Habitu virginum.—251: de Unitate ecclesiae; de Lapsis.—252: de Oratione dominica; de Mortalitate; Exhort. ad Martyrium.—253: Lib. ad Demetrianum.—254: de Opere et Eleemosynis.—255: de Bono Patientiae.—256: de Zelo et Livore. Besides these 83 letters, Opp. ed. Nic. Rigaltius. Paris. 1648. fol. Joannes Fell. Oxon. 1682. (Bremae. 1690. Amstel. 1700.) fol. Steph. Baluzius. Paris. 1726. (Venet. 1728.) fol. Opp. genuina cur. D. J. H. Goldhorn. P. ii. Lips. 1838. 39, 8.

[5] Ed. Ed. Welchmann. Oxon. 1724. (iter. 1728.) 8. Also appended to Rigalt's edition of Tertullian. Bähr, S. 47.

[6] Instructiones, ed. Nic. Rigaltius. Tulli Leuc. 1650. 4. Bibl. PP. Lugd. t. xxvii. p. 12, C. S. Schurzfleisch. Viteberg. 1705.

[7] Hieron. Cat. 79, in Chronico ad ann. xx. imperii Constantini. His work ed. cum recensione viri celeberrimi (Cl. Salmasii) et integris omnium commentariis. Lugd. Bat. 1651. 4—recogn. Jo. Conr. Orellius, P. ii. Lips. 1816. Additamentum. Lips. 1817. 8. Des Africaners Arnob. 7 Bücher wider die Heiden, übers u. erläutert v. E. A. v. Besnard. Landshut. 1842. 8. P. K. Meyer de ratione et argumento apologetici Arnobiani. Havniae. 1815. 8. Bähr, S. 66.

[8] Besides this: Epitome div. institt., de opificio Dei, de ira Dei. In a MS. Colbert. Baluzius found Lucii Cecilii liber de Mortibus persecutorum, and first published it in Miscellan. tom. ii. p. 1 (1679). He correctly pronounced it the book of Lactantius, which Jerome mentions, Cat. c. 80, as de Persecutione lib., and therefore it has been taken into all the later editions of Lactantius. Against le Nourry (Lucii Cecilii lib. de Mortibus persec. ad MS. denuo emendatus, acc. dissert. de libri auctore. Paris. 1710. 8), who wishes to distinguish this Lucius Cecilius from Lactantius, see particularly N. de Lestocq disquis. in the edition of le Brun prefixed to tom. ii. p. 48, ss. Opp. ed. J. L. Bünemann. Lips. 1739. 8. Jo. Bapt. le Brun et Nic. Lenglet Dufresnoy. Paris. 1748. Tom. ii. 4. O. F. Fritzsche. P. ii. Lips. 1842, 44. 8. Bähr, S. 72.

harmless. It is true that *Hermogenes*, when he asserted the eternity of matter too strenuously, found an opponent in Tertullian;[9] but *Arnobius* gave utterance to Platonic and gnostic opinions respecting the soul and evil, without being molested;[10] and his disciple *Lactantius* taught a suspicious dualism,[11] without being attacked on account of it. As this indicates a certain theological rudeness in the western theology, so is the same peculiarity also exhibited in the sensuous mode of treating the traditional doctrines. Even in definitions of the essence of God, the western writers of this period are not able to disentangle themselves from the forms of a sensuous conception. They thought of the Deity himself as corporeal, and of the soul as literally his breath.[12] They also firmly maintained

[9] Tertullianus adv. Hermogenem. Ritter's Gesch. d. christl. Philos. i. 178.

[10] For example, Arnobius, ii. c. 15: Nihil est, quod nos fallat,—quod a novis quibusdam dicitur viris,—animas immortales esse, Deo rerum ac principi gradu proximas dignitatis genitore illo ac patre prolatas, etc. Cap. 62: Servare animas alius nisi Deus omnipotens non potest: nec praeterea quisquam est, qui longaevas facere, perpetuitatis possit et spiritum subrogare. (Comp. Platonis Timaeus, ed. Bip. p. 325. Justinus, Tatianus, Theophilus, see Münscher's Dogmengesch. Bd. 2, S. 101, ff.)—Cap. 46, it is called immanis et scelerata persuasio, ut—Deus—aliquid fecerit claudum: and hence it is inferred, ut in sacrilegae crimen impietatis incurrat, quisquis ab eo conceperet hominem esse prognatum. Cap. 36: Discite ab eo, qui novit et protulit in medium, Christo, non esse animas regis maximi filias, nec ab eo, quemadmodum dicitur, generatas coepisse se nosse;—sed alterum quempiam genitorum his esse, dignitatis et potentiae gradibus satis plurimis ab Imperatore disjunctum, ejus tamen ex aula et eminentium nobilem sublimitate natalium (doubtless the Logos). Cap. 47: Non enim, si negemus, muscas, scarabeos, et cimices, nitedulas, curculiones, et tineas omnipotentis esse opus regis, sequaciter postulandum a nobis est, ut quis ea fecerit, institueritque dicamus. Possimus enim nulla cum reprehensione nescire, quis et illis originem dederit, et obtinere, non esse Deo a superiore prolata tam supervacua, tam vana, tam ad nullas pertinentia rationes, quinimo aliquando et noxia, et necessarias importantia laesiones. Cf. cap. 48, 58, 61, 62. Comp. above, § 44, notes 4, 5. On the theology of Arnobius see Meyer de ratione Apol. Arnob. p. 278.

[11] Lactant. Institutt. div. ii. 8: Deus—antequam ordiretur hoc opus mundi, produxit similem sui spiritum, qui esse virtutibus Dei Patris praeditus. Deinde fecit alterum, in quo indoles divinae stirpis non permansit. Itaque suapte invidia tanquam veneno infectus est, et ex bono ad malum transcendit, suoque arbitrio, quod illi a Deo liberam datum fuerat, contrarium sibi nomen ascivit. Unde apparet, cunctorum malorum fontem esse livorem. Invidit enim illi antecessori suo, qui Deo Patri perseverando cum probatus, tum etiam carus est. Hunc ergo ex bono per se malum effectum Graeci διάβολον appellant, nos criminatorem vocamus, quod crimina, in quae ipse illicit, ad Deum deferat. God divided the dominion of the world with him, so that there fell to his share occidens, septentrio, tenebrae, frigus, etc., c. 9. H. J. Alt de Dualismo Lactantiano diss. Vratislav. 1839. 8.

[12] Tertull. adv. Prax. 7: Quis enim negavit, deum corpus esse, etsi deus spiritus est? Spiritus enim corpus sui generis in sua effigie. Sed et si invisibilia illa, quaecunque sunt, habent apud deum et suum corpus et suam formam, per quae soli deo visibilia sunt: quanto magis quod ex ipsius substantia missum est (namely the λόγος), sine substantia non erit? C. 5: Es animal rationale, a rationali scilicet artifice non tantum factus, sed etiam ex substantia ipsius animatus. Lactant. de ira Dei, c. 2: Aliter de unica illa

the resurrection of the same body, the millennium, which appears here almost in its most sensual form,[13] the condemnation of all who are not Christians, and the eternity of hell punishments. With regard to the Logos, they retained the old emanistic notions, both as to its origin, which was conceived for the most part in a very coarse form,[14] and also as to its relation to the Father.[15]

majestate sentiunt, quam veritas habet, qui aut figuram negant habere ullam Deum, aut nullo affectu commoveri putant (he holds the doctrine of God's wrath to be a fundamental truth of religion). In this the Stoics had set the example, who regarded every thing which had efficiency as body. Comp. Tennemann's Gesch. d. Philol. iv. 39, 283. Seneca Epist. 106, 117, quod facit, corpus est. The soul was universally looked upon as corporeal, with the exception of Origen.

[13] Commodiani Instruct. 43, 44, 80, ex. gr. Instr. 44:—

De coelo descendet civitas in anastasi prima,—
Venturi sunt illi quoque sub Antichristo qui vincunt
Robusta martyria, et ipsi toto tempore vivunt,—
Et generant ipsi per annos mille nubentes.

Instr. 80:—

Digniores, stemmate et generati praeclaro,
Nobilesque viri sub Antichristo devicto,
Ex praecepto Dei rursum viventes in aevo
Mille quidem annis ut serviant sanctis et Alto,
Sub jugo servili, ut portent victualia collo,
Ut iterum autem judicentur regno finito.

Comp. Lactant. Institutt. div. vii. c. 14–25. Among other things he says, c. 14: Tum qui erunt in corporibus vivi, non morientur, sed per eosdem mille annos infinitam multitudinem generabunt, et erit soboles eorum sancta et Deo cara. Qui autem ab inferis suscitabuntur, ii praeerunt viventibus velut judices. Gentes vero non extinguentur omnino: sed quaedam relinquentur in victoriam Dei, ut triumphentur a justis, ac subjugentur perpetuae servituti.

[14] Cf. Lactant. Instit. divin. iv. 8: Quomodo igitur procreavit? Primum nec sciri a quoquam possunt, nec narrari opera divina, sed tamen sanctae literae docent, in quibus cautum est, illum Dei filium esse Dei sermonem, itemque ceteros angelos Dei spiritus esse. Nam sermo est spiritus cum voce aliquid significante prolatus. Sed tamen quoniam spiritus et sermo diversis partibus proferuntur, siquidem spiritus naribus, ore sermo procedit; magna inter hunc Dei filium ceterosque angelos differentia est. Illi enim ex Deo taciti spiritus exierunt, qui non ad doctrinam Dei tradendam, sed ad ministerium creabantur. Ille vero quum sit et ipse spiritus, tamen cum voce ac sono ex Dei ore processit. sicut verbum, &c.—Merito igitur sermo et verbum Dei dicitur, quia Deus procedentem de ore suo vocalem spiritum, quem non utero sed mente conceperat, inexcogitabili quadam majestatis sua virtute ac potentia, in effigiem, quae proprio sensu ac sapientia vigeat, comprehendit, et alios item spiritus suos in angelos figuravit.

[15] Tertull. adv. Hermogenem, c. 3: Et pater deus est, et judex deus est: non tamen ideo pater et judex semper, quia deus semper. Nam nec pater potuit esse ante filium, nec judex ante delictum. Fuit autem tempus, cum ei delictum et filius non fuit, quod judicem et qui patrem dominum faceret. Cap. 18: Ut (Deus sophiam) necessariam sensit ad opera mundi, statim eam condit et generat in semetipso. Adv. Praxean, c. 26: Nulla res alicujus ipsa est, cujus est.—Et ideo spiritus Deus, et sermo Deus, quia ex Deo, non tamen ipse ex quo est. Quodsi deus, Dei tanquam substantiva res, non erit ipse Deus (αὐτόθεος): sed hactenus deus, quia ex ipsius Dei substantia, qua et substantiva res est, et ut portio aliqua totius.—Patrem et ipse adorat—ignorans et ipse diem et horam ultimam, soli patri notam: disponens regnum discipulis, quo modo et sibi dispositum dicit a patre, etc. Adv. Marcionem, ii. c. 27: Quaecunque exigitis Deo digna, habebuntur in patre invisibili, incongressibili, et placido, et, ut ita dixerim, philosophorum Deo. Quaecunque

A remarkable stage of development as concerns this dogma, is exhibited by *Dionysius*, bishop of Rome (259–270) whose education was Grecian, and who unites the Origenist idea of an eternal generation of the Logos with those emanistic notions.[16]

FOURTH CHAPTER.

ECCLESIASTICAL LIFE.

§ 67.

The changes in ecclesiastical life originated especially from certain ideas, the germs of which appeared in the second century, though not completely developed till the third. The idea of one catholic church out of which there is no salvation, received its full development from *Cyprian*,[1] and strove to give

autem ut indigna reprehenditis, deputabuntur in filio, et viso, et audito, et congresso, arbitro patris et ministro, etc. Comp. Martini Gesch. d. Dogma v. d. Gottheit Christi in d. vier ersten Jahr. S. 100, ff. With Tertullian agree Cyprian (see Martini, S. 248, ff.), Novatian (l. c. S. 257, ff.), Lactantius (l. c. S. 268, ff.).

16 Dionysii Rom. Adv. Sabellianos fragmentum (apud Athanasius de Decretis Nicaen. syn. c. 26: also in Constant. Epist. Rom. Pont. ed. Schoenemann, p. 194, ss. Routh. Reliqu. Sacr. iii. p. 175, ss.). First of all he rejects *τοὺς διαιροῦντας καὶ κατατέμνοντας —τὴν μοναρχίαν εἰς τρεῖς δυνάμεις τινὰς καὶ μεμερισμένας ὑποστάσεις καὶ θεότητας τρεῖς*, and asserts in opposition: *Ἡνῶσθαι γὰρ ἀνάγκη τῷ θεῷ τῶν ὅλων τὸν θεῖον λόγον· ἐμφιλοχωρεῖν δὲ τῷ θεῷ καὶ ἐνδιαιτᾶσθαι δεῖ τὸ ἅγιον πνεῦμα· ἤδη καὶ τὴν θείαν τριάδα εἰς ἕνα, ὥσπερ εἰς κορυφήν τινα (τὸν θεὸν τῶν ὅλων τὸν παντοκράτορα λέγω) συγκεφαλαιοῦσθαί τε καὶ συνάγεσθαι πᾶσα ἀνάγκη.* Then he censures *τοὺς ποίημα τὸν υἱὸν εἶναι δοξάζοντας, καὶ γεγονέναι τὸν κύριον, ὥσπερ ἕν τι ὄντως γενομένων, νομίζοντας.—Βλάσφημον οὖν οὐ τὸ τυχὸν, μέγιστον μὲν οὖν, χειροποίητον τρόπον τινὰ λέγειν τὸν Κύριον. Εἰ γὰρ γέγονεν υἱὸς, ἦν ὅτε οὐκ ἦν· ἀεὶ δὲ ἦν, εἴ γε ἐν τῷ πατρί ἐστιν, ὡς αὐτός φησι, καὶ εἰ λόγος καὶ σοφία καὶ δύναμις ὁ Χριστός.—ταῦτα δὲ δυνάμεις οὖσαι τοῦ θεοῦ τυγχάνουσιν· εἰ τοίνυν γέγονεν ὁ υἱὸς, ἦν ὅτε οὐκ ἦν ταῦτα· ἦν ἄρα καιρὸς, ὅτε χωρὶς τούτων ἦν ὁ θεός· ἀτοπώτατον δὲ τοῦτο.* The expression *κύριος ἔκτισέ με ἀρχὴν ὁδῶν αὐτοῦ*, Prov. viii. 22, means: *ἐπέστησε τοῖς ὑπ' αὐτοῦ γεγονόσιν ἔργοις, γεγονόσι δὲ δι' αὐτοῦ τοῦ υἱοῦ.—Ὦ ῥιψοκίνδυνοι ἄνθρωποι! ποίημα ὁ πρωτότοκος πάσης κτίσεως, ὁ ἐκ γαστρὸς πρὸ ἑωσφόρου γεννηθεὶς* (Ps. cix. 3), *ὁ εἰπὼν ὡς σοφία* (Prov. viii. 26)· *πρὸ δὲ πάντων βουνῶν γεννᾷ με; καὶ πολλάχου δὲ τῶν θείων λογίων γεγεννῆσθαι, ἀλλ' οὐ γεγονέναι τὸν υἱὸν λεγόμενον εὕροι τις ἄν.* We should therefore believe *εἰς θεὸν πατέρα παντοκράτορα, καὶ εἰς Χριστὸν Ἰησοῦν τὸν υἱὸν αὐτοῦ, καὶ εἰς τὸ ἅγιον πνεῦμα· ἡνῶσθαι δὲ τῷ θεῷ τῶν ὅλων τὸν λόγον· ἐγὼ γάρ, φησι, καὶ ὁ πατὴρ ἕν ἐσμεν* (Joh. x. 30)· *καὶ ἐγὼ ἐν τῷ πατρὶ, καὶ ὁ πατὴρ ἐν ἐμοί. Οὕτω γὰρ ἂν καὶ ἡ θεία τριὰς, καὶ τὸ ἅγιον κήρυγμα τῆς μοναρχίας διασώζοιτο.* Comp. Martini, l. c. S. 227, ff. Baur's Lehre v. d. Dreieinigkeit, i. 311.

1 There are certainly found, even in the older fathers, strong passages to the effect that

itself an outward expression in the unity of every thing belonging to the church. Since religious faith was made interchangeable with the intelligent expression of it in doctrine, men began also to consider the unity of the latter as necessary to the unity of the church, and to limit freedom of inquiry more and more. How an endeavor was made to carry out an agreement in regard to ecclesiastical usages, with this very view, may be seen from Victor's conduct respecting the celebration of Easter in Asia (§ 59); and after his example, the constant effort to bring about uniformity, even in external usages, is obvious, particularly in the western church. The idea of this unity naturally led still farther, to a closer external union among the separate churches; and since the bishops, as successors of the apostles, were looked upon as the center of ecclesiastical unity, that connection was effected by their more intimate attachment to one another; and the episcopal dignity obtained not a little elevation in consequence. Another idea which exerted much influence on ecclesiastical life was this, that the constitution of the Christian church was a nobler copy of the Jewish temple-worship, and therefore, that the Mosaic laws relative to public worship, particularly the priesthood, were still valid in the church (§ 53). No less fruitful in alterations in the worship of God was finally the idea of a *disciplina arcani*[2] which began to be current toward the conclusion of the second century. After the Christians had always been compelled to keep their worship

salvation is to be found only in the catholic church. Even Origen Hom. iii. in Josuam, § 5, says: Nemo semetipsum decipiat: extra hanc domum, i. e., extra ecclesiam nemo salvatur. Nam si quis foras exierit, mortis suae ipse fit reus. See Rothe die Anfänge der christl. Kirche, i. 578. He expresses himself elsewhere, however, more mildly, just as Clement of Alexandria. See Rothe, i. 624. Thus, while he does not allow to the virtuous heathen and the Jews vitam aeternam or regnum coelorum, which can be obtained only through faith in Christ, he yet asserts, Comm. in Ep. ad Rom. ii. 7: Tamen gloria operum ejus et pax et honor poterit non perire. On the other hand Cyprianus de Unitate ecclesiae: Quisquis ab ecclesia segregatus adulterae jungitur, a promissis ecclesiae separatur. Nec perveniet ad Christi praemia, qui relinquit ecclesiam Christi. Alienus est, profanus est, hostis est. Habere jam non potest Deum patrem, qui ecclesiam non habet matrem. Si potuit evadere quisquam, qui extra arcam Noë fuit, et qui extra ecclesiam foris, fuerit, evadet.—Tales etiamsi occisi in confessione nominis fuerint, macula ista nec sanguine abluitur.—Esse martyr non potest, qui in ecclesia non est. Occidi talis potest, coronari non potest, etc. H. E. Schmieder on Cyprian's treatise respecting the unity of the church in Stäudlin's and Tzschirner's Archiv. f. Kirchengesch. v. ii. 417. Rettberg's Cyprianus, S. 297, 348, 355. Rothe, i. 635. Cyprian's Lehre, v. d. Kirche von J. G. Huther. Hamb. u. Gotha. 1839. 8.

[2] This appellation of the Christian mysteries is new, and appears to have been first used by G. Th. Meier de Recondita veteris ecclesiae theologia. Helmst. 1679. 4.

private, through fear of persecution and profanation; they now began to find a reason for this secrecy in the nature of their holy transactions, by virtue of which they must be kept secret as *mysteries* from all unbaptized persons (τελεταί, Orig. c. Cels. iii. p. 147),[3] an idea which arose out of, and was fostered by the preference for mysteries exhibited at this period, and the example of the heathen mysteries (see § 37). The so-called *apostolic constitutions*[4] may be considered, after deducting later

[3] Tertull. de Praescr. haeret. c. 41: Non omittam ipsius etiam conversationis haereticae descriptionem, quam futilis, quam terrena, quam humana sit, sine gravitate, sine auctoritate, sine disciplina, ut fidei suae congruens. In primis, quis catechumenus quis fidelis, incertum est: pariter adeunt, pariter orant, etiam ethnici, si supervenerint: sanctum canibus, et porcis margaritas, licet non veras jactabunt. Cf. Apologet. c. 7. But this secrecy was still limited to the non-admission of the unbaptized to holy ordinances. The fathers of the third century speak without reserve as yet of these transactions, as of all the doctrines of Christianity, and Tertullian even reproaches the Valentinians in the following language, adv. Val. 1: Nihil magis curant quam occultare, quod praedicant. It was not till the fourth century when this mysterious tendency became general, that even the positive doctrines of Christianity began to be treated as mysteries. Catholic writers have been inclined to explain the non-appearance of their peculiar institutions and dogmas in antiquity by the aid of this disciplina arcani. This is done particularly by Em. a Schelstrate de Disciplina arcani. Rom. 1685. 4. Of late works see Th. Lienhart de Antiquis liturgiis et de Discipl. arcani. Argentor. 1829. J. A. Toklot de Arcani disciplina, quae antiqua in ecclesia fuit in usu. Colon. 1836. 8. Comp. on the other side, G. E. Tentzel Diss. de disciplina arcani in his Exercitt. select. Lips. 1692. 4. G. C. L. Th. Frommann de Disciplina arcani, quae in vetere Ecclesia christ. obtinuisse fertur. Jenae. 1833. 8. R. Rothe de Disciplinae arcani, quae dicitur, in Eccl. christ. origine. Heidelberg. 1841. 4. Besides this disciplina arcani excluded only the unbaptized, and is, therefore, of a different nature from that disciplina agreeably to which, Clement of Alexandria and Origen wished to withhold their gnosis even from Christians. (§ 63, note 4, ff.)

[4] The Apostolic Constitutions and Canons (the best edition of them is in Cotelerii Patr. apostolicis, vol. i.) are records of the ecclesiastical customs regarded as apostolic, in the form of apostolic prescriptions (cf. Hieron. Epist. 52 ad Lucinium; Unaquaeque provincia abundet in sensu suo, et praecepta majorum leges apostolicas arbitretur. Augustin. contra Donatist. iv. 24: Quod universa tenet ecclesia, nec conciliis institutum, sed semper retentum est, id nonnisi apostolica auctoritate traditum certissime credatur). The apostolic constitutions, διατάξεις τῶν Ἀποστόλων, consist of eight books, and probably belong to Syria. The first six books presenting instructions embracing the entire range of Christian life, were written toward the end of the third century, and are probably the books which Eusebius, H. E. iii. c. 25, quoted as διδαχαὶ τῶν Ἀποστόλων, Athanasius in Ep. festali; and in Synopsi sacrae Script. as διδαχὴ τῶν Ἀποστόλων. The seventh book is an independent shorter manual of the same kind. Hence it generally treats of the same subjects as the first six books, and probably belongs to the beginning of the fourth century. The eighth book refers solely to the holy transactions (τὰ μυστικά), contains agenda in addition to the appropriate canonical prescriptions, and was put together in the middle of the fourth century as a pontifical book for the use of the clergy. This book had the title διατάξεις, which, after the work had been soon after put along with the other books, was transferred to the whole. Epiphanius often quotes it as διατάξεις or διάταξις τῶν Ἀποστόλων. After Epiphanius there must, however, have been some interpolations, the most important of which are those by which the prescriptions respecting the festival of Christ's birth (v. 13), and the easter festival (v. 17, cf. Epiphan. Haer. xxx. 10), have been altered agreeably to the later form of observance. Krabbe assumes that after Epiphanius

interpolations, as an evidence of the constitution of the church at the present time. *The apostolic canons* belong to the fifth and sixth centuries.[5]

§ 68.

HISTORY OF THE HIERARCHY.

After the number of the Christians had greatly increased in the country, separate churches in the country were now frequently formed which attached themselves either to the district (*παροικία*) of the nearest town-bishop, and received from him a presbyter or deacon;[1] or chose their own bishops (*χωρεπίσκοποι*) who, however, soon came, in part, to be in a certain state of dependence on the nearest town-bishop.[2] The power of the

many interpolations were made, even doctrinal ones, favorable to the Arians and the Macedonians, and that the eighth book was first appended after the time of that father; but in opposition to his opinion see Drey, p. 154, 177. Comp. Dr. O. Krabbe über den Ursprung u. den Inhalt d. apost. Constitutionen des Clemens Romanus. Hamburg. 1829; especially Dr. J. S. v. Drey's neue Untersuchungen über die Constitutionen und Kanones d. Apost. Tübingen. 1832. 8. According to Baur (über den Ursprung des Episcopats, S. 125, ff. 131, ff.), the constitutions are of Ebionitish origin and anti-Pauline tendency, and originated in Rome (p. 134.)

[5] Canones Apostolorum, *κανόνες ἐκκλησιαστικοὶ τῶν ἁγίων Ἀποστόλων* among the Greeks 85, among the Latins 50. Every ecclesiastical fundamental law, whether recorded or not, was at first called *κανὼν ἀποστολικός* (Alexander Ep. Alex., about 318, in Theodoret. H. E. i. 3), *κανών* (Conc. Nicaeni Can. 5, 9), *κανὼν ἐκκλησιαστικός* (ibid. Can. 2, 10): in this sense the expression *οἱ ἀποστολικοὶ κανονες* was also used at the Council of Constantinople, ann. 394, without, however, supposing that our present collection is meant. (Drey, p. 396.) The first fifty canons were gathered soon after the middle of the fifth century, under the name of Clement (who, known as the organ of the apostles, by means of the Clementines and Recognitions (§ 58), appeared the most suitable person for this purpose), from the apostolic constitutions, and from the canons of several synods of the fourth century (in particular the Synod of Antioch, 341). Dionysius Exiguus translated them, and the Latin church holds fast by them alone. But after the commencement of the sixth century, 35 were added among the Greeks, the canons were appended to the constitutions, and the name of Clement transferred to these also. Drey, p. 203, ff. M. E. Regenbrecht de Canonibus Apostolorum et codice Ecclesiae Hispanae diss. Vratislav. 1828. 8. O. Krabbe Diss. de codice Canonum qui Apostolorum nomine circumferuntur. Gotting. 1829. 4.

[1] Thus mention is made by Dionys. Alex. ap. Euseb. H. E. vii. 24, 4, of *πρεσβυτέρους καὶ διδασκάλους τῶν ἐν ταῖς κώμαις ἀδελφῶν*: by the Conc. Illiberitanum, ann. 305, can. 77, of Diaconum regentem plebem sine Episcopo et Presbytero: Conc. Neocaesar. ann. 315, can. 13. of *ἐπιχωρίους πρεσβυτέρους*.

[2] Thus they are called in the Epist. Syn. Antioch. ann. 270, apud. Euseb. H. E. vii. 30, 6, *ἐπισκόπους τῶν ὁμόρων ἀγρῶν*. In the Conc. Ancyranum, ann. 315, can. 13: *Χωρεπισκόποις μὴ ἐξεῖναι, πρεσβυτέρους ἢ διακόνους χειροτονεῖν*. Cf. Bingham, i. p. 192, ss.

bishops was enlarged, not only by this enlargement of their districts, but also by an institution which now arose, in consequence of which the bishops came into a closer and more regular union among themselves. We allude to *Provincial Synods*, which were always becoming more frequent since the end of the second century, and were held in several provinces once or twice in the year.[3] As they were for the most part convened in the principal city of the province, under the presidency of the bishop of that city; and since the latter was, as it were, the medium in relation to the other smaller bishops, by which alone they stood in connection with the rest of the church, the bishops of the principal cities (*μητροπολίτης*, Metropolitanus)[4] came gradually to obtain a kind of superintendence over the other bishops of their province (*ἐπαρχία*). As yet, however, this metropolitan constitution was general only in *the east*. In *the west*, it is true, *Rome* was elevated to be the ecclesiastical

Planck's Gesellschaftsverf. i. S. 73, ff. In Africa, where the country bishops were particularly numerous, they were not at all distinguished from others, not even by a peculiar name. Cf. St. A. Morcelli Africa christiana (Partes iii. Brixiae. 1816. 4), P. I. p. 43.

[3] Firmiliani Epist. ad Cyprian. (in Epist. Cyprian. 75): Qua ex causa necessario apud nos fit, ut per singulos annos seniores et praepositi in unum conveniamus ad disponenda ea, quae curae nostrae commissa sunt, ut si qua graviora sunt communi consilio dirigantur. What had hitherto been usual only in some provinces, was made a universal regulation by the Council of Nice, Can. 5: *Καλῶς ἔχειν ἔδοξεν, ἑκάστου ἐνιαυτοῦ καθ' ἑκάστην ἐπαρχίαν δὶς τοῦ ἔτους συνόδους γίνεσθαι.* On the origin of Synods see above, § 53, note 6. The regular provincial Synods had, in most of the provinces, their natural type in the *κοινόν*, Commune, i. e., the union of the civitates of the provinces which met from time to time, by deputies, in the metropolis, and gave advice in common matters. So we find frequently on coins *Κοινόν 'Ασίας*, K. *Βειθυνίας*, etc., see Eckhel Doctrina numorum vett. t. iv. p. 428, ss. Such assemblies were also called concilium, provinciale concilium, see Cod. Theodos. lib. xii. tit. 12, and Gothofredi paratitlon prefixed to this title. Dirksen's civilistische Abhandl. Bd. 2, S. 16. And vice versa the ecclesiastical provincial synod is called, Can. Nic. 5, *τὸ κοινὸν τῶν 'Επισκόπων*.

[4] The principle which gradually arose by custom was afterward expressed in the Conc. Antiocheni (341) can. 9: *Τοὺς καθ' ἑκάστην ἐπαρχίαν ἐπισκόπους εἰδέναι χρὴ, τὸν ἐν τῇ μητροπόλει προεστῶτα ἐπίσκοπον καὶ τὴν φροντίδα ἀναδέχεσθαι πάσης τῆς ἐπαρχίας, διὰ τὸ ἐν τῇ μητροπόλει πανταχόθεν συντρέχειν πάντας τοὺς πράγματα ἔχοντας. "Οθεν ἔδοξε καὶ τῇ τιμῇ προηγεῖσθαι αὐτὸν, μηδέν τε πράττειν περιττὸν τοὺς λοιποὺς ἐπισκόπους ἄνευ αὐτοῦ, κατὰ τὸν ἀρχαῖον κρατήσαντα τῶν πατέρων ἡμῶν κανόνα ἢ ταῦτα μόνα ὅσα τῇ ἑκάστου ἐπιβάλλει παροικίᾳ, καὶ ταῖς ὑπ' αὐτὴν χώραις· ἕκαστον γὰρ ἐπίσκοπον ἐξουσίαν ἔχειν τῆς ἑαυτοῦ παροικίας, διοικεῖν τε κατὰ τὴν ἑκάστῳ ἐπιβάλλουσαν εὐλάβειαν, καὶ πρόνοιαν ποιεῖσθαι πάσης τῆς χώρας τῆς ὑπὸ τὴν ἑαυτοῦ πόλιν, ὡς καὶ χειροτονεῖν πρεσβυτέρους καὶ διακόνους, καὶ μετὰ κρίσεως ἕκαστα διαλαμβάνειν· περαιτέρω δὲ μηδὲν πράττειν ἐπιχειρεῖν δίχα τοῦ τῆς μητροπόλεως ἐπισκόπου, μηδὲ αὐτὸν ἄνευ τῆς τῶν λοιπῶν γνώμης.* Bacchinii libb. iii. de Origine hierarchiae ecclesiasticae. Mutinae. 1704. 4. A history of the metropolitan constitution in W. C. S. Ziegler's pragmat. Geschichte der kirchl. Verfassungsformen in den ersten 6 Jahrh. der Kirche. Leipzig. 1798, S. 61–164.

metropolis of a great part of Italy; and even in Africa a somewhat similar, though peculiar, provincial constitution had been adopted;[5] but in the remaining parts of the west, the Christians had not yet reached such hierarchical associations, on account of the small number of Christian churches.[6]

By this establishment of large ecclesiastical bodies, the entire organization of the church became more compact and united. Through the medium of the metropolitans the testimonials and papers of the separate churches[7] were better attested and more safely forwarded; accounts of all important ecclesiastical events and resolutions were more expeditiously and generally circulated; and thus each community was always acquainted with the state of the whole church.

The bishops of the three great cities of the Roman empire, *Rome*, *Alexandria*, and *Antioch*, had, at the same time, the largest provinces. Hence they were regarded as the principal bishops of Christendom; and their assent in all general affairs was looked upon as of special importance. Still, however, at this time, great stress was laid on the fact that all bishops were perfectly alike in dignity and power; and that each in his own diocese was answerable only to God for his conduct.[8] They

[5] Every African province had a primate at the head of it, who, in Mauritania and Numidia was usually the oldest bishop (not always the oldest, see Hüllmann's Ursprünge d. Kirchenverfassung des Mittelalters, Bonn. 1831, p. 101), (hence senex see Bingham, vol. i. p. 214, Hüllmann, p. 106), and in proconsular Africa was the bishop of Carthage. This last was at the same time the head of all the provinces, and could summon general councils. Cf. Cypriani Epist. 45: Latius fusa est nostra provincia: habet enim Numidiam et Mauritaniam sibi cohaerentes. Ziegler in Henke's Neuem Magazin, i. 172, ff. Münteri Primordia Eccl. Afr. p. 43, ss. This regulation was copied from the political one, because all these provinces were under the proconsul in Carthage, under whom the two Mauritanias were managed by procurators. See Mannert's Geographie d. Griechen u. Römer, x. ii. 233, 391.

[6] Comp. the Ballerini Observatt. ad Quesnelli diss. v. p. ii. in their edition of the Opp. Leonis, tom. ii. p. 1030, ss. Ziegler's Gesch. der kirchl. Verfassungsformen, S. 79, ff.

[7] Literae communicatoriae appear first in the Concil. Illiberit. can. 58, but their use is certainly much older. The *κανονικὰ γράμματα* (*ὡς κατὰ κανόνα γινόμενα*, Zonaras ad Can. Laodic. 22), literae formatae (cf. formalis epistola, Sueton. in Domit. c. 13, cf. Beveregius ad Can. Apost. 12), which served as testimonials for individuals, were partly *ἐπιστολαί συστατικαί*, partly *εἰρηνικαί* (literae pacis), partly *ἀπολυτικαί* (literae dimissoriae). There were besides *ἐπιστολαὶ κοινωνικαί* (literae communicatoriae), (afterward *ἐνθρονιστικαί*), *ἐπιστολαὶ συνοδικαί*, *ἐγκύκλιοι* (literae circulares), etc. F. B. Ferrarii de Antiquo epistolarum ecclesiasticarum genere libb. iii. Mediol. 1613, (ed. G. Th. Meier. Helmst. 1678. 4.) Ph. Priorii de Literis canonicis diss. Paris. 1675. 8. J. R. Kiesling de Stabili primitivae ecclesiae ope literarum communicatoriarum connubio. Lips. 1745. 4.

[8] Cyprian. de Unitate ecclesiae: Quam unitatem firmiter tenere et vindicare debemus, maxime episcopi, qui in ecclesiae praesidemus, ut Episcopatum quoque ipsum unum atque

could the less believe in the superior authority of the Romish bishop, because the idea of his being Peter's successor just began to be developed;[9] and besides, no higher power was attributed to Peter than to the other apostles.[10] In the west, indeed,

indivisum probemus.—Episcopatus unus est, cujus a singulis in solidum pars tenetur. Ej. Epist. 52: Episcopatus unus episcoporum multorum concordi numerositate diffusus. Ej. Allocutio in Conc. Carthag. (in the year 256: Superest, ut de hac ipsa re quid singuli sentiamus, proferamus, neminem judicantes, aut a jure communionis aliquem, si diversum senserit, amoventes. Neque enim quisquam nostrum episcopum se esse episcoporum constituit, aut tyrannico terrore ad obsequendi necessitatem collegas suos adigit, quando habeat omnis Episcopus pro licentia libertatis et potestatis suae arbitrium proprium, tanquam judicari ab alio non possit, cum nec ipse possit alterum judicare. Sed expectemus universi judicium domini nostri Jesu Christi, qui unus et solus habet potestatem et praeponendi nos in ecclesiae suae gubernatione, et de actu nostro judicandi. Comp. his letters to two Roman bishops, ad Cornelium (Ep. 55, see below, note 11), ad Stephanum (Ep. 72): Caeterum scimus, quosdam quod semel imbiberint nolle deponere, nec propositum suum facile mutare, sed salvo inter collegas pacis et concordiae vinculo quaedam propria, quae apud se semel sint usurpata, retinere. Qua in re nec nos vim cuiquam facimus aut legem damus, quando habeat in ecclesiae administratione voluntatis suae arbitrium liberum unusquisque praepositus, rationem actus sui Domino redditurus.

9 The fiction of Peter being first bishop of Rome proceeded from the Clementines (§ 58, note 9), and was propagated in the Catholic Church by the Recognitions. Cyprian is the first who designates the Romish chair the locum Petri (Ep. 52 ad Antonianum) and Petri cathedram; but at the same time he takes all bishops to be successors of Peter (see note 10). Thus he was of the same opinion as Eusebius, Rufinus, and Epiphanius (§ 27, note 6), that Peter during his stay at Rome, had the supreme direction of the church there, without having been connected with it as bishop. In Rome itself, however, many went farther, as may be seen from Firmiliani Ep. ad Cyprianum (Ep. Cypr. 75): Stephanus qui sic de Episcopatus sui loco gloriatur, et se successionem Petri tenere contendit.

10 Comp. Clemens. Alex. above, § 26, note 4. Origenes ad Matth. xvi. 18 (Comment. in Matth. t. xii. § 10): *Πέτρα γὰρ πᾶς ὁ Χριστοῦ μαθητὴς—καὶ ἐπὶ πᾶσαν τὴν τοιαύτην πέτραν οἰκοδομεῖται ὁ ἐκκλησιαστικὸς πᾶς λόγος, καὶ ἡ κατ' αὐτὸν πολιτεία.* § 11: *Εἰ δὲ ἐπὶ τὸν ἕνα ἐκεῖνον Πέτρον νομίζεις ὑπὸ τοῦ θεοῦ οἰκοδομεῖσθαι τὴν πᾶσαν ἐκκλησίαν μόνον, τί ἂν φήσαις περὶ Ἰωάννου τοῦ τῆς βροντῆς υἱοῦ, ἢ ἑκάστου τῶν Ἀποστόλων; Ἄλλως τε ἄρα τολμήσωμεν λέγειν, ὅτι Πέτρου μὲν ἰδίως πύλαι ᾅδου οὐ κατισχύσουσι, τῶν δὲ λοιπῶν Ἀποστόλων, καὶ τῶν τελείων κατισχύσουσιν; ἆρα δὲ τῷ Πέτρῳ μόνῳ δίδονται ὑπὸ τοῦ κυρίου αἱ κλεῖδες τῆς τῶν οὐρανῶν βασιλείας, καὶ οὐδεὶς ἕτερος τῶν μακαρίων αὐτὰς λήψεται; Παρώνυμοι γὰρ πέτρας πάντες οἱ μιμηταὶ Χριστοῦ. Χριστοῦ μέλη ὄντες παρώνυμοι ἐχρημάτισαν Χριστιανοὶ, πέτρας δὲ Πέτροι. καὶ πρὸς πάντας τοὺς τοιούτους ἂν λέγοιτο ἀπὸ τοῦ σωτῆρος τὸ λέγον· σὺ εἶ Πέτρος καὶ τὰ ἑξῆς.* Hence § 14: *Λέλεκται τῷ Πέτρῳ καὶ παντὶ Πέτρῳ.* Cyprian. Ep. 27: Dominus noster—episcopi honorem et ecclesiae suae rationem disponens in evangelio loquitur et dicit Petro: Ego tibi dico, quia tu es Petrus, etc. (Matth. xvi. 18, 19). Inde per temporum et successionum vices episcoporum ordinatio et ecclesiae ratio decurrit, ut ecclesia super episcopos constituatur, et omnis actus ecclesiae per eosdem praepositos gubernetur:—Cyprian. de Unitate ecclesiae: Loquitur Dominus ad Petrum: "Ego tibi dico," inquit, "quia tu es Petrus," etc. (Matth. xvi. 18, 19). [Et iterum eidem post resurrectionem suam dicit: "Pasce oves meas" (Joan. xxi. 15). Super illum unum aedificat ecclesiam suam, et illi pascendas mandat oves suas]: et quamvis Apostolis omnibus post resurrectionem suam parem potestatem tribuat et dicat: "sicut misit me pater," etc. (Joh. xx. 21, 23): tamen ut unitatem manifestaret [unam cathedram constituit, et] unitatis ejusdem originem ab uno incipientem sua auctoritate disposuit. Hoc erant utique et caeteri Apostoli, quod fuit Petrus, pari consortio praediti et honoris et potestatis: sed exordium ab unitate proficisci-

a certain superior honor was paid to the Church of Rome as the largest and only apostolic church; but actual rights over the other churches were by no means conceded to it.[11] Still less, of course, was this the case in the east.[12]

tur [et primatus Petro datur, ut una Christi ecclesiae et cathedra una monstretur. Et pastores sunt omnes, et grex unus ostenditur, qui ab Apostolis omnibus unanimi consensione pascatur], ut ecclesia Christi una monstretur.—Hanc ecclesiae unitatem qui non tenet, tenere se fidem credit? Qui ecclesiae renititur et resistit [qui cathedram Petri, super quem fundata est ecclesia, deserit], in ecclesia se esse confidit? The passages in brackets are wanting in the oldest MSS., and are Romish interpolations. See especially Rigaltii Observatt. ad Cyp. p. 162, ss., and Baluzii notae 11–15 to the libb. de unit. eccl. (which last, however, have been very much abridged by the Benedictine editors). Even the words still admitted by Rigaltius: super illum unum aedificat ecclesiam, are wanting in the oldest MSS. Cf. Edm. Richerii Defensio lib. de eccles. et polit. potestate, i. p. 115. These additions have quite another sense in the mouth of Cyprian than the interpolators meant. For example, what is denoted by the expression in Cyprian, primatus Petro datur, is clear from his Epist. 71: Nam nec Petrus, quem primum Dominus elegit, et super quem aedificavit ecclesiam suam, cum secum Paulus de circumcisione postmodum disceptaret, vindicavit sibi aliquid insolenter aut arroganter assumsit, ut diceret, se primatum tenere, et obtemperari a novellis et posteris sibi potius oportere.

[11] Cypriani Epist. 55, ad Cornelium Episc. Romanum, who had received the excommunicated Felicissimus as embassador of the Carthaginian archbishop Fortunatus:—Satis miratus sum, cum animadvertissem, te minis atque terroribus eorum, qui venerant, aliquantum esse commotum, cum te, secundum quod scripsisti, agressi essent, cum summa desperatione comminantes, quod si litteras quas attulerant non accepisses, publice eas recitarent, et multa turpia ac probrosa et ore suo digna proferrent. Quod si ita res est, frater carissime, ut nequissimorum timeatur audacia—actum est de episcopatus vigore, etc. Quibus etiam satis non fuit ab evangelio recessisse—foris sibi extra ecclesiam et contra ecclesiam constituisse conventiculum perditae factionis.—Post ista adhuc insuper pseudoepiscopo sibi ab haereticis constituto navigare audent et ad Petri cathedram, atque ad ecclesiam principalem, unde unitas sacerdotalis exorta est, a schismaticis et profanis litteras ferre, nec cogitare, eos esse Romanos, quorum fides apostolo praedicante laudata est (Rom. i. 8), ad quos perfidia habere non possit accessum. Quae autem causa veniendi et pseudoepiscopum contra episcopos factum nuntiandi? Aut enim placet illis quod fecerunt: et in suo scelere perseverant: aut si displicet et recedunt, sciunt quo revertantur. Nam cum statutum sit ab omnibus nobis, et aequum sit pariter ac justum, ut uniuscujusque causa illic audiatur, ubi est crimen admissum; et singulis pastoribus portio gregis sit adscripta, quam regat unusquisque et gubernet, rationem sui actus Domino redditurus: oportet utique eos quibus praesumus non circumcursare, nec episcoporum concordiam cohaerentem sua subdola et fallaci temeritate collidere, sed agere illic causam suam, ubi et accusatores habere et testes sui criminis possint; nisi si paucis desperatis et perditis minor videtur esse auctoritas episcoporum in Africa constitutorum, qui jam de illis judicaverunt. Jam causa eorum cognitia est, jam de eis dicta sententia est: nec censurae congruit sacerdotum mobilis atque inconstantis animi levitate reprehendi, cum Dominus doceat et dicat: Sit sermo vester, est est, non non (Matth. v. 37). Cyprian, in his letters, constantly calls the Roman bishops frater and collega. What gave the latter a predominance in the west is evident from Synodi Arelatensis (in the year 314) Epist. ii. ad Sylvestrum Papam: Placuit etiam ante scribi ad te, qui majores dioceses tenes, et per te potissimum omnibus insinuari. Quid autem sit, quod senserimus, scripto nostrae mediocritatis subjunximus.

[12] Firmiliani Ep. ad Cypr. (l. c.): Eos autem, qui Romae sunt, non ea in omnibus observare, quae sint ab origine tradita, et frustra Apostolorum auctoritatem praetendere, scire quis etiam inde potest, quod circa celebrandos dies Paschae et circa multa alia

As all bishops were supposed to be perfectly alike in dignity and power, so also they believed that they had the same general duties toward the whole church in addition to those peculiar duties they owed to their respective churches.[13] Accordingly they all asserted equally the right of interfering, in cases where other bishops had departed from the fundamental rules of the church, by admonitions, reprimands, and even ecclesiastical punishment.[14] This common right was of course principally exercised by the most distinguished and powerful bishops.

divinae rei sacramenta videat esse apud illos aliquas diversitates, nec observari illic omnia aequaliter, quae Hierosolymis observantur.

[13] See especially Cypriani Epist. 67, below, note 14.

[14] L. E. du Pin de Antiqua Ecclesiae disciplina dissertt. hist. Paris. 1686. p. 141, ss. For example the condemnation of Paul of Samosata (§ 60, cf. du Pin, p. 154). Reprimand of Dionysius of Alexandria (§ 64, note 8, du Pin, p. 152.) With reference to Marcian, bishop of Arles, who had gone over to the Novatians, Cyprian. Ep. 67, ad Stephan. Ep. Rom. writes: Cui rei nostrum est consulere et subvenire, frater carissime. Quapropter facere te oportet plenissimas litteras ad coepiscopos nostros in Galliis constitutos, ne ultra Marcianum pervicacem—collegio nostro insultare patiantur, quod necdum videatur a nobis abstentus.—Dirigantur in provinciam et ad plebem Arelate consistentem a te litterae, quibus abstento Marciano alius in locum ejus substituatur, et grex Christi, qui in hodiernum ab illo dissipatus et vulneratus contemnitur, colligatur. Sufficiat multos illic ex fratribus nostris annis istis superioribus excessisse sine pace. Vel ceteris subveniatur qui supersunt. Iccirco enim, frater carissime, copiosum corpus est sacerdotum concordiae mutuae glutino atque unitatis vinculo copulatum, ut si quis ex collegio nostro haeresim facere et gregem Christi lacerare et vastare tentaverit, subveniant caeteri, et quasi pastores utiles et misericordes oves dominicas in gregem colligant. Quid enim si in mari portus aliquis munitionibus suis ruptis infestus et periculosus esse navibus coeperit, nonne navigantes ad alios proximos portus naves suas dirigunt, ubi sit tutus accessus et salutaris introitus et statio secura? Quod nunc esse apud nos debet, frater carissime, ut fratres nostros, qui jactati Marciani scopulis petunt ecclesiae portus salutares, suscipiamus ad nos prompta et benigna humanitate. Nam etsi pastores multi sumus, unum tamen gregem pascimus, et oves universas, quas Christus sanguine suo et passione quaesivit, colligere et fovere debemus, etc. In the matter of the Spanish bishops Basilides and Martial (in the year 256), Cyprian, called upon to interfere, declares the interposition of Stephanus, bishop of Rome, in favor of those deposed bishops to be exceptionable, Epist. 68, ad clerum et plebes in Hispania consistentes: Nec rescindere ordinationem (Sabini) jure perfectam potest, quod Basilides post crimina sua detecta et conscientiam etiam propria confessione nudatam, Romam pergens, Stephanum collegam nostrum longe positum et gestae rei ac veritatis ignarum fefellit, ut exambiret reponi se injuste in episcopatum, de quo fuerat jure depositus. Etsi aliqui de collegis nostris exstiterint (namely, Stephanus), fratres dilectissimi, qui deificam disciplinam negligendam putant, et cum Basilide et Martiale temere communicant, conturbare fidem nostram res ista non debet, etc. Cf. du Pin, p. 150.

§ 69.

(CONTINUATION.) HIERARCHY IN THE SEPARATE CHURCHES.

After the idea of the Mosaic priesthood had been adopted in the Christian church, the clergy, as was natural, elevated themselves far above the laity. A peculiar mystic influence was ascribed to the old rite of consecration, when considered as an *ordinatio*; and they now appeared in the character of persons appointed by God himself to be the medium of communication between Him and the Christian world.[1]

For the inferior services of the church particular offices were appointed, different, however, in the Greek and Latin churches. In the former, *ὑπηρέται* (or *ὑποδιάκονοι*), *ψαλτῳδοί* (or *ψάλται*), *ἀναγνῶσται* and *πυλωροί*:[2] in the latter, Subdiaconi, Acoluthi,

[1] Cypriani Epist. 55: Nam cum scriptum sit: Qui dixerit fratri, suo, fatue, etc. (Matth. v. 22), quomodo possunt censuram Domini ultoris evadere, qui talia ingerunt, non solum fratribus, sed et sacerdotibus, quibus honor tantus de Dei dignatione conceditur, ut quisquis sacerdoti ejus et ad tempus hic judicanti non obtemperaret, statim necaretur. Neque enim aliunde haereses obortae sunt, aut nata sunt schismata, quam inde quod sacerdoti Dei non obtemperatur, nec unus in ecclesia ad tempus sacerdos et ad tempus judex vice Christi cogitatur. Epist. 69, ad Florent. Pupianum: Animadverto te—in mores nostros diligenter inquirere, et post Deum judicem, qui sacerdotes facit, te velle, non dicam de me (quantus enim ego sum?) sed de Dei et Christi judicio judicare. Hoc est in Deum non credere, hoc est rebellem adversus Christum et adversus evangelium ejus existere, ut —tu existimes, sacerdotes Dei sine conscientia ejus in ecclesia ordinari.—Quamobrem, frater, si majestatem Dei, qui sacerdotes ordinat, cogitaveris, si Christum, qui arbitrio et nutu ac praesentia sua et praepositos ipsos et ecclesiam cum praepositis gubernat, aliquando respexeris, si temeritatis—tuae agere vel sero poenitentiam coeperis, si Deo et Christo ejus—plenissime satisfeceris; communicationis tuae poterimus habere rationem: manente tamen apud nos divinae censurae respectu et metu, ut prius Dominum meum consulam, an tibi pacem dari, et te ad communicationem ecclesiae suae admitti sua ostensione et admonitione permittat. Memini enim, quid jam mihi sit ostensum, immo quid sit servo obsequenti et timenti de dominica et divina auctoritate praeceptum: qui inter caetera quae ostendere et revelare dignatus est, et hoc addidit: Itaque qui Christo non credit sacerdotem facienti, et postea credere incipiet sacerdotem vindicanti. Cf. Epistt. 45, 52, 65. On the dignity of the priests, and particularly of the bishops, see Const. Ap. ii. 26, ss. As spiritual fathers, they are to be regarded as higher than earthly parents, c. 33, higher than kings and princes, c. 34: *Τούτους ἄρχοντας ὑμῶν καὶ βασιλεῖς ἡγεῖσθαι νομίζετε, καὶ δασμοὺς ὡς βασιλεῦσι προσφέρετε. Ὅσῳ τοίνυν ψυχὴ σώματος κρείττων, τοσούτῳ ἱερωσύνη βασιλείας· δεσμεύει γὰρ αὐτὴ καὶ λύει τοὺς τιμωρίας ἢ ἀφέσεως ἀξίους· διὸ τὸν ἐπίσκοπον στέργειν ὀφείλετε ὡς πατέρα, φοβεῖσθαι ὡς βασιλέα, τιμᾷν ὡς κύριον.*

[2] So Constitutt. Apost. iii. 11, vi. 17. Those who are called in the first six books *ὑπηρέται* are denominated *ὑποδιάκονοι* in viii. 28 (*ὑπηρέται γάρ εἰσι διακόνων*): a *ὑποδιάκονος* is also named by Athanasius in Epist. ad solitariam vitam agentes. Many

Exorcistae, Lectores, and Ostiarii[3] (afterward called ordines minores). All oppressed and helpless persons, especially widows, orphans, and virgins,[4] were referred to the clergy for assistance. The bishop (*Papa*, Tert. de Pudic. 13. Πάπα ἱερώτατος, Gregor. Thaum. Epist. can. i., Praepositus, Cyprian, note 1) exercised this support, as well as the administration of the entire wealth of the church, by *the deacons*.[5] In like manner, supported by his clergy, he was umpire in all disputes between the members of his church.[6] The bishops greatly increased in reputation and revenues, both by the enlargement of their dioceses and the clergy subject to them, and by the operation of synods. But in this very way many were now led astray unto pride, ambition, and avarice;[7] sometimes even into an immoderate ostenta-

communities, however, had different regulations. In the enumeration contained in Const. Apost. ii. 28, the ὑπηρέται are wanting, in the eighth book the πυλωροί. On the other hand, in viii. 11, the deacons have to watch the doors of the men, the subdeacons those of the women (cf. Conc. Laodic. in the fourth century, can. 22: Ὅτι οὐ δεῖ ὑπηρέτην τὰς θύρας ἐγκαταλιμπάνειν). Thus the ὑποδιάκονοι and the πυλωροί were sometimes the same, sometimes different individuals. Respecting the readers and singers, see Socrates Hist. eccl. v. 22: Ἐν Ἀλεξανδρείᾳ ἀναγνῶσται καὶ ὑποβολεῖς ἀδιάφορον, εἴτε κατηχούμενοι εἰσὶν, εἴτε πιστοί. The Greek church never adopted Acoluthi and Exorcists, comp. Constitutt. Apost. viii. 26: Ἐπορκιστὴς οὐ χειροτονεῖται. His gift is a free favor bestowed by God; and should he wish to assume the clerical office, he is ordained a bishop, presbyter, or deacon.

[3] First the Lectores mentioned in Tertullian de Praescr. 41. The others are found first in Cyprian and in Epist. Cornelii (bishop of Rome, 252) ap. Euseb. vi. 43, according to whose account there were in Rome, 46 presbyters, 7 deacons, 7 subdeacons, 42 acoluthi, and 42 exorcists, lectores, and ostiarii.

[4] Const. Ap. ii. 26: Αἵ τε χῆραι καὶ ὀρφανοὶ εἰς τύπον τοῦ θυσιαστηρίου λελογίσθωσαν ὑμῖν· αἵ τε παρθένοι εἰς τύπον τοῦ θυμιατηρίου τετιμήσθωσαν καὶ τοῦ θυμιάματος.

[5] Constitt. Apost. ii. 44: Ἔστω ὁ διάκονος τοῦ ἐπισκόπου ἀκοὴ, καὶ ὀφθαλμὸς καὶ στόμα, καρδία τε καὶ ψυχὴ, ἵνα μὴ ᾖ τὰ πολλὰ μεριμνῶν ὁ ἐπίσκοπος, ἀλλὰ μόνα τὰ κυριώτερα.

[6] As the Jews were accustomed to decide their disputes by umpires chosen from among the people, agreeably to the Mosaic law (Jos. Antt. xiv. 10, 17, xvi. 6), so from the beginning the Christians also, according to 1 Cor. vi. 1, ff., in order to establish the relations subsisting among them by the gospel, not by a heathen tribunal. The Roman jurisprudence favored generally procedure by arbitration, as Digest. lib. iv. tit. 8: De receptis, qui arbitrium receperunt, ut sententiam dicant, and in order to make the arbitration sentence secure, prescribed a penal clause to be inserted in the compromise. The Christians were accustomed to choose their bishops as umpires. Their decisions required no such safeguard, but were sufficiently protected by religious awe. Respecting this point, see Const. App. ii. 45–53. According to chapter 47, Monday is said to be the episcopal judicial day on which the bishop, surrounded by his presbyters and deacons, hears the contending parties, and also complaints regarding unchristian conduct. First of all, the other clergy attempt to reconcile the parties, and if this proves ineffectual, the episcopal sentence succeeds. But the bishop ἐν τῷ δικαστηρίῳ σύμψηφον ἔχει καὶ συνίστορα τῆς δίκης τὸν χριστὸν τοῦ θεοῦ.

[7] Origines in Exod. Hom. xi. § 6: Quis autem hodie eorem, qui populis praesunt, non

tion.[8] Still, however, their power continued to be restricted in many ways. Although the provincial bishops exercised a decided influence on the choice of a bishop, yet the election depended in a great degree on the church.[9] The bishop himself, it is true, nominated the inferior clergy, but the presbyters had

dico si jam aliqua ei a Deo revelata sunt, sed in legis scientia aliquid meriti habet, consilium dignatur inferioris saltem sacerdotis accipere? nedum dixerim laici vel gentilis. Idem in Matthaeum, tom. xvi. § 8 (on Luke xxii. 25, 26): Ἡμεῖς—τοιοῦτοί ἐσμεν, ὡς ἐνίοτε καὶ τὸν τῶν κακῶς ἀρχόντων ἐν τοῖς ἔθνεσιν ὑπερβάλλειν τύφον, καὶ μονονουχὶ ζητεῖν ὡς οἱ βασιλεῖς δορυφόρους, καὶ φοβεροὺς ἑαυτοὺς καὶ δυσπροσίτους μάλιστα τοῖς πένησι κατασκευάζοντες, τοιοῦτοί ἐσμεν πρὸς αὐτοὺς ἐντυγχάνοντας ἡμῖν, καὶ περί τινων ἀξιοῦντας, ὡς οὐδὲ οἱ τύραννοι, καὶ ὠμότεροι τῶν ἀρχόντων πρὸς τοὺς ἱκέτας. Καὶ ἔστι γε ἰδεῖν ἐν πολλαῖς νομιζομέναις ἐκκλησίαις, καὶ μάλιστα ταῖς τῶν μειζόνων πόλεων, τοὺς ἡγουμένους τοῦ λαοῦ τοῦ θεοῦ μηδεμίαν ἰσολογίαν ἐπιτρέποντας, ἔσθ' ὅτε καὶ τοῖς καλλίστοις τῶν Ἰησοῦ μαθητῶν, εἶναι πρὸς αὐτούς. καὶ ταῦτα πάντα μοι λέλεκται βουλομένῳ κατὰ τὸν λόγον παραστῆσαι, ὅτι οὐ μιμητέον τῷ ἄρχοντι τῆς ἐκκλησίας τὸν ἄρχοντα τῶν ἐθνῶν, κ. τ. λ. Cf. ejusd. in Matth. Commentariorum series, § 9: Sicut autem super cathedram Moysi—sic et super cathedram ecclesiasticam sedent quidam dicentes, quae facere oporteat unumquemque, non autem facientes, et alligantes onera gravia et imponunt super humeros hominum, ipsi nec digito volentes ea movere (Matth. xxiii. 2, 3). Ibid. § 10, 12, 14, 61, in Num. Hom. ii. 1, in Esaiam Hom. vii. 3. Cyprian. de Lapsis: Episcopi plurimi, quos et hortamento esse oportet caeteris et exemplo, divina procuratione contemta, procuratores rerum saeculariam fieri; derelicta cathedra, plebe deserta, per alienas provincias oberrantes, negotiationis quaestuosae nundinas aucupari; esurientibus in ecclesia fratribus, habere argentum largiter velle, fundos insidiosis fraudibus rapere, usuris multiplicantibus fenus augere.

[8] Compare the objections which were made to Paul of Samosata, in the writing of the synod at Antioch, which had been assembled against him, ap. Euseb. vii. 30. He drew from his episcopal jurisdiction unlawful gain, in the exercise of it imitated civil rulers, by causing to be erected for himself a *βῆμα καὶ θρόνον ὑψηλόν*, by having a *σήκρητον*, like worldly judges, and frequently giving himself up to the greatest violence. In the church he caused applause to be dealt out to him by the waving of handkerchiefs and clapping of hands. This was justly condemned; but since the clapping of hands, by way of applause, was universal in the fourth century, it may be assumed that Paul was not the only bishop of his time who willingly put up with it.

[9] Comp. § 30, note 12. Cyprian. Epist. 68: Plebs ipse maxime habet potestatem vel eligendi dignos sacerdotes, vel indignos recusandi. Quod et ipsum videmus de divina auctitorate descendere, ut sacerdos plebe praesente sub omnium oculis deligatur, et dignus atque idoneus publico judicio ac testimonio comprobetur, sicut in Numeris Dominus Moysi praecepit dicens: Apprehende Aaron fratrem et Eleazarum filium ejus, et impone eos in montem coram omni synagoga, etc. (Num. xx. 25.) Coram omni synagoga jubet Deus constitui sacerdotem, id est, instruit et ostendit, ordinationes sacerdotales non nisi sub populi assistentis conscientia fiere oportere, ut plebe praesente vel detegantur malorum crimina vel bonorum merita praedicentur, et sit ordinatio justa et legitima, quae omnium suffragio et judicio fuerit examinata. Propter quod diligenter de traditione divina et apostolica observatione servandum est et tenendum, quod apud nos quoque et fere per provincias universas tenetur; ut ad ordinationes rite celebrandas ad eam plebem, cui praepositus ordinatur, episcopi ejusdem provinciae proximi quique conveniant, et episcopus deligatur plebe praesente, quae singulorum vitam plenissime novit, et uniuscujusque actum de ejus conversatione perspexit. Origenes in Levit. Hom. vi. c. 3. Hence in Cyprian: Episcopus factus de Dei et Christi ejus judicio, de clericorum testimonio, de plebis suffragio (Epist. 52, cf. Ep. 41), cf. Lamprid. in Sev. Alex. c. 45 (§ 56, note 6) F. A. Staudenmaier's Gesch. der Bischofswahlen. Tübingen. 1830. S. 20.

first to be approved by the church.[10] In the discharge of his duties the bishop had not only to consult his presbyters,[11] but even in certain cases to ask the opinion of the whole church.[12] There were even yet cases in which laymen learned in the Scriptures publicly taught in the church with permission of the bishops.[13]

[10] Cyprian. Ep. 65. Diaconi ab episcopis fiunt. Ep. 33, ad Clerum et plebem Carthag. In ordinationibus clericis, fratres carissimi, solemus vos ante consulere, et mores ac merita singulorum communi consilio ponderare. Cornelii Ep. ad Fabium (ap. Euseb. vi. 43, 7): At the ordination of Novatian as presbyter *ὁ ἐπίσκοπος διακωλυόμενος ὑπὸ παντὸς τοῦ κλήρου, ἀλλὰ καὶ λαϊκῶν πολλῶν, ἠξίωσε συγχωρηθῆναι αὐτῷ τοῦτον μόνον χειροτονῆσαι.* Cf. Vales. ad h. l.

[11] In Cyprian often, consulere presbyterium, consilio communi res tractare, etc. Comp. Conc. Carthagin. gener. iv. v. J. 398, can. 23 (Mansii, iii. p. 953): Episcopus nullus causam audiat absque praesentia clericorum suorum: alioquin irrita erit sententia Episcopi, nisi clericorum sententia confirmetur. Concerning the right of voting at synods, see Ziegler in Henke's Neuem Magazin, Bd. 1, S. 165, ff.

[12] Cyprian. Ep. 5, ad Presbyt. et Diac.: Quando a primordio episcopatus mei statuerim, nihil sine consilio vestro et sine consensu plebis mea privatim sententia gerere. So particularly at the readmittance of the lapsed. Cypriani Ep. 11, ad Plebem: Exspectent (lapsi) regressionem nostram, ut—convocati episcopi plures secundum Domini disciplinam, et Confessorum praesentiam, et vestram quoque sententiam beatorum martyrum litteras et desideria examinare possimus. Ep. 13, ad Clerum: Hoc enim et verecundiae et disciplinae et vitae ipsi omnium nostrum convenit, ut praepositi cum clero convenientes, praesente etiam stantium plebe, quibus et ipsis pro fide et timore suo honor habendus est, disponere omnia consilii communis religione possimus. Ep. 17, ad Presbyt. et Diac.: Quae res cum omnium nostrum consilium et sententiam exspectet, praejudicare ego et soli mihi rem communem vindicare non audeo. Ep. 28, ad Eosdem: Cui rei non potui me solum judicem dare, cum—haec singulorum tractanda sit et limanda plenius ratio, non tantum cum collegis meis, sed et cum plebe ipsa universa. That the same principles were acted on at Rome is clear from Ep. Cleri Rom. ad Cypr. (Ep. Cypr. 31).—Cypriani Ep. 9, ad Clerum: Presbyters who have admitted the lapsed to church communion must agere et apud nos, et apud confessores ipsos, et apud plebem universam causam suam. Cf. du Pin de Ant. Eccl. disc. p. 246, ss. J. H. Boehmeri xii. Dissert. juris eccl. ant. ed. ii. p. 149, ss.

[13] Epist. Alexandri Episc. Hierosol. et Theoctisti Caesariensis ad Demetrium Alexandr. (ap. Euseb. vi. 19, 7). In the case of Origen: *Προσέθηκας δὲ τοῖς γράμμασιν, ὅτι τοῦτο οὐδέ ποτε ἠκούσθη, οὐδὲ νῦν γεγένηται, τὸ, παρόντων ἐπισκόπων λαϊκοὺς ὁμιλεῖν, οὐκ οἶδ᾽ ὅπως προφανῶς οὐκ ἀληθῆ λέγων. Ὅπου γοῦν εὑρίσκονται οἱ ἐπιτήδειοι πρὸς τὸ ὠφελεῖν τοὺς ἀδελφοὺς, καὶ παρακαλοῦνται τῷ λαῷ προσομιλεῖν ὑπὸ τῶν ἁγίων ἐπισκόπων· ὥσπερ ἐν Λαράνδοις Εὔελπις ὑπὸ Νέωνος, καὶ ἐν Ἰκονίῳ Παυλῖνος ὑπὸ Κέλσου καὶ ἐν Συννάδοις Θεόδωρος ὑπὸ Ἀττικοῦ τῶν μακαρίων ἀδελφῶν· εἰκὸς δὲ καὶ ἐν ἄλλοις τόποις τοῦτο γίνεσθαι, ἡμᾶς δὲ μὴ εἰδέναι.* So also Constitt. Apost. viii. c. 32: *Ὁ διδάσκων, εἰ καὶ λαϊκὸς ᾖ, ἔμπειρος δὲ τοῦ λόγου, καὶ τὸν τρόπον σεμνὸς, διδασκέτω· ἔσοντα γὰρ πάντες διδακτοὶ θεοῦ* (Jo. vi. 45): and Conc. Carthag. gener. iv. c. 98 (Mansi, iii. p 959): Laicus praesentibus clericis nisi ipsis jubentibus docere non audeat.

§ 70.

DIVINE SERVICE.

In the third century the traces of buildings devoted exclusively to Christian worship become more frequent and obvious;[1] and as early as the peaceful times between the Valerian and Diocletian persecutions, splendid edifices had been erected for this purpose.[2] These were called προσευκτήριον, κυριακόν, dominicum, οἶκος ἐκκλησίας and simply ἐκκλησία. From the time of Constantine they were also styled ναός, templum, but never fanum and delubrum. In imitation of the temple of Jerusalem, a part of the interior was inaccessible to the people (ἁγίασμα, βῆμα, chorus), where the wooden table for the Lord's Supper τράπεζα, mensa sacra) stood beside the seats of the clergy (καθέδρα, θρόνοι).[3] Though the Christians were fond of certain religious symbols on many of their household utensils,[4] yet nothing of this kind was allowed in the churches.[5]

At the time of Origen, the Christians had no other general festivals besides Sunday, than the *parasceve* (preparation) the *passover*, and the feast of *pentecost*.[6] Soon, after, however, there appears to have been added to them the feast of *the ascension* (ἡ ἑορτὴ τῆς ἀναλήψεως τοῦ Κυρίου).[7] So also in Egypt,

[1] Under Severus Alexander (§ 56, note 6) then in Cyprian, Dionysius of Alexandria, etc. Comp. above, § 53, note 10.

[2] Euseb. H. E. viii. 1, 2: Μηδαμῶς ἔτι τοῖς παλαιοῖς οἰκοδομήμασιν ἀρκούμενοι, εὐρείας εἰς πλάτος ἀνὰ πάσας τὰς πόλεις ἐκ θεμελίων ἀνίστων ἐκκλησίας.

[3] A prescription respecting the planning of churches is found in Constitt. Apost. ii. 57. A description of the church at Tyre apud Euseb. x. 4, 15, ss.

[4] So on the seal-rings, a dove, a ship, a lyre, an anchor, a fish, etc. Clem. Alex. Paedag. iii. p. 289. Tertullianus de Pudic. c. 7, mentions the picturae calicum representing the ovis perdita a Domino requisita, et humeris ejus revecta, but does not seem (cap. 10), to approve of it. Münter's Sinnbilder der alten Christen. Heft 1, S. 7, f.

[5] Can. Illiberit. 36: Placuit, picturas in ecclesia esse non debere, ne quod colitur et adoratur, in parietibus depingatur. The older Catholic theologians, for example Baronius, Bellarmine, Perronius, etc., tried many ways of evading the force of this canon; on the contrary, the true meaning of it, with its historical consequences, has been acknowledged by Petavius Dogm. theol. lib. xv. c. 13, no. 3. Pagius Crit. ad ann. 55, no. 4. 18, especially Natalis Alexander ad Hist. eccl. saec. iii. Diss. 21, Art. 2.

[6] Origen. contra Cels. viii. p. 392.

[7] First mentioned in the Constitt. Apostol. v. 19; and considered by Augustine (Ep. 118 ad Januar.) as an ancient festival. See Krabbe über die apost. Constitutionen, S. 176, ff.

toward the end of the third century, they began to observe, after the example of Basilides' followers,[8] the *epiphany* (τὰ ἐπιφάνια) on the sixth of January, but according to the orthodox view of the appearance of the Logos on earth (ἡ ἐπιφάνεια) not simply as the festival of his baptism, but also as that of his birth. The arrangement of Divine worship at this time is found in the Constitt. Apost. ii. 57. At the agapae, the clergy and poor were particularly remembered (l. c. ii. 28).

The respect paid to martyrs still maintains the same character as in the second century, differing only in degree, not in kind, from the honor shown to other esteemed dead. As the churches held the yearly festivals of their martyrs at the graves of the latter,[9] so they willingly assembled frequently in the burial places of their deceased friends,[10] for which they used in many places even caves (cryptae, catacumbae).[11] At the cele-

[8] Comp. § 45, note 2. So also Jablonski de Orig. festi nativ. Christi diss. i. § 7. (Opusc. ed. te Water, iii. p. 328, ss.) Differently Neander gnost. Systeme, S. 49, 81, and Kirchengesch. i. i. S. 519. On the other side see Hallische A. L. Z. April, 1823, S. 836.

[9] Comp. § 53, note 46. A remarkable accommodation of Gregory Thaumaturgus, see Vita S. Gregorii Thaumat. per Gregor. Nyssenum (ed. G. Vosii, p. 312): *Συνιδὼν ὅτι ταῖς σωματικαῖς θυμηδίας τῇ περὶ τὰ εἴδωλα πλάνῃ παραμένει τὸ νηπιῶδες τῶν πολλῶν καὶ ἀπαίδευτον· ὡς ἂν τὸ προηγούμενον τέως ἐν αὐτοὶς μάλιστα κατορθωθείη τὸ πρὸς τὸν θεὸν ἀντὶ τῶν ματαίων σεβασμάτων βλέπειν, ἐφῆκεν αὐτοῖς ταῖς τῶν ἁγίων μαρτύρων ἐμφαιδρύνεσθαι μνήμαις καὶ εὐπαθεῖν καὶ ἀγάλλεσθαι.*

[10] Constitt. Apost. v. c. 8: *Συναθροίζεσθε ἐν τοῖς κοιμητηρίοις, τὴν ἀνάγνωσιν τῶν ἱερῶν βιβλίων ποιούμενοι, καὶ ψάλλοντες ὑπὲρ τῶν κεκοιμημένων μαρτύρων καὶ πάντων τῶν ἀπ' αἰῶνος ἁγίων, καὶ τῶν ἀδελφῶν ὑμῶν τῶν ἐν κυρίῳ κεκοιμημένων· καὶ τὴν ἀντίτυπον τοῦ βασιλείου σώματος Χριστοῦ δεκτὴν εὐχαριστίαν προσφέρετε ἔν τε ταῖς ἐκκλησίαις ὑμῶν, καὶ ἐν τοῖς κοιμητηρίοις.* Hence Aemilianus, governor of Egypt, said to the Christians brought before him in the Decian persecution (Dionys. Alex. ap. Euseb. vii. 11, 4): *Οὐδαμῶς δὲ ἐξέσται ὑμῖν—ἢ συνόδους ποιεῖσθαι, ἢ εἰς τὰ καλούμενα κοιμητήρια εἰσιέναι.* So also the proconsul of Africa (Acta proconsularia S. Cypriani, c. 1). Gallienus removed this prohibitory rule (see above, § 56, note 14); but Maximinus afterward renewed it (Euseb. ix. c. 2). These burial-places were called *χοιμητήριον*, dormitorium.

[11] Christian catacombs are found in Rome, Naples, Syracuse, and Malta. In the year 1844 they were also discovered on the island Melos. Respecting the Roman catacombs, Hieronymus in Ezechiel. c. 40: Dum essem Romae puer, et liberalibus studiis erudirer, solebam cum caeteris ejusdem aetatis et propositi diebus dominicis sepulchra Apostolorum et Martyrum circuire: crebroque cryptas ingredi, quae in terrarum profunda defossae, ex utraque parte ingredientium per parietes habent corpora sepulturarum, et ita obscura sunt omnia, ut propemodum illud propheticum compleatur: descendant ad infernum viventes, etc. Cf. Prudentius *περὶ στεφ.* hymn. xi. Passio Hippolyti, v. 153, ss.—Modern descriptions of the catacombs in Rome, Pauli Aringhi Roma subterranea novissima. Paris. 1659. 2 voll. fol. M. A. Boldetti Osservazioni sopra i Cimiteri de SS. Martiri, ed antichi Cristiani di Roma. 1720. 2 t. fol. See farther the works of Bottari, Ciampini, etc. (see Münter's Sinnbilder d. alten Christen. Heft. 1, S. 24). Volkmann's histor. krit. Nachrichten v. Italien. (Leipz. 3 Bde. 1777), iii. 67. A description of the city of Rome by Platner, Bunsen, Gerhard, and Röstell (Stuttgart and Tübingen. 1830. i. 355); Respecting those

bration of the Lord's Supper, both the living who brought oblations, as well as the dead, and the martyrs for whom offerings were presented, especially on the anniversary of their death, were included by name in the prayer of the church.[12] Inasmuch as the re-admission of a sinner into the church was thought to stand in close connection with the forgiveness of sin, an opinion was associated with the older custom of restoring to church communion the lapsed who had been again received by the martyrs, that the martyrs could also be serviceable in obtaining the forgiveness of sins.[13] In doing so they set out in part with the idea, which is very natural, that the dead prayed for the living, as the living prayed for the dead,[14] but that the intercession of martyrs abiding in the society of the Lord, would be of peculiar efficacy on behalf of their brethren:[15] while they partly thought that the martyrs, as assessors in the last decisive judgment, were particularly active (1 Cor. vi. 2, 3).[16]

in Naples: Pellicia de Christ. eccl. politia. tom. iii. P. ii. Diss. 5. Chr. F. Bellermann über die ältesten christl. Begräbnisstätten, u. bes. die Katakomben zu Neapel mit ihren Wandgemälden. Hamburg. 1839. 4: Respecting those in Sicily, see Bartel's Briefe über Calabrien u. Sicilien. (Götting. 3 Th. 1787–91), iii. 203. Münter's Nachrichten v. Neapel und Sicilien, S. 344.—By the "Congregation of Relics and Indulgences," the symbol of the palm and the pretended blood-vessels (which were more probably used in the celebration of the eucharist) have been established as marks of the graves of martyrs; but that they are not sufficient marks is shown by Eusebius Romanus (Mabillon) de cultu Sanctorum ignotorum. Paris. 1688. 4. In the second edition, however, he was obliged to yield. 1705. (The church in the Catacombs, by Dr. C. Maitland. London, 1846. 8vo).

[12] These registers of names, since they were not always the same, were inscribed for each occasion on the writing-tables then used (diptycha, δίπτυχα), and afterward erased. Hence the appellation diptycha was used of the lists of names of persons to be mentioned at the communion service, though these lists afterward assumed a more permanent character after all the offerentes were no longer called by name. This, and the peculiar names diptycha episcoporum, dipt. vivorum, dipt. mortuorum, first occur in the fifth century. Chr. A. Salig. de Diptychis veterum tam profanis quam sacris. Halae. 1731. 4.

[13] Against this notion great zeal is shown by Tertull. de Pudicitia, c. 22: In ipsa securitate et possessione martyrii quis permittit homini donare quae Deo reservanda sunt?—Sufficiat martyri propria delicta purgasse. Ingrati vel superbi est in alios quoque spargere, quod pro magno fuerit consecutus. On the other hand, even Cyprian, Ep. 12 and 13, admits, Christianos auxilio Martyrum adjuvari apud Dominum in delictis suis posse.

[14] Cypriani Epist. 57 ad Cornelium: Memores nostri invicem simus,—utrobique pro nobis semper oremus,—et si quis istinc nostrum prior divinae dignationis celeritate praecesserit, perseveret apud Dominum nostra dilectio, pro fratribus et sororibus nostris apud misericordiam patris non cesset oratio.

[15] Cyprian writes to confessors, Ep. 15: Vox illa purificatione confessionis illustris—impetrat de domini bonitate quod postulat; and Ep. 77: Nunc vobis in precibus efficacior sermo est, et ad impetrandum quod in pressuris petitur facilior oratio est.

[16] Cyprianus de Lapsis: Credimus quidem posse apud judicem plurimum Martyrum merita et opera justorum: sed cum judicii dies venerit, cum post occasum saeculi hujus et mundi ante tribunal Christi populos ejus adsteterit. Martyrs are, according to Dionysius

Origen attributed very great value to that intercession, in expecting from it great help toward sanctification;[17] but he went beyond the ideas hitherto entertained in attributing to martyrdom an importance and efficacy similar to the death of Christ.[18] Hence he feared the cessation of persecution as a misfortune.[19] The more the opinion that value belonged to the intercession of martyrs was established,[20] the oftener it may have happened that persons recommended themselves to the martyrs yet living for intercession, i. e. after their death.[21] On the other hand, no trace is found of in-

Alex. ab. Euseb. H. E. vi. 42, 3: *Οἱ νῦν τοῦ Χριστοῦ πάρεδροι καὶ τῆς βασιλείας αὐτοῦ κοινωνοὶ, καὶ μέτοχοι τῆς κρίσεως αὐτοῦ, καὶ συνδικάζοντες αὐτῷ.*

[17] Origenes in Cant. Cant. lib. iii. ed. de la Rue. t. iii. p. 75: Sed et omnes sancti, qui de hac vita decesserunt, habentes adhuc charitatem erga eos qui in hoc mundo sunt si dicantur curam gerere salutis eorum et juvare eos precibus suis atque interventu suo apud Deum non erit inconveniens.—In libr. Jesu Nave, Hom. xvi. 5: Ego sic arbitror, quod omnes illi, qui dormierunt ante nos, patres pugnent nobiscum et adjuvent nos orationibus suis. Ita namque etiam quemdam de senioribus magistris audivi dicentem in eo loco, in quo scriptum est in Numeris (xxii. 4), quia ablinget synagoga illa hanc synagogam, sicut ablingit vitulus herbam viridem in campo. Dicebat ergo: Quare hujusmodi similitudo assumpta est, nisi quia hoc est, quod intelligendum est in hoc loco, quod synagoga Domini, quae nos praecessit in sanctis, ore et lingua consumit adversariam synagogam, i. e., orationibus et precibus adversarios nostros absumit?—in epist. ad Rom. lib. ii. 4: Jam vero si etiam extra corpus positi vel sancti, qui cum Christo sunt, agunt aliquid, et laborant pro nobis ad similitudinem angelorum, qui salutis nostrae ministeria procurant: vel rursum peccatores etiam ipsi extra corpus positi agunt aliquid secundum propositum mentis suae, ad angelorum nihilominus similitudinem sinistrorum, cum quibus et in aeternum ignem mittendi dicuntur a Christo: habeatur et hoc quoque inter occulta Dei, nec chartulae committenda mysteria.

[18] Origenis Exhort. ad Martyr. c. 30: *'Επίστησον εἰ τὸ κατὰ τὸ μαρτύριον βάπτισμα, ὥσπερ τὸ τοῦ σωτῆρος καθάρσιον γέγονε τοῦ κόσμου, καὶ αὐτὸ ἐπὶ πολλῶν θεραπείᾳ καθαιρόμενον γίνεται. ὡς γὰρ οἱ τῷ κατὰ τὸν Μωσέως νόμον θυσιαστηρίῳ προσεδρεύοντες διακονεῖν ἐδόκουν δι' αἵματος ταυρῶν καὶ τράγων ἄφεσιν ἁμαρτημάτων ἐκείνοις οὕτως αἱ ψυχαὶ τῶν πεπελεκισμένων ἕνεκεν τῆς μαρτυρίας 'Ιησοῦ μὴ μάτην τῷ ἐν οὐρανοῖς θυσιαστηρίῳ παρεδρεύουσαι διακονοῦσι τοῖς εὐχομένοις ἄφεσιν ἁμαρτημάτων.* Cap. 50: *Ταχα δὲ καὶ ὥσπερ τιμίῳ αἵματι τοῦ 'Ιησοῦ ἠγοράσθημεν,—οὕτως τῷ τιμίῳ αἵματι τῶν μαρτύρων ἀγορασθήσονταί τινες.* Cf. in Numeros Hom. xxiv. 1.

[19] Origenes in Num. Hom. x. 2: Et quidem quod Dominus noster J. Chr venerit, ut tolleret peccatum mundi, et morte sua peccata nostra deleverit, nullus, qui Christo credit, ignorat. Quomodo autem et filii ejus auferant peccata sanctorum, i. e., Apostoli et Martyres, si poterimus, ex scripturis divinis probare tentabimus. (He appeals to 2 Cor. xii. 15, 2 Tim. iv. 6, Apoc. vi. 9.) Unde ergo vereor, ne forte, ex quo Martyres non fiunt, et hostiae sanctorum non offeruntur pro peccatis nostris, peccatorum nostrorum remissionem non mereamur. Et ideo etiam diabolus, sciens, per passionem Martyrii remissionem fieri peccatorum, non vult nobis publicas Gentilium persecutiones movere.

[20] The Origenist Eusebius refers on this point, Praep. evang. xii. c. 3, first to Plato de Legg. lib. xi., then: *Καὶ ἐν τῇ βίβλῳ δὲ τῶν Μακκαβαίων* (2 Macc. xv. 14) *λέγεται 'Ιερεμίας ὁ προφήτης μετὰ τὴν ἀπαλλαγὴν τοῦ βίου εὐχόμενος ὁρᾶσθαι ὑπὲρ τοῦ λαοῦ, ὡς φροντίδα ποιούμενος τῶν ἐπὶ γῆς ἀνθρώπων. Δεῖ δέ φησι καὶ ὁ Πλάτων τούτοις πιστεύειν.*

[21] So Eusebius de Martyr. Palaest. cap. 7, relates that a maiden, Theodosia in Caesarea was added to the Martyrs expecting their death, *ὁμοῦ φιλοφρονουμένη, καὶ οἷα εἰκὸς ὑπὲρ οὗ μνημονεύειν αὐτῆς πρὸς τὸν κύριον γενομένους παρακαλοῦσα.*

vocation of the dead, since the idea was not yet entertained of the living being able to make known their requests to them.

§ 71.

CHURCH DISCIPLINE.

Memorials of the ecclesiastical discipline of this period exist in the Epistolae canonicae of Dionysius bishop of Alexandria, of Gregory Thaumaturgus (both about 260), and Peter, bishop of Alexandria, A.D. 306; the canons of the councils of Illiberis (305 ?), Arles (314), Ancyra (315), and Neo-Caesarea (315). All these are found in collections of the councils, and in Routh's Reliquiae Sacrae.

After the holiest transactions of public worship began to be treated as mysteries, the mode of admission to Christianity naturally assumed another form. A preparatory course preceded it, in which the catechumens (*κατηχούμενοι*) were instructed by suitable teachers (catechistes, doctor audientium)[1] and prepared for baptism through different classes (*ἀκροώμενοι*, audientes, *γονυκλίνοντες*, genuflectentes, *βαπτιζόμενοι*, *φωτιζόμενοι*, competentes).[2] The condition of catechumen usually continued several years; but the catechumens often deferred even baptism as long as possible, on account of the remission of sins by which it was to be accompanied.[3] Hence it was often necessary to baptize the sick; and for them the rite of sprinkling was introduced (baptismus clinicorum, *τῶν κλινικῶν*).[4] The baptism of children was more common.[5] The exorcism of those about to be baptized is

[1] At this time the positive doctrines had not yet been kept secret from the catechumens. See the rule respecting their instructions in Const. Apost. vii. 39.

[2] In Tertullian and Cyprian the audientes and catechumeni are synonymous. In Origen contra Cels. iii. 481. ed. de la Rue, Boehmer christl. Kirchl. Alterthumswissenschaft, ii. 287, and Rothe de Disciplinae arcani origine p. 13 find three classes of catechumens. See, on the other side C. F. W. Hasselbach de Catechumenorum ordinibus, quot fuerint in vetere Eccl. graeca et lat., 1839, and Redepenning's Origenes, i. 358. The *γονυκλίνοντες* are first mentioned by Conc. Neocaesar. can. 5. Nicaen. can. 14. Tob. Pfanner de Catechumenis antiquae ecclesiae. Francof. et Goth. 1688. 12. Bingham Antiquitt. lib. x. (vol. iv.).

[3] Disapproved, Constit. Apost. vi. 15: *Ὁ δὲ λέγων, ὅτι ὅταν τελευτῶ, βαπτίζομαι, ἵνα μὴ ἁμαρτήσω καὶ ῥυπανῶ τὸ βάπτισμα, οὗτος ἄγνοιαν ἔχει θεοῦ, καὶ τῆς ἑαυτοῦ φύσεως ἐπιλήσμων τυγχάνει.*

[4] Cf. Cypriani Ep. 76. ad Magnum, that the baptism of them ought not to be regarded as invalid, eo quod aqua salutari non loti sunt, sed perfusi.

[5] Comp. § 53, note 20. Origen found the baptism of children already existing in his circle, and defended it. Walli Hist. Baptism. Infant. P. i. p. 72, ss.—Fidus, an African bishop, believed, considerandam esse legem circumcisionis antiquae, ut intra octavum diem eum, qui natus est, baptizandum et sanctificandum non putaret. On the other hand, Cyprian,

now distinctly mentioned;[6] and all baptized persons, even children, received the eucharist. When the congregations became larger presbyters and deacons baptized in addition to the bishop. In the west, however, the baptized had to receive from the bishop the imposition of hands.[7] In the east the baptizing presbyters performed this ceremony.[8]

As those who were excommunicated were universally supposed to be under the dominion of the devil,[9] as much as the unbaptized, they had to undergo, as poenitentes, a similar though more severe probation-period than the catechumens, before they could be again received (pacem dare, reconciliare).[10] The No-

with his provincial synod (Epist. 64 ad Fidum), a baptismo atque a gratia Dei, qui omnibus et misericors, et benignus, et pius est, neminem per nos debere prohiberi. Wall. l. c. p. 94, ss.

[6] Comp. § 53, note 24. Vincentius a Thibari (in Conc. Carth. in the year 256): Ergo primo per manos impositionem in exorcismo, secundo per baptismi regenerationem, tunc possunt ad Christi pollicitationem venire.

[7] Cyprianus Ep. 73. ad Jubajanum: Nunc quoque apud nos geritur, ut qui in Ecclesia baptizantur praepositis Ecclesiae offerantur, et per nostram orationem ac manus impositionem Spiritum Sanctum consequantur et signaculo dominico consummentur. Conc. Illib. can. 38, 67.

[8] Constit. Apost. vii. 43, 44.

[9] The expression παραδοῦναι τῷ Σατανᾷ, 1 Cor. v. 5, 1 Tim. i. 20, referred to excommunication. Origines in lib. Judic. Hom. ii. § 5, in Jer. Hom. xviii. § 14, Selecta in Jer. xxix. 4.

[10] In what relation this admission was supposed to stand to the forgiveness of sins may be seen from Firmiliani Ep. ad Cypr. (Ep. Cypr. 75): Per singulos annos seniores et praepositi in unum convenimus,—ut si qua graviora sunt, communi consilio dirigantur, lapsis quoque fratribus et post lavacrum salutare a diabolo vulneratis per poenitentiam medela quaeratur: non quasi a nobis remissionem peccatorum consequantur, sed ut per nos ad intelligentiam delictorum suorum convertantur, et Domino plenius satisfacere cogantur. Cyprian. de Lapsis: Nemo se fallat, nemo se decipiat. Solus Dominus misereri potest: veniam peccatis, quae in ipsum commissa sunt, solus potest ille largiri, qui peccata nostra portavit.—Homo Deo esse non potest major; nec remittere aut donare indulgentia sua servus potest quod in Dominum delicto graviore commissum est, Dominus orandus est, Dominus nostra satisfactione placandus est, qui negantem negare se dixit, qui omne judicium de patre solus accepit.—Confiteantur singuli, quaeso vos, fratres dilectissimi, delictum suum, dum adhuc qui deliquit in saeculo est, dum admitti confessio ejus potest, dum satisfactio et remissio facta per sacerdotes apud Dominum grata est.—Rogamus vos, ut pro vobis Deum rogare possimus. Preces ipsas ad vos prius vertimus, quibus Deum pro vobis ut misereatur, oramus. (Later, Leo I. about 450, Ep. 89: Sic divinae bonitatis praesidia ordinata, ut indulgentia Dei nisi supplicationibus sacerdotum nequeat obtineri). Farther Cypriani Ep. 52: Pignus vitae in data pace percipiunt:—accepta pace commeatus a Deo datur. Comp. above, § 67, note 1. The reconciliation was no actus ordinis, but jurisdictionis, and could therefore be transferred from the bishop himself to a deacon. Cypr. Ep. 12, directs, ut qui libellos a martyribus acceperunt, et praerogativa eorum apud Deum adjuvari possunt (Ep. 13, et auxilio eorum adjuvari apud Dominum in delictis suis possunt), si incommodo aliquo et infirmitatis periculo occupati fuerint, non expectata praesentia nostra, apud presbyterum quemcunque praesentem, vel si presbyter repertus non fuerit, et urgere exitus coeperit, apud diaconum quoque exomologesin facere delicti sui possint: ut manu eis in poenitentiam imposita veniant ad Dominum cum pace, quam dari martyres litteris ad nos factis desideraverunt.

vatian disputes occasioned the orientals to appoint a *πρεσβύτερος ἐπὶ τῆς μετανοίας* in the separate churches;[11] and this seems to have had an influence in bringing it about that public penance, even at the end of the third century, had a succession of grades similar to the probation-period of the catechumens.[12] The four gradus or stationes poenitentiae were *πρόσκλαυσις, ἀκρόασις, ὑπόπτωσις, σύστασις* (*προσκλαίοντες, χειμάζοντες*, flentes, hiemantes, *ἀκροώμενοι*, audientes, *γονυκλίνοντες, ὑποπίπτοντες*, genuflectentes, substrati, *συνιστάμενοι*, consistentes). Excommunication fell only on public, gross offenses. Other sinners were referred to the admonition of the more experienced brethren.[13]

[11] Socrates, v. c. 19: *'Αφ' οὗ Ναυατιανοὶ τῆς ἐκκλησίας διεκρίθησαν,—οἱ ἐπίσκοποι τῷ ἐκκλησιαστικῷ κανόνι τὸν πρεσβύτερον τὸν ἐπὶ τῆς μετανοίας προσέθεσαν, ὅπως ἂν οἱ μετὰ τὸ βάπτισμα πταίσαντες ἐπὶ τοῦ προβληθέντος τούτου πρεσβυτέρου ἐξομολογῶνται τὰ ἁμαρτήματα.* Cf. Sozomenus, viii. c. 16.

[12] Cyprian knows nothing of these grades. He sets forth the arrangement to be pursued with the penitent, Epist. 11: Nam cum in minoribus delictis, quae non in Deum committuntur, poenitentia agatur justo tempore, et exomologesis fiat inspecta vita ejus qui agit poenitentiam, nec ad communicationem venire quis possit, nisi prius illi ab episcopo et clero manus fuerit imposita: quanto magis in his gravissimis et extremis delictis caute omnia—observari oportet: In like manner they are not found in the course prescribed for penitents in Const. Apost. ii. 16. The grades are first mentioned in (since Gregor. Thaumat. Epist. canonica, can. ii., as Morinus de Poen. lib. vi. c. 1, § 9, has shown, is spurious, and arose from Basilii Epist. 217, or Canonica, iii. c. 75, see Routh Reliqu. Sacr. ii. p. 458, ss.) Conc. Ancyr. c. 4. Conc. Nicaen. c. 11. J. Morinus de Disciplina in administratione sacramenti poenitentiae. Paris 1651. fol. J. Dallaeus de Sacramentali s. auriculari Latinorum confessione. Genev. 1661. 8. Sam. Basnagii Annales politico-eccles. t. ii. p. 475. Bingham, lib. xviii. in vol. viii.

[13] Origenes in Psalm. xxxvii. Hom. ii. § 6: Oportet peccatum non celare intrinsecus. Fortassis enim sicut ii, qui habent intus inclusam escam indigestam, aut humoris vel phlegmatis stomacho graviter et moleste immanentis abundantiam, si vomuerint, relevantur: ita etiam hi qui peccaverunt, si quidem occultant, et retinent intra se peccatum, intrinsecus urgentur et propemodum suffocantur a phlegmate vel humore peccati: si autem ipse sui accusator fiat, dum accusat semetipsum et confitetur, simul evomit et delictum, atque omnem morbi digerit causam. Tantummodo circumspice diligentius, cui debeas confiteri peccatum tuum. Proba prius medicum cui debeas causam languoris exponere, qui sciat infirmari cum infirmante, flere cum flente, qui condolendi et compatiendi noverit disciplinam: ut ita demum, si quid ille dixerit, qui se prius et eruditum medicum ostenderit et misericordem, si quid consilii dederit, facias, et sequaris, si intellexerit et praeviderit, talem esse languorem tuum, qui in conventu totius Ecclesia exponi debeat et curari, ex quo fortassis et ceteri aedificari poterunt, et tu ipse facile sanari: multa hoc deliberatione, et satis perito medici illius consilio procurandum est. Of course application was especially made to the clergy: hence Origenes in Levit. Hom. ii. § 4: Est—per poenitentiam remissio peccatorum, cum lavat peccator in lacrymis stratum suum,—et cum non erubescit sacerdoti Domini indicare peccatum suum, et quaerere medicinam. In Levit. Hom. v. § 4: Discant sacerdotes Domini, qui Ecclesiis praesunt, quia pars eis data est cum his, quorum delicta repropitiaverint. Quid autem est repropitiare delictum? Si assumseris peccatorem, et monendo, hortando, docendo, instruendo adduxeris eum ad poenitentiam ab errore correxeris, a vitiis emendaveris, et effeceris eum talem, ut ei converso propitius fiat Deus pro delicto, repropitiasse diceris.

The time of penance usually continued several years—sometimes even to the hour of death.[14] In Africa and Spain, re-admission was forever forbidden in case of certain offenses.[15] This strictness was relaxed only when confessors interceded on behalf of the lapsed.[16] But during the Decian persecution, the martyrs in Africa abused this privilege granted them by custom, so much that Cyprian was obliged to oppose them.[17] Yet this

[14] The determinations Constitt. Apost. ii. 16, 21–24, are distinguished by great mildness, Comp. Drey über die Constit. S. 51.

[15] Comp. § 53, note 39, § 59, note 10. So also Cyprian before the Decian persecution, Testim. adv. Judaeos, iii. c. 28: Non posse in ecclesia remitti ei, qui in Deum deliquerit. On the contrary in Rome the penitent lapsi were admitted on the sick bed. Ep. Cleri Rom. ad Cler. Carthag. Among Cyprian's letters, Ep. 2.

[16] Comp. above, § 53, note 44. Dionysius Alex. ap. Euseb. H. E. vi. 42, 3: *Οἱ θεῖοι μάρτυρες,—οἱ νῦν τοῦ Χριστοῦ πάρεδροι καὶ τῆς βασιλείας αὐτοῦ κοινωνοὶ, καὶ μέτοχοι τῆς κρίσεως αὐτοῦ, καὶ συνδικάζοντες αὐτῷ, τῶν παραπεπτωκότων ἀδελφῶν—τὴν ἐπιστροφὴν καὶ μετάνοιαν ἰδόντες, δεκτήν τε γενέσθαι δυναμένην τῷ θεῷ—δοκιμάσαντες, εἰσεδέξαντο καὶ συνήγαγον καὶ συνέστησαν, καὶ προσευχῶν αὐτοῖς καὶ ἑστιάσεων ἐκοινώνησαν.—τί ἡμῖν πρακτέον; σύμψηφοι καὶ ὁμογνώμονες αὐτοῖς καταστῶμεν, καὶ τὴν κρίσιν αὐτῶν καὶ τὴν χάριν φυλάξωμεν, καὶ τοῖς ἐλεηθεῖσιν ὑπ' αὐτῶν χρηστευσώμεθα; ἢ τὴν κρίσιν αὐτῶν ἄδεκτον ποιησώμεθα, καὶ δοκιμαστὰς αὐτοὺς τῆς ἐκείνων γνώμης ἐπιστήσωμεν, καὶ τὴν χρηστότητα λυπήσωμεν; καὶ τὴν τάξιν ἀνασκευάσωμεν;*

[17] On these cases see Cypriani Epist. 10, 11, 14, 29. Epist. Luciani (Cyprian. 21): Cum benedictus martyr Paulus adhuc in corpore esset, vocavit me et dixit mihi: Luciane, coram Christo dico tibi, ut si quis post arcessitionem meam abs te pacem petierit, da in nomine meo. Epist. 16: Universi Confessores Cypriano Papae, Salutem! Scias, nos universis, de quibus apud te ratio constiterit, quid post commissum egerint, dedisse pacem, et hanc formam per te et aliis Episcopis innotescere voluimus. Optamus te cum sanctis Martyribus pacem habere. Praesente de Clero et Exorcista et Lectore, Lucianus scripsit.—Cyprian. Epist. 22, ad Clerum Romanum: Quae res majorem nobis conflat invidiam, ut nos cum singulorum causas audire et excutere coeperimus, videamur multis negare, quod se nunc omnes jactant a Martyribus et Confessoribus accepisse. Denique hujus seditionis origo jam coepit. Nam in provincia nostra per aliquot civitates in Praepositos impetus per multitudinem factus est, et pacem, quam semel cuncti a martyribus et Confessoribus datam clamitabant, confestim sibi repraesentari coëgerunt, territis et subactis Praepositis suis, qui ad resistendum minus virtute animi et robore fidei praevalebant. Apud nos etiam quidam turbulenti, qui vix a nobis in praeteritum regebantur, et in nostram praesentiam differebantur, per hanc epistolam (Confessorum Ep. 16) velut quibusdam facibus accensi, plus exardescere, et pacem sibi datem extorquere coeperunt. Cyprian's decisions regarding the praerogativa Martyrum (see Ep. 12, above, note 10.) Lib. de Lapsis: Credimus quidem posse apud judicem plurimum Martyrum merita et opera justorum; sed cum judicii vies venerit, cum post occasum saeculi hujus et mundi ante tribunal Christi populus ejus adstiterit. Caeterum si quis praepropera festinatione temerarius remissionem peccatorum dare se cunctis putat posse, aut audet Domini praecepta rescindere, non tantum nihil prodest, sed et obest lapsis. Provocasse est iram non servasse sententiam nec misericordiam prius Dei deprecandum putare, sed contempto Domino de sua facultate praesumere.—Mandant martyres aliquid fieri? sed si justa, si licita;—ante est, ut sciamus illos de Deo impetrasse quod postulant, tunc facere quod mandant. Cyprian deferred the final decision respecting the lapsed to a council which was to be held after persecution had ceased, and after his return (Ep. 9, 11); but he allowed that before this those lapsi furnished with libellis pacis might be readmitted on the sick bed. Ep. 12, 13, see above, note 10. Comp. Rettberg's Cyprianus S. 64.

dispute, as well as the great number of the lapsed, occasioned a renunciation of the principle, of always refusing reconciliation with the church to the lapsed, immediately after the Decian persecution, in Africa.[18] On the other hand, this Montanistic rigor continued in its greatest extent beyond this period, in Spain.[19]

[18] Respecting the Synod held at Carthage on this account, 251, and in justification of it, see Cypriani Ep. 52 ad Antonianum: Et quidem primum, quoniam de meo quoque actu motus videris, mea apud te et persona et causa purganda est, ne me aliquis existimet a proposito meo leviter recessisse, et cum evangelicum vigorem primo et inter initia defenderim, postmodum videar animum meum a disciplina et censura priore flexisse, ut his, qui libellis conscientiam suam maculaverint, vel nefanda sacrificia commiserint, laxandam pacem putaverim. Quod utrumque non sine librata diu et ponderata ratione a me factum est. Nam cum—proelium gloriosi certaminis in persecutione ferveret, toto hortatu et pleno impetu militum vires fuerant excitandae, et maxime lapsorum mentes—fortiter animandae, ut poenitentiae viam non solum precibus et lamentationibus sequerentur, sed —ad confessionis potius ardorem et martyrii gloriam nostris increpiti vocibus provocarentur.—Secundum quod tamen ante fuerat destinatum, persecutione sopita, copiosus Episcoporum numerus—in unum convenimus, et scripturis divinis ex utraque parte prolatis, temperamentum salubri moderatione libravimus, ut nec in totum spes communicationis et pacis lapsis denegaretur, ne plus desperatione deficerent, nec tamen rursus censura evangelica solveretur, ut ad communicationem temere prosilirent; sed traheretur diu poenitentia, et rogaretur dolenter paterna clementia, et examinarentur causae et voluntates et necessitates singulorum.—Ac si minus sufficiens Episcoporum in Africa numerus videbitur, etiam Romam super hac re scripsimus ad Cornelium collegam nostrum; qui et ipse cum plurimis coëpiscopis habito concilio in eandem nobiscum sententiam pari gravitate et salubri moderatione consensit.—Nec putes, frater carissime, hinc aut virtutem fratrum minui aut martyria deficere, quod lapsis laxata sit poenitentia, et quod poenitentibus spes pacis oblata.—Nam et moechis a nobis poenitentiae tempus conceditur et pax datur (comp. § 53, note 39, § 59, note 4). Non tamen iccirco virginitas in ecclesia deficit, etc.—Miror autem quosdam sic obstinatos esse, ut dandam non putent lapsis poenitentiam, aut poenitentibus existiment veniam denegandam, cum scriptum sit: Memento unde cecideris, et age poenitentiam, et fac priora opera (Apoc. ii. 5). After quoting many similar passages: Quod legentes scilicet et tenentes neminem putamus a fructu satisfactionis et spe pacis arcendum, cum sciamus juxta scripturarum divinarum fidem, auctore et hortatore ipso Deo, et ad agendam poenitentiam peccatores redigi, et veniam atque indulgentiam poenitentibus non denegari. In this sense it was even made a general church law by the Conc. Nicaen. c. 13: Ὥστε, εἴ τις ἐξοδεύοι, τοῦ τελευταίου καὶ ἀναγκαιοτάτου ἐφοδίου μὴ ἀποστερεῖσθαι.

[19] Comp. Concil. Illiberit. above § 59, note 10. So says Pacian, bishop of Barcelona, about 370, in his book of capital sins: Paraeneticus ad poenitentiam (Bibl. PP. max. t. iv.) peccatis capitalibus: Reliqua peccata meliorum operum compensatione curantur. Haec quicunque post fidem fecerit, Dei faciem non videbit. Cf. Innocentii I. Epist. 6, ad Exsuperium Episc. Tolosanum (in the year 405) c. 2: Et hoc quaesitum est, quid de his observari oporteat, qui post baptismum omni tempore incontinentiae voluptibus dediti, in extremo fine vitae suae poenitentiam simul et reconciliationem communionis exposcunt. De his observatio prior durior, posterior interveniente misericordia inclinatior. Nam consuetudo prior tenuit, ut concederetur poenitentia, sed communio negaretur.

§ 72.

(CONTINUATION.) CONTROVERSY CONCERNING MATTERS OF CHURCH DISCIPLINE.

1. *The schism of Felicissimus in Carthage.*[1] A party already dissatisfied with the selection of *Cyprian* as bishop, afterward continued in a divided and hostile relation to the bishop, who was extremely jealous of his dignity. The Decian persecution put an end to the dispute arising between Cyprian and the presbyter *Novatus.*[2] But during that trying time, some presbyters readmitted the lapsed (Cypriani Ep. 9) solely on the strength of the libelli pacis of the martyrs, which were too freely granted, without regard to the bishop of Carthage, who had been obliged to leave his church. Cyprian found fault with this. But the party of the dissatisfied increased in consequence, at whose head the deacon *Felicissimus* appeared, and to which several confessors also were now added. This party now refused to obey the commands of the bishop, who had fled from persecution,[3] and went on adding to its numbers by the reception of the lapsed.[4] After Cyprian's return (251) they were excommunicated, and chose Fortunatus for their bishop, but do not appear to have long survived.

[1] Sources: Cyprian. Ep. 38, 39, 40, 42, 55. Walch's Ketzerhist. ii. 288. Rettberg's Cyprianus, S. 89.

[2] At the time of the Novatian controversy Cyprian says of him, Ep. 49: Idem est Novatus, qui apud nos primum discordiae et schismatis incendium seminavit, qui quosdam istic ex fratribus ab Episcopo segregavit, qui in ipsa persecutione ad evertendas fratrum mentes alia quaedam persecutio nostris fuit. Ipse est, qui Felicissimum satellitem suum, Diaconum, nec permittente me, nec sciente, sua factione et ambitione constituit.—Urgentibus fratribus imminebat cognitionis dies, quo apud nos causa ejus ageretur, nisi persecutio antevenisset.

[3] In particular, Felicissimus withstood a commission sent by Cyprian to inquire about the condition of the poor. Cypr. Ep. 38.

[4] Cypriani Epist. 40 ad Plebem: Conjurationis suae memores, et antiqua illa contra Episcopatum meum, imo contra suffragium vestrum et Dei judicium venena retinentes, instaurant veterem contra nos impugnationem suam, et sacrilegas machinationes insidiis solitis denuo revocant. Hi fomenta olim quibusdam confessoribus et hortamenta tribuebant, ne concordarent cum episcopo suo, ne ecclesiasticam disciplinam cum fide et quiete juxta praecepta dominica continerent, etc.—nunc se ad lapsorum perniciem venenata sua deceptione verterunt, ut aegros et saucios—a medela vulneris sui avocent, et intermissis precibus et orationibus, quibus Dominus longa et continua satisfactione placandus est, ad exitiosam temeritatem mendacio captiosae pacis invitent.

2. *Novatian schism.*[5] The presbyter *Novatian* (in *Eusebius* Νοουάτος) was dissatisfied with the choice of the bishop *Cornelius* at Rome (251) because Cornelius, in his opinion, had conducted himself with too great lenity toward the lapsed. In the controversy that now ensued, in which the Carthaginian presbyter *Novatus* proved particularly active in favor of Novatian,[6] the latter returned to the old principle that none of the lapsed ought to be admitted to church communion.[7] Hence arose a division in the church. Novatian was chosen bishop by his party at Rome. Though the other bishops, particularly *Cyprian* at Carthage, and *Dionysius* at Alexandria, stood on the side of Cornelius, yet many in different countries joined the strict party.[8] At first the Novatians (καθαροί) declared themselves only against the re-admission of the lapsi;[9] but afterward they fully returned to the old African notion, that all who had defiled themselves by gross sins after baptism should be forever excluded from the church,[10] because the church itself would be tainted if they were received again. In accordance with

[5] Sources: Cyprian. Epist. 41–52. Cornelii Rom. Ep. ad Fabium Antioch. (ap. Euseb. vi. 43), Dionys. Alex. Ep. ad Novatianum (ib. c. 45), et ad Dionysium Rom. (ibid. vii. 8). Walch's Ketzerhist. ii. 185.

[6] Although he had formerly ordained Felicissimus deacon (note 2), it does not thence follow that he afterward was of the same opinion with him regarding the readmission of the lapsed, and still later that he came over to the opposite view at Rome. See Mosheim de rebus Christ. ante C. M. p. 518. Perhaps it was even dissatisfaction with his party that urged him to go from Carthage to Rome.

[7] Formerly Novatian's opinion was milder, in the letter written by him, Epist. Cleri Rom. ad Cypr. (Ep. Cypr. 31), cf. Cypr. Ep. 52.

[8] Even Fabius, bishop of Antioch, was ὑποκατακλινόμενος τῷ σχίσματι (Euseb. vi. 44), and at a Synod in Antioch τοῦ Νοουάτου κρατύνειν τινὲς ἐπεχείρουν τὸ σχίσμα (l. c. 46). Cf. Socrat. iv. 28. Respecting Marcian, bishop of Arles, see § 68, note 14.

[9] So Novatian, in a circular-letter, required all the churches (Socrates, iv. 28), μὴ δέχεσθαι τοὺς ἐπιθυκότας εἰς τὰ μυστήρια· ἀλλὰ προτρέπειν μὲν αὐτοὺς εἰς μετάνοιαν, τὴν δὲ συγχώρησιν ἐπιτρέπειν θεῷ, τῷ δυναμένῳ καὶ ἐξουσίαν ἔχοντι συγχωρεῖν ἁμαρτήματα. Hence Cyprian, Ep. 52, accuses Novatian of inconsistency: Aut si se cordis et renis scrutatorum constituit et judicem, per omnia aequaliter judicet, et—fraudatores et moechos a latere atque a comitatu suo separet, quando multo et gravior et pejor sit moechi quam libellatici causa. O frustrandae fraternitatis irrisio, O miserorum—caduca deceptio!—hortari ad satisfactionis poenitentiam, et subtrahere de satisfactione medicinam: dicere fratribus nostris: plange et lacrimas funde, et diebus ac noctibus ingemisce, et pro abluendo et purgando delicto tuo largiter et frequenter operare, sed extra ecclesiam post omnia ista morieris: quaecumque ad pacem pertinent facies, sed nullam pacem, quam quaeris, accipies.

[10] Acesius, a Novatian bishop, at the Council of Nice, says (Socrates, i. 10): Οὐ χρὴ τοὺς μετὰ τὸ βάπτισμα ἡμαρτηκότας ἁμαρτίαν, ἣν πρὸς θάνατον καλοῦσιν αἱ θεῖαι γραφαί, τῆς κοινωνίας τῶν θείων μυστηρίων ἀξιοῦσθαι· ἀλλ' ἐπὶ μετάνοιαν μὲν αὐτοὺς προτρέπειν, ἐλπίδα δὲ τῆς ἀφέσεως μὴ παρὰ τῶν ἱερέων, ἀλλὰ παρὰ τοῦ θεοῦ ἐκδέχεσθαι, τοῦ δυναμένου καὶ ἐξουσίαν ἔχοντος συγχωρεῖν ἁμαρτήματα.

this view they declared all other churches to have forfeited the rights of a Christian church; and baptized anew those who came over to them.[11] This party was widely extended, and continued for a long time.[12] In Phrygia they united with the remnant of the Montanists.[13]

3. *Controversy concerning the baptism of heretics.*[14] The custom prevalent in Africa, Egypt, Syria, and Asia Minor, of regarding reclaimed heretics as unbaptized, was considered objectionable at Rome,[15] where they were prepared for re-admission without baptism, by passing through the *gradus poenitentiae;* especially since the time the Novatians began to re-baptize the Christians who had joined them. In Africa, too, there arose doubts regarding it; but two Carthaginian councils (255, 256) confirmed the old practice. When the second council informed *Stephen,* bishop of Rome (253–257) of its decisions, in a synodical letter (Ep. Cypr. 72), it received from him a haughty reply, disapproving of them.[16] This led to an interchange of violent letters between Stephen and Cyprian.[17] The

[11] Such also was the practice of the African church. So Tertullian de Baptismo, 15, de Praesc. 12, de Pudicit. 19, and a council in Carthage under Agrippinus, about 200 (Cypr. Ep. 71, 73). Cf. Münteri primordia Eccl. Afric. p. 150, ss.

[12] Constantine's forbearance toward them, Cod. Theodos. lib. xvi. tit. 5, l. 2: Novatianos non adeo comperimus praedamnatos, ut iis, quae petiverunt, crederemus minime largienda. Itaque ecclesiae suae domos, et loca sepulchris apta sine inquietudine eos firmiter possidere praecipimus, etc. (A.D. 326). The mildness of the Nicene council toward them, Can. Nic. 8: *Καθαροὺς χειροθετουμένους μένειν οὕτως ἐν τῷ κλήρῳ.*

[13] Comp. especially Socrates, iv. 28. The Phrygian Novatians forbade second marriage (ibid. v. 22), and celebrated the passover with the Quartodecimani (iv. 28, v. 21).

[14] Walch's Ketzerhist. ii. 310. Rettberg's Cyprianus, S. 156.

[15] The testimonies for Africa, see note 11. For Egypt Clemens Alex. Strom. i. 375: Τὸ *βάπτισμα τὸ αἱρετικὸν οὐκ οἰκεῖον καὶ γνήσιον ὕδωρ.* Comp. Dionysius Alex., below, note 20. For Syria, Constit. Apost. vi. 15. For Asia Minor, the two councils in Iconium (in the year 235, see Firmilian. in Epist. Cypr. 75), and Synnada, cf. Dionys. Alex. ap. Euseb. vii. 7, 3.

[16] Cyprian's principle was (Ep. 70): Neminem foris baptizari extra Ecclesiam posse, cum sit baptisma unum in sancta Ecclesia constitutum. On the other hand Stephen (Ep. 74): Si quis ergo a quacunque haeresi venerit ad vos, nihil innovetur nisi quod traditum est, ut manus illi imponatur in poenitentiam.—Qui in nomine Jesu Christi ubicunque et quomodocunque baptizantur, innovati et sanctificati judicentur. Cyprian adds: In tantum Stephani fratris nostri obstinatio dura prorupit, ut etiam de Marcionis baptismo, item Valentini et Apelletis, et caeterorum blasphemantium in Deum patrem contendat filios Deo nasci.

[17] The earlier letters of Cyprian on this affair are Ep. 70–73. Notices of the controversial writings between him and Stephen are found in Cypr. Epist. 74, ad Pompeium and Firmiliani Ep. ad Cypr. (Ep. Cypr. 75). Cyprian says of Stephen's letter (Ep. 74): Caetera vel superba vel ad rem non pertinentia, vel sibi ipsi contraria, quae imperite atque improvide scripsit, etc.—Quae ista obstinatio est, quaeve praesumtio, humanum traditionem divinae dispositioni anteponere, nec animadvertere, indignari et irasci Deum,

former broke off all communion with the Africans; but notwithstanding this they repeated in the most emphatic terms their opinions at a third council at Carthage (1st Sept. 256).[18] *Firmilian*, bishop of Caesarea, in Cappadocia, assured them (Epist. Cypr. 75) with bitter observations on Stephen,[19] of the full assent of the churches in his province; and Dionysius also, bishop of Alexandria, decidedly condemned the conduct of Stephen.[20] After Stephen's death, peace was immediately restored to the

quoties divina praecepta solvit et praeterit humana traditio.—Nec consuetudo, quae apud quosdam obrepserat, impedire debit, quominus veritas praevaleat et vincat. Nam consuetudo sine veritate vetustas erroris est. On the other hand (Ep. 75): Non pudet Stephanum—Cyprianum pseudochristum et pseudoapostolum et dolosum operarium dicere. The consequences to be deduced from this controversy respecting the papal supremacy afterward asserted, may be seen in J. La Placette Observatt. historico-eccl., quibus eruitur veteris ecclesiae sensus circa Pontif. Rom. potestatem in definiendis fidei rebus. Amsterd. 1695. 8, p. 102, ss.

[18] The Acts of it in Augustini de Baptismo contra Donatistas, lib. vi. et vii.—Also in Cypriani Opp.

[19] Ex. gr. gratiam referre Stephano in isto possumus, quod per illius inhumanitatem nunc effectum sit, ut fidei et sapientiae vestrae experimentum caperemus.—Sed haec interim, quae a Stephano gesta sunt, praetereantur, ne dum audaciae et insolantiae ejus meminimus, de rebus ab eo improbe gestis longiorem moestitiam nobis inferamus.—Atque ego in hac parte juste indignor ad hanc tam apertam et manifestam Stephani stultitiam, quod qui sic de Episcopatus sui loco gloriatur, et se successionem Petri tenere contendit, super quem fundamenta Ecclesiae collocata sunt, multas alias petras inducat.—Lites et dissensiones quantas parâsti (Stephane) per ecclesias totius mundi? Peccatum vero quam magnum tibi exaggerasti, quando te a tot gregibus scidisti? Exscidisti enim temet ipsum: noli te fallere. Siquidem ille est vere schismaticus, qui se a communione Ecclesiasticae unitatis apostatam fecerit (consequently not from a Roman centrum unitatis). Dum enim putas omnes a te abstinere posse, solum te ab omnibus abstinuisti, etc. This letter, so unpleasant to the Romish see (extant in 26 codd.), was purposely omitted in the edition of Cyprian. Romae ap. Paul. Manutium. 1563, and first printed in that of Guil. Morellii. Paris. 1564, who is bitterly censured for it by Latinus and Pamelius. Christ. Lupus (ad Tertull. libr. de Praescr. Bruxell. 1675. 4) first denied the authenticity of the letter. A Franciscan Raimund Missori (in duas celeberr. epist. Firm. et Cypr. disputt. crit. Venet. 1733. 4), the Jesuit R. J. Tournemine (Mémoires de Trévoux de 1734, p. 2246, ss), the Franciscan Marcellinus Molkenbuhr (in two dissertations. Münster. 1790 and 1793. 4), and A. Ant. Morcelli Africa christiana, ii. 138, declare, moreover, that Cyprian's letters respecting the baptism of heretics are forged. These arbitrary assumptions, which none else has thought fit to repeat, have been refuted by J. H. Sbaralea germana S. Cypr. et Afrorum necnon Firmiliani opinio de haereticorum baptism. Bonon. 1741. 4, and in Academic dissertations by G. G. Preu. Jenae. 1738, and D. Cotta. Tüb. 1740.

[20] Dion. Ep. ad Sixtum II. (successor of Stephen, 257) ap. Euseb. vii. 5: 'Επεστάλκει (Στέφανος) *μὲν οὖν πρότερον καὶ περὶ* 'Ελένου *καὶ περὶ* Φιρμιλιανοῦ *καὶ πάντων τῶν τε ἀπὸ τῆς* Κιλικίας *καὶ* Καππαδοκίας *καὶ* Γαλατίας, *καὶ πάντων τῶν ἑξῆς ὁμορούντων ἐθνῶν, ὡς οὐδὲ ἐκείνοις κοινωνήσων διὰ τὴν αὐτὴν ταύτην αἰτίαν, ἐπειδὴ τοὺς αἱρετικούς, φησιν, ἀναβαπτίζουσι.* Καὶ *σκόπει τὸ μέγεθος τοῦ πράγματος.* Ὄντως *γὰρ δόγματα περὶ τούτου γέγονεν ἐν ταῖς μεγίσταις τῶν ἐπισκόπων συνόδοις, ὡς πυνθάνομαι, ὥστε τοὺς προσίοντας ἀπὸ αἱρέσεων προκατηχηθέντας, εἶτα ἀπολούεσθαι καὶ ἀνακαθαίρεσθαι τὸν τῆς παλαιᾶς καὶ ἀκαθάρτου ζύμης ῥύπον.* Καὶ *περὶ τούτων αὐτοῦ πάντων δεόμενος, ἐπέστειλα.* Hieronymus Catal. c. 69: Dionysius—in Cypriani et Africanae synodi dogma consentiens de haereticis rebaptizandis.

church,[21] although difference of opinion on the disputed point continued for a long time.[22] In the mean time, even now, an intermediate opinion had arisen in the western church,[23] which afterward became the prevailing one.

4. *Meletian schism.* During the Diocletian persecution, *Meletius, bishop of Lycopolis* in Thebais, maintained that the lapsed should not be admitted to penance before peace should have been restored. On this ground he withdrew from his metropolitan *Peter of Alexandria* (306), and began to assume the duties of the metropolitan's office among the churches of his party.[24] This schism continued more than a century.

5. *Donatist schism.*[25] As early as the Diocletian persecution there arose at Carthage a fanatical party in opposition to the bishop *Mensurius* and his archdeacon *Caecilianus*, because *they* had contended against the perverseness with which many Christians sought for martyrdom partly from fanaticism, and partly from still more impure motives.[26] When, therefore, after

[21] Pontius in Vita Cypriani, where he speaks of his martyrdom: Jam de Xisto (successor of Stephen), bono et pacifico Sacerdote, ac propterea beatissimo Martyre, ab Urbe nuncius venerat.

[22] Accordingly, the Greek fathers, even of the fourth century, reject the baptism of heretics. See below, § 101, note 10.

[23] Can. Arelat. 8: De Afris, quod propria lege sua utuntur ut rebaptizent, placuit, ut si ad ecclesiam aliquis de haeresi venerit, interrogent eum symbolum; et si perviderint, eum in Patre, et Filio, et Spiritu Sancto esse baptizatum, manus ei tantum imponatur, ut accipiat Spiritum Sanctum. Quod si interrogatus non responderit hanc trinitatem, baptizetur.

[24] Some original documents relating to this controversy, especially a letter from four Egyptian bishops to Meletius, have been communicated to the public by Scipio Maffei Osservazioni letterarie, t. iii. p. 11, ss. (Verona. 1738). The account of Epiphanius Haer. 68, which is favorable to Meletius, agrees best with this letter. Different, but partial against Meletius, is the representation of Athanasius Apologia contra Arianos, § 59, which Socrates, Sozomen, and Theodoret for the most part follow. Walch, iv. 355. Neander, ii. i. 463.

[25] Sources: Optatus (bishop of Mileve about 368) de schismate Donatistarum libb. vii. (vi.?) ed. L. E. du Pin. Paris. 1700 (in which edition also: Monumenta vetera ad Donatist. hist. pertinentia and historia Donatistarum). Augustinus in several works (all contained in the 9th part of the Benedictine edition, in its appendix are also Excerpta et scripta vetera ad Donatistarum historiam pertinentia), for example contra Epistolam Parmeniani libb. 3, de Baptismo libb. 7, contra literas Petiliani libb. 3, contra Cresconium libb. 4, breviculas collationum contra Donatistas libb. 3, etc.—Cf. Valesius de schismate Donatist. diss. (appended to his edition of Eusebius). Melchior Leydecker Historia Eccles. Africanae. Ultraj. 1690. 4. p. 467. Historia Donatistarum ex Norisianis schedis excepta in H. Norisii Opp. om. ed. a Petro et Hieron. fratribus Balleriniis. (Veron. 1729. 1732. 4 t. fol.) Tom. iv. Walch, iv. 3. Neander, ii. i. 387.

[26] Comp. the contents of a letter addressed by Mensurius to Secundus, bishop of Tigisis, in Augustin. brevicul. collat. diei iii. c. 23, note 25: Eos, qui se offerrent persecutionibus non comprehensi, et ultro dicerent, se habere scripturas, quas non traderent, a quibus hoc nemo quaesierat, displicuisse Mensurio, et ab eis honorandis eum prohibuisse Christianos. Quidam etiam in eadem epistola facinorosi arguebantur et fisci debitores, qui

Mensurius's death (311), Caecilianus was chosen his successor, this party set up in opposition to him *Majorinus*, who was soon succeeded by *Donatus the great* (313). In this proceeding they were supported by the Numidian bishops, particularly Secundus, bishop of Tigisis, and Donatus, bishop of Casae Nigrae. The pretext was, that Caecilianus had been consecrated by a "traditor," *Felix, bishop of Aptunga*. This *pars Majorini*, afterward called *pars Donati*, *Donatistae*, who gained many adherents in Africa, on account of their attaching great value to purity in the church, brought their complaint against Caecilian before Constantine: the first example of spiritual affairs being laid before a civil ruler for his decision. Constantine at first intrusted Miltiades, bishop of Rome, along with three Gallic bishops (313) with an inquiry into the affair; and afterward a council was assembled at Arles for the purpose of investigating it (314). Both decisions, as well as the judgment of the emperor himself (316) occasioned by a new appeal, proved unfavorable to the Donatists. But though severe laws also had been passed against them, yet they persisted in their opposition, and continued full of enmity toward the catholic church, for more than a century in Africa.

§ 73.

ASCETICISM.

In this division of time, we still find in the church a living consciousness of Christian freedom, which was manifested, espe-

occasione persecutiones vel carere vellent onerosa multis debitis vita, vel purgare se putarent, et quasi abluere facinora sua vel certe adquirere pecuniam, et in custodia deliciis perfrui de obsequio Christianorum. With this coincides what had been objected to Caecilian immediately after his election (l. c. cap. 14, no. 26): Cum esset diaconus, victum afferri martyribus in custodia constitutis prohibuisse dicebatur. There is manifestly great exaggeration in the Donatist Actis Saturnini presbyteri, Felicis, Dativi, Ampelii et aliorum, c. 17 (in Baluzii Miscellan. t. ii. p. 72, du Pin Monumenta, p. 156: On the other hand, this appendix is left out in the Actis SS. and apud Ruinart where he is called): (Mensurius) tyranno saevior, carnifice crudelior, idoneum sceleris sui ministrum diaconum suum elegit Caecilianum: idemque lora et flagra cum armatis ante fores carceris ponit, ut ab ingressu atque aditu cunctos, qui victum potumque in carcerem martyribus afferebant, gravi affectos injuria propulsaret. Et caedebantur a Caeciliano passim qui ad alendos martyres veniebant, sitientibus intus in vinculis confessoribus, pocula frangebantur ante carceris limina, cibi passim lacerandi canibus spargebantur, etc.

cially at the beginning of the period, in opposition to the ascetic precepts of the Montanists.[1] Fasting continued to be left to the free choice of each; except that ecclesiastical custom had determined certain days as especially appropriate for that purpose, which were very different in different churches.[2] Besides, on particular occasions the churches were summoned by their bishops to a general fast;[3] and in like manner certain fasts were imposed on the penitents.[4] External asceticism generally

[1] Tertull. de Jejuniis, c. 2: Certe in evangelio illos dies jejuniis determinatos putant (Psychici), in quibus ablatus est sponsus, et hos esse jam solos legitimos jejuniorum Christianorum, abolitis legalibus et propheticis vetustatibus. Itaque de caetero indifferenter jejunandum, ex arbitrio, non ex imperio novae disciplinae, pro temporibus et causis uniuscujusque. Sic et Apostolos observasse, nullum aliud imponentes jugum certorum et in commune omnibus obeundorum jejuniorum: proinde nec stationum, quae et ipsae suos quidem dies habeant, quartae feriae et sextae, passive tamen currant, neque sub lege praecepti—cum fides libera in Christo ne Judaicae quidem legi abstinentiam quorundam ciborum debeat, semel in totum macellum ab Apostolo admissa, detestatore eorum, qui sicut nubere prohibeant, ita jubeant cibis abstinere a Deo conditis: et ideo nos (the Montanists) esse jam tunc praenotatos in novissimis temporibus abscedentes a fide, intendentes spiritibus mundi seductoribus, doctrinis mendaciloquorum inustam habentes conscientiam (1 Tim. iv. 1, 2). Sit et cum Galatis nos quoque percuti ajunt observatores dierum et mensium et annorum (Gal. iv. 10, cf. c. 14: Galaticamur plane). Jaculantur interea et Esaiam pronunciasse: non tale jejunium Dominus elegit, id est, non abstinentiam cibi, sed opera justitiae, quae subtexit (Is. lviii. 5, 6). Et ipsum Dominum in Evangelio ad omnem circa victum scrupulositatem compendio respondisse, non his coinquinari hominem, quae in os inferantur, sed quae ex ore proferantur, cum et ipse manducaret et biberet usque in nationem: Ecce homo vorator et potator (Matth. xi. 19). Sic et Apostolum docere, quod esca nos Deo non commendet: neque abundantes, si edamus, neque deficientes, si non edamus (1 Cor. viii. 8). Comp. Neander's Antignosticus, S. 279, ff.

[2] Origenes Hom. x. in Levitic. § 2: Habemus enim quadragesimae dies jejuniis consecratos. Habemus quartam et sextam septimanae dies, quibus solemniter jejunamus. Is this translation of Rufinus correct? Cf. Dionys. Epist. can. ad Basilid. can. 1: *Μηδὲ τὰς ἓξ τῶν νηστειῶν ἡμέρας ἴσως, μηδὲ ὁμοίως πάντες διαμένουσιν· ἀλλ' οἱ μὲν καὶ πάσας ὑπερτιθέασιν* (i. e., fasting all days successively. Respecting these *ὑπερθέσεις*, superpositiones see Bingham, vol. ix. p. 229. Routh Reliqu. Sacr. ii. p. 419), *ἄσιτοι διατελοῦντες, οἱ δὲ δύο, οἱ δὲ τρεῖς, οἱ δὲ τέσσαρας, οἱ δὲ οὐδεμίαν.—εἰ δὲ τινες οὐχ ὅπως οὐχ ὑπερτιθέμενοι, ἀλλὰ μηδὲ νηστεύσαντες ἢ καὶ τρυφήσαντες τὰς προαγούσας τέσσαρας, εἶτα ἐλθόντες ἐπὶ τὰς τελευταίας δύο καὶ μόνας ἡμέρας, αὐτὰς ὑπερτιθέντες, τήν τε παρασκευὴν καὶ τὸ σάββατον, μέγα τι καὶ λαμπρὸν ποιεῖν νομίζουσιν, ἂν μέχρι τῆς ἕω διαμείνωσιν, τούτους οὐκ οἶμαι τὴν ἴσην ἄθλησιν πεποιῆσθαι τοῖς τὰς πλείονας ἡμέρας προησκηκόσι.* Const. Apost. v. 18: *Ἐν ταῖς ἡμέραις οὖν τοῦ Πάσχα νηστεύετε ἀρχόμενοι ἀπὸ δευτέρας μέχρι τῆς παρασκευῆς καὶ σαββάτου ἓξ ἡμέρας, κ. τ. λ.*

[3] Tertull. de Jejun. c. 13, comp. § 53, note 33. The bishops sometimes showed themselves ambitious even here. Origenes in Matth. Commentariorum series, § 10: Qui docent etiam abstinere a cibis, et alia hujusmodi, ad quae non omnino oportet cogere homines fideles, alligant per verbum expositionis suae onera gravia, citra voluntatem Christi dicentis: Jugum meum suave est, et onus meum leve est: et imponunt ea, quantum ad verbum suum, super humeros hominum, curvantes eos et cadere facientes sub pondere gravium mandatorum eos, qui bajulare ea non sufferunt. Et frequenter videre est, eos qui talia docent, contraria agere sermonibus suis, etc.

[4] Even it would seem, of forty days, in imitation of Jesus. Petri Alex. can. 1.

was progressively and increasingly valued;[5] and there were very many ascetics of both sexes, although they were bound by no irrevocable vow.[6] The Alexandrian distinction of a higher and lower virtue had a special influence in recommending this asceticism.[7] It is true that the renouncing of sensual enjoyments (ἐγκρατεία), according to *Clement of Alexandria*, was only the means for attaining to that higher virtue, *i. e.*, to that passionless state (ἀπάθεια) whereby man is made like to God and united to Him;[8] so that whoever has reached this point has no more need of that renunciation of sensual gratification;[9] but afterward, the opinion that the higher virtue must manifest itself especially in external asceticism[10] obtained currency, after the example of *Origen*, in the Christian school at Alexandria, as well as among the new Platonists.[11] To the high

[5] Cf. Cyprianus de Habitu virginum; Methodii convivium decem virginum (in Combefisii Auctarium novissimum biblioth. Graecorum Patrum. P. i. p. 64, ss.), and the two supposititious letters to virgins that pass under the name of Clement of Rome, which probably appeared about this time, and were first communicated to the public in the Syriac language by Wetstein N. T. tom. ii. (Moehler, Patrologie, i. 67, declares them genuine.)

[6] Cypriani Epist. 62: Quod si (virgines) ex fide se Christo dicaverunt, pudicae et castae sine ulla fabula perseverent, et ita fortes et stabiles praemium virginitatis exspectant. Si autem perseverare nolunt, vel non possunt melius est ut nubant, quam in ignem delictis suis cadant. Certe nullum fratribus aut sororibus scandalum faciant, etc. Concil. Illiberit. can. 13, is directed against the lustful excesses of the virgins, quae se Deo dicaverint, and consequently does not belong to our present purpose. On the other hand, Conc. Ancyran. can. 19: Ὅσοι παρθενίαν ἐπαγγελλόμενοι, ἀθετοῦσι τὴν ἐπαγγελίαν, τὸν τῶν διγάμων ὅρον ἐκπληρούτωσαν. Bigamists according to Basilii. Ep. can. iv. were subjected to the penance of a year.

[7] See above, § 63, note 25.

[8] See § 63, note 27. Daehne de γνώσει Clementis, p. 107.

[9] Clem. Alex. Strom. iv. p. 626 of the γνωστικός: Οὐκ ἐγκρατὴς οὗτος ἔτι, ἀλλ' ἐν ἕξει γέγονεν ἀπαθείας. vii. p. 874: Διὸ καὶ ἐσθίει καὶ πίνει καὶ γαμεῖ (ὁ γνωστικὸς), οὐ προηγουμένως ἀλλὰ ἀναγκαίως. τὸ γαμεῖν δὲ, ἐὰν ὁ λόγος ἐρῃ, λέγω, καὶ ὡς καθήκει. Γενόμενος γὰρ τέλειος (maritus) εἰκόνας ἔχει τοὺς Ἀποστόλους, καὶ τῷ ὄντι ἀνὴρ οὐκ ἐν τῷ μονήρῃ ἐπανελέσθαι δείκνυται βίον, ἀλλ' ἐκεῖνος ἄνδρας νικᾷ, ὁ γάμῳ καὶ παιδοποιΐᾳ, καὶ τῇ τοῦ οἴκου προνοίᾳ ἀνηδόνως τε καὶ ἀλυπήτως ἐγγυμνασάμενος, μετὰ τῆς τοῦ οἴκου κηδεμονίας ἀδιάστατος τῆς τοῦ θεοῦ γενόμενος ἀγάπης, καὶ πάσης κατεξανιστάμενος πείρας, τῆς διὰ τέκνων καὶ γυναικὸς, οἰκετῶν τε καὶ κτημάτων προσφερομένης. Τῷ δὲ ἀοίκῳ τὰ πολλὰ εἶναι συμβέβηκεν ἀπειράστῳ. Cf. lib. iii. p. 546, etc. De Wette Geschicht. d. christl. Sittenlehre, i. 224.

[10] Tzschirner's Fall des Heidenthums, i. 435, ff.

[11] Origenes in Ep. ad. Rom. lib. iii. (ed. de la Rue, iv. p. 507: Donec quis hoc facit tantum quod debet, i. e., ea quae praecepta sunt, inutilis servus est (according to Luc. xvii. 10). Si autem addas aliquid praeceptis, tunc non jam inutilis servus eris, sed dicetur ad te: Euge serve bone et fidelis (Matth. xxv. 21). Quid autem sit quod addatur praeceptis, et supra debitum fiat, Paulus Apostolus dicit: De virginibus autem praeceptum Domini non habeo: consilium autem do, tamquam misericordiam consecutus a Domino (1 Cor. vii. 25). Hoc opus super praeceptum est. Qui ergo completis praeceptis addiderit etiam hoc, ut virginitatem custodiat, non jam inutilis servus, sed servus bonus et fidelis vocabitur. Et iterum praeceptum est, ut hi qui Evangelium annunciant, de Evangelio vivant. Paulus tamen dicit, quia nullo horum usus sum; et ideo non inutilis erat servus,

estimation of celibacy, increased by the cause just mentioned, which sometimes bordered almost upon contempt of the married state,[12] was attached very naturally the notion of its being especially becoming in priests to renounce the marriage intercourse.[13] And though no general ecclesiastical law was yet enacted on the subject,[14] yet as the priests had already been forbidden to marry a second time (§ 53, note 28), a regulation was now made in addition, that they should only keep the woman whom they had married before ordination; while in office itself, they should not marry;[15] and that the person whom they

sed fidelis et prudens. Euseb. Demonstrat. evang. i. c. 8: *Οἱ μαθηταὶ* (*τοῦ* Χριστοῦ)—*ὅσα μὲν ἅτε τὴν ἕξιν διαβεβηκόσι πρὸς τοῦ τελείου διδασκάλου παρήγγελτο, ταῦτα τοῖς οἵοις τε χωρεῖν παρεδίδουν· ὅσα δὲ τοῖς ἔτι τὰς ψυχὰς ἐμπαθέσι, καὶ θεραπείας δεομένοις ἐφαρμόζειν ὑπελάμβανον, ταῦτα συγκατιόντες τῇ τῶν πλειόνων ἀσθενείᾳ—φυλάττειν παρεδίδοσαν· ὥστε ἤδη καὶ τῇ* Χριστοῦ *ἐκκλησίᾳ δύο βίων νενομοθετῆσθαι τρόπους· τὸν μὲν ὑπερφυῆ, καὶ τῆς κοινῆς καὶ ἀνθρωπίνης πολιτείας ἐπέκεινα, οὐ γάμους, οὐ παιδοποιΐας, οὐδὲ κτῆσιν, οὐδὲ περιουσίας ὕπαρξιν παραδεχόμενον, ὅλον δὲ δι' ὅλου τῆς κοινῆς καὶ συνήθους ἁπάντων ἀνθρώπων ἀγωγῆς παρηλλαγμένον, καὶ μόνῃ τῇ τοῦ θεοῦ θεραπείᾳ προσῳκειωμένον καθ' ὑπερβολὴν ἔρωτος οὐρανίου. Οἱ δὴ τόνδε μετιόντες τὸν τρόπον, τῶν θνητῶν βίον τεθνάναι δοκοῦντες, καὶ αὐτὸ μόνον τὸ σῶμα φέροντες ἐπὶ γῆς, φρονήματι δὲ τὴν ψυχὴν εἰς οὐρανὸν μετενηνεγμένοι, οἷά τινες θεοὶ, τὸν τῶν ἀνθρώπων ἐφορῶσι βίον, ὑπὲρ τοῦ παντὸς γένους ἱερωμένοι τῷ ἐπὶ πάντων θεῷ, οὐ βουθυσίαις καὶ αἵμασιν,—δόγμασι δὲ ὀρθοῖς ἀληθοῦς εὐσεβείας, ψυχῆς τε διαθέσει κεκαθαρμένης, καὶ προσέτι τοῖς κατ' ἀρετὴν ἔργοις τε καὶ λόγοις. οἷς τὸ θεῖον ἐξιλεούμενοι, τὴν ὑπὲρ σφῶν αὐτῶν καὶ τῶν σφίσιν ὁμογενῶν ἀποτελοῦσιν ἱερουργίαν.* Τοιόσδε *μὲν οὖν καθέστηκεν ὁ ἐντελὴς τῆς κατὰ τὸν χριστιανισμὸν πολιτείας τρόπος.* 'Ο *δ' ὑποβεβηκὼς ἀνθρωπινώτερος, οἷος καὶ γάμοις συγκατιέναι σώφροσι καὶ παιδοποιΐαις, κ. τ. λ.—*Καί *τις τούτοις δεύτερος εὐσεβείας ἀπενεμήθη βαθμός, κ. τ. λ.*

[12] Origenis in Num. Hom. vi. (ed. de la Rue, t. ii. p. 288): Ego, licet non usquequaque pronunciem, puto tamen quod sint nonnulla etiam communium hominum gesta, quae quamvis peccato careant, non tamen digna videantur, quibis interesse putemus Spiritum sanctum. Ut verbi gratia dixerim, connubia quidem legitima carent quidem peccato, nec tamen tempore illo, quo conjugales actes geruntur, praesentia sancti Spiritus dabitur, etiamsi propheta esse videatur, qui officio generationis obsequitur: namely, Comm. in Matth. t. xvii. (t. iii. p. 827), *ἐν μολυσμῷ πως ὄντων καί ἀκαθαρσίᾳ τινὶ τῶν χρωμένων ἀφροδισίοις.*

[13] Euseb. Demonstr. evang. i. c. 9: *Χρῆναι γὰρ, φησὶν ὁ λόγος, τὸν ἐπίσκοπον γεγονέναι μιᾶς γυναικὸς ἄνδρα. πλὴν ἀλλὰ τοῖς ἱερωμένοις, καὶ περὶ τὴν τοῦ θεοῦ θεραπείαν ἀσχολουμένοις ἀνέχειν λοιπὸν σφᾶς αὐτοὺς προσήκει τῆς γαμικῆς ὁμιλίας.*

[14] It was only the rigid council at Illiberis that ordained, Can. 33: Placuit in totum prohibere episcopis, presbyteris et diaconibus vel omnibus clericis positis in ministerio, abstinere se a conjugibus suis, et non generare filios: quicunque vero fecerit, ab honore clericatus exterminetur. The meaning is ambiguous, but the true sense is probably this, that conjugal intercourse is forbidden bishops, presbyters, and deacons wholly (in totum), and to the inferior clergy as long as they are engaged in the active service of the church. These latter might live together with their wives, can. 65: Si cujus clerici uxor fuerit moechata, et—maritus—non eam statim projecerit, nec in finem accipiat communionem. Examples of married bishops and presbyters, belonging to this period, may be found in Calixtus de Conjugio clericorum, ed. Henke, p. 201.

[15] Const. Ap. vi. 17, Canon Ancyr. x.: *Διάκονοι, ὅσοι καθίστανται, παρ' αὐτὴν τὴν κατάστασιν εἰ ἐμαρτύραντο καὶ ἔφασαν χρῆναι γαμῆσαι, μὴ δυνάμενοι οὕτως μένειν·*

had married must have been a virgin.[16] Among ascetics, the dangerous practice arose of taking to themselves virgins for the purpose of living with them in pure spiritual communion, vanquishing all temptations. They called them ἀδελφαί, sorores,[17] Others gave them the appellations συνείσακτοι,[18] subintroductae, ἀγαπηταί, extraneae. Against this practice, which prevailed principally among the unmarried clergy, Cyprian first declared himself, and after him several synods.[19]

Hitherto the ascetics had lived scattered among other Christians without external distinction; but the Decian persecution was the cause of some Egyptian Christians[20] fleeing into the desert, and there in solitariness giving themselves up to an asceticism in the highest degree extravagant (ἐρημῖται, μοναχοί). This new asceticism began to make greater noise, when, during Maximin's persecution (311), the hermit *Anthony*[21] appeared in a wild procession at Alexandria. But a season of perse-

οὗτοι μετὰ ταῦτα γαμήσαντες, ἔστωσαν ἐν τῇ ὑπηρεσίᾳ, διὰ τὸ ἐπιτραπῆναι αὐτοὺς ὑπὸ τοῦ ἐπισκόπου. Τοῦτο δὲ εἴ τινες σιωπήσαντες, καὶ καταδεξάμενοι ἐν τῇ χειροτονίᾳ μένειν οὕτως, μετὰ ταῦτα ἦλθον ἐπὶ γάμον, πεπαῦσθαι αὐτοὺς τῆς διακονίας. Can. Neocaesar. 1: Πρεσβύτερος ἐὰν γήμῃ, τῆς τάξεως αὐτὸν μετατίθεσθαι.

16 According to Const. Ap. vi. 17, not ἑταίραν, ἢ οἰκέτιν, ἢ χήραν, ἢ ἐκβεβλημένην, as well as Levit. xxi. 7, 14. Ezek. xliv. 22.

17 So previously among the Gnostics. Irenaeus, i. 1, § 12, says of some Valentinians: Ὡς μετὰ ἀδελφῶν προσποιούμενοι συνοικεῖν, προϊόντος τοῦ χρόνου ἠλέγχθησαν, ἐγκύμονος τῆς ἀδελφῆς ὑπὸ τοῦ ἀδελφοῦ γενηθείσης. Perhaps also in the case of Marcion. See Hall. A. L. Z. April, 1823, S. 850. Epiphanius, Haer. 47, c. 3, accuses the Encratites of the same thing. The first trace of it among the Catholics is in Hermae Pastor, lib. iii. sim ix. § 11, where the virgins say of Hermas: Nobiscum dormies ut frater, non ut maritus: frater enim noster es, et de caetero tecum habitare paratae sumus: valde enim carum te habemus, &c. Tertullian also, de Jejuniis, c. 17, appears to blame the catholics for the same reason: Apud te agape in cacabis fervet, fides in culinis calet, spes in ferculis jacet. Sed major his est agape, quia per hanc adolescentes tui cum sororibus dormiunt (an allusion to 1 Cor. xiii. 13). From the time of Cyprian the thing occurs more frequently. See below, note 19. Those ascetics appealed to the example of Jesus, John, and the apostles (Lib. de Singularit. cleric. c. 20. Epiphan. Haer. 78, c. 11), and named the young women, after 1 Cor. ix. 5, Sorores (Conc. Ancyr. c. 19, Cod. Theodos. xvi. 2, 44). Comp. Observationum selectarum, tom. vi. (Halae. 1702) p. 230, ss. Dodwell Diss. Cyprian. iii. L. A. Muratori Anecdota graeca, p. 218, ss. Heinichen ad Euseb. H. E. excurs. xiii. t. iii. p. 418, ss.

18 Euseb. vii. 30, 6: Τὰς συνεισάκτους γυναῖκας, ὡς Ἀντιοχεῖς ὀνομάζουσι. Perhaps the περιακτοί, 1 Cor. ix. 5, gave rise to that appellation proceeding from Antiochian wit. Perhaps, too, it originated from John xix. 27; ἔλαβεν αὐτὴν εἰς τὰ ἴδια i. e., συνεισήγαγεν.

19 Cyprian. Epist. 5, 6, especially 62. Can. Illib. 27, Ancyr. 19, Nicaen. 3. The two Syriac letters falsely attributed to Clement also censure this abuse (note 5). The later work, de Singularitate clericorum, in Opp. Cypriani, is directed entirely against the practice.

20 Comp. Dionys. Alex. ap. Euseb. H. E. vi. 42.

21 He lived on a rock in the mountain desert at the Red Sea, a day's journey from it. See vita S. Hilarionis by Jerome, Et. Quatremère Mémoires géographiques et historiques sur l'Egypte. (Paris, 2 tomes, 1811) i. 152.

cution, which so readily engenders fanaticism, in addition to enthusiasm, was peculiarly adapted to procure approbation even for such oddities. Hence, Antony found imitators; and, since the following time favored such undertakings, in another point of view, he was in the sequel regarded as the father of *Monachism.*[22]

§ 74.

MORAL CHARACTER OF CHRISTIANITY IN THIS PERIOD.

Though Christian freedom at this time had been fettered only by a few ecclesiastical laws, and the teachers, for the most part, were still able rightly to distinguish the essence of Christian virtue from its forms, yet it can not but be perceived, that germs were already developed in the church, from which its moral corruption afterward arose. The notion of the church's external unity, with its consequences, led men to set too high a value on orthodoxy of the letter,[1] and on external connection with the church. Heretics were universally hated as men wholly corrupt and lost.[2] On the contrary, even an Origen was of opinion that, in the communion and at the intercession of the church, even gross sinners might be accepted of God.[3] To

[22] Sozomenus H. E. i. 12, 13. Vita Antonii by Athanasius (either spurious or greatly interpolated, see Oudini Comm. de scriptor. eccles. ant. vol. i. p. 358).

[1] Origenes in Matth. Commentar. series § 33: Et malum quidem est, invenire aliquem secundum mores vitae errantem, multo autem pejus arbitror esse in dogmatibus aberrare et non secundum verissimam regulam scripturarum sentire. Quoniam sicut in peccatis mortalibus, puniendi sumus amplius propter dogmata falsa peccantes.

[2] Orig. Selecta in Job. ed. de la Rue, p. 501: *Καὶ ὁ αἱρετικὸς ὅταν εὔξηται—ὅταν δοκῇ κατεστηρίχθαι, τότε εἰς τέλος ἀπολεῖται· ἡ γὰρ εὐχὴ αὐτοῦ λογίζεται αὐτῷ εἰς ἁμαρτίαν.* Cyprian. de Unit. eccles.: Tales etiamsi occisi in confessione nominis fuerint, macula ista nec sanguine abluitur. Esse martyr non potest, qui in ecclesia non est. Comp. the vota at the council of Carthage in the year 256 (in Cypriani Opp. ed Baluz. p. 334, ss.): Lucius a Thebeste: Haereticos blasphemos atque iniquos—execrandos censeo. Vincentius a Thibari: Haereticos scimus esse pejores quam ethnicos. Lucianus a Rucuma: Si potest luci et tenebris convenire, potest nobis et haereticis aliquid esse commune. Heretics are called, Const. Apost. vi. 13: *Ψευδόχριστοι καὶ ψευδοπροφῆται, καὶ ψευδαπόστολοι, πλάνοι καὶ φθορεῖς, ἀλωπέκων μερίδες καὶ χαμαιζήλων ἀμπελώνων ἀφανισταί.* C. 18: *Οἱ διαφθείροντες τὸ ποίμνιον, καὶ μολύνοντες τὴν κληρονομίαν, οἱ δοξόσοφοι καὶ παμπόνηροι.* Hence it was thought that heretics must have only the worst motives, and be guilty of the worst deeds. This was the source of so many distorted descriptions and fabrications respecting them.

[3] Origenes in libr. Jesu Nave, Hom. x. 1, on the narrative of the Gibeonites, Jos. 9:

this was added the error of estimating many virtues as well as errors too much according to external circumstances, since the temptation was easy to confound the ecclesiastical estimate of them,[4] which could only proceed upon the external form of the transactions, with the moral standard. The distinction between a higher and lower virtue did not, indeed, develop for a long time all the germs of corruption which it bore within itself; yet it must even already have perplexed the ideas of morality, since men began to place the higher virtue chiefly in certain external asceticism.[5] As too great value was attributed to this external asceticism, so also the steadfast endurance of persecution for the sake of Christianity was overvalued.[6] Although it is certain that many had worked themselves up to undergo martyrdom, from motives not wholly pure,[7] and although the confessors also were not always morally good men,[8] yet it was a general opinion that by the external fact of suffering, they not only blotted out

Isti ergo veniunt ad Jesum cum omnibus vetustatibus suis, et orant ab eo hoc tantum ut salventur. In quorum figura tale mihi aliquid videtur ostendi. Sunt quidam in Ecclesia credentes quidem et habentes fidem in Deum, et acquiescentes in omnibus divinis praeceptis: quique etiam erga servos Dei religiosi sunt, et servire iis cupiunt, sed et ad ornatum Ecclesiae, vel ministerium satis promti paratique sunt, in actibus vero suis et conversatione propria obscoenitatibus et vitiis involuti, nec omnino deponentes veterem hominem cum actibus suis—praeter hoc, quod in Deum credunt, et erga servos Dei, vel Ecclesiae cultum videntur esse devoti, nihil adhibent emendationis vel innovationis in moribus. Istis ergo Jesus Dominus noster salutem quidem concedit, sed quodammodo salus ipsa eorum notam non evadit infamiae. Cf. c. 3. In Matthaeum commentariorum series, c. 120 (ad Matth. xxvii. 15): Illud quaeramus, si tale aliquid fiat et in judicio Dei, ut omnis Ecclesiae petere possit aliquem peccatorem, ut solvatur a condemnatione peccati, maxime autem si quando habeat perditionis caetera opera, ad benefaciendum autem Ecclesiae impiger sit. Tales enim invenies saepe in potentibus constitutos, alias quidem peccatores, tamen pro Christianis, quantum possibile iis est, multa agentes. Hoc si videtur alicui dignum requisitione, requiret. Quod autem manifestum est, omnes curare tentemus, ut ex petentibus inveniamur esse, et in ordine eorum, qui bene vixerunt, magis quam ex illis, pro quibus petitur, quasi pro hominibus malis. Nam etsi concedatur aliquis peccatorum ad preces Ecclesiae, non tamen justum est gloriam et beatitudinem consequi eum, qui hujusmodi est: sufficit enim quod a poena dimittitur.

4 Comp. especially the Canones Illiberitani, de Wette's Geschichte der christl. Sittenlehre. Erste Hälfte, S. 176, ff.

5 See § 73, note 11.

6 De Wette, l. c. S. 184, ff.

7 Clem. Strom. vii. p. 871: *Οἱ μὲν γὰρ φιλοδοξίᾳ (ἐμμένουσιν ὁμολογίᾳ), οἱ δὲ εὐλαβείᾳ κολάσεως ἄλλης δριμυτέρας, οἱ δὲ διά τινας ἡδονὰς καὶ εὐφροσύνας τὰς μετὰ θάνατον ὑπομένοντες, παῖδες ἐν πίστει.* Comp. above, § 72, note 26.

8 Cyprian de Unit. eccl.: Caeterum numquam in confessoribus fraudes et stupra et adulteria postmodum viderimus, quae nunc in quibusdam videntes ingemiscimus et dolemus. Epist. 7, ad Rogatianum presb. et caeteros confessores: Cum quanto enim nominis vestri pudore delinquitur, quando aliquis temulentus et lasciviens demoratur, alius in eam patriam; unde extorris factus est, regreditur, ut apprehensus non jam quasi Christianus sed quasi nocens pereat. Cf. Epist. 6, ad Clerum suum.

their own sins before God, but were likewise able to atone for the sins of others.[9] Hence, the fanatical self-devotion to martyrdom (profiteri) always found admirers,[10] although it was disapproved by most.[11] On the other hand, in times of peace, many attached themselves to the church,[12] allured in part by external advantages, who were internally at a distance from it,[13] both regarding their relation to it as a thing simply external, and showing themselves lukewarm and indifferent.[14]

While we can not overlook these moral defects, we still find

[9] See above, § 70, note 15, ff.

[10] Comp. above, § 53, note 48. Euseb. de Martyr. Palaest. c. 3. eccl. vii. c. 12.

[11] Comp. § 53, note 49. Cyprian. Ep. 83. Petri Alex. Epist. canon. c. 9. Mensurius, bishop of Carthage, see § 72, note 26. Can. Illiberitan. c. 60 : Si quis idola fregerit, et ibidem fuerit occisus, quatenus in evangelio scriptum non est, neque invenitur ab Apostolis unquam factum placuit in numero eum non recipi martyrum.

[12] Origines c. Cels. i. p. 53 : Τὸ ὄνομα τοῦ Ἰησοῦ—ἐμποιεῖ θαυμασίαν τινὰ πρᾳότητα, καὶ καταστολὴν τοῦ ἤθους, καὶ φιλανθρωπίαν, καὶ χρηστότητα, καὶ ἡμερότητα ἐν τοῖς μὴ διὰ τὰ βιωτικὰ ἤ τινας χρείας ἀνθρωπικὰς ὑποκριναμένοις, ἀλλὰ παραδεξαμένοις γνησίως τὸν περὶ Θεοῦ καὶ Χριστοῦ καὶ τῆς ἐσομένης κρίσεως λόγον.

[13] On the time before the Decian persecution Cyprianus de Lapsis writes : Dominus probari familiam suam voluit, et quia traditam nobis divinitus disciplinam pax longa corruperat, jacentem fidem et paene dixerim dormientem censura coelestis erexit.—Studebant augendo patrimonio singuli, et—insatiabili cupiditatis ardore ampliandis facultatibus incubabant. Non in sacerdotibus religio devota, non in ministris fides integra, non in operibus misericordia, non in moribus disciplina.—Jungere cum infidelibus vinculum matrimonii, prostituere gentilibus membra Christi : non jurare tantum temere, sed adhuc etiam pejerare, caet. Origenes in Jerem. Hom. iv. 3 : Καὶ ἀληθῶς ἐὰν κρίνωμεν τὰ πράγματα ἀληθείᾳ, καὶ μὴ ὄχλοις,—ὀψόμεθα νῦν, ὡς οὐκ ἐσμὲν πιστοί· ἀλλὰ τότε ἦσαν πιστοὶ, ὅτε τὰ μαρτύρια τῇ γενεᾷ ἐγίνοντο, κ. τ. λ.—Τότε ἦσαν πιστοὶ ὀλίγοι μὲν, πιστοὶ δὲ ἀληθῶς.—Νῦν δὲ, ὅτε γεγόναμεν πολλοὶ,—ἐκ τοῦ πλήθους τῶν ἐπαγγελλομένων θεοσέβειαν σφόδρα εἰσὶν ὀλίγοι, οἱ καταντῶντες ἐπὶ τὴν ἐκλογὴν τοῦ θεοῦ καὶ τὴν μακαριότητα. On the peaceful times before the Diocletian persecution, Eusebii H. E. viii. 1 : Ἄλλας ἐπ' ἄλλαις προσετιθέμεν κακίας.

[14] Origenes in Gen. Hom. x. 1 : Ubi vel quando vestrum tempus inveniam (ad distribuendam in tempore tritici mensuram Luc. xii. 42) ? Plurimum ex hoc, imo paene totum tempus mundanis occupationibus teritis in foro, aliud in negotiatione consumitis : alius agro, alius litibus vacat, et ad audiendum Dei verbum nemo, aut pauci admodum vacant. Sed quid vos de occupationibus culpo ? Quid de absentibus conqueror ? Praesentes etiam et in Ecclesia positi non estis intenti, sed communes ex usu fabulas teritis, verbo Dei vel lectionibus divinis terga convertitis.—Sine intermissione orandum Apostolus praecipit. Vos, qui ad orationes non convenitis, quomodo impletis sine intermissione, quod semper omittitis ?—quid faciunt hi, qui diebus tantum solemnibus ad Ecclesiam conveniunt ? In Num. Hom. xii. 2 : Aliqui vestrum ut recitari audierint, quae leguntur, statim discedunt.—Alii ne hoc ipsum quidem patienter expectant, usque quo lectiones in Ecclesia recitentur. Alii vero nec si recitantur, sciunt, sed in remotioribus dominicae domus locis saecularibus fabulis occupantur. Hom. xiii. 3 : Quanti modo hic praesentes sumus, et sermo Dei tractatur ? Sunt, qui concipiunt corde, quae lecta sunt, sunt, qui omnino non concipiunt, quae dicuntur, sed est mens eorum et cor aut in negotiis, aut in actibus saeculi, aut supputationibus lucri : et praecipue mulieres quomodo, putas, corde concipiunt, quae tantum garriunt, quae tantum fabulis obstrepunt, ut non sinant esse silentium ? Jam quid de mente earum, quid de corde discutiam, si de infantibus suis, aut de lana cogitent, aut de necessariis domus ?

in the church a living Christianity prevailing, and in consequence thereof, fine moral phenomena which are sought for in vain out of its pale at this period.[15] In particular, that philanthropy which Christianity awakened in its professors,[16] deserves so much the more honorable mention,[17] as it was not confined

[15] Origines c. Celsum, i. p. 21: Εἰ δ' ὁ εὐγνωμόνως ταῦτα κατανοῶν συγκαταθήσεται τῷ, μηδὲν κρεῖττον ἐν ἀνθρώποις γεγονέναι ἀθεεί· πόσῳ πλέον τὸ τοσοῦτον περὶ τοῦ Ἰησοῦ θαῤῥῶν ἀποφανεῖται, συνεξετάζων πολλῶν προσερχομένων αὐτοῦ τῷ λόγῳ ἀρχαιοτέρους βίους μεταγενεστέροις, καὶ κατανοῶν, ἐν ὅσαις μὲν ἀκολασίαις, ὅσαις δὲ ἀδικίαις καὶ πλεονεξίαις ἕκαστος τῶνδε ἦν, πρὶν, ὥς φησι Κέλσος,—ἀπατηθῶσι·— ἐξ οὗ δὲ παρειλήφασι τὸν λόγον, τίνα τρόπον γεγόνασιν ἐπιεικέστεροι καὶ εὐσταθέστεροι; P. 50: Οἱ κατήγοροι τοῦ Χριστιανισμοῦ οὐχ ὁρῶσιν, ὅσων πάθη, καὶ ὅσων χύσις κακίας καταστέλλεται, καὶ ὅσων ἄγρια ἤθη ἡμεροῦται προφάσει τοῦ λόγου. Arnobius adv. Gentes, ii. 4: Nonne vel haec saltem fidem vobis faciunt argumenta credendi, quod jam per omnes terras in tam brevi temporis spatio immensi nominis hujus sacramenta diffusa sunt? quod nulla jam natio est tam barbari moris, et mansuetudinem nesciens, quae non ejus amore versa molliverit asperitatem suam, et in placidos sensus assumpta tranquillitate migraverit?

[16] Thus the Roman church, in the middle of the third century, had (Cornelius Ep. Rom. ap. Euseb. vi. 43, 5,) χήρας σὺν θλιβομένοις ὑπὲρ τὰς χιλίας πεντακοσίας, οὓς παντας ἡ τοῦ δεσπότου χάρις καὶ φιλανθρωπία διατρέφει, and sent help besides even to the churches in Syria, Arabia (see Dionys. Alex. b. Euseb. vii. 5, 1), and Cappadocia (Basil. M. Ep. 70). Comp. above, § 53, note 9. Cyprian in exile, Ep. 36, ad Clerum: Viduarum infirmorum et omnium pauperum curam peto diligenter habeatis. Sed et peregrinis, si qui indigentes fuerint, sumptus suggeratis de quantitate mea propria, quam apud Rogatianum compresbyterum nostrum dimisi. Quae quantitas ne forte jam universa erogata sit, misi eidem—aliam portionem, ut largius et promptius circa laborantes fiat operatio. Epist. 60. He sends to the Numidian bishops to ransom the captive brethren from the barbarians, sestertia centum millia nummorum, which he had collected in his church. Et optamus quidem nihil tale de caetero fieri:—si tamen—tale aliquid acciderit, nolite cunctari nuntiare haec nobis literis vestris, pro certo habentes, ecclesiam nostram et fraternitatem istic universam ne haec ultra fiant precibus orare, si facta fuerint, libenter et largiter subsidia praestare. Epist. 61, ad Euchratium, bishop of Thenis, in reference to a converted actor who had been obliged to give up his employment: Quod si illic ecclesia non sufficit ut laborantibus praestet alimenta, poterit se ad nos transferre, et hic quod sibi ad victum atque ad vestitum necessarium fuerit accipere.

[17] Comp. Vita S. Cypriani per Pontium Diac. c. 9, on the conduct of Cyprian and his church on occasion of a desolating plague: Aggregatam primo in loco uno plebem de misericordiae bonis instituit, docens divinae lectionis exemplis, quantum ad promerendum Deum prosint officia pietatis. Tunc deinde subjungit, non esse mirabile, si nostros tantum debito caritatis obsequio foveremus: eum perfectum posse fieri, qui plus aliquid publicano vel ethnico fecerit: qui malum bono vincens, et divinae clementiae instar exercens, inimicos quoque dilexerit: qui pro persequentium se salute, sicuti, Dominus monet et horatur, orarit. Oriri Deus facit jugiter solem suum, et pluvias subinde nutriendis seminibus impertit, exhibens cuncta ista non suis tantum, sed etiam alienis: et qui se Dei etiam filium esse profitetur, cur non exemplum patris imitatur? Respondere, inquit, nos decet natalibus nostris, et quos renatos per Deum constat, degeneres esse non congruit; sed probare potius in sobole traducem boni patris aemulatione bonitatis. Cap. 10: Multa alia, et quidem magna praetereo.—Quod si illa gentiles pro rostris audire potuissent, forsitan statim crederent. Quid christiana plebs faceret, cui de fide nomen est? Distributa sunt ergo continuo pro qualitate hominum atque ordinum ministeria. Multi qui angustia paupertatis beneficia sumtus exhibere non poterant, plus sumtibus exhibebant, compensantes proprio labore mercedem divitiis omnibus cariorem.—Fiebat itaque exuberantium operum

merely to the Christian brethren, but manifested itself in noble traits toward the heathen.

largitate, quod bonum est ad omnes, non ad solos domesticos fidei, etc. Dionysius Alex. ap. Euseb. vii. c. 22, gives a similar account of the conduct of the Alexandrian Christians at the time of a pestilence. Among other things, *οἱ γοῦν πλεῖστοι τῶν ἀδελφῶν ἡμῶν δι' ὑπερβάλλουσαν ἀγάπην καὶ φιλαδελφίαν ἀφειδοῦντες ἑαυτῶν καὶ ἀλλήλων ἐχόμενοι, ἐπισκοποῦντες ἀφυλάκτως τοὺς νοσοῦντας, λιπαρῶς ὑπηρετούμενοι, θεραπεύοντες ἐν Χριστῷ, συναπηλλάττοντο ἐκείνοις ἀσμενέστατα τοῦ παρ' ἑτέρων ἀναπιμπλάμενοι πάθους, καὶ τὴν νόσον ἐφ' ἑαυτοὺς ἕλκοντες ἀπὸ τῶν πλησίων, καὶ ἑκόντες ἀναμασσόμενοι τὰς ἀλγηδόνας.—Τὰ δέ γε ἔθνη πᾶν τοὐναντίον· καὶ νοσεῖν ἀρχομένους ἀπωθοῦντο, καὶ ἀπέφευγον τοὺς φιλτάτους, κἂν ταῖς ὁδοῖς ἐῤῥίπτουν ἡμιθνῆτας· καὶ νεκροὺς ἀτάφους ἀπεσκυβαλίζοντο, τὴν τοῦ θανάτου διάδοσιν καὶ κοινωνίαν ἐκτρεπόμενοι.*

SECOND PERIOD.

FROM CONSTANTINE TO THE BEGINNING OF THE CONTROVERSIES CONCERNING IMAGE WORSHIP. A.D. 324-726.

For the general history of the middle ages: Ed. Gibbon History of the Decline and Fall of the Roman Empire. London. 1776-88. 4to. Translated into German with remarks, by F. A. W. Wenk, K. G. Schreiber, and Ch. D. Beck. Leipz. 1788-1807. 19 Theile 8vo.—F. Ch. Schlosser's Weltgeschichte in zusammenhängender Erzahlung. Frankf. a. M. 1815, ff. 8. from the second volume onward. Fr. Rehm's Handbuch. d. Geschichte des Mittelalters, 4 Bde. Marburg. 1821-39. 8. H. Leo's Lehrbuch der. Gesch. des Mittelalters, 2 Theile. Halle. 1830. 8.

FIRST DIVISION.

TO THE COUNCIL OF CHALCEDON. A.D. 324-451.

SOURCES.

1. Greek ecclesiastical historians: The continuators of Eusebius: Socrates Scholasticus, of Constantinople, Hist. Eccl. libb. vii. from 306–439. Hermias Sozomenus, lawyer in Constantinople, Hist. Eccl. libb. ix. 323–423. (Both edited by H. Valesius. Paris. 1668. Mogunt. 1677. Amst. 1700. fol.) Theodoretus, bishop of Cyprus, Hist. Eccl. libb. v. 322–429 (in Theodoreti Opp. ed. Jac. Sirmondus. Paris. 1642, ss. fol. tom. 3, p. 2—in edit. Schulzii cura J. A. Noesselt, t. 3, p. 719, ss. Halae. 1771. 8).[1] The Arian Philostorgius, Hist. Eccl. libb. xii. 318–425 (preserved only in the extracts of Photius Cod. 40. ed. Jac. Gothofredus. Genev. 1643. 4.)

Farther continuators: Theodorus Lector in Constantinople made extracts from Socrates, Sozomen, and Theodoret, in two books, and continued the history in two books more till A.D. 518. (Fragments of the continuation have been pre-

[1] F. A. Holzhausen comm. de fontibus, quibus Socrates, Sozomenus, ac Theodoretus in ecribenda historia sacra usi sunt, adjuncta eorum epicrisi. Gotting. 1825. 4.

served chiefly in Nicephorus Callistus, who, about 1330, compiled a church history in twenty-three books down to 911, of which history the first eighteen books, reaching to 610, are extant. Ed. Fronto Ducaeus. Paris. 1630. 2 voll. fol. Old and new fragments in J. A. Cramer anecdota Graeca, e Codd. Paris. Oxon. 1839. ii. 101.) Evagrius Scholasticus in Antioch, Hist. Eccl. libb. vi. from 431–594.[2] Editions. Theodoreti et Evagrii Schol. Hist. Eccl. item excerpta ex historiis Philostorgii et Theodori Lectoris, ed. H. Valesius. Paris. 1673. Mogunt. 1679. Amst. 1695. fol. Eusebii Pamphili, Socratis Schol., Herm. Sozomeni, Theodoreti et Evagrii, item Philostorgii et Theodori Lectoris, quae exstant graece et latine. H. Valesius emendavit, latine vertit, et annotationibus illustravit: criticis plurium eruditorum observationibus locupletavit Guil. Reading. Cantabrig. 1720. 3 t. fol. (a faulty reprint, August. Taurin 1747.)

Chronicon Paschale (falsely called Alexandrinum) from the creation of the world to 628, ed. Car. du Fresne, Dom. du Cange. Paris, 1688. fol. ad exemplar Vatic. rec. L. Dindorfius, voll. ii. Bonnae. 1832. 8.[3]

2. Latin ecclesiastical historians: Severus Sulpicius, presbyter in the diocese of Agen, Histor. Sacra, libb. ii. a mundo cond. –400. p. C. (opp. ed. Jo. Clericus. Lips. 1709. 8. Hieron. de Prato, Veron. 1741, 44. 2 voll. 4). Rufinus, presbyter in Aquileia, translated Eusebius in nine books, and continued the history in two books, to 395 (Socrates H. E. ii. 1, pronounces a judgment on the continuation), ed. P. Th. Cacciari. Romae. 1740, 41. 4.—Historia tripartita, libb. xii. compiled by Cassiodorus and Epiphanius Scholasticus, about 550, from Socrates, Sozomen, and Theodoret. This, and Rufinus's church history were the historical sources for the middle ages; published together by Beatus Rhenanus. Basil. 1523, and frequently in the 16th century.

[2] G. Dangers Comm. de fontibus, indole et dignitate librorum, quos de hist. eccl. scripserunt Theodorus Lector et Evagrius. Gottingae. 1841. 4.

[3] According to the opinion which originated with Luc. Holstenius (ed. Bonn. ii. 16), the proper Chron. Pasch. reaches only to 314, while the following part belongs to a later continuator. But even in that first part we find very many allusions to later persons and things, so that it must have suffered a thorough interpolation. For example, the festival of the annunciation is mentioned, i. 373; Chrysostom, and under this very name too, 437; Eutyches, 445; Cyrillus, 450, etc.

Hieronymi de Viris Illustribus lib. (written 392) and the continuation under the same title by Gennadius (about 495), both in J. A. Fabricii Bibliotheca Ecclesiastica. Hamb. 1718. fol.

3. Latin chronicles: Jerome translated the Chronicon of Eusebius into Latin, and continued it to 379 (in Eusebii Chron ed. Jos. Scaliger. Ludg. Bat. 1606, and Amstelod. 1658. fol.). After him we have) in succession the chronicles of Prosper of Aquitania to 455 (444 ?), of the Spanish bishop Idatius, to 469, and of Marcellinus Comes, to 534. The contents of these chronicles are arranged according to years, from 379 till 455, and published in Chronica medii aevi post Eusebium atque Hieron. res saec. iv. v. et vi. exponentia, ed. Chr. F. Roesler. t. 1. Tubingae. 1798. 8.

4. Acts of councils in the Collect. Concill. The canons of the councils in H. Th. Bruns Biblioth. eccles. vol. i. (Canones Apostol. et Concill. saec. iv.–vii. in 2 Part.). Berolini. 1839. 8. G. D. Fuchs Library of the ecclesiastical councils of the fourth and fifth centuries. Leipz. 1780–84. 4 parts, 8vo. Synodicon vetus, a short account of the councils up to the year 869, prim. ed. Jo. Pappus. Argent. 1601. 4, also in G. Voelli et H. Justelli Bibl. juris canon. veteris, t. ii. p. 1166, ss., and in Fabricii Bibl. graeca vol. xi. p. 185, ed. nov. vol. xii. p. 360, ss. belongs here from cap. 34–90.

5. Imperial decrees: Codex Theodosianus (compiled in 438, partly lost) cum comm. Jac. Gothofredi, cur. Jo. Dan. Ritter. Lips. 1737, ss. 6 voll. fol. with the recently found books and fragments edited by G. Haenel. Bonnae. 1842. 4.—Codex Justinianeus compiled by Tribonianus in 529, codex repetitae praelectionis 534 (in the numerous editions of the Corpus juris civilis).

6. Heathen historians: Ammianus Marcellinus, Rerum gestarum libb. xxxi. only libb. 14–31 are extant (from the year 353–378), ed. Jac. Gronov. Lugd. Bat. 1693. fol. J. A. Ernesti. Lips. 1773. 8.—Zosimus, *ἱστορία νέα* libb. vi. (to 410), ed. Chr. Cellarius. Cizae. 1679. 8. J. F. Reitemeier. Lips. 1784. 8.[4]

[4] There are different opinions concerning the historical value of Zosimus's history. It is very favorably judged by Jo. Leunclavius (Apologia pro Zosimo in his Romanae hist. scriptt. minores. Francof. 1590. fol., reprinted in the edition of Cellarius) and Reitemeier

FIRST CHAPTER.

STRUGGLE BETWEEN CHRISTIANITY AND PAGANISM.

J. G. Hoffmann Ruina superstitionis paganae variis observatt. ex. historia eccl. saec. iv. et v. illustrata. Vitemb. 1738. 4. S. Th. Rüdiger de Statu et conditione paganorum sub. Impp. christianis post Constantinum. Vratislav. 1815. 8. Histoire de la Destruction du Paganisme en Occident par A. Beugnot. 2 Tomes. Paris. 1835. 8 (a Prize Essay).

§ 75.

THE FAVORS SHOWN TO CHRISTIANITY UNDER CONSTANTINE AND HIS SONS.

Martini über die Enführung der christl. Religion als Staatsrelig. im röm. Reiche durch d. Kaiser Constantin. München. 1813. 4. S. 29, ff.

Although Constantine, after his victory over Licinius, gave full toleration to all religions,[1] protected the heathen priests in their prerogatives,[2] reserved to himself the dignity of a pontifex maximus,[3] and not till shortly before his death († 337) received the rite of baptism from Eusebius, bishop of Nicomedia;[4] yet he openly professed Christianity immediately after that victory,[5] seeking to make it more acceptable to his subjects by recommendation and persuasion,[6] and attractive toward the Christians

(disquis. de Zosimo prefixed to his edition): quite unfavorable is the judgment of the older church historians, and of Guil. de Sainte-Croix Observations sur Zosime in his Mémoires de l'Acad. des Inscriptions, t. 49 (1808), p. 466, ss.

1 Eusebius de vit. Const. ii. 56, 60.

2 Cod. Theodos. xii. i. 21, A.D. 335, and xii. v. 2, A.D. 337.

3 See below, § 78, note 2. Constantine appears on many coins with the insignia of the pontifex maximus, see Mionnet de la raretó et du prix des medailles romaines (Paris. 1827. 2 vol. 8.), ii. 236.

4 Eusebius de vita Const. iv. c. 61, 62.

5 When later heathen asserted (Juliani Caesares, at the conclusion, Zosimus, ii. 29, Sozomen, i. 5) that a conscience, troubled on account of the murder of his son Crispus, and his wife Fausta, impelled the emperor to Christianity, which was the only religion that promised full forgiveness of sin, even chronology is against the assertion. Comp. Manso's Leben Constantins d. G. Breslau. 1817. 8. S. 119. Hug's Denkschrift zur Ehrenrettung Constantins d. G. in d. Zeitschrift f. d. Geistlichkeit des Erzbisth. Freiburg. Heft 3, S. 75, ff.

6 See his rescripts to the oriental provinces in Euseb. de vita Const. ii. 24–42, 48–60. Respecting his speeches in recommendation of Christianity, cf. iv. 29, 32, 55. The one which he wrote, ὃν ἔγραψε τῷ τῶν ἁγίων συλλόγῳ, is appended to Eusebius's life of him. In it he lays peculiar stress on the prophecies of the Sybil, and the fourth eclogue of Virgil, which he also refers to Christ.

by favors;[7] engaging with zeal in the erection of many, and in part, splendid churches,[8] and in furnishing them with revenues out of the common fund of the cities.[9] Since paganism continued to prevail in Rome,[10] he transferred the seat of his government to Byzantium, and changed this city into a chiefly Christian *New-Rome* (afterward Constantinople).[11] But yet the

[7] Euseb. de vita Const. iv. 28: *Ταῖς δ' ἐκκλησίαις τοῦ θεοῦ καθ' ὑπεροχὴν ἐξαίρετον πλεῖσθ' ὅσα παρεῖχεν· ὧδε μὲν ἀγροὺς, ἀλλαχόθι δὲ σιτοδοσίας, ἐπὶ χορηγίᾳ πενήτων ἀνδρῶν, παίδων τ' ὀρφανῶν, κ. τ. λ.* Comp. the emperor's direction to the bishops, how they should use the new means put into their hands for the conversion of the heathen, l. c. iii. c. 21: *Οἱ μὲν γὰρ ὡς πρὸς τροφὴν χαίρουσιν ἐπικαιρούμενοι· οἱ δὲ τῆς προστασίας ὑποτρέχειν εἰώθασιν· ἄλλοι τοὺς δεξιώσεσι φιλοφρονουμένους ἀσπάζονται· καὶ ξενίοις τιμώμενοι ἀγαπῶσιν ἕτεροι· βραχεῖς δ' οἱ λόγων ἀληθεῖς ἐρασταὶ, καὶ σπάνιος αὖ ὁ τῆς ἀληθείας φίλος. Διὸ πρὸς πάντας ἁρμόττεσθαι δεῖ, ἰατροῦ δίκην ἑκάστῳ τὰ λυσιτελῆ πρὸς σωτηρίαν ποριζομένους· ὥστ' ἐξ ἅπαντος τὴν σωτήριον παρὰ τοῖς πᾶσι δοξάζεσθαι διδασκαλίαν.* In this way he himself converted the pagan inhabitants of Heliopolis in Phoenicia, l. c. iii. 58: *Προνοῶν—ὅπως ἂν πλείους προσίοιεν τῷ λόγῳ, τὰ πρὸς ἐπικουρίαν τῶν πενήτων ἔκπλεα παρεῖχε, καὶ ταύτῃ προτρέπων ἐπὶ τὴν σωτήριον σπεύδειν διδασκαλίαν· μονονουχὶ τῷ φάντι παραπλησίως εἰπὼν ἂν καὶ αὐτός· "εἴτε προφάσει, εἴτ' ἀληθείᾳ Χριστὸς καταγγελλέσθω* (Phil. i. 18!)." Rewards bestowed on the places which declared in favor of Christianity, l. c. iv. 38 and 39.

[8] See his letter to all bishops, Euseb. de vit. Const. ii. 46, in which he directs them, *σπουδάζειν περὶ τὰ ἔργα τῶν ἐκκλησιῶν· καὶ ἢ ἐπανορθοῦσθαι τὰ ὄντα, ἢ εἰς μείζονα αὔξειν, ἢ ἔνθα ἂν χρεία ἀπαιτῇ, καινὰ ποιεῖν. Αἰτήσεις δὲ—τὰ ἀναγκαῖα παρά τε τῶν ἡγεμόνων, καὶ τῆς ἐπαρχικῆς τάξεως· τούτοις γὰρ ἐπεστάλθη, πάσῃ προθυμίᾳ ἐξυπηρετήσασθαι τοῖς ὑπὸ τῆς σῆς ὁσιότητος λεγομένοις.* On the rescripts to the Praesides Prov. see ii. 45.—Churches which Constantine himself caused to be built: one at the holy sepulcher in Jerusalem (*τὸ Μαρτύριον· ἡ ἐκκλησία τῆς τοῦ Σωτῆρος ἀναστάσεως*, built from 326-335. Euseb. l. c. iii. 25-40; iv. 43-45. Comp. E. F. Wernsdorfi Hist. templi Constantiniani propter resurrectionis Christi locum exstructi, and de Templi Constantiniani etc. solemni dedicatione. Viteberg. 1740. 4.), on the Mount of Olives and in Bethlehem (both built by Helena, l. c. iii. 41-43), in Nicomedia and Antioch (iii. 50), in Mambre (iii. 51), in Heliopolis (iii. 58), many churches in Constantinople (iii. 48), especially the church of the Apostles (iv. 58-60). Cf. Jo. Ciampinus de Sacris aedificiis a Const. M. exstructis. Romae. 1693. fol.

[9] Sozomenus, i. c. 8: *'Εκ δὲ τῆς οὔσης ὑποφόρου γῆς καθ' ἑκάστην πόλιν ἐξελὼν τοῦ δημοσίου ῥητὸν τέλος, ταῖς κατὰ τόπον ἐκκλησίαις καὶ κλήροις ἀπένειμε, καὶ τὴν δωρεὰν εἰς τὸν ἅπαντα χρόνον κυρίαν εἶναι ἐνομοθέτησε.* v. c. 5: *'Εκ τῶν ἑκάστης πόλεως φόρων τὰ ἀρκοῦντα* (shortly before it is called *τὰ σιτηρέσια*, ap. Theodoret. iv. 4: *σύνταξις σίτου*) *πρὸς παρασκευὴν ἐπιτηδείων ἀπένειμε τοῖς πανταχοῦ κλήροις.* The unfortunate consequences of these measures and the exemption of the clergy, on the state of municipal affairs, are shewn by F. Roth de re municipali Romanorum, lib. ii. Stuttg. 1801, p. 32, ss. Hegewisch hist. Versuch über d. röm. Finanzen. Altona. 1804. S. 324, ff.

[10] In the year 331 the temple of Concordia was restored by the senate. The erection, also, of several altars happened at this time. Comp. Beugnot Hist. de la destruction du Paganisme, i. 106.

[11] Euseb. de vita Const. iii. 48: *Τὴν πόλιν—καθαρεύειν εἰδωλολατρίας ἁπάσης ἐδικαίου· ὡς μηδαμοῦ φαίνεσθαι ἐν αὐτῇ τῶν νομιζομένων θεῶν ἀγάλματα ἐν ἱεροῖς θρησκευόμενα, ἀλλ' οὐδὲ βωμοὺς λύθροις αἱμάτων μιαινομένους, οὐ θυσίας ὁλοκαυτουμένας πυρὶ, οὐ δαιμονικὰς ἑορτὰς, οὐδ' ἕτερόν τι τῶν συνήθων τοῖς δεισιδαίμοσιν.* Constantine besides beautified his new city with works of art, even with statues of the gods, which were every where pillaged and brought together here. The *ναοὶ δύο*, with the images of

greater number of the principal families of the kingdom remained pagan still, and hence he was obliged to have many heathen about his person, and in the higher offices of state,[12] although he most readily advanced Christians to posts of honor.[13] The more violent measures of Constantine against paganism were confined to his confiscating in the east many less frequented temples, whose revenues he converted to the use of Christian churches, or the building of Constantinople,[14] and his prohibiting the rites of worship connected with immoralities.[15] The law by which he is said to have interdicted all sacrifices was not at least carried out into operation.[16] After his death he was, according to custom, placed by the senate among the gods.[17]

After the death of *Constantine II.* († 340) *Constantius* ruled

Rhea and the Fortuna Romae, ap. Zosimus, ii. 31, were probably only niches. When Constantine caused his gilded statue to be set up at the dedication of the city, with the *Τύχη τῆς πόλεως* on the right, which was to be honored at the yearly festival of the birthday of the existing emperor (Chron. paschale, p. 285): this merely proves that as yet no suitable Christian symbolism had been formed for such solemnities (comp. Manso, l. c. S. 77). It is an analogous case when we find frequently on the coins of the first Christian emperors Victoria with the Labarum. The later tradition (ap. Zonaras, Cedrenus, etc.), that Constantine dedicated his city to the mother of God, is ridiculous.

12 Euseb. l. c. ii. 44: *Τοῖς κατ' ἐπαρχίας διῃρημένοις ἔθνεσιν ἡγεμόνας κατέπεμπε, τῇ σωτηρίῳ πίστει καθωσιωμένους τοὺς πλείους· ὅσοι δ' ἑλληνίζειν ἐδόκουν, τούτοις θύειν ἀπείρητο* (cf. iv. 52).

13 Cf. Rüdiger de statu et conditione Paganorum, p. 14, ss.

14 Euseb. l. c. iii. 54. Libanius in several passages (see below, note 16). Martini, S. 38. Rüdiger, p. 21, ss.

15 So the worship of Venus in Phoenicia, Euseb. l. c. iii. 55, 58, iv. 37, 38, the scandalous worship of the Nile, iv. 25. So also he threw down the temple of Exeulopius in Cilicia, on account of the fraud carried on there, iii. 56. Martini, S. 36, f. Rüdiger, p. 23, ss.

16 As Constantius (below, note 18) refers to such a law, so Eusebius, l. c. ii. 45, speaks expressly of a *νόμος εἴργων τὰ μυσαρὰ τῆς—εἰδωλολατρίας, ὡς μήτε ἐγέρσεις ξοάνων ποιεῖσθαι τολμᾷν, μήτε μαντείαις καὶ ταῖς ἄλλαις περιεργίαις ἐπιχειρεῖν, μήτε μὴν θύειν καθόλου μηδένα.* In like manner, iv. 23, 25, and the following Christian writers, the later of whom, ex. gr. Theophanes, speak even of capital punishments which Constantine enacted against heathenism. See Martini, p. 34. Annot. 67. On the other hand, it is striking that this law is nowhere to be found, and that only expressions of his are extant which assure toleration to heathenism (see note 1), and that Libanius asserts of him, Orat. pro templis, § 3 (ed. Reiske, vol. ii. p. 161): *Εἰς μὲν τὴν τῆς πόλεως, περὶ ἣν ἐσπούδασε, ποίησιν τοῖς ἱεροῖς ἐχρήσατο χρήμασι, τῆς κατὰ νόμους δὲ θεραπείας ἐκίνησεν οὐδὲ ἕν.* According to Gothofredus (ad. Cod. Theod. lib. xvi. tit. 10, l. 3) such a law was actually passed, but in the last years of the emperor. Martini, p. 40, is of opinion that Constantine and Eusebius in those passages refer merely to the laws against immoral rites: Rüdiger thinks that a general prohibition of sacrifice was issued by Constantine, but afterward recalled. Perhaps it was published shortly before his death, and was not therefore carried into execution.

17 Eutropii Breviarum, x. 4: Inter Divos meruit referri. There is still a calendar existing in which the festivals instituted in honor of him are enumerated. See de la Bastie in the Mémoires de l'Acad. des Inscr. xv. 106. Beugnot Hist. de la destruction du Paganisme, i. 109.

the east, and *Constans* the west. Both declared themselves decided opponents to paganism.[18] *Constans*, however could not proceed very strictly in opposition to it in the west, but had to act with some respect toward Rome in particular, still addicted as it was to the sanctuaries of the ancient religion.[19] But under these emperors the Christians sometimes forgot the principles of religious toleration on which they had so loudly insisted during former persecutions,[20] and fanatical voices calling for the violent extinction of paganism were raised among them.[21] When the whole empire devolved on Constantius after Constans' death († 350), all sacrifices were prohibited for the first time on pain of death.[22] This law could not, however, be fully

[18] Cod. Theodos. lib. xvi. tit. 10, l. 2 (A.D. 341): Cesset superstitio, sacrificiorum aboleatur insania. Nam quicunque contra legem divi principis parentis nostri, et hanc nostrae mansuetudinis jussionem ausus fuerit sacrificia celebrare, competens in eum vindicta et praesens sententia exseratur.

[19] Cod. Theod. xvi. 10, 3, ad Catullinum Praef. Urbi (A.D. 342): Quamquam omnis superstitio penitus eruenda sit, tamen volumus, ut aedes templorum, quae extra muros sunt positae, intactae incorruptaeque consistant. Nam cum ex nonnullis vel ludorum, vel circensium, vel agonum origo fuerit exorta, non convenit ea convelli, ex quibus populo Romano praebeatur priscarum solennitas voluptatum. About 347 an unknown traveler (Vetus Orbis descriptio, ed. J. Gothofredi. 1628, p. 35) found in Rome not only seven Vestal virgins, but the worship of Jupiter, Sol, and the Mater Deum still entire. Comp. Gothofredi, note p. 40, ss. Testimonies respecting the Pagan worship at this time may be derived from inscriptions in Beugnot Hist. de la destruction du Paganisme, i. 154.

[20] For example Justin. Apol. maj. c. 2, 4, 12. Tertull. ad Scapulam, c. 2. So also as yet even under Constantine, Lactant. Institt. v. 19: Religio cogi non potest: verbis potius quam verberibus res agenda est, ut sit voluntas. Nihil est tam voluntarium, quam religio. C. 20: Nos non expetimus, ut Deum nostrum, qui est omnium, velint nolint, colat aliquis invitus: nec, si non coluerit, irascimur. Epitome, c. 24: Religio sola est, in qua libertas domicilium collocavit. Res est enim praeter caeteras voluntaria, nec imponi cuiquam necessitas potest, ut colat quod non vult. Potest aliquis forsitan simulare, non potest velle.

[21] Julius Firmicus Maternus lib. de errore profanarum religionum, dedicated to the two emperors, between 340 and 350 (ed. F. Münter. Havn. 1826. 8. p. 118). Among other things it is said: Vobis, sacratissimi Imperatores, ad vindicandum et puniendum hoc malum necessitas imperatur, et hoc vobis Dei summi lege praecipitur, ut severitas vestra idololatriae facinus omnifarium persequatur. Audite et commendate sanctis sensibus vestris, quid de isto facinore Deus jubeat. (Here follows: Deut. xiii. 6–10. Then it is added:) Nec filio jubet parci, nec fratri, et per amatam conjugem gladium vindicem ducit. Amicum quoque sublimi severitate persequitur, et ad discerpenda sacrilegorum corpora omnis populus armatur. Integris etiam civitatibus, si in isto fuerint facinore deprehensae, decernunter excidia: et ut hoc Providentia Vestra manifestius discat, constitutae legis sententiam proferam, etc.

[22] Cod. Theod. xvi. 10, 4, (A.D. 353): Placuit, omnibus locis atque urbibus universis claudi protinus templa, et accessu vetitis omnibus, licentiam delinquendi perditis abnegari. Volumus etiam, cunctos sacrificiis abstinere. Quodsi quis aliquid forte hujusmodi perpetraverit, gladio ultore sternatur. Facultates etiam perempti fisco decernimus vindicari, et similiter affligi rectores provinciarum, si facinora vindicare neglexerint. Comp. L. 5, (A.D. 353,) and L. 6, (A.D. 356). However the heathen priesthood were restored in cases of vacancy, xii. 1, 46, (A.D. 358).—A prohibition of the adoption of Judaism, Cod. Th. xvi. 8,

carried out in Rome and Alexandria.[23] Every where else heathenism from this time forward was obliged to conceal itself in the country, in remote corners[24] (hence Pagani. Paganismus).[25] Constantius died in 361.

These violent measures had certainly the effect of opening the eyes of the heathen people to the impotency of their gods and the fraud of their priests;[26] but with nobler patriotic spirits they tended rather to increase the prejudices against Christianity, so partisan as it appeared to be, and favored by measures so unjust. Whatever truth they discovered in it appeared to them to have been already taught by the ancient philosophers.[27] They regarded the positive doctrines of it as barbarian superstitions, while the theological controversies concerning these doctrines brought suspicion on Christianity, and turned its professors into

7, (A.D. 357): Si quis, lege venerabili constituta, ex Christiano Judaeus effectus sacrilegis coetibus aggregetur, cum accusatio fuerit comprobata, facultates ejus dominio fisci jussimus vindicari.

[23] The prefects of the city at this time were heathen. See Rüdiger p. 31, s.—Symmachus, lib. x. Ep. 61, (also in Opp. S. Ambrosii, ed. Benedict. t. iii. p. 872. Comp. the remarks of the Benedictine editor) says with reference to the presence of Constantius in Rome in the year 357: Nihil decerpsit sacrarum virginum privilegiis, decrevit nobilibus sacerdotia, Romanis caeremoniis non negavit impensas, et per omnes vias aeternae urbis laetum secutus senatum, vidit placido ore delubra, legit inscripta fastigiis deum nomina, percontatus est templorum origines, miratus est conditores. Cumque alias religiones ipse sequeretur, has servavit imperio. A calendar of the year 354 (in Graevii Thes. antiqu. Rom. viii. 95,) gives all the heathen festivals as constantly observed.

[24] Especially on account of the spies which now appeared, curiosi, see Valesius ad Ammian. Marc. xv. 3, 8.

[25] The expression is first found in a law of Valentinian, A.D. 368, (Cod. Theodos. lib. xvi. tit. 2, l. 18,) and about the same time in Marius Victorinus de ὁμοουσίῳ recipiendo (Graeci, quos Ἕλληνας vel Paganos vocant, multos Deos dicunt), and in his comm. in Ep. ad Galatas in A. Maji Script. vett. nova collectio, t. iii. P. ii. p. 29. Under Theodosius this name is the usual one. For the explanation of it see Paulus Orosius (about 416) histor. praef. qui ex locorum agrestium compitis et pagis pagani vocantur. Prudentius (about 405) has for it Peristeph. x. 296: pago dediti; in Symmachum, i. 620: pago impliciti, cf. Severi Sancti Endelechii (about 400) Carmen de mortibus boum, v. 105: Signum, quod perhibent esse crucis Dei, magnis qui colitur solus in urbibus. See T. Flav. Clementis Hymn. in Christum servatorem. Sev. Sancti Endel. Carmen bucol. de mortibus boum, ed. F. Piper (Gottingae. 1835. 8). p. 85.

[26] Eusebius de vita Const. iii. 57: Πάντες δ' οἱ πρὶν δεισιδαίμονες, τὸν ἔλεγχον τῆς αὐτῶν πλάνης αὐταῖς ὄψεσιν ὁρῶντες, τῶν θ' ἁπανταχοῦ νεῶν τε καὶ ἱδρυμάτων ἔργῳ θεώμενοι τὴν ἐρημίαν, οἱ μὲν τῷ σωτηρίῳ προσέφευγον λόγῳ οἱ δ', εἰ καὶ τοῦτο μὴ ἔπραττον, τῆς γοῦν πατρῴας κατεγίνωσκον ματαιότητος, ἐγέλων τε καὶ κατεγέλων τῶν πάλαι νομιζομένων αὐτοῖς θεῶν.

[27] Augustinus Ep. 34 mentions libros beatissimi Papae Ambrosii,—quos adversus nonnullos imperitissimos et superbissimos, qui de Platonis libris Dominum profecisse contendunt, (de Doctr. christ. ii. 43: qui dicere ausi sunt, omnes Domini nostri J. Chr. sententias, quas mirari et praedicare coguntur, de Platonis libris eum didicisse) diligentissime et copiosissime scripsit.

ridicule.[28] On the other hand, paganism gained in this respect, that the ancient classic culture and literature, containing a religious doctrine at once pure and national, seemed chiefly to belong to it and to be intrusted to its keeping.[29] The most celebrated schools of rhetoric and philosophy in Alexandria, Athens,[30] etc., had heathen preceptors. The new platonic philosophy was silently working in favor of paganism,[31] *Jamblichus* († 333), the great orators *Libanius* († 395), *Himerius* († 390), and *Themistius* († 390), were heathen;[32] while there were few Christian scholars who could rival them, like the two *Apollinaris* in Laodicea in Syria; and these had to struggle with the prejudices against all heathen learning, which were increased by monachism.[33] Thus the most distinguished spiritual orators among the Christians were obliged to receive their education in heathen schools.

Under these circumstances it can not appear strange that we should find most attachment to paganism in the higher ranks;[34]

[28] Euseb. de vita Constant. ii. c. 61. *Εἰς τοσοῦτον δὴ ἤλαυνεν ἀτοπίας ἡ τῶν γινομένων θέα ὥστ' ἤδη ἐν αὐτοῖς μέσοις τῶν ἀπίστων θεάτροις τὰ σεμνὰ τῆς ἐνθέου διδασκαλίας τὴν αἰσχίστην ὑπομένειν χλεύην.* Gregor. Naz. Orat. i. p. 34: *Μισούμεθα ἐν τοῖς ἔθνεσι·—ἃ κατ' ἀλλήλων ἐπινοοῦμεν, κατὰ πάντων ἔχουσι· καὶ γεγόναμεν θέατρον καινὸν—πᾶσι μικροῦ τοῖς πονηροῖς, καὶ ἐπὶ παντὸς καιροῦ καὶ τόπου, ἐν ἀγοραῖς, ἐν πότοις.—ἤδη δὴ προήλθομεν καὶ μέχρι τῆς σκηνῆς,—καὶ μετὰ τῶν ἀσελγεστάτων γελώμεθα, καὶ οὐδὲν οὕτω τερπνὸν τῶν ἀκουσμάτων καὶ θεαμάτων, ὡς Χριστιανὸς κωμῳδούμενος, ταῦτα ἡμῖν ὁ πρὸς ἀλλήλους πόλεμος, κ. τ. λ.*

[29] Libanius in his Apologeticus, ed. Reiske, vol. iii. p. 437, dates from the persecution of heathenism by Constantine *τὴν ἀπὸ τῶν ἱερῶν ἐπὶ τοὺς λόγους ἀτιμίαν.—οἰκεῖα γάρ, οἶμαι, καὶ συγγενῆ ταῦτα ἀμφότερα, ἱερὰ καὶ λόγοι.*

[30] Respecting them see Schlosser in his Archive für Geschichte und Literatur, Bd. 1. (Frankf. a. M. 1830,) S. 217. On the school at Athens see Ullmann's Gregorius von Nazianz. (Darmstadt 1825) S. 27, ff. Gregorii Nazianz. Orat. xx. p. 321, (ed. Bened. Orat. xliii. p. 787): *Βλαβεραὶ μὲν—Ἀθῆναι, τὰ εἰς ψυχήν· καὶ γὰρ πλουτοῦσι τὸν κακὸν πλοῦτον, τὰ εἴδωλα, μᾶλλον τῆς ἄλλης Ἑλλάδος, καὶ χαλεπὸν μὴ συναρπασθῆναι τοῖς τούτων ἐπαινέταις καὶ συνηγόροις.*

[31] Eunapius in vita Aedesii (in the beginning): *Κωνσταντῖνος ἐβασίλευε, τά τε τῶν ἱερῶν ἐπιφανέστατα καταστρέφων, καὶ τὰ τῶν Χριστιανῶν ἀνεγείρων, οἰκήματα· τὰ δὲ ἴσως καὶ τὸ τῶν ὁμιλητῶν ἄριστον πρὸς μυστηριώδη τινὰ σιωπὴν καὶ ἱεροφαντικὴν ἐχεμυθίαν ἐπιῤῥεπὲς ἦν καὶ συνεκέκλειτο.*

[32] See an account of them in Dr. A. Westermann's Gesch. d. griech. Beredsamkeit. (Leipzig. 1833). S. 239.

[33] They were for some time excommunicated because they kept up intercourse with the heathen sophist Epiphanius, and had been present when he read a hymn to Bacchus. (Socrates, ii. 46. Sozom. vi. 25.)

[34] Comp. the steadfastness of Aristophanes in heathenism, Libanii Orat. pro Arist. ed. Reiske, vol. i. p. 447, s. Hence the rhetorician Victorinus did not venture at first to make his conversion public: Augustini Confess. viii. 3: Idolis sacrisque sacrilegis tunc tota fere romana nobilitas inflata inspirabat populos. 4: Amicos suos reverebatur offendere superbos daemonicolas, quorum ex culmine babylonicae dignitatis, quasi ex cedris

or that we should hear even from Christian writers, that among the great numbers which certainly passed over to Christianity at this time, the majority were unfortunately led to that step merely by external considerations.[35] Others, on the contrary, wavered between the old and new religion, hoping to find the truth between. From this tendency even new sects sprang up, of which the *Massalians* (*Euchites*, *Euphemites*, *θεοσεβεῖς*) in Phoenicia and Palestine,[36] and the *Hypsistarii* in Cappadocia,[37]

Libani, quas nondum contriverat Dominus, graviter ruituras in se inimicitias arbitrabatur.

35 Eusebius vita Const. iv. 54: *Καὶ γὰρ οὖν ἀληθῶς δύο χαλεπὰ ταῦτα κατὰ τοὺς δηλουμένους τούτους καὶ αὐτοὶ κατενοήσαμεν· ἐπιτριβὴν ἀπλήστων καὶ μοχθηρῶν ἀνδρῶν τῶν πάντα λυμαινομένων βίον· εἰρωνείαν τ' ἄλεκτον τῶν τὴν ἐκκλησίαν ὑποδυομένων καὶ τὸ Χριστιανῶν ἐπιπλάστως σχηματιζομένων ὄνομα. Τὸ δ' αὐτοῦ* (Κωνσταντίνου) *φιλάνθρωπον καὶ φιλάγαθον—ἐνῆγεν αὐτὸν πιστεύειν τῷ σχήματι τῶν Χριστιανῶν εἶναι νομιζομένων.* Such apparent Christians are described by Libanius Orat. pro templis (ed. Reiske vol. ii. p. 177), in the church: *Καταστάντες δὲ εἰς σχῆμα τὸ τῶν εὐχομένων, ἢ οὐδένα καλοῦσιν, ἢ τοὺς θεοὺς, οὐ καλῶς μὲν ἐκ τοῦ τοιούτου χωρίου, καλοῦσι δ' οὖν. Ὥσπερ οὖν ἐν ταῖς τραγῳδίαις ὁ τὸν τύραννον εἰσιὼν οὐκ ἐστὶ τύραννος, ἀλλ' ὅπερ ἦν πρὸ τοῦ προσωπείου. οὕτω καὶ ἐκείνων ἕκαστος τηρεῖ μὲν αὑτὸν ἀκίνητον, δοκεῖ δὲ τούτοις κεκινῆσθαι.*

36 Epiphanius Haer. lxxx. Massalianorum, § 1. *Μασσαλιανοὶ, Εὐφημῖται—ἐξ Ἑλλήνων ὡρμῶντο, οὔτε Ἰουδαϊσμῷ προσανέχοντες, οὔτε Χριστιανοὶ ὑπάρχοντες, οὔτε ἀπὸ Σαμαρειτῶν, ἀλλὰ μόνον Ἕλληνες ὄντες δῆθεν· καὶ θεοὺς μὲν λέγοντες, μηδενὶ μηδὲν προσκυνοῦντες, ἑνὶ δέ μόνον δῆθεν τὸ σέβας νέμοντες καὶ καλοῦντες παντοκράτορα· τινὰς δὲ οἴκους ἑαυτοῖς κατασκευάσαντες, ἢ τόπους πλατεῖς, φόρων δίκην, προσευχὰς ταύτας ἐκάλουν.* § 2: *Ἐν ἄλλοις δὲ τόποις φύσει καὶ* (leg. *προσευχὰς*) *Ἐκκλησίας ὁμοιώματι ἑαυτοῖς ποιήσαντες καθ' ἑσπέραν καὶ κατὰ τὴν ἕω, μετὰ πολλῆς λυχναψίας καὶ φώτων συναθροιζόμενοι, ἐπὶ πολύ τε καταλεγμάτια* [leg. *καταληγμάτια* cantiunculas] *τινα ὑπὸ τῶν παρ' αὐτοῖς σπουδαίων, καὶ εὐφημίας τινὰς δῆθεν εἰς τὸν θεὸν ποιούμενοι—ὥσπερ θεὸν ἐξιλεούμενοι ἑαυτοὺς ἀπατῶσιν.* Cyrillus Alex. de adoratione in spiritu et veritate lib. iii. (ed. Auberti, t. i. p. 92) says of the religion of those who were not the children of Abraham in the old world, Jethro, Melchisedek, etc. *Προσεκύνουν μὲν γὰρ—ὑψίστῳ θεῷ—προσεδέχοντο δὲ καὶ ἑτέρους τάχα που θεοὺς, ἐναριθμοῦντες αὐτῷ τὰ ἐξαίρετα τῶν κτισμάτων, γῆν τε καὶ οὐρανὸν, ἥλιον καὶ σελήνην, καὶ τὰ τῶν ἄστρων ἐπισημότερα. Καὶ πλημμέλημα μὲν ἀρχαῖον ἡ ἐπὶ τῷδε καταφθορὰ καὶ πλάνησις, διήκει δὲ καὶ εἰς δεῦρο καὶ παρατείνεται· φρονοῦσι γὰρ ὧδε παραληροῦντες ἔτι τῶν ἐν τῇ Φοινίκῃ καὶ Παλαιστίνῃ τινὲς, οἱ σφᾶς μὲν αὐτοὺς θεοσεβεῖς ὀνομάζουσιν, οἶμον δέ τινα θρησκείας διαστείχουσι μέσην, οὔτε τοῖς Ἰουδαίων ἔθεσι καθαρῶς, οὔτε τοῖς Ἑλλήνων προσκείμενοι, εἰς ἄμφω δὲ ὥσπερ διαῤῥιπτούμενοι καὶ μεμερισμένοι.* To these, too, Libanius perhaps refers, Lib. Ep. ad Priscianum Praesidem Palaest. (ed. Vales. in note ad Socr. 1, 22. Lib. Ep. ed. Wolf, p. 624): *Οἱ τὸν ἥλιον οὗτοι θεραπεύοντες ἄνευ αἵματος, καὶ τιμῶντες θεὸν προσηγορίᾳ δευτέρᾳ, καὶ τὴν γαστέρα κολάζοντες, καὶ ἐν κέρδει ποιούμενοι τὴν τῆς τελευτῆς ἡμέραν, πολλαχοῦ μὲν εἰσὶ τῆς γῆς, πανταχοῦ δὲ ὀλίγοι, καὶ ἀδικοῦσι μὲν οὐδένα, λυποῦνται δὲ ὑπ' ἐνίων· Βούλομαι δὲ τοὺς ἐν Παλαιστίνῃ τούτων διατρίβοντας τὴν σὴν ἀρετὴν ἔχειν καταφυγὴν, καὶ εἶναι σφίσιν ἄδειαν, καὶ μὴ ἐξεῖναι τοῖς βουλομένοις εἰς αὐτοὺς ὑβρίζειν.* Valesius supposes the Manichaeans to be meant here.

37 Concerning this sect, see especially Gregory of Nazianzum in the funeral oration on his father Gregory, who had at first belonged to them, Orat. xviii. (al. xix.) § 5. He designates the party as *ἐκ δυοῖν ἐναντιωτάτοιν συγκεκραμένη, ἑλληνικῆς τε πλάνης καὶ νομικῆς τερατείας ὧν ἀμφοτέρων τὰ μέρη φυγὼν, ἐκ μέρων συνετέθη· τῆς μὲν γὰρ τὰ εἴδωλα καὶ τὰς θυσίας ἀποπεμπόμενοι, τιμῶσι τὸ πῦρ καὶ τὰ λύχνα. τῆς δὲ τὸ σάββατον*

of nearly the same sentiments, appeared in the first half of the fourth century. Toward the end of the same century, the Caelicolae in Africa arose.[38] None of these parties, however, attained to much importance or continued long.

§ 76.

JULIAN THE APOSTATE.

A. Neander über den Kaiser Julianus und sein Zeitalter. Leipzig. 1812. 8. (Compare Schlosser's review in the Jen. A. L. Z. Jan. 1813. S. 121, ff.) Neander's Kirchengesch. ii. i. 75. C. Ullmann's Gregorius v. Nazianz, der Theologe. Darmst. 1825. 8. S. 72, ff. C. H. van Herwerden de Juliano Imp. relig. christ. hoste, eodemque vindice. Ludg. Bat. 1827. 8. Julian d. Abtrünnige, v. D. G. Fr. Wiggers, in Illgen's Zeitschr. f. hist. Theol. vii. 1, 115. Gfrörer's Kirchengesch. ii. 1, 155.

The injustice which Julian had to endure from the first Christian emperors, the strict education by which Christianity was attempted to be forced upon him, and his early private acquaintance with new-platonic philosophers, especially *Maximus*, had early disposed him toward heathenism, whose dead forms he saw animated with so much life by the new-platonists.[1] When he attained to the imperial dignity (361), he declared himself

αἰδούμενοι, καὶ τὴν περὶ τὰ πρόβατα (leg. τὸ περὶ τὰ βρώματα) ἔς τινα μικρολογίαν, τὴν περιτομὴν ἀτιμάζουσι. Ὑψιστάριοι τοῖς ταπεινοῖς ὄνομα, καὶ ὁ παντοκράτωρ δὴ μόνος αὐτοῖς σεβάσμιος. Gregorius Nyss. contra Eunom. (Opp. i. 12): Ὑψιστιανῶν αὕτη ἐστὶν ἡ πρὸς τοὺς Χριστιανοὺς διαφορὰ, τὸ θεὸν μὲν αὐτοὺς ὁμολογεῖν εἶναί τινα, ὃν ὀνομάζουσιν ὕψιστον, ἢ παντοκράτορα· πατέρα δὲ αὐτὸν εἶναι μὴ παραδέχεσθαι. Information respecting the Hypsistarians, Massalians, θεοσεβεῖς, etc.: C. Ullmann de Hypsistariis comm. Heidelb. 1823. 4. Guil. Boehmer de Hypsistariis, opinionibusque quae super eis propositae sunt. Berol. 1824. 8. Ullmann in the Heidelb. Jahrb. 1824, no. 17. A reviewer in the Jen. A. L. Z. Dec. 1824. S. 455. Ullmann Gregorius v. Nazianz. Darmst. 1825. S. 558. Böhmer einige Bemerkungen zu den v. d. H. Prof. Ullmann und mir aufgestellten Ansichten über den Ursprung und den Charakter der Hypsistarier. Hamburg. 1826. 8. Ullmann explains the origin of the Hypsistarii from a blending together of Judaism and Parsism; Böhmer, following Cyril (see above, note 36), regards them as the same party as the Massalians and θεοσεβεῖς, and perceives in them the remnant of a monotheism derived from primitive revelation, but afterward disfigured by Sabaeism. Gesenius Monum. Phoeniciae, i. 135, ii. 384, puts along with them the Abellonii, ap. Augustin. de Haer. c. 87. אבעלינים from אב עליון; but the Abellonii are manifestly a Christian sect.

[38] There are two laws of Honorius against them, Cod. Theod. lib. xvi. tit. 5, l. 43, A.D. 408 (Caelicolae, qui nescio cujus dogmatis novi conventus habent), and lib. xvi. tit. 8, l. 19, A.D. 409. Comp. Gothofredus on the last law, and J. A. Schmid Hist. Caelicolarum. Helmst. 1704.

[1] Henke de theologia Juliani diss. 1777 (reprinted in his Opusc. academ. Lips. 1802, p. 353, ss.).

openly in favor of the ancient national religion, to which he endeavored to impart a more moral and religious form, even by introducing many practices borrowed from Christianity,[2] while he himself thought that he was only restoring the worship of the gods to its original purity, and practiced it with greater zeal.[3] He took away their privileges from the Christians,[4] and forbade them to appear as public teachers of the national literature;[5] but he promised them full toleration in other respects. He was guilty, however, of many acts of injustice toward them, often, it is true, provoked by their intemperate zeal.[6] But they

2 Juliani Epist. 49, ad Arsacium Pontif. Galatiae, on the morals and conduct of priests (comp. especially Fragmentum in Juliani Opp. ed. Spanh. p. 298. Ullmann's Gregor. v. Nazianz, S. 527, ff.), support of the poor, and erection of houses for the reception of strangers. Ep. 52, concerning penitents. Julian established hierarchical gradations among the priests (Ep. 62), and wished them to receive higher honor than civil officers (Fragmentum, p. 296, Ep. 49). Sozomenus v. 16 says of him: Ὑπολαβὼν, τὸν Χριστιανισμὸν τὴν σύστασιν ἔχειν ἐκ τοῦ βίου καὶ τῆς πολιτείας τῶν αὐτὸν μετιόντων, διενοεῖτο πανταχῆ τοὺς ἑλληνικοὺς ναοὺς τῇ παρασκευῇ καὶ τῇ τάξει τῆς Χριστιανῶν θρησκείας διακοσμεῖν· βήμασί τε, καὶ προεδρίαις, καὶ ἑλληνικῶν δογμάτων καὶ παραινέσεων διδασκάλοις τε καὶ ἀναγνώσταις, ὡρῶν τε ῥητῶν καὶ ἡμερῶν τεταγμέναις εὐχαῖς, φροντιστηρίοις τε ἀνδρῶν καὶ γυναικῶν φιλοσοφεῖν ἐγνωκότων (Julian led even an ascetic life, cf. Misopogon, in Opp. p. 345, 350. Ammianus Marcellin. xxv. 4), καὶ καταγωγίοις ξένων καὶ πτωχῶν, καὶ τῇ ἄλλῃ τῇ περὶ τοὺς δεομένους φιλανθρωπίᾳ τὸ ἑλληνικὸν δόγμα σεμνύναι· ἑκουσίων τε καὶ ἀκουσίων ἁμαρτημάτων κατὰ τὴν τῶν Χριστιανῶν παράδοσιν ἐκ μεταμελείας σύμμετρον τάξαι σωφρονισμόν. Οὐχ ἥκιστα δὲ ζηλῶσαι λέγεται τὰ συνθήματα τῶν ἐπισκοπικῶν γραμμάτων, κ. τ. λ. Cf. Gregorii Nazianz. adv. Julian. Orat. iii. p. 101, ss.

3 In a manner too zealous even for cultivated heathens, Ammianus Marcell. xxv. 4: Praesagiorum sciscitationi nimiae deditus—superstitiosus magis, quam sacrorum legitimus observator, innumeras sine parsimonia pecudes mactans, ut aestimaretur, si revertisset de Parthis, boves jam defuturos.

4 The law concerning the restoration of possessions held by them in the cities has strangely enough found its way into the Cod. Theod. lib. x. tit. 3, l. 1. Cf. Sozom. v. 25.

5 Juliani Epist. 42: Ἄτοπον εἶναί μοι φαίνεται διδάσκειν ἐκεῖνα τοὺς ἀνθρώπους, ὅσα μὴ νομίζομσιν εὖ ἔχειν· ἀλλ' εἰ μὲν οἴονται σοφὰ, ὧν εἰσιν ἐξηγηταὶ, καὶ ὧν ὥσπερ προφῆται κάθηνται, ζηλούτωσαν αὐτῶν πρῶτον τὴν εἰς τοὺς θεοὺς εὐσέβειαν. εἰ δὲ [del. εἰς] τοὺς τιμιωτάτους ὑπολαμβάνουσι πεπλανῆσθαι, βαδιζόντων εἰς τὰς τῶν Γαλιλαίων ἐκκλησίας, ἐξηγησόμενοι Ματθαῖον καὶ Λουκᾶν, κ. τ. λ. Socrates, iii. 12, 16. Sozomenus, v. 18. Ammian. Marcellin. xxii. 10: Illud autem erat inclemens, obruendum perenni silentio, quod arcebat docere magistros rhetoricos et grammaticos, ritus christiani cultores (cf. xxv. 4). The sacred national literature appeared to him to be profaned by the contradictory and scoffing Christian interpretation. But there is no ground in this to attribute to him the design of degrading the Christians into a state of ignorance, as has been frequently done by writers. For there were so few Christian grammarians, on account of the prejudices with which they had to contend among their brethren of the same faith (see § 75, note 27), that Christians had almost their only opportunity of studying the ancient literature under heathen preceptors, a thing which they might yet do without prohibition. In the mean time, however, some Christian authors, especially the two Apollinaris, and Gregory of Nazianzum, were led by that prohibition to attempt imitations of heathen works in poetry and eloquence with biblical materials, Socrat. iii. 16. Sozom. v. 18.

6 Juliani Ep. 52, ad Bostrenos, concerning the Christian bishops: Ὅτι μὴ τυραννεῖν

had still more to suffer from the heathen governors and people. Hence it was natural that many who had hitherto been Christian professors for the sake of external advantages, should now go back to heathenism from the same motives.[7] The Jewish religion was respected by Julian as an ancient national faith; and on his march against the Persians, he even gave permission for the temple at Jerusalem to be rebuilt, though it was soon after destroyed.[8] On this same expedition he composed in Antioch, where he bore the scoffs of the Christian populace with philosophical indifference, his work *against Christianity*.[9] Soon after this he was killed in a battle with the Persians (363).[10]

ἔξεστιν αὐτοῖς,—παροξυνόμενοι πάντα κινοῦσι λίθον, καὶ συνταράττειν τολμῶσι τὰ πλήθη, καὶ στασιάζειν.—Οὐδένα γοῦν αὐτῶν ἄκοντα πρὸς βωμοὺς ἐῶμεν ἕλκεσθαι· διάῤῥήδην δὲ αὐτοῖς προσαγορεύομεν, εἴ τις ἑκὼν χερνίβων καὶ σπονδῶν ἡμῖν ἐθέλει κοινωνεῖν, καθάρσια προσφέρεσθαι πρῶτον, καὶ τοὺς ἀποτροπαίους ἱκετεύειν θεούς.—Τὰ γοῦν πλήθη τὰ παρὰ τῶν λεγομένων Κληρικῶν ἐξηπατημένα πρόδηλον ὅτι ταύτης ἀφαιρεθείσης στασιάζει τῆς ἀδείας. Οἱ γὰρ εἰς τοῦτο τετυραννηκότες,—ποθοῦντες δὲ τὴν προτέραν δυναστείαν, ὅτι μὴ δικάζειν ἔξεστιν αὐτοῖς, καὶ γράφειν διαθήκας, καὶ ἀλλοτρίους σφετερίζεσθαι κλήρους, καὶ τὰ πάντα ἑαυτοῖς προσνέμειν, πάντα κινοῦσιν ἀκοσμίας κάλων—εἰς διάστασιν ἄγοντες τὰ πλήθη.

[7] Of them speaks (sometimes in the manner of Julian) Asterius ep. Amaseae orat. adv. avaritiam (in Combefisii Auctar. novum p. 56): *Λαβόντες ὑποσχέσεις παρὰ τῶν ἀθέων καὶ ἀσεβῶν, ἢ ζωῆς ἀρχοντικῆς, ἢ περιουσίας τῆς ἐκ βασιλικῶν ταμιείων, ὥσπερ ἱμάτιον ταχέως τὴν θρησκείαν μετημφιέσαντο.—ὅτι γὰρ ὁ βασιλεὺς ἐκεῖνος—αὐτός τε ἀναιδῶς ἔθυεν δαίμοσιν, καὶ τοῖς τοῦτο βουλομένοις ποιεῖν πολλὰ προετέθη τὰ γέρα, πόσοι τὴν ἐκκλησίαν ἀφέντες ἐπὶ τοὺς βωμοὺς ἔδραμον; πόσοι δὲ, τὸ τῶν ἀξιωμάτων δέλεαρ εἰσδεξάμενοι, μετ' ἐκείνου κατέπιον τὸ τῆς παραβάσεως ἄγκιστρον;* Cf. Themistii Oratio consularis ad Jovianum, ed. Petav. p. 278: *Ἐλεγχόμεθα πάνυ γελοίως ἁλουργῖδας, οὐ θεὸν θεραπεύοντες, καὶ ῥᾷον Εὐρίπου μεταβαλλόμενοι τὰς ἁγιστείας. καὶ πάλαι μὲν εἷς Θηραμένης, νῦν δὲ ἅπαντες κόθορνοι, μικροῦ δεῖν χθὲς ἐν τοῖς δέκα, σήμερον δὲ ἐν τοῖς πεντήκοντα, οἱ αὐτοὶ πρὸς βωμοῖς, πρὸς ἱερείοις, πρὸς ἀγάλμασι, πρὸς τραπέζαις.*

[8] Juliani Epist. 25.—An earthquake and flames of fire prevented the workmen. Gregor. Nazianz. Orat. iv. Chrysostomus Homil. iii. adv. Judaeos. Ammianus Marcellinus, xxiii. 1. Socrates, iii. 20. Sozom. v. 22. Theodoret, iii. 15. In like manner, fire burst forth when Herod wished to penetrate farther into the sepulcher of David (Joseph. Antiq. xvi. 7. 1.) These phenomena are explained by the bituminous soil. Comp. Michaelis on the vaults under the temple-mountain in Lichtenberg's and Forster's Götting. Magazin, 3tem Jahrg. (1783) S. 772.

[9] According to Hieron. Ep. 84, ad Magnum 7, and Cyrillus adv. Jul. prooem. 3 books. Fragments in Cyrilli Alexandr. adv. Julianum libb. x. published separately: Défense du Paganisme par l'empereur Julien par M. le Marquis d'Argens. Berlin. 1764. ed. 3. 1769. 8. (Comp. the review in Ernesti's n. theol. Bibl. Th. 8. S. 551, ff.)

[10] Comp. Ammianus Marcellinus, xxv. 3. Eutropii Breviar. x. 8, both of whom accompanied the expedition.—Libanius *ἐπιτάχιος ἐπ' Ἰουλιανῷ* (ed. Reiske, vol. i. p. 614) hints that he was killed by a Christian, cf. Sozomenus, vi. 1, 2. Juliani Imp. Opera (Orationes viii. Caesares, *Μισοπώγων*, Epistolae 65) et Cyrilli contra impium Julianum lib. x. ed. Ezechiel Spanhemius. Lips. 1696. fol.

§ 77.

GENERAL TOLERATION TILL 381.

The reign of *Jovian* († 364) was in so critical times that he found it advisable to allow full freedom to all religions,[1] although he himself was a zealous Christian.[2] But this very disposition of the emperor encouraged the Christians in many places not only to demand restitution for injuries actually suffered under the preceding reign, but also to exhibit their hatred against the pagans, which had been increased by Julian's measures.[3] The legal toleration of all religions also continued under the following emperors, *Valentinian I.* (in the west † 375),[4] and *Valens* (in the east † 378 [5]), although they forbade bloody sacrifices;[6] in like manner, in the first years of the emperors *Gratian* and *Valentinian II.* in the west, and *Theodosius* in the east, till the year 381; while the continued irruptions of barbarous nations and internal commotions compelled them to avoid every thing by which disturbances might have been increased still more.

1 Themistii Oratio consularis ad Jovianum, ed. Petav. p. 278: *Τά τε ἄλλα αὐτοκράτωρ ὤν τε καὶ εἰς τέλος ἐσόμενος, τὸ τῆς ἁγιστείας μέρος ἅπαντος εἶναι νομοθετεῖς· καὶ τοῦτο ζηλῶν τὸν θεὸν ὃς τὸ μὲν ἔχειν πρὸς εὐσέβειαν ἐπιτηδείως, τῆς φύσεως κοινὸν ἐποίησε τῆς ἀνθρωπίνης· τὸν τρόπον δὲ τῆς θεραπείας ἐξῆψε τῆς ἐν ἑκάστῳ βουλήσεως.*

2 He restored all rights to the churches and clergy, Sozom. vi. 3, also the *σύνταξις τοῦ σίτου* (comp. § 53, note 9, § 76, note 4), but by way of preliminary only the third part, on account of a famine. Theodoret. iv. 4.

3 To this refers Libanius Epitaph. in Julianum ed. Reiske, vol. i. p. 619. The shutting up of the temples, and the withdrawment of the priests and philosophers, of which Socrates, iii. 24, speaks, was the consequence of fear.

4 Cod. Theodos. lib. ix. tit. 16, l. 9. (A.D. 371): Haruspicinam ego nullum cum maleficiorum causis habere consortium judico, neque ipsam, aut aliquam praeterea concessam a majoribus religionem genus esse arbitror criminis. Testes sunt leges a me in exordio imperii mei datae, quibus unicuique, quod animo imbibisset, colendi libera facultas tributa est. Nec haruspicinam reprehendimus, sed nocenter exerceri vetamus. Cf. Ammian. Marcell. xxx. 9. Rüdiger de statu Pagan. p. 42, ss. Evidences of heathen worship at this time may be derived from inscriptions. Beugnot, i. 270.

5 Themistii Oratio ad Valentem de religionibus, known only in the Latin translation of Andreas Duditius (ed. Petav. p. 499), with the similar contents of the Orat. ad Jovin. (note 1).

6 According to Libanii Orat. de templis, ed. Reiske, vol. ii. p. 163: *Τὸ θύειν ἱερεῖα— ἐκωλύθη παρὰ τοῖν ἀδελφοῖν, ἀλλ' οὐ τὸ λιβανωτόν.*

§ 78.

SUPPRESSION OF PAGANISM BY THEODOSIUS.

Rüdiger de statu Paganorum sub Impp. christ. p. 47. Jan. Henr. Stuffken Diss. de Theodosii M. in rem. christianam meritis. Lugd. Bat. 1828. 8. p. 16. A. Beugnot Hist. de la déstruction du Paganisme en Occident, i. 345.

After Theodosius had secured the east against the Goths, he directed his greatest energies to the suppression of paganism. In the same year in which he summoned the second oecumenical synod at Constantinople (381), he forbade apostasy to paganism,[1] but still allowed the other rites of heathen worship to be practiced except sacrifice. The two emperors of the west followed his example. *Gratian* laid aside the dignity of pontifex maximus,[2] commanded the altar of Victoria to be removed from the senate-house, and took away all privileges from the pagan worship,[3] although he was obliged to allow in Rome the sacrifices elsewhere forbidden, as Theodosius had to do at Alexan-

[1] Cod. Theodos. lib. xvi. tit. 7. l. 1: His, qui ex Christianis Pagani facti sunt, eripiatur facultas jusque testandi. Omne defuncti, si quod est, testamentum, submota conditione, rescindatur. Gratian and Valentinian made the same regulation in the west. L. 3 (382). —Lib. xvi. tit. 10. l. 7 (381): Si qui vetitis sacrificiis, diurnis nocturnisque, velut vesanus ac sacrilegus incertorum consultor (animum) immerserit, fanumque sibi aut templum ad hujuscemodi sceleris excusationem assumendum crediderit, vel putaverit adeundum, proscriptioni se noverit subjugandum, cum nos justa institutione moneamus, castis Deum precibus excolendum, non diris carminibus profanandum.

[2] According to Zosimus, iv. c. 36, who alone speaks of the circumstance, he might have refused it as soon as it fell to him, that is, after the death of Valens (for only the first Augustus was pontifex maximus). This supposition, however, is contradicted by the fact that Gratian bore the same title for some time. See Ausonii Gratiarum actio pro consulatu, and the inscriptions in Orelli Inscriptionum latinarum amplissima collectio, vol. i. p. 245. The usual assumption that Gratian merely declined the priestly dress offered to him, but yet bore the title, is arbitrary; for Zosimus speaks in express terms of the refusal of the dress and of the title. Hence, it must be maintained that Gratian wore that dignity for some years, and then laid it aside. J. A. Bosius de pontificatu maximo Impp. praecipue christianorum, in Graevii Thesaur. antiquitt. Rom. t. v. p. 271, ss. De la Bastie du souverain pontificat des empereurs Romains in the Mémoires de l'Acad. des Inscr. t. xv. p. 75, ss. Jos. Eckhel Doctr. numor. vett. P. ii. vol. 8. p. 386, ss. Birger Thorlacius de Imp. Rom., qui religioni Christi nomen dederunt, pontificatu maximo. Havn. 1811.

[3] He took away Vestalium virginum praerogativam, Sacerdotii immunitatem (which Valentinian I. had confirmed even in 371, Cod. Theod. xii. i. 75) caused the real estates belonging to the temples (agros virginibus et ministris deficientium voluntate legatos) to be drawn into the exchequer (cf. Theod. xvi. 10, 20), and deprived the vestal virgins and priests of victum modicum justaque privilegia. Symmachus, lib. x. Ep. 61. Ambros. Ep. 17

dria.[4] In Rome, paganism continued to be predominant,[5] particularly among families of distinction;[6] but yet the attempts made by the prefect of the city, *Q. Aurelius Symmachus*, to have these imperial decrees abolished, and in particular the altar of Victoria re-erected, had no influence upon *Gratian* († 383), *Valentinian II.*, and *Theodosius.*[7] In the east, the Christians proceeded far beyond the imperial ordinances. Enterprising bishops led mobs of hirelings or fanatics against the temples;[8] and the monks especially often combined for the destruction of all heathen sanctuaries.[9] The appeal *ὑπὲρ τῶν ἱερῶν* (388–

[4] Libanius *ὑπὲρ τῶν ἱερῶν* (ed. Reiske, vol. ii. p. 181): *Οὐ τοίνυν τῇ Ῥώμῃ μόνον ἐφυλάχθη τὸ θύειν, ἀλλὰ καὶ τῇ τοῦ Σαράπιδος, τῇ πολλῇ τε καὶ μεγάλῃ καὶ πλῆθος κεκτημένῃ νεῶν, δι' ὧν κοινὴν ἁπάντων ἀνθρώπων ποιεῖ τὴν τῆς Αἰγύπτου φοράν. Αὐτὴ δὲ ἔργον τοῦ Νείλου, τὸν Νεῖλον δὲ ἑστιᾷ ἀναβαίνειν ἐπὶ τὰς ἀρούρας πειθοῦσα. ὧν οὐ ποιουμένων, ὅτε τε χρὴ, καὶ παρ' ὧν, οὐδ' ἂν αὐτὸς ἐθελήσειεν, ἅ μοι δοκοῦσιν εἰδότες οἱ καὶ ταῦτα ἂν ἡδέως ἀνελόντες οὐκ ἀνελεῖν, ἀλλ' ἀφεῖναι τὸν ποταμὸν εὐωχεῖσθαι τοῖς παλαιοῖς νομίμοις, ἐπὶ μισθῷ τῷ εἰωθότι.*

[5] According to Hieronymus in Epist. ad Gal. iv. 3, the Romans were omnium superstitionum sentina.

[6] Respecting the heads of Paganism at Rome, Praetextatus, Symmachus, Flavianus, Caecina Albinus, etc., who are introduced speaking in the Saturnalia of Macrobius, see Alph. Mahul sur la vie et les ourvages de Macrobe in the Classical Journal, xxxi. 81. Beugnot, i. 438.

[7] Two embassies, with Symmachus at the head, the first in 382 to Gratian, the second in 384 to Valentinian II. See Symmachi Epist. lib. x. Ep. 61. On the other side, Ambrosii Epist. 17 and 18, ad Valentinianum. Respecting the two later equally fruitless embassies, the one to Theodosius, when he was staying at Milan, the other to Valentinian, see Ambros. Ep. 57, ad Eugenium. Beugnot, i. 410.

[8] So Eulogius, bishop of Edessa (see Libanius pro templis, ed. Reiske, vol. ii. p. 192, ss. Gothofredus ad Cod. Theod. xvi. 10, 8); Marcellus, bishop of Apamea (Sozom. vii. 15. Theodoret. v. 21); but particularly Theophilus, bishop of Alexandria. See below, note 12. Rüdiger, l. c. p. 58, ss.

[9] Libanius *ὑπὲρ τῶν ἱερῶν* (ed. Reiske, vol. ii. p. 164): *Σὺ μὲν οὖν οὔθ' ἱερὰ κεκλεῖσθαι (ἐκέλευσας), οὔτε μηδένα προσιέναι· οὔτε πῦρ, οὔτε λιβανωτὸν, οὔτε τὰς ἀπὸ τῶν ἄλλων θυμιαμάτων τιμὰς ἐξήλασας τῶν νεῶν, οὐδὲ τῶν βωμῶν. οἱ δὲ μελανειμονοῦντες οὗτοι καὶ πλείω μὲν τῶν ἐλεφάντων ἐσθίοντες, πόνον δὲ παρέχοντες τῷ πλήθει τῶν ἐκπωμάτων τοῖς δι' ᾀσμάτων αὐτοῖς παραπέμπουσι τὸ ποτὸν, συγκρύπτοντες δὲ ταῦτα ὠχρότητι τῇ διὰ τέχνης αὐτοῖς πεπορισμένῃ, μένοντος, ὦ βασιλεῦ, καὶ κρατοῦντος τοῦ νόμου, θέουσιν ἐφ' ἱερὰ, ξύλα φέροντες καὶ λίθους καὶ σιδηρὸν, οἱ δὲ καὶ ἄνευ τούτων, χεῖρας καὶ πόδας. ἔπειτα Μυσῶν λεία καθαιρουμένων ὀροφῶν, κατασκαπτομένων τοίχων, κατασπωμένων ἀγαλμάτων, ἀνασπωμένων βωμῶν. τοὺς ἱερεῖς δὲ ἢ σιγᾶν, ἢ τεθνᾶναι δεῖ. τῶν πρώτων δὲ κειμένων, δρόμος ἐπὶ τὰ δεύτερα καὶ τρίτα. καὶ τρόπαια τροπαίοις ἐναντία τῷ νόμῳ συνείρεται. τολμᾶται μὲν οὖν κἀν ταῖς πόλεσιν, τὸ πολὺ δὲ ἐν τοῖς ἀγροῖς.* P. 168. *Ἐστὶ δὲ οὗτος ὁ πόλεμος πόρος τῶν μὲν τοῖς ναοῖς ἐγκειμένων, τῶν δὲ τὰ ὄντα τοῖς ταλαιπώροις (γεώργοις) ἁρπαζόντων, τά τε κείμενα αὐτοῖς ἀπὸ τῆς γῆς, καὶ ἃ τρέφουσιν, ὥστ' ἀπέρχονται φέροντες οἱ ἐπελθόντες τὰ τῶν ἐκπεπολιορκημένων. τοῖς δ' οὐκ ἀρκεῖ ταῦτα, ἀλλὰ καὶ γῆν σφετερίζονται, τὴν τοῦ δεῖνος ἱερὰν εἶναι λέγοντες, καὶ πολλοὶ τῶν πατρῴων ἐστέρηνται δι' ὀνόματος οὐκ ἀληθοῦς. οἱ δὲ ἐκ τῶν ἑτέρων τρυφῶσι κακῶν, οἱ τῷ πεινῆν, ὥς φασι, τὸν αὐτῶν θεραπεύοντες θεόν. ἢν δὲ οἱ πεπορθημένοι παρὰ τὸν ἐν ἄστει ποιμένα (καλοῦσι γὰρ οὕτως ἄνδρα οὐ πάνυ χρηστόν), ἢν οὖν ἐλθόντες ὀδύρωνται, λέγοντες ἃ ἠδίκηνται, ὁ ποιμὴν οὗτος τοὺς μὲν ἐπῄνεσε, τοὺς δὲ ἀπήλασεν, ὡς ἐν τῷ μὴ μείζω*

390)[10] of the eloquent *Libanius*, addressed to Theodosius, had no effect; the heathen were immediately afterward forbidden by imperial laws even to repair to the temples;[11] and the destruction of the splendid temple of Serapis 391)[12] by the violent Theophilus, bishop of Alexandria, after a bloody contest, announced the total overthrow of paganism in the east.

When Theodosius had become sole master of the entire Roman empire after the death of *Valentinian II.* († 392), he forbade all kinds of idolatry by the most severe punishments (392);[13] and during his abode at Rome (394) he brought pub-

πεπονθέναι κεκερδακότας· καίτοι τῆς μὲν σῆς ἀρχῆς, ὦ βασιλεῦ, καὶ οὗτοι, τοσούτῳ δὲ χρησιμώτεροι τῶν ἀδικούντων αὐτοὺς, ὅσῳ τῶν ἀργούντων οἱ ἐργαζόμενοι. αἱ μὲν γὰρ ταῖς μελίτταις, οἱ δὲ τοῖς κηφῆσιν ἐοίκασι. κἂν ἀκούσωσιν ἀγρὸν ἔχειν τι τῶν ἁρπασθῆναι δυναμένων, εὐθὺς οὗτος ἐν θυσίαις τέ ἐστι, καὶ δεινὰ ποιεῖ, καὶ δεῖ στρατείας ἐπ' αὐτόν, καὶ πάρεισιν οἱ σωφρονισταί, κ. τ. λ. Cf. Theodoretus, v. 21.

10 Still incomplete in Reiske, but complete for the first time in Novus SS. Patrum Graecorum saeculi quarti delectus, rec. et adnotatione instruxit Lud. de Sinner. Paris. 1842. 8.

11 Valentinian's law for the west, of the 27th February, 391. Cod. Theodos. xvi. 10, 10: Nemo se hostiis polluat, nemo insontem victimam caedat, nemo delubra adeat, templa perlustret, et mortali opere formata simulacra suscipiat. Judices quoque hanc formam contineant, ut si quis—templum uspiam—adoraturus intraverit, quindecim pondo auri ipse protinus inferre cogatur. The same was decreed for the east by Theodosius, L. 11, 17th June, 391.

12 Socrates, v. 16. Sozom. vii. 15. Theodoret. v. 22. Eunapius in vita Aedesii, ed. Schotti, p. 63, ss. Zosimus, v. 23, especially Rufinus, who was at that time in Palestine, Hist. eccl. xi. 22–30. Many impositions of the priests were hereby detected, Theodor. l. c., Rufinus, l. c. 23–25. The heathens were particularly and deeply impressed by the circumstance that the expectation, quod si humana manus simulacrum illud (Serapis) contigisset, terra dehiscens illico solveretur in chaos, caelumque repente rueret in praeceps (Rufin. l. c. 23), had not been fulfilled at the destruction of the statue, and the fear which still remained, Serapin injuriae memorem aquas ultra et affluentiam solitam non largiturum (Rufin. l. c. 30, cf. Libanius, above, note 4), was contradicted by an ample inundation of the Nile.

13 Cod. Theodos, xvi. 10, 12. Impp. Theodosius, Arcadius et Honorius AA. ad Rufinum, Pf. P.: Nullus omnino, ex quolibet genere, ordine hominum, dignitatum, vel in potestate positus, vel honore perfunctus, sive potens sorte nascendi, seu humilis genere, conditione, fortuna, in nullo penitus loco, in nulla urbe, sensu carentibus simulacris vel insontem victimam caedat, vel secretiore piaculo larem igne, mero genium, penates nidore veneratus, accendat lumina, imponat thura serta suspendat. § 1. Quodsi quispiam immolare hostiam sacrificaturus audebit, aut spirantia exta consulere, ad exemplum majestatis reus licita cunctis accusatione delatus, excipiat sententiam competentem, etiamsi nihil contra salutem principum, aut de salute quaesierit. Sufficit enim ad criminis molem, naturae ipsius leges velle rescindere, illicita perscrutari, occulta recludere, interdicta tentare, finem quaerere salutis alienae, spem alieni interitus polliceri. § 2. Si quis vero mortali opere facta et aevum passura simulacra imposito thure venerabitur, ac, ridiculo exemplo metuens subito, quae ipse simulaverit, vel redimita vittis arbore, vel erecta effossis ara cespitibus vanas imagines, humiliore licet muneris praemio, tamen plena religionis injuria honorare tentaverit, is, utpote violatae religionis reus, ea domo seu possessione multabitur, in qua eum gentilitia consterit superstitione famulatum. Namque omnia loca, quae thuris constiterit vapore fumasse (si tamen ea in jure fuisse thurificantium probabuntur), fisco

lic sacrifices to an end by interdicting the defraying of them out of the imperial treasury. At that time, he even called upon the senate to declare themselves in favor of Christianity; but the slavish tokens of subjection with which they responded to him had so little serious consequence,[14] that even heathen honors were offered to this zealous Christian emperor after his death.[15]

§ 79.

TOTAL SUPPRESSION OF PAGANISM IN THE EAST.—ITS STRUGGLE IN THE WEST AFTER THEODOSIUS.

Rüdiger, l. c. p. 70, ss. Beugnot, l. c. ii. 1, ss.

Paganism was at present only an external ceremonial, which retained its hold upon a few noble spirits with a feeling of pa-

nostro associanda censemus. § 3. Sin vero in templis fanisve publicis, aut in aedibus agrisve alienis tale quispiam sacrificandi genus exercere tentaverit, si ignorante domino usurpata constiterit, xxv. librarum auri mulctae nomine cogetur inferre, conniventem vero huic sceleri par ac sacrificantem poena retinebit. § 4. Quod quidem ita per judices ac defensores et curiales singularum urbium volumus custodiri, ut illico per hos comperta in judicium deferantur, per illos delata plectantur. Si quid autem ii tegendum gratia, aut incuria praetermittendum esse crediderint, commotioni judiciariae subjacebunt. Illi vero moniti si vindictam dissimulatione distulerint, xxx. librarum auri dispendio mulctabuntur: officiis quoque eorum damno parili subjugandis. Dat. vi. Id. Nov. Constantinopoli, Arcadio. A. II. et Rufino Coss.

14 Comp. the narrative Prudent. in Symmachum, i. 409, ss. Especially from 699, ss.:

Adspice, quam pleno subsellia nostra senatu
Decernant, infame Jovis pulvinar et omne
Idolium longe purgata ex urbe fugandum:
Qua vocat egregii sententia principis, illuc
Libera tum pedibus, tum corde frequentia transit.

A different account, and one more accordant with later phenomena, is given by Zosimus, iv. 59, in his representation of the effect of Theodosius's discourse in the senate: *Μηδενὸς δὲ τῇ παρακλήσει πεισθέντος, μηδὲ ἑλομένου τῶν ἀφ' οὗπερ ἡ πόλις ᾠκίσθη παραδεδομένων αὐτοῖς πατρίων ἀναχωρῆσαι, καὶ προτιμῆσαι τούτων ἄλογον συγκατάθεσιν (ἐκεῖνα μὲν γὰρ φυλάξαντας ἤδη διακοσίοις καὶ χιλίοις σχεδὸν ἔτεσιν ἀπόρθητον τὴν πόλιν οἰκεῖν· ἕτερα δὲ ἀντὶ τούτων ἀλλαξαμένους τὸ ἐκβησόμενον ἀγνοεῖν)· τότε δὴ ὁ Θεοδόσιος βαρύνεσθαι τὸ δημόσιον ἔλεγε τῇ περὶ τὰ ἱερὰ καὶ τὰς θυσίας δαπάνῃ, βούλεσθαί τε ταῦτα περιελεῖν, κ. τ. λ.* (That is to say, the usurper Eugenius had given back again the legacies of the heathen sanctuaries (see note 3) which had been confiscated by Gratian. See Ambros. Ep. 57, ad Eugenium). The consequence, Zosim. v. 38: *Ὅτε Θεοδόσιος ὁ πρεσβύτης, τὴν Εὐγενίου καθελὼν τυραννίδα, τὴν Ῥώμην κατέλαβε, καὶ τῆς ἱερᾶς ἁγιστείας ἐνεποίησε πᾶσιν ὀλιγωρίαν, τὴν δημοσίαν δαπάνην τοῖς ἱεροῖς χορηγεῖν ἀρνησάμενος, ἀπηλαύνοντο μὲν ἱερεῖς καὶ ἱέρειαι, κατελιμπάνετο δὲ πάσης ἱερουργίας τὰ τεμένη.*

15 Beugnot, i. 487. Hence the heathen poet, Claudianus de tertio Consulatu Honorii, v. 162, ss., who lived at this time, represents the death of the emperor as an ascent to the gods.

triotism; but with the mass it was kept up merely from unreflecting custom or superstitious fear. With almost all, however, its ancient doctrine was obliged to sink under the pressure of new ideas.[1] Hence the victory of Christianity over paganism internally dead, could not be matter of doubt;[2] although the former often carried on the contest more by external means than by its inward power.[3] Many heathen could not resist

[1] Orosius Hist. vi. 1: Deum quilibet hominum contemnere ad tempus potest, nescire in totum non potest. Unde quidam, dum in multis Deum credunt, multos Deos indiscreto timore finxerunt. Sed hinc jam vel maxime, cum auctoritate veritatis operante, tum ipsa etiam ratione discutiente, discessum est. Quippe cum et philosophi eorum—unum Deum auctorem omnium repererunt, ad quem unum omnia referrentur; unde etiam nunc pagani, quos jam declarata veritas de contumacia magis quam de ignorantia convincit, cum a nobis discutiuntur, non se plures Deos sequi, sed sub uno Deo magno plures ministros venerari fatentur. Restat igitur de intelligentia veri Dei per multas intelligendi suspiciones confusa dissensio, quia de uno Deo omnium paene una opinio est. The heathen said (Augustini Enarr. in Psalm xcvi. § 12): Non colimus mala daemonia: Angelos quos dicitis, ipsos et nos colimus, virtutes Dei magni et ministeria Dei magni. The heathen grammarian, Maximus of Madaura, writes to Augustine (August. Ep. 43): Olympum montem Deorum esse habitaculum, sub incerta fide Graecia fabulatur. At vero nostrae urbis forum salutarium numinum frequentia possessum nos cernimus et probamus. Equidem unum esse Deum summum sine initio, sine prole, naturae ceu patrem magnum atque magnificum, quis tam demens, tam mente captus neget esse certissimum? Hujus nos virtutes per mundanum opus diffusas multis vocabulis invocamus, quoniam nomen ejus cuncti, proprium videlicet, ignoramus. Nam Deus omnibus religionibus commune nomen est. Ita fit, ut, dum ejus quasi quaedam membra carptim variis supplicationibus prosequimur, totum colere profecto videamur. No one could endure that the Christian martyrs should be preferred to these deities, qui conscientia nefandorum facinorum, specie gloriosae mortis,—dignum moribus factisque suis exitum maculati reperiunt.—Sed mihi hac tempestate propemodum videtur bellum Actiacum rursus exortum, quo Aegyptia monstra in Romanorum Deos audeant tela vibrare, minime duratura. In Macrobii (about 410) Saturnalium, i. 17. A Praetextatus (comp. § 78, note 6) declares the sun to be the one supreme God. Si enim sol, ut veteribus placuit, dux et moderator est luminum reliquorum, et solus stellis errantibus praestat; ipsarum vero stellarum cursus ordinem rerum humanarum—pro potestate disponunt:—necesse est, ut solem, qui moderatur nostra moderantes, omnium, quae circa nos geruntur, fateamur auctorem. Et sicut Maro, cum de una Junone diceret, *Quo numine laeso*, ostendit, unius Dei effectus varios pro variis censendos esse numinibus; ita diversae virtutes solis nomina Diis dederunt; unde *ἓν τὸ πᾶν* sapientum principes prodiderunt.

[2] Chrysostomus de S. Babyla contra Julianum et gentiles § 3. (Opp. ed. Montf. ii. 540), *Ὑπ' οὐδενὸς ἐνοχληθεῖσά ποτε τῆς Ἑλληνικῆς δεισιδαιμονίας ἡ πλάνη ἀφ' ἑαυτῆς ἐσβέσθη, καὶ περὶ ἑαυτὴν διέπεσε, καθάπερ τῶν σωμάτων τὰ τηκηδόνι παραδοθέντα μακρᾷ, καὶ μηδενὸς αὐτὰ βλάπτοντος αὐτόματα φθείρεται, καὶ διαλυθέντα κατὰ μικρὸν ἀφανίζεται.*

[3] Augustinus in Evang. Joannis tract. 25. § 10: Quam multi non quaerunt Jesum nisi ut illis faciat bene secundum tempus! Alius negotium habet, quaerit intercessionem clericorum: alius premitur a potentiore, fugit ad ecclesiam: alius pro se vult interveniri apud eum, apud quem parum valet: ille sic, ille sic: impletur quotidie talibus ecclesia. Vix quaeritur Jesus propter Jesum. Cf. Id. de Catechizandis rudibus c. 17. Hieronymus Comm. in Esaiam, lib. xvii.: Quod sequitur: Et venient ad te curvi,—qui detraxerant tibi (Es. lx. 14), de his debemus intelligere, qui non voluntate, sed necessitate sunt Christiani, et metu offensae regnantium timentibus animis inclinantur.

the external advantages presented by it. Few were ready to suffer for their religion.[4] But it is true, that in this manner also the number of merely external Christians was increased—men who still entertained heathen modes of thought and disposition; and the value of Christianity was by no means so generally manifested in the practices of its confessors as before.[5]

In the empire of *the east* (*Arcadius*, 395–408, *Theodosius II.* till 450), which was less disturbed from without, the ordinances of Theodosius against paganism could be strictly enforced.[6] Crowds of monks were sent about through the provinces with full power from the emperors, for the purpose of destroying all traces of idolatry.[7] Even misdeeds and murders were allowed to pass unheeded by the emperors; such as the horrible murder of the female philosopher *Hypatia* in Alexandria (416).[8] The new-platonic philosophers at Athens, and among them even the celebrated *Proclus* († 485),[9] were forced to conceal themselves most carefully, because they rejected Christianity. As early as

4 Augustini Enarr. in Psalm. cxli. § 20: Quis eorum comprehensus est in sacrificio, cum his legibus ista prohiberentur, et non negavit? Quis eorum comprehensus est adorare idolum, et non clamavit, non feci, et timuit ne convinceretur? Tales ministros Diabolus habebat. He then contrasts with them the steadfastness of the Christian martyrs. Chrysostom de S. Babyla, § 7, says of the heathen priests, μᾶλλον δεσποτῶν καὶ τῶν εἰδώλων δὲ αὐτῶν τοὺς βασιλεῖς θεραπεύουσι, and describes the neglected state in which the temples, altars, and images of the gods were, in consequence, under Christian emperors.

5 Thus Augustinus Enarr. in Psalm. xxv. § 14, makes a heathen reply: Quid mihi persuades ut Christianus sim? Ego fraudem a Christiano passus sum, et nunquam feci: falsum mihi juravit Christianus, et ego nunquam. Chrysostom. in 1 Epist. ad Tim. Hom. x. § 3. (Opp. xi. 602): Οὐδεὶς ἂν ἦν Ἕλλην, εἰ ἡμεῖς ὤμεν Χριστιανοὶ, ὡς δεῖ.—Οὐδεὶς πρόσεισιν. οἱ γὰρ διδασκόμενοι πρὸς τὴν τῶν διδασκάλων ἀρετὴν ὁρῶσι. καὶ ὅταν ἴδωσι καὶ ἡμᾶς τῶν αὐτῶν ἐπιθυμοῦντας,—τοῦ ἄρχειν, τοῦ τιμᾶσθαι, πῶς δυνήσονται θαυμάσαι τὸν Χριστιανισμόν; Ὁρῶσι βίους ἐπιληψίμους, ψυχὰς γηΐνας, κ. τ. λ.

6 Cod. Theod. xvi. 10, 13, ss. By L. 14 their privileges were taken from the priests.

7 So Chrysostom (Theodoret. v. 29): Μαθὼν τὴν Φοινίκην ἔτι περὶ τὰς τῶν δαιμόνων τελετὰς μεμηνέναι, ἀσκητὰς μὲν ζήλῳ θείῳ πυρπολουμένους συνέλεξε, νόμοις δὲ αὐτοὺς ὁπλίσας βασιλικοῖς, κατὰ τῶν εἰδωλικῶν ἐξέπεμψε τεμένων. These νόμοι are without doubt Cod. Theod. xvi. 10, 16, A.D. 399: Si qui in agris templa sunt, sine turba ac tumultu diruantur. Cf. Chrysostom. Epistt. 28, 51, 53, 54, 55, 59, 69, 123, 126, 221. Chrysostom worked in the same way in other countries also. See Procli (Episc. Constantinop. 434–445) laudatio S. Jo. Chrys. (Orat. xx. in Combefisii Nov. auctarium, i. 468): In Epheso artem Midae nudavit, in Phrygia Matrem quae dicebatur deorum sine filiis fecit, in Caesarea publicana meretricia honoris vacua despoliavit, in Syria Deum impugnantes synagogas evacuavit, in Perside verbum pietatis seminavit.

8 Socrates, vii. 15. Damascius ap. Suidam, s. v. Hypatia. The article Hypatia of Alexandria in E. Münch's vermischte hist. Schrifte. Bd. 1. Ludwigsburg. 1828. 8.

9 Vita Procli scriptore Marino ed. J. A. Fabricius. Hamb. 1700. 8. His eighteen ἐπιχειρήματα κατὰ Χριστιανῶν are contained and refuted in Johannis Philoponi libb. 18, de Aeternitate mundi (graece ex Trincavelli officina. Venet. 1535. fol. lat. vert. Joh Mahatius. Lugd. 1557. fol.).

423, all visible traces of paganism had disappeared in the east.[10]

It was otherwise in *the west*, notwithstanding the want of all living attachment to paganism in this quarter of the world also. So little hold had it on the minds of the people, that even in Rome, its continued center, where many families of note were still heathen, and many of the highest places were still occupied by heathen,[11] sacrifices were totally discontinued, after the cost of public oblations had ceased to be defrayed by the state. Under the feeble reign of *Honorius* (395–423), the earlier laws against paganism still remained in force, and were even increased by the addition of several new enactments; but the emperor was obliged at times to limit their operation,[12] to acknowledge heathen priesthood as public offices,[13] and to put a check to the destruction of temples,[14] for the sake of preserving some degree of tranquillity. The struggle, however, between Christianity and paganism often proceeded here and there to acts of violence, in which the one party prevailed at one time, the other at another.[15] As the heathen had always been accustomed to

[10] Theodosius II. in Cod. Theodos. xvi. 10, 22. (A.D. 423): Paganos, qui supersunt, quanquam jam nullos esse credamus, promulgatarum legum jamdudum praescripta compescant.

[11] Thus Florentinus, A.D. 397, and Flavianus, 399, were Praef. urbis, Valerius Messala, 396, Praef. praet. Italiae, Atticus Consul, 397 (Beugnot, ii. 6). Praefecti urbis were Rutilius Numatianus, A.D. 413, Albinus, 414, Symmachus, 418: Praef. praet. Ital. 429 Volusianus (l. c. p. 127).

[12] Honorius had issued, in the year 408, the law Cod. Theod. xvi. 5, 42: Eos qui Catholicae sectae sunt inimici, intra palatium militare prohibemus. Nullus nobis sit aliqua ratione conjunctus, qui a nobis fide et religione discordat. But when he afterward wished to nominate the heathen Generidus commander in Rhoetia, the latter did not undertake the office ἕως ὁ βασιλεὺς, αἰδοῖ τε ἅμα καὶ χρείᾳ συνωθούμενος, ἔπαυσεν ἐπὶ πᾶσι τὸν νόμον, ἀποδοὺς ἑκάστῳ, τῆς αὐτοῦ ὄντι δόξης, ἄρχειν τε καὶ στρατεύεσθαι. Zosimus, v. 46.

[13] Cod. Theod. xii. i. 166 ad Pompejanum Procons. Africae, A.D. 400.

[14] The African bishops resolved at the Concil. Africanum, A.D. 399, to make the following propositions to the emperors, Can. 25 (Cod. Eccl. Afric. c. 58. Mansi, iii. p. 766): Ut reliquias idolorum per totum Africam jubeant penitus amputare—et templa eorum, quae in agris vel in locis abditis constituta nullo ornamento sunt, jubeantur omnimodo destrui. Can. 27 (Cod. Afric. c. 60): Ut quoniam contra praecepta divina convivia multis in locis exercentur, quae ab errore gentili attracta sunt—vetari talia jubeant, etc. But thereupon Honorius, A.D 399, enacted two laws of an opposite character, Cod. Theodos. lib. xvi. tit. 10, l. 17: Ut profanos ritus jam salubri lege submovimus, ita festos conventus civium et communem omnium laetitiam non patimur submoveri. L. 18: Aedes, inlicitis rebus vacuas, nostrarum beneficio sanctionum, ne quis conetur evertere.

[15] Regarding the destruction of temples which Martin, bishop of Tours, A.D. 375–400, undertook, with violent opposition on the part of the heathen, see Sulpic. Severus de vita b. Martini, c. 13–15. In Anaunia, a valley of the Rhoetian Alps, the missionaries Sisin

lay the blame of all misfortune on the Christians, so since the west of Europe had been inundated by barbarous people, and even Italy had been several times devastated by such hordes, they were especially loud in declaring all these disasters to be punishments sent by the gods,[16] and in predicting the speedy downfall of Christianity.[17] Against these accusations the writings of *Augustine*[18] and the Spanish presbyter *Oro-*

nius, Martyrius, and Alexander, were horribly murdered, A.D. 397, by the heathen during the Pagan festival of the Ambarvalia, and the church built by them destroyed. See Acta SS. (ad d. 29 Maj.) Maji, t. vii. p. 38. In Suffecte, in Africa, the Christians had demolished a statue of Hercules, and the heathen killed sixty of them for it (August. Ep. 268 ad Suffectanos). How at Calama, in Numidia, the heathen, during one of their festivals in the year 408, attacked the church there, and persecuted the Christians, may be seen in Augustin. Ep. 202 ad Nectarium.

[16] When the Gothic king Rhadegaisus, 405, broke into Italy, the heathen said (Augustin. de civ. Dei, v. 23), quod ille diis amicis protegentibus et opitulantibus, quibus immolare quotidie ferebatur, vinci omnino non posset ab eis, qui talia diis Romanis sacra non facerent, nec fieri a quoquam permitterent. When Rome was subsequently besieged by Alaric, 409 (Sozom. ix. 6), *ἀναγκαῖον ἐδόκει τοῖς ἑλληνίζουσι τῆς συγκλήτου, θύειν ἐν τῷ Καπιτωλίῳ καὶ τοῖς ἄλλοις ναοῖς.* And Zosimus, v. 41, asserts: Ὁ *δὲ* Ἰ*ννοκέντιος τὴν τῆς πόλεως σωτηρίαν ἔμπροσθεν τῆς οἰκείας ποιησάμενος δόξης, λάθρα ἐφῆκεν αὐτοῖς ποιεῖν ἅπερ ἴσασιν.* Comp. Beugnot, ii. 55. Zosimus, iv. 59: Τ*οῦ θυηπολικοῦ θεσμοῦ λήξαντος, καὶ τῶν ἄλλων, ὅσα τῆς πατρίου παραδόσεως ἦν, ἐν ἀμελείᾳ κειμένων, ἡ* Ῥ*ωμαίων ἐπικράτεια κατὰ μέρος ἐλαττωθεῖσα, βαρβάρων οἰκητήριον γέγονε, ἢ καὶ τέλεον ἐκπεσοῦσα τῶν οἰκητόρων εἰς τοῦτο κατέστη σχήματος, ὥστε μηδὲ τοὺς τόπους, ἐν οἷς γεγόνασιν αἱ πόλεις, ἐπιγινώσκειν.*

[17] Many Christians believed that Christ should return 365 years after his first appearance, and the end of the world take place. Philastr. Haer. 106: Alia est haeresis de anno annunciato ambigens, quod ait Propheta Esaias: Annuntiare annum Dei acceptabilem et diem retributionis. Putant ergo quidam, quod ex quo venit Dominus usque ad consummationem saeculi non plus nec minus fieri annorum numerum, nisi ccclxv. usque ad Christi Domini iterum de caelo divinam praesentiam. To this Christian expectation the heathen gave another application. Augustin. de civ. Dei, xviii. 53: Excogitaverunt nescio quos versus Graecos tanquam consulenti cuidam divino oraculo effusos, ubi Christum quidem ab hujus tanquam sacrilegii crimine faciunt innocentem, Petrum autem maleficia fecisse subjungunt (namely, scelere magico puer, ut dicunt, anniculus occisus, et dilaniatus, et ritu nefario sepultus est), ut coleretur Christi nomen per ccclxv. annos, deinde completo memorato numero annorum sine mora sumeret finem. In the work de Promissionibus et Praedictionibus Dei lib. (inserted in Prosper's works, and written by an African, about 450), it is related, P. iii. prom. 38, how the bishop Aurelius at Carthage had converted the long-closed temple of Caelestis (the Phoenician Astarte) into a Christian church, which, however, soon after (420) had been destroyed for the purpose of obviating a heathen illusion. Cum a quodam pagano falsum vaticinium, velut ejusdem Caelestis proferretur, quo rursum et via et templa prisco sacrorum ritui redderentur—verus Deus—sub Constantio et Augusta Placidia, quorum nunc filius Valentinus pius et christianus imperat, Urso insistente tribuno, omnia illa ad solum usque perducta agrum reliquit in sepulturam scilicet mortuorum.

[18] Augustin. Retractat. ii. 43: Interea Roma Gothorum irruptione agentium sub rege Alarico, utque impetu magnae cladis eversa est, cujus eversionem deorum falsorum multorumque cultores, quos usitato nomine Paganos vocamus, in christianam religionem referre conantes, solito acerbius et amarius Deum verum blasphemare coeperunt. Unde ego exardescens zelo domus Dei, adversus eorum blasphemias vel errores libros de

sius[19] could do but little; but they must have become dumb of themselves when even the German conquerors became converts to Christianity, and persecuted heathenism.[20] Hence even *Valentinian III.* (423–455), with all his powerlessness, could appear again as a decided opponent to paganism.[21] Still it was kept up more or less privately amid the confusion of migrations.[22]

civitate Dei scribere institui. Hoc autem de civitate Dei grande opus tandem xxii. libris est terminatum. Quorum quinque primi eos refellunt, qui res humanas ita prosperari volunt, ut ad hoc multorum deorum cultum, quos Pagani colere consueverunt, necessarium esse arbitrentur: et quia prohibetur, mala ista exoriri atque abundare contendunt. Sequentes autem quinque adversus eos loquuntur, qui fatentur haec mala nec defuisse unquam, nec defutura mortalibus, et ea nunc magna, nunc parva, locis, temporibus, personisque variari, sed deorum multorum cultum, quo eis sacrificatur, propter vitam post mortem futuram esse utilem disputant. His ergo decem libris duae istae vanae opiniones christianae religioni adversariae refelluntur. Sed ne quisquam nos aliena tantum redarguisse, non autem nostra asseruisse reprehenderet, id agit pars altera operis hujus, quae libris xii. continetur. Duodecim ergo librorum sequentium primi quatuor continent exortum duarum civitatum, quarum est una Dei, altera hujus mundi. Secundi quatuor excursum earum sive procursum. Tertii vero, qui et postremi, debitos fines. Augustini de civitate Dei lib. xxii. cum commentario Jo. Lud. Vivis. Basil. 1522. fol.; cum. comm. Leon. Coquaei. Paris. 1636. fol.; cum comm. Vivis et Coquaei sumt. Zach. Hertelii. Hamburg. 1661. 2 tom. 4. Jo. van Goens Disp. hist. theol. de Aurel. Augustino Apologeta secundum libros de civitate Dei. Amstelod. 1838. 8.

[19] Pauli Orosii adversus Paganos historiarum libb. vii. rec et illustr. Sigeb. Havercampus. Lugd. Bat. 1738. 4. Th. de Moerner de Orosii vita ejusque hist. libris. Berol. 1844. 8.

[20] So the Goths under Alaric at the sacking of Rome, 410 (Augustin. de civ. Dei, v. 23), qui—ad loca sancta confugientes, christianae religionis reverentia, tuerentur, ipsisque daemonibus atque impiorum sacrificiorum ritibus—sic adversarentur pro nomine christiano, ut longe atrocius bellum cum eis quam cum hominibus gerere viderentur. Cf. i. 1.

[21] Cod. Theod. xvi. 5, 63, A.D. 425: Omnes haereses omnesque perfidias, omnia schismata superstitionesque gentilium, omnes catholicae legis inimicos insectamur errores. It is decreed, sacrilegae superstitionis auctores, participes, conscios proscriptione plectendos.

[22] So in upper Italy Maximus Ep. Taurinensis (about 440, ed. Rom. 1784. fol.) Serm. 96, p. 655: Ante dies commonueram caritatem vestram, fratres, ut—idolorum omnem pollutionem de vestris possessionibus auferretis, et erueretis ex agris universum gentilium errorem. Nec se aliquis excusatum putet, dicens, non jussi fieri, non mandavi—tacendo enim, et non arguendo consensum praebuit immolanti.—Tu igitur, frater, cum tuum sacrificare rusticum cernis, nec prohibes immolare, peccas. Cum cellam ingressus fueris, reperies in ea pallentes cespites, mortuosque carbones. Et si ad agrum processeris, cernis aras ligneas et simulacra lapidea. Cum maturius vigilaveris, et videris saucium vino rusticum, scire debes, quoniam, sicut dicunt, aut dianaticus (a worshiper of Diana), aut aruspex est:—talis enim sacerdos parat se vino ad plagas deae suae, ut dum est ebrius poenam suam ipse non sentiat. Nam ut paulisper describamus habitum vatis hujusce: est ei adulterinis criniculis hirsutum caput, nuda habens pectora, pallio crura semicincta, et more gladiatorum—ferrum gestat in manibus, nisi quod gladiatore pejor est, quia ille adversus alterum dimicare cogitur, iste contra se pugnare compellitur. So also Maximus contra Paganos (Opp. p. 721) is directed against the still existing idolatry. Comp. his Sermo 77, p. 610: Principes quidem tam boni christiani leges pro religione promulgant, sed eas executores non exerunt competenter. In Gaul, Conc. Arelat. ii. ann. 443, c. 23: Si in alicujus Episcopi territorio infideles aut faculas accendunt, aut arbores, fontes vel saxa venerantur, si hoc eruere neglexerit, sacrilegii reum se esse cognoscat. Here persecutions of the Christians must still have taken place once and again, for chapter 10 contains penitence-decisions de his qui in persecutione praevaricati sunt, si voluntarie

Particular heathen customs, which had become of value to the people or had gained their superstitious confidence, were maintained, notwithstanding all the conversions to Christianity.[23]

fidem negaverint; and chapter 11 respecting those, qui dolore victi et pondere persecutionis negare vel sacrificare compulsi sunt. In Africa: de Promiss. et Praedict. Dei libb. P. iii. prom. 38 (comp. above, note 17): Novi quoque ipse, in quadam parte Mauretaniae provinciae de spelaeis et cavernis ita antiqua producta simulacra, quae fuerant absconsa ut omnis illa cum clericis in sacrilegio perjurii civitas teneretur. In Corsica Paganism continued predominant, and sacrifices were publicly offered. A female Christian named Julia was crucified by the exasperated heathens (between 440–445), because she would not take part in a sacrifice. See Acta SS. Maj. viii. 167 (ad 22 Maj.).

[23] In Rome, too, such practices as had a certain political importance were kept up. See Salvianus (presbyter in Marseilles, about 440. Salv. et Vincent. Lir. Opp. ed. Baluzius. Paris. 1684. 8. Bremae. 1688. 4) de gubernatione Dei lib. vi. ed. Brem. p. 106: Numquid, non Consulibus et pulli adhuc gentilium sacrilegorum more pascuntur, et volantis pennae auguria quaeruntur, ac paene omnia fiunt, quae etiam illi quondam pagani veteres frivola atque irridenda duxerunt?—haec propter Consules tantum fiunt. The fights with wild beasts were continued, Salvianus, vi. p. 105: Nihil ferme vel criminum, vel flagitiorum est, quod in spectaculis non sit; ubi summum deliciarum genus est mori homines, aut, quod est morte gravius acerbisque, lacerari, expleri ferarum alvos humanis carnibus, comedi homines cum circumstantium laetitia, conspicientium voluptate.—Atque ut hoc fiat, orbis impendium est; magna enim cura id agitur et elaboratur.—Sed haec, inquis, non semper fiunt. Certum est, et praeclara erroris est excusatio, quia non semper fiunt! P. 113: Si quando evenerit,—ut eodem die et festivitas ecclesiastica et ludi publici agantur, quaero ab omnium conscientia, quis locus majores christianorum virorum copias habeat, cavea ludi publici, an atrium Dei?—Non solum ad Ecclesiam non veniunt qui Christianos se esse dicunt; sed si qui inscii forte venerint, dum in ipsa Ecclesia sunt, si ludos agi audiunt, Ecclesiam derelinquunt.—Maximus Taurin. Hom. c. p. 334: Ante dies plerosque—circa vesperum tanta vociferatio populi extitit, ut irreligiositas ejus penetraret ad caelum. Quod cum requirerem, quid sibi clamor hic velit; dixerunt mihi, quod laboranti lunae vestra vociferatio subveniret, et defectum ejus suis clamoribus adjuvaret. It was believed (Hom. ci. p. 337), lunam de caelo magorum carminibus posse deduci. The heathen festival of the Kalendae Januariae was universally observed. Ambrose, Augustine, Leo the Great, and Peter Chrysologus, bishop of Ravenna, express themselves with zeal against it; also Maximus Hom. ciii. p. 343: Quis sapiens, qui dominici Natalis sacramentum colit, non ebrietatem condemnet Saturnalium, non declinet lasciviam Kalendarum?—Sunt plerique, qui trahentes consuetudinem de veteri superstitione vanitatis, Kalendarum diem pro summa festivitate procurent.—Nam ita lasciviunt, ita vino et epulis satiantur, ut qui toto anno castus et temperans fuerit, illa die sit temulentus atque pollutus.—Illud autem quale est, quod surgentes mature ad publicum cum munusculo, h. e., cum strenis unusquisque procedit, et salutaturus amicos, salutat praemio antequam osculo? caet. Most striking is that which Salvianus de gub. Dei viii. p. 165, writes of Africa: Quis non eorum, qui Christiani appellabantur, Caelestem illam (see note 17) aut post Christum adoravit, aut, quod est pejus multo, ante quam Christum? Quis non daemoniacorum sacrificiorum nidore plenus, divinae domus limen introiit, et cum foetore ipsorum daemonum Christi altare conscendit?—Ecce quae Afrorum, et maxime nobilissimorum, fides, quae religio, quae christianitas fuit!—At, inquis, non omnes ista faciebant, sed potentissimi quique, ac sublimissimi. Adquiescamus hoc ita esse, *caet.*

SECOND CHAPTER.

HISTORY OF THEOLOGY.

J. Chr. F. Wundemann Gesch. d. christl. Glaubenslehren vom Zeitalter des Athanasius bis auf Gregor. d. G. 2 Theile. Leipz. 1798, 99. 8. Munscher's Dogmengeschichte. Bd. 3, 4.

§ 80.

INTRODUCTION.

The universally received articles of the Christian faith in the beginning of this period were still so simple as to admit of ince to reason for free inquiry. How manifold were the theological views which arose, may be seen particularly from a comparison of the different schools, the speculative Origenist, the traditional, and the historico-exegetical, which now first began. And a still greater contrast of systems might be expected from the inclination of the Greek Christians to speculation and argument,[1] when external tranquillity was afforded them, after the cessation of persecution.

Thus theological controversies were unavoidable, though they would have had none other than a salutary influence on the development of reason, if parties had abided by the old distinction between πίστις and γνῶσις with clear consciousness; and if debated questions belonging to theology had not been drawn into the province of religion and the church. But the very simplicity of the older articles of faith frequently invited the disputants to appeal to them in their own favor, and so to accuse their opponents of deviating from the faith. If the accused also wished to lay claim for themselves to that freedom of speculation on the basis of the πίστις, the hierarchy, on the other hand, was a natural enemy to such liberty as would withdraw from its guardianship any department affecting the church, and had, of course, an interest in bringing all theological matters of debate from the

[1] Cicero de Orat. i. 11: Graeculos homines contentionis cupidiores quam veritatis.

province of theology into the province of religious faith, in order to be able to lay claim to the right of decision. This interest now appeared the more reckless in proportion as opposition to the heathen ceased to be a formidable thing, requiring a forbearing patience within the church, and in proportion as the hierarchy was now supported by worldly power.

Thus religious controversies assumed at the present time a very different character. While they were *formerly* limited to particular provinces, the whole Christian world was *now* divided by theological disputes into two parties. To put an end to the division by a final ecclesiastical decision the emperors called *general councils* (*σύνοδοι οἰκουμενικαί*), elevated their decisions into laws of the realm, and applied worldly power to enforce them universally. In earlier times, the councils summoned against heretics contented themselves merely with warding off the false doctrine by denials; but now the general councils, feeling their ecclesiastical importance, and supported by the imperial power, began to exalt positive decisions regarding disputed points, into ecclesiastical articles of faith.[2] Thus the development of doctrines proceeded more rapidly, while the field left to free speculation was always narrowed in proportion. On this very account, too, opponents presented a much more obstinate opposition, and the schisms became greater and more stiff-necked. The struggle had the most important influence on the development of the internal relations of the church, and was even of great political moment, from the circumstance of the emperors themselves taking a share in it. Hence, from this time forward, the history of theological disputes forms the central point not only of the whole history of the church, but sometimes also of the political history of the Roman empire.

[2] Hilarius de Trinitate, ii. 1: Sufficiebat quidem credentibus Dei sermo,—cum dicit Dominus: Euntes nunc docete omnes gentes, baptizantes eos in nomine Patris et Filii et Spiritus sancti, etc.—Sed compellimur haereticorum et blasphemantium vitiis illicita agere, ardua scandere, ineffabilia eloqui, inconcessa praesumere. Et cum sola fide expleri quae praecepta sunt oporteret, adorare scilicet Patrem, et venerari cum eo Filium, sancto Spiritu abundare: cogimur sermonis nostri humilitatem ad ea quae inenarrabilia sunt extendere, et in vitium vitio coarctamur alieno; ut quae contineri religione mentium oportuisset, nunc in periculum humani eloquii proferantur.

I. PERIOD OF THE ARIAN DISPUTES.

Walch's Historie der Ketzereien, ii. 385, ff. J. A. Möhler's Athanasius d. Grosse u. d. Kirche seiner Zeit, bes. im Kampfe mit dem Arianismus. 2 Th. Mainz. 1827. 8. Baur's Lehre von d. Dreieinigkeit u. Menschwerdung Gottes in ihrer geschichtl. Entwickelung, i. 320. G. A. Meier's Lehre von der Trinität in ihrer histor. Entwickelung, i. 134. Ritter's Gesch. d. christl. Philosophie, ii. 18.

§ 81.

BEGINNING OF THE ARIAN CONTROVERSY TO THE SYNOD OF NICE (325).

Storia critica della vita di Arrio, scritta da Gaetano Maria Travasa, Cler. Reg. Teatino. Venezia. 1746. 8. Der Arianismus in s. ursprungl. Bedeutung u. Richtung von L. Lange, in Illgen's Zeitschr. f. d. hist. Theol. iv. ii. 75.

While endeavors were made in vain to reunite the Donatists and Meletians with the church, the progressive development of the doctrine of the Logos gave rise to a new controversy, which soon became more general and violent than any that had preceded it. The common doctrine of the Logos, after the expulsion of the Monarchians, was, that he is the mediator of all Divine agency in the finite, by the will of the Father, and less than he. Regarding his origin, the emanistic idea had been by far the most general. In opposition to it, the school of Origen represented him as an eternal ray of the Divine glory. This bringing forth of the Logos outside of the Divine essence by the will of the Father was still, however, a creation; and that this creating could not be eternal, was already perceived, when Dionysius of Alexandria, in opposition to Sabellius, gave greater prominence to the fact that the Son was created.[1] But the emanists also took offense at this conclusion; for with them the Logos was eternal, though not as a person, yet still in the essence of God from whom he had proceeded. Dionysius at that time prevented a controversy by yielding; but now *Arius*, a

[1] See Divis. I. § 64, notes 7, 8, § 66, note 16. The Romish Dionysius merely infers from the expressions of the Alexandrian the non-eternity of the Logos; the latter denies this, a proof that he did not express it as his opinion. If, however, the Logos was a creature, he was not eternal. Hence the Arians referred even to Dionysius in favor of this doctrine. See § 14, note 7. Athanasius de sententia Dionysii endeavors to excuse him; but Basil the Great, Ep. ix. 2, finds in him the germ of Arianism.

presbyter in Alexandria, who, in the school of Lucian, by a historico-exegetical training had received the love of intelligible clearness, wished to remove the latent contradiction in Origen's doctrine, by teaching that the Logos is a created, and consequently not an eternal being.[2] When he fell into a dispute

[2] Writings of Arius: Epist. ad Eusebium Nicomediensem ap. Epiphan. Haer. 69, § 6, and Theodoret. Hist. Eccl. 1, 4, Epist. Alexandrum ap. Athanasius de synodis Arim. et Seleuc. c. 16, and Epiphanius Haer. 69, § 7, *Θαλεία* (*ἐμφερὴς τῇ χαυνότητι τοῖς Σωτάδου ᾄσμασιν*, Sozom. i. 21), not extant, except fragments in Athanasius. According to Athanasius c. Arian. Or. ii. 24, Arius, Eusebius, and Asterius, in their works, inculcated these sentiments respecting the creation of the world *ὡς ἄρα θέλων ὁ θεὸς τὴν γενητὴν κτίσαι φύσιν, ἐπειδὴ ἑώρα μὴ δυναμένην αὐτὴν μετασχεῖν τῆς τοῦ πατρὸς ἀκράτου (χειρὸς), και τῆς παρ' αὐτοῦ δημιουργίας, ποιεῖ καὶ κτίζει πρώτως μόνος μὸνον ἕνα καὶ καλεῖ τοῦτον υἱὸν καὶ λόγον, ἵνα τούτου μέσου γενομένου οὕτως λοιπὸν καὶ τὰ πάντα δι' αὐτοῦ γενέσθαι δυνηθῇ.* Arius's own explanations, Epist. ad Euseb.: *Ὅτι ὁ υἱὸς οὐκ ἔστιν ἀγέννητος, οὐδὲ μέρος ἀγεννήτου κατ' οὐδένα τρόπον, οὐδὲ ἐξ ὑποκειμένου τινός· ἀλλ' ὅτι θελήματι καὶ βουλῇ ὑπέστη πρὸ χρόνων καὶ πρὸ αἰώνων πλήρης θεὸς, μονογενῆς, ἀναλλοίωτος, καὶ πρὶν γεννηθῇ, ἤτοι κτισθῇ, ἢ ὁρισθῇ, ἢ θεμελιωθῇ, οὐκ ἦν· ἀγέννητος γὰρ οὐκ ἦν. διωκόμεθα, ὅτι εἴπαμεν, ἀρχὴν ἔχει ὁ υἱὸς, ὁ δὲ θεὸς ἄναρχός ἐστι. διὰ τοῦτο διωκόμεθα. καὶ ὅτι εἴπαμεν, ὅτι ἐξ οὐκ ὄντων ἐστὶν. οὕτω δὲ εἴπαμεν, καθότι οὐδὲ μέρος θεοῦ, οὐδὲ ἐξ ὑποκειμένου τινός.* Epist. ad Alex.: *Οἴδαμεν ἕνα θεὸν, μόνον ἀγέννητον,—τοῦτον θεὸν γεννήσαντα υἱὸν μονογενῆ πρὸ χρόνων αἰωνίων, δι' οὗ καὶ τοὺς αἰῶνας, καὶ τὰ λοιπὰ πεποίηκε· γεννήσαντα δὲ οὐ δοκήσει, ἀλλ' ἀληθείᾳ, ὑποστήσαντα δὲ ἰδίῳ θελήματι, ἄτρεπτον καὶ ἀναλλοίωτον, κτίσμα τοῦ θεοῦ τέλειον, ἀλλ' οὐχ ὡς ἓν τῶν κτισμάτων, γέννημα, ἀλλ' οὐχ ὡς ἓν τῶν γεννημάτων, οὐδ' ὡς Οὐαλεντῖνος προβολὴν τὸ γέννημα τοῦ πατρὸς ἐδογμάτισεν, οὐδ' ὡς ὁ Μανιχαῖος μέρος ὁμοούσιον τοῦ πατρὸς τὸ γέννημα εἰσηγήσατο, οὐδ' ὡς Σαβέλλιος τὴν μονάδα διαιρῶν, υἱοπάτορα εἶπεν, οὐδ' ὡς Ἱεράκας λύχνον ἀπὸ λύχνου, ἢ ὡς λαμπάδα εἰς δύο, οὐδὲ τὸν ὄντα πρότερον, ὕστερον γεννηθέντα, ἢ ἐπικτισθέντα εἰς υἱόν·—ἀλλ' ὡς φαμὲν, θελήματι τοῦ θεοῦ πρὸ χρόνων καὶ πρὸ αἰώνων κτισθέντα, καὶ τὸ ζῆν καὶ τὸ εἶναι παρὰ τοῦ πατρὸς εἰληφότα, καὶ τὰς δόξας συνυποστήσαντος αὐτῷ τοῦ πατρὸς. οὐ γὰρ ὁ πατὴρ, δοὺς αὐτῷ πάντων τὴν κληρονομίαν, ἐστέρησεν ἑαυτὸν, ὧν ἀγεννήτως ἔχει ἐν ἑαυτῷ. πηγὴ γάρ ἐστι πάντων. Ὥστε τρεῖς εἰσιν ὑποστάσεις, καὶ ὁ μὲν θεὸς αἴτιος τῶν πάντων τυγχάνων, ἔστιν ἄναρχος μονώτατος. ὁ δὲ υἱὸς ἀχρόνως γεννηθεὶς ὑπὸ τοῦ πατρὸς, καὶ πρὸ αἰώνων κτισθεὶς καὶ θεμελιωθεὶς, οὐκ ἦν πρὸ τοῦ γεννηθῆναι· οὐδὲ γάρ ἐστιν ἀΐδιος, ἢ συναΐδιος, ἢ συναγέννητος τῷ πατρί.—εἰ δὲ τὸ ἐξ αὐτοῦ, καὶ τὸ ἐκ γαστρὸς, καὶ τὸ ἐκ τοῦ πατρὸς ἐξῆλθον καὶ ἥκω, ὡς μέρος αὐτοῦ ὁμοούσιον, καὶ ὡς προβολὴ ὑπό τινων νοεῖται, σύνθετος ἔσται ὁ πατὴρ καὶ διαίρετος, καὶ τρεπτὸς, καὶ σῶμα κατ' αὐτοὺς, καὶ τὸ ὅσον ἐπ' αὐτοῖς τὰ ἀκόλουθα σώματι πάσχων, ὁ ἀσώματος θεός.* From the Thaleia (ap. Athanas. contra Arianos, Orat. ii. c. 9): *Οὐκ ἀεὶ ὁ θεὸς πατὴρ ἦν, ἀλλ' ὕστερον γέγονεν. οὐκ ἀεὶ ἦν ὁ υἱὸς, οὐ γάρ ἦν, πρὶν γεννηθῇ. οὐκ ἔστιν ἐκ τοῦ πατρὸς, ἀλλ' ἐξ οὐκ ὄντων ὑπέστη καὶ αὐτός. οὐκ ἔστιν ἴδιος τῆς τοῦ πατρὸς οὐσίας, κτίσμα γάρ ἐστι καὶ ποίημα. καὶ οὐκ ἔστιν ἀληθινὸς θεὸς ὁ Χριστός, ἀλλὰ μετοχῇ καὶ αὐτὸς ἐθεοποιήθη· οὐκ οἶδε τὸν πατέρα ἀκριβῶς ὁ υἱὸς, οὔτε ὁρᾷ ὁ λόγος τὸν πατέρα τελείως, καὶ οὔτε συνιεῖ, οὔτε γινώσκει ἀκριβῶς ὁ λόγος τὸν πατέρα· οὐκ ἔστιν ὁ ἀληθινὸς καὶ μόνος αὐτὸς τοῦ πατρὸς λόγος, ἀλλ' ὀνόματι μόνον λέγεται λόγος καὶ σοφία, καὶ χάριτι λέγεται υἱὸς καὶ δύναμις· οὐκ ἔστιν ἄτρεπτος, ὡς ὁ πατὴρ, ἀλλὰ τρεπτός ἐστι φύσει, ὡς τὰ κτίσματα, καὶ λείπει αὐτῷ εἰς κατάληψιν τοῦ γνῶναι τελείως τὸν πατέρα.* When the Son is sometimes called *τρεπτός*, sometimes *ἄτρεπτος*, that is explained by a preceding fragment (Orat. ii. c. 5): *Τῇ μὲν φύσει, ὥσπεο πάντες, οὕτω καὶ αὐτὸς ὁ λόγος ἐστι τρεπτὸς, τῷ δὲ ἰδίῳ αὐτεξουσίῳ, ἕως βούλεται, μένει καλός. ὅτε μέντοι θέλει, δύναται τρέπεσθαι καὶ αὐτὸς, ὥσπερ καὶ ἡμεῖς, τρεπτῆς ὢν φύσεως. Διὰ τοῦτο γάρ, φησι, καὶ προγινώσκων ὁ θεὸς ἔσεσθαι*

with his bishop *Alexander* on the point (318), who excluded him and his followers from church-fellowship, many bishops in Syria and Asia Minor declared themselves in favor of Arius; some, especially *Eusebius*, bishop of *Nicomedia* (Συλλουκιανιστά, Arius ad Euseb. ap. Theodoret. i. 4, see above, § 65, note 5), because they adopted his views; others, as *Eusebius*, bishop of *Caesarea*,[3] because they held that the faith of the church was at least not violated by the doctrine of Arius. The most important writer who endeavored to defend the Arian principles was the sophist *Asterius* of Cappadocia, also a disciple of Lucian († about 330).[4] Thus the controversy communicated itself to the whole east. After Constantine had in vain endeavored to induce the contending parties to give up the dispute, by rational representations,[5] he called *the first oecumenical council at Nice* (325).[6] As the number of Arian bishops was much smaller than that of their opponents, the party of Alexander prevailed, their cause being pleaded by *Athanasius*, deacon in Alexandria, and *Marcellus, bishop of Ancyra.* The Arian doctrine was rejected; but the ancient emanistic notion was confirmed, and was merely developed farther by the decision

καλὸν αὐτὸν, προλαβὼν ταύτην αὐτῷ τὴν δόξαν δέδωκεν, ἣν ἂν καὶ ἐκ τῆς ἀρετῆς ἔσχε μετὰ ταῦτα.

[3] Comp. the fragment of his letter to Alexander, bishop of Alexandria, in the Acts of the Conc. Nicaeni ii. ann. 787. Actio vi. ap. Mansi, xiii. p. 316.

[4] Fragments of his *σύνταγμα* in Athanasius.

[5] Epist. Constantini ad Alexandrum et Arium in Eusebii vit. Const. ii. 64–72. Among other things we find, c. 69: *Οὔτε ἐρωτᾷν ὑπὲρ τῶν τοιούτων ἐξ ἀρχῆς προσῆκον ἦν, οὔτε ἐρωτώμενον ἀποκρίνεσθαι. τὰς γὰρ τοιαύτας ζητήσεις, ὁπόσας μὴ νόμου τινὸς ἀνάγκη προστάττει, ἀλλ' ἀνωφελοῦς ἀργίας ἐρεσχελία προστίθησιν, εἰ καὶ φυσικῆς τινὸς γυμνασίας ἕνεκα γίγνοιτο, ὅμως ὀφείλομεν εἴσω τῆς διανοίας ἐγκλείειν, καὶ μὴ προχείρως εἰς δημοσίας συνόδους ἐκφέρειν, μηδὲ ταῖς τῶν δήμων ἀκοαῖς ἀπρονόητως πιστεύειν.*—C. 70: *Διόπερ καὶ ἐρώτησις ἀπροφύλακτος, καὶ ἀπόκρισις ἀπρονόητος ἴσην ἀλλήλαις ἀντιδότωσαν ἐφ' ἑκατέρῳ συγγνώμην.*—C. 71: *Καὶ λέγω ταῦτα, οὐχ ὡς ἀναγκάζων ὑμᾶς ἐξάπαντος τῇ λίαν εὐήθει, καὶ οἵα δή ποτέ ἐστιν ἐκείνη ἡ ζήτησις, συντίθεσθαι. δύναται γὰρ καὶ τὸ τῆς συνόδου τίμιον ὑμῖν ἀκεραίως σώζεσθαι, καὶ μία καὶ ἡ αὐτὴ κατὰ πάντων κοινωνία τηρεῖσθαι, κἂν τὰ μάλιστά τις ἐν μέρει πρὸς ἀλλήλους ὑμῖν ὑπὲρ ἐλαχίστου διαφωνία γένηται.*

[6] According to Eusebius de vita Constantini, this council numbered more than 250 bishops. In later times 318 were usually reckoned to it, and it was called the council *οἱ τιη'*. The first persons who have the latter number expressly refer to the 318 servants of Abraham, in whom Barnabas, so early as his day, had found a prediction relating to Christ, c. 9, Hilary de Synodis, c. 86: Et mihi quidem ipse ille numerus hic sanctus est, in quo Abraham victor regum impiorum ab eo, qui aeterni sacerdotii est forma, benedicitur. Liberius ap. Socrat. iv. 2. Ambrosius de Fide, lib. i. prolog. § 5. Doubtless this sacred number was arbitrarily assumed for the purpose of conferring honor on the council of the Nicenes. Gelasius, however, Hist. Conc. Nic. and an anonymous author in the Spicilegium Romanum, t. vi. (Romae. 1841. 8.) p. 608, give the number 300.

that the Son is of the same essence with the Father (ὁμοούσιος τῷ πατρί).[7] This expression, which had been till now regarded as Sabellian, was very suspicious in the eyes of the oriental bishops.[8] The most of them, however, yielded to the imperial authority, and subscribed the new creed.[9] None but the two Egyptian bishops *Theonas* and *Secundus* refused, who were therefore banished with *Arius* to Illyria. The Nicene decrees were universally proclaimed as imperial law; and when the bishops *Eusebius of Nicomedia*, and *Theognis of Nice*, departed from them, they were sent into exile to Gaul (325).

7 The history of the Nicene Synod, written by Maruthas, bishop of Tagrit in Mesopotamia, at the end of the fourth century (see Assemani Bibl. Orient. t. i. p. 195), is no longer extant. Gelasii Cyziceni (bishop of Caesarea in Palestine, about 476) σύνταγμα τῶν κατὰ τὴν ἐν Νικαίᾳ ἁγίαν σύνοδον πραχθέντων, libb. 3 (the third lost), prim. ed. Rob. Balforeus Scotus. Paris. 1600. 8, also in the collection of the decrees of Councils ap. Mansi, ii. p. 759, (translated in Fuchs, i. 416).—Th. Ittigii Historia Concilii Nicaeni (ed. Christianus Ludovici). Lips. 1712. 4. Fuchs Bibliothek der Kirchenversammlungen des vierten u. fünften Jahrh. i. 350.—Symbolum Nicaenum (cf. Chr. G. F. Walchii Bibliotheca symbolica vetus. Lemgov. 1770. 8, p. 75, ss.): *Πιστεύομεν εἰς ἕνα θεὸν, πατέρα παντοκράτορα, πάντων ὁρατῶν τε καὶ ἀοράτων ποιητήν. Καὶ εἰς ἕνα κύριον Ἰησοῦν Χριστὸν, τὸν υἱὸν τοῦ θεοῦ, γεννηθέντα ἐκ τοῦ πατρὸς μονογενῆ, τουτέστιν, ἐκ τῆς οὐσίας τοῦ πατρὸς, θεὸν ἐκ θεοῦ, φῶς ἐκ φωτὸς, θεὸν ἀληθινὸν ἐκ θεοῦ ἀληθινοῦ, γεννηθέντα, οὐ ποιηθέντα, ὁμοούσιον τῷ πατρί. δι' οὗ τὰ πάντα ἐγένετο, τά τε ἐν τῷ οὐρανῷ καὶ τὰ ἐν τῇ γῇ. τὸν δι' ἡμᾶς τοὺς ἀνθρώπους καὶ διὰ τὴν ἡμετέραν σωτηρίαν κατελθόντα καὶ σαρκωθέντα, καὶ ἐνανθρωπήσαντα, παθόντα καὶ ἀναστάντα τῇ τρίτῃ ἡμέρᾳ, ἀνελθόντα εἰς τοὺς οὐρανούς, καὶ ἐρχόμενον κρῖναι ζῶντας καὶ νεκρούς. Καὶ εἰς τὸ ἅγιον πνεῦμα. Τοὺς δὲ λέγοντας, ὅτι ἦν ποτε ὅτε οὐκ ἦν, καὶ πρὶν γεννηθῆναι οὐκ ἦν, καὶ ὅτι ἐξ οὐκ ὄντων ἐγένετο, ἢ ἐξ ἑτέρας ὑποστάσεως ἢ οὐσίας φάσκοντας εἶναι, ἢ κτιστὸν, τρεπτὸν, ἢ ἀλλοιωτὸν τὸν υἱόν τοῦ θεοῦ, ἀναθεματίζει ἡ καθολικὴ ἐκκλησία.* Concerning the composition of this creed: Athanasius Epist. de decretis synodi Nicaenae, and Eusebii Caesar. Epist. ad Caesarienses, most complete as appended to Athanasii Epist. cit. and in Theodoreti H. E. i. 11. The εἷς θεὸς is here the Father alone, consequently the sameness of essence between Him and the Son is not a numerical unity of essence. See Münscher über den Sinn der Nic. Glaubensformel, in Henke's neuem Magazin, vi. 334. Even here the sentiment, that the Son exists by the will of the Father, and is less than he, is not spoken against.

8 See Divis. I. § 60, note 13.

9 How actively Constantine employed his influence in accomplishing it may be seen in Eusebius vita Const. iii. 13. Since his view had previously been different (see note 5), and his great object was simply the restoration of peace, Gfrörer's (K. G. ii. i. 210) conjecture is not improbable that *he* had been gained over by Hosius, and *the latter* during his abode at Alexandria; consequently the epithet ὁμοούσιος was of Alexandrian origin, where it had been already set forth in opposition to Dionysius (Div. I. § 64, note 8), and had been again rejected expressly by Arius. (See above, note 2.)

§ 82.

OPPOSITION OF THE EUSEBIANS TO THE NICENE COUNCIL TILL THE SECOND SYNOD AT SIRMIUM (357).

H. J. Wetzer, Restitutio verae chronologiae rerum ex controversiis Arianis inde ab anno 325 usque ad annum 350 exortarum. Francof. ad M. 1827. 8.

The opponents of Arianism declared it to be polytheism. On the contrary, the Arians charged the *ὁμοούσιος* with Sabellianism,[1] and succeeded in spreading this view in the east so generally that Constantine thought he could effect a general union on the disputed dogma only by giving up the expression. Accordingly, the banished were recalled, not only *Eusebius* and *Theognis*, but *Arius* too (328–29) his orthodoxy being acknowledged by the emperor, as expressed in general terms, in a confession of faith which he gave in. Eusebius of Nicomedia obtained a decided influence over Constantine. Several bishops who obstinately adhered to the Nicene decrees, and refused to hold church communion with the recalled, were banished, particularly *Eustathius*, bishop of Antioch (330).[2] Athanasius himself, now bishop of Alexandria, was deposed by a council held at *Tyre* (335), and banished into Gaul by Constantine; and Arius, immediately after, was solemnly received again into church communion at *Jerusalem*. He died not long after at Constantinople (336).[3] Thus the east was separated from the western church; the latter adopting the *ὁμοούσιος*, and espousing the cause of Athanasius, which the former rejected. This division continued after the death of Constantine († 337), when *Con-*

[1] Socrates, i. 24: *Οἱ μὲν τοῦ ὁμοουσίου τὴν λέξιν ἐκκλίνοντες τὴν Σαβελλίου καὶ Μοντανοῦ δόξαν εἰσηγεῖσθαι αὐτὴν τοὺς προσδεχομένους ἐνόμιζον, καὶ διὰ τοῦτο βλασφήμους ἐκάλουν, ὡς ἀναιροῦντας τὴν ὕπαρξιν τοῦ υἱοῦ τοῦ θεοῦ. οἱ δὲ πάλιν τῷ ὁμοουσίῳ προσκείμενοι, πολυθείαν εἰσάγειν τοὺς ἑτέρους νομίζοντες, ὡς Ἑλληνισμὸν εἰσάγοντας ἐξετρέποντο.* Augustin. Opus imperf. v. 25: Ariani Catholicos Sabellianos vocant. On the other hand, Athanasius Expos. fidei (ed. Ben. i. 100): *Οὔτε γὰρ υἱοπάτορα φρονοῦμεν, ὡς οἱ Σαβέλλιοι, λέγοντες μονοούσιον καὶ οὐχ ὁμοούσιον, καὶ ἐν τούτῳ ἀναιροῦντες τὸ εἶναι υἱόν.* So far as the Nicenes also explained *ὁμοούσιος* by *ταυτοούσιος*, as Theodoret. Dial. v. in fine (cf. conc. Ancyr. below, § 83, note 5), they strengthened the suspicion of Sabellianism.

[2] Socrates, i. 24. Sozom. ii. 19. Theodoret. i. 21. Athanasius Hist. Arian. § 4, cf Eusebius de vita Const. iii. 59, ss.

[3] On the death of Arius see Walch's Ketzerhist. Th. 2. S. 500–511.

stans had become sovereign of the west, and *Constantius* of the east, and that all the more readily, inasmuch as *Eusebius*, bishop of Nicomedia, gained the same influence over Constantius as he had formerly over Constantine, and was appointed bishop of Constantinople (338). The prevailing doctrine of the east respecting the Son was the old emanistic doctrine,[4] as had been set forth at the council of *Antioch* (341), according to which both the Arian formulae and the Nicene *ὁμοούσιος* were looked upon as objectionable extremes.[5] The Arians, of whom there

[4] The confession of faith of the first council at Antioch is thus prefaced (ap. Socrat. ii. 10): *Ἡμεῖς οὔτε ἀκόλουθοι Ἀρείου γεγόναμεν (πῶς γὰρ ἐπίσκοποι ὄντες ἀκολουθήσομεν πρεσβυτέρῳ;) οὔτε ἄλλην τινὰ πίστιν παρὰ τὴν ἐξ ἀρχῆς ἐκτεθεῖσαν ἐδεξάμεθα.* All the four Antiochian formulae in Athanasius de Synodis, § 22–25. Cf. Walch Bibl. symbol. p. 109, ss. Fuchs Biblioth. d. Kirchenvers. ii. 76. In the formula Antiochena i. we read: *Εἰς ἕνα υἱὸν τοῦ θεοῦ μονογενῆ, πρὸ πάντων τῶν αἰώνων ὑπάρχοντα καὶ συνόντα τῷ γεγεννηκότι αὐτὸν πατρὶ, δι' οὗ τὰ πὰντα ἐγένετο, κ. τ. λ.* In the formula Ant. ii.: *Εἰς ἕνα κύριον Ἰησοῦν Χριστὸν, τὸν υἱὸν αὐτοῦ, τὸν μονογενῆ θεὸν, δι' οὗ τὰ πὰντα, τὸν γεννηθέντα πρὸ τῶν αἰώνων ἐκ τοῦ πατρὸς, θεὸν ἐκ θεοῦ, ὅλον ἐξ ὅλου, μόνον ἐκ μόνου, τέλειον ἐκ τελείου, βασιλέα ἐκ βασιλέως, κύριον ἐκ κυρίου, λόγον ζῶντα, σοφίαν ζῶσαν, φῶς ἀληθινὸν, ὁδὸν, ἀλήθειαν, ἀνάστασιν, ποιμένα, θύραν, ἄτρεπτόν τε καὶ ἀναλλοίωτον τῆς θεότητος, οὐσίας τε καὶ βουλῆς, καὶ δυνάμεως καὶ δόξης τοῦ πατρὸς ἀπαράλλακτον εἰκόνα· τὸν πρωτότοκον πάσης τῆς κτίσεως, τὸν ὄντα ἐν ἀρχῇ πρὸς τὸν θεὸν, θεὸν λόγον, κατὰ τὸ εἰρημένον ἐν τῷ εὐαγγελίῳ· "καὶ θεὸς ἦν ὁ λόγος." δι' οὗ τὰ πάντα ἐγένετο, καὶ ἐν ᾧ τὰ πάντα συνέστησε· τὸν ἐπ' ἐσχάτων τῶν ἡμερῶν κατελθόντα ἄνωθεν. εἴ τις παρὰ τὴν ὑγιῆ τῶν γραφῶν ὀρθὴν πίστιν διδάσκει, λέγων, ἢ χρόνον, ἢ καιρὸν, ἢ αἰῶνα ἢ εἶναι, ἢ γεγονέναι πρὸ τοῦ γεννηθῆναι τὸν υἱὸν, ἀνάθεμα ἔστω· καὶ εἴ τις λέγει τὸν υἱὸν κτίσμα ὡς ἓν τῶν κτισμάτων, ἢ γέννημα ὡς ἓν τῶν γεννημάτων, ἢ ποίημα ὡς ἓν τῶν ποιημάτων— ἀνάθεμα ἔστω.* In the formula Ant. iii. (Theophronii Episc. Tyanensis): *Εἰς τὸν υἱὸν αὐτοῦ τὸν μονογενῆ, θεὸν λόγον, δύναμιν καὶ σοφίαν, τὸν κύριον ἡμῶν Ἰησοῦν Χριστὸν, δι' οὗ τὰ πάντα, τὸν γεννηθέντα ἐκ τοῦ πατρὸς πρὸ τῶν αἰώνων, θεὸν τέλειον ἐκ θεοῦ τελείου, καὶ ὄντα πρὸς τὸν θεὸν ἐν ὑποστάσει, ἐπ' ἐσχάτων δὲ τῶν ἡμερῶν κατελθόντα. Εἰ δέ τις παρὰ ταύτην τὴν πίστιν διδάσκει, ἢ ἔχει ἐν ἑαυτῷ, ἀνάθεμα ἔστω. καὶ Μαρκέλλου τοῦ Ἀγκύρας, ἢ Σαβελλίου, ἢ Παύλου τοῦ Σαμοσατέως, ἀνάθεμα ἔστω καὶ αὐτὸς, καὶ πάντες οἱ κοινωνοῦντες αὐτῷ.* In the formula iv. (sent to Constans in Gaul some months after the council): *Εἰς τὸν μονογενῆ αὐτοῦ υἱόν, τὸν κύριον ἡμῶν Ἰησοῦν Χριστὸν, τὸν πρὸ πάντων τῶν αἰώνων ἐκ τοῦ πατρὸς γεννηθέντα, θεὸν ἐκ θεοῦ, φῶς ἐκ φωτὸς, δι' οὗ ἐγένετο τὰ πάντα ἐν τοῖς οὐρανοῖς καὶ ἐπὶ τῆς γῆς, τὰ ὁρατὰ καὶ τὰ ἀόρατα, λόγον ὄντα καὶ σοφίαν, καὶ δύναμιν, καὶ ζωὴν, καὶ φῶς ἀληθινόν. Τοὺς δὲ λέγοντας ἐξ οὐκ ὄντων τὸν υἱὸν ἢ ἐξ ἑτέρας ὑποστάσεως, καὶ μὴ ἐκ θεοῦ, καὶ ἦν ποτε χρόνος ὅτε οὐκ ἦν, ἀλλοτρίους οἶδεν ἡ καθολικὴ ἐκκλησία.* According to Sozomen, iii. 5 (where only two Antiochian formulae are mentioned), the second was given out as the Symb. Luciani Martyris (Div. I. § 65, note 6); and from Theodoret it is clear that this is the still so-called formula Antioch. ii. Athanasius, Hilary, and Socrates, who give the formulae, say nothing of it. The anathema at the end is therefore a later addition.

[5] Comp. Eusebius de Fide adv. Sabellium (in Sirmondi Opp. 1. u. Bibl. PP. Ludg. iv.) written according to Philo über die Schriften des Euseb. v. Alex. u. Euseb. v. Emisa. Halle. 1832. S. 64, 76, by Eusebius of Emisa (A.D. 341), ap. Sirmond. i. 11: Confitere ea, quae de Patre et Filio scripta sunt, et noli curiosius ea, quae non sunt scripta, requirere. Utinam autem solum legeremus! utinam solis scripturis contenti essemus! et lis nulla fiebat. Cf. p. 18, 20, 27. Comp. Cyrillus Hierosolym. in his catacheses held about the year 348, ex Gr. Catech. ad Competentes, xv. § 9: *Νῦν δὲ ἔστιν ἡ ἀποστασία. ἀπέστησαν*

were certainly many, must have concealed their peculiar sentiments behind emanistic formulae.[6] Thus the Orientals were unjustly styled Arians by the Nicenes. More appropriate was the title *Eusebians*,[7] from their head Eusebius, bishop of Nicomedia. In order to remove the schism between the east and west, Constantius and Constans united in summoning a new general council at *Sardica* (347).[8] But here the matter went so far as to issue in an entire separation. The westerns remained alone in Sardica; the orientals assembled in the neighboring town *Philippopolis*. Both parties confirmed their former acts; and in the east Eusebianism continued as prevalent under Constantius as the Nicene faith in the west under Constans.

The prejudice of the Eusebians, that Homousianism led to Sabellianism,[9] was not a little favored by the case of *Marcellus*, bishop of Ancyra, one of the principal defenders of the Nicene council. By representing the Logos as the eternal wisdom of God, and contending that the incarnate Logos alone could be called Son of God, this bishop manifestly came near Sabellianism; and when deposed from his office (336), was nevertheless declared orthodox by the westerns, and taken under their protection.[10] A pupil of Marcellus, *Photinus*, bishop of Sirmium,

γὰρ οἱ ἄνθρωποι τῆς ὀρθῆς πίστεως· καὶ οἱ μὲν υἱοπατορίαν καταγγέλλουσιν, οἱ δὲ τὸν Χριστὸν ἐξ οὐκ ὄντων εἰς τὸ εἶναι παρενεχθέντα λέγειν τολμῶσι. Καὶ πρότερον μὲν ἦσαν φανεροὶ οἱ αἱρετικοὶ, νῦν δὲ πεπλήρωται ἡ ἐκκλησία κεκρυμμένων αἱρετικῶν. Compare Touttée on this passage, and his Diss. i. cap. 4, § 17, ss., prefixed to his edition of Cyril.

[6] Respecting the *θεὸν ἐκ θεοῦ* in the Antiochian formulae they said (Socrat. ii. 45): *Οὕτως εἴρηται τὸ ἐκ θεοῦ, ὡς εἴρηται παρὰ τῷ Ἀποστόλῳ· τὰ δὲ πάντα ἐκ τοῦ θεοῦ* (1 Cor. xi. 12). Only the Nicene *ἐκ τῆς οὐσίας τοῦ θεοῦ* was not susceptible of an Arian import.

[7] So Athanasius frequently *οἱ περὶ Εὐσέβιον*.

[8] That it was held in 347, not 344, is proved by Wetzer Restit. verae chron. p. 47, against Mansi Coll. conc. iii. 87.

[9] Even Hilarius de Synodis § 67, confesses: Multi ex nobis ita unam substantiam Patris et Filii praedicant, ut videri possint non magis id pie quam impie praedicare: habet enim hoc verbum in se et fidei conscientiam, et fraudem paratam.—Unum, in quo par significatur, non ad unicum vendicetur.

[10] Marcellus's chief work was de Subjectione domini Christi. (Fragments of it in Marcelliana ed. et animadvers. instruxit Chr. H. G. Rettberg. Goett. 1794. 8). He was answered by Asterius, Eusebius of Caesarea, Acacius (fragments in Epiphanius Haer 72, § 5-9), Apollinarius and Basil of Ancyra. Of these are extant only Eusebii contra Marcellum libb. ii. and de Ecclesiast. theologia libb. iii. (both appended to Eusebii Demonstr. evang. Paris. 1828. fol.) His orthodoxy was acknowledged by Julius, bishop of Rome (epist. ad Episcop. Eusebianos Antiochiae congregatos, in Athanasii Apol. contra Arianos, n. 21-35), Athanasius in several passages, and the Synod of Sardica. On the contrary, the later catholic fathers, Basil the Great, Chrysostom, Sulpicius Severus, and others, judged of him unfavorably. The majority of the moderns, Baronius, Petavius, Schelstrate,

taught Sabellianism in a fully developed form.[11] His doctrine was rejected not only by the Eusebians at the second *council of Antioch* (345),[12] but also by the westerns at a *council at Milan* (347); and at the first *council of Sirmium* (351),[13] he was deposed by the Eusebians. The party of *the Photinians* continued, however, till the reign of Theodosius the younger.

In the mean time, Constans had died (350). Constantius became master of the whole Roman empire, after his victory over *Magnentius* (353), and now endeavored to introduce Eusebianism by force into the west also. At the synods of *Arles* (353) and *Milan* (355), the bishops were forced to subscribe the condemnation of Athanasius; all who refused being deposed and banished. Among these were *Lucifer*, bishop of *Calaris; Hilary*, bishop of Poictiers; and *Liberius*, bishop of Rome.[14]

&c., hold him also to be a heretic. His most important defender is Montfaucon Diatr. de causa Marcelli Ancyrani (in ej. Collect. nova Patrum, t. ii. p. 51, ss. Paris. 1706. fol.; reprinted in J. Vogt Biblioth. hist. haeresiologiae, t. i. fasc. ii. p. 293, ss. Hamb. 1724. 8). Comp. Walch's Ketzerhist. iii. 229. Klose's Gesch. u. Lehre des Marcellus u. Photinus. Hamburg. 1837. 8. Baur's Lehre v. d. Dreieinigkeit, i. 525.

11 Walch, iii. 3. Klose and Baur, l. c.

12 In the formula Antioch. *μακρόστιχος* (ap. Athanasius de Synodis § 26, and Socrates ii. 19, cf. Walchii Bibl. symb. p. 115): *Βδελυσσόμεθα δὲ πρὸς τούτοις καὶ ἀναθεματίζομεν καὶ τοὺς λόγον μὲν μόνον αὐτὸν ψιλὸν τοῦ θεοῦ καὶ ἀνύπαρκτον ἐπιπλάστως καλοῦντας, ἐν ἑτέρῳ τὸ εἶναι ἔχοντα, νῦν μὲν ὡς τὸν προφορικὸν λεγόμενον ὑπό τινων, νῦν δὲ ὡς τὸν ἐνδιάθετον· Χριστὸν δὲ αὐτὸν καὶ υἱὸν τοῦ θεοῦ καὶ μεσίτην καὶ εἰκόνα τοῦ θεοῦ μὴ εἶναι πρὸ αἰώνων θέλοντας, ἀλλ' ἔκτοτε Χριστὸν αὐτὸν γεγονέναι καὶ υἱὸν τοῦ θεοῦ, ἐξ οὗ τὴν ἡμετέραν ἐκ τῆς παρθένου σάρκα ἀνείληφε, πρὸ τετρακοσίων οὐχ ὅλων ἐτῶν. ἔκτοτε γὰρ τὸν Χριστὸν ἀρχὴν βασιλείας ἐσχηκέναι ἐθέλουσι. καὶ τέλος ἕξειν αὐτὴν μετὰ τὴν συντέλειαν καὶ τὴν κρίσιν. Τοιοῦτοι δέ εἰσιν οἱ ἀπὸ Μαρκέλλου καὶ Φωτεινοῦ* (Athan. *Σκοτεινοῦ*) *τῶν Ἀγκυρογαλατῶν, οἳ τὴν προαιώνιον ὕπαρξιν τοῦ Χριστοῦ καὶ τὴν θεότητα καὶ τὴν ἀτελεύτητον αὐτοῦ βασιλείαν ὁμοίως Ἰουδαίοις ἀθετοῦσιν, ἐπὶ προφάσει τοῦ συνίστασθαι δοκεῖν τῇ μοναρχίᾳ.*

13 Baronius placed the first Sirmian Synod in the year 357. On the other hand, Petavius (in Annot. ad Epiphan. p. 300 and Diss. de Photino haeretico ejusque damnatione, annexed to the third edition of the Rationar. temp. Par. 1636) correctly in the year 351. See his controversy on the subject with Sirmond, who defended Baronius. Petavius has been followed by Matth. Lorroquanus (de la Roque) Diss. duplex. i. de Photino haeret. ii. de Liberio Pontif. Rom. Genev. 1670. 8. P. de Marca de tempore syn. Sirm. in his dissertatt. ed. Francof. p. 319. Pagi and Tillemont. Mansi, on the contrary, in the treatise before cited (note 8), places the Sirmian Council in the year 358. The confession of faith of the first Sirmian Synod (ap. Athanas. de Syn. § 27) is the formula Antioch iv., to which, however, instead of one, twenty-seven anathemas are appended. Of these, Nos. 4–22 are directed against Photinus. Among other things, No. vi. says: *Εἴ τις τὴν οὐσίαν τοῦ θεοῦ πλατύνεσθαι ἢ συστέλλεσθαι φάσκοι, ἀνάθεμα ἔστω.* vii.: *Εἴ τις πλατυνομένην τὴν οὐσίαν τοῦ θεοῦ τὸν υἱὸν λέγοι ποιεῖν, ἢ τὸν πλατυσμὸν τῆς οὐσίας αὐτοῦ υἱὸν ὀνομάζοι, ἀ. ἔ.* viii.: *Εἴ τις ἐνδιάθετον ἢ προφορικὸν λόγον λέγοι τὸν υἱὸν τοῦ θεοῦ, ἀ. ἔ.*

14 Many others, both those who were banished and those who yielded, are named in Faustini et Marcellini Libellus precum ad Impp. in Bibl. pp. Lugd. v. 654.

§ 83.

DISSENSIONS AMONG THE EUSEBIANS TILL THE SUPPRESSION OF ARIANISM (381).

After the Eusebians had become the predominant party, and those who were internally separated were no longer held together by the necessity of contending together against the Homousiasts, the variety of their opinions, which had been hitherto concealed, began to appear. A strict Arian party came forth among them, which was named sometimes after its leaders, *Aetius* of Antioch (ἄθεος),[1] *Eunomius* of Cappadocia,[2] and *Acacius*, bishop of Caesarea; sometimes from its principles (Ἀνόμοιοι, Ἐξουκόντιοι).[3] In opposition to it, the majority, under the leadership of *Basil*, bishop of Ancyra, and *Georgius*, bishop of Laodicea, held fast by the old emanistic doctrine, adopted the farther development of it which had formerly appeared among the Eusebians, viz., that the Son is of *similar* essence with the Father (ὁμοιούσιος τῷ πατρί), and were hence called Ὁμοιουσιάσται, Ἡμιάρειοι, Semiariani. The emperor Constantius was attached to the Semiarians; but a powerful party about his court exerted themselves with no less cunning than perseverance in favor of the Anomoeans. And because they could not publicly vindicate their formula, they persuaded the emperor that in order to restore peace, the formulas of the two other parties also must be prohibited; which measure they brought about at *the second*

[1] A συνταγμάτιον by him may be found in Epiphan. Haer. lxxvi. 10. Other fragments in A. Maji Script. vett. nova collectio, vii. i. 71, s. 202. Respecting him and Eunomius see Select Homilies of John Chrysostom, translated into German by Ph. Mayer. Nürnberg. 1820. p. 147. Lange in Illgen's Zeitschr. f. d. hist. Theol. v. i. 33. Baur's Dreieinigkeit, i. 361.

[2] Concerning him see Basnage in Canisii Lectiones antt. vol. i. p. 172, ss. Ullmann's Gregorius v. Nazianz. S. 318. ff. Neander's Kirchengesch. ii. 2, 852, ff. Mayer, Lange, and Baur, see note 1. Klose's Gesch. u. Lehre des Eunomius. Kiel. 1833. 8. His ἔκθεσις τῆς πίστεως prim. ed. H. Valesius in notis ad Socrat. v. 10 ap. Basnage, l. c., and in Fabricii Bibl. gr. vol. viii. p. 253. Ἀπολογητικός e cod. Hamburg. prim ed. Fabricius, l. c. viii. 262 (prologus and epilogus e cod. Tenisoniano also in Cave Hist. lit. i. 220). A fragment ἐκ τοῦ περὶ υἱοῦ τρίτου λόγου ap. Majus, vii. i. 202.

[3] According to the church-fathers, these Arians rested for support particularly on the Aristotelian philosophy. So also Baur, i. 387. Of a contrary opinion is Ritter Gesch. d. christl. Philos. ii. 65, who denies emphatically that Eunomius was an Aristotelian.

synod of Sirmium (357).[4] On the other hand, *Basil*, bishop of Ancyra, called together *a synod at Ancyra* (358), which established the Semiarian creed in a copious decree, and rejected the Arian.[5] Constantius allowed himself to be easily convinced that that Sirmian formula favored the Anomoeans; and therefore the confession of faith adopted at the second must now be rejected at a *third synod of Sirmium* (358), and the anathemas of the synod of Ancyra be subscribed.[6] The Anomoeans, for

[4] Formula Sirmiensis ii. (in the Latin original ap. Hilarius de Synodis § 11, translated into Greek, Athanas. de Synod. § 28. Walch. Bibl. symb. p. 133, comp. Fuchs, ii. 196): Unum constat Deum esse omnipotentem et patrem, sicut per universum orbem creditur, et unicum filium ejus Jesum Christum, dominum salvatorem nostrum, ex ipso ante saecula genitum. Quod vero quosdam aut multos movebat de substantia, quae graece *usia* adpellatur, id est, ut expressius intelligatur, *homousion* aut quod dicitur *homoeusion*, nullam omnino fieri oportere mentionem, nec quemquam praedicare: ea de causa et ratione, quod nec in divinis scripturis contineatur, et quod super hominis scientiam sit, nec quisquam possit nativitatem filii enarrare, de quo scriptum est: generationem ejus quis enarrabit? Scire autem manifestum est solum patrem, quomodo genuerit filium suum, et filium, quomodo genitus sit a patre. Nulla ambiguitas est, majorem esse patrem. Nulli potest dubium esse, patrem honore, dignitate, claritate, majestate et ipso nomine patris majorem esse filio, ipso testante: qui me misit, majore me est. Et hoc catholicum esse, nemo ignorat, duas personas esse patris et filii, majorem patrem: filium subjectum cum omnibus his, quae ipsi pater subjecit. Patrem initium non habere, invisibilem esse, immortalem esse, impassibilem esse. Filium autem natum esse ex patre, deum ex deo, lumen ex lumine. Cujus filii generationem, ut ante dictum est, neminem scire, nisi patrem suum, caet.

[5] The decrees of this Synod ap. Epiphan. Haer. 73, § 2–11. Comp. Fuchs, ii. 213. § 9: *Ὡς ἐν ὁμοιώματι ἀνθρώπων, καὶ ἐν ὁμοιώματι σαρκὸς ἁμαρτίας, οὐκ ἐπὶ τὴν ταυτότητα ἤγετο τοῦ ἀνθρώπου, ἀλλ' ἐπὶ τὴν τῆς σακρὸς οὐσίας ὁμοιότητα· οὕτως οὐδὲ ὁ υἱὸς, ὅμοιος κατ' οὐσίαν γενόμενος τῷ γεννήσαντι πατρὶ, εἰς ταυτότητα ἄξει τοῦ πατρὸς τὴν ἑαυτοῦ οὐσίαν, ἀλλ' ἐπὶ τὴν ὁμοιότητα.* § 10: *Καὶ εἴ τις—μὴ—τὴν ὁμοιότητα καὶ κατ' οὐσίαν τοῦ υἱοῦ πρὸς πατέρα ὁμολογοίη, ὡς ψευδωνύμως λέγων τόν πατέρα καὶ τὸν υἱὸν, καὶ μήτε πατέρα λέγων ἀληθῶς μήτε υἱὸν, ἀλλὰ κτιστὴν καὶ κτίσμα—ἀνάθεμα ἔστω.* § 11: *Καὶ εἴ τις τὸ ἔκτισέ με, καὶ τὸ γεννᾷ με παρ' αὐτοῦ ἀκούων, τὸ γεννᾷ με μὴ ἐπὶ τοῦ αὐτοῦ καὶ κατ' οὐσίαν ἐννοεῖ, ἀλλὰ ταὐτὸν λέγοι τὸ γεννᾷ με τῷ ἔκτισέ με, ὡς μὴ λέγων τὸν υἱὸν τὸν ἀπαθῶς τέλειον ἐκ τῶν δύο ὀνομάτων, τοῦ ἔκτισέ με καὶ τοῦ γεννᾷ με, κτίσμα μόνον ὁμολογῶν καὶ μηκέτι υἱὸν, ὡς παραδέδωκεν ἡ σοφία ἐκ τῶν δύο εὐσεβῶς τὴν ἔννοιαν, ἀ. ἔ. Καὶ εἴ τις τοῦ υἱοῦ τὴν μὲν κατ' οὐσίαν πρὸς τὸν ἑαυτοῦ πατέρα ὁμοιότητα ἡμῖν ἀποκαλύπτοντος, δι' ὧν φησι· ὥσπερ γὰρ ὁ πατὴρ ζωὴν ἔχει ἐν ἑαυτῷ, οὕτως καὶ τῷ υἱῷ ἔδωκε ζωὴν ἔχειν ἐν ἑαυτῷ* (Joh. v. 26)· *τὴν δὲ κατ' ἐνέργειαν, δι' ὧν παιδεύει· ἃ γὰρ ἂν ὁ πατὴρ ποιῇ, ταῦτα καὶ ὁ υἱὸς ὁμοίως ποιεῖ* (Joh. v. 19), *μόνην τὴν κατ' ἐνέργειαν ὁμοιότητα διδοὺς, τῆς κατ' οὐσίαν, ἥ ἐστι τὸ κεφαλαιωδέστατον ἡμῶν τῆς πίστεως, ἀποστεροίη τὸν υἱὸν—ἀ. ἔ.* (so according to a correction). *Εἰ τις—ἀνόμοιον λέγοι κατ' οὐσίαν τὸν υἱὸν τῷ πατρὶ, ἀ. ἔ. Εἴ τις τὸν πατέρα πρεσβύτερον χρόνῳ λέγοι τοῦ ἐξ ἑαυτοῦ μονογενοῦς υἱοῦ, νεώτερον δὲ χρόνῳ τὸν υἱὸν τοῦ πατρὸς, ἀ. ἔ.* But also finally: *Εἴ τις ἐξουσίᾳ καὶ οὐσίᾳ λέγων τὸν πατέρα πατέρα τοῦ υἱοῦ, ὁμοούσιον δὲ ἢ ταυτοούσιον λέγοι τὸν υἱὸν τῷ πατρὶ, ἀ. ἔ.*

[6] Concerning Liberius, bishop of Rome, who in the year 358 subscribed two Eusebian formulas in succession, for the purpose of regaining his episcopal dignity, see Larroquani, § 82, Diss. cited, note 13, and Jo. la Placette Observationes hist. eccles., quibus eruitur veteris ecclesiae sensus circa Pont. Rom. potestatem in definiendis fidei rebus. Amstel. 1695. p. 137–150.

the purpose of uniting in appearance with the Semiarians, and yet establishing their own doctrine, now adopted the formula, *τὸν υἱὸν ὅμοιον τῷ πατρὶ κατὰ πάντα, ὡς αἱ ἅγιαι γραφαὶ λέγουσί τε καὶ διδάσκουσι,*[7] and succeeded in convincing the emperor that all parties might be most easily united in it. For this purpose all bishops were now prepared, and then the westerns were summoned to a council at *Ariminum*, the easterns to another at *Seleucia*, simultaneously (359). After many efforts, the emperor at last succeeded in getting most of the bishops to adopt that formula. But along with this external union, not only did the internal doctrinal schism continue, but there were besides differences among such as had been like-minded, according as they had gone in with that union or not. Thus Constantius at his death left all in the greatest confusion.[8]

The interference of emperors, so foreign to the object in discussion, now ceased, at least for some time. *Julian* (361–363) was of course equally indifferent to all Christian sects, and restored all banished bishops to their sees.[9] *Jovian* also († 364) and his successors in the west, *Valentinian I.* († 375), then *Gratian* and *Valentinian II.* maintained general toleration. On the contrary, *Valens*, emperor of the east (364–378), was a zealous Arian, and persecuted the Homousiasts and Semiarians.

Since the last years of Constantius, various causes had been always tending to increase in the east the number of adherents to the Nicene council. When, in its greatest strictness, Arianism wished to regain the ascendency, the majority of the ori-

[7] The same is found in the formula Sirmiensis tertia, which was composed by some Arians at Sirmium, and was submitted at Ariminum (in Athanasii de Synodis Arimini et Seleuciae celebratis epist. c. 8), in the formula Nices condita which was received at the end at Ariminum (in Theodoreti Hist. eccl. ii. 21) in the formula Seleuciensis (ap. Athanas. de Syn. c. 29) and the Constantinopolitana (ap. Athanas. l. c. c. 30), all belonging to the year 359. Comp. Fuchs, ii. 201, 259, 271, 273.

[8] There is a correct estimate of his character in Ammian. Marcellin. xxi. 16: Christianam religionem absolutam et simplicem anili superstitione confudens; in qua scrutanda perplexius, quam componenda gravius, excitavit discidia plurima, quae progressa fusius aluit concertatione verborum: ut catervis Antistitum jumentis publicis ultro citroque discurrentibus per Synodos, quas appellant, dum ritum omnem ad suum trahere conatur arbitrium rei vehiculariae succideret nervos.

[9] Ammian. Marc. xxii. 5: Utque dispositorum roboraret effectum, dissidentes Christianorum Antistites cum plebe discissa in palatium intromissos monebat civilius, ut discordiis consopitis quisque nullo vetante religioni suae serviret intrepidus. Quod agebat ideo obstinate, ut dissensiones augente licentia, non timeret unanimantem postea plebem; nullas infestas hominibus bestias, ut sunt sibi ferales plerique Christianorum, expertus. Saepeque dictitabat: Audite me quem Alemanni audierunt et Franci.

entals, who held fast by the emanation of the Son from the Father, must have felt a most decided aversion to it; while the Nicene decrees were naturally allied to those older notions, as fuller developments of them. Besides, the unity of the Nicenes, as contrasted with the constant wavering of the Eusebians, could do nothing less than make a most favorable impression. To this was added, finally, the influence of monachism, which, having now arisen in Egypt, and speedily excited universal admiration, was closely connected with Athanasius; and in all countries where it was diffused, was busy in favor of the Nicene council.[10]

First of all, *Meletius* declared himself in favor of the Nicene confession, immediately after he had been nominated bishop of Antioch, A.D. 361.[11] But the old Nicene community which had still existed in Antioch from the time of Eustathius (§ 82, note 2), and was now headed by a presbyter *Paulinus*, refused to acknowledge the former Eusebian as bishop; and this *Meletian* schism[12] soon found a ground for itself also in the doctrinal distinction that the Meletians believed they must abide by three *Hypostases* in the Trinity, while the old Nicenes would only acknowledge in it three *Prosopa*.[13] *The council of Alexandria,*

[10] Hence the frequent persecutions of the monks in Egypt by the Arians. Cf. Athanasii, Encyclica, c. 3, Hist. Arianorum, c. 70, 72, and often. In like manner under Valens, Socrat. iv. 22 and 24. Thus the the monks of Cappadocia, in the year 363, broke off church communion with Gregory, bishop of Nazianzum, father of the theologian, because he had subscribed an ambiguous formula. See Ullmann's Gregor. v. Nazianz. S. 61. Gregory of Nazianzum, Orat. xxi. p. 388, says of the monks in reference to that occurrence: Οἳ κὰν τἄλλα ὦσιν εἰρηνικοί τε καὶ μέτριοι, τοῦτό γε οὐ φέρουσιν ἐπιεικεῖς εἶναι, θεὸν προδιδόναι διὰ τῆς ἡσυχίας. ἀλλὰ καὶ λίαν εἰσὶν ἐνταῦθα πολεμικοί τε καὶ δύσμαχοι—καὶ θᾶττον ἂν τι μὴ δέον παρακινήσαιεν, ἢ δέον παραλίποιεν.

[11] Epiphan. Haer. lxxiii. c. 28, 34. Socrat. ii. 44. Sozom. iv. 26. Theodoret. ii. 27. Soon after (363) many other Semiarian bishops joined him in a Synod at Antioch (Socrat. iii. 25).

[12] Respecting this schism, see Walch's Ketzerhistorie, Th. 4, S. 410, ff.

[13] The Nicene Synod considered *οὐσία* and *ὑπόστασις* as synonymous when it anathematized the formula *ἐξ ἑτέρας ὑποστάσεως ἢ οὐσίας εἶναι*. The old Nicenes, the Egyptians, and Westerns, held fast by this. So Athanasius Ep. ad Afros, c. 4: Ἡ *ὑπόστασις οὐσία ἐστὶ, καὶ οὐδὲν ἄλλο σημαινόμενον ἔχει, ἢ αὐτὸ τὸ ὄν· ἡ γὰρ ὑπόστασις καὶ ἡ οὐσία ὕπαρξίς ἐστιν. ἔστι γὰρ καὶ ὑπάρχει.* Gregory of Nazianzum (Orat. xxi.) derives this interchange of the terms from the poverty of the Latin language, which certainly translated both by substantia. We might venture to suppose here that the Nicene creed originated especially under the influence of a Latin, Hosius (see § 81, note 9). Hence the expression *τρεῖς ὑποστάσεις*, as well as *τρεῖς οὐσίαι*, in Rome and Alexandria was regarded as Arian, and Meletius and Eusebius, bishops of Samosata, were here accustomed *τοῖς Ἀρειομανίταις συγκατηριθμῆσθαι* (Basil. Ep. 266). Basil may be considered the representative of the opposite view. Ep. 236: *Οὐσία καὶ ὑπόστασις ταύτην ἔχει τὴν διαφορὰν, ἣν ἔχει τὸ*

assembled by Athanasius (362), sought, indeed, not only to smooth the way generally for the Arians to join their party by mild measures, but endeavored particularly to settle this dispute;[14] but *Lucifer*, bishop of Calaris, gave firm footing to the Meletian schism about the same time, by consecrating *Paulinus* as bishop of the Eustathians. Although *Lucifer*, from dissatisfaction with the mildness of the Alexandrian synod, separated with his followers from the church,[15] he had nevertheless put a great obstacle in the way of uniting the old and new Nicenes by the step taken in consecrating Paulinus. The westerns and Egyptians acknowledged *Paulinus;* the oriental Nicenes, *Meletius*, as the orthodox bishop of Antioch. If the emperor *Valens* (364–

κοινὸν πρὸς τὸ καθ' ἕκαστον. (Comp. similar explanations by others in Maji Scriptt. vett. nova coll. vii. 1, 11.) He declares it therefore to be a matter of the highest importance to acknowledge *τρεῖς ὑποστάσεις*, since even Sabellius taught *μίαν ὑπόστασιν* and *τρία πρόσωπα.* Comp. especially Basilii Ep. 38: also Ep. 125, 210, 214. (Klose's Basil. d. Gr. S. 28.) Consequently he is delighted with his explanation *τὸ τρεῖς ἀναγκαῖον εἶναι τὰς ὑποστάσεις ὁμολογεῖν*, Epist. 258 ad Epiphanium. In Epist. 263 ad Occidentales, he accuses Paulinus of a leaning *πρὸς τὸ Μαρκέλλου δόγμα, οὔτε υἱὸν ἐν ἰδίᾳ ὑποστάσει ὁμολογοῦν, ἀλλὰ προενεχθέντα, καὶ πάλιν ὑποστρέψαντα εἰς τὸν ὅθεν προῆλθεν.* The Orientals generally had entertained the same suspicion against the Latins. See Basilii Ep. 69, ad Athanasium, A.D. 371: *'Επιζητεῖται δὲ κἀκεῖνο παρὰ τινῶν τῶν ἐντεῦθεν ἀναγκαίως, ὡς καὶ αὐτοῖς ἡμῖν καταφαίνεται, τὸ τὴν Μαρκέλλου αἵρεσιν αὐτοὺς* (Occidentales)—*ἐξορίσαι. ἐπεὶ μέχρι τοῦ νῦν ἐν πᾶσιν οἷς ἐπιστέλλουσι γράμμασι τὸν μὲν δυσώνυμον Ἄρειον ἄνω καὶ κάτω ἀναθεματίζοντες—οὐ διαλείπουσι. Μαρκέλλῳ δὲ, τῷ κατὰ διάμετρον ἐκείνῳ τὴν ἀσεβείαν ἐπιδειξαμένῳ, καὶ εἰς αὐτὴν τὴν ὕπαρξιν τῆς τοῦ μονογενοῦς θεότητος ἀσεβήσαντι—οὐδεμίαν μέμψιν ἐπενεγκόντες φαίνονται.* A milder judgment is given by Gregor. Naz. Or. xxi.: *Τῆς μιᾶς οὐσίας καὶ τῶν τριῶν ὑποστάσεων λεγομένων μὲν ὑφ' ἡμῶν εὐσεβῶς νοουμένων δὲ καὶ παρὰ τοῖς 'Ιταλοῖς ὁμοίως, ἀλλ' οὐ δυναμένης διά στενότητα τῆς παρ' αὐτοῖς γλώττης καὶ ὀνομάτων πενίαν διελεῖν ἀπὸ τῆς οὐσίας τὴν ὑπόστασιν, καὶ διὰ τοῦτο ἀντεισαγούσης τὰ πρόσωπα, ἵνα μὴ τρεῖς οὐσίαι παραδεχθῶσι· τὶ γίνεται ὡς λίαν γελοῖον ἢ ἐλεεινόν; πίστεως ἔδοξε διαφορὰ ἡ περὶ τὸν ἦχον σμικρολογία.*

[14] Epistola synodica Conc. Alex. (ap. Mansi, iii. p. 345, ss.): *Πάντας τοίνυν τοὺς βουλομένους εἰρηνεύειν πρὸς ἡμᾶς, μάλιστα τοὺς ἐν τῇ παλαιᾷ συναγομένους* (the Meletians) *καὶ τοὺς ἀπὸ τῶν 'Αρειανῶν, προσκαλέσασθε παρ' ἑαυτοῖς, καὶ ὡς μὲν πατέρες υἱοὺς προσλάβεσθε, ὡς δὲ διδάσκαλοι καὶ κηδεμόνες ἀποδείξασθε, καὶ συνάψαντες ἑαυτοὺς τοῖς ἀγαπητοῖς ἡμῶν τοῖς περὶ Παυλῖνον, μηδὲν πλεῖον ἀπαιτήσητε παρ' αὐτῶν, ἢ ἀναθεματίζειν μὲν τὴν 'Αρειανὴν αἵρεσιν, ὁμολογεῖν δὲ τὴν παρ' αὐτῶν ἁγίων πατέρων ὁμολογηθεῖσαν ἐν Νικαίᾳ πίστιν.* Then an explanation of the dispute respecting the hypostases. The one party teaches that there are three hypostases *διὰ τὸ εἰς ἁγίαν τριάδα πιστεύειν οὐκ ὀνόματι τριάδα μόνον, ἀλλ' ἀληθῶς οὖσαν καὶ ὑφεστῶσαν, πατέρα τε ἀληθῶς ὄντα καὶ ὑφεστῶτα, καὶ υἱὸν ἀληθῶς ἐνούσιον ὄντα καὶ ὑφεστῶτα, καὶ πνεῦμα ἅγιον ὑφεστὸς καὶ ὑπάρχον.* The others, on the contrary, taught that there was one hypostasis, *ἡγούμενοι ταὐτὸν εἶναι εἰπεῖν ὑπόστασιν καὶ οὐσίαν.* Those who were present of both parties might have mutually acknowledged one another as orthodox and agreed, *βελτίονα καὶ ἀκριβεστέραν εἶναι τὴν ἐν Νικαίᾳ παρὰ τῶν πατέρων ὁμολογηθεῖσαν πίστιν, καὶ τοῦ λοιποῦ τοῖς ταύτης ἀρκεῖσθαι μᾶλλον καὶ χρῆσθαι ῥήμασιν.*

[15] On the Luciferian schism see Walch's Ketzerhist. Th. 3, S. 338, ff. E. A. Frommanni de Lucifero Calaritano olim praesule epistola. Coburgi. 1767. 4.

378), had now favored the Semiarians instead of the Arians, he might, perhaps, have considerably checked the further spread of the Nicene party; but since he tried to make Arianism alone predominant by horribly persecuting all who thought differently,[16] he drove by this means the Semiarians who did not sink under persecution, to unite still more closely with the Nicenes. Thus a great part of the Semiarians (or, as they were now also called, *Macedonians*, from Macedonius, bishop of Constantinople, who had been deposed at the instigation of the Arians, 360),[17] declared themselves, at several councils of Asia Minor, in favor of the Nicene confession, and sent an embassy to Rome to announce their assent to it (366).[18] However much the Arians, supported by the emperor Valens, endeavored to counteract this new turn of affairs, yet the Macedonians were always passing over more and more to the Nicene creed; and for this the three great teachers of the church in particular, *Basil the Great, Gregory of Nazianzum, and Gregory of Nyssa*, began now to work. These new oriental Nicenians did not believe their faith changed by their assent to the Nicene formula, but thought they had merely assumed a more definite expression for it in the rightly understood *ὁμοούσιος*.[19] They

[16] The *λόγος προσφωνητικός*, by which Themistius about 372 in Antioch is said to have disposed the emperor to milder measures, Socrat. iv. 32, Sozom. vi. 36, is lost, and must not be confounded with the Orat. de religionibus (§ 77, note 5), Neander, ii. 1, 149, A.

[17] Socrat. ii. 45.

[18] Socrat. iv. 12: *Φόβῳ μᾶλλον καὶ βίᾳ στενοχωρούμενοι, κατὰ πόλεις διεπρεσβεύοντο πρὸς ἀλλήλους, δηλοῦντες δεῖν ἐξ ἀνάγκης καταφεύγειν περί τε τὸν ἀδελφὸν τοῦ βασιλέως* (Valentinianum I.), *καὶ ἐπὶ Λιβέριον τῆς* Ῥώμης Ἐπίσκοπον, *ἀσπάζεσθαί τε τῶν ἐκείνων πίστιν μᾶλλον ἢ κοινωνεῖν τοῖς περὶ* Εὐδόξιον. Cf. Sozom. vi. 10.

[19] Syn. Antioch. ann. 363, Epist. ad Jovianum (ap. Socr. iii. 25): *Τὸ δοκοῦν ξένον τισὶν ὄνομα, τὸ τοῦ ὁμοουσίου* signifies, *ὅτι ἐκ τῆς οὐσίας τοῦ πατρός ὁ υἱὸς ἐγεννήθη, καὶ ὅτι ὅμοιος κατ' οὐσίαν τῷ πατρί.* Those sent by Macedonius to Liberius (Sozom. vi. 10) *τὸ ὁμοούσιον ὄνομα δέχονται, ὡς τῷ ὁμοίῳ κατ' οὐσίαν τὰ αὐτά σημαῖνον.* In like manner Basilius Ep. ix. ad Maximum: *'Εγὼ δὲ—τὸ ὅμοιον κατ' οὐσίαν—δέχομαι τὴν φωνὴν, ὡς εἰς ταὐτὸν τῷ ὁμοουσίῳ φέρουσαν, κατὰ τὴν ὑγιῆ δηλονότι τοῦ ὁμοοσίου διάνοιαν.* Basil had belonged to the Semiarians (Klose's Basilius d. G. Stralsund. 1835. S. 21), and with its leaders, such as Basil of Ancyra, and Eustathius of Sebaste, had been active at the theological disputations in Constantinople, 359. (Gregor. Nyss. contra Eunom. i. p. 301. Philostorg. iv. c. 12.) He writes, however, of himself, Epist. 223, § 3: *"Εν γε τοῦτο τολμῶ καυχᾶσθαι ἐν κυρίῳ, ὅτι οὐδέ ποτε πεπλανημένας ἔσχον τὰς περὶ θεοῦ ὑπολήψεις, ἢ ἑτέρως φρονῶν μετέμαθον ὕστερον.—"Ωσπερ γὰρ τὸ σπέρμα αὐξανόμενον μεῖζον μὲν ἀπὸ μικροῦ γίνεται, ταὐτὸν δέ ἐστιν ἐν ἑαυτῷ, οὐ κατὰ γένος μεταβαλλόμενον, ἀλλὰ κατ' αὔξησιν τελειούμενον· οὕτω λογίζομαι καὶ ἐμοὶ τὸν αὐτὸν λόγον διὰ τῆς προκοπῆς ηὐξῆσθαι, οὐχὶ δὲ ἀντὶ τοῦ ἐξ ἀρχῆς ὄντος τὸν νῦν ὑπάρχοντα γεγενῆσθαι.* In this sense Athanasius, de Synodis § 41, passes judgment also on the Semiarians: *Πρὸς δὲ τοὺς ἀποδεχομένους τὰ μὲν ἄλλα πάντα τῶν ἐν Νικαίᾳ γραφέντων, περὶ δὲ μόνον τὸ ὁμοούσιον ἀμφιβάλλοντας, χρὴ μὴ ὡς πρὸς ἐχθροὺς διακεῖσθαι· καὶ γὰρ καὶ*

abided by the three hypostases of their Semiarianism, and attached themselves to the Meletians; but on this very account they could not keep church communion with the old Nicenes, notwithstanding all the efforts made by Basil to effect that object.[20] Since they supposed that they had unchangeably remained steadfast to their faith, they also continued to consider their Eusebian and Semiarian forefathers as orthodox, although condemned by the old Nicenes.[21] Thus the canons of the oriental councils held during the schism, constantly remained in force, particularly those of *the council of Antioch*, A.D. 341,[22]

ἡμεῖς οὐχ ὡς πρὸς Ἀρειομανίτας, οὐδ' ὡς μαχομένους πρὸς τοὺς πατέρας ἐνιστάμεθα, ἀλλ' ὡς ἀδελφοὶ πρὸς ἀδελφοὺς διαλεγόμεθα, τὴν αὐτὴν μὲν ἡμῖν διάνοιαν ἔχοντας, περὶ δὲ τὸ ὄνομα μόνον διστάζοντας. In like manner Hilarius de Synodis, § 76, ss.

[20] Comp. Basilii Ep. 69, ad Athanasium, Ep. 70, ad Damasum, both A.D. 371 (see Garnier vita Basilii, p. 94, prefixed to tom. iii. Opp. Bas.). Then A.D. 372, Ep. ad Occidentales; Ep. 91, ad Valerianum Illyric. Episc., Ep. 92, ad Italos et Gallos (Garnier, p. 110).—A.D. 376: Ep. 242, Orientalium ad Occidentales, Ep. 243, Basilii ad Episc. Italos et Gallos (Garnier, p. 159).—A.D. 377: Ep. 263, Orientalium ad Occidentales (Garnier, p. 165). Concerning these negotiations with the *Δυτικοῖς* Basil affirms, Ep. 239, ad Euseb. Episc. Samosatorum, A.D. 376: *Ἐμοὶ μὲν γὰρ τὸ τοῦ Διομήδους* (Iliad, ix. 698, 699) *ἐπέρχεται λέγειν· μὴ ὄφελες λίσσεσθαι· διότι, φησὶν, ἀγήνωρ ἐστὶν ὁ ἀνήρ. Τῷ ὄντι γὰρ θεραπευόμενα τὰ ὑπερήφανα ἤθη ἑαυτῶν ὑπεροπτικώτερα γίνεσθαι πέφυκε. Καὶ γὰρ ἐὰν μὲν ἱλασθῇ ἡμῖν ὁ κύριος, ποίας ἑτέρας προσθήκης δεόμεθα; ἐὰν δὲ ἐπιμείνῃ ἡ ὀργὴ τοῦ θεοῦ, ποία βοήθεια ἡμῖν τῆς δυτικῆς ὀφρύος; οἳ τὸ ἀληθὲς οὔτε ἴσασιν οὔτε μαθεῖν ἀνέχονται, ψευδέσι δὲ ὑπονοίαις προειλημμένοι, ἐκεῖνα ποιοῦσι νῦν, ἃ πρότερον ἐπὶ Μαρκέλλῳ. πρὸς μὲν τοὺς τὴν ἀλήθειαν αὐτοῖς ἀπαγγέλλοντας φιλονεικήσαντες. τὴν δὲ αἵρεσιν δι' ἑαυτῶν βεβαιώσαντες. Ἐγὼ μὲν γὰρ αὐτὸς, ἄνευ τοῦ κοινοῦ σχήματος, ἐβουλόμην αὐτῶν ἐπιστεῖλαι τῷ κορυφαίῳ, περὶ μὲν τῶν ἐκκλησιαστικῶν οὐδὲν, εἰ μὴ ὅσον παραινίξασθαι, ὅτι οὔτε ἴσασι τῶν παρ' ἡμῖν τὴν ἀλήθειαν, οὔτε τὴν ὁδὸν, δι' ἧς ἂν μανθάνοιεν, καταδέχονται.* J. E. Feisser Diss. de vita Basilii M. Groning. 1828. 8, p. 96, ss. Klose's Basilius d. G. S. 183, 201, 238.

[21] The Bishop Dianius, one of the predecessors of Basil in Caesarea, had played a principal part among the Eusebian bishops at the councils of Antioch and Philippopolis; yet Basil praises him very much notwithstanding, Ep. 51, and assures us, Ep. 140: *Ἔστι τοίνυν ἐκ πατέρων ἐμπολιτευομένη τῇ ἐκκλησίᾳ ἡμῶν ἡ γραφεῖσα παρὰ τῶν ἁγίων πατέρων πίστις τῶν κατὰ τὴν Νίκαιαν συνελθόντων.* In like manner Gregor. Naz. Orat. iii. Sozom. v. 10, Theodoret, H. E. iii. 3, praise the Semiarian Marcus bishop of Arethusa as a Christian martyr under Julian.

[22] Innocentius I. Ep. 7, ad Constantinopolitanos, A.D. 405, designates these 25 canons as composed by heretics,—non solum non sequendos, verum etiam una cum haereticis et schismaticis dogmatibus condemnandos: yet the orientals held them fast. The council of Chalcedon appeals to them, Act. 4. Soon after they were translated in the prisca versio with the Greek Codex Canonum, were transferred for the greater part into the Canones Apostolorum (See Divis. I. § 67, note 5), and enjoyed from this time forward, even in the west, undisputed authority. Pope Zacharias, Ep. 7, ad Pipinum, calls them beatorum patrum sanctiones; Nicolaus I. Ep. 9, ad Michaelem Imp. venerabiles Antiochenos et sacros canones. On this account modern Catholic historians have wished to make two Antiochian councils, a Catholic and a Eusebian one. Eman. a Schelstrate sacr. Antiochenum concil. pro Arianorum conciliabulo passim habitum, nunc vero primum ex antiquitate auctoritati suae restitutum. Antverp. 1681. 4. P. et H. fratres Ballerinii de antiquis collectionibus canonum, P. i. c. 4, § 2 (in the appendix to the Opp. Leonis M. Venet. 1757.

and of *Laodicea* (perhaps A.D. 363),[23] which canons afterward passed over from the oriental to the occidental church.

During this time new schisms had been made by new disputes on points of doctrine. The doctrine of the Holy Spirit, amid the controversies respecting the Logos, had for a long time remained untouched, and very different views respecting it were in consequence entertained.[24] But when in the east not only the Semiarians, but also many of the new Nicenians could not get rid of the Arian idea that the Holy Spirit is a creature and servant of God,[25] the other Nicenes took great offense at this, and opposed these errorists as Πνευματομάχους.[26] But they were

Reprinted in A. Gallandii de Vetustis canonum collectionibus dissertationum sylloge Venet. 1778. fol. Mongunt. 1790. tomi ii. 4.

23 Because Gratian Decreti, P. i. Dist. 16, c. 11, says of the Laodicean canons: Quorum auctor maxime Theodosius Episcopus extitit, Gothofredus ad Philost. and Pagi Crit. ann. 314, note 25, conjecture that the Eunomian Theodosius, bishop of Philadelphia in Lydia, brought about this synod. Cf. Philostorg. viii. c. 4.

24 Gregorii Naz. Orat. theol. v. de Spir. S. § 5 (Orat. 31, formerly 37): Τῶν δὲ καθ' ἡμᾶς σοφῶν οἱ μὲν ἐνέργειαν τοῦτο (τὸ πνεῦμα ἅγιον) ὑπέλαβον, οἱ δὲ κτίσμα, οἱ δὲ θεὸν, οἱ δὲ οὐκ ἔγνωσαν ὁπότερον τούτων, αἰδοῖ τῆς γραφῆς, ὥς φασιν, ὡς οὐδὲν ἕτερον σαφῶς δηλωσάσης.—οἱ μὲν ἄχρι διανοίας εἰσὶν εὐσεβεῖς, οἱ δε τολμῶσιν εὐσεβεῖν καὶ τοῖς χείλεσιν, κ. τ. λ. Hilarius de Trin. ii. 29: Cum dicunt, per quem sit (Sp. S.), et ob quid sit, vel qualis sit; si responsio nostra displicebit dicentium: "per quem omnia, et ex quo omnia sunt, et quia Spiritus est Dei, donum fidelium;" displiceant et Apostoli et Prophetae, hoc tantum de eo quod esset loquentes. On the following dispute see Baur's Dreieinigkeit, i. 490.

25 Fragm. Arianum xiv. in Maji Script. vett. nova coll. iii. ii. 229: Spir. S. est primum et majus Patris per Filium opus, creatum per Filium. Maximinus, Ep. Arianus (about 382), in G. Waitz über d. Leben u. die Lehre des Ulfila. Hannover. 1840. 4. S. 19: Spiritum Sanctum—a Patre per Filium ante omnia factum—ab ingenito per unigenitum in tertio gradu creatum, is proved by Joh. i. 3: Omnia per ipsum facta sunt, and 1 Cor. viii. 6: Unus Deus Pater, ex quo omnia, et unus dominus J. Chr., per quem omnia.

26 They were first attacked by Athanasius Epist. iv. ad Serapionem Episc. Thmuitanum (between 358 and 360), after Serapion had informed him (Epist. l. init.) ὡς ἐξελθόντων μέν τινων ἀπὸ τῶν 'Αρειανῶν διὰ τὴν κατὰ τοῦ υἱοῦ τοῦ θεοῦ βλασφημίαν, φρονούντων δὲ κατὰ τοῦ ἁγίου πνεύματος καὶ λεγόντων αὐτὸ μὴ μόνον κτίσμα, ἀλλὰ καὶ τῶν λειτουργικῶν πνευμάτων ἓν αὐτὸ εἶναι, καὶ βαθμῷ μόνον αὐτὸ διαφέρειν τῶν ἀγγέλων. Epist. Synod. Conc. Alex. A. D. 362,—Basilii M de Spiritu S. lib. ad Amphilochium, A. D. 374.—Gregorii Nazianz. Orat. 37 et 44 (comp. Ullmann's Gregorius v. Naz. S. 378, ff.) Epiphanius adv. Haer. (about 374) Haer. lxxiii. τῶν 'Ημιαρείων. § 1: Οἱ δὲ αὐτοὶ καὶ περὶ τοῦ ἁγίου πνεύματος ἴσως τοῖς Πνευματομάχοις εἰσὶν ἔχοντες. Haer. lxxiv. τῶν Πνευματομάχων. § 1. 'Απὸ τούτων τῶν 'Ημιαρείων, καὶ ἀπὸ ὀρθοδόξων τινὲς, ὡς εἰπεῖν, τέρας τισὶ [leg. τεράστιοι] γεννηθέντες ἄνθρωποι—βλασφημοῦσι τὸ πνεῦμα τὸ ἅγιον. Philastrius (about 380) de Haeresibus, c. 67: Semiariani sunt quoque. Hi de Patre et Filio bene sentiunt—Spiritum autem non de divina substantia, nec Deum verum, sed factum atque creatum Spiritum praedicantes, ut eum conjungant et comparent creaturae. In all these writers Pneumatomachi is still the exclusive appellation of these errorists. On the contrary the Semiarians were at that time called Macedonians. At the time of the first council of Constantinople (381), Constantinople was the chief seat of the Semiarians (cf. Gregorii Naz. vita a Gregor. Presb. conscripta. Socrat. ii. 45: Οἱ περὶ Μακεδόνιον

not yet all prepared to style the Holy Spirit God.[27] Finally, the number of sects was increased by a zealous adherent of the Nicene council, *Apollinaris*, bishop of Laodicea, who, misled, perhaps, by his aversion to Origen,[28] believed that he was necessarily obliged to concede to the Arians the position,[29] that the Logos in Christ supplied the place of the rational soul *νοῦς* or *ψυχὴ λογική*,[30] and from about 371 gathered round him the ad-

εἰς τὸν Ἑλλήσποντον πλεονάζουσι). Hence the appellations Semiariani, Pneumatomachi and Macedoniani (can. 1 and 7) were used as synonymous by this council. Inasmuch as the peculiarity of this party regarding the doctrine of the Son was unimportant, nothing but their views of the Holy Spirit remained to make them heretical. Hence, by an easy transition, Macedonius came to be considered the author of this heresy, as is the case so early as Sozom. iv. 27: *Ἐπειδὴ Μακεδόνιος ἀφῃρέθη τὴν Κωνσταντινουπόλεως ἐκκλησίαν, εἰσηγεῖτο τὸν υἱὸν θεὸν εἶναι, κατὰ πάντα τε καὶ κατ' οὐσίαν ὅμοιον τῷ πατρί· τὸ δὲ ἅγιον πνεῦμα ἄμοιρον τῶν αὐτῶν πρεσβείων ἀπεφαίνετο, διάκονον καὶ ὑπηρέτην καλῶν, καὶ ὅσα περὶ τῶν θείων ἀγγέλων λέγων τὶς οὐκ ἂν ἁμάρτοι.* Hence, from this time onward the usual name for those who were heretical in their views of the Holy Ghost was Macedoniani, instead of Pneumatomachi; although it is unquestionable that Macedonius, though he entertained those sentiments, like all the Semiarians, was not the author of them.

[27] Eustathius, bishop of Sebaste, who had been at the head of that Semiarian embassy to Rome (see note 18), and had since become a Nicenian, declared: *Ἐγὼ οὔτε θεὸν ὀνομάζειν τὸ πνεῦμα τὸ ἅγιον αἱροῦμαι, οὔτε κτίσμα καλεῖν τολμήσαιμι* (Socrat. ii. 25). It is true that subsequently the orientals accused him before the Occidentals of having gone over to the Arians, and having become *πρωτοστάτης τῆς τῶν πνευματομάχων αἱρέσεως* (Basilii, Ep. 263, § 3). In conformity with that earlier declaration of Eustathius was the conduct also of his friend at that time, Basil the Great. He would have all admitted to church-fellowship, Ep. 113, *τοὺς μὴ λέγοντας κτίσμα τὸ πνεῦμα τὸ ἅγιον.* But he himself abstained from calling the Holy Ghost God, on which Gregory of Nazianzum was obliged to hear reproaches (Gregor. Ep. 26, ad Basil.), and exculpated Basil in this way: *Πολὺς περὶ αὐτὸν ὁ πόλεμος, ζητούντων λαβέσθαι τῶν αἱρετικῶν γυμνῆς τῆς φωνῆς* (namely *περὶ τοῦ πνεύματος, ὡς εἴη θεός*)—*ἵν' ὁ μὲν ἐξωσθῇ τῆς ἐκκλησίας, ῥιζωθῇ δὲ τὸ κακὸν ἐν τῇ πόλει.* So also in his laudatory address to Basil, Orat. xx. p. 364. The monks in Caesarea were particularly indignant against Basil, but in opposition to them he was justified by Athanasius Ep. ad Palladium: *Αὐτὸς μὲν γὰρ, ὡς τεθάῤῥηκα, τοῖς ἀσθενοῦσιν ἀσθενὴς γίνεται, ἵνα τοὺς ἀσθενεῖς κερδήσῃ.* Cf. Garnier vita Basilii, p. 95, ss. That Basil made up his view of the Holy Spirit from Plotinian ideas of the ideal world, and the world of soul, is shown by A. Jahn, Basilius Magnus plotinizans. Bernae. 1838. 4. When Gregory of Nazianzum preached the deity of the Holy Spirit openly, it was objected to him (Orat. theol. v. de Spir. S. § 1): *Πόθεν ἡμῖν ἐπεισάγεις ξένον θεὸν καὶ ἄγραφον;* and he admitted, § 26: *Ἐκήρυσσε φανερῶς ἡ παλαιὰ τὸν Πατέρα, τὸν Υἱὸν ἀμυδρότερον· ἐφανέρωσεν ἡ καινὴ τὸν Υἱὸν, ὑπέδειξε τοῦ Πνεύματος τὴν θεότητα· ἐμπολιτεύεται νῦν τὸ Πνεῦμα, σαφεστέραν ἡμῖν παρέχον τὴν ἑαυτοῦ δήλωσιν.*

[28] See below, § 84, note 24.

[29] Cf. Eudoxii Ariani fragm. (in Maji Scriptt. vett. nova coll. vii. 1, 17): *Πιστεύομεν— εἰς ἕνα κύριον,—σαρκωθέντα, οὐκ ἐνανθρωπήσαντα· οὔτε γὰρ ψυχὴν ἀνθρωπίνην ἀνείληφεν, ἀλλὰ σὰρξ γέγονεν·—οὐ δύο φύσεις· ἐπεὶ μὴ τέλειος ἦν ἄνθρωπος, ἀλλ' ἀντὶ ψυχῆς θεὸς ἐν σαρκί.* Lucii Alexandrini Ariani fragm. l. c.: *Διὰ τοῦτο βοᾷ τὴν ἀλήθειαν Ἰωάννης· ὁ λόγος σὰρξ ἐγένετο, ἀντὶ τοῦ, συνετέθη σαρκὶ, οὐ μὴν ψυχῇ.—Εἰ δὲ καὶ ψυχὴν εἶχεν,—μάχεται τὰ κινήματα θεοῦ καὶ ψυχῆς· αὐτοκίνητον γὰρ τούτων ἑκάτερον, καὶ πρὸς ἐνεργείας διαφόρους ἀγόμενον.* Fragm. Arian. xiii. Majus, l. c. iii. ii. 228.

[30] Comp. Baur's Dreieinigkeit, i. 559. So early as in the epist. synod. Conc. Alex. A.D. 362, in which even delegates of Apollinaris took part, we find, but without the name of

vocates of this sentiment (Apollinaristae, Συνουσιασταί, Διμοιριταί.)[31]

Thus *Theodosius*, who as a Spaniard was a zealous adherent of the Nicene council, found at his accession to the throne, in

the latter, the polemic declaration: Ὡμολόγουν γὰρ καὶ τοῦτο, ὅτι οὐ σῶμα ἄψυχον, οὐδ' ἀναίσθητον, οὐδ' ἀνόητον εἶχεν ὁ σωτήρ. This opinion is also contradicted by Athanasius, especially in Epist. ad Epictetum (371), contra Apollinarium libb. ii. (372), yet without naming Apollinaris (see Möhler's Athanasius, Th. 2. S. 263, ff.), although Epiphanius Haer. 77, considers those works as refutations of it. Basil the Great heard of the heresy of Apollinaris in 373 (Ep. 129 ad Meletium), and wrote about it 374 (Ep. 264 ad Occidentales, and Ep. 265 ad Aegyptios). Fragments of the writings of Apollinaris belonging to the present subject (περὶ ἐνσαρκώσεως, περὶ πίστεως) are preserved chiefly in Gregory of Nyssa and Theodoret. Fragments of several epistles of Apollinaris are found in Leontius Byzant. (about 590) adv. fraudes Apollinaristarum libb. 2. (ex. lat. vers. Turriani in Canisii Lectt. ant. ed. Basnage, i. 608, ss. Gallandii Bibl. PP. xii. 706). Scattered fragments of every kind are in Majii Scriptt. vett. nova coll. tom. vii. P. i. Answers to Apollinaris were written by Diodorus Tarsensis, Theodotus Antiochenus, and the two bishops of Alexandria, Theophilus and Cyril. Still extant are Gregorii Naz. Ep. ad Nectarium, or Orat. 46, and Ep. ii. ad Cledonium, or Orat. 51 and 52 (Ullmann's Greg. von Naz. S. 401, ff.): and the far more important Gregorii Nysseni ἀντιῤῥητικὸς πρὸς τὰ Ἀπολλιναρίου (prim. ed. Zacagnius Monim. veter. eccl. Gr. and in Gallandii Bibl. PP. vi. 517). Nemesius de Natura hominis, c. 1. Τινὲς μὲν, ὧν ἐστι καὶ Πλωτῖνος, ἄλλην εἶναι τὴν ψυχὴν, καὶ ἄλλον τὸν νοῦν δογματίσαντες, ἐκ τριῶν τὸν ἄνθρωπον συνεστάναι βούλονται, σώματος, καὶ ψυχῆς, καὶ νοῦ. Οἷς ἠκολούθησε καὶ Ἀπολλινάριος, ὁ τῆς Λαοδικείας γενόμενος ἐπίσκοπος· τοῦτον γὰρ πηξάμενος τὸν θεμέλιον τῆς ἰδίας δόξης, καὶ τὰ λοιπὰ προσῳκοδόμησε· κατὰ τὸ οἰκεῖον δόγμα. Apollinarius ap. Greg. Nyss. c. 35: Ὁ ἄνθρωπος εἷς ἐστιν ἐκ πνεύματος καὶ ψυχῆς καὶ σώματος.—C. 9: Τὸ δὴ πνεῦμα, τουτέστι τὸν νοῦν, θεὸν ἔχων ὁ Χριστὸς μετὰ ψυχῆς καὶ σώματος, εἰκότως ἄνθρωπος ἐξ οὐρανοῦ λέγεται (1 Cor. xv. 47, ss.)—C. 7: Θεὸς μέν (ἐστι) τῷ πνεύματι τῷ σαρκωθέντι, ἄνθρωπος δὲ τῇ ὑπὸ τοῦ θεοῦ προσληφθείσῃ σαρκί.—C. 23: Οὐκ ἄνθρωπος, ἀλλ' ὡς ἄνθρωπος (Phil. ii. 7), διότι οὐχ ὁμοούσιος τῷ ἀνθρώπῳ κατὰ τὸ κυριώτατον.—C. 39: Εἰ ἀνθρώπῳ τελείῳ συνήφθη θεὸς τέλειος, δύο ἂν ἦσαν.—C. 42: Εἷς μὲν φύσει υἱὸς θεοῦ, εἷς δὲ θετός.—C. 48: Εἰ ἐκ πάντων τῶν ἴσων ἡμῖν ἐστι τοῖς χοϊκοῖς ὁ ἐπουράνιος ἄνθρωπος (ὥστε καὶ τὸ πνεῦμα ἴσον ἔχειν τοῖς χοϊκοῖς), οὐκ ἐπουράνιος, ἀλλ' ἐπουρανίου θεοῦ δοχεῖον.—C. 44: Ἡ σὰρξ τοῦ Κυρίου προσκυνεῖται, καθὸ ἕν ἐστι, πρόσωπον καὶ ἓν ζῶον μετ' αὐτοῦ. Μηδὲν ποίημα προσκυνητὸν μετὰ τοῦ Κυρίου, ὡς ἡ σὰρξ αὐτοῦ. From this resulted the principle of one nature in Christ, Apoll. fragm. ap. Majum, vii. i. 16: Μιᾷ δὲ συγκράτῳ τῇ φύσει ἄνθρωπον τὸν κύριον λέγομεν, μιᾷ δὲ συγκράτῳ τῇ φύσει σαρκικῇ τε καὶ θεϊκῇ. In another fragment Apollinaris designates the entire spiritual principle in man as ψυχή, and makes the place of it in Christ be supplied by the Logos. Ap. Majum, vii. i. 203: Ὁ Ἰωάννης—εἰπὼν, ὅτι ὁ λόγος σὰρξ ἐγένετο, οὐ προσέθηκε, καὶ ψυχή· ἀδύνατον γὰρ δύο νοερὰ καὶ θελητικὰ ἐν τῷ ἅμα κατοικεῖν, ἵνα μὴ τὸ ἕτερον κατὰ τοῦ ἑτέρου ἀντιστρατεύηται διὰ τῆς οἰκείας θελήσεως καὶ ἐνεργείας. Οὐκοῦν οὐ ψυχῆς ἀνθρωπίνης ἐπελάβετο ὁ λόγος, ἀλλὰ μόνου σπέρματος Ἀβραάμ· τὸ γὰρ τοῦ σώματος Ἰησοῦ ναὸν προδιέγραψεν ὁ ἄψυχος καὶ ἄνους καὶ ἀθελὴς τοῦ Σολομῶντος ναός. Some of his disciples, especially Polemius (Polemiani) taught ἐκ τῶν οὐρανῶν κατεληλυθέναι τοῦ Κυρίου τὸ σῶμα, ὁμοούσιον τὸ σῶμα τ. Χρ. τῇ θεότητι. Epiph. Haer. 77, § 2, 20. Theodoret. Haer. fab. iv. 9. Chr. A. Salig. de Eutychianismo ante Eutychen. Guelpherb. 1723. 4.—From this time forward the threefold division of man began to be considered heterodox. Keilii Opusc. acad. t. ii. p. 641, ss.

[31] Συνουσιασταί, because they taught, συνουσίωσιν γεγενῆσθαι καὶ κρᾶσιν τῆς θεότητος καὶ τοῦ σώματος (Theodoret. Haer. fab. comp. iv. 9). Hence Theodotus of Antioch, and Diodorus of Tarsus, wrote κατὰ Συνουσιαστῶν. Dimoeritae apud Epiphan. Haer. 77.

the west (379) universal toleration; in the east Arianism prevalent, the Homousiasts persecuted, and besides them the parties of the Photinians, Macedonians, and Apollinarists, with innumerable older sects. After conquering the Goths, he began forthwith to declare Homousianism to be the catholic faith, and to persecute other parties.[32] The more effectually to remove existing evils, he summoned *a general council at Constantinople* (381),[33] by which the schism between the Nicenes was peaceably removed,[34] and the Nicene creed enlarged with additions directed against heretics who had risen up since its origin.[35]

[32] A law of the year 380, Cod. Theod. xvi. 1, 2: Cunctos populos, quos clementiae nostrae regit temperamentum, in tali volumus religione versari, quam divinum Petrum Apostolum tradidisse Romanis religio usque nunc ab ipso insinuata declarat, quamque pontificem Damasum sequi claret, et Petrum Alexandriae episcopum, virum apostolicae sanctitatis: hoc est ut secundum apostolicam disciplinam evangelicamque doctrinam Patris et Filii et Spiritus Sancti unam deitatem sub parili majestate et sub pia trinitate credamus. Hanc legem sequentes Christianorum catholicorum nomen jubemus amplecti, reliquos vero dementes vesanosque judicantes, haeretici dogmatis infamiam sustinere, nec conciliabulo eorum ecclesiarum nomen accipere, divina primum vindicta, post etiam motus nostri, quem ex caelesti arbitrio sumserimus, ultione plectendos. Ullmann's Gregor. v. Naz. S. 220, ff. Stuffken Diss. de Theodos. M. in rem Christ. meritis. Lugd. Bat. 1828. 8, p. 135, ss.

[33] *οἱ ρν'*. Respecting it see Fuchs Bibl. d. Kirchenverf. ii. 390. Ullmann, S. 238. Stuffken, p. 142.

[34] To this Synod Meletius, as bishop of Antioch, was summoned, not Paulinus, with whom the westerns communicated, and was even a *πρόεδρος* of the council (Gregorii Naz. Carmen de vita sua, v. 1514). When he died during the council, Flavianus was appointed to succeed him, without reference to Paulinus (Ullmann, S. 245). The schism did not entirely disappear till A.D. 413 (Theodoret. v. 35).

[35] Symb. Nicaeno-Constantinopolitanum: *Πιστεύομεν εἰς ἕνα θεὸν, πατέρα παντοκράτορα, ποιητὴν οὐρανοῦ καὶ γῆς, ὁρατῶν τε πάντων καὶ ἀοράτων, καὶ εἰς ἕνα κύριον Ἰησοῦν Χριστὸν, τὸν υἱὸν τοῦ θεοῦ τὸν μονογενῆ, τὸν ἐκ τοῦ πατρὸς γεννηθέντα πρὸ πάντων τῶν αἰώνων, φῶς ἐκ φωτὸς, θεὸν ἀληθινὸν ἐκ θεοῦ ἀληθινοῦ, γεννηθέντα οὐ ποιηθέντα, ὁμοούσιον τῷ πατρὶ δι' οὗ τὰ πάντα ἐγένετο. Τὸν δι' ἡμᾶς τοὺς ἀνθρώπους καὶ διὰ τὴν ἡμετέραν σωτηρίαν κατελθόντα ἐκ τῶν οὐρανῶν, καὶ σαρκωθέντα ἐκ πνεύματος ἁγίου καὶ Μαρίας τῆς παρθένου, καὶ ἐνανθρωπήσαντα· σταυρωθέντα τε ὑπὲρ ἡμῶν ἐπὶ Ποντίου Πιλάτου, καὶ παθόντα καὶ ταφέντα καὶ ἀναστάντα ἐν τῇ τρίτῃ ἡμέρᾳ κατὰ τὰς γραφάς· καὶ ἀνελθόντα εἰς τοὺς οὐρανοὺς, καὶ καθεζόμενον ἐκ δεξιῶν τοῦ πατρὸς, καὶ πάλιν ἐρχόμενον μετὰ δόξης κρῖναι ζῶντας καὶ νεκρούς· οὗ τῆς βασιλείας οὐκ ἔσται τέλος. Καὶ εἰς τὸ ἅγιον πνεῦμα, τὸ κύριον* (according to 2 Cor. iii. 17. See Theodoret. ad h. l.), *τὸ ζωοποιὸν* (according to Joh. vi. 63), *τὸ ἐκ τοῦ πατρὸς ἐκπορευόμενον* (according to Joh. xv. 26), *τὸ σὺν πατρὶ καὶ υἱῷ συμπροσκυνούμενον καὶ συνδοξαζόμενον, τὸ λαλῆσαν διὰ τῶν προφητῶν· εἰς μίαν ἁγίαν καθολικὴν καὶ ἀποστολικὴν ἐκκλησίαν. Ὁμολογοῦμεν ἓν βάπτισμα εἰς ἄφεσιν ἁμαρτιῶν· προσδοκῶμεν ἀνάστασιν νεκρῶν καὶ ζωὴν τοῦ μέλλοντος αἰῶνος· Ἀμήν.* J. C. Suicer Symbolum Nicaeno Constantinopol. expositum et ex antiquitate ecclesiastica illustratum. Traj. ad Rhen. 1718. 4. Already, about 375, a Roman synod under Damasus had declared Sp. S. cum Patre et Filio unius potestatis esse atque substantiae (Mansi, iii. 482), and an Illyrian synod, *ὁμοούσιον εἶναι τὴν τριάδα Πατρὸς, Υἱοῦ καὶ ἁγίου Πνεύματος* (Theodoret. iv. 8): But in Constantinople they did not yet venture to give utterance to any unbiblical formulas respecting the Holy Spirit, in order not to stir up new controversies in the east, where there were still so many opponents of his deity.—Immediately after the

Valentinian II. allowed the Arians in the west to enjoy freedom of religion some years longer;[36] but the case was quite altered by Theodosius,[37] and a universal suppression of the sect ensued. The last traces of its existence in the Byzantine empire appear under the emperor Anastasius at Constantinople, 491–518.[38]

The subject of the controversy was merely the point of sameness in essence between the three persons. The unity and equality of the persons, which necessarily resulted from holding sameness of essence, was not fully acknowledged at once even by the Nicenians,[39] but continued to be more clearly perceived,[40] until at last it was expressed by *Augustine* for the first time with decided logical consequence.[41]

close of the council, Theodosius passed the law of the 30th July, 381. (Cod. Theodos. xvi. 1, 3): Episcopis tradi omnes Ecclesias mox jubemus, qui unius majestatis atque virtutis Patrem et Filium et Spiritum Sanctum confitentur, ejusdem gloriae, claritatis unius; nihil dissonum profana divisione facientes, sed Trinitatis ordinem, personarum adsertionem, et divinitatis unitatem: quos constabit communione Nectarii Episc. Constantinopolitanae Ecclesiae, Timothei necnon intra Aegyptum Alexandrinae urbis Episcopi esse sociatos: quos etiam in Orientis partibus Pelagio Ep. Laodicensi, et Diodoro Ep. Tarsensi; in Asia necnon proconsulari atque Asiana dioecesi Amphilochio Ep. Iconiensi, et Optimo Ep. Antiocheno (of Antioch in Pisidia); in Pontica dioecesi Helladio Ep. Caesariensi, et Otrejo Meliteno, et Gregorio Ep. Nysseno; Terennio Ep. Scythiae, Marmario Ep. Marcianop. communicare constiterit: hos ad obtinendas catholicas Ecclesias ex communione et consortio probabilium sacerdotum oportebit admitti, etc. In like manner there followed laws against heretics, which were often repeated. See Cod. Theodos. xvi. 5, de Haereticis L. 6-14, 16, 17, 19, 21–23.

36 At the instance of his Arian mother Justina, Cod. Th. xvi. 1, 4 (A.D. 386), cf. Ambros. Epist. 20, 21, 22. Rufini Hist. Eccl. ii. 15. In the mean time, however, but a small number of Arians had gathered around the empress at Milan. Cf. Epist. ii. Conc. Aquilej. ann. 381, ad Impp. ap. Mansii, iii. p. 623: Per occidentales partes duobus in angulis antum, hoc est in latere Daciae Ripensis ac Moesiae fidei obstrepi videbatur.

37 When driven away by Maximus, he found refuge with Theodosius. His law against the heretics, A.D. 388, see Cod. Theod. xvi. 5, 15. Cf. Gothofred. ad h. legem. Soon after even an Arian in the west wrote in defense of his doctrinal creed. See the interesting reliquiae tractatus in Lucae Evang. and fragmenta sermonum in Ang. Maji Scriptorum veterum nova collectio, t. iii. P. ii.

38 Theodorus Lector, ii. p. 562, fragm. p. 582.

39 Comp. especially Hilarii de Trin. iii. 12: Et quis non Patrem potiorem confitebitur, ut ingenitum a genito, ut Patrem a Filio, ut eum qui miserit ab eo qui missus sit, ut volentem ab eo qui obediat? Et ipse nobis erit testis: Pater major me est. iv. 16: Dicit ergo fieri Deus ex quo omnia sunt, et facit Deus per quem omnia (according to 1 Cor. viii. 6). Haec distinctio jubentis Dei, et facientis Dei.

40 Athanasius had rejected the old proposition that the Son exists by the will of the Father, Orat. adv. Arianos i. (formerly ii.) 29: Τὸ δὲ γέννημα οὐ βουλήσει ὑπόκειται, ἀλλὰ τῆς οὐσίας ἐστὶν ἰδιότης.

41 Augustinus de Trin. vii. 11: Non major essentia est Pater et Filius et Spiritus Sanctus simul, quam solus Pater, aut solus Filius: sed tres simul illae substantiae (ὑποστάσεις) sive personae, si ita dicendae sunt, aequales sunt singulis: quod animalis homo non percipit. 12: Pater, et Filius, et Spiritus Sanctus unus Deus. Id. contra sermonem Arianorum § 4: Unus Deus est ipsa Trinitas, et sic unus Deus, quomodo unus creator:

§ 84.

HISTORY OF THE THEOLOGICAL SCIENCES DURING THE ARIAN DISPUTES.

Among the theological schools of this period the most distinguished were *that of Origen*, and *the Syrian historico-exegetical*, whose origin belongs to the preceding period. *Origen* enjoyed the highest esteem, and it is to be attributed to the wide-extended influence of his writings that notwithstanding these furious theological disputes, some freedom in theology was still preserved. In the great question of the time, both parties could appeal to him.[1] When the Arians referred to the declaration in his own writings, and in those of his disciples Dionysius and Theognostus, that the son is a creature, Athanasius, on the contrary, drew from the same source arguments for the eternal generation of the Logos.[2] Men were the less perplexed by contrary passages in his writings, inasmuch as they knew and already practiced many expedients for the purpose of making such expressions of the fathers as were contradictory to the more modern views, powerless and void.[3] Thus Origen had adherents among both parties. Among the Eusebians, he had in particular *Eusebius Pamphili*, bishop of Caesarea, in Palestine († 340), a man distinguished alike for his love of peace and his merits as a church historian.[4] Among the Nicenians, were

quid est quod dicunt, jubente Patre creasse omnia Filium, tanquam Pater non creaverit, sed a Filio creari jusserit? Formant sibi in phantasmate cordis sui quasi duos aliquos, etsi juxta invicem, in suis tamen locis constitutos, unum jubentem, alterum obtemperantem. Nec intelligunt, ipsam jussionem Patris, ut fierent omnia, non esse nisi Verbum Patris, per quod facta sunt omnia. Against the old opinion that the Father is absolutely invisible, and that the Logos alone can appear, see de Trin. ii. 15, ss. Cf. § 35: Ipsa natura, vel substantia, vel essentia, vel quolibet alio nomine appellandum est id ipsum quod Deus est, quidquid illud est, corporaliter videri non potest: per subjectam vero creaturam non solum Filium vel Spiritum Sanctum, sed etiam Patrem corporali specie sive similitudine mortalibus sensibus significationem sui dare potuisse credendum est.

1 Hence the contradictory opinions concerning him. Epiphanius Haer. 64, c. 4, declares him to be the father of Arianism; and Socrates, vii. 6, wonders how Timotheus could have been at the same time an admirer of Origen and an Arian, since Origen συναΐδιον πανταχοῦ ὁμολογεῖ τὸν υἱὸν τῷ πατρί.

2 See Div. I. § 63, note 18. Compare Münscher's Dogmengeschichte. Bd. 3. S. 416, 418, ff.

3 See Münscher, l. c. S. 156, ff. 422, ff.

4 His biography, composed by his successor Acacius (Socrat. ii. 4), is lost He is called

Athanasius, the father of orthodoxy, from the year 328[8] bishop of Alexandria, frequently banished and again recalled († 373); [5] *Basil* the Great, from the year 370 bishop of Caesarea in Cappadocia († 379); [6] his brother *Gregory*, from 370 bishop of Nyssa in Cappadocia († about 394); [7] *Gregory of Nazianzum*, ὁ θεόλογος, the intimate friend of Basil, bishop of Constantinople

an Arian by Athanasius, Epiphanius, Hilary, Jerome, etc., defended by Socrat. ii. 21, and Gelasius Histor. Synod. Nic. ii. 1. The first are followed by most historians, as Baronius, Petavius (Dogmat. theolog. de trin. lib. ii. c. 11), Arnold, Jac. Basnage, etc. On the contrary, he is declared to be orthodox by Valesius, Bull, du Pin, Sam. Basnage. There was a controversy on the subject between Jo. Le Clerc, who accuses him of Arianism (Bibliothèque univers. tom. x. p. 380. Epistolae criticae s. Artis criticae, vol. iii. p. 28, ss.), and W. Cave, who, on the other hand, defends him (Diss. de Eusebii Arianismo in the append. ii. Hist. literar. script. eccl. p. 42, and Epist. apolog. ibid. p. 61, ss.) A more correct opinion is given by Chr. D. A. Martini Eusebii Caes. de Divinitate Christi sententia. Rostoch. 1795. 4. J. Ritter Eusebii Caes. de Divinitate Christi placita. Bonnae. 1823. 4. Writings: Hist. eccl. lib. x. Chronicon s. παντοδαπὴ ἱστορία (ex. vers. Armen. ed. J. Bapt. Aucher. Venet. 2 t. 1818. 4. Ang. Majus et J. Zohrab. Mediol. 1818. 4, integrius et emendatius ed. Ang. Majus in Scriptt. vet. nova coll., tom. viii. Romae. 1833. 4). Προπαρασκευὴ εὐαγγελικὴ libb. 15, ed. F. Vigerus. Paris. 1628. fol. F. A. Heinichen. 2 t. Lips. 1842. 8. Εὐαγγελικὴ ἀπόδειξις lib. 20 (of this lib. i.–x. ed. Par. 1628. fol. The beginning of the first and close of the tenth book, which are there wanting, have been supplied by J. A. Fabricius in his Delectus argumentorum et syllabus scriptt. qui veritatem relig. christ. adseruerunt. Hamb. 1725. 4. p. 1, ss.). Contra Hieroclem liber (C. Gu. Haenell de Euseb. Caes. religionis christ. defensore. Gottingae. 1843. 8). Contra Marcellum libb. 2. De Ecclesiastica theologia libb. 3 (all appended to the Demonstr. evangel.) Περὶ τῶν τοπικῶν ἐν τῇ θείᾳ γραφῇ (cum. vers. Hieronymi ed. J. Clericus. Amst. 1707. fol.) Oratio de laudibus Constantini. De vita Constantini lib. 4 (annexed to the Hist. eccl.) Canones sacr. Evangeliorum x. (in bibl. PP.) Comm. in Cant. Canticorum, in Psalmos, in Esaiam. Eclogae propheticae e cod. Vindebon. primum ed. Thom. Gaisford. Oxon. 1842. 8. Cf. Fabricii Bibl. Gr. ed. Harles. vol. vii. p. 335, ss.

[5] See particularly Ἀπολογητικὸς κατὰ Ἀρειανῶν (about 349). Ἀπολογία πρὸς τὸν βασιλέα Κωνστάντιον (356). Ἀπολογία περὶ τῆς φυγῆς αὐτοῦ (357). Ἐπιστολὴ τοῖς τὸν μονήρη βίον ἀσκοῦσι s. historia Arianorum ad Monachos (358). Κατὰ Ἀρειανῶν λόγοι δ'. Ἐπιστολὴ περὶ τῶν γενομένων ἐν τῇ Ἀριμίνῳ τῆς Ἰταλίας καὶ ἐν Σελευκείᾳ τῆς Ἰσαυρίας συνόδων (359), etc. Opp. ed Bern. de Montfaucon. Paris. 1698. 3 t. fol. N. A. Justiniani. Patav. 1777. 4 t. fol. Cf. Fabricius-Harles, viii. 171. J. A. Möhler's Athanasius d. G. u. die Kirche seiner Zeit. 2 Th. Mainz. 1827. 8.

[6] Ἀντιῤῥητικὸς τοῦ Ἀπολογητικοῦ τοῦ δυσσεβοῦς Εὐνομίου libb. v. Περὶ τοῦ ἁγίου πνεύματος (comp. § 83, note 27). Homilies (C. Gu. van der Pot de Basilio M. oratore sacro. Amstel. 1835. 8. Paniel's Gesch. d. christl. Beredsamkeit, i. 464). Ascetic writings, letters. Opp. ed. Fronto Ducaeus. Paris. 1618. 2 voll. fol. Jul. Garnier. Par. 1721, ss. 3 voll. fol. ed. ii. cur. L. de Sinner. Paris. 1839. 3 tomi 8. A. Jahnii Animadversiones in S. Basilii M. opera. Bernae et S. Galli. 1842, fasc. 1. Cf. Fabricius-Harles, ix. 1. J. E. Feisser Diss. de vita Basilii M. Groningae. 1828. 8. Basilius d. G. nach s. Leben u. s. Lehre dargestellt von Dr. C. R. W. Klose. Stralsund. 1835. 8.

[7] Κατὰ Εὐνομίου libb. xiii. Contra Apollinarem, see § 83, note 29. Περὶ τῆς ἑξαημέρου. Λόγος κατηχητικὸς ὁ μέγας. (Oratio catechetica, rec. G. Krabinger. Acc. ejusdem Gregorii oratio funebris in Meletium Episc. Antiochenum. Monachii. 1835. 8). De anima et resurrectione (ed. Krabinger. 1837). De Precatione oratt. v. (ed. Krabinger. 1840). Respecting his homilies see Paniel, i. 520. Opp. ed. F. Morellius. Paris. 1615. 2 voll. Append. add. J. Gretser. Ibid. 1618. fol. Cf. Fabricius-Harles, ix. 98. Gregor's des Bisch. v. Nyssa Leben u. Meinungen, von Dr. J. Rupp. Leipzig. 1834. 8.

[8] The "Festal Letters" make this date certain.

from 380–381 († 390);[8] and *Didymus*, president of the catechetical school in Alexandria († 395).[9] Even toward the west also, where they were accustomed to derive their knowledge uninterruptedly from the Greek literature,[10] Origen's influence had extended, and the most important occidental writers of this period, *Hilary*, bishop of Poictiers from A.D. 350, living an exile in Phrygia from 356–360 († 368);[11] the Luciferian *Hilary*, deacon in Rome (about 380),[12] and *Ambrose*, bishop of Milan from 374 († 397),[13] honored and employed him as a teacher. So also the two distinguished western monks living in Palestine, *Tyrannius Rufinus* of Aquileia,[14] who had been six years a pupil of Didymus in Egypt, but, since the year 378, had led an ascetic life on the Mount of Olives († 410), and *Sophronius Eusebius Hieronymus* of *Stridon*, the first scriptural expositor

[8] Regarding his orations (among which must be particularly distinguished de Theologia oratt. v.), see Paniel, i. 493. Letters, poems. Opp. ed. F. Morellius. Paris. 1630 (Colon. 1690) 2 voll. fol. ed. Clemencet, tom. i. Paris. 1778. Tom. ii. ed. D. A. B. Caillau. Paris. 1840. fol. Cf. Fabricius-Harles, viii. 383. Gregorius v. Nazianz, der Theologe, von D. C. Ullmann. Darmstadt. 1825. 8.

[9] Respecting him see Guerike de Schola Alex. P. i. p. 92, ss. His biblical commentaries, and his Comm. in libros Origenis περὶ ἀρχῶν, are, with many other writings, no longer extant. Still extant: Lib. de Spiritu S., according to the Latin version of Jerome (in Hieron. Opp. ed. Martian. t. iv. P. i. p. 494, ss.); lib. adv. Manichaeus (gr. et. lat. in Combefisii auctarium graec. PP. P. ii. p. 21, and in Canisii Lectt. ant. ed. Basnage. vol. i. p. 204, ss.); de Trinitate libb. iii. (prim. ed. J. A. Mingarelli. Bonon. 1769. fol.); brevis enarratio in epistt. canonicas, preserved, in the Latin translation composed at the request of Cassiodorus, by Epiphanius Scholasticus (see Cassiod. de Instit. div. scr. c. 8), among others in the Bibl. max. PP. t. iv. p. 319, ss., best of all in Lücke Quaestiones ac vindiciae Didymianae. Gotting. 1829–32. 4 particulae. 4, where it is accompanied by the Greek text, partially restored from the Scholia of Matthaei.

[10] Paniel's Gesch. d. christl. Beredsamkeit, i. 663.

[11] De Trinitate libb. xii. Ad Constantium lib. De Synodis adv. Arianos. De Synodis Ariminensi et Seleuciensi (fragments). Various commentaries. Of the comm. in Psalmos plurimos, Hieron. Cat. c. 100: In quo opere imitatus Origenem, nonnulla etiam de suo addidit: respecting the treatises no longer extant called tractatus in Job: quos de Graeco Origenis ad sensum transtulit, cf. Rosenmüller Hist. interpret. libr. sacr. in eccl. christ. P. iii. p. 301, ss. Paniel, i. 697. Bähr's christl. römische Theologie, S. 113. Opp. edd. Monachi Congreg. S. Mauri (P. Coustant). Paris. 1693. Sc. Maffeus. Veron. 1730. 2 voll. fol.

[12] The author of the Comm. in xiii. epistt. b. Pauli in the works of Ambrose (hence Ambrosiaster), and probably, too, of the Quaestiones vet. et novi test. in the works of Augustine (in the Appendix of tom. iii. P. ii. Benedictine edition). Comp. R. Simon Hist. crit. des principaux commentateurs du N. T. p. 133.

[13] De Officiis ministrorum libb. 3 (ed. Dr. R. O. Gilbert. Lips. 1839. 8). Hexaëmeron (ed. Gilbert. Lips. 1840. 8). De Fide libb. 5. De Spiritu Sancto libb. 3. A useless commentary on some of the Psalms, in Lucam libb. 10 (cf. Rosenmüller l. c. p. 315, ss.). Epistolae 92, etc. Opp. edd. Mon. Congreg. S. Mauri. Paris. 1686, 90. 2 voll. fol. Comp. Bähr, S. 142.

[14] Respecting his writings, see below, § 85, note 4.

of his day, who lived at the head of a society of monks in Bethlehem from A.D. 386 († 420).[15]

In addition to the Origenist school, the Syrian *historico-exegetical* school in the east had many friends.[16] To it belonged, among the Eusebians, *Theodore*, bishop of Heraclea († about 358),[17] *Eusebius*, bishop of Emesa († 360),[18] and *Cyril*, bishop of Jerusalem, who afterward adopted the decrees of the Nicene council, and was present at the council of Constantinople (381) († 386).[19] Among the oriental Nicenians, *Apollinaris*, bishop

[15] At that time Jerome wrote to Paula respecting Origen (Rufin. Invectiv. in Hieron. lib. ii. see Hieron. Opp. ed. Martianay, vol. iv. t. ii. p. 68 and 480): Quis enim unquam tanta legere potuit, quanta ipse conscripsit: Pro hoc sudore, quid accepit pretii? Damnatur a Demetrio episcopo: exceptis Palaestinae et Arabiae et Phoenices atque Achajae sacerdotibus in damnationem ejus consentit (add. orbis): urbs Roma ipsa contra hunc cogit senatum, non propter dogmatum novitatem, non propter haeresin, ut nunc adversum eum rabidi canes simulant, sed quia gloriam eloquentiae ejus et scientiae ferre non poterant, et illo dicente omnes muti putabantur. See a notice of his writings in § 85, note 5.

[16] Cf. J. A. Ernesti Narratio crit. de interpretatione prophetiarum messian. in Opp. theol. p. 498, ss. F. Münter über die antiochen. Schule in Staudlin's and Tzschirner's Archiv. f. Kirchengesch. i. i. 13. Caes. a Lengerke de Ephraemi Syri Arte hermeneutica liber. Regimontii Pruss. 1831. 8. p. 60.

[17] Hieronymi Catal. c. 90: Theodorus Heracliae Thraciarum Episcopus, elegantis apertique sermonis, et magis historicae intelligentiae, edidit sub Constantio Principe commentarios in Matthaeum, et in Joannem, et in Apostolum, et in Psalterium. The commentary on the Psalms in Corderis Catena in Psalmos. Antv. 1643: other exegetical fragments in the Catenae. The most are to be found in Corderii Catena in Matthaeum. Antverp. 1642. H. F. Massmann (Skeireins, Auslegung, d. Ev. Joh. in goth. Sprache München. 1834. 4) considers the fragments published by him to be the remains of a Gothic version of Theodore's commentary on John. Of a contrary opinion Dr. Julius Loebe Beiträge zur Textberichtigung u. Erklärung der Skeireins. Altenburg. 1839. 8. S. 4.

[18] Respecting him see Socrates, ii. 9, and Sozomenus, iii. 6. Both say of him: Ὑπέμεινε δὲ καὶ αὐτὸς μέμψιν, ὡς τὰ Σαβελλίου φρονῶν. On the contrary, he is called in Jerome in Chron. ad ann. x. Constantii: Arianae signifer factionis. Cf. Hieron. Cat. c. 91: Eusebius Emesenus Episcopus, elegantis et rhetorici ingenii, innumerabiles, et qui ad plausum populi pertinent, confecit libros, magisque historiam secutus, ab his qui declamare volunt, studiosissime legitur: e quibus vel praecipui sunt adv. Judaeos, et Gentes, et Novatianos, et ad Galatas libb. x., et in Evangelia homiliae breves sed plurimae. His exegetical character is more distinctly drawn, c. 119 (see below, note 22). Thilo (über die Schriften des Eusebius v. Alexandrien u. d. Eusebius v. Emesa. Halle. 1832. 8) shows that the three discourses published by Augusti (Euseb. Emes. quae supersunt Opuscula. Elberfeldi. 1829. 8) do not belong to Eusebius of Emesa, but, along with many others, to one Eusebius of Alexandria, belonging to the fifth or sixth century (an old life of this Alexandrian and several discourses are extant in the Spicilegium Romanum, t. ix. Romae. 1843. 8). Among the extant writings of Eusebius of Emesa (on them see Thilo, p. 56), the most important would be the two books de fide adv. Sabellium in the Opuscula, xiv. Eusebii Pamph. ed. J. Sirmond, Paris. 1643 (also in Bibl. PP. Lugd. iv. 1), if it could be proved that they really belong to him. Thilo makes it probable, p. 64.

[19] Catecheses xviii. ad Competentes, Catecheses mystagogicae v., probably delivered in the year 347 (their authenticity has been denied especially by Oudinus de Scriptt. eccl. ant. vol. i. p. 459, ss.), but proved by Touttée (in the Dissert. Cyrill. p. xciii. prefixed to his edition), ed. Th. Milles. Oxon. 1703. fol. A. A. Touttée. Paris. 1720. fol. Comp. J. J. van

of Laodicea (between 370 and 390),[20] known by his heresy respecting the person of Christ; *Ephraem*, deacon in Edessa, the prophet of the Syrians († 378);[21] and *Diodore*, presbyter in Antioch, bishop of Tarsus from 378 († before 394),[22] were attached to it. From the school of the latter proceeded *John Chrysostom*, deacon from 381, 386 presbyter in Antioch, from 398 bishop of Constantinople († 407),[23] and *Theodore*, presbyter in Antioch,

Vollenhoven Spec. theol. de Cyrilli Hier. catechesibus. Amstelod. 1837. 8. Paniel's Gesch. der christl. Beredsamkeit, i. 419. Against the Semiarianism of the saint, which is acknowledged by Touttée Dissertt. Cyrill. p. xi. ss. (which Epiphanius Haer. lxxiii. c. 28, also expressly attests) appeared the Jesuit Mémoires de Trevoux (mois de Dec. 1721), but they were refuted by (Prudentius Maranus) Diss. sur les Sémiariens. Paris. 1722. 8, reprinted in Vogt Bibl. hist. haeresiolog. ii. 115. Respecting his exposition of Scripture in the Catecheses, see Catech. xiii. c. 9: Συνεληλύθαμεν γὰρ, οὐ γραφῶν ἐξήγησιν θεωρητικὴν ποιήσασθαι νῦν, ἀλλὰ πιστοποιηθῆναι μᾶλλον περὶ ὧν πεπιστεύκαμεν. Cf. Fabricius-Harles, viii. 437. Tzschirner Opusc. acad. p. 253, ss. v. Cölln in Ersch u. Gruber's Encyclopädie, xxii. 143.

[20] His writings (adv. Porphyrium, libb. xxx., contra Eunomium, etc.) are all lost. Many of his interpretations of Scripture are preserved in the Catenae. Philostorgius ap. Suidam, s. v. Apollinaris prefers him to Basil and Gregory of Nazianzum: Οὗτος γὰρ δὴ καὶ τῆς Ἑβραΐδος διαλέκτου ἐπαΐειν οἷός τε ἦν. Cf. Fabricius-Harles, vol. viii. p. 588, ss.

[21] Homilies (cf. Tzschirner Opusc. acad. p. 262, ss.), Ascetic writings, Hymns. Particularly important are his Syriac commentaries on the Old Testament. Cf. Caesar a Lengerke Comm. crit. de Ephraemo Syro S. S. interprete. Halis. 1828. 4. Ejusd. de Ephr. Syri Arte hermeneutica lib. Regimontii Pruss. 1831. 8. Paniel's Gesch. d. christl. Beredsamkeit, i. 438. Opp. graeca et syr. ed. St. Evod. Assemanus. Romae. 1732–45. 6 voll. fol. Cf. Fabricius-Harles. vol. viii. p. 217, ss.

[22] Hieron. Cat. c. 119: Diodorus Tarsensis Episcopus, dum Antiochiae esset presbyter, magis claruit. Extant ejus in Apostolum commentarii, et multa alia, ad Eusebii magis Emeseni characterem pertinentia: cujus cum sensum secutus sit eloquentiam imitari non potuit propter ignorantiam saecularium litterarum. Socrat. vi. 3: Πολλὰ βιβλία συνέγραψε, ψιλῷ τῷ γράμματι τῶν θείων προσέχων γραφῶν, τὰς θεωρίας αὐτῶν ἐκτρεπόμενος. For his orthodoxy, which was afterward called in question, see Facundi Ep. Hermianensis (about 548) pro defensione trium Capitulorum lib. iv. c. 2. His writings, which have been all lost, and among them commentaries on most of the biblical books, whose loss must be chiefly regretted, are enumerated by Theodore Victor ap. Suidas, s. v. Διόδωρος, and by Ebedjesu in Assemani Bibl. orient. iii. i. 28. Cf. Fabricius-Harles, ix. 278, ss. Fragments are found in Marius Mercator, Photius (Cod. 122) and others. Among the Chaldean Christians, who held him in great repute (see Assemani, iii. ii. 224), many of his writings may have been preserved in translation.

[23] Although he had been previously distinguished by similar honorable surnames (thus he is called in Proclus, bishop of Constantinople after 437, περὶ παραδόσεως τῆς θείας λειτουργίας, in Gallandii Bibl. PP. ix. 681: ὁ τὴν γλῶτταν χρυσοῦς Ἰωάννης), yet the surname Chrysostom first occurs in Johannes Moschus (about 630) pratum spirit. c. 131, and is generally employed after Concil. vi. in the year 680. His works are: Orations, among which the homilies on the New Testament writings are also of exegetical importance. Comp. Des Joh. Chrys. auserwählte Homilien (v. d. Unbegreiflichkeit Gottes, 5 Hom. wider die Anomöer (übers. u. mit einer Einleit. über Joh. Chrys. den Homileten von Dr. Ph. Mayer. Nürnberg. 1830. Paniel's Gesch. d. christl. Beredsamkeit, i. 590. Ascetic writings, letters. Περὶ ἱερωσύνης libb. vi. (ed. J. A. Bengel. Stuttg. 1725. 8. übers. v. K. F. Hasselbach. Stralsund. 1820. 8. von. J. Ritter. Berlin. 1821. 8). Opp. ed. B. de Montfaucon, Paris. 1718–38. 13 voll. fol. ed. 2. emendata et aucta. Paris. 1834–39.

from 393 bishop of Mopsuestia († 429),[24] the most eminent exegetical writer of the Syrian school.

The difference of the exegetical principles of the two schools gave expression to itself even in controversial writings.[25] This dispute however had an entirely scientific character, and did not prevent them recognizing each other's merit. As the Origenist Jerome made diligent use of the interpreters of the Syrian school, so also Origen for the most part stood in high estimation with the Syrians.[26] But small traces of doctrinal controversies are

13 Tomi. 8. Cf. Fabricius-Harles, viii. 454. A. Neander der h. Joh. Chrysostomus u. d. Kirche bes. des. Orients in dessen Zeitalter. Berlin. 1821, 22. 2 Bde. 8.

[24] His noted biblical commentaries have been unfortunately lost with the rest of his writings, except some fragments. Recently, complete works of his have been published in the original. See Comm. in Prophetas, xii. minores taken from a Vienna MS. in: Theod. Antiocheni Mopsv. Episc. quae supersunt omnia, ed. A. F. V. a Wegnern, vol. i. Berol. 1834. 8. from a Vatican MS. in A. Maji Scriptt. vett. nova coll. t. vi. p. i. Romae. 1832; and Comm. in epist. ad Romanos, edited by Angelo Mai in the Spicilegium Romanum, tom. iv. (Romae. 1840. 8) p. 499. The Chaldean Christians who call him, by way of eminence, the interpreter (Assemani, l. c. t. iii. P. i. p. 36), and have declared in the decrees of councils his expositions to be a standard (Assem. l. c. t. iii. P. ii. p. 227), have still much of his in translations. A catalogue of his works by Ebedjesu ap. Assemani, iii. i. 30, cf. Fabricius-Harles, x. 346. R. E. Klener Symbolae literariae ad Theodorum Antiochenum Mopsvestiae Episc. pertinentes. Gotting. 1836. 8. O. F. Fritzsche de Theod. Mopsvesteni vita et scriptis comm. Halae. 1836. 8. Respecting Theodore as an interpreter, see Ernesti Opusc. theol. p. 502, ss. Rosenmüller Hist. interpret. iii. 250. Münter in Stäudlin's und Tzschirner's Archive f. K. G. i. i. 17. F. L. Sieffert Theodorus Mopsv. veteris Test. sobrie interpretandi vindex comm. Regiomonti. 1827. 8. Comp. among the accusations of Leontius against Theodore (in Gallandii Bibl. PP. xii. 686, s.): xii. aggreditur—gloriam Spiritus Sancti, cum omnes quidem scripturas altas, quas sancti afflatu ejus tradiderunt, humiliter et demisse interpretans, tum vero a numero sacracum scripturarum—eas separans. xiv. Epistolam Jacobi et alias deinceps aliorum catholicas abrogat et antiquat. xv. Inscriptiones Hymnorum, et Psalmorum, et Canticorum penitus ejecit, et omnes Psalmos judiace ad Zorobabelem et Ezechiam retulit, tribus tantum ad Dominum rejectis. xvi. Immo et sanctorum sanctissimum Canticum Canticorum—libidinose pro sua et mente et lingua meretricia interpretans, sua supra modum incredibili audacia ex libris sacris abscidit. xvii. Duos libros Paralipomenon—et insuper Esdram repudiavit.

[25] The Origenists endeavored, after the example of Origen to prove the insufficiency of the grammatical interpretation, and the necessity of the allegorical. For example Gregorius Nyssenus Prooem. in Cant. Cant., Jerome in many places. On the other side wrote Theodore according to Suidas s. v. Διόδωρος· τίς διαφορὰ θεωρίας καὶ ἀλληγορίας. Comp. on this treatise Ernesti Opusc. theol. p. 499. Still more energetically did Theodore of Mopsuestia attack the Origenists (Facundas, iii. c. 6): in libro de allegoria et historia, quem contra Origenem scripsit, unde et odium Origenianorum incurrit. Ebedjesu cites among Theodore's works quinque tomos adv. Allegoricos (Assemani, iii. i. 34, cf. p. 19).

[26] So with the author of the Ἀποκρίσεις πρὸς τοὺς ὀρθοδόξους in Justin Martyr's works, who belongs to Syria, about the year 400 (D. W. Gass Abhandlung über diese Schrift, in Illgen's Zeitschr. f. d. hist. Theol. 1842. iv. 34. Comp. S. 143, 103), and with Chrysostom (see Ernesti Opusc. theol. p. 512, and the programm by J. W. Meyer de Chrysostomo literarum sacr. interprete, p. i. Altorf. 1806. 8. De Ch. l. s. i. ejusque interpretandi modo in V. T. libris hist. obvio. Norimb. 1806. 8. Nova comm. de Chr. l. s. i. p. ii. Erlang. 1814, 15. 4, respecting his exposition of the poetical books of the Old Testament).

now to be found between the two schools.[27] Those orthodox Origenists did not adopt all the peculiar doctrinal sentiments of their master; nor were these doctrines all reckoned damnable. A pretty wide field for free investigation was still left to reason,[28] and the passion with which the question of the relation of the Son to the Father was discussed, made this doctrine so much the test of orthodoxy, almost indeed exclusively so, that they never thought during the Arian controversy of limiting freedom of inquiry on other subjects. *Gregory of Nyssa*[29] and *Didymus*[30] were known as Origenists. Many others held to single points of Origen's creed[31] without being attacked on that account. *Chalcidius*[32] and *Synesius* came to adopt still more remarkable opinions by joining new-Platonism with Christianity; yet the latter was consecrated bishop of Ptolemais by Theophilus, bishop of Alexandria, although he gave public expression to his convictions (410).[33] The belief in the inalienable capability of

[27] Theophili Alex. lib. paschalis, i. Hieronymo interprete (Hier. Opp. ed. Martian. t. iv. P. ii. p. 694): Licet (Apollinaris) adversus Arianos, et Eunomianos scripserit, et Origenem, aliosque haereticos sua disputatione subverterit, tamen, etc. So Apollinaris also defended millennarianism in a work *περὶ ἀναστάσεως*. Basil. Ep. 263. (al. 74) § 4, Hieron. Prooem. in libr. xviii. Jesaiae. Epiph. Haer. lxxvii. § 36.

[28] Gregor. Naz. Orat. 33 (de Theol. i.) in fine: *Φιλοσόφει μοι περὶ κόσμου ἢ κόσμων, περὶ ὕλης, περὶ ψυχῆς, περὶ λογικῶν φύσεων βελτιόνων τε καὶ χειρόνων, περὶ ἀναστάσεως, κρίσεως, ἀνταποδόσεως, Χριστοῦ παθημάτων. Ἐν τούτοις γὰρ καὶ τὸ ἐπιτυγχάνειν οὐκ ἄχρηστον, καὶ τὸ διαμαρτάνειν ἀκίνδυνον.* Even in the west the doctrine of the pre-existence of souls was not yet regarded as heretical. Augustine de Libero arbitrio, iii. 21: Harum autem quatuor de anima sententiarum, utrum de propagine veniant, an in singulis quibusque nascentibus novae fiant, an in corpora nascentium jam alicubi existentes vel mittantur divinitus, vel inde sua sponte labantur, nullam temere affirmare oportebit. Cf. Hieron. Epist. 126 (al. 82), ad Marcellinam et Anapsychiam.

[29] See Jo. Dallaeus de Poenis et Satisfactionibus humanis (libb. vii. Amst. 1649. 4), lib. iv. c. 7, p. 368, ss. Münscher's Dogmengesch. iv. 439, 465. Wundemann's Gesch. d. christl. Glaubenslehren, ii. 463. Rupp's Gregor v. Nyssa, S. 243.

[30] On this theology see Guerike de schola Alex. P. ii. p. 332, ss., especially on the pre-existence of souls, p. 361, and the possible conversion of the devil, p. 359, 368, especially Lücke Quaestiones ac vindiciae Didymianae P. i. p. 9, ss. Against the former, Gregory of Nazianzum declares himself very decidedly (see Ullmann, p. 414, ff.).

[31] The doctrine of Hilary regarding the humanity of Christ, de trin. x., was made up from the opinions of Clement of Alexandria and Origen. See my Comm., qua Clementis Alex. et Origenis doctrinae de corpore Christi exponuntur. Gotting. 1837. 4; that of C. Marius Victorinus philos. (about 368) in Comm. in ep. ad Ephes. i. 4 (Maji Scriptt. vett. nova collect. iii. ii. 90, 93, s.), animas nostras et ante mundi constitutionem fuisse, quippe cum sua substantia in aeternis semper extiterint, is Origenistic.

[32] Cf. Chalc. Comm. in Timaeum Platonis in Hippolyti Opp. ed. Fabricius, ii. 225 Mosheim ad Cudworth Syst. intell. p. 732, regards him as a heathen syncretist. See on the other side Fabricii bibl. lat. i. 556, Brucker Hist. philos. iii. 477.

[33] Synesius Ep. 105, ad fratrem Euoptium announces why he felt it a hazardous thing to assume the office of a bishop, which had been offered him. Among other things, it is

improvement in all rational beings, and the limited duration of future punishment[34] was so general even in the west[35] and among the opponents of Origen,[36] that, even if it may not be said to have arisen without the influence of Origen's school, it had become entirely independent of his system. On the other hand, millennarianism, although it had been abandoned by most theologians, had still many friends among the people, without their being considered as heretics on account of it.[37]

said: Χαλεπόν ἐστιν, εἰ μὴ καὶ λίαν ἀδύνατον, εἰς ψυχὴν τὰ δι' ἐπιστήμης εἰς ἀπόδειξιν ἐλθόντα δόγματα σαλευθῆναι· οἶσθα'δ' ὅτι πολλὰ φιλοσοφία τοῖς θρυλλουμένοις τούτοις ἀντιδιατάττεται δόγμασιν. ἀμέλει τὴν ψυχὴν οὐκ ἀξιώσω ποτὲ σώματος ὑστερογενῆ νομίζειν· τὸν κόσμον οὐ φήσω καὶ τἄλλα μέρη συνδιαφθείρεσθαι· τὴν καθωμιλημένην ἀνάστασιν ἱερόν τι καὶ ἀπόῤῥητον ἥγημαι, καὶ πολλοῦ δέω ταῖς τοῦ πλήθους ὑπολήψεσιν ὁμολογῆσαι.—ἢ τοῖς ὀφθαλμιῶσι τὸ σκότος ὠφελιμώτερον, ταύτῃ καὶ τὸ ψεῦδος ὄφελος εἶναι τίθεμαι δήμῳ, καὶ βλαβερὸν τὴν ἀλήθειαν τοῖς οὐκ ἰσχύουσιν ἐνατενίσαι πρὸς τὴν τῶν ὄντων ἐνάργειαν. εἰ ταῦτα καὶ οἱ τῆς καθ' ἡμᾶς ἱερωσύνης συγχωροῦσιν ἐμοί νόμοι, δυναίμην ἂν ἱερᾶσθαι, τᾶ μὲν οἴκοι φιλοσοφῶν, τὰ δ' ἔξω φιλομυθῶν.—οὐ βούλομαι δὲ καταλελεῖφθαί τινα περὶ ἐμοῦ λογὸν, ὡς ἀγνοηθεὶς ἥρπασα τὴν χειροτονίαν· ἀλλ' εἰδὼς ὁ θεοφιλέστατος πατὴρ Θεόφιλος, καὶ ὡς ἐπίσταται, σαφές μοι ποιήσας, οὕτω βουλευσάσθω περὶ ἐμοῦ. Cf. Evagrius, i. c. 15. Photius Cod. 26. Comp. Synesius des Kyrenäers Rede an Arkadios, griesch. u. deutsch v. Krabinger. München. 1825. 8. Einl. S. xix., ff. Even when bishop, Synesius continued true to his philosophical system. Cf. Luc. Holstenii diss. de Synesio, in the app. of Theodoretus, etc., ed. Valesii, p. 202. Aem. Th. Clausen de Synesio philosopho, Libyae Pentapoleos metropolita. Hafniae. 1831. 8.

34 Hieronymus ad Gal. v. 22: Nullam rationabilium creaturarum apud Deum perire perpetuo. Cf. ad Eph. iv. 16. Ambrosiaster in Eph. iii. 10. J. A. Dietelmair Commenti fanatici de rerum omnium Ἀποκαταστάσει hist. antiquior. Altorfii. 1769. 8. p. 160, ss.

35 Augustini Enchirid. ad Laurent. c. 112: Frustra nonnulli, immo quam plurimi, aeternam damnatorum poenam et cruciatus sine intermissione perpetuos humano miserentur affectu, atque ita futurum esse non credunt: non quidem scripturis divinis adversando, sed pro suo modo dura quaeque molliendo et in leniorem flectendo sententiam, quae putant in eis terribilius esse dicta quam verius. Non enim obliviscetur, inquiunt, misereri Deus, aut continebit in ira sua miserationes suas. (Ps. lxxvii. 10).

36 In Diodore of Tarsus and Theodore of Mopsuestia, whose expressions on the subject have been preserved by Salomo, bishop of Bassora (about 1222), in Assemani Bibl. Or. iii. i. 323. Respecting Theodore comp. Photii Cod. 81, Marius Mercator. p. 346, ed. Baluzii.

37 Hieronymus Prooem. in lib. xviii. in Esaiam: Nec ignoro, quanta inter homines sententiarum diversitas sit. Non dico de mysterio trinitatis, cujus recta confessio est ignoratio scientiae: sed de aliis ecclesiasticis dogmatibus, de resurrectione scilicet, et de animarum et humanae carnis statu, de repromissionibus futurorum, quomodo debeant accipi, et qua ratione intelligenda sit Apocalypsis Johannis, quam si juxta literam accipimus, judaizandum est; si spiritualiter, ut scripta est, disserimus, multorum veterum videbimur opinionibus contraire, Latinorum Tertulliani, Victorini, Lactantii, Graecorum, ut caeteros praetermittam, Irenaei tantum Lugdunensis Episcopi faciam mentionem. Adversum quem vir eloquentissimus Dionysius Alexandrinae Ecclesiae Pontifex elegantem scribit librum, irridens mille annorum fabulam.—Cui duobus voluminibus respondit Apollinarius, quem non solum suae sectae homines, sed et nostrorum in hac parte duntaxat plurima sequitur multitudo, ut praesaga mente jam cernam, quantorum in me rabies concitanda sit. Cf. Idem. lib. iv. in Jeremiam (on Cap. 19): qua (millennarian opinions) licet non sequamur, damnare tamen non possumus, quia multi ecclesiastioorum virorum et martyrum ista dixerunt. Unusquisque in suo sensu abundet, et Domini cuncta reserventur judicio.

A thorough opposition between the two schools was established by the circumstance that the Syrian school acknowledged Holy Scripture alone as the source of doctrine,[38] while the disciples of Origen advocated their Gnostic tradition as a second source.[39] But they did not attain to a scientific examination of these two positions, since all scientific free movement in the province of theology was soon checked from another quarter. In the same degree as monachism prevailed, there spread also a prejudice against having any thing to do with worldly science and heathen writers.[40] By this means there was formed and strengthened a crowd of *traditional* theologians, who, inimical to all free inquiry, would endure no opinion which could not be pointed out in the fathers. *Epiphanius*, bishop of Constantia in Cyprus, from the year 367 († 403),[41] may be regarded as the representative of this tendency. Even in his Panarion (Haer. 63 and 64), he made himself known as a bitter enemy of Origen; and when the *Arian* controversy was at an end, he began an open war against Origenism. While this contest put a stop to all free inquiry in the east, the western world was contemporaneously bound in spiritual fetters by Augustine; and free science every where banished from the church as a thing which causes mischief.

[38] Cyrilli Hieros. Cat. iv. c. 17: Δεῖ γὰρ περὶ τῶν θείων καὶ ἁγίων τῆς πίστεως μυστηρίων μηδὲ τὸ τυχὸν ἄνευ τῶν θείων παραδίδοσθαι γραφῶν, καὶ μὴ ἁπλῶς πιθανότησι καὶ λόγων κατασκευαῖς παραφέρεσθαι. Μηδὲ ἐμοὶ τῷ ταῦτά σοι λεγοντι ἁπλῶς πιστεύσῃς, ἐὰν τὴν ἀπόδειξιν τῶν καταγγελλομένων ἀπὸ τῶν θειῶν μὴ λάβῃς γραφῶν. So in many places of his catecheses. See Touttée Diss. ii. prefixed to his edition of Cyril, p. 129, s. In like manner, it is said in the work de fide (see above, note 18) lib. i. (Sirmondi Opp. i. 11), which probably belongs to Eusebius Emesenus: Confitere ea, quae de Patre et Filio scripta sunt, et noli curiosius ea, quae non sunt scripta, requirere.—Utinam solis scripturis contenti essemus! et lis nulla fiebat. Lib. ii. p. 20: Si quid scriptum non est, ne quidem dicatur: si quid autem scriptum est, ne deleatur.

[39] Comp. Div. I. § 63, note 4. Basilius de Spir. S. c. 27: Τῶν ἐν τῇ Ἐκκλησίᾳ πεφυλαγμένων δογμάτων καὶ κηρυγμάτων τὰ μὲν ἐκ τῆς ἐγγράφου διδασκαλίας ἔχομεν, τὰ δὲ ἐκ τῆς τῶν Ἀποστόλων παραδόσεως διαδοθέντα ἡμῖν ἐν μυστηρίῳ παρεδεξάμεθα, ἅπερ ἀμφότερα τὴν αὐτὴν ἰσχὺν ἔχει πρὸς τὴν εὐσέβειαν. Thus also Gregory of Nazianzum Orat. theol. v. § 1 (see § 83, note 27) could assume that the doctrine of the Holy Spirit had now come over from the obscurity of gnostic tradition into faith (πίστις).

[40] As it is expressed in the dream of Jerome, viz., that he was punished with stripes before the most high judge, because he had read Cicero too often (Hier. Epist. 22, ad Eustochium). Comp. Münscher's Dogmengesch. iii. 47.

[41] His writings: Ἀγκυρωτός s. de fide sermo. Πανάριον s. adv. haereses.—Opp. ed. D. Petavius. Paris. 1622. (Colon. 1682.) 2 voll. fol.

II. PERIOD OF THE ORIGENISTIC AND PELAGIAN CONTROVERSIES.

§ 85.

ORIGENISTIC CONTROVERSIES.

Walch's Hist. d. Ketzereien. Th. 7. S. 427, ff.

Shortly after the termination of the Arian controversies, Palestine was the chief seat of Origen's followers. Among them the most distinguished were *John*, bishop of Jerusalem (386–417), and the two monks, *Rufinus* and *Jerome*. Here Epiphanius made his appearance in the year 394, and demanded with zeal the condemnation of Origen. John and Rufinus resisted him: while Jerome, who was anxiously alive to his orthodoxy, yielded, and broke off communion with the church of Jerusalem.[1] By the efforts of *Theophilus*, bishop of Alexandria, he was indeed induced to renew it, 397. In the mean time, in the same year, Rufinus went back to Rome, and endeavored, by a revised translation of the writings of Origen,[2] which were as yet little known, to procure a more favorable opinion of him in the west. By this means a violent controversy was created between him and

1 Cf. Kimmel de Rufino Eusebii interprete (Gerae. 1838). p. 57. Hieronymi lib. ad Pammachium contra Joann. Hieros. (ap. Martianay Epist. 38). Here the following erroneous doctrines are attributed to Origen (comp. Div. I. § 64, note 15): 1. In libro περὶ ἀρχῶν (i. 1. § 8) loquitur: Sicut enim incongruum est dicere, quod possit filius videre patrem, ita inconveniens est opinari, quod spiritus s. possit videre filium, 2. quod in hoc corpore quasi in carcere sunt animae religatae, et, antequam homo fieret in paradiso, inter rationales creaturas in coelestibus commoratae sunt, 3. quod dicat, et diabolum et daemones acturos poenitentiam aliquando, et cum sanctis ultimo tempore regnaturos, 4. quod tunicas pelliceas humana corpora interpretetur, quibus post offensam et ejectionem de paradiso Adam et Eva induti sunt, 5. quod carnis resurrectionem, membrorumque compagem, et sexum, quo viri dividimur a foeminis, apertissime neget, 6. quod sic Paradisum, allegorizet, ut historiae auferat veritatem, pro arboribus angelos, pro fluminibus virtutes coelestes intelligens, totamque paradisi continentiam tropologica interpretatione subvertat, 7. quod aquas, quae super caelos in scripturis esse dicuntur, sanctus supernasque virtutes; quae super terram et infra terram, contrarias et daemoniacas esse arbitretur, 8. quod imaginem et similitudinam dei, ad quam homo conditus fuerat, dicit ab eo perditam, et in homine post paradisum non fuisse.

2 Anastasii I. Epist. ad Joh. Hierosol. A.D. 401 (ap. Coustant, p. 719): Origines autem, cujus in nostram linguam [Rufinus] composita derivavit, antea et quis fuerit, et in quae processerit verba, nostrum propositum [studium?] nescit. Augustini Ep. ad Hieron. 40: Illud de prudentia doctrinaque tua desiderabam, et adhuc desidero, ut nota nobis facias ea ipsa ejus [Origenis] errata, quibus a fide veritatis ille vir tantus recessisse convincitur.

Jerome.[3] Origen, however, having been condemned in Egypt, *Anastasius*, bishop of Rome, condemned him also. Rufinus retreated to Aquileia, and continued his meritorious services in the translation of Greek works († 410).[4] *Jerome*, on the other hand, gained for himself great merit by his continued labors on the translation of the Bible into Latin, and his commentaries († 420).[5]

Soon after these controversies in Palestine, the ambitious and violent *Theophilus*, bishop of Alexandria (385–412), came forth as the enemy of Origen.[6] The Nitrian monks were divided into two parties, the *Origenists* and the *Anthropomorphists*. Moved by personal hatred to some individuals of the first, and afraid of the fanaticism of the latter, Theophilus caused Origen to be condemned (399, 400),[7] then demanded the most noted bishops to do the same, and persecuted,[8] with the greatest cruel-

[3] Rufini Praefatio ad Orig. περὶ ἀρχῶν.—(Pammachii et Oceani Ep. ad Hieron. ap Martianay Ep. 40, ap. Vallarsi Ep. 83). Hieronymus ad Pammachium et Oceanum de erroribus Origenis (Martian. Ep. 41, Vallarsi Ep. 84.)—Rufini Apologia s. invectivarum in Hieronym. libb. ii.—Hieronymi Apologia adv. Rufinum libb. ii.—(Rufini Ep. ad Hieron. lost).—Hieronymi Responsio s. Apologiae l. iii., cf. Kimmel de Rufino, p. 64.

[4] Origenes libb. περὶ ἀρχῶν et homiliae, Pamphili apol. pro Origene, Josephi Opp.—Eusebii Hist. Eccl.—Clementis Recognitiones.—Basilii M. et Gregor. Naz. Opp. nonnulla.—Vitae Patrum. Besides Expositio symboli apostolici, Hist. Eccl. libb. ii., Comm. in Hoseam, Joel, caet.—Comp. Jo. Franc. B. Mar. de Rubeis Monumenta eccl. Aquilejensis. Argentinae. 1740. fol. p. 80, ss. Idem de Turannio s. Tyrannio Rufino. Venetiis. 1754.

[5] Revision of the Latin translation of the New Testament (cf. Epistola ad Damasum s. Hieron. in Evangelistas ad Damasum praef.).—Psalterium Romanum (382).—Psalterium Gallicanum:—New Translation of the Old Testament (385–405).—Comm. in Ecclesiasten, Prophetas, in Evang. Matthaei, in ep. ad Galatas, Ephesios, ad Titum, ad Philemonem.—Catalogus script. eccles. A.D. 392 (in J. A. Fabricii Biblioth. eccles. Hamb 1718. fol.). Interpretatio nominum Hebraicorum (388).—Polemic works: adv. Helvidium, Jovinianum, Vigilantium, Luciferianos, Pelagianos, caet.—Letters, translations: Euseb. de Situ et Nominibus locorum Hebr. (gr. et lat. ed. J. Clericus. Amst. 1707. fol.), Chronicon. Origenis Homil. ii. in Cant. Cant.—Letters of Theophilus and Epiphanius. Opp. ed. Jo. Martianay. Paris. 1693–1706, t. 5. fol. Dom. Vallarsi. Veron. 1734–42, voll. xi. fol. with single improvements. Venetiis. 1762–72, t. xi. 4.—Jerome's Life by John Stilting. (Act. SS. Sept. t. viii. p. 413, ss.), best of all by Vallarsi, in tom. xi. of his edition. Comp. v. Cölln in Ersch and Gruber's Encyclop. Sect. ii. Th. 8. S. 72.

[6] Sources for the following history: Palladii Episc. Helenopolit. Dial. de vita S. Joh. Chrysostomi (prim. graece ed. Emer. Bigot. Paris. 1680. 4, in Chrysost. Opp. ed. Montfaucon, t. 13). Socrates, vi. 3–18. Sozomenus, viii. 7–20.—Joh. Stilting de S. Chrysostomo Comm. historicus, in Act. SS. Sept. t. iv. p. 401, ss. Neander's Chrysostomus, ii. 163.

[7] Theophilus, according to Palladius ap. Montfaucon, xiii. 20, had the distinguishing surname Ἀμφαλλάξ.

[8] Theophili Epist. synodalis (rather encyclica) ex vers. Hieronymi, first edited from an Ambrose MS. by Vallarsi (Hier. Opp. vol. i. Epist. 92. Mansi Conc. coll. t. iii. p. 979). The judgment of Postumianus ap. Sulpic. Sever. Dial. i. c. 6, 7, is more moderate.—The disgustful triumphing of Jerome Ep. ad Theophilum (Martianay, Ep. 57. Vallarsi, Ep

ties, the monks who had adopted the peculiar views of Origen. These unfortunate persons repaired at last to Constantinople, where *John Chrysostom* of Antioch had been bishop, contrary to the wishes of Theophilus,[9] since 398, as much beloved by the better part of his clergy as he was hated by the more corrupt, by the luxurious court, and the empress *Eudoxia*. Theophilus directed his deadly hatred against Chrysostom, because the latter received the banished, and made representations to Theophilus on their behalf, and because by their complaints they procured from the emperor a summons commanding the bishop of Alexandria to appear in person at Constantinople before Chrysostom. After some delay, Theophilus appeared in Constantinople (403), and there succeeded in uniting the foes of Chrysostom, in procuring false accusers, and causing sentence of deposition and exile to be pronounced upon him at a synod (Syn. ad. Quercum).[10] It is true Chrysostom had to be recalled in a few days, on account of an uproar among the people, but he was as quickly displaced, chiefly through the influence of Eudoxia,[11] and died in exile at Pontus († 407).[12] Though the Romish bishop Innocent greatly condemned these acts of violence, he could not succeed in bringing Theophilus to account.[13] In consequence of such conduct,

86): Breviter scribimus, quod totus mundus exultet, et in tuis victoriis glorietur, erectumque Alexandriae vexillum crucis, et adversus haeresin trophaea fulgentia gaudens populorum turba perspectet. Macte virtute, macte zelo fidei! Ostendisti, quod hucusque taciturnitas dispensatio fuit, non consensus. Libere enim Reverentiae tuae loquor. Dolebamus te nimium esse patientem, et ignorantes magistri gubernacula, gestiebamus in interitum perditorum: sed, ut video, exaltasti manum diu, et suspendisti plagam, ut ferires fortius. Jerome translated into Latin all the writings that appeared against the Origenists (in particular Theophili Libri paschales, iii., with a new catalogue of Origen's heresies). These translations, with the correspondence between Jerome and Theophilus, are most fully given in Vallarsi, vol. i. Ep. 86, ss. How little Theophilus acted on this occasion according to his conviction is proved even by his subsequent conduct to Synesius. See § 84, note 33.

[9] Socrates, vi. 2. Palladius, p. 18.

[10] An extract from the Acts of this Synod is given in Photii Bibl. cod. 59.

[11] Beginning of a sermon of Chrysostom (according to Socrat. vi. 18. Sozom. viii. 20): *Πάλιν Ἡρωδιὰς μαίνεται, πάλιν ταράσσεται, πάλιν ὀρχεῖται, πάλιν ἐπὶ πίνακι τὴν κεφαλὴν Ἰωάννου ζητεῖ λαβεῖν.*

[12] Chrysostom's own account of the events in Constantinople, Ep. ad Innocentium I. A.D. 404 ap. Palladius Ep. ad eundem, from exile A.D. 407 (both in Constant. Innoc. P. Epist. 4 et 11). Isidore, abbot in Pelusium, passed a judgment on these proceedings soon after Chrysostom's death (lib. i. Epist. 152): Ἡ *γείτων Αἴγυπτος συνήθως ἠνόμησε, Μωσέα παραιτουμένη, τὸν Φαραὼ οἰκειουμένη.—Τὸν λιθομανῆ καὶ χρυσολάτρην προβαλλομένη Θεόφιλον, τέσσαρσι συνεργοῖς, ἢ μᾶλλον συναποστάταις ὀχυρωθέντα, τὸν θεοφιλῆ καὶ θεολόγον κατεπολέμησεν ἄνθρωπον.—Ἀλλ' οἶκος Δαβὶδ κραταιοῦται, ἀσθενεῖ δὲ ὁ τοῦ Σαούλ.*

[13] His epistles and those of Honorius are in Mansi Conc. coll. iii. 1095.

Rome broke off all church communion with Constantinople; and in the latter city itself, a great part of the church remained faithful to Chrysostom (Johannites), and kept themselves apart from his successors, whom they looked upon as intruders, until the wrong that had been done to him was atoned by the solemn bringing back of his bones (438).

§ 86.

CONTROVERSIES WITH HERETICS IN THE WEST.

During the Arian disturbances, the *Manichaeans* had been *silently* spreading in the west, because for the most part they conformed externally to the catholic church. In Spain, they coincided with the Gnostics,[1] and from contact with them arose the doctrine with which *Priscillian* (about 379) came forth in Spain.[2] His most violent opponents, the bishops *Idacius* and *Ithacius*, first obtained the condemnation of his doctrines at the synod of *Caesaraugusta* (380); and next they prevailed on the usurper *Maximus* to put him to death at Treves (385.) The

[1] Jerome often alludes to the spreading of Basilides's followers into Spain (Comm. in Esaiam lib. xvii. ad Es. lxiv. 4, Ep. 120, ad Hedibiam: Basilidis Haeresin et Iberas naenias. Prolog. in Genesin: Iberae naeniae. Comm. in Amos. c. 3: Iberae ineptiae), and in Ep. 53 ad Theodoram derives the doctrine of Priscillian from him. With him agrees Sulpic. Severus, ii. 46, representing Priscillian's doctrine as derived from Egypt (infamis illa Gnosticorum haeresis), as first brought to Spain by one Marcus, a native of Memphis, communicated by him to Agape and Helpidius, and as having come through them to Priscillian. It is not denied hereby that a new development of doctrine originated with Priscillian, and it is expressly acknowledged by others that Manichaeism had an influence upon it. The emperor Maximus, in Ep. ad Siricium ap. Baronius 387, no. 66, calls the Priscillianists nothing more nor less than Manichaeans; Hieronymus Ep. 43, ad Ctesiphontem, calls Priscillian partem Manachaei; Augustinus Ep. 36 ad Casulan, says that the Priscillianists were very like the Manichaeans, and de Haeres. c. 70: Maxime Gnosticorum et Manichaeorum dogmata permixta sectantur. There were many, however, who were inclined to perceive orthodox doctrine under a strange garb. Hieronymus Catal. c. 121: Priscillianus a nonnullis gnosticae, i.e., Basilidis et Marcionis haereseos accusator, defendentibus aliis, non ita eum sensisse ut arguitur.

[2] His history Sulpic. Sever. Hist. sacr. ii. 46–51, who calls the Priscillianists Gnosticorum haeresis. Something of their doctrine, but unsatisfactory, is found in P. Orosii Consultatio s. Commonitorium ad Augustinum de errore Priscillianistarum et Origenistarum, and in Leonis M. Epist. 93 ad Turibium Episc. Asturic. Priscilliani canones (doctrinal consequences) ad S. Pauli Epistt. cum prologo, published in the Spicilegium Romanum, t. ix. (Romae. 1843) P. ii. p. 1, have been altered by a bishop called Peregrinus juxta sensum fidei catholicae, and accordingly are no longer a source whence we may derive a knowledge of Priscillian's doctrine. Walch's Ketzerhist. iii. 378. Neander, ii. iii. 1477. Dr. J. H. B. Lübkert de haeresi Priscillianistarum. Havniae. 1840. 8.

Priscillianists, however, continued to exist in spite of all persecutions till the sixth century.

At the same time, the persecution of the *Manichaeans*, who were especially hated for various reasons, was also renewed. *Valentinian I.*, who tolerated all other sects, forbade them to assemble in public for their worship, in 372; and succeeding emperors enacted new and still more rigorous laws against them.[3] But their most zealous adversary was *Aurelius Augustinus*, born at Tagaste, in Numidia, who had himself belonged to the Manichaeans for a considerable time, but had been converted at Milan by Ambrose (387). Afterward, as bishop of *Hippo Regius* in Numidia (from 395 to 430), he became as formidable an opponent of heretics, as he exercised an incalculable influence on his own and subsequent times, by his doctrinal and polemical writings.[4] His energies were directed in a high degree against

[3] Lex Valentiniani I. A.D. 372 (Cod. Theod. xvi. 5, 3): Ubicunque Manichaeorum conventus, vel turba hujusmodi reperitur, Doctoribus gravi censione multatis, domus et habitacula, in quibus profana institutione docetur, fisci viribus indubitantur adsciscantur. Theodosii M. A.D. 381 (eod. tit. l. 7): Manichaeis, sub perpetua justae infamiae nota, testandi ac vivendi jure Romano omnem protinus eripimus facultatem, neque eos aut relinquendae aut capiendae alicujus haereditatis habere sinimus potestatem, etc. L. 9, A.D. 382: Caeterum quos Encratitas prodigiali appellatione cognominant, cum Saccoforis sive Hydroparastatis (namely the electi of the Manicheans)—summo supplicio et inexpiabili poena jubemus affligi. L. 18, A.D. 389: Ex omni quidem orbe terrarum, sed quam maxime de hac urbe pellantur sub interminatione judicii. Honorii. L. 35 A.D. 399. L. 40, A. D. 407: Volumus esse publicum crimen, quia, quod in religionem divinam committitur, in omnium fertur injuriam. Quos honorum etiam publicatione persequimur, quae tamen cedere jubemus proximis quibusque personis, etc. L. 43, A.D. 408, Theodosii II. L. 59 and xvi. x. 24, both A.D. 423. xvi. v. 62, 64, 65.

[4] Besides the numerous writings against heretics, biblical commentaries (cf. Clausen Aurel. Augustinus sacrae scripturae interpres. Hafn. 1827. 8.), [Davidson's Hermeneutics p. 133], sermons (Paniel's Gesch. d. christl. Beredsamkeit, i. 781), Ascetic writings, letters, the following are to be especially noted: de Civitate Dei libb. xxii. (comp. § 79, note 18). De Doctrina christiana libb. iv. (ed. J. Chr. B. Teegius. Lips. 1769. 8. C. H. Bruder, ed. stereot. Lips. 1839. Paniel, i. 684). Confessiones libb. xiii. (c. praef. A. Neander. Berol. 1823. 8.) Retractationes libb. ii. Opp. ed. Monachi Benedictini e Congreg. St. Mauri. Paris 1679–1700. xi. voll. recus. cum appendice cura Jo. Clerici. Antwerp. 1700–1703. xii. voll. Venetiis. 1729–35. xi. vol. fol. Operum supplem. i. cura D. A. B. Caillau et D. B. Saint-Yves. Paris. 1836. fol. Opp. emend. et aucta. Paris 1836, ss. xi. voll. 8. The more all parties had occasion to appeal to the writings of Augustine, in consequence of the high authority in which they stood, the greater was the danger of their undergoing intentional and unintentional corruptions. Even so early as the ninth century Hincmar (about 860), de non trina deitate (Opp. i. 450), unjustly accuses others of what he is disposed to do himself, i. e., of corrupting them. The doctrinal position of the editor had its influence also on the earlier editions. It is even proclaimed in the title of the Opp. Venet. 1584: In quo curavimus removeri ea omnia, quae fidelium mentes haeretica pravitate possent inficere. The Benedictines were the first who proceeded critically in their edition, but by this they gave offense to the Jesuits, who asserted they had falsified the Codd. Corbejenses. On the other side wrote Mabillon Supplementum libri de re diplomatica c. 13. On this came forth the Jesuit

the Manichaeans.[5] Several were converted by him, but many still remained in Africa. Even in Rome, there were secret Manichaeans at that time; but their numbers were very much increased there after the conquest of Africa by the Vandals (429). Hence *Leo the Great*, bishop of Rome (440–461), exerted himself to the utmost to detect and convert them.[6] His zeal, supported by imperial ordinances, was not ineffectual;[7] but yet single Manichaean opinions continued to exist till far into the middle ages.

There were still more furious controversies in Africa in the fourth century against *the Donatists*,[8] among whom the fanati-

Barth. Germon de veterum regum Franc. diplomat. discept. ii. p. 314. (App.) Now, too, the Benedictine Pet. Coustant Vindiciae Codd. MSS. Paris. 1707. On the contrary side B. Germon de vett. haereticis ecclesiasticorum Codd. corruptoribus. Paris. 1713. 8. And again P. Coustant Vindiciae vett. Codd. confirmatae. Paris. 1715. 8. The life of Augustine by his disciple Possidius, completed in Caillau et Saint-Yves, Suppl. i. On his life and character see Wiggers Darstellung des Augustinismus u. Pelagianismus (Berlin. 1821) S. 7 [translated by Emerson. Andover, 1840. 8]. Ritter's Gesch. d. christl. Philosophie, ii. 153. E. Bindemann's der h. Augustinus, Bd. 1. Berlin. 1844.

[5] His writings against the Manichaeans, see Div. I. before § 61.

[6] Leonis Opp. omnia (sermones et epistolae) ed. Paschas. Quesnell. Paris, 1675. 2 voll. 4. Petr. et Hier. fratres Ballerini. Venetiis. 1755–57. 3 t. fol. Against the Manichaeans sermo iv. de Quadragesima: Among other things he writes: Nemo ambigat esse Manichaeos, qui in honorem solis ac lunae die Dominico et secunda feria deprehensi fuerint jejunare—Cumque ad tegendum infidelitatem suam nostris audeant interesse mysteriis, ita in sacramentorum communione se temperant, ut interdum tutius lateant: ore indigne Christi corpus accipiunt, sanguinem autem redemtiones nostrae haurire omnino declinant. Quod ideo Vestram volumus scire Sanctitatem, ut vobis hujuscemodi homines et his manifestentur indiciis, et quorum deprehensa fuerit sacrilega simulatio, notati et proditi a sanctorum societate sacerdotali auctoritate pellantur. Sermo iv. de Epiphania, after enumerating the most striking of the Manichcean doctrines: Nihil ergo cum hujusmodi hominibus commune sit cuiquam Christiano, neminem fallant discretionibus ciborum, sordibus vestium, vultumque palloribus (cf. Hieron. Epist. 22, ad Eustochium: quam viderint pallentem atque tristem, miseram et Manichaeam vocant). Sermo v. de Jejunio decimi mensis: Residentibus itaque mecum Episcopis ac Presbyteris ac in eundem consessum Christianis viris ac nobilibus congregatis, Electos et Electas eorum jussimus praesentari. Qui cum de perversitate dogmatis sui, et de festivitatum suarum consuetudine multa reserarent, illud quoque scelus, quod eloqui verecundum est, prodiderunt. Quod tanta diligentia investigatum est, ut nihil minus credulis, nihil obtrectoribus relinqueretur ambiguum. Aderant enim omnes personae, per quas infandum facinus fuerat perpetratum, puella scilicet, ut multum decennis, et duae mulieres, quae ipsam nutrierant et huic sceleri praepararant. Praesto erat etiam adoles centulus vitiator puellae, et Episcopus ipsorum detestandi criminis ordinator. Omnium par fuit horum et una confessio, et patefactum est execratum, quod aures nostrae vix ferre potuerunt. De quo ne apertius loquentes castos offendamus auditus gestorum documenta sufficiunt, quibus plenissime docetur, nullam in hoc secta pudicitiam, nullam honestatem, nullam penitus reperiri castitatem, in qua lex est mendacium, diabolus religio, sacrificium turpitudo. Cf. Leonis Epist. viii. ad Episcopus per Italiam, Epist. xv. ad Turibium. Papst Leo's Leben u. Lehren v. Ed. Perthel. Jena. 1843, S. 15.

[7] Valentiniani III. Novell. tit. xvii. ed. Haenel, v. t. 445.

[8] Sources and works see Div. I. § 72, note 25.

cal *Agonistici*, called by the catholic Christians *Circumcelliones*, appeared, for the purpose of rendering their cause victorious by external force.[9] The most formidable opponent of the Donatists was *Augustine*,[10] who at last effected, by the emperor's interference, a conference with them in *Carthage* (411),[11] at which they were completely vanquished, in the judgment of the

[9] Concerning the time of the origin of the Agonistici or Circumcelliones, see Optatus, iii. c. 4: Veniebant Paulus et Macarius (sent by the emperor about 348), qui pauperes ubique dispungerent, et ad unitatem singulos hortarentur: et cum ad Bagajensem civitatem proximarent, tunc alter Donatus—ejusdem civitatis Episcopus, impedimentum unitati et obicem venientibus supra memoratis opponere cupiens, praeconis per vicina loca et per omnes nundinas misit, Circumcelliones Agonisticos nuncupans, ad praedictum locum ut concurrerent, invitavit: et eorum illo tempore concursus est flagitatus, quorum dementia paullo ante ab ipsis Episcopis impie videbatur esse succensa. Described by Augustini de Haeres. lib. c. 69: Ad hanc (Donatistarum) haeresim in Africa et illi pertinent, qui appellantur Circumcelliones, genus hominum agreste et famosissimae audaciae, non solum in alios immania facinora perpetrando, sed nec sibi eadem insana feritate parcendo. Nam per mortes varias, maximeque praecipitiorem et aquarum et ignium, se ipsos necare consuerunt, et in istum furorem alios quos potuerint sexus utriusque seducere aliquando, ut occidantur ab aliis, mortem nisi fecerint comminantes. Verumtamen plerisque Donatistarum (non) displicent tales, nec eorum communione contaminari se putant. Idem contra Crescon, iii. § 46: Quotidie vestrorum incredibilia patimur facta Clericorum et Circumcellionum, multo pejora quam quorumlibet latronum atque praedonum. Namque horrendis armati cujusque generis telis, terribiliter vagando, non dico ecclesiasticam, sed ipsam humanam quietem pacemque perturbant, nocturnis agressionibus clericorum catholicorum invasas domos nudas atque inanes derelinquunt: ipsos etiam raptos et fustibus tunsos, ferroque concisos, semivivos abjiciunt. Insuper—oculis eorum calcem aceto permixto infundentes—excruciare amplius eligunt quam citius excaecare. § 47: Circumcelliorum vestrorum. nobilis furor horrendum praebens vestris clericis satellitium usquequaque odiosissime innotuit. Idem contra Gaudentium, i. § 32: Cum idololatriae licentia usquequaque ferveret—isti Paganorum armis festa sua frequentantibus irruebant (cf. Epist. 185, § 12: quando adhuc cultus fuerat idolorum, ad Paganorum celeberrimas sollemnitates ingentia turbarum agmina veniebant, non ut idola frangerent, sed ut interficerentur a cultoribus idolorum: doubtless in the time from Julian to Gratian).—Praeter haec sunt saxa immania et montium horrida praerupta, voluntariorum creberrimis mortibus nobilitata vestrorum; aquis et ignibus rarius id agebant, praecipitiis greges consumebantur ingentes. Quis enim nescit hoc genus hominum in horrendis facinoribus inquietum, ab utilibus operibus otiosum, crudelissimum in mortibus alienis, vilissimum in suis, maxime in agris territans, ab agris vacans et victus sui causa cellas circumiens rusticanas, unde et Circumcellionum nomen accepit? Ejusd. Enarratio in Psalm. cxxxii. § 3: Quando vos recte haereticis de Circumcellionibus insultare coeperitis—illi vobis insultant de Monachis. Primo si comparandi sunt, vos videte. Comparentur ebriosi cum sobriis, praecipites cum consideratis, furentes cum simplicibus, vagantes cum congregatis. § 6: Fortasse dicturi sunt nostri non vocantur Circumcelliones: vos illos ita appellatis contumelioso nomine. Agonisticos eos vocant. Sic eos, inquiunt appellamus propter agonem. Certant enim, et dicit Apostolus: certamen bonum certavi (2 Tim. iv. 7). Quia sunt qui certant adversus diabolum et praevalent milites Christi, Agonistici appellantur. Utinam ergo milites Christi essent, et non milites diaboli, a quibus plus timetur Deo laudes quam fremitus leonis. Hi etiam insultare nobis audent, quia fratres, cum vident homines, Deo gratias dicunt. Vos *Deo gratias* nostrum ridetis: *Deo laudes* vestrum plorant homines (cf. contra literas Petiliani, ii. § 146: considerate paululum, quam multis, et quantum luctum dederint *Deo laudes* armatorum vestrorum).

[10] Adr. Roux Diss. de Aur. Augustino adversario Donatistarum. Lugd. Bat. 1838. 8.

[11] Gesta collationis Carthagine habitae prim. ed. Papirius Masson, Paris 1589. 8, accord-

imperial commissioner. This victory, and the imperial ordinances[12] that followed, very much weakened the party, though remnants of it are found as late as the seventh century.

§ 87.

PELAGIAN CONTROVERSY.

G. J. Vossii Hist. de controversiis, quas Pelagius ejusque reliquiae moverunt libb. vii. Lugd. Bat. 1618. 4. auct. ed. G. Voss. Amst. 1655. 4 (in Vossii Opp. t. vi.). Henr. Norisii Hist. Pelagiana et Dissert. de Synodo v. oecumenica. Patavii. 1673. fol. (in Norisii Opp. t. 1. Veron. 1729). Joh. Garnier diss. vii., quibus integra continetur Pelagianorum Hist. (in his edition of Marii Mercatoris Opp. 1, 113, Praefatio in tom. x. Opp. Augustini edit. Monach. Benedict. Walch's Ketzerhistorie, iv. 519. Wundemann's Gesch. d. christl. Glaubenslehren, ii. 44. Münscher's Dogmengesch. iv. 170. G. F. Wiggers Pragmat. Darstell. des Augustinismus u. Pelagianismus. 2 Th. Berlin. 1821, 33. 8. Neander's Kirchengesch, ii. iii. 1194. Ritter's Gesch. d. christl. Philos. ii. 337.

Augustine exerted the greatest influence on the theology especially of the occidental church, by his system of the relation of Divine grace to the human will, which he developed in the Pelagian controversy. The freedom of the will, the evil consequences of the fall, and the necessity of Divine grace, had always been admitted in the church, without any attempt having been made to define, by ecclesiastical formulas, the undefinable in these doctrines.[1] Since Tertullian, an opinion had been peculiar to the Latin fathers which was wholly unknown to the Greek church, that the sin of Adam had been transferred as a peccable principle to his posterity, by generation (tradux animae, tradux peccati). This must necessarily have had some influence on the doctrines of free will and Divine grace.[2] *Pelagius* and *Caeles-*

ing to the corrected edition of Baluzius in du Pin Monim. ad hist. Donatist. p. 225, and Mansi Concil. coll. t. iv. p. 1. Augustini breviculus collationis cum Donatistis (Opp. t. ix. p. 371).

12 After several other laws against them, Cod. Theod. xvi. 5, 52, Honorius ordered a general fine to be exacted of them. Also: Servos etiam dominorum admonitio, vel colonos. verberum crebrior ictus a prava religione revocabit.—Clerici vero ministrique eorum ac perniciosissimi sacerdotales ablati de Africano solo quod ritu sacrilego polluerunt, in exilium viritim ad singulas quasque regiones sub idonea prosecutione mittantur, ecclesiis eorum vel conventiculis praediisque, si qua in eorum ecclesias haereticorum largitas prava contulit, proprietati potestatique Catholicae (sicut jam dudum statuimus) vindicatis. In addition to all this, 414 L. 54: Evidenti praeceptione se agnoscant et intestabiles, et nullam potestatem alicujus ineundi habere contractus, sed perpetua inustos infamia, a coetibus honestis et a conventu publico segregendos.

1 Horn. Comm. de sententiis eorum Patrum, quorum auctoritas ante Augustinum plurimum valuit, de peccato originali. Goetting. 1801. 4. Wiggers, i. 403, ff. How groundlessly Augustine appealed in support of his theory to Gregory of Nazianzum is shown by Ullmann in his work Gregor. v. Naz. S. 438, ff. 446, ff.

2 Hilarius Pictav. in Matth. c. 18, § 6: In unius Adae errore omne hominum genus

tius, two monks universally esteemed for their morals, had distinguished themselves even during their abode at *Rome* (till 409), by giving peculiar prominence to the doctrine of free will for the promotion of personal virtue.[3] Afterward they repaired to Africa (411), whence Pelagius soon passed over into Palestine. But Caelestius, when he became a candidate for the office of presbyter in Carthage, was accused of various errors which had proceeded from the tendency to exalt free will,[4] and was excluded from church communion by a *synod at Carthage* (412); on which he went to *Ephesus*.

The doctrines of Caelestius, however, had gained many friends, and therefore Augustine was induced to oppose them, although personally he had no share in the transactions of the synod by which Caelestius was condemned. His attention was soon drawn to the writings of Pelagius, as the teacher of Caelestius, which he refuted, but always as yet with respect and forbearance.[5] But after *Jerome*, in Palestine, had begun to raise suspicions

aberravit. Ambrosius Expos. Evang. Lucae, l. vii. p. 434: Fuit Adam, et in illo fuimus omnes. Periit Adam, et in illo omnes perierunt. L. vii. § 27: Deus quos dignat vocat, quos vult religiosos facit. Comp. Neander, ii. iii. 1188.

[3] Particularly did Pelagius disapprove the address to God, in Augustini Confess. x. 29: Da quod jubes, et jubes quod vis, see August. de Dono perseverantiae, c. 20.

[4] Marius Mercator has preserved from the Gestis Concilii the seven points of accusation (Commonitorium i. ed. Baluz. p. 3, Comm. ii. p. 133): I. Adam mortalem factum, qui sive peccaret, sive non peccaret, fuisset moriturus. II. Quoniam peccatum Adae ipsum solum laesit, et non genus humanum. III. Quoniam infantes, qui nascuntur, in eo statu sunt, in quo Adam fuit ante prevaricationem. IV. Quoniam neque per mortem vel praevaricationem Adae omne genus hominum moriatur, neque per resurrectionem Christi omne hominum genus resurgat. V. Quoniam infantes, etiamsi non baptizentur, habeant vitam aeternam. VI. Quoniam lex sic mittit ad regnum coelorum, quomodo et evangelium. VII. Quoniam et ante adventum Domini fuerunt homines impeccabiles, id est sine peccato (p. 3: Posse esse hominem sine peccato et facile Dei mandata servare, quia et ante Christi adventum fuerunt homines sine peccato). Cf. Augustin. de Gestis Pelagii 11. Caelestius's defense of the second and third points in Augustin. de Pecc. orig. c. 3, 4 (from the Synodical acts): Dixi, de traduce peccati dubium me esse, ita tamen, ut cui donavit Deus gratiam peritiae, consentiam; quia diversa ab eis audivi, qui utique in ecclesia catholica constituti sunt presbyteri. Sanctus presbyter Rufinus (perhaps the celebrated, see Norisius Hist. Pelag. i. 2, and de Syn. quint. c. 13) Romae qui mansit cum sancto Pammachio: ego audivi illum dicentem, quia tradux peccati non sit.—Licet quaestionis res sit ista, non haeresis. Infantes semper dixi egere baptizari: quid quaerit aliud?

[5] Augustine's controversial writings till 415: Sermones, 170, 174, 175, 293, 294; Epist. 140 ad Honoratum; 157 ad Hilarium (in reply to his information of Pelagians in Sicily in Epist. 156); especially de peccatorum meritis et remissione (s. de baptismo parvulorum), libb. iii. ad Marcellinum (in the third book against Pelagii expositiones in Pauli Epist.); and de spiritu et littera ad eundem. These writings from 412–414. De natura et gratia against Pelagii lib. de natura (Ep. 169, § 13, adversus Pelagii haeresim) and de perfectione justitiae hominis Epist. s. liber ad Eutropium et Paullum, against Caelestii definitiones, both in the year 415.

against Pelagius of being an Origenist,[6] for he hated him from some trifling causes; and after *Orosius*,[7] a presbyter sent by Augustine, had failed in his attempt to procure the condemnation of the Pelagian doctrine, with John, bishop of Jerusalem, and also with the *synod at Diospolis* (*Lydda*, 415),[8] Augustine laid aside all forbearance, and opposed Pelagianism severely and bitterly in many works.[9] The African bishops solemnly condemned the heresy[10] at the synods of *Mileve* and *Carthage* (416), and *Innocent I.*, bishop of Rome, fully agreed with them.[11] After Innocent's death († 417), Pelagius and Caelestius applied to his successor Zosimus, by whom they were declared orthodox;[12]

[6] Hieron. praef. libri i. in Jerem.: Nuper indoctus calumniator erupit, qui commentarios meos in epistolam Pauli ad Ephesios reprehendendos putat (cf. Augustin. contra Julianum, ii. 36: De illo sancto presbytero (Hieronymo)—non solet Pelagius jactitare, nisi quod ei tamquam aemulo inviderit). Praef. lib. iv. in Jerem.: Subito haeresis Pythagorae et Zenonis ἀπαθείας καὶ ἀναμαρτησίας id est impassibilitatis et impeccantiae, quae olim in Origene, et dudum in discipulis ejus, Grunnio, Evagrioque Pontico, et Joviniano jugulata est, coepit reviviscere, et non solum in Occidentis, sed in Orientis partibus sibilare. Jerome wrote against Pelagius the Epist. ad Ctesiphontem (ap. Martianay Ep. 43, ap. Vallarsi Ep. 133) and the dialogi contra Pelagianos, libb. iii. in the years 414 and 415. Against the dialogues, although the doctrinal system in them is much nearer the Pelagian than the Augustinian, wrote Theodorus Mopsvestenus πρὸς τοὺς λέγοντας, φύσει, καὶ οὐ γνώμῃ, πταίειν τοὺς ἀνθρώπους, libb. v., cf. Photius Cod. 177, and Ebedjesu in Assemani Bibl. Or. iii. i. 34. Latin fragments in Marius Mercator ed. Baluz. p. 339, ss.

[7] August. Epist. 169, § 13: Scripsi etiam librum ad sanctum presbyterum Hieronymum de animae origine (is Ep. 166), consulens eum, quomodo defendi possit illa sententia, quam religiosae memoriae Marcellino suam esse scripsit, singulas animas novas nascentibus fieri, ut non labefactetur fundatissima ecclesiae fides, quae inconcusse credimus, quod in Adam omnes moriuntur, et nisi per Christum liberentur, quod per suum Sacramentum etiam in parvulis operatur, in condemnationem trahuntur. Occasionem quippe cujusdam sanctissimi et studiosissimi juvenis presbyteri Orosii, qui ad nos ab ultima Hispania, id est ab Oceani littore, solo sanctarum scripturarum ardore inflammatus advenit, amittere nolui, cui, ut ad illum quoque pergeret, persuasi.

[8] See the narrative in Orosii Apologeticus contra Pelagium de arbitrii libertate.

[9] In the year 416: de Gestis Pelagii s. de Gestis Palaestinis (at the same time the chief source respecting the Synod of Diospolis). 418: contra Pelagium et Caelestium lib. ii. i. de Gratia Christi, ii., de Peccato originali, a standard work. 419: de Nuptiis et Concupiscentia libb. ii., de Anima ejusque origine. 420: contra duas Epistolas Pelagianorum libb. iv. ad Bonifacium Rom. eccl. Episcopum. 421: contra Julianum haer. Pelagianae defensorem libb. vi. 426, 427 (compare below, note 45): de Gratia et libero arbitrio ad Monachos Adrumetinos. De Correptione et gratia ad eosdem (in which the doctrine of predestination is most plainly brought forward). 417–430: contra Secundam Juliani responsionem imperfectum opus, libb. vi.

[10] A synodical letter to Innocent I. from Carthage, in Epist. Augustini, Ep. 175, from Mileve in Ep. 176. Both also in Coustant.

[11] His reply to Carthage August. Epist. 181, to Mileve Ep. 182, and in Coustant.

[12] See especially Caelestii symb. ad Zosim. below note 19. The three letters of Zosimus ad Aurelium et caeteros Epist. Afric., the first two of Sept. 417, the third of 21 March, 418, may be found in Coustant. In the first it is said: Ipsum sane Caelestium, et quicunque in tempore ex diversis regionibus aderant sacerdotes, admonui, has tendiculas quaestionum et inepta certamina, quae non aedificant, sed magis destruunt, ex illa curiosa-

but the Africans adhered still to their judgment in *the synod at Carthage* (417),[13] and *the general synod* held at the same place (418),[14] and succeeded in obtaining from *Honorius* a *sacrum rescriptum* against the Pelagians.[15] Zosimus now also yielded, and condemned Pelagianism in the *Epistola tractoria*.[16] The Italian bishops were compelled to subscribe this; and eighteen who refused were deposed. Among them also was *Julian*, bishop of Eclanum, who continued to defend Pelagianism in various works, against which Augustine wrote several in refutation.

The Pelagians did not form an ecclesiastical, but simply a theological party. They had also no common type of doctrine, and therefore deviated from one another in particular points. Their opinions,[17] which are to be found without disfigurement only in their own works,[18] may be reduced to the following arti-

itatis contagione profluere, dum unusquisque ingenio suo et intemperanti eloquentia supra scripta (i. e., Scripturam S.) abutitur, etc.

[13] Fragment of the Synod's letter to Zosimus in Prosperi l. contra collatorum, c. 15: Constituimus, in Pelagium atque Caelestium per venerabilem episcopum Innocentium de beatissimi apostoli Petri sede prolatam manere sententiam, donec apertissima confessione fateantur, gratia Dei per Jesum Christum Dominum nostrum, non solum ad cognoscendam, verum etiam ad faciendam justitiam nos per actus singulos adjuvari, etc.

[14] Mansi, iv. 377. The eight (or nine see Norisius, l. c. p. 135, the Benedictine preface in t. x. Opp. Aug. § 18, and App. t. x. p. 71) Canones against the Pelagians are in the collection of the decrees of councils put erroneously as the first of the synod at Mileve, A.D. 416, ap. Mansi, iv. 325.

[15] See Opp. August. ed Benedict. t. x. Appendicis pars ii. continens varia scripta et monumenta ad Pelagianorum historiam pertinentium, p. 105 (ed. Venet.). The Edictum of the three Praeff. Praetorio consequent thereon, p. 106.

[16] Fragments of it in Appendix p. 108 and ap. Coustant. That the tractoria was not issued before the African council and the sacrum rescriptum, as is supposed by Baronius, Norisius, Garnier and others, but after both, is proved by Tillemont, t. xiii. p. 738, 739, and the Benedictines, praef. ad t. x. opp. Aug. § 18. Hence August. contra duas epist. Pelag. ii. c. 3: Quin etiam (Pelagiani) Romanos clericos arguunt, scribentes, "eos jussionis terrore perculsos non erubuisse praevaricationis crimen admittere, ut contra priorem sententiam suam, qua gestis catholico dogmati adfuerant, postea pronuntiarent, malam hominum esse naturam."

[17] Besides the works already referred to comp. J. G. Voigt Comm. de theoria Augustiniana, Pelagiana, Semipelagiana et synergistica in doctrina de peccato originali, gratia et libero arbitrio. Gottingae. 1829. 4. J. H. Lentzen de Pelagianorum doctrinae principiis diss. Coloniae ad Rh. 1833. 8. Die Lehre des Pelagius v. Lic. J. L. Jacobi. Leipzig. 1842. 8.

[18] Three works of Pelagius have been preserved complete by the circumstance of their having fallen among those of Jerome, viz., Pelagii expositiones in epist. Pauli, before the year 410. (That Pelagius is the author is proved by J. G. Vossius Hist. Pelag. i. 4. Probably Cassiodorus emended doctrinally nothing but the commentary on the Ep. to the Romans. Comp. Rosenmüller Hist. Interpret. iii. 505).—Epistola ad Demetriadem A.D. 413 (cum aliis aliorum epistolis ed. J. S. Semler. Hal. 1775. 8. Cf. Rosenmüller l. c. p. 522, ss.)—Libellus fidei ad Innocent. I. A.D. 417 (taken into libros Carolinos de imag. cultu iii. c. 1, as confessio fidei, quam a SS. Patribus accepimus, tenemus et puro corde credimus;

cles. "There is no original sin.[19] Man can by his free will choose good as well as evil.[20] Every one therefore can obtain salvation (salus s. vita aeterna). In Christianity a still higher salvation is presented, for which baptism is a necessary condition (regnum coelorum).[21] As the law was formerly given to

as late as 1521 cited by the Sorbonne in their Articulis against Luther as sermo Augustini, often falsely called Hieronymi Symboli explan. ad Damasum; cf. Jo. Launojus de auctore vero professionis fidei, quae Pelagio, Hieronymo, Augustino tribui vulgo solet Diss. Paris. ed. 2. 1663. 8. in his Opp. ii. ii. 302. Walchii Bibl. symb. vetus p. 192, ss.)—Fragments of Pelagii lib. de natura ap. August. de nat. et gratia. Of the lib. iv. de libero arbitrio and the epist. ad Innocent I. fragments ap. August. de gratia Christi and de peccato originali. Capitula s. eclogae fragments in Hieron. dial. i. contra Pelagianos and ap. August. de gestis Pelagii.—Caelestii definitiones fragments ap. August. de perfectione justitiae hominis. Symbolum ad Zosimum fragments ap. August. de peccato origin. (cf. Walchii Bibl. symb. vetus, p. 198, ss.)—Juliani libb. iv ad Turbantium Episc. contra Augustini primum de nuptiis, fragments ap. August. contra Julianum, and in M. Mercatoris subnotationes. Libb. viii. ad Florum contra Augustini secundum de nuptiis, fragments in Aug. opus imperfect. and ap. Marius Mercator l. c.—A Pelagian creed falsely called by Garnier Symb. Juliani, see Walch. Bibl. symb. vet. p. 199, ss.

[19] Caelestii Symb. fragm. i.: Infantes autem debere baptizari in remissionem peccatorum secundum regulam universalis ecclesiae et secundum evangelii sententiam, confitemur, quia Dominus statuit, regnum caelorum nonnisi baptizatis posse conferri: quod quia vires naturae non habent, conferri necesse est per gratiae libertatem. In remissionem autem peccatorum baptizandos infantes non idcirco diximus, ut peccatum ex traduce (or peccatum naturae, peccatum naturale) firmare videamur, quod longe a catholico sensu alienum est. Quia peccatum non cum homine nascitur, quod postmodum exercetur ab homine: quia non naturae delictum, sed voluntatis esse demonstratur. Et illud ergo confiteri congruum, ne diversa baptismatis genera facere videamur, et hoc praemunire necessarium est, ne per mysterii occasionem, ad creatoris injuriam, malum, antequam fiat ab homine, tradi dicatur homini per naturam. Pelagii ep. ad Demetr. C. 4: Ferat sententiam de naturae bono ipsa conscientia bona.—Quid illud obsecro est, quod ad omne peccatum aut erubescimus, aut timemus? et culpam facti nunc rubore vultus, nunc pallore monstramus?—e diverso autem in omni bono laeti, constantes, intrepidi sumus?—Est enim inquam in animis nostris naturalis quaedam (ut ita dixerim) sanctitas, quae velut in arce animi praesidens exercet boni malique judicium. But comp. c. 8: Neque vero alia nobis causa difficultatem bene faciendi facit, quam longa consuetudo vitiorum, quae nos infecit a parvo, paulatimque per multos corrupit annos, et ita postea obligatos sibi et addictos tenet, ut vim quodammodo videatur habere naturae.

[20] Pelagius ap. August. de Pecc. orig. 14: Omne bonum ac malum, quo vel laudabiles vel vituperabiles sumus, non nobiscum oritur, sed agitur a nobis: capaces enim utriusque rei, non pleni nascimur, et ut sine virtute, ita et sine vitio procreamur: atque ante actionem propriae voluntatis, id solum in homine est, quod Deus condidit. Epist. ad Demetr. c. 3: Volens namque Deus rationabilem creaturam voluntarii boni munere et liberi arbitrii potestate donare, utriusque partis possibilitatem homini inserendo proprium ejus fecit, esse quod velit: ut boni ac mali capax, naturaliter utrumque posset, et ad alterutrum voluntatem deflecteret. Hence Caelestii definitiones are proofs, hominem sine peccato esse posse. Among other things it is said, def. 2: Iterum quaerendum est, peccatum voluntatis an necessitatis est? Si necessitatis est, peccatum non est, si voluntatis, vitari potest. 5. Iterum quaerendum est, utrumne debeat homo sine peccato esse. Procul dubio debet. Si debet, potest: si non potest, ergo non debet. Et si non debet homo esse sine peccato, debet ergo cum peccato esse; et jam peccatum non erit, si illud deberi constiterit.

[21] August. de Pecc. merit. et remiss. i. 30: Sed quia non ait, inquiunt, "Nisi quis

facilitate the bringing about of goodness, so now the instructions and example of Christ, and the particular operations of grace. The latter, however, always follow the free purpose to be good.[22] God's predestination therefore is founded solely on his foreknowledge of human actions."

Though Augustine had formerly in his controversy with the Manicheans conceded much to free will, and taken a very different view of predestination,[23] he had long before Pelagius adopted a stricter view,[24] which was for the first time developed in the controversy with the Pelagians[25] in the following system.

renatus fuerit ex aqua et spiritu, non habebit salutem, vel vitam aeternam," tantummodo autem dixit "non intrabit in regnum Dei" (Jo. iii. 5): ad hoc parvuli baptizandi sunt, ut sint etiam cum Christo in regno Dei, ubi non erunt, si baptizati non fuerint: quamvis et sine baptismo si parvuli moriantur, salutem vitamque aeternam habituri sint, quoniam nullo peccati vinculo obstricti sunt. In like manner, Origen ad Rom. ii. 7, see Div. I. § 67, note 1.

[22] Pelagius de Libero arbitrio (ap. Aug. de grat. Chr. 7): Hic nos imperitissimi hominum putant injuriam divinae gratiae facere, quia dicimus eam sine voluntate nostra nequaquam in nobis perficere sanctitatem: quasi Deus gratiae suae aliquid imperaverit, et non illis, quibus imperavit, etiam gratiae suae auxilium subministret, ut quod per liberum homines facere jubentur arbitrium, facilius possent implere per gratiam. Quam nos non, ut tu putas, in lege tantummodo, sed et in Dei esse adjutorio confitemur. Adjuvat enim nos Deus per doctrinam et revelationem suam, dum cordis nostri oculos aperit; dum nobis, ne praesentibus occupemur, futura demonstrat; dum diaboli pandit insidias; dum nos multiformi et ineffabili dono gratiae caelestis illuminat. Ejusdem ep. ad Innoc. (ibid. c. 31): Ecce apud beatitudinem tuam epistola ista me purget, in qua pure atque simpliciter ad peccandum et ad non peccandum integrum liberum arbitrium habere nos dicimus, quod in omnibus bonis operibus divino adjuvatur semper auxilio. Quam liberi arbitrii potestatem dicimus in omnibus esse generaliter, in Christianis, Judaeis, atque Gentilibus. In omnibus est liberum arbitrium aequaliter per naturam, sed in solis Christianis juvatur a gratia.

[23] August. de Praedest. Sanct. c. 3: Quo praecipue testimonio (1 Cor. iv. 7) etiam ipse convictus sum, cum similiter errarem, putans fidem, qua in Deum credimus, non esse donum Dei, sed a nobis esse in nobis, et per illam nos impetrare Dei dona, quibus temperanter et juste et pie vivamus in hoc saeculo. Neque enim fidem putabam Dei gratia praeveniri, ut per illam nobis daretur, quod posceremus utiliter, nisi quia credere non possemus, si non praecederet praeconium veritatis: ut autem praedicato nobis Evangelio consentiremus, nostrum esse proprium, et nobis ex nobis esse arbitrabar. Quem meum errorem nonnulla opuscula mea satis indicant ante episcopatum meum scripta (in particular the expositio quarundam propositionum in Ep. ad Rom. c. 60 and 61, other works against the Manichaeans. See Wundemann, ii. 79 and 91. Neander's Kirchengesch. ii. iii. 1205). Cf. Retractt. i. 23.

[24] Comp. lib. de diversis quaestionibus 83 (written A.D. 388–395). Qu. lxviii. § 4–6. De diversis quaestionibus ad Simplicianum, l. i. Qu. 2 (A.D. 397). Münscher's Dogmengesch. iv. 200.

[25] See Wiggers, i. 264, ff. Even Duns Scotus (Quaest. in Lombard. lib. ii. Dist. 33) says: Frequenter sancti extinguendo contra se haereses pullulantes excessive locuti sunt volentes declinare ad aliud extremum:—sicut Augustinus contra Arium videtur quasi declinare ad Sabellium et e converso, similiter videtur contra Pelagium declinare ad Arium (leg. Manichaeum) et e converso. So also Cornelius Mussus Episc. Bitontinus († 1574) Comm. in epist. ad Rom. c. 5, p. 270. Cf. Jo. Fabricii Diss. de Scylla theologica in ejusd.

"By the sin of Adam human nature became physically and morally corrupt.[26] From it evil lust (concupiscentia) has come, which, since it has become the inheritance of all men by generation, has come to be original sin, in itself damnatory (peccatum originale, vitium originale, vitium haereditarium),[27] and prevails so much over the will of the natural man that he can no longer will what is good, as he should do, out of love to God, but sins continually, however his actions may externally appear.[28] From

amoenitatibus theoll. c. 9. On the other hand Norisius in the Vindiciis Augustinianis c. 5, § 5, seeks to defend him.—The Augustinian system is very differently represented, because the most opposite parties wished to find their own sentiments in it. It is most correctly described by the Reformed, the Dominicans, Augustines, and Jansenists; most misrepresented by the Jesuits.

[26] Wiggers, i. 106.

[27] Comp. especially the books de Peccato originali and de Nuptiis et Concupiscentia.—De civ. Dei xiv. 1: A primus hominibus admissum est tam grande peccatum, ut in deterius eo natura mutaretur humana, etiam in posteros obligatione peccati et mortis necessitate transmissa. De Peccat. merit. et remiss. i. 9: Ille, in quo omnes moriuntur, praeter quod eis qui praeceptum Domini voluntate transgrediuntur, imitationis exemplum est, occulta etiam tabe carnalis concupiscentiae suae tabificavit in se omnes de sua stirpe venientes. De Nuptiis et Concupiscentia, i. 24: Ex hac carnis concupiscentia, tanquam filia peccati, et quando illi ad turpia consentitur, etiam peccatorum matre multorum, quaecunque nascitur proles, originali est obligata peccato, nisi in illo renascatur, quem sine ista concupiscentia virgo concepit: propterea, quando nasci est in carne dignatus, sine peccato solus est natus. De Corrept. et Gratia 10: Quia vero (Adam) per liberum arbitrium Deum deseruit, justum judicium Dei expertus est, ut cum tota sua stirpe, quae in illo adhuc posita tota cum illo peccaverat, damnaretur (de Peccat. merit. et remiss. i. 10, Rom. v. 12 is cited for this purpose, in quo omnes peccaverunt, ἐφ' ᾧ πάντες ἥμαρτον, quando omnes ille unus homo fuerunt). Quotquot enim ex hac stirpe gratia Dei liberantur, a damnatione utique liberantur, qua jam tenentur obstricti. Unde etiam si nullus liberaretur, justum Dei judicium nemo juste reprehenderet. Quod ergo pauci in comparatione pereuntium, in suo vero numero multi liberantur, gratia fit, gratis fit, gratiae sunt agendae, quia fit, ne quis velut de suis meritis extollatur, sed omne os obstruatur, et qui gloriatur, in Domino glorietur. De Pecc. orig. 31: Unde ergo recte infans illa perditione punitur, nisi quia pertinet ad massam perditionis, et juste intelligitur ex Adam natus, antiqui debiti obligatione damnatus, nisi inde fuerit, non secundum debitum, sed secundum gratiam liberatus? Hence the Pelagians accused him of holding the doctrine of a tradux animae and tradux peccati (Traduciani). Inclined as he may have been to that view, he left the question of the origin of souls undecided. Cf. de Anima et ejus origine libb. iv. Opus imp. iv. 104: Arguo de origine animarum cunctationam meam, quia non audeo docere vel affirmare quod nescio (cf. de Peccat. merit. et remiss. ii. 36).

[28] Contra duas epistt. Pelagianorum, i. 2: Quis autem nostrum dicat, quod primi hominis peccato perierit liberum arbitrium de humano genere? Libertas quidem periit per peccatum, sed illa quae in paradiso fuit, habendi plenam cum immortalitate justitiam; propter quod natura humana divina indiget gratia, dicente Domino: si vos Filius liberaverit, tunc vere liberi eritis (John viii. 36), utique liberi ad bene justeque vivendum. Nam liberum arbitrium usque adeo in peccatore non periit, ut per illud peccent, maxime omnes qui cum delectatione peccant et amore peccati: hoc eis placet, quod eis libet. De gratia Christi 26: Quid autem boni faceremus, nisi diligeremus? Aut quomodo bonum non facimus, si diligamus? Etsi enim Dei mandatum videtur aliquando non a diligentibus, sed a timentibus fieri: tamen ubi non est dilectio, nullum bonum opus imputatur, nec recte bonum opus vocatur, quia omne quod non ex fide est, peccatum est, et fides per dilectionem

this corrupt mass of humanity (perditionis massa) God resolved from eternity to save some through Christ, and leave the rest to deserved perdition. Though baptism procures forgiveness of sin, even of original sin, it does not remove the moral corruption of man.[29] Therefore Divine grace alone, and irresistibly, works faith in the elect, as well as love and power to do good.[30] The others,

operatur. Ac per hoc gratiam Dei, qua caritas Dei diffunditur in cordibus nostris per Spiritum sanctum, qui datus est nobis, sic confiteatur, qui vult veraciter confiteri, ut omnino nihil boni sine illa, quod ad pietatem pertinet veramque justitiam, fieri posse non dubitet. Wiggers, i. 121. J. G. L. Duncker Hist. doctrinae de ratione quae inter peccatum originale et actuale intercedit apud Irenaeum, Tertullianum, Augustinum. Gottingae. 1836. 8.

[29] De Nupt. et Concupisc. i. 26: In eis ergo qui regenerantur in Christo, cum remissionem accipiunt prorsus omnium peccatorum utique necesse est, ut reatus etiam hujus licet adhuc manentis concupiscentiae remittatur, ut in peccatum, sicut dixi, non imputetur,—manet actu, praeterit reatu. De Peccat. de meritis et remiss. i. 19: Caeterum quis ignorat, quod baptizatus parvulus, si ad rationales annos veniens non crediderit, nec se ab illicitis concupiscentiis abstinuerit, nihil ei proderit, quod parvus accepit? Verumtamen si percepto baptismate de hac vita emigraverit, soluto reatu, cui originaliter erat obnoxius, perficietur in illo lumine veritatis, quod incommutabiliter manens in aeternum, justificatos praesentia creatoris illuminat.

[30] In the beginning of the controversy Augustine still thought of these operations of grace as resistibiles, see De Spiritu et Litera, c. 34: Agit Deus, ut velimus, et ut credamus, sive extrinsecus per evangelicas exhortationes,—sive intrinsecus, ubi nemo habet in potestate quid ei veniat in mentem, sed consentire vel dissentire propriae voluntatis est. His ergo modis quando Deus agit cum anima rationali, ut ei credat (neque enim credere potest quodlibet libero arbitrio, si nulla sit suasio vel vocatio cui credat), profecto et ipsum velle credere Deus operatur in homine, et in omnibus misericordia ejus praevenit nos: consentire autem vocationi Dei, vel ab ea dissentire, sicut dixi, propriae voluntatis est. But in his later works they appear as irresistibly acting. De Corrept. et Grat. 7: Quicunque ergo ab illa originali damnatione ista divinae gratiae largitate discreti sunt, non est dubium, quod et procuratur eis audiendum evangelium; et cum audiunt, credunt; et in fide, quae per delectionem operatur, usque in finem perseverant; et si quando exorbitant, correpti emendantur; et quidam eorum, etsi ab hominibus non corripiantur, in viam quam reliquerant redeunt; et nonnulli accepta gratia, in qualibet aetate, periculis hujus vitae mortis celeritate subtrahuntur. Haec enim omnia operatur in eis, qui vasa misericordiae operatus est eos, qui et elegit eos in filio suo ante constitutionem mundi per electionem gratiae. De Gratia Christi, c. 24: Non lege atque doctrina insonante forinsecus, sed interna atque occulta mirabili ac ineffabili potestate operari Deum in cordibus hominum non solum veras revelationes, sed etiam bonas voluntates. De Corrept. et Grat. c. 9: Quicunque ergo in Dei providentissima dispositione praesciti, praedestinati, vocati, justificati, glorificati sunt, non dico etiam nondum renati, sed etiam nondum nati, jam filii Dei sunt, et omnino perire non possunt. Ibid. 12: Ac per hoc nec de ipsa perseverantia boni voluit Deus sanctos suos in viribus suis, sed in ipso gloriari.—Tantum quippe Spiritu sancto accenditur voluntas eorum, ut ideo possint, quia sic volunt; ideo sic velint, quia Deus operatur, ut velint.—Subventum est igitur infirmitati voluntatis humanae, ut divina gratia indeclinabiliter et insuperabiliter ageretur. Ibid. 14: Non est itaque dubitandum, voluntati Dei, qui in caelo et in terra omnia, quaecunque voluit, fecit, et qui etiam illa, quae futura sunt, fecit, humanas voluntates non posse resistere, quo minus faciat ipse quod vult: quandoquidem etiam de ipsis hominum voluntatibus, quod vult, cum vult, facit. These moral effects of grace Augustine comprehends under Justificatio, cf. Opus imperfect. contra Jul. ii. c. 168: Justificat impium Deus, non solum dimittendo, quae mala facit, sed etiam donando caritatem, quae declinat a malo et facit bonum per Spiritum sanctum.

to whom the grace of God is not imparted[31] have no advantage from Christ, and fall into condemnation,[32] even an eternal one."[33]

Such were the opposing systems, apart from the consequences with which the misrepresentations of the combatants reproached

[31] For the most part Augustine uses the expression Praedestinatio only of predestination to happiness, but sometimes also of condemnation. Tract. 110, in Joan. distinguishes duplicem mundum, unum damnationi praedestinatum, alterum ex inimico amicum factum et reconciliatum. Enchirid. ad Laur. c. 100: Haec sunt magna opera Domini, ut, cum angelica et humana creatura peccasset,—etiam per eandem creaturae voluntatem, qua factum est quod Creator noluit, impleret ipse quod voluit: bene utens et malis, tamquam summe bonus, ad eorum damnationem, quos juste praedestinavit ad poenam, et ad eorum salutem, quos benigne praedestinavit ad gratiam. Cf. de Grat. et Lib. arbitr. c. 21: Operari Deum in cordibus hominum ad inclinandas eorum voluntates quocunque voluerit, sive ad bona pro sua misericordia, sive ad mala pro meritis eorum. Ratramnus de Praedest. ii. (in Vett. auctorum, qui ix. saec. de praedest. et gratia scripserunt opera, cura Gilb. Mauguin, i. 62) has collected several passages of this kind. Comp. however Wiggers, i. 305.

[32] De Peccat. merit. et remiss. iii. 4: Quoniam nihil agitur aliud, cum parvuli baptizantur, nisi ut incorporentur ecclesiae, id est, Christi corpori membrisque socientur, manifestum est, eos ad damnationem, nisi hoc eis collatum fuerit, pertinere. De Gratia et Lib. arbitr. 3: Sed et illa ignorantia, quae non est eorum, qui scire nolunt, sed eorum, qui tanquam simpliciter nesciunt, neminem sic excusat, ut sempiterno igne non ardeat, si propterea non credidit, quia non audivit omnino quid crederet; sed fortasse, ut mitius ardeat (cf. contra Julianum, iv. 3. Absit, ut sit in aliquo vera virtus, nisi fuerit justus. Absit autem, ut sit justus vere, nisi vivat ex fide. Minus enim Fabricius quam Catalina punietur, non quia iste bonus, sed quia ille magis malus: et minus impius, quam Catilina, Fabricius, non veras virtutes habendo, sed a veris virtutibus non plurimum deviando).—De Corrept. et Grat. 7: Ac per hoc et qui Evangelium non audierunt, et qui eo audito in melius commutati perseverantiam non acceperunt, et qui Evangelio audito venire ad Christum, hoc est, in eum credere noluerunt, quoniam ipse dixit, Nemo venit ad me, nisi ei datum fuerit a Patre meo (John vi. 66), et qui per aetatem parvulam nec credere potuerunt, sed ab originali noxa solo possent lavacro regenerationis absolvi, quo tamen non accepto mortui perierunt; non sunt ab illa conspersione discreti, quam constat esse damnatam, euntibus omnibus ex uno in condemnationem. Ibid. 13: Propter hujus ergo utilitatem secreti credendum est, quosdam de filiis perditionis non accepto dono perseverandi usque in finem, in fide, quae per dilectionem operatur, incipere vivere, et aliquamdiu fideliter ac juste vivere, et postea cadere, neque de hac vita, priusquam hoc eis contingat, auferri. De Praedest. Sanct. 8: Cur autem istum potius, quam illum liberet, inscrutabilia sunt judicia ejus et investigabiles viae ejus (Romae xi. 33). Melius enim et hic audimus aut dicimus: O homo, tu quis es, qui respondeas Deo (Rom. ix. 20). How much perplexity the passage, 1 Tim. ii. 4, qui omnes vult homines salvos fiere, occasioned Augustine, is proved by his numerous and all very forced attempts to explain it. So de Corrept. et Grat. c. 14. Contra Jul. iv. c. 8: Omnes i. q. multos; Enchirid. ad Laur. 103: Omnes i. q. omnis generis. De Corrept. et Gratia, c. 15: Omnes homines Deus vult salvos fieri, quoniam nos facit velle. Enchirid. l. c. tanquam diceretur, nullum hominem fieri salvum, nisi quem fieri salvum ipse voluerit.

[33] De Civ. Dei, xxi. c. 23. Enchirid. ad Laur. c. 112 (see above, § 84, note 35). The last passage is against those who inferred from Psalm lxxvii. 10, that the punishment of hell will have an end. Still he concedes to them: Sed poenas damnatorum certis temporum intervallis existiment, si hoc eis placet, aliquatenus mitigari. Etiam sic quippe intelligi potest manere in illis ira Dei (Jo. iii. 36), h. e. ipsa damnatio—ut in ira sua, h. e. manente ira sua, non tamen contineat miserationes suas (Ps. lxxvii. 10): non aeterno supplicio finem dando, sed levamen adhibendo vel interponendo cruciatibus. In the Enarrat in Psalm cv. § 2, however, he declares even this conjecture too bold.

one another,[34] for the purpose of exciting universal abhorrence of the enemy's doctrine. The sentiments of Augustine were ecclesiastically confirmed by the decisions of African synods and by Zosimus in the west; although their author himself felt how dangerous they might be made to morals, and was able to bring them forward in popular instruction in no other than an inconsequential way.[35] The Greek Church could not but stumble at them; but it troubled itself little about such controversies.[36] The exiled western bishops hoped, therefore, that they would so

[34] So the Pelagians palmed on Augustine the opinion, per diabolum aliquid substantiae creatum in hominibus (Augustin. de Nuptiis et Concupisc. ii. 34), quasi malum naturale cum Manichaeis sapiat, qui dicit, infantes secundum Adam carnaliter natos contagium mortis antiquae prima nativitate contrahere. On the contrary, Augustinus contra Julianum, lib. i. and ii. But Pelagianism also was not less misrepresented by its opponents. August. de Pecc. mer. et rem. ii. 2, designates the Pelagians as tantum praesumentes de libero humanae voluntatis arbitrio, ut ad non peccandum nec adjuvandos nos divinitus opinentur. C. 5: Dicunt, accepto semel liberae voluntatis arbitrio nec orare nos debere, ut Deus nos adjuvet, ne peccemus. Epist. Conc. Carthag. ad Innocent. (Aug. Epist. 175) § 6: Parvulos etiam propter salutem, quae per salvatorem Christum datur, baptizandos negant—promittentes, etiamsi non baptizentur, habituros vitam aeternam.

[35] De Dono perseverantiae, c. 22: Dolosi vel imperiti medici est, etiam utile medicamentum sic alligare, ut aut non prosit, aut obsit. One should not say to the church: Ita se habet de praedestinatione definita sententia voluntatis Dei, ut alii ex vobis de infidelitate, accepta obediendi voluntate, veneritis ad fidem. Quid opus est dici, alii ex vobis? Si enim Ecclesiae Dei loquimur, si credentibus loquimur, cur alios eorum ad fidem venisse dicentes caeteris facere videamur injuriam? cum possimus congruentius dicere: Ita se habet de praedestinatione definita sententia voluntatis Dei, ut ex infidelitate veneritis ad fidem accepta voluntate obediendi, et accepta perseverantia permaneatis in fide? Nec illud quod sequitur est omnino dicendum, i. e. caeteri vero qui in peccatorum delectatione remoramini, ideo nondum surrexistis, quia necdum vos adjutorium gratiae miserantis erexit: cum bene et convenienter dici possit et debeat: si qui autem adhuc in peccatorum damnabilium delectatione remoramini, apprehendite saluberrimam disciplinam: quod tamen cum feceritis, nolite extolli quasi de operibus vestris aut gloriari, quasi hoc non acceperitis; Deus est enim, qui operatur in vobis et velle et operari pro bona voluntate—de ipso autem cursu vestro bono rectoque condiscite vos ad praedestinationem divinae gratiae pertinere. Augustine is inconsistent when he, Epist. 194, c. 4, in accordance with his system, declares prayer to be an effect of Divine grace, and, Epist. 157, c. 2, says, we receive Divine grace humiliter petendo et faciendo, and, Op. imperf. iii. 107: Homines quando audiunt vel legunt, unumquemque recepturum secundum ea, quae per corpus gessit, non debent in suae voluntatis virtute confidere, sed orare potius talem sibi a Domino preparari voluntatem, ut non intrent in tentationem.

[36] Comp. the refutation of Augustine's doctrines by Theodore of Mopsuestia, ap. Marius Mercator, ed. Baluz. p. 399, ss. ex. gr. p. 342: Nihil horum prospicere potuit mirabilis peccati originalis assertor, quippe qui in divinis scripturis nequaquam fuerit exercitatus, nec ab infantia, juxta b. Pauli vocem, sacras didicerit literas.—Novissime vero in hanc dogmatis recidit novitatem, qua diceret, quod in ira atque furore Deus Adam mortalem esse praeceperit, et propter ejus unum delictum cunctos etiam necdum natos homines morte multaverit. Sic autem disputans non veretur nec confunditur ea sentire de Deo, quae nec de hominibus sanum sapientibus et aliquam justitiae curam gerentibus unquam quis aestimare tentavit, caet. The Greek church historians are altogether silent concerning the Pelagian controversy.

much the more readily obtain protection in Constantinople, as they believed they had wholly in their favor the works of Chrysostom, which were highly esteemed in that place.[37] Hence they applied particularly to Nestor, who had been bishop of the see of Constantinople since 428. But since very prejudicial representations of Pelagianism had been disseminated from the west, especially by *Marius Mercator*,[38] who was personally present in Constantinople,[39] Nestorius saw the necessity of giving prominence to the ruinous consequences of the fall and the necessity of baptism, which the Pelagians were said to deny.[40] But on the other hand, he found the Pelagians themselves who had fled to him, so little heterodox, that he asked from the Romish bishop Caelestine (429) an explanation respecting the grounds of their condemnation.[41] This very relation of the Pe-

[37] So Julian appealed to Chrysostom. See August. contra Jul. i. c. 6, s. With the same view Annianus, doubtless the Annianus Pseudodiaconus Celedensis who is mentioned by Hieron. ad August. (August. Ep. 202) as a writer in favor of Pelagianism, and who was also present at the synod of Diospolis (see Garnerii Diss. i. ad Marium Mercat. c. 7), translated into Latin numerous homilies of Chrysostom, of which Hom. viii. in Matth. and Hom vii. de laudibus S. Pauli still exist. Comp. his Prologus ad Orontium Episc. (who was condemned at Ephesus for being a Pelagian) prefixed to the Hom. in Matth. (Chrysost. Opp. ed. Montfaucon, t. vii. init.): Quid enim vel ad prudentiam eruditius, vel ad exercitationem ignitius, vel ad dogma purgatius nostrorum auribus offeratur, quam praeclara haec tam insignis animi ingeniique monumenta? Et hoc maxime tempore, quo per occasionem quarundam nimis difficilium quaestionum aedificationi morum atque ecclesiasticae disciplinae satis insolenter obstrepitur. Quid pressius ille commendat, quam ingenitae nobis a Deo libertatis decus cujus confessio praecipuum inter nos gentilesque discrimen est, qui hominem, ad imaginem Dei conditum, tam infeliciter fati violentia et peccandi putant necessitate devinctum, ut is etiam pecoribus invidere cogatur? Quid ille adversus eosdem magistros potius insinuat, quam Dei esse possibilia mandata, et hominem totius vel quae jubetur vel suadetur a Deo capacem esse virtutis? Quo quidem solo et iniquitas ab imperante propellitur, et praevaricanti reatus affigitur. Jam vero iste eruditorum decus cum de gratiae Dei disserit, quanta illam ubertate, quanta etiam cautione concelebrat? Non enim est in alterutro aut incautus, aut nimius, sed in utroque moderatus. Sic liberas ostendit hominum voluntates, ut ad Dei tamen mandata facienda divinae gratiae necessarium ubique fateatur auxilium: sic continuum divinae gratiae auxilium commendat, ut nec studia voluntatis interimat. Chrysost. in Epist. ad Rom. Hom. x. expressly rejects, as an absurdity, the opinion that by Adam's disobedience another person becomes a sinner. On the relation of grace to freedom he speaks in Epist. ad Hebr. Hom. xii.

[38] Opera ed. Jo. Garnerius, Paris. 1673. fol., better Steph. Baluzius, Par. 1684. 8 (reprinted in Gallandii Bibl. vett. Patr. viii. 613). In the Commonitorium adv. haeresin Pelagii et Caelestii vel etiam scripta Juliani, ed. Baluz. p. 1. Commonitorium super nomine Caelestii (429, presented to the emperor Theodosius II.) p. 132.

[39] Marius Mercator always gives special prominence to the tenets of Caelestius (see note 4), though Pelagius had rejected most of them at the synod of Diospolis.

[40] Nestorii Sermones iv. contra Pelagium (Latin, partly in nothing but an extract in Marius Mercator, p. 120. The four discourses in the original among Chrysostom's orations ed. Montfaucon, x. p. 733) are not aimed directly against Pelagius.

[41] Marius Merc. p. 119: Contra haeresin Pelagii seu Caelestii—quamvis recte sentiret

lagians to Nestorius was ruinous to them in the west; an internal necessary connection between Pelagianism and Nestorianism was hunted out,[42] and at the third general council at Ephesus (431) Pelagianism was condemned along with Nestorianism.[43] Yet the Augustinian doctrine of grace and predestination was never adopted in the east.[44]

But even in the west, where this doctrine had been ecclesiastically ratified, there were never more than a few who held to it in its fearful consequences. Its injurious practical effects could not be overlooked, and appeared occasionally in outward manifestation.[45] The monks in particular were naturally opposed to a view which annihilated all the meritoriousness of their monastic exercises.[46] Hence Augustine soon found his doctrine disputed even by opponents of the Pelagians.[47] The monks of *Massilia* especially, adopted a view of free grace between that of Augustine and that of Pelagius, which seems to have originated chiefly with *John Cassian* († soon after 432),[48]

et doceret, Julianum tamen ex Episcopo Eclanensi cum participibus suis hujus haeresis signiferum et antesignanum, olim ab apostolica sententia exauctoratum atque depositum, in amicitiam interim censuit suscipiendum. Spem enim absolutionis promittens, ipsum quoque Caelestium litteris suis—consolatus est. This writing follows, p. 131. On this account Nestorius applied, in the year 429, to the Romish bishop Caelestine, in two letters (ap. Baronius ad ann. 430, no. 3, ap. Coustant among the Epistt. Caelest. Ep. vi. and vii.). In the first: Julianus, caet.—saepe—Imperatorem adierunt, ac suas causas defleverunt, tanquam orthodoxi temporibus orthodoxis persecutionem passi saepe eadem et apud nos lamentantes.—Sed quoniam apertiore nobis de causis eorum notitia opus est,—dignare nobis notitiam de his largiri, caet.

42 See below, § 88, note 18.

43 See below, § 88, note 27.

44 Münscher's Dogmengeschichte, iv. 238.

45 Comp. the memorable controversy among the monks of Adrumetum, 426 and 427. August. Epistt. 214–216. Retractt. ii. 66, 67. Some (Ep. 214) sic gratiam praedicant, ut negent hominis esse liberum arbitrium, et, quod est gravius, dicant, quod in die judicii non sit redditurus Deus unicuique secundum opera ejus. They said accordingly (Retr. ii. 67), neminem corripiendum, si Dei praecepta non facit, sed pro illo ut faciat, tantummodo orandum (different after all only in the form, not essentially, from the doctrines of Augustine!) Others (Ep. 215) asserted, like the Semipelagians, secundum aliqua merite humana dari gratiam Dei. A strictly Augustinian party stood between. Against the first Augustine wrote de Correptione et Gratia; against the second de Gratia et libero Arbitrio. Comp. Walch's Ketzerhist. 245, ff.

46 Comp. for example Cassiani Coll. xix. 8: Finis quidem Coenobitae est, omnes suas mortificare et crucifigere voluntates, ac secundum evangelicae perfectionis salutare mundatum nihil de crastino cogitare. Quam perfectionem prorsus a nemine, nisi a Coenobita impleri posse certissimum est.

47 Joh. Geffcken Hist. Semipelagianismi antiquissima. Gotting. 1826. 4. Wiggers Darstellung des Augustinismus u. Pelagianismus, 2ter Th.—On the differences between him and Vitalis see August. Epist. 217. Walch, v. 9. Geffcken, p. 40, ss. Wiggers, ii. 198.

48 His works: De institutis Coenobiorum libb. xii. Collationes Patrum xxiv. De

a disciple of Chrysostom.[49] Augustine received the first account of these *Massilians*, or, as they were first named by the Scholastics, *Semipelagians*, from his zealous adherents *Prosper* of Aquitania, and *Hilary* (429),[50] and attempted to bring them over to his views in his last two works (429, 430).[51] After Augustine's death, *Prosper* († 460)[52] continued the controversy

Incarnatione Christi adv. Nestorium libb. vii.—Opp. ed. Alardus Gazaeus. Duaci. 1616 3 t. 8, auct. Atrebati. 1628. fol. (Reprinted Francof. 1722, and Lips. 1733. fol.)—Cf. G. F. Wiggers de Joanne Cassiano Massiliensi, qui Semipelagianismi auctor vulgo perhibetur, Comm. iii. Rostochii, 1824 and 25. 4. The same author's Augustinismus u. Pelag. ii. 7. Jean Cassien, sa vie et ses écrits, thèse par L. F. Meyer. Strasbourg. 1840. 4.

49 Comp. especially Collat. xiii. (according to Wiggers, ii. 37, written between 428 and 431, according to Geffcken, p. 6, somewhat before 426). Among other things we find, in c. 9: Propositum namque Dei, quo non ob hoc hominem fecerat ut periret, sed ut in perpetuum viverit, manet immobile. Cujus benignitas cum bonae voluntatis in nobis quantulamcunque scintillam emicuisse perspexerit, vel quam ipse tamquam de dura silice nostri cordis excusserit, confovet eam et exsuscitat, suaque inspiratione confortat, volens omnes homines salvos fieri, et ad agnitionem veritatis venire (1 Tim. ii. 4).—Qui enim ut pereat unus ex pusillis non habet voluntatem, quomodo sine ingenti sacrilegio putandus est, non universaliter omnes, sed quosdam salvos fieri velle pro omnibus?—C. 8: Adest inseparabiliter nobis semper divina prosectio, tantaque est erga creaturam suam pietas creatoris, ut non solum comitetur eam, sed etiam praecedat jugi providentia.—Qui cum in nobis ortum quendam bonae voluntatis inspexerit, illuminat eam confestim, atque confortat, et incitat ad salutem, incrementum tribuens ei, quam vel ipse plantavit, vel nostro conatu viderit emersisse.—Et non solum sancta desideria benignus inspirat, sed etiam occasiones praestruit vitae, et opportunitatem boni effectus ac salutaris viae directionem demonstrat errantibus.—C. 9: Ut autem evidentius clareat, etiam per naturae bonum, quod beneficio creatoris indultum est, nonnunquam bonarum voluntatum prodire principia, quae tamen nisi a Domino dirigantur, ad consummationem virtutum pervenire non possunt, Apostolus testis est dicens: Velle adjacet mihi, perficere autem bonum non invenio (Rom. vii. 18).—C. 11: Haec duo, i. e., vel gratia Dei, vel liberum arbitrium, sibi quidem invicem videntur adversa, sed utraque concordant, et utraque nos pariter debere suscipere, pietatis ratione colligimus, ne unum horum homini subtrahentes, ecclesiasticae fidei regulam excessisse videamur. C. 12: Unde cavendum est nobis, ne ita ad Dominum omnia sanctorum merita referamus, ut nihil nisi id quod malum atque perversum est humanae adscribamus naturae.—Dubitari ergo non potest, inesse quidem omni animae naturaliter virtutum semina beneficio creatoris inserta, sed nisi haec opitulatione Dei fuerint excitata, ad incrementum perfectionis non poterunt pervenire. Collat. iii. c. 12. Nullus justorum sibi sufficit ad obtinendam justitiam, nisi per momenta singula titubanti ei et corruenti fulcimenta manus suae supposuerit divina clementia. Wiggers, ii. 47.

50 Ep. Prosperi ad August. among Augustine's epistles, Ep. 225, Ep. Hilarii, 226. Wiggers, ii. 153.

51 De Praedestinatione Sanctorum liber ad Prosperum. De Dono perseverantiae liber ad Prosperum et Hilarium (s. liber secundus de Praedest. Sanct.)

52 Works: Epistola ad Rufinum de gratia et libero arbitrio. Carmen de ingratis. Epigrammata ii. in Obtrectatorem S. Augustini, all belonging to 429 and 430.—Epitaphium Nestorianae et Pelagianae haereseos, 431. Comp. Wiggers, ii. 169. Against new opponents (comp. Walch, v. 67. Geffcken, p. 32. Wiggers, ii. 184): Pro Augustino responsiones ad capitula objectionum Gallorum calumniantium. Pro Augustini doctrina resp. ad capitula objectionum Vincentianarum (doubtless Vinc. Lirin.). Pro Augustino respons. ad excepta, quae de Genuensi civitate sunt missa. De gratia Dei et libero Arbitrio lib. s. contra Collatorem (about 432, Wiggers, ii. 138). Besides see Chronicon

with greater violence, but could not prevent the Semipelagian doctrines from spreading farther, especially in Gaul. To these Semipelagians also belonged *Vincentius* Lirinensis († 450) whose *Commonitorium*, composed in the year 434, was one of the works most read in the west as a standard book of genuine Catholicism.[53]

III. CONTROVERSIES CONCERNING THE PERSON OF CHRIST.

§ 88.

NESTORIAN CONTROVERSY.

SOURCES: Nestor's own account (Evagrius Hist. eccl. i. 7) was made use of by Irenaeus (Comes, then from 444 to 448, bishop of Tyre) in his Tragoedia s. comm. de rebus in synodo Ephesina, ac in Oriente toto Gestis. This last work of Irenaeus is lost; but the original documents appended to it were transferred in the sixth century, in a Latin translation, to the Synodicon (Variorum Epist. ad Conc. Eph. pertinentes ex MS. Casin. ed. Chr. Lupus. Lovan. 1682. 4, in an improved form ap. Mansi, v. 731, and in Theodoreti Opp. ed. Schulze, v. 608). Marius Mercator also has many fragments of Acts, Opp. P. ii. (see above, § 87, note 38). A complete collection of all the Acts is given in Mansi, iv. p. 567, ss. and t. v.—Account of this controversy by Ibas, bishop of Edessa, in the Epist. ad Marin Persam (mostly contained in the Actis Conc. Chalced. Act. x. ap. Mansi, vii. p. 241, ss.).—Liberatus's (archdeacon in Carthage about 553) Breviarum causae Nestorianorum et Eutychianorum (ed. Jo. Garnerius. Paris. 1675. 8, ap. Mansi, ix. p. 659, and in Gallandii Bibl. PP. xii. p. 119).—Besides Socrates, vii. c. 29, ss. Evagrius, i. c. 7, ss.

Walch's Ketzerhistorie, v. 289. Wundemann's Gesch. d. Glaubenslehre, ii. 265. Münscher's Dogmengeschichte, iv. 53. Neander's Kirchengesch. ii. iii. 927. Baur's Lehre v. d. Dreieinigkeit u. Menschwerdung Gottes in ihrer geschichtl. Entwickelung, i. 693.

In the Arian controversy the doctrine concerning Christ's person had been touched upon, but without being fully developed. When the Arians inferred from the Catholic doctrine of a human soul in Christ that there were two persons,[1] the

(till 454).—Opp. ed. Jo. le Brun de Marette et D. Mangeaut. Paris. 1711. fol. cum var. lectt. ex Cod. Vatic. Romae. 1758. 8.

[53] Commonitorium pro catholicae fidei antiquitate et universitate adv. profanas omnium haereticor. novitates. Often published among others, cum August de Doctr. christ. ed. G. Calixtus. Helmst. 1629. 8 (ed. ii. 1655. 4) cum Salviani Opp. ed. St. Baluzius. (Paris. 1633. ed. ii. 1669. ed. iii. 1684. 8) ed. Engelb. Klüpfel. Viennae. 1809. Herzog. Vratisl. 1839. 8, comp. Wiggers, ii. 208. That this Vincentius is the one who was attacked by Prosper, and that even in the Commonitorium Semipelagian traces are found, has been proved by Vossius, Norisius, Natalis, Alexander, Oudinus de Scriptt. eccl. i. 1231. Geffcken, p. 53. Wiggers, ii. 195. On the contrary side, Act. SS. Maji, vol. v. p. 284, ss. Hist. littéraire de la France, t. ii. p. 309.

[1] See § 83, note 28.

Orientals indeed could not be led astray by this means from holding fast the human in Christ, as long as they remained true to their historico-exegetical principles;[2] but the Nicenians in Egypt and the west began to give strong prominence to the unity of his Divine person, for the purpose of obviating that Arian objection,[3] and to consider Christ accordingly in all rela-

[2] So Eusebius of Emesa (§ 84, note 18) in the fragments in Theodoreti Eranistes Dial. iii. (Opp. ed. Schulze, iv. 258), and in the work de Fide adv. Sabellium, in so far as we can venture to ascribe this work to him. See Thilo über die Schriften des Euseb. v. Alex. u. des Euseb. v. Emisa, S. 75.

[3] Athanas. de Incarnat. verbi (Opp. ed. Montfaucon, ii. 1, ap. Mansi, iv. 689): Ὁμολογοῦμεν καὶ εἶναι αὐτὸν υἱὸν τοῦ θεοῦ καὶ θεὸν κατὰ πνεῦμα, υἱὸν ἀνθρώπου κατὰ σάρκα· οὐ δύο φύσεις τὸν ἕνα υἱὸν, μίαν προσκυνητὴν καὶ μίαν ἀπροσκύνητον· ἀλλὰ μίαν φύσιν τοῦ θεοῦ λόγου σεσαρκωμένην, καὶ προσκυνουμένην μετὰ τῆς σαρκὸς αὐτοῦ μιᾷ προσκυνήσει. Since Cyril, a follower of Athanasius, appeals to this passage (lib. de recta fide ad Imperatrices, § 9), it has by this means the most important external testimony in its favor. Several writings were assigned to the Romish bishop Julius I., in which the unity existing in Christ was strongly expressed. There are still extant the Epist. ad Dionysium (ap. Mansii, ii. 1191. A. Maji Scriptt. vett. nova coll. vii. i. 144), cited as genuine by Gennadius (about 490), in which the μία φύσις is expressly and plainly asserted; the Epist. ad Prosdocium (ex. cod. Oxon. ed. J. G. Ehrlich. Lips. 1750. 4), regarded as genuine by the council of Ephesus, by Cyril, Marius Mercator, Facundus, and Ephraem bishop of Antioch about 526 (Photii Cod. 229), which rejects the phrase ἄνθρωπος ὑπὸ θεοῦ προσληφθείς, and three fragments lately published by Majus, l. c. vii. i. 165, the first and third of which are mentioned by Ephraem, l. c. How strongly also Hilary was inclined to the doctrine of one nature may be seen in Münscher's Dogmengesch. iv. 16. Baur's Dreieinigkeit, i. 681. By this means the mode of expression in the writings of Julius is rendered more intelligible from the general tendency of the west at that time. —After Eutyches and the later Monophysites continually appealed to Athanasius, the Romish bishop Felix (270–275), and Julius (337–352), and to Gregory Thaumaturgus, as unam naturam Dei verbi decernentes post unitionem, whose testimonia Cyrillus in libb. adv. Diodorum et Theodorum has put together; (see Collatio Catholicorum cum Severianis, A. D. p. 531, Mansi, viii. 820; a Jacobite collection of this kind translated from the Arabic, see Spicilegium, Rom. iii. 694), many Catholics began to assert that these testimonies have been interpolated by Apollinarists (see Collatio, l. c. p. 821. Leontius de Sectis, act. viii. Justinianus Imp. contra Monophys. in Maji Scriptt. vett. nov. coll. vii. i. 302), notwithstanding Ephraem bishop of Antioch, about 526 (Photii Cod. 229), and Eulogius bishop of Alexandria, about 580 (Phot. Cod. 230), admit the genuineness of the passage of Athanasius and of the Ep. Julii ad Prosdocium. Leontius (contra Monophys. ap. Majus, vii. i. 143, s.) appeals to the testimony of Polemon, a disciple of Apollinaris, as proof that the passage ascribed to Athanasius belongs to Apollinaris. The place in question in Polemon may be completely put together from the two quotations p. 143 and p. 16, but it says something quite different. Polemon speaks against the inconsistency of those who asserted μίαν φύσιν τοῦ λόγου σεσαρκωμένην, and yet assume in Christ θεὸν τέλειον and ἄνθρωπον τέλειον, while Apollinaris had rightly rejected the two natures, and taught εἶναι αὐτὸν υἱὸν τοῦ θεοῦ (as above in the passage of Athanasius). In short, Polemon meant to say, Athanasius had borrowed that doctrine from Apollinaris, but fell into an inconsistency with himself in so doing. Ap. Majus, l. c. p. 16, there is also a fragment of Apollinarii Epist. ad Jovian., in which that passage has been interpolated word for word as above; but it does not at all suit the construction, a sign that it has been inserted.—The moderns, however, especially Catholic writers, have retained the view that all those writings proceeded from Apollinaris. It has been defended in reference to the letters of Julius, particularly by Muratori Anecdota graeca, p. 341, ss.; and with regard to all those

tions only as God.[4] When Apollinaris, following this tendency still farther, denied to Christ a reasonable human soul, his opponents, it is true, were united in asserting that Christ is perfect God and man in one person, but in the east they were now accustomed to distinguish the two natures, and the predicates used to describe them, with greater care; and the two most eminent men of the Antiochenian school, *Diodore*, bishop of Tarsus,[5] and *Theodore*, bishop of Mopsuestia,[6] confirmed the accuracy of this distinction by their writings, which were highly esteemed in the whole east; while in Egypt the formula of Athanasius, of one Divine nature made flesh, was maintained. On the other hand,[7] *Ambrose*[8] and *Augustine*[9] in the west endeavored, after

passages above named by Le Quien Dissert. Damasc. ii. prefixed to his edition of Joannes Damasc. t. i. p. xxxii. ss. Comp. on the other side Salig de Eutychianismo ante Eutychen. Guelpherbyt. 1723. p. 112, ss. p. 365, ss.

4 Thus Mary is called *θεοτόκος* by Eusebius de vita Const. iii. 43. Cyrillus Hieros. Catech. x. p. 146. Athanasius Orat. iii. contra Arian. c. 14, 33. Didymus de Trin. i. 31, 94; ii. 4, 133, and Gregory of Nazianzum goes so far as to declare the man godless who will not employ this appellation. Heschyius, presbyter in Jerusalem († 343), calls David *θεοπάτωρ* (Photius Cod. 275). In many apocryphal writings James is called *ἀδελφόθεος* (see Thilo Acta Thomae in the Notit. upon p. x. ss. Cf. Photius Cod. 142).

5 Comp. § 84, note 21. See the fragments ap. Leontius contra Eutychianos et Nestorianos, in Canisii Thesaur. monum. eccl. ed. Basnage, i. 591).

6 See § 84, note 24. In Theodore's confession of faith (Act. Conc. Ephesini, Act. vi. ap. Mansi, t. iv. p. 1347, in Latin in Marius Mercator, see Walch Bibl. symb. vetus, p. 203, ss.): *Χρὴ δὲ καὶ περὶ τῆς οἰκονομίας, ἣν ὑπὲρ τῆς ἡμετέρας σωτηρίας ἐν τῇ κατὰ τὸν δεσπότην Χριστὸν οἰκονομίᾳ ὁ δεσπότης ἐξετέλεσε θεὸς, εἰδέναι, ὅτι ὁ δεσπότης θεὸς λόγος ἄνθρωπον εἴληφε τέλειον, ἐκ σπέρματος ὄντα Ἀβραὰμ καὶ Δαυὶδ,—ἐκ ψυχῆς τε νοερᾶς καὶ σαρκὸς συνεστῶτα ἀνθρωπίνης ὃν ἄνθρωπον ὄντα καθ' ἡμᾶς τὴν φύσιν, πνεύματος ἁγίου δυνάμει ἐν τῇ τῆς παρθένου μήτρᾳ διαπλασθέντα, γενόμενον ὑπὸ γυναικὸς καὶ γενόμενον ὑπὸ νόμον—ἀποῤῥήτως συνῆψεν ἑαυτῷ. θανάτου μὲν αὐτὸν κατὰ νόμον ἀνθρώπων πειρασθῆναι κατασκευάσας, ἐγείρας δὲ ἐκ νεκρῶν, καὶ ἀναγαγὼν εἰς οὐρανὸν, καὶ καθίσας ἐκ δεξιῶν τοῦ θεοῦ, ὅθεν δὴ ὑπεράνω πάσης ὑπάρχων ἀρχῆς, καὶ ἐξουσίας—τὴν παρὰ πάσης τῆς κτίσεως δέχεται προσκύνησιν, ὡς ἀχώριστον πρὸς τὴν θείαν φύσιν ἔχων τὴν συνάφειαν, ἀναφορᾷ θεοῦ καὶ ἐννοίᾳ πάσης αὐτῷ τῆς κτίσεως τὴν προσκύνησιν ἀπονεμούσης. Καὶ οὔτε δύο φαμὲν υἱοὺς, οὔτε δύο κυρίους. ἐπειδὴ εἷς θεὸς κατ' οὐσίαν ὁ θεὸς λόγος—ᾧπερ αὐτος συνημμένος τε καὶ μετέχων θεότητος κοινωνεῖ τῆς υἱοῦ προσηγορίας τε καὶ τιμῆς· καὶ κύριος κατ' οὐσίαν ὁ θεὸς λόγος, ᾧ συνημμένος οὗτος κοινωνεῖ τῆς τιμῆς.—Ἕνα τοίνυν τὸν κύριόν φαμεν καὶ κύριον Ἰησοῦν Χριστὸν, δι' οὗ τὰ πάντα ἐγένετο· πρωτοτύπως μὲν τὸν θεὸν λόγον νοοῦντες, τὸν κατ' οὐσίαν υἱὸν θεοῦ καὶ κύριον, συνεπινοοῦντες δὲ τὸ ληφθὲν, Ἰησοῦν τὸν ἀπὸ Ναζαρὲθ, ὃν ἔχρισεν ὁ θεὸς πνεύματι καὶ δυνάμει, ὡς ἐν τῇ πρὸς τὸν θεὸν λόγον συναφείᾳ υἱότητός τε μετέχοντα καὶ κυριότητος. Ὃς καὶ δεύτερος Ἀδὰμ κατὰ τὸν μακάριον καλεῖται Παῦλον, κ. τ. λ.* Comp. the fragments of this confession in the acts of the fifth general council at Constantinople, A.D. 553, ap. Mansi, ix. 203, and in Leontii contra Eutych. et Nestor. lib. iii. ap. Canisius-Basnage, i. 585. The latter fragments, published only in Latin by Canisius, were published in the Greek original by Majus Scriptt. vett. nova coll. vi. 300.

7 Münscher's Dogmengesch. iv. 32. Baur's Dreieinigkeit, i. 653.

8 Comp. especially the fragments in Theodoreti Dial. ii. (ed. Schulze, iv. 139).

9 Augustini Ep. 169, ad Evodium. § 7: Homo—in unitatem personae Verbi Dei—

the example of the two Gregorys, to avoid the two rocks of this doctrine, viz. the division into two persons, and the non-recognition of two natures; and thus the Gallic monk *Leporius*, in Africa (about 426), occasioned the prelude of the Nestorian controversy, while forced to retract assertions by which the unity of Christ's person appeared to be endangered.[10]

Nestorius, a presbyter of Antioch, by his elevation to the see of Constantinople, came into a difficult position (428), as far as he had both to contend against envious rivals, and was also obliged, by his extraction and position,[11] to undertake the task of completing the incipient restoration of Chrysostom's honor, which *Cyril*,[12] the nephew and worthy successor of Theophilus,[13]

coaptatus est, permanente tamen Verbo in sua natura incommutabiliter. § 8: Sicut in homine—anima et corpus una persona est, ita in Christo Verbum et homo una persona est. Et sicut homo, verbi gratia, philosophus non utique nisi secundum animam dicitur, nec ideo tamen absurde—dicimus philosophum caesum, philosophum mortuum—cum totum secundum carnem accidat, non secundum illud, quod est philosophus: ita Christus Deus—et tamen recte dicitur Deus crucifixus, cum hoc eum secundum carnem passum esse, non secundum illud, quo Dominus gloriae est, non habeatur incertum. Ep. 137 ad Volusianum, § 9: Ita inter Deum et homines mediator apparuit, ut in unitate personae copulans utramque naturam, et solita sublimaret insolitis, et insolita solitis temperaret. § 11: Ergo persona hominis mixtura est animae et corporis: persona autem Christi mixtura est Dei et hominis. Enchiridion ad Laur. c. 34, 36.

[10] Comp. epistola Episcop. Africae ad Episc. Galliae and Leporii libellus emendationis (prim. ed. Jac. Sirmond. Paris. 1530. Mansi, iv. 517). In the latter it is said: Tametsi Christum filium Dei tunc etiam natum de sancta Maria non negaremus, sicut ipsi recordamini; sed minime attendentes ad mysterium fidei, non ipsum Deum hominem natum, sed perfectum cum Deo natum hominem dicebamus; pertimescentes scilicet, ne divinitati conditionem adsignaremus humanam. His present faith: Confitemur dominum ac Deum nostrum Jesum Christum unicum filium Dei, qui ante saecula natus ex patre est, novissimo tempore de Spiritu sancto et Maria semper virgine factum hominem, Deum natum: et confitentes utramque substantiam carnis et Verbi, unum eundemque Deum atque hominem inseparabilem pia fidei credulitate suscepimus; et ex tempore susceptae carnis sic omnia dicimus, quae erant Dei, transisse in hominem, ut omnia, quae erant hominis, in Deum venirent; ut hac intelligentia verbum factum sit caro, non ut conversione aut mutabilitate aliqua coeperit esse quod non erat, sed ut potentia diviniae dispensationis Verbum patris, nunquam a patre discedens, homo proprie fieri dignaretur, incarnatusque sit unigenitus secreto illo mysterio, quod ipse novit. Nostrum namque est, credere, illius nosse. Ac sic, ut ipse Deus Verbum, totum suscipiens quod est hominis, homo sit, et adsumtus homo, totum accipiendo quod est Dei, aliud quam Deus esse non possit. Cf. Cassianus de Incarnatione Christi, i. 5.

[11] Thus, for instance, against Proclus and Philip, presbyters in Constantinople, both of whom had expectations of being raised to the episcopate. Socrates, vii. 26, 29.

[12] His writings: Commentaries of no value. Adv. Nestorium libb. 5. New controversial works against Nestorius in Maji Nova coll. viii. ii. 59. Contra Julianum lib. 10. Homiliae (among others paschales 30). Epistolae 61, etc. Opp. ed. Jo. Aubert. Paris. 1638. t. vii. fol.

[13] The admonition addressed to him by the pious Isidore, abbot of Pelusium, serves to characterize him (lib. i. Ep. 370): *Παῦσον τὰς ἔριδας· μὴ* [add *εἰς*] *οἰκείας ὕβρεως ἄμυναν ἣν παρὰ θνητῶν κεχρεώστησαι, ζῶσαν ἐκκλησίαν μεθόδευε, καὶ αἰώνιον αὐτῇ διχόνοιαν εν*

bishop of Alexandria († 444), considered derogatory to the honor of his see.[14] He soon gave an opportunity to the malevolent watcher of his proceedings by denying the propriety of calling Mary θεοτόκος.[15] A bitter but fruitless correspondence took place between them.[16] Cyril resolved to make a bishop of Con-

προσχήματι εὐσεβείας κατασκεύαζε. It may refer to that affair of Chrysostom, or to the commencement of the controversy with Nestorius.

14 The bishop of Constantinople, Atticus, about 420, had been obliged to introduce Chrysostom's name into the Diptychs, after the example of Antioch and at the pressing request of the people, and invited Cyril to do the same (Attici Ep. ad Cyrillum, in Cyrilli Op. v. iii. 201). The latter, however, refused to comply with the suggestion, desiring that the sentence pronounced on Chrysostom should be righteously maintained (l. c. p. 204). However, immediately after Nestor's elevation, new demonstrations of honor were added, Marcellinus Comes (about 534) in Chronico ad ann. 428 (Chronica medii aevi ed. Roesler, i. 262): Beatissimi Joannis Episcopi dudum malorum Episcoporum invidia exulati apud Comitatum (at the imperial court) coepit memoria celebrari mense Sept. d. xxvi. That Cyril continued to regard the condemnation of Chrysostom as a righteous measure is shown by his Epistola ad Acaciam (ap. Mansi, v. 832. Theodoreti Opp. ed. Schulze, v. 699).

15 Extracts from Nestor's discourses in the Greek original are given in the Actis Syn. Ephesin. b. Mansi, iv. 1197. Nestorii Sermones in a Latin version ap. Marius Mercator (ed. Baluz. p. 53, ss.). From the first address: θεοτόκος i. e., puerpera Dei s. genitrix Dei Maria, an autem ἀνθρωποτόκος i. e. hominis genitrix? Habet matrem Deus? Ergo excusabilis gentilitas matres diis subintroducens. Paulus ergo mendax de Christi deitate dicens ἀπάτωρ, ἀμήτωρ, ἄνευ γενεαλογίας (Hebr. vii. 3). Non peperit creatura increabilem, sed peperit hominem deitatis instrumentum. Non creavit Deum Verbum Spiritus sanctus—sed Deo verbo templum fabricatus est, quod habitaret, ex virgine (according to John ii. 21). Est, et non est mortuus incarnatus Deus, sed illum, in quo incarnatus est, suscitavit: inclinatus est elevare, quod ruerat, ipse vero non cecidit. Si jacentem elevare volueris, nonne continges corpus corpore, et te ipsum illi conjungendo elisum eriges, atque ita illi conjunctus ipse manes quod eras? Sic et illud incarnationis aestima sacramentum. Propter utentem illud indumentum, quod utitur, colo, propter absconditum adorans quod foris videtur: inseparabilis ab eo, qui oculis paret, est Deus. Divido naturas, sed conjungo reverentiam. Dominicam itaque incarnationem intremiscamus, τὴν θεοδόχον τῷ θεῷ λόγῳ συνθεολογῶμεν μορφὴν, i. e. susceptricem Dei formam una ac pari qua Deum Verbum deitatis ratione veneremur, tanquam divinitatis vere inseparabilis simulacrum, tanquam imaginem absconditi judicis. Duplicem confiteamur, et adoremus ut unum: duplum enim naturarum unum est propter unitatem. Sermo iii. (ib. p. 71): Ego natum et mortuum Deum et sepultum adorare non queo. Qui natus est et per partes incrementorum temporibus eguit, et mensibus legitimis portatus in ventre est, hic humanam habet naturam, sed Deo sane conjunctam. Aliud est autem dicere, quia nato de Maria conjunctus erat Deus ille, qui est Verbum patris, caet. Comp. the extracts in the Actis Syn. Eph. p. 1197: Ὅταν οὖν ἡ θεία γραφὴ μέλλῃ λέγειν ἢ γέννησιν τοῦ Χριστοῦ τὴν ἐκ Μαρίας τῆς παρθένου, ἢ θάνατον, οὐδαμοῦ φαίνεται τιθεῖσα τὸ θεὸς, ἀλλ' ἢ Χριστὸς, ἢ υἱὸς, ἢ κύριος. τὸ προελθεῖν τὸν θεὸν λόγον ἐκ τῆς χριστοτόκου παρθένου, παρὰ τῆς θείας ἐδιδάχθην γραφῆς· τὸ δὲ γεννηθῆναι θεὸν ἐξ αὐτῆς, οὐδαμοῦ ἐδιδάχθην.

16 Cyril proclaimed Nestor's erroneous doctrine on all sides. Thus he said to Acacius, bishop of Berhoea, that a zealous adherent of Nestorius had said in a church of Constantinople: εἴ τις λέγει θεοτόκον τὴν Μαρίαν, ἀνάθεμα ἔστω. The hoary Acacius sought in vain to exorcise the storm (Epist. ad Cyril. in Cyrilli Opp. v. iii. 63): it was the duty of bishops, καταστεῖλαι τὴν ἐξαγγελθεῖσαν φωνὴν, ὅπως μὴ πρόφασις δοθῇ τοῖς διασχίζειν καὶ διατέμνειν τὴν ἐκκλησίαν τοῦ θεοῦ ἑτοίμως ἔχουσι. Many in Constantinople συνηγορεῖν δοκοῦσι τῷ ῥηθέντι ῥητῷ, οὐκ ἐναντίως ἔχοντι κατὰ διάνοιαν τῇ ἀποστολικῇ πίστει, etc.

stantinople once more feel the superior weight of Alexandria. By misrepresenting the doctrines of Nestor to *Caelestine*, bishop of Rome,[17] he created the prejudice among the westerns, or at least strengthened it, that Nestorianism was only an offshoot of Pelagianism,[18] which at once sealed Nestor's fate in the west.

[17] Cyrilli Epist. ad Caelestium and Commonitorium datum Possidonio (his messenger) ap. Mansi, iv. 1012, ss. and p. 548, and ap. Coustant. In this last we read: Ἡ Νεστορίου πίστις, μᾶλλον δὲ κακοδοξία, ταύτην ἔχει τὴν δύναμιν. Φησὶν ὅτι ὁ θεὸς λόγος προεγνωκὼς, ὅτι ὁ ἐκ τῆς ἁγίας παρθένου γεννώμενος ἅγιος ἔσται καὶ μέγας, εἰς τοῦτ' ἐξελέξατο αὐτὸν, καὶ παρεσκεύασε μὲν γεννηθῆναι δίχα ἀνδρὸς ἐκ τῆς παρθένου, ἐχαρίσατο δὲ αὐτῷ τὸ καλεῖσθαι τοῖς αὐτοῦ ὀνόμασιν, καὶ ἤγειρεν αὐτόν. Ὥστε κἂν ἐνανθροπήσας λέγηται ὁ μονογενὴς τοῦ θεοῦ λόγος, ὅτι συνῆν ἀεὶ, ὡς ἀνθρώπῳ ἁγίῳ τῷ ἐκ τῆς παρθένου, διὰ τοῦτο λέγεται ἐνανθρωπῆσαι. Ὥσπερ δὲ συνῆν τοῖς προφήταις, οὕτω, φησί, καὶ τούτῳ κατὰ μείζονα συνάφειαν. Διὰ τοῦτο φεύγει πανταχοῦ τὸ λέγειν τὴν ἕνωσιν, ἀλλ' ὀνομάζει συνάφειαν, ὥσπερ ἐστιν ὃς ἔξωθεν, καὶ ὡς ἂν λέγῃ πρὸς 'Ιησοῦν, ὅτι καθ' ὡς ἦν μετὰ Μωϋσῆ, οὕτως ἔσομαι μετὰ σοῦ (Jos. i. 5). Κρύπτων δὲ τὴν ἀσέβειαν λέγει, ὅτι ἐκ μήτρας συνῆν αὐτῷ. Διὰ τοῦτο οὔτε θεὸν ἀληθινὸν αὐτὸς εἶναι λεγει, ἀλλ' ὡς ἐν εὐδοκίᾳ τοῦ θεοῦ κεκλημένον οὕτως· κἂν κύριος ὠνομάσθῃ, οὕτως πάλιν αὐτὸν βούλεται κύριον, ὡς τοῦ θεοῦ λόγου χαρισαμένου αὐτῷ τὸ καλεῖσθαι καὶ οὕτω. Μὴ φησὶν, ὅτι, ὅπερ λέγομεν, ἀποθανεῖν ὑπὲρ ἡμῶν τὸν υἱὸν τοῦ θεοῦ, καὶ ἀναστῆναι· ὁ ἄνθρωπος ἀπέθανε, καὶ ὁ ἄνθρωπος ἀνέστη, καὶ οὐδὲν τοῦτο πρὸς τὸν τοῦ θεοῦ λόγον.—καὶ ἐν τοῖς μυστηρίοις σῶμά ἐστιν ἀνθρώπου τὸ προκείμενον· ἡμεῖς δὲ πιστεύομεν, ὅτι τοῦ λόγου ἐστὶ σάρξ ζωοποιεῖν ἰσχύουσα διὰ τοῦτο, ὅτι τοῦ τὰ πάντα ζωοποιοῦντος λόγου γέγονε σὰρξ καὶ αἷμα. Nestor replies to this (Synodicon, c. vi. Mansi, v. 762): Ille vero (Cyrillus), omittens mihi per epistolam declarare, si quid ei tamquam blasphemum vel impium videbatur debere notari, convictionum terrore permotus, et adjutrices ob hoc perturbationes exquirens, ad Romanum Caelestinum convertitur, quippe ut ad simpliciorem quam qui posset vim dogmatum subtilius penetrare. Ed ad haec inveniens viri illius simplicitatem, circumfert pueriliter aures ejus illusionibus literarum, olim quidem nostra conscripta transmittens, quasi ad demonstrationem convictionem, quibus contradici non posset, tanquam ego Christum purum hominem definirem: qui certe legem inter ipsa meae ordinationis initia contra eos, qui Christum purum hominem dicunt, et contra reliquas haereses innovavi (Cod. Theod. xvi. v. 65). Excerptiones vero intertexens sermonum conscripta composuit, ne societatis compactione detegeretur illata calumnia, et quaedam quidem allocutionibus nostris adjiciens, aliquorum vero partes abrumpens, et illa contexens, quae a nobis de dominica humanatione sunt dicta, velut de puro ea homine dixerimus, etc.

[18] In the year 430 Cassian wrote, desired by the Romish archdeacon (subsequently bishop) Leo, his libb. vii. de Incarn. Christi adv. Nestorium (cf. Wiggers de Jo. Cassiano, p. 28, s.), although it is probable he was acquainted with Nestor's heresy merely from that Egyptian description of it. Lib. i. c. 3, he says of a new heresy which had broken out at Bellay (Beligarum urbe), to which, according to chap. iv., Leporius also belonged: Peculiare re proprium supradictae illius haereseos, quae ex Pelagiano vixisse, eo progressi sunt, ut assererent, homines, si velint, sine peccato esse posse. Consequens enim existimabant, ut si homo solitarius Jesus Christus sine peccato fuisset, omnes quoque homines sine Dei adjutorio esse possint, quicquid ille homo solitarius sine consortio Dei esse potuisset.—Unde advertit novus nunc jam, non novae haereseos auctor, qui Dominum Salvatoremque nostrum solitarium hominem natum esse contendit, idem se omnino dicere, quod Pelagianistae ante dixerunt: et consequens errori suo esse, ut qui utique sine peccato solitarium hominem Jesum Christum vixisse asserit, omnes quoque per se homines sine peccato posse esse blasphemet.—Nec dubium id est, re ipsa penitus declarante. Hinc enim illud est, quod intercessionibus suis Pelagianistarum querelas fovet, et scriptis suis causas illorum asserit, quod subtiliter his, vel ut verius dixerim, subdole patrocinatur, et consanguinae sibi improbitati improbo suffragatur affectu, etc. Comp. § 87, note 41.

In vain did Nestor represent to Caelestine that he rejected the expression θεοτόκος only in its false acceptation.[19] He was declared a heretic at synods held at *Rome* and *Alexandria* (430), and *Cyril* published twelve *anathemas*, in which he sought to establish the true doctrine of Christ's person against Nestor's heresy.[20] These anathemas were not only answered by Nestor

Hence Lib. v. c. 1, haeresim illam Pelagianae haereseos discipulam atque imitatricem; and c. 2, to Nestor: Ergo vides, Pelagianum te virus vomere, Pelagiano te spiritu sibilare. In like manner Prosperi epitaphium Nestoriani et Pelagiani:

Nestoriana lues successi Pelagianae,
Quae tamen est utero progenerata meo.
Infelix miserae genetrix et filia natae,
Prodivi ex ipso germine, quod peperi, etc.

[19] Nestorii Epist. iii. ad Caelestin. (ap. Mansi, iv. 1021, v. 725, ap. Coustant, among the Epp. Caelest. no. vi. vii. and xv.) From the Epist. 1: Unde et nos non modicam corruptionem orthodoxiae apud quosdam hic reperientes, et ira et lenitate circa aegros quotidie utimur. Est enim aegritudo non parva, sed affinis putredini Apollinaris et Arii. Dominicam enim in homine unionem ad cujusdam contemperationis confusionem passim commiscent: adeo ut et quidam apud nos clerici—aperte blasphement Deum Verbum Patri homousion, tamquam originis initium de Christotoco virgine sumsisset, et cum templo suo aedificatus esset, et consepultus. Carnem dicunt post resurrectionem suam non mansisse carnem, sed in naturam transiisse deitatis.—Si quis autem hoc nomen Theotocon propter natam humanitatem conjunctam Deo Verbo, non propter parientem proponet; dicimus quidem hoc vocabulum in ea, quae peperit, non esse conveniens (oportet enim veram matrem de eadem esse essentia ac ex se natum): ferri tamen potest hoc vocabulum—eo quod solum nominetur de virgine hoc verbum propter inseparabile templum Dei Verbi ex ipsa (natum), non quia ipsa mater sit Verbi Dei: nemo enim antiquiorem se parit. From Epist. iii.: Ego autem ad hanc quidem vocem, quae est θεοτόκος, nisi secundum Apollinaris et Arii furorem ad confusionem naturarum proferatur, volentibus dicere non resisto: nec tamen ambigo, quin haec vox θεοτόκος illi voci cedat, quae est χριστοτόκος, tamquam prolatae ab Angelis et Evangeliis.—Placuit, vero, Deo adjuvante etiam synodum inexcusabiliter totius orbis terrarum indicere propter inquisitionem aliarum rerum ecclesiasticarum: nam dubitatione verborum non aestimo habituram inquisitionem difficultates, nec impedimentum esse ad tractatum divinitatis Domini Christi.

[20] With the synodical letter relating to the same in Cyrilli Opp. v. iii. 67. Mansi, iv. 1067. Baumgarten's theol. Streitigk. ii. 770. Cf. Salig de Eutychianismo ante Eutychen, p. 324: i. *Εἴ τις οὐχ ὁμολογεῖ θεὸν εἶναι κατὰ ἀλήθειαν τὸν Ἐμμανουὴλ, καὶ διὰ τοῦτο θεοτόκον τὴν ἁγίαν παρθένον· γεγέννηκε γὰρ σαρκικῶς σάρκα γεγονότα τὸν ἐκ θεοῦ λόγον· ἀνάθεμα ἔστω.* ii. *Εἴ τις οὐχ ὁμολογεῖ, σαρκὶ καθ' ὑπόστασιν ἡνῶσθαι τὸν ἐκ θεοῦ πατρὸς λόγον, ἕνα τε εἶναι* Χριστὸν *μετὰ τῆς ἰδίας σαρκὸς, τὸν αὐτὸν δηλονότι θεόν τε ὁμοῦ καὶ ἄνθρωπον, ἀ. ἔ.* iii. *Εἴ τις ἐπὶ τοῦ ἑνὸς* Χριστοῦ *διαιρεῖ τὰς ὑποστάσεις μετὰ τὴν ἕνωσιν, μόνῃ συνάπτων αὐτὰς συναφείᾳ τῇ κατὰ τὴν ἀξίαν, ἤγουν αὐθεντίαν ἢ δυναστείαν, καὶ οὐχὶ δὴ μᾶλλον συνόδῳ τῇ καθ' ἕνωσιν φυσικὴν, ἀ. ἔ.* iv. *Εἴ τις προσώποις δυσὶν, ἤγουν ὑποστάσεσι, τάς τε ἐν τοῖς εὐαγγελικοῖς καὶ ἀποστολικοῖς συγγράμμασι διανέμει φωνὰς, ἢ ἐπὶ* Χριστῷ *παρὰ τῶν ἁγίων λεγομένας, ἢ παρ' αὐτοῦ περὶ ἑαυτοῦ, καὶ τὰς μὲν ὡς ἀνθρώπῳ παρὰ τὸν ἐκ θεοῦ λόγον ἰδικῶς νοουμένῳ προσάπτει, τὰς δὲ ὡς θεοπρεπεῖς μόνῳ τῷ ἐκ θεοῦ πατρὸς λόγῳ, ἀ. ἔ.* v. *Εἴ τις τολμᾷ λεγειν θεοφόρον ἄνθρωπον τὸν* Χριστὸν, *καὶ οὐχὶ δὴ μᾶλλον θεὸν εἶναι κατὰ ἀλήθειαν, ὡς υἱὸν ἕνα καὶ φύσει, καθὸ γέγονε σὰρξ ὁ λόγος, καὶ κεκοινώνηκε παραπλησίως ἡμῖν αἵματος καὶ σαρκὸς, ἀ. ἔ.* vi. *Εἴ τις τολμᾷ λέγειν θεὸν ἢ δεσπότην εἶναι τοῦ* Χριστοῦ *τὸν ἐκ θεοῦ πατρὸς λόγον, καὶ οὐχὶ δὴ μᾶλλον τὸν αὐτὸν ὁμολογεῖ θεὸν ὁμοῦ τε καὶ ἄνθρωπον, ὡς γεγονότος σαρκὸς τοῦ*

in as many anti-anathemas,[21] but they also excited great commotion among the Syrian bishops. Nestor had explained himself satisfactorily to *John*, bishop of Antioch, concerning the admissibility of the expression *θεοτόκος*: while Cyril seemed entirely to do away with the distinction of natures in Christ.

λόγου κατὰ τὰς γραφὰς, ἀ. ἔ. vii. *Εἴ τίς φησιν, ὡς ἄνθρωπον ἐνεργῆσθαι παρὰ τοῦ θεοῦ λόγου τὸν Ἰησοῦν, καὶ τὴν τοῦ μονογενοῦς εὐδοξίαν περιῆφθαι, ὡς ἕτερον παρ' αὐτὸν ὑπάρχοντα, ἀ. ἔ.* viii. *Εἴ τις τολμᾷ λέγειν, τὸν ἀναληφθέντα ἄνθρωπον συμπροσκυνεῖσθαι δεῖν τῷ θεῷ, λόγῳ, καὶ συνδοξάζεσθαι καὶ συγχρηματίζειν θεὸν, ὡς ἕτερον ἑτέρῳ (τὸ γὰρ "Σύν" ἀεὶ προστιθέμενον, τοῦτο νοεῖν ἀναγκάζει) καὶ οὐχὶ δὴ μᾶλλον μιᾷ προσκυνήσει τιμᾷ τὸν Ἐμμανουὴλ, καὶ μίαν αὐτῷ τὴν δοξολογίαν ἀναπέμπει, καθὸ γέγονε σὰρξ ὁ λόγος, ἀ. ἔ.* ix. *Εἴ τις φησι, τὸν ἕνα κύριον Ἰησοῦν Χριστὸν δεδοξάσθαι παρὰ τοῦ πνεύματος, ὡς ἀλλοτρίᾳ δυνάμει τῇ δι' αὐτοῦ χρώμενον, καὶ παρ' αὐτοῦ λαβόντα τὸ ἐνεργεῖν δύνασθαι κατὰ πνευμάτων ἀκαθάρτων, καὶ τὸ πληροῦν εἰς ἀνθρώπους τὰς θεοσημείας, καὶ οὐχὶ δὴ μᾶλλον ἴδιον αὐτοῦ τὸ πνεῦμά φησι, δι' οὗ καὶ ἐνήργησε τὰς θεοσημείας, ἀ. ἔ.* x. *Ἀρχιερέα καὶ ἀπόστολον τῆς ὁμολογίας ἡμῶν γεγεννῆσθαι Χριστὸν ἡ θεία λέγει γραφὴ, προσκεκομικέναι τε ὑπὲρ ἡμῶν ἑαυτὸν εἰς ὀσμὴν εὐωδίας τῷ θεῷ καὶ πατρὶ. εἴ τις τοίνυν ἀρχιερέα καὶ ἀπόστολον ἡμῶν γεγεννῆσθαί φησιν οὐκ αὐτὸν τὸν ἐκ θεοῦ λόγον, ὅτε γένονε σὰρξ καὶ καθ' ἡμᾶς ἄνθρωπος, ἀλλ' ὡς ἕτερον παρ' αὐτὸν ἰδικῶς ἄνθρωπον ἐκ γυναικός· ἢ εἴ τις λέγει, καὶ ὑπὲρ ἑαυτοῦ προσενεγκεῖν αὐτὸν τὴν προσφορὰν, καὶ οὐχὶ δὴ μᾶλλον ὑπὲρ μόνων ἡμῶν· οὐ γὰρ ἂν ἐδεήθη προσφορᾶς ὁ μὴ εἰδὼς ἁμαρτίαν· ἀ. ἔ.* xi. *Εἴ τις οὐχ ὁμολογεῖ τὴν τοῦ κυρίου σάρκα ζωοποιὸν εἶναι, καὶ ἰδίαν αὐτοῦ τοῦ ἐκ θεοῦ πατρὸς λόγου, ἀλλ' ὡς ἑτέρου τινὸς παρ' αὐτὸν, συνημμένου μὲν αὐτῷ κατὰ τὴν ἀξίαν, ἤγουν ὡς μόνην θείαν ἐνοίκησιν ἐσχηκότος· καὶ οὐχὶ δὴ μᾶλλον ζωοποιὸν, ὡς ἔφημεν, ὅτι γέγονεν ἰδία τοῦ λόγου τοῦ τὰ πάντα ζωογονεῖν ἰσχύοντος, ἀ. ἔ.* xii. *Εἴ τις οὐχ ὁμολογεῖ τὸν τοῦ θεοῦ λόγον παθόντα σαρκὶ, καὶ ἐσταυρωμένον σαρκὶ, καὶ θανάτου γευσάμενον σαρκὶ, γεγονότα τε πρωτότοκον ἐκ τῶν νεκρῶν, καθὸ ζωή τέ ἐστι καὶ ζωοποιὸς ὡς θεὸς, ἀ. ἔ.* Cyril's own doctrine is most apparent from his second letter to Succensus (Opp. v. iii. 141). The Logos became a perfect man, but continued notwithstanding unaltered, one and the same. The two natures must be distinguished only *κατὰ μόνην τὴν θεωρίαν.* P. 145: *Ἔστω δὲ ἡμῖν εἰς παράδειγμα ὁ καθ' ἡμᾶς ἄνθρωπος. δύο μὲν γὰρ ἐπ' αὐτοῦ νοοῦμεν τὰς φύσεις, μίαν μὲν τῆς ψυχῆς, ἑτέραν δὲ τοῦ σώματος· ἀλλ' ἐν ψιλαῖς διελόντες ἐννοίαις—οὐκ ἀνὰ μέρος τίθεμεν τὰς φύσεις—ἀλλ' ἑνὸς εἶναι νοοῦμεν· ὥστε τὰς δύο μηκέτι μὲν εἶναι δύο, δι' ἀμφοῖν δὲ τὸ ἓν ἀποτελεῖσθαι ζῶον. Οὐκοῦν, κἂν εἰ λέγοιεν ἀνθρωπότητος φύσιν καὶ θεότητος ἐπὶ τοῦ Ἐμμανουὴλ, ἀλλ' ἡ ἀνθρωπότης γέγονεν ἰδία τοῦ λόγου, καὶ εἷς υἱὸς νοεῖται σὺν αὐτῇ.*

21 Ap. Marius Mercator, ed. Baluz. p. 142, ss. Baumgarten's theol. Streitigk. ii. 774. I. Si quis eum, qui est Emmanuel, Deum verbum esse dixerit, et non potius nobiscum Deum, hoc est, inhabitasse eam quae secundum nos est naturam, per id quod unitus est massae nostrae, quam de Maria virgine suscepit: matrem etiam Dei verbi, et non potius ejus, qui Emmanuel est, sanctam virginem nuncupaverit, ipsumque Deum verbum in carnem versum esse, quam accepit ad ostentationem Deitatis suae, ut habitu inveniretur ut homo, anath. sit. II. Si quis in verbi Dei conjunctione, quae ad carnem facta est, de loco in locum mutationem divinae essentiae dixerit esse factam; ejusque divinae naturae carnem capacem dixerit, ac partialiter unitam carni: aut iterum in infinitum incircumscriptae naturae coextenderit carnem ad capiendum Deum, eandemque ipsam naturam et Deum dicat et hominem, anath. sit. IV. Si quis eas voces, quae tam in evangelicis quam in epistolis apostolicis de Christo, qui est ex utraque natura, scriptae sunt, accipiat tanquam de una natura: ipsique Dei verbo tentat passiones tribuere, tam secundum carnem, quam etiam deitatem, anath. sit. VI. Si quis post incarnationem Deum verbum alterum quempiam praeter Christum nominaverit; servi sane formam initium non habere a Deo Verbo, et increatam, ut ipse est, dicere tentaverit, et non magis ab ipso creatam confiteatur, tamquam a naturali domino et creatore et Deo, quam et suscitare propria virtute promisit

Hence Cyril's anathemas were generally rejected as erroneous in the east. *Andrew*, bishop of Samosata, and *Theodoret*, bishop of Cyprus († 457),[22] wrote refutations of them.[23]

Under these circumstances, Theodosius II. called *a general council* at *Ephesus* (431).[24] Cyril hastened hither with a numerous band of adherents. The bold remonstrances of the honest

Solvite, dicens, templum hoc, et in triduo suscitabo illud (Jo. ii. 19), anath. sit. VIII. Si quis servi formam pro se ipso, hoc est secundum propriae naturae rationem, colendam esse dixerit, et rerum omnium dominam: et non potius per societatem, qua beatae et ex se naturaliter dominicae unigeniti naturae conjuncta est, veneratur; anath. sit. XI. Si quis unitam carnem verbo Dei ex naturae propriae possibilitate vivificatricem esse dixerit; ipso Domino et Deo pronunciante: Spiritus est, qui vivificat, caro nihil prodest (Jo. vi. 64); anath. sit. Spiritus est Deus, a Domino pronunciatum est. Si quis ergo Deum Verbum carnaliter secundum substantiam carnem factum esse dicat (hoc autem modo et specialiter custodite: maxime Domino Christo post resurrectionem suam discipulis suis dicente: Palpate et videte, quia spiritus ossa et carnem non habet, sicut me videtis habere, Luc. xxiv. 39); anath. sit.

[22] His works: valuable commentaries, especially on the Epistles of Paul (J. F. Chr. Richter de Theodoreto Epist. Paulin. interprete comm. Lips. 1822. 8). Historical writings, Hist. Eccl. libb. 5. *Φιλόθεος ἱστορία* s. historia religiosa. Haereticarum fabularum libb. 5. Polemic: *Ἐρανιστὴς ἤτοι Πολύμορφος* libb. iv. *Ἑλληνικῶν θεραπευτικὴ παθημάτων* disputt. xii. (ad codd. MSS. rec. Thom. Gaisford. Oxon. 1839. 8). Epistles—Opp. ed. Jac. Sirmond. Paris. 1642. voll. iv. fol. v. s. auctarium add. Joh. Garnier. Paris. 1684. Ed. J. L. Schulze et J. A. Noesselt. Halae. 1769–1774. t. v. 8.

[23] That of Andrew in Latin ap. Mercator, p. 220, ss. Greek fragments in Cyrilli Apologeticus.—That of Theodoret see in his works, Opp. ed. Schulze, t. v. p. 1, ss. In the latter we read: Ad. i. *Ἡμεῖς δὲ—οὐ σάρκα φύσει γεγονέναι, οὐδὲ εἰς σάρκα μεταβληθῆναι τὸν θεὸν λόγον φαμέν.—ἀλλ' ἀνέλαβε σάρκα καὶ ἐσκήνωσεν ἐν ἡμῖν,—οὐκ αὐτὸς φύσει ἐκ τῆς παρθένου γεγέννηται συλληφθεὶς, καὶ διαπλασθεὶς,—ἀλλ' ἑαυτῷ ναὸν ἐν τῇ παρθενικῇ γαστρὶ διαπλάσας, συνῆν τῷ πλασθέντι καὶ γεννηθέντι· οὗ χάρι καὶ τὴν ἁγίαν ἐκείνην παρθένον θεοτόκον προσαγορεύομεν, οὐχ ὡς θεὸν φύσει γεννήσασαν, ἀλλ' ὡς ἄνθρωπον, τῷ διαπλάσαντι αὐτὸν, ἡνωμένον θεῷ.* Ad. ii.—*Τὴν καθ' ὑπόστασιν ἕνωσιν παντάπασιν ἀγνοοῦμεν, ὡς ξένην.—εἰ δὲ τοῦτο βούλεται λέγειν διὰ τῆς καθ' ὑπόστασιν ἑνώσεως ὁ ταῦτα γεννήσας, ὡς κρᾶσις σαρκὸς καὶ θεότητος γέγονεν, ἀντεροῦμεν σὺν πάσῃ προθυμίᾳ καὶ τὴν βλασφημίαν ἐλέγξομεν.* Ad. iii. *Συνάφεια καὶ σύνοδος οὐδενὶ διαφέρουσιν.—ἓν μὲν πρόσωπον καὶ ἕνα υἱὸν καὶ Χριστὸν ὁμολογεῖν εὐσεβές· δύο δὲ τὰς ἑνωθείσας ὑποστάσεις, εἴτουν φύσεις λέγειν, οὐκ ἄτοπον, ἀλλὰ κατ' αἰτίαν ἀκόλουθον.* Ad. iv.—*Τὰ μὲν θεοπρεπῶς εἰρημένα καὶ πεπραγμένα τῷ θεῷ λόγῳ προσάψομεν· τὰ δὲ ταπεινῶς εἰρημένα καὶ πεπραγμένα δούλου μορφῇ προσαρμόσομεν.* Ad. v. *Τὸν θεοφόρον ἄνθρωπον, ὡς πολλοῖς τῶν ἁγίων πατέρων εἰρημένον, οὐ παραιτούμεθα·—καλοῦμεν δὲ θεοφόρον ἄνθρωπον, οὐχ ὡς μερικήν τινα θείαν χάριν δεξάμενον, ἀλλ' ὡς πᾶσαν ἡνωμένην ἔχοντα τοῦ υἱοῦ τὴν θεότητα.* Ad. xii. *Ἔπαθε ἡ τοῦ δούλου μορφὴ, συνούσης αὐτῇ δηλονότι τῆς τοῦ θεοῦ μορφῆς,—οἰκειουμένης δὲ διὰ τὴν ἕνωσιν τὰ παθήματα.* From Cyril's Apology in answer to Theodoret. Ad. i.—*Εἰ λέγοιμεν σάρκα γενέσθαι τὸν λόγον, οὐ σύγχυσιν, οὐ φυρμὸν, οὐ τροπὴν, οὐκ ἀλλοίωσιν συμβῆναι περὶ αὐτὸν φαμέν· ἡνῶσθαι δὲ μᾶλλον ἀφράστως καὶ ἀποῤῥήτως σώματι ψυχὴν ἔχοντι νοεράν.* Ad. iii.—*Ἄνθρωπον συνῆφθαι θεῷ σχετικῶς διατείνοντα, κατὰ μόνην τὴν ἀξίαν, ἤγουν αὐθεντίαν, καὶ κατὰ τὴν τῆς υἱότητος ὁμωνυμίαν.—κατὰ φύσιν, τοῦτ' ἔστιν, οὐ σχετικῶς, ἀλλὰ κατὰ ἀλήθειαν.* Theodoret wrote besides, Pentalogium s. libb. v. Incarnationi Verbi adv. Cyrillum et Patres Conc. Ephesini (Fragments ap. Mercator).

[24] On the history of it, see Salig de Eutychianismo ante Eutychen, p. 234. Fuchs Bibliothek. d. Kirchenversamml. des 4ten u. 5ten Jahrh. iv. 1.

Isidore, abbot of Pelusium († 440),[25] had no effect upon him;[26] but listening only to the promptings of revenge he proceeded to condemn Nestor without waiting for the arrival of the eastern bishops.[27] When they arrived, however, they assembled with *John* at their head, and deposed Cyril and his principal assistant, *Memnon*, bishop of *Ephesus*. The weak Theodosius had been incensed at Cyril till now, but the latter not only contrived to bring over to his side the impetuous monks at Constantinople,[28] but also to make many friends at court by bribes and other artifices. The emperor at first confirmed the three depositions; but was afterward prevailed on to re-instate Cyril and Memnon in their offices. Nestor, on the other hand, was obliged to withdraw into his former cloister at Antioch.

The consequence of these measures was a division between the east and the other provinces, especially Egypt. The Orientals, however, were not sufficiently united to withstand their opponents, backed as the latter were by the court. *Rabulas*, bishop of Edessa, went over to Cyril's party, and even began to show

[25] Isid. Pelus. Epistolarum libb. iv. ed. Conr. Rittershusius. Heidelb. 1605. fol. Epistt. hactenus ineditae ed. ab A. Schotto. Antv. 1623. 8, and Francof. 1629. fol. Editions of all together: Isid. Pelus. de Interpretatione divinae scripturae epistolarum libb. v. Paris. 1638 (incorrect). Venet. 1745. fol. Cf. H. A. Niemeyer de Isidori Pelusiotae vita, scriptis et doctrina. Halae. 1825. 8. Thirteen letters in an old Latin version have been put into the Synodicon, as bearing on this controversy (prim. ed. Mansi, v. p. 758). See the originals, lib. i. Ep. 25, 102, 310, 311, 323, 324, 370, 404, 405, 419; iv. 166, 211; v. 268.

[26] Lib. i. Ep. 310 (Latin in the Synodicon, l. c.): *Προσπάθεια μὲν οὐκ ὀξυδορκεῖ, ἀντιπάθεια δὲ ὅλως οὐχ ὁρᾷ. εἰ τοίνυν ἑκατέρας λήμης βούλει καθαρεῦσαι, μὴ βιαίας ἀποφάσεις ἐκβίβαζε, ἀλλὰ κρίσει δικαίᾳ τὰς αἰτίας ἐπίτρεψον. Πολλοὶ γάρ σε κωμῳδοῦσι τῶν συνειλεγμένων εἰς Ἔφεσον, ὡς οἰκείαν ἀμυνόμενον ἔχθραν, ἀλλ' οὐ τὰ Ἰησοῦ Χριστοῦ ὀρθοδόξως ζητοῦντα. ἀδελφιδοῦς ἐστί, φασι, Θεοφίλου, μιμούμενος ἐκείνου τὴν γνώμην· ὥσπερ γὰρ ἐκεῖνος μανίαν σαφῆ κατεσκέδασε τοῦ θεοφόρου καὶ θεοφιλοῦς Ἰωάννου, οὕτως ἐπιθυμεῖ καυχήσασθαι καὶ οὗτος, εἰ καὶ πολὺ τῶν κρινομένων ἐστὶ τὸ διάφορον.* Cf. lib. i. Ep. 370. Concerning Isidore's own doctrine see Niemeyer, l. c. p. 173, ss. 22, s. Vater in the kirchenhist. Archiv. 1825. S. 248, ff.

[27] The sentence may be seen in Mansi, iv. 1212: *Ὁ βλασφημηθεὶς τοίνυν παρ' αὐτοῦ κύριος ἡμῶν Ἰησους Χριστὸς ὥρισε διὰ τῆς παρούσης ἁγιωτάτης συνόδου, ἀλλότριον εἶναι τὸν αὐτὸν Νεστόριον τοῦ ἐπισκοπικοῦ ἀξιώματος, καὶ παντὸς συλλόγου ἱερατικοῦ.* The Egyptian party (comp. the decisions p. 1139, ss.) thought they had in their favor the express words of the Nicene creed, namely, *θεὸν—ἐνανθρωπήσαντα, παθόντα*, etc. Subsequently, the adherents of Caelestius and Pelagius were often condemned with those of Nestorius, without express notification of their doctrine. See Mansi, iv. 1320, 1328, 1334, 1338, 1472, 1474.

[28] From the epistle of Epiphanius, archdeacon of Cyril, to Maximinian the new bishop of Constantinople (Mansi, v. 987. Theodoreti Opp. ed. Schulze, v. 869), it is clear that many presents were sent from Alexandria (*εὐλογίαι*) to the empress, her ladies, and influential courtiers. Clerici, qui hic sunt, contristantur, quod Ecclesia Alexandrina nudata sit hujus causa turbelae, et debet praeter illa, quae hinc transmissa sunt, Ammonio Comiti auri libras mille quingentas.

his zeal by also attacking the writings of *Theodore of Mopsuestia*, so much valued in the east, as the proper sources of Nestor's error. Even *John* made peace with Cyril (433). The latter accommodated himself so far as to subscribe the Antiochene confession of faith;[29] the former sacrificed his friend Nestor. The

[29] See Mansi, v. 305 (it was the creed put forth by Theodoret in Ephesus, and presented to the emperor by the Oriental party. Synodicon, c. 17 ap. Mansi, v. 783, comp. Alexandri Epist. ad Theodoret. in Synod. c. 96, ibid. p. 878): *'Ομολογοῦμεν τοιγαροῦν τὸν κύριον ἡμῶν 'Ιησουν Χριστὸν, τὸν υἱὸν τοῦ θεοῦ, τὸν μονογενῆ, θεὸν τέλειον καὶ ἄνθρωπον τέλειον ἐκ ψυχῆς λογικῆς καὶ σώματος· πρὸ αἰώνων μὲν ἐκ τοῦ πατρὸς γεννηθέντα κατὰ τὴν θεότητα, ἐπ' ἐσχάτων δὲ τῶν ἡμερῶν τὸν αὐτὸν δι' ἡμᾶς, καὶ διὰ τὴν ἡμετέραν σωτηρίαν ἐκ Μαρίας τῆς παρθένου κατὰ τὴν ἀνθρωπότητα· ὁμοούσιον τῷ πατρὶ τὸν αὐτὸν κατὰ τὴν θεότητα, καὶ ὁμοούσιον ἡμὶν κατὰ τὴν ἀνθρωπότητα· δύο γὰρ φύσεων ἕνωσις γέγονε· διὸ ἕνα Χριστὸν, ἕνα υἱὸν, ἕνα κύριον ὁμολογοῦμεν. Κατὰ ταύτην τὴν τῆς ἀσυγχύτου ἐνώσεως ἔννοιαν ὁμολογοῦμεν τὴν ἁγίαν παρθένον θεοτόκον, διὰ τὸ τὸν θεὸν λόγον σαρκωθῆναι καὶ ἐνανθρωπῆσαι, καὶ ἐξ αὐτῆς τῆς συλλήψεως ἐνῶσαι ἑαυτῷ τὸν ἐξ αὐτῆς ληφθέντα ναόν· τὰς δὲ εὐαγγελικὰς καὶ ἀποστολικὰς περὶ τοῦ κυρίου φωνὰς, ἴσμεν τοὺς θεολόγους ἄνδρας, τὰς μὲν κοινοποιοῦντας, ὡς ἐφ' ἑνὸς προσώπου, τὰς δὲ διαιροῦντας, ὡς ἐπὶ δύο φύσεων· καὶ τὰς μὲν θεοπρεπεῖς κατὰ τὴν θεότητα τοῦ Χριστοῦ, τὰς δὲ ταπεινὰς κατὰ τὴν ἀνθρωπότητα αὐτοῦ παραδιδόντας.* Many Egyptians were dissatisfied with this formula. Liberatus Breviar. c. 8: Culpaverunt Cyrillum, cur susceperit ab orientalibus Episcopis duarum confessionem naturarum, quod Nestorius dixit et docuit. To this must be referred Isidori lib. i. Ep. 324, ad Cyrillum, because the latter has been taken into the Synodicon (Mansi, v. 759): *Χρή σε, θαυμάσιε, ἄτρεπτον μένειν ἀεὶ, οὔτε φόβῳ προδιδόντα τὰ οὐράνια, οὔτε σαυτῷ ἐναντίον φαινόμενον. εἰ γὰρ τὰ νῦν γεγραμμένα σοι τοῖς προτέροις ἀντεξετάσειας, ἢ κολακείας φανήσῃ ὑπεύθυνος, εὐχερείας ἢ διάκονος, κενῆς μὲν δόξης ἡττώμενος, τῶν μεγάλων δὲ ἁγίων ἀθλητῶν τούς ἀγῶνας οὐ μιμησάμενος, οἳ τὸν ἅπαντα βίον ἐπ' ἀλλοτρίας κακουχεῖσθαι ὑπέμειναν, ἢ κακόδοξον φρόνημα κἂν μέχρις ὤτων εἰσδέξασθαι.* Against such charges Cyril defends himself at greatest length in the Epist. ad Acacium Episc. Melitenae (Opp. v. iii. 105. Mansi, v. 310: besides in Epist. ad Eulogium Presb. Constantinop. (Opp. v. iii. 123), ad Rufum Ep. Thessalonic. and ad Maximum Diac. Antioch. (in Maji Scriptt. vet. nova coll. viii. ii. 138). In the two latter he confesses he had accommodated himself to the prevailing notions. The orientals accordingly perceived in the adoption of that confession of faith a retraction on the part of Cyril. See Ibae Epist. ad Marin. in Actis Conc. Chalc. act. x. Mansi, vii. 247, especially Theodoreti Ep. ad Joannem Episc. Antioch, A.D. 433 (Ep. 171 in Theod. Opp. ed. Schulze, iv. 1354, a complete copy in Latin in Synodico, l. c. v. 747): *'Εν κοινῷ ἀναγνόντες τὰ Αἰγύπτια γράμματα, καὶ ἐξετάσαντες αὐτῶν ἀκριβῶς τὴν διάνοιαν, εὕρομεν σύμφωνα τοῖς εἰρημένοις (ὑφ' ἡμῶν) τὰ ἐκεῖθεν ἀπεσταλμένα, καὶ ἄντικρυς ἐναντία τοῖς δώδεκα κεφαλαίοις, οἷς μέχρι τοῦ παρόντος, ὡς ἀλλοτρίοις τῆς εὐσεβείας, πολεμοῦντες διετελέσαμεν. 'Εκεῖνα μὲν γὰρ εἶχε, σαρκικῶς σάρκα γεγονότα τὸν ἐκ Θεοῦ Λόγον, κ. τ. λ. ἀπηγόρευσε δὲ καὶ τῶν περὶ τοῦ Κυρίου φωνῶν τὴν διαίρεσιν. Τὰ δὲ νῦν ἀπεσταλμένα τῇ εὐαγγελικῇ εὐγενείᾳ καλλύνεται· Θεὸς γὰρ τέλειος καὶ ἄνθρωπος τέλειος ὁ Κύριος ἡμῶν 'Ι. Χρ. ἀναδείκνυται ἐν αὐτοῖς· καὶ φύσεις δύο, καὶ τούτων διαφορὰ, καὶ ἕνωσις ἀσυγχυτος—καὶ τῶν φύσεων τὰς ἰδιότητας ἀκρατῶς διαφυλάξασα· καὶ ἀπαθὴς μὲν ὁ Θεὸς Λόγος, καὶ ἄτρεπτος, παθητὸς δὲ ὁ ναός. κ. τ. λ.* Altera vero diffamata sunt quaedam, quae nos nimium turbaverunt. Dicunt enim, quod is, qui hic poenitudine usus sit, non solum dejectionis s. damnationis subscriptionem a vestra Sanctitate nitatur exigere, sed anathematismum quoque doctrinae sanctissimi et Deo amicissimi episcopi Nestorii. Quodsi id verum est—simile aliquid facit, tanquam si quis vix tandem perductus ad consubstantialem Deo et Patri Filium confitendum, mox iterum anathemate feriat eos, qui hoc a principio sapuerunt atque docuerunt, etc. Cyril himself says, Cyrillus ad Acacium, ap. Mansi, v. 314, 315, that even the Nestorians considered that confession as consonant with their

unfortunate Nestor, who had never asserted aught inconsistent with that very confession of faith now signed by Cyril, was first banished to Oasis; then in Thebais was dragged from one place of banishment to another, till his death about 440.[30] To justify his condemnation, his contemporaries were obliged to misrepresent his doctrinal system,[31] and it was so handed down to posterity, till men of more enlarged and clearer views recognized the truth.[32]

The Syrian bishops were now compelled to assent to the peace concluded between John and Cyril. The greatest opposition was made by *the theological school in Edessa*, which had long been the place of education for the Persian clergy, when Rabulas prohibited the writings of Diodorus and Theodore. Several of the teachers were interdicted, and betook themselves to Persia. One of them, *Barsumas* (Barsauma) became bishop of Nisibis (435–489) and confirmed the Persian Christians in their attachment

faith. It is certain that Alexander, bishop of Hierapolis the most violent opponent of Cyril, was also against that confession, because it had adopted the expression θεοτόκος (Ep. ad Theodoret. ap. Mansi, v. 878. Schulze, v. 750: Quia hoc est quasi arx totius ejus haereseos); but he does not reject it absolutely, but merely expresses his disapprobation of the doctrinal use of it under existing circumstances (Mansi, v. 875. Schulze, v. 746: post corruptionem totius orbis, et ex quo praedicari nunc coepit passibilis Deus ab impiis Cyrilli capitulis, dogmatice poni solam vocem—theotocon, absque illa—anthropotocon, nihil est aliud, nisi ea quae Cyrilli sunt praedicari). Even the later Monophysites accused Cyril of apostatizing from his doctrine. See Timothei Aeluri fragm. ap. Mansi, vii. 841, and Maji Coll. nov. vii. i. 1, 138, which fragment, if not belonging to Timothy (as Walch Ketzerhist. vi. 682, shows), proceeded at least from a Monophysite. Hence when Vater (kirchenhist. Archiv. 1825. ii. 211) and Baur (Dreieinigkeit, i. 786) deny the inconsistency of Cyril, they have, at least, the universal voice of that period against them.

30 See Nestor's own account, ap. Evagrius, i. 7.

31 Ex. gr. Cassianus above, note 18. Leo in Epist. ad Leonem Aug. (Quesn. 135, Baller. 165): Anathematizetur ergo Nestorius, qui beatam virginem Mariam non Dei, sed hominis tantummodo credidit genitricem, ut aliam personam carnis faceret, aliam deitatis: nec unum Christum in Verbo Dei et carne sentiret, sed separatim atque sejunctim alterum filium Dei, alterum hominis praedicaret. Still more misrepresented is the appendix to Augustin. de Haeresibus, c. 91: Nestoriani a Nestorio episcopo, qui contra catholicam fidem dogmatizare ausus est, Dominum nostrum J. C. hominem tantum: nec id, quod mediator Dei et hominum effectum est, in utero virginis de Spiritu S. fuisse conceptum, sed postea Deum homini fuisse permixtum, etc. Such were the sources from which the middle ages drew their ideas of Nestorianism.

32 First Luther (respecting councils in Walch's Ausg. Th. xvi. S. 2718). After him many others (P. Bayle, S. and J. Basnage, Christ. Kortholt, also Rich. Simon, L. Ell. du Pin, L. Maraccius, and others) reckoned it to be a mere dispute of words. So also P. E. Jablonski de Nestorianismo. Berol. 1724. 8, and Chr. A. Salig de Eutychianismo ante Eutychen. Guelpherb. 1723. 4. p. 284, 307. Controversial writings against Jablonski by P. Berger, J. Wessel, and especially C. G. Hoffmann, may be seen in Walchii Bibl. theol. iii. 773. Comp. J. Vogt de Recentissimis Nestorii defensoribus, in the Bibl. haeresiol. i. iii. 456.

to the doctrinal system of Theodore, and their aversion to the council of Cyril at Ephesus. The successor of Rabulas in Edessa, *Ibas*, (bishop from 436 to 457) was indeed, though at peace with Cyril, a zealous friend of the views of the Antiochenian theology, and even translated *Theodore's* works into Syriac; but persecution was afterward renewed against the adherents of these principles; the school of Edessa was destroyed (489); and its few remaining friends fled into Persia. The Persian church had now broken off all connection with the church of the Roman empire, and the kings of Persia from *Pherozes* onward (461–488) favored this separation for political reasons. These Christians, who had the bishop of *Seleucia* and *Ctesiphon* as their Catholicus (Jacelich), were called by their opponents *Nestorians*, though they called themselves *Chaldaean Christians*, and in India *Thomas-Christians*. They have not only diffused themselves extensively in Asia, but have also acquired great merit by conveying much of the learning of Greece into that part of the world, as well as by founding schools and hospitals. At a later period they became the instructors of the Arabians.[33]

§ 89.

EUTYCHIAN CONTROVERSY.

SOURCES: Breviculus historiae Eutychianistarum s. Gesta de nomine Acacii[1] reaching to the year 486, according to the conjecture of Ballerinus, by Pope Gelasius (ap. Mansi, vii. 1060).—Liberati breviarium and the last pieces of the Synodicon (see notices prefixed to § 88).—Evagrius, i. c. 9, ss.—Collection of Acts of Councils, ap. Mansi, vi. and vii.

Walch's Ketzerhistorie, vi. 1–640. Wundemann's Geschichte d. Glaubenslehre, ii. 305. Münscher's Dogmengesch. iv. 79. Neander's Kirchengesch. ii. iii. 1073. Baur's Lehre v. d. Dreieinigkeit u. Menschwerdung Gottes, i. 800.

Notwithstanding the external union between *Cyril* and *John*, the internal schism between Egypt (which Palestine followed) and the east, as to the person of Christ, still continued. The Egyptians perceived Nestorianism[2] in the doctrine of two na-

[33] The leading work is: Jos. Sim. Assemanus de Syris Nestorianis (Bibliothecae orient. t. iii. P. ii. Rom. 1728. fol.) Ebedjesu (a Nestorian metropolitan of Soba or Nisibis † 1318) liber Margaritae de Veritate fidei (in Ang. Maji Scriptt. vett. nova coll. x. ii. 317) is a discussion and justification of the Nestorian faith.

[1] Concerning the three editions of this Breviculus, see Ballerini de Antt. collection. cann. P. ii. c. 12 (in Gallandii Sylloge ed. Mogunt. t. i. p. 457), and Walch's Ketzerhistorie, Th. 6, S. 23, f. and 891, f.

[2] Notwithstanding his subscription of the Antiochenian symbol, Cyril still held fast the

tures; while the orientals, in the doctrine of one nature discovered Apollinarianism.[3] The former party, however, continued to be favored by the court; and of this favor Cyril's successor, the violent *Dioscurus* (bishop from 444 till 451) availed himself extensively for the purpose of putting down the most zealous oriental bishops as Nestorians, and of forcing the Egyptian doctrines on the east.[4]

On the other hand, a zealous adherent of Cyril, the old Archimandrite (abbot) *Eutyches* in Constantinople[5] was accused of holding these very doctrines, and condemned at a *σύνοδος ἐνδημοῦσα* by his bishop *Flavian* (448).[6] *Leo*, bishop of Rome,

Athanasian formula: *Μίαν φύσιν τοῦ θεοῦ λόγου σεσαρκωμένην.* Cf. Epistolae ii. ad Successum, Opp. v. ii. 137 and 143. Acacii Epist. ad Cyrillum in the Synodicon (Mansi, v. 860 and 998, and in Theodoreti Opp. ed. Schulze, v. 730 and 880): Cogatur unusquisque publice anathematizare Nestorii et Theodori dogmata, praecipue hos, qui dicunt duas naturas post unitionem, proprie unamquamque operantem. A copious declaration in Acacii Epist. ad Successum (in the Synod. Mansi, v. 999. Schulze, v. 881). Ex. gr.: Videmus, quod is qui ex Deo patre est sermo, inhumanatus est et incarnatus, et non sibi ex divina natura sanctum illud corpus plasmavit, sed magis ex virgine id accepit. Alioquin quomodo factus est homo, nisi quia corpus portavit humanum? Advertentes igitur, ut dixi, inhumanationis modum, videmus, quia duae naturae ad invicem convenerunt unitione indisrumpibili, inconfuse atque inconvertibiliter. Et ex duabus naturis factum fuisse dicentes, veruntamen post unitionem non dividimus naturas ab invicem, nec in duos incidemus Christum sed unum asserimus filium, et ut patres dixerunt, unam naturam verbi incarnatam. Ergo factus est homo, non hominem recepit, ut videtur Nestorio. Eranistes in Theodoreti Dial. ii. (ed. Schulze, iv. 83) says: *Τὸ δὲ γέ ἄνθρωπον ἀποκαλεῖν τῆς οἰκουμένης τὸν σωτῆρα, σμικρύνειν ἐστὶ τοῦ δεσπότου τὴν δόξαν.* P. 106 and 114: *'Ο δύο λέγων φύσεις δύο λέγει υἱούς.* P. 114: *'Εγὼ τὴν θεότητα λέγω μεμενηκέναι, καταποθῆναι δὲ ὑπὸ ταύτης τὴν ἀνθρωπότητα, ὡς ἡ θάλασσα μέλιτος προσλαβοῦσα σταγόνα. Φροῦδος γὰρ εὐθὺς ἡ σταγὼν ἐκείνη γίνεται, τῷ τῆς θαλάττης ὕδατι μιγνυμένη* (the same figure in Gregor. Nyss. Antirrhet. adv. Apollinar. § 42. Münscher's Dogmengesch. Bd. 4. S. 37). Some went still farther. See Isidor. Pelus. lib. i. Epist. 496, ad Constantinum: *Οὐκ ἔστιν ὁ ζῆλός σου κατ' ἐπίγνωσιν. τοὺς τὸ θεῖον εὐσεβῶς πρεσβεύοντας διώκεις ἐμμανῶς, σύγχυσίν τινα καὶ ἀνάκρασιν καὶ τροπὴν τὴν εἰς σάρκα τοῦ θεοῦ λογὸν κατηχῶν, ἢ ἀλλοιῶν τὴν θείαν φύσιν εἰς σάρκα καὶ ὀστέα, ἢ τήν ἀλήθειαν τῆς σαρκὸς ἀθετῶν.* Cf. Epist. 419.

[3] About this time Theodoret wrote against the Egyptians his Apologia pro Diodoro et Theodoro Mopsuest., now lost, and Eranistes (ed. Schulze, t. iv. p. 1, ss.).

[4] Deposition of Irenaeus, bishop of Tyre (Theodosii ii. lex. ap. Mansi, v. 417, and Theodoreti Epist. 110), persecution of Ibas (Liberati Breviar. c. 10), and of Theodoret (Theodoreti Epist. 79, ss.). Theodoreti Epist. 101: *Πάντων ὁμοῦ τῶν τῆς ἀνατολῆς θεοφιλεστάτων ἐπισκόπων κατέχεαν τὴν λοιδορίαν οἱ τοῦ ψεύδους ἐργάται, καὶ τὰς ἐκκλησίας ζάλης ἐνέπλησαν.* Epist. 95 ad Antioch. Praefectum: *'Επαμυνάτω τοίνυν αὐτοῖς (τοῖς ἐπισκόποις) τὸ ὑμέτερον μέγεθος, καὶ τῆς συκοφαντουμένης ἑῴας κηδόμενον, καὶ τῆς ἀποστολικῆς προμηθούμενον πίστεως.*

[5] He appears as an assistant of Cyril against Nestorius in Epiphanii Epist. ad Maximianum above, § 88, note 28.

[6] The acts of this synod are in the acts of the council of Chalcedon, actio i. ap. Mansi, vi. 649, ss. Eutyches complains, p. 700, that he has been accused of saying, *ὅτι γε δὴ ἐξ οὐρανοῦ τὴν σάρκα ὁ θεὸς λόγος κατενήνοχεν, ὡς αὐτὸς ἀνεύθυνος τυγχάνει τῆς τοιαύτης*

not only approved of this proceeding, but in his Epistola ad Flavianum[7] gave also a doctrinal development of the disputed point,

λοιδορίας. To the question, p. 741: Ὁμολογεῖς ὁμοούσιον τῷ πατρὶ κατὰ τὴν θεότητα, καὶ ὁμοούσιον τῇ μητρὶ κατὰ τὴν ἀνθρωπότητα τὸν αὐτὸν ἕνα υἱὸν τὸν κύριον ἡμῶν Ἰησοῦν Χριστόν. He answers: Ἐπειδὴ ὁμολογῶ θεόν μου, καὶ κύριον οὐρανοῦ καὶ γῆς, ἕως σήμερον φυσιολογεῖν ἐμαυτῷ οὐκ ἐπιτρέπω. ὁμοούσιον δὲ ἡμῖν ἕως νῦν οὐκ εἶπον πρὸ τούτου, ὁμολογῶ. ἕως σήμερον οὐκ εἶπον τὸ σῶμα τοῦ κυρίου καὶ θεοῦ ἡμῶν ὁμοούσιον ἡμῖν, τὴν δὲ ἁγίαν παρθένον ὁμολογῶ εἶναι ἡμῖν ὁμοούσιον, καὶ ὅτι ἐξ αὐτῆς ἐσαρκώθη ὁ θεὸς ἡμῶν. When the remark was made upon this: Τῆς μητρὸς ὁμοούσιον ἡμῖν οὔσης, πάντως καὶ ὁ υἱὸς ὁμοούσιος ἡμῖν ἐστιν, he rejoined: Ἕως σήμερον οὐκ εἶπον· ἐπειδὴ γὰρ σῶμα θεοῦ αὐτὸ ὁμολογῶ (προσέσχες), οὐκ εἶπον σῶμα ἀνθρώπου τὸ τοῦ θεοῦ σῶμα, ἀνθρώπινον δὲ τὸ σῶμα, καὶ ὅτι ἐκ τῆς παρθένου ἐσαρκώθη ὁ κύριος. εἰ δὲ δεῖ εἰπεῖν ἐκ τῆς παρθένου, καὶ ὁμοούσιον ἡμῖν, καὶ τοῦτο λέγω, κύριε. To the question, p. 744: Ὁμοούσιον, καὶ ἐκ δύο φύσεων μετὰ τὴν ἐνανθρώπησιν τὸν κύριον ἡμῶν τὸν ἐκ τῆς παρθένου λέγεις ἢ οὔ, he gave the reply in explanation: Ὁμολογῶ ἐκ δύο φύσεων γεγεννῆσθαι τὸν κύριον ἡμῶν πρὸ τῆς ἑνώσεως· μετὰ δὲ τὴν ἕνωσιν, μίαν φύσιν ὁμολογῶ. When he refused to acknowledge the two natures, and to anathematize the contrary opinion, the decision was passed, p. 748: Διὰ πάντων πεφώραται Εὐτυχὴς ὁ πάλαι πρεσβύτερος καὶ ἀρχιμανδρίτης—τὴν Οὐαλεντίνου καὶ Ἀπολιναρίου κακοδοξίαν νοσῶν. ὅθεν ἐπιδακρύσαντες, καὶ στενάξαντες ἐπὶ τῇ παντελεῖ ἀπωλείᾳ αὐτοῦ, ὡρίσαμεν διὰ τοῦ κυρίου ἡμῶν Ἰησοῦ Χριστοῦ τοῦ ὑπ' αὐτοῦ βλασφημηθέντος, ἀλλότριον αὐτὸν εἶναι παντὸς ἱερατικοῦ τάγματος, καὶ τῆς πρὸς ἡμᾶς κοινωνίας, καὶ τοῦ προεστάναι μοναστηρίου. Comp. Epist. Eutychetis ad Leonem Papam (in the Synodicon ap. Mansi, v. 1015. Schulze, v. 897): Expetebar duas naturas fateri, et anathematizare eos, qui hoc negarent. Ego autem metuens definitionem a synodo, nec adimere nec addere verbum contra expositam fidem a sancta synodo Nicaena (cf. § 88, note 27), sciens vero sanctos et beatos patres nostros Julium, Felicem, Athanasium, Gregorium sanctissimos episcopos refutantes duarum naturarum vocabulum, etc. In the confession of faith annexed (ibid. c. 223): Ipse enim, qui est verbum Dei, descendit de coelo sine carne, et factus est caro in utero sanctae virgini ex ipsa carne virginis incommutabiliter et inconvertibiliter, sicut ipse novit et voluit. Et factus est, qui est semper Deus perfectus ante saecula, idem et homo perfectus in extremo dierum propter nos et nostram salutem. None but opponents have charged Eutychianism with the doctrine of an apparent body, or the transformation of the Logos into flesh. So Theodoret. Haer. fab. comp. iv. 13. Gelasius de duabus naturis in Christo adv. Eutychem et Nestorium. Eutyches is defended by the Jesuit Gabriel Vasquez (Commentarii in Thomam. Ingolst. 1606. fol. in part. iii. Thomae Disp. xiv. c. 1), Archibald Bower (History of the Popes, vol. ii. p. 31, 61, ss.) and others.

[7] Ed. Quesnell. Ep. 24, ed. Baller. Ep. 28, c. 2, ap. Mansi, v. 1359: Fecunditatem virgini Spiritus S. dedit, veritas autem corporis sumta de corpore est; et aedificante sibi sapientia domum (Prov. ix. 1) Verbum caro factum est, et habitavit in nobis: hoc est, in ea carne, quam assumsit ex homine, et quam spiritu vitae rationalis animavit. C. 3: Salva igitur proprietate utriusque naturae et substantiae, et in unam coeunte personam, suscepta est a majestate humilitas, a virtute infirmitas, ab aeternitate mortalitas: et ad resolvendum conditionis nostrae debitum natura inviolabilis natura est unita passibili: ut, quod nostris remediis congruebat, unus atque idem mediator Dei et hominum, homo Jesus Christus, et mori posset ex uno, et mori non posset ex altero. In integra ergo veri hominis perfectaque natura verus natus est Deus, totus in suis, totus in nostris. Assumsit formam servi sine sorde peccati, humana augens, divina non minuens. Tenet enim sine defectu proprietatem suam utraque natura: et sicut formam servi Dei forma non adimit, ita formam Dei servi forma non minuit. C. 4: Nova autem nativitate generatus: quia inviolata virginitas, quae concupiscentiam nescivit, carnis materiam ministravit. Assumta est de matre Domini natura, non culpa: nec in Domino Jesu Christo, ex utero virginis genito, quia nativitas est mirabilis, ideo nostri est natura dissimilis. Qui enim verus est Deus, idem verus est homo: et nullum est in hac unitate mendacium, dum invicem sunt

which was by no means favorable to the Egyptians. It is true that Dioscurus now procured the summoning of a *general synod at Ephesus* (449) and there, as president, compelled by violent measures the bishops to pronounce in favor of Eutyches and the Egyptian doctrines (*σύνοδος ληστρική*, *Theophanis Chronograph.* p. 86.—Latrocinium Ephesinum, Leo ad Pulcheriam Ep. 75, ed. Quesnel);[8] but the death of Theodosius II. († 450) altered at once the state of affairs. The new rulers *Pulcheria* and *Marcian*, who was elevated to the throne by marrying her, were as partial to Leo as they were hostile to Dioscurus.[9] Hence, a new *general council* was called at *Chalcedon* (451), at which Dioscurus was deposed for many misdeeds, the persecuted eastern bishops, and with them Cyril, too,[10] for the purpose of sparing the Egyptians, were declared orthodox, Leo's *Epist. ad Flavianum*, made the rule of faith on the point in dispute, and at the same time a more minute explanation of it given on the part of the council.[11] But though the decrees of the synod re-

et humilitas hominis et altitudo Deitatis. Sicut enim Deus non mutatur miseratione, ita homo non consumitur dignitate. Agit enim utraque forma cum alterius communione quod proprium est: Verbo scilicet operante, quod Verbi est, et carne exequente quod carnis est. Unum horum coruscat miraculis, aliud succumbit injuriis. Et sicut Verbum ab aequalitate paternae gloriae non recedit, ita caro naturam nostri generis non relinquit. Unus enim idemque est, quod saepe dicendum est, vere Dei filius et vere hominis filius. Quem itaque sicut hominem diabolica tentat astutia, eidem sicut Deo angelica famulantur officia. Esurire, sitire, lassescere, atque dormire evidenter humanum est. Sed v. panibus v. millia hominum satiare, et largiri Samaritanae aquam vivam, cujus haustus bibenti praestet, ne ultra jam sitiat; supra dorsum maris plantis non desidentibus ambulare, et elationes fluctuum increpata tempestate consternere: sine ambiguitate divinum est. Sicut ergo, ut multa praeteream, non ejusdem naturae est, flere miserationis affectu amicum mortuum, et eundem remoto quatriduanae aggere sepulturae, ad vocis imperium excitare redivivum: ita non ejusdem naturae est, dicere: Ego et pater unum sumus (Jo. x. 30) et dicere: Pater major me est (Jo. xiv. 28). Leo here proceeded a little further on the same path as Ambrose and Augustine. See above, § 88, notes 8 and 9. J. J. Griesbach Diss. locos communes theologicos, collectos ex Leone M. sistens. Halae. 1768. Sect. iii. (in ejusd. Opusc. acad. ed. Gabler, i. 45). Epistolam, etc. ed. H. Ph. C. Henke. Helmst. (The prologue is also in Henke Opusc. acad. Lips. 1802. p. 59, ss.) Henke properly calls attention to the circumstance that there is no mention whatever of Nestor in the letter. Baur's Dreieinigkeit, i. 809.

8 Lewald die sogen. Räubersynode, in Illgen's Zeitschr. f. hist. Theol. viii. 139.

9 The Alexandrian Sophronius even accused Dioscurus in Chalcedon of having opposed the acknowledgment of Marcian in Egypt (Mansi, vi. 1033), *ἑαυτὸν γὰρ μᾶλλον βασιλεύειν ἤθελε τῆς Αἰγυπτιακῆς διοικήσεως*. No notice, however, was taken of this accusation by the synod, nor is there a trace of it to be found elsewhere.

10 How little convinced the prevailing party was of Cyril's orthodoxy is clear from the fact that Gennadius, patriarch of Constantinople, after 458, wrote against his twelve anathemas. See Facundus pro defens. iii. capitulorum, ii. 4. Salig de Eutychianismo ante Eutychen, p. 316.

11 Concerning the remarkable circumstances, and the opposition of the Roman legates,

ceived imperial confirmation and support by punitory laws, they were looked upon as Nestorian by many in Egypt and Palestine, and this proved, soon after, the beginning of the tedious *Monophysite* controversy.

§ 90.

OF THE THEOLOGICAL AUTHORITY OF THE OECUMENICAL SYNODS.

In this period the utterances of the *oecumenical* councils,[1] as the last and highest ecclesiastical decisions, began to assume an important place among the sources of theological knowledge. As all synods prior to the present time were supposed to be under the peculiar direction of the Holy Spirit, without on that account claiming infallibility,[2] so also the doctrinal decisions of general councils were derived from a special co-operation of the Holy Spirit,[3] but so far were men as yet from attributing to them

see the protocol actio v. ap. Mansi, vii. 97, ss.—P. 108: *῞Ορος τῆς ἐν Χαλκηδόνι τετάρτης Συνόδου.* P. 116: *Ἑπόμενοι τοίνυν τοῖς ἁγίοις πατράσιν, ἕνα καὶ τὸν αὐτὸν ὁμολογεῖν υἱὸν τὸν κύριον ἡμῶν Ἰησοῦν Χριστὸν συμφώνως ἅπαντες ἐκδιδάσκομεν, τέλειον τὸν αὐτὸν ἐν θεότητι καὶ τέλειον τὸν αὐτὸν ἐν ἀνθρωπότητι, θεὸν ἀληθῶς καὶ ἄνθρωπον ἀληθῶς τὸν αὐτὸν ἐκ ψυχῆς λογικῆς καὶ σώματος, ὁμοούσιον τῷ πατρὶ κατὰ τὴν θεότητα, καὶ ὁμοούσιον τὸν αὐτὸν ἡμῖν κατὰ τὴν ἀνθρωπότητα, κατὰ πάντα ὅμοιον ἡμῖν χωρὶς ἁμαρτίας· πρὸ αἰώνων μὲν ἐκ τοῦ πατρὸς γεννηθέντα κατὰ τὴν θεότητα, ἐπ' ἐσχάτων δὲ τῶν ἡμερῶν τὸν αὐτὸν, δι' ἡμᾶς καὶ διὰ τὴν ἡμετέραν σωτηρίαν, ἐκ Μαρίας τῆς παρθένου τῆς θεοτόκου κατὰ τὴν ἀνθρωπότητα, ἕνα καὶ τὸν αὐτὸν Χριστὸν, υἱὸν, κύριον, μονογενῆ, ἐκ δύο φύσεων* (leg. *ἐν δύο φύσεσι*) *ἀσυγχύτως, ἀτρέπτως, ἀδιαιρέτως, ἀχωρίστως γνωριζόμενον· οὐδαμοῦ τῆς τῶν φύσεων διαφορᾶς ἀνῃρημένης διὰ τὴν ἕνωσιν, σωζομένης δὲ μᾶλλον τῆς ἰδιότητος ἑκατέρας φύσιως καὶ εἰς ἓν πρόσωπον, καὶ μίαν ὑπόστασιν συντρεχούσης, οὐκ εἰς δύο πρόσωπα μεριζόμενον, ἢ διαιρούμενον, ἀλλ' ἕνα καὶ τὸν αὐτὸν υἱὸν καὶ μονογενῆ, θεὸν λόγον, κύριον Ἰησοῦν Χριστόν· καθάπερ ἄνωθεν οἱ προφῆται περὶ αὐτοῦ, καὶ αὐτὸς ἡμᾶς ὁ κύριος Ἰησοῦς Χριστὸς ἐξεπαίδευσε, καὶ τὸ τῶν πατέρων ἡμῖν παραδέδωκε σύμβολον.* That the true reading must be *ἐν δύο φύσεσι* (as all the Latins have in duabus naturis) is shown by Mansi, vii. 775. Walch. Bibl. symb. vetus, p. 106, to which we have also to add the testimonies of the Monophysite Severus Patr. Ant. (ap. Mansi, vii. 840), Evagrius, H. E. ii. c. 4. Leontius Bys. de Sectis. Actio, v. c. 7. Agathonis P. Ep. ad Constantem II. (in the Act. Conc. oecum. vi. Act. 4, ap. Mansi, xi. 256). Baur's Dreieinigkeit, i. 820, defends the reading *ἐκ. δ. φ.*

1 The name *σύνοδος οἰκουμενική* first in Conc. Constant. ann. 381, can. 6.

2 According to Acts xv. 28. Conc. Carthag. ann. 252 (in Opp. Cypriani): Placuit nobis sancto Spiritu suggerente et Domino per visiones multas et manifestas admonente. To what an extent this form of speech proceeded may be seen in Concil. Ephes. ann. 431, above, § 88, note 27. But in a similar formula spake also a partial council at Constantinople, which condemned Eutyches. See above, § 89, note 6.

3 Constantini Epist. ad Eccl. Alexandr. (Socrates, i. 9): In reference to the Nicene council: *῞Ο γὰρ τοῖς τριακοσίοις ἤρεσεν Ἐπισκόποις, οὐδέν ἐστιν ἕτερον, ἢ τοῦ θεοῦ γνώμη, μάλιστά γε ὅπου τὸ ἅγιον πνεῦμα, τοιούτων καὶ τηλικούτων ἀνδρῶν ταῖς διανοίαις*

an exclusive infallibility dependent only upon their conformity to certain external conditions,[4] that they were put in the same rank with other orthodox synods,[5] and in answering opponents, men did not endeavor to prove that the council was oecumenical, but that its decision was true according to Scripture and tradition.[6]

ἐγκείμενον, τὴν θείαν βούλησιν ἐξεφώτισεν. Basilii Ep. 114 (al. 204): Οἱ τριακόσιοι δέκα καὶ ὀκτὼ—οὐκ ἄνευ τῆς τοῦ ἁγίου πνεύματος ἐνεργείας ἐφθέγξαντο (τὴν πίστιν). Socrat. i. 9, against the Macedonian historian Sabinus, who had pronounced the Nicene fathers ignorant men: Οὐκ ἐνθυμεῖται, ὡς, εἰ καὶ ἰδιῶται ἦσαν οἱ τῆς Συνόδου, κατελάμποντο δὲ ὑπὸ τοῦ θεοῦ, καὶ τῆς χάριτος τοῦ ἁγίου πνεύματος, οὐδαμῶς ἀστοχῆσαι τῆς ἀληθείας ἐδύναντο. Thus Isidore Pelus. lib. iv. Ep. 99, calls the Nicene council θεόθεν ἐμπνευσθεῖσα.

4 Epist. Synodi Nicaene ad Alexandrinos (Theodoret. i. 8) in fine: Εὔχεσθε δὲ καὶ ὑπὲρ ἡμῶν ἁπάντων, ἵνα τὰ καλῶς ἔχειν δόξαντα βέβαια μένοι διὰ τοῦ κυρίου ἡμῶν Ἰησοῦ Χριστοῦ, κατ' εὐδοκίαν γεγενημένα, ὥς γε πεπιστεύκαμεν, τοῦ θεοῦ καὶ πατρὸς ἐν πνεύματι ἁγίῳ. In Socrates, i. c. 9 this passage has been altered. Augustinus de Baptismo contra Donatistas, ii. 3: Quis autem nesciat, sanctam scripturam canonicam—omnibus posterioribus Episcoporum literis ita praeponi, ut de illa omnino dubitari et disceptari non possit, utrum verum vel utrum rectum sit, quidquid in ea scriptum esse constiterit: Episcoporum autem literas—per sermonem forte sapientiorem—et per aliorum Episcoporum graviorem auctoritatem—et per concilia licere reprehendi, si quid in eis forte a veritate deviatum est: et ipsa concilia, quae per singulas regiones vel provincias fiunt, plenariorum conciliorum auctoritati, quae fiunt ex universo orbe christiano, sine ullis ambagibus cedere: ipsaque plenaria saepe priora posterioribus emendari, quum aliquo experimento rerum aperitur quod clausum erat, et cognoscitur quod latebat, sine ullo typho sacrilegae superbiae, sine ulla inflata cervice arrogantiae, sine ulla contentione lividae invidiae, cum sancta humilitate, cum pace catholica, cum caritate christiana.

5 Constantinus Epist. ad Episcopos, qui Conc. Nicaeno non interfuerunt (Euseb. de vita Const. iii. 20, and Socrates, i. 9) says generally: Πᾶν γὰρ, εἴ τι δ' ἂν ἐν τοῖς ἁγίοις τῶν ἐπισκόπων συνεδρίοις πράττηται, τοῦτο πρὸς τὴν θείαν βούλησιν ἔχει τὴν ἀναφοράν. Thus Athanasius places the Concil. Antiochen. A.D. 269, to which his opponents appealed in defense of their rejection of the term ὁμοούσιον, on an equality with the Nicene in point of theological authority. De Synodis, c. 43: Συγκρούειν μὲν γὰρ τούτους πρὸς ἐκείνους ἀπρεπές· πάντες γάρ εἰσι πατέρες· διακρίνειν δὲ πάλιν, ὡς οὗτοι μὲν καλῶς, ἐκεῖνοι δὲ τοὐναντίον εἰρήκασιν, οὐχ ὅσιον· οἱ πάντες γὰρ ἐκοιμήθησαν ἐν Χριστῷ. Οὐ χρὴ δὲ φιλονεικεῖν, οὐδὲ τῶν συνελθόντων τὸν ἀριθμὸν συμβάλλειν, ἵνα μὴ δοκῶσιν οἱ τριακόσιοι τοὺς ἐλάττονας ἐπικρύπτειν· οὐδ' ἂν πάλιν τὸν χρόνον ἀναμετρεῖν, ἵνα μὴ δοκῶσιν οἱ προλαβόντες ἀφανίζειν τοὺς μετὰ ταῦτα γενομένους· οἱ πάντες γὰρ καθὰ προείρηται πατέρες εἰσί.

6 Augustinus contra Maximinum Arian. ii. 14, 3: Sed nunc nec ego Nicaenum, nec tu debes Ariminense tamquam praejudicaturus proferre concilium. Nec ego hujus auctoritate, nec tu illius detineris: Scripturarum auctoritatibus, non quorumque propriis, sed utrisque communibus testibus, res cum re, causa cum causa, ratio cum ratione concertet.

THIRD CHAPTER.

HISTORY OF THE HIERARCHY.

Planck's Geschichte der christl. kirchl. Gesellschaftsverfassung, i. 276. C. Riffel's gesch. Darstellung des Verhältnisses zwischen Kirche u. Staat. Mainz. 1836. 8. i. 114.

§ 91.

GROWING IMPORTANCE OF THE CLERGY.

The Christian emperors enlarged the privileges already granted by Constantine to the church and the clergy (Div. I. § 56, note 30, ff.), by new tokens of their favor. They released church lands and the clergy from *certain civil liabilities*,[1] but by no means from *all* taxes;[2] gave a legal confirmation to the decisions which the bishops pronounced in *ecclesiastical* affairs,[3] and which they also gave as chosen umpires in *civil disputes*,[4]

[1] Besides the municipal offices (see Div. I. § 56, note 30), both the clergy and church property were freed from the muneribus sordidis and extraordinariis (cf. Cod. Theod. lib. xi. tit. 15, de extraordinariis sive sordidis muneribus and Gothofredi paratitlon), from the metatis (Cod. Th. l. vii. t. 8, de metatis), the angariis and parangariis (Cod. Th. l. vii. t. 5, de cursu publico, angariis et parangariis), and finally the immunity of the clerici negotiantes from the lustralis conlatio (Cod. Th. l. xiii. t. 1, de lustrali conlatione comp. Hegewisch Hist. Versuch über die röm. Finanzen, S. 307, ff.). Comp. besides the works cited Cod. Theod. l. xvi. ii. 8, 19, etc. Comp. Binghami Origg. eccl. vol. ii. p. 227. Planck, i. 289.

[2] Constantine had indeed at first, in the year 315, also released the church lands from the tributis ordinariis (Cod. Theod. xi. i. 1), but they were soon after again subjected to this tribute, and when the council of Ariminum (A.D. 359) applied to Constantius, ut juga, quae videntur ad Ecclesiam pertinere, a publica functione cessarent, inquietudine desistente, he flatly denied the request, Cod. Theod. xvi. ii. 15. Gratian even subjected the church lands to the extraordinariis collationibus (Cod. Theod. xi. xvi. 15). So also Theodosius, l. c. l. 18. Honorius released them from the extraordinaria, l. c. l. 21, 22. Theodosius II. subjected them again to the angariis and parangariis. Cod. Justin. i. ii. 11. Comp. Ambrosii Orat. de basilicis non tradendis haereticis: Si tributum petit Imperator, non negamus. Agri ecclesiae solvunt tributum. Si agros desiderat Imperator, potestatem habet vindicandorum, nemo nostrum intervenit, etc. Riffel, i. 153.

[3] Euseb. de vita Const. iv. c. 27. See below, note 4. Comp. the law of Honorius A.D 399 (Cod. Theod. xvi. xi. 1): Quotiens de religione agitur, Episcopos convenit judicare, caeteras vero causas, quae ad ordinarios cognitores, vel ad usum publici juris pertinent, legibus oportet audiri.

[4] Respecting these episcopal arbitration-decisions comp. Div. I. § 69, note 6. It had been always reckoned unchristian to depart from them, and thus public opinion demanded for them the preference, so that they laid the foundation of an actio rei judicatae. This privilege has been usually ascribed to Constantine, with reference to Eusebius de vita Const. iv. 27: Τοὺς τῶν ἐπισκόπων ὅρους τοὺς ἐν συνόδοις ἀποφανθέντας ἐπεσφραγίζετο

allowed *the clergy* to be bound by these judicial decisions, [5] and even put them in cases of discipline under spiritual courts,[6] without however conceding to the bishops a civil jurisdiction.[7]

ὡς μὴ ἐξεῖναι τοῖς τῶν ἐθνῶν ἄρχουσι, τὰ δόξαντα παραλύειν· παντὸς γὰρ εἶναι δικαστοῦ τοὺς ἱερεῖς τοῦ θεοῦ δοκιμωτέρους: in which *σύνοδος* according to Conc. Carthag. iv. c. 23 (see Div. I. § 69, note 11) is understood of the presbytery. These arbitrations, however were not pronounced by the collegia, but by the bishop, and by him sometimes committed to individual presbyters and deacons; by Sylvanus bishop of Troas, even wholly to an honest layman (Socrates, vii. 37); see Bingham. vol. i. p. 130; and thus that passage appears to refer to the decisions and sentences of the provincial synods. Sozomen i. c. 9 is indeed more distinct: Τῶν *δὲ* 'Επισκόπων *ἐπικαλεῖσθαι τὴν κρίσιν ἐπέτρεψε* (Κωνσταντῖνος) *τοῖς δικαζομένοις, ἣν βούλωνται τοὺς πολιτικοὺς ἄρχοντας παραιτεῖσθαι· κυρίαν δὲ εἶναι τὴν αὐτῶν ψῆφον, καὶ κρείττω τῆς τῶν ἄλλων δικαστῶν, ὡσανεὶ παρὰ τοῦ* Βασιλέως *ἐξενεχθεῖσαν· εἰς ἔργον δὲ τὰ κρινόμενα ἄγειν τοὺς ἄρχοντας, καὶ τοὺς διακονουμένους αὐτοῖς στρατιώτας· ἀμετατρέπτους τε εἶναι τῶν* Συνόδων *τοὺς ὅρους.* Still this seems to be only an amplified interpretation of that passage in Eusebius. The oldest law extant on the subject is A.D. 408 (Cod. Justin. i. iv. 8). Honor. et Theod. AA. Theodoro P. P. Episcopale judicium ratum sit omnibus, qui se audiri a Sacerdotibus elegerint: eamque illorum judicationi adhibendam esse reverentiam jubemus, quam vestris deferri necesse est potestatibus, a quibus non licet provocare. Per judicum quoque Officia, ne sit cassa episcopalis cognitio, definitioni executio tribuatur. Cf. Augustin. in Psalm xxv. § 13 (about 415): Principes saeculi tantum detulerunt Ecclesiae, ut quidquid in ea judicatum fuerit, dissolvi non possit. But as a like privilege was granted to the Jewish patriarchs as early as 398 (Cod. Theod. ii. i. 10), we may fairly assume that the Christian bishops also were earlier possessed of it. H. M. Hebenstreit Hist. jurisdictionis ecclesiasticae ex legibus utriusque codicis illustrata, diss. iii. Lips. 1773, ss. 4. B. Schilling de Origine jurisdictionis ecclesiasticae in causis civilibus. Lips. 1825. 4. C. F. A. Jungk de Originibus et progressu episcopalis judicii in causis civilibus laicorum usque ad Justinianum. Berol. 1832. 8.

[5] Conc. Carthag. iii. ann. 397, c. 9: Item placuit, ut quisquis Episcoporum, Presbyterorum, et Diaconorum, seu Clericorum, cum in Ecclesia ei crimen fuerit intentatum, vel civilis causa fuerit commota, si relicto ecclesiastico judicio, publicis judiciis purgari voluerit, etiamsi pro ipso fuerit prolata sententia, locum suum amittat, et hoc in criminali judicio. In civili vero perdat quod evicit, si locum suum obtinere voluerit. Cui enim ad eligendos judices undique patet auctoritas, ipse se indignum fraterno consortio judicat, qui de universa Ecclesia male sentiendo de judicio seculari poscit auxilium, cum privatorum Christianorum causas Apostolus ad Ecclesiam deferri, atque ibi terminari praecipiat. Conc. Chalced. c. 9: *Εἴ τις κληρικὸς πρὸς κληρικὸν πρᾶγμα ἔχει, μὴ καταλιμπανέτω τὸν οἰκεῖον* 'Επίσκοπον, *καὶ ἐπὶ κοσμικὰ δικαστήρια κατατρεχέτω.—εἰ δέ τις παρὰ ταῦτα ποιήσει, κανονικοῖς ὑποκείσθω ἐπιτιμίοις.*

[6] Lex Constantii (Cod. Theod. xvi. xi. 12), A.D. 355: Mansuetudinis nostrae lege prohibemus, in judiciis Episcopos accusari.—Si quid est igitur querelarum, quod quispiam defert, apud alios potissimum Episcopos convenit explorari. Gratiani (ibid. l. 23,) A.D. 376: Qui mos est causarum civilium, idem in negotiis ecclesiasticis obtinendus est: ut si qua sunt ex quibusdam dissensionibus, levibusque delictis, ad religionis observantiam pertinentia, locis suis, et a suae Dioeceseos Synodis audiantur: exceptis quae actio criminalis ab ordinariis extraordinariisque judicibus, aut illustribus potestatibus audienda constituit. Honorii (ibid. l. 41,) A.D. 412: Clericos non nisi apud Episcopos accusari convenit. Valentiniani iii. (ibid. l. 47, A.D. 425): Clericos—episcopali audientiae reservamus: fas enim non est, ut divini muneris ministri temporalium potestatum subdantur arbitrio.

[7] The limits of episcopalis audientia are definitely given by Valentiniani iii. novella de episcopali judicio A.D. 442, (ed. Gothofred. nov. Val. tit. xii. ed. Haenell nov. xxxiv.): De episcopali judicio diversorum saepe causatio est. Ne ulterius querela procedat, necesse est praesenti lege sanciri. Itaque cum inter clericos jurgium vertitur, et ipsis litigatoribus

But the old ecclesiastical rights of the clergy, particularly *the right of superintending morals*, and *the duty of interference on behalf of all the unfortunate*, received quite another importance after they had been recognized by the state, by the elevation of Christianity into the state religion. The persons of magistrates also now became subject to them as inspectors of the public morals; yea, even the emperors themselves, as far as they were Christians;[8] and the duty of interference on behalf

convenit, habeat, Episcopus licentiam judicandi, praeeunte tamen vinculo compromissi. Quod et laicis, si consentiant, auctoritas nostra permittit. Aliter eos judices esse non patimur, nisi voluntas jurgantium interposita, sicut dictum est, conditione praecedat: quoniam constat, Episcopos et Presbyteros forum legibus non habere, nec de aliis causis, secundum Arcadii et Honorii divalia constituta, quae Theodosianum corpus ostendit, praeter religionem, posse cognoscere. Sin vero petitor laicus, seu in civili seu criminali causa, cujuslibet loci Clericum adversarium suum, si id magis eligat, per auctoritatem legitimam in publico judicio respondere compellat. Quam formam etiam circa Episcoporum personam observari oportere censemus. Ut si in hujuscemodi ordinis homines actionem pervasionis et atrocium injuriarum dirigi necesse fuerit, per procuratorem solemniter ordinatum apud judicem publicum inter leges et jura confligant, judicati exitu ad mandatores sine dubio reversuro. Quod iis religionis et sacerdotii veneratione permittimus. Nam notum est, procurationem in criminalibus negotiis non posse concedi. Sed ut sit ulla discretio meritorum, Episcopis et Presbyteris tantum id oportet impendi. In reliquis negotiis criminalibus juxta legum ordinem per se judicium subire coguntur.

[8] Conc. Arelatense, ann. 314, c. 7: De praesidibus, qui fideles ad praesidatum prosiliunt, placuit ut, cum promoti fuerint, literas accipiant ecclesiasticas communicatorias (Comp. Div. I. § 41, note 5): Ita tamen ut in quibuscunque locis gesserint, ab Episcopo ejusdem loci cura de illis agatur, et cum coeperint contra diciplinam agere, tum demum a communione excludantur. Similiter et de his qui rempublicam agere volunt. Gregor. Naz. Orat. xvii. p. 271, thus addresses the *δυνάσται καὶ ἄρχοντες: ὁ τοῦ Χριστοῦ νόμος ὑποτίθησιν ὑμᾶς τῇ ἐμῇ δυναστείᾳ καὶ τῷ ἐμῷ βήματι ἄρχομεν γὰρ καὶ αὐτοὶ, προσθήσω δ' ὅτι καὶ τὴν μείζονα καὶ τελεωτέραν ἀρχήν. ἢ δεῖ τὸ πνεῦμα ὑποχωρῆσαι τῇ σαρκὶ, καὶ τοῖς γηίνοις τὰ ἐπουράνια;* Thus Athanasius excommunicated a governor of Libya on account of cruelty and excesses; and Basil the Great assures him (Ep. 61,) after he had made known this excommunication in his church, *ἀποτρόπαιον αὐτὸν πάντες ἡγήσονται, μὴ πυρὸς, μὴ ὕδατος, μὴ σκέπης αὐτῇ κοινωνοῦντες.* Comp. the excommunication which Synesius bishop of Ptolemais, uttered against the prefect Andronicus, Synesii Epist. 58: *'Ανδρονίκῳ καὶ τοῖς αὐτοῦ μηδὲν ἀνοιγνύσθω τέμενος τοῦ θεοῦ· ἅπας αὐτοῖς ἱερὸς ἀποκεκλείσθω καὶ σηκὸς καὶ περίβολος· οὐκ ἔστι τῷ Διαβόλῳ, μέρος ἐν Παραδείσῳ ὃς κἂν λάθῃ διαδὺς, ἐξελαύνεται. Παραινῶ μὲν οὖν καὶ ἰδιώτῃ παντὶ καὶ ἄρχοντι, μήτε ὁμορόφιον αὐτῷ, μήτε ὁμοτράπεζον γίνεσθαι· ἱερεῦσι δὲ διαφερόντως, οἳ μήτε ζῶντας αὐτοὺς προσεροῦσι, μήτε τελευτήσαντας συμπροπέμψουσιν, κ. τ. λ.* Cf. Clausen de Synesio. Hafn. 1831. 8, p. 152, ss. The bishops of Alexandria, in particular, made themselves objects of fear to the officials of that place. Cyril obtained this see by fighting, although the leader of the army there was against him. Socrates vii. 7: *Καὶ γὰρ ἐξ ἐκείνου ἡ 'Επισκοπὴ 'Αλεξανδρείας παρὰ τῆς ἱερατικῆς τάξεως κατάδυναστεύειν τῶν πραγμάτων ἔλαβε τὴν ἀρχήν.* Comp. Socrates, vii. c. 13, on the disputes between Cyril and Orestes, prefect of Egypt: *'Ορέστης δὲ καὶ πρότερον μὲν ἐμίσει τὴν δυναστείαν τῶν ἐπισκόπων, ὅτι παρῃροῦντο πολὺ τῆς ἐξουσίας τῶν ἐκ βασιλέως ἄρχειν τεταγμένων· μάλιστα δὲ ὅτι καὶ ἐποπτεύειν αὐτοῦ τὰς διατυπώσεις· Κύριλλος ἐβούλετο.*—Theodosius I. was compelled to do penance by Ambrose (Rufinus, xi. 18; Sozom. vii. 25; Theodoret. v. 17. Comp. Neander's K. G. ii. i. 384). Of Theodosius II. Theodoret, v. 36, relates that a monk came to him, *περί τινος δεόμενος, ἐπειδὴ δὲ τοῦτο δράσας πολλάκις οὐκ ἔτυχε, τῆς ἐκκλησιαστικῆς αὐτὸν κοινωνίας ἐκώλυσε, καὶ τὸν δεσμὸν*

of the unfortunate established a right of intercession with the civil power,[9] which often exhibited itself in a very stormy way in cases where the punishment of death, which the Christians of that time regarded with horror, was decreed.[10] In like manner the acknowledgment of this right of the clergy facilitated the transfer of the *right of asylum* from heathen temples to the Christian churches.[11] All these rights had long since grown

ἐπιθεὶς ὑπεχώρησε. Nor had the emperor any rest till this fanatic had again freed him from the sentence.

[9] (As the vestals had formerly exercised it, see Cicero pro Fontejo in fine. Sueton. Jul. Caesar, c. i., Tiber. c. 2). Conc. Sardic. c. 8, below, § 92, note 11. Ambrosius de Offic. ministr. ii. c. 21: Adjuvat hoc quoque ad profectum bonae existimationis, si de potentis manibus eripias inopem, de morte damnatum eruas, quantum sine perturbatione fieri potest, ne videamur jactantiae magis causa facere, quam misericordiae, et graviora inferre vulnera, dum levioribus mederi desideramus. Cap. 29: Egregie hinc vestrum enitescit ministerium, si suscepta impressio potentis, quam vel vidua vel orphani tolerare non queant, Ecclesiae subsidio cohibeatur, si ostendatis plus apud vos mandatum Domini, quam divitis valere gratiam. Meministis ipsi, quoties adversus regales impetus pro viduarum, immo omnium, depositis certamen subierimus. Commune hoc vobiscum mihi. Cf. Thomassini Vetus et nova Ecclesiae disiplina de beneficiis, p. ii. l. iii. c. 87, and c. 95, 96. Bingham. lib. ii. c. 8.

[10] Macedonius, vicar of the diocese of Africa, writes respecting it to Augustine (August. Ep. 152): Officium sacerdotii vestri esse dicitis intervenire pro reis, et nisi obtineatis, offendi, quasi quod erat officii vestri, minime reportetis. Hic ergo vehementer ambigo, utrum istud ex religione descendat. Nam si a Domino peccata adeo prohibentur, ut ne poenitendi quidem copia post primum tribuatur; quemadmodum nos possumus ex religione contendere, ut nobis qualecumque illud crimen fuerit, dimittatur? quod utique, cum impunitum volumus, probamus, etc. To this Augustine replies, Ep. 153, ex. gr. § 3: Morum corrigendorum nullus alius quam in hac vita locus est.—Ideo compellimur humani generis caritate intervenire pro reis, ne istam vitam sic finiant per supplicium, ut ea finita non possint finire supplicium. Noli ergo dubitare hoc officium nostrum ex religione descendere, etc. Comp. the intercession for the Circumcelliones who were to have been executed for murders, August. Ep. 133, ad Marcellinum Tribunum: Si non audis amicum petentem, audi Episcopum consulentem. Quamvis quoniam Christiano loquar, maxime in tali causa, non arroganter dixerim, audire te Episcopum convenit jubentem. Against violent interferences of the clergy, as they took place for example in Antioch (Chrysostomi Ep. ad Olympiadem and Orat. ad popul. Antioch. 17,) Theodosius I. A.D. 392, and Arcadius, A.D. 398, enacted laws (Cod. Theod. ix. xl. 15 and 16.) The latter: Addictos supplicio, et pro criminum immanitate damnatos, nulli Clericorum vel Monachorum—per vim atque usurpationem vindicare liceat ac tenere. Quibus in causa criminali humanitatis consideratione, si tempora suffragantur, interponendae provocationis copiam non negamus.—Reos tempore provocationis emenso ad locum poenae sub prosecutione pergentes, nullus aut teneat aut defendat.—Si tanta Clericorum ac Monachorum audacia est, ut bellum potius quam judicium futurum esse existimetur, ad Clementiam Nostram commissa referantur, ut nostro mox severior ultio procedat arbitrio. Ad Episcoporum sane culpam redundabit, si quid forte in ea parte regionis, in qua ipsi populo christianae religionis, doctrinae insinuatione, moderantur, ex his quae fieri hac lege prohibemus, a Monachis perpetratum esse cognoverint, nec vindicaverint.

[11] At first merely through custom (examples Ammian. Marcell. xxvi. 3. Zosimus. iv. 40; v. 8. Gregor. Naz. Orat. xx. in laudem Basilii, Opp. i. 353, etc.) which is referred to as already in existence in the restrictive laws of Theodosius I. and Arcadius (Cod. Theod. ix. 45, 1–3), and formally confirmed and strictly defined by Theodosius II. in the year 431 (ibid. l. 4). Bingham, vol. iii. p. 353 ss. (Abele) Magazin für Kirchenrecht u. Kirchengesch. St. 1. (Leipz. 1778. 8.) S. 189, ss.

naturally out of the old ecclesiastical notions before the emperors began to confirm them severally by laws.[12]

On the other side, ecclesiastical possessions became very considerable, partly by the liberality of the emperors,[13] partly by the legal permission to accept of inheritances and gifts, which alas, was often abused by the clergy, so as to become legacy-hunting.[14] All these external advantages attracted many to the spiritual profession,[15] the number of clergy was swelled beyond measure, and to the already existing classes were added parabolani, copiatae.[16] The emperors were obliged to meet this

[12] So Constantini lex A.D. 329. (Cod. Justin. i. iv. 25): Quae de alea, sive ut vocant cottis, ac de eorum prohibitione a nobis sancita sunt, ea liceat Dei amicissimis Episcopis et perscrutari, et cohibere, si fiant, et flagitiosos per clarissimos Praesides provinciarum, et Patres defensoresque civitatum ad modestiam reducere. Honorii A.D. 408. (Cod. Theod. xvi. x. 19), in reference to all kinds of idolatry: Episcopis quoque locorum haec ipsa prohibendi ecclesiasticae manus tribuimus facultatem; A.D. 409 (Cod. Theod. ix. iii. 7), after the judges had been admonished to treat the prisoners more humanely: Nec deerit Antistitum christianae religionis cura laudabilis quae ad observationem constituti judicis hanc ingerat monitionem. Cf. Cod. Theod v. v. 2; v. vii. 2; xv. viii. 2; cf. C. W. de Rhoer Dissertt. de effectu religionis christ. in jurisprudentiam Rom. (Fasc. i. Groningae. 1776. 8.) p. 94, ss.

[13] Particularly out of the parochial property of the cities (see § 75, note 9), the property of the heathen temples (Cod. Theod. xvi. 20) and of heretical churches Cod. Theod. xvi. v. 43, 52, 57, 65, etc.). Hilarius contra Constantium jam vita defunctum, c. 10: Auro reipublicae sanctum Dei honoras, et vel detracta templis vel publicata edictis, vel exacta poenis Deo ingeris.

[14] So Gregory Naz. Ep. 80 remarks, while admonishing Aërius and Alypius to pay the legacy of their mother into the church, *ὅτι πολλοὶ καὶ ὅλων οἴκων ἐμποιουμένων εἰς Ἐκκλησίας ἠνέσχοντο, οἱ δὲ καὶ παρ' ἑαυτῶν πᾶσαν προσήγοντο τὴν περιουσίαν καὶ τὴν καλλίστην ἐπραγματεύσαντο πραγματείαν, γενέσθαι διὰ τὸν ἐκεῖ πλοῦτον πένητες μὴ τοίνυν σπείρητε φειδομένως, ἵνα πλουσίως θερήσητε,—πάντα μεθ' ἡδονῆς καὶ φαιδρότητος ἐπιδόντες, ἢ ἀποδόντες ὡς οἰκεῖα τὰ τοῦ θεοῦ.* On the other hand, Valentiniani I. lex A.D 370, ad Damasum Episc. urbis Rom. (Cod. Theod. xvi. ii. 20): Ecclesiastici, aut ex Ecclesiasticis, vel qui continentium se volunt nomine nuncupari, viduarum ac pupillarum domos non adeant: sed publicis exterminentur judiciis, si posthac eos adfines earum vel propinqui putaverint deferendos. Censemus etiam, ut memorati nihil de ejus mulieris, cui se privatim sub praetextu religionis adjunxerint, liberalitate quacunque, vel extremo judicio possint adipisci, et omne in tantum inefficax sit, quod alicui horum ab his fuerit derelictum, ut nec per subjectam personam valeant aliquid, vel donatione vel testamento, percipere, etc. On this subject Jerome Epist. 34 (al. 2) ad Nepotianum: Nec de lege conqueror, sed doleo cur meruerimus hanc legem. Cauterium bonum est sed quo mihi vulnus, ut indigeam cauterio? Provida severaque legis cautio, et tamen nec sic refraenatur avaritia. Comp. the laws of Theodosius II. l. c. l. 27 and 28.

[15] In a one-sided way Athanasius Hist. Arian. ad Monachos, c. 78, designates only the Meletian clergy as *οἱ μὲν ἐξ εἰδώλων ἐλθόντες, οἱ δὲ ἐκ τοῦ βουλευτηρίου, καὶ τῆς πρώτης πολιτείας, διὰ τὴν ταλαίπωρον ἀλειτουργησίαν καὶ προστασίαν.* Basilius Ep. 54, blames his country bishops on account of their subservience to men, *τῶν πλείστων φόβῳ τῆς στρατολογίας εἰσποιούντων ἑαυτοὺς τῇ ὑπηρεσίᾳ.*

[16] In the work entitled de Septem ordinibus Ecclesiae (Opp. ed. Martian. v. 100), ascribed to Jerome, the copiatae appear under the name fossarii as the lowest order of the clergy. According to a law of Theodosius II. A.D. 416 (Cod. Theod. xiv. ii. 42) no more than 500 parabolani were to be in Alexandria. In the year 418 he permitted 600

pressure, which became dangerous to the state, with stringent laws.[17]

Under these circumstances the power of the bishops particularly rose. At the head of a numerous clergy completely subject to them, they alone had power to decide on the appropriation of the church estates,[18] and controlled ecclesiastical legislation by their exclusive privilege of having a voice at synods. Hence they continued to make the country bishops more subservient to them;[19] to the other churches in cities and in the country (ecclesia plebana, titulus), except the head church (eccl. cathedralis) they sent according to their own free choice, presbyters (parochus, plebanus),[20] to conduct the worship of God, who were entirely dependent on them even in the matter of maintenance. The first person next to the bishop was *the archdeacon*,[21] who helped him to manage the revenues. *The arch-presbyters*,[22] an order which arose about the same time, were of far inferior rank. All the lower clergy and the presby-

(ibid. i. 43). The same emperor reduced the number of copiatae in Constantinople from 1100 to 950 (Cod. Just. i. ii. 4).

[17] Constantine's law to this effect before the year 320 (Cod. Theod. xvi. ii. 3): Nullum deinceps Decurionem, vel ex Decurione progenitum, vel etiam instructum idoneis facultatibus, atque obeundis publicis muneribus opportunum, ad Clericorum nomen obsequiumque confugere: sed eos de cetero in defunctorum duntaxat Clericorum loca subrogari, qui fortuna tenues, neque muneribus civilibus teneantur obstricti. Constantius allowed in 361 (Cod. Th. xii. i. 49) every curialis admission into the clerical office, curia promente consensum, maxime si totius populi vocibus expetatur: otherwise he should give over his property to his children, or relatives, or the senate. This resigning of goods became afterward a general law (Cod. Th. xii. i. 59, 99, 104, 115, 121, 123, 163, 172, etc.). Riffel, i. 164.

[18] Riffel, i. 128.

[19] See Div. I. § 68, note 2. Conc. Antioch. ann. 341, can. 10: Τοὺς χωρεπισκόπους, εἰ καὶ χειροθεσίαν εἶεν ἐπισκόπων εἰληφότες, ἔδοξε τῇ ἁγίᾳ συνόδῳ—καθιστᾷν ἀναγνώστας καὶ ὑποδιακόνους καὶ ἐφορκιστὰς,—μήτε δὲ πρεσβύτερον μήτε διάκονον χειροτονεῖν τολμᾷν δίχα τοῦ ἐν τῇ πόλει ἐπισκόπου, ᾗ ὑπόκεινται αὐτός τε καὶ ἡ χώρα,—χωρεπίσκοπον δὲ γίνεσθαι ὑπὸ τοῦ τῆς πόλεως, ᾗ ὑπόκειται, ἐπισκόπου. Conc. Laodiceni (between 320 and 372) Can. 57: Ὅτι οὐ δεῖ ἐν ταῖς κώμαις, καὶ ἐν ταῖς χώραις καθίστασθαι ἐπισκόπους, ἢ ἀλλὰ περιοδευτάς· τοὺς μέντοι ἤδη προκατασταθέντας μηδὲν πράττειν ἄνευ γνώμης τοῦ ἐπισκόπου τοῦ ἐν τῇ πόλει. ὡσαύτως δὲ καὶ τοὺς πρεσβυτέρους μηδὲν πράττειν ἄνευ τῆς γνώμης τοῦ ἐπισκόπου. Probably it was not meant by this canon to do away with the existing country bishops, but only to prevent the establishment of new bishoprics. Accordingly we find frequent mention of country bishops long after. Basil the Great had fifty in his diocese (Gregor. Naz. de vita sua, p. 8), Theodoret, Ep. 113, names two of his suburbans, etc.

[20] Thomassini Vetus et nova eccles. disciplin. p. i. lib. 2, c. 21, ss. Bingham, lib. ix. c. 8, vol. iii. p. 590.

[21] Thomassini, p. i. lib. 2, c. 17. Bingham, vol. i. p. 338. J. G. Pertsch Abhandl. v. d. Ursprunge der Archidiaconen, 2 c. Hildesheim. 1743. 8.

[22] Thomassini, p. i. lib. 2, c. 3. Bingham, vol. i. p. 301.

ters too were now chosen by the bishop alone. The choice of bishops mostly depended on the other bishops of the provinces, except when the emperors interfered. Still, however, the consent of the people was required, and was not without weight, especially in the west.[23]

Under these external advantages, it is not surprising that the prevailing notions of priestly dignity, and especially of the bishops' authority rose higher and higher; and that the bishops externally enjoyed the highest demonstrations of respect, their claims as the vicars of Christ and the successors of the apostles being capable of indefinite development.[24] Yet their overweening pride often gave just cause for complaint [25]

[23] The bishop was chosen Ἐπισκόπων συνόδῳ, ψήφῳ κληρικῶν, αἰτήσει λαῶν (Petri Alex. Epist. in Theodoreti H. E. iv. 19). The person elected by the clergy was either accepted by the voice of the people crying out Ἄξιος, bene meritus, bene dignus; or they cried Ἀνάξιος (Augustini Epist. 110. Philostorgius, ix. 10. Constitut. Apost. viii. 4). Leo Epist. 10, c. 3: Qui praefuturus est omnibus, ab omnibus eligatur. Thomassini, p. ii. lib. 2, c. 2 and 3. Bingham, vol. ii. p. 90, ss. Staudenmaier's Gesch. d. Bischofswahlen, S. 24. Riffel, i. 574.

[24] The assertion, so pregnant with consequences, that the priesthood stands above royalty, in which during the third century nothing but a secret pride could take delight (Div. I. § 69, note 1), was not only repeated (see Chrysost. Homil. 4, de verbis Isaiae, de Sacerdotio, iii. c. 1, Homil. 15, in Epist. ii. ad Corinth. comp. Gregor. Naz. above, note 8), but was now also outwardly manifested in the conduct. Standing titles of the bishops were Dominus beatissimus (comp. Wiggers' Augustinismus, ii. 37) or sanctissimus, reverendissimus, δεσπότης ὁσιώτατος, αἰδεσιμώτατος, Beatitudo, Sanctitas tua, ἡ σὴ χρηστότης, μακαριότης or ἁγιότης. Marks of reverence which were paid them even by emperors were the ὑποκλίνειν κεφαλὴν and καταφιλεῖν τὰς χεῖρας. See Bingham, vol. i. p. 134. When Eusebia, spouse of the emperor Constantius, did not observe such things in receiving the salutations of the bishops, the Eusebian bishop of Tripolis, Leontius, declared to her (Philostorgius, ap. Suidam, s. v. Λεόντιος), that he would appear before her only under the following conditions: Ἵν' εἰσέλθοιμι μὲν ἐγὼ, σὺ δ' αὐτίκα τοῦ θρόνου τοῦ ὑψηλοῦ κατάβασα, μετ' αἰδοῦς ὑπαντήσειας ἐμοὶ, καὶ τὴν κεφαλὴν ὑπόσχῃς ταῖς ἐμαῖς χερσὶν, εὐλογιῶν ἀξιουμένη· κἄπειτα καθεσθείην μὲν ἂν ἐγὼ, σὺ δ' ἂν ἑστήκοις αἰδουμένη, ὁπόταν δὲ κελεύσαιμι, καθεδουμένη, ἡνίκα δοίην τὸ σύνθημα. Εἰ οὕτως αἱρήσῃ, ἀφικοίμην παρά σε, κ. τ. λ. Comp. the conduct of bishop Martinus at the court of Maximus. At table the emperor ordered the cup to be first presented to him (Sulp. Severus de vita Mart. c. 20), expectans atque ambiens, ut ab illius dextera poculum sumeret. Sed Martinus ubi ebibit, pateram presbytero suo tradidit, nullum scilicet existimans digniorem, qui post se biberet. At another time the empress waited on him at table (Sulp. Severi Dial. ii. 6). Comp. generally: Chrysost. de Sacerdotio. The work de Dignitate, found among the writings of Ambrose, is not by him, but by Gerbert (Sylvester II. about 1000). See Mabillon Analecta, p. 103.

[25] Hieronym. ad Tit. c. 1: De episcopatu intumescunt, et putant se non dispensationem Christi sed imperium consecutos.—Sciat episcopus et presbyter sibi populum conservum esse, non servum.

§ 92.

DEPENDENCE OF THE HIERARCHY ON THE STATE.

Notwithstanding these outward honors enjoyed by the hierarchy, they could the less escape from a dependence on the state in many ways,[1] as they presented a vulnerable side to it by their acquisition of property;[2] and as the government of the Roman emperors, since the removal of their residence to the east, began to assume an oriental despotic character.[3]

The first occasion of interference in ecclesiastical matters was offered by the hierarchy itself when involved in an uninterrupted series of controversies.[4] The emperors wished, and also ought, according to the desire of the hierarchy, to tolerate only the catholic church;[5] but as this name was claimed exclusively by so many parties, the emperors were obliged to decide to which it belonged, and what doctrine accordingly should be considered the catholic doctrine.[6] To this end they summoned councils, allowing them to consult under the superintendence of their commissioners;[7] and then gave imperial confirmation to their

[1] The two Luciferians Faustinus and Marcellinus in libello precum first complained of this (Bibl. PP. Lugd. v. 656): Imperatoris arbitrio Episcopi nunc ex catholicis fiunt haeretici, et iidem Episcopi ex haereticis ad fidem catholicam revertuntur. Isidorus Pelus. lib. v. Ep. 268, ad Cyrill. Episc.: *Πάλαι μὲν ἡ ἱερωσύνη πταίουσαν τὴν βασιλείαν διωρθοῦτο καὶ ἐσωφρόνιζε, νῦν δὲ ὑπ' ἐκείνην γέγονεν, κ. τ. λ.* Socrates, lib. iv. Proem.: *'Αφ' οὗ χριστιανίζειν ἤρξαντο (οἱ βασιλεῖς), τὰ τῆς 'Εκκλησίας πράγματα ἤρτητο ἐξ αὐτῶν, καὶ αἱ μέγισται Σύνοδοι τῇ αὐτῶν γνώμῃ γεγόνασί τε καὶ γίνονται.*

[2] Faustinus and Marcellinus, l. c. p. 654, respecting the bishops who had fallen away under Constantius (see § 82, note 14): Non dignantur pro Christo Filio Dei exilium perpeti, cum propriis sedibus et Ecclesiarum perniciossimis possessionibus oblectantur. —Episcopi plus iram regis terreni timuerunt quam Christum.

[3] C. W. de Rhoer Dissert. de effectu relig. christ. in jurisprudentiam Romanam, p. 40, ss.

[4] First by the Donatists. See Div. I.

[5] Constantine's law, A.D. 326 (Cod. Theod. xvi. v. 1): Privilegia, quae contemplatione religionis indulta sunt, catholicae tantum legis observatoribus prodesse oportet. Haereticos autem, atque schismaticos non tantum ab his privilegiis alienos esse volumus, sed etiam diversis muneribus constringi et subjici.

[6] Comp. the law of Theodosius I. A.D 380, Cod. Theod. xvi. 1, 2, see above § 83, note 32.

[7] Eusebius de vita Const. i. 44: *'Εξαίρετον τῇ ἐκκλησίᾳ τοῦ θεοῦ τὴν παρ' αὐτοῦ νέμων φροντίδα, διαφερομένων τινῶν πρὸς ἀλλήλους κατὰ διαφόρους χώρας, οἷά τις κοινὸς ἐπίσκοπος ἐκ θεοῦ καθεσταμένος, συνόδους τῶν τοῦ θεοῦ λειτουργῶν συνεκρότει.* Constant. Epist. ad Syn. Tyriam (ibid. iv. 42): *'Απέστειλα πρὸς οὓς ἐβουλήθητε τῶν ἐπισκόπων, ἵνα παραγενόμενοι, κοινωνήσωσιν ὑμῖν τῶν φροντισμάτων· ἀπέστειλα Διονύσιον τὸν ἀπὸ ὑπατικῶν, ὃς καὶ τοὺς ὀφείλοντας εἰς τὴν σύνοδον ἀφικέσθαι μεθ' ὑμῶν ὑπομνήσει, καὶ τῶν πραττομένων, ἐξαιρέτως δὲ τῆς εὐταξίας κατάσκοπος παρέσται· ἐὰν γάρ τις, ὡς ἐγὼ οὐκ οἴομαι, τὴν ἡμετέραν κέλευσιν καὶ νῦν διακρούσασθαι πειρώμενος,*

decrees.[8] But when the controversy was not terminated by this means, as usually happened, the emperors were often led by political, often by religious motives, often by court cabals, to step in with new decisions, sometimes taking a middle course, sometimes giving the superiority to the party formerly condemned.[9] The party favored by the emperor then appeared to look upon the civil power as exercised only for the protection of the church,[10] and none but the defeated maintained that matters of faith should not be submitted to the emperor's decision, but to the bishops.[11]

Besides these great party questions, individuals among the clergy had also many particular cases in which the interference of the emperors was solicited, although councils soon forbade

μὴ βουληθῇ παραγενέσθαι, ἐντεῦθεν παρ' ἡμῶν ἀποσταλήσεται, ὅς ἐκ βασιλικοῦ προστάγματος αὐτὸν ἐκβαλὼν ὡς οὐ προσῆκεν ὅροις αὐτοκράτορος ὑπὲρ τῆς ἀληθείας ἐξενεχθεῖσιν ἀντιτείνειν, διδάξει. The emperor gave full powers to the tribune Marcellinus to decide the controversy between the Catholics and Donatists, A.D. 411. See Gesta Collationis Carthaginensis diei i. c. 4 (annexed to Optatus Milev. ed. du Pin, p. 247): Cui quidem disputationi principe loco te judicem volumus residere, omnemque vel in congregandis Episcopis, vel evocandis, si adesse contemserint, curam te volumus sustinere, ut et ea, quae ante mandata sunt, et quae nunc statuta cognoscis, probata possis implere solertia: id ante omnia servaturus, ut ea quae circa catholicam legem vel olim ordinavit antiquitas, vel parentum nostrorum auctoritas religiosa constituit, vel nostra serenitas roboravit, novella subreptione submota, integra et inviolata custodias. Comp. Fuch's Bibl. der Kirchenversammlungen, Th. 3, S. 166.

[8] Epist. Conc. ii. oecumen. (Constantinop. ann. 381) ad Theodosium Imp. (Mansi, iii. p. 557): Δεόμεθα τοίνυν τῆς σῆς ἡμερότητος γράμματι τῆς σῆς εὐσεβίας ἐπικυρωθῆναι τῆς συνόδου τὸν ψῆφον· ἵν' ὥσπερ τοῖς τῆς κλήσεως γράμμασι τὴν ἐκκλησίαν τετίμηκας, οὕτω καὶ τῶν δοξάντων ἐπισφραγίσῃς τὸ τέλος. Cf. de Marca de concord. Sac. et Imp. lib. ii. c. 10, § 10, ss. lib. vi. c. 22.

[9] Thus Athanasius Hist. Arian. ad Mon. c. 33, puts into the mouth of Constantius, in reply to the bishops assembled in Milan (355) these words: Ὅπερ ἐγὼ βούλομαι, τοῦτο κανὼν νομιζέσθω· οὕτω γάρ μου λέγοντος ἀνέχονται οἱ τῆς Συρίας λεγόμενοι ἐπίσκοποι. ἢ τοίνυν πείσθητε, ἢ καὶ ὑμεῖς ὑπερόριοι γενήσεσθε.

[10] To the Donatists, who reported the imperial decisions with the words (Optatus Milev. i. 22): Quid Christianis cum Regibus? aut quid Episcopis cum palatio? and (ibid. iii. 3): Quid est Imperatori cum Ecclesia? Optatus replies (l. c.): Non Respublica est in Ecclesia, sed Ecclesia in Republica est, i. e., in Imperio Romano.—Cum super Imperatorum non sit nisi solus Deus, qui fecit Imperatorem, dum se Donatus super Imperatorem extollit, jam quasi hominum excesserat metas, ut prope se Deum, non hominem aestimaret, non reverendo eum, qui post Deum ab hominibus timebatur.

[11] Hosii Epist. ad Constantium (in Athanasii Hist. Arianorum ad Monachos, c. 44): Μὴ τίθει σεαυτὸν εἰς τὰ ἐκκλησιαστικὰ, μηδὲ σὺ περὶ τούτων ἡμῖν παρακελεύου· ἀλλὰ μᾶλλον παρ' ἡμῶν σὺ μάνθανε ταῦτα. σοὶ βασιλείαν ὁ θεὸς ἐνεχείρισεν, ἡμῖν τὰ τῆς ἐκκλησίας ἐπίστευσε. καὶ ὥσπερ ὁ τὴν σὴν ἀρχὴν ὑποκλέπτων ἀντιλέγει τῷ διαταξαμένῳ θεῷ· οὕτω φοβήθητι, μὴ καὶ σὺ τὰ τῆς ἐκκλησίας εἰς ἑαυτὸν ἕλκων ὑπεύθυνος ἐγκλήματι μεγάλῳ γένῃ. So, too, Athanasius, lib. cit. in various passages. Leontius bishop of Tripolis said to Constantius (Suidas, s. v. Λεόντιος): Θαυμάζω, ὅπως ἕτερα διέπειν ταχθεὶς, ἑτέροις ἐπιχειρεῖς, στρατιωτικῶν μὲν καὶ πολιτικῶν πραγμάτων προεστηκὼς, Ἐπισκόποις δὲ περὶ τῶν εἰς μόνους Ἐπισκόπους ἡκόντων διαταττόμενος.

such supplications to the emperor.[12] The clergy indeed endeavored, backed as they were by imperial privileges, to make themselves as independent as possible of the other authorities of the state,[13] but they still acknowledged the emperor to be their highest judge,[14] so much so that the Roman bishop regarded it a distinction to be judged only by the emperor.[15] None ventured to call in question the supreme authority of the emperor, as far as it did not violate the rights of conscience;[16] and the imperial laws, even when they touched the church, were received by the bishops with implicit obedience.[17] The great influence exercised by the emperors, partly in filling up the most

[12] Conc. Antioch. ann. 341, c. 12: Εἴ τις ὑπὸ τοῦ ἰδίου 'Επισκόπου καθαιρεθεὶς πρεσβύτερος, ἢ διάκονος, ἢ καὶ 'Επίσκοπος ὑπὸ συνόδου, ἐνοχλῆσαι τολμήσειε τὰς βασιλέως ἀκοὰς, δέον ἐπὶ μείζονα 'Επισκόπων σύνοδον τρέπεσθαι, καὶ ἃ νομίζει δίκαια ἔχειν προσαναφέρειν πλείοσιν ἐπισκόποις, καὶ τὴν αὐτῶν ἐξέτασίν τε καὶ ἐπίκρισιν ἐκδέχεσθαι· εἰ δὲ τούτων ὀλιγωρήσας ἐνοχλήσειε τῷ βασιλεῖ, καὶ τοῦτον μηδεμιᾶς συγγνώμης ἀξιοῦσθαι, μηδὲ χώραν ἀπολογίας ἔχειν, μηδὲ ἐλπίδα ἀποκαταστάσεως προσδοκᾷν. This is repeated by the Conc. Constantin. ann. 381, c. 6.—Conc. Antioch. c. 11, forbids all the clergy to go to the emperor ἄνευ γνώμης καὶ γραμμάτων τῶν ἐν τῇ ἐπαρχίᾳ ἐπισκόπων, καὶ μάλιστα τοῦ κατὰ τὴν μητρόπολιν. Conc. Sardic. can. latinus 8 (graec. 7): Quidam non cessant comitatum ire Episcopi, et maxime Afri:—ut non solum ad comitatum multas et diversas Ecclesiae non profuturas perferant causas, neque ut fieri solet aut oportet, ut pauperibus, aut viduis, aut pupillis subveniatur: sed et dignitates saeculares et administrationes quibusdam postulent. Haec itaque pravitas olim non solum murmurationes, sed et scandala excitavit. Honestum est autem, ut Episcopi intercessionem his praestent, qui iniqua vi opprimuntur, aut si vidua affligatur, aut pupillus exspolietur: si tamen ista omnia justam habeant causam, aut petitionem. Si ergo vobis fratres carissimi, placet, decernite, ne Episcopi ad comitatum accedant, nisi forte hi, qui religiosi Imperatoris literis vel invitati, vel evocati fuerint.—Universi dixerunt: Placet, et constituatur.

[13] See above, § 91, note 5.

[14] Thus Athanasius asked of Constantine (Athanas. Apol. contra Arianos, c. 9), νόμιμον ἐπισκόπων σύνοδον συγκροτηθῆναι, ἢ καὶ αὐτὸν (βασιλέα) δέξασθαι τὴν ἀπολογίαν, ὧν ἐπήγαγον αὐτῷ, and came for this purpose after the synod of Tyre in person to Constantinople. Socrates, i. 33, ss.

[15] Epistola Rom. Concilii ad Gratianum et Valentinianum Impp. A.D. 378 (in J. Sirmondi append. Cod. Theodos. p. 78, and ap. Coustant among Damasi Epistt. no. 6): Accipite aliud quoque, quod vir sanctus (Damasus) vestrae magis conferre pietati, quam sibi praestare desiderat, nec derogare cuiquam, sed principibus adrogare; quoniam non novum aliquid petit, sed sequitur exempla majorum: ut Episcopus Romanus, si concilio ejus causa non creditur, apud concilium se imperiale defendat. Nam et Sylvester Papa a sacrilegis accusatus, apud parentem vestrum Constantinum causam propriam prosecutus est. Et de scripturis similia exempla suppeditant: quod cum a praeside sanctus Apostolus vim pateretur. Caesarem appellavit, et ad Caesarem missus est.

[16] See Optatus, above, note 10. Ambrosius Apolog. David. c. 10: Nullis David legibus tenebatur, quia liberi sunt Reges a vinculis delictorum, nec enim ullis ad poenam vocantur legibus, tuti Imperii Majestate.

[17] To the law Cod. Theod. xvi. ii. 20, ad Damasum Episc. urbis Rom. (see above, § 91, note 14) the remark is annexed: lecta in ecclesiis Rom. (comp. the evasive remarks of Baronius, ann. 370, no. 123). Gothofredus ad h. l. gives several examples of the reading of the imperial laws in churches.

important episcopal sees, partly in even deposing and appointing bishops without farther ceremony,[18] naturally secured to them the obedience of the clergy, and with it the direction of ecclesiastical affairs. The slavish Greeks now began to attribute to them a priestly character.[19] A strict theory respecting the limits of the ecclesiastical and civil power was not yet laid down.[20]

§ 93.

ORIGIN OF PATRIARCHS, ESPECIALLY IN THE EAST.

Traité historique de la Primauté en l'église par D. Blondel. Genève. 1641. fol.—Jo. Morini Exercitatt. ecclesiasticae et biblicae. Paris. 1669. fol. (diss. i. de Patriarcharum et Primatum origine).—L. E. du Pin de Antiqua eccles. disciplina dissertt. Paris. 1686. 4. Diss. i.—L. Thomassini Vetus et nova Ecclesiae disciplina lib. i. cap. 7–20.—Bingham Origg. eccl. lib. ii. cap. 17.—J. W. Janus de Origine Patriarcharum christianorum diss. ii. Viteb. 1718. 4.—W. C. L. Ziegler's pragm. Gesch. der kirchl. Verfassungsformen in den ersten sechs Jahrh. Leipzig. 1798. 8. S. 164, ff.—Planck's Gesch. d. christl. kirchl. Gesellschaftsverfassung. Bd. 1. S. 598, ff.

In the preceding period it has been already seen, that the three great metropolitans of *Rome*, *Alexandria*, and *Antioch*,

18 Especially in Constantinople. Thomassini Vetus et nova Eccl. discipl. p. ii. lib. 2, c. 6. Riffel, i. 589.

19 Assent at the synod of Constantinople in the year 448 (Mansi, vi. 733): *Πολλὰ τὰ ἔτη τῷ ἀρχιερεῖ βασιλεῖ.* The later emperors seriously laid claim to the priestly dignity by virtue of their being anointed. Thus the abbot Maximus in Constantinople 655, is asked (Mansi, xi. 6): Ergo non est omnis christianus Imperator etiam sacerdos? to which indeed he replies, Non est. Leo the Isaurian about 730 writes to Pope Gregory II. (Mansi, xii. 976): *Βασιλεὺς καὶ ἱερεύς εἰμι.* The throne of the emperor in the church was at first beside that of the bishop at the choir, till Ambrose assigned it a place close to the choir. Sozom. vii. 25). Yet the emperor ventured to lay his oblations on the altar himself. Conc. Quinisext. A.D. 692, can. 69.

20 Eusebius de vita Const. iv. 24, relates the following, after he had spoken of Constantine's activity against Paganism: *Ἔνθεν εἰκότως αὐτὸς ἐν ἑστιάσει ποτὲ δεξιούμενος ἐπισκόπους, λόγον ἀφῆκεν, ὡς ἄρα εἴη καὶ αὐτὸς ἐπίσκοπος. ὧδέ πῃ αὐτοῖς εἰπὼν ῥήμασιν ἐφ' ἡμετέραις ἀκοαῖς· "ἀλλ' ὑμεῖς μὲν τῶν εἴσω τῆς ἐκκλησίας, ἐγὼ δὲ τῶν ἐκτὸς ὑπὸ θεοῦ καθεσταμένος ἐπίσκοπος ἂν εἴην." ἀκόλουθα δ' οὖν τῷ λόγῳ διανοούμενος, τοὺς ἀρχομένους ἅπαντας ἐπεσκόπει, προὔτρεπέ τε ὅσῃ περ ἂν ἡ δύναμις τὸν εὐσεβῆ μεταδιώκειν βίον.* Different explanations of these words of Constantine may be seen in Ch. G. F. Walch de *τοῖς εἴσω τῆς ἐκκλησίας* et *τοῖς ἐκτὸς* Constantini M. in the Commentationes Soc. Gottingensis, vol. vi. p. 81, ss. Heinichen Excurs. iv., annexed to his edition of Euseb. de vita Const. p. 537. Since an expression like *ἐπίσκοπος πραγμάτων* can not be pointed out, and there follows immediately after *ἐπισκοπεῖν ἀρχομένους*, Constantine probably did not mean *τὰ ἐκτός*, but *τοὺς ἐκτός*. *Οἱ ἐκτός* and *οἱ ἀρχόμενοι ἅπαντες* must be the same, and thus we obtain the following explanation: "Be ye the overseers of those who belong to the church, and so far as they belong to it: let me be the overseer of those without the church, and in so far as they are out of it (whether it be wholly as heathen, or partly, i. e., Christians in their civil relations).

were distinguished from the other metropolitans by having several provinces under their oversight. This institution came up for discussion at *the council of Nice*, probably on occasion of the Meletian schism in Egypt; and was confirmed by the 6th can.[1] At the same time provincial synods were still acknowledged at this council as the highest ecclesiastical authority.[2]

But during the subsequent Arian commotions, the provincial synods were too weak to be able to withstand, in the eternal party-strife, powerful opponents who were often supported by state authority. By this means the bishops were induced to form still larger hierarchical associations by which they might individually obtain greater security. In the political, often

[1] Can. Nic. vi.: *Τὰ ἀρχαῖα ἔθη κρατείτω, τὰ ἐν Αἰγύπτῳ καὶ Λιβύῃ καὶ Πενταπόλει, ὥστε τὸν Ἀλεξανδρείας ἐπίσκοπον πάντων τούτων ἔχειν τὴν ἐξουσίαν· ἐπειδὴ καὶ τῷ ἐν τῇ Ῥώμῃ ἐπισκόπῳ τοῦτο σύνηθές ἐστιν· ὁμοίως δὲ καὶ κατὰ τὴν Ἀντιόχειαν, καὶ ἐν ταῖς ἄλλαις ἐπαρχίαις τὰ πρεσβεῖα σώζεσθαι ταῖς ἐκκλησίαις. Καθόλου δὲ πρόδηλον ἐκεῖνο, ὅτι εἴ τις χωρὶς γνώμης τοῦ μητροπολίτου γένοιτο ἐπίσκοπος, τὸν τοιοῦτον ἡ μεγάλη σύνοδος ὥρισε μὴ δεῖν εἶναι ἐπίσκοπον.* The Romans made what they inferred from this canon in favor of their church the superscription of it in their oldest Cod. canonum (see it ap. Mansi, vi. 1186; comp. Labbei observ. ap. Mansi, ii. 688), which afterward was incorporated with the canon. So the Roman legates cited it at the council of Chalcedon (Mansi, vii. 444): Ecclesia Romana semper habuit primatum. Teneat autem et Aegyptus, Libya, et Pentapolis, ita ut Episcopus Alexandriae harum omnium habeat potestatem: quoniam et Romano Episcopo haec est consuetudo, etc. But on the other hand, in the Prisca, which dates immediately after the council of Chalcedon (Mansi, vi. 1127): Antiqui moris est, ut urbis Romae Episcopus habeat principatum, ut suburbicaria loca et omnem provinciam suam sollicitudine gubernet. Quae vero apud Aegyptum sunt, Alexandriae Episcopus omnium habeat sollicitudinem. Similiter autem et circa Antiochiam, et in caeteris provinciis privilegia propria serventur metropolitanis ecclesiis, etc. Nicolaus I. (A.D. 863) Ep. viii. ad Michaelem (ap. Mansi, xv. 206) explains the canon thus: Denique si instituta Nicaenae synodi diligenter inspiciantur, invenietur profecto, quia Romanae Ecclesiae nullum eadem Synodus contulit incrementum: sed potius ex ejus forma, quod Alexandriae Ecclesiae tribuerit particulariter, sumpsit exemplum. On the other hand Bellarmine de Romano Pontifice, lib. ii. c. 13: Alexandrinum debere gubernare illas provincias, quia Romanus Episcopus ita consuevit, id est, quia Romanus Episcopus ante omnem Conciliorum definitionem consuevit permittere Episcopo Alexandrino regimen Aegypti, Libyae, et Pentapolis, sive consuevit per Alexandrinum Episcopum illas provincias gubernare. In later times, the only point of dispute has been whether in this canon, as the Greek canonists Johannes Scholasticus, Theod. Balsamon, and Zonaras assume, patriarchal rights (so Sirmond, Em. Schelstrate, Natalis Alexander, etc.), or metropolitan rights (so J. Launoy, Sam. Basnage, etc.), are spoken of. The copious literature on the subject may be seen in Sagittarii Introduct. in Hist. Eccl. ii. 1224, ss.

[2] Can. Nic. 4 confirms to the provincial synod its influence in the election of bishops. Canon 5 recognizes it as the highest court of appeal in cases of excommunication. Conc. Antioch. ann. 341, c. 15: *Εἴ τις ἐπίσκοπος ἐπί τισιν ἐγκλήμασιν κατηγορηθεὶς, κριθείη ὑπὸ πάντων τῶν ἐν τῇ ἐπαρχίᾳ ἐπισκόπων, πάντες τε σύμφωνοι μίαν κατ' αὐτοῦ ἐξενέγκοιεν ψῆφον· τοῦτον μηκέτι παρ' ἑτέροις δικάζεσθαι, ἀλλὰ μένειν βεβαίαν τὴν σύμφωνον τῶν ἐπὶ ἐπαρχίας ἐπισκόπων ἀπόφασιν.* In case of division among the provincial bishops, the metropolitan, according to canon 14, is empowered to summon bishops from the neighboring province.

ecclesiastical separation of the east and west, this new hierarchical development proceeded in a different mode in the two empires.

In *the east*, the political division of the provinces had been followed from the first in the development of the metropolitan institution, and the fundamental principle became more and more established, that the ecclesiastical should constantly follow the political division of provinces.[3] Accordingly, in the formation of larger hierarchical bodies,[4] they adhered to the political distribution of the realm into dioceses, which had been made by Constantine.[5] The bishops of every diocese became more closely connected with each other; the bishop of the chief city in the diocese was their common president, and was elevated by this means above the other metropolitans. Yet his rights were defined according to earlier ecclesiastical relations, and for this reason were not alike in all dioceses. In Egypt, *the bishop of Alexandria* had almost monarchical power;[6] the power of *the bishop of Antioch* in the east was less;[7] less still was that of

[3] Conf. Conc. Antiochen. can. 9, see Div. I. § 68, note 4. When Cappadocia was divided into two provinces, A.D. 371, Basil was disposed to resist the application of this principle against the bishop of Tyana, Gregor. Naz. Orat. xliii. c. 58 (ed. Coloni, Orat. xx. p. 355). Ullmann's Gregorius v. Naz. S. 118, ff. On the other hand, Conc. Chalcedon. can. 17: *Εἰ δέ τις ἐκ βασιλικῆς ἐξουσίας ἐκαινίσθη πόλις, ἢ αὖθις καινισθείη, τοῖς πολιτικοῖς καὶ δημοσίοις τύποις καὶ τῶν ἐκκλησιαστικῶν παροικιῶν ἡ τάξις ἀκολουθείτω.* Comp. below, note 14.

[4] The first appearance of such larger synods, Conc. Antioch. ann. 341, can. 12, see above, § 92, note 12.

[5] Zosimus, ii. 33. Notitia dignitatum utriusque imperii, probably written in the reign of Theodosius II. (cum G. Panzirolli Comm. in Graevii Thes. antiquitt. Roman. vol. vii. p. 1309, ss.) I. PRAEFECTURA ORIENTIS, 1. Dioecesis Orientis (chief city Antioch); 2. Aegypti (Alexandria); 3. Asiae (Ephesus); 4. Ponti (Caesarea Cappadociae); 5. Thraciae (Heraclea, then Constantinople). II. PRAEF. ILLYRICI ORIENTALIS, after 379 separated from the west, with the chief city Thessalonica. 1. Dioec. Macedoniae; 2. Daciae. III. PRAEF. ITALIAE, 1. Dioec. Romae (Rome); 2. Italiae (Mediolanum); 3. Illyrici occidentalis (Sirmium); 4. Africae (Carthage). IV. PRAEF. GALLIARUM, 1. Dioec. Galliae (Augusta Trevirorum); 2. Hispaniae; 3. Britanniae. Over the prefectures were placed Praefecti Praetorio; over the dioceses or vicariates Vicarii; over the provinces Rectores, with different titles, as consulares, correctores, usually praesides.

[6] Epiphanius Haer. 68, § 1: *Τοῦτο γὰφ ἔθος ἐστὶ, τὸν ἐν τῇ Ἀλεξανδρείᾳ Ἀρχιεπίσκοπον πάσης τε Αἰγύπτου καὶ Θηβαΐδος, Μαραιώτου τε καὶ Λιβύης, Ἀμμονιακῆς Μαραιώτιδός τε καὶ Πενταπόλεως ἔχειν τὴν ἐκκλησιαστικὴν διοίκησιν.* Cf. Clausen de Synesio Hafn. 1831. p. 173.

[7] Hieronymi ad Pammachium contra errores Joann. Hierosol. (A.D. 397) c. 15: Tu qui regulas quaeris ecclesiasticas, et Nicaeni concilii canonibus uteris:—responde mihi: ad Alexandrinum episcopum Palaestina quid pertinet? Ni fallor, hoc ibi decernitur, ut Palaestinae Metropolis Caesarea sit, et totius Orientis Antiochia. Aut igitur ad Caesariensem Episcopum referre debueras—aut si procul expetendum judicium erat, Antiochiam potius literae dirigendae.

the bishop of Ephesus in the Asiatic, and that of *the bishop of Caesarea Cappadociae*, in the Pontian diocese. In the Thracian diocese, *Constantinople* had become the political capital instead of Heraclea, and as it was also the chief city of the empire, the power of the bishop of Constantinople, supported by his influence with the emperor, and the consent of the numerous bishops who were always assembled at court (*σύνοδος ἐνδημοῦσα*),[8] soon extended far beyond the Thracian diocese; but the degree of power depended very much on the personal relations of the reigning patriarch. Such was the state of things when *the second general council* (381), approved of those relations between the bishops of one diocese (can. 2), elevated the diocesan synods above the provincial synods so as to be the highest ecclesiastical court (can. 6), and gave the bishop of *Constantinople* the first rank after the bishop of Rome (can. 3).[9]

Thus in the east the bishops of *Constantinople*, *Alexandria*, *Antioch*, *Ephesus*, and *Caesarea*, had obtained an important elevation above the other metropolitans, for they had subjected to themselves the other metropolitans of their dioceses. They received the distinctive names: *Ἔξαρχος*, *Ἀρχιεπίσκοπος*,[10] and shortly before the council of Chalcedon, the appellation *Πατρι-*

[8] Anatolius, bishop of Constantinople, says at the council of Chalcedon, actio iv. (ap. Mansi, vii. 92): *Συνήθεια ἄνωθεν κεκράτηκε, τοὺς ἐνδημοῦντας τῇ μεγαλωνύμῳ πόλει ἁγιωτάτους ἐπισκόπους, ἡνίκα καιρὸς καλέσῃ, περὶ ἀνακυπτόντων τινῶν ἐκκλησιαστικῶν πραγμάτων συνεῖναι, καὶ διατυποῦν ἕκαστα, καὶ ἀποκρίσεως ἀξιοῦν τοὺς δεομένους.*

[9] Canon II.: *Τοὺς ὑπὲρ διοίκησιν ἐπισκόπους ταῖς ὑπερορίοις ἐκκλησίαις μὴ ἐπιέναι, μηδὲ συγχέειν τὰς ἐκκλησίας· ἀλλὰ κατὰ τοὺς κανόνας τὸν μὲν Ἀλεξανδρείας ἐπίσκοπον τὰ ἐν Αἰγύπτῳ μόνον οἰκονομεῖν· τοὺς δὲ τῆς Ἀνατολῆς ἐπισκόπους τὴν Ἀνατολὴν μόνην διοικεῖν, φυλαττομένων τῶν ἐν τοῖς κανόσι τοῖς κατὰ Νικαίαν πρεσβείων τῇ Ἀντιοχέων ἐκκλησίᾳ· καὶ τοὺς τῆς Ἀσιανῆς διοικήσεως ἐπισκόπους τὰ κατὰ τὴν Ἀσίαν μόνην οἰκονομεῖν· καὶ τοὺς τῆς Ποντικῆς τὰ τῆς Ποντικῆς μόνον· καὶ τοὺς τῆς Θρᾴκης τὰ τῆς Θρᾳκικῆς μόνον οἰκονομεῖν. Φυλαττομένου δὲ τοῦ προγεγραμμένου περὶ τῶν διοικήσεων κανόνος, εὔδηλον ὡς τὰ καθ' ἑκάστην ἐπαρχίαν ἡ τῆς ἐπαρχίας σύνοδος διοικήσει κατὰ τὰ ἐν Νικαίᾳ ὡρισμένα.* Can. III.: *Τὸν μέντοι Κωνσταντινουπόλεως ἐπίσκοπον ἔχειν τὰ πρεσβεῖα τῆς τιμῆς μετὰ τὸν τῆς Ῥώμης ἐπίσκοπον, διὰ τὸ εἶναι αὐτὴν νέαν Ῥώμην.* (Cf. P. de Marca de Constantinopolitani Patriarchatus institutione (in Boehmer's edition, p. 155, ss.) Can. VI.: *Εἰ δέ συμβαίη ἀδυνατῆσαι τοὺς ἐπαρχιώτας πρὸς διόρθωσιν τῶν ἐπιφερομένων ἐγκλημάτων τῷ ἐπισκόπῳ, τότε αὐτοὺς προσιέναι μείζονι συνόδῳ τῶν τῆς διοικήσεως ἐπισκόπων ἐκείνης, ὑπὲρ τῆς αἰτίας ταύτης συγκαλουμένων.*

[10] According to the Canon Sardic. vi., every metropolitan is *ὁ ἔξαρχος τῆς ἐπαρχίας*. On the other hand, shortly before the council of Chalcedon, the bishop of Antioch is called *ὁ ἔξαρχος τῆς ἀνατολικῆς διοικήσεως* (Conc. Chalcedon. actio xiv.). *Ἀρχιεπίσκοπος* first applied to the bishop of Alexandria, ap. Athanas. Apol. ii. Epiphan. Haer. 68. In the acts of the first council of Ephesus it is very frequently given to the bishops of Rome and Alexandria.

ἀρχῆς[11] was appropriated to them exclusively. But political relations and hierarchical ambition soon altered this arrangement. The bishops of *Constantinople*, favored by their position, soon gained an influence over the affairs of other dioceses also,[12] which manifested itself decidedly in the neighboring dioceses of Asia and Pontus in particular.[13] At first, indeed, they met with resistance; but since it was of moment to the emperors of the eastern Roman empire to make the bishop of their chief city powerful, as being their principal instrument in ruling the church and to make him equal in rank to the bishop of the capital of the western Roman empire, the council of Chalcedon formally invested the patriarch of Constantinople with the same rank as the bishop of Rome, the superintendence over those three dioceses,[14] and the right of receiving complaints from all

[11] In the fourth century a name of respect given to every bishop. Gregor. Nazianz. Orat. 20, 32, 41. Gregor. Nyss. Orat. funebr. in Meletium. See Suiceri Thes. eccl. ii. 640. First to the higher bishops by Socrates, v. 8, then by Conc. Chalced.

[12] Theodoret. Haer. fab. comp. iv. 12: *Νεστόριος—τῆς κατὰ Κωνσταντινούπολιν τῶν ὀρθοδόξων καθολικῆς Ἐκκλησίας τὴν προεδρίαν πιστεύεται, οὐδὲν δὲ ἧττον καὶ τῆς οἰκουμένης ἁπάσης.*

[13] Comp. Ziegler, l. c. S. 184, ff.

[14] Can. Chalced. 28 (Actio xv. ap. Mansi, t. vii. 369): *Πανταχοῦ τοῖς τῶν ἁγίων πατέρων ὅροις ἑπόμενοι, καὶ τὸν ἀρτίως ἀναγνωσθέντα κανόνα τῶν ρν΄ θεοφιλεστάτων ἐπισκόπων γνωρίζοντες, τὰ αὐτὰ καὶ ἡμεῖς ὁρίζομεν, καὶ ψηφιζόμεθα περὶ τῶν πρεσβείων τῆς ἁγιωτάτης ἐκκλησίας Κωνσταντινουπόλεως, νέας Ῥώμης. Καὶ γὰρ τῷ θρόνῳ τῆς πρεσβυτέρας Ῥώμης, διὰ τὸ βασιλεύειν τὴν πόλιν ἐκείνην, οἱ πατέρες εἰκότως ἀποδεδώκασι τὰ πρεσβεῖα, καὶ τῷ αὐτῷ σκοπῷ κινούμενοι οἱ ρν΄ θεοφιλέστατοι ἐπίσκοποι τὰ ἴσα πρεσβεῖα ἀπένειμαν τῷ τῆς νέας Ῥώμης ἁγιωτάτῳ θρόνῳ, εὐλόγως κρίναντες, τὴν βασιλείᾳ καὶ συγκλήτῳ τιμηθεῖσαν πόλιν καὶ τῶν ἴσων ἀπολαύουσαν πρεσβείων τῇ πρεσβυτέρᾳ βασιλίδι Ῥώμῃ* (cf. lex Theodos. II. ann. 421, below, § 94, note 47), *καὶ ἐν τοῖς ἐκκλησιαστικοῖς, ὡς ἐκείνην, μεγαλύνεσθαι πράγμασι, δευτέραν μετ᾽ ἐκείνην ὑπάρχουσαν· καὶ ὥστε τοὺς τῆς Ποντικῆς, καὶ τῆς Ἀσιανῆς, καὶ τῆς Θρᾳκικῆς διοικήσεως μητροπολίτας μόνους, ἔτι δὲ καὶ τοὺς ἐν τοῖς βαρβαρικοῖς ἐπισκόπους τῶν προειρημένων διοικήσεων χειροτονεῖσθαι ἀπὸ τοῦ προειρημένου ἁγιωτάτου θρόνου τῆς κατὰ Κωνσταντινούπολιν ἁγιωτάτης ἐκκλησίας· δηλαδὴ ἑκάστου μητροπολίτου τῶν προειρημένων διοικήσεων, μετὰ τῶν τῆς ἐπαρχίας ἐπισκόπων, χειροτονοῦντος τοὺς τῆς ἐπαρχίας ἐπισκόπους, καθὼς τοῖς θείοις κανόσι διηγόρευται· χειροτονεῖσθαι δὲ, καθὼς εἴρηται, τοὺς μητροπολίτας τῶν προειρημένων διοικήσεων παρὰ τοῦ Κωνσταντινουπόλεως ἀρχιεπισκόπου, ψηφισμάτων συμφώνων, κατὰ τὸ ἔθος, γενομένων, καὶ ἐπ᾽ αὐτὸν ἀναφερομένων.* Cf. Edm. Richerii Hist. Concill. generall. lib. i. c. 8. § 37, ss. Even here the Grecian principle ruled that the rank of their bishops should be determined by the political rank of the cities (see above, note 3). Rome was always *βασιλίς* or *βασιλεύουσα:* Constantinople, as being Roma Nova, received forthwith the same privileges, but was yet second in rank, *ἡ δευτέρα βασιλεύουσα* (Themistii Orat. iii. p. 41). In accordance with this, the Council of Constantinople, 381, determined the rank of the two bishops (see note 9). But after the division of the empire, the east Roman emperors would not allow their chief city to stand behind in any respect (Cod. Theod. xvi. ii. 45, A.D. 421: urbs Constantinopolitana, quae Romae veteris praerogativa laetatur). Agreeably to that opinion the position of its bishop was determined at Chalcedon. Cf. Spanhemius de Usu et praestantia

the dioceses against metropolitans.[15] Thus the exarchs of Ephesus and Caesarea were put back into the middle rank between patriarchs and metropolitans. The *bishops of Antioch* endeavored likewise to draw over Cyprus into their ecclesiastical diocese, as it belonged to the political diocese of Asia; but the Cyprian bishops received from the Alexandrian party at the council of Ephesus the assurance of their independence. *The bishops of Jerusalem*, supported by the precedence which had been conceded to them at the council of Nice,[16] after having long endeavored in vain to shake themselves free of their metropolitan in Caesarea, succeeded at last in rising to the rank of patriarchs, by an edict of Theodosius II., and by the synod of Chalcedon, the three Palestines were assigned them as their ecclesiastical domain.[17] At the close of this period, therefore, we have four patriarchs in the east, viz. of *Constantinople*, *Alexandria*, *Antioch*, *Jerusalem*.[18] In their dioceses they were looked upon as ecclesiastical centers, to which the other bishops had to attach themselves for the preservation of unity;[19] and

numismatum, p. 687. Id. in Juliani Orat. i. p. 30, 75. Jo Massonius ad Gruteri inscriptiones, p. 1080.

[15] Can. Chalced. 9: Εἰ δὲ καὶ κληρικὸς ἔχοι πρᾶγμα πρὸς τὸν ἴδιον ἐπίσκοπον, ἢ πρὸς ἕτερον, παρὰ τῇ συνόδῳ τῆς ἐπαρχίας δικαζέσθω. εἰ δὲ πρὸς τὸν τῆς αὐτῆς ἐπαρχίας μητροπολίτην ἐπίσκοπος ἢ κληρικὸς ἀμφισβητοίη, καταλαμβανέτω ἢ τὸν ἔξαρχον τῆς διοικήσεως, ἢ τὸν τῆς βασιλευούσης Κωνσταντινουπόλεως θρόνον, καὶ ἐπ' αὐτῷ δικαζέσθω. Repeated for a particular case, can. 17. An ecclesiastical oversight of the west was bestowed on the Roman bishop by Valentinian III. 445. See below, § 94, note 65.

[16] Can. Nicaen. vii.: Ἐπειδὴ συνήθεια κεκράτηκε καὶ παράδοσις ἀρχαία, ὥστε τὸν ἐν Αἰλίᾳ ἐπίσκοπον τιμᾶσθαι, ἐχέτω τὴν ἀκολουθίαν τῆς τιμῆς, τῇ μητροπόλει σωζομένου τοῦ οἰκείου ἀξιώματος. Comp. Div. I. § 68, note 12. Thus the Concil. Constant., A.D. 382, in its synodical letters (in Theodoreti Hist. eccl. v. 9), calls this church τὴν μητέρα ἁπασῶν τῶν ἐκκλησιῶν τὴν ἐν Ἱεροσολύμοις.

[17] Ziegler, l. c. S. 240, ff.

[18] Concerning their rights see Ziegler, S. 272, ff. Planck, i. 610, ff.

[19] Thus Gregorius Naz. Epist. 22 ad Caesarienses says of the church of Caesarea in Cappadocia (at the time in the highest rank of hierarchical dignity): Ἡ μήτηρ σχεδὸν ἁπασῶν τῶν Ἐκκλησιῶν ἦν τε ἀπ' ἀρχῆς, καὶ νῦν ἐστι καὶ νομίζεται, καὶ πρὸς ἣν τὸ κοινὸν βλέπει, ὡς κέντρῳ κύκλος περιγραφόμενος. When the Egyptian bishops at the council of Chalcedon, after the deposition of Dioscurus, were without a head, and yet required to subscribe Leo's Epist. ad Flavianum (Conc. Chalced. act. iv. ap. Mansi, vii. p. 53, 55) they declared: Περὶ δὲ τῆς ἐπιστολῆς τοῦ ἁγιωτάτου—Λέοντος, ἴσασι πάντες οἱ ἁγιώτατοι ἡμῶν πατέρες, ὅτι ἐν ἅπασιν ἀναμένομεν τὴν γνώμην τοῦ παρ' ἡμῖν ὁσιωτάτου ἀρχιεπισκόπου.—τοῦτο γὰρ καὶ οἱ ἐπὶ τῆς Νικαέων ἅγιοι πατέρες συναγηγερμένοι ἐκανόνισαν τιή, ὥστε ἀκολουθεῖν πᾶσαν τὴν Αἰγυπτιακὴν διοίκησιν τῷ ἀρχιεπισκόπῳ τῆς μεγαλοπόλεως Ἀλεξανδρείας, καὶ μηδὲν δίχα αὐτοῦ πράττεσθαι παρά τινος τῶν ὑπ' αὐτῷ ἐπισκόπων.—περὶ πίστεώς ἐστιν ὁ ἀγών.—παρὰ γνώμην ἀρχιεπισκόπου οὐ δυνάμεθα ὑπογράψαι. And the council allowed them a respite, Can. 30 (Mansi, vii. 372), ἄχρις ἂν χειροτονηθῇ ὁ τῆς Ἀλεξανδρέων ἀρχιεπίσκοπος.

constituted, along with their diocesan synod, the highest court of appeal in all ecclesiastical matters of the diocese; while on the other hand they were considered as the highest representatives of the church, who had to maintain the unity of the church-universal by mutual communication, and without whose assent no measures affecting the interest of the whole church could be taken.[20]

§ 94.

HISTORY OF THE ROMAN PATRIARCHS,[1] AND OF THE HIERARCHY IN THE WEST.

Blondel's Work, cited § 93. Cl. Salmasii librorum de Primatu Papae pars prima, cum apparatu. Lugd. Batav. 1645. 4. Archibald Bower's History of the Popes, 5 vols. 4to. London. J. G. Rehr's Gesch. des Papstthums. Leipz. 1801, 1802. 2 Th. 8. Planck. i. 624, ff.

The bishop of Rome stood pre-eminent above all his brethren at the very commencement of this period, inasmuch as he was bishop of the only apostolic congregation of the west and of the richest church,[2] metropolitan of several provinces, viz. the ten

[20] Liberati Breviar. c. 4. Quod audiens (namely, the heresy of Nestor) Cyrillus Alexandrinus Episcopus, cui tunc dabatur primatus de talibus agendi, venerunt ad eum aliqui de populo Constantinopolitano, etc. So Eutyches at the Concil. Constantinop. (Mansi, vi. 817) *ἀναγινωσκομένης τῆς καθαιρέσεως, ἐπεκαλέσατο τὴν ἁγίαν σύνοδον τοῦ ἁγιωτάτου ἐπισκόπου Ῥώμης, καὶ Ἀλεξανδρείας καὶ Ἱεροσολύμων, καὶ Θεσσαλονίκης.* Hence he complained at the second synod of Ephesus that Flavianus had excommunicated him on his sole authority, *καίτοι μᾶλλον ὀφείλων πρὸ πάντων τοῖς ἀρχιερεῦσιν ἐπιστεῖλαι, οὓς καὶ ἐπεκαλεσάμην,* namely, the bishops of Rome and Alexandria (Mansi, vi. 641). Hence flattery invented for them in the fifth century the title universalis Episcopus (the bishop who has oversight of the entire church), which Olympius Episc. Evazensis first gives Dioscurus at the Concil. Ephes. ii. (Mansi, vi. 855).

[1] Order of succession: Sylvester I., from 314, † 335; Marcus, † 336; Julius I., † 352; Liberius, banished 355; the Arian Felix, till 358; Liberius returns, 358, † 366; Damasus, † 384; Siricius, † 398; Anastasius I., † 402; Innocentius I., † 417; Zosimus, † 418; Bonifacius I., † 422; Caelestinus I., † 432; Sixtus III., † 440; Leo I. the Great, † 461.

[2] Ammianus Marcellinus, xxvii. c. 3: Damasus et Ursinus supra humanum modum ad rapiendam Episcopatus sedem ardentes, scissis studiis asperrime conflictabantur, ad usque mortis vulnerumque discrimina adjumentis utriusque progressis: quae nec corrigere sufficiens Juventius (Praef. urbi) nec mollire, coactus vi magna secessit in suburbanum. Et in concertatione superaverat Damasus, parte quae ei favebat instante. Constatque in basilica Sicinini, ubi ritus Christiani est conventiculum, uno die cxxxvii. reperta cadavera peremtorum: efferatamque diu plebem aegre postea delinitam. Neque ego abnuo, ostentationem rerum considerans urbanarum, hujus rei cupidos ob impetrandum, quod appetunt, omni contentione laterum jurgari debere: cum id adepti, futuri sint ita securi, ut ditentur oblationibus matronarum, procedantque vehiculis insidentes, circumspecte vestiti, epulas

suburbicarian ones,[3] and at the same time, on account of his residence in the principal city of the world. The easterns, according to their political principle, could not but concede the first place among the bishops, and afterward among the patriarchs, to the bishop of the chief city; while the westerns estimated the dignity of the episcopal seat by another principle,[4] viz. the grade of its apostolic descent; and considered the *apostolic* seats as the heads and centers of the whole church.[5]

curantes profusas, adeo ut eorum convivia regales superent mensas. Qui esse poterant beati revera, si magnitudine urbis despecta quam viciis (conviciis?) opponunt, ad imitationem Antistitum quorundam provincialium viverent: quos tenuitas edendi potandique parcissime, vilitas etiam indumentorum, et supercilia humum spectantia, perpetuo numini verisque ejus cultoribus ut puros commendant et verecundos. Hieronymi Ep. 38 (al. 61), ad Pammachium: Miserabilis Praetextatus, qui designatus consul est mortuus, homo sacrilegus, et idolorum cultor (respecting him see § 78, note 6, § 79, note 1), solebat ludens beato papae Damaso dicere: "Facite me Romanae urbis episcopum, et ero protinus Christianus." Hence the arrogance of the Roman bishops as the stewards of such rich possessions, complained of even by Jerome Epist. 101, ad Evangelum, see Pseudo-Augustini perhaps Hilarii Diaconi (about 380) Quaest. Vet. et Nov. Test. (in August. Opp. t. iii. P. ii. Append.) Quaest. 101: Quia Romanae Ecclesiae ministri sunt, idcirco honorabiliores putantur, quam apud ceteras Ecclesias, propter magnificentiam urbis Romae, quae caput esse videtur omnium civitatum. Si itaque sic est, hoc debent et sacerdotibus suis vindicare: quia, si ii, qui inferiores sunt, crescunt propter magnificentiam civitatis, quanto magis, qui potiores, sublimandi sunt?

[3] Suburbicaria loca in the versio Prisca of the 6th Nicene canon, see above § 93, note 1. Rufinus Hist. Eccl. x. 6, gives this canon as follows: Et ut apud Alexandriam et in urbe Roma vetusta consuetudo servetur, ut vel ille Aegypti, vel hic suburbicariarum ecclesiarum solicitudinem gerat.—Eccles. suburbic. mean, according to Baronius and Bellarmine, Eccl. totius orbis; according to Perronius, Valesius, J. Morinus, Natalis Alexander, Eccl. occidentis; according to J. Gothofredus (Conjectura de suburbicariis regionibus et ecclesiis. Francof. 1617), Claud. Salmasius, J. Launojus, the two Basnages, etc., only the four provinces which were under Praef. urbi (intra centesimum ab urbe lapidem). On the other hand Jac. Sirmond (Censura Conjecturae anonymi script. de suburb. regg. et eccll. 1618) has justly asserted that the provinces subject to the Vicarius urbis, or the Dioecesis Romae, were, 1. Campania. 2. Tuscia et Umbria. 3. Picenum suburbicarium. 4. Sicilia. 5. Apulia et Calabria. 6. Bruttii et Lucania. 7. Samnium. 8. Sardinia. 9. Corsica. 10. Valeria. That these constituted the Roman diocese is also evident from Conc. Sardic. synodica ad Julium P. (Mansi, iii. p. 41): Tua autem excellens prudentia disponere debet, ut per tua scripta, qui in Sicilia, qui in Sardinia, et in Italia sunt fratres nostri, quae acta sunt et quae definita, cognoscant (cf. Syn. Arelat. Epist. Div. I. § 68, note ii.). Comp. du Pin. de Ant. eccl. discipl. p. 87, ss. Zeigler's Gesch. d. Kirchl. Verfassungsformen, S. 113, Anm. The numerous ancient works on this subject are enumerated in Sagittarianae Introd. in hist. eccl. ii. 1233, ss. Fabricii Salut. lux Evangelii, p. 358, ss.

[4] See Canon Constantinop. iii. and Chalced. xxviii. above § 93, notes 9 and 13.

[5] The fundamental principle of Augustine is given by Pelagius, i. ad Episcopos Tusciae, A.D. 556 (ap. Mansi, ix. 716; also in Agobardus de comparatione utriusque regiminis, c. 2): Beatissimus Augustinus dominicae sententiae memor, qua fundamentum Ecclesiae in apostolicis sedibus collocavit, in schismate esse dicit, quicumque se a praesulis [Agob. praesulum] earumdem sedium auctoritate vel communione suspenderit; nec aliam manifestat esse ecclesiam, nisi quae in pontificibus [Agob. pontificalibus] apostolicarum sedium est solidata radicibus. Hence against the Donatists Augustinus Epist. 43 (al. 162), § 7: Non de Presbyteris aut diaconibus aut inferioris ordinis clericis, sed de collegis agebatur,

Hence, even according to this principle, Rome stood pre-eminent, being a church founded by the two chief apostles, and the only apostolic community of the west.[6]

The same need of security which led the bishops of the dioceses to unite with one another during the Arian controversy in the east, procured to bishop *Julius* of Rome decisions in the *synod of Sardica* (347),[7] giving him the privilege of appointing

qui possent aliorum collegarum judicio, praesertim apostolicarum ecclesiarum, causam suam integram reservare. Idem contra litteras Petiliani, ii. 51: Verumtamen si omnes per totum orbem tales essent, quales vanissime criminaris, cathedra tibi quid fecit Ecclesiae Romanae, in qua Petrus sedit, et in qua hodie Anastasius sedet: vel Ecclesiae Hierosolymitanae, in qua Jacobus sedit, et in qua hodie Joannes sedet, quibus nos in catholica unitate connectimur, et a quibus vos nefario furore separastis? In connection with these passages the following can only be rightly explained: Contra duas Epp. Pelag. ad Bonifac. Rom. Eccl. Episcopum, i. 2: Communis omnibus nobis, qui fungimur Episcopatus officio (quamvis ipse in ea praeemineas celsiore fastigio) specula pastoralis. Epist. 43, § 7: Romana Ecclesia, in qua semper apostolicae cathedrae viguit principatus.

6 Synodi Sardicensis Epist. ad Julium Ep. Rom. (Mansi, iii. 40): Hoc enim optimum et valde congruentissimum esse videbitur, si ad caput, i. e. ad Petri Apostoli sedem de singulis quibusque provinciis Domini referant sacerdotes. Blondel de la Primauté en l'église, p. 106, and after him Bower History of the Popes, i. 192, and Fuch's Biblioth. d. Kirchenversamml. ii. 128, look upon these words as interpolated.

7 On the double originals of the canons of this council, a Greek and a Latin one, see Ballerini de Ant. collect. can. P. i. cap. 5. Spittler in Meusel's Geschichtsforscher, iv. 33.—Can. iii. (from the Dionysius Exig. cod. can. ap. Mansi, iii. 23): Osius Episcopus dixit: Quod si aliquis Episcoporum judicatus fuerit in aliqua causa, et putat se bonam causam habere, ut iterum concilium renovetur; si vobis placet, sancti Petri Apostoli memoriam honoremus, ut scribatur ab his, qui causam examinarunt, Julio Romano Episcopo: et si judicaverit renovandum esse judicium, renovetur, et det judices. Si autem probaverit, talem causam esse, ut non refricentur ea quae acta sunt; quae decreverit confirmata erunt. Si hoc omnibus placet? Synodus respondit: Placet. Can. iv.: Gaudentius Episcopus dixit: Addendum, si placet, huic sententiae, quam plenam sanctitate protulistis; ut, cum aliquis Episcopus depositus fuerit eorum Episcoporum judicio, qui in vicinis locis commorantur, et proclamaverit, agendum sibi negotium in urbe Roma: alter Episcopus in ejus cathedra, post appellationem ejus qui videtur esse depositus, omnino non ordinetur, nisi causa fuerit in judicio Episcopi Romani determinata. Can. vii. (in Graeco v.): Osius Episcopus dixit: Placuit autem, ut, si Episcopus accusatus fuerit, et judicaverint congregati Episcopi regionis ipsius, et de gradu suo eum dejecerint; si appellaverit qui dejectus est, et confugerit ad Episcopum Romanae ecclesiae, et voluerit se audiri: si justum putaverit, ut renovetur examen, scribere his Episcopis dignetur, qui in finitima et propinqua provincia sunt, ut ipsi diligenter omnia requirant, et juxta fidem veritatis definiant. Quod si is qui rogat causam suam iterum audiri, deprecatione sua moverit Episcopum Romanum, ut de latere suo Presbyterum mittat, erit in potestate Episcopi, quid velit, et quid aestimet. Et si decreverit, mittendos esse, qui praesentes cum Episcopis judicent, habentes ejus auctoritatem, a quo destinati sunt, erit in suo arbitrio. Si vero crediderit Episcopos sufficere, ut negotio terminum imponant, faciet, quod sapientissimo consilio suo judicaverit. Comp. de Marca de Concord. Sac. et Imp. lib. vii. c. 3; du Pin de Ant. eccl. disc. p. 103, ss. That this privilege was only granted to Julius personally, is shown by Richerii Hist. concill. generall. t. i. c. 3, § 4. Doubts of the authenticity of the canons of this council, see Mich. Geddes Diss. de Sardicensibus canon., in his Miscell. tract. t. ii. p. 415. Sarpi, in Le Bret's Magazin für Staaten und Kirchengesch. Th. i. (Ulm. 1771) S. 429, ff. Comp. Le Bret's remarks on the same point, p. 435, ff.

judges to hear the appeals of condemned bishops, should he look upon them as well founded. But when the divided choice between *Damasus* and *Ursicinus* (366),[8] although Valentinian I. decided in favor of the former,[9] gave rise to a tedious schism which spread into other provinces also, and to the greatest bitterness between two parties; *Gratian* gave Damasus the right of judging in the case of condemned bishops,[10] in order that the schismatic clergy might not be at the mercy of worldly, and for the most part as yet, heathen officers.[11] At the same time the emperor, at the instance of a Roman synod (378), assured him of the support of the civil power as far as it might be necessary for the bishop's purpose.[12] Both privileges conferred on Julius and Damasus were transitory, as well as the relations which gave rise to them.[13] The rights of provincial synods remained

[8] Accounts of it in favor of Damasus, Rufinus Eccl. ii. 10. Hieron. Chron. ad ann. 366. Socrates, iv. 29, in favor of Ursicinus Faustini et Marcellini libellus precum ad Impp. in Bibl. PP. Lugd. v. 637. Comp. Ammianus Marcellinus, xxvii. 3. See above, note 2.

[9] See the imperial edicts in Baronius 368, no. 2; 369, no. 3.

[10] So Maximin, a heathen (Amm. Marcell. xxviii. 1), had been enraged, ita ut causa ad clericorum usque tormenta duceretur (Rufin. H. E. ii. 10).

[11] Epist. Romanii Concilii ad Gratian. et Valentin. Impp. A.D. 378 (first published in J. Sirmondi Appendix Cod. Theodos. Paris. 1631. 8, p. 78. Mansi, iii. 624 ap. Coustant among the epistles of Damasus as Ep. 6): A principio—statuistis ad redintegrandum corpus Ecclesiae, quod furor Ursini diversas secuerat in partes, ut auctore damnato, caeterisque—a perditi conjunctione divulsis, de reliquis ecclesiarum sacerdotibus Episcopus Romanus haberet examen: ut et de religione religionis pontifex cum consortibus judicaret, nec ulla fieri videretur injuria sacerdotio, si sacerdos nulli usquam profani judicis, quod plerumque contingere poterat, arbitrio facile subjaceret.

[12] The synod (see the epistle referred to in note 11) proposed no new regulation: Statuti imperialis non novitatem, sed firmitudinem postulamus. Hence the following rescript, like the earlier one, referred only to the peculiar relations of the time. In this rescript appended to the epist. already alluded to, Gr. et Val. ad Aquilinum Vicar. Urbis, we find these words, c. 6: Volumus autem, ut quicunque judicio Damasi, quod ille cum consilio quinque vel septem habuerit Episcoporum, vel eorum, qui catholici sunt, judicio vel concilio condemnatus fuerit, si injuste voluerit ecclesiam retentare: ut qui evocatus ad sacerdotale judicium per contumaciam non ivisset, aut ab illustribus viris praefectis praetorio Galliae atque Italie, sive a proconsulibus vel vicariis, auctoritate adhibita, ad episcopale judicium remittatur, vel ad urbem Romam sub prosecutione perveniat: aut si in longinquioribus partibus alicujus ferocitas talis emerserit, omnis ejus causae dictio ad Metropolitae in eadem provincia Episcopi deducatur examen, vel si ipse Metropolitanus est, Romam necessario, vel ad eos, quos Romanus Episcopus judices dederit, sine delatione contendat, ita tamen, ut quicunque dejecti sunt, ab ejus tantum urbis finibus segregentur, in quibus fuerint sacerdotes. Minus enim graviter meritos coercemus, et sacrilegam pertinaciam lenius quam meretur ulciscimur. Quod si vel Metropolitani Episcopi vel cujuscunque sacerdotis iniquitas est suspecta, aut gratia: ad Romanum Episcopum vel ad concilium quindecim Episcoporum finitimorum accersitum liceat provocare: modo ne post examen habitum quod definitum fuerit integretur.

[13] That the canons of the council of Sardica were never applied in practice is shown by de Marca de Conc. Sac. et Impp. libb. vii. c. 11 and 12.

still inviolate, and their decrees were considered as binding even by the bishop of Rome.[14]

A permanent kind of influence was opened up to the latter by the custom of referring questions about apostolic doctrine and practices to the bishop of the only apostolic and common mother-church,[15] which happened all the more readily[16] as similar questions were also referred to distinguished bishops in the east.[17]

[14] So Siricius replied (392) to Anysius, bishop of Thessalonica, and to the other bishops in Illyria, when they had asked advice from him respecting Bonosus (Siricii Ep. 9, ap. Coustant, erroneously given among the epistles of Ambrose, as Ep. 79, and also falsely ascribed to Damasus, see Coustantii monitum): Cum hujusmodi fuerit concilii Capuensis judicium, ut finitimi Bonoso atque ejus accusatoribus judices tribuerentur, et praecipue Macedones, qui cum Episcopo Thessalonicensi de ejus factis vel cognoscerent; advertimus, quod nobis judicandi forma competere non posset. Nam si integra esset hodie synodus, recte de iis, quae comprehendit vestrorum scriptorum series, decerneremus. Vestrum est igitur, qui hoc recepistis judicium, sententiam ferre de omnibus, nec refugiendi vel elabendi vel accusatoribus vel accusato copiam dare. Vicem enim synodi recepistis, quos ad examinandum synodus elegit. Ambrose replied to Bonosus: Omnia modeste, patienter, ordine gerenda, neque contra sententiam vestram tentandum aliquid; ut quod videretur vobis justitiae convenire, statueretis, quibus hanc synodus dederat auctoritatem. Ideo primum est, ut ii judicent, quibus judicandi facultas est data: vos enim totius, ut scripsimus, synodi vice decernitis; nos quasi ex synodi auctoritate judicare non convenit.

[15] Comp. the epistolae canonicae, Div. I. preface to § 71, as similar ones were also issued in this period by the Alexandrian bishops, Athanasius, Timothy, and Theophilus, and by Basil the Great, bishop of Caesarea.

[16] But not exclusively, cf. Conc. Carthagin. iii. (ann. 397), c. 48 (Mansi, iii. 891): De Donatistis placuit, ut consulamus fratres et consacerdotes nostros Siricium (bishop of Rome) et Simplicianum (bishop of Milan) de solis infantibus, qui baptizantur penes eosdem, num—parentum illos error impediat, ne provehantur sacri altaris ministri. We have here at the same time a proof of the fact that they considered themselves bound by such opinions, as well as by a decision given by arbiters. The two bishops had answered in the affirmative; but when afterward the deficiency of priests in Africa made another rule desirable, the Conc. African. ann. 401 (Mansi, iv. 482), resolved previously to send an embassy ad transmarinas Italiae partes, ut tam sanctis fratribus et consacerdotibus nostris, venerabili sancto fratri Anastasio, sedis apostolicae Episcopo, quam etiam sancto fratri Venerio, sacerdoti Mediolanensis Ecclesiae, necessitatem ipsam ac dolorem atque inopiam nostram valeat intimare (ex his enim sedibus hoc fuerat prohibitum): quo noverint communi periculo providendum, maxime quia tanta indigentia clericorum est, etc.

[17] Innocentii I. Ep. 25, ad Decentium, A.D. 416, ap. Coustant, ap. Mansi, iii. 1028: Quis enim nesciat, aut non advertat, id quod a principe Apostolorum Petro Romanae Ecclesiae traditum est, ac nunc usque custoditur, ab omnibus debere servari; nec superduci aut introduci aliquid, quod auctoritatem non habeat, aut aliunde accipere videatur exemplum? Praesertim cum sit manifestum, in omnem Italiam, Gallias, Hispanias, Africam atque Siciliam, et insulas interjacentes, nullum instituisse Ecclesias, nisi eos, quos venerabilis Apostolus Petrus aut ejus successores constituerint sacerdotes. Aut legant, si in his provinciis alius Apostolorum invenitur, aut legitur docuisse. Qui si non legunt, quia nusquam inveniunt, oportet eos hoc sequi, quod Ecclesia Romana custodit, a qua eos principium accepisse non dubium est; ne, dum peregrinis assertionibus student, caput institutionum videantur omittere. Ambrose, however, says of the practice of feet-washing, which did not prevail at Rome, but in Milan most probably, de Sacramentis, iii. 1: In omnibus cupio sequi Ecclesiam Romanam: sed tamen et nos homines sensum habemus: ideo quod alibi rectius servatur, et nos recte custodimus.

If it was usual in the latter case, so much the more would it occur in the former, especially as it was customary before this time to consider the current laws of Rome as a standard in doubtful cases of civil jurisprudence.[18] Hence the Roman bishops took occasion to issue a great number of didactic letters (epistolae decretales),[19] which soon assumed the tone of apostolic ordinances, and were held in very high estimation in the west, as flowing from apostolic tradition. All these circumstances had the effect of bringing about such a state of things, that in the beginning of the fifth century the Roman bishops could already lay claim to a certain oversight of the western church.[20]

The *eastern* bishops, it is true, would not allow the least interference of the western in their ecclesiastical affairs. They gave a decided repulse to Julius I., when, at the head of the western bishops, he wished to interfere on behalf of the persecuted Athanasius.[21] The fundamental principle of the mutual

[18] Digest. i. tit. 3, l. 32: De quibus causis scriptis legibus non utimur, id custodiri oportet, quod moribus et consuetudine inductum est: et si qua in re hoc deficeret, tunc quod proximum et consequens ei est: si nec id quidem appareat, tunc jus, quo urbs Roma utitur, servari oportet.

[19] The first existing decretal is Siricii Epist. ad Himerium Episc. Tarraconensem, A.D. 385, but it refers to missa ad provincias a venerandae memoriae praedecessore meo Liberio generalia decreta. The expression epist. decretalis first appears in the so-called decretum Gelasii de libris recipiendis et non recip. about 500. The original designation is decretum, afterward statutum, or constitutum decretale. Decretum, in the original sources of Roman law, means the decision of a college (decretum Pontificum, Senatus, etc.). So also in the Christian church it denotes the decision of a synod (ex. gr. Conc. Carthag. ann. 397, in fine) or of a presbytery. These decreta are also to be considered as such decisions of the Roman presbytery, or of Roman synods. Comp. Spittler's Geschichte des kanon. Rechts bis auf die Zeiten des falschen Isidorus. Halle, 1778. S. 157, ff.

[20] Innocentii I. Ep. 2, ad Victricium, § 6: Si majores causae in medium fuerint devolutae, ad sedem apostolicam, sicut synodus statuit, et beata consuetudo exigit, post judicium episcopale referantur. Ejusd. Ep. 29, ad Carthag. Concil. (among Augustine's Epistles, Ep. 181), § 1: Patres non humana sed divina decrevere sententia, ut quidquid quamvis de disjunctis remotisque provinciis ageretur, non prius ducerent finiendum, nisi ad hujus sedis notitiam perveniret. The text to which these places refer is Epist. Syn. Sardic. ad Julium above, note 6. That the interpretation extends the sense very much is obvious, doubtless in consequence of the progress and development of new circumstances.

[21] The synod of Antioch (341) had first complained to Julius of his conduct in not regarding the sentence of the eastern church. Extracts from this letter are found in Sozomenus, iii. 8. Among other things they had said: *Φέρειν μὲν γὰρ πᾶσι φιλοτιμίαν τὴν Ῥωμαίων ἐκκλησίαν, ὡς ἀποστόλων φροντιστήριον, καὶ εὐσεβείας μητρόπολιν ἐξ ἀρχῆς γεγεννημένην.—οὐ παρὰ τοῦτο δὲ τὰ δευτερεῖα φέρειν ἠξίουν, ὅτι μὴ μεγέθει ἢ πλήθει ἐκκλησίας πλεονεκτοῦσιν, ὡς ἀρετῇ καὶ προαιρέσει νικῶντες, κ. τ. λ.* The answer to this Julii I. Ep. ad Syn. Antiochenam (ap. Athanasius Apol. contra Arian. c. 21, ss. Mansi, ii. 1211. Coustant-Schoenemann, p. 210, ss.): After having shown the irregularity of the proceedings against Athanasius and Marcellus, he says at the conclusion: *Εἰ γὰρ καὶ ὅλως, ὥς φατε, γέγονέ τι εἰς αὐτοὺς ἁμάρτημα, ἔδει κατὰ τὸν ἐκκλησιαστικὸν κανόνα, καὶ μὴ*

independence of the occidental and oriental church, was universally maintained in the east.[22] Still the period of the doctrinal controversies had a very important influence in promoting the power of the Roman bishop. The speculative questions which split the east into factions excited little interest in the west. On this very account the westerns united very soon and easily in the opinion to be embraced, in which they chiefly followed the bishop of Rome, who was almost the only organ of communication with the east,[23] and by means of whom they also be-

οὕτως γεγενῆσθαι τὴν κρίσιν· ἔδει γραφῆναι πᾶσιν ἡμῖν, ἵνα οὕτως παρὰ πάντων ὁρισθῇ τὸ δίκαιον. ἐπίσκοποι γὰρ ἦσαν οἱ πάσχοντες, καὶ οὐχ αἱ τυχοῦσαι ἐκκλησίαι αἱ πάσχουσαι, ἀλλ' ὧν αὐτοὶ οἱ Ἀπόστολοι δι' ἑαυτῶν καθηγήσαντο. Διατί δὲ περὶ τῆς Ἀλεξανδρέων ἐκκλησίας μάλιστα οὐκ ἐγράφετο ἡμῖν; ἢ ἀγνοεῖτε ὅτι τοῦτο ἔθος ἦν, πρότερον γράφεσθαι ἡμῖν, καὶ οὕτως ἔνθεν ὁρίζεσθαι τὰ δίκαια; Εἰ μὲν οὖν τι τοιοῦτον ἦν ὑποπτευθὲν εἰς τὸν ἐπίσκοπον τὸν ἐκεῖ, ἔδει πρὸς τὴν ἐνταῦθα ἐκκλησίαν γραφῆναι. Julius, therefore, did not pretend to pronounce judgment on Athanasius and Marcellus alone, but in conjunction with all the bishops (comp. below, note 26). This demand grew out of the western notions respecting the superior dignity of the bishops of apostolic communities (see above, note 5), as those two were. See de Marca de concord. Sac. et Imp. lib. vii. c. 4, § 2, 6, ss. On the other hand the orientals reply in the epist. synodalis Sardicensis (Philippopoli habitae) ad Donatum (in Hilarii Fragm. lib. ii. ap. Mansi, iii. 136): Hanc novitatem moliebantur inducere, quam horret vetus consuetudo ecclesiae, ut in concilio orientales Episcopi quidquid forte statuissent, ab Episcopis occidentalibus refricaretur: similiter quidquid occidentalium partium Episcopi, ab orientalibus solveretur. Sed hoc ex illo suo pravissimo sensu tractabant. Verum omnium conciliorum juste legitimique actorum decreta firmanda, majorum nostrorum gesta consignant. Nam in urbe Roma sub Novato et Sabellio et Valentino haereticis factum concilium, ab Orientalibus confirmatum est: et iterum in oriente sub Paulo a Samosatis quod statutum est, ab omnibus est signatum.—Nos vero nulli injuriam facimus, sed legis praecepta servamus. Nam injuriati et male tractati sumus ab iis qui volebant ecclesiae catholicae regulam sua pravitate turbare: sed ante oculos habentes timorem Dei, judicium Christi, verum et justum considerantes, nullius personam accepimus, neque alicui pepercimus, quo minus ecclesiasticam disciplinam servaremus. Unde Julium urbis Romae, Osium et Protogenem, et Gaudentium et Maximinum a Treveris damnavit omne concilium secundum antiquissimam legem: Julium vero urbis Romae, ut principem et ducem malorum, qui primus januam communionis sceleratis atque damnatis aperuit, ceterisque aditum fecit ad solvenda jura divina, defendebatque Athanasium praesumentur atque audaciter, hominem, cujus nec testes noverat, nec accusatores.

[22] Constantii Imp. Ep. ad Syn. Ariminensem, A.D. 359 (ap. Mansi, iii. 297): Non enim de orientalibus Episcopis in concilio vestro patitur ratio aliquid definiri. Proinde super his tantum, quae ad vos pertinere cognoscit gravitas vestra, tractare debebitis.—Quae cum ita sint, adversus orientales nihil statuere vos oportet, aut si aliquid volueritis contra eosdem praedictis absentibus definire, id quod fuerit usurpatum irrito evanescet effectu. At the Concil. Aquilejense, ann. 381, Palladius being accused of Arianism, replied (Mansi, iii. 602): Absentibus sacerdotibus nostris nos repondere non possumus. Ambrosius Episcopus dixit: Qui sunt consortes vestri? Palladius dixit: Orientales Episcopi.—Cf. Leo Allatius de Eccles. occid. et orient. perp. consens. lib. i. c. 10. Concerning the appeals from the east to Rome, see de Marca de Concord. Sac. et Imp. lib. vii. c. 6–10. Du Pin de Ant. eccl. discipl. p. 156, ss.

[23] Augustin. contra Cresconium, iii. 34: Ad Carthaginis Episcopum Romano praetermisso nunquam orientalis catholica scribit.

came acquainted with its controversies. Thus in all these controversies the west stood united and steadfast, with the bishop of Rome at its head, in contrast with the east split into parties and wavering; and when matters came to a final decision, it turned the scale in the balance of parties, when merely as a heavy weight. This phenomenon, which was constantly reappearing, was first manifested in the final victory of the Nicene faith. When these doctrines began to spread in the east likewise, under Valens, it is true the new Nicene orientals could not entirely unite with the west, and believed that they had much reason to complain of the arrogance of the westerns;[24] but yet the west was their only stay and support in opposition to all other parties. And though *the council of Constantinople* (381), afterward arranged the affairs of the oriental church without any reference to the west, and even openly took the part of the Miletians, whom the occidentals had rejected;[25] though not long after the interference of the Italian bishops, in the matter of the rival bishop of Constantinople, *Maximus*, was entirely disregarded;[26] yet it could not but be seen, that in the great theological question of the day occidental steadfastness had obtained the victory over the wavering east. But whatever influence the west gained in the east, it gained only for the reputation of the Roman bishop,[27] who, at the head of the west, was the only

[24] Basil respecting the *δυτικὴ ὀρφύς* above, § 83, note 34. [25] See above, § 83, note 34.

[26] Epist. ii. Concilii Italiae ad Theodos. Imp. (prim. ed. in J. Sirmondi app. Cod. Theod. p. 105, ap. Mansi, iii. 631): Revera advertebamus, Gregorium nequaquam secundum traditionem patrum Constantinopolitanae ecclesiae sibi sacerdotium vindicare.—At eo ipso tempore, qui generale concilium declinaverunt, Constantinopoli quae gessisse dicuntur. Nam quum cognovissent, ad hoc partium venisse Maximum, ut causam in synodo ageret suam, quod etiamsi indictum concilium non fuisset, jure et more majorum, sicut et sanctae memoriae Athanasius, et dudum Petrus Alexandrinae ecclesiae episcopi, et orientalium plerique fecerunt, ut ad ecclesiae Romanae, Italiae, et totius Occidentis confugisse judicium viderentur;—praestolari utique etiam nostram super eo sententiam debuerunt. Non praerogitavam vindicamus examinis, sed consortium tamen debuit esse communis arbitrii.—Nectarium autem cum nuper nostra mediocritas Constantinopoli cognoverit ordinatum, cohaerere communionem nostram cum orientalibus partibus non videmus.—Nec videmus eam posse aliter convenire, nisi aut is reddatur Constantinopoli qui prior est ordinatu, aut certe super duorum ordinatione sit in urbe Roma nostrum orientaliumque concilium. The Orientals replied to this in the Synodica Conc. Constantinop. ann. 382 ad Occidentales (ap. Theodoret, v. c. 9): *Περὶ δὲ τῶν οἰκονομιῶν τῶν κατὰ μέρος ἐν ταῖς ἐκκλησίαις, παλαιός τε, ὡς ἴστε, θεσμὸς κεκράτηκε, καὶ τῶν ἁγίων ἐν Νικαίᾳ πατέρων ὅρος, καθ' ἑκάστην ἐπαρχίαν τοὺς τῆς ἐπαρχίας—ποιεῖσθαι τὰς χειροτονίας. Οἷς ἀκολούθως—τῆς ἐν Κωνσταντινουπόλει—ἐκκλησίας—Νεκτάριον ἐπίσκοπον κεχειροτονήκαμεν.—οἷς ὡς ἐνθέσμως καὶ κανονικῶς παρ' ἡμῖν κεκρατηκόσι, καὶ τὴν ὑμετέραν συγχαίρειν τραρακαλοῦμεν εὐλάβειαν.*

[7] The *κορυφαῖος τῶν δυτικῶν*, § 83, note 20, comp. Theod. xvi. 1, 2, § 83, note 32

organ of direct communication with the east. From this time forth there was no important ecclesiastical controversy in the east in which each party did not endeavor to gain over the bishop of Rome, and through him the west, to its side,[28] for which purpose both flatteries were applied, and a presumptuous tone submitted to.[29] At the councils, his legates were treated with peculiar deference. Chalcedon was the first general council where they presided.[30]

As the west was accustomed to estimate the dignity of the episcopal seat according to its apostolic derivation,[31] and since the decrees of the council of Sardica imparted certain privileges to the Roman see out of deference to the apostle Peter; so also the Romish bishops derived all their claims to distinction from the position that they were the successors of Peter.[32] At the same time, they opposed the opinion universally adopted in the east, that they and the other patriarchs owed their elevation merely

[28] Socrates, ii. 8, says that there was no Roman legate at the council of Antioch *καίτοι κανόνος ἐκκλησιαστικοῦ κελεύοντος, μὴ δεῖν παρὰ τὴν γνώμην τοῦ ἐπισκόπου Ῥώμης τὰς ἐκκλησίας κανονίζειν*. He borrows this sentence expressly, ii. 17, from Julii Ep. ad Syn. Antioch. (see above, note 21), and therefore found it in these words of his · *τοῦτο ἔθος ἦν, πρότερον γράφεσθαι ἡμῖν, καὶ οὕτως ἔνθεν ὁρίζεσθαι τὰ δίκαια*, in which Sozomen, iii. 10, also finds too much when he gives as its sense: *εἶναι γὰρ νόμον ἱερατικὸν, ὡς ἄκυρα ἀποφαίνειν τὰ παρὰ γνώμην πραττόμενα τοῦ Ῥωμαίων ἐπισκόπου* (de Marca, lib. v. c. 12, § 1). Still the practice of the church in the fifth century must have given rise to such an amplifying mode of interpretation. That there was no law in existence such as these two writers refer to, is plain from Can. Constant. 3 (above, § 93, note 9), and Chalced. 28 (§ 93, note 14): the mystery is explained by the connection already pointed out in § 93.—Moreover, we have here a remarkable proof of the manner in which interpretations, very much extended and heaped upon one another, have obtained an influence over the constitution of the church as progressively developed and formed. That passage of Socrates is translated in the Historia tripartita, iv. 9, ap. 19: Non debere absque sententia Romani Pontificis Concilia celebrari. Hence Pseudo-Isidore has borrowed this sentence from him countless times, and at length introduced it into the practice of the church.

[29] Comp. the Commonitorium (instructions) of the Roman legates for the council at Ephesus, 431, ap. Mansi, iv. 556: Ad fratrem et coëpiscopum nostrum Cyrillum consilium vestrum omne convertite, et quicquid in ejus videritis arbitrio, facietis. Et auctoritatem sedis apostolicae custodiri debere mandamus.—Ad disceptationem si fuerit ventum, vos de eorum sententiis judicare debeatis, non subire certamen.

[30] On presidency at the general councils of this time, see de Marca, lib. v. c. 3–c. 6, ap. Boehmeri Observ. ad haec cap. p. 113, ss. Launoji Epist. lib. viii. Ep. 1–6. J. T. Cramer on J. U. Bossuet's Gesch. d. Welt. Th. 1, S. 612, ff. Planck's Geschichte der. kirchl Gesellschaftsverf. Bd. 1, S. 683, ff.

[31] See above, note 5.

[32] On the original signification of Vicarius Petri, see Cypriani Ep. 67, ad. Steph. Ep. Rom. Servandus est enim antecessorum nostrorum beatorum martyrum Cornelii et Lucii honor gloriosus: quorum memoriam cum nos honoremus, multo magis tu, frater carissime, honorificare—debes, qui vicarius et successor eorum factus es. Suidas and Phavorinus explain Βικάριος by διάδοχος.

to the importance of the cities in which they resided;[33] and therefore they set themselves so much against the privileges of the bishop of Constantinople, which rested only on this ground. But though, on tracing back their claims, they supported the normal authority of their church on the basis of its apostolic origin, and its parental relation to the whole western church,[34] they acknowledged notwithstanding, that the peculiar privileges of their see did not originally belong to it, but had been granted by the fathers.[35] On the idea of Peter having been the first apostle they could hardly found any particular pre-eminence in the fourth century, since there was conceded to him only a *primatus honoris*, in so far as Christ had first given him alone those rights which he afterward transferred to all the apostles, and through them to all bishops equally.[36] And as, according

[33] Epist. Innocentii ad Alexandrum Episc. Antioch. about 415 (ap. Coustant Ep. Innoc. 24): Revolventes itaque auctoritatem Nicenae synodi, quae una omnium per orbem terrarum mentem explicat sacerdotum, quae censuit de Antiochena ecclesia cunctis fidelibus, ne dixerim sacerdotibus, esse necessarium custodire, qua super diocesin suam praedictam ecclesiam, non super aliquam provinciam recognoscimus constitutam. Unde advertimus, non tam pro civitatis magnificentia hoc eidem attributum, quam quod prima primi apostoli sedes esse monstretur, ubi et nomen accepit religio christiana, et quae conventum Apostolorum apud se fieri celeberrimum meruit, quaeque urbis Romae sedi non cederet, nisi quod illa in transitu meruit, ista susceptum apud se consummatumque gauderet. The same principle was applied in Rome itself to the Metropolitans. Ibid. Quod sciscitaris, utrum divisis imperiali judicio provinciis, ut duae metropoles fiant, sic duo metropolitani episcopi debeant nominari; non esse e re visum est, ad mobilitatem necessitatum mundanarum Dei ecclesiam commutari.

[34] Innocenti I. Ep. 25, ad Decentium, see above, note 17.

[35] See above, note 20, Zosimi Ep. 2, ad Episc. Afr. § 1: His accedit apostolicae sedis auctoritas, cui in honorem beatissimi Petri patrum decreta peculiarem quandam sanxere reverentiam. Valentiniani III. Ep. ad Theodosium Aug. A.D. 450 (among Leonis M. Epistt. ed. Ballerini Ep. 55): Ὁ μακαριώτατος ἐπίσκοπος τῆς Ῥωμαίων πόλεως, ᾧ τὴν ἱερωσύνην κατὰ πάντων ἡ ἀρχαιότης παρέσχε.

[36] In the passage Matth. xvi. 18, πέτρα was usually explained as meaning the confession of Peter (Hilary, Gregory of Nyssa, Ambrose, Chrysostom, etc.), or Christ (Jerome, Augustine), less frequently, the person of Peter (Hieron. Ep. 14, al. 57, ad Damasum), Cf. Casauboni Exercit. ad Baron. xv. num. 13, ss. Suicer Thes. eccl. s. v. πέτρα. Du Pin. de Ant. eccl. discipl. diss. iv. c. 1, § 1. But as to St. Matthew, xvi. 19, the old view was universally maintained (see Div. I. § 68, note 10). Optatus Milev. lib. vii.: Praeferri Petrus caeteris Apostolis meruit, et claves regni caelorum communicandas caeteris solus accepit. Ambrosii de incarnatione Domini, c. 4: (Petrus) ubi audivit: vos autem quid me dicitis? statim loci non immemor sui primatum egit: primatum confessionis utique, non honoris, primatum fidei, non ordinis. Hoc est dicere: nunc nemo me vincat, nunc meae partes sunt, debeo compensare quod tacui, etc. Augustinus de diversis Serm. 108: Has enim claves non homo unus, sed unitas accepit ecclesiae. Hinc ergo Petri excellentia praedicatur, quia ipsius universitatis et unitatis ecclesiae figuram gessit, quando ei dictum est: tibi trado, quod omnibus traditum est. Nam ut noveritis, ecclesiam accepisse claves regni caelorum, audite in alio loco, quid Dominus dicat omnibus Apostolis suis: accipite Sp. S. et continuo: si cui dimiseritis peccata, dimmitentur ei, si cui tenueritis, tenebuntur

to this view, men did not scruple to attribute precisely the same dignity and authority to several of the other apostles,[37] the bishop

—Idem in Evang. Joannis tract. 124, § 5: Ecclesiae Petrus Apostolus propter Apostolatus sui primatum gerebat figurata generalitate personam.—Quando ei dictum est: Tibi dabo claves regni caelorum, caet., universam significabat Ecclesiam, quae in hoc saeculo diversis tentationibus—quatitur, et non cadit, quoniam fundata est super petram. unde Petrus nomen accepit, non enim a Petro petra, sed Petrus a petra, sicut non Christus a Christiano, sed Christianus a Christo vocatur. Ideo quippe ait Dominus: super hanc petram aedificabo ecclesiam meam, quia dixerat Petrus: Tu es Christus Filius Dei vivi. Super hanc ergo, inquit, petram, quam confessus es, aedificabo ecclesiam meam. Petra enim erat Christus, super quod fundamentum etiam ipse aedificatus est Petrus.—Ecclesia ergo, quae fundatur in Christo, claves ab eo regni caelorum accepit, in Petro, i. e. potestatem ligandi solvendique peccata. Hieronymus in Amos vi. 12: Petra Christus est, qui donavit Apostolis suis, ut ipse quoque petrae vocentur: Tu es Petrus, etc.—Hieronymus adv. Jovinian. lib. i.: At dicis: super Petrum fundatur ecclesia: licit idipsum in alio loco super omnes Apostolos fiat, et cuncti claves regni caelorum accipiant, et ex aequo super eos fortitudo Ecclesiae solidetur, tamen propterea unus eligitur, ut capite constituto schismatis tollatur occasio. Cf. du Pin, l. c. Diss. vi. § 1. Launoji Epistt. lib. ii. Ep. 5. Hence all bishops were considered the successors of Peter: Siricii Ep. 5, ad Episc. Africae § 1, and Innocentius I. Ep. 2, § 2: Per Petrum et Apostolatus et Episcopatus in Christo cepit exordium. Innocentius I. Ep. 29 ad Concil. Carthag. § 1: A Petro ipse Episcopatus et tota auctoritas nominis hujus emersit. Augustini Sermo 296, § 11: Ergo commendavit nobis Dominus oves suas, quia Petro commendavit. Gaudentii sermo die ordinationis habitus: Ambrosius—tanquam Petri Apostoli successor. Cf. Baluzii not. ad Servatum Lupum (ed. Paris. 1664) p. 422, ss.

[37] Especially Paul: Ambrosii Sermo ii. in festo Petri et Pauli (Sermo 66, is also met with as Augustini de Sanctis Sermo and Maximi Taurinensis Sermo 54): Ergo beati Petrus et Paulus eminent inter universos Apostolos, et peculiari quadam praerogativa praecellunt. Verum inter ipsos, quis cui praeponatur, incertum est. Puto enim illos aequales esse meritis, qui aequales sunt passione. Et in quo tandem loco iidem martyrium pertulerunt? In urbe Roma, quae principatum et caput obtinet nationum: scilicet ut, ubi caput superstitionis erat, illic caput quiesceret sanctitatis; et ubi gentilium principes habitabant, illic ecclesiarum principes morerentur. So, too, idem de Spir. Sancto, ii. c. 12: Nec Paulus inferior Petro, quamvis ille Ecclesiae fundamentum (Matth. xvi. 18), et hic sapiens architectus sciens vestigia credentium fundare populorum (1 Cor. iii. 10). Nec Paulus, inquam, indignus Apostolorum collegio cum primo quoque facile conferendus, et nulli secundus: nam qui se imparem nescit, facit aequalem (Gal. ii. 7, ss.). Augustinus de Sanctis Sermo 25: Etsi Petrum priorum, tamen ambos ditavit honore uno. Gaudentius Serm. de Petro et Paulo: Quem cui praeponere audeam nescio. Ambrosiaster ad Gal. ii. 11: Nam quis eorum auderet Petro primo Apostolo, cui claves regni caelorum Dominus dedit, resistere, nisi alius talis, qui fiducia electionis suae sciens se non imparem, constanter improbaret, quod ille sine consilio fecerat? In Theodoret's Comm. in Epistt. Pauli, the commentary on Gal. ii. 6–14, has been erased in the Codices hitherto in use, without doubt, by Latinizing Greeks (see Noesselti corollarium to the praef. in Theodoreti Opp. t. iii. Halle edition). Out of these and similar passages arose the remarkable view of Antoine Arnauld, that Peter and Paul were alike the heads of the church (see de l'autorité de St. Pierre et de St. Paul, résidant dans le Pape leur successeur. Paris. 1645. 8, and de la grandeur l'église Rom. établie sur l'autorité de saint Pierre et saint Paul. Paris. 1645, the first work by Arnauld, the second by Martin de Barcos), a doctrine which the Romish inquisition, 1647, condemned as Jansenite. See Ittigii Diss. de origine controversiae circa aequalem Petri et Pauli primatum in his heptas dissertt., annexed to the Dissertt. de haeresiarchis aevi apostolici, p. 401, ss. Other apostles, however, were also made equal to Peter. Hieronymus in Psalm lxvii. calls Petrum et Andream Apostolorum principes. Cyrilli et Syn. Alexandr. Epist. ad Nestorium, § 5 (in Actis Conc.

of Rome could the less pretend to have inherited from Peter a peculiar spiritual power reaching beyond that of the other bishops.[38]

But after the rights of the Romish bishops had become older in the west, and their authority had been so much increased in the east likewise since the end of the Arian controversy, they began at Rome in like proportion to enlarge the notion of Peter's primacy, and to regard all the honors and rights of the Romish bishop as inherited from Peter,[39] a view which appears first to have been fully developed by Leo. In the east they could not concur with this representation, because there they were accustomed to attribute the primacy to the church of Jerusalem and James, at least during the first century.[40] In Jerusalem itself they endeavored even now to establish hierarchical claims on the ground of its being the mother congregation of the whole church;[41] but in

Ephes. ap. Mansi, iv. 1073): *Πέτρος τε καὶ Ἰωάννης ἰσότιμοι ἀλλήλοις.* Concerning James see below, note 40.

[38] Hieron. Epist. 101 (al. 85) ad Evangelum: Nec altera Romanae urbis ecclesia, altera totius orbis existimanda est. Et Galliae, et Britanniae, et Africa, et Persis, et Oriens, et India, et omnes barbarae nationes unum Christum adorant: unam observant regulam veritatis. Si auctoritas quaeritur, orbis major est urbe. Ubicunque fuerit Episcopus, sive Romae, sive Eugubii, sive Constantinopoli, sive Rhegii, sive Alexandriae, sive Tanis: ejusdem meriti, ejusdem est et sacerdotii. Potentia divitiarum et paupertatis humilitas vel sublimiorem vel inferiorem Episcopum non facit. Caeterum omnes Apostolorum successores sunt. Sed dicis, quomodo Romae ad testimonium diaconi presbyter ordinatur? Quid mihi profers unius urbis consuetudinem? Quid paucitatem, de qua ortum est supercilium, in leges ecclesiae vindicas? etc.

[39] Thus the Roman legates at the Conc. Ephesin. ann. 431, ex gr. actio iii. (Mansi, iv. 1296): *Οὐδενὶ ἀμφίβολόν ἐστι, μᾶλλον δὲ πᾶσι τοῖς αἰῶσιν ἐγνώσθη, ὅτι ὁ ἅγιος καὶ μακαριώτατος Πέτρος, ὁ ἔξαρχος καὶ κεφαλὴ τῶν ἀποστόλων, ὁ κίων τῆς πίστεως, ὁ θεμέλιος τῆς καθολικῆς ἐκκλησίας, ἀπὸ τοῦ κυρίου ἡμῶν Ἰησοῦ Χριστοῦ—τὰς κλεῖς τῆς βασιλείας ἐδέξατο· καὶ αὐτῷ δέδοται ἐξουσία τοῦ δεσμεῖν καὶ λύειν ἁμαρτίας· ὅστις ἕως τοῦ νῦν καὶ ἀεὶ ἐν τοῖς αὐτοῦ διαδόχοις καὶ ζῇ, καὶ δικάζει.*

[40] Hesychii presb. Hierosolym. († 343) ap. Photius Cod. 275: *Πῶς ἐγκωμιάσω τὸν τοῦ Χριστοῦ δοῦλον καὶ ἀδελφὸν, τὸν τῆς νέας Ἱερουσαλὴμ ἀρχιστράτηγον, τὸν τῶν ἱερέων ἡγεμόνα, τῶν ἀποστόλων τὸν ἔξαρχον, τὴν ἐν κεφαλαῖς κορυφὴν, τὸν ἐν λύχνοις ὑπερλάμποντα, τὸν ἐν ἄστροις ὑπερφαίνοντα; Πέτρος δημηγορεῖ, ἀλλ' Ἰάκωβος νομοθετεῖ, καὶ ὀλίγαι λέξεις τὸ τοῦ ζητήματος συνέστειλαν μέγεθος· "ἐγὼ κρίνω μὴ παρενοχλεῖν τοῖς ἀπὸ τῶν ἐθνῶν" καὶ ἑξῆς* (Act. xv. 19). Epiphanius Haer. lxx. c. 10: *Ἔχρην τότε τῶν Ἐπισκόπων ἐκ περιτομῆς ὄντων ἐν Ἱερουσαλὴμ κατασταθέντων τὸν πάντα κόσμον τούτοις συνέπεσθαι,—ἵνα μία τις γένηται συμφωνία καὶ μία ὁμολογία.* Haer. lxxviii. § 7: *Καὶ πρῶτος οὗτος (Ἰάκωβος) εἴληφε τὴν καθέδραν τῆς ἐπισκοπῆς, ᾧ πεπίστευκε κύριος τὸν θρόνον αὐτοῦ ἐπὶ τῆς γῆς πρώτῳ, ὃς καὶ ἐκαλεῖτο ὁ ἀδελφὸς τοῦ κυρίου.* Chrysostomus Hom. 33, in Acta Apost. cap. xv. praises James in allowing Peter and Paul to speak first, though himself *τὴν ἀρχὴν ἐγκεχειρισμένος.* In the *προσφώνησις ὑπὲρ τῶν πιστῶν* Constitutt. Apostol. viii. c. 10, the prayers for the three most distinguished bishops follow each other in this order: *Ὑπὲρ τοῦ ἐπισκόπου ἡμῶν Ἰακώβου καὶ τῶν παροικιῶν αὐτοῦ δεηθῶμεν· ὑπὲρ τοῦ ἐπισκόπου ἡμῶν Κλήμεντος καὶ τῶν παροικιῶν αὐτοῦ δεηθῶμεν· ὑπὲρ τοῦ ἐπισκόπου ἡμῶν Εὐοδίου καὶ τῶν παροικιῶν αὐτοῦ δεηθῶμεν.*

[41] Juvenalis Episc. Hieros. in Conc. Ephes. act. iv. (ap. Mansi, iv. 1312): *Ἐχρῆν μὲν*

the external insignificance of this see little stress could be laid on these claims, especially since the authority of churches generally, in the east, was not determined according to their original importance, but the political rank of the cities in which they existed.[42]

High as was the dignity which the Roman bishops enjoyed in *the west*, their influence was yet very different in the different provinces. They had the full rights of patriarchs only in the diocese of Rome. In the *dioecesis Italiae*, the bishop of *Milan* exercised quite independently of them a hierarchical power similar to that of the patriarchs; in addition to whom the bishop of *Aquileia* also,[43] and at a later period the bishop of *Ravenna*,[44] raised themselves to the rank of more independent hierarchs. In the mean time, the Roman bishops, by a skillful use of opportunities, succeeded in attaching *East Illyria* to their patriarchate.[45] During the Arian disputes, Illyria had belonged to the western empire, and the Illyrian church had continued true to the Nicene council,[46] attaching itself to the bishop of Rome for its defense, as did the whole west. When, therefore, Gratian, A.D. 379, divided Illyria, and annexed *Illyricum orientale* to the eastern empire, the bishops of East Illyria, who had for so long a time maintained no communion with the east, could not have much inclination to attach themselves ecclesiastically to the

Ἰωάννην τὸν εὐλαβέστατον ἐπίσκοπον Ἀντιοχείας—τὸν ἀποστολικὸν θρόνον συνεδρεύοντα ἡμῖν τῆς μεγάλης Ῥώμης τιμῆσαι, καὶ τῷ ἀποστολικῷ τῆς Ἱεροσολύμων ἁγίας τοῦ θεοῦ ἐκκλησίας ὑπακοῦσαι, παρ' ᾧ μάλιστα ἔθος αὐτὸν τῶν Ἀντιοχέων θρόνον ἐξ ἀποστολικῆς ἀκολουθίας καὶ παραδόσεως ἰθύνεσθαι καὶ παρ' αὐτῷ δικάζεσθαι. (In the editions *τιμῆσαι* is erroneously placed after *ὑπακοῦσαι*.)

[42] Even Dioscurus sought to elevate the see of Alexandria by appealing to St. Mark. Theodoretus Ep. 86, ad Flavianum Ep. Constantinop.: *Ἄνω καὶ κάτω τοῦ μακαρίου Μάρκου τὸν θρόνον προβάλλεται· καὶ ταῦτα σαφῶς εἰδὼς, ὡς τοῦ μεγάλου Πέτρου τὸν θρόνον ἡ Ἀντιοχέων μεγαλόπολις ἔχει, ὃς καὶ τοῦ μακαρίου Μάρκου διδάσκαλος ἦν, καὶ τοῦ χοροῦ τῶν Ἀποστόλων πρῶτος καὶ κορυφαῖος. Ἀλλ' ἡμεῖς τοῦ μὲν θρόνου τὸ ὕψος ἐπιστάμεθα, ἑαυτοὺς δὲ καὶ γινώσκομεν καὶ μετροῦμεν. τὴν γὰρ ἀποστολικὴν ταπεινοφροσύνην ἄνωθεν μεμαθήκαμεν.*

[43] J. F. B. M. de Rubeis Monumenta Ecclesiae Aquilejensis. Argentinae. 1740. fol. c. 19 et 20. Ziegler's Gesch. d. Kirchl. Verfassungsformen, S. 321, ss.

[44] Since, Honorius, fleeing from the Goths, had transferred his residence to Ravenna, Zosimus, v. 30.

[45] See especially Baluzius in de Marca de Concord. Sac. et Imp. v. c. 19, c. 29, and Boehmer's Appendix observ. 15, ss.

[46] When Theodosius was baptized (380) by Ascholius, bishop of Thessalonica, Sozom. vii. 4: *Ἥσθη δὲ (Θεοδόσιος) καὶ Ἰλλυριοῖς ἅπασι μὴ μετασχοῦσι τοῦ Ἀρείου δόξης· πυνθανόμενος δὲ περὶ τῶν ἄλλων ἐθνῶν, μέχρι μὲν Μακεδόνων ἔγνω τὰς Ἐκκλησίας ὁμονοεῖν,—ἐντεῦθεν δὲ τὰ πρὸς ἕω στασιάζειν, κ. τ. λ.*

east, during the strife of parties by which it was then distinguished; while the bishop of Thessalonica, the ecclesiastical head of East Illyria, must have been averse to a union of this kind, which would have made him subject to a superior so near, viz. the bishop of Constantinople.

Under these circumstances, it was easy for the Roman bishops to persuade the bishop of Thessalonica to exercise the patriarchal rights, in the new prefecture of East Illyria, as vicar of the Roman see. *Damasus* and *Siricius* made this arrangement; *Innocent I.* looked upon it as already fixed.[47] The East Illyrian bishops, indeed, who by this means were entirely at the mercy of the bishop of Thessalonica, remote as they were from Rome, soon found cause of dissatisfaction; but their attempt to procure the ecclesiastical union of their province with the patriarchate of Constantinople by an imperial law was frustrated.[48]

Another favorable opportunity for extending their power presented itself to the Roman bishops in *Gaul.*[49] When metropolitan relations began to be established here at the end of the

[47] Innocentii I. Ep. 13, ad Rufum Ep. Thessal.: Divinitus ergo haec procurrens gratia ita longis intervallis disterminatis a me ecclesiis discat (leg. dictat) consulendum, ut prudentiae gravitatique tuae committendam curam causasque, si quae exoriantur per Achajae Thessaliae, Epiri veteris, Epiri novae, et Cretae, Daciae Mediterraneae, Daciae Ripensis, Moesiae, Dardaniae et Praevali Ecclesias, Christo Domino annuente censeant (leg. censeam).—non primitus haec ita statuentes, sed praecessores nostros apostolicos imitati, qui beatissimis Ascholio et Anysio injungi pro eorum meritis ista voluerunt.—Arripe itaque, dilectissime frater, nostra vice per suprascriptas Ecclesias, salvo earum primatu, curam: et inter ipsos primatus primus, quidquid eos ad nos necesse fuerit mittere, non sine tuo postulent arbitratu. Ita enim aut per tuam experientiam quidquid illud est finietur: aut tuo consilio ad nos usque perveniendum esse mandamus. The relation was similar to the political one of a vicar to his praefectus praetorio (see § 93, note 5).

[48] Cod. Theod. xvi. ii. 45, and Cod. Justin. I. ii. 6: Theodosius Aug. Philippo Pf. P. Illyrici (A.D. 421). Omni innovatione cessante, vetustatem et canones pristinos ecclesiasticos, qui nunc usque tenuerunt, per omnes Illyrici provincias servari praecipimus: ut si quid dubietatis emerserit, id oporteat non absque scientia viri reverendissimi sacrosanctae legis antistitis urbis Constantinopolitanae, quae Romae veteris praerogativa laetatur, conventui sacerdotali sanctoque judicio reservari. At the intercession of Honorius (see Honorii Ep. ad Theodos. Aug. among the letters of Boniface I. ap. Coustant Ep. 10) Theodosius II. soon after repealed the law (Theodosii Ep. ad Honorium, ibid. Ep. 11): Omni supplicantium Episcoporum per Illyricum subreptione remota, statuimus observari quod prisca apostolica disciplina et canones veteres eloquuntur. It is remarkable that this law is found in two codices, but not its repeal. The Roman bishops were compelled continually to exhort the Illyrian bishops to obey the bishop of Thessalonica, cf. Bonifacii I. Ep. 14 ad Episcopos per Thessal., Ep. 15 ad Episcc. per Macedoniam, Achajam, etc. Sixti III. Ep. 7 ad Perigenem Episc. Corinth., Ep. 8 ad Synod. Thessalonicae congregandam. Leonis I. Ep. 5 ad Episcc. Metropolitanos per Illyricum constitutos, Ep. 13 ad eosdem. (Leo's Leben, v. Perthel. S. 21.)

[49] Concerning the Vicariatus Arelatensis see de Marca (Baluzius) l. c. lib. v. c. 30–c. 41.

fourth century,[50] the political principle of the orientals had obtained at first in the distribution of them.[51] The bishop of *Arles* long endeavored in vain to make the principle of apostolic origin tell in his favor in opposition to the oriental principle. At last he applied to Rome. *Zosimus*, seizing on the opportunity (417), declared *Patroclus* bishop of *Arles* his vicar in Gaul, and invested him with metropolitan rights in Viennensis, Narbonensis Prima and Secunda.[52] The offended metropolitans of Vienne, Narbo, and Massilia, refused, however, to accede to this arrangement in spite of all threats; and when, soon after, the bishop of *Arles* (418) began to strive after ecclesiastical dominion over the seven provinces (Septimana),[53] of which his city had been made the chief, the Roman bishops also found it their interest to take part with the old metropolitans.[54] Hilary

50 Compare the Ballerini Observatt. ad Quesnelli diss. v. P. ii. in Ballerinus's edition of the Opp. Leonis, tom. ii. p. 1030, ss. Ziegler's Gesch. d. Kirchl. Verfassungsformen, S. 79, ff.

51 Conc. Taurinense, ann. 491 (according to Baronius erroneously ann. 397), can. 2: Illud deinde inter Episcopos urbium Arelatensis et Viennensis, qui de primatus apud nos honore certabant, a S. Synodo definitum est, ut qui ex eis approbaverit suam civitatem esse metropolim, is totius provincia honorem primatus obtineat.

52 Zosimi Epist. 1. ad Episcopp. Galliae: Placuit apostolicae sedi, ut si quis ex qualibet Galliarum parte, sub quolibet ecclesiastico gradu, ad nos Romam venire contendit, vel alio terrarum ire disponit, non aliter proficiscatur, nisi metropolitani Arelatensis Episcopi formatas acceperit.—Quisquis igitur—praetermissa supradicti formata—ad nos venerit, sciat se omnino suscipi non posse.—Jussimus autem praecipuam, sicuti semper habuit, metropolitanus Episcopus Arelatensium civitatis in ordinandis sacerdotibus teneat auctoritatem. Viennensem, Narbonensem primam et Narbonensem secundam provincias ad pontificium suum revocet. Quisquis vero posthac contra apostolicae sedis statuta et praecepta majorum, omisso metropolitano Episcopo, in provinciis supradictis quemquem ordinare praesumserit, vel is qui ordinari se illicite siverit, uterque sacerdotio se carere cognoscat.—Sane quoniam metropolitanae Arelatensium urbi vetus privilegium minime derogandum est, ad quam primum ex hac sede Trophimus summus antistes, ex cujus fonte totae Galliae fidei rivulos acceperunt, directus est; idcirco quascunque paroecias in quibuslibet territoriis, etiam extra provincias suas, ut antiquitus habuit, intemerata auctoritate possideat. Ad cujus notitiam, si quid illic negotiorum emerserit, referri censemus nisi magnitudo causae etiam nostrum exquirat examen. Ejusd. Ep. 5. ad Episc. Prov. Vienn. et Narbon. rejects the decision of the Syn. Taurin. as surreptitiously obtained: Indecens ausus et in ipso vestibulo resecandus, hoc ab Episcopis ob certas causas concilium agitantibus extorquere, quod contra patrum et S. Trophimi reverentiam, qui primus metropolitanus Arelatensis civitatis ex hac sede directus est, concedere vel mutare ne hujus quidem sedis possit auctoritas. Against this assertion of the rights belonging to the church of Arles, see below, Leo, I. note 56.

53 After Treves had been plundered by the Germans, Arelate became the residence of Praefectus praetorio of Gaul, whose dominion extended from this place to seven provinces. See Honorii constitutio ap. Sirmond. in notis ad Sidonium Apoll. and in Codicis Theodosiani, libb. v. priores ed. C. F. Chr. Wenck. Lips. 1825. 8. p. 378, ss. Cf. p. 371, ss.

54 When the clergy and people of Lutuba complained to Boniface I. that Patroclus had forced a bishop upon them, he wrote Epist. 12 ad Hilarium Ep. Narbon. A.D. 422: Quod nequaquam possumus ferre patienter sanctionum diligentes esse custodes. Nulli etenim

bishop of *Arles* finally forgot his duty as vicar so far that he would not allow the sentence of deposition pronounced by him and his synod against *Celidonius* bishop of Vesontio to be submitted to a new examination in Rome.[55] On this account *Leo the Great* (445) withdrew from him all the privileges which had been granted by the Roman see,[56] though he could

videtur incognita synodi constitutio Nicaenae, quae ita praecepit, per unamquamque provinciam jus Metropolitanos singulos habere debere, nec cuiquam duas esse subjectas. Unde, frater carissime, si ita res sunt, et ecclesiam supradictam provinciae tuae limes includit, nostra auctoritate commonitus, quod quidem facere sponte deberes, desideriis supplicantium et voluntate respecta, ad eundem locum, in quo ordinatio talis celebrata dicitur, metropolitani jure munitus, et praeceptionibus nostris fretus, accede: intelligens arbitrio tuo secundum regulas patrum quaecunque facienda sunt a nobis esse concessa; ita ut peractis omnibus, apostolicae sedi quidquid statueris te referente clarescat, cui totius provinciae liquet esse mandatam. Nemo ergo eorum [patrum] terminos audax temerator excedat.—Cesset hujusmodi pressa nostra auctoritate praesumtio eorum, qui ultra licitum suae limitem dignitatis extendunt. So too Caelestinus Ep. 4, ad Episc. prov. Vienn. et Narbon. A.D. 428.

[55] Vita Hilarii Arelat. by Honoratus Ep. Massil. (about 490, ap. Surius and Acta SS. ad. d. 5. Maji) § 22: Hilary went himself to Rome and reminded Leo, aliquos (Celidonius, etc.) apud Gallias publicam merito excepisse sententiam, et in urbe sacris altaribus interesse. Rogat atque constringit, ut si suggestionem suam libenter excepit, secreto jubeat emendari; se ad officia, non ad causam venisse protestandi ordine, non accusandi, quae sunt acta suggerrere: porro autem si aliud velit, non futurum esse molestum Et quia tantorum virorum, praesertim jam ad supernam gratiam vocatorum, nec in narratione audeo judicia ventilare; hoc breviter tetigisse sufficiet, quod solus tantos sustinuit, quod nequaquam minantes expavit, quod inquirentes edocuit, quod altercantes vicit, quod potentibus non cessit, quod in discrimine vitae positus communioni ejus, quem cum tantis viris damnaverat, conjungi nullatenus acquievit. Auxiliaris, then Praefectus, wrote to him: Sanctos Nectarium et Constantium sacerdotes ex beatitudinis tuae parte venientes digna admiratione suscepi. Cum his saepius sum locutus de virtute animi atque constantia, contemptuque rerum humanarum, quo inter fragilitates nostras semper beatus es.—Locutus sum etiam cum S. Papa Leone. Hoc loco, credo, aliquantum animo perhorrescis. Sed cum propositi tui tenax sis, et semper aequalis, nulloque commotionis felle rapiaris, sicut nullis extolleris illecebris gaudiorum, ego nec minimum quidem factum Beatitudinis tuae arrogantiae memini contagione fuscari. Sed impatienter ferunt homines, si sic loquamur, quomodo nobis conscii sumus. Aures praeterea Romanorum quadam teneritudine plus trahuntur: in quam si se Sanctitas tua subinde demittat, plurimum tu nihil perditurus, acquiris. Da mihi hoc, et exiguas nubes parvae mutationis serenitate compesce. See Papst Leo I. Streit mit d. B. v. Arles, von E. G. Perthel in Illgen's Zeitschr. f. d. hist. Theol. 1843, ii. 27.

[56] Leonis M. Ep. 10 (al. 89) ad Episc. provinciae Viennensis, c. 4: Quid sibi Hilarius quaerit in aliena provincia: et id quod nullus decessorum ipsius ante Patroclum habuit, quid usurpat? cum et ipsum, quod Patroclo a sede apostolica temporaliter videbatur esse concessum, postmodum sit sententia meliore sublatum? Cap. 7: Suis unaquaeque provincia sit contenta Conciliis, nec ultra Hilarius audeat conventus indicere synodales, et sacerdotum Domini judicia se interserendo turbare. Qui non tantum noverit se ab alieno jure depulsum, sed etiam Viennensis provinciae, quam male usurpaverat, potestate privatum. Dignum est enim, fratres, antiquitatis statuta reparari, cum is, qui sibi ordinationem provinciae indebitae vindicabat, talis in praesenti etiam probatus fuerit extitisse, ut—suae tantum civitatis illi sacerdotium, pro sedis apostolicae pietate, praeceptio nostra servaverit.

not prevent Hilary and his successors from asserting their primacy.[57]

The Roman bishops were least successful in obtaining influence in *Africa*, where the ecclesiastical relations had long been firmly fixed, and there was on this account an aversion to the new development of the hierarchy.[58] Their ecclesiastical legislation, too, had been all along cultivated with an evident predilection.[59] As early as the Pelagian controversy, Zosimus had learned by experience how little his decision was respected in Africa (§ 87, notes 12–16). It is true, he procured restoration to his office for the presbyter *Apiarius* who had been then deposed by appealing to the canons of the Sardican council as *Nicene;* but his successor, *Boniface I.* (418–423), was reminded on this account of the humility suitable to him under such circumstances.[60] But when *Caelestinus I.* (323–432) wished to have the twice-deposed Apiarius restored,[61] the Africans in the

[57] See de Marca, l. c. lib. v. c. 33. Perthel, l. c. S. 36, ff.

[58] Conc. Carthag. iii. ann. 398 can. 26 (Cod. Canonum Eccl. Afric. c. 39): Ut primae sedis episcopus non appelletur princeps sacerdotum, aut summus sacerdos, aut aliquid hujusmodi, sed tantum primae sedis episcopus.

[59] On the so called Codex Canonum Ecclesiae Africanae (Voëlli et Justelli Bibl. jur. can. vet. i. 320, H. Th. Bruns Biblioth. ecclesiast. i. i. 155) compiled by Dionysius Exiguus from the acts of the Syn. Carthag. ann. 419, by which the decrees of former councils were confirmed, and new ones added: Gallandii de Vetustis canonum collectionibus sylloge, and the treatise of Coustant, c. 6 (ed. Mogunt. i. 103), P. de Marca, c. 4 (ibid. p. 180) Ballerini, P. ii. c. 3 (ibid. p. 334).

[60] Conc. Afric. Ep. ad Bonifac. A.D. 419 (ap. Coustant Epist. Bonif. ii.): § 5. Haec (namely, the decrees of the Sardican council given out as Nicene decrees) utique usque ad adventum verissimorum exemplarium Nicaeni Concilii inserta gestis sunt. Quae si ibi—continerentur, eoque ordine vel apud vos in Italia custodirentur; nullo modo nos talia, qualia commemorare jam nolumus, vel tolerare cogeremur, vel intolerabilia pateremur. Sed credimus—quod tua Sanctitate Romanae ecclesiae praesidente non sumus jam istum typhum passuri; et servabuntur erga nos, quae nobis etiam non disserentibus custodiri debeant cum fraterna caritate, quae secundum sapientiam atque justitiam, quam tibi donavit Altissimus, etiam ipse perspicis esse servanda, nisi forte aliter se habeant canones Concilii Nicaeni. This mistake was caused by the form of the collection of canons then in use, in which those of later synods were appended to the Nicene without distinction. Quesnell has published such a collection annexed to the Opp. Leonis; also Mansi, vi. 1183. Hence later canons are often cited as Nicene. See Ballerini de Ant. collect. cann. P. ii. c. 1, § 3 (in Gallandii Syll. ed. Mogunt. i. 311). Spittler in Meusel's Geschichtsforscher, iv. 72. The same author's Gesch. d. kan. Rechts, S. 106.

[61] Conc. Afric. ad Caelestinum, A.D. 425 (ap. Coustant Epist. Caelest. ii.): § 2. Praefato itaque debitae salutationis officio, impendio deprecamur, ut deinceps ad vestras aures hinc venientes non facilius admittatis, nec a nobis excommunicatos in communionem ultra velitis excipere: quia hoc etiam Nicaeno concilio definitum facile advertat Venerabilitas tua. Nam et si de inferioribus clericis vel de laicis videtur ibi praecaveri, quanto magis hoc de episcopis voluit observari? ne in sua provincia a communione suspensi, a tua Sanctitate praepropere vel indebite videantur communioni restitui. § 3. Presbyterorum

most express terms forbade all interference, and interdicted appeals to foreign bishops.[62]

At the close of this period *Leo I. the Great* was bishop of Rome (440–461),[63] who endeavored theoretically to establish the rights of the Romish see by enlarged ideas of the primacy of Peter,[64] and the inheritance derived from that source,[65] and

quoque et sequentium clericorum improba refugia, sicuti te dignum est, repellat Sanctitas tua: quia et nulla patrum definitione hoc ecclesiae derogatum est Africanae, et decreta Nicaena sive inferioris gradus clericos, sive ipsos episcopos suis metropolitanis apertissime commiserunt. Prudentissime enim justissimeque viderunt, quaecunque negotia in suis locis, ubi orta sunt, finienda, nec unicuique provinciae gratiam sancti Spiritus defuturam, qua aequitas a Christi sacerdotibus et prudenter videatur, et constantissime teneatur: maxime quia unicuique concessum est, si judicio offensus fuerit cognitorum, ad concilia suae provinciae vel etiam universale provocare. Nisi forte quisquam est qui credat, unicuilibet posse Deum nostrum examinis inspirare justitiam, et innumerabilibus congregatis in concilium sacerdotibus denegare. Aut quomodo ipsum transmarinum judicium ratum erit, ad quod testium necessariae personae vel propter sexus vel propter senectutis infirmitatem, vel multis aliis intercurrentibus impedimentis, adduci non poterunt? § 4. Nam ut aliqui tanquam a tuae Sanctitatis latere mittantur, in nulla invenimus patrum synodo constitutum; quia illud quod pridem per eundem coëpiscopum nostrum Faustinum tanquam ex parte Nicaëni concilii exinde transmisistis, in conciliis verioribus, quae accipiuntur Nicaena, a S. Cyrillo coëpiscopo nostro Alexandrinae ecclesiae, et a venerabili Attico Constantinopolitano antistite ex authentico missis—non potuimus reperire. § 5. Executores etiam clericos vestros quibusque petentibus nolite mittere, nolite concedere; ne fumosum typhum saeculi in ecclesiam Christi—videamur inducere. Cf. du Pin de Ant. disc. eccl. diss. ii. § 3, p. 174, ss.

[62] Concil. Milevitani ii. (ann 416) can. 22 (the canon of a later council, also contained in Cod. can. eccl. Afric. cap. 28 and 125): Item placuit, ut presbyteri, diaconi, vel caeteri inferiores clerici, in causis quas habuerint, si de judiciis episcoporum suorum questi fuerint vicini episcopi eos audiant, et inter eos quidquid est, finiant, adhibiti ab eis ex consensu episcoporum suorum. Quod si et ab iis provocandum putaverint, non provocent nisi ad Africani concilia, vel ad primates provinciarum suarum (for this Cod. Can. c. 28: non provocent ad transmarina judicia, sed ad primates suarum provinciarum, aut ad universale concilium, sicut et de Episcopis saepe constitutum est). Ad transmarina autem qui putaverit appellandum, a nullo intra Africam in communionem suscipiatur. For the genuineness of the addition: sicut et de Episcopis saepe constitutum est, see de Marca, lib. vii. c. 16, § 5. Similar decrees were also issued by other African councils. Comp. the citations of them in Conc. Carthag. ann. 325 (Mansi, viii. p. 644): Conc. decimo, ut episcopi ad transmarina pergere non facile debeant; Conc. undecimo, qui in Africa non communicat, si ausus fuerit in transmarinis, damnetur; Conc. sextodecimo, ad transmarina qui putaverit, etc. (same as the above Can. Milev.); Conc. vigesimo, ut nullus ad transmarina audeat appellare.

[63] Leo d. G. u. s. Zeit von W. A. Arendt, Mainz. 1835. 8 (a Catholic apologetic work). Papst Leo's Leben u. Lehren v. Ed. Perthel. Jena. 1843. 8.

[64] Comp. the characteristic expression of Auxiliaris regarding the teneritudo aurium of the Romans at this time, note 55, above.

[65] Leonis Ep. 10 (al. 89), ad Episc. provinciae Viennensis: Divinae cultum religionis —ita Dominus noster—instituit, ut veritas—per apostolicam tubam in salutem universitatis exiret.—Sed hujus muneris sacramentum ita Dominus ad omnium Apostolorum officium pertinere voluit, ut in beatissimo Petro, Apostolorum omnium summo, principaliter collocaret; et ab ipso, quasi quodam capite, dona sua velit in corpus omne manare: ut exsortem se mysterii intelligeret esse divini, qui ausus fuisset a Petri soliditate recedere. Hunc enim in consortium individuae unitatis assumtum, id quod ipse erat, voluit nominari, dicen-

also considerably extended the power of that see, both by his own personal qualities and good fortune. The controversy with *Hilary*, bishop of Arles, led him to obtain a law from *Valentinian III.* (445) by which the Romish bishop became the supreme head of the whole western church.[66] The catholic bishops of *Africa*, now oppressed by the Arian Vandals, attached themselves the more closely on this account to the Roman see, and allowed Leo to act as a patriarch in their dioceses without opposition.[67] At the council of *Chalcedon*, Leo, whose legates had the presidency there, hoped to make good his claims as head of the whole church; but he met with much opposition among the orientals,[68] which at last manifested itself decidedly

do: Tu es Petrus, etc., ut aeterni templi aedificatio, mirabili munere gratiae Dei, in Petri soliditate consisteret. Hence Epist. ad Anastasium Episc. Thessalonic. (Quesn. Ep. 12, Baller. 14), c. 1: Curam, quam universis ecclesiis principaliter ex divina institutione debemus. C. 11: Magna ordinatione provisum est, ne omnes (episcopi) sibi omnia vindicarent; sed essent in singulis provinciis singuli, quorum inter fratres haberetur prima sententia, et rursus quidam, in majoribus urbibus constituti, sollicitudinem susciperent ampliorem, per quos ad unam Petri sedem universalis ecclesiae cura conflueret, et nihil usquam a suo capite dissideret. Epist. ad Africanos (Quesn. 1, Baller. 12): Solicitudo, quam universae ecclesiae ex divina institutione dependimus. Leo's Leben, v. Perthel, S. 226.

66 Appended to the edition of the Cod. Theodos. by Gothofredus and Ritter Novell Theodosii, tit. 24, by Hanell Novell. Valentin. iii. tit. 16, in Leonis Opp. ed. Baller. Epist. 11: Cum igitur sedis apostolicae primatum sancti Petri meritum, qui princeps est episcopalis coronae, et Romanae dignitas civitatis, sacrae etiam synodi firmarit auctoritas, ne quid praeter auctoritatem sedis istius illicita praesumtio attentare nitatur. Tunc enim demum ecclesiarum pax ubique servabitur, si rectorem suum agnoscat universitas.—§ 3. Nec hoc solum, quod est maximi criminis, submovemus, verum ne levis saltem inter ecclesias turba nascatur, vel in aliquo minui religionis disciplina videatur, hac perenni sanctione censemus, ne quid tam episcopis Gallicanis, quam aliarum provinciarum contra consuetudinem veterem liceat sine viri venerabilis papae urbis aeternae auctoritate tentare. Sed hoc illis omnibusque pro lege sit, quidquid sanxit vel sanxerit apostolicae sedis auctoritas, ita aut, quisquis episcoporum ad judicium Romani antistitis evocatus venire neglexerit, per moderatorem ejusdem provinciae adesse cogatur, per omnia servatis, quae divi parentes nostri Romanae ecclesiae detulerunt.

67 Cf. Leonis Epistol. ad Episcop. African. (Quesn. i. Baller. xii). Leo's Leben, v. Perthel, S. 30.

68 In the very beginning of the council the legates had to declare (actio, i. ap. Mansi, vi. 579): Beatissime atque apostolici viri Papae urbis Romae, quae est caput omnium Ecclesiarum, praecepta habemus prae manibus, quibus praecipere dignatus est ejus Apostolatus, ut Dioscurus, Alexandrinorum Archiepiscopus, non sedeat in Concilio, sed audiendus intromittatur. Hoc nos observare necesse est. Si ergo praecipit vestra magnificentia, aut ille egrediatur, aut nos eximus. Judicii sui necesse est eum dare rationem, quia cum personam judicandi non haberet, praesumpsit, et synodum ausus est facere (the Robber synod) sine auctoritate sedis apostolicae, quod nunquam licuit, nunquam factum est. They were, however, foiled in this proposition by the imperial commissioners, since they could not be accusers and judges at the same time. Dioscurus accordingly took his seat, and the legates remained.—Subsequently, the Romish legates withstood the first drawing up of the decree respecting the question of faith, desiring either that it should be made to agree more closely with the epistle of Leo, or that this epistle should be mentioned in it.

in decreeing the bishop of Constantinople to be on an equality with the bishop of Rome. This measure Leo had foreseen, and in vain attempted to avert.[69] He protested against it;[70] and *Anatolius*, bishop of Constantinople, was actually obliged to send an humble letter to him, for the oriental emperor's sake.[71] Still the decrees of the synod continued in force; and thus began the contest of jealousy that lasted for centuries, between the bishops of Rome and Constantinople.

It is worthy of remark, that the Romish bishops were distinguished by no peculiar titles in the west. In the east, the honorable appellation of patriarchs was certainly given them; but these titles were as yet common to all bishops in the west.[72]

On this so fearful an outcry arose, that the Illyrian bishops called out (actio v. ap. Mansi, vii. 105): *Οἱ ἀντιλέγοντες Νεστοριανοί εἰσιν· οἱ ἀντιλέγοντες εἰς Ῥώμην ἀπέλθωσιν.*

69 Comp. above, § 93, note 14. The Romish legates withdrew, actio xv. was adopted, and they protested (act. xvi.) against it, producing the instructions given them by Leo (Mansi, vii. 443): Sanctorum quoque patrum constitutionem prolatam nulla patiamini temeritate violari vel imminui, servantes omnimodis personae nostra in vobis—dignitatem: ac si qui forte civitatum suarum splendore confisi, aliquid sibi tentaverint usurpare, hoc qua dignum est constantia retundatis. They appealed, moreover, to the sixth Nicene canon, with the Romish addition, Ecclesia Romana semper habuit primatum (see § 93, note 1), but were immediately obliged to have the canon read to them in its original form, and were thus repulsed with their protest.

70 Leonis Epist. ad Marcianum, ad Pulcheriam, ad Anatalium (ap. Quesn. Ep. 78–80, Baller. Ep. 104–106).

71 In Epist. Leonis ap. Quesn. appended to Epist. 105, ap. Baller. Ep. 132.

72 In the west the names Papa Apostolicus, Vicarius Christi, Summus Pontifex, Sedes Apostolica, were applied to other bishops also, and their sees (Thomassini, P. i. lib. i. c. 4. Basnage praef. ad Canisii Lectt. ant. t. i. p. 37. G. S. Cyprian's Belehrung vom Urspr. und Wachsthum des Papsthums, S. 506, ff.). So also Patriarcha, especially to the Metropolitans. (du Pin Diss. i. § 5).—Gregory I. (Epist. lib. v. 18, 20, 41, viii. 30), was mistaken in believing that at the council of Chalcedon the name universalis Episcopus was given to the bishop of Rome. He is styled *οἰκουμενικὸς ἀρχιεπίσκοπος* (Mansi, vi. 1006, 1012), only in the *Complaints* of two Alexandrian deacons against Dioscurus; other patriarchs have the same appellation (see above, § 93, note 20). But in another place the title was surreptitiously introduced into the Latin acts by the Romish legates. In the sentence passed on Dioscurus, actio iii. (Mansi, vi. 1048), the council say, *ὁ ἁγιώτατος καὶ μακαριώτατος ἀρχιεπίσκοπος τῆς μεγάλης ταὶ πρεσβυτέρας Ῥώμης Λέων*: on the contrary, in the Latin acts which Leo sent to the Gallic bishops (Leonis Ep. 103, al. 82), we read: Sanctus ac beatissimus Papa, caput universalis Ecclesiae, Leo. In the older editions the beginning of Leo's Epist. 97 (ap. Quesn. 134, Baller. 165), runs thus: Leo Romae et universalis catholicaeque ecclesiae Episcopus Leoni semper Augusto salutem Quesnel and the Ballerini, however, found in all the Codices only: Leo Episcopus Leoni Augusto. The fable, which is repeated even by the Catechismus Romanus, p. ii. c. 7, qu. 24, § 4, that Cyril, at the Council of Ephesus, styled the bishop of Rome, Archiepiscopum totius orbis terrarum Patrem et Patriarcham, first proceeded from the St. Thomae († 1274) Catena aurea in Evang. ad Matth. xvi. 18, who also, in his Opusc. contra errores Graecorum, falsely attributes many similar passages to the Greek fathers. See Launoji Epistt. lib. i. Ep. 1–3.

FOURTH CHAPTER.

HISTORY OF MONACHISM.

Rud. Hospiniani de Monachis, h. e. de Origine et Progressu Monachatus libb. vi. Tiguri. 1588. ed. ii. auct. 1609. Genev. 1669. fol.—Ant. Dadini Alteserrae Asceticῶν s. Origg rei monasticae libb. x. Paris. 1674. 4. rec. ac praef. notasque adjecit Chr. F. Glück. Halae. 1782. 8.—Edm. Martene de Antiquis monachorum ritibus. Lugd. 1690. 4.—J. Binghami Origg. lib. vii. (vol. iii. p. 1, ss.)—Hippol. Helyot Histoire des ordres monastiques, etc. Paris. 1714, 19. t. viii. 4. translated into German under the title : Ausführl. Gesch. aller geistl. u. weltl. Kloster u. Ritterorden. Leipzig. 1753, 56. 8 Bde. 4.—(Musson) Pragm. Geschichte d. vornehmsten Mönchsorden aus ihren eigenen Geschichtschreibern (Paris. 1751, ss.) i. e., deutschen Ausz. (v. L. G. Crome) mit ein. Vorrede v. Ch. W. Fr. Walch. Leipzig. 1774–84. 10 Bde. 8. J. H. Möhler's Gesch. d. Mönchthums in d. Zeit, s. Entstehung u. ersten Ausbildung, in his Schriften u. Aufsätzen herausgeg. von Döllinger, ii. 165. Neander's Kirchengesch. ii. 2, 486, ss.

§ 95.

ORIGIN AND HISTORY OF MONACHISM IN THE EAST.

Solitude and asceticism were universally looked upon in this age as means of approximation to the Deity. The New Platonists recommended them.[1] The Jewish Essenes and Therapeutae lived in this manner.[2] Thus *Anthony* (Div. I. § 73),

[1] After Plato's example in the Phaedo and Theaetetus. Plotinus recommends the μένον εἶναι, μόνον πρὸς μόνον (θεὸν) γενέσθαι. See Creuzer ad Plotini Opp. ed. Oxon. iii. 140, 276, 412. A. Jahnii Basilius Magnus plotinizans. Bernae. 1838. 4. p. 19.

[2] Still in the time of Nilus, who lived as monk on Sinai, A.D. 430. See Nili tract. ad Magnam, c. 39. (Nili tractatus ed. J. M. Suaresius, Romae. 1673. fol. p. 279), and de Monast. exercis. c. 3. (l. c. p. 2), where they are called Ἰεσσαῖοι.

appeared to have set forth the ideal of *a Christian* wise man; he soon found many imitators, and other hermits fixed themselves in his neighborhood. Many more were concealed in inaccessible places, of whom one, *Paul of Thebes* († 340), who had lived in the desert ever since the Decian persecution, is said to have become known to Anthony shortly before his death.[3] After a number of hermits had been brought into a kind of connection with one another by Anthony, *Pachomius* founded a place of habitation where they might dwell together (*κοινόβιον*, *μάνδρα*, claustrum.—Κοινοβίτης, Συνοδίτης), on the island *Tabenna* in the Nile (about 340), with a system of rules for the government of its inmates, by which strict obedience to the president (Ἀββᾶς, Ἡγούμενος, Ἀρχιμανδρίτης) was particularly enforced. At the same time *Amun* founded a society of monks on *the Nitrian mountain* (τὸ τῆς Νιτρίας ὄρος); and *Macarius* the elder[4] in the neighboring wilderness of *Sketis*.[5] Both were soon peopled by the monks, and became the most celebrated resorts. *Hilarion* assembled in the desert near Gaza, a company of monks, and from thence the system spread through Palestine and Syria.[6] The *Eusebian Eustathius*, afterward bishop of Sebaste, introduced it into Armenia and Asia Minor.[7] The peculiarities of the monkish life of this period consisted in solitariness, manual labor, spiritual exercises,[8] restraint of the bodily appetites for the pur-

[3] Vita Antonii by Athanasius, see Div. I. § 73, note 22. Vita Pauli by Jerome.

[4] Probably from him we have the Homiliae spirituales 50, ed. J. G. Pritius. Lips. 1698 and 1714. 8. Comp. Paniel's Gesch. der christl. Beredsamkeit, i. 396.

[5] Coptic Schiêt, Greek Σκήτης, Σκῆτις, ap. Ptolemy Σκίαθις, Latin Scetis, Scithis, Scytiaca, Scythium, means chiefly *the hill* on which Macarius settled, then *the surrounding desert*. Et. Quatremère Mémoires géograph. et hist. sur l'Egypte. (Paris. t. 2. 1811. 8.) i. 451.

[6] Vita Hilarionis by Jerome.—*Λαύραι* in Palestine.

[7] On the first monks generally see Socrates, iv. 23, 24. Sozomenus, i. 12-15, iii. 14, vi. 28-34. Palladii (bishop of Helenopolis, afterward of Aspona, † about 420), Historia Lausiaca in Jo. Meursii Opp. vol. viii. (Florent. 1746. fol.) p. 329. Theodoreti *φιλόθεος ἱστορία*,

[8] Even Tertullian (de Orat. c. 25, et adv. Psychicos, c. 10) and Cyprian (de Orat. domin. p. 154) recommended the hora tertia, sexta, and nona, as times of prayer, while every day, morning and evening, church service was performed. (Const. apost. ii. 59.) Among the monks different usages arose at first. The Egyptians had, on every day of the week, only two meetings for prayer (Cassianus de Instit. coenob. iii. 2, vespertinas ac nocturnas congregationes), and in their cells carried on manual labor, and prayed almost incessantly; those of the East came together for the purpose of singing psalms, hora tertia, sexta, et nona (l. c. c. 3), the matutina hora was first introduced at a later period into the monastery at Bethlehem (l. c. c. 4). Athanasius de virginitate (Opp. i. 1051, ss.), marks out for the nuns six seasons of prayer, viz., the third, sixth, ninth, twelfth hours (a more solemn assembly in the church at the last hour), *μεσονύκτιον* and *πρὸς ὄρθρον*. So also Jerome,

pose of mortifying the sensual nature, and allowing the spirit with less disturbance to be absorbed in the contemplation of divine things.[9] The rules of the monasteries made, indeed, more moderate demands on the abstinence of the inmates;[10] but the majority of the monks did more than was required, of their own free choice, and many even withdrew from the cells of the convents into the desert (*'Αναχωρηταί*), that they might suppress sensual desires by the most ingenious self-tortures, and attain the highest degree of holiness. In many cases these measures had only the contrary effect, and temptations increased;[11] many

Epitaph. Paulae Epist. 27, 10, Epist. 7 ad Laetam; according to Chrysostom. in 1 Tim. Hom. xiv. the monks had the same hours. Basil also, de Instit. monach. sermo, prescribes these six; but that there may be seven, agreeably to Psalm cxix. 164, the prayer of noon is directed to be divided into that before and that after eating. When six public hours for prayer are prescribed to the churches in the apostolic constitutions, viii. 34, the writer follows the view which arose in the fourth century, viz., that in the apostolic churches for which he pretends to write, a monastic institute prevailed. Even in his day there were daily but two religious services, as at an early period (*ἐν ἑσπέρᾳ καὶ ἐν πρωΐᾳ*, Chrysost. in 1 Tim. Hom. vi.).

[9] Respecting the Egyptian monasteries comp. Hieronymi Ep. 18 (al. 22) ad Eustochium (ed. Martian. t. iv. P. ii. p. 45). Jo. Cassiani Collationes Patrum, et de Institutis coenobiorum. On the labors cf. de Inst. coen. x. 23: Haec est apud Aegyptum ab antiquis patribus sancita sententia: operantem monachum daemone uno pulsari, otiosum vero innumeris spiritibus devastari. Cf. Alteserra, l. c. lib. v. cap. 7 et 8. Neander's Chrysostomus, B. 1, S. 80, ff.

[10] Comp. Pachomius' rule (ap. Pallad. Hist. Laus. c. 38): *Συγχωρήσεις ἑκάστῳ κατὰ τὴν δύναμιν φαγεῖν καὶ πιεῖν, καὶ πρὸς τὰς δυνάμεις τῶν ἐσθιόντων ἀνάλογα καὶ τὰ ἔργα αὐτῶν ἐγχείρησον, καὶ μήτε νηστεῦσαι κωλύσῃς μήτε φαγεῖν.*

[11] See the confessions of Jerome, Ep. 18, ad Eustochium: Ille igitur ego, qui ob gehennae metum tali me carcere ipse damnaveram, scorpionum tantum socius et ferarum, saepe choris intereram puellarum. Pallebant ora jejuniis, et mens desideriis aestuabat in frigido corpore, et ante hominem suum jam in carne praemortua, sola libidinum incendia bulliebant. Itaque omni auxilio destitutus, ad Jesu jacebam pedes, rigabam lachrymis, crine tergebam, et repugnantem carnem hebdomadarum inedia subjugabam.—Memini me clamantem, diem crebro junxisse cum nocte, nec prius a pectoris cessasse verberibus, quam rediret Domino increpante tranquillitas. Ep. 95, ad Rusticum: Dum essem juvenis, et solitudinis me deserta vallarent: incentiva vitiorum ardoremque naturae ferre non poteram: quem cum crebris jejuniis frangerem, mens tamen cogitationibus aestuabat. Ad quam edomandam cuidam fratri, qui ex Hebraeis crediderat, me in disciplinam dedi, ut —alphabetum discerem, et stridentia anhelantiaque verba meditarer. In like manner Basil admits to his friend Gregory, Ep. 2: *Κατέλιπον μὲν τὰς ἐν ἄστει διατριβὰς ὡς μυρίων κακῶν ἀφορμὰς, ἐμαυτὸν δὲ οὔπω ἀπολιπεῖν ἠδυνήθην.—ὥστε οὐδὲν μέγα τῆς ἐρημίας ἀπωνάμεθα ταύτης.* On the temptations to lust see Nilus, lib. ii. Ep. 140. (Nili Epistolarum, libb. iv. Romae. 1668. p. 179.) In the quaestt. et responsiones ad orthodoxos among Justin's works, written after 400, it is asked, qu. 21, whether sensual dreams exclude from the supper: *'Επειδὴ πολλή ἐστι περὶ τούτου καὶ παρ' αὐτῶν (τῶν μοναχῶν) ἡ ζήτησις.* Comp. Nilus, *περὶ διαφόρων πονηρῶν λογισμῶν* (Tractatus ed. Suaresii, p. 512). Basilii regulae breviores, interrog. 22. Comp. the experience of Philo, Legis allegor. lib. iii. (properly lib. ii.) p. 1102: *Εγὼ πολλάκις καταλιπὼν μὲν ἀνθρώπους, συγγενεῖς, καὶ φίλους, καὶ πατρίδα, καὶ εἰς ἐρημίαν ἔλθων, ἵνα τι τῶν θέας ἀξίων κατανοήσω, οὐδὲν ὤνησα· ἀλλὰ σκορπισθεὶς ὁ νοῦς, ἢ πάθει δηχθεὶς, ἀνεχώρησεν εἰς τἀναντία.*

monks were driven to despair by a sense of the hopelessness of their efforts;[12] in the case of others, complete madness was superinduced by that excessive asceticism, and by the pride associated with it, under the influence of a burning climate.[13] From that diseased excitement of the imagination, and that spiritual pride, arose also those strange miraculous occurrences which befel the monks only in solitude. The lesser marvelous things which they wrought in the circles of enthusiastic admirers must be explained by the impression they made on the feelings of reverence entertained toward the persons of the monks, and by the magnifying nature of tradition.[14]

Ἔστι δ' ὅτε καὶ ἐν πλήθει μυριάνδρῳ ἐρημῷ τὴν διάνοιαν, τὸν ψυχικὸν ὄχλον σκεδάσαντος θεοῦ, καὶ διδάξαντός με, ὅτι οὐ τόπων διαφοραὶ τό τε εὖ καὶ χεῖρον ἐργάζονται, ἀλλ' ὁ κινῶν θεὸς καὶ ἄγων, ᾗ ἂν προαιρῆται, τὸ τῆς ψυχῆς ὄχημα. Zimmermann on Solitude, part 2, chapters 6 and 7.

[12] So that some, like the circumcelliones (see § 86, note 9), put an end to their life, see Nilus, lib. ii. Ep. 140: *Τινὲς μὲν αὐτῶν ξενισθέντες, καὶ θορυβηθέντες τὸν νοῦν ἐξ ἀπροσεξίας καὶ ἀδιακρισίας, ἑαυτοὺς ἔσφαξαν μαχαίρᾳ, τινὲς δὲ κατεκρήμνησαν ἑαυτοὺς ἀφορήτῳ λύπῃ καὶ ἀπογνώσει συσχεθέντες, ἕτεροι δὲ τὰ γεννητικὰ μόρια κόψαντες, καὶ αὐτοφονευταὶ ἑαυτῶν τῇ προαιρέσει γεγονότες οἱ τάλανες, ὑπέπεσαν τῇ ἀποστολικῇ ἀρᾷ,—ἄλλοι δὲ καὶ γυναῖκας ἔλαβον συναρπασθέντες ὑπὸ τοῦ Σατανᾶ.* Gregor. Naz. Carm. xlvii. v. 100, ss. (Opp. t. ii. 107):

Θνήσκουσιν πολλοῖς προφρονέως θανάτοις,
Αὐτοὶ ὑπὸ σφετέρης παλάμης, καὶ γαστρὸς ἀνάγκῃ,
Οἱ δὲ κατὰ σκοπέλων βένθεσί τ' ἠὲ βρόχοις,
Μάρτυρες ἀτρεκίης· πολέμου δ' ἄπο καὶ στονόεντος
Χαίρουσιν βιότου τοῦδ' ἀπανιστάμενοι.
Ἵλαθι Χριστὲ ἄναξ πισταῖς φρεσὶν ἀφραδέουσιν!

Pachomius says, Vita Pachomii, § 61 (Acta SS. Maji, iii. 329, the Greek original is given in the app. p. 41): *Ἡ δὲ τῆς βλασφημίας ὑποβολὴ τῶν ἐχθρῶν ἐὰν εὕρῃ τινὰ μὴ νηφάλαιον, κἂν ᾖ ἀγαπῶν θεὸν,—τοῦτον ἀπολέσει. Καὶ πολλοὶ ἐθανάτωσαν ἑαυτοὺς, ὁ μὲν ἐπάνωθεν πέτρας ἑαυτὸν ῥίψας ὡς ἐκστατικὸς, καὶ ἄλλος μαχαίρᾳ ἀπέπτυξεν τὴν κοιλίαν αὐτοῦ καὶ ἀπέθανεν, καὶ ἄλλοι ἄλλως.* Cf. Chrysostomi ad Stagirium, libb. iii. (Opp. i. 153) to a monk who believed that he had been tempted by Satan to commit suicide. Others sought assistance in their struggle against desire in immoderate sleep. Nili, lib. iii. Ep. 224.

[13] Hieronymi Ep. 95 (al. 4), ad Rusticum: Sunt, qui humore cellarum, immoderatisque jejuniis, taedio solitudinis ac nimia lectione, dum diebus ac noctibus auribus suis personant, vertuntur in melancholiam, et Hippocratis magis fomentis quam nostris monitis indigent. Ejusd. Ep. 97 (al. 8) ad Demetriadem: Novi ego in utroque sexu per nimiam abstinentiam cerebri sanitatem quibusdam fuisse vexatam: praecipueque in his, qui in humectis et frigidis habitaverunt cellulis, ita ut nescirent quid agerent, quove se verterent: quid loqui, quid tacere deberent. Hence his disapprobation of extreme fasting in Ep. 57 (al. 7) ad Laetam and Jo. Cassian. Instit. v. 9.

[14] Several hints on this subject may be found in the following passages: Hieron. Ep. 50, ad Rusticum: Quosdam ineptos homines daemonum pugnantium contra se portenta confingere, ut apud imperitos et vulgi homines miraculum sui faciant, et exinde lucra sectentur. Sozomenus, i. 14: *Πολλὰ δὲ καὶ θεσπέσια ἐπ' αὐτῷ* ('Αμοῦν) *συμβέβηκεν, ἃ μάλιστα τοῖς κατ' Αἴγυπτον μοναχοῖς ἠκρίβωται, περὶ πολλοῦ ποιουμένοις, διαδοχῇ παραδόσεως*

Very soon in the east monachism was received with enthusiastic admiration, and the number of monks swelled to an enormous extent.[15] Since there were no more persecutions, and no more opportunities of martyrdom; since Christianity had even acquired external dominion; the erroneous notion was spread abroad that there was no longer an opportunity in the world for the full exercise of Christian virtue.[16] The general corruption[17] or consciousness of individual guilt caused many to seek solitude. Many sought escape from the oppressive circumstances of life.[18] Others wished to make a figure and obtain an influence. Others were attracted by sloth;[19] and lastly, others were drawn away

ἀγράφου ἐπιμελῶς ἀπομνημονεύειν τὰς τῶν παλαιοτέρων ἀσκητῶν ἀρετάς. Sulpicius Severus, dial. ii. 4, relates that St. Martin often told him, nequaquam sibi in episcopatu eam virtutum gratiam suppetisse, quam prius se habuisse meminisset. Quod si verum est, immo quia verum est, conjicere possumus, quanta fuerunt illa, quae monachus operatus est, et quae teste nullo solus exercuit, cum tanta illum in episcopatu signa fecisse, sub oculis omnium viderimus. For the physiological explanation of the frequent visions seen by these anchorites comp. D. Joh. Müller über die phantastischen Gesichterscheinungen. Coblenz. 1826. 8.

[15] Pachomius had in his convent 1300 monks, and in all upward of 7000 under his superintendence (Sozom. iii. 14). In a monastery at Thebais were 5000 monks (Cass. de Instit. iv. 1), in Nitria were fifty convents (Sozom. vi. 31), etc.

[16] A kindred notion may be found in Origen, see Div. I. § 70, note 19.

[17] Chrysostomus adv. oppugnatores vitae monast. i. 7: Ἐβουλόμην καὶ αὐτὸς—τῶν μοναστηρίων ἀναιρεθῆναι τὴν χρείαν, καὶ τοσαύτην ἐν ταῖς πόλεσι γενέσθαι τὴν εὐνομίαν, ὡς μηδένα δεηθῆναί ποτε τῆς εἰς τὴν ἔρημον καταφυγῆς· ἐπειδὴ δὲ τὰ ἄνω κάτω γέγονε, καὶ αἱ μὲν πόλεις—πολλῆς γέμουσι παρανομίας καὶ ἀδικίας, ἡ δὲ ἐρημία πολλῷ βρύει τῷ τῆς φιλοσοφίας καρπῷ οὐχ οἱ τῆς ζάλης ταύτης καὶ τῆς ταραχῆς τοὺς σωθῆναι βουλομένους ἐξάγοντες, καὶ πρὸς τὸν τῆς ἡσυχίας ὁδηγοῦντας λιμένα, δικαίως ἂν ἐγκαλοῖντο παρ' ὑμῶν.

[18] Isidorus Pelus. (see § 88, note 25) lib. i. Ep. 262. Εὐσέβιος (a bishop) καὶ τοῦτο τῇ παροικίᾳ Πηλουσίου παρέχετο, βουνόμοις τισὶ, καὶ αἰπόλοις, καὶ δραπέταις οἰκέταις ἐπιτρέπων μοναχικὰ συμπήγνυσθαι παλαιστήρια, οὐδενὶ μαθητευθεῖσι τὴν μοναχικὴν, ἢ μετελθόντων, ἢ ὅλως ἀγαπώντων, οὐδὲ ὅλως τῆς φιλοσοφίας ταύτης ἢ ἀκηκοόσιν, ἢ μέχρι σχήματος διδαχθεῖσι.

[19] Respecting the reputation which the monks possessed, compare what Chrysostom says to the heathen father of a monk, adv. oppugnatores vitae monast. ii. 4: Σὺ μὲν οὖν τῶν σαυτοῦ κύριος εἶ μόνον, ἐκεῖνος (ὁ υἱός σου) δὲ τῶν κατὰ τὴν οἰκουμένην ἅπασαν. εἰ δὲ ἀπιστεῖς,—πείσωμεν αὐτὸν κατελθόντα ἀπὸ τοῦ ὄρους—σημᾶναί τινι τῶν σφόδρα πλουτούντων καὶ εὐλαβῶν, πέμψαι χρυσοῦ σταθμὸν, ὅσον ἐθέλεις,—καὶ προθυμότερον ὄψει τὸν πλουτοῦντα ὑπακούοντα καὶ ἐκκομίζοντα, ἢ τῶν οἰκονόμων τινὰ τῶν σῶν. C. 6: Εὑρήσομεν αὐτὸν (τὸν υἱόν σου) οὐ μόνον λαμπρότερον ὄντα νῦν, ἀλλὰ καὶ δι' ἐκεῖνα τιμιώτερον, δι' ἅπερ ἄτιμον εἶναι φῂς καὶ εὐτελῆ. εἰ γὰρ βουλει, πείσαντες αὐτὸν ἀπὸ τοῦ ὄρους κατελθεῖν, πείσωμεν καὶ εἰς ἀγορὰν ἐμβαλεῖν, καὶ ὄψει πᾶσαν ἐπιστρεφομένην τὴν πόλιν, καὶ ὑποδεικνύντας αὐτὸν ἅπαντας, καὶ θαυμάζοντας, καὶ ἐκπληττομένους, ὡς ἀγγέλου τινὸς ἐξ οὐρανοῦ παραγενομένου νῦν. C. 7: Τίς μετὰ πλείονος ἐξουσίας διαλέξεται βασιλεῖ, καὶ ἐπιτιμήσει; ὁ τοσαῦτα σὺ κεκτημένος, καὶ ὑπεύθυνος ὢν διὰ ταῦτα καὶ τοῖς ἐκείνου δούλοις,—ἢ οὗτος ὁ τῶν ἐκείνου χειρῶν ἀνώτερος ὤν; βασιλεῦσι μὲν γὰρ οὗτοι μάλιστα διελέχθησαν μετ' ἐξουσίας πολλῆς, ὅσοι πάντων ἐγένοντο τῶν βιωτικῶν ἐκτός. C. 8: Εἰ ταπεινοὶ, καὶ ἐκ ταπεινῶν ὄντες τινὲς ἀγροί-

by mere imitation.[20] The measures taken by the emperor Valens[21] against the excessive tendency to this state of things were attended with no lasting consequences, since the following emperors only showed the more respect for monachism. The most distinguished teachers of the church, *Athanasius*, *Ambrose*, *Basil the Great*, *Gregory of Nazianzum*, *Chrysostom*, *Jerome*, and *Augustine*, were the most zealous panegyrists of the new mode of life (φιλοσοφία, ἀγγελικὴ διαγωγή).[22] Examples in favor of it were soon discovered even in the Old Testament;[23] and by new

κων υἱοὶ καὶ χειροτεχνῶν, ἐπὶ τὴν φιλοσοφίαν ταυτην ἐλθόντες, οὕτως ἐγένοντο τίμιοι πᾶσιν, ὡς μηδένα τῶν ἐν τοῖς μεγάλοις ὄντων ἀξιώμασιν αἰσχυνθῆναι πρὸς τὸ καταγώγιον τούτων ἐλθεῖν, καὶ λόγων μετασχεῖν καὶ τραπέζης·—πολλῷ μᾶλλον, ὅταν ἀπὸ λαμπροῦ μὲν ὁρμώμενον γένους—πρὸς ἐκείνην ἴδωσιν ἐλθόντα τὴν ἀρετὴν, τοῦτο ἐργάσονται. Nilus λόγος ἀσκητικός, c. 7 (Opusc. ed. Suaresii, p. 8): The striving of many monks was even at that time so much directed toward the attainment of possessions, ὥστε λοιπὸν τοὺς πολλοὺς πορισμὸν ἡγεῖσθαι τὴν εὐσέβειαν, καὶ δι' οὐδὲν ἕτερον ἐπιτηδεύεσθαι τὸν πάλαι ἀπράγμονα καὶ μακάριον βίον, ἢ ὅπως διὰ τῆς ἐπιπλάστου θεοσεβείας τὰς μὲν ἐπιπόνους λειτουργείας φύγωμεν, ἄδειαν δὲ ἀπολαύσεως πορισάμενοι, ἀκωλύτως ἐπὶ τὰ δοκοῦντα τὰς ὁρμὰς ἐκτείνωμεν, μετὰ πολλῆς ἀναισχυντίας καταλαζονευόμενοι τῶν ὑποδεεστέρων, ἔστι δὲ ὅτε καὶ τῶν ὑπερεχόντων, ὥσπερ ὑπόθεσιν τυραννίδος, ἀλλ' οὐχὶ ταπεινώσεως καὶ ἐπιεικείας τὸν ἐνάρετον βίον εἶναι νομίσαντες. Διὰ τοῦτο καὶ παρὰ τῶν σέβεσθαι ἡμᾶς ὀφειλόντων ὡς εἰκαῖος ὄχλος ὁρώμεθα, καὶ—γελώμεθα,—οὐκ ἐκ πολιτείας, ἀλλ' ἐκ σχήματος γνωρίζεσθαι βουλόμενοι.

[20] Comp. the judgment of Synesius, at that time still a heathen, afterward bishop of Ptolemais, in his Dion: Οἱ δὲ πλείους οὐδ' οἴκοθεν ἐκινήθησαν,—ὥσπερ δὲ ἄλλο τι τῶν εὐδοκιμούντων, τὴν γενναίαν αἵρεσιν ἐζηλώκασι, παντοδαποί τε ὄντες τὰ γένη, καὶ κατὰ χρείαν ἕκαστοι συνιστάμενοι.

[21] Cod. Theodos. xii. 1, 63 (A.D. 365): Quidam ignaviae sectatores desertis civitatum muneribus captant solitudines ac secreta, et specie religionis cum coetibus monazonton congregantur. Hos igitur atque hujusmodi, intra Aegyptum deprehensos, per comitem Orientis erui e latebris consulta praeceptione mandavimus, atque ad munia patriarum subeunda revocari, aut pro tenore nostrae sanctionis familiarium rerum carere illecebris, quas per eos censuimus vindicandas, qui publicarum essent subituri munera functionum. After the death of his milder brother (Orosii Hist. vii. 33: illico post fratris obitum), Valens became more violent against the monks, see Hieron. Chron. ann. 375: Multi monachorum Nitriae per tribunos et milites caesi. Valens enim lege data, ut monachi militarent, nolentes fustibus interfici jussit. This raised the courage of the numerous opponents of monachism, and therefore Chrysostom wrote at that time πρὸς τοὺς πολεμοῦντας τοῖς ἐπὶ τὸ μονάζειν ἐνάγουσιν libb. iii. (ed. Montf. t. i.)

[22] 'Ο τῶν ἀγγέλων βίος, τὰ οὐράνια πολιτεύματα, ἀποστολικὸς βίος (Epiph. Haer lxi. 4), ἡ ὑψηλὴ φιλοσοφία, ἔργῳ μᾶλλον ἢ λόγῳ κατορθουμένη (Gregor. Nyss. Orat catech. c. 18), ἡ κατὰ θεὸν φιλοσοφία (Nilus de Monast. exercitatione, c. 8). Serapion, bishop of Thmuis, about 350, writes in the Epist. ad monachos (Spicilegium Romanum, iv. p. liv.) to them: 'Ισάγγελοι ἐστὲ τῇ πολιτείᾳ· ὥσπερ γὰρ ἐν τῇ ἀναστάσει τῶν νεκρῶν οὔτε γαμοῦσιν οὔτε γαμίσκονται, ἀλλ' ὡς ἄγγελοι εἰσὶν ἐν οὐρανῷ οἱ δίκαιοι, τὸν αὐτὸν τρόπον καὶ ὑμεῖς οὕτω συμβιοτεύοντες, προελάβετε τῷ πόθῳ τὸ ἐσόμενον. Entering on the life of a monk is called by Jerome, Ep. 22 (al. 25), ad Paulam: Secundo quodammodo propositi se baptismo lavare. Subsequently Dionys. Areop. de Eccles. hierarch. c. 6, reckons the vow of monks (μυστήριον μοναχικῆς τελειώσεως) among the sacraments.

[23] Hieronymus in vita S. Pauli (about 365): Inter multos saepe dubitatum est, a quo

explanations of detached passages and the help of supplementing legends, the original condition of the early Christians was shown to be a completely monastic state.[24]

For a long time the monks appeared to have been able to dwell only in deserts. Individuals, indeed, sometimes showed

potissimum Monachorum eremus habitari coepta sit. Quidam enim altius repetentes, a b. Elia et Johanne sumsere principium. Quorum et Elias plus nobis videtur fuisse, quam Monachus: et Johannes ante prophetare coepisse, quam natus sit. Alii autem, in quam opinionem vulgus omne consensit, asserunt Antonium hujus propositi caput, quod ex parte verum est. Non enim tam ipse ante omnes fuit, quam ab eo omnium incitata sunt studia. Amathas vero et Macarius, discipuli Antonii, e quibus superior magistri corpus sepelivit, etiam nunc affirmant, Paulum quemdam Thebaeum principem istius rei fuisse, non nominis; quam opinionem nos quoque probamus. On the contrary, the same Jerome observed, about 395, Ep. 49 (al. 13), ad Paulinum: Nos autem habeamus propositi nostri principes Paulos et Antonios, Julianos, Hilarionem, Macarios. Et ut ad scripturarum auctoritatem redeam: noster princeps Helias, noster Helisaeus, nostri duces filii prophetarum, qui habitabant in agris et solitudinibus, et faciebant sibi tabernacula prope fluenta Jordanis. De his sunt et illi filii Rechab (Jerem. xxxv.), qui vinum et siceram non bibebant, qui morabantur in tentoriis, etc. Sozomenus, i. 12: Ταύτης δὲ τῆς ἀρίστης φιλοσοφίας ἤρξατο, ὥς τινες λέγουσιν, Ἠλίας ὁ προφήτης, καὶ Ἰωάννης ὁ βαπτιστής.

[24] The Therapeutae were regarded as Christians (Div. I. § 17, note 11), and for this purpose such passages as Acts ii. 44, iv. 32, ss. were appealed to. Hieron. Catal. c. 11: Philo—librum de prima Marci Evangelistae apud Alexandriam scribens ecclesia, in nostrorum laude versatus est (he means Philo περὶ βίου θεωρητικοῦ); non solum eos ibi, sed in multis quoque provinciis esse commemorans, et habitacula eorum dicens monasteria. Ex quo apparet, talem primam Christo credentium fuisse ecclesiam, quales nunc monachi esse nituntur et cupiunt, ut nihil cujuspiam proprium sit, nullus inter eos dives, nullus pauper; patrimonia egentibus dividuntur, orationi vacatur et psalmis, doctrinae quoque et continentiae: quales et Lucas refert primum Hierosolymae fuisse credentes. Jo Cassian. Collat. 18, c. 5: Itaque Coenobitarum disciplina a tempore praedicationis apostolicae sumsit exordium. Nam talis extitit in Hierosolymis omnis illa credentium multitudo, quae in Actibus Apostolorum ita describitur (seqq. loci Act. iv. 32, 34, 35).—Sed cum post Apostolorum excessum tepescere coepisset credentium multitudo, ea vel maxime, quae ad fidem Christi de alienigenis ac diversis gentibus confluebat,—non solum hi qui ad fidem Christi confluxerant, verum etiam illi, qui erant ecclesiae principes, ab illa districtione laxati sunt.—Hi autem, quibus adhuc apostolicus inerat fervor, memores illius pristinae perfectionis, discedentes a civitatibus suis—et ea, quae ab Apostolis per universum corpus ecclesiae generaliter meminerant instituta, privatim ac peculiariter exercere coeperunt, etc. Idem de Institut. coenob. ii. 5: Cum in primordiis fidei pauci quidem, sed probatissimi, monachorum nomine censerentur, qui sicut a beatae memoriae evangelista Marco, qui primus Alexandrinae urbi Pontifex praefuit, normam suscepere vivendi, non solum illa magnifica retinebant, quae primitus ecclesiam vel credentium turbas in Actibus Apostolorum legimus celebrasse, verum etiam his multo sublimiora cumulaverant; cf. Sozomenus, i. 12. Hence the monks were said ἀποστολικὸν βίον βιοῦν, Epiphan. Haer. 61, § 4.—Legends of the monkish chastity of the saints, of Mary especially, Protevangelium Jacobi, c. 7, ss. From a misunderstanding of Exodus xiii. 1 (2 Macc. iii. 19?) it was thought that there were in the temple virgins consecrated to God, among whom Mary had grown up (Epiphan. Ancorat. no. 60. Gregor. Nyss. Orat. de sancta Christi nativitate) with the vow of perpetual virginity (Augustinus de virginitate, c. 4). Her marriage with Joseph was only apparent, he being eighty years old (Epiph. Haer. 51, c. 10), and according to Epiph. l. c. a widower, but according to Jerome adv. Helvid. c. 9, a perpetual ascetic. Cf. J. A. Schmidii prolusiones Marianae x. Helmst. 1733. 4, p. 21, ss.—1 Cor. ix. 5, was referred to female friends of the apostles (Div. I. § 27, note 3).

themselves in cities to oppose heathens and heretics, but they always withdrew again very soon into their solitude.[25] *Basil the Great* was the first who established a company of monks in the vicinity of Caesarea in Cappadocia, in order to suppress Arianism, by their influence with the people.[26] From this time monasteries became more frequent in the neighborhood of cities; but since there were as yet no strict rules, wandering companies of monks were also found. Thus their influence in Church and State became stronger, but, at the same time, more dangerous.

It is true that the monks made a strong moral impression by their strict life, dedicated to God in solitude. Even heathens frequently repaired to them in numbers, for the sake of receiving their blessing, and were converted by them.[27] But the honor and power they possessed not unfrequently caused the passions within them, which were suppressed in regard to their sensual manifestations, to break forth still more strongly in the form of spiritual pride,[28] and wild fanaticism, against those who thought differently from themselves. From the time of Theodosius I., they opposed heathenism with fury and barbarousness;[29] and they

[25] Antony said: *Τοὺς μὲν ἰχθύας τὴν ὑγρὰν οὐσίαν τρέφειν· μοναχοῖς δὲ κόσμον φέρειν τὴν ἔρημον· ἐπίσης τὲ τοὺς μὲν ξηρᾶς ἀπτομένους τὸ ζῆν ἀπολιμπάνειν, τοὺς δὲ τὴν μοναστικὴν σεμνότητα ἀπολλύειν τοῖς ἄστεσι προσιόντας.* Sozom. i. 13.

[26] Socrates, iv. 21. Gregor. Nazianz. Orat. xx. in laudem Basilii, p. 358: *Τοῦ τοίνυν ἐρημικοῦ βίου καὶ τοῦ μιγάδος μαχομένων πρὸς ἀλλήλους ὡς τὰ πολλὰ, καὶ διϊσταμένων, καὶ οὐδετέρου πάντως ἢ τὸ καλὸν, ἢ τὸ φαῦλον ἀνεπίμικτον ἔχοντος· ἀλλὰ τοῦ μὲν ἡσυχίου μὲν ὄντος μᾶλλον, καὶ καθεστηκότος, καὶ θεῷ συνάγοντος, οὐκ ἀτύφου δὲ διὰ τὸ τῆς ἀρετῆς ἀβασάνιστον καὶ ἀσύγκριτον· τοῦ δὲ πρακτικωτέρου μὲν μᾶλλον καὶ χρησιμωτέρου, τὸ δὲ θορυβῶδες οὐ φεύγοντος· καὶ τούτους ἄριστα κατήλλαξεν ἀλλήλοις καὶ συνεκέρασεν· ἀσκητήρια καὶ μοναστήρια δειμάμενος μὲν, οὐ πόῤῥω δὲ τῶν κοινωνικῶν καὶ μιγάδων, οὐδὲ ὥσπερ τειχίῳ τινὶ μέσῳ ταῦτα διαλαβὼν, καὶ ἀπ' ἀλλήλων χωρίσας, ἀλλὰ πλησίον συνάψας καὶ διαζεύξας· ἵνα μήτε τὸ φιλόσοφον ἀκοινώνητον ᾖ, μήτε τὸ πρακτικὸν ἀφιλόσοφον.* On the Ascetica of Basil, the chief parts of which are *ὅροι κατὰ πλάτος* and *ὅροι κατ' ἐπιτομήν* (monks' rules), see Garnier in praef. ad Basil. Opp. t. ii p. xxxiv. ss.

[27] See Möhler's Schriften u. Aufsätze, ii. 219.

[28] Hieronym. Ep. 15 (al. 77), ad Marcum: Pudet dicere, de cavernis cellularum damnamus orbem, in sacco et cinere volutati de Episcopis sententiam ferimus. Quid facit sub tunica poenitentis regius animus? Catenae, sordes et comae, non sunt diadematis signa, sed fletus. Idem Ep. 95 (al. 4), ad Rusticum: In solitudine cito subrepit superbia: et si parumper jejunaverit, hominemque non viderit, putat se alicujus esse momenti. Oblitusque sui, unde, et quo venerit, intus corde, lingua foris vagatur. Judicat contra Apostoli voluntatem alienos servos: quo gula voluerit porrigit manum: dormit quantum voluerit: nullum veretur: facit quod voluerit: omnes inferiores se putat: crebriusque in urbibus, quam in cellula est: et inter fratres simulat verecundiam, qui platearum turbis colliditur. Comp. Nilus, above, note 19.

[29] Comp. Libanius, above, § 78, note 9. Zosimus, v. 23. Eunapius in Vita Aedesii: *Μοναχοὺς, ἀνθρώπους μὲν κατὰ τὸ εἶδος, ὁ δὲ βίος αὐτοῖς συώδης, καὶ εἰς τὸ ἐμφανὲς*

also mingled in ecclesiastical controversies in a manner no less violent. Since they despised all learning, and founded their judgment of orthodoxy merely on an obscure feeling of what looked like piety, and what did not,[30] it was seldom difficult for a superior head to excite their fanaticism in favor of a certain view. Thus the ambitious bishops of Alexandria, *Theophilus*, *Cyril*, and *Dioscurus*, knew well how to make use of them, partly to work upon the people, partly to overpower their opponents by acts of violence.[31] The rude mass were as easily excited, in a fanatical manner, against a Chrysostom, at the point of death,[32] as against idolaters and Arians. The limits of civil law, and the dignity of magistrates, appear to have been disregarded by them.[33] In them religious fanaticism was united with a cynical indifference to propriety or duty; and too often indolence and vice also were concealed under this mask of piety.[34]

Contemplation, which was regarded as the most important duty of the monk, as though it led him to an internal union with God, was usually, in the absence of mental cultivation, either a suffering resignation to feeling, without a distinct consciousness of it,[35] or a play of anthropomorphic images of the fancy. Hence anthropomorphism was very common among them.[36] But incessant occupation with religious subjects, over-

ἔπασχόν τε καὶ ἐποίουν μυριὰ κακὰ καὶ ἄφραστα. Ἀλλ' ὅμως τοῦτο μὲν εὐσεβὲς ἐδόκει τὸ καταφρονεῖν τοῦ θείου· τυραννικὴν γὰρ εἶχεν ἐξουσίαν τότε πᾶς ἄνθρωπος, μέλαιναν φορῶν ἐσθῆτα, καὶ δημοσίᾳ βουλόμενος ἀσχημονεῖν.

30 Sozomenus, i. 12: *Ἡ τοιαύτη φιλοσοφία μαθημάτων μὲν πολλῶν καὶ διαλεκτικῆς τεχνολογίας ἀμελεῖ, ὡς περιέργου, καὶ τὴν ἐν τοῖς ἀμείνοσι σχολὴν ἀφαιρουμένης, καὶ πρὸς τὸ βιοῦν ὀρθῶς οὐδὲν συλλαμβανομένης· μόνῃ δὲ φυσικῇ καὶ ἀπεριέργῳ φρονήσει παιδεύει τὰ παντελῶς κακίαν ἀναιροῦντα, ἢ μείονα ἐργαζόμενα.* Synesius, in his Dion, designates them by the names of *τῶν ἀμούσων, τῶν μισολόγων, τῶν βαρβάρων, τῶν ἀστεμφῶν καὶ ὑπερόπτων ῥητορικῆς καὶ ποιήσεως*, see Clausen de Synesio, p. 48.

31 Witness the insurrection of the Anthropomorphists against Theophilus, Socrates, vi. 7, of the Nitrian monks against Orestes in favor of Cyril, vii. 13. Destruction of a Valentinian temple, Ambrosius, Epist. 40 (al. 29), ad Theodosium.

32 In Caesarea, comp. Neander's Chrysost. Bd. 2. S. 238.

33 They frequently interfered violently in behalf of criminals, ex. gr. for disturbers of the public peace in Antioch, Chrysost. Orat. 17 et 18, ad popul. Antioch. Theodoreti H. E. v. 19. Law of Arcadius, A.D. 398. (Cod. Theod. ix. xl. 16), see above, § 91, note 10.

34 Comp. Neander's Chrysostomus, Bd. 2, S. 108, ff.

35 Yet Anthony said (Cassiani Collat. ix. 31): Non est perfecta oratio, in qua se Monachus, vel hoc ipsum quod orat, intelligit.

36 Theophilus, bishop of Alexandria, rejected the anthropomorphism of the monks, in his Easter letter, 399. Cassiani Coll. x. 2: Quod tanta est amaritudine ab universo propemodum genere Monachorum, qui per totam provinciam Aegypti morabantur, pro simplicitatis errore susceptum, ut e contrario memoratum pontificem, velut haeresi gravissima depravatum, pars maxima Seniorum ab universo fraternitatis corpore decerneret detestan-

strained views, and self-conceit, joined with the want of culture, occasionally led them to other aberrations also from the doctrine of the Church.[37] *Audius* in Mesopotamia was still worthy of respect, who separated from the Church on account of its corruption, and founded a sect of monks (*Audiani*) about A.D 340.[38] But the *Messalians* (מְצַלִּין) or Εὐχίται,[39] who also arose in Mesopotamia (about 360), were mere fanatics, wandering hordes of beggars, who supposed that incessant prayer could alone blot out all sins while they undervalued public worship, and were led into the most absurd notions by their coarse imagination. Even *Eustathius*, the founder of monachism in Armenia, came to reject marriage absolutely, and was, on this account, condemned with his followers by the *Synod of Gangra* (between 362 and 370).[40]

In the mean time monachism was developed in forms the most various. Many monks (*Rhemoboth* or *Sarabaitae*),[41] still continued to live in society[42] like the old ascetics, but were less

dum, quod scilicet impugnare Scripturae sanctae sententiam videretur, negans omnipotentem Deum humanae figurae compositione formatum, cum ad ejus imaginem creatum Adam Scripturae manifestissime testaretur. When Seraphin, an old monk highly esteemed, was convinced of his error, he was so smitten with remorse (cap. 3) eo quod illam Anthropomorphitarum imaginem Deitatis, quam proponere sibi in oratione consueverat, aboleri de suo corde sentiret, ut in amarissimos fletus crebrosque singultus repente prorumpens, in terramque prostratus, cum ejulatu validissimo proclamaret: heu me miserum, tulerunt a me Deum meum, et quem nunc teneam non habeo, vel quem adorem aut interpellem jam nescio. So the Anthropomorphites generally (cap. 5) nihil se retinere vel habere credentes, si propositam non habuerint imaginem quandam, quam in supplicatione positi jugiter interpellent, eamque circumferant mente, ac prae oculis teneant semper affixam. On the Anthropomorphism of Abraames see Theodoreti Hist. rel. c. 3.

37 Thus some were led to entertain contempt for public worship and the sacraments, as Valens and Heron (Palladii Hist. Lausiaca, c. 31 et 32), and the Messalians. One Ptolemy went even so far with his brooding and dreaming over divine things, as to arrive at last at Atheism (Palladius, l. c. c. 33).

38 Epiphan. Haer. 70; cf. Ancoratus, c. 14. Theodoret. H. E. iv. 9; Haer. fab. comp. iv. 10. Walch's Ketzerhist. iii. 300. Neander, ii. iii. 1464. They were Anthropomorphists and Quartodecimani.

39 Epiphan. Haer. 80; Theodoret. H. E. iv. 10; Haer. fab. iv. 11. Extracts in Photius Cod. 52. Walch, iii. 481. Neander, ii. ii. 514.

40 The acts of this synod (ap. Mansi, ii. 1095) are the chief source for the knowledge of his doctrines. Socrat. ii. 43. Sozom. iv. 24. Walch, iii. 536. In the synodical decree it is also reckoned among their errors in doctrine: Πρεσβυτέρων γεγαμηκότων ὑπερφρονοῦντες, καὶ τῶν λειτουργιῶν τῶν ὑπ' αὐτῶν γινομένων μὴ ἁπτόμενοι. On the contrary, can. iv.: Εἴ τις διακρίνοιτο παρὰ πρεσβυτέρου γεγαμηκότος, ὡς μὴ χρῆναι λειτουργήσαντος αὐτοῦ προσφορᾶς μεταλαμβάνειν, ἀνάθεμα ἔστω. On the time of the synod of Gangra, see Ballerini de Ant. collect. canonum, P. 1, cap. 4, § 1.

41 Concerning the former, Hieron. Ep. 18 (al. 22), ad Eustochium; concerning the latter, Cassian. Collat. xviii. c. 4 and 7. Walch de Sarabaitis (Novi commentarii Soc. Gotting. t. v. Comm. hist. p. 1, ss.).

42 Also with the συνείσακτα in Ambros. Sermo. 65. Gregorii Naz. Carm. in several passages. See Walch, l. c. p. 23, s. Moreover, there were still ascetics who abstained

highly esteemed. Others wandered about in companies (Βοσκόι)[43] in Mesopotamia. Those who lived together in convents were called *coenobites*, each convent having its peculiar constitution, among whom the most distinguished since the fifth century, were the ἀκοίμητοι, *watchers*, for whom *Studius*, in 460, founded one of the most celebrated convents in Constantinople (*Studitae*).[44] But among the people, the *anchorites* were reckoned the most holy, for they carried their artificial self-tortures the farthest, and vied with each other in inventing new modes of cruelty against their own persons.[45] The highest point in this art was reached by *Simeon*, who, from the year 420, dwelt on a pillar in the neighborhood of Antioch.[46] In this he was imitated by others, and although at first the example was found by individuals to be doubtful,[47] yet it was wondered at by the mass. Even so late as the twelfth century, similar pillar-saints (στυλίτης or στηλίτης) appeared in the east.

The female sex could not imitate the men in all these kinds of asceticism, though there were convents for them as early as for the male sex (Ascetriae, Monastriae, Castimoniales, Sanctimoniales, Nonnae).[48]

from certain meats, but not from marriage (*abstinentes* apud Tertullian, see Div. I. § 53, note 31); these also were now occasionally styled monks, Athanasii Epist. ad Dracontium: Πολλοὶ τῶν ἐπισκόπων οὐδὲ γεγαμήκασι, μοναχοὶ δὲ πατέρες τέκνων γεγόνασιν. Augustin. de Haeres. c. 40: Utentes conjugibus, et res proprias possidentes—habet catholica Ecclesia et Monachos et Clericos plurimos.

43 Sozom. vi. 33. Evagr. i. 21.

44 Nicephori Hist. eccl. xv. 23. J. J. Müller Studium coenob. Constantinopol. ex monum. Byzantinis illustratum, diss. Lips. 1721. 4.

45 An example in Sozom. vi. 28–34.

46 In like manner in heathen Syria, the Φαλλοβατεῖς in the temple at Hierapolis (Lucianus de Dea Syria, c. 28, 29). Respecting Simeon see Theodoreti Hist. relig. c. 25, and his biographies by his scholar *Antonius* (in Act. SS. ad d. 5. Jan.), and his contemporary Cosmas (in Assemani Act. SS. Mart. Occid. et Orient. P. ii. p. 268), cf. Stylitica: Simeonis Stylitae senioris biographiam graecam (a later one derived from that of Antonius), junioris orationem graecam prim. ed. et illustr. H. N. Clausen (in the Miscellanea Hafniensia ed. F. Münter. tom. ii. Fasc. 2. Hafn. 1824. 8. p. 227, ss.

47 Nili lib. ii. Epist. 114, to the Stylite Nicander: Ὁ ὑψῶν ἑαυτὸν ταπεινωθήσεται. Σὺ δὲ μηδὲν κατορθώσας ἐπαινούμενον πρᾶγμα, καὶ ὕψωσας σεαυτὸν ἐφ' ὑψηλοῦ τοῦ στύλου, καὶ βούλει μεγίστων τυγχάνειν εὐφημιῶν· ἀλλὰ πρόσεχε σαυτῷ, μήποτε ἐνταῦθα παρὰ ἀνθρώπων φθαρτῶν ἀκρατῶς ἐπαινεθεὶς, ἀρτίως τὸ τηνικαῦτα παρὰ τοῦ ἀφθάρτου θεοῦ ταλανισθῇς ἀθλίως παρ' ἐλπίδας, διότι ὑπὲρ τὴν ἀξίαν ἐνταῦθα ἐνεφορήθης τῶν ἀνθρωπίνων κρότων. Ep. 115, to the same: Ἄτοπον ἂν εἴη ἐφ' ὑψηλοῦ μὲν τοῦ κίονος ἵστασθαι τῷ σώματι τοῖς πᾶσι φαινόμενον ἔνδοξον, κάτω δὲ τοῖς λογισμοῖς σύρεσθαι, μηδὲν ἄξιον τῶν οὐρανίων πραγμάτων διανοεῖσθαι βουλόμενον, μόνον δὲ ταῖς γυναιξὶν ἡδέως προσλαλοῦντα ἐν ταῖς ἡμέραις ταύταις. Πρώην μὲν γὰρ τοῖς ἀνδράσιν ἐκ προθυμίας ἐφθέγγου, νῦν δὲ ὡς ἐπὶ τὸ πλεῖστον τὰ γύναια προσδέχῃ.

48 Pachomius in like manner founded the first. Pallad. Hist. Laus. c. 34, et 38.—Nonna (Hieron. Ep. 18, ad Eustoch.), νονίς (Pallad. l. c. c. 46), were names of honor, as among the monks Nonnus, according to Arnobius jun. in Psalm. cv. and cxl. the Egyptian

It is true that the resolution of devoting themselves to a monastic life was now to be declared, and penance was imposed on those who drew back; but yet the teachers of the Church looked upon this retractation not merely as possible, without farther permission, but even advisable under certain circumstances.[49]

§ 96.

MONACHISM IN THE WEST.

Jo. Mabillon Observ. de monachis in Occidente ante Benedictum. (Acta SS. Ord. Bened. Saec. I. Praef. p. 7.)

Monachism was first acknowledged in the west by *Athanasius*, although it was generally looked upon as an excrescence of oriental fanaticism, with a surprise which not unfrequently amounted to contempt and hatred. Yet it also found numerous warm friends, many of whom went as far as Egypt and Palestine, for the purpose of being initiated into the new mode of life.[1] *Ambrose* and *Jerome* were the influential promoters of it in Italy. The former established a monastery at *Milan*.[2] At

for sanctus, castus, or according to Benedicti regula, c. 63, paterna reverentia: according to Jablonski Opusc. ed. te Water, t. i. p. 176, properly Ennueneh or Nueneh, i. e., quae non est hujus saeculi, quae saeculo renunciavit.—The lady president was called mother, ἀμμάς (Pallad. l. c. c. 42).

49 Epiphan. Haer. 61, § 7: Κρεῖττον τοίνυν ἔχειν ἁμαρτίαν μίαν, καὶ μὴ περισσοτέρας. κρεῖττον πεσόντα ἀπὸ δρόμου φανερῶς ἑαυτῷ λαβεῖν γυναῖκα κατὰ νόμον, καὶ ἀπὸ παρθενίας πολλῷ χρόνῳ μετανοήσαντα εἰσαχθῆναι πάλιν εἰς τὴν ἐκκλησίαν, ὡς κακῶς ἐργασάμενον, ὡς παραπεσόντα, καὶ κλασθέντα, καὶ χρείαν ἔχοντα ἐπιδέματος, καὶ μὴ καθ' ἑκάστην ἡμέραν βέλεσι κρυφίοις κατατιτρώσκεσθαι. Hieronym. Ep. 97 (al. 8), ad Demetriadem: Sanctum virginum propositum et coelestis angelorumque familiae gloriam quarundam non bene se agentium nomen infamat. Quibus aperte dicendum est, ut aut nubant, si se non possunt continere, aut contineat, si nolunt nubere (see above § 73, note 6). Augustinus de Bono viduit. c. 10: Qui dicunt talium nuptias non esse nuptias, sed potius adulteria, non mihi videntur satis acute ac diligenter considerare quid dicant.—Fit autem per hanc minus consideratam opinionem, qua putant lapsarum a sancto proposito feminarum, si nupserint, non esse conjugia, non parvum malum, ut a maritis separentur uxores, quasi adulterae sint, non uxores: et cum volunt eas separatas reddere continentiae, faciunt maritos earum adulteros veros, cum suis uxoribus vivis alteras duxerint. Concil. Chalced. can. 16: Παρθέναν ἑαυτὴν ἀναθεῖσαν τῷ δεσπότῃ θεῷ ὡσαύτως δὲ καὶ μονάζοντα, μὴ ἐξεῖναι γάμῳ προσομιλεῖν· εἰ δὲ γε εὑρεθεῖεν τοῦτο ποιοῦντες, ἔστωσαν ἀκοινώνητοι· ὡρίσαμεν δὲ ἔχειν τὴν αὐθεντίαν τῆς ἐπ' αὐτοῖς φιλανθρωπίας τὸν κατὰ τόπον ἐπίσκοπον.

1 On this account Jerome translated the rule of Pachomius into Latin, as he says in the preface (Luc. Holstenii Codex regularum, i. 59), propterea quod plurimi Latinorum habitant in Thebaidis coenobiis et in monasterio Metanoeae, qui ignorant aegyptiacum graecumque sermonem.

2 Augustini Confess. viii. 6: Erat monasterium Mediolani plenum bonis fratribus extra

the same time convents for both sexes were founded in *Rome*,[3] notwithstanding the unfavorable opinion of the people; and the small islands near the coast,[4] *Gallinaria* (Galinara), Gorgon

urbis moenia sub Ambrosio nutritore. Id. de Moribus eccles. cath. i. 33: Vidi ego diversorium sanctorum Mediolani non paucorum hominum, quibus unus Presbyter praeerat, vir optimus et doctissimus.

[3] Hieron. Ep. 96, ad Principiam de laudibus Marcellae, A.D. 412: Nulla eo tempore nobilium feminarum voverat Romae propositum Monachorum, nec audebat propter rei novitatem ignominiosum, ut tunc putabatur, et vile in populis nomen assumere. Haec (Marcella) ab Alexandrinis sacerdotibus, Papaque Athanasio et postea Petro, qui persecutionem Arianae haereseos declinantes, quasi ad tutissimum communionis suae portum Romam confugerant, vitam beati Antonii adhuc tunc viventis, monasteriorumque in Thebaide Pachumii et virginum ac viduarum didicit disciplinam.—Hanc multos post annos imitata est Sophronia, et aliae.—Hujus amicitiis fruita est Paula venerabilis. In hujus cubiculo nutrita Eustochium, virginitatis decus, ut facilis aestimatio sit, qualis magistra, ubi tales discipulae.—Audivimus te illius adhaesisse consortio, et nunquam ab illa—recessisse.—Suburbanus ager vobis pro Monasterio fuit, et rus electum pro solitudine. Multoque ita vixistis tempore, ut, ex imitatione vestri, conversatione multarum gauderemus Romam factam Jerosolymam. Crebra virginum monasteria, Monachorum innumerabilis multitudo, ut pro frequentia servientium Deo, quod prius ignominiae fuerat, esset postea gloriae. Epist. 54 ad Pammachium, A.D. 398: Pammachius meus—*ἀρχιστρατηγὸς* Monachorum. Augustin. de Moribus eccl. cath. (388, written in Rome) i. 33: Romae plura (diversoria sanctorum) cognovi, in quibus singuli gravitate atque prudentia et divina scientia praepollentes caeteris secum habitantibus praesunt, christiana caritate, sanctitate et libertate viventibus. Ne ipsi quidem cuiquam onerosi sunt, sed Orientis more et Apostoli Pauli auctoritate, manibus suis se transigunt. Jejunia etiam prorsus incredibilia multos exercere didici, non quotidie semel sub noctem reficiendo corpus, quod est usquequaque usitatissimum, sed continuum triduum vel amplius saepissime sine cibo et potu ducere: neque hoc in viris tantum, sed etiam in foeminis, quibus item, multis viduis et virginibus simul habitantibus, et lana ac tela victum quaeritantibus, praesunt singulae gravissimae probatissimaeque, non tantum in instituendis componendisque moribus, sed etiam instituendis mentibus peritae atque paratae. These fasts which were manifestly prejudicial to the health, stirred up the people. At the burying of Blaesilla, a daughter of Paula, a young nun, supposed to have been killed by fasting, A.D. 384, the people cried out (Hieronymi Ep. 22, al. 25, ad Paulam): Quousque genus detestabile monachorum non urbe pellitur? non lapidibus obruitur? non praecipitatur in fluctus?

[4] Ambrosii Hexaëmeron, iii. c. 5: Quid enumerem insulas, quas velut monilia plerumque praetexit, id quibus ii, qui se abdicant intemperantiae saecularis illecebris, fido continentiae proposito, eligunt mundum latere, et vitae hujus declinare dubios anfractus? Hieronymus Ep. 84 (al. 30), de Morte Fabiolae about 400: Angusta misericordiae ejus Roma fuit. Peragrabat ergo insulas et totum Etruscum mare, Volscorumque provinciam et reconditos curvorum littorum sinus, in quibus monachorum consistunt chori, vel proprio corpore, vel transmissa per viros sanctos ac fideles munificentia circumibat. Comp. the itinerarium of the heathen Rutilii Numatiani (A.D. 417), i. 439, ss.:

Processu pelagi jam se Capraria tollit,
Squallet lucifugis insula plena viris.
Ipsi se monachos Grajo cognomine dicunt, etc.

and respecting Gorgon, ibid. v. 517, ss.:

Aversor scopulos, damni monumenta recentis:
Perditus hic vivo funere civis erat.
Noster enim nuper, juvenis majoribus amplis,
Nec censu inferior, conjugiove minor,
Impulsus furiis, homines divosque reliquit,

(Gorgona), *Capraria* (Capraia), *Palmaria* (Palmarola), on the west coast of Italy and the islands on the *Dalmatian* coast,[5] became important seats of monastic establishments. *Martin*[6] first established in *Gaul* a monastery at *Poictiers;*[7] and afterward, when he became bishop of *Turonum* (375–400), another in that city.[8] About 400, *Honoratus* founded the celebrated monastery on the island *Lerins* (now St. Honorat).[9] Others rose on the island *Lero*[10] (St. Marguerite), and the *Stoechades*[11] on the south coast of Gaul. *John Cassian*,[12] who was educated among the Egyptian monks, founded two cloisters in Massilia (after 410). He died after 432. In *Africa*, notwithstanding *Augustine's* most zealous encomiums on monachism, it found acceptance almost entirely with the lower classes alone;[13] and the hatred of it was kept up there longer than in any other place.[14]

Et turpem latebram credulus exsul amat.
Infelix putat illuvie coelestia pasci;
Seque premit laesis saevior ipse Deis.
Num, rogo, deterior Circaeis secta venenis?
Tunc mutabantur corpora, nunc animi.

[5] Hieron. Ep. 92, ad Julianum: Exstruis monasteria, et multus a te per insulas Dalmatiae Sanctorum numerus sustentatur.

[6] Severi Sulpicii b. Martini vita. Epistolae iii. de Martino Dialogi. iii. de virtutibus monach. orientalium et b. Martini.

[7] The monasterium Locociagense, Gregor. Turon. de miraculis S. Martini, iv. 30.

[8] Majus monasterium (Marmoutier).

[9] A. F. Silfverberg Hist. Monasterii Lerinensis usque ad ann. 731 enarrata. Havn. 1834. 8. The life of Honoratus, who became bishop of Arles in 426, by his disciple and successor Hilary, may be seen in Acta SS. ad d. 16. Jan.

[10] Plinius Nat. Hist. iii. 5, calls the two islands Lerina and Lero, Strabo, iv. 1, 10, ἡ Πλανασία καὶ Λήρων. In later authors (Sidonii Carm. xvi. 104, Ennodius in vita Epiphanii) they are called Lerinus and Lerus.

[11] To the founders of Monachism on these islands, viz., Jovinianus, Minervius, Leontius, and Theodoretus, Cassian dedicated his last seven Collations, as he had done the preceding seven to Honoratus and Eucherius. Cf. Praefatt. ad coll. xi. et xiii.

[12] Respecting him see § 87, note 48.

[13] Augustin. de Opere Monach. c. 22: Nunc autem veniunt plerumque ad hanc professionem servitutis Dei et ex conditione servili, vel etiam liberti, vel propter hoc a dominis liberati sive liberandi, et ex vita rusticana, et ex opificum exercitatione et plebejo labore. Neque enim apparet, utrum ex proposito servitutis Dei venerint, an vitam inopem et laboriosam fugientes vacui pasci atque vestiri voluerint, et insuper honorari ab eis, a quibus contemni conterique consueverant.

[14] Salvianus Massiliensis (about 450) de Gubernat. Dei, viii. 4: Ita igitur et in monachis. —Afrorum probatur odium, quia irridebant scilicet, quia maledicebant, quia insectabantur, quia detestabantur, quia omnia in illos paene fecerunt, quae in salvatorem nostrum Judaeorum impietas. Intra Africae civitates, et maxime intra Carthaginis muros, palliatum et pallidum et recisis comarum fluentium jubis usque ad cutem tonsum videre tam infelix ille populus quam infidelis sine convitio atque execratione vix poterat. Et si quando aliquis Dei servus, aut de Aegyptiorum coenobiis, aut de sacris Hierusalem locis, aut de sanctis eremi venerandisque secretis ad urbem illam officio divini operis accessit, simul

The mode of life of the western monks was far less strict than that of the eastern; partly in consequence of the climate, and partly out of regard to the general feeling of the people.[15] Another important point of difference was that the monks in the west soon abandoned mechanical labor.[16] Here also there was not uniformity among them.[17] Besides the monks and nuns who lived in convents, some wandered about,[18] others led an ascetic life, occasionally at considerable expense, in the cities,[19] others imitated the most striking asceticism of the orientals, frequently indeed only in appearance.[20]

ut populo apparuit, contumelias, sacrilegia et maledictiones excepit. Nec solum hoc, sed improbissimis flagitiosorum hominum cachinnis et detestantibus ridentium sibilis quasi taureis caedebatur.

[15] Sever. Sulp. Dial. i. 8: Edacitas in Graecis gula est, in Gallis natura. Cassian de Institut. coenob. i. 11: Nam neque caligis nos, neque colobiis, seu una tunica esse contentos hiemis permittit asperitas: et parvissimi cuculli velamen, vel melotes gestatio derisum potius, quam aedificationem ullam videntibus comparabit.

[16] Sev. Sulp. Vita Mart. c. 10, of the monastery at Turonum: Ars ibi exceptis scriptoribus nulla habebatur: cui tamen operi minor aetas deputabatur: majores orationi vacabant. Yet Augustine de Opere monachorum (cf. Retractt. ii. c. 21), and Cassian de Instit. coenob. lib. x. recommended the monks to resume manual labor.

[17] As in the east, so there were also in the west, tot propemodum typi ac regulae, quot cellae ac monasteria (Cassian. Institt. ii. c. 2). After Rufinus had translated the rules of St. Basil into Latin, they were observed in many monasteries.

[18] Cassianus de Institutione coenobiorum, x. 23: In his regionibus nulla videmus monasteria tanta fratrum celebritate fundata (as in Egypt), quia nec operum suorum facultatibus fulciuntur, ut possint in eis jugiter perdurare: et si eis suppeditari quoquomodo valeat sufficientia victus alterius largitate, voluptas tamen otii et pervagatio cordis diutius eos in loco perseverare non patitur. Augustin. de Opere monach. c. 28: Callidissimus hostis tam multos hypocritas sub habitu monachorum usquequaque dispersit, circumeuntes provincias, nusquam missos, nusquam fixos, nusquam stantes, nusquam sedentes. Alii membra martyrum, si tamen martyrum, venditant, alii fimbrias et phylacteria sua magnificant: et omnes petunt, omnes exigunt aut sumtus lucrosae egestatis, aut simulatae pretium sanctitatis. C. 31: Illi venalem circumferentes hypocrisim, timent ne vilior habeatur tonsa sanctitas quam comata, ut videlicet qui eos videt, antiquos illos quos legimus cogitet, Samuelem et caeteros qui non tondebantur.

[19] Hieron. Ep. 95 (al. 4), ad Rusticum: Vidi ego quosdam, qui postquam renunciavere saeculo vestimentis duntaxat et vocis professione, non rebus, nihil de pristina conversatione mutarunt. Res familiaris magis aucta quam imminuta. Eadem ministeria servulorum, idem apparatus convivii. In vitro et patella fictili aurum comeditur, et inter turbas et examina ministrorum nomen sibi vindicant solitarii.

[20] Hier. Ep. 18 (al. 22), ad Eustochium: Viros quoque fuge, quos videris catenatos, quibus foeminei contra Apostolum crines, hircorum barba, nigrum pallium, et nudi patientia frigoris pedes. Haec omnia argumenta sunt diaboli. Talem olim Antonium, talem nuper Sophronium Roma congemuit. Qui postquam nobilium introierunt domos, et deceperunt mulierculas oneratas peccatis, semper discentes, et nunquam ad scientiam veritatis pervenientes, tristitiam simulant, et quasi longa jejunia furtivis noctium cibis protrahunt.

§ 97.

RELATION OF THE MONKS TO THE CLERGY.

The monks, as such, belonged to the laity, the convents forming separate churches whose presbyters were usually abbots[1] standing in the same dependent relation to bishops as did the other churches with their people. As monachism was considered the perfection of Christianity, it was natural to choose clergymen from the monks. At first the stricter monks were much dissatisfied with this arrangement;[2] but the aversion to it soon ceased, and even at the end of the fourth century, monastic life was considered to be the usual preparation, and monachism the nursery for the clergy, especially for bishops.[3]

The idea of transferring monachism, as much as possible, entirely to the clergy, was natural in these circumstances; and it was especially adopted in the *west*. The venerable *Paphnutius* had prevented the celibacy of the clergy from being enacted as an ecclesiastical law, in Nicaea;[4] but now this regulation took

[1] Alteserra Ascetic. ii. 2. iii. 8. vii. 2.

[2] Cassian. de Instit. coenob. xi. 17: Quapropter haec est antiquitus patrum permanens nunc usque sententia, quam proferre sine mea confusione non potero, qui nec germanam vitare potui, nec episcopi evadere manus, omnimodo monachum fugere debere mulieres et episcopos. Neuter enim sinit eum, quem semel suae familiaritati devinxerit, vel quieti cellulae ulterius operam dare, vel divinae theoriae per sanctarum rerum intuitum purissimis oculis inhaerere. Hence monks were not seldom ordained against their will. Epiphan. Ep. ad Joh. Hierosol. Theodoret. Hist. relig. c. 13. Cf. Bingham, lib. iv. c. 7 (vol. ii. p. 189, ss.).

[3] Hieron. Ep. 95, ad Rusticum: Ita age et vive in monasterio, ut clericus esse merearis. A law of Arcadius, A.D. 398 (Cod. Theod. xvi. ii. 32): Si quos forte Episcopi deesse sibi Clericos arbitrantur, ex Monachorum numero rectius ordinabunt. Against the excess of this principle see Augustini Ep. 60: Ordini clericorum fit indignissima injuria, si desertores monasteriorum ad militiam clericatus eligantur:—nisi forte—vulgares de nobis jocabuntur dicentes: malus monachus bonus clericus est. Nimis dolendum, si ad tam ruinosam superbiam monachos surrigamus, et tam gravi contumelia clericos dignos putemus;—cum aliquando etiam bonus monachus vix bonum clericum faciat, si adsit ei sufficiens continentia, et tamen desit instructio necessaria, aut personae regularis integritas.

[4] Socrates, i. 11: *'Εδόκει τοῖς ἐπισκόποις νόμον νεαρὸν εἰς τὴν ἐκκλησίαν εἰσφέρειν, ὥστε τοὺς ἱερωμένους, λέγω δὲ ἐπισκόπους καὶ πρεσβυτέρους καὶ διακόνους, μὴ συγκαθεύδειν ταῖς γαμεταῖς, ἃς ἔτι λαϊκοὶ ὄντες ἠγάγοντο* (just as Can. Illiberit. 33, see Div. I. § 73, note 14, and therefore proposed probably by Hosius). *Καὶ ἐπεὶ περὶ τούτου βουλεύεσθαι προύκειτο, διαναστὰς ἐν μέσῳ τοῦ συλλόγου τῶν ἐπισκόπων ὁ Παφνούτιος, ἐβόα μακρὰ, μὴ βαρὺν ζυγὸν ἐπιθεῖναι τοῖς ἱερωμένοις ἀνδράσι, τίμιον εἶναι καὶ τὴν κοίτην καὶ αὐτὸν ἀμίαντον τὸν γάμον* (Hebr. xiii. 4) *λέγων, μὴ τῇ ὑπερβολῇ τῆς ἀκριβείας μᾶλλον τὴν ἐκκλησίαν προσβλάψωσιν· οὐ γὰρ πάντας δύνασθαι φέρειν τῆς ἀπαθείας τὴν ἄσκη-*

root in the west, first by the influence of *Siricius*, bishop of Rome (385),[5] whom several councils soon followed. *Eusebius*, bishop of Vercellae († 371), and *Augustine* went still farther, and united with their clergy in adopting a strictly monastic life,[6]

σιν, οὐδὲ ἴσως φυλαχθήσεσθαι τὴν σωφροσύνην τῆς ἑκάστου γαμετῆς (σωφροσύνην δὲ ἐκάλει καὶ τῆς νομίμου γυναικὸς τὴν συνέλευσιν)· ἀρκεῖσθαί τε τὸν φθάσαντα κλήρου τυχεῖν, μηκέτι ἐπὶ γάμον ἔρχεσθαι, κατὰ τὴν τῆς ἐκκλησίας ἀρχαίαν παράδοσιν· μήτε μὴν ἀποζεύγνυσθαι ταύτης, ἣν ἅπαξ ἤδη πρότερον λαϊκὸς ὢν ἠγάγετο. Καὶ ταῦτ' ἔλεγεν ἄπειρος ὢν γάμου, καὶ ἁπλῶς εἰπεῖν γυναικός. 'Εκ παιδὸς γὰρ ἐν ἀσκητηρίῳ ἀνετέθραπτο, καὶ ἐπὶ σωφροσύνῃ, εἰ καί τις ἄλλος, περιβόητος ὤν. Πείθεται πᾶς ὁ τῶν ἱερωμένων σύλλογος τοῖς Παφνουτίου λόγοις· διὸ καὶ τὴν περὶ τούτου ζήτησιν ἀπεσίγησαν, τῇ γνώμῃ τῶν βουλομένων ἀπέχεσθαι τῆς ὁμιλίας τῶν γαμετῶν καταλείψαντες. So also Sozom. i. 23. Gelasii Hist. Conc. Nic. ii. 32, and Historia tripartita, ii. 14.—The truth of it is doubted by Baronius, Bellarminus, Jo. Stilting (Act. SS. Sept. t. iii. p. 784, ss.). On the other side, Natalis Alexander Hist. eccl. saec. iv. diss. 19. Calixtus de Conj. cler. ed. Henke, p. 213, ss.

[5] Epistola ad Himerium Episc. Tarraconensem, c. 7: Ii vero, qui illiciti privilegii excusatione nituntur, ut sibi asserant veteri hoc lege concessum: noverint se ab omni ecclesiastico honore, quo indigne usi sunt, apostolicae sedis auctoritate dejectos.—Quilibet episcopus presbyter atque diaconus, quod non optamus, deinceps fuerit talis inventus, jam nunc sibi omnem per nos indulgentiae aditum intelligat obseratum: quia ferro necesse est excidantur vulnera, quae fomentorum non senserint medicinam.—C. 9: Quicumque itaque se ecclesiae vovit obsequiis a sua infantia, ante pubertatis annos baptizari, et lectorum debet ministerio sociari. Qui ab accessu adolescentiae usque ad tricesimum aetatis annum, si probabiliter vixerit, una tantum et ea, quam virginem communi per sacerdotem benedictione perceperit, uxore contentus, acolythus et subdiaconus esse debebit; postque ad diaconii gradum, si se ipse primitus continentia praeeunte dignum probarit, accedat. Unde si ultra quinque annos laudabiliter ministrarit, congrue presbyterium consequatur. Exinde, post decennium, episcopalem cathedram poterit adipisci, si tamen per haec tempora integritas vitae ac fidei ejus fuerit approbata.—C. 13: Monachos quoque, quos tamen morum gravitas et vitae ac fidei institutio sancta commendat, clericorum officiis aggregari et optamus et volumus. In the middle ages it was constantly admitted that this *lex Ecclesiastica* had been unknown to the primitive church. See Calixtus, l. c. p. 3, ss. 304. Many, however, believed it to be the meaning of Conc. Nicaeni, can. 3 (according to Dionys. Exig. translation: Interdixit per omnia magna synodus, non episcopo, non presbytero, non diacono, nec alicui omnino qui in clero est, licere subintroductam habere mulierem, nisi forte aut matrem, aut sororem, aut amitam, vel eas tantum personas, quae suspicionem effugiunt). Cf. Aelfrici canones, A.D. 970 (Wilkins. Concil. Magn. Brit. i. p. 250), c. 5: At the Nicene synod statuerunt omnes unanimi consensu, quod neque episcopus, neque presbyter, neque diaconus, nec ullus verus canonicus habeat in domo sua uxorem aliquam, nisi matrem, etc. Benedictus VIII. in Conc. Ticinensi, between 1014 and 1024 (ap. Mansi, xix. p. 344): Nicaeni patres non solum connubium, sed etiam cum mulieribus habitationem clericis omnibus interdicunt. So also Alfonsus a Castro († 1550), tit. Sacerdotium; Consuetudo, juxta quam matrimonio alligatus promovebatur ad sacerdotium, invaluit usque ad tempora Nicaeni concilii, in quo, ut fertur, generali decreto statutum est, ne aliquis uxorem habens consecretur sacerdos. Quod statutum cum ab aliquibus minime ut decebat observaretur, Siricius Papa de hac re illos acerbissime reprehendit. The Jesuits were the first, in the sixteenth century, who maintained, in opposition to the Protestants, that the celibacy of the priests originated in apostolic times. Calixtus, l. c. p. 10, ss. 28, ss. J. Gf. Körner vom Cölibat der Geistlichen. Leipzig. 1784. 8. J. A. Theiner u. A. Theiner die Einführung der erzwungenen Ehelosigkeit b. d. christl. Geistlichen u. ihre Folgen. Altenburg. 1828. 2 Bde. 8.

[6] Respecting Eusebius see Ambros. Ep. 63, ad Vercellenses, § 66: Haec enim primus

though at first they found no imitators. But we may see how difficult it was to carry out the law of celibacy, though *Jerome*, *Ambrose*, and *Augustine*, strongly advocated it, from the frequent repetition of the law, and the mildness with which it was found necessary to punish transgressors.[7] Still *Leo the Great* extended the requisition even to the sub-deacons (subdiaconi).[8]

In the east, on the other hand, the Eustathians were opposed for their very rejection of marriage in the case of priests,[9] and no law of celibacy was generally adopted. It was the custom, indeed, toward the end of the fourth century, in several prov-

in Occidentis partibus diversa inter se Eusebius sanctae memoriae conjunxit, ut et in civitate positus instituta Monachorum teneret, et Ecclesiam regeret jejunii sobrietate. Maximi Ep. Taurinensis (about 422) Sermo ix. de S. Eusebio, in Muratorii Anecdotis, t. iv. p. 88: Ut universo Clero suo spiritalium institutionum speculum se coeleste praeberet, omnes illos secum intra unius septum habitaculi congregavit, ut quorum erat unum atque indivisum in religione propositum, fieret vita victusque communis. Quatenus in illa sanctissima societate vivendi invicem sibi essent conversationis suae et judices et custodes, etc. Cf. Sermo vii. p. 82.—Respecting Augustine see Augustini vita auct. Possidio, c. 5: Factus ergo presbyter monasterium inter ecclesiam mox instituit, et cum Dei servis vivere coepit secundum modum et regulam sub sanctis Apostolis constitutam, maxime ut nemo quidquam proprium in illa societate haberet, sed eis essent omnia communia. After he had become bishop, cap. 11: In monasterio Deo servientes Ecclesiae Hipponensi clerici ordinari coeperunt. Ac deinde—ex monasterio, quod per illum memorabilem virum et esse et crescere coeperat, magno desiderio poscere et accipere episcopos et clericos pax Ecclesiae atque unitas et coepit primo, et postea consecuta est. Nam ferme decem—sanctos—viros continentes—b. Augustinus diversis Ecclesiis—rogatus dedit. Similiterque et ipsi ex illorum sanctorum proposito venientes—monasteria instituerunt, et—caeteris Ecclesiis promotos fratres ad suscipiendum sacerdotium praestiterunt. Comp. August. Sermones ii. de moribus Clericorum (at an earlier period Sermo 49 and 50 de diversis, in the Benedictine edition, Sermo 355 and 356), ex. gr. Sermo, i. c. 1: Nostis omnes,—sic nos vivere in ea domo, quae dicitur domus episcopii, ut quantum possumus imitemur eos sanctos, de quibus loquitur liber Actuum Apostolorum: Nemo dicebat aliquid proprium, sed erant illis omnia communia,—volui habere in ista domo episcopii mecum monasterium clericorum. Ejusd. Epis. 20, 149, 245. Cf. Thomassinus, P. i. lib. iii. c. 2 and 3. It is a different thing when other monks, elevated to be bishops, as Martin of Turonum, had about them establishments of monks, and continued the monastic life in them.

[7] Siricii Ep. ad Episc. Afr. (A.D. 386) c. 3. Conc. Carthag. (390) can. 2. Innocent. I. Ep. ad Vitricium (404) cap. 9. Conc. Taurin. (397) can. 8. Carthag. v. (398) can. 3. Toletan. i. (400) can. 1, etc. Conc. Turonense i. (461) can. 2: Licet a patribus nostris emissa auctoritate id fuerit constitutum, ut, quicunque sacerdos vel levita filiorum procreationi operam dare fuisset convictus, a communione dominica abstineretur: nos tamen huic districtioni moderationem adhibentes, et justam constitutionem mollientes, id decrevimus, ut sacerdos vel levita conjugali concupiscentiae inhaerens, vel a filiorum procreatione non desinens ad altiorem gradum non ascendat, neque sacrificium Deo offere vel plebi ministrare praesumat.

[8] Leo Ep. 14 ad Anastas. Episc. Thessalon. (A.D. 446) c. 4. Still this was by no means general till the times of Gregory the Great. See Calixtus, l. c. p. 380, ss.

[9] See above § 93, note 39. To this refers also Can. Apost. 5: Ἐπίσκοπος, ἢ Πρεσβύτερος, ἢ Διάκονος τὴν ἑαυτοῦ γυναῖκα μὴ ἐκβαλλέτω προφάσει εὐλαβείας· ἐὰν δὲ ἐκβάλλῃ, ἀφοριζέσθω· ἐπιμένων δὲ καθαιρείσθω. Comp. Drey über die Constitut. und Canones der Apostel, S. 339.

inces, to select the unmarried for bishops; and in some of these this was extended even to the clergy in general,[10] but in most parts, all clergymen had the liberty of living in wedlock.[11]

FIFTH CHAPTER.

HISTORY OF PUBLIC WORSHIP.

§ 98.

The church had triumphed over heathenism. It had acquired riches, external influence, and power. The effect of this was seen in the increasing splendor of its ceremonial. At the same time, a great number of those who now pressed into the church brought with them that purely external tendency peculiar to heathen religions, which turned on the sensuous forms of worship, partly with a one-sided aesthetic interest, and partly

[10] In the chief countries of Monachism. Hieronym. adv. Vigilantium: Quid facient Orientis ecclesiae? quid Aegypti et sedis Apostolicae? quae aut virgines clericos accipiunt, aut continentes, aut si uxores habuerint, mariti esse desistunt. Epiphan. Haer. 59, § 4. Expos. fidei Cath. § 21. Synesius, when about to be bishop of Ptolemais, wrote, among other things, even to his brother Euoptius (Ep. 105): *'Εμοὶ ὅ τε θεὸς, ὅ τε νόμος, ἥ τε ἱερὰ Θεοφίλου χεὶρ γυναῖκα ἐπιδέδωκε· προαγορεύω τοίνυν ἅπασι καὶ μαρτύρομαι, ὡς ἐγὼ ταύτης οὔτε ἀλλοτρώσιομαι καθάπαξ, οὔτε ὡς μοιχὸς αὐτῇ λάθρα συνέσομαι· τὸ μὲν γὰρ ἥκιστα εὐσεβὲς, τὸ δὲ ἥκιστα νόμιμον· ἀλλὰ βουλήσομαί τε καὶ εὔξομαι, συχνά μοι πάνυ καὶ χρηστὰ γενέσθαι παιδία.* Comp. above, § 84, note 33. Clausen de Synesio, p. 119.

[11] Examples of married bishops in the fourth century. Calixtus, p. 258, ss. Theiner, i. S. 263, ss. Gregory of Nazianzum was born when his father was a priest, for he makes him say, Carmen de vita sua, v. 512:

Οὔπω τοσοῦτον ἐκμεμέτρηκας βίον,
῞Οσος διῆλθε θυσιῶν ἐμοὶ χρόνος.

(Evasions of Papebrochius, Act. SS. Maji, t. ii. p. 370, against Tillemont, who explained honestly the Jesuit Mémoires de Trevoux, 1707, Avril, p. 711. Cf. Calixtus, l. c. p. 261, ss. Ullmann's Gregor v. Naz. S. 551, ss.) Whether Gregory of Nyssa was married is matter of dispute. Rupp (Gregor's v. Nyssa Leben u. Meinungen, S. 24), with Clemencet and others, denies it. Nicephorus Callistus first mentions this marriage; Tillemont also recognizes it. St. P. Heyns Disp. de Gregorio Nysseno, Lugd. Bat. 1835. 4. p. 6, defends it at length, and has even found a son called Basil. Socrates, v. 22: *῎Εγνων δὲ ἐγὼ καὶ ἕτερον ἔθος ἐν Θεσσαλίᾳ. Γενόμενος κληρικὸς ἐκεῖ, ἣν νόμῳ γαμήσας πρὶν κληρικὸς γένηται, μετὰ τὸ κληρικὸς γενέσθαι συγκαθευδήσας αὐτῇ, ἀποκήρυκτος γίνεται· τῶν ἐν ἀνατολῇ πάντων γνώμῃ ἀπεχομένων, καὶ τῶν ἐπισκόπων, εἰ καὶ βούλοιντο, οὐ μὴν ἀνάγκῃ νόμου τοῦτο ποιοῦντων. Πολλοὶ γὰρ αὐτῶν ἐν τῷ καιοῷ τῆς ἐπισκοπῆς καὶ παῖδας ἐκ τῆς νομίμης γαμετῆς πεποιήκασιν.*

with a superstitious veneration. Even those who were capable of higher views yielded to this tendency, either that the pagans might be the more readily won over to Christianity, or from a desire to show honor to a supposed pious intention.[1] But in proportion as the internal life evaporated from the Church, and its external reputation increased, the more usual did it become to impress the character of a law externally binding on ecclesiastical usages which had been gradually developed. Thus the entire ecclesiastical life was overburdened with forms which were merely tolerated at first, but finally converted into laws.[2]

§ 99.

NEW OBJECTS OF WORSHIP.

Jo. Dallaeus adversus Latinorum de cultus religiosi objecto traditionem. Genevae. 1664. 4.

Martyrdom,[1] which presented so strong a contrast to the lukewarmness of the present time, was the more highly venerated in proportion to its remoteness.[2] The heathen converts naturally enough transferred to the martyrs the honors they had

[1] This irruption of heathen usages into the church is acknowledged as early as Baptista Mantuanus in Fastis mense Febr. et Novembre, Beatus Rhenanus ad Tertull. contra Marc. lib. v. and de Corona militis, Polydorus Vergilius de Rerum inventoribus, lib. v. c. 1, Baronius ann. 58, § 76, ann. 200, § 5. It has been shown more at length by (Mussard) les Conformitez des Ceremonies modernes avec les anciennes. (Londres) 1667. 8 (new edition, Amsterd. 1744); Conyers Middleton a letter from Rome, showing an exact conformity between Popery and Paganism (London. 1755. 8); Jo. Marangonius Delle cose gentilesche e profane transportate ad uso e ad ornamento delle chiese. Rom. 1744. 4 (comp. the continuation of the same, 1752, S. 511, ss.); Ge. Christ. Hamberger Enarratio rituum, quos Romana ecclesia a majoribus suis gentilibus in sua sacra transtulit. Gotting. 1751 (reprinted in J. P. Berg Museum Duisburgense, t. i. P. ii. p. 363, ss.). John James Blunt Vestiges of ancient Manners and Customs, discoverable in modern Italy and Sicily. London. 1823.

[2] Leo M. Sermo 77, de Jejun. Pentecost. 2: Dubitandum non est, quicquid ab Ecclesia in consuetudinem devotionis est receptum, de traditione apostolica, et de Sancti Spiritus prodire doctrina.

[1] On the increased veneration paid to martyrs comp. Sagittarius de Natalitiis martyrum, cap. 5, § 19, ss. Bossuet's Gesch. v. Welt. u. v. Religion, fortgesetzt von J. A. Cramer. Erste Fortf. S. 493, ss. Dritte Fortf. S. 285, ss. 329, ss.

[2] To which even the apologists of the day contributed. Eusebius Praep. evang. xiii. c. 11, cites a passage of Plato concerning the worship of demons, and then continues: *Καὶ ταῦτα δὲ ἁρμόζει ἐπὶ τῇ τῶν θεοφιλῶν τελευτῇ, οὓς στρατιώτας τῆς ἀληθοῦς εὐσεβείας οὐκ ἂν ἁμάρτοις εἰπὼν, παραλαμβάνεσθαι. Ὅθεν καὶ ἐπὶ τὰς θήκας αὐτῶν ἔθος ἡμῖν παριέναι, καὶ τὰς εὐχὰς παρὰ ταύταις ποιεῖσθαι, τιμᾷν τε τὰς μακαρίας αὐτῶν ψυχὰς, ὡς εὐλόγως καὶ τούτων ὑφ' ἡμῶν γιγνομένων.* Comp. below, note 33.

been accustomed to pay their heroes.[3] This took place the more readily as the scrupulous aversion to excessive veneration of the creature died away in the church after the victory over heathenism; and the despotic form of government became accustomed to a slavish respect for the powerful.[4] Thus the old custom of holding meetings for public worship at the graves of the martyrs now gave occasion to the erection of altars and churches (*Μαρτύριον*, Memoria)[5] over them. In Egypt, the Christians, following an old popular custom, began to preserve the corpses of men reputed to be saints in their houses;[6] and since the

[3] Respecting the pagan belief that the relics of distinguished men afforded protection to cities and countries, see Lobeck Aglaophamus, t. i. p. 280, s. Thus Ælius Aristides (a rhetorician who lived about 170 A.D.) Orat. ii. ad Platonem, ed. Dindorf vol. ii. p. 230, calls the Greeks who had fallen in battle against the Persians, *ὑποχθονίους τινὰς φύλακας καὶ σωτῆρας τῶν Ἑλλήνων, ἀλεξικάκους καὶ πάντα ἀγαθοὺς, καὶ ῥυεσθαί γε τὴν χώραν οὐ χεῖρον ἢ τὸν ἐν Κωλωνῷ κείμενον Οἰδίπουν, ἢ εἴ τις ἄλλοθί που τῆς χώρας ἐν καιρῷ τοῖς ζῶσι κεῖσθαι πεπίστευται.* Respecting Œdipus, Valerius Maximus, v. 3, externa 3: Oedipodis ossa—inter ipsum Areopagum—et—Minervae arcem honore arae decorata, quasi sacrosancta, colis. In Greece worship was paid especially to the founders of cities, which were built for the most part over their graves. Thus Autolycus was worshiped in Sinope, Tenes in Tenedos, Æneas by the Æneates (Liv. xl. 4). See others noticed in Voss. de Idolol. i. 13, comp. Thucydides, v. 11, concerning Brasidas: *Οἱ Ἀμφιπολῖται, περιέρξαντες αὐτοῦ τὸ μνημεῖον, ὡς ἥρωί τε ἐντέμνουσι καὶ τιμὰς δεδώκασιν ἀγῶνας καὶ ἐτησίους θυσίας, καὶ τὴν ἀποικίαν ὡς οἰκιστῇ προσέθεσαν.*

[4] Compare the honors paid to the emperors: their edicts were termed divina, sacra coelestia: their statues were honored by adoration and frankincense (Zorn, in Miscell. Groning. vol. i. p. 186, ss.). Consultationum Zachaei Christ. et Apollonii Philos. (after 408) lib. i. c. 28 (in d'Archery Spicileg. i. p. 12): Apollonius: Cur imagines hominum vel ceris pictas, vel metallis defictas sub Regum reverentia etiam publica adoratione veneramini, et, ut ipsi praedicatis, Deo tantum honorem debitum etiam hominibus datis? Zacheus: Istud quidem nec debeo probare nec possum, quia evidentibus Dei dictis non Angelos, nec quoslibet coeli ac terrae vel aëris principatus adorare permittimur. Divini enim speciale hoc nomen officii est, et altior omni terrena veneratione reverentia: sed sicut in hujusmodi malum primum adulatio homines impulit, sic nunc ab errore consuetudo vix revocat; in quo tamen incautum obsequium, non aliquem divinum deprehenditis cultum. Sed propter similitudinem amabilium vultuum gaudia intenta plus faciunt, quam hi forte exigant, quibus defertur, aut perfungi oporteat deferentes; et licet hanc incautioris obsequii consuetudinem districtiores horreant Christiani, nec prohibere desinant sacerdotes, non tamen Deus dicitur cujus effigies salutatur, nec adolentur thure imagines, aut colendae aris superstant, sed memoria pro meritis exponuntur, ut exemplum factorum probabilium postéris praestent, aut praesentes pro abusione castigent. A law of Theodosius II. A.D. 425 (Cod. Theod. xv. iv. 1): Si quando nostrae statuae vel imagines eriguntur,—adsit judex sine adorationis ambitioso fastigio,—excedens cultura hominum dignitatem superno numini reservetur. Cf. de Rhoer Dissertt. de effectu relig. christ. in jurisprud. Rom. p. 41, ss.

[5] So called at first by Eusebius de vita Const. iii. 48. So also Constantine, on no higher authority, indeed, than the liber pontificalis, vita 34, Sylvestri, written about the year 870, is said to have built the basilics in Rome over the graves of the apostles Peter and Paul. Comp. Jerome, below, note 8. Afterward they were called, too, *Ἀποστολεῖον, Προφητεῖον.*

[6] A practice strongly disapproved by St. Anthony. Comp. Athanasius in vita Antonii (Opp. t. ii. p. 502): *Τῶν δέ ἀδελφῶν βιαζομένων μεῖναι αὐτὸν παρ' αὐτοῖς, κἀκεά τελειω-*

idea of communion with the martyrs was always increasingly associated with the vicinity of their mortal remains, the latter were drawn forth from their graves and placed in the churches,[7] especially under the altars.[8] Thus respect for the martyrs received a material object to center itself on, and became in consequence more extravagant and superstitious. To the old idea of the efficacy of the martyrs' intercession,[9] was now added the belief, that it was possible to communicate the desires to them directly; an opinion partly founded on the popular notion that departed souls still hovered about the bodies they had once inhabited;[10] partly on the high views entertained of the glorified

θῆναι, οὐκ ἠνέχετο,—διὰ τοῦτο δὲ μάλιστα· οἱ Αἰγύπτιοι τὰ τῶν τελευτώντων σπουδαίων σώματα, καὶ μάλιστα τῶν ἁγίων μαρτύρων φιλοῦσι μὲν θάπτειν καὶ περιελίσσειν ὀθονίοις, μὴ κρύπτειν δὲ ὑπὸ γῆν, ἀλλ' ἐπὶ σκιμποδίων τιθέναι, καὶ φυλάττειν ἔνδον παρ' ἑαυτοῖς νομίζοντες ἐν τούτῳ τιμᾷν τοὺς ἀπελθόντας. Ὁ δὲ Ἀντώνιος πολλάκις περὶ τούτου καὶ ἐπισκόπους ἠξίου παραγγέλλειν τοῖς λαοῖς· ὁμοίως δὲ καὶ λαϊκοὺς ἐνέτρεπεν, καὶ γυναιξὶν ἐπέπληττεν, λέγων, μήτε νόμιμον, μήτε ὅλως ὅσιον εἶναι τοῦτο. Καὶ γὰρ τὰ τῶν Πατριαρχῶν καὶ τῶν Προφητῶν σώματα μέχρι νῦν σώζεται εἰς μνήματα, καὶ αὐτὸ δὲ τὸ τοῦ κυρίου σῶμα εἰς μνημεῖον ἐτέθη—. Καὶ ταῦτα λέγων ἐδείκνυε, παρανομεῖν τὸν μετὰ θάνατον μὴ κρύπτοντα τὰ σώματα τῶν τελευτώντων, κἂν ἅγια τυγχάνῃ· τί γὰρ μεῖζον ἢ ἁγιώτερον τοῦ κυριακοῦ σώματος;—Αὐτὸς δὲ τοῦτο γινώσκων, καὶ φοβούμενος, μὴ καὶ τὸ αὐτοῦ ποιήσωσιν οὕτως σῶμα, ἤπειξεν ἑαυτὸν, συνταξάμενος τοῖς ἐν τῷ ἔξω ὄρει μοναχοῖς. In like manner Marcian, Theodoreti Hist. relig. c. 3 (ed. Schulz. t. iii. p. 1147, s.), and Akepsimas, ibid. c. 15, p. 1221.

7 Translations of the bodies of the saints into churches. The first instances were those of St. Andrew, Luke, and Timothy (359), at the command of Constantine. Hieron. contra Vigilant. (Comp. the discovering and transferring of the bones of Theseus, by Cimon, Plutarch in Thes. ad fin.)

8 Ambrosii Ep. 22 (al. 85, al. 54), ad Marcellinam sororem, § 13: Succedant victimae triumphales in locum, ubi Christi hostia est. Sed ille super altare, qui pro omnibus passus est: isti sub altari, qui illius redemti sunt passione. Hunc ego locum praedestinaveram mihi: dignum est enim ut ibi requiescat sacerdos, ubi offerre consuevit: sed cedo sacris victimis dexteram portionem, locus iste martyribus debebatur. Hieronymus adv. Vigilant.: Male facit ergo Romanus Episcopus, qui super mortuorum hominum Petri et Pauli, secundum nos ossa veneranda, secundum te vilem pulvisculum, offert Domino sacrificia, et tumulos eorum Christi arbitratur altaria? Sozomenus, v. 9, et 19. Cf. Goth. Voigti Thysiasteriologia, s. de altaribus vett. Christt. Hamb. 1709. 8. p. 250, ss. The passage Apoc. vi. 9, was not yet used, however, in justification of this practice. See Dallaeus adv. Latinorum de Cultus relig. objecto traditionem, lib. iv. c. 9.

9 See Div. I. § 70, notes 13–21.

10 This was the opinion of the heathen. Cf. Platonis Phaedon; Tibullus, i. 6, 15; Macrobius de Somn. Scip. i. 9, et 13; Porphyrius de Abstin. ii. 47. Lactantius, ii. 2: Vulgus existimat, mortuorum animas circa tumulos et corporum suorum reliquias oberrare. Cf. Wetstenii Nov. Test. i. p. 354. Hence Conc. Illiberitanum, c. 34: Cereos per diem placuit in coemeterio non incendi: inquietandi enim spiritus Sanctorum non sunt. Among the spiritual Origenists this idea did not naturally meet with acceptance. Cf. Macarii Politici (about 370) Sermo de Excessu justorum et peccatorum, in Cave Hist. Liter. vol. i. p. 259, and in J. Tollii Insignia itineris Italici (Traj. ad. Rhen. 1696. 4) p. 196. But comp. Ambrosii de Viduis, c. 9: Martyres obsecrandi, quorum videmur nobis quodam corporis pignore patrocinium vindicare,—isti enim sunt Dei martyres, nostri praesules, specula-

state of the martyrs[11] who alone abide with the Lord. As Origen first laid the foundation of this new kind of respect for martyrs, so the Origenists were the first who addressed them in their sermons, as if they were present and besought their intercession.[12] But though the orators were somewhat extravagant

tores vitae, actuumque nostrorum.—Pseudo-Ambrosii (perhaps Maximi Taurinensis about 430) Sermo vi. de Sanctis: Cuncti martyres devotissime percolendi sunt, sed specialter ii venerandi sunt a nobis, quorum reliquias possidemus. Illi enim nos orationibus adjuvant, isti etiam adjuvant passione: cum his autem nobis familiaritas est. Semper enim nobiscum sunt, nobiscum morantur, hoc est, et in corpore nos viventes custodiunt, et de corpore recedentes excipiunt: hic ne peccatorum labes absumat, ibi ne inferni horror invadat.

[11] So that people attributed to them a kind of omnipresence, as the heathen did to the demons (Hesiodi Opera et Dies, v. 121, ss.); cf. Hieronymus adv. Vigilantium: Tu Deo leges pones? Tu Apostolis vincula injicies, ut usque ad diem judicii teneantur custodia, nec sint cum Domino suo, de quibus scriptum est: Sequuntur agnum, quocunque vadit (Apoc. xiv. 4)? Si agnus ubique, ergo, et hi, qui cum agno sunt, ubique esse credendi sunt. Gregorii Naz. Orat. xviii. in laudem Cypriani, p. 286: Σὺ δὲ ἡμᾶς ἐποπτεύοις ἄνωθεν ἵλεως, καὶ τὸν ἡμέτερον διεξάγοις λόγον καὶ βίον, καὶ τὸ ἱερὸν τοῦτο ποίμνιον ποιμαίνοις, ἢ συμποιμαίνοις, κ. τ. λ. Prudentius Peristephanon hymn. i. v. 16, ss. ix. v. 97, and often. Sulpicius Severus Ep. ii. de Obitu b. Martini (ed. Lips. 1709, p. 371): Non deerit nobis ille, mihi crede, non deerit: intererit de se sermocinantibus, adstabit orantibus: quodque jam hodie praestare dignatus est, videndum se in gloria sua saepe praebebit, et adsidua, sicut ante paullulum fecit, benedictione nos proteget. Ep. iii. p. 381: Martinus hic pauper et modicus coelum dives ingreditur: illinc nos ut spero custodiens, me haec scribentem respicit te legentem. At first, Vigilantius (404) resisted this opinion (see below, § 106, note 6), and Jerome defended it against him (see above). On this Augustine also combated it, while he endeavored at the same time to defend independently of it, the practice of praying to the martyrs, which had been already established. Cf. Augustinus de Cura gerenda pro mortuis (A.D. 421) c. 13: Si rebus viventium interessent animae mortuorum, et ipsae nos quando eas videmus alloquerentur in somnis; ut de aliis taceam, me ipsum pia mater nulla nocte desereret, quae terra marique secuta est, ut mecum viveret.—Isaias propheta dicit (lxiii. 16): Tu es enim pater noster: quia Abraham nescivit nos, et Israel non cognovit nos. Si tanti Patriarchae quid erga populum ex his procreatum ageretur ignoraverunt, quomodo mortui vivorum rebus atque actibus cognoscendis adjuvandisque miscentur? With regard to the martyrs, he is not indisposed indeed to allow a miraculous exception (cap. 16), but proceeds: Quamquam ista quaestio vires intelligentiae meae vincit, quemadmodum opitulentur Martyres iis, quos per eos certum est adjuvari; utrum ipsi per se ipsos adsint uno tempore tam diversis locis,—sive ubi sunt eorum Memoriae, sive praeter suas Memorias ubicumque adesse sentiuntur: an ipsis in loco suis meritis congruo ab omni mortalium conversatione remotis, et tamen generaliter orantibus pro indigentiis supplicantium,—Deus—exaudiens Martyrum preces, per angelica ministeria usquequaque diffusa praebeat hominibus ista solatia, quibus in hujus vitae miseria judicat esse praebenda: et suorum merita Martyrum, ubi vult, quando vult, quomodo vult, maximeque per eorum Memorias, quoniam hoc novit expedire nobis ad aedificandum fidem Christi—mirabili atque ineffabili potestate ac bonitate commendet. Res haec altior est, quam ut a me possit attingi, et abstrusior, quam ut a me valeat perscrutari: et ideo quid horum duorum sit, an vero fortassis utrumque sit, ut aliquando fiant per ipsam praesentiam Martyrum, aliquando per Angelos suscipientes personam Martyrum, definire non audeo: mallem a scientibus ista perquirere. Cf. de Civit. Dei, xxii. c. 9. In his sermons he does not attack the usual opinion, ex. gr. sermo de Diversis 316 (al. 94): Ambo (Paulus et Stephanus) modo sermonem nostrum auditis: ambo pro nobis orate.

[12] Basilii M. Hom. 19, in xl. Martyres, § 8: Οὗτοί εἰσιν οἱ τὴν καθ' ἡμᾶς χώραν

in this respect, the poets, who soon after seized upon the same theme, found no colors too strong to describe the power and glory of the martyrs.[13] Even relics soon began to work miracles, and to become valuable articles of commerce on this account, like the old heathen instruments of magic.[14]

In proportion as men felt the need of such heavenly intercessors, they sought to increase their number. Not only those persons who were inscribed in the Diptycha * for services done to the church, but also the pious of the Old Testament, and particularly distinguished monks,[15] were taken into the cata-

διαλαβόντες, οἱονεὶ πύργοι τινὲς συνεχεῖς, ἀσφάλειαν ἐκ τῆς τῶν ἐναντίων καταδρομῆς παρεχόμενοι· οὐχ ἑνὶ τόπῳ ἑαυτοὺς κατακλείσαντες, ἀλλὰ πολλοῖς ἤδη ἐπιξενωφέντες χωρίοις, καὶ πολλὰς πατρίδας κατακοσμήσαντες. Καὶ τὸ παράδοξον, οὐ καθ' ἕνα διαμερισθέντες τοῖς δεχομένοις ἐπιφοιτῶσιν, ἀλλ' ἀναμιχθέντες ἀλλήλοις, ἡνωμένως χορεύουσιν· ὢ τοῦ θαύματος!—οὔτε ἐλλείπουσι τῷ ἀριθμῷ, οὔτε πλεονασμὸν ἐπιδέχονται· ἐὰν εἰς ἑκατὸν αὐτοὺς διέλῃς, τὸν οἰκεῖον ἀριθμὸν οὐκ ἐκβαίνουσιν· ἐὰν εἰς ἓν συναγάγῃς, τεσσαράκοντα καὶ οὕτω μένουσι, κατὰ τὴν τοῦ πυρὸς φύσιν· καὶ γὰρ ἐκεῖνο καὶ πρὸς τὸν ἐξάπτοντα μεταβαίνει, καὶ ὅλον ἐστὶ παρὰ τῷ ἔχοντι· καὶ οἱ τεσσαράκοντα, καὶ πάντες εἰσὶν ὁμοῦ, καὶ πάντες εἰσὶ παρ' ἑκάστῳ·—ὁ θλιβόμενος ἐπὶ τοὺς τεσσαράκοντα, καταφεύγει, ὁ εὐφραινόμενος ἐπ' αὐτοὺς ἀποτρέχει. ὁ μὲν, ἵνα λύσιν εὕρῃ τῶν δυσχερῶν· ὁ δὲ, ἵνα φυλαχθῇ αὐτῷ τὰ χρηστότερα. ἐνταῦθα γυνὴ εὐσεβὴς ὑπὲρ τέκνων εὐχομένη καταλαμβάνεται, ἀποδημοῦντι ἀνδρὶ τὴν ἐπάνοδον αἰτουμένη, ἀῤῥωστοῦντι τὴν σωτηρίαν· μετὰ μαρτύρων γενέσθω τὰ αἰτήματα ὑμῶν·—Ὢ χορὸς ἅγιος! ὢ σύνταγμα ἱερόν! ὢ συνασπισμός! ὢ κοινοὶ φύλακες τοῦ γένους τῶν ἀνθρώπων! ἀγαθοὶ κοινωνοὶ φροντίδων, δεήσεως συνεωργοὶ, πρεσβευταὶ δυνατώτατοι, ἀστέρες τῆς οἰκουμένης, ἄνθη τῶν ἐκκλησιῶν! ὑμᾶς οὐχ ἡ γῆ κατέκρυψεν, ἀλλ' οὐρανὸς ὑπεδέξατο, κ. τ. λ. Cf. Hom. xxiii. in Mamantem Martyrem. Gregorii Naz. Orat. xviii. in laudem Cypriani. Gregorii Nysseni Orat. in Theodorum Mart. Daniel's Gesch. v. christl. Beredsamkeit i. 281. In the west Ambrose goes farther in extolling the martyrs, Daniel i. 658.

13 So especially the Spanish writer Aurelius Prudentius Clemens (about 405. Poemata ed. Nic. Heinsius. Amst. 1667. 12. Chr. Cellarius. Halae. 1703. 8.) in his lib. *περὶ στεφανῶν*, containing fourteen hymns to the martyrs, comp. H. Middeldorpf Comm. de Prudentio et Theologia Prudentiana in Illgen's Zeitschr. f. hist. Theol. ii. ii. 187; and Pontius Paulinus, bishop of Nola († 431. Letters and poems ed. J. B. le Brun. Paris. 1685, t. ii. 4, in Bibl. max. PP. t. vi. p. 163, ss.), especially in the ten natales S. Felicis.

14 See Augustine, above, § 96, n. 18. The law of Theodosius I. A.D. 386 (Cod. Theod. ix. xvii. 7): Humatum corpus nemo ad alterum locum transferat: nemo martyrem distrahat, nemo mercetur. Habeant vero in potestate, si quolibet in loco sanctorum est aliquis conditus pro ejus veneratione, quod martyrium vocandum sit, addant quod voluerint fabricarum.

15 Joannes Cassianus Collat. vi. c. 1: In Palaestinae partibus juxta Tecuae vicum—solitudo vastissima est usque ad Arabiam ac mare mortuum.—In hac summae vitae ac sanctitatis monachi diutissime commorantes, repente sunt a discurrentibus Saracenorum latrunculis interempti. Quorum corpora—tam a Pontificibus regionis illius quam ab universa plebe Arabum tanta veneratione praerepta, et inter reliquias martyrum condita, ut innumeri populi e duobus oppidis concurrentis gravissimum sibi certamen indixerint, et usque ad gladiorum conflictum, pro sancta rapina sit eorum progressa contentio, dum pia inter se devotione decertant, quinam justius eorum sepulturam ac reliquias possiderent,

* *Diptycha.* In Rees's Cyclopaedia, Diptycha are explained to be "a double catalogue, in one whereof were written the names of the living, and in the other those of the dead, which were to be rehearsed during the office."

logue; and thus a still more comprehensive *saint-worship* arose out of the veneration paid to martyrs.[16] Martyrs before unknown announced themselves also in visions; others revealed the places where their bodies were buried. Till the fifth century, prayers had been offered even for the dead saints;[17] but at that time the practice was discontinued as unsuitable.[18] It is true that the more enlightened fathers of the church insisted on a practical imitation of the saints in regard to morality as the most important thing in the new saint-worship,[19] nor were

aliis scilicet de vicinia commorationis ipsorum, aliis de originis propinquitate gloriantibus. Comp. the dispute about the body of James, Theodoreti Hist. relig. c. 21 (ed. Schulz. 3, p. 1239).

16 Thus Ambrose discovered the bodies of *Protasius* and *Gervasius*. Ambrose, Epist. 22, ad sororem, August. de Civ. Dei, xxii. 8. The populace were inclined to regard every ancient unknown grave as the grave of a martyr, *Sulpicius Severus* de vita Martini, c. 11.

17 Epiphan. Haer. 75, § 7: *Καὶ γὰρ δικαίων ποιούμεθα τὴν μνήμην, καὶ ὑπὲρ ἁμαρτωλῶν·—ὑπὲρ δὲ δικαίων, καὶ πατέρων, καὶ Πατριαρχῶν, Προφητῶν, καὶ Ἀποστόλων, καὶ Εὐαγγελιστῶν, καὶ Μαρτύρων, καὶ Ὁμολογητῶν, Ἐπισκόπων τε καὶ Ἀναχωρητῶν, καὶ παντὸς τοῦ τάγματος, ἵνα τὸν κύριον Ἰησοῦν Χριστὸν ἀφορίσωμεν ἀπὸ τῆς τῶν ἀνθρώπων τάξεως,—ἐν ἐννοίᾳ ὄντες, ὅτι οὐκ ἔστιν ἐξισούμενος ὁ κύριος τινὶ τῶν ἀνθρώπων, κἂν τε μυρία καὶ ἐπέκεινα ἐν δικαιοσύνῃ ἕκαστος ἀνθρώπων.* Cf. Constitt. Apostol. viii. c. 12. Cyrill. Hieros. Catech. Mystag. v. § 8. Such intercessions, in their more ancient form, are preserved in the liturgies of the Nestorians, ex. gr. liturgia Theodori Interpretis (in Renaudotii Liturgiarum orientalium collectio, tom. ii. p. 620): Domine et Deus noster, suscipe a nobis per gratiam tuam sacrificium hoc gratiarum actionis, fructus scilicet rationabiles labiorum nostrorum, ut sit coram te memoria bona justorum antiquorum, Prophetarum sanctorum, Apostolorum beatorum, Martyrum et Confessorum, Episcoporum, Doctorum, Sacerdotum, Diaconorum, et omnium filiorum Ecclesiae sanctae catholicae, eorum qui in fide vera transierunt ex hoc mundo, ut per gratiam tuam, Domine, veniam, illis concedas omnium peccatorum et delictorum, quae in hoc mundo, in corpore mortali, et anima mutationi obnoxia peccaverunt aut offenderunt coram te, quia nemo est qui non peccet. So too Liturgia Nestorii ap. Renaudot, l. c. p. 633. Cf. Bingham, lib. xv. c. 3, § 16, 17 (vol. vi. p. 330, ss.).

18 Augustin. Serm. 17: Injuria est enim pro martyre orare, cujus nos debemus orationibus commendari (quoted by Innocent III., as sacrae scripturae auctoritas to justify, decretal Gregorii lib. iii. tit. 41, c. 6, the change of the old formula, annue nobis, Domine, ut animae famuli, tui Leonis haec prosit oblatio, into the modern, annue, nobis, quaesumus, Domine, ut intercessione b. Leonis haec nobis prosit oblatio).

19 Augustin. de Vera religione, c. 55: Non sit nobis religio cultus hominum mortuorum: quia, si pie vixerunt, non sic habentur, ut tales quaerant honores; sed illum a nobis coli volunt, quo illuminante laetantur, meriti sui nos esse consortes. Honorandi sunt ergo propter imitationem, non adorandi propter religionem, contra Faustum, xx. 21: Populus christianus Memorias Martyrum religiosa solemnitate concelebrat, et ad excitandam imitationem, et ut meritis eorum consocietur, atque orationibus adjuvetur: ita tamen, ut nulli Martyrum, sed ipsi Deo Martyrum, quamvis in Memoriis Martyrum, constituamus altaria. Quis enim antistitum in locis sanctorum corporum adsistens altari, aliquando dixit: offerimus tibi, Petre, aut Paule, aut Cypriane? sed quod offertur, offertur Deo, qui Martyres coronavit, ut ex ipsorum locorum admonitione major adfectus exsurgat ad acuendam caritatem, et in illos, quos imitari possumus, et in illum, quo adjuvante possumus. Colimus ergo Martyres eo cultu dilectionis et societatis, quo in hac vita coluntur sancti homines Dei, quorum cor ad talem pro evangelica veritate passionem paratum esse

exhortations to address prayer directly to God also wanting;[20] but yet the people attributed the highest value to the intercession of the saints whose efficacy was so much prized.[21] Many heathen customs were incorporated with this saint-worship. Churches, under whose altars their bodies rested, were dedicated to their worship.[22] As gods and heroes were formerly chosen

sentimus. At vero illo cultu, qui graece λατρεία dicitur, latine uno verbo dici non potest, cum sit quaedam proprie divinitati debita servitus, nec colimus, nec colendum docemus, nisi unum Deum.

[20] Ambrosiaster ad Rom. i. 22, against those who adored the elements, the stars, etc.: Solent tamen pudorem passi, neglecti Dei misera uti excusatione, dicentes per istos posse iri ad Deum, sicut per comites pervenitur ad regem. Age, numquid tam demens est aliquis, aut salutis suae immemor, ut honorificentiam regis vindicet comiti, cum de hac re si qui etiam tractare fuerint inventi, jure ut rei damnentur majestatis? Et isti se non putant reos, qui honorem nominis Dei deferunt creaturae, et relicto Domino conservos adorant; quasi sit aliquid plus, quod reservetur Deo. Nam et ideo ad regem per tribunos aut comites itur, quia homo utique est rex, et nescit quibus debeat republicam credere. Ad Deum autem, quem utique nihil latet (omnium enim merita novit), promerendum suffragatore non opus est, sed mente devota. Ubicumque enim talis loquutus fueret ei, respondebit illi. So Chrysostomus in Matth. Hom. 52 (al. 53), § 3, annexes to the history of the woman of Canaan (Matth. xv. 21), the admonition: *Σὺ δέ μοι σκόπει, πῶς τῶν ἀποστόλων ἡττηθέντων καὶ οὐκ ἀνυσάντων, αὕτη ἤνυσε. τοσοῦτον ἐστι προσεδρεία εὐχῆς· καὶ γὰρ ὑπὲρ τῶν ἡμετέρων παρ' ἡμῶν βούλεται μᾶλλον τῶν ὑπευθύνων ἀξιοῦσθαι ἢ παρ' ἑτέρων ὑπὲρ ἡμῶν.* Cf. de Poenitentia orat. iv. 4: (*ὁ θεὸς*) *χωρὶς μεσίτου παρακαλεῖται.* Comp. Cramer's dritte Forts. and Bossuet, S. 350, ss.

[21] Ambrosius de Viduis, c. 9: Aegri, nisi ad eos aliorum precibus medicus fuerit invitatus, pro se rogare non possunt. Infirma est caro, mens aegra est et peccatorum vinculis impedita, ad medici illius sedem debile non potest explicare vestigium. Obsecrandi sunt Angeli pro nobis, qui nobis ad praesidium dati sunt, martyres obsecrandi, quorum videmur nobis quoddam corporis pignore patrocinium vindicare. Possunt pro peccatis rogare nostris, qui proprio sanguine etiam si qua habuerunt peccata laverunt. Isti enim sunt Dei martyres, nostri praesules speculatores vitae actuumque nostrorum. Non erubescamus eos intercessores nostrae infirmitatis adhibere, etc. Even Chrysostom recommends (de Sanctis martyr. Serm. 68, Opp. v. 872), the worship of martyrs and their relics as a means of procuring the forgiveness of sins, and virtues.

[22] The churches were still named in different ways, many after their founders (so in Carthage the basilicae Fausti, Florentii, Leontii, in Alexandria the eccl. Arcadii (the old Serapeum), in Rome the basilicae Constantini and Justiniani), others from other circumstances, thus in Carthage basilica restituta, in Alexandria the Caesareum, in Rome the eccl. triumphalis (the old Church of Peter), eccl. Laterana (because on the site of the palace of Lateranus, a contemporary of Nero), see Bingham, vol. iii. p. 329. Thus although originally the calling of churches after martyrs did not denote that they were dedicated to them, yet the meaning attached to the names came gradually to be so understood, and even the distinctions made by Augustine admit of this acceptation, comp. de Civitate Dei, xxii. 10: An dicent, etiam se habere deos ex hominibus mortuis, sicut Herculem, sicut Romulum, sicut alios multos, quos in deorum numerum receptos opinantur? Sed nobis Martyres, non sunt dii.—Nos Martyribus nostris non templa sicut diis, sed memorias sicut hominibus mortuis, quorum apud Deum vivunt spiritus, fabricamus; neque ibi erigimus altaria, in quibus sacrificemus Martyribus, sed uni Deo et Martyrum et nostro sacrificia immolamus: ad quod sacrificium, sicut homines Dei, qui mundum in ejus confessione vicerunt, suo loco et ordine nominantur, non tamen a sacerdote qui sacrificat invocantur. Deo quippe, non ipsis, sacrificat, quamvis in memoria sacrificet eorum. Cf. viii. 27.

for patrons, so patron-saints were now selected.[23] And since the heathen had been so bitterly accused at an earlier period by the Christians of worshiping dead men,[24] they could not now be blamed in their turn for ridiculing the new saint-worship.[25]

In the fourth century no peculiar reverence above other saints was as yet shown to *the Virgin Mary*. In consequence of monastic ideas (see § 95, note 23), the Christians merely attributed a high value to her perpetual virginity; and for this reason began to declare the opinion that she had afterward borne children to Joseph[26] to be heretical; as, for instance, Epiphanius

[23] Theodoreti Graec. affect. curat. disp. 8 (ed. Schultze, t. iv. p. 902): *Αἱ μὲν γενναῖαι τῶν νικηφόρων ψυχαὶ περιπολοῦσι τὸν οὐρανὸν,—τὰ δὲ σώματα, οὐχ εἷς ἑνὸς κατακρύπτει τάφος ἑκάστου· ἀλλὰ πόλεις καὶ κῶμαι ταῦτα διανειμάμεναι, σωτῆρας καὶ ψυχῶν καὶ σωμάτων, καὶ ἰατροὺς ὀνομάζουσι; καὶ ὡς πολιούχους τιμῶσι καὶ φύλακας· καὶ χρώμενοι πρεσβευταῖς πρὸς τὸν τῶν ὅλων δεσπότην, διὰ τούτων τὰς θείας κομίζονται δωρεάς.* Page 921: *Οἱ δέ γε τῶν καλλινίκων μαρτύρων σηκοὶ, λαμπροὶ καὶ περίβλεπτοι, καὶ μεγέθει διαπρεπεῖς, καὶ παντοδαπῶς πεποικιλμένοι, καὶ κάλλους ἀφιέντες μαρμαρυγάς· εἰς δὲ τούτους οὐχ ἅπαξ ἢ δίς γε τοῦ ἔτους ἢ πεντάκις φοιτῶμεν· ἀλλὰ πολλάκις μὲν πανηγύρεις ἐπιτελοῦμεν, πολλάκις δὲ καὶ ἡμέρας ἑκάστης τῷ τούτων Δεσπότῃ τοὺς ὕμνους προσφέρομεν· καὶ οἱ μὲν ὑγιαίνοντες αἰτοῦσι τῆς ὑγείας τὴν φυλακήν· οἱ δέ τινι νόσῳ παλαίοντες, τὴν τῶν παθημάτων ἀπαλλαγήν· αἰτοῦσι δὲ καὶ ἄγονοι παῖδας, καὶ στέριφαι παρακαλοῦσι γενέσθαι μητέρες.—καὶ οἱ μὲν εἴς τινα ἀποδημίαν στελλόμενοι, λιπαροῦσι τούτους ξυνοδοιπόρους γενέσθαι, καὶ τῆς ὁδοῦ ἡγεμόνας· οἱ δὲ τῆς ἐπανόδου τετυχηκότες, τὴν τῆς χάριτος ὁμολογίαν προσφέρουσιν· οὐχ ὡς θεοῖς αὐτοῖς προσιόντες, ἀλλ' ὡς θείους ἀνθρώπους ἀντιβολοῦντες, καὶ γενέσθαι πρεσβευτὰς ὑπὲρ σφῶν παρακαλοῦντες. ὅτι δὲ τυγχάνουσιν ὧνπερ αἰτοῦσιν οἱ πιστῶς ἐπαγγέλλοντες, ἀναφανδὸν μαρτυρεῖ τὰ τούτων ἀναθήματα, τὴν ἰατρείαν δηλοῦντα· οἱ μὲν γὰρ ὀφθαλμῶν, οἱ δὲ ποδῶν, ἄλλοι δὲ χειρῶν προσφέρουσιν ἐκτυπώματα· καὶ οἱ μὲν ἐκ χρυσοῦ, οἱ δὲ ἐξ ὕλης ἀργύρου πεποιημένα·* Page 923: *Τοὺς γὰρ οἰκείους νεκροὺς ὁ Δεσπότης ἀντεισῆξε τοῖς ὑμετέροις θεοῖς· καὶ τοὺς μὲν φρούδους ἀπέφηνε, τούτοις δὲ τὰ ἐκείνων ἀπένειμε γέρα· ἀντὶ γὰρ δὴ τῶν Πανδίων, καὶ Διασίων, καὶ Διονυσίων, καὶ τῶν ἄλλων ὑμῶν ἑορτῶν, Πέτρου καὶ Παύλου καὶ Θωμᾶ καὶ Σεργίου—καὶ τῶν ἄλλων μαρτύρων, ἐπιτελοῦνται δημοθοινίαι, κ. τ. λ.* Comp. Neander's Chrysostomus, Bd. 2, S. 128, f.

[24] Arnobius adv. Gentiles, vi. 6: Multa ex his templa—comprobatur, contegere cineres atque ossa, et functorum esse corporum sepulturas, etc.

[25] Julianus ap. Cyrill. adv. Jul. x. p. 335: *Ὅσα δὲ ὑμεῖς ἐξῆς προσευρήκατε, πολλοὺς ἐπεισάγοντες τῷ πάλαι νεκρῷ τοὺς προσφάτους νεκροὺς, τίς ἂν πρὸς ἀξίαν βδελύξηται; Πάντα ἐπληρώσατε τάφων καὶ μνημάτων.—Εἰ ἀκαθαρσίας Ἰησοῦς ἔφη εἶναι πλήρεις τοὺς τάφους* (Matth. xxiii. 27), *πῶς ὑμεῖς ἐπ' αὐτῶν ἐπικαλεῖσθε τὸν θεόν;* Cf. vi. p. 201. Misopogon, p. 344. Eunapius in vita Aedesii, ed. Genev. 1616, p. 65. Ammian. Marcell. xii. 11. Comp. Maximus, § 79, note 1.

[26] Basilius M. Hom. in sanctam Christi generationem, c. 5 (Opp. t. ii. p. 598), remarks, however, on Matth. i. 25: *Οὐκ ἐγίνωσκε αὐτὴν, ἕως οὗ ἔτεκε τὸν υἱὸν αὐτῆς τὸν πρωτότοκον* the following *τοῦτο δὲ ἤδη ὑπόνοιαν παρέχει, ὅτι μετὰ τὸ καθαρῶς ὑπηρετήσασθαι τῇ γεννήσει τοῦ κυρίου τῇ ἐπιτελεσθείσῃ διὰ τοῦ πνεύματος τοῦ ἁγίου, τὰ νενομισμένα τοῦ γάμου ἔργα μὴ ἀπαρνησαμένης τῆς Μαρίας· ἡμεῖς δὲ, εἰ καὶ μηδὲν τῷ τῆς εὐσεβείας παραλυμαίνεται λόγῳ (μέχρι γὰρ τῆς κατὰ τὴν οἰκονομίαν ὑπηρεσίας ἀναγκαία ἡ παρθενία, τὸ δ' ἐφεξῆς ἀπολυπραγμόνητον τῷ λόγῳ τοῦ μυστηρίου), ὅμως διὰ τὸ μὴ καταδέχεσθαι τῶν φιλοχρίστων τὴν ἀκοὴν, ὅτι ποτὲ ἐπαύσατο εἶναι παρθένος ἡ θεοτόκος, ἐκείνας ἡγούμεθα τὰς μαρτυρίας αὐτάρκεις.*

(Haer. 78) against the Ἀντιδικομαριανῖται, in Arabia (367); Jerome against *Helvidius*, in Rome (383);[27] and the Macedonian bishops against *Bonosus*, bishop of Sardica (392);[28] while it was also shown in what way she did not cease to be a virgin, notwithstanding the birth of Christ.[29] Besides, the teachers of the Church in the fourth century did not refrain from speaking of the faults of Mary;[30] and Epiphanius includes certain enthusiastic women in his catalogue of heretics for their extravagant adoration of the Virgin (Κολλυριδιανοί).[31] The Nestorian controversy first led men to set her at the head of the host of saints, as the mother of God, θεοτόκος.

Though it was the general belief that *angels* guarded men, and presented their prayers to God, it was still thought unal-

[27] Hieron. adv. Helvidium, lib. in Opp. ed. Martianay, t. iv. P. ii. p. 129, ed. Vallarsi, t. ii. Concerning the Antidicomarianites and Helvidius see Walch's Ketzerhist. iii. 577.

[28] Siricii Ep. 9 (comp. above, § 94, note 14). Walch, iii. 598.

[29] Tertullianus de Carne Christi, c. 23: Agnoscimus ergo signum contradicibile (according to Luc. ii. 34) conceptum et partum virginis Mariae; de quo Academici isti: peperit, et non peperit; virgo, et non virgo.—Peperit, enim, quae ex sua carne: et non peperit, quae non ex virili semine. Et virgo, quantum a viro; non virgo, quantum a partu. Clemens Alex. Strom. vii. p. 889: Τοῖς πολλοῖς καὶ μέχρι νῦν δοκεῖ ἡ Μαριὰμ λεχὼ εἶναι διὰ τὴν τοῦ παιδίου γένησιν, οὐκ οὖσα λεχώ· καὶ γὰρ μετὰ τὸ τεκεῖν αὐτὴν μαιωθεῖσαν φασί τινες παρθένον εὑρεθῆναι. Epiphanius, Haer. lxxviii. § 19, does not hesitate to say, in reference to Luke ii. 23, Exod. xiii. 2: Οὗτός ἐστιν ἀληθῶς ἀνοίγων μήτραν μητρός. On the contrary, Ambrosius, Ep. 42 (al. 81, al. 7), ad Siricium P.: Haec est virgo, quae in utero concepit: virgo, quae peperit filium. Sic enim scriptum est: Ecce virgo in utero accipiet, et pariet filium (Es. vii. 14), non enim concepturam tantummodo virginem, sed et parituram virginem dixit. Quae autem est illa porta sanctuarii, porta illa exterior ad Orientem, quae manet clausa; et nemo, inquit, pertransibit per eam, nisi solus Deus Israel (Ezech. xliv. 2)? Nonne haec porta Maria est, per quam in hunc mundum redemtor intravit? . . . de qua scriptum est, quia Dominus pertransibit per eam, et erit clausa post partum; quia virgo concepit et genuit. Hieronymus adv. Pelagianos, lib. ii. (Opp. ed. Martian. t. iv. P. ii. p. 512): Solus enim Christus clausas portas vulvae virginalis aperuit quae tamen clausae jugiter permanserunt. Haec est porta orientalis clausa, per quam solus Pontifex ingreditur et egreditur, et nihilominus semper clausa est.

[30] After the example of Irenaeus, iii. 18. Tertull. de Carne Christi, 7. Origines in Luc. Hom. 17:—Basilius Ep. 260 (al. 317) ad Optimum. Chrysostomus Hom. 45 in Matth. et Hom. 21 in Joh. On the other hand, Augustin. de Nat. et Grat. c. 36: Excepta sancta virgine Maria, de qua propter honorem Domini nullam prorsus, cum de peccatis agitur, haberi volo quaestionem,—si omnes illos sanctos—congregare possemus, et interrogare, utrum essent sine peccato, quid fuisse responsuros putamus?

[31] Concerning them Epiphan. Haer. 78, § 23. Haer. 79. Anacephal. c. 79. Comp. Walch's Ketzerhistorie, iii. 625. F. Münter de Collyridianis in the Miscellanea Hafniensia, t. i. fasc. 2. Hafn. 1818. p. 153, ss. Their heresy was: Ἀντὶ θεοῦ ταύτην παρεισάγειν σπουδάζοντες,—ὡς εἰς ὄνομα τῆς ἀειπαρθένου κολλυρίδα τινὰ ἐπιτελεῖν, καὶ συνάγεσθαι ἐπὶ τὸ αὐτὸ,—καὶ εἰς ὄνομα αὐτῆς ἱερουργεῖν διὰ γυναικῶν. This usage is perhaps explained by Jerem. xliv. 19, where the women offer cakes to the Queen of Heaven; perhaps by Conc. Quinisexti, can. 79: "The birth of the Virgin was ἀλόχευτος: hence no cake (σεμίδαλις) shall be presented after the birthday of Christ προφάσει τιμῆς λοχειῶν τῆς ἀχράντου παρθενομήτορος."

lowable to address them, because of the passages, *Coloss.* ii. 18, *Revelation of John* xix. 10; xxii. 8, 9.[32] *Ambrose* is the first who recommends seeking the intercession of the *guardian* angel;[33] but as yet the Christians had not adopted a more general worship of angels.[34]

The cross, always a highly honored symbol among Christians,[35] had been more superstitiously venerated ever since the time when Constantine believed that he owed to it his victory over Maxentius.[36] But after the tradition had spread, from the end of the fourth century, that Helena (326) had discovered the true cross of Christ,[37] relics and even imitations of it began to

[32] Concil. Laodic. can. 35: *Ὅτι οὐ δεῖ Χριστιανοὺς ἐγκαταλείπειν τὴν ἐκκλησίαν τοῦ θεοῦ καὶ ἀπιέναι καὶ ἀγγέλους ὀνομάζειν*, κ. τ. λ. Dionys. Exig. translates: Atque angelos (var. lect. angulos) nominare. Cf. Theodoret. ad Coloss. ii. 18: *Οἱ τῷ νομῳ συνηγοροῦντες, καὶ τοὺς ἀγγέλους σέβειν αὐτοῖς εἰσηγοῦντο, διὰ τούτων λέγοντες δεδόσθαι τὸν νόμον. ἔμεινε δὲ ταῦτο τὸ πάθος ἐν τῇ Φρυγίᾳ καὶ Πισιδίᾳ μέχρι πολλοῦ· οὗ δὴ χάριν καὶ συνελθοῦσα σύνοδος ἐν Λαοδικείᾳ τῆς Φρυγίας νόμῳ κεκώλυκε τὸ τοῖς ἀγγέλοις προσεύχεσθαι· καὶ μέχρι δὲ τοῦ νῦν εὐκτήρια τοῦ ἁγίου Μιχαὴλ παρ' ἐκείνοις καὶ τοῖς ὁμόροις ἐκείνων ἐστὶν ἰδεῖν. τοῦτο τοίνυν συνεβούλευον ἐκεῖνοι γίνεσθαι, ταπεινοφροσύνῃ δῆθεν κεχρημένοι, καὶ λέγοντες, ὡς ἀόρατος ὁ τῶν ὅλων θεὸς ἀνέφικτός τε καὶ ἀκατάληπτος, καὶ προσήκει διὰ τῶν ἀγγέλων τὴν θείαν εὐμένειαν πραγματεύεσθαι.* Augustini Confess. x. 42: Quem invenirem, qui me reconciliaret tibi? Abeundem mihi fuit ad angelos? Multi conantes ad te redire, neque per se ipsos valentes, sicut audio, tentaverunt haec, et inciderunt in desiderium curiosarum visionum, et digni habiti sunt illusionibus. Cf. Keilii Opusc. acad. t. ii. p. 548, ss.

[33] Ambros. de Viduis, c. 9: Obsecrandi sunt angeli, qui nobis ad praesidium dati sunt. See note 21.

[34] Augustini Collatio cum Maximino, c. 14 (Opp. viii. 467): Nonne si templum alicui sancto Angelo excellentissimo de lignis et lapidibus faceremus, anathematizaremur a veritate Christi et ab Ecclesia Dei, quoniam creaturae exhiberemus eam servitutem, quae uni tantum debetur Deo? In the time of Sozomen there was, it is true, a church in Constantinople, named *Μιχαήλιον*, but solely for this reason (Sozom. ii. 3): *Καθότι πεπίστευται ἐνθάδε ἐπιφαίνεσθαι Μιχαὴλ τὸν θεῖον Ἀρχάγγελον.*

[35] But Minucius Felix, c. 29: Cruces nec colimus, nec optamus.

[36] Euseb. de vit. Constant. i. 40; ii. 6–9, 16; iv. 21. Sozom. i. 8, in fine.

[37] This story is false. Eusebius de vita Const. iii. 25, relates at great length how the holy sepulcher was cleared out at the command of Constantine, not of Helena, and the church of the resurrection built over it, but says nothing of the discovery of the cross. Then not till c. 41, ss. does he speak of the journey of Helena to Palestine, and how she built churches at the spot where Christ was born in Bethlehem, and on the locality of the ascension on the Mount of Olives. The Gaul also, who was in Jerusalem A.D. 333, and mentions all the holy objects in the city in his Itinerarium (Vetera Rom. Itineraria, ed. P. Wesseling, p. 593), knew nothing of the holy cross and its finding. The oldest testimony alleged for it, but which notwithstanding does not speak of Helena, in Cyrilli Hieros. Epist. ad Constantium, professedly written about A.D. 351, is a later interpolation. It can not have been known before the fifth century, for Jerome, in Catal. s. v. Cyrillus, does not mention it, and Ambrose Orat. de obitu Theodosii, Jo. Chrysostomus Hom. 85 (al. 84), Paulinus Nolanus Epist. 31 (al. 11), Rufinus Hist. eccl. x. 7, 8, Socrates, i. 17, Sulpic. Sever. Hist. sacr. ii. 34, are ignorant of it; since otherwise they would not have related the circumstances of the finding, and especially the recognition of the true cross so differently. The

work miracles,[38] became objects of the highest adoration, and were finally put on altars.[39]

Helena set the first example of a pilgrimage to Palestine, which was soon extensively imitated.[40] By this means ideas of *the holiness of that country* had increased so much, even to the grossest superstition,[41] that many teachers of the Church openly discouraged these pilgrimages.[42]

Aversion to pictures ceased among Christians in the fourth century. They allowed not merely likenesses of emperors,[43]

credulous Sozomen (ii. 1) first speaks of this letter of Cyril. The conclusion of it, in which the emperor is designated as δοξάζων τὴν ὁμοούσιον τριάδα is decidedly adverse to its authenticity. For Cyril, in the time of Constantius, was not an adherent of the Nicene faith, and that this emperor was not so might have been unknown a considerable time after, in different places. Comp. Dallaeus adv. Latinorum de cultus religiosi objecto traditionem. Genevae. 1664. 4. p. 704. Witsii Miscellan. sacra, ii. 364.

38 Paulinus Nolanus Ep. 31 (al. 11): The bishop of Jerusalem alone could bestow splinters of the cross, ad magnum fidei et benedictionis gratiam. Quae quidem crux in materia insensata vim vivam tenens, ita ex illo tempore innumeris paene quotidie hominum votis lignum suum commodat, ut detrimenta non sentiat, et quasi intacta permaneat.

39 First mentioned by Sozomen, ii. 3, and Nilus. See note 48. Cf. Bingham, vol. iii. p. 236.

40 Partly in order to be baptized in Jordan (Euseb. de locis Ebr. s. v. Βηθαβαρά), which was also the purpose of Constantine (Euseb. de vit. Const. iv. 62); but also attracted by the marvelous and the love of relics. Paulinus Nol. Ep. 11: The holy cross was shown only at Easter, nisi interdum religiosissimi postulent, qui hac tantum causa illo peregrinati advenerint, ut sibi ejus revelatio quasi in pretium longinquae peregrinationis deferatur. Epist. 36: Religiosa cupiditas est loca videre, in quibus Christus ingressus et passus est, et resurrexit, et unde conscendit: et aut de ipsis locis exiguum pulverem, aut de ipso Crucis ligno aliquid saltem festucae simile sumere et habere, benedictio est. As the wood of the cross suffered no diminution (note 38), so also the footsteps of the Lord at his ascension were not worn away. Sulpic. Sever. Hist. sacr. ii. 33: Cum quotidie confluentium fides certatim Domino calcata diripiat, damnum tamen arena non sentit: et eadem adhuc sui speciem, velut impressis signata vestigiis terra custodit.

41 Ex. gr. Augustin. de Civ. Dei, xxii. 8. Respecting the wonderful power of the terra sancta de Hierosolymis allata.

42 Hieron. Ep. 13, ad Paulinum: Non Hierosolymis fuisse, sed Hierosolymis bene vixisse laudandum est.—Et de Hierosolymis et de Britannia aequaliter patet aula coelestis.—Beatus Hilarion cum Palaestinus esset et in Palaestina viveret: uno tantum die vidit Hierosolymam, ut nec contemnere loca sancta propter viciniam, nec rursus, dominum loco claudere videretur. (On the other hand, Epist. 47, ad Desiderium: adorasse, ubi steterunt pedes Domini, pars fidei est, et quasi recentia nativitatis et crucis ac passionis vidisse vestigia.) Especially zealous is Gregorii Nysseni Epist. περὶ τῶν ἀπιόντων εἰς Ἱεροσόλυμα against these pilgrimages (reprinted also as an appendix to J. H. Heidegger de Peregrinationibus religiosis. Turici. 1670. 8). We see from his letters that even then Jerusalem was remarkable for corruption of morals, as places of pilgrimage usually are: Εἰ ἦν πλέον ἡ χάρις ἐν τοῖς κατὰ Ἱεροσόλομα τόποις οὐκ ἂν ἐπεχωρίαζε τοῖς ἐκεῖ ζῶσιν ἡ ἁμαρτία. Νῦν μέντοι οὐκ ἔστιν ἀκαθαρσίας εἶδος, ὃ μὴ τολμᾶται παρ' αὐτοῖς, καὶ πονηρίαι, καὶ μοιχεῖαι, καὶ κλοπαὶ, καὶ εἰδωλολατρεῖαι, καὶ φαρμακεῖαι, καὶ φθόνοι, καὶ φόνοι.

43 Likenesses of Constantine and his children were affixed to the Labarum, Euseb de vita Const. i. 31, iv. 69, comp. above, note 4.

but also of other distinguished men.[44] On the other hand, it was still reckoned a heathen practice to represent objects of worship by *pictures*.[45] At first, allegorical representations of sacred doctrines, and historical pictures taken from the Scriptures or from the history of martyrs, were allowed in the churches. Of these the earliest instances in the east are mentioned by *Gregory* of Nyssa;[46] in the west, by *Paulinus*, bishop of Nola (409–

[44] Thus the Christians of Antioch had likenesses of their bishop Meletius († 381) even during his lifetime, on the seals, rings, vessels, and walls. See Chrysostomi Orat. encomiastica in S. Meletium, Opp. ii. 519.

[45] See Div. I. § 70, note 5. Euseb. Caesariensis Ep. ad Constantium. (Conc. Nicaeni, ii. actio 6. Published more complete by J. Boivin in the notes to Nicephori Gregorae Byzant. Histor. ed. Bonn. t. ii. p. 1301): *Ἐπεὶ δὲ καὶ περί τινος εἰκόνος ὡς δὴ τοῦ Χριστοῦ γέγραφας, εἰκόνα βουλομένη σοι ταύτην ὑφ' ἡμῶν πεμφθῆναι· τίνα λέγεις καὶ ποίαν ταύτην, ἣν φῂς τοῦ Χριστοῦ εἰκόνα;—πότερον τὴν ἀληθῆ καὶ ἀμετάλλακτον, καὶ φύσει τοὺς αὐτοῦ χαρακτῆρας φέρουσαν· ἢ ταύτην ἣν δι' ἡμᾶς ἀνείληφε, τῆς τοῦ δούλου μορφῆς περιθέμενος τὸ σχῆμα;—ἀλλὰ τοῦ πρὸ τῆς μεταβολῆς σαρκίου αὐτοῦ δὴ τοῦ θνητοῦ τὴν εἰκόνα φῂς παρ' ἡμῶν αἰτεῖν· ἆρα γὰρ τοῦτό σε μόνον διέλαθεν τὸ ἀνάγνωσμα, ἐν ᾧ ὁ θεὸς νομοθετεῖ μὴ ποιεῖν ὁμοίωμα μήτε τῶν, ὅσα ἐν τῷ οὐρανῷ, μήτε τῶν, ὅσα ἐν τῇ γῇ κάτω; ἢ ἔστιν ὅτε ἐν ἐκκλησίᾳ τὸ τοιοῦτον ἢ αὐτὴ, ἢ καὶ παρ' ἄλλου τοῦτο ἤκουσας; οὐχὶ δὲ καθ' ὅλης τῆς οἰκουμένης ἐξώρισται καὶ πόῤῥω τῶν ἐκκλησιῶν πεφυγάδευται τὰ τοιαῦτα, μόνοις τε ἡμῖν μὴ ἐξεῖναι τὸ τοιοῦτον ποιεῖν παρὰ πᾶσι βεβόηται;—οὐκ οἶδα γὰρ, ὅπως γύναιόν τι μετὰ χεῖράς ποτε δύο τινὰς φέρουσα καταγεγραμμένους, ὡς ἂν φιλοσόφους, ἀπέῤῥιψε λόγον, ὡς ἂν εἶεν Παύλου καὶ τοῦ Σωτῆρος· οὐκ ἔχω λέγειν, οὔτε ὁπόθεν λαβοῦσα, οὔτε ὅθεν τοῦτο μαθοῦσα· ἵνα μηδὲ αὐτὴ, μηδὲ ἕτεροι σκανδαλίζοιντο, ἀφελόμενος ταύτην παρ' ἐμαυτὸν κατεῖχον, οὐχ ἡγούμενος καλῶς ἔχειν εἰς ἑτέρους ὅλως ἐκφέρειν ταῦτα, ἵνα μὴ δοκῶμεν δίκην εἰδωλολατρούντων τὸν θεὸν ἡμῶν ἐν εἰκόνι περιφέρειν.* Epiphanius Ep. ad Johannem Hierosol. ex vers. Hieronymi (Epiph. Opp. ii. 317) relates, that when he had come into the church in Anablatha, a village of Palestine, inveni ibi velum pendens in foribus ejusdem Ecclesiae tinctum atque depictum, et habens imaginem, quasi Christi, vel sancti cujusdam. Non enim satis memini, cujus imago fuerit. Cum ergo hoc vidissem, in Ecclesia Christi contra auctoritatem Scripturarum hominis pendere imaginem, scidi illud, et magis dedi consilium custodibus ejusdem loci, ut pauperem mortuum eo obvolverent et efferrent. He promises them a new velum which he herewith sends and asks John, deinceps praecipere, in Ecclesia Christi ejusmodi vela, quae contra religionem nostram veniunt, non appendi. Asterius, bishop of Amasea (about 400. See Homilies in the auctarium PP. ed. Combefisii) Hom. in Divitem et Lazarum: *Μὴ γράφε τὸν Χριστόν. ἀρκεῖ γὰρ αὐτῷ ἡ μία τῆς ἐνσωματώσεως ταπεινοφροσύνη, ἣν αὐθαιρέτως δι' ἡμᾶς κατεδέξατο· ἐπὶ δὲ τῆς ψυχῆς σου βαστάζων νοητῶς τὸν ἀσώματον λόγον περίφερε.* Cf Suiceri Thes. eccl. i. 1014. Jo. Dallaei de Imaginibus libb. iv. Lugd. Bat. 1642. 8. p. 163, ss. Frid. Spanhemii Hist. imaginum. Lugd. Bat. 1686. 8. (Opp. iii. 707). Neander's Chrysostomus, ii. 143.

[46] Greg. Nyss. Orat. de laudibus Theodori Mart. c. 2 (Opp. ii. 1011), in describing the church built in honor of Theodore: *Ἐπέχρωσε δὲ καὶ ζωγράφος τὰ ἄνθη τῆς τέχνης ἐν εἰκόνι διαγραψάμενος, τὰς ἀριστείας τοῦ μάρτυρος, τὰς ἐνστάσεις, τὰς ἀλγηδόνας, τὰς θηριώδεις τῶν τυράννων μορφὰς, τὰς ἐπηρείας, τὴν φλογοτρόφον ἐκείνην, κάμινον τὴν μακαριωτάτην τελείωσιν τοῦ ἀθλητοῦ, τοῦ ἀγωνοθέτου Χριστοῦ τῆς ἀνθρωπίνης μορφῆς τὸ ἐκτύπωμα· πάντα ἡμῖν, ὡς ἐν βιβλίῳ τινι γλωττοφόρῳ διὰ χρωμάτων τεχνουργησάμενος σαφῶς διηγόρευσε τοὺς ἀγῶνας τοῦ μάρτυρος.* In the Orat. de deitate Filii et Spir. S. (l. c. p. 908), he describes a picture of the sacrifice of Isaac. (Augustin. contra Faustum, xxii. 73: Factum ita nobile,—ut tot linguis cantatum, tot locis pictum, et aures et oculos

431, A.D.).[47] Such pictures were not intended to be worshiped, but were merely for instruction and stimulus.[48] The likenesses of individuals only were capable of leading the minds of the illiterate astray, so as to worship them. The first pictures of this kind which we find in a Gallic Church at the end of the fifth century do not, it is true, imply that they were worshiped;[49] but soon after, superstition connected itself with the likenesses of miracle-working persons, which were placed in houses.[50] Under Leo the Great, we find the first picture of Christ in a Romish Church.[51]

dissimulantis feriret.) Comp. Cramer's Forts. v. Bossuet's Weltgesch. Th. 4, S. 442, ss. Münter's Sinnbilder u. Kunstvorstellungen der alten Christen. Heft 1, S. 9, ss.

47 Paulin. Natal. ix. Felicis:

> Propterea visum nobis opus utile, totis
> Felicibus domibus pictura illudere sancta:
> Si forte attonitas haec per spectacula mentes
> Agrestum caperet fucata coloribus umbra, etc.

Cf. Natalis vii. et x. Epist. 30 (al. 12). Prudentius περὶ στεφανῶν, hymn ix. v. 10, hymn xi. v. 127. Münter, i. 18.

48 Nilus (see § 85, note 1) advised the Eparch Olympiodorus who intended to build a Martyrion and to adorn it with a number of pictures (lib. iv. Ep. 61): Ἐν τῷ ἱερατείῳ μὲν κατὰ ἀνατολὰς τοῦ θειοτάτου τεμένους ἕνα καὶ μόνον τυπῶσαι σταυρόν· δι' ἑνὸς γὰρ σωτηριώδους σταυροῦ τὸ τῶν ἀνθρώπων διασώζεται γένος, καὶ τοῖς ἀπηλπισμένοις ἐλπὶς πανταχοῦ κηρύσσεται· ἱστοριῶν δὲ παλαιᾶς καὶ νέας διαθήκης πληρῶσαι ἔνθεν καὶ ἔνθεν χειρὶ καλλίστου ζωγράφου τὸν ναὸν τὸν ἅγιον, ὅπως ἂν οἱ μὴ εἰδότες γράμματα, μηδὲ δυνάμενοι τὰς θείας ἀναγινώσκειν γραφὰς τῇ θεωρίᾳ τῆς ζωγραφίας μνήμην τε λαμβάνωσιν τῆς τῶν γνησίως τῷ ἀληθινῷ θεῷ δεδουλευκότων ἀνδραγαθίας, καὶ πρὸς ἅμιλλαν διεγείρωνται τῶν εὐκλεῶν καὶ ἀοιδίμων ἀριστευμάτων, δι' ὧν τῆς γῆς τὸν οὐρανὸν ἀπηλλάξαντο.

49 Severus caused pictures of Martin of Tours and Paulinus of Nola to be brought into the baptistery of the church in Bourges, while the former was probably alive, the latter, certainly so. Pauli Nol. Ep. 32. Cf. Bingham, vol. iii. p. 305.

50 Thus Augustine mentions pictures of Peter and Paul (de Consensu evangel. i. 10), but says of them: Sic omnino errare meruerunt, qui Christum et Apostolos ejus non in sanctis codicibus, sed in pictis parietibus quaesierunt. Comp. de Moribus eccl. cath. i. 34: Novi, multos esse sepulchrorum et picturarum adoratores. Nunc vos illud admoneo, ut aliquando Ecclesiae catholicae maledicere desinatis, vituperando mores hominum, quos et ipsa condemnat, et quos quotidie tanquam malos filios corrigere studet. According to Theodoreti Hist. relig. c. 26 (ed. Schultze, iii. 1272), Simeon Stylites was held in such honor at Rome even during his lifetime, ὡς ἐν ἅπασι τοῖς τῶν ἐργαστηρίων προπυλαίοις εἰκόνας αὐτῷ βραχείας ἀναστῆσαι, φυλακήν τινα σφίσιν αὐτοῖς καὶ ἀσφάλειαν ἐντεῦθεν πορίζοντας.

51 According to Severianus (about 400) an opponent of Chrysostom, subsequently bishop of Gabala (Tract. in s. crucem in S. Jo. Chrysost. de Educandis liberis, lib. etc. ed. Franc. Combefis. Paris. 1656. 8. p. 129), the cross is ἡ τοῦ ἀθανάτου βασιλέως εἰκών. In the churches of Paulinus of Nola, Christ appears only in the symbolic form of the lamb at the foot of the cross. In the mosaic picture belonging to the S. Maria Maggiore, the oldest extant, which was made under Sixtus III., 432–440, a throne with a book roll, and behind it a cross, forms the central point. In the background, Christ appears only as a child, in historical representations from the accounts of his childhood. In the Basilica of St. Paul, which was built under Leo I., in the picture of the triumphal arch he is first made to occupy the exact center as a Savious (see die bildl. Darstellungen im Sanctuarium d.

§ 100.

PLACES AND TIMES OF PUBLIC WORSHIP.

Since *basilicae*[1] had frequently been converted into churches after the time of Constantine, and churches had been built in the form of *basilicae*,[2] the name *basilica* was also the more readily transferred to the churches themselves,[3] because it was susceptible in this instance of a signification so appropriate. The churches, now large and splendid, were divided into three parts: the νάρθηξ (πρόναος, ferula) *porch*, from which the *beautiful gates*, πύλαι ὡραῖαι (according to Acts iii. 2–10), led into the *body* of the church, ναός, navis (where was the ἄμβων, pulpitum), which again was divided from the βῆμα, sacrarium, *sacristy*, by cancelli, κιγκλίδες, a lattice-work. There were usually other buildings attached to the churches, and especially a baptistery, βαπτιστήριον, with the font, piscina, fons, κολυμβήθρα. All the buildings were situated in an inclosed court (αἴθριον, αὐλή, atrium), in which was also a *reservoir* or large vessel of water (κρήνη, cantharus) for washing the hands before entering the church, after the ancient, originally Jewish fashion.

christl. Kirchen vom 5ten bis zum 14ten Jahrh. von J. G. Müller. Trier. 1835. 8. S. 42, ss.). These Salvator-pictures continue for a long time the only ones. Pictures of the crucified, the Ecce-homo, the dead Christ in the bosom of the mother, belong to the middle ages. The caput radiatum or the nimbus was taken from heathen and transferred to Christian art. See Schoepflini Comment. hist. et crit. p. 69, Münter's Sinnbilder, ii. 28.—The Thomas-Christians in India suppose that Cyril introduced the to them hateful pictures. See La Croze Hist. du Christianisme des Indes, a la Haye, 1724. 4. p. 243. Assemanus Bibl. Orient. iii. ii. 401, endeavors indeed to prove that this tradition can not be very old; but it is a remarkable fact that it is also related by the Copt *Elmacin* (about 1250) on whose authority it is repeated by Makriz (about 1400). (See Renaudot Hist. Patr. Alex. p. 114, Makrizii Hist. Coptorum ed. Wetzer. Solisb. 1828. 8. p. 53.) On any supposition, it is historically established that pictures were introduced into churches in the time of Cyril.

[1] The Roman basilica, an imitation of the στοὰ βασιλική in Athens, consisted partly of an oblong four-cornered space, which served principally for a place of merchandise, and partly of a second space situated over against the entrance which formed a semicircle, and in which a court was held, the so called *tribunal*. See Vitruv. v. i. Hirt's Baukunst, iii. 180. Dr. F. Kugler's Handbuch der Kunstgeschichte. Stuttgart. 1842.

[2] On the form of the churches, see the description of the city of Rome by Platner, Bunsen, Gerhard, and Röstell, i. 419. Die Basiliken des christl. Roms. Kupfertafeln u Erklärung (von Bunsen). München. 1843. fol.

[3] Hieronymus Ep. 35; epitaph. Nepotiani: basilicas ecclesiae.

Fasts, hitherto voluntary, were now prescribed by the Church.[4] *Festival days* were more regularly arranged, and, at the same time, multiplied. In the east, *the Epiphany* was celebrated as the festival[5] both of the birth and baptism of our Lord; in the west, the 25th December had been adopted as the birth-day ever since the middle of the fourth century;[6] the cus-

[4] The older and more liberal view (see Div. I. § 73, note 1) is still maintained by Victor Antiochenus (about 400), Comm. in Ev. Marci, c. 2 (Bibl. PP. max. t. iv.): Enimvero inter eos, qui in Moysis, et eos rursum, qui in gratiae lege jejuniis dant operam, hoc praeter caetera interest, quod illi quidem jejunia a Deo praefinita habebant, quae proinde modis omnibus explere obligabantur, etiamsi alias noluissent; hi vero virtutis amore, liberaque voluntatis electione jejunant verius, quam ulla legis coactione. Quodsi vero quadragesimale vel aliud quodcunque jejunium definitum habemus, propter ignavos et negligentes, quo nimirum quoque ii officium faciant, praefinitum habemus. Chrysostomus Hom. lii. in eos qui primo Pascha jejunant. Cassianus Collat. xxi. c. 30: Sciendum sane hanc observantiam quadragesimae, quamdiu ecclesiae illius primitivae perfectio inviolata permansit, penitus non fuisse. Non enim praecepti hujus necessitate nec quasi legali sanctione constricti, arctissimis jejuniorum terminis claudebantur, qui totum anni spatium aequali jejunio concludebant. Socrates, v. 22. On the contrary Epiphanius Haer. lxxv. 6, Expos. fidei, c. 22, derives the Wednesday and Friday fasts from an apostolic arrangement. Hieronymus Ep. 27 (al. 54), ad Marcellam: Nos unam quadragesimam secundum traditionem Apostolorum, toto nobis orbe congruo, jejunamus. Leo P. Serm. 43, de Quadrages. 6: Apostolica institutio xl. dierum jejunio impleatur. While in the Oriental church all fasting was prohibited on the Saturday, the custom of fasting on this day arose in the west, especially in Rome, perhaps even in the third century (Neander, i. i. 510: Tertullian de Jejun. c. 14, does not, however, prove this. See my remarks in the Theol. Stud. und Kritik. 1833, iv. 1149). In the fourth century, Saturday as a fast day entirely took the place of Wednesday at Rome (Innocent I. Ep. 25, ad Dicentium. c. 4. Augustini Ep. 36, ad Casulanum). Cf. Quesnel. Diss. de Jejunio Sabbati in Eccl. Rom. observato, in his edition of the Opp. Leonis, ii. 544.

[5] Cassian. Collat. x. c. 2: Intra Aegypti regionem mos iste antiqua traditione servatur, ut peracto Epiphaniorum die, quem provinciae illius sacerdotes vel dominici baptismi, vel secundum carnem nativitatis esse definiunt, et idcirco utriusque sacramenti solemnitatem non bifarie, ut in occiduis provinciis, sed sub una diei hujus festivitate concelebrant, epistolae pontificis Alexandrini per universas dirigantur Aegypti ecclesias, quibus et initium quadragesimae et dies paschae non solum per civitates omnes, sed etiam per universa monasteria designentur.

[6] According to Epist. Johannis Episc. Nicaeni, in the auctar. Bibl. Patr. ed. Combefisius, t. ii. p. 297, and an Anonymus ap. Cotelerius ad Constitt. Apost. v. 13, which, however, are too modern to be regarded as proper witnesses, although they certainly come near the truth, this day was established by Julius, bishop of Rome (337–352). An expression of his successors, Liberius (352–366) in Salvatoris Natali is adduced by Ambrosius de Virginibus, iii. c. 1. Even an ancient Syrian in Assemani Bibl. orient. ii. 164, states that the natalis solis invicti falling on this day (Winter-solstice, according to the erroneous reckoning of the Julian calendar on the 25th December, see Ideler's Chronologie, ii. 24), was the reason why the natalis Christi was assigned to the same day. So also Jo. Harduin (Acta SS. Junii iv. 702, D.) and especially Jablonski de Origine festi nativit. Christi. diss. ii. § 2 (Opusc. ed. te Water, iii. 348). Even so late as the times of Leo the Great, there were many in Rome quibus haec die solemnitatis nostrae non tam de nativitate Christi, quam de novi, ut dicunt, solis ortu honorabilis videatur (Leonis M. Sermo xxi. c. 6). According to Credner de Natalitiorum Christi et rituum in hoc festo celebrande solemnium origine, in Illgen's Zeitschr. f. d. hist. Theol. iii. ii. 228, this festival began in Egypt in the fourth century.

tom proceeding from Rome and spreading into the different parts of the empire. This festival began now to obtain in the east;[7] and at last, also (shortly before 431) in Egypt.[8] The Epiphany was observed in addition as the day of baptism, and came to be kept as such even in the west.[9] The celebration of the passover, as customary in Asia Minor, had been rejected at the council of Nice;[10] and since that time, those who still retained it were regarded as heretics, Τεσσαρεσκαιδεκατῖται, Quartodecimani.[11] With respect to the appointment of the Easter festival, they followed for the most part the patriarch of Alexandria;[12] yet not always, especially in the west; and thus Easter was sometimes observed on different Sundays in different provinces.[13] The Paschal festival, which was announced at the

[7] For example, in Antioch about 380. Chrysost. Hom. 31, de Natali Christi (ed. Montfauc. ii. 355): *Οὔτω δέκατόν ἐστιν ἔτος, ἐξ οὗ δήλη καὶ γνώριμος ἡμῖν αὕτη ἡ ἡμέρα γεγέννηται.* What follows furnishes a remarkable illustration of the ease with which customs of a recent date could assume the character of apostolic institutions: *Παρὰ μὲν τοῖς τὴν ἑσπέραν οἰκοῦσιν ἄνωθεν γνωριζομένη—παλαιὰ καὶ ἀρχαία ἐστὶ, καὶ ἄνωθεν τοῖς ἀπὸ Θρᾴκης μέχρι Γαδείρων οἰκοῦσι κατάδηλος καὶ ἐπίσημος γέγονε.*

[8] Comp. Cassian Collat. x. 2, above, note 5. On the other hand, in the Acts of the Ephesian council (ap. Mansi, iv. 293) Pauli Episc. Emiseni homilia *λεχθεῖσα κθ' Χοιὰκ* (25 Dec.) *ἐν τῇν μεγάλῃ ἐκκλησίᾳ 'Αλεξανδρείας—εἰς τὴν γέννησιν τοῦ Κυρίου, κ. τ. λ.* About the same time under bishop Juvenalis the festival was also adopted in Jerusalem, which was united with Alexandria against Antioch. See Basilides Seleuc. de S. Stephano, in S. Joannis Chrysostomi de Educandis liberis lib. ejusdem tractatus alii quinque, etc. ed. Franc. Combefis. Paris. 1656. 8. p. 302.

[9] The first trace of it is in 360, when Julian, according to Ammian. Marcell. xxi. c. 2, celebrated the Epiphany in the church at Vienne. In the west, the commemoration of the arrival of the Magi (i. e., three kings, according to Psalm lxxii. 10) and the first miracle in Cana were united with this feast. Bingham, vol. ix. p. 80. Neander, ii. ii. 657, ss.

[10] Comp. Div. I. § 60, note 15. Constantini Epist. ad ecclesias de decretis syn. Nic. (ap. Eusebius de vita Const. iii. 18) et Epist. Syn. Nic. ad eccl. Alexandr. ap. Socrates, i. 9: *'Ως πάντας τοὺς ἐν τῇ ἑῴᾳ ἀδελφοὺς τοὺς μετὰ τῶν 'Ιουδαίων τὸ πρότερον ποιοῦντας, συμφώνως 'Ρωμαίοις καὶ ἡμῖν—τὸ πάσχα ἐκ τοῦ δεῦρο ἄγειν.* There is nothing more precise on the subject. This Nicene decree was confirmed by the Conc. Antioch. ann. 341, can. 1.

[11] The name first occurs in Conc. Laodic. (about 364) can. 7. Conc. Constant. oec. ii. ann. 381, c. 2. Epiphan. Haer. 50. On the other hand, Philastrius Haer. 87, knows nothing of it.

[12] Leonis Ep. 121 (ed. Quesn. 94): Paschale festum—quamvis in primo semper mense celebrandum sit, ita tamen est lunaris cursus conditione mutabile, ut plerumque sacratissimae diei ambigua occurrat electio, et ex hoc fiat plerumque quod non licet, ut non simul omnis Ecclesia quod nonnisi unum esse oportet observet. Studuerunt itaque sancti Patres occasionem hujus erroris auferre, omnem hanc curam Alexandrino Episcopo delegantes (quoniam apud Aegyptios hujus supputationis antiquitus tradita esse videbatur peritia), per quem quotannis dies praedictae solemnitatis Sedi apostolicae indicaretur, cujus scriptis ad longinquiores Ecclesias indicium generale percurreret.

[13] Ambrosii Ep. 23 (al. 83). On the different paschal cycles see Bingham, vol. ix. p. 99. Ideler's Chronologie, Bd. 2, S. 200, ss. In Alexandria a cycle of nineteen years invented by Anatolius was used (*ἐννεακαιδεκαετηρίς*). In Rome, to the time of Leo the Great,

Epiphany, was preceded by the Quadragesima (τεσσαρακοστή)[14] and divided into the πάσχα σταυρώσιμον, hebdomas magna, *the great week*, in which the feria quinta (ἡ ἁγία πέμπτη), the παρασκευή, and the Sabbatum magnum were distinguished from one another; and into the πάσχα ἀναστάσιμον, *the week of the resurrection*, which ended with the Dominica in albis (καινὴ κυριακή). This festival was followed by the Quinquagesima (πεντηκοστή), which included the ascension (ἀνάληψις), and ended with pentecost (πεντηκοστή).

The nightly service (vigiliae, παννυχίδες) which preceded the Easter festival was observed with great splendor;[15] but now similar vigils were also annexed to other festivals, especially to those in honor of martyrs.

§ 101.

RITES AND CEREMONIES OF WORSHIP.

Christian worship was now invested with a splendor hitherto unknown. The clergy began to wear a peculiar costume while engaged in holy things.[1] In some of the services lights were

and in the west, the cycle of eighty-four years. With the Alexandrians, Easter festival must fall between 22d March and 25th April; with the Latins, between the 18th March and the 21st April. Hence there was a difference in the keeping of Easter, and hence arose the discussions respecting it. Ideler, ii. 254, ff. For this reason, Leo M. Ep. 121 (see note 12), applied to the emperor Marcian: Obsecro clementiam vestram, ut studium vestrum praestare dignemini, quatenus Aegyptii, vel si qui sunt alii, qui certam hujus supputationis videntur habere notitiam, scrupulum hujus solicitudinis absolvant, ut in eum diem generalis observantia dirigatur, qui nec paternarum constitutionum normam relinquat, nec ultra praefixos terminos evagetur. Quicquid autem pietas vestra de hac consultatione cognoverit, ad meam jubeat mox notitiam pervenire, ut in divinis mysteriis nulla dissonantiae culpa nascatur.

[14] Among the Orientals seven weeks, among the Westerns who fasted also on the Sabbath (see above, note 6) six; in both cases, therefore, thirty-six days. Cassiani Collat. xxi. 24, 25 (qui substantiarum nostrarum omniumque fructuum decimas offerre praecipimur, multo magis necesse est, ut ipsius quoque conversationis nostrae, et humani usus, operumque nostrorum decimas offeramus, quae profecto in supputatione quadragesimae implentur), 27, 28. Comp. Socrates, v. 22.

[15] Euseb. de vit. Const. iv. 22. Gregor. Nyss. Orat. 5, de Paschate Gregor. Naz. Orat. 19 et 42.

[1] All the clergy wore the στιχάριον (vestis alba tunica); bishops, presbyters, and deacons wore over that the ὠράριον (according to Jo. Morinus de sacris Ecclesiae ordinationibus, p. 174, ὡράριον, according to Suicer. Thes. eccl. ii. 498, ὀράριον lat. orarium, afterward Stola), bishops and presbyters over that the φελόνης or φαίλονης (planeta, casula; comp. Morinus, p. 176. Suicer. ii. 1422). The ὠμοφόριον (pallium) distinguished the bishops in

also used in the day-time;[2] and in the fifth century frankincense began to be employed.[3] More attention was paid to the music. The custom of singing in responses, first introduced into the Church at Antioch,[4] soon spread in the east, and was transferred to the Western Church by Ambrose.[5] The *disciplina arcani* (distinction between the initiated and uninitiated) reached its highest development in the fourth century,[6] but afterward gradually disappeared as heathenism ceased. Public worship (*λειτουργία*,[7] missa)[8] was divided on account of it into several

the east; in the west it was not yet in use (cf. Pertsch de Origine, usu et auctoritate pallii archiepiscopalis. Helmst. 1754. 4. p. 91, ss). That no tonsure was ever practiced either by monks or clergymen may be inferred from Hieronymus ad Ezech. xliv. 20: Quod sequitur; caput suum non radent neque comam nutrient, sed tondentes attondebunt capita sua, perspicue demonstratur, nec rasis capitibus, sicut sacerdotes cultoresque Isidis ac Serapis nos esse debere, nec rursum comam demittere, quod proprie luxuriosorum est, barbarorumque et militantium, sed ut honestus habitus sacerdotum facie demonstretur, etc. Comp. Bingham, vol. ii. p. 413, iii. 50.

2 Before the relics of martyrs, and in the east also during the reading of the Gospel. See Hieronymus adv. Vigilantium. Lactantius (Institutt. vi. 2) still mocks the heathens on account of it.

3 The first certain trace of it is found in Pseudo-Dionys. Areop. de Eccl. hier. c. 3. It had been used before as a mark of honor to the emperors. See § 99, note 4.

4 According to Theodoretus H. E. ii. 19. Flavianus and Diodorus, two monks in Antioch, in the time of Constantius, were its originators: *Οὗτοι πρῶτοι, διχῇ διελόντες τοὺς τῶν ψαλλόντων χοροὺς, ἐκ διαδοχῆς ᾄδειν τὴν Δαυτικὴν ἐδίδαξαν μελῳδίαν· καὶ τοῦτο ἐν Ἀντιοχείᾳ πρῶτον ἀρξάμενον πάντοσε διέδραμε, καὶ κατέλαβε τῆς οἰκουμένης τὰ τέρματα.* According to Theodore of Mopsvestia in Nicetae Acomin. Thesaurus orthodoxiae, v. 30, they first only translated Antiphonies from the Syriac into Greek: and Socrates, vi. 8, attributes the first introduction of this kind of music to Ignatius (Augusti Diss. de hymnis Syrorum. Vratisl. 1814. 8. Hahn über den Gesang in der syrischen Kirche, in the Kirchenhist. Archive für 1823, iii. 52). The custom of singing in responses was especially diffused by the monks (*τὸ ἀντίφωνον, ἀντίφωνοι ὕμνοι*). Comp. generally M. Gerbertus de Cantu et musica sacra (tomi ii. typis San-Blasianis, 1774. 4), i. 40. Schöne's Geschichtsforschungen über die kirchl. Gebräuche, ii. 191.

5 Augustini Confess. ix. 6, 7. Paulinus in vita Ambros. p. iv. On the musical character of the Ambrosian singing see Kiesewetter's Gesch. d. europäisch-abendländischen Musik. Leipzig. 1834. 4. S. 3.

6 Comp. Div. I. § 67, note 3. Basilius de Spir. sancto, c. 27. Comp. especially Cyrilli Hieros. catecheses. Hence the formula so frequent among the orators, *ἴσασιν οἱ μεμυημένοι* or *οἱ συμμύσται*, in opposition to the *ἀμύητοι*: in Augustine, norunt fideles: Frommann de Disciplina arcani, p. 43.

7 Comp. Suiceri Thes. eccl. ii. 220. Bingham, v. 16, particularly the solemnity of the Lord's Supper, but in other respects every religious service too.

8 Missa, i. e. missio: as remissa, offensa, for remissio, offensio. Avitus (archbishop of Vienne about 490) in Epist. i.: In Ecclesiis, Palatiisque, sive Praetoriis missa fieri pronunciatur, cum populus ab observatione dimittitur. In the first part of the service, which consisted of psalms, readings, and sermon, even the unbelieving portion of the people were permitted to join. After their retiring, the proper missa catechumenorum followed, which was a series of prayers, whereby the catechumens, penitents, and possessed, were dismissed in classes (by the call *οἱ ἀκοινώνητοι περιπατήσατε. μή τις τῶν κατηχουμένων*), etc. (Cf. Conc. Carthag. iv. ann. 398, can. 84: Ut Episcopus nullum prohibeat ingredi

parts (missa catechumenorum, and missa fidelium),[9] and received more definite formularies.[10]

Baptism, now preceded by unction, was frequently delayed as long as possible.[11] Against this abuse several teachers of the Church zealously remonstrated.[12] The baptism of infants did

Ecclesiam, et audire verbum Dei, sive gentilem, sive haereticum, sive Judaeum, usque ad missam catechumenorum. Augustini Sermo 49, § 8 : Ecce post sermonem fit missa catechumenis : manebunt fideles, venietur ad locum orationis). According to this analogy, the last part of public worship was called missa fidelium, i. e., the service with which the fideles were dismissed, and which ended with the call *ἀπολύεσθε*, ite, missa est (this dismissal was among the Greeks, *ἡ ἀπόλυσις τῆς ἐκκλησίας*). Since the last part was the most important, it was also called in particular missa (cf. Ambrosii Ep. 20, al. 14, ad Marcellinam sororem: post lectiones atque tractatum dimissis catechumenis—missam facere coepi). Finally the name was transferred to every public service. Thus it is applied to the meetings of the monks for prayer, Cassian. Institt. ii. c. 13, missa nocturna, iii. c. 5, missa canonica.

[9] See note 8. The Greeks distinguished the parts of public worship in a different manner. See Conc. Laodic. can. 19 : *Περὶ τοῦ δεῖν ἰδίᾳ πρῶτον μετὰ τὰς ὁμιλίας τῶν Ἐπισκόπων, καὶ τῶν κατηχουμένων εὐχὴν ἐπιτελεῖσθαι, καὶ μετὰ τὸ ἐξελθεῖν τοὺς κατηχουμένους τῶν ἐν μετανοίᾳ τὴν εὐχὴν γίνεσθαι, καὶ τούτων προσελθόντων ὑπὸ χεῖρα καὶ ὑποχωρησάντων οὕτως τῶν πιστῶν τὰς εὐχὰς γίνεσθαι τρεῖς,—καὶ μετὰ τὸ Πρεσβυτέρους δοῦναι τῷ Ἐπισκόπῳ τὴν εἰρήνην, τότε τοὺς Λαϊκοὺς τὴν εἰρήνην διδόναι, καὶ οὕτω τὴν ἁγίαν προσφορὰν ἐπιτελεῖσθαι.*

[10] The arrangement of public worship and single formularies had been already established for a long time ; but now there were added to them formularies of prayer too ; complete liturgies were made, and those of the apostolic churches were soon derived from their founders. Proclus Episc. Constantinop. (about 440) de traditione divinae Missae (in Gallandii Bibl. PP. ix. 680 : *Πολλοὶ μὲν τινὲς καὶ ἄλλοι τῶν τοὺς ἱεροὺς Ἀποστόλους διαδεξαμένων θεῖοι ποιμένες καὶ διδάσκαλοι τῆς Ἐκκλησίας τὴν τῆς μυστικῆς λειτουργίας ἔκθεσιν ἐγγράφως καταλιπόντες, τῇ Ἐκκλησίᾳ παραδεδώκασιν. ἐξ ὧν δὲ πρῶτοι οὗτοι καὶ διαπρύσιοι τυγχάνουσιν ὅ,τε μακάριος Κλήμης, ὁ τοῦ κορυφαίου τῶν Ἀποστόλων μαθητὴς καὶ διάδοχος, αὐτῷ τῶν ἱερῶν Ἀποστόλων ὑπαγορευσάντων.* (This is the liturgy found in the Constitut. apost. viii. 16, the oldest extant.) *καὶ ὁ θεῖος Ἰάκωβος, ὁ τῆς Ἱεροσολυμιτῶν Ἐκκλησίας τὸν κλῆρον λαχών.—Ὁ δὲ μέγας Βασίλειος μετὰ ταῦτα τὸ ῥάθυμον καὶ κατωφερὲς τῶν ἀνθρώπων θεωρῶν, καὶ διὰ τοῦτο τὸ τῆς λειτουργίας μῆκος ὀκνούντων, —ἐπιτομώτερον παρέδωκε λέγεσθαι.—Μετ' οὐ πολὺ δὲ πάλιν ὁ ἡμέτερος πατὴρ ὁ τὴν γλῶτταν χρυσοῦς Ἰωάννης—εἰς τὴν τῆς ἀνθρωπίνης φύσεως ῥαθυμίαν ἐφορῶν—τὰ πολλὰ ἐπέτεμε, καὶ συντομώτερον τελεῖσθαι διετάξατο.* In the fifth century the liturgy of Basil had been spread almost over all the east. But in addition to it, that of Chrysostom also, proceeding from Constantinople, gradually obtained acceptance. The Alexandrians derived their liturgy from Mark, the Romans from Peter, the Milanese from Barnabas and Ambrose. No liturgy of this period, with the exception of that in the Constitutt. apost., has been preserved free from alteration. Comp. Leonis Alatii de Libris ecclesisticis Graecorum, diss. ii. Paris. 1645. 4. (with Fabricius' remarks in the old edition of his Biblioth. graeca, appended to vol. v.) Jac. Goar *εὐχολόγιον* s. rituale Graecorum. Paris. 1647, and Venet. 1730. fol. Eus. Renaudotii Liturgiarum orientalium collectio, t. ii. Paris. 1716. 4. J. A. Assemani Codex liturgicus Eccl. universae, p. vi. Romae. 1749, ss. 4.

[11] Constitutt. apostoll. vii. c. 41. Cyrill. Hieros. Catech. myst. ii. c. 3 et 4. This unction was with *ἐλαίῳ ἁγίῳ*; the unction after baptism, which had been practiced before (see Div. I. § 53, note 25), with *μύρῳ* or *χρίσματι*, see Suicer. Thes. eccl. i. 1077, ii. 1534. Bingham, vol. iv. p. 303.

[12] Gregor. Nazianz. Orat. 40. Comp. Ullmann's Gregor v. Naz. S. 466, ss. (On the baptism of children: *Δίδωμι γνώμην, τὴν τριετίαν ἀναμείναντας—ἡνίκα καὶ ἀκοῦσαί τι*

not become universal until after the time of Augustine. The baptism of heretics was still, in the fourth century, rejected for the most part in the east; and afterward the baptism of single parties only was excepted.[13] On the contrary Augustine established the milder practice of the west on firm principles.[14]

As to *the Lord's Supper*, the Christians of that period recognized in it the flesh and blood of Christ, and even spoke of a transformation; but only in a figurative sense.[15] As this rite

μυστικὸν, καὶ ἀποκρίνεσθαι δυνατὸν,—οὕτως ἁγιάζειν.) Basilii M. Orat. 13. (Walli Hist. bapt. infant. i. 136, 181.) Gregorii Nyss. Orat. in eos qui differunt baptismum. Chrysostom (Neander's Chrys. i. 74).

[13] Comp. Div. I. § 72, note 22. Athanasius, Cyril of Jerusalem, and Basil rejected it. Münscher's Dogmengesch. iv. 368. The Synod of Laodicea, can. 7, and the second oecumenical Synod of Constantinople, can. 7, made exceptions, whose consistency is not obvious. Comp. Drey über apost. Constit. S. 260. Gass, in Illgen's Zeitschr. f. hist. Theol. 1842, iv. 120.

[14] Augustinus de Baptismo contra Donatistas, vi. 47: Dicimus, baptismum Christi, i. e. verbis evangelicis consecratum, ubique eundem esse, nec hominum quorumlibet et qualibet perversitate violari. C. 61: Manifestum est, iniquos, quamdiu iniqui sunt, baptismum quidem posse habere; sed salutem, cujus sacramentum baptisma est, habere non posse. C. 78: Dicimus, accipientibus non prodesse (baptismum), cum in haeresi accipiunt consentientes haereticis: et ideo veniunt ad catholicam pacem atque unitatem, non ut baptismum accipiant, sed ut eis prodesse incipiat quod acceperant.

[15] We find the expressions: μεταβολή, μεταβάλλεσθαι, μεταμορφοῦσθαι, μεταστοιχειοῦσθαι (similar expressions with regard to the consecrated oil, Münscher, iv. 387, and the baptismal water, same author, p. 352. Wundemann, ii. 417), and again, τύπος, ἀντίτυπον, figura, signum. Hence all churches appeal to the fathers in their favor. Comp. especially the dispute between A. Arnauld, P. Nicole (chief work, la Perpétuité de la foi de l'église catholique touchant l'eucharistie, 3 t. 1669–1672; t. 4 et 5, par Eus. Renaudot, 1711–1713. 4), and J. Claude (Résponse aux deux traités intitulés: la Perpétuité, etc. Charent. 1666. Réponse au livre de M. Arnauld intitulé: la Perpétuité, etc. Charent. 1671. 2 voll. 8). Clear passages on this subject are: Augustinus Epist. 98 (al. 23), ad Bonifacium, § 9: Nempe saepe ita loquimur, ut Pascha propinquante dicamus crastinam vel perendinam Domini passionem, cum ille ante tam multos annos passus sit, nec omnino nisi semel illa passio facta sit.—Nonne semel immolatus est Christus in se ipso, et tamen in sacramento non solum per omnes Paschae solemnitates, sed omni die populis immolatur, nec utique mentitur, qui interrogatus eum responderit immolari? Si enim sacramenta quandam similitudinem earum rerum, quarum sacramenta sunt, non haberent, omnino sacramenta non essent. Ex hac autem similitudine plerumque etiam ipsarum rerum nomina accipiunt. Sicut ergo secundum quendam modum sacramentum corporis Christi corpus Christi est, sacramentum sanguinis Christi sanguis Christi est, ita sacramentum fidei fides est. Contra Adimantum Manich c. 12: Non enim Dominus dubitavit dicere hoc est corpus meum, cum signum daret corporis sui. Ad Ps. iii: Figuram corporis et sanguinis sui, in Joan. tract. xxvi. 18: Qui non manet in Christo, et in quo non manet Christus, procul dubio nec manducat carnem ejus, nec bibit ejus sanguinem, etiamsi tantae rei sacramentum ad judicium sibi manducet et bibat (so all MSS. The editions have interpolations). Cf. contra Faustum, xx. c. 18 and 21. De Doctrina christiana, iii. 16. A fragment in Fulgentius in Bibl. max. PP. t. ix. p. 177, s. While the Catholic theologians endeavor to explain away these passages by a forced interpretation, P. de Marca, in his Traité du sacrament de l'Eucharistie (published after his death by his relative, the abbot Paul Faget, Paris, 1668, and though suppressed soon, reprinted in the Netherlands), can-

was looked upon in the light of a sacrifice,[16] the idea was naturally suggested, that God could be propitiated by it, and in this way it was even already abused, and that frequently, by superstition.[17] The Agapae had been, for a considerable time past, in most countries separated from the Supper,[18] and converted

didly acknowledged that the fathers, to Chrysostom, and particularly Augustine, did not teach the doctrine of transubstantiation. Very clear passages on this subject are furnished by the polemical demonstrations against Eutyches and the Monophysites, so far as they had been always accustomed to compare the union of the earthly with the heavenly in the Supper, with the incarnation of Christ, and now borrowed a proof from the rite in favor of the fact, that the human nature in Christ did not cease to exist after the union. So Theodoreti Eranistes, Dial. ii. (ed. Schulze, t. iv. p. 126): *Οὐδὲ μετὰ τὸν ἁγιασμὸν τὰ μυστικὰ σύμβολα τῆς οἰκειας ἐξίσταται φύσεως· μένει γὰρ ἐπὶ τῆς προτέρας οὐσίας καὶ τοῦ σχήματος, καὶ τοῦ εἴδους·—νοεῖται δὲ ἅπερ ἐγένετο, καὶ πιστεύεται καὶ προσκυνεῖται, ὡς ἐκεῖνα ὄντα ἅπερ πιστεύεται.* First to this controversy is to be assigned Chrysostom's Epis. ad Caesarium, although even Leontius Hierosolym. (or Byzantium, about 600) in Maji Scriptt. vett. coll. vii. i. 130, 135, Joannes Damasc., and others, cite this letter as belonging to Chrysostom. The same is preserved in Latin, in a codex Florentinus, and was first discovered and employed by Peter Martyr. The first edition by Bigot (appended to Palladii vita Chrysostom, see above, § 85, note 6), was torn out of the copies by royal command (see Chaufepié and Bayle, in their Dictionnaires, art. Bigot). The second edition appeared, according to a copy of Scipio Maffei, with Greek fragments, in Canisii Lectt. ant ed. Basnage, i. 235. Comp. especially Salig de Eutychianismo ante Eutychen, p. 367. In this letter it is said: Antequam sanctificetur panis, panem nominamus, divina autem illum sanctificante gratia, mediante sacerdote, liberatus est quidem appellatione panis, dignus autem habitus est dominici corporis appellatione, etiamsi natura panis in ipso permansit. Comp. R. Hospiniani Historia sacramentaria (t. ii. Tiguri. 1602. Genev. 1681. fol.). J. A. Ernesti Antimuratorius, 1755 (Opusc. theol. p. 1). Münscher, iv. 377. Wundemann, ii. 419. How value was still attributed to the fact, that the laity also received the cup, may be seen from Leo I. Sermo iv. de Quadrages. (§ 86, note 6). Chrysostom. in Epist. ii. ad Cor. Hom. 18: *Ἔστι δὲ ὅπου οὐδὲ διέστηκεν ὁ ἱερεὺς τοῦ ἀρχομένου, οἷον ὅταν ἀπολαύειν δέῃ τῶν φρικτῶν μυστηρίων· ὁμοίως γὰρ πάντες ἀξιούμεθα τῶν αὐτῶν· οὐ καθάπερ ἐπὶ τῆς παλαιᾶς τὰ μὲν ὁ ἱερεὺς ἤσθιε, τὰ δὲ ὁ ἀρχόμενος, καὶ θέμις οὐκ ἦν τῷ λαῷ μετέχειν, ὧν μετεῖχεν ὁ ἱερεύς· ἀλλ' οὐ νῦν· ἀλλὰ πᾶσιν ἓν σῶμα πρόκειται, καὶ ποτήριον ἕν.*

[16] How far, see Münscher, iv. 400. Wundemann, ii. 441. Neander's K. G. ii. ii. 707.

[17] Especially as the bread was often taken home (in Egypt universally, see Basilii Ep. 93, ad Caesarium). Thus Satyrus, brother of Ambrose, during a shipwreck, took the holy bread, ligari fecit in orario, et orarium involvit collo, utque ita se dejecit in mare:—his se tectum atque munitum satis credens, alia auxilia non desideravit (Ambrosius de Obitu fratris sui Satyri, c. 13): A certain Acatius (August. Opus imp. contra Julian. iii. c. 162), related to Augustine that he had been born blind, and a surgeon was about to perform an operation for him, neque hoc permisisse religiosam matrem suam, sed id effecisse impositio ex Eucharistia cataplasmate. Comp. Gregor. Naz. Orat. xi. in laudem Gorgoniae, p. 186, s. Epist. 240. Comp. Münscher, iv. 403. Wundemann, ii. 446. Neander, ii. ii. 705. In like manner the heathen, cf. Etym. Magn.: *Ὑγίειαν καλοῦσιν Ἀττικοὶ τὰ πεφυραμένα οἴνῳ καὶ ἐλαίῳ ἄλφιτα καὶ πᾶν ὅ,τι ἐξ ἱεροῦ φέρεται, οἷον θαλλόν τινα ἢ ἄλειμα.* Simplicius (about 530) Comm. ad Epictet. c. 38, ed. Schweigh. p. 351: *Τὰ προσαγόμενα καὶ ἀνατιθέμενα—μεταλαμβάνει καὶ αὐτὰ τῆς θείας ἀγαθότητος, ὡς καὶ θείας ἐνεργείας ἐπιδείκνυσθαι. καὶ γὰρ ἐπιληψίας τις ὡμολόγησεν ἀπηλλάχθαι καὶ τῆς τῶν τοιούτων μεταλήψεως, καὶ χαλάζας καὶ θαλάσσης κλύδωνας ἔπαυσε.* Cf. Lobeck Aglaophamus, i. p. 766, ss.

[18] As it was now an ecclesiastical law that the Lord's Supper should be taken fasting,

into entertainments which families prepared on the death of relatives, churches on the anniversaries of martyrs, and at which clergy and poor were regular guests.[19] But because the heathen notions of the people found in them the reappearance of their Parentalia and sacrificial festivals, drunkenness soon pervaded them.[20] Hence they began to be discountenanced and opposed,

so it was also believed that even in the time of the Apostles the agapae were observed after the Supper. Chrysost. Hom. xxvii. in 1 Cor. (on xi. 27); Pelagius in 1 Cor. xi. 20; Theodoret. in 1 Cor. xi. 16.—Remains of the old custom were still found in several parts of Egypt, in which the Lord's Supper was observed on the Sabbath, after the evening meal, Socrates, v. 22; Sozom. vii. 19; and in the African mode to celebrate the Supper after the evening meal on the Thursday before Easter. Conc. Carthag. iii. ann. 397, c. 29: Ut sacramenta altaris nonnisi a jejunis hominibus celebrentur, excepto uno die anniversario, quo coena domini celebratur. Cf. Augustin. Ep. 54, ad Januarium, c. 9.

[19] Comment. in Job (among the works of Origen, belonging to the fourth century), lib. iii. p. 437: Celebramus (diem mortis) religiosos cum sacerdotibus convocantes, fideles una cum clero, invitantes adhuc egenos et pauperes, pupillos et viduas saturantes, ut fiat festivitas nostra in memoriam requiei defunctis animabus, quarum memoriam celebramus, nobis autem efficiatur in odorem suavitatis in conspectu aeterni Dei. Augustini Ep. xxii. ad Aurelium, c. 6: Istae in coemeteriis ebrietates et luxuriosa convivia non solum honores martyrum a carnali et imperita plebe credi solent, sed etiam solatia mortuorum. Id. contra Faustum, xx. 20: Agapes nostrae pauperes pascunt sive frugibus, sive carnibus—plerumque in agapibus etiam carnes pauperibus erogantur. Theodoret. Graec. affect. curat. disp. viii. (ed. Schulze, iv. 923): Ἀντὶ τῶν Πανδίων καὶ Διασίων καὶ Διονυσίων καὶ τῶν ἄλλων ὑμῶν ἑορτῶν, Πέτρου καὶ Παύλου—καὶ Ἀντωνίνου καὶ Μαυρικίου καὶ τῶν ἄλλων μαρτύρων ἐπιτελοῦνται δημοθοινίαι· καὶ ἀντὶ τῆς πάλαι πομπείας καὶ αἰσχρουργίας—σώφρονες ἑορτάζονται πανηγύρεις, οὐ μέθην ἔχουσαι, καὶ κῶμων, καὶ γέλωτα, ἀλλ' ὕμνους θείους, καὶ ἱερῶν λογίων ἀκρόασιν, καὶ προσευχὴν ἀξιεπαίνοις κοσμουμένην δακρύοις. Juliani Imp. fragm. (ed. Spanhem. p. 305): Ὥσπερ οἱ τὰ παιδία διὰ τοῦ πλακοῦντος ἐξαπατῶντες—πείθουσιν ἀκολουθεῖν ἑαυτοῖς—τὸν αὐτὸν καὶ αὐτοὶ πρόπον ἀρξάμενοι (οἱ δυσσεβεῖς Γαλιλαῖοι) διὰ τῆς λεγομένης παρ' αὐτοῖς ἀγάπης καὶ ὑποδοχῆς καὶ διακονίας τραπεζῶν—πιστοὺς ἐπήγαγον εἰς τὴν ἀθεότητα. The use of these Agapae was defended by the council of Gangra against the darker asceticism of the Eustathians. Can. 11: Εἴ τις καταφρονοίη τῶν ἐκ πίστεως ἀγάπας ποιούντων καὶ διὰ τιμὴν τοῦ κυρίου συγκαλούντων τοὺς ἀδελφοὺς, καὶ μὴ ἐθέλοι κοινωνεῖν ταῖς κλήσεσι, διὰ τὸ ἐξευτελίζειν τὸ γινόμενον, ἀνάθεμα ἔστω.

[20] Even teachers of the church compared them with those heathen festivities. See Theodoret, note 19. Chrysostom (Hom. xlvii. in S. Julianum) advises his hearers to partake of the meal to be appointed in honor of the martyr beside his church (τοῦ μαρτυρίου πλησίον ὑπὸ συκὴν ἢ ἄμπελον), instead of joining in the heathen feasts in Daphne, a suburb of Antioch. Hence some even supposed that they had been appointed by their ancestors as a substitute for those heathen banquets. See Gregorius Nyss. in vita Gregor. Thaumat. Div. I. § 70, note 9. So also Augustine explains the origin of them to his church (Ep. xxix. ad Alypium, c. 9): Post persecutiones—cum facta pace turbae gentilium in christianum nomen venire cupientes hoc impedirentur, quod dies festos cum idolis suis solerent in abundantia epularum et ebrietate consumere, nec facile ab his—voluptatibus se possent abstinere, visum fuisse majoribus nostris, ut huic infirmitatis parti interim parceretur, diesque festi post eos quos relinquebant alii in honorem SS. Martyrum vel non simili sacreligio, quamvis simili luxu celebrarentur. On the drunkenness at these meals, Ambrosius de Elia et Jejunio, c. 17: Calices ad sepulchra Martyrum deferunt, atque illic ad vesperam bibunt, et aliter se exaudiri posse non credunt. Augustin Ep. 22, ad Aurelium, c. 3: Comessationes et ebrietates ita concessae et licita putantur, ut in honorem etiam

and even banished from the Church where it could be done without offense, while the clergy were forbidden to take part in them.[21] Thus these festivals ceased in most countries, though in some they still continued beyond the present period.[22]

beatissimorum Martyrum non solum per dies solemnes, sed etiam quotidie celebrentur. Gregorius Naz. Carm. ccxvii. thus addresses those who took part in such feasts:

Νῦν δὲ τί τάρβος ἔχει με, ἀκούσατε ὦ φιλόκωμοι,
Πρὸς τοὺς δαιμονικοὺς αὐτομολεῖτε τύπους.

On the festivals of the martyrs, traders sold in the sanctuary that which was necessary for the feasts, Basilii M. regula major, qu. xl.: Ἀλλ' οὐδὲ τὰς ἐν τοῖς μαρτυρίοις γινομένας ἀγορασίας οἰκείας ἡμῖν ὁ λόγος δείκνυσιν (he then mentions how Christ drove the sellers out of the temple). Paulinus Nol. nat. S. Felicis ix.: Divendant vina tabernis. Sancta precum domus est Ecclesia. Thus the Manichaean Faustus, not without reason, reproached the Catholics (Augustin. contra Faust. xx. 4): Sacrificia eorum (gentilium) vertistis in agapas, idola in Martyres, quos votis similibus colitis: defunctorum umbras vino placatis et dapibus.

21 In the east, the Laodicean council enacted (probably 363) can. 28: Ὅτι οὐ δεῖ ἐν τοῖς κυριακοῖς ἢ ἐν ταῖς ἐκκλησίας τὰς λεγομένας ἀγάπας ποιεῖν, καὶ ἐν τῷ οἴκῳ τοῦ θεοῦ ἐσθίειν καὶ ἀκούβιτα στρωννύειν. Accordingly they were, even in Antioch, celebrated beside the places dedicated to the martyrs. See Chrysostom, note 20. About 392 they were no longer observed in the greatest part of the west out of Africa. See Augustini Ep. xxii. ad Aurelium, c. 4: Per Italiae maximam partem, et in aliis omnibus aut prope omnibus transmarinis Ecclesiis partim nunquam facta sunt, partim vel orta vel inveterata—Episcoporum diligentia et animadversione exstincta atque deleta sunt. In Milan, Ambrose had forbidden them (Augustin. Confess. vi. 2, ne ulla occasio se ingurgitandi daretur ebriosis, et quia illa quasi parentalia superstitioni gentilium essent simillima). In Rome, Alethius, at the funeral of his wife, entertained all the poor in the basilica S. Petri (Paulinus Nol. Ep. 33); Pammachius on the contrary gave rich alms on a similar occasion (Hieron. Ep. 26, ad Pammach. c. 2). In Nola they kept vigils on the festival of the birth of St. Felix, while all the night through they ate and drank in the church of the saint. Paulinus, since he could not abrogate this practice, endeavored by means of pictures which he brought into the church to give a more serious direction to the joy (Paulini nat. Felicis ix. Compare above § 99, note 47). In Africa, where those festivals were universal (August. de Moribus eccl. cath. i. 34): Novi—multos esse qui luxuriosissime super mortuos bibant, et epulas cadaveribus exhibentes, super sepultos se ipsos sepeliant, et voracitates ebrietatesque suas deputent religioni. Augustine used his influence against them. He first of all motioned for their abolition from Aurelius, bishop of Carthage, in the Epist. xxii. ad Aurelium, cf. c. 6: Mihi videtur facilius illic dissuaderi posse istam foeditatem,—si—oblationis pro spiritibus dormientium, quas vere aliquid adjuvare credendum est, super ipsas memorias non sint sumtuosae, atque omnibus petentibus sine typho et cum alacritate praebeantur: neque vendantur (that is, when that which was intended to serve as oblations is not offered for sale there), sed si quis pro religioni aliquid pecuniae offerre voluerit, in praesenti pauperibus eroget. Afterward he effected their abrogation in Hippo; in what way is related by him Ep. xxix. ad Alypium, in the year 395. Finally it was enacted by the Conc. Carthag. iii. ann. 397, c. 30: Ut nulli Episcopi vel Clerici in Ecclesia conviventur, nisi forte transeuntes hospitiorium necessitate illic reficiantur: populi etiam ab hujusmodi conviviis quantum fieri potest prohibeantur.

22 In Syria they are mentioned at a time so late as that of Theodoret, without blame, see note 19, and Theodoret's Hist. eccles. iii. 11, where he relates how the martyrs, Juventinus and Maximinus in Antioch, were honored, μέχρι δὲ τήμερον ἐτησίῳ δημοθοινίᾳ γεραίρονται.—The council Quinisextum, A.D. 692, repeats can. 74 of the can. Laodic. 28 (see note 21).—L. A. Muratori de Agapis sublatis, in his Anecd. graeca. Patav. 1709. 4. p. 241. Bingham, vol. vi. p. 516, ix. 147, x. 69. Drescher de Agapis comm. Giessae, 1824. p. 39.

SIXTH CHAPTER.

HISTORY OF MORALS.

§ 102.

HISTORY OF CHRISTIAN ETHICS.[1]

Stäudlin's Gesch. d. Sittenlehre Jesu, Bd. 3.—De Wette Gesch. d. christl. Sittenlehre. Erste Hälfte, S. 334, ss.

The disposition already manifested in the preceding period to lay too much stress on certain forms of external discipline, had now been much increased by the influence of monachism. Fasting and almsgiving,[2] as well as prayer, were regarded as expiatory of sins. The theater, dancing, and other amusements,[3] were branded as absolutely sinful; oaths,[4] the taking of interest for money lent,[5] every kind of self-defense,[6] capital punishments,[7] and second marriages,[8] were rejected. In the fourth century,

[1] There is an old controversy concerning the morals of the fathers occasioned by the unfavorable view taken of them by J. Barbeyrac in the preface to the translation of Puffendorf: le Droit de la Nature et des Gens. Amst. 1712. 4. On the other side, Remig. Ceiller Apologie de la morale des pères de l'église contre J. Barb. Paris. 1718. 4. J. F. Buddeus Isag. ad univers theolog. p. 620. Replied to by Barbeyrac Traitè de la morale des pères de l'église. Amst. 1728. 4.

[2] Münscher's Dogmengesch. iv. 314, de Wette, i. 354. Ambrosius de Elia et Jejuno, c. 20: Pecuniam habes, redime peccatum tuum. Non venalis est Dominus, sed tu ipse venalis es: redime te operibus tuis, redime te pecunia tua. Vilis pecunia, sed pretiosa est misericordia (according to Dan. iv. 24: Peccata tua eleemosynis redime et iniquitates tuas misericordiis pauperum). Salvianus (about 450) adv. Avaritiam libb. iv. expressly makes generosity to churches and convents the surest redemtio peccatorum.

[3] De Wette, i. 349. Stäudlin's Gesch. d. Vorstellungen, v. d. Sittlichkeit des Schauspiels. Gött. 1823.

[4] Jerome, Basil, especially Chrysostom. See Stäudlin's Gesch. d. Sittenlehre Jesu, iii. 111, 220, 244, same author's Gesch. der Vorstellungen und Lehren vom Eide. Gött. 1824. Hence the Lex Marciani, A.D. 456 (Cod. Justin. i. 3, 25): ecclesiasticis regulis, et canone a beatissimis Episcopis antiquitus instituto, clerici jurare prohibentur.

[5] Basilius M. in Ps. xiv. et contra foeneratores. Gregor. Nyss. ep. can. ad Letojum can. 6. Ambrosius de Tobia, c. 2, ss.

[6] Ambrosius, Augustinus, Basilius, see Stäudlin's Gesch. der Sittenlehre Jesu, iii. 65, 149, 219.

[7] Ambrosius Ep. 25 and 26 (al. 51 and 52). Augustin. Ep. 153, ad Macedonium.

[8] Forbidden by Ambrose and Jerome, disadvised by Chrysostom, only made second to a state of widowhood by Augustine, cf. Cotelerius ad Hermae Pastor. lib. ii. Mand. 4. c.

indeed, those who had been legally divorced were still universally allowed to marry again,[9] though this was discouraged as well as second marriages generally; but in the fifth century, the Latin church began to forbid the divorced person to marry as long as the other party lived.[10] So prevalent was now the spirit of monachism, that the married state began to be considered as something impure,[11] and only a tolerated evil.[12] Even certain kinds of food were forbidden.[13]

By means of such excrescences, whose foundations could not be shown in the moral consciousness of mankind, Christian

4, and in Constit. apost. iii. 2. Stäudlin, iii. 60, 92, 141, 146. Hence penances were imposed on those who married twice. Conc. Neocaesar. can. 1, 3; Laodic. can. 1; Basilii Epist. 188 (Ep. can. 1), can. 4. Comp. Ep. can. ii. c. 50, respecting those who married three times, and Ep. can. iii. c. 80, respecting those who married more than three times.

[9] Ambrosiaster in 1 Cor. vii. 15: Si infidelis discesserit, liberum habebit arbitrium, si voluerit, nubere legis suae viro. Contumelia enim creatoris solvit jus matrimonii circa eum, qui relinquitur, etc. Epiphan. Haer. 59, § 4: Ὁ δὲ μὴ δυνηθεὶς τῇ μιᾷ ἀρκεσθῆναι τελευτησάσῃ, [ἢ] ἕνεκέν τινος προφάσεως, πορνείας ἢ μοιχείας, ἢ κακῆς αἰτίας χωρισμοῦ γενομένου, συναφθέντα δευτέρᾳ γυναικὶ ἢ γυνὴ δευτέρῳ ἀνδρὶ, οὐκ αἰτιᾶται ὁ θεῖος λόγος, οὐδὲ ἀπὸ τῆς ἐκκλησίας καὶ τῆς ζωῆς ἀποκηρύττει, ἀλλὰ διαβαστάζει διὰ τὸ ἀσθενὲς, οὐχ ἵνα δύο γυναῖκας ἐπὶ τὸ αὐτὸ σχῇ ἔτι περιούσης τῆς μιᾶς, ἀλλ' ἀπὸ μιᾶς ἀποσχεθεὶς δευτέρᾳ, εἰ τύχοιεν, νόμῳ συναφθῆναι. Cf. Asterius, below, § 105, note 18. Bingham, vol. ix. p. 301, ss. 349, ss.

[10] The transition to this view may be traced in Augustinus de Fide et Opere, c. 19: In ipsis divinis sententiis ita obscurum est, utrum et iste cui quidem sine dubio adulteram licet dimittere, adulter tamen habeatur, si alteram duxerit, ut, quantum existimo, venialiter ibi quisque fallatur. Still the Conc. Milevitanum, ii. ann. 416, at which also Augustine was present resolved, quite unanimously, can. 17: Placuit, ut secundum evangelicam et apostolicam disciplinam, neque dimissus ab uxore neque dimissa a marito, alteri conjugantur: sed ita maneant, aut sibimet reconcilientur. Quod si contempserint, ad poenitentiam redigantur. In qua causa legem imperialem petendam promulgari. Such too was the opinion of Innocentius I. Epist. 6, ad Exsuperium, c. 6: De his etiam requisivit dilectio tua, qui interveniente repudio alii se matrimonio copularunt. Quos in utraque parte adulteros esse manifestum est, etc.

[11] As Origen. See Div. I. § 73, note 12. Hence Conc. Carthag. iv. c. 13, enacts that the newly-married pair, cum benedictionem acceperint, eadem nocte pro reverentia ipsius benedictionis in virginitate permaneant.

[12] Hieronymus adv. Jovinian. i. 4, with reference to 1 Cor. vii. 1: Si bonum est mulierem non tangere, malum est ergo tangere: nihil enim bono contrarium est nisi malum. Si autem malum est, et ignoscitur; ideo conceditur, ne malo quid deterius fiat.—Oro, te quale illud bonum est, quod orare prohibet? quod corpus Christi accipi non permittit? Quamdiu impleo mariti officium, non impleo Christiani. Yet he was obliged in the Epist. 30 (al. 50) ad Pammachium, pro libris adv. Jovinianum apologia to make some concession. Among other things he writes: Cum toties et tam crebro lectorem admonuerim,—me ita recipere nuptias, continentes viduas virginesque praeferrem: debuerat prudens et benignus lector etiam, ea, quae, videntur dura, aestimare de caeteris, etc. Augustine is more moderate in the work called forth by this very controversy between Jovinian and Jerome, de Bono conjugali. Among other things, he writes. c. 8: Duo bona sunt connubium et continentia, quorum alterum est melius. Cap. 10: Certe dubitare fas non est, nuptias non esse peccatum. Non itaque nuptias secundum veniam concedit Apostolus (1 Cor. vii. 6).

[13] Against the use of flesh and wine Hieronymus adv. Jovinian. lib. ii.

morals now assumed the aspect of a series of arbitrary, divine, despotic commands.[14] And since those rigorous principles were not at all observed by most people, they promoted the spirit of indifference toward the divine precepts generally, and prepared the way for the unfortunate distinction between a higher virtue, which was solely for the monks, and a lower, which was sufficient for common Christians.[15]

It seems at first sight contradictory to this external strictness, yet it is in fact intimately connected with it, that most of the church fathers of this period maintained, in addition to that apparent moral severity,[16] lax principles concerning veracity, which threatened the very foundations of genuine virtue.[17]

§ 103.

MORALS OF THE CLERGY.

As ecclesiastical offices were no longer attended with dangers and persecutions, but with honor and power, there was a general

14 Comp. de Wette, i. 340. 15 Münscher's Dogmengesch. iv. 311; de Wette, i. 346.

16 See Div. I. § 63, note 7.

17 Ex. gr. Hieronymus Epist. 30 (al. 50), ad Pammachium: Aliud esse γυμναστικῶς scribere, aliud δογματικῶς. In priori vagam esse disputationem, et adversario respondentem nunc haec nunc illa proponere, argumentari ut libet, aliud loqui, aliud agere, panem, ut dicitur, ostendere, lapidem tenere. In sequenti autem aperta frons, et ut ita dicam, ingenuitas necessaria est, etc. In particular they stretched the limits of allowed accommodation quite too far (οἰκονομία), and believed that they could attribute it in the same extent even to Jesus and the apostles. Comp. Suicer, s. v. συγκατάβασις, ii. 1067. Münscher's Dogmengesch. iv. 154, s. Jahn's Nachträge zu s. theolog. Werken. Tübingen. 1821. S. 15, ss. 28, ss. In this way Jerome Comm. ad Gal. ii. 11, ss., thought that he could explain the transaction between Peter and Paul by a mere accommodation, but was opposed by Augustine who held stricter principles. (Comp. his writings de Mendacio and contra Mendacium.) Comp. the correspondence between them on this subject in Epistt. Hieron. Ep. 65, 67–73, 76; see Jahn, l. c. p. 31, ff. Even Chrysostom lays down very questionable principles respecting the allowableness of deception and lying, in certain cases. In this he is followed by his disciple John Cassian, Coll. xvii. 8, ss. ex. gr. cap. 17: Itaque taliter de mendacio sentiendum, atque ita eo utendum est, quasi natura ei insit hellebori. Quodsi imminente exitiali morbo sumtum fuerit, fit salubre: caeterum absque summi discriminis necessitate perceptum praesentis exitii est.—Non enim Deus verborum tantum actuumque nostrorum discussor et judex, sed etiam propositi ac destinationis inspector est. Qui si aliquid causa salutis aeternae ac divinae contemplationis intuitu ab unoquoque vel factum viderit vel promissum, tametsi hominibus durum atque iniquum esse videatur; ille tamen intimam cordis inspiciens pietatem, non verborum sonum, sed votum dijudicat voluntatis quia finis operis et affectus considerandus est perpetrantis: quo potuerunt quidam, ut supra dictum est, etiam per mendacium justificari (for example, Rahab, Josh. ii.), et alii per veritatis assertionem peccatum perpetuae mortis incurrere (Delilah, Judg. xvi.).

pressing toward them:[1] all the arts of unworthy flattery and low intrigue were put in requisition to obtain them, and to rise from a lower to a higher station.[2] In this way not merely the unprepared, but even many absolutely immoral pushed themselves into the clerical office;[3] an objectionable, worldly spirit pervaded the whole order, which frequently perverted what was holy to its own purposes;[4] and since that monkish morality re-

[1] Comp. above, § 91, note 15. Cf. Gregorius Naz. below, note 4.

[2] Gregor. Naz. Orat. xliii. (al. xx.) in laudem Basilii, c. 26 (ed. Colon. p. 335): Νῦν δὲ κινδυνεύει τὸ πάντων ἁγιώτατον τάγμα τῶν παρ' ἡμῖν παντῶν εἶναι καταγελαστότατον· οὐ γὰρ ἐξ ἀρετῆς μᾶλλον, ἢ κακουργίας ἡ προεδρία· οὐδὲ τῶν ἀξιωτέρων, ἀλλὰ τῶν δυνατωτέρων οἱ θρόνοι. Ullmann's Gregor. v. Naz. S. 511, ss. Conc. Sardic. c. 1 and 2, against the striving of the bishops for better and richer bishoprics. Basilius Ep. 76, ad Episcopos suos, against simony in the choice of bishops. Can. Chalced. 2, and Can. Apost. 30, against simony generally.

[3] Hieron. in Ep. ad Titum i. 8 (Opp. iv. p. 417): Vere nunc est cernere—in plerisque urbibus, Episcopos, sive Presbyteros, si laïcos viderint hospitales, amatores bonorum, invidere, fremere, excommunicare, de Ecclesia expellere, quasi non liceat facere quod Episcopus non faciat; et tales esse laïcos damnatio Sacerdotum sit. The Can. Apost. 26, 64, 71, are directed against roughnesses and common offenses in the clergy, which, in fact, must have occurred at this time, See Drey Apost. Constitut. S. 339, 344.

[4] Comp. Hieronymus Ep. 34 (al. 2), ad Nepotianum, concerning the law of Valentinian against underhand dealing with inheritances, given above, § 91, note 14. He then continues: Ignominia omnium Sacerdotum est, propriis studere divitiis. Natus in paupere domo, et in tugurio rusticano, qui vix milio et cibario pane rugientem saturare ventrem poteram, nunc similam et mella fastidio. Novi et genera et nomina piscium, in quo littore concha lecta sit calleo: saporibus avium discerno provincias; et ciborum preciosorum me raritas, ac novissime damna ipsa delectant. Audio praeterea in senes et anus absque liberis quorumdam turpe servitium. Ipsi apponunt matulam, obsident lectum, purulentiam stomachi et phlegmata pulmonis manu propria suscipiunt. Pavent ad introitum medici, trementibusque labiis, an commodius habeant, sciscitantur: et si paululum senex vegetior fuerit, periclitantur: simulataque laetitia, mens intrinsecus avara torquetur. He describes the life of rich widows, Ep. 18 (al. 22), ad Eustochium: Plena adulatoribus domus, plena conviviis. Clerici ipsi, quos in magisterio esse oportuerat doctrinae pariter et timoris, osculantur capita matronarum, et extenta manu, ut benedicere eos putes velle, si nescias, pretia accipiunt salutandi. In an oration of that time, which is found among the sermons of Ambrose (Sermo in dominicam xxii. post Pentecosten, and of Augustine (tom. v. app. Sermo 82), it is said on Luke iii. 14: Si (clericus) non contentus stipendiis fuerit, quae de altario, Domino jubente, consequitur; sed exercet mercimonia, intercessiones vendit, viduarum munera libenter amplectitur: hic negotiator magis potest videri, quam clericus. Gregorii Naz. Carmen de se ipso et adv. Episcopos, v. 331, ss. (in J. Tollii Insignia itineris Italici. Traj. ad Rhen. 1696. 4. p. 34, ss.):

331. Ἄγνοια γὰρ κακὸν μὲν, ἀλλ' ἧσσον κακόν.
Τί δ' ἂν τις εἴποι καὶ κακῶν μεμνημένος;
Εἰσὶν γὰρ, εἰσὶν ἀθλιώτεροί τινες,
Δύστην', ἀπευκτὰ τοῦ βίου κυβεύματα,
Τὴν πίστιν ἀμφιδέξιοι, καιρῶν νόμους,
Οὐ τοὺς θεοῦ σέβοντες, εὔριποι λόγων
Παλιῤῥοοῦντες, ἢ κλάδων μετακλίσεις,
Θῶπες γυναικῶν, τερπνὰ δηλητήρια,
Μικροῖς λέοντες, τοῖς κρατοῦσι δ' αὖ κύνες,
Πάσης τραπέζης εὐφυεῖς ἰχνεύμονες,

quired of the clergy many external things to keep up the appearance of spirituality, low hypocrisy pervaded the clerical

341. Θύρας κρατούντων ἐκτρίβοντες, οὐ σοφῶν.....
361. Αἰσχρὸν μὲν εἰπεῖν, ὡς ἔχει, φράσω δ' ὅμως.
Ταχθέντες εἶναι τοῦ καλοῦ διδάσκαλοι,
Κακῶν ἁπάντων ἐσμὲν ἐργαστήριον·
Σιγῇ βοῶντες, κἂν δοκῶμεν μὴ λέγειν·
Πρόεδρος ἡ κακία, πονείτω μηδὲ εἷς·
Κακὸν γίνεσθαι, τοῦτο συντομώτατον,
367. Καὶ λῷον.....
375. Ἡμεῖς δὲ πάντας ῥᾳδίως καθίζομεν,
Ἐὰν μόνον θέλωσι, λαοῦ προστάτας,
Οὐδὲν σκοποῦντες τῶν νέων, ἢ τῶν πάλαι,
378. Οὐ πρᾶξιν, οὐ λόγον τιν' οὐ συνουσίαν.....
382. Εἰ γὰρ τόδ' ἴσμεν, ὡς τὸν ἐξειλεγμένον
Χείρω τίθησιν ὡς τὰ πολλ' ἐξουσία.
384. Τίς ἂν προβάλοιτ' εὖ φρονῶν, ὃν ἀγνοεῖ;....
393. Ὁ δὲ πρόεδρος ῥᾳδίως εὑρίσκεται,
Μηδὲν πονηθεὶς, πρόσφατος τὴν ἀξίαν.
395. Ὦ τῆς ταχείας τῶν τρόπων μεταστροφῆς!
402. Χθὲς ἦσθα μίμων καὶ θεάτρων ἐν μέσῳ,
(Τὰ δ' ἐκ θεάτρων ἄλλος ἐξεταζέτω)
Νῦν αὐτὸς ἡμῖν εἶ ξένη θεωρία.
Πρώην Φίλιππος, καὶ θεῷ πέμπων κόνιν,
406. Ὡς ἄλλος εὐχὰς, ἢ νοήματ' εὐσεβῆ.....
411. Νῦν εὐσταλής τις, καὶ βλέπων αἰδῶ μόνην,
412. Πλὴν εἰ λαθών που πρὸς ἀρχαῖον δράμοις.....
415. Χθὲς ῥητορεύων τὰς δίκας ἀπημπόλεις,
416. Στρέφων ἄνω τε καὶ κάτω τὰ τῶν νόμων.....
419. Νῦν μοι δικαστὴς, καὶ Δανιήλ τις ἀθρόως.
Χθές μοι δικάζων σὺν ξίφει γυμνουμένῳ
Τὸ βῆμ' ἐποίεις ἔννομον λῃστήριον,
Κλέπτων, τυραννῶν, καὶ πρὸ πάντων τοὺς νόμους.
Ὡς ἥμερός μοι σήμερον! οὐδ' ἐσθῆτά τις
Οὕτως ἀμείβει ῥᾳδίως, ὡς σὺ τρόπον·
Χθὲς ἐν χορευταῖς ἐστρέφου θηλυδρίαις,
Γάμων δὲ κήρυξ ἦσθα Λυδαῖς ἐν μέσαις,
Ὠιδὰς λυρίζων, καὶ ποτοῖς γαυρούμενος.
Νῦν σωφρονιστὴς παρθένων καὶ συζύγων.
Ὡς σου τὸ καλὸν ὕποπτον ἐκ τοῦ πρὶν τρόπου!
Σίμων μάγος χθὲς, σήμερον Πέτρος Σίμων!
431. Φεῦ τοῦ τάχους! φεῦ, ἀντ' ἀλώπεκος λέων!

The remark is worthy of attention, v. 382, s. comp. v. 634, ss.:

Οὗτοι μέν οὕτως· καὶ τάχ' ἂν καὶ βελτίους
Αὐτῶν γενόμενοι κωλύονται τοῖς θρόνοις.
Τὸ γὰρ κρατεῖν τὸν ἄφρανα ποιεῖ χείρονα.

Gregorii Naz. Orat. ii. (al. 1) Apologeticus de fuga sua (ed. Col. p. 4, s.): Ὅσοι μηδεν τῶν πολλῶν ὄντες βελτίους, μέγα μὲν οὖν εἰ καὶ μὴ πολλῷ χείρους, ἀνίπτοις χερσὶν, ὃ δὴ λέγεται, καὶ ἀμυήτοις ψυχαῖς, τοῖς ἁγιωτάτοις ἑαυτοὺς ἐπεισάγουσι, καὶ πρὶν ἄξιοι γενέσθαι προσιέναι τοῖς ἱεροῖς, μεταποιοῦνται τοῦ βήματος, θλίβονταί τε καὶ ὠθοῦνται περὶ τὴν ἁγίαν τράπεζαν, ὥσπερ οὐκ ἀρετῆς τύπον, ἀλλ' ἀφορμὴν βίου τὴν τάξιν ταύτην εἶναι νομίζοντες, οὐδὲ λειτουργίαν ὑπεύθυνον, ἀλλ' ἀρχὴν ἀνεξέταστον. Isidor. Pelus. lib. v. Ep. 21: Μεταπεπτωκέναι λοιπὸν τὸ ἀξίωμα ἔδοξεν ἀπὸ ἱερωσύνης εἰς τυραννίδα, ἀπὸ ταπεινοφροσύνης εἰς ὑπερηφανίαν, ἀπὸ νηστείας εἰς τρυφὴν, ἀπὸ οἰκονομίας εἰς δεσποτείαν. οὐ γὰρ ὡς οἰκονόμοι ἀξιοῦσι διοικεῖν, ἀλλ' ὡς δεσπόται σφετερίζεσθαι.

order.[5] This corruption of the clergy was not a little increased by the interference of the emperors with ecclesiastical disputes. While, on the one side, the clergy were always carrying their spiritual pride higher,[6] on the other, they frequently changed their opinions at the beck of the court. Synods were the theater on which this new pharisaism of the Christian clergy, along with a rough passionateness, was chiefly exhibited.[7]

[5] Especially as monachism led them to place so great value on external forms. Gregor. Naz. Carmen de se ipso, et adv. Episc. v. 647, ss., thus describes the spiritual hypocrite:

647. Ἔπειτα χαλκὸς χρυσὸν ἠμφιεσμένος,
Ἢ καὶ χαμαιλέοντος ἔκστασις χρόας,
Πώγων, κατηφὲς ἦθος, αὐχένος κλάσις,
Φωνὴ βραχεῖα, πιστὸς ἐσκευασμένος,
651. Νωθρὸν βάδισμα, πάντα, πλὴν φρενὸς, σοφός.
696. Αἰσχρῶν μὲν οὖν αἴσχιστον ἡ τρόπου πλάσις.

Thus it became the custom, especially in consequence of the example of the monks (see Bingham, vol. ii. p. 189, ss.), seemingly to decline receiving ecclesiastical honors when presented. Cf. lex Leonis, A.D. 469 (Cod. Justin. i. 3, 31): Nemo gradum sacerdotii pretii venalitate mercetur:—Cesset altaribus imminere profanus ardor avaritiae, et a sacris adytis repellatur piaculare flagitium.—Nec pretio, sed precibus ordinetur antistes. Tantum ab ambitu debet esse sepositus, ut quaeratur cogendus, rogatus recedat, invitatus effugiat: sola illi suffragetur necessitas excusandi. Profecto enim indignus est sacerdotio, nisi fuerit ordinatus invitus. This priestly decorum led of course, very frequently, merely to a mock reluctance and hesitation. Cf. Gregorius Naz. Orat. xvii. de se ipso, p. 466: Οὐ γὰρ ἵνα ζητηθῶμεν ἀποκρυπτόμεθα· οὐδ' ἵνα πλείονος ἄξιοι δόξωμεν τιμῆς.

[6] See above, § 91, note 24.

[7] Comp. the ironical discourse of Gregory of Nazianzum, at the second oecumenical council (Carmen de vita sua, Opp. ii. 27):

.... ὅς θέλει δεῦρ' εἰσίτω,
Κἂν δίστροφός τις ἢ πολύστροφος τύχῃ·
Πανήγυρις ἕστηκεν, ἀπίτω μηδεὶς
Ἀπραγμάτευτος. ἂν μεταστραφῇ κύβος
(Καιροῦ γὰρ οὐδέν ἐστιν εὐστροφώτερον),
Ἔχεις τὸ τεχνύδριον, ἔκδραμε πάλιν·
Οὐκ εὐμαθὲς πίστει τὸ προσκεῖσθαι μιᾷ,
Βίων δὲ πολλὰς εἰδέναι διεξόδους.

Comp. Carmen de se ipso, et adv. Episc. v. 152 (ap. Tollius, p. 18), on the same council:

.... καὶ γὰρ ἦν αἶσχος μέγα,
Τούτων τιν' εἶναι τῶν καπήλων πίστεως.

In like manner he calls the bishops (Carmen de vita sua, p. 28) Χριστέμποροι. When he was invited to the synod at Constantinople, A.D. 382, he replied, Epist. 55, ad Procopium: Ἔχω μὲν οὕτως, εἰ δεῖ τἀληθὲς γράφειν, ὥστε πάντα σύλλογον φεύγειν ἐπισκόπων, ὅτι μηδεμιᾶς συνόδου τέλος εἶδον χρηστὸν, μηδὲ λύσιν κακῶν μᾶλλοι ἐσχηκυίας, ἢ προσθήκην. Αἱ γὰρ φιλονεικίαι καὶ φιλαρχίαι (ἀλλ' ὅπως μήτε φορτικὸν ὑπολάβῃς οὕτω γράφοντα) καὶ λόγου κρείττονες· καὶ θᾶττον ἄν τις ἐγκληθείη κακίαν ἑτέραν δικάζων, ἢ τῶν ἐκείνων λύσειε. Διὰ τοῦτο εἰς ἐμαυτὸν συνεστάλην, κ. τ. λ.—Carmen x. v. 92, ss. (Opp. ii. 81):

Οὐδέ τί που συνόδοισι ὁμόθρονος ἔσσομ' ἔγωγε
Χηνῶν ἢ γεράνων ἄκριτα μαρναμένων·
Ἔνθ' ἔρις, ἔνθα μόθος τε, καὶ αἴσχεα κρυπτὰ πάροιθεν
Εἰς ἕνα δυσμενέων χῶρον ἀγειρόμενα.

Comp. Ullmann's Gregor v. Naz. S. 269, s.

In the mean time, however, zeal for morality among the clergy was not rare. This zeal for morality fearlessly found fault with sin where it existed, opposed with spirit tyrannical barbarity,[8] took under its powerful protection all that needed help,[9] and left behind even permanent monuments of benevolence and concern for the public good.[10]

§ 104.

MORAL INFLUENCE OF THE CHURCH ON THE PEOPLE.

The clergy thus sinking into degeneracy were now called to solve the most difficult problem that could ever, perhaps, be presented to an order of Christian teachers. A highly cultivated people, but one sunk in unbelief and superstition of every kind, now crowded into the church,[1] impelled, for the most part, by interested motives; a people either for the most part fully devoted to paganism in their heart,[2] or apprehending Christianity from a heathen point of view,[3] and transferring into it even

[8] See § 91, note 8.

[9] See § 91, note 9.

[10] *Ξενῶνες* or *ξενοδοχεῖα, πτωχοτροφεῖα, γηροκομεῖα, νοσοκομεῖα, ὀρφανοτροφεῖα*. The institution which Basil founded in Caesarea for strangers and the sick was very large. After him it was called Βασιλειάς (Basil. Ep. 94. Gregor. Naz. Orat. 30 and 27). Basil also caused to be established smaller ones of the same kind, in the country (Basil. Ep. 142, 143). Theodoret got colonnades and bridges built, and a canal made (Theod. Ep. 81). See Neander, ii. i. 292.

[1] See above, § 75, notes 7 and 35.

[2] Chrysost. in Ep. ad Ephes. c. 3, Hom. vii. (Opp. xi. 44): *Οἱ μὲν γὰρ ὀρθῶς βιοῦντες—τὰς κορυφὰς τῶν ὀρίων κατειλήφασι, καὶ ἐκ μέσου γεγόνασιν* (the monks).—*φθόροι δὲ καὶ μυρίων γέμοντες κακῶν εἰσεπήδησαν εἰς τὰς ἐκκλησίας.—Εἴ τις κατὰ τὴν ἡμέραν τοῦ Πάσχα πάντας τοὺς προσιόντας—ἐξήτασε σὺν ἀκριβείᾳ,—πολλὰ ἂν εὑρέθη βαρύτερα τῶν Ἰουδαϊκῶν κακῶν. καὶ γὰρ οἰωνιζομένους, καὶ φαρμακείαις καὶ κληδονισμοῖς καὶ ἐπῳδαῖς κεχρημένους, καὶ πεπορνευκότας, καὶ μοιχεύσαντας, καὶ μεθύσους, καὶ λοιδόρους, εὗρεν ἄν.*

[3] P. E. Müller Comm. hist. de genio, moribus et luxu aevi Theodosiani (P. ii. Lips. 1797, 98. 8), P. i. p. 33, ss. Neander's Chrysostomus, Bd. 1, S. 236, ss. Abuse of holy things as charms. Cf. Hieronymus in Matth. xxiii. (ed. Martian. iv. p. 109: Haec in corde portanda sunt, non in corpore. Hoc apud nos superstitiosae mulierculae in parvulis Evangeliis et in crucis ligno et istiusmodi rebus usque hodie factitant. Chrysostom. ad. Pop. Antioch. Hom. xix. (t. ii. p. 197): *Αἱ γυναῖκες καὶ τὰ μικρὰ παιδία ἀντὶ φυλακῆς μεγάλης εὐαγγέλια ἐξαρτῶσι τοῦ τραχήλου, καὶ πανταχοῦ περιφέρουσιν, ὅπου περ ἂν ἀπίωσιν.* See above § 99, notes 38, 41, 50; § 101, note 17. Many of the clergy made use of and fostered this superstition. Cf. Conc. Laodic. c. 36: *Ὅτι οὐ δεῖ ἱερατικοὺς, ἢ κληρικοὺς, μάγους ἢ ἐπαοιδοὺς εἶναι, ἢ μαθηματικοὺς, ἢ ἀστρολόγους, ἢ ποιεῖν τὰ λεγόμενα φυλακτήρια.* Heineccius Abbildung der alten u. neuen griech. Kirche. Leipzig. 1711. 5. Th. 3, S. 461. Du Resnel treatise on the pagan sortes Homericae, sortes Virgilianae, etc., and the Christian sortes Sanctorum in the Mémoires de l'Acad. des Inscriptions, t. xix. p. 287, ss.

heathen customs or Jewish practices.[4] In addition to this, the new converts were demoralized by all the vices which follow in the train of over-refinement, and confirmed in them by the example of the court which had been growing more corrupt ever since its removal to the east, and by the example of the nobility.[5] Christian knowledge and Christian faith, in place of unbelief and superstition, and piety for vice, had to be infused into this spiritually dead mass. To be successful, the Gospel needed to be proclaimed in its spiritual aspect with apostolic zeal; but the greater portion of the clergy depended for the most part on external means; and thereby gave Christianity the character of a compulsory institute, promoting the superstitious and external view of it.

The Christians soon forgot the principles of religious toleration which they had so prominently exhibited and insisted on in their former persecutions;[6] and fanatical voices were raised among them calling for a violent suppression of paganism.[7] It

[4] See especially Chrysostomi adv. Judaeos Oratt. viii. Bingham, vol. vii. p. 274, ss. Neander's Chrysostomus, Bd. 1, S. 256, ss.

[5] Comp. the description of the court at Julian's accession, Ammian. Marcell. xxii. 4: Namque fatendum est pleramque eorum (Palatinorum) partem vitiorum omnium seminarium effusius aluisse, ita ut rempublicam inficerent cupiditatibus pravis, plusque exemplis quam peccandi licentia laederent multos. Pasti enim ex his quidam templorum spoliis, et lucra ex omni odorantes occasione, ab egestate infima ad saltum sublati divitiarum ingentium, nec largiendi, nec rapiendi, nec absumendi tenuere aliquem modum, aliena invadere semper adsuefacti. Unde fluxioris vitae initia pullularunt, et perjuria, et nullus existimationis respectus, demensque superbia fidem suam probrosis quaestibus polluebat. Inter quae ingluvies et gurgites crevere praerupti conviviorum, etc. An orator of the day (Augustini, tom. v. app. Sermo 82, also in Ambrosii Opp. as Sermo in dom. xxii. post Pentecosten) complains: Usque adeo autem hoc inolevit malum, ut jam quasi ex consuetudine vendantur leges, corrumpantur jura, sententia ipsa venalis sit, et nulla jam causa possit esse sine causa. Salvianus de Gubern. Dei is particularly full of complaints of the corruption of his time, ex. gr. iv. 5, 7; vi. 11; vii. 12, 15.

[6] For example, Justin. Apol. i. 2, 4, 12. So still under Constantine, Lactantius Institutt. v. 19: Religio cogi non potest: verbis potius quam verberibus res agenda est, ut sit voluntas.—Nihil est tam voluntarium, quam religio. C. 20: Nos non expetimus, ut Deum nostrum, qui est omnium, velint, nolint, colat aliquis invitus: nec, si non coluerit, irascimur. Epitome c. 54: Religio sola est, in qua libertas domicilium collocavit. Res est enim praeter caeteras voluntaria, nec imponi cuiquam necessitas potest, ut colat quod non vult. Potest aliquis forsitan simulare, non potest velle.

[7] So even Julius Firmicus Maternus under Constantine. See § 75, note 21. Hilarii Pictav. contra Auxentium Mediol. liber. init. Ac primum misereri licet nostrae aetatis laborem et praesentium temporum congemiscere: quibus patrocinari Deo humana creduntur, et ad tuendam Christi Ecclesiam ambitione saeculari laboratur. Oro vos, Episcopi, qui hoc vos esse creditis, quibusnam suffragiis ad praedicandum Evangelium Apostoli usi sunt? Quibus adjuti potestatibus Christum praedicaverunt, gentesque fere omnes ex idolis ad Deum transtulerunt? Anne aliquam sibi assumebant e palatio dignitatem, hymnum Deo in carcere, inter catenas, et post flagella cantantes? Edicitisque Regis

was not without the co-operation of the Christian clergy that the prohibitions of *heathenism* were always assuming a stricter tone, and that the laws against *Judaism* were more and more circumscribing.[8] The treatment of heretics, too, became more severe.[9] At first the Catholic Christians were contented to render them innocuous by interdicting their meetings or by banishment.[10] The execution of Priscillian (§ 86) was still universally regarded with abhorrence.[11] At the same time, however, Augustine allowed himself to be persuaded that corporal punishments against heretics were allowable and fit;[12] and Leo

Paulus cum in theatro spectaculum ipse esset, Christo ecclesiam congregabat?—Aut non manifesta se tum Dei virtus contra odia humana porrexit: cum tanto magis Christus praedicaretur, quanto magis praedicari inhiberetur? At nunc, proh dolor! divinam fidem suffragia terrena commendant: inopsque virtutis suae Christus, dum ambitio nomini suo conciliatur, arguitur. Terret exiliis et carceribus Ecclesia, credique sibi cogit, quae exiliis et carceribus est credita: pendet a dignatione communicantium, quae persequentium est consecrata terrore: fugat sacerdotes, quae fugatis est sacerdotibus propagata: diligi sese gloriatur a mundo, quae Christi esse non potuit, nisi eam mundus odisset. Haec de comparatione traditae nobis olim Ecclesiae, nunc quam deperditae, res ipsa, quae in oculis omnium est atque ore, clamavit.

[8] C. W. de Rhoer Dissertt. de effectu relig. christianae in jurisprudentiam Romanam, p. 157, ss. Meysenbug de Christ. relig. vi et effectu in jus civile. Gottingae. 1828. 4. p. 42.

[9] Bingham, vol. vii. p. 285, ss.; De Rhoer, p. 170, ss.; Meysenbug, p. 38; Riffel geschichtl. Darstellung des Verhältnisses zwischen Kirche und Staat, i. 669.

[10] It is true that Julianus (ap. Cyrill. c. Jul. lib. vi. ed. Spanh. p. 206) accuses the Christians, even in his time: *'Απεσφάξατε οὐχ ἡμῶν μονον τοὺς τοῖς πατρῴοις ἐμμένοντας, ἀλλὰ καὶ τῶν ἐξίσης ὑμῖν πεπλανημένων αἱρετικῶν τοὺς μὴ τὸν αὐτὸν τρόπον ὑμῖν τὸν νεκρὸν θρηνοῦντας.* Epist. 52, that under Constantius *τοὺς πολλοὺς αὐτῶν καὶ φυγαδευθῆναι, καὶ διωχθῆναι, καὶ δεσμευθῆναι· πολλὰ δὲ ἤδη καὶ σφαγῆναι πλήθη τῶν λεγομένων αἱρετικῶν· ὡς ἐν Σαμοσάτοις, καὶ Κυζίκῳ, καὶ Παφλαγονίᾳ, καὶ Βιθυνίᾳ, καὶ Γαλατίᾳ, καὶ πολλοῖς ἄλλοις ἔθνεσιν ἄρδην ἀνατραπῆναι πορθηθείσας κώμας.* Perhaps, however, this should be understood of extra-judicial murders.

[11] Not only by Latinus Pacatus, in his Panegyricus Theodosio dictus, c. 29, but also by bishops: Sulpic. Severus Hist. sacr. ii. 50: Namque tum Martinus (bishop of Turonum) apud Treveros constitutus, non desinebat increpare Ithacium, ut ab accusatione desisteret: Maximum orare, ut sanguine infelicium abstineret: satis superque sufficere, ut Episcopali sententia haeretici judicati Ecclesiis pellerentur: novum esse et inauditum nefas, ut causam Ecclesiae judex saeculi judicaret. How he behaved when he came again to Treves, after the murder of Priscillian may be seen in Sulpic. Sever. Dial. iii. c. 11–13. Maximus wished that the persecution of the Priscillianists should be continued in Spain; but pia erat solicitudo Martino, ut non solum Christianos, qui sub illa erant occasione vexandi, sed ipsos etiam haereticos liberaret. Besides cavit cum illa Ithacianae partis communione misceri. Ambrose, too, who was with Maximus as embassador from Valentinian II., A.D. 387, endeavored there (Ambros. Ep. 24, ad Valentin.) abstinere ab episcopis,—qui aliquos devios licet a fide ad necem petebant. Cf. Ep. 26. Indeed, at that time every kind of capital punishment was pretty generally regarded as forbidden.

[12] Augustini Ep. 93, ad Vincentium § 17: Mea primitus sententia non erat, nisi neminem ad unitatem Christi esse cogendum, verbo esse agendum, disputatione pugnandum, ratione vincendum, ne fictos catholicos haberemus, quos apertos haereticos noveramus. Sed haec opinio mea non contradicentium verbis, sed demonstrantium superabatur exemplis. Nam primo mihi opponebatur civitas mea, quae cum tota esset in parte Donati, ad unitatem catholicam timore legum imperialium conversa est, quam nunc videmus ita

the Great went so far as to approve the putting of them to death.[13] Besides, the bishops endeavored by means of ecclesiastical laws, not only to prevent all contact of the faithful with the opponents of the church,[14] but ventured even to absolve individuals from the obligation of duties which they manifestly owed to heretics.[15]

At the same time, the church did not the less deviate from the

hujus animositatis perniciem detestari, ut in ea nunquam fuisse credatur, etc. Cf. Retractt. ii. 5. How the Donatists attack these new principles, and how Augustine defends them, may be seen in ejusd. contra litt. Petiliani lib. ii. Contra Gaudentium lib. i. Epist. 185, ad Bonifacium, among other things, § 21, it is written: Melius est quidem—ad Deum colendum doctrina homines duci, quam poenae timore vel dolore compelli. Sed non quia isti meliores sunt, ideo illi qui tales non sunt, negligendi sunt. Multis enim profuit (quod experimentis probavimus et probamus) prius timore vel dolore cogi, ut postea possent doceri. Then he refers, § 24 the cogite intrare (Luc. xiv. 23) to this point: ipse Dominus ad magnam coenam suam prius adduci jubet convivas, postea cogi.—In illis ergo, qui leniter primo adducti sunt, completa est prior obedientia, in istis autem, qui coguntur, inobedientia coërcetur. Still Epist. 100, ad Donatum, Procons. Africae: Unum solum est, quod in tua justitia, pertimescimus, ne forte—pro immanitate facinorum, ac non potius pro lenitatis christianae consideratione censeas coërcendum, quod te per Jesum Christum ne facias obsecramus.—Ex occasione terribilium judicum ac legum ne in aeterni judicii poenas incidant, corrigi eos cupimus, non necari; nec disciplinam circa eos negligi volumus, nec suppliciis, quibus digni sunt, exerceri. So, too, Epist. 139, ad Marcellinum: Poena sane illorum, quamvis de tantis sceleribus confessorum, rogo te, ut praeter supplicium mortis sit, et propter conscientiam nostram, et propter catholicam mansuetudinem commendandam. Cf. Ph. a Limborch Historia inquisitionis. (Amst. 1692. fol.) lib. i. c. 6. J. Barbeyrac Traité de la morale des pères, c. 16, § 19. Jerome, however, says, Epist. 37 (al. 53) ad Riparium, adv. Vigilantium: Non est crudelitas pro Deo pietas. Unde et in lege dicit: si frater tuus et amicus et uxor, quae est in sinu tuo, depravare te voluerit a veritate, sit manus tua super eos, et effunde sanguinem eorum, et auferes malum de medio Israel (Deut. xiii. 6, ss.). Chrysostom, indeed, recommends Christian love toward heretics and heathen (Hom. 29 in Matth.), but would yet have them restrained, and their assemblies forbidden, and declares himself only against putting them to death (Hom. 46 in Matth.). Thus also, he caused their churches to be taken from the Novatians, Quartodecimani, and other heretics in Asia, and many considered his misfortunes a righteous retribution for this. Socrates, vi. 19.—Stäudlin's Gesch. d. Sittenlehre Jesu iii. 238. De Wette Gesch. d. christl. Sittenlehre, i. 344.

[13] The first law of a Christian emperor, authorizing capital punishment against certain heretics, is that of Theodosius I. A.D. 382, against the Manichaeans. Sozomen, however, vii. 12, says of all the laws of this emperor against heretics: *Χαλεπὰς τοῖς νόμοις ἐπέγραφε τιμωρίας, ἀλλ' οὐκ ἐπεξῄει· οὐ γὰρ τιμωρεῖσθαι, ἀλλ' εἰς δέος καθιστᾷν τοὺς ὑπηκόους ἐσπούδαζεν.* (Cf. Socrates, v. 20): and Socrates, vii. 3, still maintains: *Οὐκ εἰωθὸς διώκειν τῇ ὀρθοδόξῳ ἐκκλησίᾳ.* On the other hand, Leo M. Epist. 15, ad Turribium:—Etiam mundi principes ita hanc sacrilegam amentiam (Priscillianistarum) detestati sunt, ut auctorem ejus cum plerisque discipulis legum publicarum ense prosternerent.—Profuit diu ista districtio ecclesiasticae lenitati, quae etsi sacerdotali contenta judicio, cruentas refugit ultiones, severis tamen christianorum principum constitutionibus adjuvatur, dum ad spiritale nonnumquam recurrunt remedium, qui timent corporale supplicium.

[14] Bingham, vol. vii. p. 276, ss. 294, ss.

[15] For example, Concil. Carthag. iii. ann. 397, can. 13: Ut Episcopi vel clerici, in eos qui catholici Christiani non sunt, etiamsi consanguinei fuerint, nec per donationes, nec per testamentum rerum suarum aliquid conferant.

right path, in her measures instituted for the purpose of gaining over the masses of external professors to the side of Christianity internally. She endeavored to give her *service* the external attractions of the heathen worship, and thus only strengthened the tendency to externalities; thus she herself invited men to substitute for a genuine interest in religion and the service of God a feeling quite foreign to piety. On the one hand, many were confirmed in the heathenish, superstitious notion of looking for works acceptable to God in the external rites of his worship; on the other hand, there were not a few, especially in the cities, who went to the churches as if to the theater, with a mere aesthetic interest; and followed the spiritual orators as they would rhetoricians;[16] while, on the contrary, they did not remain to be present at the Lord's Supper,[17] a circumstance which necessarily led to the command to partake of it.[18] Meetings for public worship began to be even abused, as occasions for sensual excesses.[19] Finally, *the theological disputes* of this period were also an important obstacle in pre-

[16] Gregor. Naz. Orat. 42 (ed. Colon. Or. 22, p. 596): *Οὐ γὰρ ζητοῦσιν ἱερεῖς, ἀλλὰ ῥήτορας.* How the clergy themselves promoted this tendency may be seen in Orat. 36 (ed. Col. Or. 27, p. 465): *Ὁρῶ πολλοὺς τῶν νῦν ἱερατεύειν ὑπισχνουμένων, οἳ τὴν ἁπλῆν καὶ ἄτεχνον ἡμῶν εὐσέβειαν ἔντεχνον πεποιήκασι, καὶ πολιτικῆς τι καινὸν εἶδος ἀπὸ τῆς ἀγορᾶς εἰς τὰ ἅγια μετενηνεγμένης, καὶ ἀπὸ τῶν θεάτρων ἐπὶ τὴν τοῖς πολλοῖς ἀθέατον μυσταγωγίαν, ὡς εἶναι δύο σκηνὰς, εἰ δεῖ τολμήσαντα τοῦτο εἰπεῖν, τοσοῦτον ἀλλήλων διαφερούσας, ὅσον τὴν μὲν πᾶσιν ἀνεῖσθαι, τὴν δὲ τισί· καὶ τὴν μὲν γελᾶσθαι, τὴν δὲ τιμᾶσθαι· καὶ τὴν μὲν θεατρικὴν, τὴν δὲ πνευματικὴν ὀνομάζεσθαι.* Chrysostom. de Sacerdot. v. 1, of the hearers of sermons: *Οὐ πρὸς ὠφέλειαν, ἀλλὰ πρὸς τέρψιν ἀκούειν εἰθίσθησαν οἱ πολλοὶ, καθάπερ τραγῳδῶν ἢ κιθαρῳδῶν καθήμενοι δικασταί.* Id. Hom. 30, in Act. Apost. Hieronym. adv. Luciferianos (Opp. iv. 296): Ex litteratis quicunque hodie ordinantur, id habent curae, non quomodo Scripturarum medullas ebibant: sed quomodo aures populi declamatorum flosculis mulceant. Id. praef. in lib. iii. comm. in epist. ad Ephes. Comp. Neander's Chrysostomus, i. 118, 320, ss. 327. Ullmann's Gregor. v. Naz. S. 155, ss. Daniel's Gesch. d. christl. Beredsamkeit, i. 331. Concerning the applause by clapping of hands during the sermon, see B. Ferrarii de Ritu sacrarum eccl. vet. concionum. (Mediolani. 1621, c. praef. J. G. Graevii. Ultraj. 1692. 8.) lib. ii. c. 24. Bingham, vol. vi. p. 187, ss. Daniel, i. 334, 605, 677.

[17] Chrysostom. Hom. iii. in epist. ad Ephes. (Opp. xi. 23): *Εἰκῇ θυσία καθημερινὴ, εἰκῇ παρεστήκαμεν τῷ θυσιαστηρίῳ, οὐδεὶς ὁ μετέχων.* Id. de incomprehensibili hom. iii. 6 (Opp. i. 462).

[18] Conc. Antioch. (341) can. 2. Can. apost. 8 and 9. See Drey, über die Apost. Constitutionen, S. 255.

[19] Hieronymus adv. Vigilantium (ed. Martian. t. iv. P. ii. p. 285), says de vigiliis et pernoctationibus in basilicis Martyrum celebrandis in defense of them: Error autem et culpa juvenum vilissimarumque mulierum, qui per noctem saepe deprehenditur, non est religiosis hominibus imputandus: quia et in vigiliis Paschae tale quid fieri plerumque convincitur, et tamen paucorum culpa non praejudicat religioni, etc.

venting Christianity from exercising its full power on the men of the age. While they were contending about definitions, as if the essence of Christianity consisted in them; the interest of the understanding being in a one-sided way excited in favor of it;[20] it was no wonder that among many Greeks the interest in favor of Christianity was of the same nature with an interest in sophistical problems;[21] the holiest relations being torn asunder at the same time by hatred and discord.[22] And then, again, as the prevailing systems changed, sometimes one and sometimes another being enforced by wordly power, it was almost an unavoidable consequence that the people should either be made suspicious of Christianity and indifferent to it, or else tempted to employ falsehood and hypocrisy in the most sacred things.[23]

It is true that *monachism* appeared likely to subordinate every thing to a striving after the highest, by means of its example in giving a wholesome stimulus to the enervated race;[24] but it was itself too impure in most of its manifestations to be able to give pure impressions, while it brought confusion into moral ideas by its arbitrary mode of worship. In former times, this external strictness of morals had found a corresponding internal basis in the minds of men; but now it was to be made prominent, in a degree much increased by monachism, among a people devoid of faith. Of course the people endeavored to make the pressure of the new law as light as possible,[25] to which

[20] Hilarius ad Constantium, ii. 5: Dum in verbis pugna est, dum de novitatibus quaestio est,—dum de studiis certamen est, dum in consensu difficultas est, dum alter alteri anathema esse coepit; prope jam nemo Christi est.

[21] Gregor. Naz. Orat. xxxiii. p. 530: Ὡς ἕν τι τῶν ἄλλων καὶ τοῦτο φλυαρεῖται ἡδέως, μετὰ τοὺς ἱππικοὺς, καὶ τὰ θέατρα, καὶ τὰ ᾄσματα, καὶ τὴν γαστέρα, καὶ τὰ ὑπὸ γαστέρα, οἷς καὶ τοῦτο μέρος τρυφῆς, ἡ περὶ ταῦτα ἐρεσχελία καὶ κομψεία τῶν ἀντιθέσεων. Cf. Orat. xxi. p. 376, or. xxvi. Gregor. Nyss. Orat. de deitate Fil. et Spir. Sancti, Opp. iii. 466. The law of Theodosius, A. D. 388 (Cod. Theod. xvi. iv. 2): Nulli egresso ad publicum vel disceptandi de religione, vel tractandi, vel consilii aliquid deferendi patescat occasio (cf. Gothofred. ad h. l.), of Marcian, A. D. 452 (in Actis Conc. Chalced. ap. Mansi, vii. 476, and Cod. Justin. i. 1, 4). Neander's Chrysost. ii. 118. Ullmann's Gregor. v. Naz. S. 158, ss.

[22] Gregor. Naz. Orat. xxxii. 4, says of the theological controversies: Καὶ τοῦτό ἐστιν, ὡς ἐπὶ τὸ πλεῖστον, ὃ διέσπασε μέλη, διέστησεν ἀδελφοὺς, πόλεις ἐτάραξε, δήμους ἐξέμηνεν, ὥπλισεν ἔθνη [ἐπὶ] βασιλεῖς, ἐπανέστησεν ἱερκεῖς λαῷ καὶ ἀλλήλοις, λαὸν ἑαυτῷ καὶ ἱερεῦσι, γονεῖς τέκνοις, τέκνα γονεῦσιν, ἄνδρας γυναιξὶ, γυναῖκας ἀνδράσι.

[23] Gregorii Naz. Carmen de se ipso et adv. Episc. v. 333, ss., above, § 103, note 4.

[24] Neander's Chrysost. Bd. 1, S. 78, 90.

[25] Chrysostom. Orat. de baptismo Christi (Opp. ii. 366), complains that many went to the churches, οὐ καθ' ἑκάστην σύναξιν, ἀλλ' ἐν ἑορτῇ μόνον ἅπαξ ἢ δεύτερον μόλις τοῦ παντὸς ἐνιαυτοῦ. Id. Hom. in Princip. Act. i. (Opp. iii. 50). Salvianus de Gubern. Dei, lib. vi. p. 113: Nos Ecclesiis Dei ludicra anteponimus, nos altaria spernimus et theatra

monachism itself contributed most readily by making a distinction between a higher and a lower virtue.[26] To introduce a Christian morality into the life of society, the church began to extend its penance to smaller offenses likewise,[27] and at the numerous councils an extensive code of laws was formed, which fixed certain ecclesiastical punishments for different ecclesiastical and moral transgressions, according to their external form. In the eastern church, this penance was left to the free-will of the transgressors, in the case of private offenses; particularly after *Nectarius*, bishop of Constantinople, had abolished (about 391) the *πρεσβύτερος ἐπὶ τῆς μετανοίας* (see Div. I. § 71, note 11).[28] But in the western church, they began to consider it a necessary condition of forgiveness for all gross sins,[29] and in order

honoramus.—Omni enim feralium ludicrorum die si quaelibet Ecclesiae festa fuerint, non solum ad Ecclesiam non veniunt qui Christianos se esse dicunt; sed si qui inscii forte venerint, dum in ipsa Ecclesia sunt, si ludos agi audiunt, Ecclesias derelinquunt.

[26] Comp. an unknown preacher of the day (Augustini, tom. v. app. Sermo 82, also in Ambrosii Opp. as Sermo in dom. xxii. post Pentecost.) on Luc. iii. 12, ss.: Nonnulli fratres, qui aut militiae cingulo detinentur, aut in actu sunt publico constituti, cum peccant graviter, hac solent a peccatis suis prima se voce excusare, quod militant.—Illud autem quale est, quod cum ob errorem aliquem a senioribus arguuntur, et imputatur, alicui de illis, cur ebrius fuerit, cur res alienas pervaserit, caedem cur turbulentur admiserit; statim respondeat: Quid habebam facere, homo saecularis et miles? Numquid monachum sum professus aut clericum? Quasi omnis, qui clericus non est aut monachus, possit ei licere, quod non licet. Chrysostom frequently inveighs against the abuses of this distinction; for example, de Lazaro Orat. iii. (Opp. i. 737) in Ep. ad Hebr. Hom. vii. c. 4 (Opp. xii. 79). Neander's Chrysost. i. 95. Augustin. in Psalm xlviii. Sermo ii. § 4: Cum coeperit Deo quisque vivere, mundum contemnere, injurias suas nolle ulcisci, nolle hic divitias, non hic quaerere felicitatem terrenam, contemnere omnia, Dominum solum cogitare, viam Christi non deserere; non solum a paganis dicitur insanit, sed quod magis dolendum est, quia et intus multi dormiunt, et evigilare nolunt, a suis, a Christianis audiunt *quid pateris?* in Psalm xc. Sermo i. § 4: Quomodo inter Paganos qui fuerit Christianus, a Paganis audit verba aspera,—sic inter Christianos qui voluerint esse diligentiores et meliores, ab ipsis Christianis audituri sunt insultationes,—dicunt: magnus tu justus, tu es Elias, tu es Petrus, de caelo venisti. Insultant; quocumque se verterit, audit hinc atque inde verbum asperum.

[27] Cramer's Fort. v. Bossuet's Weltgesch. Th. 5, Bd. 1, S. 379, ss.

[28] Socrates, v. 19. Sozomenus, vii. 16. According to Socrates, the decree was: *Περιελεῖν μὲν τὸν ἐπὶ τῆς μετανοίας πρεσβύτερον· συγχωρῆσαι δὲ, ἕκαστον τῷ ἰδίῳ συνειδότι τῶν μυστηρίων μετέχειν.* So Chrysost. in Ep. ad Hebr. Hom. 31, c. 3 (Opp. xii. 289): *Μὴ ἁμαρτωλοὺς καλῶμεν ἑαυτοὺς μόνον, ἀλλὰ καὶ τὰ ἁμαρτήματα ἀναλογιζώμεθα, κατ' εἶδος ἕκαστον ἀναλέγοντες. οὐ λέγω σοι "ἐκπόμπευσον σαυτόν," οὐδὲ παρὰ τοῖς ἄλλοις κατηγόρησον, ἀλλὰ πείθεσθαι συμβουλεύω τῷ προφήτῃ λέγοντι "ἀποκάλυψον πρὸς κύριον τὴν ὁδόν σου"* (Psalm xxxvi. 5). *ἐπὶ τοῦ θεοῦ ταῦτα ὁμολόγησον, ἐπὶ τοῦ δικαστοῦ ὁμολόγει τὰ ἁμαρτήματα, εὐχόμενος, εἰ καὶ μὴ τῇ γλωττῃ, ἀλλὰ τῇ μνήμῃ.* In like manner ad Illuminandos catech. ii. c. 4 (Opp. ii. 240), de Poenitentia Hom. vi. c. 5 (ibid. p. 326): Non esse ad gratiam concionandum, c. 3 (ibid. p. 663), in Ep. i. ad Corinth. Hom. 28, c. 1, ad 1 Cor. xi. 28 (Opp. x. 250), et passim.

[29] Augustinus Serm. 351 (de Poenitentia, 1) § 2, ss., distinguishes tres actiones poenitentiae. Una est, quae novum hominem parturit, donec per baptismum salutare omnium

to set aside all difficulties, to change public confession into a private one in the case of private sins.[30]

It can not be denied, that this system of penance promoted a certain external propriety of conduct; and as little can it be disallowed that the church awakened and animated a sympathy, which had almost entirely disappeared from paganism,[31] by its care

praeteritorum fiat ablutio peccatorum.—Altera,—cujus actio per totam istam vitam, qua in carne mortali degimus, perpetua supplicationis humilitate subeunda est.—Tertia, quae pro illis peccatis subeunda est, quae legis decalogus continent. Respecting the latter: § 9: Implicatus igitur tam mortiferorum vinculis peccatorum detrectat, aut differt, aut dubitat confugere ad ipsas claves Ecclesiae, quibus solvatur in terra, ut sit solutus in caelo: et audet sibi post hanc vitam, quia tantum Christianus dicitur, salutem aliquam polliceri? —Judicet ergo se ipsum homo—et mores convertat in melius. Et cum ipse in se protulerit severissimae medicinae, sed tamen medicinae sententiam, veniat ad antistites, per quos illi in Ecclesia claves ministrantur: et tamquam bonus jam incipiens esse filius, maternorum membrorum ordine custodito, a praepositis sacramentorum accipiat satisfactionis suae modum.—Ut si peccatum ejus non solum in gravi ejus malo, sed etiam in tanto scandalo aliorum est, atque hoc expedire utilitati Ecclesiae videtur antistiti, in notitia multorum, vel etiam totius plebis agere poenitentiam non recuset, non resistat, non letali et mortiferae plagae per pudorem addat tumorem. However, de Symbolo ad Catechumenos, c. 7: Illi, quos videtis agere poenitentiam, scelera commiserunt, aut adulteria, aut aliqua facta immania: inde agunt poenitentiam. Nam si levia peccata (above: venialia, sine quibus vita ista non est, and: levia, sine quibus esse non possumus) ipsorum essent, ad haec quotidiana oratio delenda sufficeret. Leo M. Epist. 108, ed. Ball. (83, ed. Quesn.) ad Theodorum, c. 2: Multiplex misericordia Dei ita lapsibus subvenit humanis, ut non solum per baptismi gratiam, sed etiam per poenitentiae medicinam spes vitae, reparetur aeternae, ut qui regenerationis dona violassent, proprio se judicio condemnantes, ad remissionem criminum pervenirent: sic divinae bonitatis praesidiis ordinatis, ut indulgentia Dei nisi supplicationibus Sacerdotum nequeat obtineri. Mediator enim Dei et hominum homo Christus Jesus hanc praepositas Ecclesiae tradidit potestatem, ut et confitentibus actionem poenitentiae darent: et eosdem salubri satisfactione purgatos ad communionem sacramentorum per januam reconciliationis admitterent. Cui utique operi inaccessibiliter ipse Salvator intervenit, nec umquam ab his abest, quae ministris suis exequenda commisit, dicens: Ecce ego vobiscum sum, etc. (Matth. xxviii. 20), ut si quid per servitutem nostram bono ordine et gratulando impletur effectu, non ambigamus per Spiritum Sanctum fuisse donatum. Cf. Hieronymus Comm. in Matth. xvi. 19: Istum locum: Et dabo tibi claves regni caelorum, Episcopi et Presbyteri non intelligentes, aliquid sibi de Pharisaeorum assumunt supercilio, ut vel damnent innocentes, vel solvere se noxios arbitrentur, cum apud Deum non sententia sacerdotum, sed eorum vita quaeratur.

[30] Leo M. Epist. 168, ed. Ball. (ed. Quesn. 136), c. 2: Illam etiam contra apostolicam regulam praesumtionem, quam nuper agnovi a quibusdam illicita usurpatione committi, modis omnibus constituo submoveri. De poenitentia scilicet, quae a fidelibus postulatur, ne de singulorum peccatorum genere libello scripta professio publice recitetur: cum reatus conscientiarum sufficiat solis sacerdotibus indicari confessione secreta.—Quia non omnium hujusmodi sunt peccata, ut ea, qui poenitentiam poscunt, non timeant publicare; removeatur tam improbabilis consuetudo: ne multi a poenitentiae remediis arceantur, dum aut erubescunt, aut metuunt inimicis suis sua facta reserari, quibus possint legum constitutione percelli. Sufficit enim illa confessio, quae primum Deo offertur, tum etiam, Sacerdoti, qui pro delictis poenitentium precator accedit. Tunc enim demum plures ad poenitentiam poterunt provocari, si populi auribus non publicetur conscientia confitentis.

[31] Comp. § 91, note 9; § 103, note 10. Thomassinus, p. ii. lib. 3, c. 87, and c. 95, s. Stäudlin's Gesch. d. Sittenlehre Jesu, iii. 404.

for the oppressed and suffering part of humanity, for the poor, the captives, the sick, widows and orphans. But yet by this new system of legislation, Christian freedom, and genuine morality which has its root in it, were robbed of their true life. A comparison of the present with earlier times, in this particular, would present none but melancholy results.[32]

§ 105.

INFLUENCE OF THE CHURCH ON LEGISLATION.

C. W. de Rhoer Dissertt. de Effectu religionis christianae in jurisprudentiam Romanam. Fasc. I. Groningae. 1776. 8. H. O. Aem. de Meysenbug de Christianae religionis vi et effectu in jus civile, speciatim in ea, quae Institutiones in primo libro tractant. Gotting. 1828. 4. De l'Influence du Christianisme sur le droit civil des Romains, par M. Troplong. Paris. 1843. 8.

Though the great changes which had taken place in Roman legislation since Constantine had not been effected by Christianity alone,[1] yet Christian principles and Christian customs, even respect to the Mosaic law,[2] had an important influence on it; while several laws were directly owing to representations made by the bishops.[3] A stay was put to sensual excesses,[4] rape was punished with death,[5] immoral *plays* were abolished or checked.[6] *Contests of gladiators*, which had been already pro-

[32] E. g. Chrysostomus Hom. 26, in Epist. ii. ad Corinth. (Opp. x. 623): *Ἂν τὰ ἡμέτερά τις ἐξετάσῃ τὰ νῦν, ὄψεται ἡλίκον τῆς θλίψεως τὸ κέρδος. νῦν μὲν γὰρ εἰρήνης ἀπολαύοντες ἀναπεπτώκαμεν, καὶ διεῤῥύημεν, καὶ μυρίων τὴν ἐκκλησίαν ἐνεπλήσαμεν κακῶν· ὅτε δὲ ἠλαυνόμεθα, καὶ σωφρονέστεροι, καὶ ἐπιεικέστεροι, καὶ σπουδαιότεροι· καὶ περὶ τοὺς συλλόγους τούτους ἦμεν προθυμότεροι, καὶ περὶ τὴν ἀκρόασιν· ὅπερ γὰρ τῷ χρυσίῳ τὸ πῦρ, τοῦτο ἡ θλίψις ταῖς ψυχαῖς, κ. τ. λ.* Hieronymus in vita Malchi, init.: Scribere disposui,—ab adventu Salvatoris usque ad nostram aetatem,—quomodo et per quos Christi Ecclesia nata sit, et adulta, persecutionibus creverit, et martyriis coronata sit: et postquam ad christianos principes venerit, potentia quidem et divitiis major, sed virtutibus minor facta sit. Verum haec alias. Salvianus de Avaritia, i. 1. Cf. Rittershusius Sacr. lectt. vi. c. 17. Venema Hist. eccl. t. iv. p. 260, ss.

[1] De Rhoer. p. 39, ss.

[2] De Rhoer, p. 65, 77, s.

[3] De Rhoer, p. 89, s.—On the influence of Christianity on Constantine's laws (*νόμους ἐκ παλαιῶν ἐπὶ τὸ ὁσιώτερον μεταβάλλων ἀνενεοῦτο*) cf. Euseb. de vita Const. iv. 26.

[4] Cod. Theodos. lib. xv. tit. 8, de lenonibus. Riffel's Gesch. Darstellung des Verhältnisses zwischen Kirche und Staat, i. 108. Laws for lessening concubinage. Meysenbug, p. 51.

[5] Cod. Theod. lib. ix. tit. 24, de raptu virginum vel viduarum. Riffel, i. 110.

[6] Comp. the laws Cod. Theodos. lib. xv. t. 5, de spectaculis; tit. 6, de Majuma; tit. 7, de scenicis. Stäudlin's Gesch. d. Sittenlehre Jesu, Bd. 3, S. 388. Yet it is evident from the law, Cod. Justin. iii. 12, 11. A.D. 469, that at that time, in addition to the scena theatralis and the circense theatrum, the ferarum lacrymosa spectacula also still continued:

hibited by Constantine, still continued, it is true, at Rome;[7] but they were entirely abolished by Honorius. Classes of society which had been heretofore almost unrecognized by the laws, were now embraced within their operation. The condition of *slaves*[8] and of *prisoners*[9] was improved; the unlimited *power of fathers over their children* abridged;[10] *women*, who had been kept till now in a very inferior position, were invested with greater rights;[11] and the *widow* and *orphan* protected.[12] On the other hand, legislation did not comply every where, or in every respect, with the peculiar requirements of the Christian morals of this age. The laws became *more bloody* and strict than before.[13] The *oath* assumed Christian forms, but was more frequently administered.[14] And though *restrictions upon certain marriages* were established, agreeably to Christian principles,[15] the laws against *celibacy* abolished,[16] and *second marriages* rendered difficult,[17] yet the old *liberty of divorce* was but partially limited; and from fear of still greater crimes, the emperors were obliged to admit many causes of valid separation, besides unfaithfulness to the marriage contract.[18]

probably only in the west, for in the east, they appear to have ceased even before Theodosius I. See Müller Comm. de genio, moribus et luxu aevi Theodosiani. Havn. 1797 P. ii. p. 87.

[7] Cod. Theod. lib. xv. tit. 12, de gladiatoribus. The self-sacrifice of Telemachus, Theodoret, Hist. eccl. v. 26. Comp. Neander's Chrysost. i. 383.

[8] De Rhoer, p. 117, ss. Meysenbug, p. 34.

[9] Cod. Theod. lib. ix. tit. 3, de custodia reorum. De Rhoer, p. 72.

[10] De Rhoer, p. 137, s. Meysenbug, p. 45.

[11] De Rhoer, p. 124. [12] De Rhoer, p. 111. [13] De Rhoer, p. 59, ss.

[14] J. F. Malblanc Doctrina de jurejurando e genuinis fontibus illustrata. Norimberg 1781. ed. 2. Tübing. 1820. 8. p. 342. C. F. Stäudlin's Gesch. der Lehren vom Eide. Göttingen. 1824. 8. S. 81.

[15] Cod. Theod. lib. iii. tit. 12, de incestis nuptiis, on forbidden degrees of affinity. De Rhoer, p. 248. Besides, marriage between Christians and Jews was forbidden (l. c. iii. 7, 2). A proposal of marriage made to a nun was punished with death (ix. 25, 2).

[16] Cod. Theod. viii. 16, 1. See Div. I. § 56, note 35.

[17] On the poenas secundarum nuptiarum, see de Rhoer, p. 240; Meysenbug, p. 61; v Löhr in the Archive f. d. civilistische Praxis, Bd. 16 (1833), S. 32.

[18] Cod. Theodos. lib. iii. tit. 16, de repudiis. Theodosii II. Novell. tit. 12. Bingham, vol. ix. p. 356, ss. De Rhoer, p. 287, ss. Asterii Amaseni (about 400) Homil. v. (in Combefisii Auct. nov. i. 82): Ἀκούσατε δὲ νῦν οἱ τούτων κάπηλοι, καὶ τὰς γυναῖκας ὡς ἱμάτια εὐκόλως μετενδυόμενοι· οἱ τὰς παστάδας πολλάκις καὶ ῥᾳδίως πηγνύντες, ὡς πανηγύρεως ἐργαστήρια.—Οἱ μικρὸν παροξυνόμενοι καὶ εὐθὺς τὸ βιβλίον τῆς διαιρέσεως γράφοντες. οἱ πολλὰς χήρας ἐν τῷ ζῆν ἔτι καταλιμπάνοντες· πείσθητε, ὅτι γάμος θανάτῳ μόνῳ καὶ μοιχείᾳ διακόπτεται. Hieronymi Epist. 84 (al. 30) ad Oceanum de Morte Fabiolae, c. 1: Aliae sunt leges Caesarum, aliae Christi: aliud Papinianus, aliud Paulus noster praecipit, etc.

SEVENTH CHAPTER.

ATTEMPTS AT REFORMATION.

§ 106.

The new tendencies of Christian life could not slide in unnoticed, especially as it is certain that the Catholic church was frequently reproached with them by the older Christian parties.[1] Nor were the morally dangerous aspects of these tendencies entirely overlooked by the more acute; though they were too often exculpated on the ground of pious intentions.[2] The men who

[1] Faustus (ap. Augustin. contra Faust. xx. 4): Vos, qui desciscentes a gentibus monarchiae opinionem primo vobiscum divulsistis, id est, ut omnia credatis ex Deo; sacrificia vero eorum vertistis in agapas, idola in Martyres, quos votis similibus colitis; defunctorum umbras vino placatis et dapibus; solemnes gentium dies cum ipsis celebratis, ut calendas, et solstitia; de vita certe mutastis nihil; estis sane schisma, a matrice sua diversum nihil habens nisi conventum. The Novatians also rejected the worship of martyrs and relics. See Eulogius Patr. Alex. (about 580) contra Novatianos lib. Vto. (ap. Photius Cod. 280; cf. Cod. 182): perhaps also Eustathius (Conc. Gangr. c. 20, comp. however, Dallaeus adv. Latinorum de cultus religiosi objecto tradit. p. 151). Eunomius was an opponent of martyr-worship (auctor hujus haereseos. Hieron. adv. Vigilant.) and of monachism (Gregor. Nyssen. contra Eunom. lib. ii.).

[2] As Hieronym. adv. Vigilant. (Opp. iv. ii. p. 284): Cereos autem non clara luce accendimus, sicut frustra calumniaris, sed ut noctis tenebras hoc solatio temperemus.—Quod si aliqui per imperitiam et simplicitatem saecularium hominum, vel certe religiosarum feminarum, de quibus vere possumus dicere: confiteor, zelum Dei habent, sed non secundum scientiam (Rom. x. 1) hoc pro honore Martyrum faciunt, quid inde perdis? Causabantur quondam et Apostoli, quod periret unguentum; sed Domini voce correpti sunt (Matth. xxvi. 8, ss.). Neque enim Christus indigebat unguento, nec Martyres lumine cereorum: et tamen illa mulier in honore Christi hoc fecit, devotioque mentis ejus recipitur; et quicumque accedunt cereos, secundum fidem suam habent mercedem, dicente Apostolo: unusquisque in suo sensu abundet (Rom. xiv. 5). Augustin. ad Januarium lib. ii. (Epist. 55) § 35: Quod autem instituitur praeter consuetudinem, ut quasi observatio sacramenti sit, approbare non possum, etiamsi multa hujusmodi propter nonnullarum vel sanctarum vel turbulentarum personarum scandala devitanda, liberius improbare non audeo. Sed hoc nimis doleo, quod multa, quae in divinis libris saluberrime praecepta sunt, minus curantur; et tam multis praesumtionibus sic plena sunt omnia, ut gravius corripiatur, qui per octavas suas terram nudo pede tetigerit (namely neophytus, cf. Tert. de Cor. mil. c. 3. See Div. I. § 53, note 25), quam qui mentem vinolentia sepelierit. Omnia itaque talia, quae neque sanctarum scripturarum auctoritatibus continentur, nec in conciliis episcoporum statuta inveniuntur, nec consuetudine universae ecclesiae roborata sunt, sed pro diversorum locorum diversis moribus innumerabiliter variantur, ita ut vix aut omnino nunquam inveniri possint causae, quas in eis instituendis homines secuti sunt, ubi facultas tribuitur, sine ulla dubitatione resecanda existimo. Quamvis enim neque hoc inveniri possit, quomodo contra fidem sint: ipsam tamen religionem, quam

looked into the ecclesiastical and religious errors of the time more profoundly, and attacked them publicly, were declared heretics by the offended hierarchy; and their voice soon died away without being able to give another direction to the incipient development of ecclesiastical life. To these latter belonged *Aërius*, presbyter in Sebaste, and friend of bishop Eustathius (about 360);[3] *Jovinian*, monk at Rome (about 388), first condemned there by Siricius, afterward by Ambrose at Milan;[4] some of

paucissimis et manifestissimis celebrationum sacramentis misericordia Dei esse liberam voluit, servilibus oneribus premunt, ut tolerabilior sit conditio Judaeorum, qui, etiamsi tempus libertatis non agnoverunt, legalibus tamen sarcinis, non humanis praesumtionibus subjiciuntur. Sed ecclesia Dei inter multam paleam multaque zizania constituta, multa tolerat, et tamen quae sunt contra fidem vel bonam vitam non approbat, nec tacet nec facit. Id. contra Faustum, xx. 21: Aliud est quod docemus, aliud quod sustinemus, aliud quod praecipere jubemur, aliud quod emendare praecipimur, et donec emendemus, tolerare compellimur. Alia est disciplina Christianorum, alia luxuria vinolentorum, vel error infirmorum.

[3] Only authority Epiphan. Haer. 75. His doctrines, ib. § 3: 1. *Τί ἐστιν ἐπίσκοπος πρὸς πρεσβύτερον; οὐδὲν διαλλάττει οὗτος τούτου· μία γάρ ἐστι τάξις, καὶ μία τιμὴ καὶ ἓν ἀξιώμα* (proofs from New Testament passages, § 5). 2. *Τί ἐστι τὸ πάσχα, ὅπερ παρ' ὑμῖν ἐπιτελεῖται;—οὐ χρὴ τὸ πάσχα ἐπιτελεῖν· τὸ γὰρ πάσχα ὑμῶν ἐτύθη Χριστός* (1 Cor. v. 7).—3. *Τίνι τῷ λόγῳ μετὰ θάνατον ὀνομάζετε ὀνόματα τεθνεώτων;—εἰ δὲ ὅλως εὐχὴ τῶν ἐνταῦθα τοὺς ἐκεῖσε ὤνησεν, ἄρα γοῦν μηδεὶς εὐσεβείτω, μηδὲ ἀγαθοποιείτω, ἀλλὰ κτησάσθω φίλους τινάς,—καὶ εὐχέσθωσαν περὶ αὐτοῦ, ἵνα μή τι ἐκεῖ πάθῃ.*—4. *Οὔτε νηστεία ἔσται τεταγμένη· ταῦτα γὰρ Ἰουδαϊκά ἐστι, καὶ ὑπὸ ζυγὸν δουλείας.—εἰ γὰρ ὅλως βούλομαι νηστεύειν, οἵαν δ' ἂν αἱρήσομαι ἡμέραν ἀπ' ἐμαυτοῦ νηστεύω διὰ τὴν ἐλευθερίαν.* The Protestants were frequently accused of the heresy of Aërius. Walch's Ketzerhist. iii. 321.

[4] Siricii Epist. ad diversos episcopos adv. Jovinianum (about 389) ap. Coustant. Epist. 7 Ambrosii Rescriptum ad Siricium (Epist. 42, ap. Coustant. Ep. Siric. 8). Hieronymi libb. ii. adv. Jovinianum A.D. 392. Augustinus de Haeres. c. 82, and in other writings. Doubtless Jovinian was greatly strengthened by the prevailing prejudice at Rome against monachism, and by the death of Blaesilla (384). See § 96, note 3. He was thus excited to reflection, and was brought to deny the advantages which the monastic state claimed in its favor. Hence also he met with so much acceptance in Rome. See his doctrines in Jerome, i. 2: Dicit, virgines, viduas et maritatas, quae semel in Christo lotae sunt, si non discrepent caeteris operibus, ejusdem esse meriti (August. l. c. virginitatem etiam sanctimonialium, et continentiam sexus virilis in sanctis eligentibus caelibem vitam conjugiorum castorum atque fidelium meritis adaequabat: ita ut quaedam virgines sacrae provectae jam aetatis in urbe Roma, ubi haec docebat, eo audito nupsisse dicantur). Nititur approbare, eos, qui plena fide in baptismate renati sunt, a diabolo non posse subverti (farther below:—non posse tentari: quicunque autem tentati fuerint, ostendi, eos aqua tantum et non spiritu baptizatos, quod in Simone mago legimus: more accurately Jerome adv. Pelag. ii.: Posse hominem baptizatum, si voluerit, nequaquam ultra peccare: i. e., divine grace is communicated fully to man in baptism, and is not increased by the monastic state). Tertium proponit, inter abstinentiam ciborum et cum gratiarum actione perceptionem eorum nullam esse distantiam. Quartum, quod et extremum, esse omnium, qui suum baptisma servaverint, unam in regno caelorum remunerationem. Augustine adds, l. c.: Omnia peccata, sicut stoici philosophi, paria esse dicebat. (Jovinian said: Hieron. adv. Jov. ii. 20: Qui fratri dixerit fatue et raca, reus erit Geenae: et qui homicida fuerit et adulter, mittetur similiter in Geennam), and virginitatem Mariae destruebat, dicens eam pariendo fuisse corruptam.—Comp. Augustin. Retract. ii. 22:

whose opinions were soon after adopted by two monks of Milan, *Sarmatio* and *Barbatianus* (about 396);[5] but especially *Vigilantius* (shortly before 404) of Calagurris in Gaul (now Caseres in the district Commenges in Gascogne), presbyter in Barcelona.[6]

Remanserant autem istae disputationes ejus (Joviniani) in quorundum sermunculis ac susurris, quas palam suadere nullus audebat:—jactabatur, Joviniano responderi non potuisse cum laude, sed cum vituperatione nuptiarum (cf. § 102, note 12). Propter hoc librum edidi, cujus inscriptio est de bono conjugali. Walch, iii. 655. Neander's K. G. ii. ii. 574. Gu. B. Lindner de Joviniano et Vigilantio diss. Lips. 1839. 8. p. 10.

[5] Ambrosii Epist. 63 (al. 82, al. 25) ad Vercellensem ecclesiam: Audio venisse ad vos Sarmationem et Barbatianum, vaniloquos homines, qui dicunt nullum esse abstinentiae meritum, nullum frugalitatis, nullam virginitatis gratiam, pari omnes aestimari pretio, delirare eos, qui jejuniis castigent carnem suam, et menti subditam faciant etc.

[6] Concerning his earlier abode in Palestine (396), and his disputes with Jerome, whom he considered to be a follower of Origen, Hieron. Ep. ad Vigilantium (ap. Martian, Ep. 36, ap. Vallarsi Ep. 61).—Against the later assertions of Vigilantius Hieron. Ep. ad Riparium, A.D. 404 (ap. Martian. Ep. 37, ap. Vallarsi Ep. 109), adv. Vigilantium lib. A.D. 406.—In the latter it is said: Martyrum negat sepulchra veneranda (in Ep. ad Riparium: Ais, Vigilantium, qui κατ' ἀντίφρασιν hoc vocatur nomine, nam Dormitantius rectius diceretur, os foetidum rursus aperire, et putorem spurcissimum contra sanctorum martyrum proferre reliquias: et nos, qui eas suspicimus, appellare cinerarios et idololatras, qui mortuorum hominum ossa veneremur), damnandas dicit esse vigilias nunquam nisi in pascha alleluja cantandum (cf. Bingham, vol. vi. p. 41, ss.), continentiam haeresin, pudicitiam libidinis seminarium.—Proh nefas, episcopos sui sceleris dicitur habere consortes, si tamen episcopi nominandi sunt, qui non ordinant diaconos, nisi prius uxores duxerint, nulli caelibi credentes pudicitiam. Extracts from the writings of Vigilantius: Quid necesse est, te tanto honore non solum honorare, sed etiam adorare illud nescio quid, quod in modico vasculo transferendo colis?—Quid pulverem linteamine circumdatum adorando oscularis?—Prope ritum gentilium videmus sub praetextu religionis introductum in ecclesiis, sole adhuc fulgente moles cereorum accendi, et ubicunque pulvisculum nescio quod in modico vasculo pretioso linteamine circumdatum osculantes adorant. Magnum honorem praebent hujusmodi homines beatissimis martyribus, quos putant de vilissimis cereolis illustrandos, quos agnus, qui est in medio throni cum omni fulgore majestatis suae illustrat.—Vel in sinu Abrahae, vel in loco refrigerii, vel subter aram Dei animae Apostolorum et Martyrum consederunt, nec possunt suis tumulis, et ubi voluerint, adesse praesentes.—Dum vivimus, mutuo pro nobis orare possumus: postquam autem mortui fuerimus, nullius est pro alio exaudienda oratio. Jerome adds still farther: Praeterea iisdem ad me relatum est epistolis, quod contra auctoritatem Pauli—tu prohibeas, Hierosolymam in usus sanctorum aliqua sumtuum solatia dirigi;—hoc unumquemque posse in patria sua facere; nec pauperes defuturos, qui ecclesiae opibus sustentandi sint.—Asseris, eos melius facere, qui utuntur rebus suis, et paulatim fructus possessionum suarum pauperibus dividunt, quam illos, qui possessionibus venumdatis—semel omnia largiuntur.—Dicis: si omnes se clauserint et fuerint in solitudine: quis celebrabit ecclesias? quis saeculares homines lucrifaciet? quis peccantes ad virtutes poterit cohortari? Comp. the writings quoted in § 102, note 1. Barbeyrac pref. p. 48. Ceillier, p. 339, ss. Barbeyrac Traité, p. 251, ss. —Bayle Diction. s. v. Vigilantius. Walch de Vigilantio haeretico orthodoxo. Goett. 1756 (in Pottii Syll. comm. theol. vii. 326). Walch, iii. 673. Lindner de Joviniano et Vigilantio, p. 40.

EIGHTH CHAPTER.

SPREAD OF CHRISTIANITY.

§ 107.

IN THE EAST.

In *Persia*, where there were numerous churches under the metropolitan bishop of *Seleucia* and *Ctesiphon*, Christianity had become an object of suspicion ever since it had prevailed in the Roman empire. The recommendation of Constantine, therefore, in favor of the Persian Christians, had no permanent or good influence with the king (*Sapor II.* 309–381).[1] When a war broke out soon after between the Romans and Persians, Sapor began a tedious and horrible persecution of the Christians with the execution of *Simon, bishop of Seleucia* and *Ctesiphon* (343), under the pretense of his being a spy of the Romans.[2] After *Sapor's* death, indeed, this persecution ceased, *Jezdegerd I.* (400–421) being at first even a friend to the Christians; but the fanatic *Abdas, bishop of Susa*, by the destruction of a fire-temple (414) brought on another persecution as severe, which was finally extinguished by Theodosius II. making war on the Persians (422).[3] The Persian church was always in close connection with the Syrian, and exhibited the same theological tendency. When, therefore, Nestorianism in its native land was forced to give way to violence, it found a secure asylum among Persian Christians; from which time the Persian church separated itself from that of the Roman empire.[4]

Christianity had also been introduced into *Armenia* as early as the second century.[5] In the time of Diocletian, it was spread

1 Constantini Epist. ad regem Persarum ap. Euseb. de vit. Const. iv. 9–13, et ap. Theodoret. i. 24.

2 Sozomen. ii. 9–41. Steph. Evod. Assemani Acta sanctorum Martyrum orientalium et occidentalium. Romae. 1784. fol. Neander's K. G. ii. i. 222.

3 Theodoretus, v. 38. Socrates, vii. 18–21. Neander, S. 235, ss.

4 § 88, at the end.

5 Dionysius Corinthius according to Eusebius, vi. 46, wrote *τοῖς κατὰ 'Αρμενίαν περὶ μετανοίας, ὧν ἐπεσκόπευε Μερουζάνης.*

more widely by *Gregory the Illuminator*,[6] who gained over king *Tiridates* himself to its side, and was consecrated first metropolitan of Armenia in 302 by Leontius, bishop of Caesarea.[7] The long contests that followed, with the adherents of the old religion, had an important political character, so far as the one party was supported by the Persian, the other by the Roman emperors.[8] But when, after the greatest part of Armenia had come under the Persian dominion (428), the Persian kings wished to procure by violence a victory for the Zend-doctrine over Christianity, they found such determined opposition, that they were at last obliged to allow the Christians the free exercise of their religion, after a lengthened war (442–485).[9] In the fifth century, *Mesrop* gave the Armenians their alphabet and a version of the Bible.[10]—Christianity was carried into *Iberia* under Constantine the Great.[11]

At the same time it was introduced into *Ethiopia* by *Frumentius;* first at court, and, very soon after, throughout the country.[12] In *southern Arabia* among the *Homerites*, Constantius endeavored to establish Christianity by means of *Theophilus* (about 350).[13] He seems, however, not to have produced any considerable effect.

[6] Armenian, Lusaworitsch, illuminator. Respecting him see C. F. Neumann's Gesch. der armen. Literatur. Leipzig. 1836. S. 13.

[7] Sozomenus, ii. 8. Mosis Chorenensis (about 440) Historiae Armeniacae libb. iii. ed. Guilelmus et Georgius Guil. Whistoni filii. Londini. 1736. 4. p. 256, ss. Bekehrung Armeniens durch d. heil. Gregor Illuminator, nach nationalhistor. Quellen bearbeitet von P. Mal. Samueljan. Wien. 1844. 8.

[8] Mémoires historiques et géographiques sur l'Armenie par M. J. Saint-Martin (t. ii. Paris. 1818, 19. 8), t. i. p. 306, ss.

[9] A history of these persecutions, from 439–451, and of the general of the Armenians, Wartan, written by a contemporary, Elisã, bishop of the Amadunians, is: The History of Vartan, by Elisaeus, bishop of the Amadunians, translated from the Armenian by C. F. Neumann. Lond. 1830. 4. Comp. St. Martin, i. 321. The proclamation in commendation of the Zend-religion, issued before the beginning of the persecution by the Persian general Mihr-Nerseh, is especially deserving of notice, ap. Saint-Martin, ii. 472, more correctly in the history of Vartan, p. 11.

[10] Goriun's (a disciple of Mesrop) Lebensbeschr. des. heil. Mesrop, aus d. Arm. übersetzt u. erläutert von Dr. B. Welte (Programm.) Tübingen. 1841. 4. Neumann's Gesch. d. arm. Literatur, S. 30. Concerning the many Armenian versions of Greek writers in the succeeding period see Saint-Martin, i. 7. Neumann, S. 71.

[11] Rufini Hist. eccl. x. 10. Socrates, i. 20. Sozomenus, ii. 7. Theodoretus, i. 23 Moses Chorenensis, ii. c. 83.

[12] Rufinus, x. 9. Socrates, i. 19. Sozomenus, ii. 24. Theodoretus, i. 22. Hiobi Ludolfi Historiae Aethiopicae libb. iv. Francof. 1681. fol. lib. iii. c. 2. Ejusdem Commentarius ad hist. Aethiopicam. Ibid. 1691. fol. p. 283, ss.

[13] Philostorgius, ii. 6; iii. 4. Since it was an Arian Christianity, orthodox historians are silent on the subject.

§ 108.

IN THE WEST.

In the preceding period Christianity had been known among the *Goths* (Div. I. § 57), and there was even a Gothic bishop at the council of Nice.[1] After Arianism had been fathered upon them by their ecclesiastical connection with Constantinople,[2] *Ulphilas*, who was consecrated bishop in 348 at Constantinople, became their apostle.[3] When the Christian Goths were oppressed by a persecution, he led a great multitude of them into the habitation about Nicopolis in Moesia, which Constantius had assigned them (355), where, after inventing the Gothic alphabet, he translated the Bible into Gothic.[4] Afterward, Frithigern broke off from Athanarich, the leader of the Visigoths, who persecuted the Christians, with a part of the people, was supported by Valens, and spread Christianity among his subjects. And when the Huns pressed upon the Goths, this portion of the Visigoths received a place of residence from Valens, in Thrace, on condition of their becoming Christians (375); and Ulphilas was especially active in their conversion. Soon after, Arianism was overthrown by Theodosius. Ulphilas died in Constantinople (388), where he endeavored in vain to revive it. Efforts were now made at Constantinople to procure acceptance for the Nicene confession among the Goths, but without much success.

[1] Among the signatures preserved in Latin: Theophilus Gothorum Metropolis (sc. Episc). Socrates also mentions the signature of *Θεόφιλος τῶν Γότθων ἐπίσκοπος*.

[2] According to Theodoret. H. E. iv. 33, Ulfila led away the Goths to Arianism, while he told them *ἐκ φιλοτιμίας γεγενῆσθαι τὴν ἔριν, δογμάτων δὲ μηδεμίαν εἶναι διαφοράν*. It is true, indeed, that the Goths had such a view of the controversy.

[3] Respecting him, Socrates, iv. 33; Sozomenus, vi. 37; Theodoretus, iv. 33; Philostorgius, ii. 5; Jordanis (about 550 in the Eastern Roman Empire, incorrectly called Jornandes, and reckoned a bishop of Ravenna) de Rebus Geticis (in Muratorii Rerum Italicarum scriptores, i. p. 187), c. 25. More exact information respecting him was first furnished by the letter of Auxentius, bishop of Dorostorus, his disciple, which, transferred to a work of the Arian bishop Maximin, has been again found along with it in a cod. Paris, and printed and explained in: G. Waitz über das Leben u. die Lehre des Ulfila. Hannover. 1840. 4.

[4] The most complete edition: Ulfilas. Veteris et Novi Test. versionis gothicae fragmenta quae supersunt, edd. H. C. de Gabelentz et Dr. J. Loebe. Altenburgi et Lips. vol. i. and vol. ii. P. i. 1836, 1843. 4. Comp. Hug's Einleit. in d. N. T. i. 492.

Arian Christianity was diffused by the *Visigoths* with surprising rapidity among the other wandering German tribes, while it was suppressed in the Roman empire.[5] The fact of the Arian doctrine being more easily apprehended, and hatred to the Romans, procured the confidence of the Germans in Arianism; and it soon obtained the reputation of being as generally the Christianity of the Germans as Homousianism was of the Romans.

The *Ostrogoths* and *Vandals* first received Arian Christianity from their countrymen.[6] The *Burgundians* had passed indeed into the Catholic Church after their wandering into Gaul (413); but they afterward (about 450) adopted Arianism, along with their kings, belonging to the Visigothic race. In like manner, Catholic Christianity had been at first received by the *Suevi* in Spain; but Arianism was subsequently disseminated among them by the Visigoths (469). The older Catholic inhabitants of the countries in which these German tribes had settled suffered oppression only from the *Visigoths* and *Vandals*.[7] They were especially persecuted by the latter in a most horrible manner after Africa (431–439) had been conquered by them under their first two kings, *Genseric* († 477) and *Hunerich* († 484).[8] The Christianity of the Germans was still mixed, to a considerable degree, with heathenism: what rude notions they entertained of the former may be seen in the practice of buying off crimes with money, which they soon transferred to Christian repentance.[9]

5 Walch's Ketzerhistorie, Th. 2. S. 553, ss. Cf. Prosper in Chron. Imperiali ad ann. 404. (Chronica medii aevi ed. Roesler. Tübing. 1798. 8. t. i. p. 199): Radagaius Rex Gothorum Italiae limitem vastaturus transgreditur. Ex quo Ariani, qui Romano procul fuerant orbe fugati, barbararum nationum, ad quas se contulere, praesidio erigi coepere.

6 Jordanis, c. 25: Sic quoque Vesegothae a Valente Imp. Ariani potius quam Christiani effecti. De caetero tam Ostrogothis quam Gepidis parentibus suis per affectionis gratiam evangelizantes hujus perfidiae culturam edocentes, omnem ubique linguae hujus nationem ad culturam hujus sectae invitavere.

7 Sidonius Apollinaris (Episc. Arvernorum 472) lib. vii. Ep. 6.

8 Victor Episc. Vitensis wrote, 487, Hist. persecutionis Africanae sub Genserico et Hunnerico Vandalorum regibus, reprinted in Th. Ruinarti Historia persecutionis Vandalicae. Paris. 1694. 8. (Venet. 1732. 4.) Neander's Denkwürdigkeiten, iii. 1, S. 3, ff. F. Papencordt's Gesch. d. vandal. Herrschaft in Afrika. Berlin. 1837. S. 66, 113, 269.

9 Cf. Homilia de haereticis peccata vendentibus, in Mabillon Museum Italicium, t. i. P. ii. p. 27 (according to Mabillon's conjecture, p. 6, belonging to Maximus Taurinensis, about 440): Nec mirari debemus, quod hujusmodi haeretici in nostra aberrare coeperint regione.—Nam ut eorum interim blasphemias seponamus, retexamus, quae sint ipsorum praecepta vivendi. Praepositi eorum, quos Presbyteros vocant, dicuntur tale habere mandatum, ut si quis laicorum fassus fuerit crimen admissum, non dicat illi: age poenitentiam, deplora

Christianity in Britain (Div. I. § 57) was in the mean time very much retarded by the Anglo-Saxons, who had established themselves there from A.D. 449. The Britons still held out in *Wales*, in the mountains of *Northumberland* and *Cornwall*, where alone Christianity was preserved. Shortly before this, Christianity had been established in Ireland by *St. Patrick*[10] (about 430) and spread with rapidity over the island.[11] The seat of the bishop soon arose at *Armagh*.

facta tua, defle peccata; sed dicat: pro hoc crimine da tantum mihi, et indulgetur tibi.—Suscipit ergo dona Presbyter, et pactione quadam indulgentiam de salvatore promittit. Insipiens placitum, in quo dicitur, minus deliquisse Domino, qui plus contulerit Sacerdoti. Apud hujusmodi praeceptores semper divites innocentes, semper pauperes criminosi.

[10] According to Ussher, belonging to Kilpatrick in Dumbarton in Scotland; according to John Lanigan Ecclesiastical History of Ireland (2 ed. Dublin. 1829. 4 voll.), i. 93, belonging to Bonavem Taverniae, i. e., Boulogne in Picardy.

[11] Respecting him see particularly his Confessio (in Patricii Opusculis ed. Jac. Waraeus. Lond. 1658. 8; and Acta SS. Mart. ii. 517, after an older text in Betham, P. ii. App. p. xlix.). In this work nothing is found about his journey to Rome, nor of a Papal authorization of a mission to Ireland, of which we find a relation first of all in Hericus Vita S. Germani, i. 12. (Act. SS. Jul. vii.) about 860. Jocelin, in the 12th century, has introduced still more fables in his vita Patricii (Acta SS. Mart. ii. 540). Jac. Usserii Britanicarum ecclesiarum antiquitates, Dublin. 1639. 4. auctius Lond. 1687. fol. Neander's Denkwürdigkeiten, iii. ii. 19. Irish Antiquarian Researches by Sir Will. Betham, P. ii. Dublin. 1826 and 27. 8.

SECOND DIVISION.

FROM THE COUNCIL OF CHALCEDON TO THE BEGINNING OF THE MONOTHELITIC CONTROVERSIES, AND THE TIME OF MUHAMMED. A.D. 451–622.

SOURCES.

I. *Ecclesiastical historians:* The works of the two Monophysites are lost, viz., the presbyter John Aegeates, Hist. eccles. lib. x., of which the first five books comprised the period between 428 and 479 (see Photius Cod. 41, cf. 55); and of Zacharias Rhetor, bishop of Meletina in Lesser Armenia, an excerpt from Socrates and Theodoret, and a continuation to 547 (Greek fragments in Evagrius: 19 Syrian fragments, of which Assemanus Bibl. orient. ii. 53, gave an account, communicated in A. Maji Scriptt. vett. nova coll. x. 361); as also of the Nestorian Basil of Cilicia (presbyter in Antioch, Photius Cod. 107), Eccles. hist. libb. iii. from 450 to 518 (Photius Cod. 42).

Still extant are: Theodorus Lector, in fragments, Evagrius Scholasticus, Nicephorus Callistus (comp. the preface of division 1).

Gennadius, presbyter in Marseilles, † after 495, and Isidore, bishop of Hispalis, † 636, de scriptoribus ecclesiasticis, both in Fabricii Bibliotheca eccles. Hamb. 1718. fol.

II. Profane historians: Procopius Caesariensis († after 522, de bello Persico libb. ii., de bello Vandalico libb. ii., de bello Gothico libb. iv., historia arcana Justiniani, de aedificiis Justiniani Imp. libb. vi. Opp. ex rec. Gu. Dindorfii, voll. iii. Bonnae. 1833–38. 8).—Agathias Myrinaeus (Historiarum libb. v., written about 580, ed. B. G. Niebuhr. Bonnae. 1828. 8).

Chronicon paschale (comp. the preface of division 1).

Theophanes Confessor († 817, Chronographia from 285 to 813, ex rec. Jo. Classeni, voll. ii. Bonnae. 1839, 41. 8.

III. Latin chroniclers (comp. preface to division 1): Marcellinus Comes, till 534, continued by another till 566 (in Sirmondi

Opp. ii. Bibl. PP. Lugd. ix. 517). Victor, bishop of Tunnuna, from 444 till 566 (ap. Canisius-Basnage, i. 321, best printed in Henr. Florez Espanna Sagrada, vi. 382). Isidore, bishop of Seville, from the creation of the world till 614 (in Esp. Sagr. vi. 445).

IV. Imperial decrees: Codex Justinianeus, see preface to division 1.—Novellae (νεαραὶ διατάξεις μετὰ τὸν κώδικα).

FIRST CHAPTER.

ENTIRE SUPPRESSION OF PAGANISM IN THE ROMAN EMPIRE.

§ 109.

In *the east*, the remains of paganism disappeared under Justinian I. (527–565), who abolished the New Platonic school at Athens (529),[1] and compelled the heathen to submit to baptism.[2] Only the free Maenotts in the Peloponnesus clung obstinately to it.[3] Even in *the west* it was not yet completely extirpated. Theodoric was obliged to prohibit sacrifices to the gods on pain of death;[4] and at the end of the fifth century many heathen practices were still continued at Rome, and could not be abolished without resistance.[5] Still longer did various

[1] Joh. Malala (about 600) Historia chronica (libb. xviii. from the creation of the world to the death of Justinian I.) ex. rec. Lud. Dindorfii. Bonnae. 1831. 8. p. 451. Exile of the philosophers Damascius, Isidorus, Simplicius, Eulamius, Hermias, Diogenes, and Priscian, into Persia, Agathias, ii. 30. Cf. Wesselingii Observationum variarum (Traj. ad Rhen. 1740. 8), lib. i. c. 28.

[2] Cod. Justin. lib. i. tit. xi. (de paganis et sacrificiis et templis) l. 10. Theophanes, i. 276, activity of Johannes Episc. Asiae (probably a missionary bishop for the conversion of the heathen in Asia Minor) see Assemani Bibl. Orient. ii. 85. As late as the year 561 heathens were discovered in Constantinople (Joh. Malala, p. 491).

[3] Till the ninth century. See Div. I. § 44.—According to J. Ph. Fallmerayer Gesch. d. Halbinsel Morea während des Mittelalters (2 Th. Stuttg. u. Tübingen. 1830. 36), i. 169, 189, heathen Slavonians had seized upon, from 578 till 589, the interior of Macedonia, Thessaly, Hellas, and the Peloponnesus; but this first happened about 746, though single Slavonian colonies in those parts may have been older. See J. W. Zinkeisen's Gesch. Griechenlands v. Anfange geschichtl. Kunde bis auf unsere Tage. Th. 1 (Leipzig. 1832), S. 689, 741.

[4] See Lindenbrogii Cod. legum antt. p. 255.

[5] Cf. Salvianus Massil. above § 79, note 23. Gelasius P. (492–496) adv. Andromachum Senatorem caeterosque Romanos, qui Lupercalia secundum morem pristinum colenda constituebant (ap. Mansi, viii. p. 95, ss.). He shows of what a sacrilege he is guilty, qui cum se Christianum videri velit, et profiteatur, et dicat, palam tamen publiceque prae-

superstitions adhere to those heathen temples which were not destroyed.[6] In many distant places paganism was maintained for a long time undisturbed. Sacrifices were offered in a temple of Apollo on Mount Cassinum, until Benedict (529) transformed it into a chapel of St. Martin.[7] In Sicily,[8] but especially in Sardinia[9] and Corsica,[10] there were still many heathen about A.D. 600. Even Gregory the Great did not hesitate now to advise violent measures, with the view of effecting their conversion.[11]

dicare non horreat, non refugiat, non pavescat, ideo morbos gigni, quia daemonia non colantur, et deo Februario non litetur.—Quando Anthemius Imperator Romam venit (about 470), Lupercalia utique gerebantur—dum haec mala hodieque perdurant, ideo haec ipsa imperia defecerunt, ideo etiam nomen Romanorum, non remotis etiam Lupercalibus, usque ad extrema quaeque pervenit. Et ideo nunc ea removenda suadeo.—Postremo si de meorum persona praescribendum aestimas praedecessorum: unusquisque nostrorum administrationis suae redditurus est rationem.—Ego negligentiam accusare non audeo praedecessorum, cum magis credam fortasse tentasse eos, ut haec pravitas tolleretur, et quasdam extitisse causas et contrarias voluntates, quae eorum intentionibus praepedirent: sicut ne nunc quidem vos istos absistere insanis conatibus velle perpenditis. Beugnot Hist. de la déstruction du Paganisme en Occident, ii. 273.

[6] Palladium in the temple of Fortune, Procop. de Bello Goth. i. 15. The temple of Janus, i. 25. The Pantheon continued till 610 with its idololatriae sordibus, Paulus Diac. Hist. Longob. iv. 37. Beugnot, ii. 288.

[7] Gregorii M. Dialog. lib. ii. Beugnot, ii. 285. At a still later period heathen rites of worship in holy groves were practiced in the diocese of Terracina. Gregorii M. viii. Ep. 18, ad Agnellum Episc. Terracin.

[8] Gregor. M. lib. iii. Epist. 62.

[9] Gregor. M. lib. iv. Epist. 26; and lib. ix. Epist. 65; ad Januar. Episc. Caralitanum, lib. v.; Epist. 41, ad Constantinam Augustam.

[10] Gregor. M. lib. viii. Epist. 1.

[11] He prescribes, lib. iv. Ep. 26, in case a peasant should obstinately persist in heathenism: Tanto pensionis onere gravandus est, ut ipsa exactionis suae poena compellatur ad rectitudinem festinare. And lib. ix. Epist. 65: Contra idolorum quoque cultores vel aruspices atque sortilegos Fraternitatem vestram vehementius pastorali hortamur invigilare custodia, atque publice in populo contra hujus rei viros sermonem facere, eosque a tanti labe sacrilegii et divini intentatione judicii, et praesentis vitae periculo, adhortatione suasoria revocare. Quos tamen si emendare se a talibus atque corrigere nolle repereris, ferventi comprehendere zelo te volumus: et siquidem servi sunt, verberibus cruciatibusque quibus ad emendationem pervenire valeant, castigare. Si vero sunt liberi, inclusione digna districtaque sunt in poenitentiam dirigendi; ut qui salubria et a mortis periculo revocantia audire verba contemnunt, cruciatus saltem eos corporis ad desideratum mentis valeat reducere sanitatem.

SECOND CHAPTER.

HISTORY OF THEOLOGY.

§ 110.

MONOPHYSITE CONTROVERSIES.

Sources: Fragments of Acts of Councils collected by Mansi, vii. 481.–ix. 700. Liberati Breviarum (see preface to § 88).—Breviculus Hist. Eutych. (see preface to § 89).—Leontii Byzantini (about 600?) de sectis liber, in x. actiones distributus (prim. ed. Jo. Leunclavius in Legat. Manuelis Comneni ad Armenos. Basil. 1578. 8, in Gallandii Bibl. PP. t. xii. p. 621, ss.), actio v.–x. Ejusdem contra Eutychianos et Nestorianos, libb. iii. (lat. ex. Fr. Turriani versione ap. Canisius-Basnage, i. 535; ap. Gallandius xii. 658; in Greek Ang. Maji Spicileg. roman. x. ii. 1). Zachariae Rhet., et Theodori Lect., Hist. eccl. fragmenta.—Evagrius, ii. 5, ss. Theophanes, ed. Paris. p. 92, ss.
Works: Walch's Ketzerhistorie, vi. 461, vii. and viii. Baur's Lehre, v. d. Dreieingkeit und Menschwerdung Gottes, ii. 37.

The decisions of the council of Chalcedon were regarded by the Egyptian party as completely Nestorian.[1] There was therefore an insurrection of monks in *Palestine*, led on by one of their number, Theodosius, against Juvenal, bishop of Jerusalem, and favored by the widowed empress Eudoxia, which was finally crushed after much bloodshed (451–453).[2] But in *Alexandria*, a considerable party, headed by the presbyter, *Timothy* ὁ αἴλουρος, and the deacon *Peter* ὁ μογγός (*i. e.*, blaesus, Liberat. c. 16), separated from the newly-appointed bishop Proterius. The

[1] So also the Monophysites related that Leo the Great and Theodoret had been completely reconciled to Nestorius; that the latter had been invited to the Synod of Chalcedon by the Emperor Marcian, but had died on the way. See Zachariae Hist. eccl. in Maji Scriptt. vett. nova coll. x. 361, and Xenayas, bishop of Mabug, about 500, in Assemani Bibl. or. ii. 40. On the other hand, it is remarked by Evagrius, ii. 2, that Nestorius had died previously.

[2] Zachariae Fragm. ap. Majus, x. 363. Vita S. Euthymii Abbatis († 472) by Cyril of Scythopolis (about 555), in an enlarged form, by Simeon Metaphrastes in Cotelerii Monum. Eccles. Graec. ii. 200; in a shorter, perhaps a genuine form, in the Analectis Graecis (ed. Benedictini mon. Jac. Lopinus, B. Montfaucon, Ant. Pugetus. Paris. 1688. 4), p. 1, ss. Juvenal had before sided with the Egyptians, and was also at first at Chalcedon on the side of Dioscurus: but (Zacharias, l. c.) accepta demum ab Imperatore promissione de subjiciendis tribus Palaestinae sedibus honori cathedrae hierosolymitanae, mentis oculos sibi obstruxit, solum destituit in certamine Dioscorum, et adversariorum in partes transiit.

greatest part of this faction continued to maintain the doctrine of one nature, rejected the council of Chalcedon, and considered Dioscurus as unjustly deposed;[3] while, on the contrary, they

[3] The most important representative of this tendency which we have is Severus, Monophysite patriarch of Antioch, from A.D. 513. (See below, note 19.) Comp. my Comm. qua Monophysitarum veterum variae de Christi persona opiniones imprimis ex ipsorum effatis recens. editis illustrantur (Partic. ii. Gotting. 1835, 38. 4), i. 9, ss. Severi locus (prim. ed. Mansi, vii. 831. Gallandius, xii. 733, is, according to Maji Scriptt. vett. nova coll. vii. i. 136, from Severi lib. contra Grammaticum, Joannem Ep. Caesareae): *Δύο τὰς φύσεις ἐν τῷ Χριστῷ νοοῦμεν, τὴν μὲν κτιστὴν, τὴν δὲ ἄκτιστον· ἀλλ' οὐδεὶς ἐγράψατο τὴν ἐν Χαλκηδόνι σύνοδον τὴν ἄλογον ταύτην γραφὴν, τί δήποτε δύο φύσεις ὠνόμασαν περὶ τῆς τοῦ 'Εμμανουὴλ ἑνώσεως διαλαμβάνοντες. οὐδεὶς ταύτην ἔστησε τὴν κατηγορίαν, ἀλλ' ἐκείνην μάλα δικαίως, τί δήποτε μὴ ἀκολουθήσαντες τῷ ἁγίῳ Κυρίλλῳ ἐκ δύο φύσεων ἔφασαν εἶναι τὸν Χριστόν. Οὐ παυσόμεθα λέγοντες, ὡς δειξάτω τις τὴν ἐν Χαλκηδόνι σύνοδον ἢ τὸν τόμον Λέοντος τὴν καθ' ὑπόστασιν ἕνωσιν ὁμολογήσαντας, ἢ σύνοδον φυσικὴν, ἢ ἐξ ἀμφοῖν ἕνα Χριστὸν, ἢ μίαν φύσιν τοῦ θεοῦ λόγου σεσαρκωμένην· καὶ τότε γνωσόμεθα, ὡς κατὰ τὸν σοφώτατον Κύριλλον θεωρίᾳ μόνῃ ἀνακρίνοντες τὴν οὐσιώδη διαφορὰν τῶν συνενεχθέντων ἀποῤῥήτως εἰς ἓν ἴσασι· καὶ ὡς ἑτέρα ἡ τοῦ λόγου φύσις, καὶ ἑτέρα ἡ τῆς σαρκὸς, καὶ ὡς δύο τὰ ἀλλήλοις συνενηνεγμένα καθορῶσι τῷ νῷ, διϊστῶσι δὲ οὐδαμῶς.* Ex ejusd. ad Jo. Grammat. lib. ii. c. 1, ap. Majum, l. c. p. 138: *Καὶ τῶν, ἐξ ὧν ἡ ἕνωσις, μενόντων ἀμειώτων καὶ ἀναλλοιώτων, ἐν συνθέσει δὲ ὑφεστώτων καὶ οὐκ ἐν μονάσιν ἰδιοσυστάτοις.* Ex ejusd. epist. iii. ad Joannem ducem ap. Majum, l. c. p. 71: *"Εως ἂν οὖν εἷς ἐστιν ὁ Χριστὸς, μίαν ὡς ἑνὸς αὐτοῦ τήν τε φύσιν καὶ τὴν ὑπόστασιν καὶ τὴν ἐνέργειαν σύνθετον ἐπ' ὄρους ὑψηλοῦ, τὸ δὴ λεγόμενον, ἀναβάντες κηρύττομεν, ἀναθεματίζοντες καὶ πάντας τοὺς ἐπ' αὐτοῦ μετὰ τὴν ἕνωσιν δυάδα φύσεων καὶ ἐνεργειῶν δογματίζοντας.*—Collatio Catholicorum cum Severianis habita Constantinop. anno 531, ap. Mansi, viii. 822: Quod ex duabus quidem naturis dicere unam significat Dei verbi naturam incarnatam, secundum b. Cyrillum et SS. Patres: in duabus autem naturis duas personas et duas subsistentias significat. At the same time they allowed that Christ is *κατὰ σάρκα ὁμοούσιος ἡμῖν* (Leontius de Sectis, act. 5. Evagrius, iii. 5).—Severus ap. Anastasius Sinaita (about 560) in the *'Οδηγὸς* adv. Acephalos (prim. ed. J. Gretser. Ingolst. 1606. 4), c. 18: *"Ωσπερ ἐπὶ τῆς μιᾶς τοῦ ἀνθρώπου φύσεως μέρος μὲν ταύτης ἐστὶν ἡ ψυχὴ, μέρος δὲ τὸ σῶμα, οὕτω καὶ ἐπὶ τοῦ Χριστοῦ, καὶ τῆς μιᾶς αὐτοῦ φύσεως, μέρους τάξιν ἐπέχει ἡ θεότης, καὶ μέρους τὸ σῶμα.* This comparison was frequently used by the Monophysites generally after Cyril's example (see Ep. ad Succensum, above § 88, note 21), and in like manner by Philoxenus or Xenayas, bishop of Mabug (488–518) in Assemani Bibl. orient. ii. 25. Gelasius I. (bishop of Rome, 492–496) de duabus naturis in Christo adv. Eutychen et Nestorium (in Bibl. PP. and in Jo. Heroldi Haereseologia. Basil. 1556. p. 686): Adhuc autem etiam illud adjiciunt, ut sicut ex duabus rebus constat homo, id est ex anima et corpore, quamvis utriusque rei sit diversa natura, sicut dubium non habetur, plerumque tamen usus loquendi singulariter pronunciet, simul utrumque complectens, ut humanam dicat naturam, non humanas naturas: sic potentiam in Christi mysterio, et unitionem divinitatis atque humanitatis unam dici vel debere vel posse naturam: non considerantes, quia cum una natura dicatur humana, quae tamen ex duabus constet, id est ex anima et corpore principaliter, illa causa est, quia nec initialiter anima alibi possit existere, quam in corpore, nec corpus valeat constare sine anima: et merito, quae alterutro sibi sit causa existendi, pariter unam abusive dici posse naturam, quae sibi invicem causam praebeat, ut ex alterutro natura subsistat humana, salva proprietate duntaxat duarum. According to the decrees of the synod at Chalcedon, *φύσις* and *οὐσία* are synonymous, while *τὸ ἄτομον* and *ἡ ὑπόστασις* are different from them. But the Monophysites took *φύσις*, *ὑπόστασις*, and *ἄτομον* synonymously, and separated *ἡ οὐσία* from them. See Maji Scriptt. vett. nova coll. vii. 1, 11, ss.; my Comm. i. 11. That this was also the phraseology employed by Cyril is acknowledged by Eubulus, bishop of Lystra, ap. Majus, l. c. p. 31, who endeavors to exculpate him on that account. And that this controversy was more about correctness

approved of the condemnation of Eutyches, for his supposed Docetism.[4] But as the doctrine of one nature had before led, in some cases, to the idea of considering the body of Jesus as something superhuman,[5] so also now, many attributed peculiar excellencies to it.[6] To the most influential advocates of the doctrine of one nature, Athanasius and Cyril, was now added *Pseudo-Dionysius, the Areopagite*, whose writings were doubtless composed in Egypt toward the end of the fifth century,[7] and there-

of expression than of idea, even the monk Eustathius, with all his bitterness against Severus, is obliged to allow. See Majus, l. c. p. 291, and my Comm. i. 23.

[4] Collatio Cathol. cum Severianis apud Mansi, t. viii. p. 818: Qualem opinionem de Eutyche habetis? Orientales dixerunt: Tanquam haereticus, magis autem princeps haeresis. Zacharias (ap. Evagrium, iii. 5): *Οἱ τὴν Εὐτυχοῦς φαντασίαν νοσοῦντες ἀνὰ τὴν βασιλεύουσαν, καὶ τὸν μονήρη διώκοντες βίον, ὥσπερ ἑρμαίῳ τινὶ περιτυχεῖν οἰηθέντες* Τιμοθέῳ (Aeluro),—*δρομαῖοι παρ' αὐτὸν ἀφικνοῦνται, καὶ ὡς διελεγχθέντες πρὸς* Τιμοθέον, *ὁμοούσιον ἡμῖν εἶναι κατὰ σάρκα τὸν τοῦ θεοῦ λόγον, καὶ τῷ πατρὶ ὁμοούσιον κατὰ τὴν θεότητα, ἐς τοὐπίσω ἀνεχώρουν.* Prevailing notion respecting the doctrine of Eutyches: Hormisdae P. Epist. 30, ad Caesarium: Eutyches carnis negans veritatem,—ut Manichaeam phantasiam ecclesiis Christi—insereret, etc. Justinianus in Codice, i. i. 5: (anathematizamus) et Eutychetem mente captum, *phantasiam inducentem.* Vigilius Tapsensis (about 484) adv. Eutychen, libb. v. (Opp. ed. P. F. Chiffletius. Divione. 1664. 4), in the beginning of lib. iii.: Eutychiana haeresis in id impietatis prolapsa est errore, ut non solum verbi et carnis unam credat esse naturam, verum etiam hanc eandem carnem non de sacro Mariae virginis corpore adsumtam, sed de coelo dicat, juxta infandum Valentini et Marcionis errorem, fuisse deductam. Ita pertinaciter verbum carnem adserens factum, ut per virginem, ac si aqua per fistulam, transisse videatur, non tamen ut de virgine aliquid, quod nostri sit generis, adsumsisse credatur. Liberatus, c. 11, Samuel, presbyter in Edessa, went so far as to attempt to prove to the Eutychians veram humani generis carnem a Deo assumtam, et non de coelo exhibitam, nec crassi aëris substantiam in carne incessisse formatam (Gennadius de vir. illustr. c. 82).

[5] See Theodoreti Eranistes, et Isidor. Pelus. § 89, note 2.

[6] So said Dioscurus (in Maji Nova coll. vii. i. 289): 'Ι. Χρ. *γενόμενος ἄνθρωπος—τοῖς ἀνθρωπίνοις κεκοινώνηκε πάθεσιν οὐ κατὰ φύσιν, ἀλλὰ κατὰ χάριν.* And *μὴ γένοιτο ἑνὸς τῶν κατὰ φύσιν λέγειν ἡμᾶς ὁμοούσιον τὸ αἷμα Χριστοῦ.* Timotheus Aelurus (l. c. p. 277): *Φύσις δὲ Χριστοῦ μία μόνη θεότης* (consequently not as according to Severus: *φύσις σύνθετος*), and: *Εἰ γὰρ ἦν ἄνθρωπος κατὰ φύσιν καὶ νόμον ὁ μέλλων ἀποτελεῖσθαι ἄνθρωπος ἐν μήτρᾳ τῆς παρθένου, οὐκ ἂν ἐτέχθη ἐξ αὐτῆς εἰ μὴ πρῶτον τῆς παρθενίας διαλυθείσης.*

[7] De hierarchia coelesti, de hierarchia ecclesiastica, de nominibus divinis, de theologia mystica, epistolae (ed. Paris. 1644, 2 voll. fol.) falsely ascribed to the Dionysius mentioned in Acts xvii. 34, who, according to Dionys. Corinth. ap. Euseb. iii. 4, iv. 23, was the first bishop of Athens. The first trace of these writings which has been preserved to us, belongs to the beginning of the sixth century, when Joannes Scythopolitanus wrote scholia on them (Le Quien dissertt. Damasc. prefixed to his edition of Joannes Damasc. i. fol. xxxviii. verso). The Monophysite patriarch of Antioch, Severus, cites them (see note 8), and the no less respectable orthodox writer Ephraemius, who, from 526, was patriarch of Antioch, refers to them (ap. Photius Cod. 229, ed. Hoeschel. p. 420). When, however, in the collatio Catholicorum cum Severianis, in the year 531, the Monophysites appealed to them (Mansi, viii. 817), Hypatius, archbishop of Ephesus, judged, ostendi non posse, ista vera esse, quae nullus antiquus memoraverit. Subsequently many were found in the Greek church, who always asserted the spuriousness of these writings (Maximi Prol. in schol. Dionys. p. 45, Photius Cod. 1). In the Latin church, in which they had been widely diffused from

fore coincided with the mode of expounding the doctrine of Christ's person adopted by Cyril.[8] Among the many heretical names which the party received from its opponents,[9] the appellation Μονοφυσῖται was the most common. On the other hand they called the opposite party Δυοφυσῖται, or Διφυσῖται.[10]

The death of Marcian († 457) inspired the Monophysites with new hopes. At *Alexandria*, Proterius was killed in an insurrection; and *Timotheus Aelurus*, chosen bishop. The emperor, *Leo I.* (457–474) actually requested a new decision of the bishops respecting adherence to the decrees of the council of Chalcedon. But as the majority declared themselves in favor of the synod,[11] Timotheus Aelurus was banished, and *Timotheus*

the ninth century, Laurentius Valla († 1457) was the first that detected the imposition He was followed in his opinion by the ablest scholars of the day; and Jo. Dallaeus de Scriptis, quae sub Dionysii Areop. et Ignatii Ant. nominibus circumferentur. Genevae. 1666. 4, finally exhibited in a copious form the evidence of their spuriousness. Cf. le Quien l. c. Salig de Eutychianismo ante Eutychen. Wolfenbuttelae. 1723. 4, p. 159, ss. J. G. V. Engelhardt Diss. de Dionysio Plotinizante. Erlang. 1820. 8. Id. de Origine scriptorum Areopagiticorum. Erl. 1823. 8. The same writer's Die angebl. Schriften des Areopagiten Dionysius, übers. u. m. Abhandlungen begleitet. Sulzbach. 1823, 2 Theile. 8. Baumgarten-Crusius de Dionysio Areop. comm. 1823 (Opusc. theol. p. 261), departing from the opinions of others, attributes these writings to the third century, and thinks they were written with the object of transferring the Greek mysteries to Christianity. See against this hypothesis Ritter Gesch. d. christl. Philos. ii. 519.

[8] He combats the excrescences of it, the doctrines of a confusion and transmutation, de Eccles. hierarchia, c. 3 (Opp. i. 297, 299), de Divinis nominibus, c. 2 (l. c. p. 501). The principal passage is in Epist. iv. ad Cajum (Opp. ii. 75): *Οὐδὲ ἄνθρωπος ἦν, οὐχ ὡς μὴ ἄνθρωπος, ἀλλ' ὡς ἐξ ἀνθρώπων, ἀνθρώπων ἐπέκεινα, καὶ ὑπὲρ ἄνθρωπον ἀληθῶς ἄνθρωπος γεγονώς. Καὶ τὸ λοιπὸν, οὐ κατὰ Θεὸν τὰ θεῖα δράσας, οὐ τὰ ἀνθρώπεια κατὰ ἄνθρωπον, ἀλλ' ἀνδρωθέντος Θεοῦ, καινήν τινα τὴν θεανδρικὴν ἐνέργειαν ἡμῖν πεπολιτευμένος.* The last words of this passage are addressed by Severus, Epist. ad Joannem ducem, in Maji Collect. vii. 1, 71, as a *φωνὴν τοῦ πανσόφου Διονυσίου τοῦ* 'Αρεοπαγητικοῦ, and enlarged by the addition of *τὸν ἀνδρωθέντα θεὸν, τὸν ταύτην (ἐνέργειαν) καινοπρεπῶς πεπολιτευμένον, μίαν ὁμολογοῦμεν φύσιν τε καὶ ὑπόστασιν θεανδρικὴν, ὥσπερ καὶ τὴν μίαν φύσιν τοῦ θεοῦ λόγου σεσαρκωμένην.* The Monophysites obtained from Dionysius a new formula in addition to the old Athanasian one.

[9] At different times and places, for example, Acephali, Severiani, Aegyptii, Jacobitae, Timotheani, etc.—Facundus Episc. Hermianensis (about 540) pro defensione iii. capitulorum (libb. v. prim. ed. Jac. Sirmond. Paris. 1629. 8. ap. Gallandius, t. xi. p. 655), lib. i. c. 5, et iv. c. 3: Acephali vocantur a Graecis, quos significantius nos Semieutychianos possumus appellare. This name, however, never became usual.

[10] So Timotheus Aelurus, in Maji Coll. vii. 1, 277.

[11] The letters are collected in the Codex encyclius. Mansi, t. vii. p. 777, ss., gives their form, and the writings themselves also in the same volume, p. 521, ss. Most remarkable is the Epist. Episcoporum Pamphyliae. Ibid. p. 573, ss.: Doctrina—quae a S. Niceano concilio gratia spiritali prolata est—omnia complet et omnibus valde sufficit—Nos et Nicaenum synodum debito honore veneramur, et Chalcedonensum quoque suscipimus, veluti scutum eam contra haereticos opponentes, et non anathema (leg. mathema, *μάθημα*) fidei existentem. Non enim ad populum a papa Leone et a S. Chalcedonensi concilio scripta est, ut ex hoc debeant scandalum sustinere, sed tantummodo sacer-

σαλοφακίαλος nominated in his place (460), who succeeded in maintaining the tranquillity of Alexandria by his prudent, conciliating conduct toward the opposite party. It is true, that new commotions arose soon after even in Antioch. *Peter* the Fuller (ὁ γναφεύς), a monk of Constantinople, and an enemy of the council of Chalcedon, endeavored to carry through here the favorite formula of the Monophysites θεὸς ἐσταυρώθη, and even to introduce it into the *Trisagion*;[12] succeeded in gaining over the monks to his party; and put himself in the place of the deposed patriarch; but not long after he was banished by an imperial decree (about 470), and there was hope of seeing the schism gradually disappear and be every where forgotten. But it proved incurable when *Basiliscus*, having driven the emperor Zeno Isauricus from the throne (476, 477), declared in favor of the Monophysites, reinstated Timotheus Aelurus and Peter the Fuller in their dignities, and by the *Encyclion*, required all bishops (476) to condemn the synod of Chalcedon.[13]

dotibus, ut habeant quo possint repugnare contrariis. Duarum namque naturarum sive substantiarum unitatem in uno Christo declaratam invenimus a pluribus apud nos consistentibus sanctis et religiosissimis patribus, et nequaquam veluti mathema aut symbolum his qui baptizantur hoc tradimus, sed ad bella hostium reservamus. Si vero propter medelam eorum, qui per simplicitatem scandalizati noscuntur, placuerit vestrae potentiae, Christo amabilis imperator, S. Leoni Rom. civ. episcopo, nec non aliorum pariter sanctitati, propter istorum (sicut dixi) condescensionem et satisfactionem, quatenus idem sanctissimus vir literis suis declaret, quia non est symbolum neque mathema epistola, quae tunc ab eo ad sanctae memoriae nostrum archiepiscopum Flavianum directa est, et quod a sancto concilio dictum est, sed haereticae pravitatis potius increpatio: simul et illud, quod ab eis est dictum, "in duabus naturis," quod forte eis dubium esse dignoscitur, dum a patre prolatum sit propter eos, qui veram Dei verbi incarnationem negant, his sermonibus apertius indicatum, ita tamen, ut in nullo sanctae synoda fiat injuria Nihil enim differt, sive duarum naturarum unitas inconfusa dicatur, sive ex duabus eodem modo referatur. Sed neque si una dicatur verbi natura, inferatur autem incarnata, aliud quid significat, sed idem honestiori sermone declarat. Nam et invenimus saepius hoc dixisse SS. patres. Apud vestrae pietatis imperium, quod significat vestra potentia decenter ago, quia ipsa synodus permanebit, sicut ecclesiae membra discerpta copulabuntur hoc sermone curata, et ea, quae contra sacerdotes nefanda committuntur, cessabunt, et ora haereticorum contra nos aperta damnabuntur, et omnia reducentur ad pacem, et fiet, sicut scriptum est, unus grex et unus pastor. Quoniam et dominus Christus multa condescensione circa nos usus, et humanum salvavit genus: et quia cum dives esset, utique divinitate, pauper factus est pro nobis, secundum quod homo fieri voluit, ut nos illa paupertate ditaremur, sicut b. Paulus edicit, etc.

[12] The elder τρισάγιον consisted of the words Is. vi. 3; cf. Constitt. apost. viii. 12. Miraculous origin of the later one under Theodosius II. (Felicis Papae Ep. ad Petrum, Full. ap. Mansi, vii. 1041. Acacii Ep. ad. eund. ibid. p. 1121): Ἅγιος ὁ θεὸς, ἅγιος ἰσχυρὸς, ἅγιος ἀθάνατος (ὁ σταυρωθεὶς δι' ἡμᾶς), ἐλέησον ἡμᾶς. Cf. Suiceri Thes. ii. 1310. Bingham, vi. p. 37, ss. Walch's Ketzerhistorie, vii. 239.

[13] In the Ἐγκύκλιον (ap. Evagrius, iii. 4), it is said: Θεσπίζομεν τὴν κρηπῖδα καὶ βεβαίωσιν τῆς ἀνθρωπίνης εὐζωΐας, τουτέστι τὸ σύμβολον τῶν τιη' ἁγίων πατέρων τῶν

It was not long, indeed, before the persevering *Acacius*, patriarch of Constantinople, succeeded in exciting a popular tumult, which was the means of restoring *Zeno Isauricus* to the throne (477–491); but in the mean time, the principles of the Monophysites had been so firmly established in Egypt by these occurrences, that Zeno, by the advice of Acacius, issued the *Henoticon*[14] (482), in which both parties were to be brought into a state of peace and union by reducing the points at issue to more general principles. *Peter Mongus* was patriarch of Alexandria, and subscribed the Henoticon. Many Monophysites, however, displeased at this, separated from him, and were called Ἀκέφαλοι, without a head.[15] *Peter the Fuller* was once more

ἐν Νικαίᾳ πάλαι μετὰ τοῦ ἁγίου πνεύματος ἐκκλησιασθέντων—μόνον πολιτεύεσθαι και κρατεῖν ἐν πάσαις ταῖς ἁγιωτάταις τοῦ θεοῦ ἐκκλησίαις τὸν ὀρθόδοξον λαὸν, ὡς μόνον τῆς ἀπλανοῦς πίστεως ὅρον, καὶ ἀρκοῦν εἰς ἀναίρεσιν μὲν καθόλου πάσης αἱρέσεως, ἕνωσιν δὲ ἄκραν τῶν ἁγίων τοῦ θεοῦ ἐκκλησιῶν· ἐχόντων δηλαδὴ τὴν οἰκείαν ἰσχὺν, καὶ τῶν εἰς βεβαίωσιν αὐτοῦ τοῦ θείου συμβόλου πεπραγμένων ἔν τε τῇ βασιλευούσῃ πόλει ταύτῃ—παρὰ τῶν ρν′ ἁγίων πατέρων, ἔτι δὲ καὶ πάντων τῶν πεπραγμένων ἐν τῇ Ἐφεσίων μητροπόλει κατὰ τοῦ δυσσεβοῦς Νεστορίου, καὶ τῶν μετὰ ταῦτα τὰ ἐκείνου φρονησάντων· τὰ δὲ διελόντα τὴν ἕνωσιν καὶ εὐταξίαν τῶν ἁγίων τοῦ θεοῦ ἐκκλησιῶν καὶ εἰρήνην τοῦ κόσμου παντὸς, δηλαδὴ τὸν λεγόμενον τόμον Λέοντος, καὶ πάντα τὰ ἐν Χαλκηδόνι ἐν ὅρῳ πίστεως ἢ ἐκθέσει συμβόλων—εἰρημένα καὶ πεπραγμένα εἰς καινοτομίαν κατὰ τοῦ μνημονευθέντος ἁγίου συμβόλου τῶν τιη′ ἁγίων πατέρων, θεσπίζομεν ἐνταῦθά τε καὶ πανταχοῦ καθ' ἑκάστην ἐκκλησίαν παρὰ τῶν ἁπανταχοῦ ἁγιωτάτων ἐπισκόπων ἀναθεματίζεσθαι, καὶ πυρὶ παραδίδοσθαι παρ' οἷς ἂν εὑρίσκηται.—θεσπίζομεν τοὺς πανταχοῦ ἁγιωτάτους ἐπισκόπους ἐμφανιζομένῳ τῷ θείῳ τούτῳ ἡμῶν ἐγκυκλίῳ γράμματι καθυπογράφειν σαφῶς καταμηνύοντας, ὅτι δὴ μόνῳ τῷ θείῳ στοιχοῦσι συμβόλῳ τῶν τιη′ ἁγίων πατέρων, ὅπερ ἐπεσφράγισαν οἱ ρν′ πατέρες ἅγιοι, ὡς ἔδοξεν ὁριστικῶς καὶ τοῖς μετὰ ταῦτα συνελθοῦσι κατὰ τὴν Ἐφεσίων μητρόπολιν ὀρθοδόξοις καὶ ὁσίοις πατράσιν. Cf. J. Gu. Berger Henotica Orientis. Vitemb. 1723. 4. p. 1, ss.

14 Ap. Evagrius, iii. 14: Αὐτοκράτωρ Καῖσαρ Ζήνων—τοῖς κατὰ Ἀλεξάνδρειαν καὶ Αἴγυπτον, καὶ Λιβύην καὶ Πεντάπολιν, κ. τ. λ.—γινώσκειν ὑμᾶς ἐσπουδάσαμεν, ὅτι καὶ ἡμεῖς καὶ αἱ πανταχοῦ ἐκκλησίαι ἕτερον σύμβολον, ἢ μάθημα, ἢ ὅρον πίστεως, ἢ πίστιν πλὴν τοῦ εἰρημένου ἁγίου συμβόλου τῶν τιη′ ἁγίων πατέρων, ὅπερ ἐβεβαίωσαν οἱ μνημονευθέντες ρν′ ἅγιοι πατέρες, οὔτε ἐσχήκαμεν, οὔτε ἔχομεν, οὔτε ἕξομεν.—ᾧ καὶ ἐξηκολούθησαν οἱ ἅγιοι πατέρες οἱ ἐν τῇ Ἐφεσίων συνελθόντες, οἳ καὶ καθελόντες τὸν ἀσεβῆ Νεστόριον, καὶ τοὺς τὰ ἐκείνου μετὰ ταῦτα φρονοῦντας· ὅντινα καὶ ἡμεῖς Νεστόριον ἅμα καὶ Εὐτυχῆ, τἀναντία τοῖς εἰρημένοις φρονοῦντας, ἀναθεματίζομεν, δεχόμενοι καὶ τὰ ιβ′ κεφάλαια τὰ εἰρημένα παρὰ τοῦ τῆς ὁσίας μνήμης γενομένου Κυρίλλου ἀρχιεπισκόπου τῆς Ἀλεξανδρέων ἁγίας καθολικῆς ἐκκλησίας. Ὁμολογοῦμεν δὲ τὸν μονογενῆ τοῦ θεοῦ υἱὸν καὶ θεὸν τὸν κατὰ ἀλήθειαν ἐνανθρωπήσαντα, τὸν κύριον ἡμῶν Ἰησοῦν Χριστὸν, τὸν ὁμοούσιον τῷ πατρὶ κατὰ τὴν θεότητα καὶ ὁμοούσιον ἡμῖν τὸν αὐτὸν κατὰ τὴν ἀνθρωπότητα, κατελθόντα καὶ σαρκωθέντα ἐκ πνεῦματος ἁγίου καὶ Μαρίας τῆς παρθένου καὶ θεοτόκου, ἕνα τυγχάνειν καὶ οὐ δύο· ἑνὸς γὰρ εἶναι φαμὲν τά τε θαύματα καὶ τὰ πάθη, ἅπερ ἑκουσίως ὑπέμεινε σαρκί. τοὺς γὰρ διαιροῦντας, ἢ συγχέοντας, ἢ φαντασίαν εἰσάγοντας οὐδὲ ὅλως δεχόμεθα· ἐπείπερ ἡ ἀναμάρτητος κατὰ ἀλήθειαν σάρκωσις ἐκ πῆς θεοτόκου προσθήκην υἱοῦ οὐ πεποίηκε.—πάντα δὲ τὸν ἕτερόν τι φρονήσαντα, ἢ φρονοῦντα, ἢ νῦν ἢ πώποτε, ἢ ἐν Χαλκηδόνι, ἢ οἵᾳ δήποτε συνόδῳ, ἀναθεματίζομεν. Berger Henotica Orientis, p. 42, ss.

15 These considered Timothy Aelurus as the last legitimate patriarch. See Eustathii

appointed patriarch of Antioch (485); though many Syrian bishops were deposed because they would not subscribe the Henoticon. The most decided opposition to church fellowship with the Monophysites was presented by the Roman patriarchs, who had become entirely independent of the emperor since the downfall of the western empire (476). All remonstrances proving vain, *Felix II.* issued an anathema (484)[16] against Acacius, and communion between the Eastern and Western churches was broken off.

But even in the east, the Henoticon proved but a weak bond of union, since the questions left indeterminate in it, were continually employing the minds of men. At Constantinople, the council of Chalcedon stood high in estimation; and *the Acoemetae* even continued in communion with the Church of Rome. In Alexandria, the decrees of this council were rejected. In the east, opinions on the subject were divided. Among all these churches, it is true, external fellowship was for the most part maintained by the Henoticon; but it could not be otherwise than that there should be coldness between the parties, which often led to open quarrels. Such was the situation of affairs at the accession of the emperor *Anastasius* (491–518). He adopted the principle of avoiding all interference in religious matters, except to protect the peace of the citizens against fanaticism.[17]

Mon. Epist. ad Timoth. Scholasticum, in Maji Coll. vii. 1, 277: Τούτῳ (Τιμοθέῳ Αἰλούρῳ) *καὶ τοῖς ἀπ' αὐτοῦ μέχρι τῆς σήμερον οὐ κοινωνοῦσιν οἱ Σευήρου, ἀκεφάλους αὐτοὺς προσαγορεύοντες.* However, Timotheus himself seems to have died before the division, since Severus esteems him highly. See his words, l. c.: *Διοσκόρου δὲ καὶ Τιμοθέου τῶν τῆς ἀληθείας ἀγωνιστῶν—τοὺς ἀγῶνας τιμῶ καὶ ἀσπάζομαι.* It might be expected that the strictest Monophysites should have belonged to the Acephali, who considered even the body of Jesus as something higher, and these found passages in Timotheus Aelurus, which agreed with them (see note 6), though he had maintained that the body of Christ is of like essence with our own.

16 Felicis Epist. ad Acacium ap. Mansi, vii. p. 1053. The conclusion: Habe ergo cum his, quos libenter amplecteris, portionem ex sententia praesenti, quam per tuae tibi direximus ecclesiae defensorem, sacerdotali honore, et communione catholicae, nec non etiam a fidelium numero segregatus; sublatum tibi nomen et munus ministerii sacerdotalis agnosce, S. Spiritus judicio et apostolica auctoritate damnatus, numquamque anathematis vinculis exuendus.—Theophanes, p. 114: *'Ακάκιος δὲ ἀναισθήτως ἔσχε περὶ τὴν καθαίρεσιν, καὶ τὸ ὄνομα αὐτοῦ (τοῦ Φίλικος) ἐξῆρε τῶν διπτύχων.*

17 Evagrius, iii. 30: *Οὗτος ὁ 'Αναστάσιος εἰρηναῖος τις ὢν, οὐδὲν καινουργεῖσθαι παντελῶς ἠβούλετο, διαφερόντως περὶ τὴν ἐκκλησιαστικὴν κατάστασιν.—'Η μὲν οὖν ἐν Χαλκηδόνι σύνοδος ἀνὰ τούτους τοὺς χρόνους οὔτε ἀναφανδὸν ἐν ταῖς ἁγιωτάταις ἐκκλησίαις ἐκηρύττετο, οὔτε μὴν ἐκ πάντων ἀπεκηρύττετο. ἕκαστοι δὲ τῶν προεδρευόντων, ὡς εἶχον νομίσεως, διεπράττοντο. Κἂν ἔνιοι μὲν τῶν ἐκτεθειμένων αὐτῇ μάλα γεννικῶς ἀντείχοντο, καὶ πρὸς οὐδεμίαν ἐνεδίδοσαν συλλαβὴν τῶν ὁρισθέντων παρ' αὐτῆς οὐ*

But he could not prevent all outbreaks of the latter. In Constantinople itself, he was threatened by the seditious *Vitalianus*, who put himself forth as a defender of the Chalcedonian synod (514), and was obliged to promise to him that he would effect a restoration of communion with Rome. But all negotiations to bring this about were frustrated by the extravagant demands of the Roman see; and Anastasius carried with him to the grave the hatred, of all the friends of the council of Chalcedon, as may be seen by many narratives written after his death.[18]

Under *Justin I.* (518–527), a popular tumult finally compelled the general and solemn adoption of the Chalcedonian council at Constantinople, and the renewal of Church-communion with Rome (519). The same measures were soon after taken in the east; the Monophysite bishops were deposed, particularly *Severus*, patriarch of Antioch,[19] *Xenayas* or *Philoxe-*

μὴν γράμματος ἀλλαγὴν παρεδέχοντο, ἀλλὰ καὶ μετὰ πολλῆς ἀπεπήδων τῆς παῤῥησίας, καὶ κοινωνεῖν παντελῶς οὐκ ἠνείχοντο τοῖς μὴ δεχομένοις παρ' αὐτῆς τὰ ἐκτιθέμενα. Ἕτεροι δὲ οὐ μόνον οὐκ ἐδέχοντο τὴν ἐν Χαλκηδόνι σύνοδον καὶ τὰ παρ' αὐτῆς ὁρισθέντα, ἀλλὰ καὶ ἀναθέματι περιέβαλον αὐτήν τε καὶ τὸν Λέοντος τόμον. Ἄλλοι τοῖς ἑνωτικοῖς Ζήνωνος ἐνισχυρίζοντο καὶ ταῦτα πρὸς ἀλλήλους διεῤῥωγότες τῇ τε μιᾷ καὶ ταῖς δύο φύσεσιν, οἱ μὲν τῇ συνθήκῃ τῶν γραμμάτων κλαπέντες, οἱ δὲ καὶ πρὸς τὸ εἰρηνικώτερων μᾶλλον ἀποκλίναντες· ὡς πάσας τὰς ἐκκλησίας εἰς ἰδίας ἀποκριθῆναι μοίρας, καὶ μηδὲ κοινωνεῖν ἀλλήλοις τοὺς προεδρεύοντας.—Ἅπερ ὁ βασιλεὺς Ἀναστάσιος θεώμενος τοὺς νεωτερίζοντας τῶν ἐπισκόπων ἐξωθεῖτο, εἴ που κατειλήφει ἢ παρὰ τὸ εἰωθὸς τοῖς τόποις τινὰ τὴν ἐν Χαλκηδόνι σύνοδον κηρύττοντα, ἢ ταύτην ἀναθέματι περιτιθέντα.

[18] Evagrius, iii. 32: *Ὁ Ἀναστάσιος δόξαν μανιχαϊκῆς (νομίσεως) παρὰ τοῖς πολλοῖς εἶχεν.* Theodor. Lect. ii. 6: *Μανιχαῖοι καὶ Ἀρειανοὶ ἔχαιρον Ἀναστασίῳ. Μανιχαῖοι μὲν, ὡς τῆς μητρὸς αὐτοῦ ζηλούσης αὐτοὺς* (Symmachi P. Ep. ad Orientales, ap. Mansi, viii. p. 220: Declinemus sacrilegum Eutychetis errorem cum Manichaea malitia congruentum), *Ἀρειανοὶ δὲ ὡς Κλέαρχον τὸν θεῖον πρὸς μητρὸς Ἀναστασίου ὁμόδοξον ἔχοντες.* Victor Episc. Tununensis (about 555) in his Chronicon (in Canisii Lectt. ant. ed. Basnage, vol. i. p. 326): Messala V. C. Cos. Constantinopoli, jubente Anastasio Imperatore, sancta Evangelia, tamquam ab idiotis Evangelistis composita, reprehenduntur et emendantur. (P. Wesselingii Diss. de Evangeliis jussu Imp. Anast. non emendatis, append. to his diatribe de Judaeorum Archontibus. Traj. ad Rh. 1738.) On the contrary, Liberati Breviarium, c. 19: Hoc tempore Macedonius Constantinopolitanus episcopus ab imperatore Anastasio dicitur expulsus, tamquam evangelia falsasset, et maxime illud Apostoli dictum: qui apparuit in carne, justificatus est in spiritu (1 Tim. iii. 16). Hunc enim immutasse, ubi habet ΟΣ id est Qui, monosyllabum graecum, littera mutata Ο in Θ, vertisse et fecisse ΘΣ, id est Deus, ut esset: Deus apparuit per carnem. Tamquam Nestorianus ergo culpatus expellitur per Severum monachum.—P. E. Jablonski Exercit. de morte tragica Anastasii Dicori, Francof. ad Viadr. 1744. (Opusc. ed. te Water, t. iv. p. 353.) Among the Monophysites Zeno and Anastasius were reckoned orthodox. See Zachariae Hist. Eccl. in Maji Coll. x. i. 366.

[19] To the fragments of his works which were known before (a list is given in Cave, i. 500), many new ones have been added, which are scattered through A. Maji Scriptt. vett. nova coll. vii. i. Fragments of his Comm. in Lucam, and in Acta Apost. are given in Maji Classicorum auctorum, x. 408. Fragments and a Confession of Faith, addressed to the Emperor Anastasius, out of the Arabic in the Spicilegium romanum, t. iii. (Romae,

nus, bishop of Mabug, *Julian*, bishop of Halicarnassus ; and the greater number of them fled to Alexandria ; for in Egypt, Monophysitism was so generally prevalent, that Justin durst not undertake any thing against it there.

This very congregating of so many bishops in Alexandria now led to internal divisions among the Monophysites themselves.[20] From the controversy between Severus and Julian respecting the question whether the body of Christ was subject to that corruption, *τῇ φθορᾷ*, and was therefore *φθαρτόν τι*, or not,[21] which has come upon human bodies by the fall, arose the first and most obstinate dispute, that of the *Severians* (Theodosiani,[22] Φθαρτολάτραι) and the *Julianists*[23] (Gajanitae, Ἀφθαρτοδοκῆται, Phantasiastae.) Soon after there sprang from the former the Ἀγνοηταί, or Themistiani.[24] On the other hand, the Julianists were divided into the Ἀκτιστηταί and Κτιστολάτραι. About 530, the celebrated *John Philoponus*[25] promulgated his errors respecting the Trinity[26] and the resurrec-

1840. 8) p. 722. Liber ad Julian. Episc. Halicarn. out of the Syriac in the Spicileg. rom. x. 169.

[20] Concerning them as a peculiar source: Timotheus presb. de Variis haereticis ac diversis eorum in Ecclesiam recipiendi formulis, in Cotelerii Monum. Eccles. gr. iii. 377. Comp. Walch's Ketzerhist, viii. 520. Baur's Dreieinigkeit, ii. 73.

[21] Comp. my Comm. qua Monophysitarum variae de Christi persona opiniones illustrantur. Partic. ii. Gotting. 1835, 38. 4.

[22] A fragment of Theodosius, Patriarch of Alexandria, which extends over this disputed question, is given out of the Arabic in the Spicileg. rom. iii. 711. Among other things it is written: Nisi Christus—in sua carne eas qualitates habuisset, quae sine peccato consistere possunt, scil. nisi ejus caro par nostrae esset, tum quod ad essentiam attinet, tum etiam quod ad patiendum ;—nunquam stimulus mortis destructus fuisset, i. e., peccatum. Comp. especially Severi liber ad Julianum, quo demonstrat, quid sacri libri doctoresque Ecclesiae docuerint circa incorruptibilitatem corporis J. Chr. out of the Syriac in the Spicileg. rom. x. 169.

[23] Juliani anathematismi, x. in Syriac in J. S. Assemani Biblioth. Vatic. Codd. Mss. Catal.,P. i. t. iii. (Romae. 1759. fol.) p. 223, in Lat. in my Comm. ii. 5.

[24] Fragments of Themistius in Maji Coll. vii. 1, 73. In order to perceive his view, the following sentences are of importance: Μία τοῦ Λόγου θεανδρικὴ ἐνέργειά τε καὶ γνῶσις. But τὰ μὲν θεϊκῶς, τὰ δὲ ἀνθρωπίνως ὁ αὐτὸς ἐνήργησεν (consequently also ἐγίνωσκεν).

[25] That a great part of his life does not belong to the seventh century, as has been usually assumed, is shown by Ritter Gesch. d. christl. Philos. ii. 501, and confirmed by a letter which he wrote, when an old man, to the Emperor Justinian. See Spicileg. rom. iii. 739. His writings were: In Hexaëmeron, Disp. de Paschate (ed. B. Corderius. Vienn. 1630. 4, more correctly printed in Gallandius, xii. 471), de Aeternitate mundi contra Proclum lib. (Venet. 1535), Commentaries on Aristotle.—Among other lost book was one adv. Synod. Chalcedonensem (Photius Cod. 55). Fabricii Bibl. gr. vol. ix. p. 359, ss. (ed. Harles, vol. x. p. 639, ss.)

[26] Leontius de Sectis act. v. § 6, makes Philoponus say to the church: Εἰ δύο λέγετε φύσεις ἐν τῷ Χριστῷ, ἀνάγκη ὑμᾶς καὶ δύο ὑποστάσεις εἰπεῖν.—ναὶ ταὐτό ἐστι φύσις καὶ ὑπόστασις. Εἶτα πάλιν ἡ ἐκκλησία· εἰ ταὐτό ἐστι φύσις καὶ ὑπόστασις, οὐκοῦν λέγομεν

tion,[27] drawn from the Aristotelian philosophy, among the Monophysites (Philoponiaci, Tritheitae; on the other side, Condobauditae and Cononitae) in opposition to whom *Damian*, patriarch of Alexandria, appeared to fall into the Sabellian error (Damianitae). At the same time, the doctrine of *Stephanus Niobes*, who removed all distinction of natures in Christ after their union, was condemned by the other Monophysites (Niobitae).[28]

§ 111.

CONTROVERSIES UNDER JUSTINIAN I.

Justinian I. (527–565), a zealous adherent of the council of Chalcedon[1] endeavored to restore unity and order both in state and church by means of laws; for which purpose he tried to bring back the Monophysites in particular, into the church. These endeavors were turned to advantage by a secret Monophysite court party, at whose head stood his spouse, *Theodora*,[2] who exercised great influence over him, and who, in the hope of bringing the Catholic Church, step by step, to Monophysitism, persuaded the emperor that the Monophysites took offense simply at points in the Catholic Church, which could be removed without a violation of orthodoxy. But since the dominant church had also its representatives at court, the emperor was led sometimes by the one party, sometimes by the other, to enact regulations, whose natural consequence was to increase rather than remove the causes of dispute.

καὶ τῆς ἁγίας τριάδος τρεῖς φύσεις, ἐπειδὴ ὁμολογουμένως τρεῖς ὑποστάσεις ἔχει.—*'Απεκρίνατο ὁ Φιλόπονος· ὅτι καὶ ἔστω τρεῖς φύσεις λέγειν ἡμᾶς ἐπὶ τῆς ἁγίας τρίαδος. Ἔλεγε δὲ ταῦτα λαβὼν τὴν ἀφορμὴν ἀπὸ τῶν 'Αριστοτελικῶν· ὁ γὰρ 'Αριστοτέλης φησὶν, ὅτι εἰσὶ τῶν ἀτόμων καὶ μερικαὶ οὐσίαι, καὶ μία κοινή· οὕτως οὖν καὶ ὁ Φιλόπονος ἔλεγεν, ὅτι εἰσὶ τρεῖς μερικαὶ οὐσίαι ἐπὶ τῆς ἁγίας τριάδος, καὶ ἔστι μία κοινή.* Comp. the important fragments out of Philoponi dial. *Διαιτητὴς* ap. Joh. Damascenus de Haeresibus, c. 83.—His book on the Trinity against John, patriarch of Constantinople (Photius Cod. 75), is lost. J. G. Scharfenberg de Joh. Philop. Tritheismi defensore diss. Lips. 1768. 4. Joh. Philoponus, eine dogmenhist. Eröterung von F. Trechsel, in the Theol. Studien. u. Kritiken, 1835. i. 95. Baur's Dreieinigkeit, ii. 13. Ritter, ii. 512.

[27] Timotheus in Cotelerii Monum. eccl. gr. iii. 413. Philoponus's book *περὶ ἀναστάσεως* (Photius Cod. 21) is lost. Ritter, ii. 511.

[28] Dionysius Patr. Antioch. in Assemani Bibl. orient. ii. 72. Timotheus, l. c. p. 397, 407, ss. 417, ss. Baur, ii. 92.

[1] A new memorial of it is his *λόγος δογματικὸς πρὸς τοὺς ἐν τῷ ἐνάτῳ τῆς 'Αλεξανδρέων μοναχούς*, which Majus Scriptt. vett. nova coll. vii. i. 292, has published.

[2] Respecting her see Procopii Hist. arcana, c. 9.

The conferences between Catholic and Monophysite bishops, which Justinian[3] caused to be held, were, on the whole, fruitless. The original Monophysite formula—"God was crucified"—which had been approved of by many, even among the Catholics in the east (θεοπασχῖται),[4] but which some Scythian monks under Justin I. had in vain attempted to introduce both at Rome and Constantinople (519–521),[5] was declared orthodox by Justinian (533), with the evident purpose of conciliating the Monophy-

[3] The protocol of the one A.D. 531: Collatio Catholicorum cum Severianis, ap. Mansi, viii. 817.—Johannes Episc. Asiae speaks of several in Assemani Bibl. orient. ii. 89.

[4] See Walch's Ketzerhist. vii. 261, 311, ff.

[5] Walch, vii. 262. Under Anastasius the addition in the Trishagion (see § 110, note 12), was also introduced at Constantinople (see Zachariae Hist. eccl. ap. Assemani Bibl. or. ii. 59, and in Maji Nova coll. x. 375, comp. Dioscuri Diac. Ep. ad Hormisdam ap. Mansi, viii. 480). Its abrogation during the reaction under Justin doubtless occasioned the monks to defend the formula. Hormisdae Ep. Rom. Epist. ad Possessorem Episc. Afric. Constantinopoli exulantem (ap. Mansi, viii. 498): Ubi non varie tentationis aculei? Quales per hunc fere jugem annum quorundam Scytharum, qui monachos prae se ferebant specie non veritate, professione non opere, subtili tectas calliditate versutias, et sub religionis obtentu famulantia odiis suis venena pertulimus.—Nunquam apud eos caritas novo commendata praecepto, nunquam pax dominico relicta discessu: una pertinacis cura propositi, rationi velle imperare, non credere: contemtores auctoritatum veterum, novarum cupidi quaestionum; solam putantes scientiae rectam viam, qualibet concepta facilitate sententiam: eo usque tumoris elati, ut [ad] arbitrium suum utriusque orbis putent inclinandum esse judicium, etc. The answer of one of the Scythian monks to this, Joh. Maxentii ad Epist. Hormisdae responsio (Bibl. PP. Lugdun. t. ix. p. 539, ss.):—Non est facile credendum, hanc esse epistolam cujus fertur nomine titulata, praesertim cum in ea nihil, ut diximus, rationis aut consequentiae reperiatur, sed tota criminationibus obtrectationibusque vanis—videatur referta.—Quod monachis responsum quaerentibus Romanus Episcopus dare omnino distulerit, eosdemque post multa maris pericula, longique itineris vexationem, nec non etiam afflictionem prolixi temporis, quo eos apud se detinuit, vacuos et sine ullo effectu ad has partes venire compulerit, quod omnibus paene catholicis notum est, nec ipsi queunt haeretici denegare.—Nam et ipsi haeretici ad hoc ubique hanc ipsam, cui respondimus, epistolam proferunt, quatenus et saepedictis monachis invidiam concitent, et omnes quasi ex auctoritate ejusdem Romani Episcopi prohibeantur Christum filium Dei unum confiteri ex trinitate. Sed quis hanc sententiam catholicam non esse ausus est profiteri, quam universa veneratur et amplectitur Dei ecclesia? Confidenter etenim dicere audeo, non quod, si per epistolam, seu quod, si viva voce hic in praesenti positus idem Romanus prohiberet Episcopus Christum filium Dei unum confiteri ex sancta et individua trinitate, nunquam eidem Dei ecclesia acquiesceret, nunquem ut Episcopum catholicum veneraretur, sed omnino ut haereticum penitus execraretur. Quia quisquis hoc non confitetur non est dubium, quod Nestorianae perfidiae tenebris excaecatus, quartum et extraneum a sancta et ineffabili Trinitate eum, qui pro nobis crucem sustinuit, praedicare contendat.—An forte illos rationi credere, non imperare judicat, qui Christum unam personam quidem ex Trinitate, non autem unum ex Trinitate esse fatentur? Sed hi qui hoc dicunt, potius rationi velle imperare, non credere, penitus convincuntur, etc. The Episcopi Africani in Sardinia exules also sided with the Scythian monks: comp. their book composed by Fulgentius Ruspensis lib. de incarnatione et gratia Dom. nostri J. C. ad Mon. Scyth. (Fulgentii Opera ed. Paris. 1684. 4. p. 277, ss.). Fulgentius Ferrandus Diac. Carthag. ad Anatolium Diac. Rom. Dionysius Exiguus praef. ad versionem epistolae Procli Archiep. Const. ad Armenos (ap. Mansi, v. 419).

sites.[6] This step, however, was without success. In Egypt the Monophysites continued to be the prevailing party, though Justinian (536) again appointed a Catholic patriarch of Alexandria, *Paul*. But, on the other hand, the secret endeavors of Theodora to spread Monophysitism in Rome and Constantinople were equally fruitless. *Anthimus*, who had been promoted to the see of Constantinople by her (535), was soon after (536) deposed for being a Monophysite.[7] *Vigilius*, elevated to the see of Rome, with the secret understanding[8] that he was to de-

[6] The Monophysites accused the orthodox, before the emperor, of not acknowledging dominum passum carne, vel unum eum esse de sancta Trinitate, nec ejusdem esse personae tam miracula quam passiones (cf. collatio Cathol. cum Sever. ap. Mansi, viii. 832). The Acoemetae did really deny esse confitendum, b. Mariam vere et proprie Dei genetricem; et unum de Trinitate incarnatum et carne passum (Liberatus, c. 20), evidently misled by their adherence to Rome (Sam. Basnage Annal. politico-eccles. iii. 701). Justiniani lex A.D. 533 (Cod. i. i. 6).—Unius ac ejusdem passiones et miracula, quae sponte pertulit in carne, agnoscentes. Non enim alium Deum Verbum, et alium Christum novimus, sed unum et eundem.—Mansit enim Trinitas et post incarnatum unum ex Trinitate Dei verbum: neque enim quartae personae adjectionem admittit sancta Trinitas.—Anathematizamus—Nestorium anthropolatram, et qui eadem cum ipso sentiunt—qui negant nec confitentur Dominum nostrum J. C. filium Dei et Deum nostrum incarnatum et hominem factum et crucifixum unum esse ex sancta et consubstantiali Trinitate.—Epist. Joannis Ep. Romae ad Justin.) ibid. l. 8, et ap. Mansi, viii. 797): Comperimus, quod fidelibus populis proposuistis Edictum amore fidei pro submovenda haereticorum intentione, secundum apostolicam doctrinam, fratrum et Coëpiscoporum nostrorum interveniente consensu. Quod, quia apostolicae doctrina convenit, nostra auctoritate confirmamus. The formula, however, was still suspected in the west of being Monophysite, and Bishop Cyprian of Toulon (about 550) was obliged to defend himself against Bishop Maximus of Geneva, quod beatitudo Vestra imperitiam nostram judicat esse culpandam, eo quod Deum hominem passum dixerim (the document is communicated by Schmidt in Vater's Kirchenhist. Archive für 1826, S. 307). The addition to the Trishagion (§ 110, note 12) continued to be used by the Catholics in Syria (see Ephraem. Patr. Antioch. about 530, apud Photius Cod. 228. Assemani Bibl. Orient. i. 518), till it was rejected by the Conc. Quinisextum, can. 81. After that time it was retained only by the Monophysites and Monothelites (Walch's Ketzerhist. ix. 480). Among the Catholics the idea arose that a quaternity, instead of a Trinity, was introduced by it. See Jo. Damasc. de Fide orthod. iii. 10. See Royaards in the Nederlandsch Archief voor kerkel. Geschiedenis, ii. 263 (1842).

[7] Acta Syn. Constantinop. ann. 530 ap. Mansi, viii. 873, ss.

[8] Liberatus, c. 22. In him and in Victoris Tunun. Chronic. (ap. Canisius-Basnage, i. 330), is found the Epist. Vigilii to the Monophysite bishops, Theodosius, Anthimus, and Severus, where we read, among other things: Me eam fidem, quam tenetis, Deo adjuvante et tenuisse et tenere significo.—Oportet ergo, ut haec, quae vobis scribo, nullus agnoscat, sed magis tanquam suspectum me sapientia vestra ante alios existimet habere, ut facilius possim haec, quae coepi, operari et perficere. In the Confession of Faith appended to it in Liberatus: Non duas Christum confitemur naturas, sed ex duabus naturis compositum unum filium, unum Christum, unum Dominum. Qui dicit in Christo duas formas, unaquaque agente cum alterius communione, et non confitetur unam personam, unam essentiam, anathema. Qui dicit: quia hoc quidem miracula faciebat, hoc vero passionibus succumbebat (Leo, § 89, note 7): et non confitetur miracula et passiones unius ejusdemque, quas sponte sua sustinuit, carne nobis consubstantiali, anathema sit. Qui dicit, quod Christus velut homo misericordia dignatus est, et non dicit ipsum Deum Verbum

clare in favor of Monophysite doctrines (538), soon found it expedient to break through his agreement.

In the mean time, these theological affrays were increased by the revival of *the Origenist controversy.* Origen had, by degrees, obtained many devoted admirers among the monks in Palestine. One of them, *Theodorus Ascidas*, bishop of Caesarea in Cappadocia, who had come to court, and gained the confidence of the emperor, protected the Origenists in propagating their doctrines in Palestine, sometimes by violent means.[9] But at last the opposite party prevailed, by the aid of *Mennas*, patriarch of Constantinople, and obtained from Justinian a condemnation of the Origenist errors (about 544).[10] It was more with the design of diverting attention from Origenism than of being revenged on his orthodox opponents, that Theodorus now persuaded the emperor[11] that the reconciliation of the Monophysites with the orthodox would be much facilitated by a public condemnation not only of *Theodore of Mopsuestia*,[12] who had

et crucifixum esse, ut misereatur nobis, anathema sit. Anathematizamus ergo Paulum Samosatenum, Dioscorum (leg. Diodorum), Theodorum, Theodoritum et omnes, qui eorum statuta coluerint, vel colunt. Soon after this, however, he proved his orthodoxy to the Emperor and the Patriarch of Constantinople. Epist. ad Justinian. ap. Mansi, ix. 35, ad Mennam, ibid. p. 38.

[9] Chief authority, Vita s. Sabae by Cyrillus Scythopolitanus (in Cotelerii Monum. Eccles. graec. t. iii.) from cap. 36. Cf. Walch de Sabaitis (Novi comm. Soc. Gotting. vii. 1).

[10] In the Epist. ad Mennam Archiepisc. Const. adv. impium Origenem ap. Mansi, ix. 487. Here, p. 524, Mennas is ordered *συναγαγεῖν ἅπαντας τοὺς ἐνδημοῦντας κατὰ ταύτην τὴν βασιλίδα πόλιν ὁσιωτάτους ἐπισκόπυς, καὶ τοὺς—μοναστηρίων ἡγουμένους, καὶ παρασκευάσαι πάντας—τὸν—Ὠριγένην—ἀναθεματίσαι*, and from this *σύνοδος ἐνδημοῦσα* proceeded, without doubt, the fifteen canons against Origen (prim. ed. Petr. Lambecius in Comment. bibl. August. Vindob. viii. 435, ap. Mansi, ix. 395), though their title favors the fifth oecumenical council. See M. Le Quien Oriens christianus, iii. 210. Walch's Ketzerhist. vii. 660.

[11] The Origenist Domitian, bishop of Ancyra, himself admitted in libello ad Vigilium (in Facundi Episc. Hermianensis pro defens. trium capitul. lib. iv. c. 4): Prosiluerunt ad anathematizandos sanctissimos et gloriosissimos doctores sub occasione eorum, quae de praeexistentia et restitutione mota sunt, dogmatum, sub specie quidem Origenis, omnes autem, qui ante eum et post eum fuerunt, sanctos anathematizantes. Hi vero, qui proposuerant hujusmodi dogma defendere, id implere nullo modo voluerunt: sed talem relinquentes conflictum, conversi sunt, ut moverent adversus Theodorum, qui fuit Mopsvestenus episcopus, et moliri coeperunt, quatenus anathematizaretur et ille, ad abolitionem, ut putabant, eorum, quae contra Originem mota constiterant. Liberatus, c. 24: Theodorus Caesareae Cappadociae episcopus, dilectus et familiaris principum—cognoscens Originem fuisse damnatum, dolore damnationis ejus, ad ecclesia conturbationem, damnationem molitus est in Theodorum Mopsvestenum, eo quod Theodorus multa opuscula edidisset contra Originem, exosusque et accusabilis haberetur ab Origenistis.

[12] The enmity of the abbot Sabba to him, Vita Sabae (see note 9), c. 72, 74.—A Synod convened for the purpose at Mopsuestia by the imperial command (550), came to the conclusion: Theodorum veterem, qui per istam civitatem fuit episcopus, in antiquis temporibus

been long in somewhat evil repute among the orthodox, but also of *Theodoret's* writings against Cyril and the letter of *Ibas* to Maris, though the two latter had been expressly pronounced orthodox by the council of Chalcedon.[13] Justinian accordingly condemned, in an edict (544), the Three Chapters (τρία κεφάλαια, tria capitula).[14] In the east they very easily coincided with this measure; but in the west it was so much the more obstinately resisted.[15] On this account Justinian summoned *Vigilius*, bishop of Rome, to Constantinople (546), and prevailed on him there to condemn, in like manner, the Three Chapters (518)[16] in a document called *Judicatum*. But Vigilius was soon induced to hesitate, by the decided opposition of the greater number of the western bishops;[17] and he refused to adopt the emperor's second edict against the Three Chapters (551).[18]

Justinian now convened *the fifth oecumenical council at*

extra praedicationem divini mysterii fuisse, et sacris diptychis ejectum esse: et—in illius vocabulum, inscriptum esse Cyrillum sanctae memoriae (see Mansi, ix. 286). The testimonies of the ancients against Theodorus, collected in the collatio v. of the fifth oecumenical council, must be very cautiously received; for instance, Theodore's name, in the two laws of Theodosius II. against Nestorius (p. 249, ss.), is a later addition.

[13] Theodoret, in the actio viii. (ap. Mansi, vii. 189). Ibas, after a long investigation, act ix. and x. after which the Roman embassadors expressly declare: Ἀναγνωσθείσης τῆς ἐπιστολῆς αὐτοῦ (that very Epist. ad Marin.) ἐπέγνωμεν αὐτὸν ὑπάρχειν ὀρθόδοξον.

[14] I. e., three points, articles: not as J. H. Mücke de tribus capitulis concilii Chalced. Lips. 1766. 4. p. 6, thinks, the three decrees of the council of Chalcedon, for there was no such decree respecting Theodore. The first edict of Justinian is lost, except fragments in Facundus, ii. 3, iv. 4. See Norisii Diss. de synodo quinta, c. 3. Walch's Ketzerhist. viii. 150.

[15] Their leading reasons are given by Fulgentius Ferrandus Epist. vi. ad Pelagium et Anatolium, at the conclusion of the following sentences: Ut concilii Chalcedonensis, vel similium nulla retractatio placeat, sed quae semel statuta sunt, intemerata serventur. Ut pro mortuis fratribus nulla generentur inter vivos scandala. Ut nullus libro suo per subscriptiones plurimorum dare velit auctoritatem, quam solis canonicis libris ecclesia catholica detulit.

[16] The particulars are related by Facundus, lib. contra Mocianum scholast.—The Judicatum is no longer extant, except in a fragment in the Latin translation of the Epist. Justin. ad Concilium oecum. v. (ap. Mansi, ix. 181).

[17] Victor. Tunun. in Chron. (l. c. p. 332): Post Consulatum Basilii V. C. anno ix. (549). Illyriciana Synodus in defensione iii. capitum Justiniano Aug. scribit, et Benenatum, primae Justinianae Civitatis episcopum, obtrectatorem eorundem iii. capitum condemnat. —Post Cons. Bas. V. C. anno x. (550) Africani Antistites Vigilium Romanum Episcopum, damnatorem iii. Capitulorum synodaliter a catholica communione, reservato ei poenitentiae loco, recludunt, et pro defensione memoratorum iii. Capitulorum literas satis idoneas Justiniano Principi per Olympium Magistrianum mittunt. Also defenses of the three chapters by Facundus and Rusticus.

[18] Or the ὁμολογία πίστεως Ἰουστ. Αὐτοκράτορος, preserved in the Chronic. Alexandr. ed. du Fresne, p. 344, ss. ap. Mansi, ix. 537.—Concerning the conduct of Vigilius see especially Epistola legatis Francorum, qui Constantinopolim proficiscebantur, ab Italiae clericis directa, A.D. 551, ap. Mansi, xi. 151.

Constantinople (553),[19] at which Vigilius not only refused to attend, but even defended the three chapters in the so-called *Constitutum*.[20] The Synod, therefore, broke off all Church communion with him,[21] and approved without qualification all the decrees of the emperor hitherto made respecting religion.[22] No farther notice was taken of the Origenists,[23] a circumstance which we shall not be far from the truth in attributing to the artful management of Theodorus Ascidas, who was the leading person at the council. Vigilius at length (554) assented to the decisions of the council,[24] to which step he was doubtless influenced chiefly by the success of the imperial arms in Italy under Narses. Immediately after, he set out on his return to Rome, but died by the way, in Syracuse (555). His successor,

19 Acta in Mansi, ix. 157, ss. Natalis Alexander Hist. eccl. saec. vi. t. v. p. 502, ss. J. Basnage Histoire de l'église, liv. x. c. 6. Norisii Diss. de synodo v. (Patav. 1673. Opp. ed. Ballerini, Veron. 1729. t. i. p. 437). Against him Garnerii Diss. de syn. v. (first appended to his Liberatus. Paris. 1675, improved in the auctar. Opp. Theodoreti, p. 493, also in Theodoret. ed. Schultze, v. 512). On the other side the Ballerini: Defensio diss. Noris. adv. Garn. (in Noris. Opp. iv. 985).

20 Ap. Mansi, ix. 61-106.

21 Justinian declared, with reference to Vigilius, to the synod in a rescript (in the Acta of the Synod, collatio vii. ap. Mansi, ix. 367): Ipse semetipsum alienum catholicae ecclesiae fecit, defendens praedictorum capitulorum impietatem, separans autem semetipsum a vestra communione. His igitur ab eo factis, alienum Christianis judicavimus nomen ipsius sacris diptychis recitari [leg. resecari], ne eo modo inveniamur Nestorii et Theodori impietati communicantes.—Unitatem vero ad apostolicam sedem et nos servamus, et certum est quod et vos custodietis. Without sufficient reason the Ballerini, in their defensio (Norisii Opp. iv. 1035), declare this writing to be spurious.

22 The thirteen anathemas appended to Justinian's *ὁμολογία* (ap. Mansi, ix. 557) are for the most part verbally repeated in the fourteen anathemas of the Synod (l. c. p. 376, ss). So also the 6th imperial anathema in the 10th of the council: *Εἴ τις οὐχ ὁμολογεῖ τὸν ἐσταυρωμένον σαρκὶ κύριον ἡμῶν Ἰησοῦν Χριστὸν εἶναι. θεὸν ἀληθινὸν καὶ κύριον τῆς δόξης, καὶ ἕνα τῆς ἁγίας τριάδος, ὁ τοιοῦτος ἀνάθεμα ἔστω.*

23 Though as early as Cyrillus Scythopolit. in vita Sabae, c. 90, and Evagrius, iv. 37, the formal condemnation of Origen is attributed to the 5th council by confounding it with the synod under Mennas (see note 10), as was afterward generally believed. See on the other side Walch's Ketzerh. viii. 280.

24 Vigilii Epist. ad Eutychium Archiepisc. Constant. prim. ed. P. de Marca in Diss. de decreto Papae Vigilii pro confirmatione v. Syn. (in ejusd. dissertt. iii. a Baluzio editis. Paris. 1669. 8, and appended to Boehmer's edition of the concord. Sac. et Imp. p. 227), ap. Mansi, ix. 413, ss. The remarkable commencement: *Τὰ σκάνδαλα, ἅπερ ὁ τοῦ ἀνθρωπίνου γένους ἐχθρὸς τῷ σύμπαντι κόσμῳ διήγειρεν, οὐδεὶς ἀγνοεῖ, οὕτως ὡς τὸ οἰκεῖον βούλημα πρὸς τὸ ἀνατρέψαι τὴν τοῦ θεοῦ ἐκκλησίαν—πληρῶσαι οἵῳ δήποτε τρόπῳ σπουδάζοντα, οὐ μόνον ἐξ ὀνόματος ἰδίου, ἀλλὰ καὶ ἐξ ἡμετέρου καὶ ἐξ ἄλλων, διὰ τοῦ λέγειν ἢ τοῦ γράφειν, διάφορα πλάσασθαι πεποίηκεν· εἰς τοσοῦτον, ὅτι ἡμᾶς μετὰ τῶν ἀδελφῶν καὶ συνεπισκόπων ἡμῶν—ἐν τῇ τῶν τεσσάρων συνόδων μιᾷ καὶ τῇ αὐτῇ πίστει ἀμώμως διατελοῦντας, τοῖς σοφίσμασι τῆς οὕτω πονηρᾶς πανουργίας, αὐτῶν ἐπεχείρισε διελεῖν.—Ἀλλ' ἐπειδὴ Χριστὸς ὁ θεὸς ἡμῶν—πάσης, συγχύσεως τῆς ἡμῶν διανοίας ἀποκινηθείσης πρὸς εἰρήνην τὴν οἰκουμένην ἀνεκλέσατο, κ. τ. λ.*

Pelagius I., acknowledged at once the authority of the fifth Synod,[25] which led to a tedious schism between several Western Churches and Rome. Among the writers who, during this controversy, opposed the condemnation of the Three Chapters, the most distinguished are *Fulgentius Ferrandus*, deacon in Carthage († before 551);[26] *Facundus*, bishop of Hermiane († about 570);[27] *Rusticus*, deacon in Rome;[28] *Liberatus*, deacon in Carthage (about 553);[29] *Victor*, bishop of Tununa († after 565).[30]

Shortly before his death (564), Justinian was misled by his excessive desire to bring back the Monophysites to the Church, so as to elevate to the rank of orthodoxy the doctrine of the *Aphthartodocetae*. *Eutychius*, patriarch of Constantinople, was deposed for his opposition to this measure; and the like fate awaited *Anastasius Sinaita*, patriarch of Antioch; when the death of the emperor (565) became the death likewise of the new doctrine.[31]

§ 112.

DEVELOPMENT OF MONOPHYSITE CHURCHES.

The efforts of Justinian to reunite the Monophysites with the Catholic Church were so far from successful, that the sect

[25] Victor Tunun. in Chron. Post consulatum Basilii V. C. anno xviii. Pelagius Romanus archidiaconus, trium praefatorum defensor Capitulorum, Justiniani principis persuasione de exsilio redit: et comdemnans ea, quae dudum constantissime defendebat Romanae Ecclesiae Episcopus a praevaricatoribus ordinatur.

[26] Opp. ed. Fr. Chiffletius. Divione. 1649. Bibl. PP. Lugd. t. ix. Bibl. PP. Gallandi, xi. 329. Among his letters the most remarkable are those in answer to questions addressed to him from Rome, ad Anatolium, quod unus de Trinitate passus dici possit, et ad Pelagium et Anatolium [546] pro tribus capitulis.

[27] By whom is the chief work in favor of the three chapters pro defensione iii. Capitulorum, libb. xii. (about 548), and contra Mocianum scholasticum (Opp. prim. ed. Jac. Sirmond. Paris. 1629. 8, emendatius in Bibl. PP. Gallandii, xi. 665).

[28] Lib. adv. Acephalos ad Sebastianum (in Bibl. PP. apud Gallandius, xii. 37).

[29] Breviarum causae Nestorianorum et Eutychianorum (ed. Jo. Garnerius. Paris. 1675, 8. Ap. Mansi, ix. 659, and ap. Gallandius, xii. 119).

[30] Chronicon ab orbe condito, only the second part is extant, from 444 to 565 (ap. Canisius-Basnage, i. 321, plur. in locis restitut. ap. Gallandius, xii. 221).

[31] Evagrius, iv. 38–40. Eutychii vita, composed by one of his adherents, Eustathius or Eustratius (in the Greek original, Acta SS. April. tom. i. append. p. 59), has been dressed out with praises even to the miraculous. Walch's Ketzerhist. viii. 578. According to Eustathius, Justinian was misled by Origenists.

was always becoming more distinct under his reign, and internally established. The later dominion of the Arabians, by which the Monophysites were especially favored, rendered the breach incurable.

Only a small part of the Egyptians followed the Catholic patriarch of Alexandria, who had been appointed by Justinian. The more numerous Monophysites chose another patriarch; and thus they continue till the present day under the name of *Copts.*[1] The *Æthiopian Church* was always in connection with them.[2]

The Christians in *Armenia*[3] also attached themselves ecclesiastically in the fifth century to the Greek emperors, by whose aid they held out against the Persians, and accordingly agreed to the Henoticon of Zeno.[4] After Monophysitism had obtained acceptance among them, in consequence of these proceedings, they remained all the more faithful to it from the time of Justin I., since the Persians favored all parties separated from the Greek Church. In vain did Kyrion, patriarch of Georgia, endeavor to procure an approval of the council of Chalcedon in Armenia also;[5] a Synod at *Twin* (595)[6] declared itself decid-

1 Taki-eddini Makrizii (a lawyer in Cairo † 1441) Hist. Coptorum Christianorum in Aegypto. arab. et lat. ed. H. J. Wetzer. Solisbaci 1828. 8. (A complete and more accurate edition, with a translation, may be shortly expected from Prof. Wüstenfeld.) Eusebii Renaudot Historia patriarcharum Alexandrinorum Jacobitarum. Paris. 1713. 4. Michael. Le Quien Oriens christianus in iv. patriarchatus digestus, quo exhibentur ecclesiae patriarchae caeterique praesules totius Orientis. (Paris. 1740. 8. t. fol.) t. ii. p. 357.

2 Jobi Ludolf Historia Aethiopica. Francof. ad M. 1681. Commentarius ad Hist. Aeth. 1691, and appendix ad Hist. Aeth. 1993. All in fol.—Maturin Veyssier la Croze Histoire du Christianisme d' Ethiopie et d'Arménie, à la Haye. 1739. S.

3 The older literature respecting Armenian church history in Clem. Galani Hist. Armena eccl. et polit. Colon. 1686. Francof. et Lips. 1701. 8 (a reprint of vol. i. of the Conciliatio eccl. Armenae cum Romana. Romae. 1651. 3 voll. fol.), la Croze, le Quien, l. c. almost useless, since the Mechitarists, united Armenian monks, have begun to publish on the island of St. Lazzaro at Venice, the numerous Armenian historians, and to prepare an Armenian history. Their principal work is the history of Armenia by P. Michael Tschamtschean († 1823) in the Armenian language, 3 volumes, 4to. 1784. With it are connected the works of Saint-Martin and C. F. Neumann. Comp. Mémoires sur l'Arménie par J. Saint-Martin, tomes ii. Paris. 1828, 29. Histoire d' Arménie par le patriarche Jean VI., dit Jean Catholicos († 925) trad. de l'arménien en français par J. Saint-Martin. Paris. 1841. 8. C. F. Neumann's Gesch d. armen. Literatur. Leipzig. 1836. 8.

4 In the year 491, at a synod at Edschmiadsin, the Henoticon was adopted, and the decrees of the council of Chalcedon rejected, Tschamtschean, ii. 225. Mémoires sur l'Arménie par J. Saint-Martin, i. 329.

5 See respecting him, Neumann's Gesch. d. arm. Lit. S. 94.

6 Twin (also written Thevin or Thovin), in the province of Ararat, at that time the residence of the Armenian kings and patriarchs. Galanus Hist. arm. c. 10, Le Quien, i.

edly in favor of Monophysitism; and thus the *Armenian Church* still continues, to the present day, as a sect separated from the other Monophysite Churches,[7] merely by peculiar customs.

In *Syria* and *Mesopotamia* the Monophysites had nearly become extinct by persecution and want of a clergy, when *Jacob Baradai*, or Zanzalus, by unwearied diligence (from 541 to 578), set in order their churches, and supplied them with pastors. From him the Syrian Monophysites received the name *Jacobites*.[8]

§ 113.

CONTROVERSY BETWEEN AUGUSTINISM AND SEMIPELAGIANISM.

G. F. Wiggers Pragm. Darstellung des Augustinismus und Pelagianismus. Th. 2. (Hamburg. 1833.) S. 224.

The Western Churches were but little disturbed by the Monophysite controversy. On the other hand, the struggle between Augustinism and Semipelagianism continued, especially in Gaul (comp. § 87, note 47, and following) though without leading to actual schisms in the Church. At first the Semipelagians had so much the advantage that their most distinguished defender *Faustus*, formerly abbot of the monastery at Lerins, afterward *bishop* of *Reji* (*Reis*) († after 490), compelled a certain presbyter, *Lucidus*, to retract the Augustinian doctrines,[1] and his Semipelagian creed was generally approved at the councils of *Arles* and *Lyons* (475).[2] Hence *Arnobius* the younger,[3] author of the *Praedestinatus*[4] (both about 460), and

1360, and other older writers, place this synod earlier. Comp. however, Ang. Majus in the Spicilegium Rom. x. ii. 450, annotation 3.

[7] Comp. Eccl. Armeniacae canones selecti in Ang. Maji vett. Scriptt. nova coll. x. ii. 269. Among the most remarkable of these customs are these, that the Armenians use unmixed wine at the Lord's Supper, p. 303, and keep the day of Epiphany as the festival of the birth and baptism of Jesus, p. 307.

[8] Assemani Bibl. orient. t. ii.—Le Quien, l. c. t. ii.

[1] Fausti Rejensis Epist. ad Lucidum, and Lucidi errorem emendantis libellus ad Episcopos ap. Mansi, vii. 1008. Comp. Walch's Ketzerhist. v. 90.

[2] His chief work de Gratia Dei et humanae mentis libero arbitrio libb. 2 (Bibl. Patr. Lugd. viii. 525), was subscribed there. His creed is given by Wiggers, ii. 235.

[3] See his Comm. in Psalmos (Bibl. PP. Lugd. viii. 238). Wiggers, ii. 348.

[4] Prim. ed. J. Sirmond. Paris. 1643. 8 (recus. in Bibl. PP. Lugd. xxvii. 543. Bibl. PP. Gallandii, x. 357). The first book contains a short sketch of 90 heresies (the 90th that of the Praedestinatorum), the second a liber sub nomine Augustini conflictus, in which the Augustinian doctrine was presented with great exaggeration (as it had been previously

Gennadius, presbyter at Massilia († after 495),[5] express these sentiments without disguise. They had even penetrated to Upper Italy; and *Magnus Felix Ennodius* bishop of Pavia (from 511 to 521), professed them.[6]

Augustinism was hated in Gaul, especially on account of the doctrine of an unconditional decree of God, which, in the form it had there assumed, distorted by the consequences drawn from it by its obstinate defenders on the one hand, and still more by its too eager opponents on the other,[7] was completely and necessarily fatal to all morality.[8] Some, indeed, did not hesitate to attribute these errors directly to Augustine;[9] but for the

in the capitulis calumniantium, which Prosper refuted, see § 87, note 52. Wiggers, ii. 184), the third a refutation of this book. Walch, v. 227. Wiggers, ii. 329. Perhaps Arnobius was the anthor, as Sirmond and the Benedictines, Histoire litéraire de la France, ii. 349, suppose. Comp. however, Wiggers, ii. 349.

[5] De Scriptoribus ecclesiasticis, continuation of Jerome (in Biblioth. eccl. J. A. Fabricii. Hamb. 1718): de Fide s. de Dogmatibus ecclesiasticis liber ad Gelasium Papam (ed. Elmenhorst. Hamburg. 1614. 4). Wiggers, ii. 351.

[6] Cf lib. ii. Epist. 19 (see Opera, best in Sirmondi Opp. t. i.). Wiggers, ii. 356.

[7] Lucidus was forced to condemn the following propositions: Quod praescientia Dei hominem violenter compellat ad mortem, vel quod cum Dei pereant voluntate, qui pereunt,—alios deputatos ad mortem, alios ad vitam praedestinatos. The Pseudo-Augustinus Praedestinatus lib. ii. says: Quem voluerit Deus sanctum esse, sanctus est, aliud non erit: quem praescierit esse iniquum, iniquus erit, aliud non erit. Praedestinatio enim Dei jam et numerum justorum, et numerum constituit peccatorum, et necesse erit constitutum terminum praeteriri non posse.—De Deo Apostolus dicit: Quos vocavit, hos praedestinavit (Rom. viii. 30). Si praescientem et praedestinantem et vocantem in Apostolo legitis; nobis ut quid impingitis crimen ob hoc, quod dicimus, praedestinasse Deum homines sive ad justitiam sive ad peccatum?—Invictus enim in sua voluntate permanet Deus, cum homo adsidue superetur. Si ergo invictum confitemini Deum, confitemini et hoc, quia quod eos voluit ille, qui condidit, aliud esse non possunt. Unde colligimus apud animum, quia quos Deus semel praedestinavit ad vitam, etiamsi negligant, etiamsi peccent, etiamsi nolint, ad vitam perducentur inviti: quos autem praedestinavit ad mortem, etiamsi currant, etiamsi festinent, sine causa laborant. Cf. § 87, note 31.

[8] Praefatio Praedestinati:—Quis hanc fidem habens sacerdotum benedictionibus caput inclinare desideret, et eorum sibi precibus et sacrificiis credat posse succurri? Si enim haec nec prodesse volentibus, nec obesse nolentibus incipiant credi, cessabunt omnia Dei sacerdotum studia, et universa monitorum adminicula vana videbuntur esse figmenta: atque ita unusquisque suis erit vitiis occupatus, ut criminum suorum delectationem Dei praedestinationem existimet, et ad bonum a malo transitum, nec per sacerdotum Dei (studia?), nec per conversionem suam, nec per legem dominicam se possere invenire confidat.

[9] Faustus only alludes to him (if Lucidus be not meant, as Wiggers, ii. 232, assumes) de Grat. Dei et hum. ment. lib. arb. i. 4: Si ergo unus ad vitam, alter ad perditionem, ut asserunt, deputatus est, sicut quidam Sanctorum dixit, non judicandi nascimur, sed judicati. Ibid. c. 11: Igitur dum liberi interemtor arbitrii in alterutram partem omnia ex praedestinatione statuta et definita esse pronunciat, etc.—Gennadius de Script. eccl. c. 38, speaking of Augustine: Quis tanto studio legat quanto ille scripsit? Unde et multa loquenti accidit, quod dixit per Salomonem Spir. S.: In multiloquio non effugies peccatum (Prov. x. 19).—Error tamen illius sermone multo, ut dixi, contractus, lucta

most part it was usual, in order not to tread too closely on the honored man, to distinguish between himself and his adherents at that time,[10] that these last could be the more safely condemned as heretics under the name of *Predestinarians.*[11]

In Rome and Africa, on the other hand, the doctrines of Augustine were strictly followed.[12] Thus Gallic Semipelagianism was threatened with extinction from this quarter, and that the more readily, inasmuch as even in Gaul were many adherents of Augustine, and among them two distinguished bishops, *Avitus*, archbishop of Vienne (490–523), and *Caesarius*, bishop of Arles (502–542).[13] Those same Scythian monks who had raised so much disturbance by their efforts to introduce the formula, "one of the Trinity was crucified" (§ 111, note 5), also renewed the struggle against Pelagianism, which seemed to them to be closely connected with Nestorianism, and against Semipelagianism.[14] After they had been banished from Rome, because Hormisdas had pronounced judgment too indefinitely on Faustus, they brought the question of the latter's orthodoxy before the African bishops living in Sardinia (523); in whose name *Fulgentius*, bishop of Ruspe († 533), now defended Augustine against the writings of Faustus.[15] In consequence of this, Semipelagianism was rejected in Gaul also, under the leader-

hostium exaggeratus, necdum haeresis quaestionem dedit.—Ennodius, lib. ii. Ep. 19, contradicts the doctrine that man has freedom only to do evil, and adds: Video, quo se toxica libycae pestis extendant: arenosus coluber non haec sola habet perniciosa, quae referat.

[10] So particularly Praedestinatus. In the praef.: Silerem—si non etiam audacter sub Augustini nomine libros ederent.—Quis enim nesciat, Augustinum orthodoxum semper fuisse doctorem, et tam scribendo quam disputando omnibus haereticis obviasse?

[11] Violent controversy in the 17th century on the question whether there ever was a particular sect of the Praedestinarians, as the Jesuits (particularly J. Sirmond Historia Praedestinatiana. Paris. 1648, in ej. Opp. t. iv., and in Gallandii Bibl. PP. x. 401) and the older Lutherans asserted, while the Jansenists (especially G. Mauguin Accurata historiae Praedestinatianae J. Sirmondi confutatio, in his Vindiciis praedestinationis et gratiae, p. 443, ss.), Dominicans, and Reformed, denied it. Modern impartial historians agree with the latter (comp. Semler in the historical introduction prefixed to Baumgarten's Polemik, iii. 312).—Comp. Sagitarii Introd. in hist. eccl. i. 1148. Walch's Ketzerhist. v. 218.

[12] Wiggers, ii. 365.

[13] Alcimi Ecdicii Aviti Opera (poems, letters, homilies), ed. J. Sirmond. Paris. 1643. (Bibl. PP. Lugd. ix. 560). Caesarii Opp. (especially homilies, many incorrectly attributed to him) in the Bibl. PP. Lugd. viii. 819, 860; xxvii. 324. Wiggers, ii. 368.

[14] Walch, v. 117. Wiggers, ii. 394.

[15] Epistola synodica Episc. Afric. in Sardinia exulum ad Jo. Maxentium, etc. ap. Mansi, viii. 591.—Fulgentii Ruspensis libb. iii. de Veritate praedestinationis et gratia Dei (his libb. vii. adv. Faustum are lost) together with his other works (libb. iii. ad Monimum—several writings against the Arians, and other doctrinal treatises) published. Paris. 1684. 4; in Bibl. PP. Lugd. ix. 16.

ship of *Caesarius* at the synod of *Arausio* (Oranges, 529), and the Augustinian system adopted, though in a form essentially modified.[16] Thus also no teacher of Semipelagianism was condemned by name;[17] and not long after the principles were again taught without giving offense,[18] although even rigid Augustinism continued to have its adherents.[19]

§ 114.

HISTORY OF THE THEOLOGICAL SCIENCES.

After the Roman Empire had been annoyed and overrun by barbarians, the necessity of struggling against paganism no longer calling forth spiritual activity, and the study of the so-called heathen sciences having become increasingly suspicious, especially in the eyes of the monks, scientific cultivation deriorated more and more, inasmuch as the free movement of the spirit was hindered by the narrowing down of orthodoxy, and attention exclusively directed to single barren speculations, by the disputes carried on with so much zeal.[1] How narrowly

[16] The 25 capitula of the Synod, to which a sketch of the doctrine of grace, in the form of a Confession of Faith, is annexed, ap. Mansi, viii. 711. Here the Augustinian doctrines of original sin, and of grace as the only source of all that is good, are introduced; afterward it is said in the Confession of Faith: Quam gratiam—omnibus, qui baptizari desiderant, non in libero arbitrio haberi, sed Christi novimus simul et credimus largitate conferri.—Hoc etiam secundum fidem catholicam credimus, quod accepta per baptismum gratia omnes baptizati, Christo auxiliante et cooperante, quae ad salutem animae pertinent possint et debeant, si fideliter laborare voluerint, adimplere. If sufficient grace be granted to all in baptism, it depends on man to embrace or to resist it, and there is no gratia irresistibilis and no decretum absolutum. These latter, therefore, do not result, as Wiggers, ii. 441, supposes, as necessary consequences from the positions of the Synod. The Synod does not teach them, because it does not recognize them.

[17] Hence Faustus is still honored in Provence as a saint, which is indeed censured by some (for example, Baronius, ad ann. 490, § 42), but defended by others. Comp. J. Stilting de S. Fausto comm. hist. in Actis SS. Sept. vii. 651.

[18] So by the African bishop Junilius (about 550), de partibus divinae legis (Bibl. PP. Lugd. x.) ii. 12, 15, by Gregory, archbishop of Tours († 595) Miraculorum (Bibl. PP. xi.) ii 1, vii. 1, 2, 9, 11, 13, by Gregory the Great, bishop of Rome († 604). Comp. G. F. Wiggers, de Gregorio M. ejusque placitis anthropologicis comm. ii. Rostochii. 1838-40. 4.

[19] To these belong Fulgentius Ferrandus—see § 111, note 26. Comp. his Paraeneticus ad Reginum comitem; Facundus, bishop of Hermiane—see § 111, note 27, contra Mocianum ap. Gallandius, xi. 811; Isidore, archbishop of Seville († 636), Sententt. ii. 6.

[1] Bossuet's Weltgesch. continued by J. A. Cramer, v. ii. 52. L. Wachler's Handbuch der Geschichte der Literatur. (Zweite Umarbeit. Frankf. a. M. 1823), ii. 5. Münscher's Dogmengesch. iii. 44.

they began in the west to judge of the writings of the older fathers, according to the standard of the new orthodoxy, is proved by the so-called Decretum Gelasii de libris recipiendis et non recipiendis.[2]

The writers who were engaged in the various controversies have been already named. In the Western Church, *Faustus Rejensis* (§ 113, notes 1, 2), *Fulgentius Ruspensis* (§ 113, note 15), *Fulgentius Ferrandus*, *Facundus Hermianensis*, *Liberatus* (§ 111, note 26, ff.); among the Orientals, *Leontius Byzantinus* (preface to § 110), and *Johannes Philoponus* (§ 110, note 25).

There was now less and less of independent investigation; and instead of it men were content with compilations from the highly esteemed older fathers.[3] By way of exegesis began the series of the so-called catenae;[4] in the east with *Procopius of Gaza* (about 520),[5] in the west with *Primacius*, bishop of

[2] In some MSS. it is attributed to Damasus (366–384), in the Spanish MSS. to Hormisdas (514–523), but commonly to a Roman Synod under Gelasius (496). On the contrary, it is wanting in the Dionysian collection of decrees (525), and in the Spanish (about 600) is placed entirely at the end, behind the decrees of Gregory the Great, which points to a later addition. It is afterward first mentioned, but without the name of an author, by the English bishop Adhelmus (about 680) de virginitate, c. 11, first attributed to Gelasius by Hincmar, archbishop of Rheims (about 860) Opusc. l. capitulorum, c. 24. That it was gradually enlarged is shown by the different existing texts (three in Mansi, viii. 153). In like manner, the difference of authors may be inferred from the fact that the Opera Cypriani are placed both among the libris recipiendis and the non-recipiendis. At the time of Hormisdas the basis of this list was already in existence (Horm. Ep. ad Possessorem ap. Mansi, viii. 499: Non improvide veneranda patrum sapientia fideli potestati quae essent catholica dogmata definiit, certa librorum etiam veterum in auctoritatem recipienda, sancto Spiritu instruente, praefigens), but not in the form of a decree, since, in the latter case, Dionysius would have adopted it. At the time of Hormisdas the Opera Fausti were also not yet in it, since Hormisdas hesitates to condemn Faustus. The decree, however, must have received its present form substantially in the first half of the sixth century, because in it no writings and heretics of this century whatever are mentioned, and only the first four general councils. Single interpolations were indeed made afterward. Thus, in Hincmar's time the canones Apostolorum were not yet adduced among the Apocryphis. Cf. Mansi, viii. 145, 151. Regenbrecht de Canonibus Apostolorum et codice Eccl. hispanae diss. Vratisl. 1828. 8. p. 52.—In this decree, among others, the Historia Eusebii Pamph. the Opuscula Tertulliani, Lactantii, Clementis Alex., Arnobii are reckoned among the libris apocrpyhis, qui non recipiuntur.

[3] Cassiodorus Institt. div. praef.: Quapropter tractores vobis doctissimos indicasse sufficiat, quando ad tales remisisse competens plenitudo probatur esse doctrinae. Nam et vobis quoque erat praestantius praesumpta novitate non imbui, sed priscorum fonte satiari.

[4] J. F. S. Augustin de Catenis PP. graec. in N. T. observationes. Halae. 1762 (in J. A. Noesselti iii. Commentatt. ad Hist. Eccl. pertinent. Halae. 1817. 8. p. 321, ss.).

[5] Comm. in Octateuchum, in Esaiam, Proverbia, in xii. Proph. minores, etc. Cf. Fabricii Bibl. gr. vol. vi. p. 259 (ed. Harles, vol. vii p. 563). Augustin, l. c. p. 385. In Ang. Maji Classicorum auctorum e Vaticanis codd. editorum, t. vi. (Romae. 1834. 8) are published besides comm. in Genesin usque ad cap. xviii. and fragm. in Cant. Salomonis; t. ix. (1837) Comm. in Salom. Proverbia, Catena in Cant. Cant.

Adrumetum (about 550).[6] Most of the works, too, of *Magnus Aurelius Cassidorus Senator* († after 562),[7] and of *Isidore, bishop of Seville* († 636),[8] are written in this compilation method. The χριστιανικὴ τοπογραφία of the Nestorian *Cosmas Indicopleustes* (about 535), in its remarkable theologico-geographical part, is only a compilation, chiefly from the works of Diodorus of Tarsus and Theodorus of Mopsuestia.[9]

Distinguished as an independent thinker, in this age of imitation and authorities, was the Aristotelian philosopher *Anicius Manlius Torquatus Severinus Boethius* († 525), who, however, in his philosophical writings,[10] refers so little to Christianity, that one is led to doubt not only of the authenticity of the theological works[11] ascribed to him, but even whether he could have been a Christian.[12]

[6] Comm. in Epistolas Pauli.

[7] Thus his Comment. in Psalmos is drawn from Augustine; his Historia eccl. tripartita in twelve books (see preface to § 1).—De institutione divinarum literarum libb. ii. (a more correct title is: Institutiones quemadmodum divinae et humanae debeant intelligi lectiones libb. ii. See Credner's Einl. in d. R. T. i. i. 15). Historically important are his variae epistolae libb. xii. Of his de rebus gestis Gothorum libb. xii. there remains only the extract by Jordanis (see § 108, note 3). His book de vii. disciplinis was much used in the middle ages. Opp. ed. J. Garetius. Rothomagi. 1679. (Venet. 1729.) 2 vol. fol. La vie de Cassiodore par F. D. de Ste Marthe. Paris. 1694. 12. Cassiodorus by Stäudlin, in the Kirchenhist. Archive for 1825, p. 259, ff. and 381, ff. Ritter's Gesch. d. christl. Philos. ii 598. Bähr's christl. römische Theologie, S. 418.

[8] Comm. in libros hist. Vet. Test.—De ecclesiasticis officiis libb. ii.—Sententiarum s. de summo bono libb. iii. (important for the middle ages. Sententiarii.)—Regula Monachorum.—De Scriptoribus eccles.—and many others. See the chief work Originum s. Etymologiarum libb. xx.—Hist. Gothorum, Vandalorum et Suevorum in Hispania.—Opp. ed. J. Grial. Madr. 1599 (Paris. 1601. Colon. 1617). fol. Faust. Arevalo. Romae. 1797. vii. voll. 4. Bähr. S. 455.

[9] Prim. ed. B. de Montfaucon in Collect. nov. PP. Graec. t. ii. (Paris. 1706): recus. in Gallandii Bibl. PP. t. xi. p. 401, ss. The Nestorianism of Cosmas was first pointed out by La Croze Hist. du Christianisme des Indes, t. i. p. 40, ss. Cf. Semler Hist. eccl. selecta capita, i. p. 421, ss.

[10] His principal work: de Consolatione philosophiae libb. v. Besides this, translations from the writings of Porphyry and Aristotle, and commentaries on the same. He laid the foundation of the predilection for the Aristotelian philosophy in the west, as John Philoponus did at the same time in the east (§ 110, note 25).

[11] Adv. Eutychen et Nestor. de duabus naturis et una persona Christi.—Quod Trinitas sit unus Deus et non tres dii ad Symmachum.—Utrum Pater, Filius, et Sp. S. de divinitate substantialiter praedicentur. Comp. Hand, in the Encyclopädie of Ersch and Gruber, xi 283. Bähr's christl. römische Theologie, S. 423. On the other hand, Gust. Baur. de A. M. S. Boëthio christianae doctrinae assertore, Darmst. 1841. 8, is in favor of the authenticity.

[12] Much used in the schools of the middle ages. In the eighth century he was even enrolled among the saints, and in addition to two other Severini, worshiped on the 23d October. That he was a Christian is denied by Gottf. Arnold (Kirchen u. Ketzerhist. Th. i. B. 6, cap. 3, § 7), and Hand, l. c. On the contrary, G. Baur asserts that he was at least outwardly a Christian. Comp. Ritter's Gesch. d. christl. Philos. ii. 580.

The prevailing dialectic development of Christian doctrine must have been as unsatisfactory as it was injurious to deeper religious spirits, and therefore mysticism, in opposition to it, obtained a fuller and better developed form in the works of *Pseudodionysius Areopagita*,[13] which appeared toward the end of the fifth century. These writings, banishing the divine essence, in the manner of the New Platonists, beyond all being and knowledge, and representing all things as proceeding in regular gradation out of it as their essence, proposed to teach how man, rightly apprehending his own position in the chain of being, might elevate himself through the next higher order to communion with still higher orders, and finally with God himself. At present they spread but gradually in the oriental church, till they penetrated in the middle ages into the west also, and so became the basis of all the later Christian mysticism.

There were now but few institutions for the advancement of theological learning any where; in the west none whatever.[14] The monkish contempt displayed by *Gregory the Great*,[15] bishop

[13] Comp. § 110, note 7, and Engelhardt's works there quoted. Ritter's Gesch. d. christl. Philosophie, ii. 515. Die Christl. Mystik in ihrer Entwickelung u. in ihren Denkmalen von A. Helfferich (2 Th. Gotha. 1842) i. 129; ii. 1.

[14] Cassiodor. de. Inst. div. lit. praef.: Cum studia saecularium literarum magno desiderio fervere cognoscerem (comp. Sartorius Versuch über die Regierung der Ostgothen während ihrer Herrschaft in Italien. Hamburg. 1811. S. 152, ss. Manso Gesch. des ostgoth. Reichs in Italien. Breslau. 1824. S. 132), ita ut multa pars hominum per ipsa se mundi prudentiam crederet adipisci; gravissimo sum (fateor) dolore permotus, quod scripturis divinis magistri publici deessent, cum mundani auctores celeberrima procul dubio traditione pollerent. Nisus sum ergo cum b. Agapito Papa urbis Romae, ut sicut apud Alexandriam multo tempore fuisse traditur institutum, nunc etiam in Nisibi civitate Syrorum ab Hebraeis sedulo fertur exponi (see below, § 122, note 5), collatis expensis in urbe Romana professos doctores scholae potius acciperent christianae, unde et anima susciperet aeternam salutem, et casto atque purissimo eloquio fidelium lingua comeretur. Sed cum per bella ferventia et turbulentia nimis in Italico regno certamina desiderium meum nullatenus valuisset impleri: quoniam non habet locum res pacis temporibus inquietis; ad hoc divina caritate probor esse compulsus, ut ad vicem magistri introductorios vobis libros istos, Domino praestante, conficerem, etc. What substitute was adopted may be seen from Conc. Vasense, iii. ann. 529, can. 1: Hoc enim placuit, ut omnes presbyteri, qui sunt in parochiis constituti, secundum consuetudinem, quam per totam Italiam satis salubriter teneri cognovimus, juniores lectores—secum in domo—recipiant: et eos—psalmos parare, divinis lectionibus insistere, et in lege domini erudire contendant: ut sibi dignos successores provideant. In Spain we find the first trace of a kind of episcopal seminaries, Conc. Tolet. ii. ann. 531, can. 1: De his, quos voluntas parentum a primis infantiae annis clericatus officio manciparit, hoc statuimus observandum, ut mox detonsi vel ministerio lectorum cum traditi fuerint, in domo Ecclesiae sub episcopali praesentia a praeposito sibi debeant erudiri.

[15] Pauli Warnefridi (about 775) de Vita S. Gregor. Papae, libb. iv. (prim. ed. Jo. Mabillon in the Annales Ord. S. Bened. saec. i. p. 385) and Johannis Eccl. Rom. Diaconi (about 875) Vita S. Greg. libb. iv. both in tome iv. of the Benedictine edition of Gregory's works.

of Rome (from 590–604), for the liberal sciences,[16] contributed much to the daily increasing neglect of them; but the later traditions of his hostility to all literature, are not to be fully believed.[17]

New fields were now opened to ecclesiastical writers in collecting and arranging *the saints' traditions*, in which *Gregory, archbishop of Tours* (573–595),[18] and *Gregory the Great*,[19] led the way; and in the cultivation of *ecclesiastical law*.[20] In

Comp. the life composed by the Benedictines, and given in that volume. G. F. Wiggers de Gregorio M. ejusque placitis anthropologicis, comm. ii. Rostoch. 1838. 4. p. 11.—Gregory's most important works (see Bähr's christl. röm. Theologie, S. 442. Wiggers, p. 35): Expositionis in Job. s. Moralium libb. xxxv.—Liber pastoralis curae ad Joh. Ravennae Episc. (by Anastasius Sinaita, patriarch of Antioch, immediately translated into Greek).—Dialogorum de vita et miraculis Patrum Ital. et de aeternitate animarum, libb. iv. (translated into Greek by Pope Zacharias, about 744).—Epistolarum libb. xiv. (according to the older arrangement, libb. xii.).—Liber Sacramentorum de circulo anni s. Sacramentarium. —Antiphonarius s. gradualis liber.—Opp. ed. Petr. Gussanvillaeus. voll. iii. Paris. 1675. fol. studio et labore Monachorum Ord. S. Bened. e Congr S. Mauri, voll. iv. Paris. 1705. fol. locupletata a J. B. Gallicciolì. Venet. 1768, ss. voll. xvii. 4. Concerning the modern abbreviators of Gregory see Oudinus de Scriptt. eccl. ant. i. 1544.

16 For example, in the epistola ad Leandrum prefixed to his Exposit. libri Jobi: Non barbarismi confusionem devito, situs motusque praepositionum casusque servare contemno, quia indignum vehementer existimo, ut verba caelestis oraculi restringam sub regulis Donati.—Lib. xi. Epist. 54, ad Desiderium, Episc. Viennensem: Pervenit ad nos, quod sine verecundia memorare non possumus, Fraternitatem tuam grammaticam quibusdam exponere. Quam rem ita moleste suscepimus, ac sumus vehementius aspernati, ut ea, quae prius dicta fuerant, in gemitus et tristitiam verteremus: quia in uno se ore cum Jovis laudibus Christi laudes non capiunt, etc.

17 Joannes Sarisburiensis (about 1172) in his Policraticus, lib. ii. c. 26: Doctor sanctus ille Gregorius—non modo Mathesin jussit ab aula, sed, ut traditur a majoribus, incendio dedit probatae lectionis scripta Palatinus quaecumque recepit Apollo. Lib. viii. c. 19, fertur b. Gregorius bibliothecam combussisse gentilem, quo divinae paginae gratior esset locus, et major auctoritas, et diligentia studiosior. Barthol. Platina (about 1480) de Vitis Pontificum, in Vita Gregorii: Neque est cur patiamur, Gregorium hac in re a quibusdam —carpi, quod suo mandato veterum aedificia sint dirupta, ne peregrini et advenae—posthabitis locis sacris, arcus triumphales et monumenta veterum cum admiratione inspicerent. Platina tries to defend him from the charge. Id. in Vita Sabiniani: Paululum etiam abfuit, quin libri ejus (Gregorii) comburerentur, adeo in Gregorium ira et invidia exarserat homo malevolus. Sunt qui scribant, Sabinianum instigantibus quibusdam Romanis hoc in Gregorium molitum esse, quod veterum statuas tota urbe, dum viveret, et obtruncaverit et disjecerit, quod quidem ita vero dissonum est, ut illud, quod de abolendis aedificiis majorum in vita ejus diximus. Against the credibility of these stories see P. Bayle Dictionnaire hist. et crit. Art. Gregoire, not. H. and M. Jo. Barbeyrac de la Morale des Pères, c. 17 § 16. What Brucker, Hist. Phil. iii. 560, says in their defense is of no importance.

18 De Gloria Martyrum libb. ii., de Gloria Confessorum lib. i., de Virtutibus et Miraculis S. Martini libb. iv., de Vitis Patrum lib. i., in his Opp. ed. Theod. Ruinart. Paris. 1699. fol (comp. Div. I. § 53, note 46). Dr. C. G. Kries de Greg. Tur. Episc. vita et scriptis. Vratisl. 1839. 8.

19 Dialogorum libb. iv.; see above, note 15.

20 A. Gallandii de Vetustis canonum collectionibus dissertationum sylloge (Dissertations of Coustant, de Marca, the Ballerini, Berard, Quesnell, etc.). Venetiis. 1778. fol. recus. Mogunt. 1790, t. ii. 4. (L. T. Spittler's) Geschichte des kanonischen Rechts bis auf die Zeiten des falschen Isidorus. Halle. 1778. 8.

the Greek Church,[21] soon after the council of Chalcedon, appeared the so-called *apostolic canons*,[22] claiming to form the unalterable basis of all ecclesiastical arrangements. About the same time the Christians began to put together the decrees of councils in the order of the subjects, instead of in the old chronological way. The oldest collection of this kind now extant is that of *Johannes Scholasticus* of Antioch (afterward patriarch of Constantinople, † 578),[23] which was in great repute for several centuries. Justinian's code was also so rich a source for ecclesiastical matters, that particular collections of church laws were made soon after his time, out of his Institutes.[24] Those of John Scholasticus were at a later period adapted to Justinian's by a new arrangement of the collection of canons,[25] and thus arose the first *Nomocanon*.[26]

In the Latin Church there was not even a tolerably complete chronological collection of the canons till that made after the council of Chalcedon, since known as the *prisca translatio*.[27] A still fuller collection was afterward made by *Dionysius Exiguus* (about 500)[28] in a better translation, to which was added, in a second part, a collection of the papal decretals. In *Spain* there had been a collection of canons, between 633 and 636, on the model of that by Dionysius (the Greek ones in a peculiar version), and of papal decretals for the use of the Spanish

[21] Jos. Sim. Assemani Bibliotheca juris orientalis, civilis et canonici. Romae. 1762–66. t. v. 4. (incomplete, contains merely the Codex canonum eccl. Graecae and the Codex juris civilis eccl. Graecae). F. A. Biener de collectionibus canonum Eccl. Graecae schediasma litterarium. Berol. 1827. 8.

[22] See Div. I. § 67, note 5.

[23] Published in Guil. Voëlli et H. Justelli Bibliotheca juris canonici veteris (t. ii. Paris. 1661. fol.) ii. 449.

[24] The Collectio lxxxvii. capitulorum, collected by Johannes Scholasticus from the Novellae; the Coll. xxv. capitt. from the Codex and Novellae (published in G. E. Heimbach. Anecdota, t. ii. Lips. 1840. 4); and that erroneously published under the name of Theod. Balsamon in Voëlli et Justelli Bibl. juris ii. 1223 collectio constitt. ecclesiasticarum, which was compiled at the time of Heraclius, perhaps also of Justin II. from the Pandects, Codex, and Novellae. Comp. F. A. Biener's Gesch. d. Novellen Justinians. Berlin. 1824 8. S. 166.

[25] In this form it is found in Voëlli et Justelli Bibl. ii. 603.

[26] Though this name is much more modern. See Biener's Gesch. d. Novellen, S. 194 Heimbach Anecd. t. ii. Prolegom. p. lv.

[27] Best edition that of the Ballerini Opp. Leonis, iii. 473, from which Mansi, vi. 1105 Concerning it comp. Ballerini de Ant. collectionibus canonum (before t. iii. Opp. Leonis and in Gallandii Sylloge), P. ii. cap. 2, § 3. Spittler, S. 129.

[28] Published in Voëlli et Justelli Biblioth. i. 101. Ballerini, l. c. P. iii. cap. 1–3. Spittler, S. 134. According to Drey, über die Constit. u. Kanones d. Apostel, p. 203, even before the end of the fifth century.

Church,[29] which was afterward called the collection of *Isidore*,[30] because it was erroneously ascribed to the most celebrated man of that time, Isidore, archbishop of Seville († 636). The laws respecting penance had gradually become so numerous as to require a separate work. *Johannes Jejunator* (ὁ νησευτής), patriarch of Constantinople (from 585–593), wrote the ἀκολουθία καὶ τάξις ἐπὶ ἐξομολογουμένων,[31] the first libellus poenitentialis (rules of penance).

THIRD CHAPTER.

HISTORY OF THE HIERARCHY.

§ 115.

PRIVILEGES OF THE CLERGY.

The clergy, and particularly the bishops, received new privileges from *Justinian.* He intrusted the latter with civil jurisdiction over the monks and nuns, as well as over the clergy.[1] Episcopal *oversight of morals*, and particularly *the duty of providing for all the unfortunate* (§ 91, notes 8–10), had been established till the present time only on the foundation of ecclesiastical laws: but Justinian now gave them a more

[29] Published by Ant. Gonzalez in 2 Div. Collectio canonum Eccl. Hispanae. Matriti. 1808, and Epistolae decretales ac rescripta Rom. Pontiff. Matriti. 1821. fol.; comp. Ballerini, l. c. P. ii. cap. ii. § 2; P. iii. c. 4. M. E. Regenbrecht de Cann. Apostolorum et codice Eccl. Hispaniae diss. Vratisl. 1828. 8. Eichhorn on the Spanish collection of the sources of ecclesiastical jurisprudence, in the Transactions of the Royal Academy of Sciences at Berlin for the year 1834. (Berlin. 1836. 4to.) Historical and Philosophical Class, p. 89.

[30] According to Eichhorn, p. 113, since Pseudo-Isidore.

[31] Afterward variously interpolated; published in J. Morini Comm. Hist. de disciplina in administratione Sacramenti Poenitentiae. Paris. 1651. fol. in append.

[1] Novellae Justin. 79 et 83 (both A.D. 539). More particular notices are given in Nov. 123, cap. 21: Si quis autem litigantium intra x. dies contradicat iis, quae judicata sunt, tunc locorum judex causam examinet.—Si judicis sententia contraria fuerit iis, quae a Deo amabili Episcopo judicata sunt: tunc locum habere appellationem contra sententiam judicis.—Si vero crimen fuerit, quod adversus quamlibet memoratarum reverendissimarum personarum inferatur,—judex ultionem ei inferat legibus congruentem. Further, in a criminal accusation: Si Episcopus distulerit judicare, licentiam habeat actor civilem judicem adire. Cf. B. Schilling de Origine jurisdictionis eccles. in causis civilibus. Lips. 1825. 4. p. 41, ss.

general basis, by founding them on the civil law also.[2] He made it the duty of the bishops, and gave them the necessary civil qualifications, to undertake the care of *prisoners, minors, insane persons, foundlings, stolen children,* and *women*;[3] and invested them with the power of upholding good morals[4] and impartial administration of justice. It is true that he established a mutual inspection of the bishops and of the civil magistrates; but he gave in this respect to the latter considerably smaller privileges than to the former.[5] For example, he gave the bishops a legal influence over the choice of magistrates,[6] and security against general oppression on their part;[7] allowed them to interfere in case of refusal of justice;[8] and, in special instances, even constituted them judges of those official personages.[9] In like manner, he conveyed to them the right of concurrence in the choice of city officials,[10] and a joint oversight of the administration of city funds, and the maintenance of public establishments.[11] Thus the bishops became important personages even in civil life; and were farther honored by Justinian, in freedom from parental authority,[12] from the necessity of appearing as witnesses, and from taking oaths.[13]

[2] C. W. de Rhoer de Effectu relig. christ. in jurisprudentiam rom. fasc. 1. Groningae, 1776. 8. p. 94. C. Riffel's geschichtl. Darstellung des Verhältnisses zwischen Kirche und Staat. (Mainz. 1836) i. 622.

[3] Cod. Justin. lib. i. tit. iv. de episcopali audientia (i. e. judicio) l. 22.—l. 30.—l. 27. l. 28. —l. 24.—l. 33.

[4] In addition to their former powers against pimps (Cod. Th. xv. viii. 2) and sorcerers (Cod. Th. ix. xvi. 12), Justinian gave them also the privilege of interfering against gaming (Cod. Just. i. iv. 25).

[5] The Praesides provinciarum were obliged to see to it that bishops observed ecclesiastical laws relating to ecclesiastical things (Cod. Just. i. iii. 44, § 3, Nov. cxxxiii. c. 6), particularly those relating to the unalienableness of church possessions (Nov. vii. in epil.) and the regular holding of synods (Nov. cxxxvii. c. 6). They could only, however, put the bishops in mind of their duty, and then notify the emperor.

[6] Nov. cxlix. c. 1.

[7] Cod. Just. i. iv. 26, Nov. cxxxiv. c. 3.

[8] Nov. lxxxvi. c. 1.

[9] Nov. lxxxvi. c. 4 (A.D. 539): Quodsi contingat aliquem ex subditis nostris ab ipso clarissimo provinciae praeside injuria affici, jubemus eum sanctissimum illius urbis Episcopum adire, ut ille inter cl. praesidem, eumve, qui se ab eo injuria affectum putat, judicet. If the president (of a province) were condemned, and gave no satisfaction, the matter was referred to the emperor, and in case he found the episcopal sentence just, the president was condemned to death. According to Nov. viii. c. 9, cxxviii. c. 23, every magistrate, after laying down his office, was obliged to remain fifty days in the province to satisfy any claims that might be made against him. If he removed sooner, every one injured might complain to the bishop.

[10] Cod. Just. i. iv. 17, Nov. cxxviii. 16.

[11] Cod. Just. i. iv. 26.

[12] Novell. lxxxi.

[13] Novell. cxxiii. c. 7.

Finally, *Heraclius* committed to them jurisdiction over the clergy in criminal cases also (628).[14]

§ 116.

DEPENDENCE OF THE HIERARCHY ON THE STATE.

Notwithstanding these great privileges, the hierarchy became still more dependent on the State. As the emperors sent their civil laws to be promulgated by the Praetorian prefects, so, in like manner, ecclesiastical laws went forth from them to the patriarchs,[1] and the magistrates were directed to watch the observance of them by the bishops.[2] None doubted the emperor's right to enact laws touching the external relations of the Church, and even subjects connected with its internal constitution;[3] but it was more suspicious when the emperors began

[14] The law issued to the patriarch of Constantinople, Sergius, of which merely the contents are given in the Constitutt. Imper. appended to the Codex Justin. is found complete in Jo. Leunclavii Juris Graeco Romani (tomi ii. Francof. 1596. fol.), i. 73, and in Voëlli et Justelli Biblioth. juris can. ii. 1361: The offenses (ἐγκλήματα) of clergymen are to be judged by the bishop *κατὰ τοὺς θείους κανόνας. εἰ δέ γε νομίσοι σφοδροτέρας ἐπεξελεύσεως ἄξιον καθιστάναι τὸν κρινόμενον, τηνικαῦτα τὸν τοιοῦτον—τοῦ περικειμένου κελεύομεν γυμνοῦσθαι σχήματος, καὶ τοῖς πολιτικοῖς ἄρχουσι παραδιδόσθαι, τὰς τοῖς ἡμετέροις διωρισμένας νόμοις τιμωρίας ὑποσχησόμενον.*

[1] For example, Nov. 6, epilogus: Sanctissimi igitur Patriarchae cujusque diocesis haec in sanctissimis Ecclesiis sub se constitutis proponant, et Dei amantissimis Metropolitanis quae a nobis sancita sunt nota faciant. Hi vero ipsi in sanctissima Ecclesia metroplitana haec rursus proponant, et Episcopis, qui sub ipsis sunt, manifesta faciant. Quilibet vero illorum in Ecclesia sua haec proponat, ut nemo in nostra sit republica, qui ea—ignoret. F. A. Biener's Gesch. der Novellen Justinian's. Berlin. 1824. S. 31, f. comp. S. 25, ss.

[2] See § 115, note 5.

[3] Biener, l. c. S. 157, ss. 161, ss. Thus Justinian, Nov. 123, c. 3, where he fixes the amount to be given by the bishops pro inthronisticis, uses the expression: Κελεύομεν *τοίνυν τοὺς μὲν μακαριωτάτους ἀρχιεπισκόπους καὶ πατριάρχας, τουτέστι τῆς πρεσβυτέρας* Ῥώμης, *καὶ* Κωνσταντινουπόλεως, *καὶ* Ἀλεξανδρείας, *καὶ* Θεουπόλεως, *καὶ* Ἱεροσολύμων. When the Emperor Maurice had made a law, ut quisquis publicis administrationibus fuerit implicatus, ei neque ad ecclesiasticum officium venire, neque in monasterium converti liceat: Gregory the Great, lib. iii. Ep. 65, ad Mauricium Aug. remonstrated against the second part of the prohibition. Ex. gr. Ego vero haec Dominis meis loquens, quid sum nisi pulvis et vermis? Sed tamen quia contra auctorem omnium Deum hanc intendere constitutionem sentio, Dominis tacere non possum.—Ad haec ecce per me servum ultimum suum et vestrum respondebit Christus dicens: Ego te de notario comitem excubitorum, de comite excubitorum, Caesarem, de Caesare Imperatorem, nec solum hoc, sed etiam patrem Imperatorum feci. Sacerdotes meos tuae manui commisi, et tu a meo servitio milites tuos subtrahis? Responde, rogo, piissime Domine, servo tuo, quid venienti et haec dicenti responsurus es in judicio Domino tuo?—Ego quidem jussioni subjectus eandem legem per diversas terrarum partes transmitti feci: et quia lex ipsa

now to decide questions of faith by edicts, and when Synods were assembled almost entirely for the purpose of adopting imperial articles of faith. The Greek bishops became more and more accustomed to sacrifice their conviction to circumstances;[4] but the bishops of Italy, favored by the political condition of their country, were able for the most part to assert a firmer position.

§ 117.

HISTORY OF THE PATRIARCHS.

Ever since the beginning of the Monophysite controversy in the East, the sees of Alexandria and Antioch had become so weak, that the patriarchs of Constantinople only, upheld by the privileges granted them at the council of Chalcedon,[1] were able to vie with the Roman patriarchs.[2] But while the former were dependent on imperial caprice, and constantly harassed by the Greek spirit of controversy, the latter enjoyed the most perfect freedom in ecclesiastical things, and the advantage of standing at the head of the west, which was less inclined to controversies about faith, and therefore more united.[3] After the extinction of the West Roman empire (476), by which, however, they had never been molested, but often furthered,[4] the Roman

omnipotenti Deo minime concordat, ecce per suggestionis meae paginam serenissimis Dominis nuntiavi. Utrobique ergo quae debui exsolvi, qui et Imperatori obedientiam praebui, et pro Deo quod sensi minime tacui.

[4] Epistola Legatis Francorum, qui Constantinopolim proficiscebantur, ab Italiae clericis directa, A.D. 551, ap. Mansi, ix. p. 153: Sunt graeci Episcopi habentes divites et opulentas ecclesias, et non patiuntur duos menses a rerum ecclesiasticarum dominatione suspendi: pro qua re secundum tempus, et secundum voluntatem principum, quidquid ab eis quaesitum fuerit, sine altercatione consentiunt. Comp. § 92, notes 1 and 2.

[1] The Monophysite party which predominated under Basiliscus, suspended these privileges in part, Evagrius, iii. 6: (Timotheus Aelurus) *ἀποδίδωσι τῇ Ἐφεσίων καὶ τὸ πατριαρχικὸν δίκαιον, ὅπερ αὐτὴν ἀφεῖλεν ἡ ἐν Χαλκηδόνι σύνοδος*: but by the law Cod. Justin. i. ii. 16 (by Zeno, not, as the title has it, by Leo), the decrees of Chalcedon were revived, to be in force ever after.

[2] Order of the Roman bishops: Leo I. the Great † 461, Hilary † 468, Simplicius † 483, Felix II. † 492, Gelasius I. † 496, Anastasius II. † 498, Symmachus † 514, Hormisdas † 523, John I. † 526, Felix III. † 530, Boniface II. † 532, John II. † 535, Agapetus I. † 536, Silverius banished by Belisarius 537, Vigilius † 555, Pelagius I. † 560, John III. † 573, Benedict I. † 578, Pelagius II. † 590, Gregory I. the Great † 604, Sabinianus † 606, Boniface III. † 607, Boniface IV. † 615, Deusdedit † 618, Boniface V. † 625.

[3] See vol. i. pp. 383, 384.

[4] See above, § 94, notes 12 and 66.

bishops became subject to German princes, who left them at perfect liberty to manage all affairs within the Church according to their pleasure. This was particularly the case with *Theoderich*, king of the Arian Ostrogoths (493–526),[5] to whom the schism between Rome and Constantinople gave sufficient security from all dangerous combinations of the Catholic hierarchy. And when, on the death of Bishop Anastasius, there was a contested election between Symmachus and Laurentius (498),[6] he waited till required by both parties to decide,[7] and then quietly allowed a Roman synod under Symmachus to declare all interference of the laity in the affairs of the Roman Church entirely inadmissible.[8]

[5] On the course pursued by the Ostrogoth kings toward the church, see G. Sartorius Versuch über die Regierung der Ostgothen während ihrer Herrschaft in Italien. Hamburg. 1811. S. 124, ss. 306, ss. J. C. F. Manso Gesch. des ostgoth. Reichs in Italien. Breslau. 1824. S. 141, ss. Theoderich says (Cassiodori Variarum, lib. ii. Ep. 27): Religionem imperare non possumus: quia nemo cogitur, ut credat invitus. King Theodahat to the emperor Justinian (ibid. x. Ep. 26): Cum divinitas diversas patiatur religiones esse, nos unam non audemus imponere. Retinemus enim legisse nos, voluntarie sacrificandum esse Domino, non cujusquam cogentis imperio. Quod qui aliter facere tentaverit, evidenter caelestibus jussionibus obviavit.

[6] According to Theodorus Lector, lib. ii. (ed. Vales. Amstelod. p. 560) Laurentius was chosen by an imperial party on condition of subscribing the Henoticon. Cf. Anastasii Lib. pontificalis, c. 52, in vita Symmachi.

[7] Anastasii Lib. pontificalis, c. 52, in vita Symmachi: Et facta contentione hoc constituerunt partes, ut ambo ad Ravennam pergerent ad judicium Regis Theodorici. Qui dum ambo introissent in Ravennam, hoc judicium aequitatis invenerunt, ut qui primo ordinatus fuisset, vel ubi pars maxima cognosceretur, ipse sederet in sede apostolica. Quod tandem aequitas in Symmacho invenit.

[8] Synodus Romana iii. sub Symmacho (in the collections cited erroneously as the Syn. Rom. iv. s. palmaris, see Pagi ad ann. 502 num. 3, ss.) ap. Mansi, viii. 266, ss. The protocol of a synod held after the death of Pope Simplicius was here read, and the decrees passed at it declared nugatory as proceeding from a layman. This protocol is given in the Acta of the Synod referred to, and runs thus: Cum in unum apud b. Petrum Apostolum resedissent, sublimis et eminentissimus vir, praefectus praetorio atque patricius, agens etiam vices praecellentissimi regis Odoacris, Basilius dixit: Quamquam studii nostri et religionis intersit, ut in episcopatus electione concordia principaliter servetur ecclesiae, ne per occasionem seditionis status civitatis vocetur in dubium: tamen admonitione beatissimi Papae nostri Simplicii, quam ante oculos semper habere debemus, hoc nobis meministis sub obtestatione fuisse mandatum, ut propter illum strepitum, et venerabilis ecclesiae detrimentum, si eum de hac luce transire contigerit, non sine nostra consultatione cujuslibet celebretur electio. Nam et cum quid confusionis atque dispendii venerabilis ecclesia sustineret, miramur praetermissis nobis quidquam fuisse tentatum, cum etiam sacerdote nostro superstite nihil sine nobis debuisset assumi. Quare si amplitudini vestrae vel sanctitati placet, incolumia omnia, quae ad futuri antistitis electionem respiciunt, religiosa honoratione servemus, hanc legem specialiter praeferentes, quam nobis haeredibusque nostris christianae mentis devotione sancimus: Ne unquam praedium, seu rusticum seu urbanum, vel ornamenta aut ministeria ecclesiarum—ab eo qui nunc antistes sub electione communi fuerit ordinandus, et illis qui futuris saeculis sequentur, quocumque titulo atque commento alienentur. Si quis vero aliquid eorum alienare voluerit, inefficax atque irritum

Thus the Roman bishops were so far from being hindered by any superior power, that it proved an advantageous circumstance to them in the eyes of their new civil rulers, that they steadfastly resisted innovations of faith made in Constantinople, till they gained a new victory over the changeable Greeks under the Emperor Justin. The natural consequence of this was, that while the patriarchs of Constantinople were constantly sinking in ecclesiastical esteem on account of their vacillation in these controversies, the bishops of Rome still maintained their ancient reputation of being the defenders of oppressed orthodoxy.[9]

Under these favorable circumstances, *the ecclesiastical* pretensions of the Roman bishops, who now formed the only center of Catholic Christendom in the west, in opposition to the Arian conquerors, rose high, without hindrance. They asserted that not only did the highest ecclesiastical authority in the west belong to them, but also superintendence of orthodoxy and maintenance of ecclesiastical laws throughout the whole Church. These claims they sometimes founded on imperial edicts[10] and decrees of synods;[11] but for the most part on the peculiar rights

judicetur; sitque facienti vel consentienti, accipientique anathema, etc. At this enactment the following voices were now raised at the synod under Symmachus: Perpendat s. Synodus, uti praetermissis personis religiosis, quibus maxime cura est de tanto pontifice, electionem laici in suam redegerint potestatem, quod contra canones esse manifestum est. —Scriptura evidentissimis documentis constat invalida. Primum quod contra patrum regulas a laicis, quamvis religiosis, quibus nulla de ecclesiasticis facultatibus aliquid disponendi legitur unquam attributa facultas, facta videtur. Deinde quod nullius praesulis apostolicae sedis subscriptione firmata docetur. The arrangement was declared null, and, on the contrary, another of similar import was passed by the synod to secure ecclesiastical property.

[9] Cod. Just. i. i. 7, below, note 23.

[10] Hilarii P. Epist. xi. (Mansi, viii. 939): Fratri enim nostro Leontio nihil constituti a sanctae memoriae decessore meo juris potuit abrogari:—quia Christianorum quoque principum lege decretum est, ut quidquid ecclesiis earumque rectoribus—apostolicae sedis antistes suo pronunciasset examine, veneranter accipi tenaciterque servari, cum suis plebibus caritas vestra cognosceret: nec unquam possent convelli, quae et sacerdotali ecclesiastica praeceptione fulcirentur et regia.

[11] Epist. synod. Rom. ad Clericos et Monachos Orient. A.D. 485 (Mansi, vii. 1140): Quotiens intra Italiam propter ecclesiasticas causas, praecipue fidei, colliguntur domini sacerdotes, consuetudo retinetur, ut successor praesulum sedis apostolicae ex persona cunctorum totius Italiae sacerdotum juxta solicitudinem sibi ecclesiarum omnium competentem cuncta constituat, qui caput est omnium; Domino ad b. Petrum dicente: Tu es Petrus etc. Quam vocem sequentes cccxviii. sancti patres apud Nicaeam congregati confirmationem rerum atque auctoritatem sanctae Romanae ecclesiae detulerunt (comp. above, § 94, notes 28, 35, 60): quam utramque usque ad aetatem nostram successiones omnes, Christi gratia praestante, custodiunt. Gelasii Ep. iv. ad Faustum (Mansi, viii. 19): Quantum ad religionem pertinet, nonnisi apostolicae sedi juxta canones debetur summa judicii totius. Ejusd. Ep. xiii. ad Episc. Dardaniae (Mansi, viii. 54): Non reticemus

conferred on Peter by the Lord.[12] After the *synodus palmaris*, called by Theoderich to examine the charges newly raised by the Laurentian party against Symmachus (503), had acquitted him without examination, in view of the circumstances;[13]

autem, quod cuncta per mundum novit ecclesia, quoniam quorumlibet sententiis ligata pontificum, sedes b. Petri Apostoli jus habeat resolvendi, utpote quod de omni ecclesia fas habeat judicandi, neque cuiquam de ejus liceat judicare judicio, siquidem ad illam de qualibet mundi parte canones appellari voluerint, ab illa autem nemo sit appellare permissus.

[12] Gelasii decretum de libris recipiendis et non recipiendis (Mansi, viii. 157; comp. on it § 114, note 2): Quamvis universae per orbem catholicae diffusae ecclesiae unus thalamus Christi sit, sancta tamen Romana ecclesia nullis synodicis constitutis caeteris ecclesiis praelata est, sed evangelica voce Domini et Salvatoris nostri primatum obtinuit: Tu es Petrus, etc. Cui data est etiam societas b. Pauli Apostoli,—qui non diverso, sicut haeretici garriunt, sed uno tempore, uno eodemque die gloriosa morte cum Petro in urbe Roma sub Caesare Nerone agonizans, coronatus est. Et pariter supradictam s. Romanam ecclesiam Christo domino consecrarunt, aliisque omnibus in universo mundo sua praesentia atque venerando triumpho praetulerunt. (Gregorii M. lib. iv. in 1 Reg. v. ed. Bened. iii. ii. 250: Saulus ad Christum conversus caput effectus est nationum, quia obtinuit totius ecclesiae principatum. Comp. above, § 94, note 37.)

[13] Syn. Rom. iv. sub Symmacho s. palmaris, in the collections falsely cited as Syn. iii. See Pagi ad ann. 503, num. 2, ss. C. L. Nitzschii Disp. de Synodo palmari. Viteberg. 1775 (reprinted in Pottii Sylloge commentt. theoll. iv. 67).—The Acts ap. Mansi, viii. 247. After Symmachus had been in danger of his life at the synod, from his enemies, he declared (relatio Episcopp. ad Regem, p. 256): Primum ad conventum vestrum—sine aliqua dubitatione properavi, et privilegia mea voluntati regiae submisi, et auctoritatem synodi dedi: sicut habet ecclesiastica disciplina, restaurationem ecclesiarum regulariter poposci: sed nullus mihi a nobis effectus est. Deinde cum venirem cum clero meo, crudeliter mactatus sum. Ulterius me vestro examini non committo: in potestate Dei est, et domini regis, quid de me deliberet ordinare. (Compare above, § 92, note 15.) The synod having reported this to the king, he answered (l. c. p. 257): Miramur denuo fuisse consultum: cum si nos de praesenti ante voluissemus judicare negotio, habito cum proceribus nostris de inquirenda veritate tractatu, Deo auspice, potuissemus invenire justitiam, quae nec praesenti saeculo, nec futurae forsitan displicere potuisset aetati.—Nunc vero eadem, quae dudum, praesentibus intimamus oraculis.—Sive discussa, sive indiscussa causa, proferte sententiam, de quae estis rationem divino judicio reddituri: dummodo, sicuti saepe diximus, haec deliberatio vestra provideat, ut pax Senatui populoque Romano, submota omni confusione, reddatur. For the further proceedings of the synod see their protocol, p. 250: Dei mandata complentes Italiae suum dedimus rectorem, agnoscentes nullum nobis laborem alium remansisse, nisi ut dissidentes cum humilitate propositi nostri ad concordiam hortaremur. They proceed to consider quanta inconvenienter et praejudicialiter in hujus negotii principio contigissent:—maxime cum illa quae praemisimus inter alia de auctoritate sedis obstarent: quia quod possessor ejus quondam b. Petrus meruit, in nobilitatem possessionis accessit:—maxime cum omnem paene plebem cernamus ejus communioni indissociabiliter adhaesisse; and therefore concluded: Ut Symmachus Papa sedis apostolicae praesul, ab hujusmodi propositionibus impetitus, quantum ad homines respicit (quia totum causis obsistentibus superius designatis constat arbitrio divino fuisse dimissum), sit immunis et liber.—Unde secundum principalia praecepta, quae nostrae hoc tribuunt potestati, ei, quidquid ecclesiastici intra sacram urbem Romam vel foris juris est, reformamus totamque causam Dei judicio reservantes, etc. Just as before also the Conc. Cirtense, A.D. 305 (see Augustin. contra Cresonium, iii. 27), put down the accusation against several bishops of their being Traditores, with the asseveration: habent Deum, cui reddant rationem.

the apologist of this synod, *Ennodius*, bishop of Pavia (511), first gave utterance to the assertion, that the bishop of Rome is subject to no earthly judge.[14] Not long after an attempt was made to give a historical basis to this principle by supposititious *Gesta* (acts) of former popes;[15] and other falsifications of older documents in favor of the Roman see now appeared in like manner.[16] Still the Roman bishops (or as they were already called in Italy, by way of distinction, *Papa*)[17] did not yet demand any other kind of honor than was paid to the other apostolic sees,[18] acknowledging that they were subject to gen-

[14] Magni Felicis Ennodii (Opp. ed. J. Sirmond. Paris. 1611, recusa in Gallandii Bibl. PP. xi. 47) libellus apologeticus pro Synodo iv. Romana (Mansi, viii. 274): Non nos b. Petrum, sicut dicitis, a Domino cum sedis privilegiis, vel successores ejus, peccandi judicamus licentiam suscepisse. Ille perennem meritorum dotem cum haereditate innocentiae misit ad posteros: quod illi concessum est pro actuum luce, ad illos pertinet, quos par conversationis splendor illuminat. Quis enim sanctum esse dubitet, quem apex tantae dignitatis attollit? in quo si desint bona acquisita per meritum, sufficiunt quae a loci decessore praestantur: aut enim claros ad haec fastigia erigit, aut qui eriguntur illustrat. Praenoscit enim, quid Ecclesiarum fundamento sit habile, super quem ipsa moles innititur. P. 284: Aliorum forte hominum causas Deus voluerit per homines terminare: sedis istius presulem suo, sine quaestione, reservavit arbitrio, in direct contradiction to the Epist. Rom. Conc. A.D. 378, above, § 92, note 15.

[15] Namely Conc. Sinuessanum de Marcellini P. condemnatione (quod thurificasset) pretended to be held A.D. 303. (Mansi, i. 1249, ss. The bishops say to him: Tu eris judex: ex te enim damnaberis, et ex te justificaberis, tamen in nostra praesentia.—Prima sedes non judicabitur a quoquam): Constitutio Silvestri Episc. urbis Romae et Domini Constantini Aug. in Concil. Rom. pretended to be in 324 (Mansi, ii. 615, ss. Cap. 20: Nemo enim judicabit primam sedem, quoniam omnes sedes a prima sede justitiam desiderant temperari. Neque ab Augusto, neque ab omni clero, neque a regibus, neque a populo judex judicabitur): Synodi Rom. (alleged to be held A.D. 433) acta de causa Sixti III. stupro accusati, et de Polychronii Hierosolym. accusatione (Mansi, v. 1161). Comp. P. Coustant. Diss. de antiquis canonum collectionibus, § 97–99 (in Gallandii de Vetustis canonum collectionibus dissertationum sylloge, i. 93).

[16] Thus the passage in Cyprian's lib. de unit. eccl. (see Div. I. § 68, note 10) appears already corrupted in Pelagii II. Ep. vi. ad Episc. Istriae (Mansi, ix. 898).

[17] Thus, for instance, as early as in the councils held under Symmachus (see above, notes 8 and 13) and in Ennodius (see note 14. Sirmond ad Ennod. lib. iv. Ep. 1): In the other regions of the west, however, the title Papa continued for a long time to be a name of honor applied to every bishop (Walafrid Strabo, about 840, de Rebus eccl. c. 7, in Hittorp's Collection, p. 395: Pabst a Papa, quod cujusdam paternitatis nomen est, et Clericorum congruit dignitati) till Gregory VII. forbade it, A.D. 1075. Comp. Jo. Diecmann de vocis Papae aetatibus diss. ii. Viteberg. 1671. 4. In the east Πάπας was especially the title of the patriarchs of Rome and Alexandria.—Just so in Italy the see of Rome was especially Sedes apostolica; in other countries of the west every episcopal see was so styled; cf. Gregorii Tur. Hist. Franc. iv. 26: Presbyter—Regis praesentiam adiit et haec effatus est: Salve, Rex gloriose, Sedes enim apostolica eminentiae tuae salutem mittit uberrimam. Cui ille, numquid, ait, Romanam adisti urbem, ut Papae illius nobis salutem deferas? Pater, inquit Presbyter, tuus Leontius (Ep. Burdegalensis) cum provincialibus suis salutem tibi mittit.

[18] Pelagius I. ad Valerianum (Mansi, ix. 732): Quotiens aliqua de universali synodo aliquibus dubitatio nascitur, ad recipiendam de eo quod non intelligunt rationem,—ad apos-

eral councils,[19] and that the bishops were bound by duty to hear them only in case of delinquency. In other respects, they admitted that these bishops were equal to them in dignity.[20]

tolicas sedes pro recipienda ratione conveniant.—Quisquis ergo ab apostolicis divisus est sedibus, in schismate eum esse non dubium est. Comp. above, § 94, note 5. Gregorii M. lib. vii. Ep. 40, ad Eulogium Episc. Alexandr.: Suavissima mihi Sanctitas vestra multa in epistolis suis de S. Petri Apostolorum principis cathedra locuta est, dicens, quod ipse in ea nunc usque in suis successoribus sedeat.—Cuncta quae dicta sunt in eo libenter accepi, quod ille mihi de Petri cathedra locutus est, qui Petri cathedram tenet. Et cum me specialis honor nullo modo delectet, valde tamen laetatus sum, quia vos, sanctissimi, quod mihi impendistis, vobismetipsis dedistis.—Cum multi sint Apostoli, pro ipso tamen principatu solo Apostolorum principis sedes in auctoritate convaluit, quae in tribus locis unius est. Ipse enim sublimavit sedem, in qua etiam quiescere, et presentem vitam finire dignatus est (Rome); ipse decoravit sedem, in qua Evangelistam discipulum misit (Alexandria); ipse firmavit sedem, in qua septem annis, quamvis discessurus, sedit (Antioch). Cum ergo unius atque una sit sedes, cui ex auctoritate divina tres nunc Episcopi praesident quidquid ego de vobis boni audio, hoc mihi imputo. Si quid de me boni creditis, hoc vestris meritis imputate, quia in illo unum sumus, qui ait: Ut omnes unum sint, etc. (Jo. xvii. 21). Cf. Wiggers de Gregorio M. ejusque placitis anthropologicis comm. ii. Rostoch. 1838. 4. p. 29. The flattery of Eulogius may be explained by his straitened condition, which Gregory relieved even by presents (cf. lib. vi. Ep. 60; vii. 40; viii. 29). Isidorus Hisp. Etymol. vii. 12 (in Gratiani Decreto, dist. xxi. c. 1): Ordo Episcoporum quadripartitus est, id est in Patriarchis, Archiepiscopis, Metropolitanis atque Episcopis. Patriarcha graeca lingua summus patrum interpretatur, quia primum, i. e. apostolicum retinet locum: et ideo quia summo honore fungitur, tali nomine censetur, sicut Romanus, Antiochenus et Alexandrinus. Here, therefore, the pope still stands in the same rank completely with the other patriarchs.

[19] Gelasius Ep. xiii. (Mansi, viii. 51): Confidimus, quod nullus jam veraciter Christianus ignoret, uniuscujusque synodi constitutum, quod universalis ecclesiae probavit assensus, non aliquam magis exsequi sedem prae caeteris oportere, quam primam, quae et unamquamque synodum sua auctoritate confirmat, et continuata moderatione custodit, pro suo scilicet principatu, quem b. Petrus apostolus domini voce perceptum, ecclesia nihilominus subsequente, et tenuit semper et retinet.

[20] Gregorii M. lib. ix. Epist. 59, ad Joh. Episc. Syracus.: Si qua culpa in Episcopis invenitur, nescio quis ei (Sedi apostolicae) subjectus non sit: cum vero culpa non exigit, omnes secundum rationem humilitatis aequales sunt. Lib. xi. Ep. 37, ad Romanum defensorem: Pervenit ad nos, quod si quis contra clericos quoslibet causam habeat, despectis eorum Episcopis, eosdem clericos in tuo facias judicio exhiberi. Quod si ita est, quia valde constat esse incongruum, hac tibi auctoritate praecipimus, ut hoc denuo facere non praesumas.—Nam si sua unicuique Episcopo jurisdictio non servatur, quid aliud agitur, nisi ut per nos, per quos ecclesiasticus custodiri debuit ordo, confundatur? (Lib. ii. Ep. 52: Mihi injuriam facio, si fratrum meorum jura perturbo).—Lib. viii. Ep. 30, ad Eulogium Episc. Alexandr.: Indicare quoque vestra Beatitudo studuit, jam se quibusdam (the patriarch of Constantinople) non scribere superba vocabula, quae ex vanitatis radice prodierunt, et mihi loquitur, dicens: sicut jussistis. Quod verbum jussionis peto a meo auditu removere, quia scio, qui sum, qui estis. Loco enim mihi fratres estis, moribus patres. Non ergo jussi, sed quae utilia visa sunt, indicare curavi. Non tamen invenio vestram Beatitudinem hoc ipsum, quod memoriae vestrae intuli, perfecte retinere voluisse. Nam dixi, nec mihi vos, nec cuiquam alteri tale aliquid scribere debere: et ecce in praefatione epistolae, quam ad me ipsum qui prohibui direxistis, superbae appellationis verbum, universalem me Papam dicentes, imprimere curastis. Quod peto dulcissima mihi Sanctitas vestra ultra non faciat, quia vobis subtrahitur, quod alteri plus quam ratio exigit praebetur. —Nec honorem esse deputo, in quo fratres meos honorem suum perdere cognosco.—Si enim universalem me Papam vestra Sanctitas dicit, negat se hoc esse, quod me fatetur

After ecclesiastical peace had been restored between Rome and Constantinople, the kings of the Ostrogoths became suspicious of their Catholic subjects generally, and, in particular, of the Romish bishops, who still had unbroken communication with Constantinople. *John I.*, indeed, in his capacity of regal embassador, procured the restoration of their Churches to the Arians in the Greek Church; yet he was obliged to end his life in prison.[21] The kings maintained a strict oversight of the choice of the Catholic bishops, reserving to themselves the confirmation, or absolute appointment of them.[22] Yet even now the Gothic rule was not so dangerous to the papacy as the Byzantine, which latter began after the conquest of Italy (553–554). It is true that Justinian honored the Roman see,[23] but he also distinguished the Constantinopolitan with no less favor;[24] and

universum. Sed absit hoc. Recedant verba, quae vanitatem inflant et caritatem vulnerant.

[21] Anastasii lib. pontific. c. 54, in vita Joannis. Historia miscella, lib. 15 (in Muratori Scriptt. Ital. i. 103). Manso Gesch. d. ostgoth. Reiches in Italien, S. 163, ss.

[22] Thus Theoderich appointed the Roman bishop, Felix III. Cassiodori Variarum, lib. viii. Ep. 15. Comp. Sartorius Vers. über die Regierung der Ostgothen in Italien, S. 138, ss. 308, s.—Athalarich's edict addressed to John II. against bribery at the election of popes and bishops, A.D. 533. Cassiod. Variar. ix. Ep. 15, with a commentary ap. Manso, l. c. p. 416, ff.

[23] Justinian, A.D. 533, to the patriarch of Constantinople. Cod. Justin. i. i. 7: *Οὔτε γὰρ ἀνεχόμεθά τι τῶν εἰς ἐκκλησιαστικὴν ὁρώντων κατάστασιν, μὴ καὶ τῇ αὐτοῦ (τοῦ πάπα τῆς πρεσβυτέρας Ῥώμης καὶ πατριάρχου) ἀναφέρεσθαι μακαριότητι, ὡς κεφαλῇ οὔσῃ πάντων τῶν ὁσιωτάτων τοῦ θεοῦ ἱερέων, καὶ ἐπειδὴ, ὁσάκις, ἐν τούτοις τοῖς μέρεσιν αἱρετικοὶ ἀνεφύησαν, τῇ γνώμῃ καὶ ὀρθῇ κρίσει τοῦ ἐκείνου σεβασμίου θρόνου κατηργήθησαν.* Ibid. l. 8, Justinianus ad Joannem II. P.: Nec enim patimur quicquam, quod ad Ecclesiarum statum pertinet, quamvis manifestum et indubitatum sit, quod movetur, ut non etiam vestrae innotescat sanctitati, quae caput est omnium sanctarum Ecclesiarum. Per omnia enim (ut dictum est) properamus, honorem et auctoritatem crescere vestrae sedis.

[24] Cod. Justin. i. ii. 25: Ἡ *ἐν Κωνσταντινουπόλει ἐκκλησία πασῶν τῶν ἄλλων ἐστὶ κεφαλή.* On the other hand, the right of the highest ecclesiastical court, which was conveyed to the patriarch of Constantinople at Chalcedon (comp. above, § 93, note 15), if indeed it ever extended beyond the dioceses of Pontus, Asia, and Thrace, appears to have fallen into oblivion. The right of appeal is thus fixed by Justinian Cod. i. iv. 29: Bishop—Metropolitan and his Provincial synod—Patriarch. From the decision of the last, as from that of the Praetorian prefect, there could be no appeal (Cod. Just. vii. lxii. 19). No complaint is to be brought before the patriarch first, *πλὴν εἰ μὴ τὴν αἰτίασίν τις ἐπὶ τούτῳ θείη, ἐφ' ᾧτε παραπεμφθῆναι τὴν ὑπόθεσιν τῷ τῆς χώρας θεοφιλεστάτῳ ἐπισκόπῳ· τηνικαῦτα γὰρ ἄδεια μὲν ἔσται τὴν αἰτίασιν ὑποτίθεσθαι καὶ παρὰ τοῖς θεοφιλεστάτοις πατριάρχαις*, i. e., unless accompanied with the petition that the matter shall be delegated to the bishop of the province. For in that case it shall be allowed to bring the complaint before the patriarch. Then, § 2: Εἰ *μέντοι παραπεμφθείσης τῆς ὑποθέσεως παρὰ τοῦ θεοφιλεστατου πατριάρχου ἤ τινι τῶν θεοφιλεστάτων μητροπολιτῶν, ἢ ἄλλῳ τῶν θεοφιλεστάτων ἐπισκόπων, ἐνεχθείη ψῆφος, καὶ μὴ στερχθείη παρὰ θατέρου μέρους, ἐκκλητός τε γένηται· τηνικαῦτα ἐπὶ τὸν ἀρχιερατικὸν θρόνον* (*Vers. lat.* ad Archiepiscopalem hanc sedem) *φέρεσθαι τὴν ἔφεσιν, κἀκεῖσε κατὰ τὸ μέχρι νῦν κρατοῦν ἐξετάζεσθαι*, i. e.,

endeavored in the end to convert both merely into instruments to enable him to rule both in church and state. Two of his creatures, *Vigilius* and *Pelagius I.*, successively filled the Roman see; and in the controversy concerning the three chapters it soon became apparent how hazardous to Rome this dependence on Byzantium was. For a long time in the Western Church the rejection of the Three Chapters was considered a violation of orthodoxy; and on this account the bishops of the diocese of Italy broke off communion with Rome. The bishops of *Milan* and *Ravenna* were indeed reconciled; when, oppressed by the Arian Lombards, they were compelled to set greater value on communion with the Catholic Church (570–580); but the archbishop of *Aquileia* (who, since the incursions of the Lombards into Italy (568), resided on the island Grado) and the Istrian bishops were more obstinate, and did not renew their fellowship with Rome till the year 698.[25]

But even this dangerous period of dependence on Byzantium ceased for Rome, after the incursion of the Lombards into Italy (568). From that time the Greek dominions in this country were confined to *the exarchate of Ravenna, the Duchy of Rome and Naples, the cities on the coast of Liguria, and the extreme provinces of Lower Italy.* Continually threatened by the Lombards, and often forsaken by the Greek emperors, these districts were frequently obliged to protect themselves. At the head of all measures for defense appeared the popes, as the richest possessors,[26] whose own interest it was to avert the rule

if the complaint is delegated by the patriarch to a metropolitan or another bishop, and a sentence passed which the one party is dissatisfied with, and an appeal is made; then the appeal shall be to the archbishop (consequently with the omission of some intermediate courts, according to the rule Cod. Just. vii. lxii. 32, § 3: Eorum sententiis appellatione suspensis, qui ex delegatione cognoscunt, necesse est eos aestimare—qui causas delegaverint judicandas). Ὁ ἀρχιερατικὸς θρόνος, is every delegating patriarch, not exclusively (as has been assumed after the Latin translation of Anton. Augustinus, which in this law is entirely false) the patriarch of Constantinople. Even Ziegler Geschich. der kirchl. Verfassungsformen, S. 232, ss. has entirely misunderstood this law.

[25] J. F. B. M. de Rubeis de Schismate eccl. Aquilejensis diss. hist. Venet. 1732. 8. Republished in an enlarged form in ejusd. monimenta eccl. Aquilejensis. 1740. fol. Walch's Ketzerhist. viii. 331. N. C. Kist de Kerk en het Patriarchaat van Aquileja in the Archief voor kerkelijke Geschiedenis, i. 118.

[26] As the emperors called their fortunes patrimonium (namely patrimonium privatum s. dominicum their private property, and patrim. sacratum s. divinae domus, their domains. See Gutherius de offic. dom. Aug. lib. iii. c. 25. Pancirolius ad notit. dignatatum Imp. orient. c. 87), so the churches called their possessions patrimonia of their saints. That of the Roman church was therefore patrimonium S. Petri: at the same time also the single

of those Arian barbarians. Thus they not only gained great political influence in Grecian Italy,[27] but also obtained a more independent position in ecclesiastical matters in relation to the Greek emperors. As citizens, they remained subject to the Greek emperors, and their representatives, the exarchs of Ravenna.[28]

Toward the end of this period the flame of controversy was again kindled between the two first patriarchs of Christendom, when *John Jejunator* began to assume the title of a Patriarcha

estates which were managed by defensoribus or rectoribus were called patrimonia. Cf. Zaccaria diss. de patrimoniis s. Rom. Eccl. in his commentationes de rebus ad hist. atque antiquitt. Ecclesiae pertinentibus dissert. latinae (Fulginiae. tomi. ii. 1781. 4.) ii. 68. Planck's Gesch. d. christl. kirchl. Gesellschaftsverf. i. 629. C. H. Sack de patrimoniis Eccl. Rom. circa finem saeculi vi. in his Commentationes, quae ad theol. hist. pertinent, tres. Bonnae. 1821. 8. p. 25, ss. For an account of the activity of the Popes in protecting Italy, comp. Gregorii M. lib. v. Ep. 21, ad Constantinam Aug.: Viginti autem jam et septem annos ducimus, quod in hac urbe inter Langobardorum gladios vivimus. Quibus quam multa hac ab Ecclesia quotidianis diebus erogantur, ut inter eos vivere possimus, suggerenda non sunt. Sed breviter indico, quia sicut in Ravennae partibus Dominorum Pietas apud primum exercitum Italiae saccellarium habet, qui causis supervenientibus quotidianas expensas faciat, ita et in hac urbe in causis talibus eorum saccellarius ego sum. Et tamen haec Ecclesia, quae uno eodemque tempore clericis, monasteriis, pauperibus, populo, atque insuper Langobardis tam multa indesinenter expendit, ecce adhuc ex omnium Ecclesiarum premitur afflictione, quae de hac unius hominis (Johannis Jejunat.) superbia multum gemunt, etsi nihil dicere praesumunt.

[27] Gregorii M. lib. ii. Ep. 31, ad cunctos milites Neapolitanos: Summa militiae laus inter alia bona merita haec est, obedientiam sanctae Reipublicae utilitatibus exhibere, quodque sibi utiliter imperatum fuerit, obtemperare: sicut et nunc devotionem vestram fecisse didicimus, quae epistolis nostris, quibus magnificum virum Constantium Tribunum custodiae civitatis deputavimus praeesse, paruit, et congruam militaris devotionis obedientiam demonstravit. Unde scriptis vos praesentibus curavimus admonendos, uti praedicto viro magnifico Tribuno, sicut et fecistis, omnem debeatis pro serenissimorum Dominorum utilitate, vel conservanda civitate obedientiam exhibere, etc. Comp. the excerpt from the acts of Honorius I. (625, 638) by Muratori, Antiquitt. Ital. v. 834, from Cencii Camerarii lib. de censibus, and published more fully by Zaccaria, l. c. p. 131, from the collect Cann. of Cardinal Deusdedit. Idem in eodem (i. e., Honorius in suo Registro) Gaudisso Notario et Anatolio Magistro militum Neapolitanam civitatem regendam committit, et qualiter debeat regi, scriptis informat. It does not follow from these passages, as Dionysius de Ste Marthe in vita Gregorii, lib. iii. c. 9, no. 6 (Gregg. Opp. iv. 271), and Zaccaria, l. c. p. 112, 131, conclude from them that the city of Naples belonged to the patrimonium S. Petri; but that the popes who had important possessions there (a patrimonium Neapolitanum and Campanum, Zaccaria, p. 111), when the city was hard pressed (cf. Gregor. M. lib. ii. Ep. 46, ad Johannem Episc. Ravennae: De Neapolitana vero urbe, excellentissimo Exarcho instanter imminente, vobis indicamus, quia Arigis—valde insidiatur eidem civitati, in quam si celeriter dux non mittatur, omnino jam inter perditas habetur), and required speedy aid, took the necessary measures instead of the exarch. Cf. Sack. l. c. p. 52.

[28] Cf. Gregorii M. lib. iii. Ep. 65, above, § 116, note 3. For the official authorities concerning the relations of the ecclesiastical to the civil power, especially concerning the right of the exarchs to confirm the choice of a pope, see the liber diurnus Romanorum Pontiff. See on this subject on the following period.

universalis, οἰκουμενικός (587).[29] Even *Pelagius II.* grew very warm respecting it,[30] and still more *Gregory the Great.* These popes rejected that appellation altogether, as anti-Christian and devilish; without, however, making the desired impression on the Emperor Maurice and the court patriarch.[31] So much the more, therefore, did Gregory thank Providence when *Maurice's* murderer *Phocas* (602) ascended the throne;[32] and Phocas

[29] At first applied by flatterers to all patriarchs. See § 93, note 20, § 94, note 72. Ziegler Gesch. der kirchl. Verfassungsformen, S. 259. Justinian gives the patriarch of Constantinople the title, τῷ ἁγιωτάτῳ καὶ μακαριωτάτῳ ἀρχιεπισκόπῳ τῆς βασιλίδος ταύτης πόλεως καὶ οἰκουμενικῷ πατριάρχῃ. Cod. i. 1, 7. Novell. iii. v. vi. vii. xvi. xlii.

[30] Gregorii M. lib. v. Ep. 18, 43, ix. 68. The letter viii. Pelagii ad universos Episcc. (Mansi, ix. 900) relative to this point is Pseudo-Isidorian. See Blondelli Pseudo-Isidorus, p. 636, ss.

[31] Gregorii M. lib. v. Ep. 18, ad Johann.—Si ergo ille (Paulus) membra dominici corporis certis extra Christum quasi capitibus, et ipsis quidem Apostolis subjici partialiter evitavit (1 Cor. i. 12, ss.): tu quid Christo, universalis scilicet Ecclesiae capiti, in extremi judicii es dicturus examine, qui cuncta ejus membra tibimet conaris universalis appellatione supponere? Quis, rogo, in hoc tam perverso vocabulo, nisi ille ad imitandum proponitur, qui despectis Angelorum legionibus secum socialiter constitutis, ad culmen conatus est singularitatis erumpere, ut et nulli subesse et solus omnibus praeesse videretur? Certe Petrus Apostolorum primus, membrum sanctae et universalis Ecclesiae, Paulus, Andreas, Johannes, quid aliud quam singularium sunt plebium capita? et tamen sub uno capite omnes membra. Numquid non—per venerandum Chalcedonense Concilium hujus apostolicae sedis Antistites, cui Deo disponente deservio, universales oblato honore vocati sunt? (Comp. § 94, note 72.) Sed tamen nullus umquam tali vocabulo appellari voluit, nullus sibi hoc temerarium nomen arripuit: ne si sibi in Pontificatus gradu gloriam singularitatis arriperet, hanc omnibus fratribus denegasse videretur. Ep. 19, ad Sabinianum Diac. (Apocrisiarium.) Ep. 20, ad Mauricium Aug. Ep. 21, ad Constantinam Aug. Ep. 43, ad Eulogium Ep. Alexandr. et Anastasium Antiochenum. Lib. vii. Ep. 4, 5, and 31, ad Cyriacum Ep. Constant. Ep. 27, ad Anastas. Antioch. Ep. 33, ad Mauricium Aug.: De qua re mihi in suis jussionibus Dominorum Pietas praecipit, dicens, ut per appellationem frivoli nominis inter nos scandalum generari non debeat. Sed rogo, ut Imperialis Pietas penset, quia alia sunt frivola valde innoxia, atque alia valde nociva. Numquidnam cum se Antichristus veniens Deum dixerit, frivolum valde erit, sed tamen nimis perniciosum? Si quantitatem sermonis attendimus, duae sunt syllabae; si vero pondus iniquitatis, universa pernicies. Ego autem fidenter dico, quia quisquis se universalem Sacerdotem vocat, vel vocari desiderat, in elatione sua Antichristum praecurrit, quia superbiendo se caeteris praeponit. Nec dispari superbia ad errorem ducitur, quia sicut perversus ille Deus videri vult super omnes homines: ita quisquis iste est, qui solus Sacerdos appellari appetit, super reliquos Sacerdotes se extollit. Ep. 34, ad Eulogium Alex. et Anastas. Ant. How earnestly Gregory rejected for himself this title, may be seen in lib. viii. Ep. 30, ad Eulogium Ep. Alex. above, note 18. According to Johannes Diac. (about 825) in vita Greg. M. ii. 1, Gregory may have assumed the title servus servorum Dei, to put to shame the patriarch of Constantinople. Even Augustine calls himself, Ep. 130 and 217, servus servorum Christi, Fulgentius Ep. 4, servorum Christi famulus. Among Gregory the Great's letters, there are now only three before which he so styles himself. But even so late as the eleventh century other bishops too, as well as kings and emperors, employed this title. See du Fresne Glossar. ad scriptt. med. et. inf. lat. s. v. servus.

[32] Comp. the congratulatory letter of Gregory, lib. xiii. Ep. 31, ad Phocam Imp., Ep. 38, ad Leontiam Aug.

repaid the pope's favor by taking his part against the patriarch,[33] though after him that disputed title was constantly used by the see of Constantinople.[34]

At this time the popes also began to bestow the pallium (which all bishops in the east received at their consecration)[35] on the most distinguished bishops of the west, for the purpose of symbolizing and strengthening their connection with the Church of Rome.[36]

33 The patriarch Cyriacus was an adherent of Maurice (Theophanes, i. 446, 453). Anastasius de vitis Pontific. c. 67, Bonifacius, iii.: Hic obtinuit apud Phocam Principem, ut Sedes apostolica b. Petri Apostoli caput esset omnium ecclesiarum, i. e., Ecclesia Romana, quia Ecclesia Constantinopolitana primam se omnium Ecclesiarum scribebat. With the same words Paulus Warnefridi de Gestis Longob. iv. 37. Doubted by J. M. Lorenz Examen decreti Phocae de primatu Rom. Pont. Argent. 1790. Schröckh, xvii. 72. Remarkable is the view of the subject taken by the Ghibelline Gotfridus Viterbiensis (about 1186), in his Pantheon, p. xvi. (Pistorii Rer. Germ. scriptt. ed. Struve, ii. 289):

> Tertius est Papa Bonifac us ille benignus,
> Qui petit a Phoca munu per secula dignum,
> Ut sedes Petri prima sit; ille dedit.
> Prima prius fuerat Constantinopolitana;
> Est modo Romana, meliori dogmate clara.

34 Even Heraclius, successor of Phocas, in his laws gives again this title to the patriarch of Constantinople. See Leunclavii Jus Graeco-Romanum, t. i. p. 73, ss.

35 See above, § 101, note 1. Against the opinion almost universally adopted from Petrus de Marca de conc. Sac. et Imp. lib. vi. c. 6, that the old pallium, a splendid mantle, was a part of the imperial dress, and therefore bestowed only by the emperors, or with their permission by the patriarchs, see J. G. Pertsch de Origine, usu, et auctoritate, pallii archiepiscopalis. Helmst. 1754. 4. p. 56, ss.

36 The oldest document on the subject is Symmachi P. Ep. ad Theodorum Laureacensem (Mansi, viii. p. 228) about 501: Diebus vitae tuae palli usum, quem ad sacerdotalis officii decorem et ad ostendendam unanimitatem, quam cum b. Petro Apostolo universum gregem dominicarum ovium, quae ei commissae sunt, habere dubium non est, ab apostolica sede, sicut decuit, poposcisti, quod utpote ab eisdem Apostolis fundatae ecclesiae majorum more libenter indulsimus ad ostendendum te magistrum et archiepiscopum, tuamque sanctam Laureacensem ecclesiam provinciae Pannoniorum sedem fore metropolitanam. Idcirco pallio, quod ex apostolica caritate tibi destinamus, quo uti debeas secundum morem ecclesiae tuae, solerter admonemus pariterque volumus, ut intelligas, quia ipse vestitus, quo ad missarum solemnia ornaris, signum praetendit crucis, per quod scito te cum fratribus debere compati ac mundialibus illecebris in affectu crucifigi, etc. (The formula in the liber diurnus, cap. iv. tit. 3, is abbreviated from this epistle.) According to Vigilii P. Ep. vii. ad Auxanium Arelatensem (Mansi, ix. p. 42), Symmachus also invested Caesarius, bishop of Arles, with the pallium. These investitures became more frequent under Gregory the Great, not only of metropolitans, as John of Corinth, Leo of Prima Justinianea, Vigilius of Arles, Augustine of Canterbury, but also simple bishops, as of Donus of Messina, John of Syracuse, John of Palermo, etc. See Pertsch. l. c. p. 134, ss. Though Vigilius P. Ep. vi. ad Auxanium Arelatensem (Mansi, ix. p. 40), writes: De his vero, quae Caritas vestra tam de usu pallii, quam de aliis sibi a nobis petiit debere concedi, libenti hoc animo etiam in praesenti facere sine dilatione potuimus, nisi cum christianissimi Domini filii nostri imperatoris hoc, sicut ratio postulat, voluissemus perficere notitia; and Gregorius i. lib. ix. Ep. 11, ad Brunichildem Reginam, while he mentions to Synagrius, bishop of Autun, gifted with the pallium, the necessity of the imperial approbation; yet it was probably sought for only when hostile relations existed with the kingdom to which the

FOURTH CHAPTER.

HISTORY OF MONACHISM.

§ 118.

THE LITERATURE MAY BE SEEN IN THE PREFACE TO § 95.

In the east, monachism continued in its manifold forms.[1] Justinian favored it by his laws,[2] though he endeavored to restrain the irregular wanderings of the Coenobites.[3] While

pallium was sent. See Pertsch, l. c. p. 196, ss. That a tax was early connected with this investiture, see Gregorii i. lib. v. Ep. 57, ad Johannem Episc. Corinth. (also ap. Gratianus dist. C. c. 3): Novit autem fraternitas vestra, quia prius pallium nisi dato commodo non dabatur. Quod quoniam incongruum erat, facto Concilio tam de hoc quam de ordinationibus aliquid accipere sub districta interdictione vetuimus. The decree referred to is in Mansi, ix. p. 1227.

[1] Comp. the description, Evagrius, i. 21. The spirit of the oriental monks of this period may be gathered from Johannis Moschi (about 630) *λειμών*, pratum spirituale (in Latin in Herib. Rosweydi Vitae patrum. Antverp. 1615. fol. p. 855, ss. The Greek original, though defective is found in Frontonis Ducaei Auctarium bibl. PP. ii. 1057. The chasms are supplied in Cotelerii Monum. Eccl. Gr. ii. 341). Even here complaints of the decay of monachism appear, ex. gr. c. 130: *Οἱ πατέρες ἡμῶν τὴν ἐγκράτειαν καὶ τὴν ἀκτημοσύνην μέχρι θανάτου ἐτήρησαν, ἡμεῖς δὲ ἐπλατύναμεν τὰς κοιλίας ἡμῶν καὶ βαλάντια, κ. τ. λ.* Cf. cap. 52 and 168.

[2] Cod. Justin. i. 3, 53 (A.D. 532), forbids, *μηδένα παντελῶς, μήτε βουλευτὴν μήτε ταξεώτην ἐπίσκοπον ἢ πρεσβύτερον τοῦ λοιποῦ γίνεσθαι*, but adds: *Πλὴν εἰ μὴ ἐκ νηπίας ἡλικίας, καὶ οὔπω τὴν ἔφηβον ἐκβάσης, ἔτυχε τοῖς εὐλαβεστάτοις μοναχοῖς ἐγκαταλελεγμένος, καὶ διαμείνας ἐπὶ τούτου τοῦ σχήματος· τηνικαῦτα γὰρ ἐφίεμεν αὐτῷ καὶ πρεσβυτέρῳ γενέσθαι, καὶ εἰς ἐπισκοπὴν ἐλθεῖν,—τὴν τετάρτην μέντοι μοῖραν τῆς αὐτοῦ περιουσίας ἁπάσης παρέχων τοῖς βουλευταῖς, καὶ τῷ δημοσίῳ.* § 3: *Ἔτι θεσπίζομεν, εἴτε ἀνὴρ ἐπὶ μονήρη βίον ἐλθεῖν βουληθείη, εἴτε γυνὴ τὸν ἄνδρα καταλιποῦσα πρὸς ἄσκησιν ἔλθοι, μὴ τοῦτο αὐτὸ ζημίας παρέχειν πρόφασιν, ἀλλὰ τὰ μὲν οἰκεῖα πάντως λαμβάνειν.* Cf. Novell. cxxiii. c. 40: *Εἰ δὲ συνεστῶτος ἔτι τοῦ γάμου ὁ ἀνὴρ μόνος ἢ ἡ γυνὴ μόνη εἰσέλθῃ εἰς μοναστήριον, διαλυέσθω ὁ γάμος, καὶ δίχα ῥεπουδίου.* (On the other hand Gregorius M. lib. xi. Ep. 45: Si enim dicunt, religionis causa conjugia debere dissolvi, sciendum est, quia etsi hoc lex humana concesssit, divina lex tamen prohibuit. Cf. Bingham, vol. iii. p. 45.) Cod. Just. i. 3, 55: Ut non liceat parentibus impedire, quominus liberi eorum volentes monachi aut clerici fiant, aut eam ob solam causam exheredare (cf. Nov. cxxiii. c. 41). Nov. v. c. 2, allows slaves to go into convents contrary to the will of their masters.

[3] Novella v. de Monachis (A.D. 535), cap. 4: *Εἰ δέ τις ἅπαξ ἑαυτὸν καθιερώσας τῷ μοναστηρίῳ, καὶ τοῦ σχήματος τυχὼν, εἶτα ἀναχωρῆσαι τοῦ μοναστηρίου βουληθείη, καὶ ἰδιώτην τυχὸν ἑλέσθαι βίον· αὐτὸς μὲν ἴστω, ποίαν ὑπὲρ τούτου δώσει τῷ θεῷ τὴν ἀπολογίαν, τὰ πράγματα μέντοι ὁπόσα ἂν ἔχοι ἡνίκα εἰς τὸ μοναστήριον εἰσῄει, ταῦτα τῆς δεσποτείας ἔσται τοῦ μοναστηρίου καὶ οὐδ' ὁτιοῦν παντελῶς ἐξάξει.* Cap. 7: *Εἰ δὲ ἀπο-*

the Stylites in the east still attracted the highest wonder, especially one *Daniel*,[4] in the neighborhood of Constantinople, under the Emperors Basiliscus and Zeno, an attempt in the neighborhood of Treves to imitate them was interdicted by the bishops of the place.[5] On the other hand, the *κατειργμένοι* of the east, found many admirers especially in Gaul, (Reclausi, Recluses).[6]

§ 119.

BENEDICTINES.

Jo. Mabillonii Annales ordinis S. Benedicti, vi. tomi (the 6th, edited by Edm. Martene, reaches to the year 1157). Paris. 1703–1739. auct. Luccae. 1739–1745. fol.—Lucae Dacherii et Jo. Mabillonii acta Sanctorum Ord. S. Benedicti (six centuries to 1100), ix. voll. 1668–1701. fol.

In the west, *Benedict*, a native of Nursia in Umbria,[1] gave a new form to the monastic life. After he had long lived a hermit's life, he founded a convent on a mountain in Campania, where the old castrum Cassinum was situated (hence called monasterium Cassinense, monte Cassino). Here he introduced a new system of rules (529)[2] which mitigated the extreme

λιπὼν τὸ μοναστήριον, καθ' ὅπερ τὴν ἄσκησιν εἶχεν, εἰς ἕτερον μεταβαίνοι μοναστήριον, καὶ οὕτω μὲν ἡ αὐτοῦ περιουσία μενέτο τε καὶ ἐκδικείσθω ὑπὸ τοῦ προτέρου μοναστηρίου, ἔνθα ἀποταξάμενος τοῦτο κατέλιπε. προσῆκον δέ ἐστι τοὺς εὐλαβεστάτους ἡγουμένους μὴ εἰσδέχεσθαι τὸν τοῦτο πράττοντα.

4 Acta Danielis, ap. Surium ad d. 11 Dec.

5 Gregor. Turon. Hist. Franc. viii. 15.

6 Ex. gr., Gregor. Tur. ii. 37, v. 9, 10, vi. 6.

1 His biographer is Gregorius M. in Dialogorum lib. secundo.

2 Regula Benedicti in 73 capp. in Hospinian and many others, best in Luc. Holstenii Codex regularum monastic. et canon. (Romae. 1661. iii. voll. 4), auctus a Marian. Brockie (August. Vindel. 1759. vi. tomi fol.) i. 3, and thence in Gallandii Bibl. PP. xi. 298. Among the numerous commentaries the best are by Edm. Martene, Paris. 1690. 4, and by Augustin Calmet, Paris. 1734. t. ii. 4. General regulations: Cap. 64: In Abbatis ordinatione illa semper consideretur ratio, ut hic constituatur, quem sibi omnis concors congregatio secundum timorem Dei, sive etiam pars, quamvis parva, congregationis, saniori consilio, elegerit. Cap. 65: Quemcunque elegerit Abbas cum consilio fratrum timentium Deum, ordinet ipse sibi Praepositum. Qui tamen Praepositus illa agat cum reverentia, quae ab Abbate suo ei injuncta fuerint, nihil contra Abbatis voluntatem aut ordinationem faciens. Cap. 21: Si major fuerit congregatio, eligantur de ipsis fratres boni testimonii et sanctae conversationis, et constituantur Decani, qui solicitudinem gerant super Decanias suas. Cap. 3: Quoties aliqua praecipua agenda sunt in monasterio, convocet Abbas omnem congregationem, et dicat ipse unde agitur. Et audiens consilium fratrum, tractet apud se, et quod utilius judicaverit faciat. Si qua vero minora agenda sunt in monasterii utilitatibus, seniorum tantum utatur consilio. Cap. 5: Primus humilitatis gradus est obedientia sine mora. Haec convenit iis, qui nihil sibi Christo carius aliquid existimant; propter servitium sanctum, quod professi sunt, seu propter metum gehennae, vel gloriam

rigor of the eastern monks,[3] prescribed a variety of suitable employments,[4] but was distinguished especially by this, that it exacted a promise from all who entered, never to leave the monastery again, and strictly to observe its rules.[5] This system was soon diffused in Italy, Gaul, and Spain. Instead of the former diversity of monasteries, unity now appeared; and thus arose the first proper monastic order or association of many monasteries under a peculiar rule. The straitening of vows in this Benedictine rule was followed by the declaration of marriage being invalid in the case of monks;[6] while the monks and nuns

vitae aeternae, mox ut aliquid imperatum a majore fuerit, ac si divinitus imperetur, moram pati nesciunt in faciendo.

[3] Cap. 39, appoints for the daily food cocta duo pulmentaria (ut forte, qui ex uno non poterit edere, ex alio reficiatur). Et si fuerint inde poma aut nascentia leguminum, addatur et tertium. Farther panis libra una, and, cap. 40, hemina vini (different opinions concerning the hemina, see in Martene Comm. in Reg. S. Bened. p. 539, ss.). On the other hand, carnium quadrupedum ab omnibus abstineatur comestio, praeter omnino debiles et aegrotos. Cap. 36: Balneorum usus infirmis, quoties expedit, offeratur. Sanis autem, et maxime juvenibus, tardius concedatur.

[4] Cap. 48: Otiositas inimica est animae: et ideo certis temporibus occupari debent fratres in labore manuum, certis iterum horis in lectione divina. Between these the horae canonicae, namely the Nocturnae vigiliae, Matutinae, Prima, Tertia, Sexta, Nona, Vespera, and Completorium (see respecting them cap. 8-19). Cap. 16 justified by Ps. cxix. 164: Septies in die laudem dixi tibi, and v. 62: Media nocte surgebam ad confitendum tibi. Comp. § 95, note 8.

[5] Cap. 58: After ordering a probation time of the noviter venientis ad conversionem: si habita secum deliberatione promiserit se omnia custodire et cuncta sibi imperata servare, tunc suscipiatur in congregatione, sciens se jam sub lege regulae constitutum, quod ei ex illa die non liceat egredi de monasterio, nec collum excutere de subjugo regulae, quam sub tam morosa deliberatione licuit aut excusare, aut suscipere. Suscipiendus autem in oratorio coram omnibus promittat de stabilitate sua, et conversione morum suorum, et obedientia coram Deo et sanctis ejus, ut si aliquando aliter fecerit, ab eo se damnandum sciat, quem irridet. De qua promissione sua faciat petitionem ad nomen Sanctorum, quorum reliquiae ibi sunt, et Abbatis praesentis. Quam petitionem manu sua scribat, aut certe, si non scit literas, alter ab eo rogatus scribat, et ille novitius signum faciat, et manu sua eam super altare ponat. Cap. 59: Si quis forte de nobilibus offert filium suum Deo in monasterio, si ipse puer minori aetate est, parentes ejus faciant petitionem, quam supra diximus. Et cum oblatione ipsam petitionem et manum pueri involvant in palla altaris, et sic eum offerant. Cap. 66: Monasterium autem, si possit fieri, ita debet construi, ut omnia necessaria, id est aqua, molendinum, hortus, pistrinum, vel artes diversae intra monasterium exerceantur, ut non sit necessitas Monachis vagandi foras, quia omnino non expedit animabus eorum.

[6] The older appointment (see § 95, note 49), that the breaking of the vow should be punished with church-penance, is still repeated by Leo I. Ep. 90, ad Rusticum, c. 12, (Propositum monachi—deseri non potest absque peccato. Quod enim vovit Deo, debet et reddere. Unde qui relicta singularitatis professione ad militiam vel ad nuptias devolutus est, publicae poenitentiae satisfactione purgandus est), and Gelasius I. Ep. 5, ad Episc. Lucaniae (ap. Gratian. Causa xxvii. Qu. 1, c. 14). Also Conc. Aurelian. i. ann. 511, c. 21, pre-supposes the validity of marriage. (Monachus si in monasterio conversus vel pallium comprobatus fuerit accepisse, et postea uxori fuerit sociatus, tantae praevaricationis reus nunquam ecclesiastici gradus officium sortiatur.) On the contrary, first, the

who had left their monasteries began to be violently brought back into them.[7]

Of literary pursuits among the monks we find no trace, either in Benedict's rule, or among the first Benedictines.[8] It was *Cassiodorus* who made the first attempt of this kind in the convent built by him called *Vivarium* (Coenobium Vivariense, 538) near Squillacci in Bruttia, whither he had withdrawn;[9] and where in addition to other useful employments, an endeavor was made to introduce learned occupations also into a monastery.[10] The Benedictines, already accustomed to a well regulated ac-

Conc. Turonicum ii. ann. 567, c. 15: (Monachus) si—uxorem duxerit, excommunicetur, et de uxoris male societae consortio etiam judicis auxilio separetur.—Qui infelix monachus, —et illi, qui eum exceperint ad defensandum, ab ecclesia segregentur, donec revertatur ad septa monasterii, et indictam ab Abbate—agat poenitentiam, et post satisfactionem revertatur ad gratiam.

7 Thus Gregory the Great ordered, with reference to a married nun (ap. Gratian. c. xxvii. Qu. 1, c. 15), and with reference to another who had merely returned ad saecularem habitum, lib. vii. Ep. 9, ad Vitalianum Ep. A.D. 597 (ap. Gratian. l. c. c. 18): Instantiae tuae sit, praedictam mulierem una cum Sergio defensore nostro comprehendere, et statim non solum ad male contemptum habitum sine excusatione aliqua revocare, sed etiam in monasterio, ubi omnino districte valeat custodiri, detrudere. And lib. i. Ep. 40, A.D. 591: Quia aliquos Monachorum usque ad tantum nefas prosiliisse cognovimus, ut uxores publice sortiantur, sub omni vigilantia eos requiras, et inventos digna coërcitione in monasteriis, quorum monachi fuerant, retransmittas.

8 See Rich. Simon Critique de la bibliothèque de M. Ell. du Pin. (Paris. 1730. 4. tom. 8.) i. 212.

9 That he introduced the rules of Benedict into his convent, as the Benedictines (see Garetius in the vita Cass. prefixed to his Opp. p. 27) supposed, has been justly denied by Baronius ad ann. 494.

10 For this purpose he wrote in particular his works de Institutione divinarum litterarum, and de Artibus ac disciplinis liberalium litterarum, comp. § 114, note 7. He exhorts, above all things, to study the Holy Scriptures and the fathers. But then he adds, de Instit. div. litt. c. 28: Verumtamen nec illud Patres sanctissimi decreverunt, ut saecularium litterarum studia respuantur: quia exinde non minimum ad sacras scripturas intelligendas sensus noster instruitur.—Frigidus obstiterit circum praecordia sanguis, ut nec humanis nec divinis litteris perfecte possit erudiri: aliqua tamen scientiae mediocritate suffultus, eligat certe quod sequitur:

Rura mihi et rigui placeant in vallibus amnes.

Quia nec ipsum est a Monachis alienum hortos colere, agros exercere, et pomorum foecunditate gratulari. Cap. 30: Ego tamen fateor votum meum, quod inter vos quaecumque possunt corporeo labore compleri, Antiquariorum mihi studia (si tamen veraciter scribant) non immerito forsan plus placere; quod et mentem suam relegendo scripturas divinas salubriter instruant, et Domini praecepta scribendo longe lateque disseminent. (Comp. the directions for copying and revising manuscripts, cap. 15, and the treatise de orthographia.)—Cap. 31: Sed et vos alloquor fratres egregios, qui humani corporis salutem sedula curiositate tractatis, et confugientibus ad loca sanctorum officia beatae pietatis impenditis. Et ideo discite quidem naturas herbarum, commixtionesque specierum sollicita mente tractate. He recommends to them the writings of Dioscorides, Hippocrates, and Galen. Comp. Stäudlin in the Kirchenhist. Archive für 1825, S. 413, ss.

tivity, very soon followed this example; and thus they could now be useful to the west in many ways.

They reclaimed many waste lands, actively advanced the cause of education,[11] handed down to posterity the history of their time in chronicles, and preserved to it by their copyists, for the most part indeed as dead treasures, the writings of antiquity.[12]

§ 120.

RELATION OF THE MONKS TO THE CLERGY.

Though the clergy continued to be very often chosen from among the monks, yet there were in the convents no more ordained monks than were required by the necessities of the monks' congregation; and many convents had no presbyter whatever.[1] The old rule that all convents should be under the inspection of the bishops of the dioceses in which they were situated,[2] was first departed from in Africa, where many put themselves under the superintendence of distant bishops, especially the bishop of Carthage, to keep themselves secure against oppression.[3] In the remaining part of the west, the duty of the

[11] The permission to undertake the care of pueros oblatos, given by Benedict in his rule c. 59 (see above, note 5), was soon and often taken advantage of. See Gregory M. dial. ii. cap. 3: Coepere etiam tunc ad eum Romanae urbis nobiles et religiosi concurrere, suosque ei filios omnipotenti Deo nutriendos dare. For these pueri oblati in particular, the monastery schools were erected, of which the first intimation is found in the so-called Regula Magistri, c. 50 (ap. Holstenius-Brockie, t. i. p. 266), composed about 100 years after Benedict, where it is prescribed that in the three hours from the first to the third, infantuli in decada sua in tabulis suis ab uno litterato litteras meditentur.

[12] Cf. Mabillon acta SS. Ord. Ben. t. i. Praef. no. 114 et 115.

[1] Presbyters were sent into the convents by the bishops (directi, deputati) ad missas celebrandras. Gregor. M. lib. vi. Ep. 46, vii. 43.—Abbots prayed and received permission in monasterio Presbyterum, qui sacra Missarum solemnia celebrare debeat, ordinari. Ibid. vi. 42, ix. 92: or a presbyter was appointed to the convent, quem et in monasterio habitare, et inde vitae subsidia habere necesse fuit, ibid. iv. 18.—On the other hand Gregory libb. vi. Ep. 56, praises a convent of which he had heard, et Presbyteros et Diaconos cunctamque congregationem unanimes vivere ac concordes.

[2] Conc. Chalced. c. 4:—Ἔδοξε *μηδένα μὲν μηδαμοῦ οἰκοδομεῖν μηδὲ συνιστᾷν μοναστήριον ἢ εὐκτήριον οἶκον παρὰ γνώμην τοῦ τῆς πόλεως* Ἐπισκόπου· *τοὺς δὲ καθ' ἑκάστην πόλιν καὶ χώραν μονάζοντας ὑποτετάχθαι τῷ* Ἐπισκόπῳ. Can. 8: Οἱ *κληρικοὶ τῶν πτωχείων καὶ μοναστηρίων καὶ μαρτυρίων ὑπὸ τῶν ἐν ἑκάστῃ πόλει* Ἐπισκόπων *τὴν ἐξουσίαν, κατὰ τὴν τῶν ἁγίων πατέρων παράδοσιν, διαμενέτωσαν, καὶ μὴ καταυθαδιάζεσθαι ἢ ἀφηνιᾷν τοῦ ἰδίου* Ἐπισκόπου.

[3] Conc. Carthag. ann. 525, dies secunda (ap. Mansi, viii. 648). The prayer of Abbas

monasteries to be spiritually subject to the diocesan bishops was still strictly enforced.[4] On the other hand, synods and popes took them under their protection, in opposition to episcopal oppression, and made it a fundamental principle that the bishops should not interfere with their internal administration.[5] *Gregory the Great*, in particular, was distinguished for his protection of convents.[6]

Petrus to Bishop Boniface of Carthage, p. 653:—Humiles supplicamus, ut—a jugo nos clericorum, quod neque nobis neque patribus nostris quisquam superponere aliquando tentavit, eruere digneris. Nam docemus, monasterium de Praecisu, quod in medio plebium Leptiminensis ecclesiae ponitur, praetermisso eodem Episcopo vicino, Vico Ateriensis ecclesiae Episcopi consolationem habere, qui in longinquo positus est.—Nam et de Adrumetino monasterio nullo modo silere possumus, qui praetermisso ejusdem civitatis Episcopo de transmarinis partibus sibi semper presbyteros ordinaverunt.—Et cum sibi diversa monasteria, ut ostenderent libertatem suam, unicuique prout visum est, a diversis Episcopis consolationem quaesierint: quomodo nobis denegari poterit, qui de hac sede sancta Carthaginensis ecclesiae, quae prima totius Africanae ecclesia haberi videtur, auxilium quaesivimus? etc. Cf. Concil. Carthagin. ann. 534 (Mansi, viii. 841). Cf. Thomassinus P. i. l. iii. c. 31.

[4] Conc. Aurelian. i. (511) can. 19. Epaonense (517) can. 19. Arelatense v. (554) can. 7.

[5] So first Concil. Arelatense, iii. A.D. 456 (Mansi, vii. 907), which limited the rights of the bishop of the diocese in the convent of Lerins as follows: Ut clerici, atque altaris ministri a nullo, nisi ab ipso, vel cui ipse injunxerit ordinentur; chrisma non nisi ab ipso speretur; neophyti si fuerint, ab eodem confirmentur; peregrini clerici absque ipsius praecepto in communionem, vel ad ministerium non admittantur. Monasterii vero omnis laica multitudo ad curam Abbatis pertineat: neque ex ea sibi Episcopus quidquam vindicet, aut aliquem ex illa clericum, nisi abbate petente, praesumat. Hoc enim et rationis et religionis plenum est, ut clerici ad ordinationem Episcopi debita subjectione respiciant: laica vero omnis monasterii congregatio ad solam ac liberam Abbatis proprii, quem sibi ipsa elegerit, ordinationem dispositionemque pertineat; regula, quae a fundatore ipsius monasterii dudum constituta est, in omnibus custodita.

[6] Comp. especially Greg. M. lib. viii. Ep. 15, ad Marinianum Ravennae Episc.: Nullus audeat de reditibus vel chartis monasterii minuere.—Defuncto Abbate non extraneus nisi de eadem congregatione, quem sibi propria voluntate congregatio elegerit, ordinetur.—Invito Abbate ad ordinanda alia monasteria aut ad ordines sacros tolli exinde monachi non debent.—Descriptio rerum aut chartarum monasterii ab Ecclesiasticis fieri non debet.—Quia hospitandi occasione monasterium temporibus decessoris vestri nobis fuisse nunciatum est praegravatum: oportet ut hoc Sanctitas vestra decenter debeat temperare. He orders a bishop to restore what he had taken from a convent xenii quasi specie, lib. viii. Ep. 34. On the other hand he admonishes all bishops to keep a strict watch over the discipline and morals of the convents, lib. vi. Ep. 11; viii. Ep. 34.—Other privileges which Gregory is alleged to have granted to convents, for instance the celebrated privilegium monasterii S. Medardi in Soissons (see appendix to his letters in the Benedictine edition, no. 4) are spurious. Cf. Launoji Opp. iii. ii. 90. Thomassinus, P. i. lib. iii. c. 30.

FIFTH CHAPTER.

HISTORY OF PUBLIC WORSHIP.

§ 121.

How much the sensuous tendency of public worship,[1] of which we have already spoken, was farther developed in this period, and how many new superstitious notions sprung from it,[2] is best seen in the writings of *Gregory the Great*, a man who, with much real piety, had also very many monkish prejudices and great credulity; while by his high reputation in the Western Church, he did much to introduce new forms of worship, and diffuse a multitude of superstitions.

The chief part of the reverence paid to saints came more and more to consist in the superstitious worship of relics,[3] of whose

[1] For it there is a decree, Gregorii M. (Opp. ed. Maur. ii. 1298. Mansi, x. 434, also in Gratianus dist. 92, c. 2) characteristically: In sancta Romana Ecclesia—dudum consuetudo est valde reprehensibilis exorta, ut quidam ad sacri altaris ministerium Cantores eligantur et in Diaconatus ordine constituti modulationi vocis inserviant, quos ad praedicationis officium eleemosynarumque studium vacare congruebat. Unde fit plerumque, ut ad sacrum ministerium dum blanda vox quaeritur, quaeri congrua vita negligatur, et cantor minister Deum moribus stimulet, cum populum vocibus delectat. He therefore arranges that not deacons but sub-deacons and minores ordines should be employed in the singing.

[2] Comp. Neander's Denkwürdigkeiten aus der Gesch. des Christenthums. Bd. 3, Heft 1. (Berlin. 1824) S. 132, ss.

[3] Gregor. M. lib. iv. Ep. 30, ad Constantinam Aug. (Serenitas vestra—caput S. Pauli Apostoli, aut aliud quid de corpore ipsius, suis ad se jussionibus a me praecepit debere transmitti.—Major me moestitia tenuit, quod ille praecipitis, quae facere nec possum, nec audeo. Nam corpora, SS. Petri et Pauli App. tantis in Ecclesiis suis coruscant miraculis atque terroribus, ut neque ad orandum sine magno illuc timore possit accedi.—Examples. Among other things, that in opening the grave of Laurentius monachi et mansionarii, qui corpus ejusdem Martyris viderunt, quod quidem minime tangere praesumserunt, omnes intra x. dies defuncti sunt (Exod. xxxiii. 20).—Romanis consuetudo non est, quando Sanctorum reliquias dant, ut quidquam tangere praesumant de corpore: sed tantummodo in pyxide *brandeum* mittitur, atque ad sacratissima corpora Sanctorum ponitur. Quod levatum in Ecclesia, quae est dedicanda, debita cum veneratione reconditur: et tantae per hoc ibidem virtutes fiunt, ac si illuc specialiter eorum corpora deferantur (in like manner Gregor. Turon. de gloria Martyr. i. 28). Unde contigit, ut b. recordationis Leonis P. temporibus, sicut a majoribus traditur, dum quidam Graeci de talibus reliquiis dubitarent, praedictus Pontifex hoc ipsum brandeum allatis forficibus inciderit, et ex ipsa incisione sanguis effluxerit. In Romanis namque vel totius Occidentis partibus omnino intolerabile est atque sacrilegum, si Sanctorum corpora tangere quisquam fortasse voluerit. Quod si praesumserit, certum est, quia haec temeritas impunita nullo modo remanebit.—Sed quia

miraculous power the most absurd stories were told. The consequence of this was, that *the moral aspect* of saint-reverence was still farther lost sight of by an age which longed only for the marvelous. As this tendency now began to give rise to imposture in introducing false relics,[4] it had also the effect of developing the legends of the saints, to a greatly increased extent, in consequence of the love of the miraculous. The old martyrs, of whom for the most part the names alone were handed down,[5] were furnished with new descriptions of their lives, while the new saints were dressed out with wonderful narratives; even martyrs, with the histories of martyrs, were entirely fabricated anew.[6]

In the worship of saints, *angels* were now without hesitation made to participate, to whom also churches were dedicated.[7]

serenissimae Dominae tam religiosum desiderium esse vacuum non debet, de catenis, quas ipse S. Paulus Ap. in collo et in manibus gestavit, ex quibus multa miracula in populo demonstrantur, partem aliquam vobis transmittere festinabo, si tamen hanc tollere limando praevaluero, namely, quibusdam petentibus, diu per catenas ipsas ducitur lima, et tamen ut aliquid exinde exeat non obtinetur.—Lib. ix. Ep. 122, ad Recharedum Wisigoth. Regem: Clavem vero parvulam a sacratissimo b. Petri Ap. corpore vobis pro ejus benedictione transmisimus, in qua inest ferrum de catenis ejus inclusum; ut quod collum illius ad martyrium ligaverat, vestrum ab omnibus peccatis solvat. Crucem quoque dedi latori praesentium vobis offerendam, in qua lignum Dominicae crucis inest, et capilli b. Joannis Baptistae. Ex qua semper solatium nostri Salvatoris per intercessionem praecursoris ejus habeatis. Cf. lib. iii. Ep. 33. A number of similar miraculous stories are found in the works of Gregory of Tours, see note 6.

4 Gregor. M. lib. iv. Epist. 30, ad Constantinam Aug.: Quidam Monachi Graeci huc ante biennium venientes nocturno silentio juxta ecclesiam S. Pauli corpora mortuorum in campo jacentia effodiebant, atque eorum ossa recondebant, servantes sibi dum recederent. Qui cum tenti, et cur hoc facerent diligenter fuissent discussi, confessi sunt quod illa ossa ad Graeciam essent tanquam Sanctorum reliquias portaturi. Concil. Caesaraugust. ii. (592) can. 2: Statuit S. Synodus ut reliquiae in quibuscunque locis de Ariana haeresi inventae fuerint, prolatae, a Sacerdotibus, in quorum ecclesiis reperiuntur, pontificibus praesentatae igne probentur (the old German ordeal).

5 Gregor. M. lib. viii. Ep. 29, see Div. I. § 53, note 46.

6 The writings of Gregory, archbishop of Tours, afford abundant proofs of all this. See above § 114, note 18. Among many other things we find also in him for the first time (de Gloria mart. i. 95), the legend belonging to the Decian persecution de septem dormientibus apud urbem Ephesum. It had been derived from an old tradition which is even found in Pliny Nat. hist. vii. 52; but which being afterward transferred to Christian martyrs, was differently localized. Thus it appears in the Koran (Surat 18) to be transplanted into Arabia, subsequently it was carried into Gaul (Pseudo-Gregor Tur. Epist. ad Sulpic. Bituric.), to Germany (Nicephori Call. Hist. eccl. v. 17), and also to the north (Paulus Diac. de Gestis Longob. i. 4).

7 Comp. § 99, note 34. As presents had been made to the deities in heathen Rome, so now they were frequently made to saints and angels. Cf. lex Zenonis (Cod. Just. i. ii. 15): Si quis donaverit aliquam rem—in honorem Martyris, aut Prophetae, aut Angeli, tanquam ipsi postea oratorium aedificaturus,—cogitur opus, quamvis nondum inchoatum fuerit, perficere per se vel per heredes. Justiniani, A.D. 530 (l. c. l. 26): In multis jam testamentis invenimus ejusmodi institutiones, quibus aut ex asse quis scripserat Dominum nostrum Jesum Christum heredem: then the inheritance of the church of the place was to

Pictures became more common in the churches. In the east authentic likenesses of Christ now appeared in public,[8] and were the principal means of establishing there the worship of images;[9] but in the west the latter was still rejected.[10]

Justinian was distinguished for building splendid *churches*.[11]

To the festivals were added the two feasts of Mary, *festum purificationis* (ὑπαπαντή) on the second of February; and *festum annunciationis* (ἡ τοῦ εὐαγγελισμοῦ ἡμέρα) on the 25th of March.[12]

On the three days before the ascension (jejunium rogationum), *Mamercus* or *Mamertus*, bishop of Vienne (452), had instituted solemn rites of penance and prayer, accompanied by fasting and public worship (litaniae, rogationes), appointed for the three days

be applied to the benefit of the poor. Si vero quis unius ex Archangelis meminerit, vel venerandorum Martyrum, in that case the nearest church dedicated to him shall be heir.

8 The picture of Christ by Luke first mentioned by Theodorus Lector about 518, which was soon followed by pictures of other holy persons from the same hand. But after this appeared the *εἰκόνες ἀχειροποίητοι*, a counterpart of the *ἀγάλματα διοπετῆ* of heathenism, first noticed in Evagrius, iv. 27. See Div. I. § 21, note 4.

9 Comp. especially the fragment of Leontii (bishop of Neapolis in Cyprus † about 620) Apologia pro Christianis adv. Judaeos in the Acts of the Conc. Nic. ii. ann. 787, Act. 4 (Mansi, xiii. 43), where he defends *προσκύνησις* before the pictures, mentions even *αἱμάτων ῥύσεις ἐξ εἰκόνων* and designates the pictures as *πρὸς ἀνάμνησιν καὶ τιμὴν καὶ εὐπρέπειαν ἐκκλησιῶν προκείμενα καὶ προσκυνούμενα.* Neander's Kirchengesch. ii. ii. 627, ss.

10 Gregorii Magni lib. ix. Ep. 105, ad Serenum Massiliensem Ep.: Praeterea indico dudum ad nos pervenisse, quod Fraternitas vestra, quosdam imaginum adoratores adspiciens, easdem in Ecclesiis imagines confregit atque projecit. Et quidem zelum vos, ne quid manufactum adorari posset, habuisse laudavimus, sed frangere easdem imagines non debuisse indicamus. Idcirco enim pictura in Ecclesiis adhibetur, ut hi, qui litteras nesciunt, saltem in parietibus videndo legant, quae legere in codicibus non valent (as Paulinus Nilus, § 99, notes 47 and 48). Tua ergo Fraternitas et illas servare, et ab earum adoratu populum prohibere debuit: quatenus et litterarum nescii haberent, unde scientiam historiae colligerent, et populus in picturae adoratione minime peccaret. Lib. xi. Ep. 13, ad eundem: Quod de scriptis nostris, quae ad te misimus, dubitasti, quam sis incautus apparuit. Amplification of the above. Among other things, frangi ergo non debuit, quod non ad adorandum in ecclesiis, sed ad instruendas solummodo mentes fuit nescientium collocatum. Cf. lib. ix. Ep. 52, ad Secundinum: Imagines, quas tibi dirigendas per Dulcidum Diaconum rogasti, misimus. Unde valde nobis tua postulatio placuit: quia illum toto corde, tota intentione quaeris, cujus imaginem prae oculis habere desideras, ut te visio corporalis quotidiana reddat exercitatum: ut dum picturam illius vides, ad illum animo inardescas, cujus imaginem videre desideras. Ab re non facimus, si per visibilia invisibilia demonstramus. Scio quidem, quod imaginem Salvatoris nostri non ideo petis, ut quasi Deum colas, sed ob recordationem filii Dei in ejus amore recalescas, cujus te imaginem videre desideras. Et nos quidem non quasi ante divinitatem ante illam prosternimur, sed illum adoramus, quem per imaginem aut natum, aut passum, sed et in throno sedentem recordamur.

11 Procopius Caesariensis de Aedificiis Justiniani libb. vi.

12 Bingham vol. ix. p. 170, ss. J. A. Schmidii Prolusiones Marianae sex. Helmst. 1733. 4. p. 116, ss. 103, ss.

before the ascension (jejunium rogationum).[13] To this festival *Gregory the Great* added new ceremonies (litania septiformis).[14] He also improved the church-music (cantus Gregorianus).[15]

Justinian first transferred to the spiritual relationship (cognatio spiritualis) between the god-father and the god-child, the civil consequences arising from corporeal affinities.[16]

Gregory the Great, in his *Sacramentarium*, gave that form to the Roman *liturgy relative to the Lord's Supper*, which it has substantially preserved ever since.[17] The earlier notions of this rite, and of its atoning power, became more exaggerated in proportion as the idea became general, which was thrown out by *Augustine* as a conjecture,[18] that men would be sub-

[13] Sidonius Apollinaris Ep. Arvernorum († 482) Epistolarum lib. vii. Ep. 1, lib. v. Ep. 14. Gregor. Tur. ii. 34. Bingham, vol. v. p. 21.

[14] Appendix ad Gregorii Epistolas, no. iii. and Sermo tempore mortalitatis (in the older edition, lib. xi. Ep. 2).

[15] Joannes Diac. de vit. Gregorii, lib. ii. c. 7. Martin. Gerbert de Cantu et musica sacra (Bambergae et Frib. 1774, t. ii. 4), t. i. p. 35, ss. Jos. Antony's archäologisch-liturg. Lehrbuch d. gregorian. Kirchengesanges. Münster. 1829. 4.

[16] Ideas of regeneration in baptism, of spiritual generation, of the brotherly relation of Christians, had before led men to compare the relations of the baptizer, of the godfather, and the baptized, with corporeal relationship. Cf. Fabii Marii Victorini (about 360) Comm. in Ep. ad Gal. (in Maji Scriptt. vett. nova coll. iii. ii. 37) : Per baptismum, cum regeneratio fit, ille qui baptizatum perficit, vel perfectum suscipit, pater dicitur. Cf. Gothofr. Arnoldi Hist. cognationis spiritualis inter Christianos receptae. Goslar. 1730. 8. p. 44, ss. From this now proceeded the decree of Justinian, Cod. lib. v. tit. 4, de nuptiis, l. 26 : Ea persona omnimodo ad nuptias venire prohibenda, quam aliquis—a sacrosancto suscepit baptismate : cum nihil aliud sic inducere potest paternam affectionem et justam nuptiarum prohibitionem, quam hujusmodi nexus, per quem Deo mediante animae eorum copulatae sunt. The relation was considered as a sort of adoption. See du Fresne Glossar. s. v. Adoptio et Filiolatus.

[17] Joannes Diac. de vita Greg. ii. 17 : Sed et Gelasianum codicem, de missarum solemniis multa subtrahens, pauca convertens, nonnulla superadjiciens, in unius libelli volumine coarctavit. Jo. Bona Rerum liturg. libb. ii. Colon. 1764. 8, and frequently. Best edited in his Opp. omnibus. Antverp. 1723. fol. Th. Christ. Lilienthal de Canone Missae Gregoriano. Lugd. Bat. 1740. 8.

[18] Entirely distinct from the purifying fire of the last day, the belief in which has been frequent since Origen (see Div. I. § 63, note 12), and in which even Augustine seems to believe, August. de Civ. Dei, xx. 25, apparere in illo judicio quasdam quorundam purgatorias poenas futuras. On the other hand, liber de viii. quaestionibus ad Dulcitium, § 13 : Tale aliquid (ignem, tribulationis tentationem) etiam post hanc vitam fieri incredibile non est, et utrum ita sit, quaeri potest, et aut inveniri aut latere, nonnullos fideles per ignem quendam purgatorium, quanto magis minusve bona pereuntia dilexerunt, tanto tardius citiusve salvari. De Civ. Dei, xxi. 26 : Post istius sane corporis mortem, donec ad illum veniatur, qui post resurrectionem corporum futurus est damnationis et remunerationis ultimus dies, si hoc temporis intervallo spiritus defunctorum ejusmodi ignem dicuntur perpeti,—non redarguo, quia forsitan verum est. Dallaei de Poenis et satisfactionibus humanis libb. vii. Amst. 1649. 4. J. G. Chr. Hoepfner de Origine dogmatis de purgatorio. Hal. 1792. 8. Münscher's Dogmengeschichte, Th. 4 S. 425.

jected to a purifying fire immediately after death.[19] *Gregory the Great* did much to confirm these notions by descriptions of the tortures of departed souls, and the mitigation of such tortures by the sacrifice offered in the Supper.[20] In proportion as the latter assumed the form of a *tremendum mysterium*, the more seldom did the people partake of it, so that it was necessary for the Church to enact laws on the subject.[21] In other respects the ideas of the nature of the elements in the Supper suffered no change (§ 101, note 15).[22]

[19] Caesarius Arelat. Hom. viii. on 1 Cor. iii. 11–15 (in Bibl. PP. Lugd. viii. 826), has the Augustinian distinction between peccata capitalia and minuta, and teaches that the latter are expiated by an ignis transitorius or purgatorius ; but yet he places the latter in the time of the final judgment. Ille ipse purgatorius ignis durior erit, quam quicquid potest poenarum in hoc saeculo aut cogitari, aut videri, aut sentiri. Et cum de die judicii scriptum sit, quod erit dies unus tanquam mille anni, et mille anni tanquam dies unus : unde scit unusquisque, utrum diebus aut mensibus, an forte etiam et annis per illum ignem sit transiturus. Et qui modo unum digitum suum in ignem mittere timet, quare non timeat, ne necesse sit tunc non parvo tempore cum animo et corpore (consequently after the resurrection) cruciari ? Et ideo totis viribus unusquisque laboret, ut et capitalia crimina possit evadere, et minuta peccata ita operibus bonis redimere, ut aut parum ex ipsis, aut nihil videatur remanere, quod ignis ille possit absumere.—Omnes sancti, qui Deo fideliter serviunt,—per ignem illum—absque ulla violentia transibunt. Illi vero, qui, quamvis capitalia crimina non admittant, ad perpetranda minuta peccata sint faciles, ad vitam aeternam—venturi sunt ; sed prius aut in saeculo per Dei justitiam vel misericordiam amarissimis tribulationibus excoquendi, aut illi ipsi per multas eleemosynas, et dum inimicis clementer indulgent, per Dei misericordiam liberandi, aut certe illo igne, de quo dixit Apostolus, longo tempore cruciandi sunt, ut ad vitam aeternam sine macula et ruga perveniant. Ille vero, qui aut homicidium, aut sacrilegium, aut adulterium, vel reliqua his similia commiserunt, si eis digna poenitentia non subvenerit, non per purgatorium ignem transire merebuntur ad vitam, sed aeterno incendio praecipitabuntur ad mortem. Cf. Oudinus de Scriptoribus eccl. i. 1514.

[20] Greg. M. Dialog. lib. iv. c. 39 : Qualis hinc quisque egreditur, talis in judicio praesentatur. Sed tamen de quibusdam levibus culpis esse ante judicium purgatorius ignis credendus est, pro eo quod veritas dicit, quia si quis in S. Spiritu blasphemiam dixerit, neque in hoc seculo remittetur ei, neque in futuro (Matth. xii. 31). In qua sententia datur intelligi, quasdam culpas in hoc seculo, quasdam seculo vero in futuro posse laxari.—Instances of such tormented souls, ibid. ii. 23, iv. 40, especially iv. 55 : Si culpae post mortem insolubiles non sunt, multum solet animas etiam post mortem sacra oblatio hostiae salutaris adjuvare, ita ut hanc nonnumquam ipsae defunctorum animae expetere videantur, with two examples. Peter, listening, artlessly asks (iv. 40) : Quid hoc est, quaeso, quod in his extremis temporibus tam multa de animabus clarescunt, quae ante latuerunt : ita ut apertis revelationibus atque ostensionibus venturum saeculum inferre se nobis atque aperire videatur ? To which Gregory replies (c. 41) : Ita est : nam quantum praesens saeculum propinquat ad finem, tantum futurum saeculum ipsa jam quasi propinquitate tangitur, et signis manifestioribus aperitur.

[21] Conc. Agathense (506) can. 18 : Saeculares, qui natale domini, pascha, et pentecosten non communicaverint, catholici non credantur, nec inter catholicos habeantur.

[22] Gelasius P. de Duabus in Christo naturis adv. Eutychen et Nestorium (cited as genuine even by his contemporaries, Gennadius de Script. c. 94, and Fulgentius Rusp. in Epist. xiv. ad Fulgentium Ferrandum, cap. 19, in Gallandii Bibl. t. xi. p. 334, and therefore doubted without reason by Baronius, Bellarminus, and others. It is found in the Bibl

SIXTH CHAPTER.

SPREAD OF CHRISTIANITY, AND ITS CONDITION WITHOUT THE ROMAN EMPIRE.

I. IN ASIA AND AFRICA.

§ 122.

During the reign of Justinian I., the people dwelling on the Black Sea, viz., the *Abasgi*, *Alani*, *Lazi*, *Zani*, and *Heruli*, declared themselves in favor of Christianity, and for the Catholic Church. But the *Nestorians* and *Monophysites* made much more important acquisitions to the cause, during this period, in Asia and Africa.

The *Nestorians*[1] not only maintained themselves in *Persia*, where they enjoyed exclusive protection (§ 88, at the end), but also spread themselves on all sides in Asia, particularly into *Arabia*[2] and *India*,[3] and it is said, in the year 636, even as

PP., in Heroldi Haereseologia. Basil. 1556. fol. p. 683, etc.): Certe sacramenta, quae sumimus, corporis et sanguinis Christi, divina res est, propter quod et per eadem divinae efficimur consortes naturae, et tamen esse non desinit substantia vel natura panis et vini. Et certe imago et similitudo corporis et sanguinis Christi in actione mysteriorum celebrantur. Satis ergo nobis evidenter ostenditur, hoc nobis in ipso Christo Domino sentiendum, quod in ejus imagine profitemur, celebramus et sumimus, ut sicut in hanc, scilicet in divinam transeant Spiritu S. perficiente substantiam permanente tamen in sua proprietate natura, sic illud ipsum mysterium principale, cujus nobis efficientiam virtutemque veraciter repraesentant. Facundus Hermian. pro defens. iii. capitul. ix. 5: Nam sacramentum adoptionis suscipere dignatus est Christus, et quando circumcisus est, et quando baptizatus est; et potest sacramentum adoptionis adoptio nuncupari, sicut sacramentum corporis et sanguinis ejus, quod est in pane et poculo consecrato, corpus ejus et sanguinem dicimus: non quod proprie corpus ejus sit panis, et poculum sanguis: sed quod in se mysterium corporis ejus et sanguinis contineant. Hinc et ipse Dominus benedictum panem et calicem, quem discipulis tradidit, corpus et sanguinem suum vocavit. Cramer's Forts. v. Bossuet, Th. 5, Bd. 1, S. 200, ff.

[1] Concerning them, compare especially Jos. Sim. Assemani Diss. de Syris Nestorianis, Part ii. tom. iii. of the Biblioth. orientalis. [2] Assemanus, l. c. p. 607, s.

[3] Cosmas Indicopleustes (about 535) Christ. topographiae, lib. iii., says that there was a Christian Church *ἐν τῇ Ταπροβάνῃ νήσῳ ἐν τῇ ἐσωτέρᾳ Ἰνδίᾳ* (namely lib. xi.: *Ἐκκλησία τῶν ἐπιδημούντων* Περσῶν *χριστιανῶν* with a *πρεσβύτερος ἀπὸ* Περσίδος *χειροτονούμενος*): *οὐκ οἶδα δὲ εἰ καὶ περαιτέρω.* So too in Male. But *ἐν τῇ* Καλλιάνᾳ—*ἐπίσκοπός ἐστιν ἀπὸ* Περσίδος *χειροτονούμενος.* So also *ἐν τῇ νήσῳ τῇ καλουμένῃ* Διοσκορίδους.—*Ὁμοίως δὲ καὶ ἐπὶ* Βάκτροις, *καὶ* Οὔννοις, *καὶ* Πέρσαις, *καὶ λοιποῖς* Ἰνδοῖς, *καὶ* Περσαρμενίοις, *καὶ* Μήδοις, *καὶ* Ἐλαμίταις *καὶ πάσῃ τῇ χώρᾳ* Περσίδος *καὶ ἐκκλησίαι ἄπειροι,*

far as *China*.[4] Along with the theological tendencies of the Syrian Church, whence they had come forth, they preserved its learning likewise; and were thus the introducers of Greek science into Asia. Their school in *Nisibis* was the only theological institution of Christendom in the sixth century.[5]

The *Monophysites*, on the other hand, spread themselves from Alexandria toward the south. Among the *Hamdschars* or *Homerites*, Christianity had been early established (§ 107); though it did not become general till the time of Anastasius.[6] But when Dhu-Nowas, a Jewish king of this people, afterward persecuted the Christians with violence (522), the Aethiopian king Elesbaan came to their aid (529); in consequence of which the Homerites were subject to Aethiopian rulers for seventy-two years.[7] As the Homerite Christians were Mono-

καὶ ἐπίσκοποι, καὶ χριστιανοὶ λαοὶ πάμπολλοι, κ. τ. λ. Hence the Christiani S. Thomae. Cf. Assemanus, l. c. p. 435, ss., again discovered in the sixteenth century by the Portuguese in Malabar (about A.D. 780, all the Persian Christians, among whom were the Indian, declared themselves disciples Thomae Apostoli. See Abulpharagius ap. Assem. l. c. p. 438).

[4] That is, if the monumentum Syro-Sinicum be genuine, which is said to have been erected A.D. 781, and discovered 1625 in the city Si-an-fu, in the province Schen-si, copies of the inscription on it having been sent to Europe by the Jesuit missionaries. First published in Athanas. Kircheri Prodromus Copticus, Rom. 1636. 4. p. 74, and in ejusd. China illustrata, ibid. 1667. fol. p. 43, ss., also in Mosheim Hist. Tartarorum eccl. Helmst. 1741. 4. App. p. 4. The genuineness of the monument has always been doubted by many. So in particular by La Croze, against whom Assemanus Bibl. Orient. iii. ii. 538, defends it. Renaudot Anciennes relations des Indes et de la Chine. Paris. 1718, p. 228; Mosheim Hist. Tart. eccl. p. 9. Deguignes Untersuchung über die in 7ten Jahrh. in Sina sich aufhaltenden Christen. Greifsw. 1769. 4; Abel Remusat Nouveaux mélanges. Paris. 1829, ii. 189; and Saint Martin on Lebeau Hist. du Bas-Empire (new edition. Paris. 1824, voll. xi.) vi. 69, hold it to be genuine. On the contrary, Beausobre (Hist. de Manichée, c. 14), Neumann in the Jahrb. f. wissen. Kritik, 1829, S. 592, and Von Bohlen (das alte Indien. Königsberg. 1830, Th. 1. S. 383), have once more declared it to be a work of the Jesuits.

[5] It was formed at the end of the fifth century out of the exiled remains of the school of Edessa (comp. § 88, at the end). Respecting it comp. Assemani Bibl. orient. iii. ii. 927, ss., cf. p. 80, and the passage of Cassiodorus given above, § 114, note 14. The African bishop, Junilius (about 550), relates in the preface to his work de partibus divinae legis respecting the origin of it, that he had become acquainted with quendam Paulum nomine, Persam genere, qui in Syrorum schola in Nisibi urbe est edoctus, ubi divina lex per magistros publicos, sicut apud nos in mundanis studiis Grammatica et Rhetorica, ordine ac regulariter traditur. He had read drawn up by him, regulas quasdam, quibus ille discipulorum animos, divinarum scripturarum superficie instructos, priusquam expositionis profunda patefaceret, solebat imbuere, ut ipsarum interim causarum, quae in divina lege versantur, intentionem ordinemque cognoscerent, ne sparsim et turbulente, sed regulariter singula discerent. These regularia instituta he gives here with some alteration of the form.

[6] Theodori Lect. Hist. eccl. ii. where they are called Ἰμμιρηνοί.

[7] Comp. the varying accounts of the contemporaries Johannis Episc. Asiae in Assemani Bibl. orient. i. 359; Simeonis Episc. in Perside Epist., preserved in Zachariae Hist. eccl. ap. Assemani, l. c. p. 364, and in Maji Coll. x. i. 376; and Procopius de Bello Persico i. c.

physites, the Monophysite doctrines were carried to other parts of Arabia.[8] Under Justinian the *Nubians* were also converted to Christianity by the Monophysites of Alexandria.[9]

II. AMONG THE GERMAN NATIONS.

Planck's Gesch. d. christl. kirchl. Gesellschaftsverfassung. B. 2.

§ 123.

SPREAD OF CHRISTIANITY AMONG THE GERMAN NATIONS.

The first German people converted to the Christianity of the Catholic Church were the *Franks*, who since 486 had been masters of the greatest part of Gaul. *Clovis*, king of the Salian Franks, influenced by his queen Clotildis, and by a vow made at the battle of *Tolbiacum* (Zülpich, 496), was baptized by Remigius, bishop of Rheims,[1] and his people followed his example.

17 and 20. Martyrium Arethae (Arethas, head of the Christian city Nadschran), hitherto known only in the work of Simeon Metaphr. but recently published in the original in J. Fr. Boissonade Anecdota graeca, v. 1 (Paris. 1833). Walchii Hist. rerum in Homeritide seculo sexto gestarum, in the Novis Commentariis Soc. Reg. Gottingensis, iv. 1. Johannsen Historia Jemanae (Bonnae. 1828) p. 88, ss. Jost's Gesch. der Israeliten, v. 253, 354. Lebeau Hist. du Bas-Empire, ed. Saint Martin, viii. 48. On the chronology, see De Sacy in the Mémoires de l'Acad. des Inscript. l. 531, 545.—Respecting Gregentius, archbishop of Taphara, who was in the highest repute under the Christian viceroy, Abraham, see Gregor. disp. cum Herbano Judaeo ed. Nic. Gulonius. Lutet. 1586. 8, and νόμοι τῶν Ὁμηριτῶν, composed by Gregentius, ap. Boissonade, v. 63.

8 Assemani Bibl. orient. iii. ii. 605. The Arab tribes among whom Christianity was propagated, are pointed out in Ed. Pocockii Spec. Hist. Arabum, ed. Jos. White. Oxon. 1806, p. 141.

9 Abulpharagius in Assem. Bibl. orient. t. ii. p. 330. Comp. Letronne Nouvel examen de l'inscription grecque du roi nubien Silco, considerée dans ses rapports avec la propagation de la langue grecque et l'introduction du christianisme parmi les peuples de la Nubie et de l'Abyssinie, in the Mémoires de l'institut royal de France, Acad. des inscriptions, t. ix. (1831) p. 128.

1 Gregorii Turonensis († 595) Historiae Francorum (libb. 10, till the year 591, best edited in Dom Martin Bouquet Rerum Gallicarum et Francicarum scriptores, t. ii. Paris. 1739, fol.) lib. ii. c. 28–31. F. W. Rettberg's Kirchengesch. Deutchslands, Bd. i. (Göttingen. 1845. 8) S. 270. Dr. C. G. Kries de Greg. Tur. vita et scriptis. Vratisl. 1839. 8. Gregor v. Tours u. s. Zeit, von. J. W. Löbell. Leipzig. 1839. 8.—Tradition of the oil-flask brought by a dove found first in Hincmar in vita Remigii, cap. 3. The Ampulla itself first came to light at the coronation of Philip II., 1179, and was broken in the year 1794, at Rhül's command. Comp. de Vertot. Diss. au sujet de la sainte ampulle (Mémoires de l'Acad. des Inscr. t. ii. Mém. p. 669). C. G. v. Murr über die heil. Ampulle in Rheims. Nürnberg u. Altdorf. 1801. 8.

From the Franks Christianity was propagated among the *Allemanni*, who were subject to them.[2]

So far as the inclination of all Romans that had been subjected to the yoke of the Germans leaned immediately to the Franks as Catholic Christians,[3] the latter obtained an important predominance of influence over the other German people. For this reason the others successively came over at this time to the Catholic Church.[4] This took place in regard to the *Burgundians*, under their King Sigismund (517); the *Suevi*, under their Kings Carrarich (550–559) and Theodemir I. (559–569);[5] the *Visigoths*, under their King Reccared at the council of Toledo (589).[6] Since under Justinian the *Vandal* kingdom in Africa (534), and that of the *Ostrogoths* in Upper Italy (553), had been destroyed, Arianism also lost its dominion in those territories.

On the contrary, it revived under the rule of the *Lombards* in Italy (from 568), and was longest maintained among this people.[7]

In other parts, the amalgamation of the German conquerors with the older inhabitants of their land,[8] and the development of the new European nations, were universally effected by similarity of faith.[9]

[2] Bishopric of Vindonissa (now Windisch in the canton Aargau) transferred to Constance in the 6th century. Sosimus, the first known bishop of Augsburg, A.D. 582. C. J. Hefele's Gesch. d. Einführung des Christenth. im südwestl. Deutschland. Tübingen. 1837, S. 112.

[3] Gregor. Tur. Hist. ii. 36: Multi jam tunc ex Gallis habere Francos dominos summo desiderio cupiebant. Unde factum est, ut Quintianus Rutenorum (Rodez) Episcopus per hoc odium ab urbe depelleretur (by the Visigoths). Dicebant enim ei: quia desiderium tuum est, ut Francorum dominatio possideat terram hanc. Hence Chlodowich gave his war against the Visigoths the appearance of being undertaken chiefly from religious zeal. He said to his people, l. c. c. 37: Valde moleste fero, quod hi Ariani partem teneant Galliarum. Eamus cum Dei adjutorio, et superatis redigamus terram in ditionem nostram.

[4] A history of Arianism among the German nations in Walch's Ketzerhist. ii. 553.

[5] The history of Carrarich's conversion in Gregor. Turon. de miraculis S. Martini, i. c. 11; but Theodemir first propagated the catholic faith among the people, and therefore Isidorus Chron. Suevorum even makes him the first catholic king of the Suevi. See Ferrera's span. Geschichte, Bd. 2.

[6] Aschbach's Gesch. d. Westgothen. Frankf. a. M. 1827, S. 220, ff.

[7] Paulus Warnefridi, Diaconus (about 774): de Gestis Longobardorum libb. vi. (best in Muratori Scriptor. Italic. Tom. i. Mediol. 1723, fol.).

[8] Formerly marriages between the two parties were universally forbidden by the Church; but among the Visigoths they were also prohibited by the civil code: See leges Visigothorum (best edition: Fuero juzgo en latin y castellano, por la real Academia española. Madrid. 1815. fol.) iii. i. 2 (a law of King Recesvinth from 649–672): Priscae legis remota sententia hac in perpetuum valitura lege sancimus, ut tam Gothus Romanam, quam etiam Gotham Romanus, si conjugem habere voluerit,—facultas eis nubendi subjaceat.

[9] H. I. Royaard's über d. Gründung u. Entwickelung der neueurop. Staaten im Mittel-

At the end of this period began the conversion of the *Anglo-Saxons* in Britain. Augustine, sent thither by Gregory the Great with forty Benedictines (596), was first received by Ethelbert, King of Kent, through the influence of his Queen Bertha, who was a Frank. From Kent Christianity was gradually diffused in the other Anglo-Saxon kingdoms.[10]

§ 124.

HIERARCHY IN THE GERMAN EMPIRE.

Eugen Montag's Gesch. der deutschen staatsbürgerlichen Freiheit. (Bamb. u. Würzb. 1812. 8.) Bd. 1, Th. 1, S. 205, ff. Th. 2, S. 1, ff. K. F. Eichhorn's deutsche Staats- u. Rechtsgeschichte. (4 Theile. 4te Ausg. Göttingen. 1834–36. 8.) i. 217, 478. Gregor v. Tours u. s. Zeit von T. W. Löbell, S. 315. S. Sugenheim's Staatsleben des Klerus im Mittelalter. Bd. 1. Berlin. 1839.

Although the ecclesiastical constitution and code which had been formed in the Roman Empire were adopted by the German nations,[1] yet the relations of the hierarchy received a peculiar form. The kings soon saw how much their power could be supported and strengthened by the reputation of the clergy;[2] and they endeavored therefore to bind more closely to themselves the heads of the clergy, the bishops and abbots. Churches and monasteries received considerable possessions from their hands,[3] while the bishops and abbots, as the temporary

alter, bes. durch d. Christenth. aus d. Archief Deel 2, übersetzt, v. G. Kinkel, in Illgen's Zeitchr. f. d. hist. Theol. v. i. 67.

[10] Beda Venerabilis († 735) Historia ecclesiastica gentis Anglorum libb. v. ed. Fr. Chiffletius. Paris. 1681. 4. Joh. Smith. Cantabrig. 1722. fol. Jos. Stevenson (Bedae Opp. hist. t. i.) Lond. 1838. 8. J. A. Giles (Bedae Opp. vol. 2 et 3). Lond. 1843. 8. Das erste Jahrh. d. engl. Kirche, od. Einführung und Befestigung des Christenthums bei den Angelsachen in Britannien, v. D. K. Schrödl. Passau. 1840. 8. [Sharon Turner's History of the Anglo-Saxons, 3 vols. 8vo. London, 1823, fourth edition. Lingard's History of the Anglo-Saxon Church, second edition, 2 vols. 8vo, 1845. Lond.]

[1] As all conquered nations lived according to their own law (Lex Ripuariorum, tit. xxxi. § 3), so the clergy, according to Roman law, Lex Ripuar. tit. lviii. § 1: Legem Romanam, qua Ecclesia vivit. Comp. Eichhorn, i. 172, 217.

[2] Chlodovaei praeceptum pro Monasterio Reomaensi, in Bouquet Rerum gall. scriptt. iv. 615: Servos Dei, quorum virtutibus gloriamur et orationibus defensamur, si nobis amicos acquirimus, honoribus sublimamus atque obsequiis veneramur, statum regni nostri perpetuo augere credimus, et saeculi gloriam atque caelestis regni patriam adipisci confidimus. Löbell, S. 318.

[3] Gregor. Turon. Hist. Franc. vi. 46: Chilperich, king in Soissons (from 561–584), ajebat plerumque: Ecce pauper remansit fiscus noster, ecce divitiae nostrae ad Ecclesias sunt translatae: nulli penitus nisi soli Episcopi regnant: periit honor noster et translatus est

possessors, became *the vassals* (ministeriales) of the king,[4] were often employed in affairs of the state, and were thus invested with a very important political influence. The possessions of the Church were only by degrees, as exceptions, freed from all taxes; but, though exempted from contributions to the royal exchequer, continued to be devoted to military services,[5] which were in some instances rendered in person.[6] Besides, the kings regarded church property as feudal tenures (beneficia), and frequently did not scruple to resume them.[7] It was stipulated by law that the choice of a bishop should be confirmed by the king;[8] but for the most part, the kings themselves appointed to vacant sees.[9]

ad Episcopos civitatum. Comp. Hüllmann's Gesch. des Ursprungs der Stände in Deutschland (2te Ausg. Berlin. 1830), S. 114, ff.

[4] Fredegarii (about 740) chron. c. 4: Burgundiae barones, tam Episcopi quam caeteri leudes. C. 76: Pontifices caeterique leudes. G. I. Th. Lau on the influence which the feudal tenure system has exercised on the clergy and papacy in Illgen's Zeitschr. f. Hist. Theol. 1841, ii. 82.

[5] Gregor. Tur. v. 27: Chilpericus rex de pauperibus et junioribus Ecclesiae vel basilicae bannos jussit exigi, pro eo quod in exercitu non ambulassent. Non enim erat consuetudo, ut hi ullam exsolverent publicam functionem. From this it does not follow, as Löbell says (p. 330), that in general the church was not required by duty to furnish troops from its estates. Rather does the *erat* show that it had not been usual only till the time of Chilperich. Comp. Planck, ii. 222. Montag, i. i. 314. Eichhorn, i. 202, 506, 516. Sugenheim, i. 315.

[6] In a battle against the Lombards (572) there were the bishops Salonius and Sagittarius, qui non cruce caelesti muniti, sed galea aut lorica saeculari armati, multos manibus propriis, quod pejus est, interfecisse referuntur. Gregor. Turon. iv. 43 (al. 37).

[7] Conc. Arvernense (at Clermont) ann. 535, c. 5. Qui reiculam ecclesiae petunt a regibus, et horrendae cupiditatis impulsu egentium substantiam rapiunt; irrita habeantur quae obtinent, et a communione ecclesiae cujus facultatem auferre cupiunt, excludantur. Comp. Conc. Parisiens. (about 557) against those qui facultates ecclesiae, sub specie largitatis regiae, improba subreptione pervaserint. Even judicial miracles take place, ex. gr. when Charibert, king of Paris (562–567) wished to take away a property belonging to the church at Tours. Gregor. Tur. de miraculis S. Martini, i. 29. Planck, ii. 206. Hüllmann, S. 123, ff.

[8] Conc. Aurelian. v. ann. 549, c. 10: Cum voluntate regis, juxta electionem cleri ac plebis—a metropolitano—cum comprovincialibus pontifex consecretur.

[9] Ex. gr. Gregor. Turon. de SS. Patrum vita c. 3, de S. Gallo: Tunc etiam et Apronculus Treverorum episcopus transiit. Congregatique clerici civitatis illius ad Theodoricum regem (king of Austrasia 511–534) S. Gallum petebant episcopum. Quibus ille ait: Abscedite et alium requirite, Gallum enim diaconum alibi habeo destinatum. Tunc eligentes S. Nicetium episcopum acceperunt. Arverni vero clerici consensu insipientium facto cum multis muneribus ad regem venerunt. Jam tunc germen illud iniquum coeperat pullulare, ut sacerdotium aut venderetur a regibus, aut compararetur a clericis. Tunc ii audiunt a rege, quod S. Gallum habituri essent episcopum.—The Concil. Paris ann. 615, wished indeed (can. 1) to have the choice by canons restored; but king Chlotarius II. modified that decree in his confirmatory edict, as follows (Mansi, x. p. 543): Episcopo decedente in loco ipsius, qui a metropolitano ordinari debet cum provincialibus, a clero et populo eligatur; et si persona condigna fuerit, per ordinationem principis ordinetur: vel certe si de palatio eligitur, per meritum personae et doctrinae ordinetur. Comp. the formulas in

Synods could not assemble without the royal permission; their decrees had to be confirmed by the king, being previously invalid. In the mean time they began to consult about the affairs of the Church, even in the meetings of the king's vassals or council (Placitum regis, Synodus regia, Synodale concilium).[10] Synods became more rare, and at length ceased entirely.

This arrangement completed the downfall of the metropolitan system, which had been already weakened in many ways. The king became the only judge of the bishops.[11] But in proportion as *they* rose higher in civil relations, the other clergy sank so much the deeper. No free man was allowed to enter the clergy without the royal permission.[12] Hence the clergy were chosen for the most part from among the serfs; and on this very account the bishop acquired an unlimited power over them, which frequently manifested itself in the most tyrannical conduct.[13] The administration of justice among the clergy was at first conducted according to Roman principles of legislation, as they were in force before Justinian (§ 91, note 5, ff.),[14] till *the Synod of Paris* (615) gave the clergy the privilege of being brought before a mixed tribunal, in all cases which hitherto belonged to

Marculfi (about 660) Formularum l. i. c. 5 (in Baluzii Capitularia Regum Franc. t. ii. p. 378): Praeceptum Regis de Episcopatu, c. 6. Indiculus Regis ad Episcopum, ut alium benedicat; and in the Formulis Lindenbrogii, c. 4: Carta de Episcopatu (ibid. p. 509). Sugenheim, i. 86. Löbell, S. 335.

[10] Just. F. Runde Abhandlung v. Ursprung der Reichsstandschaft der Bischöfe u. Aebte. Göttingen. 1775. 4. (The treatise on the same subject, appended, p. 93, is by Herder, and is also reprinted in his works on philosophy and history, Carlsruhe edition, Part 13, p. 219.) Planck, ii. 126. Hüllmann, S. 186, ff. Montag, i. ii. 54.

[11] Gregory Turon. says to king Chilperich: Si quis de nobis, o Rex, justitiae tramitem transcendere voluerit, a te corrigi potest: si vero tu excesseris, quis te corripiet? Loquimur enim tibi, sed si volueris, audis: si autem nolueris, quis te condemnabit, nisi is qui se pronunciavit esse justitiam? Gregor. Tur. Hist. Franc. v. 19.

[12] See Marculfi Formularum, lib. i. c. 19 (Baluzii Capitul. ii. p. 386), and Bignon's remarks on it (ibid. p. 901).

[13] Even before this time it appears that monks had been punished with blows by their abbots, Cassian. Collat. ii. 16. Palladii Hist. Lausiaca, c. 6, Benedicti Regula, c. 70. Bishops were now instructed by synods to punish in this manner also the offenses of the inferior clergy. See Concil. Agathense, ann. 506, can. 41. Epaonense, ann. 517, c. 15. The Concil. Matisconense, i. ann. 581, c. 8, prescribes the Mosaic number uno minus de quadraginta ictus. How the bishops often treated their clergy may be seen from Concil. Carpentoractense (527): Hujusmodi ad nos querela pervenit, quod ea quae a quibuscunque fidelibus parochiis conferuntur, ita ab aliquibus Episcopis praesumantur, ut aut parum, aut prope nihil ecclesiis, quibus collata fuerant, relinquatur. Concil. Toletanum, iii. (589) capitul. 20: Cognovimus Episcopos per parochias suas non sacerdotaliter deservire, sed crudeliter desaevire.

[14] Planck, ii. 161. Montag, i. ii. 106. Schilling de Orig. jurisdictionis eccles. in causis civilibus. Lips. 1825. 4. p. 46.

the civil judge alone.[15] A wider influence was given to the bishops by committing to them an oversight of the entire administration of justice,[16] while their spiritual punishments were made more effectual by connecting with excommunication civil disadvantages also.[17] On the other hand, in the application of their discipline they were bound to regard the intercession of the king.[18]

Under these circumstances, the popes could not directly interfere in ecclesiastical matters; and their communication with the established church of the country depended entirely on the royal pleasure.[19]

[15] In the Edictum Clotarii II., confirming this synod, we have: Ut nullus judicum de quolibet ordine clericos de civilibus causis, praeter criminalia negotia, per se distringere aut damnare praesumat, nisi convincitur manifestus, excepto presbytero aut diacono. Qui vero convicti fuerint de crimine capitali, juxta canones distringantur, et cum pontificibus examinentur. Comp. Planck, ii. 165. Rettberg's Kirchengesch. Deutschl. i. 294.

[16] Chlotarii Regis constitutio generalis, A.D. 560 (in Baluzii Capitularia Regum Franc. i. 7. Walter Corpus juris Germ. ant. ii. 2): VI. Si judex aliquem contra legem injuste damnaverit, in nostri absentia ab Episcopis castigetur, ut quod perpere judicavit, versatim melius discussione habita emendare procuret. Conc. Toletanum, iii. (589) cap. 18: Judices locorum vel actores fiscalium patrimoniorum ex decreto gloriosissimi domini nostri simul cum sacerdotali concilio autumnali tempore die Kal. Nov. in unum conveniant, ut discant, quam pie et juste cum populis agere debeant, ne in angariis aut in operationibus superfluis sive privatum onerent, sive fiscalem gravent. Sint enim prospectores episcopi secundum regiam admonitionem, qualiter judices cum populis agant; ut aut ipsos praemonitos corrigant, aut insolentias eorum auditibus principis innotescant. Quodsi correptos emendare nequiverint, et ab ecclesia et a communione suspendant.

[17] Decretio Childeberti Regis, A.D. 595: II.—Qui vero Episcopum suum noluerit audire, et excommunicatus fuerit, perennem condemnationem apud Deum sustineat, et insuper de palatio nostro sit omnino extraneus, et omnes facultates suas parentibus legitimis amittat, qui noluit sacerdotis sui medicamenta sustinere.

[18] Conc. Parisiense v. (615) can. 3: Ut si quis clericus—contemto episcopo suo ad principem vel ad potentiores homines—ambularit, vel sibi patronos elegerit, non recipiatur, praeter ut veniam debeat promereri. Chlotar II. repeats in his edict confirming this canon, but adds: Et si pro qualibet causa principem expetierit, et cum ipsius principis epistola ad episcopum suum fuerit reversus, excusatus recipiatur. Conc. Toletan. xii. ann. 681, c. 3: Quos regia potestas aut in gratiam benignitatis receperit, aut participes mensae suae effecerit, hos etiam sacerdotum et populorum conventus suscipere in ecclesiasticam communionem debebit: ut quod jam principalis pietas habet acceptum, neque a sacerdotibus Dei habeatur extraneum. Confirmed in Conc. Tolet. xiii. ann. 683, c. 9. Cf. J. G. Reinhard de Jure Principum Germaniae circa sacra ante tempora Reformationis exercito. Halae. 1717. 4. p. 359.

[19] Hence Pelagius I. was obliged to use the utmost pains in defending himself to king Childebert against the suspicion of heresy which he had drawn on himself by condemning the three chapters. Pelagii I. Ep. 16, ad Childeb. Reg. (Mansi, ix. p. 728): Since one must give no offense even to the little ones: quanto nobis studio ac labore satagendum est, ut pro auferendo suspicionis scandalo obsequium confessionis nostrae regibus ministremus; quibus nos etiam subditos esse sanctae Scripturae praecipiunt? Veniens etenim Rufinus vir magnificus, legatus excellentiae vestrae, confidenter a nobis, ut decuit, postulavit, quatenis vobis aut beatae recordationis papae Leonis tomum a nobis per omnia conservari significare debuissemus, aut propriis verbis nostrae confessionem fidei destin-

§ 125.

MORAL INFLUENCES OF CHRISTIANITY AMONG THE GERMAN NATIONS

As is usual among rude people when coming into closer contact with the more enlightened, there proceeded from the Romans, then greatly corrupted, pernicious influences rather than cultivation to the Germans, which were exhibited among the latter in the roughest form, less hidden in their case by the external rites prevalent among the Romans. Christianity, as it was then proclaimed, a series of dogmas and laws, could not restrain this corruption. Since it offered *expiations* for all offenses, along with its prohibitions of them, there was opened up to wild barbarity a way of first enjoying the lust of sin, and then of procuring exemption from the guilt of it. There was little concern for instruction. The public services of religion by means of their pomp and the use of a foreign, *i. e.*, the Latin language, awakened obscure feelings rather than right ideas. As the grossest notions were entertained of hell, so also were similar ideas prevalent respecting the power of the church, the influence of the saints,[1] the merit of ecclesiastical and monkish exercises, the value of alms to the church and to the poor.[2] These notions

are. Et primam quidem petitionis ejus partem, quia facilior fuit, mox ut dixit, implevimus.—Ut autem nullius deinceps, quod absit, suspicionis resideret occasio, etiam illam aliam partem, quam memoratus vir illustris Rufinus admonuit, facere mutavi, scilicet propriis verbis confessionem fidei, quam tenemus, exponens. Then follows a diffused confession of faith, in which, however, he mentions only four oecumenical synods, not the fifth. At the same time he writes to Sapaudus Episc. Arelat. (Ep. 15, l. c. p. 727) praying, ut, si epistola, quam—ad—Childebertum regem direximus, in qua de institutis beatissimorum patrum nostrorum fidem catholicam nostro per Dei gratiam sermone deprompsimus, tam ipsi gloriossimo regi, quam caritati tuae, vel aliis fratribus coëpiscopis nostris, placuit, rescripto tuae caritatis celerius agnoscamus. Cf. Preuves des Libertés de l'église Gallicane, c. 3. Planck, ii. 673.

[1] Even under them an aristocracy was formed. When the Huns approached Metz (Gregor. Tur. Hist. ii. 6), St. Stephen implored in the heavenly regions the Apostles Peter and Paul to protect the town, and received from them the answer: Vade in pace, dilectissime frater, oratorium tantum tuum carebit incendio. Pro urbe vero non obtinebimus, quia dominicae sanctionis super eam sententia jam processit.

[2] Cf. vita S. Eligii Episc. Noviomensis libb. iii. written A.D. 672, by his contemporary Audoënus Archiep. Rotomag. in Luc. d'Achery Spicilegium, ed. ii. tom. ii. p. 76, ss. Eligius, bishop of Noyon, was considered a man of extraordinary sanctity (Vitae, lib. ii. c. 6, p. 92: Huic itaque viro sanctissimo inter caetera virtutum suarum miracula id etiam a Domino concessum erat, ut sanctorum Martyrum corpora, quae per tot saecula abdita

were strengthened by legends and miracles, which were certainly in part an imposition of the clergy,[3] but were far from exerting any good moral influence on the people.[4] Crimes of the grossest kind were common among the clergy,[5] as well as the kings and

populis hactenus habebantur, eo investigante ac nimio ardore fidei indagante patefacta proderentur: siquidem nonnulla venerabantur prius a populo in locis, quibus non erant, et tamen quo in loco certius humata tegerentur, prorsus ignorabatur). The more remarkable, therefore, is his exhortation, contained in the Vitae, lib. ii. c. 15, p. 96, ss. He first refers to the judgment-day, then to the points of faith, then to the duty of performing opera christiana, and thus continues: Ille itaque bonus Christianus est, qui nulla phylacteria, vel adinventiones diaboli credit.—Ille, inquam, bonus Christianus est, qui hospitibus pedes lavat, et tamquam parentes carissimos diligit; qui juxta quod habet pauperibus eleemosynam tribuit; qui ad Ecclesiam frequentius venit, et oblationem quae in altari Deo offeratur exhibet; qui de fructibus suis non gustat, nisi prius Deo aliquid offerat; qui stateras dolosas et mensuras duplices non habet; qui pecuniam suam non dedit ad usuram; qui et ipse caste vivit, et filios vel vicinos docet, ut caste et cum timore Dei vivant; et quoties sanctae solemnitates adveniunt, ante dies plures castitatem etiam cum propria uxore custodit, ut secura conscientia ad Domini altare accedere possit; qui postremo symbolum vel orationem dominicam memoriter tenet, et filios ac filias eadem docet. Qui talis est, sine dubio verus Christianus est.—Ecce audistis, Fratres, quales sint Christiani boni: ideo quantum potestis cum Dei adjutorio laborate, ut nomen christianum non sit falsum in vobis. Sed ut veri Christiani esse possitis, semper praecepta Christi et cogitate in mente, et implete in operatione. Redimite animas vestras de poena, dum habetis in potestate remedia; eleemosynam juxta vires facite, pacem et charitatem habete, discordes ad concordiam revocate, mendacium fugite, perjurium expavescite, falsum testimonium non dicite, furtum non facite, oblationes et decimas Ecclesiis offerte, luminaria sanctis locis juxta quod habetis exhibete, symbolum et orationem dominicam memoria retinete, et filiis vestris insinuate.—Ad Ecclesiam quoque frequentius convenite, Sanctorum patrocinia humiliter expetite, diem dominicam pro reverentia resurrectionis Christi absque ullo servili opere colite, Sanctorum solemnitates pio affectu celebrate, proximos vestros sicut vos ipsos diligite, etc.—Quod si observaveritis, securi in die judicii ante tribunal aeterni judicis venientes dicetis: Da, Domine, quia dedimus: miserere, quia misericordiam fecimus; nos implevimus quod jussisti, tu redde quod promisisti.

[3] The Arians blamed the Catholic clergy for this. So Gregorius Turon. de Glor. mart. i. 25: Theodegisilus hujus rex regionis, cum vidisset hoc miraculum, quod in his sacratis Deo fontibus gerebatur, cogitavit intra se dicens, quia ingenium est Romanorum (Romanos enim vocitant homines nostrae religionis) ut ita accidat, et non est Dei virtus. C. 26: Est enim populus ille haereticus, qui videns haec magnalia non compungitur ad credendum, sed semper callide divinarum praeceptionum sacramenta nequissimis interpretationum garrulationibus non desinit impugnare. On the contrary, the Catholics related many impostures of miracles wrought by the Arian priests, Gregor. Tur. Hist. ii. 3, de Gloria Confess. c. 13. Comp. the miraculous histories in Löbell, p. 274, and the judgment delivered respecting them, p. 292. The reason why cures performed at the graves of saints should be credible it is impossible to perceive. The presents which those gifted with miraculous power had to expect from pious simplicity induced deception even here.

[4] Gregor. de Glor. mart. i. 26. While a person was filling his vessel with that wonder-working water from a priest, manum alterius extendit ad balteum, cultrumque furatus est.—How holy rites were made instrumental in crime may be seen from the words of the monster Fredegundis, the spouse of Chilperich, to the assassins she had hired to murder king Sigbert (575. See Gesta Regum Franc. c. 32, in Bouquet Rer. Gall. scriptt. t. ii. p. 562): Si evaseritis vivi, ego mirifice honorabo vos et sobolem vestram: si autem corrueritis, ego pro vobis eleemosynas multas per loca Sanctorum distribuam.

[5] Löbell's Gregor. v. Tours, S. 309.

the people, without shame for them being exhibited,[6] while public opinion did not declare against them in a manner conformable to the spirit of Christianity.[7] The moral influence of Christianity on the multitude was confined to the external influence of church laws and church discipline, so far as these were respected. The period of legal restraint, as a preparation for the Gospel, had now returned.

Though every thing heathen was strictly forbidden,[8] yet secret idolatry[9] and apostasy from Christianity[10] frequently appeared. It was still more common for the new Christians to be unable en-

[6] Assassination was an every-day occurrence, and even the clergy were employed as instruments: Gregor. Tur. Hist. Franc. vii. 20, viii. 29. Several Frankish kings lived in polygamy; Chlotar, for instance, with two sisters, Gregor. Tur. iv. 3. Dagobert tres habebat ad instar Salomonis reginas maxime et plurimas concubinas. Fredegarii Chronicon, c. 60. Löbell S. 21.

[7] Thus Gregory Tur. relates, without disguise, the crimes of Chlodowich, and yet he passes this judgment on him, ii. 40: Prosternebat enim quotidie Deus hostes ejus sub manu ipsius, et augebat regnum ejus, eo quod ambularet recto corde coram eo, et faceret, quae placita erant in oculis ejus. Löbell's (p. 263) exculpation of this judgment is of no avail. It is nothing but moral barbarousness, when Gregory admits and disapproves the crimes of Clovis, and yet designates him as pious on account of his confession. Comp. iii. 1: Velim, si placet, parumper conferre, quae Christianis beatam confitentibus Trinitatem prospera successerint, et quae haeriticis eandem scindentibus fuerint in ruinam.—Hanc Chlodovechus Rex confessus, ipsos haereticos adjutorio ejus oppressit, regnumque suum per totas Gallias dilatavit: Alaricus hanc denegans, a regno et populo, atque ab ipsa, quod majus est, vita multatur aeterna. Moral barbarousness is also shown in the sentiments expressed concerning Guntramnus Boso v. 14: Guntchramnus alias sane bonus, nam ad perjuria nimium praeparatus erat. Comp. ix. 10: Fuit in actu levis, avaritiae inhians, rerum alienarum ultra modum cupidus, omnibus jurans, et nulli promissa adimplens. In like manner, concerning king Theudebert, iii. 25: Magnum se atque in omni bonitate praecipuum reddidit. Erat enim regnum cum justitia regens, sacerdotes venerans, Ecclesias munerans, pauperes elevans, et multa multis beneficia pia ac dulcissima accommodans voluntate. Omne tributum, quod in fisco suo ab Ecclesiis in Arverno sitis reddebatur, clementer indulsit. Comp. de vitis Patrum, c. 17, § 2: Nam Theudebertus—(cum) multa inique exerceret, et ab eodem (Nicetio) plerumque corriperetur, quod vel ipse perpetraret, vel perpetrantes non argueret, etc.

[8] Theodorich's prohibition, see § 109, note 4. Childebert I. law, de abolendis idololatriae reliquiis A.D. 554, in Baluzii Capitul. i. 5.

[9] Even as late as the time of Gregory of Tours, an image of Diana was worshiped at Treves. (Greg. Tur. Hist. viii. 15.) In Herbadilla at Nantes, about the same time, were statues of Jupiter, Mercury, Venus, Diana, and Hercules. (Mabillon Acta SS. Ord. S. Bened. i. 683.) In like manner there was found in Luxovium, when Columbanus came thither about 590, imaginum lapidearum densitas, quas cultu miserabili rituque profano vetusta paganorum tempora honorabant (Jonas in vita Columbani, c. 17, in Mabillon Acta SS. Ord. S. Bened. ii. 13). Martinus Ep. Bracarensis (about 570) wrote de origine idolorum (ed. A. Majus Classicorum auctorum, iii. 379), pro castigatione rusticorum, qui adhuc pristina paganorum superstitione detenti, cultum venerationis plus daemoniis quam Deo persolvunt. The Roman names of deities were frequently transferred to Celtic and German deities also; and therefore the peculiar character of this worship can not always be perceived. Beugnot Hist. de la déstruction du Paganisme en Occident. (Paris. 1835) ii. 307.

[10] Conc. Aurelian, ii. ann. 533, can. 20.

tirely to lay aside reverence for their old gods, and the power they were supposed to possess.[11] Thus the remains of old pagan superstition were preserved among the people along with Christianity.[12] In civil legislation, all traces of heathenism were likewise rejected,[13] though the most extended freedom of divorce remained,[14]

[11] Thus said the Arian Agilanes, embassador of the Visigoths, to Gregory of Tours (Hist. Franc. v. 43): Sic vulgato sermone dicimus, non esse noxium, si inter gentilium aras et Dei ecclesiam quis transiens utraque veneretur.

[12] Conc. Turon. ii. ann. 567, c. 22, against the heathen mode of celebrating the Calends of January. Then: Sunt etiam, qui in festivitate cathedrae domni Petri Apostoli cibos mortuis offerunt, et post missas redeuntes ad domos proprias ad gentilium revertuntur errores, et post corpus Domini sacratas daemoni escas accipiunt. Conc. Autissiodorense ann. 578, c. 1: Non licet Kalendis Januarii vetula aut cervolo facere, vel strenas diabolicas observare. C. 4: Non licet ad sortilegos vel ad auguria respicere, non ad caragios, nec ad sortes, quas sanctorum vocant, vel quas de ligno aut de pane faciunt, adspicere. Conc. Narbon. ann. 589, c. 14: against viros ac mulieres divinatores, quos dicunt esse caragios atque sorticularios. C. 15: Ad nos pervenit, quosdam de populis catholicae fidei execrabili ritu diem quintam feriam, quae dicitur Jovis, multos excolere, et operationem non facere. On the celebration of the Kal. Jan. Isidorus Hisp. de Eccles. officiis, i. 40: Tunc miseri homines, et quod pejus est etiam fideles, sumentes species monstruosas in ferarum habitu transformantur; alii foemineo gestu demutati, virilem vultum effoeminant; nonnulli etiam de fanatica adhuc consuetudine, quibusdam ipso die observationem auguriis profanantur: perstrepunt omnia saltantium pedibus, tripudiantium plausibus, et quod his turpius est nefas, nexis inter se utriusque sexus choris, inops animi, furens vino turma miscetur. On belief in auspices and sorcery among the Franks, see Löbell's Gregor v. Tours, S. 271.

[13] On the records of ancient national privileges, the Salic law under Clovis, the Burgundian under King Gundobald, † 516, the Ripuarian under King Theoderich, 511–534, the Alemannic under Chlotar II. in 613–628, the Bavarian under Chlotar II. or Dagobert I 613–638. See Eichhorn's Deutsche Staats und Rechtsgesch. i. 220. Editions of the laws in Baluzii Capitularia Reg. Franc. t. i. J. P. Canciani barbarorum leges antiquae. Venet. 1781–92. 5 tomi fol. Walter Corp. juris Germ. ant. t. i. Cf. prologus Leg. Ripuar. (in many editions incorrectly printed as prol. Leg. Sal.): Theodoricus Rex Francorum, cum esset Cathalaunis, elegit viros sapientes;—ipso autem dictante jussit conscribere legem Francorum Alamannorum et Bojoariorum, et unicuique genti, quae in ejus potestate erat, secundum consuetudinem suam: addiditque addenda, et improvisa et incomposita resecavit; et quae erant secundum consuetudinem Paganorum, mutavit secundum legem Christianorum. Et quidquid Theodoricus Rex propter vetustissimam Paganorum consuetudinem emendare non potuit, posthaec Hildebertus rex inchoavit corrigere; sed Chlotharius rex perfecit. Haec omnia Dagobertus rex—renovavit, et omnia veterum legum in melius transtulit; unicuique quoque genti scriptam tradidit.

[14] By the lex Burgund. tit. 34, c. 3, the husband could put away an adulteram, maleficam, vel sepulcrorum violatricem without ceremony; if he does so without these reasons, he was obliged to make her indemnification (c. 2, 4, and Lex Bajuvar. tit. vii. c. 14). By agreement of both parties, however, marriage could be annulled without any difficulty. See the formulae in the formulis Andegavensibus (from the sixth century prim. ed. Mabillon Analect. iv. 234) c. 56, and Marculfi Formularum, lib. ii. c. 30. The libellus repudii adopted by Marculf runs thus: Certis rebus et probatis causis inter maritum et uxorem repudiandi locus patet. Idcirco dum et inter illo et conjuge sua illa non caritas secundum Deum, sed discordia regnat, et ob hoc pariter conversare minime possunt, placuit utriusque voluntas, ut se a consortio separare deberent. Quod ita et fecerunt. Propterea has epistolas inter se uno tenore conscriptas fieri et adfirmare decreverunt, ut unusquisque ex ipsis, sive ad servitium Dei in monasterio, aut ad copulam matrimonii se sociare voluerit, licentiam habeat, etc.

and *the ordeal*[15] still continued. The attempt of Gregory the Great to adopt into the services of the church particular heathen rites, at the time of the conversion of the Anglo-Saxons, stands quite alone.[16]

III. OLD BRITISH CHURCH.

§ 126.

Since the invasion of the Anglo-Saxons, ecclesiastical as well as social order had been subverted among the Britons, who manfully strove for their freedom.[1] But the Irish Church was still in a very prosperous state. Their convents were distinguished for their discipline and learning,[2] as well as their efforts to diffuse Christianity toward the north. The monk *Columba* in particular (about 565, † 597) converted a great part of the northern *Picts*, became their spiritual leader as abbot of the monastery

[15] Which was used even in questions belonging to Christianity itself. Comp. Can. Caesaraugust. § 121, note 4.—Gregor. Tur. de Glor. mart. i. 81: Arianorum presbyter cum diacono nostrae religionis altercationem habebat. At ille—adjecit dicens: Quid longis sermocinationum intentionibus fatigamur? Factis rei veritas adprobetur: succendatur igni aeneus, et in ferventi aqua annulas cujusdam projiciatur. Qui vero eum ex ferventi unda sustulerit, ille justitiam consequi comprobatur: quo facto pars diversa ad cognitionem hujus justitiae convertatur, etc.

[16] Gregor. M. lib. xi. Ep. 76, ad Mellitum Abbatem (also in Bedae Hist. eccl. Angl. i. 30): Cum vos Deus omnipotens ad—Augustinum Episcopum perduxerit, dicite ei, quid diu mecum de causa Anglorum cogitans tractavi, videlicet, quia fana idolorum destrui in eadem gente minime debeant, sed ipsa, quae in eis sunt, idola destruantur. Aqua benedicta fiat, in eisdem fanis aspergatur, altaria construantur, reliquiae ponantur: quia si fana eadem bene constructa sunt, necesse est ut a cultu daemonum in obsequium veri Dei debeant commutari: ut, dum gens ipsa eadem fana non videt destrui, de corde errorem deponat, et Deum verum cognescens ac adorans, ad loca, quae consuevit, familiarius concurrat. Et quia boves solent in sacrificio daemonum multos occidere, debet his etiam hac de re aliqua solemnitas immutari: ut die dedicationis vel natalitiis SS. Martyrum, quorum illic reliquiae ponuntur, tabernacula sibi circa easdem ecclesias, quae ex fanis commutatae sunt, de ramis arborum faciant et religiosis conviviis solemnitatem celebrent. Nec diabolo jam animalia immolent, sed ad laudem Dei in esum suum animalia occidant, et donatori omnium de satietate sua gratias referant: ut, dum eis aliqua exterius gaudia reservantur, ad interiora gaudia consentire facilius valeant. Nam duris mentibus simul omnia abscidere impossibile esse non dubium est: quia is, qui locum summum adscendere nititur, necesse est ut gradibus vel passibus, non autem saltibus elevetur.

[1] Gildas Badonicus (560–580) de Excidio Britanniae liber querulus (in three parts historia; epistola; increpatio in clerum), best edited in Thom. Gale Historia Britannicae, Saxon. Anglo-Danicae scriptores, xv. Oxon. 1691, thence in Gallandii Bibl. PP. xii. 189.

[2] Jo. Ph. Murray de Britannia atque Hibernia saeculis a sexto inde ad decimum litterarum domicilio, in the Novis commentariis Soc. Reg. Gotting. t. i. comm. hist. et philol. p. 72, ss.

founded by him on the island *Hy* (*St. Iona*), and transmitted this relation to his successors.[3]

Close as the union was between the British and Irish Churches, they could yet have little connection of importance, on account of their remoteness, with other Churches. Hence they had retained many old arrangements, and developed them in a peculiar way, after such usages had been altered in other countries.[4]

[3] Beda Hist. eccl. iii. 4: Habere autem solet ipsa insula rectorem semper Abbatem Presbyterum, cujus juri et omnis provincia, et ipsi etiam Episcopi, ordine inusitato, debeant, esse subjecti, juxta exemplum primi doctoris illius, qui non Episcopus, sed Presbyter exstitit et Monachus.

[4] These appear in the following controversy, and relate to (*a*) the reckoning of Easter. The Britons were by no means Quartodecimani, though they were often called so from ignorance (ex. gr. Bedae Chron. ad. ann. 4591), and appealed too, themselves, to John and the Asiatics (for example, Colman, Beda, H. E. iii. 25). Beda Hist. eccl. iii. 4: Paschae diem non semper in luna quartadecima cum Judaeis, ut quidam rebantur, sed in die quidem dominica, alia tamen quam decebat hebdomada, celebrabant. Namely, ii. 2: Paschae diem a decimaquarta usque ad vicesimam lunam observabant. Quae computatio octoginta quatuor annorum circulo continetur. The Romans on the other hand (ii. 19), adstruebant, quia dominicum Paschae diem a quintadecima luna usque ad vicesimam primam lunam oporteret inquiri. The difference therefore, was, that the Easter festival fell on different Sundays in several years. The cause of this was, that owing to the previous confusion on the subject, and for the purpose of removing it (see above, § 100, note 13), the Aquitanian Victorius first (457), and afterward the Roman abbott, Dionysius Exiguus (525), had made new Easter tables, which, in succession, were brought into use, first in Italy, and then in the other western churches (see Ideler's Chronologie, ii. 275). On the contrary, the British church had retained the old cycle of 84 years. The state of the controversy is more minutely developed by Jac. Usserius Britannicarum Ecclesiarum antiquitt. Dublin. 1639. 4. p. 925. Humphr. Prideaux Connection of Scripture History, ii. 273. Ideler's Chronol. ii. 295. (*b*) The tonsure. The Roman clergy were in coronam attonsi; the British, as also the monks elsewhere, in older times, see Paulini Nol. Ep. vii., had the fore part of the head bald. The former called their tonsure tonsuram Petri, and that of the Britons tonsuram Simonis Magi (Beda H. E. v. 21). Usserii Brit. Eccl. antiqu. p. 921. (*c*) Lanfrancus Episc. ad Terdelvacum Hibern. regem, written 1074 (in J. Usserii Vett. epistolarum hibernicarum syll. Dublin. 1632. 4. p. 72), accuses them, quod quisque pro arbitrio suo legitime sibi copulatam uxorem, nulla canonica causa interveniente, relinquit, et aliam quamlibet, seu sibi vel relictae uxori consanguinitate propinquam, sive quam alius simili improbitate deseruit, maritali seu fornicaria lege, punienda sibi temeritate conjungit. Quod Episcopi ab uno Episcopo consecrantur. Quod infantes baptismo sine chrismate consecrata baptizantur. Quod sacri ordines per pecuniam ab Episcopis dantur. But from these the abuses 1 and 4, which afterward prevailed, may have sprung. We have also to direct attention to the following peculiarities of the British-Irish church, which are not touched on in the disputes. They had (*a*) no celibacy of the priests. Patrick himself was sprung from priests, see Patricii confessio: Patrem habui Calpurnium Diaconum, filium quondam Potiti Presbyteri. Synodus Patricii about 456, can. 6 (in D. Wilkins Concilia Magnae Brittanniae et Hiberniae, i. 2): Quicunque clericus ab ostiario usque ad sacerdotem—si non more romano capilli ejus tonsi sint (i. e., cut short generally, the differences of tonsure arose subsequently), et uxor ejus si non velato capite ambulaverit, pariter a laicis contemnantur, et ab Ecclesia separentur. Synodus Hibern. in d'Achery Spicilegium, i. 493: Qui ab accessu adolescentiae usque ad trigesimum annum aetatis suae probabiliter vixerit, una tantum uxore virgine sumta contentus, quinque annis Subdiaconus, et quinque annis Diaconus, quadragesimo anno Presbyter, quinquagesimo Epis-

Since the condemnation of the Three Chapters, a great mistrust of the Romish orthodoxy had arisen here also.[5]

When *Augustine* formed a new Church with Roman arrangements among the Anglo-Saxons, he required the British clergy (Culdees)[6] to adopt the Roman ecclesiastical arrangements, especially with regard to the mode of reckoning Easter; and to yield to him, as archbishop of Canterbury, the primacy of all Britain.[7] But the negotiations at two meetings[8] (603) led to

copus stet. The Irish Clement defended the marriage of a bishop as late as the eighth century. Bonifacii Ep. 67. (*b*) A peculiar liturgy. Usser. Brit. Eccles. Antiqu. p. 916. (*c*) The monks had a peculiar system of rules. Usser. p. 918.—That the British-Irish Church derived its origin from Asia Minor, and had preserved a purer, simpler Christianity, are mere empty conjectures, which have been carried to an extravagant length, especially by Münter in the Theol. Studien u. Krit. 1833, iii. 744. The opinion that the Britons, as Quartodecimani, had the Asiatic mode of celebrating the passover, an opinion which principally lies at the foundation of that belief, is obviously false.

[5] Comp. § 111, note 25; § 117, note 25; § 124, note 19. Gregorii Magni Ep. ad Episcopos Hiberniae, A.D. 592 (lib. ii. Ep. 36): Reducat caritatem vestram tandem integritas fidei ad matrem, quae vos generavit, Ecclesiam.—Nam in Synodo, in qua de tribus capitulis actum est, aperto liquet nihil de fide convulsum esse vel aliquatenus immutatum, sed (sicut scitis) de quibusdam illic solummodo personis est actitatum.—Quod autem scribitis, quia ex illo tempore inter alias provincias maxime flagellatur Italia, non hoc ad ejus debetis intorquere exprobrium, quoniam scriptum est: quem diligit Dominus castigat.—Ut igitur de tribus capitulis animis vestris ablata dubietate possit satisfactio abundanter infundi, librum, quem ex hac re sanctae memoriae decessor meus Pelagius Papa scripserat, vobis utile judicavi transmittere. Quem si deposito voluntariae defensionis studio, puro vigilantique corde saepius volueritis relegere, eum vos per omnia secuturos, et ad unitatem nostram reversuros nihilominus esse confido. However, at a later period, Columbanus defended, with zeal, the three chapters against Boniface IV. See below, note 13.

[6] Keledei, Kyledei, Latinized Colidei, the British appellation for priests and monks (Kele-De, i. e., servus Dei, as elsewhere too, for example, in Gregory the Great, the clergy are often called servi Dei). When the Roman regulations were subsequently adopted generally in these lands, the name continued to be applied principally to the clergy, who in their corporations held fast by the old British modes. It was, however, given also to all priests to the time of the Reformation, by those who spoke in British. See Hector Boëthius Hist. Scotorum, lib. vi. p. 95: Invaluit id nomen apud vulgus in tantum, ut sacerdotes omnes ad nostra paene tempora vulgo Culdei, i. e., cultores Dei, sine discrimine vocitarentur. Comp. historical account of the ancient Culdees of Iona, and of their settlements in Scotland, England, and Ireland, by John Jamieson. Edinburgh. 1811. 4. J. W. J. Braun de Culdeis comm. Bonnae. 1840. 4.

[7] Gregory the Great had conferred this on him (lib. xi. Ep. 65. Beda H. E. i. 29: Tua vero fraternitas—omnes Britanniae sacerdotes habeat—subjectos. He derived the right of doing so from this fact, that he held the British church, as well as the Anglo-Saxon, to be a daughter of the Roman (see note 5).

[8] Respecting them, see Beda H. E. ii. 2. The Britons had not only a different mode of celebrating the Easter festival, set et alia plurima unitati ecclesiasticae contraria faciebant. Qui cum, longa disputatione habita, neque precibus, neque hortamentis, neque increpationibus Augustini ac sociorum ejus assensum praebere voluissent, sed suas potius traditiones universis, quae per orbem sibi in Christo concordant, ecclesiis praeferrent, sanctus pater Augustinus—finem fecit. At the second meeting Augustine said to them: Quia in multis quidem nostrae consuetudini, imo universalis Ecclesia, contraria geritis; et tamen si in tribus his mihi, obtemperare vultis, ut Pascha suo tempore celebretis, ut

no agreement; they gave rise rather to bitter hatred between the two parties.[9]

At this time the Irish monk *Columbanus* came into the kingdom of Burgundy (about 590), where he acquired great reputation by his strict piety and cultivated mind, and founded several convents, particularly that at *Luxovium* (Luxeuil). Here he not only introduced a peculiar system of monastic rules, but also continued faithful to the peculiarities of his mother Church, and defended the Irish mode of celebrating Easter with great zeal.[10] At length he displeased King Theodorich II., on account of his boldness; was banished (about 606); labored some years in the conversion of the Alemanni at the lake of Constance; then transferred this task to his pupil *Gallus;* founded the con-

ministerium baptizandi—juxta morem sanctae Romanae et apostolicae Ecclesiae compleatis, ut genti Anglorum una nobiscum verbum Domini praedicetis; caetera quae agitis, quamvis moribus nostris contraria, aequanimiter cuncta tolerabimus. At illi nil horum se facturos, neque illum pro Archiepiscopo habituros esse respondebant. The papal primacy was not at all a subject of dispute. The first rank among the bishops was conceded to the popes by the Britons, but they believed so in an erroneous way (see note 5). But the popes themselves did not yet lay claim to a greater ecclesiastical power than that of other apostolic sees (see § 117, notes 18-20); and so one appealed against the Britons, not to papal authority, but to the statuta canonica quaternae sedis Apostolicae, Romanae videlicet, Hierosolymitanae, Antiochenae, Alexandrinae, to the old councils, and to the universalis Ecclesiae catholicae unanimem regulam (see Cummiani Ep. ad Segienum Huensem Abbatem, in J. Usserii Vett. epistt. hibernicarum sylloge, p. 27, 28). The Britons did not consider the pope as the sole successor of Peter, but all bishops. Gildas de excidio Britanniae, P. iii. cap. 1, describes bad priests as sedem Petri Apostoli immundis pedibus usurpantes (comp. § 94, note 36). That the Britons acknowledged no ecclesiastical power of the pope over them, is proved by their opposition to the Roman regulations, an opposition which continued in Ireland down to the twelfth century. Spelman (Conc. Brit. i. 108) has published for the first time, from a Cottonian MS. in the old British language, the following declaration of Dinooth, abbot of the monastery of Bangor, which he is said to have made to Augustine: Notum sit et absque dubitatione vobis, quod nos omnes sumus et quilibet nostrum obedientes et subditi ecclesiae Dei, et Papae Romae, et unicuique vero Christiano et pio, ad amandum unumquemque in suo gradu in caritate perfecta, et ad juvandum unumquemque eorum verbo et facto fore filios Dei. Et aliam obedientiam, quam istam, non scio debitam ei, quem vos nominatis esse Papam; nec esse patrem patrum vindicari et postulari: et istam obedientiam nos sumus parati dare et solvere ei et cuique Christiano continuo. Praeterea nos sumus sub gubernatione episcopi Caerlionis super Osca, qui est ad supervidendum sub Deo super nobis, ad faciendum nos servare viam spiritualem. It is however spurious. See Döllinger's Gesch. d. christl. Kirche, i. ii. 218. Stevenson on Bedae H. E. ii. 2, p. 102.

[9] Thus Augustine's successor, Laurentius (Beda, ii. 4), complained that the Scottish bishop, Dagamus, ad nos veniens, non solum cibum nobiscum, sed nec in eodem hospitio, quo vescebamur, sumere voluit. Comp. Beda, ii. 20: Usque hodie moris est Brittonum, fidem religionemque Anglorum pro nihilo habere, neque in aliquo eis magis communicare quam paganis.

[10] Columbani Epist. i. ad Gregor. Papum (among Gregory's letters, lib. ix. Ep. 127), and Epist. ii. ad Patres Synodi cujusd. Gallicanae.

vent *Bobium* in a valley in the Apennines in Liguria, where he inspired the same desire for learning for which the monks of his country were chiefly distinguished.[11] He died A.D. 615.[12] His letter to Gregory the Great on the subject of the celebration of Easter, as well as that to Boniface IV. against the condemnation of the three chapters, still attest the free spirit of the Irish Church.[13]

[11] Cf. Antiquissimus quatuor Evangeliorum Codex Sangallensis, ed. H. C. M. Rettig. Turici. 1836. 4. praef. Hence the important discoveries of modern times in the Codd. Bobiensibus, at present very much scattered. See Amad. Peyron de bibliotheca Bobiensi comm. prefixed to his Ciceronis orationem fragmenta inedita. Stuttg. et Tubing. 1824. 4.

[12] His life by his pupil Jonas, abbot of Luxovium, in Mabillon Acta Sanct. Ord. Bened. ii. 3. Neander's Denkwürdigk. iii. ii. 37, ff. Gu. Chr. Knottenbelt Disp. hist. theol. de Columbano. Lugd. Bat. 1839. 8.—His works (regula coenobialis, sermones xvi., epistolae vi., carmina iv.), ed. Patricius Flemingus. Lovanii. 1667, recensita et aucta in Gallandii Bibl. PP. xii. 319.

[13] Ep. ad Gregor.: Forte notam subire timens Hermagoricae novitatis, antecessorum et maxime Papae Leonis auctoritate contentus es. Noli te quaeso in tali quaestione humilitati tantum aut gravitati credere, quae saepe falluntur. Melior forte est canis vivus in problemate Leone mortuo (Eccl. ix. 4). Vivus namque sanctus emendare potest, quae ab altero majore emendata non fuerint.—non mihi satisfacit post tantos, quos legi auctores, una istorum sententia Episcoporum dicentium tantum: "Cum Judaeis Pascha facere non debemus." Dixit hoc olim et Victor Episcopus, sed nemo Orientalium suum recepit commentum. Epist. 5, ad Bonifacium, iv. cap. 4: Vigila itaque quaeso, Papa, vigila, et iterum dico, vigila: quia forte non bene vigilavit Vigilius, quem caput scandali isti clamant, qui vobis culpam injiciunt. C. 10: Ex eo tempore, quo Deus et Dei filius esse dignatus est, ac in duobus illis ferventissimis Dei Spiritus equis, Petro scilicet et Paulo Apostolis—per mare gentium equitans, turbavit aquas multas, et innumerabilium populorum millibus multiplicavit quadrigas; supremus ipse auriga currus illius, qui est Christus,—ad nos usque pervenit. Ex tunc vos magni estis et clari, et Roma ipsa nobilior et clarior est; et, si dici potest, propter Christi geminos Apostolos—vos prope caelestes estis, et Roma orbis terrarum caput est ecclasiarum, salva loci dominicae resurrectionis singulari praerogativa (comp. Firmilianus, Div. I. § 68, note 12. Augustinus, § 94, note 5). Et ideo sicut magnus honor vester est pro dignitate cathedrae, ita magna cura vobis necessaria est, ut non perdatis vestram dignitatem propter aliquam perversitatem. Tamdiu enim potestas apud vos erit, quamdiu recta ratio permanserit: ille enim certus regni caelorum clavicularius est, qui dignis per veram scientiam aperit, et indignis claudit. Alioquin, si contraria fecerit, nec aperire nec claudere poterit. C. 11: Cum haec igitur vera sint, et sine ulla contradictione ab omnibus vera sapientibus recepta sint (licet omnibus notum est, et nemo est qui nesciat, qualiter Salvator noster sancto Petro regni caelorum contulit claves, et vos per hoc forte superciliosum nescio quid, prae caeteris vobis majoris auctoritatis, ac in divinis rebus potestatis vindicatis); noveritis minorem fore potestatem vestram apud Dominum, si vel cogitatis hoc in cordibus vestris: quia unitas fidei in toto orbe unitatem fecit potestatis et praerogativae; ita ut libertas veritati ubique ab omnibus detur, et aditus errori ab omnibus similiter abnegetur, etc.

THIRD DIVISION.

FROM THE BEGINNING OF THE MONOTHELITIC CONTROVERSY, AND FROM THE TIME OF MUHAMMED TO THE BEGINNING OF THE CONTROVERSY CONCERNING THE WORSHIP OF IMAGES. FROM 622–726.

FIRST CHAPTER.

RESTRAINING OF THE CHURCH IN THE EAST.

§ 127.

Though the Persians tolerated the Nestorians, they hated the Catholic Christians, as was apparent in the war which *Kesra* (Chosröes) *II. Purveez* carried on against the East Roman empire from A.D. 604, and especially in the taking of Jerusalem (614). On this account the victories of *Heraclius* from 621, ending with the dethronement of Chosröes by his son *Schirujeh* (Siröes) (628) were of importance in relation to the Church. Besides, Heraclius brought back the wood of the true cross which had been carried off; and instituted a festival in commemoration of it, the *σταυρώσιμος ἡμέρα*, festum exaltationis (14th of September).[1]

In the mean time, a far more dangerous enemy of the Church had appeared in Arabia. *Muhammed*, in the year 611, began to preach Islamism, at first in private, and then publicly among the Koreish in Mecca. At first, indeed, he was obliged to give way to his enemies (15th July, 622, *Hegira*),[2] but gained over the city *Yatschreb* (Medina al Nabi) in his favor; extended his dominion and his doctrines thence, prince and prophet in one person, till they spread far into Arabia; at length conquered Mecca (630); consecrated the *Caaba* as the chief temple of Islamism; and bequeathed to his successors (*Chalifs*) Arabia,

[1] Theophanis Chronographia p. 245–273, among other things says, of the conduct of Chosröes in the conquered lands, p. 263: *'Ηνάγκαζε τοὺς Χριστιανοὺς γενέσθαι εἰς τὴν τοῦ Νεστορίου θρησκείαν πρὸς τὸ πλῆξαι τὸν βασιλέα.*

[2] Ideler's Chronologie, Bd. 2, S. 482, ff.

as a country completely subject to their faith and their dominion († 632).[3]

Islamism, whose holy writings are contained in the *Koran*,[4] collected by Abu-Bekr, was, in its chief doctrines, a compound of Judaism and Christianity.[5] But it made the doctrine of the infinite sublimity of God its basis, in a way so one-sided that *an absolute dependence* of man on God resulted from it; and ideas of a likeness and an inward union between man and God, and consequently the fundamental principles of all the higher morality, found no place in the system. By making it a religious duty to wage war on unbelievers, by its fatalism, and its sensual promises, it excited among the rude and powerful people of the Arabs so unconquerable a spirit for war, and so wild a desire for conquest,[6] that the two neighboring kingdoms, the Persian and the Byzantine, could not withstand such resistance, amid their internal weaknesses. The provinces of the Byzantine empire, which lay nearest, were the more easily conquered, inasmuch as the greater number of the inhabitants consisted of Monophysites who joyfully met the Arabians as their deliverers. The conquest of *Syria* was begun under the first Chaliph *Abu-Bekr* († 634), and completed under the second, *Omar* (639), under whom the valiant Amru also overcame Egypt (640). Under *Othman* the Persian empire was conquered (651). Dur-

[3] Abulfeda de vita Muhammedis ed. J. Gagnier. Oxon. 1723. fol. La vie de Mohammed par J. Gagnier. Amsterd. 1732. 2 voll. 8, translated into German by Ch. F. R. Vetterlein. Köthen 1802–1804. v. Hammer-Purgstall's Gemäldesaal der Lebensbeschreibungen grosser moslimischer Herrscher. Bd. 1. Mohammed d. Prophet. Leipzig. 1837. (Comp. Umbreit in the Theol. Studien u. Krit. 1841. i. 212). Gust. Weil's Mohammed d. Prophet, s. Leben u. s. Lehre, aus handschriftl. Quellen u. d. Koran geschöpft. Stuttgart. 1843. 8.—On the miracles of Muhammed and his character, see in Tholuck's vermischten Schriften i. 1.

[4] Arab. et lat. ed. Lud. Maraccius. Patav. 1698. fol. French par Savary, Paris. 1783. 2 voll. 8. German by F. E. Boysen, Halle. 1775. 8, by F. S. G. Wahl, Halle. 1828. 8, literally translated with annotations by Dr. L. Ullmann. Bielefeld u. Crefeld, 3te Aufl. 1844. 8. G. Weil's hist. krit. Einleit. in den Koran. Bielefeld. 1844. 8. [English by G. Sale].

[5] Weil's Mohammed, see note 3. Muhammed's Religion nach ihrer innern Entwickelung und ihrem Einflusse auf das Leben der Völker, von. I. I. I. Döllinger. Regensburg. 1838. 4. Dettinger's Beiträge zu einer Theologie des Korans, in the Tübingen Zeitschr. f. Theol. 1831. iii. 1.—Was hat Mohammed aus dem Judenthume angenommen? von Abr. Geiger. Bonn. 1833. 8.—Maier's christl. Bestandtheile des Koran, in the Freiburger Zeitschr. f. Theol. Bd. 2. Heft. 1. S. 34 (1839). C. F. Gerock's Darstellung der Christologie des Koran. Hamburg und Gotha. 1839. 8.—On the relation of Islamism to the gospel, in Möhler's Schriften u. Aufsätzen, herausgeg. v. Döllinger, i. 348.

[6] See a representation of the influence of his faith on the middle ages by K. E. Oelsner. Frankf. a. M. 1810. 8. Muhammed's religion by Döllinger, see note 5.

ing the reign of the *Ommeyades*, their general *Musa*, brought first the entire northern coast of Africa (707), and then Spain also (711), under the Arabian dominion; while, on the other side, the Arabians advanced several times as far as Constantinople, and twice besieged the city for a long time (669 till 676, and 717 till 718).

Jews and Christians were tolerated by the Arabs on condition of paying a poll-tax; and though sometimes severely oppressed, yet they were not compelled to change their religion.[7] Still, however, the advantages held out to those who adopted Islamism attracted many converts; and thus Christianity not only lost all political importance in the conquered provinces, but the number of its confessors was always diminishing in proportion to that of the Moslems. The catholic patriarchates of Antioch, Jerusalem, and Alexandria, remained unoccupied; for their possessors, living in the Greek empire, were merely titulars.

[7] Muhammed was tolerant at first of other religions (cf. Sura, ii. et v.): afterward, however, he made it the duty of believers, by the 9th and 67th Surats, to carry on religious war, for the purpose of exterminating idolaters and making Jews and Christians tributary (comp. Gerock's Christologie des Koran, S. 118). Before this he had granted the Christians of some parts of Arabia, as well as the Jews and Sabaeans, letters of freedom, though doubtless both the Testamentum et pactiones initae inter Mohammedem et christianae fidei cultores (first brought from the East by the Capuchin Pacificus Scaliger, and printed at Paris 1630, 4to, and often afterward), and the Pactum Muhammedis, quod indulsit Monachis montis Sinai et Christianis in universum (in Pococke Descr. of the East, Lond. 1743. fol. i. 268, translated into German, 2d edition, Erlangen. 1771. 4. i. 393), in which distinguished privileges are secured to all Christians, are spurious. The humiliating terms under which Omar, at the taking of Jerusalem, 637, allowed freedom of religion to the Christians there (Le Beau Hist. du Bas-Empire, xii. 421), express, on the contrary, the spirit with which the subjugated Christians were treated at a later time. Cf. Th. Chr. Tychsen comm. qua disquiritur, quatenus Muhammedes aliarum religionum sectatores toleraverit, in the Commentationes Soc. Reg. Gotting. xv. 152.

SECOND CHAPTER.

HISTORY OF THE GREEK CHURCH.

§ 128.

MONOTHELITIC CONTROVERSY.

Original Documents in the Acts of the first Lateran Synod, A.D. 649 (ap. Mansi, x. 863), and the sixth General Council, A.D. 680 (ap. Mansi, xi. 190). Anastasii Bibliothecarii (about 870) collectanea de iis quae spectant ad Histor. Monothelit. (prim. ed. J. Sirmond. Paris. 1620. 8, in Sirm. Opp. t. iii. in Bibl. PP. Lugdun. xii. 833, ap. Gallandius, t. xiii. and scattered in Mansi, t. x. and xi.)

Historical authorities: Theophanes (comp. the preface to section 2).

Works: F. Combefisii Hist. haeresis Monothelitarum ac Vindiciae actorum sextae synodi, in his Nov. auctarium Patrum. ii. 3 (Paris. 1648). Walch's Ketzerhist. ix. 3. Neander's K. G. iii. 353.

A fresh attempt to bring the Monophysites back to the Catholic Church was followed by no other consequence than that of introducing into the latter a new element of controversy. When the Emperor *Heraclius* (A.D. 611–641) during his Persian campaign abode in Armenia and Syria (from 622), he thought he perceived that the Monophysites were particularly stumbled at the consequence arising from the catholic doctrine, viz., *two manifestations of will* (*ἐνέργειαι*) in the person of Christ. *Sergius*, patriarch of Constantinople, having been applied to on the point, declared that the adoption of *one active will*, and *one manifestation of will*, was not inconsistent with the received creed of the Church; and therefore the emperor, as well as several bishops, decided in favor of this opinion.[1] But when one of these bishops, *Cyrus*, whom the emperor had appointed patriarch of Alexandria, reunited (633)[2] the Severians

[1] Cyri Episc. Phasidis Epist. ad Sergium (ap. Mansi, xi. 561), mentions *κέλευσις* of Heraclius to Arcadius, archb. of Cyprus, *δύο ἐνεργείας ἐπὶ τοῦ δεσπότου ἡμῶν* 'I. X. *μετὰ τὴν ἕνωσιν λέγεσθαι κωλύουσα*. Sergius ad Cyprum (ibid. p. 525), rests on the authority of Cyril of Alexandria, who speaks of *μίαν ζωοποιὸν ἐνέργειαν*, and on Mennas' letter to Virgilius, which says, *ἓν τὸ τοῦ Χριστοῦ θέλημα καὶ μίαν ζωοποιὸν ἐνέργειαν*, though he is willing to be instructed by stronger reasons in favor of the contrary opinion. More decidedly Theodorus Episc. Pharan. (Fragments, ibid. p. 567, ss.), *εἶναι μίαν ἐνέργειαν· ταύτης δὲ τεχνίτην καὶ δημιουργὸν τὸν θεὸν, ὄργανον δὲ τὴν ἀνθρωπότητα.*

[2] Cyri Epist. altera ad Sergium (ap. Mansi, xi. 561), with the nine articles of agreement appended, p. 563. In the seventh we read: *Τὸν αὐτὸν ἕνα Χριστὸν καὶ υἱὸν ἐνεργοῦντα τὰ θεοπρεπῆ καὶ ἀνθρώπινα μιᾷ θεανδρικῇ ἐνεργείᾳ, κατὰ τὸν ἐν ἁγίοις Διονύσιον* (Dionys. Areopag. Epist. iv. ad Cajum. Comp. § 110, note 8. The orthodox read *καινῇ θεανδρικῇ ἐνεργείᾳ*).

of that place with the Catholic Church by articles of agreement, in which that doctrine of one will was expressed; *Sophronius*, a Palestinian monk, who happened to be there at the time, raised the first opposition to this doctrine, which he afterward continued with zeal after he became patriarch of Jerusalem (634).[3] Sergius now advised that nothing should be said on the disputed point.[4] Pope Honorius agreed with him, not only in this advice, but in the doctrinal view of the matter.[5] Sophronius was quieted by the incursions of the Arabs; but the spark which had fallen on spirits so susceptible of dogmatic speculation could not be extinguished. In vain did the emperor now issue the Ἔκθεσις (638),[6] composed by Sergius for the purpose of putting down the controversy. The west, too, now rose up against the new doctrine. The monk *Maximus*,[7] a

[3] Sophronii Synodica ap. Mansi, xi. 461.—His other extant writings (saints' lives, discourses, etc.), to which many have been added in the Spicilegium Romanum t. iii. and iv. (1840) do not refer to Monothelitism.

[4] Sergii Ep. ad Honorium (ap. Mansi, xi. 529), contains the most credible account of the beginning of the controversy. He assures Cyrus that his advice was, *μηκέτι τοῦ λοιποῦ τινι συγχωρεῖν, μίαν ἢ δύο προφέρειν ἐνεργείας ἐπὶ* Χριστοῦ *τοῦ θεοῦ ἡμῶν· ἀλλὰ μᾶλλον, καθάπερ αἱ ἅγιαι καὶ οἰκουμενικαὶ παραδεδώκασι σύνοδοι. ἕνα καὶ τὸν αὐτὸν υἱὸν μονογενῆ τὸν κύριον ἡμῶν* Ἰ. Χ. *τὸν ἀληθινὸν θεὸν ἐνεργεῖν ὁμολογεῖν τά τε θεῖα καὶ ἀνθρώπινα, καὶ πᾶσαν θεοπρεπῆ καὶ ἀνθρωποπρεπῆ ἐνέργειαν ἐξ ἑνὸς καὶ τοῦ αὐτοῦ σεσαρκωμένου θεοῦ λόγου ἀδιαιρέτως προϊέναι, καὶ εἰς ἕνα καὶ τὸν αὐτὸν ἀναφέρεθαι· διὰ τὸ τὴν μὲν μιᾶς ἐνεργείας φωνὴν—θορυβεῖν τὰς τινῶν ἀκοὰς, ὑπολαμβανόντων, ἐπ' ἀναιρέσει ταύτην προφέρεσθαι τῶν ἐν* Χριστῷ*—ἡνωμένων δύο φύσεων.—ὡσαύτως δὲ καὶ τὴν τῶν δύο ἐνεργειῶν ῥῆσιν πολλοὺς σκανδαλίζειν·—ἕπεσθαι ταύτῃ τὸ καὶ δύο πρεσβεύειν θελήματα ἐναντίως πρὸς ἄλληλα ἔχοντα,—δύο τοὺς τἀναντία θέλοντας εἰσάγεσθαι, ὅπερ δυσσεβές.*

[5] Honorii Ep. i. ad Serg. (ap. Mansi, xi. 537). Extracts from the Ep. ii. ad eund., ib. p. 579.

[6] Ap. Mansi, x. 992: Ὅθεν *ἕνα ἴσμεν υἱὸν τὸν κύριον ἡμῶν* Ἰ. Χ.*—καὶ ἑνὸς καὶ τοῦ αὐτοῦ τάτε θαύματα καὶ τὰ πάθη κηρύττομεν, καὶ πᾶσαν θεῖαν καὶ ἀνθρωπίνην ἐνέργειαν ἑνὶ καὶ τῷ αὐτῷ σεσαρκωμένῳ τῷ λόγῳ προσνέμομεν,—οὐδαμῶς συγχωροῦντες τινὶ τῶν πάντων μίαν ἢ δύο λέγειν ἢ διδάσκειν ἐνεργείας ἐπὶ τῆς θείας τοῦ κυρίου ἐνανθρωπήσεως, ἀλλὰ μᾶλλον, καθάπερ αἱ ἅγιαι καὶ οἰκουμενικαὶ παραδεδώκασι σύνοδοι.* What follows is word for word the same as the passage from Sergii Ep. ad Honor., given in note 4. But he continues, *εἰ γὰρ ὁ μιαρὸς* Νεστόριος *καίπερ διαιρῶν τὴν θεῖαν τοῦ κυρίου ἐνανθρώπησιν, καὶ δύο εἰσάγων υἱοὺς, δύο θελήματα τούτων εἰπεῖν οὐκ ἐτόλμησε, τοὐναντίον δέ ταυτοβουλίαν τῶν ἐπ' αὐτοῦ ἀναπλαττομένων δύο προσώπων ἐδόξασε, πῶς δυνατὸν, τοὺς τὴν ὀρθὴν ὁμολογοῦντας πίστιν, καὶ ἕνα υἱὸν τὸν κύριον ἡμῶν* Ἰ. Χ. *τὸν ἀληθινὸν θεὸν δοξάζοντας δύο καὶ ταῦτα ἐναντία θελήματα ἐπ' αὐτοῦ παραδέχεσθαι; ὅθεν τοῖς ἁγίοις πατράσιν ἐν ἅπασι καὶ ἐν τούτῳ κατακολουθοῦντες, ἓν θέλημα τοῦ κυρίου ἡμῶν* Ἰ. Χ.*—ὁμολογοῦμεν, ὡς ἐν μηδενὶ καιρῷ τῆς νοερῶς ἐψυχωμένης αὐτοῦ σαρκὸς κεχωρισμένως καὶ ἐξ οἰκείας ὁρμῆς, ἐναντίως τῷ νεύματι τοῦ ἡνωμένου αὐτῇ καθ' ὑπόστασιν θεοῦ λόγου, τὴν φυσικὴν αὐτῆς ποιήσασθαι κίνησιν, ἀλλ' ὁπότε καὶ οἵαν καὶ ὅσην αὐτὸς ὁ θεὸς λόγος ἠβούλετο.*

[7] Who is also worthy of notice as a commentator on Pseudo-Dionysius the Areopagite. See Neander's K. G. iii. 344. Ritter's Gesch. d. christl. Phil. ii. 535. His works, for the most part against the Monothelites, were edited by Franc. Combefisius. Paris. 1675. 2

former companion of Sophronius, roused up Africa against it; Pope *John IV.* refused to adopt the *Ecthesis*;[8] and Pope *Theodore* excommunicated *Paul*, patriarch of Constantinople (646). Equally unsuccessful was the attempt of *Constans II.* (A. D. 642–668) to restore internal tranquillity by means of the edict called Τύπος (648),[9] which merely recommended silence on the point, without giving a preference to either view; although that tranquillity was most desirable in the kingdom so severely oppressed from without.[10] Pope *Martin I.* at *the first Lateran synod* (649),[11] even ventured to anathematize the doctrine of one will, and the two imperial decrees relating to it. *Martin I.* indeed was now deposed, and, together with Maximus, brought to Constantinople (653), where both were condemned to end their life in exile after much severe treatment.[12] This had the effect of restoring communion between Rome and Constantinople,

voll. fol. Prefixed to the first volume is the Greek life of Maximus, important in the history of the Monothelites. The doctrines of the Duothelites and Monothelites are most clearly represented in contrast, in Maximi Disp. cum Pyrrho, Opp. ii. 159.

[8] Johannis Ep. ad Constantinum Imp. in Anastasii Collectan. ap. Mansi, x. 682.

[9] Ap. Mansi, x. 1029.—"Εγνωμεν ἐν πολλῷ καθεστάναι σάλῳ τὸν ἡμέτερον ὀρθόδοξον λαὸν, ὡς τινῶν μὲν ἓν θέλημα ἐπὶ τῆς οἰκονομίας τοῦ μεγάλου θεοῦ καὶ σωτῆρος ἡμῶν Ἰησοῦ δοξαζόντων, καὶ τὸν αὐτὸν ἐνεργεῖν τάτε θεῖα καὶ τὰ ἀνθρώπινα· ἄλλων δὲ δογματιζόντων δύο θελήματα καὶ ἐνεργείας δύο ἐπὶ τῆς αὐτῆς ἐνσάρκου τοῦ λόγου οἰκονομίας· καὶ τῶν μὲν ἐν ἀπολογίᾳ προτιθεμένων διὰ τὸ ἓν πρόσωπον ὑπάρχειν τὸν κύριον ἡμῶν Ἰ. Χ. ἐν δύο ταῖς φύσεσιν ἀσυγχύτως καὶ ἀδιαιρέτως θέλοντα καὶ ἐνεργοῦντα τάτε θεῖα καὶ τὰ ἀνθρώπινα· τῶν δὲ διὰ τὰς ἀδιαιρέτως ἐν τῷ αὐτῷ καὶ ἑνὶ προσώπῳ συνελθούσας φύσεις, καὶ τοῦ τὴν αὐτῶν σώζεσθαι καὶ μένειν διαφορὰν, καταλλήλως καὶ προσφυῶς ταῖς φύσεσι τὸν αὐτὸν καὶ ἕνα Χριστὸν ἐνεργεῖν τάτε θεῖα καὶ τὰ ἀνθρώπινα.—θεσπίζομεν, τοὺς ἡμετέρους ὑπηκόους—μὴ ἄδειαν ἔχειν πρὸς ἀλλήλους ἀπὸ τοῦ παρόντος περὶ ἑνὸς θελήματος ἢ μιᾶς ἐνεργείας, ἢ δύο ἐνεργειῶν καὶ δύο θελημάτων, οἱανδήποτε προφέρειν ἀμφισβήτησιν, ἔριν τε, καὶ φιλονεικίαν. There is said to be τὸ πρὸ τῆς ἀνωτέρω τῶν εἰρημένων ζητήσεων προελθούσης φιλονεικίας ἁπανταχοῦ φυλαχθῆναι σχῆμα. Sharp threats against those who disobey.

[10] The opponents derided the Typus as ἀνενέργητον πάντη καὶ ἀνεθέλητον, τουτέστιν ἄνουν, καὶ ἄψυχον, καὶ ἀκίνητον αὐτὸν τὸν τῆς δόξης θεὸν τὸν κύριον ἡμῶν Ἰ. Χ. ἐδογμάτισαν, τοῖς τῶν ἐθνῶν ἀψύχοις παραπλησίως εἰδώλοις (Epistola Abbatum et Monachorum in Synodo Lateranensi, ap. Mansi, x. 908). So too Martin in his address. Ibid. p. 880.

[11] The Acts in Mansi, x. 863. On the bad state of the Latin text see Walch's Ketzerhist. ix. 222. The twenty canons in the fifth Secretarius, can. x. ss. are directed against the Monothelites. Can. xiv. runs thus: Si quis secundum scelerosos haereticos cum una voluntate et una operatione, quae ab hereticis impie confitetur, et duas voluntates pariterque et operationes, hoc est, divinam et humanum, quae in ipso Christo Deo in unitate salvantur, et a sanctis patribus orthodoxe in ipso praedicantur, denegat et respuit, condemnatus sit.

[12] See Martini Epist. xv. et xvi. and the commemoratio eorum, quae saeviter acta sunt in Martinum, given together from Anastasii Collectan., in Mansi, x. 851. Neander, iii. 375. For an account of the sufferings of Maximus see acts and letters ap. Mansi, xi. 3. Anastasii Presb. Epist. ad Theodosium in Opp. Maximi, i. 67. Neander, iii. 383.

at least for a time,[13] though it was broken off again under *Constantine Pogonatus* (668–685). To remove this, the emperor summoned *the sixth general council* (680), where Pope *Agatho* triumphed in procuring a confirmation by the synod of the doctrine of two wills,[14] as copiously unfolded by him in an epistle, after an examination which terminated in peace and order.[15]

[13] Namely, between the patriarch Peter and pope Vitalianus. Cf. Acta Synodi oecum. vi. Actio xiii. ap. Mansi, xi. 572: *Ἔτι ἀνεγνώσθη—ἐπιστολὴ Πέτρου—πρὸς Βιταλιανὸν—ἧς ἡ ἀρχὴ πνευματικῆς εὐφροσύνης πρόξενον ἡμῖν τὸ γράμμα τῆς ὑμετέρας ὁμοψύχου καὶ ἁγίας ἀδελφότητος γέγονεν.*

[14] Agathonis Epistola ad Imperatores ap. Mansi, xi. 233–286.—P. 239: Cum duas naturas, duasque naturales voluntates, et duas naturales operationes confitemur in uno domino nostro J. Ch., non contrarias eas, nec adversas ad alterutrum dicimus (sicut a via veritatis errantes apostolicam traditionem accusant, absit haec impietas a fidelium cordibus), nec tanquam separatas in duabus personis, vel subsistentiis, sed duas dicimus unum eundemque dominum nostrum J. Ch., sicut naturas, ita et naturales in se voluntates et operationes habere, divinam scilicet et humanum, etc.—P. 243: Apostolica ecclesia—unum dominum nostrum J. Ch. confitetur ex duabus et in duabus existentem naturis—et ex proprietatibus naturalibus unamquamque harum Christi naturarum perfectam esse cognoscit, et quidquid ad proprietates naturarum pertinet, duplicia omnia confitetur.—Consequenter itaque—duas etiam naturales voluntates in eo, et duas naturales operationes esse confitetur et praedicat. Nam si personalem quisquam intelligat voluntatem, dum tres personae in s. Trinitate dicuntur, necesse est, ut et tres voluntates personales, et tres personales operationes (quod absurdum est et nimis profanum) dicerentur.—Ipse dominus noster J. Ch.—in sacris suis evangeliis protestatur in aliquibus humana, in aliquibus divina, et simul utraque in aliis de se patefaciens.—Orat quidem ad Patrem ut homo, ut calicem passionis transageret, quia in eo nostrae humanitatis natura absque solo peccato perfecta est, Pater, inquiens, si possibile est, etc. (Matth. xxvi. 39.) Et in alio loco, Non mea voluntas, sed tua fiat (Luc. xxii. 42). Farther, the passages Phil. ii. 8, obediens usque ad mortem; Luc. ii. 51, obediens parentibus; Jo. vi. 38, descendi de coelo, ut non faciam voluntatem meam, sed voluntatem ejus qui misit me; cf. Jo. v. 30; also from the Old Testament, Ps. xl. 9, Ut faciam voluntatem tuam, Deus meus, volui; Ps. liv. 8, voluntarie sacrificabo tibi. Then follow testimonies from the fathers. On the mode in which the two wills co-operate Agatho says nothing.

[15] The definitio (*ὅρος*) of the sixth council in the actio xviii. ap Mansi, xi. 631, ss.—P. 637: *Ἕνα καὶ τὸν αὐτὸν Χριστὸν, υἱὸν κύριον μονογενῆ, ἐν δύο φύσεσιν ἀσυγχύτως, ἀτρέπτως, ἀχωρίστως, ἀδιαιρέτως γνωριζόμενον, οὐδαμοῦ τῆς τῶν φύσεων διαφορᾶς ἀνῃρημένης διὰ τὴν ἕνωσιν, σωζομένης δὲ μᾶλλον τῆς ἰδιότητος ἑκατήρας φύσεως, καὶ εἰς ἓν πρόσωπον καὶ μίαν ὑπόστασιν συντρεχούσης.—Καὶ δύο φυσικὰς θελήσεις ἤτοι θελήματα ἐν αὐτῷ, καὶ δύο φυσικὰς ἐνεργείας ἀδιαιρέτως, ἀτρέπτως, ἀμερίστως, ἀσυγχύτως κατὰ τὴν τῶν ἁγίων πατέρων διδασκαλίαν ὡσαύτως κηρύττομεν· καὶ δύο μὲν φυσικὰ θελήματα οὐχ ὑπεναντία, μὴ γένοιτο, καθὼς οἱ ἀσεβεῖς ἔφησαν αἱρετικοὶ ἀλλ' ἑπόμενον τὸ ἀνθρώπινον αὐτοῦ θέλημα, καὶ μὴ ἀντιπίπτον, ἢ ἀντιπαλαῖον [ἀντίπαλον], μᾶλλον μὲν οὖν καὶ ὑποτασσόμενον τῷ θείῳ αὐτοῦ καὶ πανσθενεῖ θελήματι.—ὥσπερ γὰρ ἡ αὐτοῦ σὰρξ, σὰρξ τοῦ θεοῦ λόγου λέγεται καὶ ἔστιν, οὕτω καὶ τὸ φυσικὸν τῆς σαρκὸς αὐτοῦ θέλημα ἴδιον τοῦ θεοῦ λόγου λέγεται καὶ ἔστι, καθά φησιν αὐτός· "ὅτι καταβέβηκα ἐκ τοῦ οὐρανοῦ, οὐχ ἵνα ποιῶ τὸ θέλημα τὸ ἐμὸν, ἀλλὰ τὸ θέλημα τοῦ πέμψαντός με πατρὸς"* (Jo. vi. 38), *ἴδιον λέγων θέλημα αὐτοῦ τὸ τῆς σαρκὸς, ἐπεὶ καὶ ἡ σὰρξ ἰδία αὐτοῦ γέγονεν· ὃν γὰρ τρόπον ἡ παναγία καὶ ἄμωμος ἐψυχωμένη αὐτοῦ σὰρξ θεωθεῖσα* (deificata) *οὐκ ἀνῃρέθη, ἀλλ' ἐν τῷ ἰδίῳ αὐτῆς ὅρῳ τε καὶ λόγῳ διέμεινεν, οὕτω καὶ τὸ ἀνθρώπινον αὐτοῦ θέλημα θεωθὲν οὐκ ἀνῃρέθη, σέσωσται δὲ μᾶλλον κατὰ τὸν θεολόγον Γρηγόριον λέγοντα· "τὸ γὰρ ἐκείνου θέλειν τὸ κατὰ τὸν σωτῆρα νοούμενον οὐδὲ ὑπεναντίον θεῷ θεωθὲν, ὅλον." δύο δὲ φυσικὰς ἐνεργείας ἀδιαιρέτως,*

An anathema was pronounced on all *Monothelites*,[16] and also on Honorius;[17] and thus Church unity was restored in the Roman empire.

§ 129.

CONCILIUM QUINISEXTUM.

At the last two general councils, no attention had been paid to the laws affecting the constitution of the Church. To supply this defect, and to obtain a complete synodical code, the emperor *Justinian II.* (reigned from 685–695, and from 705–711), called a new oecumenical council in the Trullus at Con-

ἀτρέπτως, ἀμερίστως, ἀσυγχύτως ἐν αὐτῷ τῷ κυρίῳ ἡμῶν 'Ι. Χ. *τῷ ἀληθινῷ θεῷ ἡμῶν δοξάζομεν, τουτέστι θείαν ἐνέργειαν καὶ ἀνθρωπίνην ἐνέργειαν κατὰ τὸν θεηγόρον Λέοντα τρανέστατα φάσκοντα· "ἐνεργεῖ γὰρ ἑκατέρα μορφὴ μετὰ τῆς θατέρου κοινωνίας ὅπερ ἴδιον ἔσχηκε, τοῦ μὲν λόγου κατεργαζομένου τοῦτο, ὅπερ ἐστι τοῦ λόγου, τοῦ δὲ σώματος ἐκτελοῦντος ἅπερ ἐστὶ τοῦ σώματος"* (comp. § 89, note 7).

16 The name Μονοθελῆται first in Johannes Damasc.

17 John IV., in the Epist. ad Constantin. (note 8), had endeavored to exculpate Honorius on the ground that he merely asserted quia in salvatore nostro duae voluntates contrariae, id est, in membris ipsius (cf. Rom. vii. 23) penitus non consistant, quoniam nihil vitii traxit et praevaricatione primi hominis. So too Maximus in Epist. ad Marinum ap. Mansi, x. 687, and in the disputatio cum Pyrrho, ibid. p. 739. In all the measures afterward taken in Rome against the Monothelites, no mention was made of Honorius. On the other hand, Synodus oecum. vi. actio xiii. (ap. Mansi, xi. 556), pronounces an anathema on Sergius, Cyrus, Pyrrhus, Petrus, Paulus, Theodorus, bishop of Pharan, *καὶ 'Ονώριον τὸν γενόμενον πάπαν τῆς πρεσβυτέρας 'Ρώμης διὰ τὸ εὑρηκέναι ἡμᾶς διὰ τῶν γενομένων παρ' αὐτοῦ γραμμάτων πρὸς Σέργιον κατὰ πάντα τῇ ἐκείνου γνώμῃ ἐξακολουθήσαντα καὶ τὰ αὐτοῦ ἀσεβῆ κυρώσαντα δόγματα.* This anathema was repeated act. xvi. p. 622, act. xviii. p. 655, etc. Leo II. in his Epist. ad Constant. Imp. in which he confirms the council (ap. Mansi, xi. 731): Anathematizamus—nec non et Honorium, qui hanc apostolicam ecclesiam non apostolicae traditionis doctrina lustravit, sed profana proditione immaculatam subvertere conatus est. Cf. ejusd. Epist. ad Episc. Hispaniae ap. Mansi, xi. 1052, and ad Ervigium Regem Hispaniae ibid. p. 1057. Also in the confession of faith subscribed by the following popes at their accession (liber diurnus cap. ii. tit. 9, professio 2), the anathema was pronounced against auctores novi haeretici dogmatis, Sergium, etc.—una cum Honorio, qui pravis eorum assertionibus fomentum impendit.—Anastasius Biblioth. Ep. ad Joannem Diaconum (Collectanea ed. Sirmond. p. 3), is the first that endeavors again, after the example of John IV., whose letter he reproduced, to excuse Honorius, licet huic sexta sancta Synodus quasi haeretico anathema dixerit. But later Catholic historians deny even this fact. Platina in vita Honorii I.: Ferunt Heraclium—Pyrrhi—et Cyri fraudibus deceptum in haeresim Monothelitarum incidisse.—Hos tamen postea tanti erroris auctores, hortante Honorio et veram ante oculos literis et nunciis ponente, relegavit Heraclius. According to Baronius, the acts of the sixth council have been corrupted, and instead of Honorius we should read Theodorus. Bellarmine maintains that the letters of Honorius are either spurious or interpolated. According to Pagi, Garnier, the Ballerini, and others, Honorius was not condemned for heresy, but for negligence; and according to Combefisius and others, even with the consent of Pope Agatho. Against all these evasions see Richer Historia concil. general. i. 296. Du Pin de Antiqua eccl. discipl. p. 349. Bossuet Defensio declar. Cleri Gallic. ii. 128.

stantinople (692),[1] at which 102 canons were passed, for the most part giving legal expression merely to older Church usages, and repeating older canons. It appears that the Greek bishops had expressly entertained the design, both here and at Chalcedon, of reminding the Roman patriarchs, again exalted by their new victory, of the limits of their power. Particularly unacceptable to the Romans were the six canons *concerning the Church laws to be esteemed valid*,[2] *the marriage of priests*,[3]

[1] Names: Concilium Trullanum, Σύνοδος πενθέκτη, Conc. quinisextum. The Greeks consider it merely as a continuation of the sixth council, and call its decisions κανόνες τῆς ἕκτης συνόδου. The Acts are given in Mansi, xi. 921.

[2] Can. ii. confirms 85 canones Apost., while the Roman church, after Dionysius, adopted only the first 50. This council also sanctioned, as church laws, the canons of the councils of Nice, Ancyra, Neocaesarea, Gangra, Antioch, Laodicea, Constantinople in A.D. 381, Ephesus, Chalcedon, Sardica, Carthage and Constantinople, A.D. 394. Also the canons of Dionysius Alexandrinus, Petrus Alex., Gregory Thaumaturgus, Athanasius, Basil the Great, Gregory Nyssene, Gregory of Nazianzum, Amphilochius of Iconium, Timotheus Alex., Cyril Alex., and Gennadius patriarch of Constantinople. Lastly, also, of Cyprian and his synod. All other canons are prohibited as not genuine. (Μηδενὶ ἐξεῖναι—ἑτέρους παρὰ τοὺς προκειμένους παραδέχεσθαι κανόνας ψευδεπιγράφως ὑπό τινων συντεθέντας τῶν τὴν ἀλήθειαν καπηλεύειν ἐπιχειρησάντων.) In that list, however, many western synods, and all decretals of Romish bishops, are passed over.

[3] Can. xiii.: Ἐπειδὴ ἐν τῇ Ῥωμαίων ἐκκλησίᾳ ἐν τάξει κανόνος παραδεδόσθαι διέγνωμεν, τούς μέλλοντας διακόνου ἢ πρεσβυτέρου ἀξιοῦσθαι χειροτονίας καθομολογεῖν, ὡς οὐκέτι ταῖς αὐτῶν συνάπτονται γαμεταῖς· ἡμεῖς τῷ ἀρχαίῳ ἐξακολουθοῦντες κανόνι τῆς ἀποστολικῆς ἀκριβείας καὶ τάξεως, τὰ τῶν ἱερῶν ἀνδρῶν κατὰ νόμους συνοικέσια καὶ ἀπὸ τοῦ νῦν ἐῤῥῶσθαι βουλόμεθα· μηδαμῶς αὐτῶν τὴν πρὸς γαμετὰς συνάφειαν διαλύοντες, ἢ ἀποστεροῦντες αὐτοὺς τῆς πρὸς ἀλλήλους κατὰ καιρὸν τὸν προσήκοντα ὁμιλίας. Ὥστε εἴ τις ἄξιος εὑρεθείη πρὸς χειροτονίαν ὑποδιακόνου ἢ διακόνου ἢ πρεσβυτέρου, οὗτος μηδαμῶς κωλυέσθω ἐπὶ τοιοῦτον βαθμὸν ἐκβιβάζεσθαι γαμετῇ συνοικῶν νομίμῳ, μήτε μὴν ἐν τῷ τῆς χειροτονίας καιρῷ ἀπαιτείσθω ὁμολογεῖν, ὡς ἀποστήσεται τῆς νομίμου πρὸς τὴν οἰκείαν γαμετὴν ὁμιλίας. ἵνα μὴ ἐντεῦθεν τὸν ἐκ θεοῦ νομοθετηθέντα καὶ εὐλογηθέντα τῇ αὐτοῦ παρουσίᾳ γάμον καθυβρίζειν ἐκβιασθῶμεν, τῆς τοῦ εὐαγγελίου φωνῆς βοώσης· ἃ ὁ θεὸς ἔζευξεν, ἄνθρωπος μὴ χωριζέτω (Matth. xix. 6) καὶ τοῦ ἀποστόλου διδάσκοντος τίμιον τὸν γάμον καὶ τὴν κοίτην ἀμίαντον (Heb. xiii. 4) καὶ δέδεσαι γυναικὶ, μὴ ζήτει λύσιν (1 Cor. vii. 27).—χρὴ τοὺς τῷ θυσιαστηρίῳ προσεδρεύοντας ἐν τῷ καιρῷ τῆς τῶν ἁγίων μεταχειρήσεως ἐγκρατεῖς εἶναι ἐν πᾶσιν.—Εἰ τις οὖν τολμήσοι, παρὰ τοὺς ἀποστολικοὺς κανόνας κινούμενος, τινὰ τῶν ἱερωμένων, πρεσβυτέρων φαμὲν ἢ διακόνων ἢ ὑποδιακόνων, ἀποστερεῖν τῆς πρὸς νόμιμον γυναῖκα συναφείας τε καὶ κοινωνίας, καθαιρείσθω. Ὡσαύτως καὶ εἴ τις πρεσβύτερος ἢ διάκονος τὴν ἑαυτοῦ γυναῖκα προφάσει εὐλαβείας ἐκβάλλει, ἀφοριζέσθω, ἐπιμένων δὲ καθαιρείσθω (cf. Can. Apostol. v. § 97, note 9). Bellarmin. de Cler. i. 10, supposes, respecting this subject: Tempore hujus synodi (Trullanae) coepit mos Graecorum, qui nunc est.—Besides, can. iii. forbids the clergy marrying a second time, and marriage with a widow. Can. vi. forbids marriage after ordination. Can. xii. forbids bishops to remain in the married state: Εἰς γνῶσιν ἡμετέραν ἦλθεν, ὡς ἔν τε Ἀφρικῇ καὶ Λιβύῃ καὶ ἑτέροις τόποις οἱ τῶν ἐκεῖσε θεοφιλέστατοι πρόεδροι συνοικεῖν ταῖς ἰδίαις γαμεταῖς, καὶ μετὰ τὴν ἐπ' αὐτοῖς προελθοῦσαν χειροτονίαν, οὐ παραιτοῦνται.—ἔδοξεν ὥστε μηδαμῶς τὸ τοιοῦτον ἀπὸ τοῦ νῦν γίνεσθαι· τοῦτο δέ φαμέν, οὐκ ἐπ' ἀθετήσει ἢ ἀνατροπῇ τῶν ἀποστολικῶς προνενομοθετημένων, ἀλλὰ τῆς σωτηρίας καὶ προκοπῆς τῆς ἐπὶ τὸ κρεῖττον τῶν λαῶν προμηθούμενοι, κ. τ. λ. Cf. Can. xlviii. According to Zonaras and Theod. Balsamo ad Can. Apost. v. these were the first ecclesiastical prohibitions against the marriage of

the rank of the patriarch of Constantinople,[4] *against fasting on Saturday,*[5] *against the eating of blood and things strangled,*[6] *and against pictures of the Lamb.*[7] Though the papal legates had subscribed them, yet Pope *Sergius I.* refused to accept them. Justinian meant to have him brought to Constantinople, but was prevented by the rebellion of the garrison of Ravenna, and soon after by his deposition.[8] Thus this council was acknowledged only in the east, but not in the west;[9] and was the first public step which led to the separation of the two Churches.

§ 130.

FORTUNES OF MONOTHELITISM.

The emperor *Philippicus Bardanes* (711–713) revived once more the Monothelitic doctrine, and made it the prevailing faith, though merely for a short time.[1] Only Rome withstood him.[2] But the Greek bishops were as ready to subscribe a Monothelitic

bishops, though Justinian had forbidden them by a civil law (Cod. i. iii. 48). Cf. Calixtus de Conjugio Clericorum ed. Henke, p. 389, ss.

[4] Can. xxxvi., referring to Can. Constant. iii. (§ 93, note 9), and Can. Chalced. xxviii. (ibid. note 14), and in the same words as the latter. So, too, in Can. xxxviii. the 17th canon of Chalced. (ibid. note 3) is repeated word for word.

[5] Can. lv.: Ἐπειδὴ *μεμαθήκαμεν, ἐν τῇ* Ῥωμαίων *πόλει ἐν ταῖς ἁγίαις τῆς τεσσαρακοστῆς νηστείαις τοῖς ταύτης σάββασι νηστεύειν παρὰ τὴν παραδοθεῖσαν ἐκκλησιαστικὴν ἀκολουθίαν* (comp. § 100, note 14) *ἔδοξε τῇ ἁγίᾳ συνόδῳ, ὥστε κρατεῖν καὶ ἐπὶ τῇ* Ῥωμαίων *ἐκκλησίᾳ ἀπαρασαλεύτως τὸν κανόνα τὸν λέγοντα· "εἴ τις κληρικὸς εὑρεθείη τῇ ἁγίᾳ κυριακῇ νηστεύων ἢ τὸ σάββατον πλὴν τοῦ ἑνὸς καὶ μόνου, καθαιρείσθω· εἰ δὲ λαϊκὸς, ἀφοριζέσθω."* (Can. Apostol. lxvii.)

[6] Can. lxvii.

[7] Can. lxxxii.: Ἐν *τισι τῶν σεπτῶν εἰκόνων γραφαῖς ἀμνὸς δακτύλῳ τοῦ προδρόμου δεικνύμενος ἐγχαράττεται* (according to Joh. i. 29).—*τὸν τοῦ αἴροντος τὴν ἁμαρτίαν τοῦ κόσμου ἀμνοῦ* Χριστοῦ *τοῦ θεοῦ ἡμῶν κατὰ τὸν ἀνθρώπινον χαρακτῆρα καὶ ἐν ταῖς εἰκόσιν ἀπὸ τοῦ νῦν ἀντὶ τοῦ παλαιοῦ ἀμνοῦ ἀναστηλοῦσθαι ὁρίζομεν.* See § 99, note 51.

[8] Cf. Anastas. Biblioth. in vita Sergii.

[9] Ap. Beda de Sex aetatibus and Paulus Diac. Hist. Longob. vi. 11, it is called Synodus erratica. By degrees however, several of the less offensive canons began to be cited, as Canones Syn. vi., those who did so being misled by the example of the Greeks (see note 1). Gratian (Decret. P. i. dist. xvi. c. 6) translates a Greek account of this Synod, and then naïvely adds: Ex his ergo colligitur, quod sexta synodus bis congregata est: primo sub Constantino Imp., et nullos canones constituit, secundo sub Justiniano filio ejus, et praefatos canones promulgavit. Thus, then, he also adopts several of the canons. It was not till after the Reformation that the conciliabulum pseudosextum was again discovered. Cf. Calixtus, p. 401, ss.

[1] The chief authority on this subject is the epilogus ad Acta Syn. vi. of the contemporary Agathon, deacon and librarian of the church at Constantinople (prim. ed. F. Combefisius in the Nov. auctar. PP. ii. 199, ap. Mansi, xii. 189. Farther, Theophanes, p. 319, ss. Walch's Ketzerhist. ix. 449.

[2] Anastasii Bibl. vita Constantini. Paulus Diac. Hist. Longob. vi. 33.

confession of faith as they were to return to orthodoxy at the command of the next emperor, *Anastasius II.*[3]

In Syria, however, a small party of Monothelites remained for a long time. Here all Christian parties had a political importance. The *Jacobites* were favorable to the Arabians; the *Catholics* to the Greek emperors, hence called *Melchites* (from מֶלֶךְ). On the other hand, an independent party had collected in mount Libanus, about the monastery of St. *Maro*, who adopted the Monothelitic doctrines, chose for themselves a patriarch of Antioch (the first was *John Maro*, † 701), and under the name of *Maronites*[4] continued to hold the doctrine of one will in Christ till the time of the Crusades.[5]

[3] The miserable spirit of the Greek bishops is particularly expressed in the exculpatory letter which John, who had been elevated to the see of Constantinople by Philippicus, addressed to Pope Constantine, after the state of things had been entirely changed (appended to Agathon's Epilogus ap. Combefis. p. 211, ss. Mansi, p. 195, ss.). Among other things he says: *Οἴδατε γὰρ καὶ ὑμεῖς,—ὡς οὐ λίαν ἀντιτύπως καὶ σκληρῶς ἔχειν πρὸς τὴν τῆς ἐξουσίας ἀνάγκην ἐν τοῖς τοιούτοις, ἄνευ τινὸς τέχνης καὶ περινοίας καθέστηκεν εὐμαρές· ἐπεὶ καὶ Νάθαν ὁ προφήτης οὐκ ἀπερικάλυπτον τὸν ἔλεγχον τὸν περὶ τῆς μοιχείας τε καὶ τοῦ φόνου προσήγαγε τῷ Δαβὶδ, καίτοι καὶ αὐτοῦ τοῦ Δαβὶδ προφητικῷ τετιμημένου χαρίσματι. Κατὰ τοῦτο καὶ ἡμεῖς, ὅπερ φησὶν ὁ μέγας Βασίλειος, ἐνδιδόναι μικρὸν τῷ ἤθει τοῦ ἀνδρὸς κατεδεξάμεθα, ὥστε τὴν ἐν τοῖς καιρίοις τῆς πίστεως ὁμολογίαν, εἰ καὶ μὴ λέξεσιν, ἀλλάγε ταῖς ἐννοίαις φυλάττεσθαι ἀπαράβατον. Οὐ γὰρ ἐν λέξεσιν ἡμῖν, ἀλλ' ἐν πράγμασιν ἡ ἀλήθεια, ὁ θεῖος Γρηγόριος βοᾷ· καὶ πάλιν ἱκανῶς ἄτοπον καὶ λίαν αἰσχρὸν διορίζεται, τὸ περὶ τὸν ἦχον σμικρολογεῖσθαι.—Κατὰ τοῦτον δὴ τὸν τῆς οἰκονομικῆς καὶ κατὰ περίστασιν συμβάσεως τρόπον καὶ τὰ λοιπὰ τῶν γεγενημένων προελθεῖν πειθόμενοι, ἁγιώτατοι, μὴ ἀσύγγνωστον ἡμῖν τὸ ἐπὶ τούτοις ἔγκλημα προσαγαγεῖν καταδέξησθε· ἀλλὰ κἂν τι τῆς ἀκριβείας ἡμῖν ἡμαρτῆσθαι ὑπονοῆται, τῇ παραθέσει τῶν ἐκ τῶν ἁγίων πατέρων ἡμῶν οἰκονομικῶς προελθόντων ἀπολυέσθω ἀνεύθυνον καὶ πάσης ἐλεύθερον κατακρίσεως.* He then appeals to the bishops of the Robber Synod at Ephesus, who had condemned Flavian unjustly, *καὶ ὅμως ἐν τῇ κατὰ Χαλκηδόνα ἁγίᾳ συνόδῳ ἤρκεσε τούτοις πρὸς τελείαν ἀποτροπὴν τοῦ ἐγκλήματος ἡ τῆς ὑγιοῦς ὁμολογίας σύνθεσις*, etc., and concludes that he has offered an *ἀπολογίαν ἰσχυράν τε καὶ ἔννομον.*

[4] Johann. Damasc. Lib. de vera sententia c. 8. Epist. de Hymno trishagio, c. 5. Eutychii Annal. Alex. t. ii. p. 192.

[5] The modern Maronite writers, namely, Abraham Echellensis in several works, Faustus Nayron Diss. de origine et religione Maronitarum. Rom. 1679. 8. Ejusd. Enoplia fidei catholicae. Ibid. 1694. 8. Assemani Bibl. orient. i. 496, have introduced confusion into the history of their sect, 1. By asserting that the Maronites were never Monothelites, but were always orthodox (in addition to the opposite reasons given by Renaudot Histor. patr. Alexandr. p. 149, ss. is the testimony of Germanus, patriarch of Constantinople, about 725, de Haeresibus et Synodis, in the Spicilegium Romanum, vii. 65, that the Maronites rejected the sixth synod. The grounds given by both parties my be found in M. Le Quien Oriens christ. iii. 1. Walch's Ketzerhist. ix. 474); 2. By identifying the Mardaites (whose name is erroneously derived from מָרַד) with the Maronites. On the contrary, Anquetil Duperron Recherches sur les migrations des Mardes, ancien peuple de Perse in the Mémoires de l'Acad. des Inscript. tome 50, p. 1, has shown that the Mardaites or Mards, a warlike people in Armenia, were placed as a garrison on Mount Libanus by Constantine Pogonatus A.D. 676 (Theophanes, p. 295), but withdrawn as early as 685 by Justinian II. (Theoph. p. 302, s.)

THIRD CHAPTER.

HISTORY OF THE WESTERN CHURCH.

§ 131.

ECCLESIASTICAL STATE OF ITALY.

Important for the history of this and the following period is Anastasii Bibliothecarii (about 870) Liber pontificalis, s. vitae Rom. Pontif.[1] ed. C. Annib. Fabrotus, in the Corp. hist. Byz. t. xix. Paris. 1649. fol.; Fr. Blanchini. Rom. 1718–35. iv. t. fol. Jo. Vignolius. Romae. 1724. 4, with the biographies of the later popes in L. A. Muratorii Rerum Ital. scriptor. t. iii. p. i.—Liber diurnus Roman. Pontificum, collected about 715, prim. ed. Luc. Holstenius. Rom. 1658. 8.[2] J. Garnerius. Paris. 1680. 4. (Supplementum in J. Mabillon Museum Italicum, i. i. 32. Paris. 1687. 4) reprinted in Chr. G. Hoffmanni Nova scriptorum ac monumentorum collect. t. ii. Lips. 1733. 4.

The political consequence of the *popes*[3] in Italy increased, in proportion as the Greek emperors, now pressed by the Saracens

[1] The Liber pontificalis has arisen from former Catalogi Pontificum which we know only in part. The first known catalogus, which was composed under Liberius, 354, and contains few other notices besides those relating to chronology, furnished ground for subsequently attributing to Damasus the first collection of the vitae Pontificum. The second known catalogus under Felix IV. (526–530) has taken the former into itself only in part, but enlarged it by other accounts. From these catalogues arose, at the end of the seventh century, the first edition of the Liber pontificalis, which concludes with Conon († 687) and is still extant in a Veronese and a Neapolitan MS. (see Pertz in the Archiv. d. Gesellschaft für ältere deutsche Geschichtskunde, v. 68). The second edition of it in the Cod. Vatican 5269, concludes with Constantine († 714). The lives that follow were appended successively by contemporaries, and Anastasius can only have composed the last till Nicolaus I. († 868), and have published the book anew in this form. The lives of Hadrian II. and Stephen VI. († 891), subsequently added, are attributed to one Gulielmus Bibliothecarius. From what has been said, it may be seen how even Beda, Rabanus Maurus, Walafrid Strabo, could cite the Liber pontificalis; and how Pseudo-Isidorus could use it. Just as the older shorter lives, which merely furnish notices of time, and short accounts of ordinations, church buildings, regulations and arrangements of popes, and respecting martyrdoms and heresies, have become uncertain by the mixing up of doubtful traditions with true accounts; so, on the other hand, the more copious lives, from the end of the seventh century and onward, have great historical value, as they were written by contemporaries. Cf. Emm. a Schelstrate de Antiquis Rom. pont. catalogis, ex quibus Lib. pontificalis concinnatus fuit, et de lib. pont. auctore ac praestantia. Jo. Ciampini Examen Lib. pontif. Fr. Blanchini praef. in Lib. pont., all together prefixed to Muratori's edition. See a description of the city of Rome by Platner, Bunsen, Gerhard, and Röstell, i. 206.

[2] This edition, better than that of Garnier, was immediately suppressed by the Romish censors. Its history (see especially Baluzii. not. ad de Marca de Concord Sac. et Imp. lib. i. c. ix. § 8), and an account of its variations may be seen in Schoepflini Commentt. hist. crit. Basil. 1741. 4. p. 499, ss. In addition to the two codd. used by Holsten and Garnier, a third is noticed by Launojus Diss. de Lazari et Magdal. in provinciam adpulsu cap. 10, obs. 10.

[3] Honorius I. from 625–638, Severinus † 640, John IV. † 642, Theodore † 649, Martin I.

too, were forced to leave tó them chiefly the defense of their Italian possessions against the Lombards.[4] Still they continued subjects of the emperors, had to be confirmed by them in office,[5] and paid them taxes.[6] While the Monothelitic troubles gave the popes an opportunity of appointing a vicar even in Palestine now overrun by the Saracens,[7] *Martin I.* was still made to feel bitterly the emperor's power; and *Vitalianus* was compelled to bow to Monothelitism supported by imperial patronage. But

banished 654, † 655, but even in 654 Eugenius I. was again chosen, † 657, Vitalianus † 672, Adeodatus † 676, Domnus I. † 678, Agatho † 682, Leo II. † 683, Benedict II. † 685, John V. † 686, Conon † 687, Sergius I. † 701, John VI. † 705, John VII. † 707, Sisinnius † 708, Constantine † 714, Gregory II. † 731.

[4] Comp. above, § 117, note 26. Cf. Liber diurnus cap. ii. tit. iv. Account of the Romans de electione Pontificis ad Exarchum: Et ideo supplicantes quaesumus, ut inspirante Deo celsae ejus dominationi, nos famulos voti compotes celeriter fieri praecipiat: praesertim cum plura sint capitula, et alia ex aliis quotidie procreentur, quae curae solicitudinem et pontificalis favoris expectant remedium.—Propinquantium quoque inimicorum ferocitas, quam nisi sola Dei virtus atque Apostolorum Principis per suum Vicarium, hoc est Romanum Pontificem, ut omnibus notum est, aliquando monitis comprimit, aliquando vero flectit ac modigerat hortatu, singulari interventu indiget, cum hujus solius pontificalibus monitis, ob reverentiam Apostolorum Principis, parentiam offerant voluntariam: et quos non virtus armorum humiliat, pontificalis increpatio cum obsecratione inclinat. The popes possessed already some small forts; probably erected, in the first place, for protection of their patrimony. Thus Anastasius in vita xc. Gregorii II., relates, that the Lombards had taken from him the Cumanum castrum, and that the pope having in vain required them to surrender it, John, Dux Neapolitanus, retook it from them, and gave it back to the former possessor. Pro cujus redemptione lxx. auri libras ipse Sanctissimus Papa, sicut promiserat antea, dedit.

[5] As had become customary under the Ostrogoth kings. Agatho, however, received from Constantine Pogonatus divalem jussionem, per quam relevata est quantitas, quae solita erat dari pro ordinatione Pontificis facienda: sic tamen, ut si contigerit post ejus transitum electionem fieri, non debeat ordinari qui electus fuerit, nisi prius decretum generale introducatur in regiam urbem secundum antiquam consuetudinem, et cum eorum conscientia et jussione debeat ordinatio provenire (Anastasius in vita lxxx. Agathonis). Benedict II. received from the same emperor the privilege ut persona, qui electus fuerit ad Sedem Apost. e vestigio absque tarditate Pontifex ordinetur (Anastasius in vita lxxxii. Bened.). Still, however, this did not obviate the necessity of confirmation. See the forms in Liber diurnus, cap. ii. de ordinatione Summi Pontificis. Namely, tit. 1. Nuntius ad Exarchum de transitu Pontificis. Tit. 2. Decretum de electione Pontificis. (Subscribed by totus Clerus, Optimates, et Milites seu Cives). Tit. 3. Relatio de electione Pontificis ad Principem. Tit. 4. De electione Pontificis ad Exarchum. On the same subject, tit. 5. ad Archiepisc. Ravennae, tit. 6. ad Judices Ravennae, tit. 7. ad Apocrisiarium Ravennae, to effect the speedy confirmation. Tit. 8. Ritus ordinandi Pontificis, and tit. 9. Professio pontificia.

[6] Ex. gr. Anastas. in vita lxxxiv. Cononis: Hujus temporibus pietas Imperialis relevavit per sacram jussionem suam ducenta annonae capita (i. e. capitationem), quae patrimonii custodes Brutiae et Lucaniae annue persolvebant.

[7] This was done by the popes Theodore and Martin I. during a vacancy in the see of Jerusalem, though the patriarchs of Antioch and Jerusalem protested against it. See lib. Stephani Episc. Dorensis ad Synod. Rom. (Mansi, t. x. p. 899), and Martini P. Epist. ad Johannem Episc. Philadelphiae (ibid. p. 805, ss.), comp. Walch's Ketzerhistorie, Th. 9. S. 280, comp. S. 214 and 240.

by their triumph at the sixth synod the popes strengthened anew their ancient calling as defenders of the true faith;[8] and began at this time to attribute to themselves the title *Episcopus Universalis*, which Gregory the Great had declared to be anti-christian.[9] The *Quinisextum* could no longer humble them in the west. When Justinian II. attempted to bring Pope Sergius I. to Constantinople to compel him to subscribe the decrees of the Quinisextum, the garrison of Ravenna rose in rebellion,[10] and soon after (701) the mere suspicion of such an intention caused a new uproar against the exarch.[11] Hence, in order to confirm his own authority in Italy, Justinian II. invited Pope *Constantine* to visit him, and overloaded him with exceedingly high marks of honor (710).[12] The loose connection between Rome and the empire was soon after shown in the refusal of the former to obey the heretic Philippicus Bardanes (711–713).[13]

The oppressed Church of Africa now yielded to the claims of Rome without resistance.[14] On the other hand they still met with much opposition in Italy. *The bishops of Ravenna*

[8] Comp. Agathonis P. Ep. ad Imperatores (see above, § 128, note 14) ap. Mansi, xi. p 239: Petrus spirituales oves ecclesiae ab ipso redemptore omnium terna commendatione pascendas suscepit: cujus annitente praesidio haec apostolica ejus ecclesia nunquam a via veritatis in qualibet erroris parte deflexa est, cujus auctoritatem, utpote Apostolorum omnium principis, semper omnis catholica Christi ecclesia, et universales synodi fideliter amplectentes, in cunctis secutae sunt, etc.

[9] So first in the Liber diurnus cap. iii. tit. 6, ap. Hoffmann, ii. 95, in the promissio fidei Episcopi, which falls between 682 and 685.

[10] Anastasius vit. lxxxv. Sergii says: Sed misericordia Dei praeveniente, beatoque Petro Apostolo et Apostolorum Principe suffragante, suamque ecclesiam immutilatam servante, excitatum est cor Ravennatis militiae, etc.

[11] Anastas. vit. lxxxvi. Joannis VI.

[12] Anastas. vit. lxxxix. Constant.: In die autem, qua se vicissim viderunt, Augustus Christianissimus cum regno in capite se prostravit, pedes osculans Pontificis.

[13] Anastasii vit. lxxxix. Constant.—Pauli Diac. Hist. Longobard. vi. 34.

[14] Comp. the letter of the African bishops to Pope Theodore in the Acts of the Conc. Lateran. ann. 649, Secretarius ii. (Mansi, x. 919): Magnum et indeficientem omnibus Christianis fluenta redundantem, apud apostolicam sedem consistere fontem nullus ambigere possit, de quo rivuli prodeunt affluenter, universum largissime irrigantes orbem Christianorum, cui etiam in honorem beatissimi Petri patrum decreta peculiarem omnem decrevere reverentiam in requirendis Dei rebus.—Antiquis enim regulis sancitum est, ut quidquid, quamvis in remotis vel in longinquo positis ageretur provinciis, non prius tractandum vel accipiendum sit, nisi ad notitiam almae sedis vestrae fuisset deductum, ut hujus auctoritate, juxta quae fuisset pronunciato, firmaretur, indeque sumerent caeterae ecclesiae velut de natali suo fonte praedicationis exordium, et per diversas totius mundi regiones puritatis incorruptae maneant fidei sacramenta salutis. Taken almost word for word from the letters of Innocent I. and Zosimus to the African bishops. Comp. the passages § 94, notes 20, 35.

ventured to build higher claims on the fact that their city was the seat of the exarch, in accordance with Grecian principles, and even maintained for some time the independent management of the Church of the exarchate, when Rome would not accommodate herself to the imperial Monothelitism.[15] Among the *Lombards* catholicism found many adherents since the time of Queen Theodelinda and her son King *Adelwald* (616–620); and from the time of King *Grimoald* († 671) became the prevailing system among them.[16] Still, however, they remained at variance with the popes;[17] and Upper Italy asserted its ecclesiastical independence.[18] Theological learning continued to be in a low state in Italy.[19]

§ 132.

ECCLESIASTICAL STATE OF FRANCE AND SPAIN.

The superior dignity of the Romish Church was the more readily admitted in the west on account of its being the only

[15] Anastas. vit. lxxix. Domini I. (676–678): Hujus temporibus Ecclesia Ravennatum, quae se ab Ecclesia Romana segregaverat causa autocephaliae, denuo se pristinae Sedi Apostolicae subjugavit. Vit. lxxxi. Leonis II. (683–684): Hujus temporibus percurrente divali jussione clementissimi Principis restituta est Ecclesia Ravennatis sub ordinatione Sedis Apostolicae.—Typum autocephaliae, quem sibi elicuerant, ad amputanda scandala Sedis Apostolicae restituerunt.

[16] Though always mixed with idolatry still. See vita S. Barbati (bishop of Benevent. † 682) in the Actis Sanct. Febr. iii. 139: His diebus quamvis sacri baptismatis unda Longobardi abluerentur, tamen priscum gentilitatis ritum tenentes, sive bestiali mente degebant, bestiae simulacro, quae vulgo Vipera nominatur, flectebant colla, quae debite suo debebant flectere creatori. Quin etiam non longe a Beneventi moenibus devotissime sacrilegam colebant arborem, in qua suspenso corio, cuncti qui aderant terga vertentes arbori, celerius equitabant, calcaribus cruentantes equos, ut unus alterum posset praeire, atque in eodem cursu retroversis manibus in corium jaculabantur, sicque particulam modicam ex eo comedendam superstitiose accipiebant. Et quia stulta illic persolvebant vota, ab actione nomen loco illi, sicut hactenus dicitur, Votum imposuerunt.

[17] Planck's Gesch. d. kirchl. Gesellschaftsverf. ii. 669, ff.

[18] It is true that there is also found an indiculum (sacramenti) Episcopi de Longobardia in the Liber diurnus cap. iii. tit. 8, but such an oath was taken only by the bishops of the Roman patriarchal territory (the middle and south of Italy), who were now under the Lombard dominion.

[19] This is clear, particularly from Agathonis Ep. ad Impp. in the Actis Syn. Constantinop. ann. 680, Act. iv. (ap. Mansi, xi. 235), where he repeatedly says of the legates whom he sends to the council: Non nobis eorum scientia confidentiam dedit, with the general remark: Nam apud homines in medio gentium positos et de labore corporis quotidianum victum cum summa haesitatione conquirentes, quomodo ad plenum poterit inveniri scripturarum scientia?

apostolic Church in that region, as well as the only medium of ecclesiastical connection with the east. But the greatest impression was made by the halo of holiness which surrounded that city in the eyes of the westerns; so that every thing proceeding from it was regarded as sacred.[1]

The connection of the *Frank Church* with Rome was slight since the time of Gregory the Great. The chief authority lay continuously in the hand of the king; and thus all traces of metropolitan government had disappeared. Among the political disturbances of the French empire in the seventh century, the Church also fell into great disorder; the bishops took part in the feuds of the nobles; clergy and monasteries became ungovernable; and the better few, who wished to call attention to morality and discipline, were persecuted.[2] The robbing of Churches was not uncommon; and *Charles Martel* (major-domus from 717–741) even distributed ecclesiastical revenues and offices in usufruct to valiant soldiers (as beneficium, precarium).[3]

[1] For example, Anastas. vit. xc. Gregor. II. after the account of the great victory gained by Duke Eudo of Aquitania over the Saracens at Toulouse (721): Eudo announced it to the pope, adjiciens, quod anno praemisso in benedictionem a praedicto viro eis directis tribus spongiis, quibus ad usum mensae (perhaps the altar?) Pontificis apponuntur, in hora, qua bellum committebatur, idem Eudo Aquitaniae princeps populo suo per modicas partes tribuens ad sumendum eis, nec unus vulneratus est, nec mortuus ex his, qui participati sunt.

[2] So Leodegar, bishop of Autün, who was put to death by the major-domus Ebrün, 678. Aigulf, abbot of a monastery at Lerins, wished merely to keep order among his monks, but was therefore abused, banished, and, in 675, murdered. See the lives of both in Mabillon Act. SS. Ord. Benedicti, saec. ii. p. 679, ss. 656, ss.

[3] Comp. above, § 124, note 7. Bonifacius Ep. 132 (ed. Würdtwein Ep. 51), ad Zachariam, about 742: Franci enim, ut seniores dicunt, plus quam per tempus lxxx. annorum Synodum non fecerunt, nec Archiepiscopum habuerunt, nec Ecclesiae canonica jura alicui fundabant vel renovabant. Modo autem maxima ex parte per civitates Episcopales sedes traditae sunt Laicis cupidis ad possidendum, vel adulteratis Clericis, scortatoribus, et publicanis saeculariter ad perfruendum. De Majoribus domus regiae libellus vetusti scriptoris, in du Chesne Hist. Francorum scriptt. t. ii. p. 2: Carolus—res Ecclesiarum propter assiduitatem bellorum laicis tradidit. Hadriani P. I. Ep. ad Tilpinum Archiep. Rhem. in Flodoardi Hist. eccl. Rhem. lib. ii. c. 17, and ap. Mansi, xii. p. 844. Hincmar Epist. vi. ad Episc. diocesis Remensis, c. 19: Tempore Caroli Principis—in Germanicis et Belgicis ac Gallicanis provinciis omnis religio Christianitatis paene fuit abolita, ita ut, Episcopis in paucis locis residuis, Episcopia Laicis donata et rebus divisa fuerint; adeo ut Milo quidam tonsura Clericus, moribus, habitu et actu irreligiosus laicus Episcopia, Rhemorum ac Trevirorum usurpans simul per multos annos pessumdederit, et multi jam in orientalibus regionibus (East Franks) idola adorarent et sine baptismo manerent. Cf. Chronicon Virdunense (written about 1115) in Bouquet Rer. Gall. et Franc. script. t. iii. p. 364. But for this even the clergy abused him after his death. Boniface wrote to Athelbald, king of Mercia, to deter him from a similar course (Baronius ann. 745 no. 11): Carolus quoque Princeps Francorum, multorum monasteriorum eversor, et ecclesiasticarum pe-

The *Spanish Church* appears to have gradually relaxed in humble subjection to the Roman see since catholicism had prevailed among the Goths likewise; although that subordination had been shown as long as the Church stood under the pressure of Arianism.[4] Here also the king, as feudal lord of the bishops, was the head of the Church;[5] but at the same time the bishops attained to a peculiarly great importance, both by their weighty voice in the election of the king, and by the necessity of supporting a tottering throne by means of spiritual authority.[6]

cuniarum in usus proprios commutator, longa torsione et verenda morte consumtus est. (This passage, however, is wanting in the editions of Boniface's letters, ap. Serarius, Ep. 19). A hundred years later, on the contrary, Hincmar, archbishop of Rheims, in the prologus in vitam b. Remigii (written about 854), and still more fully in his Epist. Synodi Carisiacensis ad Ludov. Germ. Regem, A.D. 858 (Capitularia Caroli Calvi, tit. xxvii. c. 7, ap. Baluzius, ii. p. 108, Bouquet, l. c. p. 659): Carolus Princeps, Pipini Regis pater, qui primus inter omnes Francorum Reges ac Principes res Ecclesiarum ab eis separavit atque divisit, pro hoc solo maxime est aeternaliter perditus. Nam S. Eucherius Aurelianensium Episc.—in oratione positus ad alterum est saeculum raptus, et inter caetera, quae Domino sibi ostendente conspexit, vidit illum in inferno inferiori torqueri. Cui interroganti ab Angelo ejus ductore responsum est, quia Sanctorum judicatione, qui in futuro judicio cum Domino judicabunt, quorumque res abstulit et divisit, ante illud judicium anima et corpore sempiternis poenis est deputatus, et recipit simul cum suis peccatis poenas propter peccata omnium, qui res suas et facultates in honore et amore Domini ad Sanctorum loca in luminaribus divini cultus, et alimoniis servorum Christi ac pauperum pro animarum suarum redemtione tradiderant. Qui in se reversus S. Bonifacium et Fulradum, Abbatem monasterii S. Dionysii, et summum Capellanum Regis Pipini ad se vocavit, eisque talia dicens in signum dedit, ut ad sepulchrum illius irent, et si corpus ejus ibidem non reperissent, ea quae dicebat, vera esse concrederent. Ipsi autem—sepulchrum illius aperientes, visus est subito exisse dracc, et totum illud sepulchrum interius inventum est denigratum, ac si fuisset exustum. Nos autem illos vidimus, qui usque ad nostram aetatem duraverunt, qui huic rei interfuerunt, et nobis viva voce veraciter sunt testati quae audierunt atque viderunt. Cf. Acta SS. Februarii, t. iii. p. 211, ss.

[4] Planck's Gesch. d. christl. kirchl. Gesellschaftsverfassung, Bd. ii. 692, ff. On the Romish vicars in Spain who appeared during the Arian period, see P. de Marca de Concordia Sac. et Imp. lib. v. c. 42. Caj. Cenni de Antiquitate Eccl. Hispanae (2 tomi. Romae. 1741. 4) i. 200.

[5] The king called councils, Cenni, ii. 89, and was supreme judge, even of bishops, ii. 153.

[6] Planck, ii. 235, 246. Gregor. Tur. Hist. Franc. iii. c. 30: Sumpserant enim Gothi hanc detestabilem consuetudinem, ut si quis eis de regibus non placuisset, gladio eum adpeterent: et qui libuisset animo, hunc sibi statuerent regem. Comp. in particular, Concil. Tolet. iv. (633) cap. 75 (ap. Mansi, x. p. 637, ss.): Post instituta quaedam ecclesiastici ordinis—postrema nobis cunctis sacerdotibus sententia est, pro robore nostrorum regum et stabilitate gentis Gothorum pontificale, ultimum sub Deo judice ferre decretum. A long admonition to maintain fidelity to the kings. Then: Nullus apud nos praesumtione regnum arripiat, nullus excitet mutuas seditiones civium, nemo meditetur interitus regum: sed et defuncto in pace principe, primates totius gentis cum *sacerdotibus* successorem regni concilio communi constituant. Then follows the solemn condemnation of every one who should resist: Anathema sit in conspectu Dei Patris et angelorum, atque ab ecclesia catholica, quam profanaverit perjurio, efficiatur extraneus, et ab omni coetu Christianorum alienus cum omnibus impietatis suae sociis, etc. Finally: Anathema sit in conspectu Christi et apostolorum ejus, atque ab ecclesia cath. etc. as above. Finally, Anathema sit

Thus the connection with Rome ceased.[7] The bishop of the royal metropolis, Toledo, was primate of the Spanish Church,[8] and raised himself to a self-reliance, which exhibited itself very decidedly even in opposition to the Roman see.[9] King *Witizia* (701–710) at length broke off all connection with it;[10] but this

in conspectu Spiritus Sancti, et martyrum Christi, etc.—But further on also: Te quoque praesentem regem, futurosque sequentium aetatum principes humilitate qua debemus deposcimus, ut moderati et mites erga subjectos existentes cum justitia et pietate populos a Deo vobis creditos regatis.—Ne quisquam vestrum solus in causis capitum aut rerum sententiam ferat, sed consensu publico, cum rectoribus, ex judicio manifesto delinquentium culpa patescat.—Sane de futuris regibus hanc sententiam promulgamus, ut si quis ex eis contra reverentiam legum, superba dominatione et fastu regio, in flagitiis et facinore, sive cupiditate crudelissimam potestatem in populis exercuerit, anathematis sententia a Christo domino condemnetur, et habeat a Deo separationem atque judicium, etc.

7 Cenni, ii. 46, 62, 154.

8 Cenni, ii. 197.

9 From Gregorii M. lib. vii. Ep. 125, 126, it is plain that the same sent the pallium to Archbishop Leander of Seville. It may be that the latter was already dead († 599) when it came to him, so that for this reason no trace is found of his receiving it, as Cenni, ii. 225, supposes. That little value generally was attributed to the Roman pallium, is proved by the fact that the succeeding archbishops did not seek for it, and that, before the invasion of the Saracens, no other Roman pallium came to Spain, Cenni, ii. 252.—That self-reliance and independence are expressed particularly in the explanations of Archbishop Julian of Toledo, respecting the remarks made by Benedict II. against his confession of faith, in Conc. Toletan. xv. (688) ap. Mansi, xii. 9. They conclude with the words, p. 17: Jam vero si post haec et ab ipsis dogmatibus patrum, quibus haec prolata sunt, in quocumque [Romani] dissentiant, non jam cum illis est amplius contendendum, sed, majorum directo calle inhaerentes vestigiis, erit per divinum judicium amatoribus veritatis responsio nostra sublimis, etiamsi ab ignorantibus aemulis censeatur indocilis.

10 Witizia is a remarkable example of the manner in which the clergy, treating of the historical persons of the middle ages, handled those who displeased them. The oldest writer of his history, Isidorus Pacensis (about 754. Chronicon in España Sagrada por Henrique Florez, t. viii. p. 282, ss.), speaks in highly commendatory terms of his reign. He notices the ecclesiastical regulations made under his sanction in two places; first at the Aera, 736 (698, p. C.), when Witiza reigned along with his father Egica, p. 296: Per idem tempus Felix, urbis Regiae Toletanae Sedis Episcopus, gravitatis et prudentia excellentia nimia pollet, et Concilia satis praeclara etiam adhuc cum ambobus Principibus agit. (To these councils also belongs Conc. Toletan. xviii. (701) at which, perhaps, the decrees above alluded to were enacted. Cf. Roderici Ximenii Hist. Hispan. iii. c. 15: Hic [Witiza] in ecclesia S. Petri, quae est extra Toletum, cum episcopis et magnatibus super ordinatione regni concilium celebravit, quod tamen in corpore canonum non habetur.) The second passage of Isidorus, p. 298: Per idem tempus (toward the end of Witiza's reign) divinae memoriae Sinderedus urbis Regiae Metropolitanus Episcopus sanctimoniae studio claret: atque longaevos et merito honorabiles viros, quos in suprafata sibi commissa Ecclesia repetit, non secundum scientiam zelo sanctitatis stimulat (probably he was zealous against unchastity) atque instinctu jam dicti Witizae Principis eos sub ejus tempore convexare non cessat. The first aspersions of Witiza appear in the Frankish Chron. Moissiacense (about 818) ad ann. 715, in Pertz Monumenta Germaniae Hist. i. 290: His temporibus in Spania super Gothos regnabat Witicha.—Iste deditus in feminis, exemplo suo sacerdotes ac populum luxuriose vivere docuit, irritans furorem Domini. Sarraceni tunc in Spania ingrediuntur. In Spain these aspersions first appear in the Chron. Sebastiani Episc. Salmanticensis seu Alphonsi III. Regis (about 866 in España Sagrada, t. xiii.) They have been extended and exaggerated by Rodericus Ximenius, archbishop of Toledo, in the historia Hispania (A.D. 1243) lib. iii. c. 15–17, and Lucas, Episc. Tudensi, in the continuation

step was attended with no important consequence, inasmuch as an incursion of the Saracens took place soon after.

§ 133.

ECCLESIASTICAL CONDITION OF THE BRITISH ISLANDS.

Among the Anglo-Saxons, Christianity had at first to struggle against heathenism with various fortune, but was afterward diffused by degrees in all the Anglo-Saxon states. Those who preached it were for the most part Roman missionaries; *Northumberland* alone being converted by the Scottish clergy, who introduced here the regulations of the ancient British Church. Old controversies between them and the Roman-English clergy were soon renewed; however, after a conference between both parties at the synod of *Strenechal* (now Whitby, not far from York, Synodus Pharensis 664), the king of Northumberland, *Oswin*, decided in favor of the Roman ordinances.[1] And since the well-ordered schools of the Irish monas-

of Isidore's Chronicon (A.D. 1236). After relating many infamous deeds of Witiza, it is stated by Rodericus, l. c. c. 16, in Andr. Schotti Hispania illustrata (Francof. 1603. 4 tomi, fol.) ii. 62: Verum quia ista sibi in facie resistebant [clerici], propter vexationem pontificis [Episc. Toletani] ad Romanum pontificem appellabant. Vitiza facinorosus timens, ne suis criminibus obviarent, et populum ab ejus obedientia revocarent, dedit licentiam, immo praeceptum, omnibus clericis, ut uxores et concubinas unam et plures haberent juxta libitum voluptatis, et ne Romanis constitutionibus, quae talia prohibent, in aliquo obedirent, et sic per eos populus retineretur. Lucas Tudensis (ibid. iv. 69): Et ne adversus eum insurgeret s. ecclesia, episcopis, presbyteris, diaconibus et caeteris ecclesiae Christi ministris carnales uxores lascivus Rex habere praecepit, et ne obedirent Romano Pontifici sub mortis interminatione prohibuit. The state of the matter appears to have been this. Witiza, in conjunction with Sinderedus, archbishop of Toledo, opposed licentiousness in priests, and perceived that it could be eradicated only by allowing them to marry. The latter had been general among the Arians, and abolished when they joined the Catholic Church (cf. Conc. Tolet. iii. ann. 589, c. 5): Compertum est a sancto Concilio, Episcopos, Presbyteros et Diaconos venientes ex haerese carnali adhuc desiderio uxoribus copulari: ne ergo de cetero fiat, etc. Thus the prejudicial alteration, which had been introduced for one hundred years by the prohibition of the council, could be clearly noticed. Hence Witiza allowed priests to marry, and declared the Roman decretals, forbidding it, to be of no binding force. Comp. a defense of King Witiza by Don Gregorio Mayans y Siscar, translated into German, from the Spanish, in Büsching's Magazin für die neue Historie und Geographie, i. 379, ff. Aschbach's Gesch. der Westgothen, S. 303, ff.

[1] Bedae Hist. eccl. gentis Anglorum, iii. 25. The remarkable conclusion of the dispute between the Scotch bishop, Colman, and the English presbyter, Wilfrid. The former appealed to Anatolius and Columba, the latter to Peter, and closed with the passage, Matth. xvi. 18: Tu es Petrus, etc. King Oswin then said: Verene, Colmane, haec illi Petro dicta sunt a Domino? Qui ait: vere, Rex. At ille: habetis, inquit, vos proferre aliquid

teries always attracted many young Anglo-Saxons to Ireland,[2] and by this means might become dangerous to the Roman regulations, Rome sent forth into England, for the purpose of giving a check to this influence, the learned *Theodore*, born at Tarsus, as archbishop of Canterbury (668–690), and the abbot *Hadrian*, who every where strengthened the Roman ordinances, and, by the erection of schools, rendered those journies to Ireland superfluous.[3] No less active in favor of the Romish Church was also *Wilfrid*, a noble Anglo-Saxon,[4] who, even when a young priest, had turned the scale at the synod of Whitby, had been afterward for a time bishop of York; and, driven thence, had preached, not without fruit, to the Frieslanders; and, lastly, had converted *Sussex* (about 680, † 709), where heathenism remained longest among the Anglo-Saxons.

tantae potestatis vestro Columbae datum? At ille ait: nihil. Rursum autem Rex: si utrique vestrum, inquit, in hoc sine ulla controversia consentiunt, quod haec principaliter Petro dicta, et ei claves regni caelorum sunt datae a Domino? Responderunt: etiam utique. At ille ita conclusit: et ego vobis dico, quia hic est ostiarius ille, cui ego contradicere nolo, sed in quantum novi vel valeo, hujus cupio in omnibus obedire statutis, ne forte me adveniente ad fores regni caelorum, non sit qui reserat, averso illo qui claves tenere probatur. Haec dicente Rege faverunt assidentes quique sive adstantes, majores una cum mediocribus, et abdicata minus perfecta institutione, ad ea quae meliora cognoverant, sese transferre festinabant.

[2] Beda, iii. 27: Multi nobilium simul et mediocrium de gente Anglorum,—relicta insula patria, vel divinae lectionis vel continentioris vitae gratia illo secesserant. Et quidam quidem mox se monasticae conversationi fideliter mancipaverunt, alii magis circumeundo per cellas magistrorum lectioni operam dare gaudebant: quos omnes Scoti libentissime suscipientes, victum eis quotidianum sine pretio, libros quoque ad legendum et magisterium gratuitum praebere curabant. Cf. Murray in Nov. Comm. Soc. Gott. (see above, § 126, note 3) t. i. p. 109.

[3] Beda, iv. 2. (Theodorus) peragrata insula tota, quaquaversum Anglorum gentes morabantur,—rectum vivendi ordinem, ritum celebrandri pascha canonicum, per omnia comitante et cooperante Adriano disseminabat. Isque primus erat archiepiscopus, cui omnis Anglorum ecclesia manus dare consentiret. Et quia literis sacris simul et saecularibus, ut diximus, abundanter ambo erant instructi, congregata discipulorum caterva, scientiae salutaris quotidie flumina irrigandis eorum cordibus emanabant: ita ut etiam metricae artis, astronomicae et arithmeticae ecclesiasticae disciplinam inter sacrorum apicum volumina suis auditoribus contraderent. Indicio est, quod usque hodie supersunt de eorum discipulis, qui latinam graecamque linguam aeque ut propriam, in qua nati sunt, norunt. Neque unquam prorsus ex quo Britanniam petierunt Angli, feliciora fuere tempora, dum et fortissimos christianosque habentes reges cunctis barbaris nationibus essent terrori, et omnium vota ad nuper audita caelestis regni gaudia penderent: et quicunque lectionibus sacris cuperent erudiri, haberent in promtu magistros qui docerent: et sonos cantandi in ecclesia—ab hoc tempore per omnes Anglorum ecclesias discere coeperunt, etc.

[4] Vita S. Wilfridi by the contemporary Eddius (Æddi), cognomento Stephanus (cantandi magister in Northumbrorum Ecclesiis, invitatus de Cantia a reverendissimo viro Wilfrido, Beda Hist. eccl. iv. 2), in Th. Gale Historiae Britannicae, Saxonicae, Anglodanicae Scriptores xv. Oxon. 1691. fol. p. 40. Lappenberg's Geschichte von England. Bd. 1 (Hamburg. 1834), S. 167.

It is true that the original missionary dependence of the Anglo-Saxon Church on Rome gradually ceased; here also the kings put themselves in possession of the same ecclesiastical privileges, which kings asserted in the other German kingdoms;[5] the Latin language, connecting with Rome, was obliged to allow along with itself, even in the Liturgy, the Anglo-Saxon tongue;[6] but notwithstanding such considerations, Rome continued to maintain an authority in the Anglo-Saxon Church which it did not now exercise in any other German Church.[7]

Emulation with the Irish institutions for educational purposes also introduced into the Anglo-Saxon schools a very great activity. Not only did they distinguish themselves by the study of the Greek language, which Theodore had established in the whole of the west, but its stimulus unquestionably contributed to the development of the Anglo-Saxon dialect, already even as a written language.[8] At the end of this period, England possessed the most learned man of the west, *the Venerable Bede*, a monk in the monastery of *Peter and Paul* at Yarrow († 735).[9] The

[5] Theodore was still in Rome when nominated Archbishop of Canterbury, after Wighard, who had been sent thither to be ordained, had died (Beda, iii. 29, iv. 1). But the decision of Rome in favor of Wilfrid, who had been expelled from the see of York (Eddius in vita Wilfridi, ap. Gale, i. 67), was not regarded; Wilfrid, on the contrary, was put in captivity (l. c. p. 69). The bishops were for the most part appointed by the kings (Lappenberg's Gesch. v. England, i. 183), who had also the power of confirming the decrees of synods, and the highest judicial power over the clergy (Lappenberg, i. 194).

[6] Lappenberg, i. 196.

[7] Planck's christ. kirchl. Gesellschaftsverf. ii. 704, ff.

[8] Caedmon, a monk in the monastery of Streaneshalh † 680 (Beda, iv. 24, non ab hominibus,—sed divinitus adjutus gratis canendi donum accepit), author of poetical paraphrases of biblical books, especially of Genesis. See Caedmon's metrical paraphrase of parts of the Holy Scriptures, in Anglo-Saxon, by Benj. Thorpe. London. 1832. 8.—Aldhelm, abbot of Malmesbury, afterward bishop of Sherborne († 709), translated the Psalms (King Alfred said of him, according to Wilhelm. Malmesb. ap. Gale, i. 339: Nulla unquam aetate par ei fuit quisquam poësin anglicam posse facere, tantum componere, eadem apposite vel canere vel dicere). As early as the year 680, there existed a version of the four gospels by Aldred. (Selden Praef. ad Scriptt. Hist. Angl. ed. Twysden, p. 25): also Ekbert, bishop of Lindisfarne, translated the gospels; Bede, the gospel of John.—Beowulf, a heroic poem, received its present form at this time from the hands of Christians (ed. G. F. Thorkelin, Kopenh. 1817. 4, translated into German by L. Ettmüller. Zurich. 1840. 8). In like manner, about the year 700, there existed a poem (by Aldhelm?) descriptive of the conversion of the Myrmidonians by the apostle Andrew, and another on the finding of the cross by the empress Helena, composed by one Cynewulf. See Andrew and Elene, published by J. Grimm. Cassel. 1840. 8vo.

[9] As a proof of his wide-spread fame is adduced Sergii P. I. Ep. ad Ceolfridum (abbot of the cloister there, A.D. 700, quoted in Guilelmi Malmsburiensis († 1143) de Reb. gestis Regum Angl. i. 3: Hortamur Deo dilectam bonitatis tuae religiositatem, ut, quia exortis quibusdam ecclesiasticarum causarum capitulis (without doubt the cloister in question), non sine examinatione longius innotescendis, opus nobis sunt ad conferendum artis literatura imbuti,—absque aliqua immoratione religiosum famulum Dei (Bedam) venerabilis

new branch of ecclesiastical literature founded by John the Faster, in his penitential law-book, had been first adopted in the west by the British Church,[10] and, after its example, was also used among the Anglo-Saxons by *Theodore*, *Bede*, and *Egbert* of York († 767).[11] On the other hand, these *libelli poenitentiales* do not seem to have as yet obtained currency any where out of England.

Endeavors were always proceeding from the Anglo-Saxon states to reconcile the Britons and Irish with the Roman Church as the common mother-church,[12] and to unite them with the Church of the Anglo-Saxons. But although the abbot *Adam*-

monasterii tui ad veneranda limina Apostolorum principum dominorum meorum Petri et Pauli, amatorum tuorum ac protectorum, ad nostrae mediocritatis conspectum non moreris dirigere. Stevenson, however, in his Introduction prefixed to Bedae Opp Hist. tom. 1, p. x., shews that the word Bedam is wanting in an old MS. of this epistle, and was inserted by William of Malmesbury, but that Bede could not have been called at that time.—Bede's writings embrace Natural Philosophy, Chronology, Philosophy, Grammar, Astronomy, Arithmetic, etc., and give a view of all the learning of the time. In particular, Historia ecclesiast. gentis Anglorum libb. v., from Julius Cæsar till 731 (ed. Fr. Chiffletius. Paris. 1681. 4. Joh. Smith. Cantabrig. 1722. fol.). De sex aetatibus mundi liber. Lives of English monks. (Opera historica ad fidem Codd. MSS. rec. Jos. Stevenson, t. ii. Lond. 1838–41. 8.) Numerous commentaries on the Holy Scriptures, homilies, letters, etc. Opp. ed. Basil. 1563. t. viii. fol. Colon. 1688. t. iv. fol. ed. J. A. Giles, 5 voll. Lond. 1843. 8. H. Gehle Disp. de Bedae Ven. vita et scriptis. Lugd. Bat. 1838. 8.

[10] These libelli poenitentiales were constantly altered, that they might continue useful in practice: on the other hand, the earlier were transferred more or less verbally into the later. Hence hardly any one has come down to us entirely free from alterations; and in many cases it is difficult to decide to what author an extant poenitentiale is to be attributed. Among the Irish the oldest known was that of Columbanus, a part of which was published in Colomb. Opp. ed. Patric. Fleming. Lovan. 1667. (See F. F. Mone's Quellen u. Forschungen zur Gesch. d. teutschen Literatur u. Sprache. Bd. 1. Aachen u. Leipzig. 1830. S. 494), another by Cumin († 661), an extract from which was published by Fleming, l. c. and Bibl. PP. Lugd. xii. 42 (see Mone, S. 490), and which is the same work as the so-called Canones poenitentiales Hieronymi (Opp. ed. Martianay, v. 5) (Mone, S. 497).

[11] Theodori Liber poenitentialis, printed in its oldest existing form in the ancient laws and institutes of England, London. 1840. fol. and taken from this in Dr. F. Kuntsmann's latein. Pönitentialbücher der Angelsachsen. Mainz. 1844. S. 43. Theodori capitula de redemptione peccatorum (ap. Kuntsmann, P. 106), give the oldest instructions how to purchase penitential seasons by singing, prayer, and by money.—Beda de remediis peccatorum (ap. Kuntsmann, S. 142), elaborated, perhaps, by Egbert; and therefore Bede's canons are also occasionally attributed to the latter, and the Ballerini de Ant. collectionibus canonum p. iv. c. 6, have assigned the whole to him. Egbert's Poenitential, Latin and Anglo-Saxon, is given in Wilkin's Conc. M. Brit. i. A fourth book was published by Mone, l. c. i. 501. Comp. Ballerini, l. c. Wasserschleben's Beiträge zur Gesch. u. Kenntnisz der Beichtbücher in dess. Beitr. zur Gesch. d. vorgratianischen Kirchenrechtsquellen. Leipzig. 1839. S. 78.

[12] Hence the fable which first appears in Beda, i. 4, that the British king, Lucius, in the second century, applied to Pope Eleutherus, obsecrans, ut per ejus mandatum Christianus efficeretur, and that the British church was thus founded. Cf. D. Thiele de Ecclesiae britann. primordiis partt. 2 (Halae. 1839. 8.) i. 10, ii. 14.

nan, at the beginning of the eighth century, had labored to effect this object, not without success among the Britons and in the south of Ireland,[13] and the monk *Ecbert* had gained over the northern Picts to the side of Rome,[14] yet the breach was not removed by this means.[15] It was not till the decline of the Irish Church amid the continued civil wars,[16] that, toward the end of the eleventh century, Dublin first came to attach itself to the archbishop of Canterbury;[17] afterward the archbishop of Armagh, *Malachy* († 1148), was active in favor of Rome;[18] till at last Ireland and Wales were conquered by Henry II.,[19] and

[13] Beda, v. 16.

[14] Beda, v. 23.

[15] Beda, v. 24, says, when he speaks of the condition of his times (735): Britones maxima ex parte domestico sibi odio gentem Anglorum et totius catholicae Ecclesiae statum pascha minus recto moribusque improbis impugnant. About the same time Gregory III. (731–741) warns the German bishops of the British errors. See an epistle among those of Boniface Ep. 129: Gentilitatis ritum et doctrinam, vel venientium Britonum abjiciatis.

[16] Bernardus Claraevall. de vita S. Malachiae, c. 10 (Opp. ed. Montfaucon, i. 673): Mos pessimus inoleverat quorundum diabolica ambitione procerum, sedem sanctam (Armachanam) obtentum iri haereditaria successione. Nec enim patiebantur episcopari, nisi qui essent de tribu et familia sua.—Et eo usque firmaverat sibi jus pravum—generatio mala,—ut etsi interdum defecissent clerici de sanguine illo, sed Episcopi nunquam. Denique jam octo exstiterant ante Celsum viri uxorati, et absque Ordinibus, literati tamen. Inde tota illa per universam Hiberniam—dissolutio ecclesiasticae disciplinae, censurae enervatio, religionis evacuatio.—Nam—sine ordine, sine ratione mutabantur et multplicabantur Episcopi pro libitu Metropolitani, ita ut unus Episcopatus uno non esset contentus, sed singulae paene Ecclesiae singulos haberent Episcopos. Hence also, perhaps, may be explained the statement of Ekkehardus († 1070, a monk in St. Gallen, to which place many Irish came at that time) in his Liber benedictionem: In Hibernia Episcopi et Presbyteri unum sunt (ex MS. in Arx Gesch. v. St. Gallen, i. 267).

[17] Lanfranc, A.D. 1074, consecrated Patricius, who was chosen bishop of Dublin, and obtained from him the promise of canonical obedience. All subsequent bishops of Dublin were consecrated by the Archbishop of Canterbury. See J. Usseri Veterum epistolarum hibernicarum sylloge, Dublinii. 1632. 4. p. 68, 118, 136, but for this very reason hated by the other Irish bishops. After this Gillebertus Ep. Lunicensis (of Limerick) endeavored as well as Anselm, Archbishop of Canterbury, to induce the other Irish also to come to the same conclusion, l. c. p. 77, ss. The church of Waterford also attached itself to England 1096, p. 92.

[18] He stood in close connection with St. Bernard, and died in a journey to Rome in Clairvaux. Bernard wrote on this lib. de vita et rebus gestis S. Malachiae (Opp. ed. Montf. i. 663). Malachy was legatus sedis Apost. per totam Hiberniam, but did not desire the pallium. In Clairvaux he educated young Irishmen, and then founded by their instrumentality, Cistercian monasteries in Ireland (vita Mal. c. 16. Usserii Vett. epist. hibern. p. 102). Immediately after him came the first pallia to Ireland. See Chronica de Mailros (ed. Edinburgi. 1835. 4) p. 74: Anno MCLI Papa Eugenius quatuor pallia per legatum suum Johannem Papirum transmisit in Hiberniam, quo nunquam antea pallium delatum fuerat.

[19] Pope Hadrian IV. made a gift of Ireland, A.D. 1155, to the king. See the Bull in Usserii Vett. epist. hib. p. 109; comp. Johannis Sarisburiensis (who, as royal embassador, had prevailed on the pope to do so) Metalogicus lib. iv. in fine. Giraldi Cambrensis (about 1190) Expugnatio Hiberniae (in the Historicis Angl. Normannicis. Francof. 1602. fol.)

thus the complete connection of the British and Irish Church with Rome was effected.

§ 134.

SPREAD OF CHRISTIANITY IN GERMANY.

Schmidt's Kirchengesch. iv. 10. Neander's Kirchengesch. iii. 72. Rettberg's Gesch. d. Kirche Deutschlands. Bd. i. Göttingen. 1845.

The attempts to convert the Germans, whether made by Franks, or by Irish and Anglo-Saxons, were as yet but partially successful.

The Irish *Kilian*[1] lost his life in the cause at Würzburg (689); as also *Emmeram*[2] at Ratisbon (654). In Bavaria, however, better success attended *Rupert*,[3] bishop of Worms, who baptized Duke Theodore II. († 696), and founded the Church of Salzburg († 718); as also *Corbinian*,[4] who gathered a church in Freisingen († 730).

On the other hand, Anglo-Saxon monks endeavored to spread Christianity among the kindred north-German races. *Wilfrid* was the first who preached among the Frieslanders († 677).[5]

M. Chr. Sprengel's Gesch. v. Grossbritannien. Th. 1 (a continuation of the Universal History of the world, part 47) S. 433.—Wales was conquered since 1157. See Giraldi Cambr. Descriptio Cambriae (in the above quoted collection). Sprengel, l. c. p. 378.

1 Acta SS. ad d. 8 Jul. C. F. Hefele's Gesch. d. Einführung des Christenth. im sud-westl. Deutschland. Tübingen. 1837. S. 372.

2 See life of Aribo, fourth bishop of Freisingen († 753). See Acta SS. ad d. 22 Sept. B. A. Winter's Vorarbeiten zur Beleuchtung d. baier. u. österr. Kirchengesch. (2 Bde. München. 1805, 1810), ii. 153. According to Winter, ii. 169, he was not a native of Pictavium, in West Franconia, as has been usually assumed, but of Petavio, now Petau, in Pannonia.

3 Act. SS. ad d. 27 Mart. Rupert came to Bavaria at the time of a Frankish King Childebert. According to the Salzburg tradition, the king was Childebert II., at the end of the sixth century; but, according to Valesius, Mabillon, Pagi, and especially Hansiz Germania sacra, ii. 51) Childebert III., a hundred years later. On the contrary, M. Filz, a Benedictine, and Professor in Salzburg, has reasserted, conformably to the ancient tradition, that Rupert came to Bavaria, A.D. 580, and died in 623. See his treatise on the true period of the apostel. Wirksamkeit d. heil. Rupert in Baiern. Salzburg. 1831. 8. The same writer in the Anzeigelblätt. d. Wiener Jahrb. d. Literatur, Bd. 64 (1833), S. 23. Bd. 80 (1837), S. 1. In the mean time, however, the younger age of Rupert is maintained by Blumberger, Benedictine in Göttweih. in the Vienna Jahr. Bd. 73. S. 242. u. Bd. 74. S. 147, and by Rudhart in the Munich gel. Anzeigen. Bd. 5. 1837. S. 587.

4 See life of Aribo, bishop of Freisingen. See Acta SS. ad d. 8 Sept.

5 See § 133, note 4. Beda Hist. eccl. v. 19. Eddius ap. Gale p. 64. H. J. Royaards Geschiedenis der invoering en vestiging van het Christendom in Nederland 3te Uitg. Utrecht. 1844. p. 127.

Afterward *Willebrord*, first bishop of Wiltaburg (Utrecht) from 696–739 labored, along with his associates,[6] with much success, under the protection of the Franks, among the West Frieslanders and the surrounding territories; but the East Frieslanders remained steadfast to paganism. The Saxons even murdered the two *Ewalds* who visited them;[7] and *Suidbert*,[8] who had at first been received among the Boructiarii, was afterward obliged to retreat, when they were subdued by the Saxons; and obtained from Pipin an island in the Rhine to establish a convent on it (Kaiserswerth) † 713.

[6] Beda Hist. eccl. v. c. 10, ss. Willebrord's life by Alcuin in Mabillonii Act. SS. Ord. Bened. Saec. iii. P. i. p. 601. Royaards, p. 159.

[7] Beda, v. c. 11. Acta SS. ad. 3 Oct. L. v. Ledebur das Land u. Volk der Bructerer. Berlin. 1827. S. 277. Royaards, p. 201.

[8] Beda, v. c. 12. Acta SS. ad. d. 1 Mart. Ledebur, S. 280. Royaards, p. 197.

ADDITIONAL REFERENCES AND NOTES,

BY THE AMERICAN EDITOR.

---

§ 1. *The Idea of the Church.*—Prof. *Leo*, of Halle, in his *Ferienschriften*, Halle, 1847, contends for the Celtic origin of the word kirche, church. In the Celtic, *cyrch* or *cylch* designates the central point, around which something is gathered, the place of assemblage. *Kurtz*, Kirchengeschichte, Bd. 1, § 1, remarks, "that the introduction of the word among the Anglo-Saxons, and through English missionaries among the Germans," is the most probable hypothesis. For the idea of the church, cf. Dr. *A. Petersen*, Die Idee d. Kirche. 3 Thle. 1843-45.—Rev. *Arthur Litton*, Church of Christ in its Idea, etc. Lond. 1851.—*W. Palmer*, on the Church, 2. 1841.—The *Princeton Repertory*, 1846, 1853, 1854.—*Field*, B. of the Church (1628), new ed. by *R. Eden*, 4. 8. 1853.—*Münchmeyer*, d. Dogma von der sichtbaren und der unsichtbaren Kirche. 1854.—*J. Müller*, d. unsichtbare Kirche, Deutsche Zeitschrift. 1851.—*Scherer*, l'Eglise. 1844.

§ 2. On the general subject of this section, the most important recent work is, *Baur's* Epochen der kirchlichen Geschichtschreibung, Tübingen, 1852, written to sustain the views of the Tübingen school.—*Hagenbach*, Neander's Services as a Church Historian, transl. in *Bib. Sacra*, vol. viii. 1851.—*Niedner*, Zeichnung des Umfangs für d. Inhalt d. Gesch. d. christl. Religion: in *Studien u. Kritiken*. 1853.

W. Brown, History of the Propagation of Christianity among the Heathen since the Reformation. New edition, 3. 8. Edinb. 1854.—*J. Wiggers*, Geschichte der evangelischen Mission, 2. 8. 1844-45.—Origin and History of Missions. By *T. Smith* and *J. O. Choules*, 2, 4. Bost. 1838.—*Henrion*, histoire générale des missions catholiques, depuis le xiii. siècle. Paris, 1844. 2. 8.

The State in its Relations with the Church. By *W. E. Gladstone*, Esq. 4th ed. 2. 8. 1841.—Dr. *Pusey* on the Royal Supremacy. 1849.

The History of Doctrines.—Dr. *Hagenbach's* History of Doctrines, transl. by *C. W. Buck*, 2. 8. 2d edition. Edinb. 1853, from the third German edition.—*Münscher's* Elements of Dogmatic History, transl. by *Jas. Murdock*, D.D. 12. New Haven, 1830.—*Theod. Kliefoth*, Einleitung in d. Dogmengesch. 8. 1839.—Of *Meier's* Dogmengesch. a new edition appeared in 1854, edited by *G. Baur*.—Dr. *F. Ch. Baur*, Lehrbuch d. christlichen Dogmengeschichte, 8. Stuttg. 1847.—Dr. *H. Klee* (Bonn) Lehrbuch der Dogmengesch. 2. 8. Mainz. 1837, '8, from the Roman Catholic point of view.—*Marheinecke*, Vorlesungen uber d. Dogmengesch.: a posthumous publication, 8. 1849.—*L. Noack*, Dogmengesch. Erlangen, 1853.—*Carl Beck*, Christl. Dogmengesch. Weimar, 1848.—Other earlier works are, *Bertholdt*, 1823; *Ruperti*, 1830; and *Lentz*, 1834.—*Vorländer*, Tabellen d. Dogmengesch. nach Neander. Hamb. 1835, '7, to A.D. 604. On the history of doctrines, *Neander's* General History is very full.

On the general subject of the *History of Doctrines* and its historians, compare *Kling*, in *Studien u. Kritiken*. 1840, 1841, 1843; *Niedner*, zur neuesten Dogmengesch. u. Dogmatik, in *Allg. Monatsschrift*. 1851; *Engelhardt*, in *Zeitschrift für d. hist. Theologie*. 1852, '3, '4, a review and criticism of the literature.—*Niedner*, d. Recht d. Dogmen im Christenthume, in the same *Zeitschrift*. 1852; *Dortenbach*, d. Methode d. Dogmengesch. in *Stu-*

dien u. Kritiken. 1852; (*Thomasius*), Aufgabe d. Dogmengesch. in *Zeitschrift für Protestantismus*, Bd. 3.—*Kling*, "Dogmengeschichte" in the *Real-Encyclop. f. Prot. Theologie.*

History of Special Doctrines.—*Corrodi*, Chiliasmus, 4 Bde. 1794.—*Baur*, Versöhnung. 1838.—*Baur*, Dreieinigkeit, 3 Bde. 1841–45.—*Dorner*, d. Person. Christi. 2te Aufl. 1845–55, 2. 2. 1 (the Reformation).—*Meier*, Trinität. 1844.—*Jacobi*, Tradition, 1. 1847.—*Kahnis*, vom heiligen Geiste, 1. 1847.—*Höfling*, Taufe, 2. 1847, '8.—*Ebrard*, Abendmahl, 2. 1846.—*Kahnis*, Abendmahl. 1851.—*Helfferich*, Mystik, 2. 1842.—*Güder*, d. Erscheinung Jesu unter d. Todten. 1853.—*F. Huydekoper*, Belief of first three Centuries on Christ's Mission to the Underworld. Boston, 1854.—*König*, Christi Höllenfahrt. 1844.—*Maywahlen*, d. Todtenreich. 1854.

History of Theology.—Dr. *W. Gass* has begun an important work on the "History of the Protestant Theology," vol. 1. 1854.—*Schweizer*, d. Protestantischen Centraldogmen in ihrer Entwickelung, Bd. 1. 1854. Earlier works are, *Heinrich*, Gesch. d. Dogmatik. 1790; *Schickedanz.* 1827; *W. Herrmann.* 1842.

Neander's "Memorials of Christian Life" have been translated in part, and published in Bohn's Library. 1853.

Christian Antiquities.—Of *Joseph Bingham's* work a new edition is in the course of preparation in England by *Richard Bingham.*—*C. S. Henry*, Compendium of Christian Antiq. Phil. 1838, is an abridgment of Bingham.—*Lyman Coleman*, Ancient Christianity exemplified, 8. Phil. 1852.—*Siegel*, Handbuch d. christlich-kirchlichen Alterthümer, 4 Bde. Leipsic, 1835–38, alphabetically arranged.—*Guericke*, Lehrbuch d. Archäologie, 8. Leips. 1847.—Cf. *M. J. E. Volbeding*, Thesaurus commentationum illustrandis antiquitat. christ. inserventium, t. i. Lips. 1847.—*J. E. Riddle*, Manual of Christian Antiquities. Lond. 1839.

History of Heresies.—*A. Sartori*, die christlichen und mit der christlichen Kirche zusammenhängenden Secten (in tabular form). Lübeck, 1855.—History of Christian Churches and Sects, Rev. *J. B. Marsden*, 5 parts published. 1854, '5.—Dr. *G. Volkmar*, Die Quellen d. Ketzergeschichte bis zum Nicänum, kritisch untersucht, Bd. 1. 1855.

Works on the General History of the Christian Church.—*Neander's* history has been admirably translated by Prof. *Joseph Torrey*, of the University of Vermont, in 5 vols. 8vo, comprising the whole of the original, including Schneider's edition of the last volume. Boston, 1849–54.—The seventh edition of Dr. *Hase's* History, translated by *C. E. Blumenthal* and *C. P. Wing*, 8. New York, 1855.—*Marheinecke*, Universal Kirchenhist. Bd. 1. 1806.—*Fleury*, Eccles. Hist., with *Tillemont's* Chronology, transl. to A.D. 870, 5. 4. 1727–32.

Niedner, Kirchengeschichte, 8. 1846: a condensed and philosophical manual.—*Fricke*, Lehrb. d. Kirchengesch. i. Leips. 1850.—*W. B. Lindner*, Lehrb. d. christl. Kirchengesch. i.–iii. 1. 1848–52, to 1648, with special respect to the history of doctrines.—*Zeller*, Gesch. d. Kirche. Stuttg. 1848.—*Kurtz*, Lehrbuch d. Kirchengesch. 2te Ausg. 1850, to be translated by Dr. *Schaeffer.* Of his *Handbuch d. K. Gesch.* only the first volume has appeared, in 3 parts, 1853, '4, completing the history of the Oriental Church to 1453.—*Schleiermacher*, Vorlesungen über d. Kirchengesch., edited by Bonnell. 1850.

Of *Böhringer's* "die Kirche Christi u. ihre Zeugen," a church history in biographies, the third division of the second volume, for the Middle Ages, has been published. 1855.

Of the later more popular manuals of church history in German, *Judä's* appeared in 1838; *Thiele*, 2d ed., 1852; *Jacobi*, Bd. 1, 1850; *Schmid*, Lehrb. 1851; *Wilcke*, 1850; *Trautmann*, 1852–54; *Huber*, Universalgesch. 1850.

The "Ecclesiastical History of *Meletius*," metropolitan of Athens in the seventeenth and eighteenth centuries, previously issued in inferior modern Greek, though written in the ancient, is issued at Constantinople, edited by Prof. *Constantine Euthybules*, first vol. 1853.

Stolberg's Geschichte is continued by *Brischar*, 1853, Bd. 49, being the 4th vol. of the continuation.—*Döllinger's* Church History to the Reformation, translated by *Ed. Cox.* Lond. 4. 8. 1848; "History of the Reformation" in German, in 1846.—*Rohrbacher*, histoire universelle de l'eglise, 29 tom. Par. 1842–49. A new edition is in the course of publication.—*Henrion*, Hist. Eccles. depuis la création jusqu'au pontificat de Pie IX. A new edition in 25 vols. is in the course of publication.—*M. I. Matter*, Hist. du Christianisme, 2d ed. Par. 1838. 2. 8.—Of *Capefigue's* Histoire de l'Eglise, the seventh vol., 1854, begins the history of the Reformation.—Abbé *Darras*, Hist. gener. de l'Eglise, 4. 8 (arranged by the chronology of the Popes). Paris, 1854.

The Annals of *Baronius* are to be continued by *Aug. Theiner* from A.D. 1572, where they were left by *Laderchi*; his History of Clement XIV. is a part of this work, which he undertook by request of Gregory XVI.—*Palma*, Praelectiones historico-ecclesiasticae. Romae. 3 voll. 1838–42.—*N. J. Cherrier* (Pesth), Epitome Hist. Eccl. Nov. Foederis, 2. 8. Vienna, 1854.

A translation of *Spanheim's* Eccles. Annals into English, from commencement of Script. to Reformation. Lond. 1829.—Of Dean *Milman's* History of Latin Christianity, a continuation of his "History," 3 vols. were published in 1854; two more complete this portion of his elaborate work. The best edition of *Milner's* Church History is by Rev. *T. Bantham*, 4. 8.—*W. Bates*, College Lectures on Eccl. History, 2d ed. 1852.—*Jortin's* Remarks on Eccl. Hist.—*Foulkes*, Manual of Church History, the first twelve centuries. 1851.—*Chs. Hardwick*, History of the Church in the Middle Ages. Camb. 1853; one of a series of Theological Manuals: the "Early Church History" and that of the "Reformation" will soon appear.—*J. C. Robertson*, History of Christian Church to 590. Lond. 1854.—*Palmer's* Compendium of Church History, new ed. 1852.—*M. Rütter's* History. New York, 1853.—State of Man before and after Promulgation of Christianity, including the Reformation, 4. 12. in "Small Books on Great Subjects." 1850–54.—*Henry Stebbing*, Hist. of the Church to Reformation, 2. 8. From 1530 to the eighteenth century, 3. 8. Lond. 1842.

Chronological Works and Tables of Church History.—Ecclesiastical Chronology, Rev. *J. E. Riddle*, 8. Lond. 1840.—Abstract of *Vater's* Tables, by *F. Cunningham*. Bost. 1831. —*Danz*. Jena, 1838.—*Douai*, 2te Aufl., 1850.—*L. Lange*. Jena, 1841.—*Schone*. Berl. 1838.—*Franke Parker*, The Church, fol. Lond. 1851.—Oxford Chronological Tables, fol. 1835–40.

§ 3. *Relation of Church History to other Historical Studies*, p. 19.—*History of Culture.* *Wachsmuth*, allg. Culturgeschichte. Leips. 1851, *sq.* und Sittengesch. 5 Bde. 1831, *sq.*—*Klemm*, allg. Culturgeschichte, 10 Bde. Leips. 1847–53.—*Karl von Raumer*, Geschichte der Pädagogik, 4. 8. (Completed 1855.)—*Robert Blakey*, Temporal Benefits of Christianity. Lond. 1849.—*Guizot's* General Hist. of Civilization in Europe, transl. by *Hazlitt.* New York, 1850.—*Hegel*, Philosophie d. Geschichte, 8.—*Schlegel*, Philosophy of History, translated by *Robertson.*

History of Religions.—*B. Constant*, De la Religion, 2. 8. Paris, 1824.—*Kraft*, die Religion aller Völker. 1845.—*Hegel*, Phil. d. Religion, herausg. *Marheinecke*, 2. 8.—*Bunsen*, Christianity and Mankind, vols. 3 and 4. 1854.

History of Philosophy.—*Ritter's* work is now completed in 12 volumes.—*Schwegler*, Gesch. d. Phil., 8. 1848.—Das Buch d. Weltweisheit, 2. 8. 1854.—*Reinhold*, 3 Bde., 4th ed. 1854.—*Tennemann's* Manual, transl. by *Morell.* Lond. 1854.—*Erdmann*, Gesch. d. neueren Philos. (Three vols. in six.) 1834.—*Chalybäus*, Hist. of German Philosophy, transl. Am. ed. 1854.

History of Literature.—*Grässe*, Lehrb. einer allgemeinen Literär-geschichte aller bekannten Völker, i.–iii., 3. 2 (to the first half of the nineteenth century). 1837–54.—*H. Hallam's* View of the State of Europe in the Middle Ages, 3. 8. tenth ed. 1853; Literature of 15th to 17th centuries, 2. 8. 1853.—*Sismondi's*, of the South of Europe.—*Quérard's*, la France littéraire.—*Ticknor's* Spanish Literature.—*Gervinus*, Gesch. d. Deutschen Literatur.

Upon the *History of Art*, in relation to Christianity, the work of Dr. *Gieseler* contains no references. Prof. Dr. *F. Piper*, Mythologie u. Symbolik der christlichen Kunst, Bd. 1. 1851.—Dr. *F. Kugler*, Hand-book of the Hist. of Art, new ed. transl. Lond. 1854.—Lord *Lindsay's* Sketches of the History of Christian Art, 3. 8. 1847.—*Didron's* Christian Iconography, 1, transl. in Bohn's Library. 1852.—Symbols and Emblems of Early and Mediaeval Christian Art, by *Louisa Twining*. Lond. 1852.—Mrs. *Jameson*, Sacred and Legendary Art, 3.—*Schnaase*, Gesch. d. bildenden Künste. 1843.—*Kinkel*, 1. 1845.—*Romberg* und *Steger*, Gesch. d. Baukunst. 1827.—*Kreuser*, 2 Bde. 1851.—*Pugin's* Gothic Specimens and Examples.—*Ruskin's* Seven Lamps of Architecture. 1848; Stones of Venice, 3, with fol. plates. 1850–54.—*Kallenbach* u. *Schmitt*, Christliche Kirchen Baukunst, 12 Hefte. 1853.—*Kiesewetter*, Gesch. d. Musik. 1846.—*Hoffmann von Fallersleben*, Gesch. d. Deutschen Kirchenlieds. 1853.—*Baur*, Gesch. d. Kirchenlieds. 1852.—*Schauer*, Gesch. d. bibl. kirchlichen Dicht und Tonkunst u. ihrer Werke. 1850.—*Koch*, Gesch. d. Kirchenlieds u. K. Gesangs, 4 Bde. 2te Aufl. 1853.

Of *Spruner's* Hist.-geog. Atlas, the ninth part of the second division, comprising the Hist. of Europe from the beginning of the Middle Ages, was published in the second edition. 1854. An abridged edition is in the course of publication in England.—*A. L. Köppen*, edition of *Spruner* on Middle Ages. New York. 1854.—*Quin's* Hist. Atlas. Lond. 1851.—Atlas geographique, histor., universelle, *V. Durny*. Paris, 1842.—*Carl v. Ritter*, die Erdkunde im Verhältniss zur Natur u. zur Geschichte des Menschen, xvii. Thl. 2te Ausg. (the 17th in 1854).—*Ritter's* geogr.-statistisches Lexicon, 4te Aufl. v. *Hoffmann*, etc. 1852.

Chronology.—Sir *Harris Nicolas*, The Chronology of History (Lardner's Cycl.).—*Petavius*, de Doctrina Temporum, ed. *Harduin*, 3. fol. 1734.—*H. Browne*, Ordo Saeclorum. 8. Lond. 1844.—*D. H. Hegewisch*, Introd. to Historical Chronology, transl. by *James Marsh*, 18. Burlington, 1837.—*Hales*, New Analysis of Chronology and Geography. Lond. 1830, 4. 8.—*Blair's* Tables, new ed. Lond. 1850.—*Piper*, Kirchenrechnung. Berl. 1841. —*S. F. Jarvis*, Chronolog. Introd. to Church History, New York, 1845, is an inquiry into the dates of the birth and death of Christ.—Rev. *Ed. Greswell*, Fasti Temporis Catholice, et Origines Kalendariae, 5. 8. and a vol. of Charts. Lond. 1852; also, Origines Kalendariae Italicae. 4. 8. 1854.—*De Morgan's* Book of Almanacs. Lond. 1851.

Geography, etc.—*J. E. S. Wiltsch*, Kirchliche Geographie und Statistik, 2. 8. Berl. 1846.—*M. le Quien*, Oriens Christianus. Par. 1760, 3 t. fol.—A System of Ancient and Mediaeval Geography. By *Charles Anthon*, 8. New York, 1850.

Works in Universal History.—*W. C. Taylor*, Manual of Ancient and Modern History, 2. 8. New York, 1846, and often.—*T. Keightley*, Outlines of History. Lond. 1836.—*Weber's* Universal History, edited by Prof. *Bowen*, 8. Bost. 1853.—*Tytler*, Elements of General History, 4. 18. New York, *Harpers*.—*J. Müller*, Hist. of World, revised by *A. H. Everett*, 4. 12. New York, 1846.—*C. von Rotteck*, General Hist. of the World, transl., 4. 8. Phil. 1842. *Cantu*, C. Histoire universelle, trad. par *E. Aroux*. Paris, 18. 8. 1843. New ed. 1852–54.—*H. Leo*, Lehrbuch d. Universal Gesch., 6. 8. Halle, 1839, *sq*.—*D. H. Dittmar*, Gesch. d. Welt vor u. nach Christus, Bd. 1–4. 4. Heidelb. 1852, *sq*. New edition of vol. 1. 1855.

§ 4. *On the Sources of Ecclesiastical History*, p. 21.—*J. G. Dowling*, Introduction to the Critical Study of Eccl. History, 8. Lond. 1838.—Dr. *Arnold's* Lectures on Modern History contain valuable directions to students for the use of original documents.—*C. W. F. Walch*, Kritische Nachricht von den Quellen d. Kirchengesch. Leips. 1770.

Biographies of the Popes.—*Bowyer*, Hist. of Popes, continued by *S. H. Cox*, 3. 8. Phil. 1840.—*De Cormenin*, Hist. Popes. Phil. 1845.—*Müller*, Abbé Prof. Phil. die römischen Päbste, 14 Bde. to 1855.—The Popes, from Linus to Pius IX. By *G. A. F. Wilks*. Lond. 1851.—*J. E. Riddle*, History of Papacy, 2. 8. Lond. 1854.—*W. Giesebrecht*, d. Quellen d. früheren Pabstgeschichte, in *Allg. Monatsschrift*. 1852.

The volume of the "*Acta Sanctorum*," for Oct. 10 and 11, was reprinted at Brussels in 1852; the vol. for Oct. 17–20, the second of the Brussels continuation, was published in 1853; the first of this continuation in 1845.—*Alban Butler's* Lives of the Saints, 12. 8. New York, 1849.

Collections of the Works of the Fathers, etc.—*L. E. Dupin*, History of Eccl. Writers to close of 16th Century, transl. by *Wm. Wotton* and *Digby Cotes*, 3. fol. Dublin, 1723.—*Cave*, Script. Eccles. etc., edited by *Henry Wharton*, best ed. Oxford, 1740, 41. *Idem*, Chartophylax Ecclesiasticus, etc. 1685, '6.

Spicilegium Solesmense, tom. 1 (to be in 10), 1853, 4; fragments from the second to the fourth century, edited by *J. Pitra.*—*Cailloü* et *Guillon*, Collectio S. Patrum. Paris, 1841, *sq.*, 148 t. with Indices.—*J. P. Migne*, Patrologiae Cursus Compl., 130 tom. to 1854. —*Martene* et *Durand*, Vet. Scriptorum Collectio. Paris, 1724–33, 9 fol.; Thesaurus Nov. Anecdot. 1747, 5 fol.—*J. E. Grabe*, Spicilegium ss. patrum., 2 fol. Oxon. 1698.—*D'Achery*, Spicilegium, 13. 4. Par. 1655.—*Mabillon*, Vetera Analecta. Par. 1723, fol.—*Baluzius*, Miscellanea. 1761, 4 fol.—*Muratori*, Anecdota. 1697, 4. 4.

J. G. Walch, Bibliotheca Patristica. 1770.—*Augusti*, Chrestomathia Patristica. 1812. —*Roesler*, Bibliothek d. K. Väter, 10 Bd. 1776.—*J. Basnage*, Thesaurus Monumentorum. Amst. 1695, 6 fol.—*A. Mai*, Patrum Nova Bibliotheca, t. 6. 1852, '3, (to be in 10 volumes); previously, Script. vet. Nova Collectio e Vat. Codd. Rom. 1825, *sq.*, 10. 4.—Bibliotheca Patr. Eccl. Lat., ed. *Gersdorf*, 13 tom. 12 (Clement, Tertull., Ambrose, Lactant., Arnobius, Minucius Felix).—*A. Mai*, Spicilegium Rom., tom. 10. 4. 1839, '44.

W. Cave, Lives of the Fathers, ed. *H. Cary*, 3. 8. Oxf. 1840.—Institutiones patrologiae, Dr. *J. Fessler*, tom. 1. 1850, 8.—*J. N. Locherer*, Lehrb. d. Patrologie. 1837.—*Winter*, Patrologie. 1814. Annegarn, 1837.—*Adam Clark*, View of Succession of Sacred Lit. vol. 2. By *J. B. B. Clark*, 2. 8. Lond. 1830, '1.—At Athens, in 1846, *Φiλoλoγικὴ καὶ κριτικὴ ἱστορία τῶν ἁγίων πατέρων, ὑπο Κωνσταντίνου Κοντογονου*, 775 p. 8, ends with John of Damascus: cf. Leips. Repertorium. Feb. 1852.

The first volume of *Hefele*, Geschichte d. Concilien, 1855, reaches to the fourth century. —*H. T. Bruns*, Bibl. Eccl. Canones Apost. et Conciliorum saec., 4. 7. Berol. 1839, 2 tom. —A Manual of Councils, with the Substance of the most important Canons, by Rev. *E. H. Landon*. Lond. 1846.—Definitions of Faith, and Canons of the Six Œcumenical Councils, by Rev. *W. A. Hammond.* Am. ed. 12. New York, 1844.—French Councils: *Sirmond*, Concilia antiq. Galliae. Par. 1629, 3 fol.; Suppl. 2 fol.—Spanish: *Gonzalez*, Coll. Can. Eccl. Hisp. Matriti, 1808, fol.—*Saenz D'Aguirre*, Coll. maxima Conc. omnium Hisp. et novi orbis. Rom. 1693, 3 fol. — Concilios provinciales de Mexico (in 1555, '65, '85), 3. 1769, '70, Mexico.—English: *H. Spelman*, Conc. Decr. ad 1066, fol. 1639.—*D. Wilkins*, Conc. Mag. Brit. et Hibern. Lond. 1727, 4 fol.—*L. Howell*, Synopsis Concil., fol. 1708. —German: *Hartzheim*, Conc. Germaniae. 1749, 10 fol.

Beveridge, Pandectae Canon. ss. et Conciliorum ab Ecclesia Graeca receptorum, etc., 2 fol. Oxon. 1672.

Cabassutii, Notitia Eccl. Hist. Concil. et Canonum, fol. Lugd. 1690. New edition, 3. 8. Par. 1838 (1690).—*A. D'Avallon*, Histoire chronol. et dogmatique des Conciles. Par. (vol. iv. issued in 1854).—*Hammond* (Ap.). Paraenesis (1656), 1841, p. 98, *sq.*

Symbolism, Confessions of Faith.—*G. B. Winer*, Comparative Darstellung ds. Lehrbegriffs d. verschiedenen christlichen Kirchenpartheien. 2te Aufl. Leips. 1837.—*Chs. Butler*, Hist. and Lit. Account of Symbol. Books, 8. Lond. 1816.—*Peter Hall*, The Harmony of Protest. Confessions, new ed. Lond. 1842.—*Guericke*, Allg. christl. Symbolik. Leips. 2te Aufl., 1846.—*Marheineke*, Christlich. Symbolik, th. 1, Katholicismus, 3 Bde. 1810–13; Institutiones Symbol. ed., 3. 1830; Vorlesungen, ed. *Matthies* u. *Vatke.* 1848.—*E. Kollner*, Symbolik christlich. Confessionen. i. Luth. K. ii. Kathol. K., 8. Hamb. 1837, *sq.*— *A. H. Baier*, Symbol. d. christl. Confess., 1; Röm. Kath. K. Leips. 1854.—*K. Matthes*, Comp. Symbolik, 8. Leips. 1854.—*G. J. Planck*, Abriss einer hist. u. vergleich. Darstellung d. dogmat. Syst. 3te Aufl. 1822.

Möhler, Symbolik, 5te Aufl. 1838. English transl. by *J. B. Robertson.* New York, 1840.—*Baur*, Gegensatz d. Kathol. u. Prot. 2te Ausg. 1836.—*Möhler*, Neue Untersuchungen. 2te Ausg. 1835. — *Nitzsch*, Prot. Beantwortung d. Symbolik Dr. *Möhler's*, 8. Hamb. 1835 (aus d. *Stud. u. Krit.*).

Bullarium Romanum, etc. Continuation by *A. Spetia.* 1835–44, 8 tom. fol. Another volume added in 1852.

P. Jaffé, Regesta Pontif. Romanorum a condita Ecclesia ad annum post Christum 1198. Berol. 1851, 4. These Regesta, from 1198 to 1572, are in the Vatican, in 2016 folios. Among the Protestants, *Pertz* is almost the only one who has been allowed to examine them, for his Monumenta Germaniae. The Regesta to 1198 are for the most part lost. Jaffé, in the above work, has collected the fragments (cf. *Kurtz*, Handbuch, 1. § 4).

Liturgies.—Codex Liturgicus Ecclesiae universae in Epitomen redactus. Curavit Dr. *H. A. Daniell.* Completed in 4 vols. 1854.—*L. A. Muratori*, Lit. Romana vetus. Venice, 1748, 2 fol.—*Mabillon*, Liturg. Gallicana. Paris, 1729.—*J. Pinius*, Liturgia Ant. Hisp. Goth. Mozarab. Rom. 1749. 2 fol. (cf. Christ. Rembr. Oct. 1853).—*J. Goar*, Rituale Graecorum. Ven. 1780.—*Guillaume Durand*, Rationale ou Manuel des divins offices. New edition. Par. 5, 8. 1854.—*Palmer, W.*, Origines Liturgicae; or, Antiq. of the Church of England, 2. 8. 1845.—*J. M. Neale*, Tetralogia Liturgica (those of James, Mark, Chrysostom, and the Mozarabic). Lond. 1848.—*Bunsen*, Analecta Ante-Nicaena, 3. 8. 1854.

Additional Works on the First Period.—1–324. Page 29.—*Eusebius:* Hist. Eccl. ad Codd. MSS. recens, *E. Burton.* Oxon. 1845; Annotationes variorum, tom. 2. 1842. Hist. Eccl. recognovit *A. Schwegler.* 1853. A new translation of *Eusebius*, by Dr. *C. F. Cruse.* New York, 4th ed. 1847, and London.—*Evagrii*, Hist. Eccl. Oxon. 1844 (ex recens. *H. Valesii*).—*Socrates'* Schol. ex recens. Valesii. Oxon. 1844. The early ecclesiastical historians, Eusebius, Socrates, Sozomen, Theodoretus, and Evagrius, have been issued in an English version, in 6 vols. 8. Lond., *Bagster*, 1845, '6.—*Theodoreti*, Ecclesiasticae historiae recensuit, *Thos. Gaisford* (a new revision of the text, from two MSS. in the Bodleian). Oxon. 1854.

Henry Milman, Hist. of Christ. Lond. 3. 8.; New York, 1841.—*E. Burton*, Lectures to Time of Constantine, 2. 8. Oxf. 1849, Works vol. iv. v.—*Maurice*, Lectures on Eccl. Hist. of first and second Cent., 8. Lond. 1854.—*Hinds*, Rise and Progress of Christianity, 2. 8. 1828.—*D. Welsh*, Elements Ch. Hist. vol. i. Edinb. 1844.—*Cave's* Lives of the Fathers, 3. 8.—*H. G. Humphrey*, Early Progress of the Gospel (Hulsean Lect.). 1850.—*Whiston's* Primitive Christ., 4. 8.—*W. Cooke Taylor*, History of Christ. to its Legal Establishment in the Roman Empire, 12. Lond. 1844.—*Jeremie*, Christ. Ch. second and third Cent. Encycl. Metr.—*Neander*, transl. by *Rose*, 8. New York, 1848.—*W. Kipp*, Early Conflicts of Christians. New York, 1850.—*B. H. Cooper*, Free Church of Ancient Christendom. Lond. 1854.—*Chs. Maitland*, The Church in the Catacombs. Lond. 1846.

F. C. Baur, d. Christenthum u. d. christl. Kirche d. drei ersten Jahr., 8. 1853.—*D. J. Hergenröther*, de Catholicae Ecclesiae primordiis recentiorum Protest. systemata expenduntur, 8. 1851.—*Ritschl*, Entstehung d. altkatholischen Kirche. Bonn, 1839.—*Hagenbach*, d. drei ersten Jahrhnd., 8. 1853.—*Biesenthal*, Gesch. aus Talmud. Quellen. Berl. 1850.—*Gfrörer*, Geschichte des Urchristenthums. Stuttg. 1831, *sq.*, 3 Bde.—The "Ecclesiastical History of *John of Ephesus*," pt. 3, edited by *Cureton*, 1853, is important for the Monophysitic discussion.

Brocklesby, Hist. of Primitive Christ. first three Centuries. 1712, 8.—*Whiston's* Primitive Christianity, 4. 8. 1711.—*W. Reeves*, Apology of Primitive Fathers, 2. 8. London, 1716.—*Wakefield*, Opinions of the three first Centuries, 8. 1755.—*C. J. Couard*, Life of early Christians of first three Centuries, transl. by *L. J. Bernays* (Edb. Bibl. Cab.).—*W. Simpson*, Epitome Hist. Christ. Church first three Cent., 2d ed. 1851.—Rev. *Chs. Smyth*, Voice of the Early Church. Lond. 1850.—*J. De Wille*, The Christ. of certain Roman Empresses before Constantine. Paris, 1853.—*W. G. Humphrey*, Early Propagation of Gospel (Hulseans). 1850.

Works on the Apostolic Age, page 30.—*Philip Schaff*, History of Apostolic Church. Transl. by *E. D. Yeomans*, 8. New York, 1853.—*Geo. Benson*, History of first Planting of Christianity, 3. 4. 1759.—*H. W. J. Thiersch*, Gesch. d. christl. Kirche, 1. 1852. English transl. by *T. Carlyle.* 1852.—*Lechler*, d. Apostolische u. nachapostol. Zeitalter. Haarlem, 1851 (prize essay).—*Schwegler*, d. Nachapostolische Zeitalter, 2. 8. Tübingen, 1846.—*J. P. Lange*, Gesch. d. Kirche i. Apostol. Zeitalter. 1853.—*M. Baumgarten*, d. Apostolgesch. u. s. w. (Transl. Edinb. 1855.)—*Dietlein*, das Urchristenthum (against *Baur*). 1845.—*Rothe*, die Anfänge d. christlichen Kirche, Bd. 1. 1837.—*Neander's* Planting and Training, etc. Transl. by *J. E. Ryland.* Philad. 1844.—*W. W. Harvey*, Ecclesiae Catholicae Vindex Catholicus, Collection of treatises, transl., 3. 8. Lond.

§ 8–14. *Condition of the Heathen Nations*, etc., page 30–44.—*Collinson's* Observations on the Preparation of Man for Christianity. Lond. 1840.—*Mosheim's* Commentaries, vol. i. p. 9–49.—*Trench*, Unconscious Prophecies of Heathenism (Hulsean Lect.). Am. ed. 1853.—*Maurice*, Religions of the World, etc. Am. ed. 1854.—State of Man before Promulgation of Christianity, in "Small Books," etc. 1848.—*Schaff*, p. 143–164.

Creuzer, Symbolik u. Mythologie. 3te Aufl. 1837.—*F. C. Baur*, Symbolik u. Mythol. 1824.—*A. Muller*, Introd. to Scientific Mythology. Transl. by *J. Leitch*. 1844.—*Stuhr*, d. Religions Systems d. Hellenen. 1838.—*G. S. Faber*, Origin and Progress of Idolatry, 3. 4. 1816.—*Warburton*, Divine Legation of Moses.—*L. Preller*, Griech. Mythol. 1854. —*J. C. Harless*, de Supernaturalismo Gentilium (Progr.). 1834.—*J. F. Sepp*, d. Heidenthum, u. seine Bedeutung, 3. 8. 1853.—*A. Wuttke*, Gesch. ds. Heidenthums, 2 Bde. 1854. —*J. Voss*, de Theolog. Gentili et Physiol. Christiana. 1675, 2. 4.—*Görres*, Mythengesch. d. Asiatischen Völker, 2. 8. 1810.

§ 15–19. *Condition of the Jewish People*, etc.—The works of Josephus, transl. into English by *W. Whiston*, in frequent editions; a new transl. by *R. Traill*, with notes by *J. Taylor*, 2. 8. 1847.—Dr. *F. Creuzer* on Josephus: *Stud. u. Krit.* 1850, 1853.—Preparation for the Gospel, as exhibited in the History of the Israelites. By *Geo. Curry* (Hulsean Lect.). 1851.—*W. H. Johnstone*, Israel in the World; or, the Mission of the Hebrews to the great military Monarchies, 12. London, 1854.—*Id.*, Israel after the Flesh, etc., 8. Lond. 1852.—*Kurtz*, Sacred History. Transl. by Dr. *Schäffer*. Philad. 1855.—*Id.*, Geschichte des alten Bundes, 1. 2 (1854).—*Lengerke*, Kenaan, 1. 1844.—Dr. *Murdock*, transl. of *Jost* on Condition of Jews, etc. *Bibl. Repos.* 1839.—*Geo. Smith*, Sacred Annals, 3. 8. Am. ed. 1850–'54.—*Isaac M. Wise*, Hist. Israel. Nation, 1. Albany, 1854.—*Is. Da Costa*, Israel and the Gentiles. New York, 1855.—*Ewald's* Gesch. d. Israeliten. 2te Ausg. 4. 8. 1851–'54.—*Leo*, Vorlesungen. 1828.—*Basnage*, Hist. d. Juifs, 15 tom. 12.—*M. De Bonnechose*, Histoire Sacrée. Paris, 1850.—Analysis and Summary of Old Test. Hist., by *J. L. Wheeler*, 2d ed. 1854.—*Jarvis*, Church of Redeemer, vol. i. Old Test., 8. New York, 1851.—*Gleig's* Hist. of Bible, 2. 18.—*Jost*, Hist. Jews: transl. by *J. H. Hopkins*. New York.—Rev. *J. Jones*, Chronological and Analytical View of the Bible. Oxf. 1836.

Thos. Stackhouse, Hist. of Bible. Ed. by Rev. *G. Gleig*, 3. 4. London, 1817.—Bishop *Hall*, Contemplations on Old and New Test. (1634) in Works. 1808.—*Samuel Shuckford*, Connection Sacred and Profane History, 3. 8.—*Russell's* Connection, 2. 1827.—*Prideaux's* Connection, 4. 8. Oxf. 1820.—*Davidson's*. New York, 1853.—*Howell's* Hist. of Bible. Edited by *Geo. Burder*. 3. 8. Lond. 1805.—*Sharon Turner's* Sacred Hist. of World, 3. 18. (*Harper's* Lib.).—Dean *Milman's* Hist. Jews, 3. 18. 1831. (*Harper's* Lib.).

J. J. F. Buddaeus, Hist. Eccles. Vet. Test., ed. 4, 2. 4. 1744.—*Vitringa*, de Synagoga. 1696; abridged by *Bernard*, 1849.—*Saurin*, Discours. Hist. Theol. Moraux, etc. 1720, *sq.* —*J. J. Hess*, Geschichte d. Israel, 12 Bde. 1776–88.—*Hävernick*, d. Theologie d. Alt. Test., 1843.—*Vatke*, Rel. d. Alt. Test., 1. 1835.—*Knobel*, d. Prophetismus. 1837.—*J. C. K. Hoffmann*, Weissagung u. Erfüllung im A. u. N. Test., 2. 8. 1841.—Spirit of Old Test., Dr. *J. Lewis's* Bibl. Repos. 1850.—*Palfrey*, Academical Lectures on Jewish Script. and Antiq., 4. 8. 1850–52.

Samaritans.—*J. Grimm*, d. Samariter, u. ihre Stellung in d. Weltgeschichte. München, 1854.—*E. Burritt*, in Am. Ecl., 2. 249. 281.—Samaritan Pentateuch, *Kitto's* Journal. July, 1853.—Christ. Exam., 28. 29 (*J. Walker*).—*M. Stuart*, in Bibl. Repos., vol. 2, and North Am., vol. 22.

The Essenes.—*Kitto's* Journal. Oct. 1852; April, 1853; Oct. 1853.—*W. Hall*, Bibl. Repos., 3d series, 3.

Philo and the Alexandrian Philosophy.—*M. Wolff*, d. Philon'sche Philosophie. Leips. 1849.—Dr. *Rubinssohn*, in Christ. Rev. Jan. 1853.—First Eng. transl. by *C. D. Yonge*, Bohn's Lib. 3 vols. published 1855.—*John Jones*, Eccles. Researches on Philo and Josephus. Lond. 1812.—*St. Paul and Philo*, Journal of Class. and Sacred Lit., 1. 1854.

§ 20, page 59.—*The Life of Jesus.*—Dr. *J. N. Sepp*, d. Leben Jesu, 4. 8. Munchen, 1843, *sq.* (French transl. 1848.)—*Ebrard*, Wiss. Kritik d. Evangel. Geschichte. 1842.—*Krabbe*, Leben Jesu. 1838.—*Weisse*, Evang. Gesch., 2. 1838, '9.—*Gfeörer*, d. Urchristenthum, 1.—*Osiander*, Apologie. 1837.—*J. P. Lange*, d. Leben Jesu, 3. 1844.—*Hoff-*

mann, d. Leben Jesu nach d. apocryphen Evangelien. 1853.—*Ewald*, Geschichte Christus und seiner Zeit. 1855.

Fleetwood's Life of Christ and the Apostles (Works, 1854).—*Henry Blunt*, Life of our Saviour. Am. ed. Phil. 1850.—Birth and Infancy of Christ, *Jl. Sacr. Lit.* 1854.—*Neander's* Life of Christ. Transl. by Prof. *Blumenthal.* New York, 1845.

J. Salvador, Jesus Christ, et sa Doctrine, 2 tomes. Paris, 1838.—*Beard*, Voice of the Church (in reply to *Strauss*). Lond. 1844.—*Alexander's* Christ and Christianity. New York edit. 1854.—*A. Norton*, Genuineness of Gospels, 3. 8. 2d ed. 1852.—*Id.*, Internal Evidence, 2. 1855.—*Da Costa*, Four Witnesses. Lond. 1851.—*Jas. Smith*, Diss. Origin Gospels. Lond. 1852.—*Jas. Strong*, A new Harmony. New York, 1852.—*Kostler*, Ursprung u. Composition d. Synopt. Evang. 1852.—*Hilgenfeld*, Evangelien nach ihrer Entstehung. 1854.

Chronological Data in Life of Christ.—*S. F. Jarvis*, Chronol. Introd. to Church History. 1845.—*Journal of Sacred Lit.*, 1825, on the Nativity.—*J. P. Mynter*, Bishop of Seeland, de Momentis Chronol. in Vita T. Xti. 1843.—*Wieseler*, Date of Birth. Transl. Bib. Sac. by Prof. *Day.*—*N. Mann*, True Years of Birth and Death of Christ. Lond. 1752.—*Ideler*, Handb. d. Chronologie, 2. 1826.—*Montacutius*, Analect. Exercit. Eccles. (Exc. ix. p. 317, *sq.*).—*Byneus*, de Natali Jesu Christi, fol. 1689.

§ 22, page 63.—*John the Baptist.*—Life, by Rev. *Wm. C. Duncan*, 12. New York, 1852.—Johannes d. Taufer in Gefangnisse, by Dr. *B. Gauss*, of Tubingen. 1853.—Verhältniss Joh. d. Taufers zum Herrn, *Luth. Zeitschrift.* 1852.

§ 26, page 76.—*Paul*, etc.—*Conybeare* and *Hewson*, Life and Epistles of Paul, 2. 4. Lond. 2. 8; New York, 1854 (cf. President *Woolsey*, in New Englander, Feb. 1854).—*J. Pearson's* Lectures on Acts and Annals of Paul. Ed. by *J. R. Crowfoot.*—*Whateley's* Difficulties in Writings of Paul. 1845.—Life of Paul, by Rev. Dr. *Addington.*—Life and Epistles, by Mr. *Bevan.* Lond.—*Tholuck*, Life of Paul. Transl. in Bibl. Cabinet, No. 28.—*Henry Blunt*, Lect. on Paul. 10th ed. London, 1851 (repr. Phil.).—*Thos. Lewin*, Life of St. Paul, 2. 8. Lond. 1851.—*A. T. Paget*, Unity and Order of St. Paul's Epistles. Lond. 1852.—*Jas. Smith*, Voyages and Shipwreck of St. Paul. Lond. 1848.—Paul and Demosthenes, by *Köster*, in *Stud. u. Kritiken*, 1854. Transl. in Bib. Sacra. 1854.—Paul and Josephus, *Journ. Sacr. Lit.*, April, 1854.—*Usteri*, d. Paul. Lehrbegriff. 5th ed. 1834.—*Dähne*, d. Paul. Lehrbeg. 1835.—*J. P. Mynster*, De ultimis annis Muneris Apostolici a Paulo gesti. 1815.—An Attempt to ascertain the Chronology of the Acts of the Apostles and of St. Paul's Epistles, by *E. Burton*, 8. Oxf. 1830 (Works, vol. 4).—*Baur*, Paulus. 1845.—*Zeller*, über d. Apostlegeschichte. Tübingen Zeitschrift, 1850, '1.—*Id.*, d. Ursprung d. Apostelgeschich. 1854.—*Lekebusch*, d. Composition und Entstehung d. Apostelgesch. v. neuem untersucht. 1854.—*Baumgarten*, von Jerusalem zu Rom., 2. 8. 1854 (to be transl. in Clark's Library).—*Schneckenburger*, Beiträge zur Erklärung d. Apostelgeschichte: *Stud. u. Krit.* 1855.

§ 27. page 80.—*History of the other Apostles.*—*Bacon's* Lives of the Apostles. New York, 1850.

Peter.—*Henry Blunt*, Nine Lectures on Peter. 18th ed. 1851.—*Mayerhoff*, Einleitung in d. Petrinsche Schriften. 1835.—*Windischmann*, Vindiciae Petrin. 1836.—*J. C. Simon*, Mission and Martyrdom of Peter; original Text of all the Passages supposed to imply a Journey to the East, 8. 1842.—*Cave's* Lives of Apostles.—*Kitto's* Journal, vol. 5.—*Allies*, Primacy of Peter, on the Basis of Passaglia. Lond. 1852. Cf. *Dublin Review*, July, 1853.

John.—*Lücke*, d. Evangelien u. Episteln (3te Aufl.), Enleitung in d. Offenbarung. 2te Aufl. 1850–'54.—*Fromman* (1839), *Köstlin* (1843), Ueber d. Lehrbegriff d. Johannes.—*Ebrard*, d. Evangel. Johannes. 1845.—*F. Trench*, Life and Character of John. London, 1850.—*J. B. Troost*, Disquisitio de Discipulo quem dilexit Jesus. Lugd. Bat.—*K. F. Th. Schneider*, Aechtheit d. Johan. Evang. 1854.—*G. K. Mayer*, Aechtheit, u. s. w. Schaffhausen, 1854.—Die Johan. Frage, by *F. C. Baur*, in Theol. Jahrb. Tübingen, 1854. 2 Heft.

Lutterbeck, d. Neutestamentliche, Lehrbegriffe. 1854.—Dr. *Grabe*, Essay on the Doctrine of the Apostles. 1711.

§ 30. *Constitution of the Church.*—*Rothe*, Die Anfänge d. christl. Kirche. 1837.—*Baur*,

Ursprung des Episcopats. 1838.—*Petersen*, d. Idee d. Kirche, 3. 1843-46.—*Palmer*, The Church, 2. 8. 1841.—*Milton's* Prelatical Episcopacy (Works).

Bingham's Origines Eccles.—*Hooker*, Laws of Eccl. Polity. Ed. by *Keble*, 2. 8.—*Bilson's* Perpetual Government. 1593.—Sir *P. King*, Primitive Church. New York, 1841. —*Sclater's* Original Draught. 1833 (Am. ed.).—*Hickes's* Two Treatises, 2. 8, 1711, and in Libr. Angl. Cath. Theol.—*Marshall's* Notes. New York, 1844.—*Bowden*, Episcopacy, 2. New York, 1808, *sq*.—*Routh*, in *Reliq. Sacrae*, vol. 4, all canons before Nice.

Whateley, on the Kingdom of Christ. New York, 1842.—*Mason*, Essays on Church. 1843.—*Wilson's* Government of Church. 1833.—*Coleman*, Apostol. Church. 1844.—Prim. Church Officers. New York. 1851.—*Woods's* Objections to Episcopacy. 1844.—*Chapin's* Prim. Church. 1842.—*Barnes's* Inquiry. 1843.—*Miller's* Letters and primitive Order.—*Smyth's* Apostol. Succession. 1844.—*King's* Church Government. 1853.—*Owen's* Works, vol. 15. 16.—*Baxter* on Episcopacy.—*Chauncey's* View of the Fathers.—*Cotton's* Keys.—*Goodwin's* Government of the Church.—*Ayton* on Church Government.—Bishop *Kaye* (Lincoln), Account of the external Discipline and Government of the Church of Christ, first three Cent. Lond. 1855.

§ 35. *The Apostolic Fathers*.—The third edition of *Hefele*, Patrum Apostol., etc. 1849. —*T. Chevallier*, Epistles of Clem., Rom., Ign., etc., transl. 2d ed. Lond. 1851.—*Ritschl*, die altkatholische Kirche.—*Hilgenfeld*, d. Apostol. Väter. 1854 (cf. Review by *Lipsius*, in *Gersdorf's* Repertorium). 1854.—*J. H. B. Lübkert*, die Theologie der Apostol. Väter: *Zeitschrift f. d. hist. Theologie*. 1854.

Archbishop *Wake's* Genuine Epistles of Apostol. Fathers (1693). New York, 1817.—*Daillé*, Right Use of the Fathers. Transl. by *S. W. Hanna*. Lond. 1838 (Phil. ed.).—*Collinson's* Bampton Lecture, Key, etc. Oxf. 1813.—*C. W. Woodhouse*, Use and Value of the Fathers (Hulsean Essay). Lond. 1842.—*Bickersteth*, The Fathers. Lond. 1845.

Ignatius, Epistles (Gk. and Eng.), by *W. Whiston*, in Prim. Christ. Revived, 1. 1711. —*W. Cureton*, Corpus Ignat. (Syriac, Greek, and Latin). London. 1848.—*Id*., Vindiciae Ignat. 1846.—*Bunsen*, Ignat. u. seine Zeit. 1847.—*Id*., Die drei ächten u. d. vier unächten Briefe ds. Ign. 1847.—*Baur*, die Ign. Briefe. 1848.—*Deuzinger*, d. Aechtheit d. Ign. Briefe. 1849. Cf. *Zeitschrift für d. Luth. Theol*., 1848-52 (abridged in *Arnold's* Theol. Critic, 1852); *Zeitschrift für d. hist. Theol*., 1851, by *Uhlhorn*; *Quarterly Rev*. (Lond.) 1851, Jan.; *Edinb. Rev*., 1849; *Church Rev*., 1849.

Clement of Rome.—*Hilgenfeld*, Kritische Untersuchungen. 1850.—Clementis Rom. quae feruntur Homiliae, etc. Ed. by *A. Dressel*, 1853; *A. Schwegler*, 1847.—*G. Uhlhorn*, d. Homilien u. Recogn. 1854.—*E. Gundert*, d. erste Brief ds. Clem. Rom., in *Zeitschr. Luth. Theol*. 1853, '4.—*E. Ecker*, Disquisitio—de Cl. Rom. prior. ad Rom. Epistola. Traj. ad Rhenum. 1853.—*Uhlhorn*, in Real. Encycl. f. Prot. Theologie.—*R. A. Lipsius*, de Clementis Rom. Epistola ad Corinthios priore Disquisitio, 8. Leipsic, 1855.

§ 40. *Celsus and Lucian*.—Transl. of Disc. of Celsus, with notes, in *Glass's* Works, vol. 4; M. *Bonhèreau*, of Dublin: transl. into French. Amsterd. 4. 1700.—*Lucian*, u. d. Christhenthum, ein Beitrag zur K. Gesch. ds. zweiten Jahr.: *Studien u. Kritiken*, 1853; transl. in *Bibl. Sacra*, 1853.—*Lucian*, ed. *Bekker*, 2. 1853.—Life and Writings of Lucian, in *Quarterly Rev*., vol. 37.

Papias, Fragments, in *Lardner's* Credibility, vol. 2.

§ 44-48. *Gnostics*, etc.—*Ed. Burton*, Inquiry into the Heresies of the Apostolic Age (Bampton Lects. 1829); Works, vol. 3. 1837.—*H. Rossel*, Theol. Untersuchungen über d. Gnost. s. 179-209.—*Id*., Syst. ds. Valentinus, s. 250-300.—On the early Forms of Gnosticism, in *Bunsen's* Hippolytus.—*Gieseler*, in *Studien u. Kritiken*. 1830.—*Möhler*, Ursprung ds. Gnosticismus. 1831.—*Baur*, in his Drei ersten Jahr.—Pistis Sophia, Opus Gnosticum Valentino adjudicatum. Edited by *J. H. Petermann*. Berl. 1852. Cf. *Köstlin*, in *Theol. Jahrb*. 1854.—*Valentinianus*, and Tertullian, Works of Bp. Hooper, 307-345.

Jacobi, Prof. Dr. *L. Basilidis*, Philos. Gnost. Sententiae ex Hippolyti libro, etc. Berl. 1852.—*E. Gundert*, d. Syst. ds. *Basilidis*, in *Zeitschft. Luth. Theol*. 1855.—*Dorner*, in his Gesch. d. Person Christi, u. s. w.—*Pusey* on *Manichees*, in "Conf. of Augustine."

A. H. L. Fuldner, Comm. de *Ophitis*. 1834.

Marcion.—*Harting*, Quaestio de Marcione, Traj. ad Rhenum. 1849.—*Ritschl*, d. Evang. Marcions. 1847.—*Volckmar*, d. Evang. Marcions. Cf. *Gersdorf*, Repert. 1852.—*Franck*, d. Evang. Marc.: *Stud. u. Krit.* 1855.—*Hilgenfeld*, d. Apostolikon Marcions, in *Ztschft. f. d. hist. Theologie.* 1855.

Melito, bishop of Sardis, p. 143.—See *Journal of Sacred Lit. and Bibl. Record*, Jan. 1855.

§ 50.—*Apologies for Christianity*, p. 145, cf. *Bolton;* The Apologists of the second and third Century. Am. ed. Boston, 1853.—Corpus Apolog. Christ. Ed. by *Otto; Justin*, 2d ed. 1850, 5 tom.; *Tatian*, 1851.—*Baur*, in his Dogmengeschichte, und Geschichte d. drei ersten Jahr.—*Clausen*, Apologetae Ecclesiae. 1837.

Theophilus Antioch, Libri tres ad Autolycum. Edit. by *G. G. Humphrey*. Lond. 1852. —The Octavius of *Minucius Felix*. Edited by Rev. *H. A. Holden*. Oxf. 1853.—Other Eng. transl. by *R. James*, Oxf. 1636; *Combe*, 1703; *W. Reeves*, 1719 (in "Apolog. of Prim. Fathers"); by *Dalrymple*. Edinb. 1781.—The Apologetics, by *T. Betty*. Oxf. 1722.

Epistola ad Diognetum.—Just. M. Epist. ad Diognetum, by *Hoffmann*. 1851. Cf. *Otto*, in *Gersdorf's* Rep. 1852.—The Epistle translated in *Kitto's* Journal, 1852, and *Princeton Review*, 1853.—Der Brief an Diogn., herausg. by *W. A. Hollenberg*. Berlin, 1853. Cf. *Gersdorf's* Rep. März, 1853.

Justin Martyr.—Bishop *Kaye*, Some Account of Opinions and Writings of Just. Mart. 2d ed.—*Lemisch* on J. M., transl. by *J. E. Ryland*, in Bibl. Cab., vol. 41. 42.—De J. M. doctrina, Diss. by *A. Kayser*. 1850.—*Volckmar*, Ueber J. M. 1853.—Just. Mart., v. *K. Otto*, reprinted from *Allg. Encyclop.* 1853.—*Duncker*, d. Logoslehre d. Just. M. 1847.—Zur charakteristik d. Just. M., v. *K. Otto*. Wien, 1852.—D. Evang. ds. Just. by *Hilgenfeld*, *Theol. Jahrb.* 1852.—*Volckmar*, die Zeit ds. Just. M., *Theol. Jahrb.* 1855.

English transl., by *W. Reeves* (the first Apol.). 2d ed. 1716.—Dialogue with Trypho, by *H. Browne*, 2. 8. Lond. 1755.—Exhort. to Gentiles, by *T. Moses*. 1757.

§ 51. *Irenaeus*, p. 148.—Opera quae supersunt. Ed. by *Stieren*, 1850.—Supposed Fragments, *Spicilegium Solesmense*, 1. 1852 (cf. *Christ. Rembr.* 1853, July).—Life and Times of Irenæus, in *The Eclectic* (Lond.), Sept. 1854.—*J. Beaven*, Life of Irenaeus, 8. Lond. 1841.

Canon of New Test.—*J. Kirchhofer*, Quellensammlung zur Geschichte d. Neutest. Canon, bis Hieron. Zurich, 1844.—*W. J. Thiersch*, d. Neutestamentliche Canon. 1845. *Cosin*, Scholastical Hist. of the Canon, 4. 1672.—*Jones* (*Jeremiah*), New and full Method of settling the Canon. Authority of New Test., 3. 8. 1726. New ed. Oxf. 1827.—*Westcott*, on the Canon. Lond. 1855.—On the "Fragmentum Muratorii," by *Wieseler*, *Studien u. Krit.* 1847; ed. by *J. Van Gilse*. Amstelod. 1852.—*Bötticher*, in *Zeitschr. Luth. Theol.* 1854.—*Dupin*, Hist. of Canon, fol. 1699.—*Whitehead*, Canon and Inspiration. 1854.—*Chr. Wordsworth*, Canon and Insp. Am. ed. 1855.—*Routh*, in *Rel. Sacrae*, tom. 5, 1848.

§ 52. *Apocryphal Writings*, p. 153.—Cf. *Whiston*, Prim. Christ., 4. 1711.—Fragmenta Act. S. Joh. Ed. by *Thilo*. 1847.—Acta Apostol. Apocr. Ed. by *Tischendorf*. 1851. Cf. *Gersdorf. Rep.* Jan. 1852.—*Id.*, de Evang. Apoc. Origine. Lugd. Bat. 1851.

Stuart, Book of Enoch, *Bibl. Repos.* 1840.—Book of Enoch. Transl. by *A. Dillmann*. 1854.—*Ewald*, Abhandlung über d. Buch Enoch. 1854.—*For. Quar. Review*, vol. 24.—Codex Apocr. Nev. Test. Edit. by *Thilo*, 1. 1832.—*Franck*, d. Evang. d. Hebräer, in *Stud. u. Krit.* 1848.—*Köstlin*, d. Pseudonym. Lit. d. ältesten Kirch. *Tüb. Zeitschft.* 1851. —*Bleeck*, d. Apocryphen: *Stud. u. Krit.* 1853.—*H. Jolowicz*, d. Himmelfahrt u. Vision ds. Jesaias. Leipsic, 1854. Cf. *Gersdorf's Rep.*, April, 1854.—*C. Tischendorf*, Pilati circa Christum judicio quid lucis afferatur ex actis Pilati. 1855.

Hoffmann, R. das Leben Jesu nach d. Apocryphen. Leips. 1851.

Sibylline Oracles.—*Mai*, published books, 9–14. in his Script. Veterum nova Collectio, vol. 3.—*Lücke*, Einleitung in d. *Offbg. Joh.* 2d ed. 1848.—*M. Stuart*, on the Apocalypse, vol. 1.—*Blondel*, on Sibyl. Orac. Transl. by *Davies*. Lond. 1661.—Sir *J. Floyer*, Lond. 1751.—Oracula Sibyllina. Ed. by *P. L. Courier*. Paris, 1854; with a German version by *Friedlob*. Leips. 1852.—*Volckmann*, de Orac. Sibyl. 1853.—An edition of the Oracula, by *Alexander*, 2 tom. Paris, 1841, '53. Cf. *Meth. Quart. Rev.*, Oct. 1854.

§ 54. *New Platonism.*—*Chs. Kingsley*, Four Lectures on Alexandria and her Schools. Lond. 1854.—*Proclus*, transl. by *T. Taylor*, 2. 4. 1816.—*Plotinus*, by *Taylor*, 8. 1834.—

Guericke, de Schola quae Alex. Flor. Cf. *R. Emerson*, in *Bibl. Repos.*, vol. 4.—*Simon*, Hist. de l'Ecole d'Alexandrie, 2. 8. Par. 1845.—*Matter*, Hist. de l'Ecole. 2d ed. 4 tomes. —*Plotinus*, Opera Omnia. Oxf., 3. 4. 1835.—*Kirchner*, d. Philos. des Plotin. 1854.—*Neander*, in his Wiss. Abhandlungen, on Plotinus. 1843.—*Vacherot*, Hist. de l'Ecole d'Alexandrie, 3 tom. Paris, 1847.—*Kirchhoff*, Plotinus de Virtutibus. Berlin, 1847.

§ 56, p. 179.—*Diocletian*, de Pretiis rerum Venalium. Herausg. b. *T. Mommsen*. Leips. 1851.

§ 58. *Elcesaites and the Clementina.*—*Ritschl*, in *Zeitschrift f. d. hist. Theol.*, 1853, on the Elcesaites, on the basis of the work of Hippolytus.—*Id.*, Bedeutung d. Pseudoclementin. Literatur, *Allg. Monatsschrift.* 1852.—The Clementina, in *Hilgenfeld*, die Clementinischen Recognitionen. Jena, 1848.—*Ritschl*, Altkathol. Kirche.—*Uhlhorn*, in *Real-Encycl. f. d. Prot. Theologie.*—*Rössel's* Theologische Schriften, Bd. 1.—Recognitions of Clement. Transl. by *Whiston.* Lond. 1712.

§ 59. *The Easter Controversy.*—*Hilgenfeld*, in *Theol. Jahrb.* Tübingen, 1849.—*Weiss*, in *Reuter's* Repertorium. 1850.—*Weitzel*, in *Studien u. Krit.*, 1848.—*Weitzel*, d. christl. Passahfeier d. drei ersten Jahrhunderte. Pforzheim, 1848.

§ 60, p. 197.—*Theology of the Fathers of second and third Centuries.*—*Ed. Burton*, Testimony of the Ante-Nicene Fathers to Trinity, Divinity of Christ, and of Holy Spirit. 1829–'31. Works, vol. 2.—*I. Bennett*, The Theology of the early Christian Church (in extracts: 8 of Congl. Lectures).—*Gfrörer*, Bd. 1.—*Ginoulhiac*, Histoire du Dogma Catholique dans les trois premiers Siècles. Paris, 2. 8. 1850.—*Reuss*, R., Hist. de la Theol. Chrétienne, 2. 8. 1853.—*Charpentier*, Etudes sur les pères de l'Eglise, 2. 8. Paris, 1853.

The Monarchians and Sabellians.—See *Baur*, Lehre v. d. Dreieinigkeit u. Menschwerdung Gottes, 3. 8. 1841, *sq.*—*Dorner*, Lehre v. d. Person Christi. 2te Aufl. 1845, *sq.*—*Meier*, Lehre v. d. Trinität. 1844.—*Lange*, Gesch. d. Unitarier. 1831.

§ 62–64, p. 208, *sq. Clement of Alexandria, and Origen.*—Clement of Alexandria, by *Baur*, in his christl. Gnosis.—*Kling*, in *Studien u. Kritiken*, 1841.—Bishop *Kaye*, Account of the Writings and Opinions of Clem. of Alex. London, 1839.—*Christ. Review*, July, 1852.—*Kitto's* Journal of Sacred Lit., 1852.—*Leutzen*, Erkennen u. Glauben, Cl. v. Alex. und Anselm v. Canterb. Bonn, 1848.—*Reinkens*, de Clem. Alex. Vratislaviae, 1851.—*Reuter*, Clem. Alex. Theologia Moralis. Berol. 1853.—The Chronol. of Cl. of Alex., in *Journ. of Class. and Sacred Philol.*, 1854.—*H. Laemmer*, Clem. Alex. de "logo" Doctrina. Commentatio Histor. Theol., 8. Leips. 1855.

Origen.—*Redepenning*, des Hieronymus wieder aufgefundenes Verzeichniss d. Schriften ds. Origen, in *Zeitschrift f. d. hist. Theol.*, 1851.—*Ritschl*, die Schriftstellerei ds. Varro u. ds. Origen. Bonn, 1847.—*Fischer*, Commentatio de Originis Theologia et Cosmologia. 1846.—*C. Ramen*, des Orig. Lehre v. der. Anferstehung des Fleisches.—*Mosheim's* Commentaries. Transl. by Dr. *Murdock*, vol. 2, p. 143–209.—*R. Emerson*, in *Bibl. Repos.*, vol. 4.—*B. Sears*, in *Bibl. Sacra*, vol. 3.—*A. Lawson*, in *Christ. Exam.*, vols. 10. 11.—*British Quarterly*, vol. 2.

§ 65. *Hippolytus*, p. 225.—*Gieseler's* modified View, in *Stud. u. Krit.*, 1853. A large addition has been made to the literature by the discovery and publication of the "Philosophumena, sive omnium Haeresium Refutatio," edited by *J. Müller*, and issued at Oxford in 1851, as a work of Origen.—*Bunsen's* Hippolytus and his Age, 4. 8; second edition, 2. 8. under the title of Christianity and Mankind.—*Jacobi*, Deutsche Zeitschrift, 1851; *Meth. Qu. Review*, 1851; *Theolog. Critic*, 1852; *Edinb. Review*, 1852 and 1853; *Christ. Remembr.* 1853; *Dublin Review*, 1853, 1854; *British Quarterly* (two articles), 1853; *Westminster*, 1853; *North British*, 1853; *Christ. Review*, 1853; *North American*, 1854.—*Ritschl*, *Volckmar* and *Baur*, in the *Theol. Jahrb.*, 1853, '4.—*Journal of Class. and Sacred Philol.*, 1854. —*New Brunswick Review*, 1854.

Besides these articles, a number of independent works have been published.—*Chr. Wordsworth*, The Church of Rome in the third Century, with Reference to Hippolytus. 1853.—*W. Elfe Tayler*, Analysis of Hippolytus. 1854.—*Lenormant*, Controverse sur les Philos. d'Origine. Par. 1853.—*Döllinger*, Hippolytus u. Kallistus. 1854.—*Cruice*, Etudes sur les Philosoph. Paris, 1853.—*C. Wordsworth*, Remarks on the Preface to the last Edition of *Bunsen*'s Hippolytus. 1855.—*Volckmar*, Hippolytus. 1855.

§ 66, p. 225. *Theology in the West; Tertullian and Cyprian.—Tertullian*, p. 226.—*Opera*, ed. *Oehler*. 1852–'4, 3 tom.—*K. Hesselberg*, Tertullian's Lehre. Dorpat, 1848.—*Neander*, Antignostiken, Geist ds. T. 2te Ausg. 1849. (Eng. transl. in part in Bohn's Library, appended to *Neander's* "Planting," etc.)—*Tertullian*, Transl. in "Libr. of Fathers," vol. 1. 2d ed.—Bishop *Kaye*, Eccl. Hist. of second and third Cent. illustr., in Tertull. 3d ed. 1848.—*Engelhardt*, Tertullian als Schriftsteller, in *Zeitshcrift f. d. hist. Theol.*, 1852. —De Corona Militis. Edit. by *G. Curry*. Camb. 1853.—Apology of T., with English notes, by *H. A. Woodham*. 2d ed. Camb.—*Leopold*, doctr. Tert. de Baptismo, in *Zeitschrift f. d. hist. Theol.*, 1854.—*Hauber*, T. gegen d. zweite Ehe, in *Stud. u. Krit.*, 1845. —Œuvres de T., trad. en Français, by *M. de Genoude*. 2d ed., 3. 8. 1852.—*Uhlhorn*, Fundamenta Chronologiae Tertullian. Götting. 1852.

English Translations.—The seconde Booke of Tertullian unto his Wyf, etc., by *John Hoper*. 1550.—Apology, by *H. B. Brown*, 4. Lond. 1655.—Tertullian's Apology, 8. 1788. Transl., preface by *W. Reeves*, 2. 8. 1716.—Prescriptions, by *T. Betty*. Oxf. 1772.—Address to Scapula Tertullus. Transl. by Sir D. Dalrymple, 12. Edinb. 1790.

Cyprian.—Life and Times of Cyprian, by *Geo. Ayliffe Poole*. Oxf. 1840.—*Shepherd*, Hist. of Ch. of Rome. 1852. He doubts the authenticity of all the letters of Cyprian.—*Id.*, Five Letters to Dr. Maitland. 1852–'54. Cf. *Christ. Remembr.*, 1853, and *Dublin Review*, 1852.—*Dodwell*, Dissertationes Cyprianicae. 1704.—Bishop *Sage*, Principles of Cyprianic Age, 2. 8. Edinb. 1846.—Libr. of Fathers, vols. 3 and 17, Cyprian's Treatises and Epistles.—Cyprian, in *Rudelbach*, christl. Biographie, and in *Böhringer*.—Dr. *Nevins*, Cyprian and his Views, in *Mercersb. Rev.*, 1852.—*M. F. Hyde*, Cypr. de Unitate. 1852.—*Gräbinger*, Cypriani libri de Unitate. Leips. 1853. Other Eng. transl.: Sweete and devoute Sermon, by Syr *Thos. Eliot*. 1534, 1539, 1560.—On the Lorde's Praier, by *T. Paynell*. 1539.—Unity of Church, by *J. Fell*. Oxf. 1681.—Disc. to Donatus, by *J. Tunstall*. 1716.—His whole Works, by *N. Marshall*. 1717.

§ 67, p. 233. *Apostolic Constitutions and Canons.*—In *Bunsen's* Hippolytus is an elaborate attempt to restore these to their original form: Analecta Ante-Nicaena.—*Wedgewood*, Apostol. Constitutions. London, 1843.—*Whiston*, Prim. Christ. revived, 4. 8. 1711.—*Chase*, The Apostol. Constitutions, *Whiston*'s Version, and *Krabbe's* Essay. New York, 1848.—*G. Ueltzen*, Constitutiones Apostolicae. Greek transl. and notes, 8. 1853. Cf. *Zeitschrift f. d. hist. Theol.*, 1854.—Apostol. Constitutions, in *Christ. Remembr.*, 1854.— —The Æthiopic Didascalia, ed. by *T. P. Platt*. Lond. 1834.

§ 68. *History of the Hierarchy*, p. 234.—*W. E. L. Ziegler*, Versuch einer pragmat. Geschichte d. Kirchlichen Verfassungsformen in d. 6 ersten Jahrhund. Leips. 1798.—*J. W. Bickell*, Gesch. ds. Kirchenrechts. 1849.—*Möhler*, die Einheit in d. Kirche, d. Kirchenverfassung d. drei ersten Jahrhunderte. 1830.—*Schmid*, d. Bisthumssynode, 2. 8. 1851. —*Callistus* (and *Zephyrinus*), in his Episcopate and character: cf. the works of *Bunsen*, *Döllinger*, and *Wordsworth*, upon Hippolytus.

§ 70. *Divine Service*, p. 244.—*Bunsen's* Hippolytus, Analecta Ante-Nicaena, 3. 8; Reliquiae Liturgicae.

SECOND PERIOD, A.D. 324–726, p. 268, *sq.*—*General Works on this Period.*—*Fleury's* Hist. of Christ. 381–451. Transl. and edited by *J. H. Newman*, 3. 8. London.—*Milman*, Hist. of Lat. Christ., 3 (to be 5), 8. Lond. 1854.—*Isaac Taylor's* Ancient Christianity, 2. 8. 4th ed. Lond. 1844.—*E. von Lasaulx*, d. Untergang des Hellenismus, und die Einziehung seiner Tempelgüter von d. christlichen Kaisern. München, 1854.

A. de Broglie, Hist. du Christianisme et de la Société Romaine au ive. Siècle, 4. 8. Par. 1855.—*Capefigue*, Hist. de l'Eglise (second portion, 2. 8). Par. 1853.

J. B. Heard, The Extinction of Christianity in the Roman Empire, in Relation to the Evidences of Christianity (Hulsean). 1851.—*Attila*, par *Amédee Thierry*, Rev. des deux Mondes. 1852.

Influence of Christianity on Greek and Roman World.—*C. Schmidt*, Essai historique sur la Société dans le monde Romain, et sur sa Transformation. Paris, 1853 (prize essay).

—Etudes Historiques sur l'Influence de la Charité durant les prem. Siècles Chrét. par *Etienne Chastel.* Paris, 1853 (prize essay).—*F. de Champagny,* la Charité Chrétienne dans les premiers Siècles. Paris, 1854.—*A. Tollemer,* Œuvres de Miséricorde, 12. Par. 1853.

Villemain, Nouveaux Essais sur l'Infl. du Christianisme dans le monde Grec et Latin. Paris, 1855.—*Ozanam,* de la Civilisation au cinquième Siècle, 2. 8. Paris, 1855.

H. J. Leblanc, Essai sur l'Etude des Lettres profanes dans les premiers Siècles. Paris, 1852.—*Troplong,* de l'Influence du Christianisme sur le droit civil des Romains. Paris, 1853.—*C. M. Kennedy,* Influence of Christianity on International Law (Hulsean). 1855.

§ 75, p. 271. *Constantine.—Burckhardt,* die Zeit Constantins des Grossen. 1853.—Rev. *B. H. Cooper,* The Free Church of ancient Christendom, and its Subjugation by Constantine. Lond. 1851.—*Id.,* Life and Times of Constantine.—Life of Constantine, by *Eusebius,* transl. Lond. 1846.—*Manso,* Leben Constantins, 8. 1817.—*Arendt,* in *Tüb. Quartalschrift,* 1834.—*Christ. Rev.,* iv.—*Lit. and Theol. Rev.,* vol. 6.—The Vision of Constantine is investigated by *Passy,* Academie des Sciences Morales et Polit. 1846.—*Polus* (Cardinal), De Baptismo Constantini Magni Imperatoris. 1556.—Panegyric of Constantine the Great, by *Const. Accopoliti,* from MSS. by *Constantine Simonides.* Lond. 1854.

§ 76. *Julian the Apostate,* p. 278.—*F. Strauss,* d. Romantiker auf d. Throne, oder Julian d. Abtrünnige. 1847.—*N. Bangs,* in *Meth. Quar. Rev.,* vol. 9.—*Neander's* Work on Julian, transl., 12. New York, 1848.—*Wiggers,* in *Zeitschrift f. hist. Theol.,* vol. 7.—*H. Schulze,* de Philos. Jul. 1839.—Life of Julian. Lond. 1682; Orations, 1693.—*Auer's* Julian, 1855.

§ 81, *sq.—The Arian Controversy,* p. 294.—*Newman's* Translation of *Fleury's* Eccl. Hist. 381–451, 3. 8. 1838.—*Id.,* The Arians of fourth Cent.—*Maimbourg,* History of Arianism, by *W. Webster,* 2. 4. 1728.—*J. A. Stark,* Versuch einer Gesch. ds. Arianismus.—*Klose,* in Real-Encycl. f. d. Prot. Theologie.—*T. G. Hassencamp,* Historia Arianae Controversiae. 1845.—Bishop *Kaye,* in his "Council of Nice." Lond. 1854.

Whitaker's Origin of Arianism.

The Council of Nice, p. 297.—Bishop *Kaye,* Some Account of the Council of Nice, in Connection with Life of Athanasius. Lond. 1853: cf. *Christ. Remembr.* 1854.—Bishop *Forbes,* Explan. of Nicene Creed. Lond. 1852.—*Marheinecke,* in his Dogmengesch. 1850. —*Baur* and *Dorner,* in their works on the Trinity and Incarnation.—*Petavius,* in his "Theol. Dogm.," 3 fol. tom. 2.—*Frohschammer,* d. Vorsitz auf. d. Synode zu N. (Beiträge zur Kirchengesch. 1850.)

Bishop *Bull,* Defensio Fid. Nicaen. in his Works, 8. 8.—*Id.,* Disc. on Doctrine of Catholic Church.—*Sherlock,* Doctrine of Trinity. 1690.—*Waterland,* Vindication of Christ's Divinity: Works. 1843.—*Hampden,* in Bampton Lects. 3d ed. 1848.

The Athanasian Creed.—History, by Dr. *Waterland*: Works, vol. 1.—*J. Redcliff,* Creed of Athanasius, illustrated from the Scriptures and Writings of the Fathers, 8. London, 1844.

§ 84, p. 314.—*Eusebius Pamph.,* bishop of Caesarea: Evang. Demonstrat., libri x. rec. *T. Gaisford,* 2. 8.—Contra Hieroclem et Marcellum, ed. by *T. Gaisford.* Oxon.—Armenian transl. of Chronicles of Eusebius, from *Niebuhr,* in *Journal of Sacr. Lit.,* 1853, '4.—*Marginalia* of *Pearson* on Eusebius, in *Journ. Class. and Sacred Philol.,* 1854.—*Hollenberg,* on *Schwegler's* and *Burton's* edition of the Eccl. Hist., in *Studien u. Kritiken,* 1855.—Theophania in the Syriac, and transl. by Dr. *Samuel Lee,* 2. 8. Lond.—Tracts by Eusebius, in *Mai's* Patrum Nova Biblioth., tom 3. 1853.—*Lawson,* in *Christ. Exam.,* vol. 18.

Athanasius.—Bishop *Kaye,* in his "Council of Nice." 1853.—Athanasius against the Arians, transl. by *Newman,* Lib. Fathers, vols. 8. 19; Historical Tracts, vol. 13.—The Festal Letters of Athanasius, from Syriac, with Notes, by *W. Cureton,* 1848; to be transl. by *H. Burgess*; German transl. by *Lasrow,* 1852: cf. *Journal Sacred Lit.,* 1855.—Orations, transl. by *Parker.* 1718.—Athanasius and Arius, in *Christ. Remembr.,* 1854; *Christian Examiner,* 1855.—Opera Dogmatica Selecta, ed. by *Thilo,* in "Bibl. Patrum Graec. Dogmatica," vol. 1. Leips. 1853.

Basil the Great.—Christian Review, July, 1854.—Opera Dogmat., in *Thilo's* Bibl. Patrum Graec. Dogm., vol. 2. 1854.—Basil, Select Passages from. Lond. 1810.—Holy Love of heavenly Wisdom, transl. by *T. Stocker.* 1594.

Gregory of Nazianzum.—*Ullmann's* Life, transl. in part by *G. V. Cox.* Lond. 1851.—*Piper's* Evang. Kalend. 1852.—*Journal Sacr. Lit.*, 1852; *Westminster Rev.*, vol. 56.—*Hergenröther*, Gregory's "Lehre v. d. Dreieinigkeit." Regensb. 1850.—*Thilo*, Bibl. Patrum Graec. Dogm., vol. 2. 1854.

Gregory of Nyssa.—Doctrina de hominis natura illustravit et cum Origeniana comparavit, by *E. G. Moeller.* Halle, 1852.

Hilary.—In the Spicilegium Solesmense, ed. by *Pitra*, 1853, fragments of a commentary on Paul are vindicated for Hilary; cf. *Christ. Remembr.*, July, 1853. Against this, and for Theodorus, *Jacobi*, in the "*Deutsche Zeitschrift*," 1854.

Jerome.—*Collembet*, l'Hist. d'Hieronyme. 1845 (in French, 1847).—Jerome and his Times, by *S. Osgood*, in *Bibl. Sacra*, vol. 5.

Ambrose.—*Rudelbach*, in "Christl. Biog." Bd. 1.—*Böhringer*, in his "Kirche Christi," and in the Real-Encycl. f. Prot. Theol.—Ambrosian MSS., *Quar. Rev.*, vol. 16.—Tract on the Holy Virginity, by *A. J. Christie.* Oxf. 1843.

Cyril.—Lectures. 3d ed. "Lib. Fathers," vol. 2.—Thirteen works in *Mai's* "Nova Bibliotheca," 1853, vol. 2.

Ephraem Syrus.—*H. Burgess*, Transl. of Hymns and Homilies. Lond. 1853; cf. *Kitto's* Journal, 1853.—*Id.*, Repentance of Nineveh. 1854.—Das Leben ds. Eph. Syr., *J. Alsleben.* 1853.—Cardinal *Wiseman*, in his "Essays," vol. 3 (from *Dublin Review*).—*North British*, Aug. 1853; *Journal of Sacred Lit.*, Jan. 1854; *Church Review*, 1852.

Theodor of Mopsuestia.—Commt. in N. T., ed. *Fritsche.* 1847.—Doctrina de imagine Dei, *Dorner*, 1844; cf. *Dorner's* Person. Christi.—Commentar. in Spicileg. Solesm. (see under *Hilary*, above).

John Chrysostom.—The first vol. of Neander's Life. Transl. by *J. C. Stapleton.* Lond. 1845.—*Böhringer*, in "Die Kirche Christi."—In the "Lib. of Fathers," Oxf., translation of Chrysostom in vols. 4. 5. 6. 7. 9. 11. 12. 14. 15. 27. 34.—Chrysostom on "Priesthood," with notes and Life, by *H. M. Mason.* Philad. 1826.—*Bibl. Sacra*, vol. 1. Life by *J. D. Butler.*—*Kitto's* Journal, vol. 1. by *Eadie.*—*S. Osgood*, in *North Amer.*, vol. 62.—*C. P. Krauth*, in *Evangel. Rev.*, vol. 1.—Sermons of Chrysostom, in *Christian Rev.*, vol. 12.—*Perthes*, Life of Chrysostom, transl. Boston, 1854.

Chrysostom, "No man is hurted but of hym-selfe." Transl. by *T. Luprette.* London, 1542.—On the "Priesthood," by *H. Hollier*, Lond. 1728; by *J. Bunce*, Lond. 1759.—"Select Passages," by *H. S. Boyd.* Lond. 1810.

Synesius.—Quae exstant Opera omnia, ed. by *J. G. Krabinger*, tom. 1. 1850.—Homilies; trad. pour la prem. fois, par *B. Kolbe.* Berl. 1850.

§ 86, p. 326.—*Priscillian.*—*J. M. Mandernach*, Geschichte ds. Priscillianismus. 1851.—Defense of Priscillian, by Dr. *Lardner;* Works, vol. 4.

§ 87. *Augustine and Pelagius.*—*Augustine*, in "Lib. of Fathers," Oxf., vol. 1. Confessions, by *S. B. Pusey* (rep. in Boston); vols. 16 and 20, Sermons; 22, Treatises; 16, 20, Sermons; 24, 25, 30, 32, Psalms; 26, 29, John.—*Trench*, Essay on Augustine as Interpreter, and Comm. on Serm. on Mount.—Life, etc., by *Schaff.* 1854.—Life and Labors. Lond. 1853. (Bagster).—*R. Emerson*, Transl. of first vol. of *Wiggers*, "Augustin. and Pelagianism." Andover.—*Princeton Rev.*, July, 1854.—Aug. and Pelag., *Am. Bib. Repos.*, vol. 3. from Neander; vol. 5. by *H. P. Tappan.*—*Christian Rev.*, vols. 5, 15; *Brit. Quar. Rev.*, vol. 6.—Augustine as Preacher, *Bibl. Repos.*, vol. 3. and vol. 7. 2d series.—*Osgood*, on Augustine and his Times, in "Studies in Christian Biogr."—*Zeller*, on Augustine's Doctrine of Sin, in *Theol. Jahrb.*, 1854.—*Ponjoulat*, Hist. de St. Aug. 3d ed. 2. Paris, 1852.—*Mozley*, Augustinian Doctrine of Predestination. London, 1855.

Two hundred new Sermons of Augustine, in *Mai*, Patrum Nova Biblioth., vol. 1.—De Civitate Dei, ed. *Strange.* Colon. 1850, '51.

L. Gangauf, Metaphys. Psychologie ds. heilig. August. Augsb. 1852.

Augustine, Of the Citie of God, with the Comm. of *L. Vives.* Englished by *J. H.* 2d ed. 1620.—Manuell, London, 1577.—Meditations, by *Stanhope.* London, 1745.—A new French transl. of the "Civitas Dei," by *Saisset*, 4. 12. 1855.

Shicksale d. Augustinischen Anthropologie von d. Verdammung ds. Semipelagianismus auf. d. Synoden zu Orange u. Valence 529 bis zur Reaction ds. Mönchs Gottschalck f. d. August, Dr. *G. F. Wiggers*, in *Zeitschrift f. d. historische Theologie*, 1854, '5.

Julius Müller, Der Pelagianismus, ein Vortrag. *Deutsche Zeitschrift.* 1855.

Vincens of Lirens, p. 343.—Commonitorium, ed. alt. Oxford, with a translation. On him, see *Hefele*, in *Theol. Quartalschrift*, 1854.

English translations: *J. Procter*, Lond. 1554; *A. P.*, Lond. 1559; *Luke*, Lond. 1611.—*W. Reeves*, with the Apolog. of Primitive Fathers, 2. 8. Lond. 1716.

§ 88. *Nestorian Controversy*, p. 343. On the Views of Nestorius, in *Zeitschrift f. d. Luth. Theol.*, 1854.—Nestorius and the Council of Ephesus, in *Christ. Exam.*, 1853.—On the present Nestorians, *T. Laurie.* Bost. 1853; *J. Perkins*, in *Journal Sacr. Lit.*, 1853. Cf. the works of *Baur*, *Dörner*, and *Meier*, on the Trinity and Incarnation.—*E. Robinson*, in *North American*, vol. 57.; in *Am. Bibl. Repos.*, vol. 6 (second series).—*G. P. Badger*, The Nestorians and their Rituals, 2. Lond. 1852.

Theodoretus, Comment. in omnes b. Pauli Epist: Pars 1. Oxon. 1852, in Bibl. Patrum Eccles. Cath., etc.

§ 94. *History of the Roman Patriarchs, and of the Hierarchy in the West*, p. 377.—On the Claims and Succession of the Papacy.—*Barrow* on the Papal Supremacy, *M'Crie's* edition.—*Riddle's* Hist. of Papacy, 2. 8. 1854 (from *Schröckh* and others); cf. *Dublin Rev.*, 1854.—*G. A. F. Wilks*, The Popes. Lond. 1851.—*Passaglia*, de Praerogativis. B. S. Petri, 2. 8. Rom. 1850.—*Allies*, Digest of Passaglia. Lond. 1853.—*Ed. Burton*, Power of the Keys; Works, 1. 1838.—*J. Pearson*, de Serie et Success. prim. Rom. Episcop. 1688.—*Dodwell* on the same subject.—*Palmer* on the Church, vol. 2. p. 451–529.—*Collette*, The Pope's Supremacy. Lond. 1852.—*André Archinaud*, Les Origines de l'Eglise Romaine, 2. 8. Geneve, 1852.

Storia dei Papi, *Bianchi-Giovini* (8 vols. published in Switzerland).

Dowling's History of Romanism. 6th ed. 8. New York, 1845.—*J. A. Wylie*, The Papacy. Lond. 1852.—*Philippe de Boni*, de la Papanté. 1852 (condemned at Rome).—*Poussel*, Origine du principat Romain. Avignon, 1852.—*F. Maassen*, d. Primat ds. Bischofs von Rom, u. d. alten Patriarchalkirchen. Bonn, 1853.—*J. Meyrick*, Papal Supremacy tested by Antiquity. Lond. 1855.—*Elliott* on Romanism, 2. 8. New York.—*Ellendorf*, d. Primat. d. Römischen Pabste, 2. 8. 1841.—*Kenrick*, The Primacy. 3d ed. 1855.

Edict of Valentinian III. on Papal Supremacy, in *Deutsche Zeitscrift*, 1855.

Routh, Tres breves Tractatus (the third, S. Irenaei illustrata ῥησις, in qua Ecclesia Romana commemoratur), Oxon. 1854; cf. *Pusey*, Notes to Sermon on the Rule of Faith. 1854.

On the States of the Church.—*John Miley*, History of. Transl. into French by *C. Quin-Lacroix.* Paris, 1851.—*Hasse* (Prof. H.), Die Vereinigung der geistlichen u. der weltlichen Obergewalt im Röm. Kaiserstaat. 1852.—*Brasseur de Bourbourg*, Hist. de la Patrimonie de St. Peter. 1853.—*Sugenheim*, Geschichte d. Entstehung u. Ausbildung des Kirchenstaats (prize essay), 8. Leips. 1854.

Daunon, Essai Hist. sur la puissance Temporelle des Papes (written at the instance of Napoleon); see *Quar. Rev.*, Oct. 1853.

Febronius, de Statu Eccles. et Legit. Potest. Rom. Pontif., 3. 4. 1763, *sq.*—*Salmasius* (Claude), de Primatu Papae, etc. Lugd. Bat. 1645.

History of Popery. London, 1837.—Temporal Power of Popes, *Christ. Rev.*, 1851.—*Brownson's* Quarterly, 1851, '2, '3.—Papal Supremacy, *Dublin Rev.*, 1852.—The Primacy, *Dubl. Rev.*, 1853.

Christ. Remembr., 1855, on the papal and royal Supremacy.

Synod of Sardica, p. 379, in *Shepherd's* Church of Rome, 1852; its Acts discussed.—*Barrow* on the Papal Supremacy (also a recently discovered treatise of *Barrow*).—*Scotch Eccl. Journal*, April and May, 1852.

Leo, p. 392.—*St. Cheron*, vie de Leo, 8. Paris (to be translated).

§ 95. *History of Monasticism*, p. 397.—De Monachatus Originibus et Causis, by *G. F. Mangold.* Marburg, 1852.—*P. Maclean*, Monks and Monasteries. London, 1854.—Early History of Monasticism, by *R. Emerson*, in *Bibl. Sacra*, vol. 1.—*Ruffner's* Fathers of the

Desert, 2. 12. 1850.—*S. P. Day*, Monastic Institutions: their Origin, etc. Lond. 1846, vol. 89.—*Isaac Taylor's* Ancient Christianity, 2. 8. 4th ed. Lond. 1844.—Eastern Monachism; Mendicants founded by Gotama Budha, from Singalese MSS., by *R. Spence Hardy*. Lond.

§ 102, p. 340. *Celibacy.*—See *Taylor's* Ancient Christianity.—*Beavan's* Hist. of Celibacy. Lond. 1841 (against Taylor).

Du Célibat, par *L. Ant. A. Pacy* (bishop of Algiers). Par. 1852.—Untersuchungen über d. Römische Ehe, *A. Rossbach*, 2 Thle. Stuttg.

§ 106, p. 455. *Attempts at Reformation.*

Jovinian and Vigilantius.—De Jovin. et Vigil. purior. Doctr.—*G. B. Lindner.* 1839.—Vigilantius and his Times, 8. Lond. 1845.

§ 108, p. 469. *Goths*, etc.—*C. J. Revillont*, de l'Arianisme des peuples Germaniques, qui ont envahi l'Empire Romain. Paris, 1850.

Ulphilas, and his Gothic Version of the Scriptures, by *S. Loewe*, in *Kitto's* Journal, vol. 3.—Gothica Versio, ed. *C. D. Castillionaeus*, 4. Mediol. 1829.—Continued, the Pauline Epistles. 1829–'35.—Gothische Bibelübersetzung, *Fulda* u. *Zahn*, 4. Weissenfels. 1805.—Versio Gothica, cum Interpret., *E. Benzelii*, ed. *E. Lye*, 4. Oxon. 1750. Fragmenta vers. Ulphil., u. *F. A. Knittell.* Upsal, 1763.—Codex argenteus s. sacrorum evangeliorum versionis Gothicae Fragmenta, quae iterum recognita, etc. Ed. Dr. Andr. *Uppström*, 4. Upsaliae, 1855.

§ 112, p. 382. *Æthiopia.*—*Geddes*, History of Church of Æthiopia. Lond. 1696.—*Id.*, Hist. of the Church of Malabar. Lond. 1694.

Armenia.—*Samuljan*, Die Bekehrung Armeniens durch d. heiligen Gregorius illuminator. 1844.—*Bodenstedt*, d. Einführung ds. Christenth. in Armenien. 1850.—*Ingigi*, Antiquitates Armen., 3. 4. 1855.—Zur Urgeschichte d. Armenier. Philol. Versuch. Berl. 1854.—Armenia, Hist. Dogm. et Liturg., etc., 8. Paris, 1855.—Die Entwickelung d. Armenischen Kirche vom Evangelio zum Evangelio, *K. N. Pischon*, in *Deutsche Zeitschrift*, Dec. 1854.

§ 114, p. 389. *Dionysius the Areopagite.*—Opera omnia quae exstant, ed. *B. Corderius.* Leips. 1854.

Boethius, De Consolatione. Transl. into English by *Chaucer;* also by Lord *Preston*, with Notes, 1695; 2d ed. 1712, by *Ridpath.* Lond. 1785.—*G. Baur*, de Boethio. Darmst. 1841.

Gregory the Great, p. 389.—Gregor. u. seine Zeit, by *G. Pfahler*, Bd. 1. Francf. 1852.—*G. F. Wiggers*, de Greg. M. ejusque placitis Anthropol. Rostock. 1838.—*Markgraf*, de G. M. Vita. Berol. 1845.—*Lau*, Greg. I., Leben, u. s. w. Leips. 1845.—*Böhringer*, in Kirche u. Zeugen. 1.—Gregory's Views on Augustinianism, by *Wiggers*, in *Zeitschrift f. d. hist. Theol.*, 1854.—Gregory's Morals on Book of Job, in *Oxf. Lib. of F.*, vols. 18, 21, 23, 31.—His Dialogues, transl. in the *Metropolitan*, Balt. 1854.—*Maimbourg*, Hist. du Pontif. de S. Grég. Paris, 1686.—King *Alfred*, transl. Gregory's Pastoral, publ. in Aelfred Regis Res Gest. Lond. 1574.—Collectanea out of Gregory and Bernard. Oxf. 1618.

Gregory of Tours, p. 390.—Kirchengesch. d. Franken, im Deutschen. Würz. 1849.—Zehn Bücher, *W. Giesebrecht*, 2. 1851.—Vie de S. Grégoire, par l'Abbé *A. Dupuy*, 8. Paris, 1854.

Canon Law.—*Wasserschleben*, Beiträge zur Geschichte des vorgratianischen Kirchenrechtsquellen. 1848.—*Bickell's* Geschichte des Kirchenrechts, 1. 1843. Cf. in *Niedner's* Kirchengeschichte.—Geddes Tracts, vol. 2.—*F. Walter*, Lehrbuch, 11th ed. 1854.

§ 119, p. 407. *Benedict* and the Benedictines, *Edinb. Rev.*, vol. 89.

§ 123, p. 419; § 134, p. 457. *Christianity in Germany, and the Franks.*—*W. Krafft*, Kirchengesch. Deutschlands, 1. 1855 (Ursprung d. Deutschen Kirche).—*Rettberg*, Kirchengesch. Deutschlands, 1. Die Franken bis auf Karl d. Gross. 1848.—*P. Roth*, Gesch. d. Beneficialwesens, bis ins 10te Jahr. Erlang. 1850; cf. *Brandes*, in *Gersdorf Rep.*, 1851.—*A. F. Ozanam*, la Civilisation Chrétienne chez les Francs. Par. 1849.—*Destombes*, Hist. de St. Amand, et du Christ. chez les Francs. Paris, 1850 (ultramontane).—*Anschar*, Life and Times, in *Böhringer*, and in *Christ. Exam.*, 1853.—*Adalbert of Prague*, Leben v. Tornwaldt, in *Zeitschrift f. d. hist. Theol.*, 1853.—The Conversion of the Northern Nations, in *New Brunswick Rev.*, 1854.—*Adalbert*, Erzb. v. Hamburg, *C. Grünhagen.* Leipsic, 1854.

Ozanam (A. F.), Etudes Germaniques, 2. 8; La Germanie avant le Christianisme, 1847.

H. Rückert, Culturgesch. ds. Deutschen Volkes, 2. 8. 1854.—*Leo*, Vorlesungen über d. Ursprung ds. Deutschen Volkes u. Reichs, vol. 1. 1852.

Luden, Gesch. d. Deutschen Volkes, 12 Bde. 1825–'37.—*Kohlrausch*, transl. by *Haas.* New York, 1847.—*Menzel*, by *G. Horrocks*, 3. 12. Lond. 1848.—*J. J. Mascon*, Hist. Ancient Germans. Transl. by *Lediard*, 2. 4. London, 1833.—*Stenzel*, Gesch. d. Deutschen unter d. Frankischen Kaisern, 2. 8. Leips. 1838.—*Pfister*, Geschich. d. Deutschen, 5. 8. Hamb. 1829–'35.—*G. H. Pertz*, Monumenta Germ. Hist., 1-14. 1826–'54.

§ 127, p. 434. *Mohammed.*—*Bush's* Life of Mohammed (*Harper's* Lib.). 1830.—*Prideaux*, Life of Mohammed. 4th ed. 1708.

Foster's Mohammedanism Unveiled. 1829.—*Weil*, Mohammed. 1843; Geschichte d. Chalifen, 3. 1851 (to A.D. 1258).—*J. L. Merrick*, Life and Religion of Mohammed, as contained in the Sheeāh Traditions of the Hyât-ul-Kooloob, from the Persian. Boston, 1850.—*Hammer-Purgstall*, Gemäldesaal d. Lebensbeschreibungen. Leips. 1837.—Life of Mohammed from original Sources, by Dr. *A. Sprenger*, pt. 1. Lond. 1832.—Mohammed and the Arab. Emp., by Prof. *Koeppen*, in *New York Quarterly*, 1854.—*F. A. Neale*, Rise and Progress of Islamism, 2. London, 1854.—*Christ. Remembr.*, Jan. and April, 1855.—*Kitto's* Journal, vol. 1, article Mohammed.—*Irving*, Mohammed and his Successors.—*North Am. Rev.*, vol. 63; *North British*, vol. 13; *Brownson's Quar.*, vol. 4; *Foreign Quar.*, vol. 12.

The Koran, transl. of Arabic text, by *Kasimirski.* New ed. Paris, 1852.—Refutation of the Koran, in *Mai's* Patr. nov. Biblioth., tom. 4. 1853.—*Sale's* Translation of the Koran, 2d ed., 2. 8. London, 1844.—Selections from the Koran, by *Lane.* 1844.—Coranus Arabice. Ed. *G. M. Redslob.* Lips. 1855.

§ 132. *Spanish Church*, p. 450.—Manual razonado de Historia y Legislation de la Iglesia desde sei Establecimienta hasta... 4. Madrid, 1845; cf. *Stud. u. Krit.*, 1848.—*Dunham*, Spain and Portugal, 5 vols. (*Lardner's* Cab. Cyclop.).—*St. Hilaire*, Hist. de l'Espagne depuis les premiers Temps. New ed., 4. 8. Paris, 1853.—Papal Dominion in Spain, *For. Rev.*, vol. 1.—Gothic Laws of Spain, *Edinb. Rev.*, vol. 31.

§ 126, p. 429; § 133, p. 452. *Old British, Irish, and Scotch Churches.*—De Ecclesiasticae Briton. Scotorumque fontibus disseruit, *C. G. Schöll.* 1851.—English Church Historians, from Bede to Foxe, 8. 8. London, 1853, *sq.*—*T. Wright*, British Lit. Biography, Anglo-Saxon and Roman Period, 2. 8. 1851.—*North British Rev.*, 1853, Account of early Works on British History.—*Dugdale's* Monasticon Anglicanum, 8 fol. 1846.—Historia Britonorum of *Nennius*, repr. *Irish Arch. Soc.*, ed. *J. H. Todd.* 1850.—Anglo-Sax. Poetae atq. Script. prosaici, edit. *L. Ettmüller.* 1850.—*J. W. Ebeling*, d. Geschichtschreiber Englands. 1852 (cf. *Lond. Athenæum*, May 6, 1852).—*Gildas* et *Nennius*, Hist. Britonorum, ed. *Stevenson*, 2. 8 (English Hist. Soc.).—*Rog. de Wendover*, Chronica, ed. *Coxe*, 4 (English Hist. Soc.).—*William Malmsb.*, Gesta rerum Angl., ed. *Hardy* (English Hist. Soc.).—*Bede*, by the same Society, 2. 8.

Rev. *B. Poste*, Britannic Researches, Rectifications of Ancient Brit. Hist., 8. 1853.—The Anglo-Saxon Legend of St. Andrew and St. Veronica, ed. for Camb. Antiq. Society by *C. W. Goodwin.* 1854.—*Polydore Virgil*, Engl. Hist., transl. by *Ellis*, 4. London, 1844 (Camden Soc.).——*Geoffrey of Monmouth*, Brit. Hist., ed. by *J. A. Giles.* London, 1842.—Surtees Publ. Society, 28 vols. to 1854, illustrating the early Eng. Eccl. History, *e. g.*, Anglo-Saxon and early English Psalter and Hymnarium; the Pontifical of *Egbert*, Archbishop of York (732–766), issued in 1853.—*H. Herbert*, Britannia, 2. 4. Lond. 1836–'41.—*Eccleston*, Introd. to English Antiquities, 8. Lond. 1847.

J. M. Kemble, Codex diplomat. aevi Saxonici (Engl. Hist. Soc.), 1–6. Lond. 1839–'48. —*Id.*, The Saxons in England, 2. 8. 1851.—*Wm. B. M'Cabe*, A Catholic Hist. of England: the Anglo-Saxon Period, 3. 8. 1850–'54.—*Sharon Turner*, Hist. Anglo-Saxons. 7th ed., 3. 8. 1851.—*J. J. A. Worsae*, The Danes and Norwegians in England. Lond. 1852.—*Sir Francis Palgrave*, Hist. of Anglo-Saxons, 12. Lond. 1847.—*Id.*, Anglo-Saxon Period, 2. 4. 1832.—*Lingard's* Antiquities of Anglo-Saxon Church, 2. 8. 1806.—*Henry*

Soames, Lat. or Rom. Church in Anglo-Saxon Times. 1848 (reply to *Lingard*).—*Thos. Wood*, Ancient Britons. 1846.—*De Bonnechose*, Hist. des quatre Conquétes d'Angleterre. 1852 (received the Montegon prize).—Remains of Pagan Saxondom, by *J. G. Akerman*. 1851 (Soc. Antiq. Lond.).—England under the Popish Yoke, by *E. C. Armstrong*. Oxf. 1850.

P. F. Tytler, Hist. of Scotland, 9. 8. London, 1842-'44.—*Burton's* Hist., 2. 8. 1854.—Analecta Scotia, 2. 8. Edinb., 1834-'37.—*Dalrymple*, Antiq. of Scotland, 4. 1800.—*D. Wilson*, The Archæology and præhistoric Annals of Scotland. Edinb. 1851 (cf. *North British*, 1852).—*Dempsteri*, Historia Eccles. gentis Scotorum, sive de Scriptoribus Scotis, 2. 4. 1829 (Bannatyne Club).—*Stuart* (A.), Caledonia Romana, 4. 2d ed. 1852.—Early Scottish History and its Exponents, *Retrosp. Rev.*, No. 3. 1853.

D'Alton, Hist. of Ireland, from earliest Period to 1245, 2. 8. Dubl. 1845.—The Annals of Ireland, ed. by *P. M'Dermott*, 4. Dublin, 1847.—*Moore's* Hist., 4. 1846.—*J. Lanigan*, Eccl. History of Ireland. 2d ed. 1829, 2. 8.—*Robert King*, Mem. Introd. to early History of Primacy of Armagh. 1854.—*Todd*, Hymns of ancient Irish Church. 1852.—*O'Donovan*, Book of Rights of ancient Kings of Ireland. 1847.—Ancient Irish Brehon Laws, to be published after the Manner of the Scotch and Welsh Collections.—Annals of Kingdom of Ireland by the *Four Masters*, to 1616; ed. by *J. O'Donovan*, 7. 4. Dublin, 1851 (cf. *Quar. Rev.*, Aug., 1853).

Annals of Ireland, by *J. Nave*, ed. by *R. Butler*. 1841.—Latin Annalists of Ireland, *Clyn* and *Dowling*, ed. by *R. Butler*. 1848.—*Shee*, Irish Church, History, etc. London, 1852.—*Williams*, Eccl. Antiquities: the Cymry.—History of Wales till incorporated with England, by *B. B. Woodward*. London, 1853.—*W. J. Reeves*, Cambro-British Saints of fifth and succeeding Centuries, from MSS. Llandoverey. 1854 (for the Welsh MSS. Society).—St. Patrick and his Birth-place, *Notes and Queries*, vol. 5.

Columban.—*Arnold's* Theol. Critic, vol. 1. 1851.—*Scotch Ecclesiastical Journal*, 1852.—Notes on the Study of the Bible by our Forefathers (Columban, Patrick, Gildas), in *Journal of Class. and Sacred Philol.*, 1854.—*Knottenbelt*, de Columbano. Lugd. 1839.

J. Jamieson, Hist. Account of the ancient Culdees of Iona, and of their Settlement in Scotland, England, and Ireland, 4. Edinb. 1811.

E. Churten, Early English Church. 1841.—*Bates*, College Lect. on Eccl. Hist. 1853. —*Jeremy Collier*, Eccl. Hist. of England. New ed., 9. 8. 1845.—*Giles*, History of Ancient Britons to the Invasion of the Saxons, 2. 8.—*Wm. Hales*, Origin of Church of British Isles.—Chronicles of the British Church previous to Augustine. 2d ed. Lond. 1853. —*Le Neve*, Fasti Anglic., ed. by *Hardy*. New edition, Clarendon press. 1854.—*Cotton's* Fasti Ecclesiae Hibernicae.—The Religion of the ancient Britons, from earliest Times to Norman Conquest, by *Geo. Smith*, 8. 2d ed. 1854.

Liber poenitentialis, Theod. (edition of the Record Commission), Untersuchungen über d. german. Pönitent. Bücher, von *K. Hildebrand*. Wurz. 1851.—Die Bussordnungen d. Abendl. Kirche, v. *F. W. H. Wasserschleben*. Halle, 1851 (cf. *Gersdorf's Rép.*, 1852).

Caedmons, des Angelsachsen, Biblische Dichtungen, ed. *K. W. Bouterwek*. Leipsic, 1851.—*A. Daniels*, de Saxonici Speculi Origine, etc., 8. Berol. 1852.

Ælfric, Remains of, ed. by *L'Isle*, 1623; with a reprint of the "Testimonie of Antiquitie," sanctioned by Archbishop Parker. 1567.

Bede.—The English Historical Society published his Historia Eccles. et Opera Hist. Minora, ed. *Stevenson*, 2. 8.—Works, in 12. 8. Edited by *J. A. Giles*. Lond. 1843, '4.—*Giles*, Life of Bede.—Historia Eccles. gentis Anglorum, ed. *R. Hussey*. 1846.—His Ecclesiastical History. Transl. by *J. A. Giles*, 1845; also his Biog. Writings and Letters. 1845.—Opera, ed. *Stephenson*. 1848.—Bede and his Biographers, *Dubl. Rev.*, July, 1854. —Bede's Eccl. Hist. Transl. by *T. Stapleton*, 4. Anto. 1565, and *St. Omer's*, 1622; from Dr. *Smith's* edition, with Notes and Life, 8. Lond. 1723.—*Smith's* edition, fol. Camb. 1722.

END OF VOL. I.